RUGBY LEAGUE 2023-2024
Changing landscape

League Express

LEAGUE
Publications Ltd

First published in Great Britain in 2023 by
League Publications Ltd, Wellington House, Briggate, Brighouse, West Yorkshire HD6 1DN

Copyright © League Publications Ltd

All rights reserved. No part of this book may be reproduced or transmitted in any form or by any means, electronic or mechanical, including photocopying, recording or by any information storage and retrieval system, without prior permission in writing from the publisher.

A CIP catalogue record for this book is available from the British Library
ISBN 978-1-901347-43-2

Designed and Typeset by League Publications Limited
Printed by H Charlesworth & Co Ltd, Wakefield

Contributing Editor
Tim Butcher

Statistics, production and design
Daniel Spencer

Contributors
Thomas Alderson
David Ballheimer
Tom Bell
Peter Bird
Aaron Bower
Steve Brady
Phil Caplan
Josh Chapman
Louis Chapman-Coombe
James Chestney
Mark Chestney
Luke Connelly
John Davidson
Gareth Davies
Daniel Fowler
Ian Golden
Thomas Grisedale
Nick Heald
Phil Hodgson
Ash Hope
Stephen Ibbetson
Andrew Jackson
Jake Kearnan
Dan Kelly
David Kuzio
Christian Lee
Callum Linford
Gareth Lyons
Lorraine Marsden
Paddy McAteer
Keith McGhie
Dave Parkinson
James Pike
Huw Richards
Ian Rigg
Martyn Sadler
Matthew Shaw
Steve Slater
Tom Smith
Sebastian Sternik
Mark Taylor
Doug Thomson
Callum Walker
Rob Wallace
Matthew Ward
Jordan Weir
Gavin Wilson
Ian Wilson
Peter Wilson

Pictures
SWPix
Dean Williams
Craig Hawkhead
Simon Hall
Craig Cresswell
Steve Jones (RLPix)
Gareth Lyons
Thomas Fynn
David Greaves
Steve Mower
Rob Terrace
Ben Challis
Alex Coleman
Steve McCormick
Steve Miller
Paul Cowan
Josh Harper
Mike Inkley
Craig Irvine
Brian King
Chris Lishman
Jackie Meredith
Matthew Merrick
Dave Murgatroyd
Paul Whitehurst
Catalans Dragons
Cornwall RLFC
Getty Images
NRL Imagery

Main cover picture
Dean Williams

CONTENTS

Acknowledgments	5
Introduction	6

1. Personalities of 2023 — 9
- James Roby — 10
- Bevan French — 11
- Lachlan Lam — 12
- Mikey Lewis — 13
- Mike Eccles — 14

2. The 2023 Season — 15
- December 2022 — 16
- January — 19
- February — 21
- March — 29
- April — 42
- May — 50
- June — 58
- July — 69
- August — 78
- September — 88
- October — 100
- Super League awards — 105

3. Championship, League One & Women 2023 — 107
- Championship — 108
- League One — 117
- Women — 124

4. World Cup 2021 — 129
- *World Cup 2021 - In Colour* — 129
- World Cup 2021 - Statistical review — 145

5. Season Down Under — 169
- NRL — 170
- State of Origin — 181

6. International Year — 185
- England v Tonga Test Series — 186
- England v France — 191
- Other Internationals — 192

7. Statistical review 2023 — 195
- Super League Players 1996-2023 — 197
- Super League XXVIII club by club — 225
- Super League XXVIII round by round — 250
- Super League Records 1996-2023 — 268
- Championship 2023 club by club — 269
- Championship 2023 round by round — 284
- League One 2023 club by club — 305
- League One 2023 round by round — 316
- Challenge Cup 2023 round by round — 326
- 1895 Cup 2023 round by round — 332
- 2023 Statistical round-up — 333

ACKNOWLEDGEMENTS

The *League Express Yearbook 2023-2024* is the 28th of League Publications Ltd's annual series of Rugby League Yearbooks, which began in the first year of Super League in 1996.

This historical record of the Rugby League year would not be possible without the hard work and dedication of all the contributors to *Rugby Leaguer & Rugby League Express*, *Rugby League World* magazine and the *totalrl.com* website.

We are able to include some wonderful action photography provided by, in particular SWPix, Dean Williams, Craig Hawkhead, Simon Hall, Craig Cresswell, Steve Jones (RLPix) and Gareth Lyons.

Thanks to the Rugby Football League for their help during the year and to the historians and statisticians at clubs who help us resolve any anomalies.

Special thanks to Neil Ormston and the Rugby League Record Keepers' club who have been an invaluable source for the crosschecking of statistics throughout the year.

Acknowledgement also to the series of Rothmans Yearbooks, compiled by our late friend Ray Fletcher, the British Rugby Records Book from London Publications and to the club officials, and some supporters, who helped us verify records.

Special thanks to Doug Thomson for the Championship round-up and to Lorraine Marsden, who wrote the League One and Women's sections.

The amazing statistical review, compiled with painstaking accuracy, is the work of my colleague Daniel Spencer, who also designed the book.

TIM BUTCHER
Contributing Editor

INTRODUCTION

The end of 2023 saw a major sea-change in Rugby League, as the first radical development from the sport's tie-up with international marketing organisation IMG came into view, two years into the twelve-year partnership. From the end of the 2024 season, all RFL clubs were to be graded, with their rank determining which division they will play in. Provisional gradings were published in October 2023 and for the record we list the gradings and on which criteria were taken into account.

Many viewed the 're-imagination of the game' as not very imaginative and a return to franchising which had been tried from 2009 and ditched after six seasons. And with a decline in the contract with Sky Sports to 21.5 million per year for three seasons from 2024 (the contract was worth 40 million ten years before), accompanied with the hangover from the Covid epidemic which led to huge losses for clubs and the central governing body, plus the withdrawal from the RFL of two clubs, London Skolars and Newcastle Thunder, the doom-mongers predicted apocalypse once again.

But there was plenty of positives in the year 2023, which provided a big chance for the sport to gain a higher profile on the back of the World Cups of the previous year, which positioned Rugby League as the most inclusive ball game in the world.

The higher exposure given by increased TV coverage during the World Cup helped the domestic game attract more spectators than any year since 2012, with average attendances showing an increase of more than 11 per cent on 2022, the fourth-best since Super League began in 1996. The second-tier Championship crowds were also up over six per cent on the previous season.

On the other side of the world the National Rugby League boomed, with an average of 19,633 fans at club games, the successful introduction of a 17th team, the Brisbane-based Dolphins and the start of a plan to expand their market into the United States of America. The 2024 NRL Premiership was to kick off at Allegiant Stadium in Las Vegas with a double header featuring Manly v South Sydney and Sydney Roosters v Brisbane Broncos.

Super League XXVIII was a thoroughly entertaining season from start to finish, beginning with St Helens' magnificent, if nail-biting World Club Challenge victory over Penrith Panthers at the foot of the Blue Mountains in New South Wales and ending with Wigan Warriors re-taking the Championship title from Saints after four years of dominance.

The Super League Grand Final win, which saw Wigan beat Catalans Dragons 10-2, was the culmination of two years of progress under head coach Matt Peet, with the Challenge Cup success of 2022 thrown in.

The Warriors were blessed by having the blistering speed of Jai Field and brilliance of 2023 Man of Steel Bevan French but around them was a set of fine players adhering to a rarely broken team spirit. The tough Grand Final wasn't the most open of games until Wigan opened up in the second half to subdue the battling Dragons.

Catalans narrowly lost their second Grand Final but it was another year of great progress by the French club, who are not resting on their laurels and, with an increased media presence, plan to expand their stadium. They already have the best matchday atmosphere in Super League and their dramatic semi-final win over St Helens in October was one of the most memorable events of the season.

Introduction

Jubilant Leigh players are joined by Leopards owner Derek Beaumont to celebrate the club's Challenge Cup Final win

The man who pulled off that most dramatic of finishes was Sam Tomkins who scored the late late try to take the Dragons to Old Trafford in his last ever game at the Stade Gilbert Brutus. Defeat the following Saturday wasn't the perfect way for him to take his playing bow but he will go down as one of the greats of the modern era.

As will James Roby, who at 37 years of age retired at the end of the campaign after 20 seasons as a one-club man. There was no fairytale finish either for him, after 551 St Helens' appearances, as Saints fell in Perpignan.

After their Word Cub Challenge heroics, St Helens had a mixed season that never reached the heights of the previous four Championship-winning years, although a late charge looked at times likely to bear fruit. Until that fateful night in the south of France.

The Challenge Cup final was back at Wembley and was won by Leigh Leopards in nail-biting circumstances as Lance Todd Trophy winner Lachlan Lam kicked a field goal in the historic golden point period to break Hull KR hearts.

Promoted Leigh were the story of 2023, not just for their Challenge Cup win but for the way they competed for a top-four spot throughout the whole season. Their pre-season re-branding as Leopards from Centurions was met with derision in some quarters and wasn't universally popular among the fans. But after proving themselves from start to finish under Coach of the Year Adrian Lam, that was all forgotten.

Introduction

Hull KR were another club to grow exponentially and ended the season by eliminating Leigh, after pinching fourth position from them, before their own elimination in the semi-final the week after at Wigan. New coach Willie Peters did a fine job in getting the best out of a playing squad that suffered more than its fair share of injuries.

Warrington Wolves were in sixth place, but only just after a stunning eight-match winning run at the start of the season. At times in mid-season they couldn't win a raffle and coach Daryl Powell, after two seasons that followed a similar pattern, was sacked after a humiliating 42-6 defeat at Wakefield at the end of July. Having star-signing prop Josh McGuire banned for a total of 19 matches, for 'discriminatory language', didn't help the cause.

Salford pushed the Wolves all the way but a late-season period where their brilliant spine of Brodie Croft, Andy Ackers and Ryan Brierley were all injured stunted their momentum.

Leeds Rhinos' collapse towards the end of the season, in at times humiliating fashion, left them miles off the pace and Huddersfield Giants and Hull FC disappointed too for the bulk of the season.

Castleford were left gasping for air until they beat Hull FC in round 25, after going through three coaches in a season, Lee Radford and Andy Last getting the push and Danny Ward, who guided the Tigers to safety, deciding not to stay on after the end of the season.

Below them Wakefield Trinity this year could not escape relegation after 25 seasons in Super League. Their season-long battle against the drop the year before, even though they eventually finished ten points clear of bottom club Toulouse, had seen a host of players lured to pastures new. Although one of them, David Fifita, was brought back from semi-retirement in Australia to lead a mini-mid-season revival that looked for a time would save their skins. But a round-22 defeat to the Tigers effectively sealed their fate.

Trinity will be replaced by London Broncos, who stunned Featherstone Rovers in the semi-final of the Championship play-offs before edging Toulouse in the final to earn promotion.

The historic end-of-season tour to England by Tonga couldn't have gone better for Shaun Wane's England side as they emerged with a 3-0 series win over a side made up of some top performers in the NRL. Encouragingly the young halfback pair of Wigan's Harry Smith and Hull KR's Mikey Lewis stood out on the international stage. Sadly, just after the series, Samoa turned down the chance to tour England the next autumn.

The whole year is related in the following pages. We hope you enjoy recalling the ups and downs of another compelling year of Rugby League.

TIM BUTCHER
Contributing Editor

PROVISIONAL CLUB GRADINGS AT END OF 2023

Seven Super League clubs achieved a provisional 'A' rating at the end of 2023, scoring 15 or higher out of a maximum possible 20 points and meaning they would be assured Super League status.

The gradings were decided through five categories - On-field Performance, Fandom, Finances, Stadium and Community.

		Category	Score
1	Leeds	A	17.49
2	Wigan	A	16.87
3	St Helens	A	16.78
4	Catalans	A	16.73
5	Warrington	A	15.75
6	Hull KR	A	15.52
7	Hull FC	A	15.05
8	Salford	B	13.80
9	Huddersfield	B	13.49
10	Toulouse	B	12.97
11	Wakefield	B	12.52
12	Leigh	B	12.45
13	Castleford	B	12.16
14	Bradford	B	12.02
15	Featherstone	B	10.65
16	Widnes	B	10.17
17	York	B	10.05
18	Newcastle	B	9.30
19	Barrow	B	9.18
20	Halifax	B	9.06
21	Batley	B	8.62
22	Sheffield	B	8.36
23	Doncaster	B	8.11
24	London Broncos	B	8.07
25	Oldham	C	7.39
26	Swinton	C	7.21
27	Dewsbury	C	7.10
28	Rochdale	C	7.03
29	Hunslet	C	6.94
30	Keighley	C	6.58
31	Workington	C	6.54
32	Whitehaven	C	6.27
33	Midlands	C	5.92
34	Cornwall	C	5.75
35	North Wales	C	5.07

The 28th League Express Yearbook contains the detailed story of the domestic year, the Australian season and matchfacts for all Super League, Challenge Cup games involving professional teams, Championship and League One games. Every player who has played Super League is also listed along with those players to have made their debuts this year. We have also selected five individuals who we judge to have made the biggest impact on Rugby League in 2023. There are scoring and attendance records for every club.

League Publications publishes the weekly newspaper Rugby Leaguer & Rugby League Express, as well as the monthly glossy magazine Rugby League World and the website 'totalrl.com'.

1
PERSONALITIES OF 2023

James Roby
St Helens

It will be a different St Helens after the retirement of one of the club's and the sports's greatest servants at the end of the 2023 season.

James Roby finally hung up his boots after squeezing out a 20th season as a one-club man. After 551 appearances for Saints there was no letting up on his standards on the field.

Thirty-seven year-old Roby changed his mind about retiring at the end of the 2022 season. And at the start of the 2023 campaign he inspired his team to a momentous World Club Championship win, defeating Penrith Panthers in their own backyard, 16 years after his first WCC title in 2007, an 18-14 win over Brisbane at Bolton.

Roby made his senior debut on Friday 19th March 2004 off the bench in a game against Widnes at Knowsley Road, aged 18. It's fair to say he was a scrawny looking kid but looks can be deceiving as it soon became apparent his extraordinary strength and agility would mark him out as the ideal dummy-half for the modern game.

In the early days he came off the bench, providing a perfect impact when replacing the starting Keiron Cunningham.

His career couldn't have taken a higher trajectory - 42 international caps, six Grand Final rings, four Challenge Cup winners' medals, two Harry Sunderland Trophies (2014 and 2020) and the Man of Steel award in 2007.

On Saturday 13th May 2023, Roby played his 532nd game for St Helens against Salford Red Devils and became the new all-time record holder for match appearances for the club, taking over from Kel Coslett, who set the record in 1976.

A 12-6 semi-final exit at Catalans prevented a perfect finish to an astonishing career but in November, James Roby was inducted into the St Helens Hall of Fame. It would be surprising if there were no plans to honour him with a statue beside that of Cunningham.

Bevan French
Wigan Warriors

It is very rare in the 28 years of the League Express Yearbook that a player or coach is considered as one of its top personalities in consecutive seasons.

Bevan French has forced his way into the reckoning again after netting the Steve Prescott MBE Man of Steel Award as the game's best player and finishing joint winner of the Albert Goldthorpe Medal, with Warrington's George Williams.

The Australian was ever-present for Champions Wigan Warriors this year, lighting up Super League with his silky skill set, whether playing winger, fullback or stand-off. French thrills the crowds whatever his role on the field.

His season began on the wing, where he had finished as Super League's top try-scorer with 31 in 2022, then, after six games, having nine games at fullback. After the return of Jai Field from injury in June and with Abbas Miski scoring tries for fun out wide, French was shifted to stand-off by head coach Matt Peet. The ploy worked a treat and French remained in that position for the remaining 15 games. Wigan won every league game bar one from that point, culminating in the 10-2 Grand Final win over Catalans.

French himself credits the work of the coaching staff, Tommy Leuluai, Sean O'Loughlin and Peet for making his transition a success.

French arrived at Wigan midway through the 2019 season from Parramatta Eels and starred at fullback in his first full season, helping the Warriors win the League Leaders' Shield and reach the Super League Grand Final. 2021 was for him a year marked by injury and a long-term return to Australia to be with his seriously ill mother.

But he bounced back from that setback and across his five years so far at Wigan, in three different roles, French has proved himself one of Super League's most exciting players.

Lachlan Lam
Leigh Leopards

Leigh Leopards didn't just buck the trend of promoted teams making an exit from Super League after one season - a fate they themselves experienced in 2017 and 2021 - they pushed the top clubs all the way from start to finish.

At the centre of it all was halfback Lachlan Lam, whose distribution, kicking and wicked sidestep created so many great tries, with former England winger Josh Charnley a major beneficiary.

The other major beneficiaries have been the people of Leigh, who bought readily into Leigh owner Derek Beaumont's outrageous (at least that what's most people thought at the time) re-imagining of the re-branded Centurions.

With the club providing excitement and entertainment on matchdays, the Leopards were rewarded with bumper crowds and a tangible buzz in the town. There can be little argument that Leigh's re-entry added greatly to Super League in 2023.

Without a winning team, it would have been a more difficult job. And that winning formula didn't happen by chance. Former Wigan coach Adrian Lam, along with Head of Rugby Chris Chester, built a team in Leigh's Championship-winning year that could compete with the best.

The coach's son was signed in mid-July of 2022 and he quickly formed a devastating spine with Kumuls hooker Edwin Ipape and ball-playing prop John Asiata. That spine continued to develop into one of the best in Super League.

Lam was ever present in 2023 and although he will one day surely return to the NRL, in August he signed a contract extension until the end of 2025.

Having come through the Sydney Roosters junior teams, representing the Australian Schoolboys in 2016 and playing junior State of Origin, Lam continues to star for Papua New Guinea.

Lam's biggest moment in 2023 was his golden-point field goal at Wembley and his selection as winner of the Lance Todd Trophy. A first Challenge Cup win since 1971 was just reward for a club determined to stay at the top table.

Mikey Lewis
Hull KR

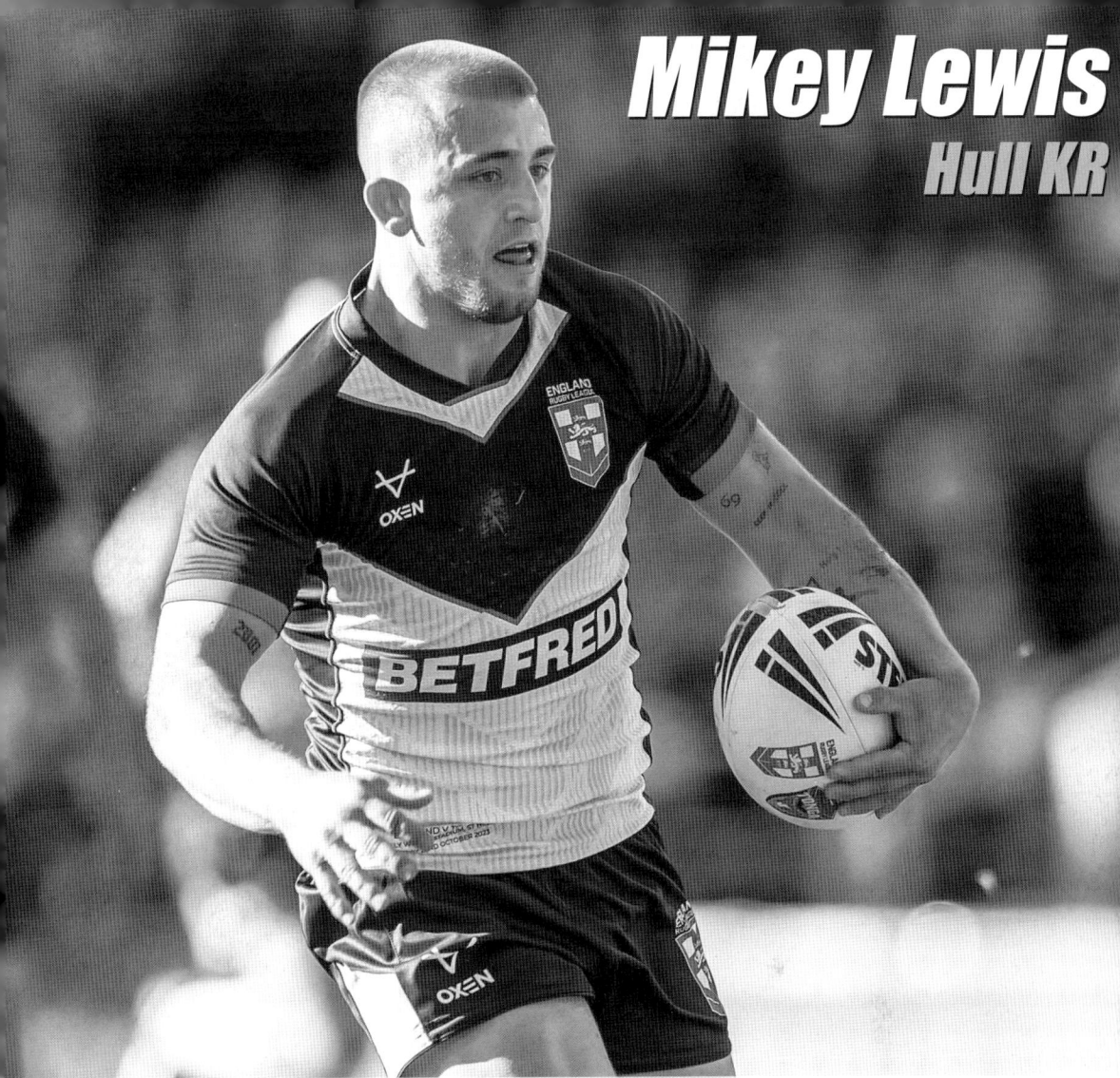

When Tonga went into the first match of their historic tour of England it was thought they might be taken by surprise by England's new halfback Mikey Lewis.

The 22-year-old was selected in the absence of captain George Williams, who missed the first two games through suspension.

Lewis didn't let England coach Shaun Wane or his country down. He stunned the powerful Tongans, scoring a try and setting up another with two superb pieces of individual play in the first half of an eventual 22-18 win.

His first highlight on the international stage set the opening try of the series in motion with a step inside that beat Tyson Frizell and break clean through. He rounded fullback Will Hopoate and was only finally tackled close to the try-line by covering right winger Starford Toa. The ball was moved swiftly left, with Toby King one of several players queuing up to score.

Then, after Tonga had fought back into the lead, Lewis received the ball on the right with winger Toluta'u Koula rapidly advancing on him from the wing. Lewis dummied him and then stepped around Moses Suli to clear the path to his first international try.

His performance in the second Test was good enough for some pundits, unsuccessfully, to call for him the retain his spot when Williams was cleared to play in the third Test.

Lewis has played a major part of Hull KR's rise, under coach Willie Peters, in 2023, making 31 appearances, helping them reach the Challenge Cup Final and coming to within 80 minutes of the Super League Grand Final. It was no surprise when in November the club secured a prize asset as he signed a new deal until the end of the 2028 season.

Combative and fearless with electrifying pace of the mark combined with a dangerous short kicking game, at the tender age of 22 Mikey Lewis has a stellar future.

Mike Eccles
London Broncos

London Broncos won promotion to Super League just a year after they were on the brink of relegation to League One, long-time strength and fitness coach Mike Eccles, recently appointed Director of Rugby, credited with guiding them to safety.

The year 2023 looked like being another season of struggle as the Broncos won only one of their first five games. But it ended with the Broncos almost unbeatable - losing only one more league game after a mid-June hammering at Featherstone.

Eccles rebuilt the Broncos with the help of the Academy he had done so much to develop and promotion was eventually won with a large core of southern, homegrown players. And the signings of former New Zealand international Dean Whare and ex-NRL star Corey Norman proved pivotal, Eccles moving smartly to sign the duo at the conclusion of the French domestic season.

Finishing fifth in the table meant there would be no home advantage in the play-offs but thumping wins at Sheffield and then previously dominant Featherstone secured their place in the Play-off Final at Toulouse. In that, a comeback from 14-4 for an 18-14 win stunned the French side. And just about everybody else.

At the end-of-season awards night, Eccles was named Championship Coach of the Year, and he was joined on the stage by utility Dean Parata, named joint Championship Player of the Year and Maidstone-born hooker Bill Leyland, the Young Player of the Year.

Within days of the Broncos being promoted, IMG revealed its provisional club gradings which at the end of the 2024 season was to determine who would play in Super League in 2025. Only the top 12 would make the cut. Broncos were ranked 24th.

It was typical of Eccles that there was disappointment at the club but a determination to improve the club's rating in 2024.

Eccles and the Broncos face a huge test. The club is now settled into its new Super League-standard stadium in Wimbledon but will operate with a mix of part-time and full-time players in their squad.

2
THE 2023 SEASON

DECEMBER 2022
A different world

The 2022 season came to a magnificent climax with the triple header of World Cup finals in mid-November finally bringing its curtain down.

The tournament finished with impressive TV audience figures, while falling short of its target for ticket sales. Tournament organisers set an ambitious aim of selling 750,000 tickets for the 61 matches across three tournaments. However, the final cumulative attendance for the World Cup was 473,851.

The organisers came under some criticism for the over-pricing of match tickets, although there was the mitigation of a cost of living crisis made worse by the invasion of Ukraine by Russia in February of 2022, the tournament being delayed by a year because of the global Covid-19 epidemic.

The men's tournament attracted aggregate crowds of 423,689, the second-highest in history but short of the 458,483 achieved when the World Cup was last played in England in 2013.

A further 30,698 people watched standalone women's fixtures, including a northern hemisphere-record crowd of 8,621 for the opening games, with many more watching women's games as part of double headers.

And the wheelchair tournament attracted an aggregate attendance of 19,464, including a world record figure of 4,526 for England's win in the final.

The numbers were more encouraging for TV audiences, with a cumulative match average audience of 29.24 million people tuning in to the BBC's coverage domestically across network and digital channels.

The biggest audience was for the men's semi-final between England and Samoa, watched by a combined peak audience of 2.8 million, a 23 per cent audience share, while England women's semi-final defeat to New Zealand attracted a combined peak of 1.4 million.

The wheelchair final was watched by a combined peak audience of 1.3 million people, while nearly a million viewers tuned in to the women's final and almost two million for the men's decider.

Organisers reported that 46 per cent of the UK viewership was based south of the Midlands, outside of the traditional Rugby League heartlands, with a further 43 per cent based in the north and the remaining share from Wales, Scotland and Northern Ireland.

'Our ambition for Rugby League World Cup 2021 was to make the tournament the biggest, best and most inclusive World Cup in the sport's 127-year history, and I think we've achieved that and more,' said RLWC2021 Chief Executive Jon Dutton.

'We overcame huge obstacles to make it happen, including the pandemic and the subsequent postponement but these numbers clearly show that the tournament was worth waiting for.

'I hope we have demonstrated the appetite for all three disciplines and laid a platform for international Rugby League to build on in the future with France 2025 and beyond.'

Ralph Rimmer left his position as RFL Chief Executive on New Year's Eve. During his tenure the RFL had ridden the Covid-19 crisis and was the first governing body to have negotiated financial support from the UK Government that saved many clubs. Rimmer also cited relocating the RFL from Media City and Red Hall to its new home on the Etihad Campus in Manchester; driving the 12-year strategic partnership with IMG; and 'working daily with Jon Dutton and his fantastic RLWC team to cope with the postponement and then the successful delivery, twelve months later, of the most inclusive World Cup ever in men's, women's and wheelchair tournaments.'

December 2022

A costly split between the RFL and Super League Europe also took place during Rimmer's tenure but its reversal was already underway. Rhodri Jones was appointed Managing Director of Rugby League Commercial (RLC), the new body charged with boosting Rugby League's income from sponsorship and other sources. IMG would have a seat on RLC and were expected to be a driving force, with a new TV contract to be negotiated from 2024 onwards.

Outgoing RFL President Clare Balding backed her successor Sir Lindsay Hoyle to do a great job. Balding was to officially hand over the ceremonial chains to Hoyle, the Speaker of the House of Commons and MP for Chorley, at the President's Ball in Leeds in January. The popular TV broadcaster took on the role in June 2020, with her term set to run for two years, but she was later granted a six-month extension to allow her to oversee the delayed World Cup. 'It has genuinely been the greatest honour of my life', she said.

December saw the confirmation that two of Super League's brightest young stars had decided to chance their arm in the National Rugby League (NRL) in Australia as Wigan's Kai Pearce-Paul and Huddersfield's Will Pryce both signed for Newcastle Knights from the end of the 2023 season.

A financial gulf between the hemispheres had been further widened by an increase in the NRL salary cap to a new record high. While Super League clubs could spend only £2.1 million on their squads (plus marquee players and other dispensations), NRL sides would have AU$12.1 million (£6.8m) to each spend on player salaries, an increase of 25 per cent on 2022, while there was a similar increase in the cap for top 30 players, to AU$11.45 million. The minimum salary for all players in an NRL club's top 30 squad was now AU$120,000 (£67,000), not far off the average salary for a Super League club's top 25 players (£84,000).

At the end of the month, England forward John Bateman finally decided he would leave Wigan immediately for a second stint in the NRL, this time with Wests Tigers, on a four-year contract. The Warriors were to receive a 'significant' transfer fee for the 29-year-old for a second time, though the club made its displeasure clear in a statement released following the news.

Interest from Down Under in England's best women's stars also grew following a 153 per cent increase in the NRLW salary cap. York Valkyrie second-rower Hollie Dodd, Leeds Rhinos fullback Fran Goldthorp and teammate Georgie Roche all made moves down under.

The Rhinos announced that from 2023 they would be making match payments to their women players and they were followed by York early in the new year.

In the men's Super League, promoted Leigh announced a controversial rebrand. Their previous Centurions identity - carried since 1995 - was replaced by Leopards, with a new club badge and playing shirt.

Some supporters' complaints over the radical alteration to the club's kit brought a re-think and a partial return to cherry and white. The grey leopard-skin imprint on the white shirt would remain but, rather than black, the shorts would be red.

An impressive list of signings was announced by Leigh in Gareth O'Brien (Castleford), Tom Briscoe and Zak Hardaker (both Leeds) and Ricky Leutele (Huddersfield), all on two-year contracts. Oliver Holmes, Jack Hughes, Rob Mulhern, Matt Davis and Jacob Gannon also joined from Warrington on two-year deals. Nathan Wilde signed from Newcastle Thunder on a one-year contract.

Adam Sidlow (Salford Red Devils), Luis Roberts (Leeds), Krisnan Inu (retired), Caleb Aekins (released), Sam Stone (Salford), Mark Ioane (Keighley Cougars), Ata Hingano (York), Kieran Dixon (Widnes) and Jy Hitchcox (retired) all left. And they were followed in December by Nene Macdonald, who signed for Leeds and Blake Ferguson, who was released on compassionate grounds to return to Australia.

Inu returned to Salford Red Devils in a coaching capacity as the 35-year-old called time on his 16-year playing career after helping Leigh to promotion. He had previously spent three seasons with the Red Devils, playing a role in their run to the Super League Grand Final in 2019 before helping them reach the Challenge Cup Final the following season.

Backrower Stone joined him along with former loanee from Featherstone Ben Hellewell, while former New Zealand international forward Elijah Taylor signed for Championship favourites Rovers.

Tim Lafai, a star of World Cup runners up Samoa, after a late call-up, extended his Red Devils contract by two years to the end of the 2025 season.

December 2022

After a year of uncertainty, Red Devils Chairman Paul King was optimistic that the proposal by Salford City Council to buy out Peel Holdings and gain complete ownership of the AJ Bell Stadium would help the club maintain its place among the elite of Rugby League. The Council currently had a 50 per cent share in the Red Devils' home with Peel Holdings and earlier in 2022 it had looked likely that the stadium would be sold to a joint venture between current co-tenants Sale Sharks rugby union and soccer club Salford City. The proposed deal would have seen the Red Devils swapping home grounds with the football club and moving to their Moor Lane home.

Warrington Wolves, on the back of a nightmare season, saw former England star Gareth Widdop leave for Castleford Tigers and promptly signed Josh Drinkwater from Catalans. And they sent out a message to NRL clubs that other halfback George Williams was not available after his fine showing for England in the World Cup. Former winger Matty Russell returned on a one-year contract.

Prolific Championship winger Theerapol 'Tee' Ritson swapped Championship side Barrow Raiders for Super League champions St Helens on a season-long loan deal, which included an option for Saints to make the move permanent at the end of the 2023 campaign. The Thailand international, who had amassed 100 tries in his career, including 55 in 46 outings across the previous two years with Barrow, was looking to fill the void left by rugby union-bound Regan Grace.

Catalans Dragons' first day of pre-season training at the end of November was a lonely affair with only a handful of players available following 12 departures from the 2002 squad and the absence of 17 internationals due to World Cup duty.

The Dragons' 13 players in the French national team were to return to the training group on December 5th and those still on duty with England (Sam Tomkins, Mike McMeeken and Michael McIlorum) wouldn't rejoin until the new year. Prop forward Romain Navarrete was an early starter after re-signing on a two-year deal.

Catalans also confirmed the signing of Sydney Roosters' 25-year-old utility back Adam Keighran on a one-year contract.

Wakefield Trinity, in relegation danger for most of 2022 before climbing to an eventual finishing position of tenth, ten points above bottom side Toulouse, had lost a string of players, including skipper Jacob Miller to neighbours Castleford, second-rower James Batchelor to Hull KR and winger Tom Johnstone to Catalans.

The club were in the midst of redeveloping their Belle Vue stadium and had a new unproven coaching team of Mark Applegarth and assistant James Ford. They did manage a 38-20 win over Leeds in the Boxing Day Wetherby Whaler Challenge, with new signings, prop Renouf Atoni from Sydney Roosters and halfback Morgan Smith from Featherstone, impressing. Former New Zealand international second-rower Kevin Proctor and Catalans centre Samisoni Langi were their other signings.

St Helens' England star Jack Welsby was voted Super League Player of the Year by League Express readers. Welsby beat runner-up Brodie Croft of Salford and Wigan pair Jai Field and Bevan French, who came third and fourth respectively, with the previous year's winner Sam Tomkins in fifth place. Welsby was also voted the Super League Young Player of the Year by a larger margin.

Inspirational duo Rob Burrow and Kevin Sinfield were honoured with awards at the end-of-year BBC's Sports Personality of the Year show. Burrow won the Helen Rollason Award, which since 1999 had been awarded for 'outstanding achievement in the face of adversity', while Sinfield received a special BBC award.

Former Leeds Rhinos and England star Burrow had helped raise awareness of motor neurone disease (MND) since being diagnosed in 2019, while his old teammate Sinfield had raised more than £7 million in the past three years for causes related to the disease through a series of fundraising challenges. His latest saw him run seven ultra-marathons in seven days, finishing at Old Trafford at half-time of the men's World Cup final.

The first step towards the construction of the Rob Burrow Centre for Motor Neurone Disease (MND) in Leeds had begun.

---

* The League One (third tier) schedule for 2023 was left in disarray by the withdrawal of West Wales Raiders from the competition five weeks after the publication of fixtures.

JANUARY
Raising awareness

Rugby League gained both civic and royal recognition in the first month of 2023.

Leeds City Council awarded its highest honour to Rob Burrow and Kevin Sinfield, giving both the former Leeds Rhinos stars the freedom of the city 'in recognition of their heroic campaigning and fundraising for all those affected by motor neurone disease (MND).'

The remarkable fundraising feats of Sinfield was the subject of a BBC documentary in early February. His support for Burrow inspired the nation.

On the 20th of the month, the Princess of Wales praised the England Wheelchair team for creating 'an incredible legacy' through their World Cup win. The squad attended a reception hosted by the Patron of the Rugby Football League in the Garden Room at Hampton Court.

There was less good news from France where relegated Toulouse Olympique were putting together a financial rescue package following significant losses incurred during their first-ever season in Super League. Reports in the French media suggested the club ran up a half-million euro deficit in 2022, which needed to be repaid by the end of March.

Long-time club President Bernard Sarrazain, who in 2022 announced that he was prepared to step down and hand the club to new owners, pledged to balance the books before he left.

Further east, Catalans Dragons were fined £25,000 - half suspended until the end of the 2023 campaign - following the behaviour of fans at their play-off defeat to Leeds the previous September. The Perpignan club was warned that any supporter misbehaviour in 2023 would result in two matches being played behind closed doors at Stade Gilbert Brutus.

Catalans acknowledged that their supporters threw items onto the pitch during the Leeds fixture, with the touch judges forced to take evasive action, that further objects were thrown at the officials as they left the field after the match and that there was 'a further aggressive incident requiring a response from security staff as the officials left the stadium'.

The Dragons pledged to launch an education campaign underlining the importance of improving spectator behaviour, specifically relating to match officials, after receiving several punishments in recent seasons for incidents of fan misbehaviour or unacceptable criticism of match officials.

The RFL's match officials department was under the temporary control of its senior coach Dave Elliott after Steve Ganson was stood down as the governing body conducted an 'internal review'.

Former Super League referee Ganson was head of match officials, having been involved with the department since hanging up his whistle in 2013 to become match officials coach and technical director. He had been in his current role for seven years.

Dragons winger Fouad Yaha's pre-season preparations were wrecked after he dislocated his shoulder at training and needed surgery. Other injury concerns were Sam Tomkins (knee and Tyrone May (dislocated hip). Mike McMeeken suffered a wrist injury in the first game for England against Samoa and he continued through the World Cup with it, but he needed surgery.

Catalans captain Ben Garcia recovered from a serious arm infection sustained in the World Cup. The French international skipper said he was pleased with the 2023 squad which included new signings Sio Siua Taukeiaho, Tom Johnstone, Romain Navarrete, Adam Keighran and Manu Ma'u.

January

Meanwhile Leigh Leopards continued their squad building with the signings of Wigan's Umlya Hanley and former Leeds prop Ava Seumanufagai

A number of testimonial games were played, with St Helens holding off an eager Widnes Vikings by 16-12 in Mark Percival's beneficiary while Sean Long-coached Featherstone Rovers' 28-0 demolition of Hull Kingston Rovers at the Millennium Stadium, in Craig Hall's testimonial, raised a few eyebrows.

Wakefield winger Lewis Murphy, named as League Express's Rookie of 2022, was the latest young star planning a move to the NRL, signing a two-year deal from the end of 2023 with Sydney Roosters.

The RFL paid tribute to its former Secretary, Chief Executive and President David Oxley CBE, who died at the age of 85. Oxley was widely credited with lifting the sport from a huge decline in the 1970s. The former Chief Executive and Chairman of BARLA Maurice Oldroyd also died in the same month.

The RFL's clampdown on a range of offences in 2022, particularly involving contact with the head and dangerous play, had drawn criticism from many sections of the game, with a glut of lengthy player suspensions and countless sin-binnings marring the competition.

In 2023 the potential length of suspension would be reduced for each grade of offence. Grade C charges would carry a suspension range of one-to-two matches instead of two-to-three, Grade D would be two-to-three, instead of three-to-five, and Grade E would be three-to-five instead of four-to-eight. For the most serious Grade F charges, the suspension range would begin at six matches, instead of eight, as in 2022.

Fines were to have a greater role, including being the only punishment available for a Grade A offence and a potential option, along with a one-match ban, for a Grade B offence.

A player's previous record would continue to be considered but players would now need three offences in the past 24 months instead of only two to receive the top-end punishment.

The controversial 'frivolous appeal' measure, whereby bans could be increased, would remain in place.

Leeds forward James Donaldson escaped a ban for his Boxing Day sin-binning against Wakefield. The 31-year-old received an early yellow card from referee Ben Thaler for a challenge on Trinity centre Oliver Pratt but rather than a suspension for his dangerous throw, was handed a £250 fine.

The introduction of an 18th player was one of three changes to the laws approved on the eve of the 2023 season. A fifth interchange could be brought on if three of the team's players had failed a head injury assessment. The system was used for the first time during the World Cup.

The Laws Committee also reinforced the protocols around the green card, which was introduced in 2022 to deter time wasting and gamesmanship. If the referee called time off for a player to receive medical treatment, the player had to leave the field for two minutes of the game before re-joining.

The final law change saw penalties awarded at scrums no longer being differential and could now be kicked for goal.

The RFL's Clinical Advisory Group also increased to twelve days, from eleven, the minimum amount of time a player had to sit out following a head injury.

FEBRUARY
On top of the world

World Club Challenge

February of 2023 will live long in the memory of British sports fans as Super League champions St Helens emulated the feat of Wigan in 1994 by winning the World Club Challenge on Australian soil.

They did it in the most dramatic of circumstances as halfback Lewis Dodd's 83rd-minute field goal clinched a fully deserved victory over back-to-back NRL champions Penrith Panthers in golden-point extra time.

A week before, St Helens had beaten an understrength St George Illawarra side by 30-18 and the Australian pundits gave them no chance in the big game. Neither did the bookies who had them at 7/1 to win.

Officials delayed the kick-off by 50 minutes to avoid the 37-degree daytime heat and sporadic torrential thunderstorms produced slippery conditions.

James Roby uncorked a vintage performance against a near-full-strength Panthers side, only missing injured duo Liam Martin and Dylan Edwards, with Joe Batchelor out for Saints after picking up an ankle injury the week before and Tommy Makinson sidelined by a head injury after 20 minutes.

Jack Welsby shone brilliantly in the opening 30 minutes, scoring a try after supporting a Curtis Sironen break from deep before setting up another for the barnstorming Konrad Hurrell. Playing fullback, Welsby made a string of try-saving tackles, including an amazing effort to turn Nathan Cleary on his back as he slid over the line.

An early second-half penalty from Mark Percival made it 12-0 but it wasn't long before Cleary put in a perfect kick to the left corner for Izack Tago to ground.

Saints gallantly protected their six-point lead and, running to the end where the travelling 800-strong Saints contingent was congregated, both Jonny Lomax and Dodd sprayed field-goal attempts that would have sealed the win inside 80 minutes.

For the second effort, referee Ashley Klein penalised St Helens for illegally blocking Penrith defenders during Dodd's shot, piggybacking the hosts up the field.

Stephen Crichton then unleashed a high ball that Welsby cruelly spilled into the path of Lindsay Smith, who sent Brian To'o away for a last-gasp four-pointer.

Needing a successful conversion to square things at 12-all, Cleary nailed his effort from

WORLD CLUB CHALLENGE

Saturday 18th February 2023

PENRITH PANTHERS 12 ST HELENS 13
(after golden point extra-time)

PANTHERS: 1 Stephen Crichton; 2 Taylan May; 3 Izack Tago; 4 Sunia Turuva; 5 Brian To'o; 6 Jarome Luai; 7 Nathan Cleary (C); 8 Moses Leota; 9 Mitch Kenny; 10 James Fisher-Harris; 11 Luke Garner; 12 Zac Hosking; 13 Isaah Yeo. Subs (all used): 14 Jack Cogger; 15 Matt Eisenhuth; 16 Spencer Leniu; 17 Jaeman Salmon; 18 Lindsay Smith.
Tries: Tago (52), To'o (79); **Goals:** Cleary 2/2.
SAINTS: 1 Jack Welsby; 2 Tommy Makinson; 4 Mark Percival; 23 Konrad Hurrell; 3 Will Hopoate; 6 Jonny Lomax; 7 Lewis Dodd; 8 Alex Walmsley; 9 James Roby (C); 10 Matty Lees; 11 Sione Mata'utia; 16 Curtis Sironen; 13 Morgan Knowles. Subs (all used): 14 Joey Lussick; 15 Louie McCarthy-Scarsbrook; 17 Agnatius Paasi; 19 James Bell; 18 Jake Wingfield.
Tries: Welsby (9), Hurrell (16); **Goals:** Makinson 1/2, Percival 1/1; **Field goal:** Dodd (83).
Rugby Leaguer & League Express Men of the Match:
Panthers: Nathan Cleary; *Saints:* Jack Welsby.
Penalty count: 6-3; **Half-time:** 0-10; **Referee:** Ashley Klein; **Attendance:** 13,873 (at BlueBet Stadium).

(Game played with five substitutes for both sides, to aid player welfare)

February

St Helens celebrate their World Club Challenge victory against Penrith Panthers

nine metres inside the right touchline.

Crichton was much less cool in extra time, spilling the ball under a heavy Hurrell tackle and gifting the Super League champions prime field position. An Alex Walmsley charge put Saints on the front foot and Dodd did the rest, booting one of the most precious points in St Helens' century-and-a-half history.

It was a superb all-round performance from a team rated as the best of the summer era.

Round 1

St Helens went into Super League XXVIII, unsurprisingly on the back of four consecutive titles, as 2/1 favourites, though their involvement down under meant their round-one game with Huddersfield had to be postponed.

Warrington, who had finished eleventh five months before, opened the season as joint 8/1 third favourites, along with 2022 runners-up Leeds, who just happened to be their round-one opponents at the Halliwell Jones Stadium.

It was all over by half-time as the re-moulded Wolves led 30-0 thanks to tries from Matt Dufty, Daryl Clark, Josh Thewlis, Danny Walker and new face Sam Kasiano; and 42-10 by the close of play.

Warrington had experienced a far from perfect build-up. They lost two newly signed props after their warm-up win over Leigh, as Gil Dudson suffered a hand injury and Australian Josh McGuire was banned for a whopping seven games. McGuire was sent off at the end of the game after a melee and the RFL tribunal found him guilty of 'verbal abuse based on disability'.

February

But their other new signings, Paul Vaughan and Kasiano in the pack and Josh Drinkwater at halfback, made a huge difference. Vaughan, alongside James Harrison, was outstanding in the middle from the very start as Leeds were well and truly put on the back foot. Drinkwater had been brought in to control the game and give George Williams the freedom to create. The early signs were positive.

The Rhinos had four debutants in wingers Luis Roberts and Derrell Olpherts and props Sam Lisone and Justin Sangaré, the Toulouse product impressing and getting a try for his efforts, Olpherts scoring Leeds' other. Harrison and Greg Minikin tries kept the Rhinos at a safe distance.

Promoted Leigh, now the Leopards, pulled out the stops to attract a crowd of over eight-and-a-half thousand for their Friday night bow against 2022 surprise packets Salford.

The pre-match entertainment brought a 40-minute set from indie band Scouting for Girls, a spectacular pyro show and a fireworks display that announced Leigh's return to Super League in some style. But the Leopards couldn't quite top the night off as the Red Devils emerged with a 20-10 win.

There was next to nothing in the contest for the most part but two periods were crucial - before half-time, when an early Leigh lead became a 10-4 deficit as the exertions of the first half told in a slack final few minutes and, following Red Devils halfback Marc Sneyd's sin-binning in the second half when Leigh could only find a penalty try in response.

The Leopards went set for set for the first 20 minutes - indeed, for most of the game - and opened the scoring immediately after Championship Player of the Year Edwin Ipape entered the action. His first good run led to a try on the next play, with Lachlan Lam passing wide for the energetic Josh Charnley to register the Leopards' first ever points in their new identity.

Only in the final eight minutes of the first half were Leigh really on the back foot as Salford had a succession of sets and made them count, firstly through Kallum Watkins running a great line to score off Brodie Croft. More pressure on the home line finished with Andy Ackers dummying and darting over and, with Sneyd converting both, the Red Devils suddenly led 12-4 going into the break.

That became 18-4, ten minutes into the second half as Croft sliced through the middle of the defence and Ryan Brierley was in support to touch down.

Brierley had to be just as sharp in defence to preserve the Salford lead and he made two brilliant try-saving tackles on Charnley and Lam. After the first, Sneyd held down too long and was shown a yellow card and, from the second, Watkins blocked Jack Hughes from running onto Gareth O'Brien's grubber and Leigh were awarded a penalty try.

With Zak Hardaker's conversion, Leigh trailed by eight points with a quarter of the game still to go. But despite attacking opportunities against both twelve and 13 men, they couldn't find another way through.

Instead the victors had the final word, a Tom Amone tip tackle allowing Sneyd to add two more points at the very end, in front of Salford's jubilant travelling support, with Amone being sin-binned. He escaped a ban, as did Jack Hughes. Both were fined for dangerous contact.

Leigh had eight players on debut in Hardaker, Ricky Leutele, Tom Briscoe, Gareth O'Brien, Matt Davis, Robbie Mulhern, Oliver Holmes and Hughes, while Salford debuted Oliver Partington and Sam Stone.

The Red Devils had been busy tying up key players on long-term contracts, Joe Burgess and Jack Ormondroyd for three years, Ackers four and Croft until the end of 2030.

On the same night 10/1 fifth favourites Catalans came away from Wakefield with a 38-24 win.

The Dragons were far from full strength, without new signing Sio Siua Taukeiaho, Sam Tomkins, Mike McMeeken and Mitchell Pearce through injury as Steve McNamara went with a new halfback pairing of César Rougé and another signing from Sydney, Adam Keighran. There was a question mark over French international Rougé but the 20-year-old kicked superbly as well as scoring an interception try on the full-time hooter. Keighran was all class in an excellent debut.

Romain Navarrete and Manu Ma'u also made debuts but it was former Trinity winger Tom Johnstone who will most remember his, finishing with three trademark tries.

February

Hull KRs Shaun Kenny-Dowall tackled by Wigan's Liam Farrell and Toby King

Samisoni Langi in the centres, Kevin Proctor, Morgan Smith and Renouf Atoni all made their debuts for Trinity, huge favourites to be relegated, who were missing injured Kelepi Tanginoa and Jordan Crowther.

It was an even game until Tom Davies' second try 12 minutes from time created a 14-point lead. Fouad Yaha, the club's all-time leading try scorer, was out long term after dislocating his right shoulder during pre-season training.

Wakefield's Belle Vue ground was undergoing reconstruction with half the ground closed off, meaning a reduced capacity.

McNamara reported a rash of grazed elbows and knees within his squad following the win on the brand new hybrid 4G playing surface.

Channel 4 began their coverage on the Saturday afternoon with a bumper crowd enjoying a home victory for Hull KR as they overcame Wigan 27-18.

Rovers captain Shaun Kenny-Dowall scored his first Super League hat-trick of tries, two from the left wing after Ryan Hall suffered a rib injury.

New coach Willie Peters gave debuts to Tom Opacic, Sauaso Sue, Rhys Kennedy and James Batchelor and they all contributed well, especially Batchelor when he moved to left centre in the second half. Matt Peet's Wigan had two new centres in Jake Wardle and Toby King

Rovers got off to a flier when 35-year-old Hall went in at the corner after Kenny-Dowall took Jordan Abdull's kick and kept the ball alive via the excellent Lachlan Coote.

But Wigan stormed back with three tries in 13 minutes, as Liam Marshall went in at the left corner after catching Harry Smith's smart chip on the full, followed by two more, set up by the other halfback, Cade Cust.

Cust's kick was knocked down by Toby King for Jai Field to score in the right corner, then he set up the third try with a clever grubber for Kai Pearce-Paul on 22 minutes.

But Smith was off target with all three kicks, to leave Rovers still in touch at only 12-6 down. And the hosts turned things round.

Kenny-Dowall forced his way over just past the half hour near the left touchline, Coote

February

converted and Abdull's one-pointer on the half-time hooter got Rovers' noses in front at 13-12.

Hall did not reappear after the break as Kane Linnett burrowed over from dummy-half. Although Coote missed that one, he earned his side a seven-point cushion after Wigan were penalised for a late tackle on Mikey Lewis. Morgan Smithies was yellow-carded for a shoulder charge and Rovers capitalised as Batchelor's good hands sent in Kenny-Dowall.

Cust sent Marshall down the left for Wardle to score on his debut, this time Smith landing the kick from out wide. But, having reduced the gap to 23-18, Kenny-Dowall's third try, after Batchelor had stolen the ball one on one from Jai Field, secured the two points for the Robins.

A 15,000-plus crowd witnessed a remarkable game on the Sunday afternoon at the MKM Stadium. Hull FC led 32-6 until the hour mark but were hanging on for dear life in the last four minutes as Castleford fought back to 32-30, Hull's desperation in defence in the final five minutes doing just enough to earn the result.

New NRL arrivals from Newcastle Knights, Tex Hoy and Jake Clifford stood out through Hull's period of dominance, picking the Tigers edges to pieces, while Brad Dwyer proved dangerous through the middle as the Airlie Birds played an eye-catching brand of rugby.

Hull took the lead early with a Darnell McIntosh try in the right corner after a great looping pass over the top from Hoy. The home side doubled their advantage on the next set, with dummy-half Dwyer splitting the Tigers' defence to send fellow debutant Liam Sutcliffe over to score.

Castleford had no answer to the early onslaught, with McIntosh showing some soccer skills to control a Ben McNamara pass and grab his second after 15 minutes.

The Tigers had to be the next to score and they did so through former Hull man Bureta Faraimo, who collected a pass out wide to score after good build-up play from Gareth Widdop. But Hull quickly hit their straps again, adding two quickfire Adam Swift tries down the left, both with Hoy playing a key role in set plays from the scrum, to give the hosts a 20-point lead at half time.

Despite an enterprising start to the second half for Castleford, it was Hull who scored first after the break, with Danny Houghton reaching the line after McNamara had pounced on a wayward McIntosh kick to put Hull in total control.

However, it was there the scoring ended for the Airlie Birds as the Tigers, sporting an impressive new halves pairing in Jacob Miller and Widdop, came alive to come roaring back into the game.

Miller hit Kenny Edwards with a great pass to score untouched before the halfback turned scorer on debut, collecting a pass from Jake Mamo to race away from long range.

The Tigers were on a roll and unpicked Hull again on the right, with Faraimo charging over out wide to make it an eight-point game. And when Mamo pin-balled through Black and White shirts to score next to the posts with five minutes to play it sent the tension into overdrive.

Hull saved their best defensive effort until the final play, however, filling the field with players to eventually force an error from Castleford to ensure they claimed the win.

The Tigers' build-up had been overshadowed by scandal after an online video emerged showing Joe Westerman involved in a sex act. The former England international was issued a 'substantial fine' by the club and issued an apology after the video made national headlines. Castleford also required the forward to undertake community service 'to educate young people on the effects of alcohol... (and) the dangers of social media when in the public eye'.

Round 2

Hull KR made it back-to-back wins for a perfect start to the new season under new coach Willie Peters with a hard-earned 24-10 success at Salford.

In the Thursday-night TV game, the Robins made clear that their opening-round win over Wigan was no fluke when they came back from an early 4-0 deficit as the Red Devils demonstrated their attacking flair, though they couldn't add one single point to their advantage before half-time.

February

Hull FC's Cameron Scott dives past Leeds' Ash Handley and Derrell Olpherts to score

Rovers halfback Jordan Abdull had a hand in all four of their second-half tries. His left-footed kicks led to scores by Ethan Ryan, Frankie Halton and Sam Wood, who had earlier touched down from Abdull's cut-out pass. The win was all the more impressive because the Robins were without four players who helped down Wigan - fullback Lachlan Coote (hamstring), winger Ryan Hall (ribs) and forwards Rhys Kennedy (concussion) and Matty Storton (toe).

Wood scored two vital tries as he deputised for Hall, while stand-in fullback Will Dagger made a telling contribution with four conversions from as many attempts

Salford coach Paul Rowley was left to reflect on a first half in which his side failed to convert territorial superiority into more than a solitary try from Ken Sio. Once they fell behind at the start of the second half, they struggled to create chances and finished well beaten.

Hull KR were second behind Warrington on points difference by the end of the round.

On the Friday night the Wolves built a lead at Huddersfield and then defended like demons to emerge 26-16 winners. They were under pressure for much of the first half but ended it 8-0 up, thanks to an early converted Peter Mata'utia try and an 18th minute Stefan Ratchford penalty. And when the outstanding James Harrison scored little more than a minute after the restart Warrington were well on their way.

Matty Ashton's spectacular double settled any nerves when the Giants belatedly rallied.

Huddersfield, whose round one game with St Helens had been postponed to accommodate the World Club Challenge, had two debutants in centres Kevin Naiqama and Esan Marsters, both among their better performers. But it was an unsatisfactory way for their wingers to mark impressive milestones - Jermaine McGillvary's 300th Giants match, and Leroy Cudjoe's 350th career appearance.

After Harrison's try, Huddersfield finally found a way through when Joe Greenwood crashed onto a short ball and Will Pryce made it 14-6, as it remained beyond the hour mark with the game still in the balance.

That was until the intervention of Ashton. First, he sped away down his left flank after Ratchford set him free, dummying Lolohea to complete a fine finish, before showing his pace over the full length of the field after intercepting a Lolohea pass.

February

Ratchford converted both for a 20-point lead, although Warrington's efforts told in a tired final five minutes which saw Pryce and Naiqama cut through their defence for consolation tries.

Hull FC also remained 100 per cent after the Friday TV game as they imposed a second straight loss on Leeds, though they had another close scrape in a 22-18 win at Headingley, prop Scott Taylor spinning over for the clinching try six minutes from time.

The Rhinos were essentially the architects of their own downfall, especially in the second half when they converted only two of six gilt-edged chances with poor final selections and then not being able to defend their own line in the closing stages on the back of an error.

Hull were more direct and decisive when they carved out opportunities, as shown by Adam Swift's fine try just after the break, whereas long-range breaks by Nene Macdonald - who was outstanding on debut - Cameron Smith and Ash Handley all came to nothing.

Hull's Chris Satae made a significant impact on both his introductions from the bench and even though there was an overall lack of fluency, the early spine link between Jake Clifford and Tex Hoy looked promising, centre Cameron Scott the stand out.

Catalans also made it four points from four on the Saturday but they had an almighty battle with Leigh Leopards in cold, grey Perpignan before escaping with a 14-6 win.

Missing influential hooker Edwin Ipape and second-rower Oliver Holmes, and suffering a blow when Jack Hughes picked up an injury in the warm-up, Leigh fell just short.

Coach Steve McNamara said the Dragons had had the 'worst week ever' as they prepared for the match, with seven players needing antibiotics to recover from infections caused by wounds sustained in the previous round at Wakefield, Trinity's new hybrid pitch coming under fire.

The late withdrawal of Matt Whitley (shoulder) and Adam Keighran (calf) ripped up McNamara's game-plan before kick-off, although the decision to play Sam Tomkins at scrum-half on his return from a knee injury was a masterstroke and he, at the side of youngster César Rougé, was the difference between the two teams.

The game was held at a scoreless stalemate until fullback Arthur Mourgue landed a penalty in the 30th minute following a high tackle on substitute prop Jordan Dezaria.

It had been set for set until that moment with little to choose between the sides. But five minutes later Tom Johnstone scored his debut home try, latching onto the end of a quick Michael McIlorum delivery from dummy-half through Tomkins, Rougé and Mourgue's quick hands to touch down in the left corner. Mourgue converted from the touchline to put Catalans ahead 8-0 at half-time.

Leigh hit back early in the second half when scrum-half Lachlan Lam caused chaos in the Catalans' defence with a kick to the line that was fumbled by Matthieu Laguerre and mopped up by second-rower Joe Wardle and grounded, with Ben Reynolds adding the conversion to put them within two points of the lead.

And the Leopards held the Dragons for long periods until Mickael Goudemand split their defence with a powerful ten-metre burst to score in the 66th-minute, which was converted by Mourgue to make it 14-6.

Wigan rebounded on the Friday night from their round-one loss at Hull KR as they never gave Wakefield an inch in a 60-0 hammering at the DW Stadium.

Liam Marshall finished with four tries out of a total of eleven as Harry Smith and Cade Cust controlled the attacks from halfback. Marshall and Bevan French both scored two tries apiece in the first half, while skipper Liam Farrell and Jai Field also got in on the act. Wigan's performance was so dominant it took Wakefield 34 minutes before they got a full set in Wigan's half.

Marshall completed his hat-trick in the 43rd minute before grabbing a fourth ten minutes later to take his career tally at Wigan to 100, while Sam Powell, Smith and Cust crossed for further tries in a clinical display.

In the Channel 4 game from the Jungle on the Sunday afternoon, St Helens won their first game of the Super League season, Alex Walmsley scoring two tries, reward for a barnstorming display in a 24-6 victory.

February

Tigers coach Lee Radford rung the changes from the loss at Hull FC with Joe Westerman, Nathan Massey, Suaia Matagi and Mahe Fonua all dropping out as Jack Broadbent, Cain Robb and Adam Milner came in. Tee Ritson made his competitive debut for Saints, with Jon Bennison starting on the other wing, as Will Hopoate and Tommy Makinson dropped out with injuries. James Roby and Agnatius Paasi also took knocks against Penrith, with Joey Lussick starting at hooker.

Saints led 6-0 at the break, courtesy of a Jack Welsby try under the posts, though the Tigers had bombed a number of chances created by the distribution of Jacob Miller and speed of Jake Mamo. Plenty of other breaks came but none could be finished off.

Ritson got his first Super League try on the end of a Jonny Lomax break before Broadbent's wonderful break for the line was ended by Welsby's high shot and a penalty try to bring the Tigers back to six points. But Walmsley's rampage swung it Saints' way.

Castleford should have had a consolation score on 75 minutes after Bureta Faraimo intercepted from deep, only for the winger, under no pressure, to inexplicably put his arm in touch a fraction before grounding the ball.

BETFRED SUPER LEAGUE
Sunday 26th February

	P	W	D	L	F	A	D	Pts
Warrington Wolves	2	2	0	0	68	26	42	4
Hull KR	2	2	0	0	51	28	23	4
Catalans Dragons	2	2	0	0	52	30	22	4
Hull FC	2	2	0	0	54	48	6	4
Wigan Warriors	2	1	0	1	78	27	51	2
St Helens	1	1	0	0	24	6	18	2
Salford Red Devils	2	1	0	1	30	34	-4	2
Huddersfield Giants	1	0	0	1	16	26	-10	0
Leigh Leopards	2	0	0	2	16	34	-18	0
Castleford Tigers	2	0	0	2	36	56	-20	0
Leeds Rhinos	2	0	0	2	28	64	-36	0
Wakefield Trinity	2	0	0	2	24	98	-74	0

MARCH
Dancing with Wolves

Round 3

Warrington's lightning start to the season looked like coming to a shuddering halt at half-time of the Thursday-night Skysports game when they trailed at home to Salford by 20-6. But the Wolves showed their mettle in the second half, applying near-relentless pressure and scoring 30 unanswered points for a 36-20 victory.

In the first 40 minutes, Salford were rampant, having responded to Ben Currie's early effort through Ellis Longstaff's four-pointer and then surged ahead with Ryan Brierley and Marc Sneyd tries, Sneyd's four goals making it a three-score lead.

The Wolves were also helped, after Matty Ashton had cut the deficit with a great finish in the left corner, by the yellow card shown to Brierley, who was adjudged to have committed a professional foul by holding Josh Drinkwater down for too long.

Salford conceded three further tries while their fullback was off the field, by Thomas Mikaele, Josh Thewlis and George Williams, as the match turned decisively on its head.

Thewlis's effort was given as an eight-point try after Red Devils prop Tyler Dupree drove his knees into the try-scorer, as was Warrington's final try by Matt Dufty for a high shot by Kallum Watkins.

There was a major surprise the night after at St Helens as a big crowd assembled to welcome back the world champions. But Leeds pooped the party as Blake Austin kicked a field goal in the last minute of normal time to secure a 25-24 win.

The Rhinos had started the season with back-to-back defeats, a mauling at the hands of Warrington in the opening round followed by a late defeat at home to Hull FC.

But they upset the form book in a rematch of the previous season's Grand Final as Austin struck the one-pointer perfectly to cap a determined Rhinos fightback, after they had trailed 24-12 early in the second half.

It was a game packed with flashpoints and controversy, including a red card for Konrad Hurrell and spells in the sin bin for both Sione Mata'utia and Curtis Sironen, all three for late shots, two on Leeds fullback Richie Myler.

The game's turning point came in the 75th minute, when a shoulder charge from Leeds' Sam Walters resulted in a penalty against Saints after Jack Welsby was adjudged by referee Chris Kendall to have caused a melee by running in and challenging Walters aggressively.

Saints had Tommy Makinson back after suffering a head injury in the win over the Panthers, while Sironen also returned after having missed the win at Castleford with illness. James Roby and Agnatius Paasi were unavailable due to injury.

It was a nip and tuck first half with Leeds opening the scoring, with Mata'utia in the sin bin, with a brilliant long-range try involving a Nene Macdonald break down the right, support from Richie Myler and a perfect inside pass for Ash Handley to turn the cover inside out. But Saints led 18-12 at the break with two Lewis Dodd tries and a typical dummy-half try from Joey Lussick, Rhyse Martin getting the Rhinos' second try.

A try for Mark Percival five minutes into the second half and Makinson's conversion stretched the home lead to 24-12 but, after Leeds lost Kruise Leeming to a foot injury and Saints

March

Leigh's Josh Charnley drives towards the Hull KR tryline

saw Sironen sin-binned, Leeds struck back on the hour when a superb Walters back-flick put Cameron Smith in by the posts. Makinson had a try-claim ruled out by video to the increasing displeasure of the home fans.

Saints had their full 13 back when the Rhinos kept the ball alive on attack and Martin stepped through on the left for his second try, which he duly converted. With two minutes left, Leeds attacked down the left and Hurrell saw red for a high, late shot, setting the scene for Austin to snatch the Rhinos' first win of the season.

Another 100 per cent record had to give on the same night and it was Hull FC's perfect start that went as Catalans took them to the cleaners in Perpignan by 38-6.

Tonga prop Sio Siua Taukeiaho made a try-scoring debut as fellow recruit from the Roosters Adam Keighran stood out, as he had in his previous game at Wakefield.

Keighran was incredible with boot (seven from eight conversions) and ball (a try and several assists).

The early loss of scrum-half César Rougé to an ankle injury was a challenge for coach Steve McNamara, who had four forwards on the bench. But the Dragons rejigged seamlessly and dominated from start to finish.

Tony Smith made three changes to the side he selected against the Rhinos with Jack Brown, Ligi Sao, and Andre Savelio coming onto the bench.

The trio, making their first appearances of the season, replaced Joe Cator and Danny Houghton, who were rested, and Scott Taylor, who served a one-match suspension for dangerous contact in the win at Leeds.

Carlos Tuimavave, Jake Trueman, Connor Wynne and Mitieli Vulikijapani were also unavailable through injury and it told as the game wore on. And Hull picked up further knocks to Ben McNamara (who missed the second half with a shoulder injury) and Tex Hoy, whose back was hurt by an accidental knee in a tackle.

Hull KR's winning run ended too as Leigh won their first game of their return to Super League, a 78th-minute try earning the Leopards a 30-25 Friday-night win at Craven Park.

Leigh, superbly led by scrum-half Lachlan Lam, were behind until that last play.

The Robins grabbed four tries through Shaun Kenny-Dowall, Mikey Lewis - a superb

March

individual break - James Batchelor and Jordan Abdull. But two scores from Tom Briscoe and others from Tom Amone and Charnley kept it tight until Charnley won the game.

Huddersfield got their first win in their second game with a tough 8-0 win at Wakefield.

The game had gone ahead after a midweek inspection of the re-laid hybrid Belle Vue pitch following concerns about its abrasive qualities. Wakefield admitted that the grass had not been given enough time to grow between the synthetic turf but the fixture was given a green light.

Wakefield had been nilled two weeks in a row but their defence was much improved from the 60-0 mauling at Wigan. But the Giants were formidable at the back too and, led by Joe Greenwood and Luke Yates up front, did enough to go home with the points.

Wakefield coach Mark Applegarth rang the changes from the side that lost to Wigan. Lee Kershaw came in for Tom Lineham with Samisoni Langi moving to the centres to replace Corey Hall. Lee Gaskell shifted back to the halves with Liam Kay at fullback in place of injured Max Jowitt. Sam Eseh made his Trinity debut from the bench and Liam Hood also came in for his first appearance of 2023.

Jake Bibby made his debut for the Giants at centre with the former Wigan man replacing the injured Kevin Naiqama in Ian Watson's only change.

After a scoreless first half, a six-again immediately after the resumption for the Giants handed them a great opportunity and, following a penalty for a late hit on Theo Fages, Tui Lolohea slotted over the first points of the game for a 2-0 lead.

And just before the hour mark, a superb last-tackle play with Esan Marsters, Lolohea and Nathan Peats involved saw Greenwood crash over next to the posts. Lolohea had the simple task of converting from in front for an 8-0 lead with a quarter of the game left.

More bad news for Trinity was a first-half ACL injury to star winger Lewis Murphy, that ended his season.

Only one other team was pointless as Castleford crashed to a 36-0 home defeat by rampant Wigan.

Liam Marshall scored a hat-trick, the week after he scored four against Wakefield, as the Warriors kept a clean sheet for the second game running.

It was only 6-0 at the break despite the Tigers losing skipper Paul McShane after six minutes with a back spasm. But Ethan Havard, Toby King and Jai Field tries added to Marshall's treble for a comfortable end result.

On the Monday it was announced that Tigers head coach Lee Radford, who it had been rumoured would be leaving his post at the end of the 2023 season, was stepping down with immediate effect by mutual agreement. Assistant Andy Last, as he had when Radford was sacked at Hull FC in 2020, took over as interim coach.

Round 4

Leigh made it clear that 2023 was the year they would establish themselves as a Super League club when, on the Friday night, they inflicted a 20-12 defeat on St Helens.

It wasn't just on the field that the Leopards were making waves as another bumper crowd turned out at Leigh Sports Village, despite freezing conditions, with 80s band T'Pau providing the pre-match entertainment for almost 8,000 fans.

The Leopards' second successive comeback win came after an early Tommy Makinson penalty goal and first-half tries from Jonny Lomax and Jon Bennison had given Saints seeming control. Leigh fought hard but it remained 12-0 at half-time.

Leigh's first try, scored by Josh Charnley on the left, was the result of a great lobbed pass from form halfback Lachlan Lam and a step inside from the winger. Zak Hardaker couldn't convert but Leigh were gaining in confidence.

The game turned completely after Saints prop Matty Lees was sin-binned for a swinging arm in a tackle on fullback Gareth O'Brien and Leigh immediately scored as Joe Mellor hoisted a kick right for Hardaker to find Tom Briscoe for his second try of the season. Again it proved too far out for Hardaker to goal.

March

The Leopards brought the house down with a third try after 74 minutes when Hardaker pirouetted and bobbed through several challenges to go under the posts. This time there was no mistake from his boot and Leigh led 14-12.

Leigh made it three tries in Lees' absence when John Asiata kicked forward and on-loan from Wigan Joe Shorrocks collected a ricochet to go over by the posts, allowing the North Stand to erupt. Hardaker added his second goal.

St Helens' second defeat in a row left them six points adrift of the leaders, although they had a game in hand.

Both the Wolves and the Dragons maintained their 100 per cent starts and both did it tough.

In the Thursday TV game, the Dragons edged the Warriors 18-10 at DW Stadium, only their third ever win in Wigan and their first since 2011.

In freezing temperatures and blustery conditions, the French side kept their cool as they frustrated Wigan for 80 minutes to grind out a narrow victory. It was a seesaw battle with both teams having periods of domination, two tries from Manu Ma'u edging the game the Dragons' way.

It was a satisfying result for the Dragons who were once again without Sam Tomkins and Mitchell Pearce, while Romain Navarrete and Cesar Rouge were absent after picking up knocks in their win over Hull FC. Adam Keighran moved from centre to the halves to replace Rougé and was excellent again, while Matthieu Laguerre was named in the centres, though he suffered an early injury and had to be replaced with youngster Ugo Tison. England backrower Mike McMeeken moved up to the front row.

Wigan coach Matt Peet went with the same 17 that ran out 36-0 winners away at Castleford Tigers, with Liam Byrne once again deployed as an unused 18th man.

The Dragons built a 12-2 lead through Ma'u and Arthur Romano tries and a conversion and penalty from Keighran but Ma'u was sin-binned for a late tackle on Cade Cust, which saw Harry Smith kick the penalty to give Wigan hope at 12-2.

Four minutes after the break Wigan took advantage of their extra man with a great try from Smith as he fed Kaide Ellis and ran around for a neat offload from the Australian forward, with the halfback racing away to score. Smith converted his own try and added an easy penalty ten minutes later to make it 12-10.

But the winning try came in the 63rd minute when Tyrone May looked like he was running out of options as he crabbed across the field. But with nothing on he put in a grubber kick and Ma'u raced through to pick up the ball, step past Jai Field and touch down. Keighran converted and the French side led 18-10 with just over 16 minutes remaining.

Former Wakefield winger Tom Johnstone didn't score for the first time in 2023 but he produced a nerve-settling try-saving tackle on Toby King as he headed for the right corner

Warrington topped the table on a small points difference after they won at Hull KR on the Friday night by the same scoreline, 18-10, a late Paul Vaughan try under the sticks sealing the victory.

Prop James Harrison missed out for the Wolves while Rovers were without skipper Shaun Kenny-Dowall, at the start of a four-game ban from the Leigh game for 'making unnecessary contact with an injured opponent', the first suspension of his outstanding career. They were also without long-term injured Kane Linnett and also influential halfback Jordan Abdull.

A superb burst from Frankie Halton put Rovers ahead on eight minutes but tries from Thomas Mikaele, off a short ball from Sam Kasiano, and Matty Nicholson, on the end of a George Williams' grubber, had the Wolves 12-6 up at half-time.

Early in the second half Rovers gained momentum and the pressure paid when Lachlan Coote sent Halton in for his second of the game. But Coote was off target with the kickable conversion attempt.

Eleven minutes from time Coote had a chance to level the scores when Sam Kasiano put what looked like a dangerous tackle on Tom Opacic. But from 20 metres out the fullback was unable to land the penalty.

March

Catalans Dragons' Manu Ma'u mobbed by teammates after scoring against Wigan

It was Rovers' final chance of the game as, with just a minute to go, Vaughan bounced up from an incomplete tackle for Stefan Ratchford to add his third conversion and put the game out of sight.

Also on Friday, Leeds got their second straight win when they finally cracked the Wakefield defence after a scoreless first half at Headingley, the Rhinos running away to a 26-0 win.

It was a night for graft in the conditions, best epitomised by Jarrod O'Connor, the joint top tackler for the Rhinos and, with Kruise Leeming out, their only designated hooker. The Leeds bench was significant, with Sam Lisone a real handful in his best performance to date after he was introduced in the second half and Sam Walters again a threat.

Harry Newman made his return and their was also a first appearance of the year for James Bentley, both coming off the bench, centre Newman scoring the second home try and Bentley twice producing try-saving tackles on his own line late on.

Wakefield finished scoreless for a third game running with star players Max Jowitt, Lewis Murphy and Kelepi Tanginoa injured. Stand-off Lee Gaskell (pectoral) and Samisoni Langi (head knock) only lasted half a game and the disruption showed.

Their lack of threat was summed up by the final try, which was Nene Macdonald's first for Leeds. On a last-tackle play, Mason Lino's impossible pass to Jay Pitts while he was surrounded fell to the floor near the Leeds line. Richie Myler scooped up and sent the PNG international racing clear down the South Stand side.

Two other sides had hit form slumps. On the same Friday night, Castleford Tigers, in the wake of the departure of head coach Lee Radford and missing captain Paul McShane, were well beaten at Huddersfield, the Giants finishing 36-6 winners and that after a George Lawler try gave the Tigers an early 6-0 lead. Chris McQueen soon hit back for the Giants, who were totally dominant thereafter.

Will Pryce and Jake Bibby tries and four goals from Oliver Russell, two from penalties, made it 20-6 at the break. McQueen's second, and further scores from Tui Lolohea and Leroy Cudjoe secured a first home win for the Giants.

March

Russell controlled the Giants brilliantly in his first appearance of the season, mostly alongside Pryce following a 12th minute calf injury to Theo Fages.

Interim Tigers coach Andy Last had a huge job on his hands to lift the Tigers' confidence and the same could be said for Hull FC coach Tony Smith, who on the Saturday afternoon watched his side crumble to a 60-14 home defeat to Salford.

The Red Devils were spectacularly good, the style of play that brought such rich rewards in 2022 on full display, their inspirational spine hitting their straps again. But Hull made it easy at times. Some of the tries were sub-standard from a defensive perspective. For Ryan Brierley's, Brodie Croft was almost waved through. Tyler Dupree faced almost no resistance down the middle for his. Tex Hoy's attempt at a tackle to deny Shane Wright's first looked half-hearted.

That was just the opening 40. After the break, there was Kallum Watkins touching down a ball he had no right to claim, simply by wanting it more than any home player. There was Marc Sneyd, on his old stomping ground, dancing around woeful 'tackles'. And in the final minute, there were more statues where defenders should have been, allowing Tim Lafai to do as he pleased.

Hull took the lead in only the third minute. Salford started with a risk too far, with Jack Ormondroyd attempting an offload that wasn't on, and paid the price when Jake Clifford dummied to cross.

But from then on, just about everything the Red Devils touched turned to gold. Sneyd and Brierley's break led, thanks to a quick switch on the next play, to Deon Cross putting them ahead, starting a run of 56 unanswered points in 48 minutes.

Chief Operating Officer Tony Sutton was appointed Chief Executive Officer of the RFL, having replaced former CEO Ralph Rimmer in an interim capacity three months before.

Round 5

Warrington made it five wins from five with a comfortable 38-20 Friday-night home win over Leigh Leopards as the calm distribution of Josh Drinkwater set the platform for runners George Williams and Matt Dufty to add the polish.

The Wolves scored four tries in the first half and three in the first eleven minutes of the second before the Leopards gained some consolation with two tries in the last ten minutes. Warrington took control with first-half Drinkwater (in the first minute), Paul Vaughan and Dufty tries in response to Tom Briscoe and Josh Charnley scores for Leigh.

Matty Ashton's second-half hat-trick in the space of ten minutes well and truly took the game away from the Leopards, who had won their last two. Tom Amone and Zak Hardaker tries showed Leigh's heart with the game gone.

In Perpignan the day after, a hat-trick of tries from Tom Johnstone kept the Dragons' 100 per cent record intact with a 26-12 win over Hull KR. Five wins from five should have put a smile on coach Steve McNamara's face, but he wasn't happy with the performance.

Rovers became the first club in Super League to use an 18th man because of a bizarre series of first-half head injuries.

Knocks to Mikey Lewis, Jordan Abdull, Dean Hadley and Frankie Halton meant coach Willie Peters had to play the spare card in Will Dagger at half-time under the new HIA rules. While Lewis passed his test, the three others did not and were set to miss Rovers' next game at Wakefield.

Johnstone put the Dragons ahead early on, finishing a near length-of-the-field effort that started with an intercept by Adam Keighran. Tom Davies' try made it 10-0 at the break, with Johnstone's second coming before Rowan Milnes responded.

Johnstone grabbed a third and Julian Bousquet completed the win before Ryan Hall went over for battling Rovers' second.

Friday night saw Wigan edge an attritional game at Huddersfield by 14-12.

It was nip and tuck throughout a first half ultimately remembered for some key errors.

March

Huddersfield kept the score at 8-6 only thanks to two missed Harry Smith conversions - in contrast, Smith's kicking in open play was often excellent - and three penalties between the other posts by Oliver Russell.

The first came after nine minutes to open the scoring, and the second in the 23rd minute, both times following high tackles. In between, Esan Marsters' fumbled a Leroy Cudjoe pass in the challenge of Toby King, leading to Wigan's opening try as Cade Cust's brilliant sharp thinking set up Bevan French with a kick.

It was 4-4 with Russell's second penalty but further disaster struck for Huddersfield only two minutes later. Bibby failed to claim a Smith kick under pressure in the corner and Jake Wardle only had to place his hand on the ball to score against the club that let him leave last year.

A four-point lead was halved after the half-time hooter though, as an offside penalty allowed Russell to stroke another goal.

The second half was more of the same, tight and tense. But the match was placed in Huddersfield's hands when, for once, it was Wigan who came up with a critical error.

Moments after Patrick Mago cheaply gave away possession, Liam Marshall failed to collect a Will Pryce kick and Kevin Naiqama was on hand to put the Giants in front. Russell improved for a 12-8 scoreline.

Wigan gave themselves numerous opportunities at the line and, although Mago and Willie Isa both lost the ball in attempting to score, they kept up the pressure and were rewarded with the match-winning try in the 61st minute.

Smith's high kick was knocked down by Wardle for French and the speedster surged for the line and evaded oncoming challenges to squeeze over for his second score of the game.

With the Smith conversion added, Wigan were back ahead and would remain so, as Huddersfield's composure let them down.

It was just as tough in St Helens as the home side returned to winning ways with a 20-12 win over Hull FC. With both sides coming into the contest on the back of consecutive defeats, it was a genuine battle from start to finish, with Saints leaving it until the 79th minute to seal the victory with a late try by Jon Bennison.

After being embarrassed by Salford last time out, Tony Smith's men had newfound energy and intensity, dominating Saints physically for large parts of the game. Despite this, they just couldn't find the killer blow and were left ruing missed chances.

It looked like the game was heading for a scoreless first half but the deadlock was eventually broken after 39 minutes by Ben Davies. Hull had to drop out from under their own posts and they tried a short kick but it backfired massively when the Saints centre climbed highest to take the ball 20 metres out and leave the defence in his wake to score.

Saints' lead was short lived as Hull opened their account after half-time when Scott Taylor barged his way through three defenders from short range to ground the ball on the line. Jake Clifford converted to put Hull up by two.

Bennison and Jack Welsby went over for converted tries but just as St Helens looked to be pulling clear, the game swung again as Hull responded almost immediately from the restart to cut the gap to four points. A stinging tackle from Brad Dwyer and Chris Satae forced an error from Jake Wingfield and Jake Clifford picked up the ball and raced away to score next to the posts.

Hull then created the chance to win the game with minutes remaining but they bombed it in spectacular fashion. Josh Griffin manufactured a kick to put Adam Swift into space and the winger chipped the ball back infield for Dwyer. But the hooker fumbled the ball to see the chance go begging.

It was a let-off that Saints duly took advantage of when they wrapped the game up with quick hands down the short side putting Bennison over for his second to seal the victory for the champions.

In the Friday-night TV game, Castleford got off the mark with a 14-8 home win over Leeds. As the full-time hooter sounded, the Tigers' victorious players joined together in embrace. On the sidelines, Andy Last jumped for joy with his coaching staff.

Bureta Faraimo scored both of the Tigers' tries, breaking the deadlock in the first half and

March

Wakefield's Sam Hewitt and Reece Lyne can't stop Marc Sneyd from kicking Salford to victory

then scoring the match-winning try from a fine scrum-play midway through the second.

For Leeds, execution particularly let them down, with only one Richie Myler try to show for their efforts. It was summed up five minutes from time when Derrell Olpherts, on his first return to Castleford since a pre-season move, dropped the ball cold when sent in for what should have been a match-winning try.

Rhinos hooker Kruise Leeming was notable for his absence and news emerged that he had asked for a release from the club to seek other opportunities.

On the Sunday, Wakefield went close to joining Castleford on two league points but a golden-point field goal from Marc Sneyd, which came after a Wakefield error on half-way four minutes into extra time, gave Salford a 14-13 home victory.

The Red Devils led after four minutes when Brodie Croft and Ryan Brierley combined to send Matty Costello through a gap for the posts.

Trinity replied through Corey Hall and Reece Lyne before Chris Atkin's dummy-half try gave Salford a 12-10 lead at the break.

Already struggling for squad depth - on-loan Huddersfield forward Sam Hewitt made his debut - Trinity lost hooker Liam Hood to a head injury on 53 minutes, although a late hit allowed Mason Lino to level with a penalty goal ten minutes later.

The Red Devils held their nerve to go in front with Sneyd's first field goal with five and a half minutes remaining. But, when Wakefield regained possession at the restart, Lino marshalled his pack and stepped up to level again with his own one-pointer.

Lino and Sneyd traded field-goal attempts before the end and when the final hooter sounded it was still locked up at 13-13.

The teams traded possessions until the otherwise impressive Jay Pitts threw a forward pass and Salford moved into position from where Sneyd's boot decided matters.

March

Round 6

After six victories on a row, Warrington went clear at the top of the table with their Friday-night win at Castleford and Catalans' defeat the day after.

The Wolves hammered coach Daryl Powell's former club Castleford, maintaining their 100 per cent record with a 38-0 win which featured a try-double by winger Matty Russell, on his second debut for the club after moving from Toulouse Olympique. By the end of the weekend they were two points clear at the top after the Dragons' 32-22 loss at Leeds on the Saturday.

Led from the front by Paul Vaughan and Sam Kasiano and moved around the park by George Williams and Matt Dufty, the Wolves looked every bit a champion team, albeit against a woeful Castleford.

The Tigers were without Mahe Fonua, who had failed his HIA against the Rhinos, as well as George Lawler with a sternum injury. In came Jordan Turner for only his second appearance of the season, with Albert Vete and George Griffin returning.

Warrington's Josh Thewlis was out with concussion, with Josh Drinkwater also dropping out as Peter Mata'utia moved into the halves and Russell and Gil Dudson made their debuts.

It was 24-0 by half-time thanks to tries from Kasiano, Thomas Mikaele and two from Russell, all converted by Stefan Ratchford. Vaughan stretched over 12 minutes after the break and Williams grabbed a four-pointer before Dufty added Warrington's seventh try.

A bumper crowd was on hand at Headingley for the Channel 4 game the next day and it was treated to a rip-roaring contest, with the Dragons leading 22-8 at half-time and looking in seeming command before the Rhinos scored 24 unanswered points, despite having two-try Harry Newman in the sin bin.

Blake Austin led the Rhinos with a virtuoso performance, best illustrated in setting up the opening score after the break, which started the shift, and an imperious 40/20 that established the position for him to set up the try that put his side back in front.

For the former, his marauding 40-metre run up the middle, brushing aside four would-be tacklers, broke the cover for Aidan Sezer to send in Richie Myler. Rhyse Martin failed with a simple conversion attempt in a run of five consecutive misses.

For the latter, having landed his second 40/20 of the season, Austin slipped Tom Holroyd in to score on the left with a superbly timed pass.

Austin also sent Derrell Olpherts brilliantly tiptoeing his way over after Nene Macdonald had snaffled a dropped Mike McMeeken ball. And his spiralling kicks in a strong swirling wind were the catalysts for scores by Rhyse Martin and Jarrod O'Connor in a complete performance.

Catalans had injuries as a mitigating factor. The loss of Mickael Goudemand before he could make an impact off the bench and then, in quick succession at the start of the second half, the influential Tyrone May with an ankle injury and Ben Garcia to a head injury, clearly disrupted them, leading to the Dragons' first loss of the campaign.

Third-placed Wigan had to dig deep to see off a stubborn Salford Red Devils at the DW Stadium on the Friday, two late tries taking them to a 20-16 victory.

The scores were level at the break at 8-8, with Ken Sio and Bevan French exchanging tries and Marc Sneyd and Harry Smith both kicking a conversion and penalty each.

The Warriors looked out of sorts in attack and were struggling to get a foothold in the game and found themselves 16-8 down heading into the final 20 minutes as Sio grabbed his second try and Sneyd kicked four more points.

The visitors were worthy of their lead and Wigan needed to change things immediately. Coach Matt Peet did that, as he brought Cade Cust off and moved Jai Field into the halves with French dropping to fullback.

That was a master stroke as the Warriors took control and French grabbed his second try before Field sent Toby King over for the match-winning score.

Champions St Helens were given a stern task at Huddersfield in the Thursday TV game before finishing 14-12 winners.

Personifying Saints' effort was Matty Lees, who played the full 80 minutes in the front row,

March

St Helens' Alex Walmsley takes on Huddersfield's Oliver Russell and Harry Rushton

a consequence of Sione Mata'utia suffering a head injury inside the very first minute which ruled him out of the rest of the game.

Lees made 68 tackles as Saints spent much of the game on the back foot, particularly in the second half as they defended a lead built by quick-fire Konrad Hurrell and Tommy Makinson tries.

Although Ashton Golding and Innes Senior responded for the Giants, a resolute goal-line defence held out when required to ensure a narrow but sweet victory.

The deciding score was a Makinson penalty goal when Sebastine Ikahihifo caught Konrad Hurrell with a high tackle.

There was a second Giants debut for Jake Connor, who came off the bench in the second half and had mixed fortunes, kicking a 40/20, only to then cough up the ball a couple of plays later.

On the Saturday, Leigh registered their third win with a surprise 24-16 victory at Hull FC. After two last-gasp victories, at Hull KR and at home to St Helens, the Leopards this time got the job done early. The course of the match, and more or less its outcome, was decided in the first twelve minutes as the Leopards scored three tries to build a 16-0 lead.

After Jake Clifford had a kick charged down in his own half, Leigh opened the scoring as Lachlan Lam put Kai O'Donnell over with a sweetly-timed pass.

Hull kicked the restart out on the full and were punished by a flowing move that saw Ricky Leutele provide for Josh Charnley. And prolific winger Charnley, who went on to score a hat-trick to take his season's tally to eight and move joint-top of the Super League scoring charts, was in again from a Gareth O'Brien cut-out pass.

It was an impressive platform and although Hull regained their composure to make a game of it, the mountain was too great to climb.

Brad Dwyer pegged it back to 16-6 by half-time but another Charnley try was enough to stave off a home fightback through Clifford and Liam Sutcliffe tries, Ben Reynolds kicking a settling penalty five minutes from time.

March

Hull KR had ended their three-match losing run the night before with a comfortable 34-6 win at point-less Wakefield.

As soon as Sam Wood opened the scoring after 13 minutes, the result seemed inevitable. Only poor goalkicking kept Wakefield in the contest as regards the scoreboard, with further tries for Louis Senior, Tom Opacic and Kane Linnett only taking Hull KR to 18-0 at half-time, but they were never in the contest in a competitive sense.

It was hardly a battle in the forwards, Trinity getting rolled time and again and that was only compounded by the sort of errors typical of a team low on confidence. In the second half they earned some attacking position at last but only Jai Whitbread's try avoided a fourth blank in five games. Meanwhile, scores from Mikey Lewis, Elliot Minchella and Opacic again condemned Trinity and their supporters to another demoralising defeat.

Trinity had a problem at fullback with Max Jowitt and Lee Gaskell both out long term. Academy player Robbie Butterworth was given a tough debut in the role. Dummy half was also a challenge as Liam Hood failed an HIA at Salford the week before, with Wigan youngster Tom Forber also on debut as a loanee.

In the days after, Wakefield swapped star young centre Corey Hall for Hull KR's Will Dagger, both on permanent deals.

Round 7

Round seven opened with a bang on the Thursday night with another big effort by Leigh attracting a record Super League crowd to the Sports Village for the televised game with neighbours Wigan.

But the Wigan supporters had most to cheer as their side romped to a 34-6 win and, after the live band and the fireworks, Bevan French was the real showstopper. The fullback's vintage display gave Wigan a classy and ultimately decisive victory.

French scored only once himself, slicing through the defence after Leigh had taken an early lead through Tom Briscoe's 200th career try. But his superb skill-set was demonstrated by his three assists in a second half that the Warriors totally dominated.

The first laid on the opening try following the break. After his initial kick was deflected back into his path, French broke down the wing and chipped another kick, over the outstretched hand of a leaping Zak Hardaker, perfectly for Joe Wardle to score.

French then brilliantly flicked on a pass, despite the incoming challenge of Ed Chamberlain, for Abbas Miski to dive in for the decisive score of the game, putting Wigan in an unassailable position.

Then, with the Warriors in full control, playing pure, free-spirited, joyful rugby, French contributed to an audacious final score in the last minute. He collected Harry Smith's chip over the top from halfway, then kicked long and wide for Miski to finish a remarkable piece of play.

Jai Field was also outstanding and scored two individual tries, although he limped off with a hamstring injury 13 minutes from time.

The Warriors had Jake Wardle in the sin bin early on for a late shot on Gareth O'Brien - who subsequently failed a head-injury assessment - in the move that brought Briscoe's try.

Key to Wigan outlasting Leigh were the resources on the bench, with Ethan Havard impressive again. Brad O'Neill was also excellent coming on at hooker as was Joe Shorrocks, back in a Warriors shirt after four weeks on loan at Leigh.

On the Saturday, Warrington kept their perfect start with a 34-6 win over Hull FC, who sank to their fifth defeat in a row.

The current gulf was laid bare in a thoroughly one-sided first half. The excellent George Williams did much of the damage to Hull, starting with the first try as his kick over the top from deep was weighted excellently to allow Matty Ashton to chase and score.

It was 14-0 by the quarter-hour mark after two more tries that showed the confidence Warrington were currently playing with.

First Peter Mata'utia drove to the line after Paul Vaughan's offload allowed the lively Matt

March

Warrington's Paul Vaughan looks for a way past Hull FC's Josh Griffin

Dufty to find the makeshift loose forward. Then Williams popped up a gorgeous chip from close to the line and Ben Currie flew through the air to score the try.

Williams' third assist was no less brilliant, breaking forward after Currie nailed Brad Fash with a tackle when defending the Wolves' goal-line. Dufty was in support to complete a wonderful length-of-the-field try and Hull were left disheartened.

That showed in the final try of the first half, as Jake Clifford and Tex Hoy were picked out in the defence and smashed through with embarrassing ease by the quietly influential Josh Drinkwater.

Stefan Ratchford converted four of the five tries - and would add another to the sole Warrington score of the second half, by Matty Nicholson - as they went into half-time 28-0 up with the two competition points long secured.

Hull finally scored past the hour-mark as Brad Dwyer surged over and Jake Clifford converted.

They were the first points conceded by the Wolves in almost 150 minutes and they would concede no more, instead having the final say when Nicholson powered through weak defence nine minutes from time.

On the same afternoon, Catalans kept within two points of Warrington with a tough 22-18 home win over the reviving Castleford Tigers.

Expectations of a French rout following Catalans' successful start to the season and Castleford's dismal run of defeats failed to materialise as the Tigers stepped up to the plate in style and could easily have come home with the points from Perpignan. But former Tigers' favourite Mike McMeeken broke the Tigers' hearts with a late try for the Dragons after a bitter slog that went right to the wire.

Castleford started without stand-off Gareth Widdop, who had been feeling unwell, and centre Alex Sutcliffe who hurt his calf in the pre-match warm-up, Muizz Mustapha called up into the starting 17. Jack Broadbent filled in in the halves and had a great game, the highlight an 80-metre sprint for his second try, which put Castleford in front ten minutes from time.

March

The Dragons were missing hooker Michael McIlorum but fullback Sam Tomkins made a second-half return from injury from the substitutes' bench.

On the Friday night, Hull KR recorded back-to-back wins with a 20-12 home win over Leeds, thanks in the main to a kicking masterclass from Jordan Abdull. His kicking on a foul wet evening led to a night to forget for Rhinos' debutant Luke Hooley and winger Derrell Olpherts, but they were not the only players to have an off night for the visitors.

Rovers dominated so much that the Rhinos didn't have a set inside the home '20' for the full first half. Another problem for Leeds was the 14th minute loss of winger David Fusitu'a with an injury to his left ankle.

BETFRED SUPER LEAGUE
Sunday 2nd April

	P	W	D	L	F	A	D	Pts
Warrington Wolves	7	7	0	0	232	82	150	14
Catalans Dragons	7	6	0	1	178	108	70	12
Wigan Warriors	7	5	0	2	192	79	113	10
St Helens	6	4	0	2	132	75	57	8
Hull KR	7	4	0	3	152	120	32	8
Huddersfield Giants	6	3	0	3	110	76	34	6
Salford Red Devils	7	3	0	4	156	143	13	6
Leeds Rhinos	7	3	0	4	131	144	-13	6
Leigh Leopards	7	3	0	4	116	159	-43	6
Hull FC	7	2	0	5	108	224	-116	4
Castleford Tigers	7	1	0	6	74	196	-122	2
Wakefield Trinity	7	0	0	7	43	218	-175	0

It was 14-0 at half-time. And Rovers' second-half kick-off was taken on the run by Sauaso Sue ending in a Kane Linnett try after just 24 seconds to make it 18-0. Winger Luis Roberts quickly replied but Lachlan Coote's penalty on 54 minutes saw Leeds needing to score three times. They managed one more try through backrower James McDonnell.

For the fourth time in seven matches this season, Wakefield Trinity failed to score a single point in their Friday night 38-0 defeat at St Helens.

The first half, and the beginning of the second, was an error-fest, the only redeeming feature being that the match was still, theoretically at least, in the balance at 12-0 after Saints scored three times through Mark Percival, Will Hopoate and Tommy Makinson, all unconverted.

Trinity had reason to regret one big chance, when Jay Pitts broke through only for the supporting Mason Lino to fumble his untidy pass. Lewis Dodd, Konrad Hurrell twice and Jonny Lomax tries, plus five goals from Percival, stretched out the final score.

In the only Sunday game, Huddersfield edged Salford at the AJ Bell Stadium by 26-16.

First-half tries to Ashton Golding - who damaged a hamstring in the act of scoring - and Owen Trout came either side of Shane Wright's score for the Red Devils, giving the Giants the half-time lead. Matt Costello's second-half score reduced arrears for Salford, but Trout stomped over for a crucial second. Chris McQueen's late try meant Kallum Watkins' score was only a consolation.

APRIL
Crowds appeal

Round 8

Billed as 'Rivals Round' the Easter weekend of derbies, with the help of some sunny weather, set a number of attendance records.

The decision to play a single round spread over four days, with all the games televised live by Sky Sports, paid off. The scrapping of the much-maligned two-round weekend was motivated largely by player welfare considerations. But it also proved a huge hit with supporters - with a total of 83,357 people attending the six matches, a new record for a single six-match round of Super League, smashing the previous record of 79,173 set on the first half of the Easter weekend in 2019.

The average attendance of 13,892 was also a record for any round of Super League stretching back to the launch of the competition in 1996, beating 13,196 for that same 2019 round.

A number of other individual records were set. The capacity crowd of 24,275 for the Good Friday derby between Wigan Warriors and St Helens was the highest at the DW Stadium for 18 years, the highest for a regular season Super League fixture since the all-time record of 31,555 for the fixture between Catalans Dragons and Wigan played at Barcelona's Camp Nou in 2019.

The crowd of 20,985 for the Hull derby at the MKM Stadium earlier on Good Friday, also a capacity, was Hull FC's highest since 2009.

And the 5,308 who were in attendance for the opening fixture of the Betfred Women's Super League season at Headingley on Easter Sunday between Leeds Rhinos and York Valkyrie set a new record for that competition, beating the 4,235 gate for the BWSL Grand Final in 2021, also at Headingley.

The action on the pitch was top class, though it started on the Thursday night with a nervy encounter between the bottom two clubs, with Castleford getting their second win of the season and opening a four-point gap over bottom club Wakefield.

Greg Eden scored two of the Tigers' three tries in a 16-4 home win as Trinity fell to their eighth loss out of eight games.

Castleford did what they needed to do, grinding out victory by any means. Their captain, Paul McShane, was the difference maker as he scored their first try, assisted their second by collecting a Will Dagger grubber and sending Eden down the left touchline; and laid the platform for their last.

In between, Wakefield competed but errors at key moments, with and without the ball, undid them, in contrast to the Tigers, who were sharp and committed in defence and clinical enough times in attack to get over the line.

Trinity were strengthened by five changes, with Liam Hood, Renouf Atoni and Kevin Proctor back from injury, Sam Hewitt back from suspension, and Nathan Mason the latest sticking plaster on loan from Huddersfield Giants.

But their start was disastrous. Although Trinity scrambled to recover from a Jack Broadbent break, they were caught out again on the next play with McShane scooting over from dummy-half, with less than three minutes gone. It was 12-0 at the break after Eden's long-range effort. Wakefield dominated the second half but could only manage one try from Samisoni Langi and Eden's second in the left corner in the 69th minute sealed it for the Tigers.

April

Hull KR's Mikey Lewis and Ryan Hall celebrate a try against Hull FC

Friday afternoon provided a bumper TV double header in front of sunlit capacity crowds. In the first, Hull KR put the cleaners through Hull FC at the MKM Stadium, the 40-0 thrashing a humiliation for the black and white side of the city.

In mitigation, FC, already without injured fullback Tex Hoy, lost halfback Jake Clifford before half-time and Jamie Shaul not long after. But they were out-enthused by a rampant Rovers.

The passion required on days like this was exemplified by Mikey Lewis, one of the outstanding performers alongside halfback partner Jordan Abdull, backrower James Batchelor and hat-trick winger Ryan Hall.

Rovers led after nine minutes, Hall scoring his first. Shaun Kenny-Dowall and Kane Linnett between them knocked down an Abdull kick for Lewis to provide it.

Cold errors were a familiar Hull theme, along with last plays to no positive effect. Abdull showed them how it should be done, sending a horrifying bomb the way of Shaul. Making his first appearance of the season, Shaul tried putting a boot to it and only gave it to Tom Opacic, who gleefully sprinted in.

After a Lachlan Coote penalty for 14-0, the period before half-time was not Rovers' finest hour. As well as having Batchelor binned for a dangerous tackle, which ended Clifford's afternoon, they might have also had Sauaso Sue similarly punished. Sue got two games and Batchelor one the following week for dangerous tackles.

Despite repeat sets, the home side failed to find a way to score. After half-time they never looked remotely in the game.

Abdull again got alarm bells ringing following the resumption, sending a kick the way of Carlos Tuimavave, which the Hull skipper knocked on. From that, Abdull put in Batchelor for the first of four tries in 13 minutes.

Coote got the next, putting Hall down the wing and then offering support to finish the move. Hall then added his second from a scrum play involving Abdull and Lewis, before a break from deep saw their roles reversed as Hall provided for Lewis.

The record derby win was secured by Hall. All three of his tries were laid on by Lewis, the final one an impressive, fired cut-out pass.

April

The Wigan-St Helens derby was a different kettle of fish which could have gone either way, the Warriors emerging with a 14-6 win after a gripping game.

All the talk before the game was who would replace injured Jai Field in the halves and Matt Peet eventually went with Joe Shorrocks. Although he was not as creative as Field or Cade Cust would have been - it was the first time he had played in that position - he played the full 80 minutes and a crucial role in helping Wigan to victory.

It was Shorrocks' last-ditch tackle that prevented Morgan Knowles from scoring a try in the second half. Had Saints scored then, no-one would have bet against them to go on and win.

In a thrilling opening half, it was Wigan who held a slender advantage thanks to a try and conversion and penalty goal from Harry Smith. Smith put Jake Wardle clear and then backed up on the inside for his try.

Saints looked certain to reply five minutes from half-time when Konrad Hurrell broke and sent Tommy Makinson for the right corner but a desperate tackle from Bevan French prevented Makinson from getting the ball down before he slid into touch.

Eleven minutes into the second half the Warriors led 14-0, thanks to a great try by Toby King off French's pass. Jonny Lomax gave Saints a glimmer of hope with a well-worked try from Lewis Dodd's grubber just after the hour mark and it could have been a different result had Knowles grounded the ball in the 69th minute.

There was some fall out from the clash as Wigan lost prop Mike Cooper for the season to an ACL injury. Morgan Knowles was subsequently banned for five games for the 'hip-drop' tackle that caused the injury. Wigan's Morgan Smithies also got one game for dangerous contact.

The Leigh-Salford Saturday-afternoon match-up was another close encounter, with the Red Devils coming away with the points from LSV for the second time in eight rounds, this time by 22-20.

Three of Salford's tries came in a nine-minute period in the first half when they hit their straps following Josh Charnley's unconverted opener and Ben Reynolds' penalty goal.

Ken Sio, Sam Stone and Brodie Croft all crossed to give the Red Devils a lead they would not let up, though Leigh's tails were up early in the second half when Tom Briscoe scored, shortly after Ryan Brierley had been sent to the sin bin for a professional foul.

But Tyler Dupree powered over at the end of the ten-minute period when Salford were a man down. And they saw out the match despite Charnley and Ben Reynolds tries providing a late scare.

Later that day there was another edge-of-the-seat thriller in Perpignan, with Warrington having to dig deep to maintain their perfect start with a 20-14 win.

Injury-hit Catalans Dragons, missing six senior players, had three try claims ruled out by video referee Marcus Griffiths, but nobody could deny the Wolves their moment in the sunshine, especially considering they finished the game with twelve men.

A moment of madness by prop Gil Dudson when he punched grounded Dragons' winger Tom Johnstone, with the game deadlocked at 14-14 in the 66th-minute, seemed to hand the initiative to the home side as their former player was sent off.

But a dazzling second try for winger Josh Thewlis gave the Wolves, with George Williams in majestic form, a famous victory.

In a nip-and-tuck opening half, Warrington tries from Thewlis and Matt Dufty - a breathtaking 90-metre kick return - came either side of Mike McMeeken's touchdown and a Catalans penalty try, as Adam Keighran was pushed by Ben Currie while attempting to ground a loose ball over the line.

Behind just 10-8, Warrington took control early in the second half when Williams exchanged passes with Sam Kasiano and regathered to score under the posts, with Ratchford's conversion pushing the Wolves 14-10 in front. But Arthur Romano dragged Catalans level before Dudson saw red and Thewlis's second edged Warrington ahead.

There was still time for Catalans to have another try, by Romano, ruled out, the video referee adjudging a teammate was offside in the build-up, to the utter dismay of French supporters.

April

Middle forward Josh McGuire finally made his competitive debut for the Wolves after serving his seven-match suspension. Dudson was banned for five matches.

Which left one game on the Sunday afternoon that ended up with closest scoreline of the round, Leeds pipping Huddersfield by 18-17 at Headingley.

Up 13-4 at the break, the Giants were shredded after the interval by a completely different Leeds side as the likes of Blake Austin and Nene Macdonald helped the Rhinos to a priceless two points.

Macdonald, Richie Myler and Ash Handley returned for Leeds, while Tui Lolohea came in for Olly Russell for Huddersfield, after the halfback tore a hamstring in training, whilst Adam O'Brien made his first appearance of the season from the bench.

Two tries in the first seven minutes from Jermaine McGillvary, after Jake Connor's grubber caused chaos, and Chris McQueen off Chris Hill's short pass gave Giants the ideal start.

Connor's penalty goal made it 12-0, after Richie Myler was harshly sin-binned for a high tackle on McGillvary and Connor snapped a field goal after Ash Handley scored Leeds' first try to give Huddersfield a 13-4 lead at the break.

The Rhinos came good again in the second half. James McDonnell strode through a huge gap to cap off an impressive display after Rhyse Martin kept the ball alive. And, following a stellar Harry Newman break, Leeds had their third try of the night, with Austin finding Martin out wide on his own on 55 minutes.

An Aidan Sezer kick was spilled by McGillvary and, with Lolohea failing to grasp possession, Cameron Smith won the race to the bouncing ball. Martin this time converted to make it 18-13 and complete the turnaround.

It had been all the Rhinos in the second half, but out of nothing, Lolohea got the Giants on the front foot, skipping through before Connor prodded a superb kick for McQueen to grab his second of the night.

Connor couldn't convert though – much to the joy of the Headingley faithful – with Leeds still leading 18-17.

The Giants fullback clearly thought his side was winning as he sent a kick into touch with four minutes remaining, which confused even his teammates.

And when Lolohea sent a field goal just wide as the clock wound down, it was going to be Leeds' night.

Round 9

Wigan ended Warrington's hundred per cent start to the season with a thrilling 13-6 win at a packed out Halliwell Jones Stadium.

The highly anticipated Friday-night TV clash drew a record crowd for the stadium and the wet conditions did little to reduce the excitement of a full-blooded clash, with Harry Smith giving a superb kicking performance to dictate field position.

Wigan opened the scoring after seven minutes when superb linking on the left between Smith and Bevan French saw the fullback fire a pinpoint pass and Jake Wardle was able to slide between two defenders. Smith hit the post with the conversion attempt and Wigan then lost Brad Singleton to a knee injury.

It resulted in a longer-than-usual stint for Kaide Ellis and the big Australian did not disappoint, going head-to-head with Warrington's in-form prop Paul Vaughan. He wasn't the only outstanding forward for Wigan, with Liam Byrne, Ethan Havard and skipper Liam Farrell also lending great support, while Josh McGuire and returning Daryl Clark battled gamely for the hosts, as did debutant Lucas Green in a short spell. But they were ultimately outdone in the middle of the field.

Wigan grabbed their second try after 27 minutes when the electric French put a reverse kick in and Brad O'Neill collected before spinning and appearing to bounce the ball down. Chris Kendall referred the touchdown to video-referee Tom Grant, who decided there was enough evidence to award the four points. Smith converted to open a 10-0 advantage for the Warriors.

April

Wigan's Brad O'Neill crashes over against Warrington

Wigan had dominated but Warrington struck before the break as George Williams, Matty Ashton and Matt Dufty combined over eighty metres before a cover tackle from Liam Marshall on Dufty stopped the Wolves. It was only a temporary respite, as Stefan Ratchford and Josh Drinkwater quickly took play right and Matty Nicholson stepped inside Smith to go over. Ratchford goaled and somehow, despite being clearly second best, the Wolves found themselves only four points down at the break.

The second half was barely four minutes old when McGuire was penalised for interference and Smith stepped up to add the penalty and increase the advantage back to six points.

Smith added a field goal in the 64th minute before the final ten minutes saw Williams come to life. Twice the Wolves thought they had scored tries but both efforts were overruled by video-referee.

Catalans missed the chance to make up ground on leaders Warrington as they lost at Huddersfield 26-14 on the same night.

The Giants of 2023 had made a habit of coming out on the wrong side of close scorelines. But they played the relentlessly wet conditions better, as their spine controlled the game more effectively than their injury-ravaged opponents. And they came up with the big plays when required to win with a margin of comfort.

Centre Sam Halsall and Harvey Livett both grew a little more into their claret and gold shirts over the course of the win, with Halsall scoring a first-half double and Livett also getting his first try for the club in what was his 100th career appearance. Another off-season recruit, Kevin Naiqama, put the seal on victory in the closing stages

The Dragons had tries from Tom Johnstone and Matthieu Laguerre that helped them stay in close contention until Naiqama's score eleven minutes from time. Jake Connor converted and finished a fine day with the boot, in general play and from the tee, with another long-range penalty after the full-time hooter.

Hull KR moved above Catalans into third spot on points difference with a 26-14 home win over St Helens.

Despite St Helens taking an early 6-0 lead the home side went on to dominate and make it four wins in a row, backing up the previous weekend's hammering of cross-city rivals Hull FC.

Lachlan Coote was imperious and kicked five goals out of five attempts and halfback Mikey Lewis scored two tries in an effervescent display.

Rovers went into the game without the suspended duo of James Batchelor and Sauaso Sue, while Sam Wood was unavailable with a minor hamstring injury. Coach Willie Peters went for a change out wide with skipper Shaun Kenny-Dowall on the wing and recent signing from Wakefield Corey Hall given his debut in the centre.

April

Saints were missing some of their influential power pack with Alex Walmsley, Curtis Sironen, Sione Mata'utia and Joe Batchelor all out through injury. They were also without loose forward Morgan Knowles, who was starting the first of a five-game ban, meaning there was a start in the front row for Louie McCarthy-Scarsbrook, with Mark Percival in the second row.

Jez Litten's try on 66 minutes, which gave Rovers an 18-point lead, was the gamebreaker.

Leeds reversed the week-two result between the sides as they beat Hull FC 34-10 at rainy Headingley.

The first half went like a dream for the Rhinos, who crossed through James McDonnell, Ash Handley and the barnstorming Tom Holroyd, all the tries converted by Rhyse Martin for an 18-0 half-time lead.

Handley's second try on 47 minutes made it 24-unanswered points, before Hull responded with Carlos Tuimavave's try. But Mikolaj Oledzki and Martin scored either side of Davy Litten's try to cap an important home success.

It was a seventh consecutive loss for Hull FC.

Which left only one game for the Sunday afternoon, as Leigh travelled to Wakefield for what the fixture planners would have positioned as a relegation battle. But the Leopards' 32-0 win illustrated they were unlikely to finish anywhere near the bottom of the table.

It was a ninth successive loss for Trinity and they had been nilled for a fifth time in nine games.

With halfback Lachlan Lam fizzing, first-half tries by Gareth O'Brien and Ben Reynolds were followed by four more after the break. Lam, Super League top try scorer at the time Josh Charnley - with two in quick succession - and Joe Mellor all crossed.

Interim Castleford coach Andy Last was hoping to land a permanent contract on the back of a win at Salford in the Thursday TV game. But the Tigers went down 14-6 at the AJ Bell Stadium, a fourth loss in six matches under his command.

They dominated the first half against the Red Devils but were limited to just six points through Greg Eden's try and Gareth Widdop's conversion.

And, three minutes before half-time, the Red Devils produced the move of the match. Kallum Watkins flicked out a pass to Ryan Brierley who shot away down the touchline and smartly kicked infield for the supporting Brodie Croft, who read the bounce of the ball to perfection and touched down under the posts.

Australian forward Shane Wright scored the only try of the second half off Marc Sneyd's short ball. And with ten minutes remaining, Salford extended their lead to eight points when Sneyd kicked a penalty from 30 metres following a late hit by Adam Milner.

The following week, Last was appointed as Tigers head coach on a two-and-a-half year contract.

Round 10

In the round before the break for the international weekend, Wigan suddenly emerged as table-toppers.

Warrington's Thursday-night 28-6 defeat at St Helens gave the Warriors the opportunity to overtake them on points difference, which they duly took the following Sunday afternoon with a second home victory over Wakefield, this time by a more modest score of 22-6.

Both Saints and the Wolves were not at full strength but despite that St Helens looked to be getting back into the groove that had seen them win four successive titles.

Warrington had James Harrison back from a six-week lay-off but were still without Joe Bullock and the suspended trio of Paul Vaughan, Joe Philbin and Gil Dudson in their pack. And they lost stand-in loose forward Daryl Clark to a knee injury after 20 minutes.

For Saints, Tommy Makinson (recurring leg issue) and Mark Percival (hamstring strain in training) were the latest big-name players to become unavailable through injury. Joe Batchelor did return from a knee injury for his first competitive match of the year and put in a typically dedicated shift, though this performance was largely about the unsung heroes.

April

Salford's Brodie Croft makes a break against Catalans Dragons

Wingers Jon Bennison and Tee Ritson came in, both scoring tries and impressing. James Bell produced another all-action display at loose forward and 19-year-old prop George Delaney underlined his potential with a big and fearless shift off the bench. Jonny Lomax pulled it all together.

A superb opening 20 minutes shaped the story of the night, the champions surging 16-0 in front. The tries of Konrad Hurrell, Jonny Lomax and Will Hopoate had the Wolves, beaten for the first time at home to Wigan the previous week, stunned, and no matter what they tried, St Helens stayed in control and stayed comfortably in the lead. Bennison and Ritson added further tries in the second half, with Matty Russell's converted try on 25 minutes the only Wolves reply.

On the Sunday afternoon, with kick-offs delayed in the three Super League fixtures because of a UK government national trial of an emergency alert via mobile phones, Wigan never looked likely to lose against win-less Wakefield.

Having already beaten Trinity 60-0 at the DW Stadium in week two, it was expected that Wigan would put up a similar scoreline. They led 18-0 at the break thanks to tries from Liam Marshall, Abbas Miski and Ethan Havard but Trinity battled hard and showed the effort and commitment that coach Mark Applegarth had been asking for. They got their only points with Jay Pitts crossing over from loanee Rowan Milnes' pass, before Bevan French's try ensured there would be no miracle comeback.

Wakefield were without hooker Liam Hood, serving the first of a two-game suspension for two separate dangerous contact offences in the defeat to Leigh.

By the end of the weekend, Hull KR had gone two points clear in third, courtesy of a hard-fought, Friday-night 12-7 win at Castleford, with seven wins from their first ten matches, representing the Robins' best ever start to a Super League season.

The Tigers, with Andy Last now installed as permanent head coach after six weeks as interim, came out fired up and Jacob Miller's try was the only one of a first half they dominated. But the impressive Corey Hall, in his second Hull KR appearance, started a fightback which man of the match Matt Parcell completed on the hour mark, just after Miller's field goal had edged the Tigers a point ahead, by sniping from dummy-half.

Catalans fell back to fourth on the Sunday as they went down at Salford 16-14.

The Red Devils had deservedly led 16-4 early in the second half but the Dragons, much improved after the break, fought back with tries from Paul Seguier and Adam Keighran to cut the deficit to just two points with a minute to play. Keighran had the chance to send the game to golden point with his conversion attempt half way between touch and the posts. But he was off target and Salford were able to celebrate a third successive victory.

Salford had gone into a 13th minute lead when prop King Vuniyayawa took a short ball from Andy Ackers at pace and proved unstoppable from close range for a try converted by Marc Sneyd to make it 6-0. Sneyd made it 8-0 after a Sio Siua Taukeiaho high shot on Shane Wright.

However, Sneyd spilled the ball from the restart and, straight from the scrum, the ball was worked to the left edge with a long Keighran pass and winger Tom Johnstone finished well from ten metres. Keighran was unable to add the conversion.

On the stroke of half-time, Salford scored their second try after turning defence into attack in the blink of an eye. Sam Tomkins kicked to the Salford in-goal on the last tackle, but the ball just rolled dead. The 20-metre tap was taken quickly by Rhys Williams and Joe Burgess took an inside pass before sprinting clear. There was a valiant chase from Johnstone, who was actually able to haul Burgess down but he just had enough momentum to reach over and score under the posts. Sneyd's goal made it 14-4 as the half-time hooter sounded.

Sneyd was gifted another shot at goal five minutes into the second half which proved the difference as the Dragons staged their valiant comeback.

The Red Devils drew level in the table with fourth-placed Catalans.

Inspired by Edwin Ipape and a power-packed prop performance from Tom Amone, Leigh Leopards survived a second-half scare to claim another notable scalp with a 20-6 home win over Leeds on the Friday.

The Leopards were 16-0 up until a minute before half-time through two Ipape tries which sandwiched one from Kai O'Donnell. But a minute from half-time, Nene Macdonald stole the ball in a one-on-one challenge with Gareth O'Brien and this inspired the Rhinos, with Blake Austin putting James Bentley over the line for Rhyse Martin's goal to make it 16-6 at the break.

After Leigh withstood a Rhinos onslaught Ben Reynolds added his third goal on 64 minutes to increase Leigh's lead to 18-6. And Leigh made the game safe with a couple of minutes remaining when the Rhinos were caught offside and Reynolds converted to secure a hard-fought 20-6 victory, the margin of which was sufficient for them to leapfrog above their opponents in the table.

On the Sunday, Hull FC ended a seven-match losing run with a 20-14 home win over Huddersfield.

Danny Houghton, who surpassed club legend Johnny Whiteley MBE in all time club appearances, was outstanding, winding back the clock to cause Huddersfield endless issues through the middle with and without the ball. And young fullback Davy Litten provided a level of security and quality at the back.

The Giants struggled to click into gear, particularly with ball in hand and were made to pay for a slow start to the second half.

Former Hull man Jake Connor had his moments at stand-off but was under immense pressure all afternoon and struggled to take control of the game alongside Tui Lolohea and Will Pryce.

Although they mounted a late comeback, the Giants couldn't produce the right play at the right time and fell to their fifth defeat of the season, missing a chance to climb into the top six.

Chris McQueen responded for Huddersfield after Liam Sutcliffe grabbed the game's first try as the sides went into half-time level at 8-8. Sutcliffe scored his second try ten minutes after Chris Satae put the hosts ahead when he charged through a huge gap at first receiver and under the posts three minutes after the break.

Sam Halsall had a try disallowed for a forward pass, though Esan Marsters went over five minutes from time. But the Airlie Birds deserved to hang on for a desperately needed win.

BETFRED SUPER LEAGUE
Sunday 23rd April

	P	W	D	L	F	A	D	Pts
Wigan Warriors	10	8	0	2	241	97	144	16
Warrington Wolves	10	8	0	2	264	137	127	16
Hull KR	10	7	0	3	230	141	89	14
Catalans Dragons	10	6	0	4	220	170	50	12
Salford Red Devils	10	6	0	4	208	183	25	12
St Helens	9	5	0	4	180	121	59	10
Leigh Leopards	10	5	0	5	188	187	1	10
Leeds Rhinos	10	5	0	5	189	191	-2	10
Huddersfield Giants	9	4	0	5	167	128	39	8
Hull FC	10	3	0	7	138	312	-174	6
Castleford Tigers	10	2	0	8	103	226	-123	4
Wakefield Trinity	10	0	0	10	53	288	-235	0

MAY
Dragons fire up

Round 11

Wigan had spent the two-week rest enforced for the England Test against France at the top of the table on points difference, on the back of a six-match winning run. But that run ended on the Thursday night at Hull FC, as the Airlie Birds built on their first win in eight matches against Huddersfield the week before the international break with a 14-10 success.

Hull looked energised, playing with a new-found belief and desperation to hold off a second-half Wigan barrage and claim consecutive victories. The Black and Whites were sharp with ball in hand in the first half, led largely by the outstanding Jake Clifford, the Warriors enjoying a mountain of possession and field position for much of the second half.

Hull started well and took the lead in the fifth minute through Darnell McIntosh, who collected a clever Clifford kick through to touch down one handed in the corner. Clifford converted brilliantly. And, ten minutes later, with the Warriors' defence retreating, the Aussie halfback took the line on himself, slamming the ball down on the line to make it a two-score lead.

The Warriors desperately tried to arrest Hull's momentum and conceded a penalty from close range, with Clifford stepping up to make it a 14-point advantage after half-an-hour.

Wigan opened their account just before half-time through Iain Thornley, back in the side after a long absence with several injuries. He finished well in the corner from a flowing scrum play and Harry Smith converted from near the touchline to cut the gap to eight points at the break.

The Cherry and Whites picked up where they left off after half-time, cutting the deficit to just four points, when Thornley got on the outside of Cameron Scott after good work from Bevan French.

As the half wore on, Wigan turned the screw, with Hull unable to get out of their own half. But the Warriors were guilty of squandering opportunities in the face of tenacious and desperate black and white defence.

The game reached a crescendo in the final minute when Jake Trueman, who was making his Hull debut after a long-term ACL injury, was sin-binned for a professional foul on Joe Shorrocks metres from Hull's line.

Wigan went for all or nothing with seconds remaining and came up with an error under pressure to see Hull defy the odds and seal a well-earned victory.

The night after, early pacesetters Warrington moved two points clear of the Warriors at the top with a 32-18 home win over Wakefield, who were still searching for their first points of the season.

It wasn't as straightforward as the final scoreline suggested. A lightning Wolves start saw them 12-0 ahead in as many minutes through two Josh Thewlis tries converted by Stefan Ratchford. But Trinity were well in the contest after tries from Morgan Smith and Kelepi Tanginoa and two Will Dagger conversions had them level at half-time.

However they were dealt a huge blow with almost half an hour remaining when Kevin Proctor was shown a red card for a high shot on Thewlis.

From that point, Warrington took control, scoring three tries in the final quarter, the last

Hull FC's Brad Fash, Carlos Tuimavave and Danny Houghton combine to bring down Wigan's Jake Wardle

one a wonderful solo effort from Matty Ashton, to run out comfortable winners.

All the other games were played on the Friday night as well, to accommodate the new king's coronation and there was a TV belter from Perpignan as Catalans ended a three-match losing run with a 24-12 win over St Helens.

The return from injury of scrum-half Mitchell Pearce, another impressive stint by Adam Keighran and a dream debut for fellow Aussie centre Matt Ikuvalu, added to killer pace provided on the wings by the two Toms, Davies and Johnstone, were key for the Dragons.

Ben Garcia's class and relentless work rate was the cornerstone of the Dragons' success, leading once again with ferocity and perfectly-timed discipline.

Garcia had to take evasive action during the warm-up, jumping the fence into the crowd to avoid a runaway bull from a pre-match parade but for the following 80 minutes he never took a backwards step.

Not even the return of Alex Walmsley and Tommy Makinson could save St Helens from another defeat in a controversial bruiser. Despite an early against-the-grain 12-0 lead thanks to two counter-attacks, Walmsley and Jack Welsby the try scorers, Saints fell apart in the face of controlled aggression and relentless pace. Arthur Mourgue and Ikuvalu tries had it back at 12-all at the break. Adam Keighran added two more goals in the second half and a Davies double took Catalans clear.

Saints dropped out of the top six to the benefit of Leigh, whose second-half home blitz saw off Castleford by 30-6.

It was 6–6 at half-time, Joe Westerman opening the scoring and Ben Reynolds replying for Leigh. After the turnaround, Kai O'Donnell put Leigh in front before prop Ava Seumanufagai got their third, with Ricky Leutele making the game safe and Matt Davis finishing it off.

Hull KR remained third with their sixth consecutive win as they mastered the wet conditions at Craven Park to end 28-0 victors over Huddersfield.

The win was achieved without influential halfback Jordan Abdull, who had been terrorising defences with his kicking game but was out for six weeks with a quad injury sustained in training. They were also missing second row forward Frankie Halton but were helped by the return, after suspension, of Sauaso Sue.

May

Giants coach Ian Watson had problems of his own, lacking key players in Theo Fages and Oliver Russell with long-term injuries plus two, in Matty English and Josh Jones, due to concussion protocols. It meant that Jake Connor had to slot in the halves with Tui Lolohea, while Sam Hewitt, Innes Senior and Kieran Rush were all called into the matchday squad.

Rovers opened up a 14-0 lead by the break after Ryan Hall's double and a Rowan Milnes penalty goal. James Batchelor scored either side of Tom Opacic's try for the Robins to complete the scoring.

Salford were another side in hot form and they registered their fifth successive win, after a supremely controlled performance produced a 22-12 win at Leeds.

Whilst the Rhinos pulled the game back just on half-time with a Richie Myler score - after conceding two converted tries through Rhys Williams and Sam Stone, when Blake Austin was in the sin bin for obstructing Brodie Croft as he followed his own kick - they were their own worst enemies as they tried to speed the game up, error-strewn early in the tackle count and undisciplined, losing the second-half penalty count 6-0.

Marc Sneyd kicked two penalty goals either side of Ellis Longstaff's converted try, meaning James Bentley's reply for Leeds was only consolation.

Round 12

Saturday afternoon was a historic day as James Roby became the St Helens club's top appearance record-holder. The Saints skipper made his 532nd club appearance in their 26-12 home win against Salford Red Devils, overtaking the previous record held by Kel Coslett.

After entering the field to a huge guard of honour from both side's players, 37-year-old Roby played 75 minutes in the baking heat, causing Salford a host of problems with his dummy-half runs and kicking from acting halfback.

Salford raced into a 12-0 lead inside the opening 20 minutes on the back of having to defend their line for long periods as Saints started the brighter.

The Red Devils turned defence into attack when King Vuniyayawa made a break up the middle and offloaded to the supporting Brodie Croft, who raced away and got the ball down despite the attempt of Tee Ritson to keep him out. Marc Sneyd converted for a 6-0 lead.

Seven minutes after, Ritson acrobatically grounded the ball in the left corner. But television replays showed the ball hit the touchline following a great cover tackle from Ryan Brierley. Salford soaked up more Saints pressure and countered brilliantly as Brierley and Kallum Watkins exchanged short passes to see the former race over under the posts. Sneyd converted and the Red Devils led 12-0.

Saints refused to go away and laid siege on the Salford line. And they were frustrated for the majority of the half before James Bell crossed from a Curtis Sironen backflick, after Roby's burst up the middle, eight minutes before the break to reduce the deficit to six points.

The home side came firing out of the blocks after half-time and punished Salford for multiple errors, with Sironen again, Jonny Lomax, Tommy Makinson and Joe Batchelor all scoring to secure victory.

Salford had a couple of key injuries that harmed their cause. In-form backrower Shane Wright had his season ended in the 23rd minute with an ankle injury suffered in a tackle off the ball by Matty Lees, who was later banned for two games. Hooker Andy Ackers failed a HIA half way through the second half, while Sironen later got a match ban for a late tackle on Croft.

Leeds' second-half comeback at the DW Stadium the night before was truly remarkable. The Rhinos were 14-0 down to a dominant Wigan with five minutes to half-time. But, with twelve men, they ended 40-18 winners.

Centre Harry Newman's two long-range interception tries were crucial. The 23-year-old had been in the news over the previous week following a reported bust-up with teammate Tom Holroyd in the aftermath of Leeds' defeat to Salford.

But in the 35th minute, Newman plucked a Harry Smith pass out of the air to race away and score what looked like being a consolation try. It ended up being a game changer, even

May

Chairman Eamonn McManus congratulates James Roby on becoming St Helens' all-time leader for appearances

though Zane Tetevano's red card shortly after for a horrible-looking late high tackle on Smith looked like ending Leeds' chances.

Tries from Abbas Miski and Bevan French - along with three goals from Smith - saw the Warriors lead. But Tetevano's exit seemed to galvanise the Rhinos and they came out for the second half a completely different team, scoring two tries in the opening ten minutes through Holroyd and Richie Myler to lead for the first time.

Iain Thornley levelled matters and it looked like Wigan would kick on and take the points but Leeds took it to another level with Newman scoring another interception try before Rhyse Martin, Cameron Smith and Liam Tindall all went over to secure a remarkable victory. Tetevano got a two-match penalty notice.

Wigan's loss, their second on a row, meant that Warrington moved four points clear at the top of the table after a comeback win of their own, by 21-14 at home over Hull KR, who were on the back of a six-match winning run.

The hosts trailed 12-6 at the break, a Josh McGuire try on 34 minutes replying to Ethan Ryan and Kane Linnett scores, but gradually turned things around, twice levelling before eventually taking the lead in the 69th minute.

Ben Currie levelled at 12-12 soon into the second half; Mikey Lewis and Stefan Ratchford exchanged penalty kicks before Matty Ashton ran in a late winner for the Wolves and George Williams sealed the win with a late field goal.

Also on the Friday, Catalans backed up the previous week's win over St Helens, announcing their return to form with one of their best displays of the season and a 46-22 win at Castleford.

They utterly dominated the Tigers in the first half, playing with too much power and pace for the hosts to handle, scoring six tries to secure the result by half-time, leading 34-6. Adam Keighran scored a first-half double alongside Jordan Dezaria, Matt Ikuvalu, Tom Johnstone and Ben Garcia tries, before Matt Whitley and Sam Tomkins also crossed in the second half.

Tigers' coach Andy Last took some pleasure from the second half, in which Bureta Faraimo scored twice and Alex Mellor completed his own double, despite losing their whole spine of Niall Evalds, Jacob Miller and Gareth Widdop to injury. But he could not hide his disappointment at all that came before.

May

A Josh Charnley brace helped Leigh make it four Super League wins on the trot with a huge 30-4 win at Huddersfield. And the five-try Leopards came within two minutes of nilling the Giants, whose supporters' pre-season optimism was on the wane.

Injuries to key playmakers Oliver Russell and Theo Fages left an obvious lack of direction from the Giants' halves, with Jake Connor and debutant Kieran Rush starting. Tui Lolohea had a nightmare at fullback, dropping the ball cold as he ran a ball back to leave Joe Mellor to pick up and crash over.

In contrast the Leopards had Ben Reynolds and Lachlan Lam running riot, as Leigh moved into fifth spot. Tries from Reynolds and Charnley put Leigh 12-0 ahead at half-time. Charnley, Lam and Mellor added further scores to underline Leigh's first win ever at the John Smith's Stadium.

It was a fourth loss in five games for Huddersfield, who went 10th as Hull FC won their third game in a row with a 26-6 victory at win-less Wakefield.

Hull's resilience in their previous week's success against Wigan was evident again, particularly in the first half when they repelled a fair amount of pressure to take a 6-0 lead through an Adam Swift try.

Whenever they attacked, they were finding open space and centres Carlos Tuimavave and Liam Sutcliffe both scored to seal the match before Scott Taylor capped a fine display with the final try.

Wakefield avoided a sixth nilling of the season with twelve minutes left when captain Matty Ashurst drove towards the line and managed to put the ball down on it, Will Dagger converting. But Trinity once again looked blunt in attack.

* *That Monday the French Federation announced they would be unable to stage the World Cup in 2025 after the French government pulled funding.*

Challenge Cup Round 6

Warrington's Wembley dreams got off to a flying start in France with a hard-fought 16-14 win over Catalans Dragons, in a tie which went right to the wire.

With nothing to choose between two teams in a disjointed, niggling game, it was the slightly more successful boot of Stefan Ratchford that proved to be the difference as he landed two conversions, compared to just one by Dragons' fullback Arthur Mourgue.

A sin-binning for Michael McIlorum mid-way through the second half could have been the Dragons' undoing but instead Catalans went ahead for the first time and went on to dominate the closing stages until a fatal defensive flaw allowed winger Matty Ashton to strike for the second time in the game, moments from the final hooter, for the winning try.

On the same Saturday afternoon, Wigan gained revenge for their league defeat by Leeds when they beat the Rhinos at sunny Headingley by 18-14.

It was a mirror-image of the clash at DW Stadium as the Rhinos started with intent, forcing errors and punishing enough of them to build a well-deserved 14-0 lead. This time it was the Warriors who came roaring back, scoring four unanswered tries to successfully begin their defence of the trophy.

Tries from Tom Holroyd and Harry Newman helped to earn Leeds their three-score first-half cushion. But Bevan French tries either side of half-time and two more from Junior Nsemba and impressive Jake Wardle proved enough, despite Harry Smith only landing one conversion.

There were three other all-Super League ties at the last-16 stage.

On the Friday night, Leigh Leopards repeated their big league win at Wakefield earlier in the season, Tom Briscoe and Kai O'Donnell both scoring braces in a 40-12 victory. And the day after an astounding game at Salford ended with the Red Devils hanging on for a 42-40 home victory over Huddersfield.

Salford led 24-0 thanks to converted tries from Matty Costello, Alex Gerrard, Kallum Watkins and Rhys Williams and looked to be on course for a smooth passage into the last eight. But the previous year's beaten finalists Huddersfield scored four tries of their own without reply,

May

Warrington's Matt Dufty driven back by Catalans Dragons' Matt Whitley

with Luke Yates leading the way with a double and others from Sam Hewitt and Jake Bibby. Three of the tries were converted by Jake Connor, meaning Huddersfield trailed only 24-22 early in the second half.

Cue Salford's second purple patch, with Joe Burgess, Williams and Marc Sneyd all scoring in a stunning 14-minute spell which re-established Salford's handsome lead to 42-22 with only 13 minutes to play. But Ian Watson's men refused to concede and fought back with a further three converted tries from Tui Lolohea, Kevin Naiqama and a hat-trick score from Yates against his former club. Connor's conversions meant that, with a minute to play, Salford's lead had been shaved to 42-40.

On Sunday, Hull FC continued their improvement with a 32-8 win at Castleford. Heavily depleted Castleford had a change in every position bar one from the previous week's team that lost at Catalans, including a halfback pairing of Joe Westerman and Paul McShane in a spine that contained George Lawler and young prop Sam Hall due to injury and suspension, meaning ex-Hull hooker Jacob Hookem made his bow off the bench.

The black and whites, in front of a vociferous following in the Railway End sun, made it to their ninth consecutive quarter-final and, by contrast, were boosted by Tex Hoy being back to replace ankle victim Davy Litten, returning Brad Fash replacing suspended Scott Taylor and with Nick Staveley on debut in a young bench.

Jake Clifford ran the show, form winger Adam Swift finishing with a try hat-trick.

There were no giant-killings as Hull KR accounted for Batley at home by 50-0, Ethan Ryan weighing in with a hat-trick of tries. And St Helens won through 26-6 at Halifax, at a cost as Morgan Knowles was red-carded a minute from time for a high tackle and subsequently got a two-game ban. Knowles was making his return from a five-match suspension.

Which left York Knights as the only Championship side in the quarter-finals after they beat London Broncos at home by 36-12, winger Olly Butterworth celebrating his return from a 16-month lay-off with a fine hat-trick on his competitive club debut.

May
Round 13

Sky television viewers were treated to two thrilling golden-point games in the last round of May.

On the Thursday night, Wigan came back to edge their clash at Craven Park 26-22. The difference between Hull KR winning a remarkable game and Wigan Warriors taking the spoils was an Abbas Miski try in the very last second of normal time, a Mikey Lewis field goal attempt rebounding off a post and a hat-trick try from Liam Farrell in the fifth minute of extra time.

With ten minutes to go, the Robins led by eight points but Wigan's resilience and the Bevan French factor won the day.

Liam Marshall's second try, when he out-jumped Shaun Kenny-Dowall from a Harry Smith kick to the corner, gave them hope and then, with the clock showing zero, the real drama began. Wigan threw caution to the wind and the move ended with Miski going over in the corner. Referee Jack Smith thought it was a try and video referee Tom Grant agreed that the ball had been grounded in the narrowest of spaces.

Smith could have won the game with the touchline conversion but instead it was to be golden point.

Rovers had the early impetus in extra time as Lewis's field-goal attempt hit the post. Matt Parcell caught the rebound offside.

Wigan came up with the decisive play with five minutes gone, as Rovers stood off their attack and allowed French to race past four defenders and find Farrell in support to score his hat-trick try. The home fans screamed for a forward pass. A draw would have been a fair result.

The night after at Headingley was just as entertaining as St Helens emerged 13-12 winners.

The contest went to the 89th-and-a-half minute before being decided by a Lewis Dodd field goal, the first success after nine goal attempts in total, one of them a 45-metre penalty attempt by Rhyse Martin that fell short.

Spectacular tries, none better than Ash Handley's in the fourth minute to set the stage, injury setbacks pushing Leeds in particular – who lost three backs in the opening half-hour and with a bench of forwards – to the limit, a red card, several missed chances and a magnificent backdrop all amounted to a wonderful sporting spectacle.

Alex Walmsley's post-contact metres among a haul of over 230 were astonishing. His final momentous drive that saw Saints go 80 metres, when it looked as though both sides would have to settle for a point each, enabled Dodd to clinch the contest was simply superb.

He was backed up by the workaholic James Bell and returning Curtis Sironen, with Saints coach Paul Wellens acknowledging that their opponents deserved something as the debate about the cruelty of golden point swamped social media for the second night running.

The Rhinos' effort was outstanding as they were hit hard with injuries. Star centre Harry Newman suffered another hamstring injury after being downed in a two-man Saints tackle. Halfback Aidan Sezer left the field in the sixth minute with a groin injury, while Morgan Gannon suffered an ankle injury. And they had James McDonnell sent off near the end of normal time for punching. He successfully appealed a two-game ban.

Handley put Leeds in front when Rhyse Martin was set away by Derrell Olpherts from deep, before Tommy Makinson, in his 300th Saints game, dived over in trademark fashion shortly after. Saints were behind again before half-time when Makinson's escort attempt obscured Jack Welsby's sight of a bomb and Cameron Smith punished his spill to score.

Sironen's burst for the line helped Saints pull within two points and a penalty goal gave Makinson the chance to square things up with Leeds creaking, that after Justin Sangaré thought he'd wrested back the initiative, juggling Tom Holroyd's offload and regathering to go over, only for the video-referee to overrule the on-field decision as the ball had hit Agnatius Paasi's hand.

Dodd missed two field-goal attempts and Leeds' Richie Myler one before full-time and a breathless extra time ensued.

Three other games went ahead that night and the one at Leigh Sports Village had a major effect as table-toppers Warrington were well beaten by the Leopards, by 30-12.

Former Wolves backs Gareth O'Brien, two tries, and Josh Charnley both crossed, along

May

St Helens' Lewis Dodd celebrates his golden point winner at Leeds

with Tom Briscoe and Ben Reynolds as Leigh moved within four points of the top, while Warrington had their lead at the top over Wigan cut to two points.

The Wolves' points came from George Williams and Joe Philbin's first-half tries but they were chasing an early 14-0 home lead. Leigh stretched away and Reynolds' try with four minutes remaining secured the Leopards' fifth league win on a row.

In the south of France, Catalans had a comfortable 36-6 win over Wakefield, who sank to their 13th straight league defeat.

Some brave first-half resistance gave the 300-or-so away supporters in the Puig Aubert Stand something to shout about on a hot and humid Friday night in Perpignan. But to compound matters, former Trinity winger Tom Johnstone scored two long-range tries. Fullback Arthur Mourgue's every move had Wakefield worried and his 16-point contribution to Catalans' win was fundamental to the game.

Huddersfield ended a three-match losing Super League run with a 20-4 home win over Castleford, themselves now on a five-match losing streak.

The Tigers made a woeful start and were 10-0 down after 22 minutes through an Esan Marsters try and three Jake Connor goals. But an unconverted Alex Mellor try had them only 10-4 down at half-time.

After the break, Innes Senior and Kevin Naiqama tries took the Giants home.

In the only Sunday game, Salford ended Hull FC's three-match winning run with a 29-22 win at the AJ Bell Stadium.

It was a terrific game, with both sides moving the ball around to test the opposition, a trademark of the Red Devils under coach Paul Rowley.

Tyler Dupree, Deon Cross and Ryan Brierley tries put the hosts 18-10 up at the break, with Hull's tries coming from Jake Clifford and Jake Trueman. Clifford's effort was superb as Adam Swift was put clear down the left wing before feeding the supporting Clifford inside.

Brierley's was the pick for Salford as Marc Sneyd kicked from deep straight from a scrum for the fullback to win the chase.

Darnell McIntosh and Josh Griffin scores had Hull back at 24-22 after half-time, but Ken Sio's converted try sealed it. Sneyd added a late field goal to put the result beyond doubt.

BETFRED SUPER LEAGUE
Sunday 28th May

	P	W	D	L	F	A	D	Pts
Warrington Wolves	13	10	0	3	329	199	130	20
Wigan Warriors	13	9	0	4	295	173	122	18
Catalans Dragons	13	9	0	4	326	210	116	18
Hull KR	13	8	0	5	294	188	106	16
Leigh Leopards	13	8	0	5	278	209	69	16
Salford Red Devils	13	8	0	5	271	243	28	16
St Helens	12	7	0	5	231	169	62	14
Leeds Rhinos	13	6	0	7	253	244	9	12
Huddersfield Giants	12	5	0	7	191	190	1	10
Hull FC	13	5	0	8	200	357	-157	10
Castleford Tigers	13	2	0	11	135	322	-187	4
Wakefield Trinity	13	0	0	13	83	382	-299	0

* The 2023 European Championships scheduled for the end of the domestic season were postponed amid uncertainty over the 2025 World Cup.

JUNE
The Magic's gone?

Round 14

Magic Weekend in Newcastle attracted a total attendance over two days of 63,269 spectators (36,943 on Saturday, 26,326 on Sunday), the highest total figure since 2018, but its future in the fixture list was unsure under IMG's plans to 're-imagine' Rugby League.

There was certainly plenty of entertainment at sunny St James' Park among a festival atmosphere, with Salford and Hull KR providing a see-saw opener that the Red Devils edged 26-16.

Salford were flying high, leapfrogging the Robins in the Super League standings with their seventh win in their past eight games in all competitions.

The game was in the balance almost all the way through, the lead changing hands no fewer than six times and the difference between the sides never more than a converted try until Chris Atkin secured it for Salford six minutes from time.

Atkin's try followed that of Ken Sio five minutes earlier, with both coming from excellent and ultimately match-winning Ryan Brierley breaks.

Hull KR were hit by injury, with a long stoppage in play before James Batchelor was stretchered off and taken to hospital with a neck injury. He was released but had to wear a neck brace for the next month. Sauaso Sue was out for three months with a hamstring injury and the returning Lachlan Coote failed a head injury assessment.

Game two was expected to be just as close but Catalans totally dominated Wigan to emerge 46-22 winners, winger Tom Johnstone scoring a hat-trick - that took his season tally to 17, in 14 Super League rounds, and in-form Matt Whitley getting two tries.

The Dragons' blistering display was masterminded by their two classy veterans Mitchell Pearce and Sam Tomkins, on their injury returns. Their eight tries were evenly split across two periods of total dominance, one in the first half and one at the beginning of the second.

After an early penalty from Arthur Mourgue, who proved reliable with the boot in converting six of the eight tries to follow, Wigan scored the first try through Jake Wardle, provided by their own returning key man, Jai Field, and Bevan French. But then they were simply blown away, outfought and out-enthused by a Dragons side seemingly keen on making a statement, in the week they signed signed Hull FC prop Chris Satae on a two-year contract from the 2024 season.

The final Saturday game was another close one with Castleford coming from ten points behind within as many minutes to defeat Leeds 26-24.

Joe Westerman led the way for the Tigers on his 400th career appearance with a towering performance, leading the tackles and almost the metres made for his side, beaten only in the latter by hugely impressive winger Elliot Wallis, the former Hull KR recruit a danger with every carry, strong on defence and rewarded with his first try for the club.

On the opposite flank, Jason Qareqare was publicly challenged by Last to be more consistent on his return from a loan spell at Bradford and he responded with the last touchdown. But what best epitomised the revived Tigers was the final tackle of the game as Leeds looked to mount a desperate charge, James Bentley being gang-tackled into touch from 20 metres out by a posse of cover defenders led by Paul McShane.

Castleford's Jason Qareqare shows his delight on scoring at the Magic Weekend against Leeds

Moving Gareth Widdop to fullback in the absence of Niall Evalds also gave Castleford an extra dimension. His two late touchline conversions and three try-assists were ultimately the difference.

Already beset by injuries, the Rhinos were not helped by a late change when form forward Tom Holroyd was ruled out in the warm-up with a leg injury. Sam Walters moved up to the starting line-up and Liam Tindall was promoted to the bench, though not used until the final minute.

Backrower James McDonnell was the Rhinos' best after having a two-match ban for punching St Helens' Jonny Lomax the week before overturned on appeal.

On Sunday, Leigh beat Wakefield for the third time in 2023, by 30-4, despite playing for 53 minutes with 12 men, and for ten minutes, eleven. The Leopards were led by the brilliant triumvirate of Lachlan Lam, Edwin Ipape and Ricky Leutele.

Wakefield were desperate after injuries to quota players Samisoni Langi, Kelepi Tanginoa, Renouf Atoni and Jai Whitbread and had sent out an SOS call to David Fifita who the previous autumn had returned home to Australia after six-and-a-half years at Belle Vue. Centre Jack Croft was also re-signed.

Fifita had an impact as Ben Reynolds was sent off for a strike to the big forward's face. It became even tougher for the Leopards when Tom Nisbet was sent to the sin bin just two minutes later for a hip-drop tackle.

Incredibly, Adrian Lam's men kept their clean sheet intact as stellar defence from the likes of Ipape and Leutele forced Wakefield errors.

Lam's dazzling sixth-minute opening try was added to by Rob Mulhern as the Leopards took a 10-0 lead.

Edwin Ipape, Josh Charnley and Lam's second try sealed the win, before Max Jowitt's late consolation for Trinity.

Wakefield's season so far was summed up when the first set of the second half saw Mason Lino kick the ball at Jordan Crowther's head, which forced the forward off the field for a HIA.

Reynolds was banned for two matches and Nisbet one.

June

Tommy Makinson bagged four tries as St Helens set Tyneside alight, smashing Huddersfield by 48-6, piling on nine tries in a one-sided affair.

Makinson also kicked six goals from nine attempts, while Konrad Hurrell grabbed a brace in what was an outstanding team performance.

Saints' last try on 74 minutes was a stunner, a 90-metre effort started by a Jack Welsby break, before the ball came to Makinson whose nonchalant back flick went to Joey Lussick for the four-pointer.

Hull FC and Warrington provided a fitting finale which the Airlie Birds won 30-18, after the Wolves had shot into an early 12-0 lead.

The returning Connor Wrench and George Williams scored the early tries, both converted by Stefan Ratchford but a Danny Houghton try moments later meant it was 12-6 at half-time.

After the break Warrington were cut apart by the Black and Whites, with the likes of Josh Griffin, Tex Hoy and Jake Clifford running riot.

The lead was wiped out and overhauled when Adam Swift and Griffin, with two, crossed for the hosts, though the Wolves replied through Wrench's second. Griffin completed a hat-trick to pull Hull clear before Tex Hoy settled it.

Warrington's signing from Australia, prop Josh McGuire, was absent, awaiting a tribunal over charges he had made discriminatory language in the defeat at Leigh.

The outcome of the weekend was that Catalans sat at the top of the table, on points difference from Warrington.

Round 15

Champions St Helens had been excellent in the big win over Huddersfield at Magic Weekend that lifted them into the top six for the first time in 2023. And they continued to show they were back to their best the following Friday when they eventually dominated Wigan in a 34-16 victory at a packed-out Totally Wicked Stadium.

Saints tore to shreds a Wigan pack missing some big players and being ruthlessly exploited for it. Alex Walmsley and Matty Lees were strong from the start but the key was the performance of the bench forwards, particularly Agnatius Paasi, who produced one of, if not the best, display of his St Helens career.

Sione Mata'utia and James Bell backed up the work of two superb backrowers, Curtis Sironen and Joe Batchelor, and the returning Morgan Knowles, to ensure there was barely a passage of the game in which the home side were not completely on top.

Jack Welsby showed some outrageous talent on his 100th appearance for the club, scoring two tries and creating another three, skipper James Roby delivering a 73-minute masterclass.

As well as Mike Cooper being ruled out for the rest of the season with a knee injury, Wigan were currently without forwards Willie Isa and Ethan Havard, through hamstring and elbow issues, plus backrower Kai Pearce-Paul (leg). Brad Singleton returned from six games out with a knee injury as coach Matt Peet dropped Sam Powell and Toby King and moved Bevan French to halfback, with Jai Field at fullback.

Field and French scored tries to have Wigan only 12-10 down after half an hour but Welsby's kick-and-chase try just before the hooter signalled the end of the Warriors' chances. Quick-fire tries from Paasi and Welsby after the break confirmed that.

The result meant Saints leapfrogged Wigan into fifth, with the Warriors hanging on in sixth.

Catalans were still top after a 38-4 win over Hull KR on a hot and humid evening in Perpignan.

The depleted Robins, already missing fullback Lachlan Coote and a string of senior players, couldn't cope with a red-hot Dragons' side who raced to a 20-0 half-time lead before finishing the job in the second half.

Battered, bruised and beaten, Rovers flew home to assess the latest additions to the injury list, with Jordan Abdull (on his return), Jack Walker (on debut) and Sam Wood all limping from the Stade Gilbert Brutus pitch.

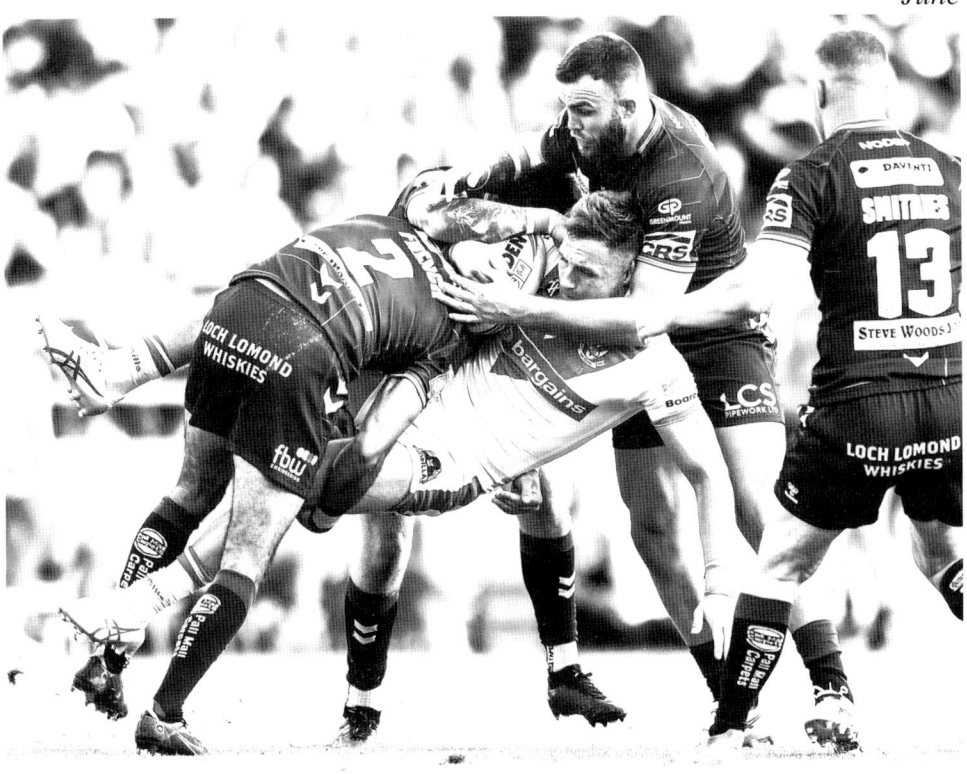

Wigan's Bevan French, Kaide Ellis and Morgan Smithies converge on St Helens' Matty Lees

Arthur Mourgue just pipped two-try Matt Whitley to the gamestar award with another dazzling display from fullback and a personal points tally of 16. Corey Hall got a consolation eight minutes from time with a brilliant long-range effort.

Warrington stayed second, behind on points difference, beating Huddersfield at home by 30-26 on the Saturday afternoon.

While the Giants allowed a Warrington attack still in decent shape to build and then maintain a lead, the Wolves in turn allowed a misfiring Giants attack several routes back into the game.

Sam Kasiano and Josh Thewlis scored tries for the Wolves either side of Jake Bibby's opener for the Giants, with George Williams and Leroy Cudjoe then exchanging converted tries before the break.

Soon after half-time, Danny Walker crossed for Warrington but quickfire tries from Kevin Naiqama and Theo Fages got the Giants back in it at 24-22.

Matt Dufty sent the hosts further ahead but Tui Lolohea's 73rd-minute try set up a tense finale.

Wolves prop Josh McGuire's future was hanging in the balance after he received one of Super League's longest-ever bans. Off-season Australian import McGuire was given a twelve-match suspension and £1,000 fine by an RFL tribunal after being found guilty of using 'unacceptable language' in Warrington's defeat to Leigh Leopards in late May.

He was considered to have used a 'derogatory and negative... term of abuse and disparagement towards disabled individuals' at Leigh winger Josh Charnley, relating to a member of Charnley's family.

McGuire, 33, had served a seven-match ban at the start of the season, also for unacceptable language that referenced disability and also in a match against Leigh, on that occasion a pre-season game. The latest incident took place in only his seventh match for the club.

June

Leigh were up to third after a Friday-night 28-16 home win over Hull FC.

Hull made a close game of it and Leigh could only breathe easy when Joe Mellor blasted past three defenders for their final try in the 78th minute.

The Leopards were indebted to a sparkling performance by Gareth O'Brien, who scored a try and created three and was a settling presence at the back, fielding every kick that went his way and kicking well from hand. Josh Charnley scored a typical brace in the left corner.

On the same night, Salford maintained fourth spot with an emphatic 42-10 win at Castleford.

Samoan international centre Tim Lafai was incredible from the outset, destroying the Castleford right-edge defence on numerous occasions as his halfback Marc Sneyd had the ball on a string. The Red Devils' professional display was a fitting tribute for Kallum Watkins' 350th career game, with wingers Rhys Williams and Ken Sio both getting a brace.

The Tigers had 12 men out from their first-team line-up and then lost Paul McShane, to a broken arm, and Mahe Fonua midway through the second half.

Young forward Aaron Willis – the Tigers academy player of the year in 2022 - made his senior debut.

Only one game was played on the Sunday as Wakefield won their first game of the season, a 24-14 home success over an equally depleted Leeds Rhinos.

Mark Applegarth enjoyed his first victory as Trinity head coach. And it was fully deserved as, even with twelve men, Wakefield rallied and showed heart and desire.

The newly signed Luke Gale was still absent, while Mason Lino was out with injury, so Morgan Smith and Will Dagger were the halves. Frenchmen Romain Franco and Hugo Salabio made their debuts after joining the club on trial, while Joe Law also made his debut off the bench late in the game.

Catalans prop Salabio was the man red-carded five minutes after half-time for a tip-tackle on Richie Myler. He had only been off the bench ten minutes and looked lively but a seven-match ban followed.

For Leeds, Leon Ruan made his Super League debut as Richie Myler again partnered Blake Austin in the halves, with Liam Tindall replacing Derrell Olpherts.

In hot conditions at Belle Vue, Trinity began strongly as winger Lee Kershaw patted down a Will Dagger kick and Jack Croft burrowed over before winger Franco marked his debut with their second try.

The ten-point lead was wiped out in short order by the Rhinos as Myler sent Cameron Smith in and former Wakefield junior Ruan powered over from another Myler pass.

The dismissal of Salabio seemed to have turned the match in Leeds' favour but after Blake Austin had kicked out on the full from a goal-line drop-out, Dagger restored the home side's lead.

Austin made amends for his sloppiness, exploiting a big gap in the Trinity defence to stride over from distance and put Leeds ahead for the first time.

But Dagger again hauled Trinity level with a penalty and when Ash Handley was sin-binned for obstruction, Matty Ashurst spun over to establish a four-point lead. Then Smith capitalised on Myler's error under a high kick and, with Dagger adding the second conversion, Wakefield were home and dry.

Challenge Cup Quarter Finals

Hull KR defied the form book and a minor injury crisis to book their place in the Challenge Cup semi-finals with a 28-10 home win over Salford.

Salford had been in electric form over the past two months, winning eight of their last nine games coming into the trip to a Robins side who had lost their last four in Super League.

Throw in a fresh batch of recent injuries and the home team were clear underdogs. But they delivered an excellent and much-needed performance that brought back to mind their early-season form.

The biggest blow of all was the loss of halfback star Jordan Abdull long-term, just after

Hull KR's Dean Hadley wrapped up by Salford's Oliver Partington and Tim Lafai

returning from a previous absence that coincided with their downturn. But Rowan Milnes not only stepped in but stepped up, putting in a controlled display.

At fullback, the loss of Lachlan Coote and new signing Jack Walker to concussion saw them put a call in to France for Catalans youngster Tanguy Zénon. Safe at the back and a real threat in attack, including scoring one of three first-half tries as his new team built an impressive 18-0 lead, he took this unexpected opportunity extremely well.

Shaun Kenny-Dowall's try on 62 minutes sealed the result and came at the end of a tricky spell of pressure that Hull KR saw out well.

Later on the Saturday on the other side of the city, St Helens had to showcase patience and composure in the second half to overcome a resilient and stubborn twelve-man Hull FC side by 32-18.

The dynamic of the contest changed completely at the break when Hull's Josh Griffin was sent off, immediately after being yellow-carded for dissent by referee Chris Kendall as the players were making their way from the field, leaving the Black and Whites a man short for the entire second half.

Saints rarely gave Hull a sniff after half-time, notching up four tries to one in the second 40 and were led exceptionally well by their spine, with Jack Welsby in particular proving a constant thorn in the side of the hosts.

It was an impressive performance from Saints, who lost both Mark Percival and Tommy Makinson to injury in the first half and played the majority of the game with a reshuffled backline.

For Hull, it was a case of what might have been. After battling back from 8-0 to take the lead, before heading into the break level at 12-all, Griffin's brain explosion as well as errors at crucial points of the game cost them.

To make matters worse, the hosts lost both Scott Taylor and Tex Hoy to injury. And Griffin was later banned for seven games for 'questioning the officials' integrity'.

June

On the Sunday, a committed performance against Warrington at the DW Stadium from Wigan saw them overcome the seventh-minute dismissal of Kaide Ellis to claim another famous Challenge Cup victory, by 14-12.

With Harry Smith in imperious kicking form and a superb effort from Ethan Havard, Liam Byrne and Liam Farrell, it was just too good for Warrington.

Josh Thewlis's try seven minutes from time brought the Wolves to within two points set up a thrilling finish. Then a superb kick return from Matt Dufty brought an excellent run from Connor Wrench but an error from Ben Currie handed possession back to Wigan with three minutes remaining.

Liam Marshall then spilled a ball and Warrington came forward again with James Harrison just stopped. Thewlis then saw a try disallowed, with Peter Mata'utia ruled to have thrown a forward pass with two minutes remaining. From that point Wigan successfully navigated their way to the win.

Ellis got three matches for a head-butt on Stefan Ratchford.

In the final game, Leigh knocked out the only remaining Championship team when they won at York Knights 34-14.

The tie ought to have been nothing other than a rout, the team third in Super League and enjoying an eight-match winning run playing the side fourth-from-bottom in the Championship. Throw in the fact that Leigh beat York 100-4 and 70-10 at the back end of the second-tier campaign in 2022 and it looked a mismatch.

It was anything but, down to two main factors, the Knights' extraordinary effort, each individual giving absolutely everything, and the Leopards' best efforts at the beginning to make it as difficult for themselves as possible, starting with Kai O'Donnell's fifth-minute red card.

It came after John Asiata fumbled the ball because of a Conor Fitzsimmons tackle, with Will Jubb collecting the loose pass and handing it to Josh Daley. Daley was met by O'Donnell and lifted up, tipped and slammed on his head.

Myles Harrison and Joe Brown tries and Harrison's three goals gave York a 14-6 lead at half-time, with Joe Mellor replying for the Leopards.

After the break, Tom Amone's try gave Leigh momentum and they took the lead for the first time when Josh Charnley scored on the hour mark. Charnley's second and Tom Briscoe's double blew out the score late on.

O'Donnell was suspended for six matches.

Round 16

Castleford picked up only their fourth win of the season, by far their most impressive, to soothe relegation nerves with a 23-14 home Friday night win over Warrington.

The Tigers showed their intentions from the start, running quicker and hitting harder than the early season pacesetters. Wingers Will Tate and Jason Qareqare scored first-half tries and three Gareth Widdop penalties made it 14-0 at the break.

Warrington only needed one bright spell to make up the difference and they got that, as Matty Ashton (twice) and Connor Wrench crossed to level the scores.

But Castleford did not drop the effort they showed all night. Instead they found a little bit more, as Widdop dropped a magnificent field goal from distance and then Jack Broadbent made certain with a try at the end.

Widdop was instrumental throughout, as were fellow pivots Jacob Miller and Joe Westerman. Broadbent too filled in at nine excellently after Nathan Massey, himself starting at hooker for broken-arm victim Paul McShane, was injured early by the tackle that saw James Harrison yellow-carded during the Tigers' fast start.

There were mitigating factors for the Wolves in terms of missing personnel. George Williams and Josh Drinkwater, so effectively controlling the team from halfback at the beginning of the year, were both out injured, while the dominant forward pack that steamrollered opposition early on had been denuded.

June

High-profile signing Josh McGuire's short time in England had come to a bitter end, with Warrington releasing the forward from his contract following his lengthy ban.

The result left Wakefield looking increasingly hopeless, six points adrift at the bottom of the table after a 28-12 defeat at Hull KR.

It had been a busy week at Trinity, former Manly winger Jorge Taufua following Lee Gaskell in leaving the club to join Championship side Bradford Bulls.

Wakefield were looking for back-to-back wins after their defeat of Leeds Rhinos. But Rovers stormed into a 22-0 lead, with Rowan Milnes filling in superbly again at halfback in the absence of Jordan Abdull. Trinity had the better of the second half but the 70th-minute sin-binning of David Fifita for questioning the referee's decision of his foul tackle, stopped their momentum dead and Mikey Lewis's 72nd-minute try took Rovers home and ended a four-league-match losing streak.

Both sides were missing significant talent with no less than seven players from each side on the sidelines but with new faces debuting for both sides. Rovers brought in Catalans winger Fouad Yaha on loan on the wing and there was finally a debut for Trinity for Luke Gale.

That week Rovers fullback Lachlan Coote had been forced to retire from the sport on medical advice. The 33-year-old, three-time Super League Grand Final winner with St Helens, planned to call time on his career at the end of this season, but had done so prematurely after suffering a series of concussions over the past year.

Hovering just above the relegation zone were Huddersfield, who on the same night were on the end of a 54-0 hammering at Headingley.

Seven out of the previous eight contests between the Rhinos and the Giants had been settled by a margin of six points or less - they couldn't be divided once even after golden-point extra-time. But on a night swelled by a tidal wave of emotion and dubbed by Leeds coach Rohan Smith 'a mini–Grand Final', with play-off hopes likely disappearing for the loser, his side rose to the occasion.

The hosts' nine-try demolition accompanied the uplifting presence of Rob Burrow and his family as part of the MND awareness round and the emotional passing of Leeds great Bev Risman.

Aidan Sezer's organisation and frequent running at the line allowed Blake Austin to become the dominant figure, while Richie Myler posed much more of a threat from fullback and wingers David Fusitu'a – back after a long absence – and Ash Handley made almost 400 metres between them.

Sam Walters, Fusitu'a and Rhyse Martin all got braces, with Richie Myler, Handley and James McDonnell scoring singles, Martin kicking nine out of ten goals.

On the Thursday night, Hull FC had put a significant dent in St Helens' top-two hopes with a 34-6 home win over the Champions.

At halfback, Jake Clifford, returning from a concussion protocol absence, was sensational in steering his side to victory on the back of tireless work from the forwards, who bullied Saints through the middle throughout the contest.

Jamie Shaul returned to the side at fullback and was excellent, while Andre Savelio and Darnell McIntosh, who had spent time in the reserves, both turned in top displays backing up from the previous Saturday's Cup defeat to Saints, in what was an outstanding performance from all 17 Hull players.

Conversely, the St Helens juggernaut was stopped in its tracks. Coming into the game in red hot form on the back of six straight wins, they were off the pace from the first set and came up with several uncharacteristic errors, which resulted in them barely firing a shot.

Paul Wellens opted to start Morgan Knowles at dummy-half, which backfired as the Saints attack stuttered. James Roby, who had started all 14 appearances, came on at half-time, by which point Hull led 22-0. Cameron Scott's second-half try just five minutes after Saints had opened their account ruled out any thoughts of a comeback.

In the only Sunday game, Wigan leapt from sixth to third with a 26-6 win at Salford.

Both teams had to battle the elements in the form of a constant downpour as well as thunder and lightning in the air but it was Wigan who handled them the better in the opening 40 minutes.

June

Catalans Dragons' Tom Johnstone bursts past Leigh's Ed Chamberlain and Gareth O'Brien

Their forwards laid the platform, with Morgan Smithies, Liam Byrne, two-try Liam Farrell and Joe Shorrocks getting through the hard yards, while Harry Smith controlled matters with his kicking game. Brad O'Neill was a stand-out filling in for Sam Powell, who had surgery on nagging shoulder injury.

The Warriors had won just one of their previous five league games and were up against an in-form Salford team, although they were without injured stars Brodie Croft and Andy Ackers and lost another as Ryan Brierley suffered a head injury. But they cracked a strong Salford defensive performance in the first half by scoring three second-half tries, in front of a club record attendance of 7,854 at the AJ Bell Stadium.

Catalans had gone two points clear at the top of the table on the Saturday night with a thrilling 38-30 home win over Leigh.

Temperatures in the south of France soared to over 35 degrees but the Leopards refused to wilt in the heat and pushed Catalans all the way in a highly competitive game. It was a breathless slug-fest illuminated by brilliance in attack and defence from both sides.

Missing four senior players to suspension (and five more to injury) Leigh coach Adrian Lam could only name an initial 18-man squad, so the Leopards were always up against it and the Dragons turned up the heat straight from kick-off, racing into a 20-0 lead after 17 minutes. But the visitors, with Edwin Ipape in brilliant form, fought back late in the first half to keep the game close and edged into a 30-26 lead with Tom Briscoe's try on 57 minutes, before the Dragons took control in the closing stages.

Ben Garcia's try augmented by Arthur Mourgue's seventh goal gave the Dragons a two-point lead. But it wasn't until Tom Johnstone's second try of the game, when he picked up a loose pass and raced 70 metres, to the posts, that the game was finally settled.

Round 17

Leigh Leopards dominated Hull KR in the Friday TV game to collect a 34-4 home win and move up into second place in the Super League table.

By this stage of the season it was obvious that the Leopards would buck the trend of promoted clubs being involved in a relegation battle. But their progress under coach Adrian Lam and Director of Football Chris Chester was staggering.

June

All Leigh's middle men were outstanding. Tom Amone, Robbie Mulhern, on-loan from St Helens Dan Norman and returning Ben Nakubuwai set the platform and Rovers couldn't match it.

Leigh led 22-0 at half-time after completing at 90 per cent through Tom Briscoe, Edwin Ipape, Ed Chamberlain and Josh Charnley tries. Ricky Leutele's penalty try and one for Mulhern, with Ben Reynolds kicking five goals made it 34-0 before Rovers, who lost Elliot Minchella and on-loan Fouad Yaha to injury at half-time, got a late consolation from Mikey Lewis.

The Leopards replaced Warrington in second spot after the Wolves had suffered a fifth defeat in six matches on the Thursday night, Leeds backing up their 54-0 thrashing of Huddersfield with a 22-6 win at the Halliwell Jones Stadium.

The Wolves players were booed off after the game, in which they were 16 points down in as many minutes.

The Rhinos delivered a near complete performance - clinical in attack, firmly resolute in defence - while the Wolves looked out of practice and one-dimensional, despite the return of Josh Drinkwater. George Williams was missing for the second week running with a hamstring injury picked up in training.

Blake Austin took the game by the scruff of the neck from the very beginning. Sam Walters' opener and Ash Handley's double put Leeds in firm control and they never really looked like letting go of their lead. Matty Ashton and Richie Myler swapped second-half tries

Walters was set to join Wigan at the end of the season as the Rhinos signed Catalans Dragons forward Mickael Goudemand for 2024.

Huddersfield had conceded nine tries the week before at Headingley but on the Friday night they showed plenty of fight at Wigan in a 22-6 loss.

Winger Abbas Miski was the hero for Wigan as his first-half try double helped his side overcome the stubborn Giants to make it back-to-back Super League wins. The Giants' forwards put in a shift in the first half but it was the Warriors that led 10-0 at the break thanks to Miski's brace.

Wigan extended their lead to 16 points shortly after the interval, with Jai Field scoring a sublime solo try. Liam Marshall then put the game to bed with a try while Wigan were down to twelve men, Ethan Havard in the bin for a shoulder charge, before Jake Bibby added a late consolation try against his former club.

Giants coach Ian Watson was full of praise for teenage forward Fenton Rogers after the Academy product came off the bench for his Super League debut.

St Helens edged into fifth spot after a 22-0 rainy Friday-night home win over Castleford.

Saints head coach Paul Wellens had labelled their thrashing at Hull FC the week before as complacent but they were anything but in a methodical win.

Sione Mata'utia, Jack Welsby, Jon Bennison and Mark Percival scored the four tries, Percival converting three, that got them over the line, while nilling the Tigers in defence. Bennison's hard work throughout personified Saints' approach as he dealt with the high ball well in wet conditions, returned it with gusto, and deserved his try in the second half.

Wellens recalled Percival, Joey Lussick and George Delaney as Tee Ritson, Joe Batchelor and Curtis Sironen all dropped out, the latter two missing with hamstring injuries.

Castleford had Jack Broadbent starting at hooker to cover for the injured Nathan Massey, who was covering for the injured Paul McShane, and debuting Warrington loanee Riley Dean started at halfback.

The Tigers were kept scoreless for the third time this season but their head coach, Andy Last, believed they deserved more out of the game.

The last of the four Friday matches saw Wakefield edge closer to eleventh placed Castleford with an emphatic 32-6 home victory over Salford, only their second win of the season, with Will Dagger and Luke Gale playing key roles.

Both players had been mid-season additions at Trinity - Dagger moved from Hull KR at the end of March, in a swap deal which saw Corey Hall transfer in the opposite direction, while Gale signed at the beginning of May from Championship side Keighley Cougars, although the Salford game was only his second appearance.

June

Wakefield's David Fifita looks to fend off Salford's Joe Burgess and Oliver Partington

Dagger had been used mostly at fullback or centre but was moved to the halves alongside former England international and Man of Steel Gale and he scored a try and eight goals, four of them penalties.

Salford were on a three-match losing streak in all competitions, their worst spell of the season so far, after defeats to Hull KR in the Cup and Wigan in the league. The Red Devils had been without England international hooker Andy Ackers throughout that run, while reigning Man of Steel Brodie Croft had missed the past two. In-form fullback Ryan Brierley too was unavailable at Wakefield. Backrower Kallum Watkins lined up at halfback.

BETFRED SUPER LEAGUE
Saturday 1st July

	P	W	D	L	F	A	D	Pts
Catalans Dragons	17	13	0	4	476	284	192	26
Leigh Leopards	17	11	0	6	400	271	129	22
Wigan Warriors	17	11	0	6	381	265	116	22
Warrington Wolves	17	11	0	6	397	300	97	22
St Helens	16	10	0	6	341	225	116	20
Salford Red Devils	17	10	0	7	351	327	24	20
Hull KR	17	9	0	8	346	298	48	18
Leeds Rhinos	17	8	0	9	367	300	67	16
Hull FC	17	7	0	10	298	437	-139	14
Huddersfield Giants	16	5	0	11	229	344	-115	10
Castleford Tigers	17	4	0	13	194	424	-230	8
Wakefield Trinity	17	2	0	15	155	460	-305	4

There was movement at the other end of the table after the Saturday game as Catalans moved four points clear at the summit with a hard-fought 28-18 win at Hull FC, their seventh victory in a row.

The Dragons were dominant in the first half against a Hull FC side far more subdued than in the previous week's crushing of St Helens, scoring four tries in the first 34 minutes, and then they closed the game out in measured fashion in the second half.

Quick-fire tries before the break from Darnell McIntosh and Adam Swift sent Hull in with just a four-point deficit after the Dragons had earlier led 22-6 through tries from Tom Johnstone, Tom Davies, Arthur Romano and Julian Bousquet, Chris Satae having opened Hull's scoring on 27 minutes.

Davies put some distance between the two sides as he worked on to Tyrone May's pass to cross for Catalans on 63 minutes. Winger Davies, as well as scoring two tries, ran for an amazing 318 metres.

Hull remained ninth in the table, six points off the play-off spots, while Catalans looked secure at the summit, Johnstone remaining as Super League's top try-scorer on 21, one ahead of Leigh's Josh Charnley.

JULY
Changing of the guard

Round 18

Despite not dominating the weekly rounds as they had in previous seasons, St Helens were up to third spot in the table after the first full round of July, after a 24-20 win at sun-bathed Warrington, in one of the best games of the season.

The defending champions had to fight back from 20-12 down in the last 20 minutes as the Wolves re-found their early season form, despite the continued absence of George Williams.

Mark Percival replied to Stefan Ratchford's penalty kick with a try off a lovely Jack Welsby pass. Matty Ashton levelled the scores from Ben Currie's cut-out pass, before James Bell put Saints ahead 12-6, though a Lewis Dodd inside pass to Welsby in the build-up looked a mile forward, Percival goaling both tries.

But Ashton scored his second try four minutes into the second half, intercepting Welsby's long pass and tearing away, Ratchford kicked another penalty and then Matt Dufty finished off a breathtaking try involving Currie and Josh Drinkwater. With Ratchford's two conversions the Wolves were eight points clear.

Jonny Lomax proved the catalyst for Saints' comeback. He shimmied through the Warrington defence, finding Welsby, who returned the ball to Lomax for a try beneath the posts.

Then a wonderful inside run, again from Welsby, having received the ball from Dodd, saw the fullback return the ball back to his scrum-half to score. With Percival converting both tries St Helens were back in front at 24-20 and managed to cling on in a frantic final ten minutes.

Saints not only leapfrogged Warrington but Wigan too after the Warriors were stunned by a 27-26 golden-point defeat at bottom side Wakefield on the same Friday night.

A dramatic late goal double from the boot of Will Dagger sparked wild Wakefield celebrations for the third home game in succession.

Dagger bisected the posts twice, either side of the final hooter, to snatch victory away from a Wigan side that had led three times but failed, often through their own mistakes, to put away rejuvenated Trinity. When the opportunity occurred, through a last-minute penalty and a field-goal three minutes into golden-point time, halfback Dagger made no mistake in denying the side that began the weekend third in the table.

It looked likely that Wigan would claim a fourth straight win when Toby King ran in the Warriors' fifth try and Harry Smith converted to edge them ahead 26-24. But the newly found belief and will to win displayed by Mark Applegarth's side kept coming and, with a little good fortune, they came away with both league points.

Back-to-back wins by Wakefield meant Castleford were now only two points clear of the bottom of Super League after a 34-16 home reverse to Leigh.

The Tigers were done for by a typical Leigh first-half blitz, led by Lachlan Lam, Tom Amone, Edwin Ipape and John Asiata.

The former two, alongside Tom Briscoe, scored tries in an eight-minute spell and although a Gareth Widdop try and an Elliot Wallis double either side of the break gave them real hope, they faded as quickly as they rose.

Instead, another two tries by the evergreen Josh Charnley and Lam completing his own

July

Huddersfield's Chris McQueen and Tui Lolohea halt the progress of Catalans Dragons' Matt Whitley

brace saw Leigh over the line with a degree of comfort.

Saturday evening saw the Catalans' seven-match winning run come to an end as Huddersfield came home from Perpignan with a 22-14 win.

Two tries from Aussie veteran second-rower Chris McQueen was the difference between the teams, his second on 60 minutes giving the Giants the lead for the last time.

Oliver Russell's perfect five from five conversions was sealed with a 69th-minute penalty that put daylight between the sides for the first time in the game.

Aidan Sezer guided Leeds to a 16-14 win at Salford on the Sunday, in the absence of the suspended Blake Austin (dangerous contact in the win at Warrington).

Salford's discipline proved to be their downfall as they were edged out of a bad-tempered affair. The Red Devils ended up conceding ten penalties, with Rhyse Martin kicking three of them in a game that saw referee Aaron Moore led off the field by stewards in the face of a group of angry home fans.

The Rhinos led 10-4 at the break, despite spending the majority of the half defending. In the first 40 minutes they had three genuine attacks at Salford's line and ended up posting points.

The opening score fell to Cameron Smith as he glided through some poor defending to touch down, while Tim Lafai got the Red Devils back in the game with a try for the hosts.

Salford threw everything at Leeds after that try but were unable to turn pressure into points. The Rhinos soaked it all up and scored a try from nothing as Richie Myler went left and sent a long ball out for Ash Handley to score, with Martin adding a penalty just before the break.

The Red Devils turned the game in their favour in the space of eight second-half minutes. Lafai – who was the best player on the field – reached out to score his second try two minutes after half-time before Ken Sio jumped the highest to grab his try.

But two Martin penalties saw the Rhinos edge two points in front and to within two league points of Salford in sixth spot.

Hull FC got revenge for their Easter derby humiliation with a 16-6 win at Hull KR, in a scrappy game that was only decided by Adam Swift's second try with three minutes to go.

Jack Walker gave Rovers a first-half lead, as they dominated. Shaun Kenny-Dowall was sin-binned for a high tackle just short of the hour and it proved a telling absence as Ligi Sao's try converted by Jake Clifford gave the Airlie Birds a 12-6 lead, after Swift had levelled from a great Cameron Scott round-the-man pass five minutes after half-time.

The result left Hull FC four points off sixth-placed Salford in the last play-off spot, with Rovers only two points ahead.

July

Round 19

Leaders Catalans had to tough it out to emerge from their Thursday-night TV clash at St Helens with a 14-12 win.

The game had everything and the Dragons, who were never behind in the contest and controlled large parts of the game, endured a frantic and nervous final quarter in which Saints almost broke their hearts in the final seconds.

With the Catalans' defence shot on the right edge and leading by just two points, the ball came to Will Hopoate, who had a chance to put Konrad Hurrell over in the right corner to win the game. But Hurrell stepped inside his centre and the pass went sailing into touch.

Led by the outstanding Michael McIlorum, the Dragons were out on their feet but withstood an avalanche of pressure to subject Saints to their seventh defeat of the season. Saints had to contend with losing captain James Roby and Mark Percival to concussions in either half, with the pair both set to miss the Challenge Cup semi-final the following week.

After Adam Keighran opened the scoring with a penalty goal, a Saints cross-field kick was brilliantly taken by Keighran, who offloaded to his flying winger all in one motion and Tom Johnstone raced 90 metres to score. Keighran converted to make it a two-score lead.

Percival broke the line from deep to set up great field position before he was quickest to react to a deft Lewis Dodd kick and he converted his own try to cut the gap to two points at the break.

It didn't take the Dragons long to click into gear in the second half as they extended their lead with a try to Matt Ikuvalu thanks to quick hands from Tyrone May. Keighran converted from wide out to re-establish an eight-point lead.

Saints eventually cracked the Catalans' defence to set up the grandstand finish. They kept the ball alive brilliantly on the last tackle, with Hopoate offloading inside for the supporting Dodd to score a converted try to reduce the deficit to two points with five minutes remaining.

On the Friday night, Kai Pearce-Paul returned from an eight-week injury lay-off to devastating effect, helping Wigan overcome Warrington at home by 26-12. The England international dominated with ball in hand and was just as impressive when he needed to defend.

It was another good effort from the Wolves after they just fell short the previous week against St Helens. They were without Matty Ashton and Josh Thewlis with calf and knee problems respectively, meaning Matty Russell and Greg Minikin started on the wings, while George Williams missed out for the fourth game in a row with a hamstring injury.

It was 12-all at half-time, James Harrison and Daryl Clark tries for the Wolves and Liam Marshall and Bevan French responding for Wigan.

Five minutes after the break, the Warriors received a penalty deep in Warrington's half when Marshall was taken out off the ball by Sam Kasiano and Harry Smith landed his third goal to make it 14-12.

The Wolves were struggling to contain Pearce-Paul and it was his run that put Wigan in the position to score their third try. The ball went left, and Jake Wardle sailed through a gap created by Jai Field's offload to touch down for a 20-12 lead.

With the clock running down, Warrington looked to close the deficit, but they blew a great chance as Ratchford's inside ball - intended for Matt Dufty - went to ground and Wigan survived.

The Warriors put the game to bed 60 seconds later. Field broke the line and drew in Dufty before sending captain Liam Farrell away to score. Smith's conversion made it 26-12 and it was game over.

There was genuine drama at Headingley on the same night as Hull KR signing from Canberra Brad Schneider, on debut, kicked a field goal in the third minute of extra time to secure a 19-18 win over Leeds.

Schneider, a former NRL Rookie of the Year, couldn't have had a much more influential debut with a try, assist and the winning one-pointer.

Off the back of three consecutive victories that had them looking at a top-six spot, Leeds clawed their way back into the contest after having gone 16-6 behind on 29 minutes after Rovers

July

Hull FC's Adam Swift celebrates scoring against Castleford

tries from Schneider, Tom Opacic and Louis Senior. Corey Johnson added to Jarrod O'Connor's try and Rowan Milnes' penalty made it 18-12 at half-time.

As they had for most of the game, Rovers controlled the early territory in the second half, with some intelligent kicking from Jez Litten backed up by a committed chase, but Ash Handley raising the siege with a 50-metre interception of Milnes' pass on the last.

The excellent Sam Luckley held up Justin Sangaré but Cameron Smith, twice, Myler, James McDonnell and Mikolaj Oledzki kept the ball moving and Aidan Sezer, with an imperious grubber to the corner, saw Ash Handley claim his 100th Super League try on his 200th appearance. Rhyse Martin's touchline goal levelled the scores with 28 minutes still to go. And there was no further scores before Schneider's golden touch.

On the same night, Huddersfield looked to be running into form with a comfortable 34-6 home win over Wakefield, who were on the back of three wins from four games.

Tries from Chris McQueen, Kevin Naiqama, Sam Halsall put the hosts in total control, 16-0 at half-time before Jermaine McGillvary and Tui Lolohea quickly added to the home lead after the break. Samisoni Langi touched down for the visitors before Lolohea got his second.

Leroy Cudjoe made his 350th appearance (all but one of them starts) for his hometown club, becoming only the second player to reach the milestone for Huddersfield in the summer era after Eorl Crabtree.

On the Saturday, Hull FC kept their play-off hopes alive with a 36-18 home win over Castleford.

The Tigers were well in the game, against a Hull side well below its best, with the scores level at 8-8 at the break. But they conceded back-to-back tries, the latter straight from the restart in spectacular fashion, Chris Satae linking with Adam Swift moments after scoring a hotly-debated try himself.

And then after pulling the deficit back to six points through a Jack Broadbent try, the same player dropped the kick-off and two more successive tries followed to Davy Litten and Cameron Scott.

Satae and Brad Dwyer made a great impact off the bench as Hull dominated, despite losing Carlos Tuimavave and Danny Houghton to injury in the first half and Darnell McIntosh in the build-up to the game with a sore heel.

Suspended Josh Griffin that week left the club to join Wakefield.

July

On the Sunday, Leigh fought back from twelve points down in the second half to record their first win at Salford since 1983 and boost their hopes of winning their first-ever League Leaders' Shield, emerging with a 24-22 victory.

The game was shrouded in controversy, with both teams probably feeling aggrieved, but it was Salford who led at the break after outscoring the Leopards by three tries to two.

The Red Devils opened the scoring through Ken Sio in the corner, but Leigh hit back through Ed Chamberlain and a controversial score from Ricky Leutele to lead 10-4.

It looked like Leigh would kick on but Salford hit back to lead at the break thanks close-range tries from King Vuniyayawa and Andy Ackers, while the home side felt they should have had a bigger lead after Joe Burgess had a runaway score brought back for a knock-on, which left the Salford faithful up in arms.

The controversy continued in the second half as, after Ben Hellewell put the Red Devils 22-10 in front, Leigh hit back and Lachlan Lam reduced the arrears following great work from Tom Amone and John Asiata.

Then a dubious pass from Lam caused confusion in the Salford defence and the loose ball was eventually pounced on by Zak Hardaker to level matters heading into the final 15 minutes.

Poor discipline from Salford saw them concede consecutive penalties, which allowed Ben Reynolds to kick a 42-metre goal and secure the victory.

It was a gutsy win from the Leopards. Boom hooker Edwin Ipape was a late withdrawal from the team due to illness. His replacement – Aaron Smith – also withdrew before kick-off through illness, with Joe Mellor filling in at dummy-half.

Challenge Cup Semi-finals

Hull KR and Leigh Leopards won through to the Challenge Cup Final at Wembley, scheduled for 12th August, after two tight semi-finals went the way of the underdogs.

The Robins won an extraordinary match against Wigan, who played the last 38 minutes with twelve men, in golden-point time at Headingley on the Sunday afternoon by 11-10.

And it was their recent Australian signing Brad Schneider who sealed victory in the 82nd minute, kicking a successful field goal from 40 metres out to seal victory.

It was the second game in succession at the same venue that Schneider had kicked a winning field goal, having despatched Leeds a week earlier to secure a 19-18 victory in the 83rd minute of a league encounter.

Rovers were hit before kick-off as Ryan Hall was forced out of the line-up when his torn calf flared up, with Mikey Lewis going in at fullback and Ethan Ryan shifting to the wing.

The Robins scored with their first attack after ten minutes of a Wigan barrage. Jai Field knocked on and a beautiful scrum move ended with Louis Senior crossing wide out.

Wigan replied on 23 minutes as Field threw a big dummy and scythed past Rowan Milnes for a brilliant individual try. Smith's conversion from wide out was equally as good and his side led 6-4. And after Pearce-Paul had the ball ripped out with the half-time hooter about to sound, Smith sent over a penalty-goal for an 8-4 lead.

It was all action at the beginning of the second half, with Joe Shorrocks seemingly hitting Lewis around the head with a shoulder charge, referee Liam Moore showing him a red card.

Shortly after, Robins skipper Shaun Kenny-Dowall was sent for a ten-minute spell in the sin bin for a professional foul on Bevan French as the latter ran through for a kick. From the penalty, Smith slotted over two points to make it 10-4 with half an hour left.

It was nip and tuck throughout and two penalties in a row helped Rovers set up their best field position of the second half, but again an error ended the attack before they did finally breach the steely Wigan defence just after the hour.

A brilliant offload from Kenny-Dowall, who had just returned from the field after his yellow card, found Matt Parcell, who in turn found Ryan wide out.

Schneider converted excellently to level the scores at 10-10 with 16 minutes remaining.

It became a test of mental and physical strength as the clock wound down, with both sides

July

Hull KR's Brad Schneider lands the winning field goal against Wigan

missing field-goal attempts.

When Smith went for a one-pointer and Wigan didn't get a repeat set despite a chargedown, Field was caught on halfway with Rovers having one last attack.

Neither Schneider nor Milnes, however, could get a field-goal away as golden point approached.

However, Schneider kept his composure in the first minute of extra time to send Rovers to Wembley.

Leigh reached their first Challenge Cup final in 52 years with a stunning 12-10 win over St Helens at Warrington.

It was a fully deserved win, despite being outplayed in the first half. The Leopards held firm to stay in the game while their backs were against the wall and then, after Oliver Holmes and Zak Hardaker tries early in the second half, they showed even greater defensive resilience to stay in a winning position.

Saints appeared to have the match in their grasp at half-time, having got on top of a gruelling physical battle and taken the lead through Joey Lussick, James Roby out on concussion protocols. But their dominance was only reflected in a 6-0 lead thanks to several missed chances and a Makinson penalty kick on the hooter that he sliced horribly wide.

Leigh's blitz after the break was a shock but Saints could still have won the match from there. They pushed while Sione Mata'utia was in the sin bin, and pushed some more in the last ten minutes when back to 13 men.

But every time they seemed to have found a way in, the Leopards slammed the door emphatically and by the time Jonny Lomax crossed in the last minute they knew Makinson's conversion was their only real hope of staying in the tie. From tight on the touchline, Makinson couldn't land the goal.

After surviving a couple of final plays, cue pandemonium.

After the game, Paul Wellens paid tribute to Lussick after the Australian hooker announced his return to join Parramatta Eels. He was to be replaced immediately by St George Illawarra Dragons' Moses Mbye on a deal until the end of 2025.

July

Leigh's Tom Amone in the thick of the action against St Helens

Round 20

There were big changes at top and bottom of the table on the last round of July. In the Saturday afternoon Channel 4 game, Wigan stopped Leigh's winning charge to leapfrog their neighbours into second spot, meaning Catalans were back in a four-point lead after their hammering of Salford. And then on the Sunday, Wakefield won their fourth game of the season with a big win over Warrington that ended with the sacking of Wolves coach Daryl Powell.

Boom prop Tyler Dupree had moved to Wigan from Salford in midweek and he made a massive debut off the bench as the Warriors took their Challenge Cup semi-final frustration out on the Leopards with a 44-18 home win. Bevan French scored twice and Lebanon's Abbas Miski bagged a fine hat-trick.

The game was in the balance until the last four minutes of the first half after Tom Amone's converted try put Leigh ahead and French equalised. But late first-half tries from Toby King and French gave Wigan a flattering 16-6 lead at the break

The second half saw Wigan dominate as French, Dupree, a fine solo, Miski, three times and Liam Marshall crossed. Tom Briscoe and Rob Mulhern responded for the Leopards.

The Dragons roasted weakened Salford by 42-0 in a heatwave at Stade Gilbert Brutus. Coach Paul Rowley's depleted side, missing a string of first-teamers (including forward King Vuniyayawa, who was turned away upon arrival in France because of visa issues) were outgunned in every department. Salford only had 18 players to choose from at the end of a week in which star prop Dupree was lured to Wigan.

Two tries each from Adam Keighran, also on his way to Wigan, but at the end of the season, and Tom Johnstone plus touchdowns for Tyrone May, Tiaki Chan (Wigan-bound too for 2024) and Sam Tomkins were too much for a depleted Red Devils.

Wakefield's 42-6 home win over the Wolves on the Sunday brought Trinity back level, on eight league points, with Castleford as the team labelled as the worst attacking side ever in Super League put the early-season pacesetters to the cleaners. Wakefield had gone from a side unable to score a point to one that ran in eight of the highest quality, with their spine of Luke Gale, Max

July

Jowitt and Mason Lino looking sensational.

And that after repelling continuous pressure from the Wolves, for whom George Williams made a return and dominated early on.

Trinity, like the Tigers, had loaned players throughout the season but none made a bigger impact than Huddersfield winger Innes Senior, on his fourth loan spell at Belle Vue, as he finished with four tries.

Gale's signing from Keighley in mid-season was the key as he orchestrated Trinity's attack, freeing Lino to provide more of a running threat and releasing Jowitt to devastating effect.

Powell left the Wolves 'by mutual consent', that night.

The weekend's events almost overshadowed what had been a fine contest on the Friday night as home side St Helens just held off Leeds by 22-18.

Jack Welsby was the difference between two sides it had been hard to separate in 2023, with two stunning second-half tries, an assist and almost 100 running metres to reignite his side's drive for five successive titles.

Welsby's touchdowns, the second a wonderful effort when shooting onto a perfectly timed pass from Jonny Lomax 35 metres out, took the eye and plaudits. But equally as good – and critical – was his instinctive close-quarters catch from Blake Austin's kick as the Rhinos mounted their final attack.

Will Hopoate also registered one try and two assists. But it was in the pack that Saints – and particularly their experienced players, Morgan Knowles, Matty Lees and the returning James Roby – really stood up, bringing the best out of Sam Royle, George Delaney and Dan Norman. The bench included debutant Moses Mbye.

Prior to Welsby's matchwinner on 65 minutes, Leeds had just clawed their way back into the game with the outstanding Nene Macdonald's determined dive into the corner from a rolling Richie Myler pass on the last, with Rhyse Martin converting from touch, only for Austin to kick out on the full from the set after scoring.

The same was true at the end of the first half, the Rhinos having overcome a slow start to lead by six points through Rhyse Martin and Sam Walters tries after Hopoate's opener, and with the clock winding towards the break, securing their second goal-line drop-out.

Conceding a penalty when chasing an Aidan Sezer grubber to the in-goal from it, by the time the teams headed for the tunnel, Saints were level after Tee Ritson went into the corner as the half-time hooter sounded.

Hull KR leapt above Warrington into fifth, collecting the Roger Millward MBE trophy, after completing a league double over Castleford Tigers with a 34-16 home win on the Friday night. It was back to business for the Robins, who named an unchanged side from their Challenge Cup victory over Wigan Warriors five days earlier and it paid off.

The Tigers went into the game after having allowed Mahe Fonua, Bureta Faraimo and Albert Vete to leave the club but with some incomings. PNG international Liam Horne and Lebanese international Charbel Tasipale both signed 18-month deals, although neither played. Greek international Billy Tsikrikas was on the bench, however, with a return to the club, also on the bench, for Alex Foster from Newcastle Thunder.

Tries from Tom Opacic, Rhys Kennedy and Kane Linnett saw Rovers open up a 16-0 lead before Castleford got back in it in the last ten minutes of the first half through Will Tate and Jack Broadbent tries.

After the break, the home side took complete control with a superb try from loose forward Elliot Minchella, after a Matt Parcell break from halfway, and further scores from James Batchelor and Ethan Ryan.

Greg Eden's try eight minutes from time was little consolation for Castleford.

On the Thursday night Huddersfield kept their faint play-off hopes alive with a gritty 19-12 home win over Hull FC.

It was a game very much designed for the middle men as Chris Hill stole the show, the England veteran rolling back the years with a powerful display that punched holes in the Hull defence. Then he unlocked it at the end with the deftest of hands.

Wakefield's Max Jowitt takes on Warrington's Josh Thewlis

With the scores stuck at 12-12 for more than 40 minutes, Hill's subtlety played in Chris McQueen for the match-winning try on 69 minutes.

The Giants opened the scoring thanks to the brilliance of Jake Connor, who kicked a 40/20 and then put Jermaine McGillvary - who later had to come off with a hamstring issue, one of several casualties in the match - into the corner.

That began a 15-minute spell of four tries, with Hull getting the next two in their only real threatening period of the match. Jake Clifford punched numerous holes with his running and the halfback, via Jordan Lane, set up a try for Adam Swift.

Brad Fash then followed in after Jake Trueman went straight through home defence that was left disoriented by Hull's play and the visitors were suddenly 12-6 up and good value for it.

But Huddersfield recovered, and Hull couldn't find the same sort of threat again for the rest of the match. Tui Lolohea levelled things back up after Davy Litten failed to deal with an Oliver Russell chip, setting up a second-half stalemate.

Until McQueen's try on 68 minutes gave the Giants a six-point lead and Russell, having converted all three of Huddersfield's tries, added a field goal a few minutes later to end the contest.

BETFRED SUPER LEAGUE
Sunday 30th July

	P	W	D	L	F	A	D	Pts
Catalans Dragons	20	15	0	5	546	318	228	30
Wigan Warriors	20	13	0	7	477	322	155	26
Leigh Leopards	20	13	0	7	476	353	123	26
St Helens	19	12	0	7	399	277	122	24
Hull KR	20	11	0	9	405	348	57	22
Warrington Wolves	20	11	0	9	435	392	43	22
Salford Red Devils	20	10	0	10	387	409	-22	20
Leeds Rhinos	20	9	0	11	419	355	64	18
Hull FC	20	9	0	11	362	480	-118	18
Huddersfield Giants	19	8	0	11	304	376	-72	16
Castleford Tigers	20	4	0	16	244	528	-284	8
Wakefield Trinity	20	4	0	16	230	526	-296	8

AUGUST
Leopards arise

Round 21

Another month, another coaching casualty as Castleford sacked head coach Andy Last in the wake of a 28-0 home Friday-night defeat by Huddersfield.

Last's tenure at Wheldon Road ended with an uninspiring performance. He was put out of his misery almost immediately after the final hooter, as the club pulled the plug on a 19-match reign that brought only four wins and left the Tigers above the relegation spot only on points difference.

For the fourth time this season, Castleford failed to score a point and on this occasion, they didn't even look like ever doing so. Their attack lacked any kind of shape or threat that could trouble Huddersfield.

Young winger Sam Halsall was quietly impressing at the Giants and his hat-trick was the standout feature for them, twice finishing from fine Jake Connor assists at the start of either half and then completing his treble with seven minutes to go from a Leroy Cudjoe offload at the line.

Cudjoe also scored himself, in the first half, as did the in-form Chris McQueen, while Adam Milner rubbed salt into Castleford's great wounds with the final try in his first appearance against the club he'd spent his entire career with until leaving in May.

The defeat actually sent Castleford bottom of the table on points difference but rivals Wakefield missed their chance to stay above them on the Sunday at Hull as the Airlie Birds put in a fine performance and ran away with a 42-4 victory that badly damaged Trinity's points difference.

Tony Smith's men needed to win to keep pace with the top six and led by just 12 points after a hard-fought first half. But they hit Wakefield with two tries in three minutes after half-time, then cut loose, to score five tries to one and move to within only two points of sixth place.

It was a win built on desperate and resilient defence and a ruthless edge in attack, particularly in the second half, led by the outstanding Jake Clifford.

Trinity certainly showed plenty of fight and reasons why they'd claimed the scalps they had in recent weeks. But ultimately they had themselves to blame at crucial times, coming up with several poor errors with and without the ball.

That week it was announced Clifford would be returning to his first NRL club, North Queensland Cowboys, at the end of the season.

The top four sides all registered wins.

Leaders Catalans won 30-10 at Warrington, who had assistant Gary Chambers in interim charge for their sixth straight loss and Thomas Mikaele back for a second debut after a mid-season sojourn at Gold Coast Titans.

But the Dragons notched a fourth consecutive win thanks to five different try scorers - Adam Keighran, Tom Davies, Mitchell Pearce, Matt Whitley and Matt Ikuvalu with the Wolves' tries, one in each half, from Ben Currie and Josh Thewlis.

Second-placed Wigan had a field day with a 64-6 home win over Hull KR as Willie Peters chose to rest his first-string side before the following week's Challenge Cup Final. Abbas Miski scored four tries and Jai Field crossed for a hat-trick.

August

Huddersfield's Adam Milner holds off Castleford's Gareth Widdop on the way to scoring against his former club

Louix Gorman, on-loan Cesar Rougé, Lennie Ellis, Isaac Shaw (on loan from Wakefield), Leo Tennison and Luke Thomas all made their debuts. Louis Senior, Rowan Milnes, Matty Storton and Jimmy Keinhorst were the only survivors from their win over Castleford Tigers.

Many predicted a cricket score before the game and Wigan were never in any danger. Hull KR never gave up but they were second best all night. They were powerless up the middle with the likes of Kaide Ellis, Patrick Mago and Kai Pearce-Paul making yards, while Miski, Field, Marshall, Smith and Bevan French burned them on the outside.

Leigh coach Adrian Lam took the opposite route to Peters and was rewarded with a 13-6 win at Headingley on the Sunday afternoon.

Lam opted only to rest former Rhino Zak Hardaker, free-scoring Josh Charnley and Oliver Holmes from their likely Wembley starting line-up, bringing in Oliver Gildart for his debut in the centre (Gildart had returned to England from the NRL Dolphins and had signed for Hull KR for 2024) and Tom Nisbet, who wasn't in their originally named squad, alongside him on the left.

Ben Reynolds controlled the encounter in impressive fashion, while Jack Hughes cemented his claims for a starting spot against Hull KR at Wembley, Edwin Ipape and Kai O'Donnell made welcome returns with typically hardworking efforts and, even though he was only on for half an hour, John Asiata set a huge lead again.

Edwin Ipape put Leigh ahead midway through the first half before Jarrod O'Connor broke through for Leeds. Tom Amone restored the Leopards' lead soon after the break, before Reynolds added a penalty after a high tackle. After O'Connor had a second try ruled out, Gareth O'Brien's cool field goal eight minutes from time to open up a two-score lead for the first time in the game finally gave the Leopards breathing space.

That week, star halfback Lachlan Lam, whose contract was due to expire at the conclusion of the season, committed to a new deal to keep him at Leigh Sports Village until the end of 2025.

Leeds halfback Blake Austin didn't play, having signed on loan for the rest of the season with Castleford.

August

Jack Welsby produced another stellar performance as St Helens came back from 15-2 down at half-time to secure an 18-15 victory at Salford.

The Red Devils were left ruing some refereeing decisions at full-time with their coach Paul Rowley laying into the match officials after the game. 'I thought the officials were a disgrace,' he said.

In the wake of a 42-0 defeat at Catalans the week before, Salford brought Tim Lafai, Andy Ackers, Marc Sneyd and debutant Brad Singleton in, the Wigan prop being part of the deal that took Tyler Dupree to Wigan, while Saints changed both centres. Konrad Hurrell and Will Hopoate (hamstring) were both missing with Mark Percival returning to the starting line-up.

Percival opened the scoring with a fifth minute penalty but the Red Devils took a 15-2 lead into the break thanks to tries from Kallum Watkins and Ryan Brierley and three goals and a field goal from Marc Sneyd. But Saints closed the deficit when Matty Lees forced his way over the line and Tommy Makinson's self-converted try drew them to within one point.

And Saints hit the front with ten minutes to go when Welsby scythed through the right centre.

A tense ten minutes ensued as Saints managed the game to the full-time hooter.

Challenge Cup Final

Leigh Leopards won the Challenge Cup for the first time since 1971 with a 17-16 win over Hull Kingston Rovers, in the first Challenge Cup Final to be decided by golden point.

At the time the Leopards were sitting in third place in the Super League table in a season in which they bucked the trend of clubs promoted from the Championship making a return downwards after a single season - which they themselves had done in 2017 and 2021.

It was a game tight, tense and full of incident. There were controversial penalties, a contentious yellow card, a try that might not have been grounded, and a video-referee decision that took an age before confirming the Matt Parcell score for Hull KR that took the match into extra time.

In the end it all came down to who would get the one-pointer. Rovers had first possession, which Kane Linnett seemed to have lost. Referee Chris Kendall changed his decision from knock-on to penalty but Brad Schneider failed to find touch with the kick. From then, the onus was all on Leigh to win it.

Gareth O'Brien, the man for a field goal in a big game, had the first attempt but sliced it narrowly wide. Hull KR came up the pitch and Schneider attempted a goal from halfway, which dribbled out of play and presented Leigh with a second chance.

The Leopards' next set-up and execution were perfect. Rob Mulhern's drive towards the posts on the penultimate play put them in position, from which the pass went initially to O'Brien again, to the right. Expecting the pressure, Lachlan Lam was positioned left, and O'Brien allowed him to write his name in Leigh folklore with a swing of his left boot. It also secured Lam the Lance Todd Trophy.

The Leopards were never behind in the game but they could never shake off their opponents. On 66 minutes they took a 16-10 lead through Tom Briscoe's converted try in the right corner in front of their own supporters, who must have started believing at that point that the game was going their way.

BETFRED CHALLENGE CUP FINAL

Saturday 12th August 2023

HULL KR 16 LEIGH LEOPARDS 17
(after golden point extra-time)

HULL KR: 20 Mikey Lewis; 2 Ethan Ryan; 3 Tom Opacic; 4 Shaun Kenny-Dowall (C); 5 Ryan Hall; 21 Rowan Milnes; 37 Brad Schneider; 15 Rhys Kennedy; 14 Jez Litten; 10 George King; 16 James Batchelor; 12 Kane Linnett; 13 Elliot Minchella. Subs (all used): 9 Matt Parcell; 17 Matty Storton; 22 Dean Hadley; 26 Sam Luckley.
Tries: Litten (15), Parcell (79); **Goals:** Schneider 4/4.
Sin bin: Minchella (31) - late challenge on Reynolds.
LEOPARDS: 17 Gareth O'Brien; 2 Tom Briscoe; 3 Ed Chamberlain; 1 Zak Hardaker; 5 Josh Charnley; 15 Ben Reynolds; 7 Lachlan Lam; 8 Tom Amone; 9 Edwin Ipape; 10 Robbie Mulhern; 24 Kai O'Donnell; 12 Jack Hughes; 13 John Asiata (C). Subs (all used): 6 Joe Mellor; 14 Ben Nakubuwai; 16 Oliver Holmes; 18 Matt Davis.
Tries: Lam (26), Briscoe (66); **Goals:** Reynolds 4/5;
Field goal: Lam (84).
Rugby Leaguer & League Express Men of the Match:
Hull KR: Mikey Lewis; *Leopards:* Lachlan Lam.
Penalty count: 3-4; **Half-time:** 8-10; **Referee:** Chris Kendall; **Attendance:** 58,213 *(at Wembley Stadium).*

August

Tom Amone and John Asiata lift the Challenge Cup following Leigh's Wembley victory against Hull KR

August

But when the Robins scored with a minute to go, with a try from Parcell that was examined forensically by video-referee Liam Moore, who was prepared, as he made clear, to take all the time in the world (and he nearly did) to reach the correct decision, their semi-final field-goal hero Schneider was up to the task of converting to take the game into golden-point time.

With Schneider's recent record of scoring late field goals to win matches, the odds moved sharply in favour of Hull KR at that point. But the League gods had already put their money on the Leopards.

The match had exploded into life four minutes in when John Asiata crashed low into the legs of George King in the manner that had recently brought vocal criticism from rival clubs. The referee did not punish the challenge but the furious reaction of the Robins players was penalised and Ben Reynolds kicked the first points of the game.

Leigh built the early momentum, finding space with Kai O'Donnell, Edwin Ipape and Tom Amone making breaks. Reynolds had another shot at goal but kicked short from distance and, moments later, Hull KR hit back with the opening try.

Elliot Minchella was the architect, breaking through the tackle of Ipape and finding Jez Litten in support for a try converted by Schneider.

Things could have got even better for the Robins but Tom Opacic found no sympathy from the video referee when he tumbled on contact with Lam in a chase for a loose ball running towards the try line.

Instead, Opacic's error at the play-the-ball allowed the Leopards to respond, as Lam put O'Donnell on a clean break and kept in touch for the return pass.

The grounding was uncertain but the try was awarded unchecked, with Reynolds kicking Leigh back in front - a two-point advantage that became four soon afterwards, from another incident that had Hull KR fans unhappy.

Minchella struck Reynolds late following a kick and further replays showed he had caught the halfback's head with his arm too. That was enough for Chris Kendall to draw the yellow card - last seen in a Challenge Cup Final in 2001 - and Hull KR were down to twelve for the remainder of the half.

Reynolds kicked the resulting penalty but the Leopards could not take any further advantage, thanks to some heroic defence during two great passages of pressure, particularly one challenge on Ed Chamberlain by Ethan Ryan and Tom Opacic, which won back possession.

That moment had greater significance when Mikey Lewis got Hull KR up the field with the final play of the half and won a penalty for the second effort by Reynolds after the tackle, allowing Schneider to cut Leigh's lead to 10-8 at half-time.

The second half began the same way, with a Schneider penalty goal following a late Ipape hit levelling at 10-10.

Leigh still looked the more dangerous side, with O'Brien and Chamberlain both stopped close to the line and Josh Charnley stopped over it after swerving around a bundle of defenders.

The pressure was rewarded in the 66th minute when Reynolds, Lam and O'Brien all combined perfectly and the latter sent a sweet pass over to Briscoe.

Reynolds' touchline kick gave Leigh a six-point advantage to cling onto until the end, and cling on they had to. Hull KR pushed hard in the last six minutes, Lewis coming to the fore in probing for an opening and finally a breakthrough was found with a minute and a half left on the clock.

Schneider delivered a huge kick from right edge to left, Zak Hardaker knocked the ball back under pressure from Kane Linnett, and Parcell touched down in front of the Hull KR fans.

After an agonising four-minute check by video, the try stood, and Schneider's goal ensured the final would have to be decided by Lam's golden boot.

Earlier in the day, St Helens had made history by winning the first Women's Challenge Cup Final to be played at Wembley, beating Leeds Rhinos 22-8. And after the men's final, Halifax Panthers beat Batley Bulldogs by 12-10 to win the 1895 Cup.

August

Round 1

On the Sunday evening after the Challenge Cup Final, St Helens leaped over Cup-winers Leigh into third in the table with a 32-18 home win over Huddersfield, in a game re-scheduled from round one to accommodate Saints participation in the World Club Challenge.

A first-half hat-trick from Tommy Makinson seemingly put the hosts in command but a thrilling fightback from the Giants closed the score to 20-18 with ten minutes remaining before tries from Lewis Dodd and Jack Welsby settled the contest.

For 25 minutes the game simmered and Saints ran red hot with two Makinson tries in the first eight minutes. Matty English was sin-binned for the Giants and ten minutes later Joe Greenwood was red-carded for use of the elbow. Greenwood escaped with a fine but the player involved in the tackle, Matty Lees, was suspended for two games.

Huddersfield responded through Matty English but Makinson completed his hat-trick just before the half-time hooter.

Ash Golding and Kevin Naiqama started Huddersfield's turnaround before Dodd and Welsby took Saints home.

Round 22

Former London Broncos coach Danny Ward was appointed head coach by Castleford Tigers on a short-term deal for the final six matches of the season. And Ward hailed the impact of Blake Austin after Castleford Tigers' critical Friday-night win, in his first game in charge, over relegation rivals Wakefield Trinity.

Castleford's 28-12 victory at Belle Vue marked a winning start for Austin and Ward, appointed as the Tigers' third head coach of the season following Andy Last's departure.

The Australian halfback's arrival on loan from Leeds Rhinos was a great surprise in transfer deadline week and he was influential in earning Castleford a first win in six and moving them two points clear of Wakefield at the foot of the table.

Ward played in the 'Battle of Belle Vue' in 2006, when the Tigers were relegated on the final day of the season. With another five matches still to go, this sequel never quite had the same jeopardy, but it wasn't too far off.

The celebrations, from when Greg Eden scored his hat-trick try on the hooter, told the story, as the Castleford supporters celebrated wildly until long after the final whistle.

The Tigers scored first through Lebanese international Charbel Tasipale and they then had the mentality to deal with adversity when Wakefield got on top in the middle of the first half.

Eden's first two tries, in the final four minutes before half-time, were pivotal in the game and both clubs' seasons. Wakefield, faced with an eight-point deficit which was soon made 14 by an Alex Foster try, played with desperation as the Tigers saw out this biggest of wins, Eden getting his hat-trick try in the finals seconds.

Josh Griffin scored two of Wakefield's three tries, Max Jowitt getting the first, making a mark on his third debut for the club after returning from Hull FC and completing a seven-game suspension.

Castleford were now two points ahead and also boosted their points difference, meaning Wakefield would likely need two more wins than the Tigers over the run-in.

On the same night, St Helens went two points clear of Leigh in third spot with a 28-6 home win over Hull KR, after a superb second half in the wind and rain, with St Helens scoring four tries to eventually ease to a comfortable victory over the committed Robins.

Sione Mata'utia got the only try of the first half in the 37th minute to give Saints a 6-0 half-time lead. But the home side charged away in the first 15 minutes of the second half, with Tommy Makinson scoring twice either side of Moses Mbye.

Mikey Lewis got the away side on the scoreboard before Ben Davies rounded off the win late on.

Defeat meant Rovers dropped out of the top six on points difference, given Salford's 32-8 victory at Huddersfield.

August

Leeds' David Fusitu'a claims a high ball above the Warrington chase

Salford's play-off hopes had been spun off course by a run of six straight Super League defeats - three of which were by three points or fewer. But they finally notched a first win since early June on the Friday night, Sam Stone scoring two of Salford's five tries, while winger Ken Sio also touched down for his 100th Super League try.

Of that tally, 77 of Sio's efforts had come for Salford, whom he joined in 2019 from Newcastle Knights after a previous spell in England with Hull KR. Sio was Super League's top try-scorer in 2021, with 19 efforts, and bettered that the following season with 26, finishing only behind Wigan Warriors' Bevan French in the scoring charts.

Leigh coach Adrian Lam admitted it could take a few weeks for his Challenge Cup heroes to come down from their Wembley high.

They returned to action on the Saturday, seven days after their triumph over Hull KR, against Super League leaders Catalans Dragons.

The Leopards impressively led at half-time but appeared to tire in the second half as 18-unanswered points saw Catalans record a 30-14 Saturday-afternoon win at Leigh Sports Village that secured a play-off spot.

Leigh led 14-12 at the end of a half which saw two Dragons sin-binned - Mike McMeeken for a shoulder charge and Michael McIlorum for a high shot.

Ben Reynolds kicked the first two points for Leigh from a penalty after a high-intensity opening 15 minutes, following the McMeeken challenge on John Asiata.

The Leopards were further in front when a neat Asiata inside ball put Tom Amone through and Reynolds' boot made it 8-0 to the hosts.

But Catalans hit back while playing with twelve men, Mitchell Pearce making his first special contribution by chasing his own cute grubber and grounding by the left upright.

Four minutes later, Paul Séguier crashed over from a classy, flat Pearce pass, and Adam Keighran's two goals (he'd go on to convert all five Dragons tries) put his side 12-8 ahead.

August

Catalans struggled under pressure at the end of the half, however, giving away three penalties in succession - one of which saw McIlorum binned for clipping Asiata late and high - before Ben Nakubuwai barged under the sticks from dummy-half and Reynolds converted to put Leigh back in front by two at the break.

But the second half was all Catalans after Tom Davies got on the end of a Tyrone May grubber to restore the Dragons' lead.

Two more tries in the space of six minutes clinched the match, the first coming from May who pushed off Reynolds to go through. Pearce then put in a low kick which Manu Ma'u pounced upon, leaving the final period of the match to fizzle out.

On the Sunday afternoon, Leeds edged Warrington at Headingley by 24-22, the difference between winning and losing for two desperate sides ultimately Wolves fullback Matt Dufty's finger.

On the final play of a game in which Warrington could have been clear at the break, the fullback just failed to pull in Stefan Ratchford's grubber with the line open.

It meant the Wolves were on a run of seven losing matches, though in the week they had been boosted by the announcement that Sam Burgess would return from Australia to take over as head coach for the 2024 season. The Rhinos meanwhile kept their own play-off hopes well and truly alive.

Superb Matty Ashton and Dufty tries edged Wire 10-6 ahead at the break, with Sam Walters replying. After the break, Ratchford kicked his second goal before David Fusitu'a touched down to tie the scores at 12-12. Ratchford and Luke Hooley traded tries before James Bentley took Leeds clear at 24-16. But they had to hold on after Matt Nicholson's late score.

An even closer game had panned out on the Friday night as it took a Harry Smith field goal in extra-time for Wigan to see off Hull FC by 13-12.

Smith, who had missed all three conversion attempts for Wigan, had a first-half extra-time field-goal attempt blocked and watched one sail wide. But he managed to compose himself long enough to nail a 40-metre field goal in the second period of golden point to secure a narrow and nervous win.

A late score from Jake Wardle had ensured the game went into golden-point extra time. Wigan had gone ahead when Liam Marshall scored on the half-hour mark but resolute defence and Adam Swift's last-minute finish gave Hull a slender 6-4 half-time lead.

Brad Dwyer extended that to 12-4 fourteen minutes after the turnaround, Toby King cut the lead shortly after and, after Hull lost Carlos Tuimavave to the sin bin, Wardle levelled with only three minutes left.

Round 23

Wigan fans celebrated late into the night in Perpignan following an unexpected 34-0 rout of the Dragons at Stade Gilbert Brutus, with a hat-trick by Abbas Miski and some Bevan French polish the highlights of a famous night for the Warriors.

The result meant that Catalans were now only two points clear of Wigan and St Helens at the top of the table. And the manner of the Warriors' victory sent a clear warning to the title contenders.

Wigan, who were nilled on their past two trips to Catalans and had already lost twice to Catalans in 2023, put on an incredible performance of total domination to turn the tables on the torn turf of the Dragons' home ground. Brown circles marred the grass at the Brutus, caused by cross-contamination from sharing lawnmowers with local rugby union side USAP.

A fungal pitch infection at Stade Aimé Giral has crossed codes and it seems the Dragons had also caught a losing habit from their 15-a-side neighbours with a lacklustre and limp display in front of their biggest crowd of the season so far.

French's kicking game, deceptive running and passing skill created tries for Miski and Toby King, while he also scored himself in a virtuoso display. Jake Wardle got the final score.

St Helens made short work of Castleford at the Jungle on the Friday night with a 34-4 win, after leading 30-0 at half-time.

August

Castleford's Jordan Johnstone looks to escape from St Helens' George Delaney and Moses Mbye

After all the excitement of the crunch win at Wakefield, in Danny Ward's first game in charge, his Castleford homecoming was derailed by five players from that match being absent. Jack Broadbent and Nathan Massey were injured during the relegation decider. Debutant Blake Austin and hat-trick hero Greg Eden picked up knocks and were pulled out. And then Suaia Matagi reported ill on the day. And so the Tigers ended up with a reshuffled line-up, headlined by Joe Westerman pitching in at halfback.

In contrast, St Helens named a completely unchanged line-up from their win over Hull KR and unsurprisingly were far too good as they secured a fifth victory in succession.

Mark Percival, Tommy Makinson and Jack Welsby in particular starred in a blistering first-half attacking performance, Makinson scoring a double and Percival registering 14 points, while Jon Bennison, Joe Batchelor and, at the start of the second half, Jonny Lomax also got on the scoreboard.

But they scored no further points in the final 35 minutes, while Castleford got their sole response through Jordan Turner.

Fortunately for Castleford, Wakefield sank to defeat at Salford, whose enthusiastic defence harassed Trinity into mistake after mistake, the Red Devils securing a 20-0 win.

Admittedly two of Salford's tries were handed to them on a plate but their first was a beauty, Ryan Brierley finishing off a long Kallum Watkins break after only four minutes. Marc Sneyd's conversion and penalty made it 8-0 at the break.

Andy Ackers was left with a clear run to the line from ten metres when Max Jowitt's short goal-line drop-out was patted back to him. And with Wakefield desperately trying their luck as they looked to break their duck in the dying minutes, a pass was intercepted by the ever-impressive Ken Sio deep inside his own half and he raced away before passing inside to Brierley, who finished it off. Sneyd kicked his fourth goal.

August

On the same night, Hull KR finally beat the Leigh Leopards at the fourth time of asking and they did it in some style with a 52-10 win at Craven Park.

The Robins ran in nine tries with Brad Schneider landing eight goals from eleven attempts. Led by a player-of-the-match performance from Elliot Minchella, Rovers dominated with a fine team performance.

In a dominant first half, Shaun Kenny-Dowall, Minchella, Ryan Hall, Louis Senior and Mikey Lewis all scored to send Rovers in 30-0 up. Lewis added a second try after the break, Josh Charnley replied, before Hall, Kane Linnett and Jez Litten added further gloss. A late Edwin Ipape try finished the scoring. Hull KR were still well and truly in the play-off race, in seventh position but level with Warrington and Salford on 24 points.

After a miserable couple of months of results involving eight straight defeats and a change of head coach, Warrington finally moved back into the winner's circle, with a tough and hard-fought 18-4 Saturday-afternoon victory at Hull FC that re-ignited their play-off hopes.

It was their first win in any competition since edging out Huddersfield in early June. Since then they had been eliminated in the Challenge Cup quarter-finals and lost seven in a row in Super League.

The forward pack, led by hooker Danny Walker, was the difference, with George Williams and Matt Dufty causing significant issues on the back of it. And in the second half, they withstood a mountain of Hull possession to restrict the Black and Whites to just one try.

Adam Swift swiped a loose ball to put Hull ahead before two superb tries from George Williams and Matt Dufty. The Wolves kept Hull out with stubborn defence before Matty Ashton went over from a looping Williams pass.

BETFRED SUPER LEAGUE
Sunday 27th August

	P	W	D	L	F	A	D	Pts
Catalans Dragons	23	17	0	6	606	376	230	34
Wigan Warriors	23	16	0	7	588	340	248	32
St Helens	23	16	0	7	511	320	191	32
Leigh Leopards	23	14	0	9	513	441	72	28
Warrington Wolves	23	12	0	11	485	450	35	24
Salford Red Devils	23	12	0	11	454	435	19	24
Hull KR	23	12	0	11	469	450	19	24
Leeds Rhinos	23	10	0	13	461	411	50	20
Huddersfield Giants	23	10	0	13	379	452	-73	20
Hull FC	23	10	0	13	420	515	-95	20
Castleford Tigers	23	5	0	18	276	602	-326	10
Wakefield Trinity	23	4	0	19	246	616	-370	8

Hull stand-off Jake Trueman's season was over as he limped off five before the break with a ruptured Achilles.

Leeds' play-off hopes were looking slim after their 21-12 defeat at Huddersfield left them four points adrift, every remaining round a must-win for both sides.

In a cup-tie atmosphere the Giants avenged their 54-0 defeat at Headingley in June, led by the charges of Chris Hill and backed up with the high work rate of Luke Yates.

Sam Halsall, Kevin Naiqama and Tui Lolohea crossed for tries in the first half, before Luke Hooley and Ash Handley hit back for Leeds to make it 16-12 at the break. Two Will Pryce goals and a field goal from Jake Connor, many thought he had missed, were enough to seal the victory for the home side in a tight second half.

The 10th-placed Giants moved to 20 points, the same amount as Hull FC in ninth and Leeds in eighth.

SEPTEMBER
Big guns fire

Round 24

The first of September, with the UK enjoying an Indian summer, was a Friday night of significant change at the top of Super League, with Wigan leapfrogging Catalans into pole position on points difference and St Helens joining the pair on 34 league points.

The weekend probably also provided the longest time to decide a game in the history of Rugby League after the floodlights failed during the second half of the Leigh versus Huddersfield fixture at Leigh Sports Village.

The Warriors backed up their stunning 34-0 win over Catalans Dragons in the south of France with another professional performance as Liam Farrell, Abbas Miski, Jake Wardle, Jai Field and Toby King all crossed for tries in a 26-8 home win over Salford.

It was a hard-fought first half with the crucial score coming right at the very end of it. It looked like Wigan would lead by ten points when Salford were given a penalty on the hooter and Marc Sneyd – who was back on after a HIA – put up a bomb to the Wigan posts. But Jai Field collected it and then raced 85 metres to score under the Salford posts. Harry Smith made it 20-4.

After the turnaround, Salford battled hard but were reduced to twelve men for ten minutes when King Vuniyayawa was sin-binned for a high tackle on Bevan French, who was brilliant at stand-off.

Wigan took advantage of the extra man, with Field and French combining before French produced a sublime flick pass for Toby King to waltz over. Smith converted and Wigan were out of sight at 26-4.

Salford kept fighting and went close through Danny Addy before they were rewarded with a late try to Ken Sio in the corner.

Catalans fell to back-to-back defeats with a 26-18 reverse at Hull KR, who were hitting their straps at the business end of the season.

Particularly impressive was fullback Jack Walker, who arrived from Bradford Bulls at the start of June in a deal until the end of the 2023 campaign. His try, two minutes into the second half, handed Rovers the initiative after a topsy-turvy first half in which overseas veterans Shaun Kenny-Dowall and Kane Linnett replied to tries from French forwards Romain Navarrete and Benjamin Garcia.

Fouad Yaha's reply for Catalans had the hosts just two points in front on the hour, before there was a key sequence of events starting when Julian Bousquet was denied a try by referee Ben Thaler, who ruled he'd lost the ball. Moments later, Manu Ma'u was sin-binned for a swinging arm and, from that, Mikey Lewis scored the final try.

St Helens had to win to keep pace at the top on the Sunday afternoon and they did so with a 32-16 success at Wakefield.

Trinity showed plenty of spirit and endeavour but in the end, a sixth consecutive win for the reigning champions always felt likely. That was particularly evident after Saints weathered a first-half storm from Wakefield to score twice in the final six minutes of the first half to lead 20-6 at the break. Paul Wellens' side never looked back.

Wakefield fullback Will Dagger's withdrawal due to a broken collar bone midway through

September

The lights go out in Leigh's clash with Huddersfield and *(inset)* John Asiata in action during the game's completion

the first half, after a late hit by Konrad Hurrell, was a big moment. On-loan Romain Franco dropped to fullback and had an error-ridden time of it.

Jonny Lomax, Tommy Makinson, James Roby and Jon Bennison all crossed for Saints in the first half, with Matty Ashurst scoring for Trinity.

Lee Kershaw hit back after the break for Wakefield but Makinson's second try and Lewis Dodd's four-pointer just before the hour mark put the visitors out of sight. Kershaw scored a late consolation but Trinity fell to a fourth straight loss and desperately needed at least one win to escape relegation. Hurrell was banned for one game.

The Saturday had seen the play-off chances of Hull FC finally ended as Leeds Rhinos beat them 28-12 at the MKM Stadium to keep their own hopes alive.

Former Gold Coast prop Sam Lisone scored an amazing hat-trick. All three of Lisone's tries were crucial in the game, the first two coming at the end of the first half to take Leeds' lead from two points to 14 after a tight opening half-hour.

Both of those short-range efforts were typical of a frontrower; the third was not. Charging onto Rhyse Martin's pass, he burst through the line 40 metres out and then sidestepped fullback Jamie Shaul.

That was the final try of the match, ending the hopes of a resurgent Hull and confirming that Leeds remained in the top-six hunt, four points off with three matches remaining.

Hull had the better of the territory in the first half but were made to pay for not taking their chances. The Rhinos struck first when Luke Hooley chased onto a James McDonnell kick after David Fusitu'a had played the backrower into space. Hull were unhappy as Liam Sutcliffe was down injured, close to the action, at the time and the centre was forced off on his 250th career appearance.

Jordan Lane moved out to replace Sutcliffe and he set up Adam Swift's response, the winger twisting over to score for a tenth consecutive Super League game.

September

But Lisone struck two crucial blows before half-time. Both tries were simple, the first coming from a James Donaldson offload and the second from Jarrod O'Connor's dummy-half pass, but he'd made the required impact off the bench - and would do so again later on.

When Fusitu'a followed in, from Rhyse Martin and McDonnell offloads, within two minutes of the restart and made it 22-4 to Leeds, it appeared to be game over.

But Hull made things interesting with a couple of tries in response, from Harvey Barron after great work by Andre Savelio to shrug off a tackle and pass wide, and then from Cameron Scott off an assist by Jake Clifford.

Clifford's failure to land a single goal meant Leeds still had a ten-point cushion, but for a period Hull had the momentum, the crowd on their side, and looked capable of completing the comeback. Strong goal-line defence ensured they didn't get any closer, and the Rhinos made certain of victory seven minutes from time as Lisone completed his most memorable of hat-tricks.

On the same day, Warrington did their play-off chances and their points difference a world of good with a 66-12 home hammering of Castleford, whose patched up side suffered three more key injuries and then the 51st minute sin-binning of Jacob Miller for a tip tackle.

The Tigers drew first blood through a beautiful short ball from Joe Westerman, which saw an outstretched Sam Hall touch down in the third minute. But 77 minutes later the rampant Wolves had registered eleven tries - Matt Dufty, Paul Vaughan and George Williams getting doubles - as well as bombing at least two more.

Miller was suspended for a game and the Tigers looked shot.

Which leaves the story of Leigh v Huddersfield, which finished on the Sunday afternoon, almost 44 hours after it originally kicked off on the Friday night and was abandoned following a floodlight failure with just 48 minutes played.

It was a fixture to remember for home winger Josh Charnley, who (on the Friday night) passed John Woods' longstanding top division Leigh record with two tries.

The Leopards went in 16-6 leaders at half-time through Charnley's brace, with Tom Briscoe registering the other score. However Jake Connor also bagged a brace, with his second coming eight minutes into the second forty, just before the floodlights went out.

The RFL board decided the game would resume on the Sunday, the last 32 minutes seeing the Leopards consolidate fourth spot in the table with a 34-16 win.

Round 25

The top three in the Super League table was decided with two games to go after St Helens beat fourth-placed Leigh at home on the Friday night of round 25.

Saints' 22-12 win combined with victories for Wigan and Catalans put the three six league points clear of Leigh, with points difference leaving the Warriors top.

St Helens just got the better of the Leopards in a bone-crunching showdown, despite Leigh missing Josh Charnley and John Asiata.

The game was poised 6-all at half-time, the Leopards first to draw blood with their first opportunity in the opposition's '20', scoring off a slick back-line spread which saw Gareth O'Brien put Oliver Gildart over untouched.

It didn't take long for Saints to hit back through Tommy Makinson to score the try of the match. In the 18th minute, a beautiful early backline shift out of their own end saw Mark Percival find the overlap to get Makinson in some space down the right edge. He fed inside for Jonny Lomax, who then found Joe Batchelor in support. He was able to draw and pass, engaging some the cover defence to allow Makinson to finish the job in the corner.

The first points of the second half came in the 51st minute through Makinson after a swirling bomb from Lewis Dodd put Leigh fullback O'Brien under pressure. He fumbled the ball, which was scooped up by James Roby and passed to Makinson, who beat two defenders to ground.

Lomax ran in another try in the 58th minute off the back of an attacking shift where Lomax dummied and went himself to score almost untouched.

September

Leigh hit back in the 64th minute when Edwin Ipape asked some questions of the Saints middle defenders, catching Moses Mbye by surprise and bursting through before putting Rob Mulhern under the sticks.

In the 74th minute the scores looked all but tied up when a Saints pass that went to ground saw O'Brien run 40 metres to score a try. But it was sent upstairs to the video referee Marcus Griffiths and called back after it was ruled that Leigh's Joe Mellor got a finger-tip to the ball causing the deflection and it was ruled a knock on.

Saints then quickly put out the fire caused by Leigh's late surge, scoring in the 74th minute when dynamo James Bell managed to get the ball free attacking the line. Joe Batchelor scooped up the ball and crossed for the decisive try.

Catalans got their first win in three with an 18-10 win at Wakefield on the same night.

Winger Tom Johnstone made it six tries in three games against his old club in 2023 to put the Dragons ahead and Adam Keighran crossed off a switch play, giving Catalans a 12-0 half-time lead. Tom Davies dived in at the right corner just after the hour mark to give them daylight in a tense game in sticky conditions.

Returning from injury Kelepi Tanginoa and Lee Kershaw crossed late on but Trinity were running out of time to save themselves from the drop. That looked increasingly unlikely and the return to Australia after the match of talisman David Fifita to be at the birth of his child was another blow.

Wigan did their chances of the League Leaders Shield a power of good on the Saturday with a 50-0 televised thrashing of Leeds at Headingley.

The Rhinos' faint hopes of the play-offs were totally extinguished as the Warriors ran riot. A seventh consecutive Super League win secured the points difference at the top of the table, built on a combination of devastatingly clinical attack and fierce defence

Leeds were struggling with injuries and they were also missing first-choice stars, either because they had been released in the last week of the transfer window without a replacement (Blake Austin) or because they were on the other side of the world (Nene Macdonald) and mysteriously not re-appearing. With no Aidan Sezer because of injury, the Rhinos' halfback pairing was 18-year-old Jack Sinfield and 19-year old backrower Morgan Gannon.

Two tries from Jake Wardle plus scores from Jai Field and Liam Marshall gave the Warriors a 22-0 lead at half-time. Kai Pearce-Paul added to their lead before Wardle waltzed over to complete his treble. Abbas Miski, Liam Farrell and Patrick Mago went over late on to complete Wigan's biggest ever win at Headingley and Leeds' heaviest competitive home defeat since losing 54-3 to Bradford Northern in 1945.

That week, there was more negative news for Leeds as prop Zane Tetevano left the club to go back to New Zealand, three months after suffering a stroke while training. He had been allowed to return home following heart surgery, after a hole in his heart was found to be the cause of the stroke.

Hull KR cemented their claim for a semi-final berth thanks to a fiery 26-18 Friday-night victory over Huddersfield at the John Smith's Stadium, the tight win moving them up into fifth spot on the Super League.

Will Pryce and Jake Connor's penalty goal had put the Giants in front but Shaun Kenny-Dowall's try and Brad Schneider's two goals sent Rovers ahead. Jordan Abdull continued the Robins' try-scoring, with Linnett adding to Hull KR's tally after the break and Schneider converting both for a 20-6 lead.

Jermaine McGillvary, his 250th career try and Sam Halsall hit back for the Giants either side of Louis Senior's score. But Schneider put the final nail in the coffin with a penalty goal in the 78th minute to finally seal a vital victory.

Abdull, returning after being injured in the 38-4 defeat by Catalans in France in June, came off the bench at loose forward and almost immediately scored the crucial try that turned the game seven minutes before half-time.

The Sunday-afternoon game was a cracker as a try from Sam Stone in golden-point extra-time boosted Salford's play-off hopes with a 24-20 home win and kept Warrington waiting to secure their own top-six spot.

September

Salford fans celebrate as Sam Stone wins the game against Warrington

In extra time, a knock-on from James Harrison gave Salford a great opportunity to win it and Sneyd let fly with a field-goal attempt that came back off the post. But the Red Devils then won it with an amazing long-range try. The ball went to the left and Brad Singleton got the ball to Tim Lafai, who sent Joe Burgess racing down the wing. He then turned the ball inside for Stone to score and win the game for Salford.

Ben Hellewell and Brodie Croft tries had put Salford 12-6 up at half-time after Matty Nicholson was gifted the opener. A Ben Currie try and Stefan Ratchford's penalty edged Warrington ahead again before Croft's second score restored Salford's lead. George Williams again put Wolves in front, only for a Marc Sneyd penalty goal to force golden point, where Stone won it.

The biggest result as a far as Castleford supporters were concerned came on the Friday night as the Tigers made almost certain of a Super League place in 2024 with a 29-12 home win over Hull FC.

Supporters were dancing on the terraces after a disjointed but ultimately gutsy and deserved win, while the players' lap of honour for their final home game of the season felt pretty close to a survival party.

Four weeks earlier, the mood could not have been any more different. Castleford had been trounced by Huddersfield to sit joint-bottom of the Super League table, fans staged a sit-in protest after the game, and Andy Last was sacked as coach within an hour of the final whistle. In came Danny Ward, tasked with saving their season.

It was far from a pretty contest, riddled with basic of errors by both teams. Hull made more, but the biggest difference was Castleford's exceptional defence, the sort they had lacked for most of the season - not least the previous week in a trouncing at Warrington.

That resilience meant Hull only scored twice, both through the prolific Adam Swift, while the Tigers scored five tries, two in the first half by Jason Qareqare - including a length-of-the-field effort - followed by Greg Eden, Alex Foster and Jordan Turner, Blake Austin potting a field goal. Gareth Widdop kicked four goals in his 300th career appearance.

September

Round 26

Wakefield were officially relegated in the penultimate round of the season as they succumbed to a 20-19 Friday night golden-point defeat at Leigh, their brave effort eventually thwarted by the boot of Gareth O'Brien.

Castleford also fell to a thumping 48-6 loss at in-form Wigan but their four-point lead over Trinity in the table was now insurmountable.

Wakefield got off to a bad start as they fell behind after just four minutes when Tom Briscoe sped onto O'Brien's grubber to the corner. But Liam Hood quickly got the away side level when he scooped up a loose ball and raced away.

Josh Charnley continued his excellent season with his 26th try of the year and Jack Hughes' bustling score, when Wakefield were down to 12 men with Kevin Proctor in the sin bin, should have opened the floodgates. But Trinity showed great character to fight back thanks to two Lee Kershaw tries in six minutes, one a long-range intercept another from a fine passing move to the right.

Ben Reynolds and Mason Lino exchanged penalties to keep the scores tied before O'Brien looked to have won it with his first field goal. But Luke Gale landed a long-range field of his own in the last minute to send the game to extra time.

Both sides managed to get into good field position and Max Jowitt saw a kick dribble underneath the posts before O'Brien came up trumps to break Wakefield hearts.

For Wakefield, the second tier beckoned for the first time since 1998.

Leigh's play-off spot was secure as they remained in fourth spot, though they could still be overtaken by last-round opponents Hull KR, who secured their own top-six place with a tight 12-0 win at home over Salford on the Saturday.

James Batchelor's score, midway through the first half, came from a fine play by Penrith-bound halfback Brad Schneider, who ran into the line and dummied a pass before releasing Tom Opacic into space, with his backrower providing the support to finish.

Schneider converted that try and added a further penalty after the hour mark but victory was only secured when Mikey Lewis superbly tipped on a Schneider pass, allowing Ryan Hall to race into the left corner with eight minutes to go.

For Salford, two encounters with their play-off rivals in successive weeks had not decided their fate. Despite their golden-point victory over Warrington, they trailed the sixth-placed Wolves on points difference and would need to better their result the following Friday.

While Warrington were due to travel to Huddersfield, Salford had to overcome League Leaders' Shield-chasing Catalans on home soil to have any chance of continuing their season.

Both Catalans and Huddersfield had big wins on the Saturday.

The Dragons roasted a dispirited Leeds side 61-0 in Perpignan.

They raced into a 28-0 lead by half-time with Adam Keighran, Ben Garcia, Tom Johnstone and two Tom Davies tries, combined with four Keighran goals embarrassing the Rhinos.

Mitchell Pearce, Johnstone and Keighran made it 46-0 after 54 minutes before Matt Ikuvalu crossed and Keighran made it a hat-trick as the Dragons romped home.

The Giants ran away in the second half to provide embarrassment for Hull FC on their own patch, running out 52-20 winners, Fijian centre Kevin Naiqama finishing with a hat-trick.

Jermaine McGillvary put the Giants ahead before Tex Hoy and Darnell McIntosh crossed for Hull. But Esan Marsters and Seb Ikahihifo gave Huddersfield a 16-10 lead at the break.

Andre Savelio's try reduced the gap to two points early in the second half before the Giants cut loose through Naiqama and second tries for Will Pryce and McGillvary.

Jake Connor was excellent from the tee, kicking eight goals as the Giants went past 50 points, before Scott Taylor's 79th-minute consolation under the sticks.

Friday night saw Wigan and St Helens maintain their run-in form.

Wigan had little trouble in beating Castleford at home, as Abbas Miski helped himself to five tries to go top of the Super League try-scoring chart (though Catalans' Tom Johnstone joined him on 27 the night after) in a 48-6 victory.

September

A despondent Luke Gale meets Wakefield fans as the club's relegation from Super League is confirmed

The Warriors crossed for ten tries – five in each half – as they increased their impressive points difference, meaning that they only needed a win over Leigh Leopards the following Friday to finish top.

Saints remained third but they were given a much tougher test, fighting hard for an 18-6 win at Warrington.

The defending champions' ability to defend their own line, especially in the second half, secured the victory, with their coach Paul Wellens marvelling at his side's ability to wrestle back momentum late in the game, Moses Mbye's dummy-half try a minute from time sealing it.

Jack Welsby was outstanding at the back, both in terms of organising the Saints' defence and making some outstanding tackles himself. His tackle on Matty Russell towards the end of the first half to save a certain try was out of the top drawer, as was his role in the charge to prevent Matty Ashton scoring in the corner on 54 minutes.

Saints led through converted tries from Curtis Sironen and Mark Percival in the first half and seemed to be cruising to a comfortable win. But the Wolves came up with a spirited reply and Daryl Clark's 56th-minute try had the home fans at the Halliwell Jones Stadium dreaming of an end to a five-match losing streak against their local rivals. But Saints held firm, despite losing Jon Bennison to the sin bin in the closing stages, with Mbye providing the killer try.

Despite an eighth win in a row, Saints remained third behind Wigan and Catalans, with huge points differences to make up to avoid a first-week eliminator.

Round 27

There was a lot resting on results going into the final round of the regular season.

With leaders Wigan, Catalans and St Helens all level on league points at the top of the table, any of the three could end the six-game Friday night programme as League Leaders. Below them, Hull KR could leap above fourth-placed Leigh to ensure they would be at home in the eliminators. And in the middle of the table, Salford were looking to edge into the play-off spots at the expense of Warrington.

September

As it unfolded, all the top-three teams won, allowing Wigan coach Matt Peet to hail the Warriors' League Leaders' Shield triumph a success for the whole club after a tense final-day 10-6 win at neighbours Leigh Leopards.

Any slip-up from Wigan would have thrown away not only the Shield but a top-two place and automatic play-off semi-final berth. But the Warriors held their nerve for their ninth win in a row in Super League, to finish ahead of their two rivals on points difference.

All the points were scored in the first half, Wigan taking the lead through an exceptional Jai Field try and a Jake Wardle score, before Lachlan Lam cut the Leopards' deficit before half-time.

The second half was no less absorbing for being scoreless. Both teams had tries controversially ruled out for obstruction, both teams defended heroically on their try-line, and both teams made frustrating errors at key times.

The end result was a third defeat from three for Leigh against their local neighbours this season, plus the pain of watching Wigan lift the Shield at their ground.

Leigh showed plenty of guts, going toe-to-toe with a rampant, in-form Warriors. Their aggressive and physical approach, epitomised by the hard-hitting Edwin Ipape, gave Wigan little room to breathe. But Wigan held on, as they defended in front of a wall of passionate Warriors fans in a sold-out Leigh Sports Village.

Catalans held onto second spot and with it a week off before the semi-finals, with a hard-fought 19-8 win at Salford, on a damp, chilly autumnal night.

Arthur Romano looked like he had put the Dragons in front after ten minutes off a smart Matt Whitley offload but Tyrone May's earlier pass was ruled forward. May made amends by sending Whitley in for the opener as Sam Tomkins converted and added another goal on the half hour before Marc Sneyd's penalty, after a dust-up between Tomkins and Amir Bourouh saw them both sin-binned, got Salford on the board just before half-time. May also saw yellow for time-wasting just before the break.

Ben Hellewell pulled Salford level just before the hour mark, crashing though off Oliver Partington's short pass for Sneyd to convert.

Tomkins edged Catalans back in front with a field goal ten minutes later and three minutes after that Julian Bousquet powered over from Mike McMeeken's smart offload, before Tomkins crossed to seal it six minutes from time.

St Helens were expected to coast at home against a Hull FC side whose play-off ambitions had long gone. It was far from vintage Saints in a 30-12 win but the reigning champions never looked like losing against an embattled Hull side who salvaged some pride in their final outing of the season.

It was a fiercely competitive game in the middle but Saints just had the extra touch of class, led by Jonny Lomax and Jack Welsby, with Mark Percival causing issues on the edge, that ultimately proved too much for Hull, who ended their year with six straight defeats.

Saints went in at half-time with an 8-0 lead thanks to a try and two goals from Percival, a lead that was extended to 14 points almost straight after the break when Lewis Dodd grounded Lomax's smart kick to the posts,

Hull bounced back with a long-range effort against the run of play. Darnell McIntosh put Jordan Lane through a gap and the backrower handed on to young debutant Lewis Martin, who stepped and powered his way over from 40 metres.

It didn't take the hosts long to click back into gear, scoring again through Lomax, who powered over the line off a short ball from Moses Mbye. Saints then made it two in two minutes, with Morgan Knowles bursting through the middle to put Welsby under the posts to end the game as a contest.

Hull wouldn't go away and stemmed the flow with another long-range try to Cameron Scott, who intercepted and raced 70 metres to score.

The hosts had the final say, however, with some trademark brilliance from Welsby, who glided through the line and held off the chasers to score from 80 metres out to round off a hard-fought win.

September

Wigan's Bevan French, Abbas Miski and Patrick Mago show off the League Leaders' Shield

Saints coach Paul Wellens heaped praise on Alex Walmsley, who defied all expectations to return to action off the bench, having previously been ruled out for the season with a knee injury.

Hull KR had to win to have a chance of going above Leigh - thereby winning the rights to a home tie for the eliminator with the Leopards - and they did so in some style with a 56-12 drubbing of already relegated Wakefield at Belle Vue, overcoming a difference of 34 points to finish in fourth position.

The triumvirate of Mikey Lewis, Brad Schneider and Jack Walker ripped Trinity's defence to shreds in a remarkable second half that saw Rovers register seven tries - three while Max Jowitt was in the sin bin - after Liam Kay's try brought Wakefield back to 18-12.

Schneider, Matty Storton and Jez Litten all scored two tries with one each for Walker, Mikey Lewis, Matty Storton, Tom Opacic and Ryan Hall.

Wakefield coach Mark Applegarth named three Super League debutants in the shape of Harvey Smith, Jordan Schofield and Oli Pratt.

Salford's loss to the Dragons meant they had no chance of improving a seventh-place finish but a win wouldn't have mattered anyway as Warrington won at Huddersfield by 20-8.

The Wolves were now set to face St Helens in an eliminator on the following Saturday at the Totally Wicked Stadium, thanks to tries from Matt Dufty and James Harrison, while Stefan Ratchford kicked a perfect six from six with the boot.

Huddersfield finished their season on a disappointing note in what was the final club appearance of veteran Jermaine McGillvary before he was released, and the final games for retiring Australian pair Nathan Peats and Chris McQueen.

The Wolves built a 12-4 lead at half-time, with Dufty and Harrison crossing, before McQueen hit back for the Giants.

Ratchford struck in the second half with three penalty goals, before Will Pryce's brilliant individual try, to claim the tight win and secure a semi-final berth.

Star prop Paul Vaughan was missing from the Wolves side after he copped four-match ban for 'making unnecessary contact with a player who is or may be injured' in Warrington's penultimate Super League regular-season game against St Helens.

At a tribunal, the player in question - Sione Mata'utia - admitted he stayed on the ground following a tackle in an act of gamesmanship, rather than due to an injury.

However, Vaughan was still found guilty.

September

There was only one match with no effect on the table and Leeds went some way to erasing the memory of their previous two huge defeats with a 46-0 home thrashing of Castleford.

David Fusitu'a's majestic finishing and the Rhinos' eight tries grabbed the headlines but it was their commitment to keep their line intact that impressed. That was best exemplified late on when Liam Horne and George Lawler were denied, indicating that although the Leeds side had been badly bent over the previous two weeks, it had not been broken.

Alfie Edgell and Tom Nicholson-Watton made their debuts off the bench for the Rhinos, while Fletcher Rooney made a sound debut at fullback for the Tigers.

BETFRED SUPER LEAGUE
Final table - Friday 22nd September

	P	W	D	L	F	A	D	Pts
Wigan Warriors	27	20	0	7	722	360	362	40
Catalans Dragons	27	20	0	7	722	420	302	40
St Helens	27	20	0	7	613	366	247	40
Hull KR	27	16	0	11	589	498	91	32
Leigh Leopards	27	16	0	11	585	508	77	32
Warrington Wolves	27	14	0	13	597	512	85	28
Salford Red Devils	27	13	0	14	494	512	-18	26
Leeds Rhinos	27	12	0	15	535	534	1	24
Huddersfield Giants	27	11	0	16	473	552	-79	22
Hull FC	27	10	0	17	476	654	-178	20
Castleford Tigers	27	6	0	21	323	774	-451	12
Wakefield Trinity	27	4	0	23	303	742	-439	8

* Warrington's George Williams and Wigan's Bevan French tied for first place in the Albert Goldthorpe Medal table, with both players earning 27 points from 27 rounds of matches.

The Eliminators

Hull KR were the first side through the elimination play-offs after a 20-6 home victory over Leigh on the last Friday night of September.

Craven Park was rocking long before kick-off and rarely stopped, through a cagey opening and then through a burst of tries around half-time by Jack Walker, Ryan Hall and, straight from the second-half restart, Sam Luckley. A sell-out crowd then carried the Robins through some nervous moments before a thoroughly deserved victory was settled.

The only points in the opening half-hour were a penalty apiece, Ben Reynolds for Leigh when Hull KR gave away a penalty in possession, Brad Schneider responding after a Joe Wardle high tackle.

In between, the hosts applied greater pressure on the try-line, with backrowers Kane Linnett and James Batchelor repelled, along with Hall, all in one set on the line.

The opening try began with a break down the left by Mikey Lewis, in combination with Shaun Kenny-Dowall, as the following play saw a shift right and Batchelor coupled a dangerous run with a perfectly-measured offload for Walker to steam over.

Matt Parcell was then pivotal to Hull KR's second try on the stroke of half-time, brilliantly ripping possession from Gareth O'Brien - who suffered a horror show, struggling under numerous high balls from Schneider and Lewis - and almost making it to the corner. On the next play, Hall twisted through a Joe Mellor tackle to ground. Mellor did his best to keep his hand between ball and ground but video referee Chris Kendall confirmed Jack Smith's on-field decision of a try.

The score became 18-2 barely a minute after the restart. Again O'Brien erred, fumbling the kick-off into touch, and from that position Hull KR scored their third try, Schneider's delayed dummy-half pass sending Luckley over. Schneider couldn't convert as he had for both first-half tries but the Robins had a healthy lead to defend and they went about the task with relish.

Walker and Lewis made pivotal tackles to hold out on one attacking set, before Mellor crossed on the next with a dummy-half scoot.

Hull KR players immediately pleaded with Smith to check the try and it soon became clear why, as Edwin Ipape had taken out marker George King after getting up from being tackled the previous play.

But Leigh finally broke through five minutes later. Batchelor stopped Josh Charnley earlier in the set but the defence could not spread back across in time when Oliver Gildart popped the winger in for his 27th try of the season.

September

Hull KR's Matt Parcell leaves Leigh's Gareth O'Brien and Ben Reynolds trailing

Home victory was assured when Hall superbly wrestled the ball from O'Brien, breaking half the length of the field, from where a Tom Briscoe high tackle gave Schneider the chance to kick two match-clinching points.

Despite their exit, there was little doubt Leigh had been the outstanding story in Rugby League in 2023, having won the Challenge Cup and been a fixture in the play-off places for almost the whole season.

They lost their home advantage for the play-offs with defeat to Wigan in the final regular-season round and that was significant, particularly when their small squad was missing John Asiata, Zak Hardaker and Ricky Leutele.

The following afternoon, St Helens kept alive their hopes of a fifth title in a row with a 16-8 home win over Warrington.

It wasn't as easy as many had anticipated, especially given the absence of Warrington's two prop forwards Paul Vaughan and Thomas Mikaele, while Saints were able to select Alex Walmsley after his recent early return from a knee injury suffered in the Challenge Cup semi-final.

Saints started well, almost scoring an excellent try after six minutes. Mark Percival and Joe Batchelor sent Tommy Makinson away down the right and the winger's kick behind was chased eagerly, only for Matty Ashton to get there first and knock the ball dead. Batchelor pulled up straight away with a hamstring pull and that was the end of his season.

The deadlock was broken after 25 minutes, through a move started and finished by Lewis Dodd. After George Williams was penalised for a late tackle on Sione Mata'utia, Dodd and James Bell put Curtis Sironen through a gap and the halfback appeared again in support to claim the opening try.

Percival converted, and added a penalty, awarded when Josh Drinkwater lifted Jack

September

St Helens' James Bell looks for a way past Warrington's Daryl Clark and Joe Philbin

Welsby upside down, three minutes from half-time for an 8-0 score that could certainly have been wider.

Within three minutes of the re-start, Matt Dufty had released Connor Wrench to go down the right. The centre rounded the defence and then just about beat Welsby, before scampering to the line after being knocked to his knees by the fullback's tackle.

Stefan Ratchford converted, and then levelled the scores ten minutes later from the tee after a high tackle by Matty Lees on Joe Philbin.

By that time St Helens were playing a man down, due to a high shot from Walmsley on Jordan Crowther that earned him ten minutes on the sidelines.

Ratchford's penalty goal would be the only Wolves points in that period and Saints stepped things up on Walmsley's return to re-take the lead with a finely-worked try which saw Welsby offload and Percival pass the ball on sharply for Makinson to step over. Percival added the conversion for a 14-8 advantage.

Things got much worse for Warrington from the restart as Lees claimed the kick, ran it in and was met by Joe Bullock's firm shoulder to his head. Referee Ben Thaler again went for the yellow card.

The Wolves barely had another sniff, with Welsby looking dangerous along with James Roby's replacement, Moses Mbye. After a break by the latter, Matty Russell hit Jon Bennison high and Percival erased any doubt over the outcome with a penalty goal.

Saints stalwart Roby, at the age of 37 and in his 550th game for St Helens, was making his last appearance at the Totally Wicked Stadium, along with Louie McCarthy-Scarsbrook.

The reigning champions' victory set up a do-or-die semi-final at Catalans the following Friday, with Hull KR travelling to League leaders Wigan in the other knock-out.

OCTOBER
Warriors all

Semi-finals

Super League XXVIII would climax with first versus second in the table as the sides with home advantage both won through their semis.

On the first Friday of October, Catalans ended St Helens' dream of a fifth consecutive title with a 12-6 win on a night of pure drama at a sold-out Stade Gilbert Brutus.

A try 80 seconds from time from Sam Tomkins, with the scores locked at 6-6, was the killer blow in a toe-to-toe slugfest. Showing the daintiness and fleet-footed flair of his early years, Tomkins turned an attempted field goal into a dazzling dash over the line, rounding Alex Walmsley and pushing off Curtis Sironen to unleash scenes of true delight on and off the pitch.

The pressure got to both sides in a brutal first half with handling mistakes littering the game and Catalans just about winning the arm-wrestle.

The Dragons were over the line first, with Tom Johnstone grounding in the left corner, only for the video referee to adjudge he pushed Jonny Lomax before touching down. Moments later, Johnstone's stellar season seemed to crumble as he fumbled a high kick in front of his own posts and put Saints on the attack. But the tackle of the match followed swiftly when Dragons' captain Ben Garcia hit Saints prop Alex Walmsley hard and low as he thundered for the line, loosening the ball and regaining the offensive for his team.

A challenge by Sione Mata'utia on Tomkins created the only score of the first half, with Adam Keighran converting a penalty from 40 metres out after what appeared to be a swinging arm to the head while Tomkins was on the floor.

The attrition continued into the second half, with both teams losing possession as the intensity took its toll, the crucial difference being the penalty count - 7-2 against Saints was crucial to the result.

It didn't seem to matter, however, when centre Will Hopoate cut through a gap created by Welsby's inside ball, to score the first try of the game in the 50th minute to put the champions 6-2 in front. But the penalty Hopoate conceded moments later with a late hit on Mitchell Pearce put Catalans back on the offensive.

A high Moses Mbye shot on Johnstone allowed Keighran to convert two more points and the fatal flaw was finally committed by prop Matty Lees, when he held on in a tackle on Johnstone for what seemed like an eternity and was sin-binned for a professional foul, meaning Saints were down to twelve men for the final eight minutes of the game.

Keighran levelled the scores with the penalty and the stage was set for a frantic finale.

Tomkins had two field-goal attempts and when he was frustrated on his third aim at goal by a charging Saints defence, he took matters into his own hands with the match-winning try.

The following afternoon, Wigan blasted their way into the Grand Final with a 42-12 home win over Hull KR.

The Warriors' momentum had been building ever since they were last beaten, in mid-June in the Challenge Cup semi-finals by Rovers. And the week off won by topping the table worked to their great advantage as they had three players suspended for offences following their last round win at Leigh. But all three, including Bevan French, were free to play in the semi-final due to a loophole in the system.

October

Sam Tomkins splits the St Helens defence to send Catalans Dragons to Old Trafford

French, along with Kaide Ellis and Harvie Hill all served their one-game suspensions on the free weekend when Wigan played in the Reserve Grand Final against St Helens.

All the damage was done by Wigan's start to each half, with three tries in the opening twelve minutes of the first - two of them before the Robins had so much as carried the ball - and the other four in the first 16 minutes after the break.

Liam Marshall scored three of their tries, in an excellent all-round display. Jai Field was sensational, scoring a flukey try in the first half but a brilliant one in the second to add to his highlight reel, while providing two assists as well.

French didn't score but he provided a hat-trick of assists, two with the boot and one with the hands. And Harry Smith rose to another big occasion, his kicks always challenging Hull KR and leading to the first two tries of the second half which sealed the win. Smith was even flawless from the tee, with seven conversions out of seven.

Two tries from Marshall and one from Field inside the first 11 minutes put Wigan into an 18-0 lead. The Warriors were almost home and dry, although the only other try before half-time came from the Robins, who gave themselves hope when Sam Luckley, freshly introduced from the bench, offloaded at the line for Matt Parcell to put Elliot Minchella over.

Within three minutes of the second-half kick-off, Wigan were back on the scoreboard and effectively in the Grand Final. The try was a wonderful piece of improvisation from French. After Hull KR failed to challenge for a Smith kick to the right edge and the ball was scrappily recycled, he saw the space a long way out wide for Marshall and arrowed a precision missile into the hands of his winger for his hat-trick.

And when another Smith bomb in the same direction was knocked back by Kai Pearce-Paul, French again found the right play, passing to Toby King on his inside to score.

Field and joint league top try-scorer Abbas Miski tries quickly followed and a rout seemed inevitable with over 20 minutes to go.

October

Wigan legend Martin Offiah celebrates with Liam Marshall following victory against Hull KR

Instead Hull KR, who had a marvellous season to appear in the Challenge Cup Final, as well as reaching a play-off semi-final with a six-match winning run, had the final say, with a fine try the type of which had illuminated their year under coach Willie Peters. Three of their pivots, Parcell, Jordan Abdull and Jez Litten, all combined to great effect down the middle to prise an opening, the latter finishing the move and mid-season import Brad Schneider adding his second conversion.

Grand Final

Wigan recorded their sixth Grand Final win with a tough 10-2 success over Catalans Dragons. It was their eleventh victory in a row, a run filled with scintillating rugby, as they finished the season as League Leaders and few doubters that they were the best team in Super League in 2023.

It was the ultimate example of Grand Final rugby - a slippery surface on a night of tension, both the temperature and the scoreline mostly staying in single figures.

Catalans battled hard for a historic first Super League triumph but they rued two sin-binnings that drained them when they needed an energy burst late on. They held Wigan at bay while Adam Keighran was sidelined for a first-half spear tackle but could not in the second half without Tom Davies, who saw yellow for a professional foul.

Left winger Liam Marshall scored the game's only try, down Davies' wing, in the 52nd minute. Jake Wardle, another outstanding player and the winner, by just a single vote from halfback Harry Smith, of the Harry Sunderland Trophy, stepped inside and slipped through the tackle of Mitchell Pearce, then found Liam Farrell. The skipper couldn't rumble all the way over but he could offload to Marshall, who was once again Wigan's man for the big occasion.

Smith's three goals helped the Warriors home, with all their points scored by homegrown talent. But it was their collective defensive efforts that stood out most of all, which was a sign of the culture allowed to flourish by head coach Matt Peet.

October

Wigan's Jai Field and Kaide Ellis show their delight at defeating Catalans Dragons at Old Trafford

October

Catalans coach Steve McNamara took particular pride in the fact his side conceded only one try. But that workload took its toll, not least when playing a quarter of the match a man light.

And in attack, there was no final piece of magic from the retiring Sam Tomkins and Mitchell Pearce. Tyrone May was the brightest threat in a first half which saw them equal Wigan's physicality but could do little to turn the game late on.

Catalans were slightly the better team in the first half when the game was 13 against 13, although chances were at a premium. They had the game's first opening when May zipped away down the left, only for his scruffy kick to run dead. But otherwise their attacks saw the forwards hammer on a Wigan door that would not open.

Keighran's tackle on Kai Pearce-Paul, lifting a leg and throwing him to the ground, opened the game up at the 20-minute mark and the Warriors dominated the following period. Farrell so very nearly charged over after slipping through, only for Pearce to produce a miraculous tackle, along with Davies, to stop the Wigan skipper.

The English side were now dominating field position but, such was the tight nature of the contest, they were happy to take two points when they were offered by a high Manu Ma'u tackle on Marshall, and Smith kicked them in front.

Keighran returned - while Wigan lost Ethan Havard, his surprise comeback from injury backfiring - and Catalans drove forward again, replying in kind when the returning man kicked a penalty of his own after Wigan were caught offside defending a scrum.

So 2-2 it was at half-time, though not without a late scare for the Dragons when the electric Jai Field burst through from the left. He ran inside with menace only to be met by a huge hit from the covering Tom Johnstone, who then chased back on the next play to defuse a Bevan French kick, at the expense of a hefty collision with the hoardings down the dangerous Old Trafford slopes.

The break was a chance for Johnstone and everybody else to rest their wounds after a bruising half. More of the same seemed in prospect - but instead Wigan returned a different team, one with their slick attacking instincts suddenly rediscovered.

BETFRED SUPER LEAGUE GRAND FINAL

Saturday 14th October 2023

CATALANS DRAGONS 2 WIGAN WARRIORS 10

DRAGONS: 29 Sam Tomkins; 2 Tom Davies; 21 Matt Ikuvalu; 3 Adam Keighran; 24 Tom Johnstone; 6 Tyrone May; 7 Mitchell Pearce; 8 Mike McMeeken; 9 Michael McIlorum; 22 Sio Siua Taukeiaho; 11 Matt Whitley; 12 Paul Seguier; 13 Benjamin Garcia (C). Subs (all used): 1 Arthur Mourgue; 10 Julian Bousquet; 16 Romain Navarrete; 26 Manu Ma'u.
Goals: Keighran 1/1.
Sin bin: Keighran (20) - dangerous challenge on Pearce-Paul; Davies (43) - obstructing Marshall.
WARRIORS: 1 Jai Field; 23 Abbas Miski; 3 Toby King; 4 Jake Wardle; 5 Liam Marshall; 2 Bevan French; 7 Harry Smith; 34 Tyler Dupree; 22 Brad O'Neill; 15 Kaide Ellis; 12 Liam Farrell (C); 17 Kai Pearce-Paul; 13 Morgan Smithies. Subs (all used): 9 Sam Powell; 11 Willie Isa; 16 Ethan Havard; 20 Patrick Mago.
Try: Marshall (52); **Goals:** Smith 3/3.
Rugby Leaguer & League Express Men of the Match:
Dragons: Tom Johnstone; *Warriors:* Harry Smith.
Penalty count: 4-6; **Half-time:** 2-2; **Referee:** Liam Moore; **Attendance:** 58,137 *(at Old Trafford, Manchester).*

The first hint came within a minute, as crisp handling put French away down the right before the Dragons closed down the threat. Soon after, Field progressed down the other flank and put Wardle through a gap, his run stopped by Sam Tomkins. But the support play from Marshall was impeded by Davies' tug of his shirt and the latter received the game's second yellow card.

Catalans held firm after the first, but couldn't this time. They had an escape when Field created another break down the left, only for his final pass to French to go forward. But they were finally beaten when Wardle and Farrell put Marshall over for the Grand Final-winning try.

Now it was about game management, and Wigan's was impeccable. French and Smith kept the Dragons on the back foot with their kicking and the latter made it a two-score lead at 10-2 when he added to his wide conversion of Marshall's try with a penalty, after a high Keighran tackle on Tyler Dupree.

Only after that goal did McNamara roll the dice, introducing Arthur Mourgue from the bench for Pearce. But it was too little, too late, as both he and Tomkins made errors in their desperate attempts to get Catalans back in the game.

Wigan were worthy winners and celebrated their first Grand Final win since 2018 as if it were their first.

SUPER LEAGUE AWARDS

STEVE PRESCOTT MAN OF STEEL
Bevan French (Wigan Warriors)

YOUNG PLAYER OF THE YEAR
Josh Thewlis (Warrington Wolves)

COACH OF THE YEAR
Adrian Lam (Leigh Leopards)

SUPER LEAGUE DREAM TEAM

			Previous selections
1	Jack Welsby	St Helens	2021, 2022
2	Josh Charnley	Leigh Leopards	2012, 2013
3	Shaun Kenny-Dowall	Hull KR	2022
4	Jake Wardle	Wigan Warriors	Debut
5	Tom Johnstone	Catalans Dragons	2018
6	Bevan French	Wigan Warriors	2020, 2022
7	Lachlan Lam	Leigh Leopards	Debut
8	Paul Vaughan	Warrington Wolves	Debut
9	Edwin Ipape	Leigh Leopards	Debut
10	Tom Amone	Leigh Leopards	Debut
11	Kallum Watkins	Salford Red Devils	2014, 2015
12	Liam Farrell	Wigan Warriors	2015, 2019, 2020, 2021, 2022
13	John Asiata	Leigh Leopards	Debut

Back row *(left to right)*: Josh Charnley, Jack Welsby, Tom Johnstone
Middle row *(left to right)*: Jake Wardle, Lachlan Lam, Bevan French, Shaun Kenny-Dowall
Front row *(left to right)*: Tom Amone, Kallum Watkins, Edwin Ipape, John Asiata, Liam Farrell, Paul Vaughan

3 CHAMPIONSHIP, LEAGUE ONE & WOMEN 2023

CHAMPIONSHIP SEASON
Capital gains

Few would have tipped **LONDON BRONCOS** to reclaim the Super League berth lost in 2019 at the midway point of 2023, never mind the start. But in one of the stories of the season, promoted, in Mike Eccles' first full campaign at the helm, they were, thanks to a stirring run of 10 wins in their final 12 regular league games. Then from a final position of fifth, impressive play-off triumphs at Sheffield, favourites Featherstone and Toulouse, where they came from ten points down, secured their return.

It was a remarkable feat, led by long-serving Eccles, previously the club's strength and conditioning coach, who blended a crop of homegrown players like fullback Alex Walker, winger Iliess Macani and centre or second rower Will Lovell with overseas signings such as Australian back Jarred Bassett (from London Skolars) and classy mid-season recruits from the French domestic league, Australia halfback Corey Norman and Kiwi centre Dean Whare.

That was recognised at the end-of-season awards at which Eccles was named Championship Coach of the Year, Aussie utility Dean Parata joint Player of the Year and hooker and local product Bill Leyland the Young Player of the Year.

Even allowing for their well-chronicled habit of coming close to promotion only to fluff their lines when under the spotlight on the big stage, the latest failure to reach Super League by **FEATHERSTONE ROVERS** was hard to fathom.

The Millennium Stadium side fairly sauntered to the League Leaders' Shield, topping the table by a 12-point margin. With a strong and well-balanced squad, and prolific try-scorers in winger Gareth Gale, hooker Connor Jones and fullback or halfback Caleb Aekins, they suffered only two defeats in 27 league matches.

Rovers reacted to those setbacks, against Toulouse and Halifax, by parting company with coach Sean Long. His replacement was from within, ex-York chief James Ford having left his post as assistant coach to Mark Applegarth at Wakefield to become Rovers' director of rugby in mid-May, in another show of top-flight intent.

Ford won six out of six - before Featherstone came unstuck in a home play-off semi-final for the second season running. Twelve months earlier Batley had done the damage - this time it was London Broncos who left the faithful stunned.

So disappointed was long-serving coach Sylvain Houlès with the relegation after one season in Super League of **TOULOUSE OLYMPIQUE** that he thought long and hard about taking on the challenge of trying to guide them back at the first attempt.

He knew there would have to be something of a squad rebuild, given the financial impact of falling through the trapdoor (it led to the need for a rescue package, with an influx of cash from sponsors and shareholders helping to re-float the club).

Eventually the former TO player, who took the reins in 2012 and led them to the top flight via success over Featherstone in the 2021 play-off final, committed to another campaign. And he came agonisingly close to achieving his objective, taking Toulouse, again driven by dependable Kiwi forward Harrison Hansen and with centre Guy Armitage grabbing tries and halfback Jake Shorrocks goals, to a final position of second.

Championship Season

Joey Leilua leads the celebrations as Featherstone get their hands on the League Leaders' Shield, but the season ultimately ended in heartbreak once more for Rovers

The unexpected play-off semi-final elimination of Featherstone left the French side, who overcame Bradford in the semi, as firm promotion favourites, especially with home advantage.

And up to the midway point of the big match at the Stade Ernest Wallon, when the Olympians were leading London Broncos 14-4, things were looking good. But the Broncos claimed 14-unanswered second-half points, and Toulouse's hopes were in tatters.

The wait for a return to Super League goes on. But **BRADFORD BULLS** came closer than at any time since 2015, when they lost out at Wakefield in the Million Pound Game in the season following their relegation from the top flight.

Much of the credit must go to Lee Greenwood, who stepped up from his role as assistant coach after the departure of Mark Dunning in May, up to which point the Odsal side had been inconsistent, winning five and losing five in the league.

As interim, Greenwood, the former Gloucestershire All Golds and Dewsbury coach, was able to call on the help of one Brian Noble, the club's football consultant.

And with centre Kieran Gill regularly among the tries and halfback Dec Patton kicking goals reliably, Bradford won 11 and drew one of their remaining 17 regular-season games to finish third.

Visitors York were seen off in the first stage of the play-offs but a semi-final against Toulouse over in France proved a step too far.

Championship Season

Sheffield's Titus Gwaze mobbed by teammates after scoring in the Eagles' home win against Newcastle Thunder

The Championship just wouldn't be the same without Mark Aston's involvement. And the single-minded **SHEFFIELD EAGLES** chief went into the 2023 season as full of vim and vigour as ever and buoyed by the knowledge it would be a first full campaign at the new-look Olympic Legacy Park, to where the club had returned midway through 2022, when they finished eighth.

Aston, with a good sprinkling of thirty-somethings like wingers Ben Jones-Bishop and Matty Dawson-Jones, centre Kris Welham and halfback Anthony Thackeray, built on those foundations by guiding his side to fourth.

But even so, they were bedevilled by inconsistency, often struggling to back up one win with another and having made the play-offs, lost at home to London Broncos in an eliminator.

Like London Broncos, **YORK KNIGHTS** were slow starters as they found their feet under Andrew Henderson, who after playing his part in Keighley's fine League One promotion of 2022 as head of rugby, arrived at the LNER Stadium that October to succeed the long-serving James Ford.

Henderson, the ex-Broncos boss and Warrington assistant coach, had a particularly tough time with injuries, which had an effect. But when things started to click and, as he put it 'the penny started to drop' in terms of his tactical requirements, the picture changed.

Having been above the relegation zone only on points difference in late June in the wake of five straight league defeats, York won 10 out of 11, including their last six, to squeeze into the play-offs at the expense of Batley, whose points difference was minus 13 (the Knights scored the same number - 557 - as they conceded).

Henderson's side were beaten in their eliminator at Bradford, but there are clear foundations on which to build.

Championship Season

By making the play-offs for the second season in succession in 2022, and then reaching the Grand Final, **BATLEY BULLDOGS** set the bar high for 2023 and ultimately fell short. But it was still a memorable campaign.

The Fox's Biscuits Stadium team, who had made such a habit of punching above their weight in recent times, missed out on the top-six play-offs on points difference to York, having earlier beaten them to seal a first-ever trip to Wembley for the 1895 Cup Final.

While Batley were edged out in a thriller by Halifax at the national stadium, Craig Lingard's spirited side were still able to show what the popular club are all about.

Lingard, having altered his squad following the departure of key men fullback Luke Hooley to Leeds and halfback Tom Gilmore to Widnes (in the event Hooley played some matches on loan for Batley), was particularly busy.

In May, he took the role of assistant (since upgraded to head) coach at Castleford – on the understanding he could continue his role at Batley until the end of the campaign, with his assistant Mark Moxon then moving up.

HALIFAX PANTHERS had a similar season to Batley, but at least had some silverware to show off at the end of it courtesy of their 1895 Cup final trip to Wembley, where the Bulldogs were beaten 12-10.

That revived memories of the heady days of the mid-1980s, when Chris Anderson's Thrum Hallers lifted the Challenge Cup the year after claiming the league title.

Panthers fans learned in mid-July that Simon Grix, coach for the previous four years, would be departing at the end of the season to take up a post in Super League (assistant coach at Hull in the event). And the obvious hope was that he could guide his charges to a third straight play-off appearance.

However Halifax, despite having a deadly finisher in winger and joint Championship Player of the Year Lachlan Walmsley (nor was fullback James Woodburn-Hall a slouch when it came to try-scoring), never quite hit their straps and finished eighth after losing 12 out of 27 league outings.

The loss of playmaker Joe Keyes to injury for a spell in the middle of the season hardly helped, while Grix several times referred to confidence issues, something his successor Liam Finn will want to address.

It was another false dawn for **WIDNES VIKINGS**, who hoped that most seasoned of Rugby League navigators, John Kear, was the man to take them closer to a return to Super League than at any time since their relegation and descent into financial difficulties in 2018.

Kear had taken over in July of the previous season, when his side finished eighth, just as they had under Simon Finnigan in 2021.

With a rejigged squad, including experienced winger Kieran Dixon, who was to prove a reliable try-grabber, Widnes started well, with three wins from four. But they were unable to maintain such a regular flow of league points and Kear departed the DCBL Stadium at the end of June.

Neil Belshaw, who had been one of his assistants, took interim control and with four wins from his first five games when steering the longship, a push for the play-offs looked on, but there were only two more from the six remaining matches, leading to a final position of ninth.

By that point, Swinton's Allan Coleman had been confirmed as the new man at the helm for the 2024 Vikings voyage.

Coach Allan Coleman left Heywood Road having guided **SWINTON LIONS** to promotion through the League One play-offs in 2022 - and kept them in the Championship thanks to an excellent 22-12 win over Halifax at The Shay on a dramatic and tense final day of the campaign.

That ninth league victory reflected both the spirit within a player pool put together on a tight budget and Coleman's assertion that with most of them available, he could field a side capable of giving any opponent a game.

Championship Season

Swinton celebrate during a dramatic last-day victory at Halifax that secured the Lions' Championship status

That was also shown by wins at Batley, at home to Toulouse, at Widnes (a month before confirmation that he would be with the Vikings for the 2024 season) and at home to Sheffield.

Especially impressive for the Lions were fullback Dan Abram, centre Andy Badrock, who made a successful step up from the community game Coleman knows so well, and Jordy Gibson, the lively halfback signed from North Wales Crusaders and another to have moved up impressively from the amateur ranks.

Swinton revealed a month before the end of the season that Coleman's coaching successor would be Hunslet's Alan Kilshaw.

Having won promotion from League One, then making the Championship play-offs, in successive seasons, it was a disappointing year for **BARROW RAIDERS**, who spent the bulk of it far too close to the drop zone for comfort and finally finished 11th, just a point above relegated Keighley.

The departure of winger Tee Ritson to St Helens, initially on loan before the deal was made permanent, pleased stalwart coach Paul Crarey, who had worked hard on the former Workington and Newcastle player's development during his four years at the club. But it also left a big try-scoring void to fill.

Having also lost Hakim Miloudi, who returned to France, Barrow brought in Andrew Bulman from Whitehaven and Greg Worthington from Halifax, among others.

Ryan Shaw provided a good return with the boot, and while there were injuries aplenty, there was no shortage of either spirit or workrate. But with only eight league wins (as well as a draw), Barrow didn't click nearly enough for Crarey's liking.

WHITEHAVEN were playing in the second tier for the third successive season, a second under coach Jonty Gorley, who as assistant to Gary Charlton had helped the outpost side to the 2021 play-offs.

While finishing 10th in 2022, Whitehaven were well clear of danger in the closing stages of that season but this time, after cash-flow issues brought worries over the club's future, the fight for survival went right to the wire.

With fullback Josh Rourke proving an astute signing from Salford, Gorley's side had the occasional highs, such as doubles over Sheffield and York, both of whom made the play-offs, and wins at Barrow and, comprehensively, at home to Widnes.

But they lost 10 of the last 11 games and all the last six, only staving off a return to the third tier because Keighley ended up with a points difference which was three worse.

Even with the departure of head of rugby Andrew Henderson to become York coach, fans of **KEIGHLEY COUGARS** had reasons to be cheerful as the 2023 season approached.

Rhys Lovegrove's side had romped to promotion as League One champions with a 100 per cent record. And the squad had been strengthened through the acquisition of such as ex-Hull and Leeds halfback Luke Gale, Hull KR threequarter Ben Crooks, Bradford hooker Thomas Doyle, Leigh prop Mark Ioane and Wakefield loose forward Brad Walker.

Second-tier consolidation looked comfortably achievable but, amid strident opposition to IMG's controversial club-grading system and subsequent cloth-cutting as other areas of necessary spending came to the fore, things started to unravel.

Lovegrove left, leaving assistant Jy-mel Coleman in caretaker control, and key players like Gale (to Wakefield), fellow pivot Dane Chisholm (back to Featherstone), prop Brenden Santi (York) and Crooks (Halifax) also exited mid-season.

Popular former player Matt Foster returned from Australia to become coach in mid-July but the Cougars dropped out of the division and back into League One on points difference after a last-day loss at London Broncos.

Having once declared their intention of being crowned Super League champions by 2030, **NEWCASTLE THUNDER** ended the 2023 campaign fighting for their existence as the stark financial reality of a return to League One hit home.

The North-East club's bold ambition had been set out shortly before elevation to the Championship through a bidding process in December 2020.

And having finished 11th the following season, they went full-time for 2022, when they ended up 12th, albeit eight points above the relegation positions.

After the end-of-season departure of Denis Betts, the director of rugby who had taken interim charge after coach Eamon O'Carroll's exit, Chris Thorman was given control of a now part-time squad.

But the former Super League, NRL and England halfback, and proud Geordie, just couldn't find the formula for staying in the Championship, and Thunder managed only 11 points, finishing five adrift at the foot of the table.

CHAMPIONSHIP AWARDS

PLAYER OF THE YEAR
Dean Parata (London Broncos) and Lachlan Walmsley (Halifax Panthers)

YOUNG PLAYER OF THE YEAR
Bill Leyland (London Broncos)

COACH OF THE YEAR
Mike Eccles (London Broncos)

Championship Season

Championship Play-offs

London Broncos only secured their place in the top-six play-offs with a tough home win over Keighley in the last regular round, so their 42-0 hammering of third-placed Sheffield Eagles in the first eliminator came as something of a shock.

It was just about all over by half-time as the Broncos led 24-0 at the Eagles' Olympic Legacy Park guided by former NRL star Corey Norman. When London stalwart Alex Walker scored three minutes after the break it was all over.

Winger Dalton Grant and Aussie centre Jarred Bassett both scored try doubles as London eased their way to a semi-final at runaway League Leaders Featherstone the week after.

The assumption for the whole season had been that Featherstone would win promotion to Super League. But, written off by all and sundry before kick-off, the Broncos produced their best performance of the season as Norman, former New Zealand centre Dean Whare and much-travelled utility Dean Parata destroyed their opponents in one of the most stunning triumphs of 2023.

The final score was 36-26 but it was 36-12 on 63 minutes after Norman, pulling the strings like a puppet master, followed up his own kick and fed scrum-half Henry Raiwalui to score under the posts.

The Broncos were through to the play-off final and Featherstone's long-term plans were in tatters.

At the other side of the draw, Bradford Bulls registered 22 unanswered points to soar into the semi-finals, progressing with a hard-fought 22-8 home win over a stubborn York side.
The Knights led 8-0 until the half-hour mark, thanks to a try from Aussie Jesse Dee and two Liam Harris goals, before Lee Greenwood's triple substitution of Eribe Doro, Keven Appo and Fenton Rogers swung the game in the Bulls' favour.

Bradford led 12-8 at half-time after converted tries from Rogers and Kevin Appo and three minutes into the second half Doro's superb break had Jordan Lilley cantering through to send Tom Holmes streaking away. Lilley was on target to make it 18-8 and kicked two more penalties to take the Bulls into a daunting semi at second-placed Toulouse.

There they met their match as TO, led by Wales international halfback Josh Ralph, won through to the final 38-20, winger Ben Laguerre scoring a brace of tries.

Championship Grand Final

London Broncos were back in Super League after completing a sensational run to and through the Championship play-offs with a comeback victory in France. The Broncos lost four of their first five games of the season and at one stage were far too close to the relegation zone for comfort.

Trailing 14-4 at half-time of the final at Stade Ernest Wallon, Mike Eccles' men scored three unanswered tries in the second half to make the top flight for the first time since 2019.

Spurred on by massive performances from ex-Toulouse halfback Corey Norman, winger Iliess Macani and fullback Alex Walker, the Broncos deserved to celebrate at full-time.

Championship Coach of the Year Eccles made just one change from the side that stunned Featherstone in the semi-finals, with

BETFRED CHAMPIONSHIP GRAND FINAL

Sunday 15th October 2023

TOULOUSE OLYMPIQUE 14 LONDON BRONCOS 18

OLYMPIQUE: 22 Zac Santo; 5 Paul Marcon; 4 Mathieu Jussaume; 18 Guy Armitage; 19 Benjamin Laguerre; 6 Josh Ralph; 7 Jake Shorrocks; 8 Lambert Belmas; 9 Calum Gahan; 10 Harrison Hansen; 12 Dominique Peyroux; 11 Maxime Stefani; 13 Anthony Marion. Subs (all used): 14 Eloi Pelissier; 15 Sitaleki Akauola; 16 Joe Bretherton; 20 Greg Richards.
Tries: Jussaume (3), Ralph (17); **Goals:** Shorrocks 3/3.
BRONCOS: 1 Alex Walker; 4 Dalton Grant; 3 Jarred Bassett; 19 Dean Whare; 5 Iliess Macani; 17 Henry Raiwalui; 20 Corey Norman; 33 Rob Butler; 9 Sam Davis; 15 Lewis Bienek; 11 Will Lovell; 12 Marcus Stock; 13 Dean Parata. Subs (all used): 8 Wellington Albert; 14 Bill Leyland; 10 Jordan Williams; 18 Emmanuel Waine.
Tries: Whare (25), Walker (52), Macani (59, 62);
Goals: Norman 1/4.
Rugby Leaguer & League Express Men of the Match:
Olympique: Zac Santo; *Broncos:* Corey Norman.
Penalty count: 4-3; **Half-time:** 14-4;
Referee: Jack Smith; **Attendance:** 3,974.

Championship Season

Toulouse's Josh Ralph takes on London Broncos' Bill Leyland and Will Lovell during the Championship Grand Final

Ethan Natoli suffering concussion in that win, leaving Marcus Stock to take his spot in the back row, as Wellington Albert featured on the bench.

The Broncos could hardly have started the match in worse fashion, as Rob Butler knocked on at a play-the-ball in the first set and Olympique struck in just the third minute, with France international Mathieu Jussaume streaking over after great work by Josh Ralph. Jake Shorrocks converted for a 6-0 lead.

Things got worse for the Broncos, with Toulouse fullback Zac Santo scything his way through lacklustre defence before feeding Ralph, who went over under the posts as the midway point of the first 40 minutes approached. Shorrocks again converted to make it 12-0.

Slowly but surely, the Broncos grew into the game and following a penalty, the capital club had their first points, with Norman sending through a wonderful grubber which was pounced on by Dean Whare. Norman, however, couldn't convert.

Shorrocks kept the TO side of the scoreboard ticking over with a penalty goal when Butler was caught in the ruck. Down 14-4 after half an hour, the Broncos couldn't capitalise on a Greg Richards knock-on from the kick-off as Wellington Albert threw a forward pass.

The big comeback started in the 52nd minute. Following a superb Dalton Grant break and offload to Jarred Bassett, the attack went left and Alex Walker managed to dot down, despite Paul Marcon's attempted tackle. Norman, again, couldn't convert.

Two Macani tries in three minutes around the hour sent the Broncos into a lead from which they never looked back.

Great passing to Whare ended with the ever-impressive Macani finishing wide out, but Norman's conversion attempt hit a post, with the Broncos still trailing 14-12.

The stunning comeback was complete on 62 minutes with Macani grabbing his second after yet more brilliant work from Norman and Whare. This time Norman was on target from the tee and the Broncos led 18-14.

A harsh high-tackle penalty against the Broncos meant the game might have swung once more but prop Lambert Belmas was held up before Ben Laguerre failed to take a Shorrocks kick.

But the Broncos were a team possessed in the second half and they held out for a remarkable victory.

Championship Season

1895 Cup Final

Halifax Panthers were winners of the fourth 1895 Cup Final, played after the Challenge Cup Final at Wembley, but they were they made to sweat until the last before emerging 12-10 winners over Batley Bulldogs.

With twelve minutes left, Halifax were as many points in front, thanks to Brandon Moore's second-minute try and four Louis Jouffret goals.

But then Batley, error-prone for much of the game, came alive, halving a 12-0 deficit through Dale Morton's try, converted by Luke Hooley, and from then on hammering at the Halifax door.

After five minutes under intense pressure, the final hooter indicated the Panthers were almost there. But having waited so long to return to Wembley - 35 years - they would have to wait a little longer to be sure of their desired outcome.

Because the Bulldogs, in turn making the first Wembley appearance of their entire, storied history, were going to go down fighting and produced one of the great tries on the greatest stage.

They kept the ball alive down the left, then down the right, then down the left again. It was desperate, desperate stuff, but then the space appeared, the overlap developed and Elliot Kear had crossed for an astounding try.

That only made it 12-10, however, and Batley needed the kick too. Fullback Hooley, back on loan from Leeds, had the thankless task from the touchline. He struck it well but the ball pulled just wide of the near post - so close that both sets of players and supporters only knew their respective fates when the flags went down rather than up.

Frenchman Jouffret controlled the game from halfback for Halifax while kicking his former club towards defeat from the tee and he was the recipient of the Ray French Award as man of the match.

AB SUNDECKS 1895 CUP - FINAL

Saturday 12th August 2023

BATLEY BULLDOGS 10 HALIFAX PANTHERS 12

BULLDOGS: 32 Luke Hooley; 22 Dale Morton; 4 Josh Hodson; 15 Elliot Kear; 21 Aidan McGowan; 14 James Meadows; 7 Josh Woods; 8 Adam Gledhill; 6 Ben White; 13 James Brown; 11 Dane Manning; 3 Kieran Buchanan; 30 Martyn Reilly. Subs (all used): 9 Alistair Leak; 16 Michael Ward; 20 Samy Kibula; 26 Nyle Flynn.
Tries: Morton (68), Kear (80); **Goals:** Hooley 1/2.
PANTHERS: 18 Brandon Pickersgill; 5 James Saltonstall; 3 Zack McComb; 22 Jake Maizen; 2 Lachlan Walmsley; 6 Louis Jouffret; 1 James Woodburn-Hall; 16 Will Calcott; 9 Brandon Moore; 10 Dan Murray; 11 Ben Kavanagh; 12 Matty Gee; 13 Jacob Fairbank. Subs (all used): 8 Adam Tangata; 19 Ryan Lannon; 31 Kevin Larroyer; 34 Adam O'Brien.
Try: Moore (2); **Goals:** Jouffret 4/4.
Rugby Leaguer & League Express Men of the Match:
Bulldogs: Josh Hodson; *Panthers:* Louis Jouffret.
Penalty count: 5-6; **Half-time:** 0-8; **Referee:** Jack Smith. *(at Wembley Stadium).*

Halifax show off the 1895 Cup after victory against Batley at Wembley

LEAGUE ONE SEASON
Ram-raid

Things are rarely straightforward in Rugby League and that was certainly the case in League One in 2023 after West Wales Raiders decided to pull out of the competition just weeks before it was due to kick off.

The Welsh club, which had struggled to make any significant on-field progress in their previous five years based at Llanelli, winning just two games and drawing once in that time, decided in mid-December to withdraw from all RFL competitions.

Owners Peter Tiffin and Andrew Thorne were ready to relinquish their roles with the club but new owners could not be found. Therefore the club folded and left the already published fixture list in disarray.

It was decided at a clubs meeting that each of the remaining teams would play out an 18-game season, facing each of their opponents home and away once. Rounds that were originally scheduled with the Raiders would be a bye as it would be too disruptive at that late stage to redraw the fixture list completely.

Discussions were had about the introduction of loop fixtures to maintain a 22-game campaign and avoid blank weekends. But with the team finishing top of the league earning automatic promotion it was felt that the introduction of loop fixtures could benefit some clubs whilst compromising the promotion prospects of others.

The extra blank weekends, plus numerous breaks for Challenge Cup rounds and the mid-season internationals meant a very stop-start nature to the season for all clubs, with some facing the prospect of no fixtures for four or five weeks at a time.

It was hardly the ideal scenario but when the action got underway **DEWSBURY RAMS** led the way by dominating right from round one to earn promotion back to the Championship at the first time of asking.

Having won just 11 games in the previous two seasons, coach Liam Finn, who had taken over from Lee Greenwood midway through 2022, simply wanted his team to enjoy winning again.

The Rams managed it in their stride, racking up the points in an eight-match winning run at the start of the season, a run that only came to a halt with a 26-26 draw at Oldham.

Dewsbury soon put that behind them and went unbeaten until the end of July when, knowing a win would secure top spot and automatic promotion, they fell to a 16-14 defeat at Hunslet. But a 38-8 win over Workington a week later finally confirmed their position at the top of the league and the champagne corks were popping.

It was an almost flawless year for the Rams, who saw stand-out seasons for many players, with Owen Restall finishing second in the league's try-scoring list, captain Reiss Butterworth, who has since earned himself a move to Super League side Hull KR, leading the side from hooker, while the likes of veteran stand-off Paul Sykes, centre Ollie Greensmith and Jimmy Beckett also impressed.

Not only were the Rams the big winners in League One, they also celebrated an awards double at the end of the season, with Finn named League One Coach of the Year and hooker Butterworth getting the Player of the Year gong.

League One Season

Dewsbury celebrate after a home win against Workington seals the League One title with two rounds to spare

The Rams will have to navigate life back in the Championship without Finn, who has taken on the head coach role at Halifax Panthers, with former Super League and Rams forward Dale Ferguson stepping into his shoes at the Tetley's Stadium.

At the third time of asking **DONCASTER** finally managed to win a play-off final and will now play in the Championship for the first time since 2015.

Having lost in both the 2021 and 2022 finals, the South Yorkshire club went into the decider against an in-form North Wales Crusaders praying it would be third time lucky.

And that proved to be the case as tries from Mahe Fonua, Loui McConnell and Sam Smeaton, plus three Connor Robinson goals saw them claim an 18-6 win and bring the Crusaders' late-season surge to a shuddering halt.

A big factor in this year's success was continuity in the side. Coach Richard Horne never faced a particular injury crisis throughout the year and by once again avoiding going down the dual registration route, changes to playing personnel during the season were minimal.

That continuity was added to the fact that very few players moved on from 2022's squad that fell to Swinton Lions at the final hurdle.

Horne used his contacts in the game to add experience to what he already had with players such as Brad Hey, Matt James, Brett Ferres, McConnell, Elliot Hall and Brad Knowles all arriving. The mid-season signings of former Super League duo Fonua and Bureta Faraimo, as well as the return of Watson Boas, who had time back in his native Papua New Guinea for family reasons, and the loan signing of Albert Vete all added an extra dimension to the club when they needed it to kick on.

After missing out on the 2022 play-offs by the narrowest of margins, **HUNSLET** went into the season determined to put that right.

And after operating on a much-reduced budget in 2022, this year saw many changes, with 19 new signings arriving at the club ahead of kick-off - including big names such as former Bradford Bulls duo Steve Crossley and Sam Hallas, as well as Michael Knowles and Adam Ryder from Dewsbury.

League One Season

That experience, coupled with the younger players that were retained, seemed to do the trick for head coach Alan Kilshaw as a steady season saw them finish second behind Dewsbury with 14 wins from 18 games.

Defeat to Doncaster and Dewsbury within the opening four games of the season was not enough to knock them off their stride, losing only once, to Oldham, in the next 13 games - a run that included a win over Dewsbury that prevented the Rams from lifting the title that day. That run also saw Hunslet remain unbeaten in league games at the South Leeds Stadium.

The same can't be said for the play-offs as a run of injuries leading into them saw Hunslet suffer defeats to both Doncaster and North Wales Crusaders, bringing Kilshaw's tenure at the club to an end.

Ryder and Hallas have since moved on as well, while Crossley has retired, but many of the other experienced heads have stayed under new coach Dean Muir.

Having only just scraped into the play-offs on points difference 12-months earlier, **OLDHAM** looked stronger candidates for a promotion push from the start this season.

A three-game unbeaten run at the start of the year, which saw them post 136 points, was temporarily halted by a 26-22 loss to Doncaster. But they bounced back and never looked in danger of dropping out of the top six.

So it was perhaps a surprise then at the end of July when Stuart Littler, who had been in charge since 2021, was relieved of his duties, with former player and coach Mike Ford, who was part of a consortium that had taken over the club in March, taking temporary charge until the end of the season.

That change came about after a run of three defeats in four games, to the sides they'd be challenging for promotion - Doncaster (again), Dewsbury and Hunslet.

Under Ford, Oldham went on to win three of their last four league games to secure a fourth-place finish and a second chance in the play-offs, but defeat to Doncaster (for a third time) and North Wales Crusaders in those knock-out games ended their season earlier than planned.

While promotion would have been nice this time around, the Roughyeds laid some real foundations in becoming a stronger club.

New owners, a new deal to move from the basic Vestacare Stadium back to a redeveloped Boundary Park, will help their off-field growth, while the appointment of Rugby League legend Sean Long as coach, and incoming players such as Jordan Turner, Joe Wardle and Craig Kopczak signing for 2024, should see them become a force to be reckoned with.

WORKINGTON TOWN had one clear aim at the start of the season and that was simply to make the play-offs. So for them to do that with a few weeks to spare will have come as an added bonus for new coach Anthony Murray.

Teams always face a tough battle when they have been relegated from the Championship, with expectations of an immediate return, or at the very least a strong showing in a battle to return.

But 2023 saw new beginnings for Workington. Not only did Murray come in to replace Newcastle Thunder-bound Chris Thorman, so did a lot of new faces as the new man in charge looked to fulfil the club's desire of a largely local squad that had local pride to play for as well as competition points.

The club also had a strong season off the field with lots of positive community events cementing them at the heart of the town, while the progress of the women's team was also very satisfying.

However, the play-off proved one game too many and, with a lot of injured bodies and others playing while carrying knocks, a meeting with a resurgent North Wales Crusaders ended in a 26-10 home defeat, which also ultimately ended their campaign.

They may not have been able to celebrate promotion but they did have something to cheer at the end of the year when Ciaran Walker was named League One Young Player of the Year.

League One Season

North Wales show their delight at play-off victory against Hunslet

NORTH WALES CRUSADERS could easily stake a claim as being League One's club of the year after an end-of-season push saw them go within 80 minutes of promotion to the Championship, despite facing many obstacles.

Suffering a string of injuries at the start of the year, the Colwyn Bay-based side had to wait until their seventh game of the season before securing their first points of the season. At that stage, they were already six points adrift of the play-offs and with continued injury concerns wreaking havoc across the squad not allowing new player-coach Carl Forster any real consistency in his matchday 17, it already looked as though the top six would be too big an ask.

Add to that the nomadic existence of the club when work on the pitch at Eirias Park overran, meaning the club had to find a new home for seven of their nine home fixtures. They subsequently moved games to Widnes, Conwy, Chester and Rhyl, meaning they never really gained any advantage from playing on their own turf.

A loss at home, which was Rhyl for the day, to Cornwall at the end of July looked to have finally ended their hopes of the play-offs. But back-to-back wins over Doncaster and London Skolars sealed what had just weeks earlier looked like an unlikely play-off spot.

A 26-10 eliminator win over Workington in Cumbria followed despite having gone into the knock-out phase of the season as underdogs.

By now fully fit, and used to playing games on the road, the Crusaders upset the odds by travelling to both Oldham and Hunslet and claiming wins to set up the Promotion final meeting with Doncaster.

Despite Toby Hughes' try, converted by Leon Hayes, Crusaders fell short at the final hurdle. But nonetheless, it was certainly a memorable year to be involved with the Crusaders.

2023 was a season of transition for **ROCHDALE HORNETS**, who faced many changes ahead of kick-off.

After taking over from Matt Calland part-way through the previous season, Gary Thornton was retained as head coach but he had to effectively rebuild his squad from scratch, with only nine players who featured in 2022 back to play any part in this campaign.

For Thornton and club chairman Andy Mazey, the main emphasis was building a squad of young, local players eager to develop their careers in Rugby League.

That is what they managed to build on a vastly reduced playing budget. But the lack of experience at key times told as Hornets once again failed to make the play-offs - for the second time in three seasons. They did stay in the race for the top six until the final few weeks.

League One Season

With the change in personnel came a change in culture and a desire to create a more professional environment.

Although their season may have finished a lot earlier than they'd have liked, Mazey and Thornton will have been left satisfied by some green shoots of progress. A number of younger players have shown real promise and their extra year's experience will do Hornets the power of good as they look to be in the mix for promotion over the next couple of years.

Another club that had a season of transition was **MIDLANDS HURRICANES**. It was their first under the sole ownership of Mike Lomas and the first at their new home at Birmingham's Alexander Stadium. And while results stayed fairly similar on the field, the new regime was keen to make the necessary changes to ensure future growth.

Head coach Richard Squires moved on and in came former Bradford Bulls boss Mark Dunning. Prior to taking the head coach role at the Bulls, Dunning had spent most of his coaching career working with players at youth, academy and reserves levels and helped develop many now first-team players in the game. With the Hurricanes' future blueprint including developing their own players, Dunning was the natural fit for Lomas and chief executive Greg Wood.

Under Dunning, the Hurricanes won three out of their last nine games and two of those were away from home against eventual play-off finishers - beating Oldham 18-10 in the final round and, perhaps more impressively, Doncaster 41-10 in July.

CORNWALL continued to show improvement throughout their second year in the competition, and were able to celebrate some special moments with the hardy bunch of fans that turned out at the Memorial Ground.

Former coach Neil Kelly, who had used his vast experience in the game to be a calming influence on the new outfit in their first season, may have gone but in Mike Abbott they had a more than adequate replacement.

Having worked under Kelly in the Choughs' first year, Abbott also had the benefit of knowing the lay of the land in the Duchy, having lived there since 2016.

Under Abbott's guidance the club picked up five wins - four more than in their maiden season. That included a first home victory (against Midlands Hurricanes), a league double over London Skolars, back-to-back wins and a first success over one of the more traditional heartland clubs when they beat Rochdale 18-12 in the final game of the campaign.

Three of those five wins came in July, so had that form continued, or even started earlier they could have been pushing for a play-off spot, which would have been far more than they could have ever dreamed of so early in their journey.

In a mirror image of the start of the year, once the campaign was completed **LONDON SKOLARS**, who had failed to win a game all season, followed in West Wales' footsteps and announced their decision to withdraw from the league.

Their decision was made for financial reasons after a proposed take over by the ARC Group failed to materialise. As the season progressed a lack of the funding that deal would have secured left the club short of playing resources, and that showed on the pitch.

Some bad luck with injuries left the Skolars struggling for numbers on more than one occasion and most weeks coach Joe Mbu was forced to used different combinations across key positions.

That lack of consistency in the side meant it was virtually impossible to get any in performances and, while the Skolars showed in glimpses that they could compete across the competition, there simply wasn't enough firepower in the squad to get the points needed to win games - scoring an average of just 14 points a game.

Defensively they found it just as tough, conceding 897 points in 18 games, 185 more than the next worse defence.

The club now plan to consolidate, rebuild and seek new investment while plying their trade in the Southern Conference League, with a view to one day fielding a League One side again.

League One Season

LEAGUE ONE AWARDS

PLAYER OF THE YEAR	YOUNG PLAYER OF THE YEAR	COACH OF THE YEAR
Reiss Butterworth (Dewsbury Rams)	Ciaran Walker (Workington Town)	Liam Finn (Dewsbury Rams)

League One Play-offs

Dewsbury Rams won automatic promotion to the Championship by virtue of finishing top of the table at the end of the regular season, with the next five teams qualifying for the play-offs to decide the other team to be promoted.

Doncaster were ultimately the club to join Dewsbury after they beat North Wales Crusaders by 18-6 in the promotion final at their own Eco-Power Stadium. Coached by Richard Horne, the Dons defended for their lives as North Wales, who had sneaked into sixth spot with only seven wins, exactly half as many as Doncaster, got the better of the territorial battle.

The hosts' first penalty of the game enabled them to register the first points of the afternoon in the 14th minute as a powerful scoot from Mahe Fonua ended with the released Castleford man crashing over from dummy-half. Connor Robinson's superb conversion made it 6-0.

Doncaster should have had another score moments later when a brilliant dribbled Robinson kick was tapped on beautifully by Fonua, only for another unwanted Tiger, Bureta Faraimo to spill possession and let North Wales off the hook, although Robinson extended the lead to 8-0 with a penalty goal not long after. Warrington loanee halfback Leon Hayes was causing Doncaster problems but the defensive effort was outstanding.

Big hits and superb goal-line defence dominated second-half proceedings before Robinson took matters into his own hands with 14 minutes to go, stepping his way through some tired bodies to send Loui McConnell over between the posts. The former converted to make it 14-0 and effectively seal a hard-fought victory.

But North Wales weren't in the final to make up the numbers and after a great run by Jake Burns, a lovely kick and chase by Toby Hughes allowed the halfback to gather and pounce for a fine individual score.

Hayes converted to make to 14-6 with just eight minutes to go. There would be no miracle finish, however, as Sam Smeaton made sure of a Doncaster victory with a strong run from ten metres out.

In week one, Workington Town had been the first team eliminated when they were beaten 26-10 by North Wales at Derwent Park.

The Crusaders finished eight points behind Workington in the final table and twice lost to them in the league but that didn't prevent Carl Forster's men from keeping their play-off campaign alive. Forster was among the Crusaders' four try-scorers, with centres Kieran Taylor and Matt Reid also on the sheet either side of replacement hooker Pat Rainford, while Hayes landed five goals from as many attempts.

League One Season

Doncaster's Mahe Fonua heads towards the North Wales tryline during the League One Promotion Final

Doncaster had finished third in the table and beat fourth-placed Oldham 36-0 in their home qualifier, with Robinson scoring 16 points and winger Tom Halliday ending with two tries.

The next week the Crusaders eliminated Oldham, the final score 13-12 after a tense contest decided by vital kicks, hooker Burns slotting a field goal from around 35 metres in the 79th minute to win his side the game.

Doncaster earned their way straight to the final with a 26-14 win at second-placed Hunslet. Watson Boas's try on 63 minutes, plus Robinson's conversion and subsequent penalty, gave the visitors an eight-point buffer after Fonua had scored two first-half tries and Johnny Campbell's 48th try for Hunslet converted by Matty Beharrell had levelled at 14-all.

Hunslet had a second bite the following week in the Final Eliminator but North Wales again upset the odds with a 25-18 win at South Leeds Stadium. The Crusaders led for much of the game but found themselves trailing 18-14 as the contest headed into the final quarter. But a spilled bomb gave Hughes the chance to send Taylor over out wide.

Hughes was unable to land the conversion and, as golden-point became a real possibility, Beharrell was wide with a field-goal attempt. North Wales fullback Owain Abel, the man of the match, made no mistake with his own effort, on 73 minutes, and victory was sealed when former Hunslet man Cole Oakley crashed over with three minutes left, Abel adding the conversion.

BETFRED LEAGUE ONE PROMOTION FINAL

Sunday 24th September 2023

DONCASTER 18 NORTH WALES CRUSADERS 6

DONCASTER: 30 Josh Guzdek; 2 Tom Halliday; 21 Brad Hey; 3 Mahe Fonua; 32 Bureta Faraimo; 6 Ben Johnston; 7 Connor Robinson; 20 Brad Knowles; 9 Greg Burns; 31 Albert Vete; 11 Sam Smeaton; 27 Brett Ferres; 13 Loui McConnell. Subs (all used): 8 Keelan Foster; 15 Alex Holdstock; 17 Matt James; 24 Watson Boas.
Tries: Fonua (14), McConnell (66), Smeaton (76);
Goals: Robinson 3/4.
CRUSADERS: 1 Owain Abel; 27 Josh Lynch; 3 Cole Oakley; 14 Kieran Taylor; 4 Matt Reid; 25 Leon Hayes; 28 Toby Hughes; 16 Jack Houghton; 9 Jake Burns; 17 Chris Barratt; 21 Ryan Ellis; 13 Matt Fletcher; 26 Carl Forster. Subs (all used): 8 Callum Hazzard; 10 Jordan Andrade; 19 Shaun Costello; 20 Pat Rainford.
Try: Hughes (72); **Goals:** Hayes 1/1.
Rugby Leaguer & League Express Men of the Match:
Doncaster: Connor Robinson; *Crusaders:* Matt Reid.
Penalty count: 4-8; **Half-time:** 8-0;
Referee: Nick Bennett; **Attendance:** 2,549.

WOMEN'S SUPER LEAGUE
Rise of the Valkyrie

In a year that saw more history made and more records broken, **YORK VALKYRIE** and **ST HELENS** were the biggest winners as the Women's Super League competition continued to grow and impress an ever-increasing audience.

A near-perfect season results-wise saw York retain the League Leaders Shield, with the only blot on their copybook proving a thrilling 16-16 draw against Leeds Rhinos in round six.

They went the rest of the league season unbeaten and after finishing top of the league - five points clear of second-placed St Helens - they still faced questions on whether this was the year they would finally take the next step and win a major final.

Under the guidance of former England international Lindsay Anfield, York had tasted defeat in the 2021 Challenge Cup Final to St Helens and last year's Grand Final to Leeds. Add to that, the Challenge Cup Finals defeats of 2018 and 2019 and the 2019 Grand Final loss while Anfield and a host of her players were at Castleford Tigers, all of which were at the hands of the Rhinos, and it's no wonder they were in determined mood heading into the play-offs.

After coming through their play-off semi-final 22-6 against Wigan Warriors, York headed into the final against Leeds with one thing and one thing only on their minds - to finally get that monkey off their backs. And in front of a record Grand Final crowd of 4,547, that is exactly what they did.

Tamzin Renouf opened the scoring after a quarter of an hour of a largely tight contest before Tara Jane Stanley crossed for a try on the hooter to give York an 8-0 lead at the break.

Both sides traded penalties after the restart before the Valkyrie started gaining dominance over last season's Champions and when Lacey Owen increased York's lead to 16-2 with just over 15 minutes left, York could feel confident they were finally getting their hands on the trophy.

The celebrations that erupted at full-time vastly outweighed any disappointment they were left with after letting Leeds in for their only try of the game in quite unusual circumstances.

As the hooter sounded at the end of the 80 minutes and York players began falling to their knees or rushing to celebrate with each other, the referee had allowed play to continue and Caitlin Casey went in unopposed for a Leeds consolation. With the game now done and the result settled, the final conversion attempt was declined and York's celebrations got underway.

WOMEN'S SUPER LEAGUE - GROUP ONE

	P	W	D	L	F	A	D	Pts
York Valkyrie	10	9	1	0	376	74	302	19
St Helens	10	7	0	3	362	116	246	14
Leeds Rhinos	10	6	1	3	394	136	258	13
Wigan Warriors	10	3	1	6	116	250	-134	7
Warrington Wolves	10	2	1	7	128	450	-322	5
Huddersfield Giants	10	1	0	9	102	452	-350	2

WOMEN'S SUPER LEAGUE - GROUP TWO

	P	W	D	L	F	A	D	Pts
Featherstone Rovers	10	8	0	2	356	103	253	16
Barrow Raiders	10	8	0	2	336	88	248	16
Leigh Leopards	10	7	1	2	271	108	163	15
Salford Red Devils	10	4	0	6	176	248	-72	8
Bradford Bulls	10	2	1	7	124	350	-226	5
Castleford Tigers	10	0	0	10	44	410	-366	0

Women's Super League

Sinead Peach leads the York Valkyrie celebrations following Grand Final victory

There were more reasons to celebrate a few days later when hooker and captain Sinead Peach got her hands on the Woman of Steel prize after being a runner-up the previous two years. Anfield was also named Coach of the Year at the same RL Awards ceremony.

While satisfied with their league double, York missed out on the chance to make even more history after suffering their only defeat of the season to Saints in the Challenge Cup semi-final.

As the tie looked to be heading for golden-point extra-time, Faye Gaskin, who had only just returned from a two-year injury nightmare that came close to ending her career, struck a field goal to ensure Saints would be making history as one of the first women's sides to run out and play on the Wembley turf. And they certainly made the most of that opportunity.

Saturday, 12th August 2023 is a date that will forever be remembered as the day that the women's game appeared on the biggest of stages at the national stadium. And by the time the hooter sounded there were over 8,000 spectators watching on as St Helens' stars, led by captain Jodie Cunningham and Emily Rudge, entered the Royal Box to collect their trophy and etch their names into history.

Opponents Leeds Rhinos went close to opening the scoring through Amy Hardcastle but a great tackle from Eboni Partington flipped the game on its head and saw Saints score three quick tries before Leeds had another meaningful touch of the ball.

Tara Jones, who went into the record books as the first female player to score a try at Wembley, Phoebe Hook and Partington, were all on the scoresheet to open up a 16-0 lead.

A try either side of half-time from Sophie Robinson and Caitlin Beevers, a sensational solo effort, saw Leeds hit back briefly before Shona Hoyle made sure of a Saints victory six minutes after the restart to secure a third straight Challenge Cup title.

Unlike in 2021 though, Saints were unable to follow that up with either of the trophies on offer in the league.

Women's Super League

Leeds' Lucy Murray tackled by Lucie Sams during St Helens' Wembley triumph

After finishing second in the table behind York with seven wins from their ten games, Saints welcomed **LEEDS RHINOS**, who were eager to avenge that Wembley defeat, in the play-off semi-final.

In what has become a tradition between these two sides, neither was willing to surrender and with the scores locked at 16-16, Amy Taylor had the chance to send Saints to the final. But her penalty goal attempt fell short sending the game into golden point.

With Saints' Shona Hoyle, one of the club's three nominations for Woman of Steel alongside Cunningham and Rudge, knocking on as extra time started, Leeds were able to pile the pressure on. A perfect kick from Casey found Sophie Robinson, who touched down in the corner to send Leeds into the Grand Final and give them the chance to retain their title.

The Rhinos had won the title from third place 12 months earlier so would have been confident to do the same this time round, but it wasn't to be on the day as York claimed the prize.

That said, appearances in two finals, another strong showing in the league and the development of some up-and-coming stars of the future can all be seen as a success for the Rhinos, who were rocked at the start of the season by star halfback Georgia Roche.

Having already lost Courtney Winfield-Hill to retirement, Roche was expected to be the linchpin for Lois Forsell's side. But a mega five-year contract with NRLW Newcastle Knights was too good to turn down and the England international didn't make a single appearance for Leeds. This meant that teenager Casey, who had been earmarked to spend this year finding her feet in Super League, was thrown in at the deep end and found herself with increased responsibility as a first-team regular.

But she stood up to the challenge exceptionally well and not only was that recognised by her club, it was by others as well as she was named as the game's Young Player of the Year and was pushing for a spot in Stuart Barrow's England squad.

Away from the top three, who again proved the leading lights in the game, **WIGAN WARRIORS** took the final play-off spot after another season of improvement under Kris Ratcliffe.

Women's Super League

Strong showings against York and Leeds in the play-off and Challenge Cup semi-finals respectively show the Warriors are not too far off competing with the leading sides. Wins over the two sides that finished below them in the league - Huddersfield twice and Warrington, as well as a draw against the Wolves - will have pleased the side, but also shows that they need to take the next step forward to become a leading competitor in the game.

They might get to do just that with club legend Denis Betts returning to the club to coach the side from 2024 after Ratcliffe stepped down due to other work commitments.

Another club that will start next season with a new coach in place is **WARRINGTON WOLVES**, who now have former player Armani Sharrock at the helm after injury forced her to retire earlier this year.

Sharrock has replaced Lee Westwood, who stood down after five years in the role, and her appointment will go some way to maintaining the continuity the club have been building over the last couple of years.

Having stepped up from Group Two last season, Warrington were always going to find it tough. But with a year's more experience under their belts, they should be able to start closing the gap on those above them relatively soon.

HUDDERSFIELD GIANTS have also found the step up to Super League difficult in recent years, but 2023 was the year they got their first win under their belts.

Having picked up victories over Oulton Raidettes and Bradford Bulls in this year's Challenge Cup group stages, as well as Hull FC and Leigh Miners (now Leopards) in last year's competition, a 20-16 victory against an understrength Leeds Rhinos side in August finally saw them register points in the league table.

A week before the Challenge Cup final meant Leeds rested a number of their bigger names and handed debuts to some future stars. But still, the victory will have done the Giants' confidence the world of good going into 2024, when they'll be boosted by the arrivals of former Bradford Bulls duo Grace Ramsden and Jess Harrop.

The competition will revert to one league from next season but will see an increased number of teams, with **FEATHERSTONE ROVERS** and **BARROW RAIDERS** both promoted to the top division after playing their part in an exciting conclusion to the Group Two season.

Going into the final round of fixtures **LEIGH LEOPARDS** were top of the league, one point clear of both that day's opponents Barrow, and Featherstone. For Leigh the equation was

WOMEN'S SUPER LEAGUE GRAND FINAL
Sunday 8th October 2023

YORK VALKYRIE 16 LEEDS RHINOS 6

VALKYRIE: 1 Tara Jane Stanley; 19 Georgie Hetherington; 30 Carrie Roberts; 3 Tamzin Renouf; 4 Emma Kershaw; 6 Sade Rihari; 7 Liv Gale; 29 Elisa Akpa; 9 Sinead Peach; 14 Aimee Staveley; 11 Lacey Owen; 12 Savannah Andrade; 8 Olivia Wood. Subs: 15 Rhiannon Marshall; 10 Jas Bell; 23 Daisy Sanderson; 16 Ashleigh Hyde (not used).
Tries: Renouf (14), Stanley (39), Owen (63); **Goals:** Stanley 2/4.
RHINOS: 31 Ruby Enright; 5 Sophie Nuttall; 11 Amy Hardcastle; 3 Caitlin Beevers; 2 Sophie Robinson; 4 Hanna Butcher; 26 Caitlin Casey; 8 Zoe Hornby; 9 Keara Bennett; 18 Izzy Northrop; 28 Lucy Murray; 24 Jenna Greening; 12 Bethan Dainton. Subs (all used): 22 Kaiya Glynn; 32 Bella Sykes; 15 Jasmine Earnshaw-Cudjoe; 16 Beth Lockwood.
Try: Casey (80); **Goals:** Enright 1/1.
Rugby Leaguer & League Express Women of the Match:
Valkyrie: Carrie Roberts; *Rhinos:* Bethan Dainton.
Penalty count: 4-6; **Half-time:** 8-0; **Referee:** Liam Rush; **Attendance:** 4,547 *(at LNER Community Stadium, York).*

WOMEN'S SUPER LEAGUE SEMI-FINALS
Saturday 23rd September 2023
York Valkyrie 22 Wigan Warriors 6
St Helens 16 Leeds Rhinos 20 *(after golden point extra-time)*

WOMEN'S SUPER LEAGUE GROUP TWO PROMOTION FINAL
Sunday 8th October 2023

BARROW RAIDERS 14 LEIGH LEOPARDS 8

RAIDERS: 1 Michelle Larkin; 18 Emma Hutchinson; 20 Leah Clough; 11 Claire Hutchinson; 5 Samantha Norman; 13 Demi Fisher; 7 Jodie Litherland; 14 Mia Dobson; 9 Beth Lindsay; 22 Jodie Morley; 12 Vanessa Temple; 4 Emily Stirzaker; 3 Leah Cottier. Subs (all used): 2 Charlotte Todhunter; 8 Hannah Sherlock; 10 Kerrie-Ann Smith; 15 Kellie Friend.
Tries: Lindsay (65), Morley (70); **Goals:** Litherland 3/3.
LEOPARDS: 1 Isla Aspden; 2 Toryn Blackwood; 6 Rhianna Burke; 3 Mackenzie Taylor; 5 Elise Gater; 32 Beth Stott; 7 Emma Knowles; 10 Mairead Quinn; 9 Kate Howard; 29 Keira McCosh; 11 Keli Morris; 27 Chantel Melvin; 13 Ellise Derbyshire. Subs (all used): 15 Rebecca Owen; 18 Grace Hill; 31 Hatice Dogus; 33 Claire Collins.
Tries: Dogus (48, 54); **Goals:** Knowles 0/2.
Rugby Leaguer & League Express Women of the Match:
Raiders: Beth Lindsay; *Leopards:* Hatice Dogus.
Penalty count: 5-6; **Half-time:** 2-0; **Referee:** Elliott Burrow.
(at LNER Community Stadium, York).

WOMEN'S SUPER LEAGUE GROUP TWO SEMI-FINALS
Sunday 24th September 2023
Barrow Raiders 62 Bradford Bulls 0
Leigh Leopards 28 Salford Red Devils 10

WOMEN'S CHALLENGE CUP FINAL
Saturday 12th August 2023

LEEDS RHINOS 8 ST HELENS 22

RHINOS: 31 Ruby Enright; 5 Sophie Nuttall; 3 Caitlin Beevers; 4 Hanna Butcher; 2 Sophie Robinson; 26 Caitlin Casey; 24 Jenna Greening; 8 Zoe Hornby; 15 Jasmine Earnshaw-Cudjoe; 10 Dannielle Anderson; 11 Amy Hardcastle; 28 Lucy Murray; 12 Bethan Dainton. Subs (all used): 19 Elle Frain; 21 Eloise Hayward; 20 Tara Moxon; 18 Izzy Northrop.
Tries: Robinson (24), Beevers (42); **Goals:** Enright 0/2.
SAINTS: 6 Zoe Harris; 3 Eboni Partington; 2 Luci McColm; 11 Paige Travis; 28 Phoebe Hook; 21 Amy Taylor; 7 Faye Gaskin; 17 Philippa Birchall; 9 Tara Jones; 10 Chantelle Crowl; 8 Shona Hoyle; 12 Emily Rudge; 13 Jodie Cunningham. Subs (all used): 14 Vicky Whitfield; 15 Lucie Sams; 4 Naomi Williams; 19 Katie Mottershead.
Tries: Jones (12), Hook (15), Partington (17), Hoyle (46); **Goals:** Taylor 3/5.
Rugby Leaguer & League Express Women of the Match:
Rhinos: Caitlin Beevers; *Saints:* Jodie Cunningham.
Penalty count: 1-4; **Half-time:** 4-16; **Referee:** James Vella. *(at Wembley Stadium).*

WOMEN'S CHALLENGE CUP SEMI-FINALS
Saturday 22nd July 2023
St Helens 17 York Valkyrie 16 *(at Halliwell Jones Stadium, Warrington)*
Sunday 23rd July 2023
Leeds Rhinos 16 Wigan Warriors 4 *(at Headingley, Leeds)*

Women's Super League

simple - win and claim the automatic promotion spot. If Barrow won, much would depend on Featherstone's result against Salford as to which of the two went up.

Playing in an earlier kick-off, Featherstone beat the Red Devils 28-18 to leapfrog Leigh at the top, meaning Barrow would need to win by more than seven points if they were to claim the top spot for themselves.

In a fiercely contested battle, Barrow put in their strongest performance of the season to date to claw their way to a 14-12 win, denying Leigh promotion but also handing it to Featherstone, who lost out in the Grand Final in the previous two seasons.

Much like in Group One, the top three led the way all season, so it was perhaps hardly surprising when Barrow and Leigh met once again in the Promotion Final - Barrow accounting for Bradford Bulls 62-0 in the semi-final and Leigh beating Salford 28-10 to progress to the Grand Final doubleheader at York.

In what was a tight contest from the kick-off. A Jodie Litherland penalty kick was the only score of the first half as Barrow led 2-0 but two unconverted touchdowns from Leigh's Hattice Dogus soon after the restart put the Leopards in the driving seat before late goaled tries from Beth Lindsay and Jodie Morley, to secured a 14-8 victory, and ultimately a spot in Super League for the Raiders.

Since rebranding from Miners Rangers, who struggled in Group Two last year, to the Leopards and linking up with the men's Super League side, Leigh have made giant strides under the coaching of former Huddersfield, Leigh and Widnes boss Kieron Purtill. And with club owner Derek Beaumont still willing to do what's needed to keep them improving, it's likely they will be one of the clubs in the frame whenever Super League expands again and welcomes more new teams into the competition.

Jodie Morley touches down in Barrow's Promotion Final win against Leigh

But for now, they, and the remaining clubs - **SALFORD RED DEVILS**, **BRADFORD BULLS** and **CASTLEFORD TIGERS**, who all struggled to keep up with the pack - will revert to playing the community game in the new structured pyramid below Super League. There they can consolidate, enjoy being in more even and competitive contests and prepare themselves in the best possible way for any future opening that arises in the top division.

Away from the two Super League groups, **HULL KR** impressed in the Championship, finishing five points clear at the top of the league with 18 wins from their 20 games and beating Oulton 30-16 in the Grand Final to claim the title. A 22-6 win over Stanningley in the League Cup Final in July meant the East Yorkshire outfit claimed the treble in 2023.

In Super League South, reigning champions **CARDIFF DEMONS** lost their grip on the title, going down 22-10 to **LONDON BRONCOS** in the Grand Final. The two sides had led the pack all season, finishing the regular season level on points, with Cardiff taking top spot on points difference.

* Last year's Yearbook wrongly claimed that London Broncos claimed the Super League South title with a 34-4 victory over Cardiff Demons. It was actually Cardiff that won that game by 34-4 to retain the title they lifted the previous year.

The 2021 Rugby League World Cup, played in the autumn of 2022 because of the Covid-19 pandemic, was the most diverse global sporting event ever, with the 16th men's tournament being played in parallel with the women's and wheelchair tournaments.

Every one of the 61 matches across three tournaments was televised by the BBC. The biggest United Kingdom TV audience was for the men's semi-final between England and Samoa, watched by a combined peak audience of 1.8 million - a 23 per cent audience share, while England women's semi-final defeat to New Zealand attracted a combined peak of 1.4 million.

The wheelchair final was watched by a combined peak UK audience of 1.3 million people, while nearly a million viewers tuned in to the women's final and almost two million for the men's decider.

Australia won both the men's tournament for the 12th and third time on a row and the women's for the third consecutive time, with England beating France in the wheelchair final, with all three finals held in Manchester on the same weekend in November 2022.

GROUP A

England strolled through the group stages with three big wins over Samoa, France and Greece.

They actually went into the tournament opener at St James's Park in Newcastle as second favourites to a Samoa side that included six players from the NRL Grand Final. The opening quarter was a contest but after three tries in the space of eleven minutes England took command, though Izack Tago's interception try six minutes before the break could have presaged a Samoa comeback.

It never happened as Kallum Watkins scored from a short-side play on 49 minutes and England blitzed increasingly demoralised Samoa with six tries in the last fifteen minutes from centre Herbie Farnworth, two from Elliott Whitehead, Tommy Makinson, George Williams and Tom Burgess. Thrilling first-half tries had come from a Dominic Young double and the opener from Jack Welsby, who then provided the passes for the winger's scores.

It was one of the best all-round performances by an England team and the 60-6 scoreline was a true reflection of their dominance.

Samoa looked ramshackle but recovered their composure to make the quarter finals as second-placed group finishers. The following Sunday they hammered Greece 72-4 in Doncaster, Penrith halfback Jarome Luai pulling the strings as the Samoa pack totally dominated. The week after in Warrington it was much the same in a 62-4 win over France, although this time it was the other halfback, two-try Anthony Milford, who stole the show, Penrith winger Taylan May finishing with four tries.

England didn't shine so bright in their second game at Bolton but they were comfortable 42-18 winners over France, Young getting another try-double, along with opposite winger Ryan Hall. A week after, Young netted four tries in a 94-4 drubbing of Greece at Bramall Lane in Sheffield, that after leading only 10-4 after 25 minutes.

Salford's Marc Sneyd scored his first England try, coupled with 13 successful conversions. That gave him not only the record for both goals and points in an England match but the best haul ever from a British player in a World Cup game, surpassing John Holmes' 50-year record.

France finished third in the group, courtesy of a 34-12 win over Greece in week one at Doncaster.

Qualifiers: England and Samoa

ABOVE: Samoa's Junior Paulo offloads despite the challenge of Greece's Adam Vrahnos

RIGHT: France's Gadwin Springer halted against Samoa

LEFT: England's Tom Burgess touches down against Greece

GROUP B

Australia guaranteed they would come top of their group, as like England they beat their nearest challenger in the first weekend, ruthlessly sweeping Fiji aside at Headingley, winger Josh Addo-Carr scoring twice in a 42-8 victory.

The Bati, beaten 50-0 by England in their warm-up match, had been disrupted by injuries, with Hull FC winger Mitieli Vulikijapani drafted in and included in the 17 alongside London Broncos halfback Sitiveni Moceidreke, Salford prop King Vuniyayawa and Leigh front-rower Ben Nakubuwai.

Melbourne pair Cameron Munster and Harry Grant were the pick of an Australian side that looked strong in every department.

Fiji bounced back from the defeat as they outclassed Italy at Kingston Park in Newcastle with Viliame Kikau and Maika Sivo both grabbing two tries in a 60-4 win. Winger Jake Maizen got Italy's consolation try. The week after at the same venue, Fiji found Scotland a much harder nut to crack but eventually hung on for a 30-14 win, Korbin Sims' try on 67 minutes ending any Scotland hopes of a comeback.

That was Scotland's best performance of the tournament as they had sunk to a 28-4 defeat against Italy at Kingston Park in Newcastle, Maizen scoring the first hat-trick of the World Cup. A week later, in Coventry, they were humbled by 84-0 by an Australian side that included NRL Grand Final players who had been rested by coach Mal Meninga in week one. Addo-Carr got four tries and centre Campbell Graham three in a brilliant exhibition that inflicted Scotland's record international defeat.

Addo-Carr was rested for the Kangaroos' final game as they made short work of Italy in a 66-6 win at St Helens.

Qualifiers: Australia and Fiji

BELOW: Scotland's Lachlan Walmsley closed down by Italy's Jake Maizen

RIGHT: Fiji's Vuate Karawalevu sprints clear of the Italy cover

ABOVE: Fiji's Korbin Sims drives into the heart of the Scotland defence

RUGBY LEAGUE MEN'S WORLD CUP ENGLAND 2021

RIGHT: Australia's Campbell Graham races away to score against Italy

LEFT: Fiji's Kevin Naiqama and Australia's Ben Hunt meet head on

BELOW: Australia's Liam Martin gets the ball away against Scotland

GROUP C

New Zealand were hot favourites to win their group and they duly did so with three wins from three. But they were pushed hard in their first game before emerging 34-12 winners over Lebanon in Warrington.

The Lebanese had threatened a remarkable upset, crossing in the first minute of the game and then clawing back to 18-12 in the second half.

But three tries in six minutes, as well as a red card for dissent to Lebanon talisman Adam Doueihi, took the Kiwis into an unassailable position. Roosters centre Joseph Manu established his fullback credentials with a perfect performance and scored an incredible second-half try that saw him evade almost half the Lebanon team.

But as they had in 2017, Lebanon, guided by Eels' halfback Mitchell Moses, ensured they would qualify for the quarter-finals, this time with a 32-14 win over Ireland in Leigh. Ireland, fired by a brilliant performance from Souths half Luke Keary, had drubbed Jamaica by 48-2 in week one at Headingley, so the Cedars had to beat them to qualify.

Ireland were far from their best and were left to rue a number of handling errors and poor discipline in a disappointing defeat. Moses paired brilliantly with young Bulldogs halfback Khaled Rajab, who slotted in seamlessly in the absence of the suspended Doueihi, on the back of terrific go-forward from the Lebanon pack.

The Irish were effectively knocked out and had it confirmed at Headingley the Friday after, although they showed plenty of spirit in a 48-10 loss to New Zealand, Melbourne halfback Jahrome Hughes in sensational form. The Kiwis were too too strong and too good but it was still a memorable night in front of over 14,000 fans, including a huge amount of Irish support. Louis Senior got Ireland's two tries.

Both New Zealand and Lebanon made short work of out-gunned Jamaica, Dallin Watene-Zelezniak scoring an 18-minute first-half hat-trick amid four tries and a 20-point haul in a 68-6 win for the Kiwis in Hull. A week after, Lebanon beat the Reggae Warriors 74-12 in Leigh. But there were wild scenes of joy when Ben Jones-Bishop claimed his country's first ever World Cup try five minutes from time against the Kiwis.

Qualifiers: New Zealand and Lebanon

ABOVE: Ireland's George King tackled by Lebanon's Elie El-Zakhem

BELOW: New Zealand's Brandon Smith dragged down against Lebanon

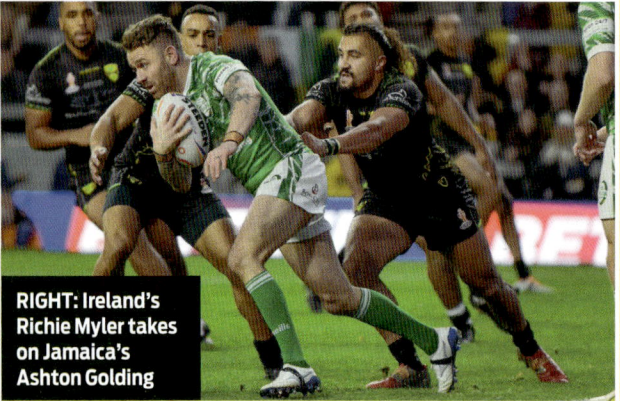

RIGHT: Ireland's Richie Myler takes on Jamaica's Ashton Golding

BELOW: Ireland's Richie Myler and James Bentley fail to stop New Zealand's Jahrome Hughes from scoring

ABOVE: Lebanon's Josh Mansour dives past Jamaica's Abevia McDonald to score

RUGBY LEAGUE MEN'S WORLD CUP ENGLAND 2021

ABOVE: Jamaica's Joel Farrell and Andrew Simpson arrive too late to prevent New Zealand's Dallin Watene-Zelezniak going over

GROUP D

Group D was the closest fought, though Tonga topped the group thanks to three wins. They had some close shaves, especially in their first game on a Tuesday night in St Helens, as it took a 77th minute try from Souths form back-rower Keaon Koloamatangi to seal a 24-18 win against the never-say-die PNG Kumuls.

Leigh hooker Edwin Ipape was at the heart of the Kumuls fight and Leeds' Rhyse Martin landed three out of three conversions to equal the world record of 41 successive successful kicks, having not missed a goal since the previous July.

The week after, Wales gave as good as they got in a brave effort before succumbing to Tonga by 32-6. They held the lead as late as the 37th minute, having opened the scoring after debutant winger Kyle Evans produced a stunning hit to win possession from Siosifa Talakai and then received the ball back from Josh Ralph to sprint over the line to score. But two Tonga tries before half-time were killers as winger Daniel Tupou finished with a hat-trick.

In Tonga's last game, Jason Taumalolo played after the completion of a three-match suspension and absolutely brutalised Cook Islands in a 92-10 win in Middlesbrough. A try in the first minute from Daniel Tupou saw Tonga never look back and they went on to score a further 14 tries.

By then the Cooks were out. They had beaten Wales 18-12 on a Wednesday night in Leigh in their first game with the experience of Brad Takairangi guiding them home when he came off the bench. But a 32-16 defeat to Papua New Guinea the Tuesday after in Warrington sealed their fate. The Cooks were only two points adrift at the turnaround and, scenting a shock second win. But PNG ran in four tries, with winger Rodrick Tai, one of a crop of players from the country's Queensland Cup side the Hunters, completing a double.

Man of the match Martin missed his first conversion attempt which would have seen him set a new outright world record for consecutive kicks.

Wales put in their worst performance of the tournament in the very last group game when PNG overpowered them 36-0 at Doncaster. Nixon Putt and winger Jimmy Ngutlik scored two tries each, with the Kumuls 24-0 up at half-time.

Qualifiers: Tonga and Wales

ABOVE: Papua New Guinea's McKenzie Yei wrapped up by the Cook Islands defence

BELOW: Wales' Joe Burke gets to grips with Cook Islands' Johnathon Ford

LEFT: Tonga's Will Penisini charges over against Cook Islands

BELOW: Tonga's Sione Katoa produces an incredible offload as Wales' Caleb Aekins moves in

RIGHT: Keaon Koloamatangi scores Tonga's late winner against Papua New Guinea

LEFT: Papua New Guinea's Jimmy Ngutlik heads for the Wales tryline

QUARTER FINALS

AUSTRALIA 48 LEBANON 4

On the Friday night of a wet weekend, Australian winger Josh Addo-Carr scored five tries as the Kangaroos hammered Lebanon 48-4 in Huddersfield.

The victory was inevitable after an opening 20 minutes in which Addo-Carr put Lebanon to the sword with his first three tries. Lebanon were supported throughout by a noisy band of fans in the stand but Australia threatened to run riot.

The Cedars got the try their grit deserved when a grubber by Mitchell Moses was touched down by Josh Mansour after Cameron Munster - shifted from halfback to fullback with captain James Tedesco taken off as a precautionary measure - failed to knock it dead.

And although Lebanon, coached by Argentine rugby union coach Michael Cheika, did not manage to score again, they frustrated Australia in limiting them to only two more tries in the closing stages.

NEW ZEALAND 24 FIJI 18

In a late Saturday game in Hull, Fiji had their hearts broken in the cruelest possible way as their quarter-final tie with New Zealand became the first World Cup game effectively to be decided by a captain's challenge, the Kiwis qualifying after a 24-18 win.

The captain's challenge – which was used in the NRL and not Super League – was brought into effect after referee Gerard Sutton ruled that Joey Manu had knocked on, with ten minutes remaining and the scores locked at 18-all.

The Kiwis challenged the ruling and although television replays suggested that Manu had dropped it with a loose carry, video referee Tom Grant did not agree and a penalty was awarded.

Jordan Rapana converted it to put New Zealand in front for the first time at 20-18 and that left Fiji shellshocked. They tried everything to retake the lead but a last-second try from Rapana sealed the win.

Fiji had raced into a 12-0 lead thanks to tries from Maika Sivo and Kevin Naiqama as they dominated the Kiwis for the opening 20 minutes. Ronaldo Mulitalo went over in the corner to get New Zealand on the board but despite camping on Fiji's line for the last ten minutes of the half they went in at half-time trailing.

The second half was just as entertaining. Naiqama grabbed his second to put Fiji 18-6 in front. The Kiwis then hit back with tries from Briton Nikora and Manu and it looked like the game would go to extra time - until that crucial challenge.

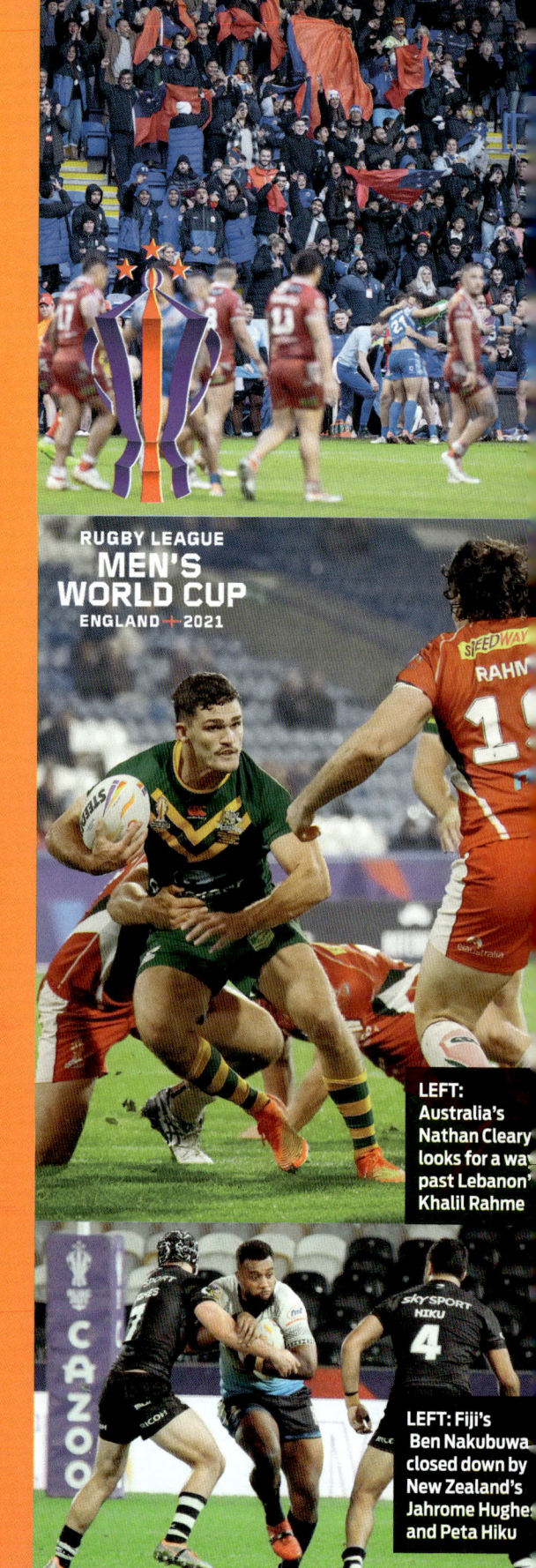

LEFT: Australia's Nathan Cleary looks for a way past Lebanon' Khalil Rahme

LEFT: Fiji's Ben Nakubuwa closed down by New Zealand's Jahrome Hughes and Peta Hiku

ABOVE: Tonga and Samoa meet head on before kick-off

BELOW: Jarome Luai dives over

ABOVE LEFT: Samoa players and fans celebrate victory

ABOVE: The Princess of Wales meets the England team before their clash with Papua New Guinea

LEFT: Tom Burgess reaches for the tryline

SAMOA 20 TONGA 18

The Tonga-Samoa clash at the Halliwell Jones Stadium on the Sunday, in the last quarter-final of the weekend, lived up to its pre-match billing in an edge-of-the-seat thriller that could have gone either way, Samoa hanging on for a 20-18 win, sealing a semi-final showdown with England in London the following Saturday.

A Stephen Crichton penalty goal separated the teams and put them into the semi-finals for the first time.

Halfbacks Anthony Milford and Jarome Luai were excellent on the back of a pack led by captain Junior Paulo and came up with the right plays at the right time, especially when Tonga mounted a late comeback.

It ended in heartbreak for Kristian Woolf's Tonga side, who had hopes of making the final four for their second successive World Cup. They had their own moments of brilliance and never gave up.

After Sione Katoa's 72nd-minute try converted by his brother Isaiya Katoa, the final few minutes were frantic, with Tonga throwing everything at the Samoa line in a desperate bid to snatch victory. But the men in blue did just enough to hold on.

ENGLAND 46 PAPUA NEW GUINEA 6

England qualified with a Saturday afternoon 46-6 win over Papua New Guinea at Wigan.

The Kumuls' direct approach was predicted to worry England but they were blitzed from the kick-off, as Wellington Albert brought the ball back and was poleaxed by a huge hit from Victor Radley.

And when England got possession, Tom Burgess gave a titanic performance, charging into the line and carrying PNG players downfield with him. He ran for 100 metres within the first 20 minutes and the Papuans looked dispirited. His front-row partner Chris Hill was almost as good.

The crucial moment early in the game was when Justin Olam knocked on a grubber kick from Sam Tomkins on four minutes. Almost exactly a minute after, Burgess scored England's first try when he was able to retain his feet in the tackle, twist and fall to the floor. Three minutes later, Tommy Makinson was in for England's second when he touched down another Tomkins grubber.

The next crucial moment was when Rodrick Tai caught a George Williams kick but Makinson, Herbie Farnworth and Elliott Whitehead bundled him into touch. The Kumuls hardly touched the ball for the next 20 minutes as England scored try after try with Makinson finishing with five tries for a new England record and five goals for 30 points in total.

SEMI-FINALS

AUSTRALIA 16 NEW ZEALAND 14

Defending champions Australia booked their place in the final with a 16-14 Friday-night win over New Zealand. Nearly 30,000 inside Elland Road in Leeds were treated to a breathtaking match.

New Zealand were the best team in the first half and deservedly led at the break. But the momentum and then the match slipped from their grasp in the second half, which featured just one try. And one of the greatest of games was settled by the simplest of scores on 53 minutes, Cameron Murray charging straight over from a tap penalty.

The Kiwis went ahead through Jahrome Hughes and although Josh Addo-Carr and Valentine Holmes responded for Australia with breathtaking finishes, Jordan Rapana's penalty and then Dylan Brown's try as he backed up Ronaldo Mulitalo's break gave the Kiwis a 14-10 half-time lead.

At the start of the second half Peta Hiku thought he had extended the lead, only for Moses Leota to be adjudged offside from a kick.

The crucial penalty before Murray's try came under the Kiwis' sticks. Referee Ashley Klein called 'play on' at a play-the-ball with a Kiwi body in the ruck. Manu did just that but was adjudged to be not square at marker. Murray went straight for the line from Nathan Cleary's tap, going over the top of Brandon Smith to stretch over.

Cleary's second conversion of the night edged Australia back in front by two and they lifted, though the Kiwis thought they had won it in the 73rd minute. Manu made a spectacular break after fielding a kick and Rapana carried it on. Hughes' subsequent kick to the corner was pounced on by Hiku but replays showed he leapt from outside the field of play and grounded on the touch-in-goal line.

It was a thrilling end to one of the greatest Test matches of all time.

SAMOA 27 ENGLAND 26

England were knocked out on the Saturday afternoon, succumbing to a nail-biting, 27-26 golden-point defeat to Samoa at the Emirates Stadium in north London.

Shaun Wane fielded almost exactly the same side that hammered the Samoans 60-6 in the opening match of the tournament in Newcastle. The only change was the selection of the then suspended John Bateman, who replaced Mike McMeeken in the second row.

Whereas everything went the host's way in Newcastle and every chance created was executed perfectly, a combination of mis-timing and heroic Samoan defence led to their downfall.

Twice England could have scored in the opening stages, George Williams stopped short and Tommy Makinson unable to catch Jack Welsby's kick to the corner.

Minutes later Salford centre Tim Lafai got on the outside of clubmate Kallum Watkins to open the scoring and when Watkins looked to have broken England's duck, with Junior Paulo in the sin bin for a tip tackle on Tom Burgess, Lafai was on hand, literally, to dislodge the ball just as Watkins touched down.

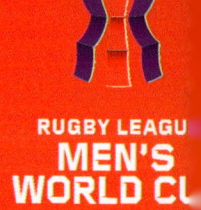

Five minutes later though England were in the lead as Williams broke up the middle and served a brilliant short ball to Elliott Whitehead for Makinson to convert. But Samoa were back in front by half-time after Hull's Ligi Sao exploited a mix up at marker between Watkins and Welsby and shot over down the blind side. Stephen Crichton converted for a 10-6 lead.

After the turnaround, Bateman gave England the lead when he picked up a kick dropped by Lafai and plonked the ball under the sticks. Makinson's boot put England in front again but Samoa hit straight back. The increasingly influential Jarome Luai toyed with the defence and found Paulo, who produced an unbelievable offload from the ground that was tapped on by Luai for Crichton to score.

Dom Young, one of the stars of the tournament, dropped a kick cold, then shot out of the line to allow Lafai his second and give Samoa an eight-point lead.

Eight points behind, England rose to the occasion to set up a thrilling conclusion. Young was denied a try when Welsby's kick bounced on the touch-in-goal line but moments later Herbie Farnworth spun round and crashed through three defenders to cross.

Makinson converted, then levelled from a penalty after a late Paulo push on kicker Sam Tomkins.

England were in attacking mode but Victor Radley threw a pass straight into the arms of Crichton, who ran half the pitch to put Samoa back in front with seven minutes to go. But, two minutes from time, up stepped Williams and Farnworth again, the former breaking through a tired defence from deep and the latter supporting for his second try and, thanks to Makinson's trusty boot, golden point.

For England, extra time could hardly have gone any worse. They had first use of the ball but Welsby's indecision over a pass saw him fumble and he was indebted to Whitehead for a heroic charge down of Anthony Milford's attempt at a match-winner.

There was no such rescue when Tomkins passed forward from dummy-half, with Crichton this time offered the chance to win it with three and half minutes of extra time gone. He made no mistake from 30 metres out.

LEFT: Jubilant Samoa players converge on Stephen Crichton following his golden point field goal against England

BELOW: Brian To'o gets a pass away under pressure from Morgan Knowles and Michael McIlorum

RIGHT: Australia's Josh Addo-Carr celebrates his try against New Zealand

ABOVE: The two sides clash as temperatures rise

FINAL

AUSTRALIA 30 SAMOA 10

Australia claimed a twelfth title from 16 global tournaments with a 30-10 win over Samoa, who became the first Pacific Island nation to make a World Cup final.

A bumper crowd of 67,502 turned out to see the final double header, Australia beating New Zealand in the women's final before the men's game, on a grey day at Old Trafford in Manchester.

The vast majority of the Australian side were debutants when they had arrived in England and coach Mal Meninga improved and developed his side as the tournament went on. Not that their squad was not made up of brilliant individuals.

Captain James Tedesco scored two of their six tries, one in the first-half burst that turned a nervy start into a solid Australian advantage, the other late in the second half to wrap up the title.

Latrell Mitchell also scored twice, taking some of the plaudits from his prolific wide man Josh Addo-Carr for once.

Samoa did still have attacking opportunities in the opening stages, but they found the Kangaroos a tough nut even for their expansive play to crack. The Kangaroos countered in a flash. Valentine Holmes' break put them on the Samoan line for the first time and, after forcing a dropout, Mitchell received a pass from Nathan Cleary and stepped away from Brian To'o before powering through Joseph Sua'ali'i to score.

The tournament's top try-scorer, Addo-Carr, settled for provider as his break set up Tedesco for his first score. Cleary, after missing the first kick, nailed the second, and from 10-0 Samoa would be chasing the game. Hanging on proved their main task.

On the half-hour mark, the challenge only got greater. Liam Martin's effort from a Harry Grant short-side dash from dummy-half was initially sent to the video-referee as no try, but the angles showed him ground the ball despite the best efforts of Tim Lafai.

Samoa's only glimmer of hope before the break came with a Taylan May break but Tedesco's pressure shut down Jarome Luai and Australia headed off with a well-earned 14-0 lead.

If the contest were to re-ignite, Samoa needed to score first in the second half. They were presented with that opportunity when Angus Crichton, following an Australian error, lifted his arm to fend Chanel Harris-Tavita and elbowed him hard in the head. Samoa needed to make the most of that time, and they were gifted enough ball to do so. But they couldn't find a try and it was the Kangaroos who scored in that period as Cleary's flat pass saw Cameron Murray ease over.

Crichton almost added to Australia's joy on his return from the bin, but he was unable to touch down from an Addo-Carr kick.

Moments later came the faintest glimmer of hope for the Samoans. Luai skipped from one side of the field to the other and sprayed out a pass that Mitchell tried and failed to intercept, allowing Kelma Tuilagi to send in To'o.

Stephen Crichton converted and Old Trafford did all it could to roar Samoa onto a comeback. Tedesco had something to say about that, however, and settled the game for certain by spotting a brilliant line to score of Cameron Munster's inside pass.

Cleary made it 26-6 and, although Samoa hit back almost immediately with a Crichton intercept, it would not have the same importance as his similar try the week before. Here he picked off Ben Hunt's dummy-half pass but he then hit the post with the conversion and the gap remained too great with too little time left.

And so Australia had the final say. Stephen Crichton looked for another interception and this time came up empty-handed, leaving space for Mitchell to score his second try.

ABOVE: Latrell Mitchell shows off the World Cup

GHT: Samoa skipper Junior Paulo leads the Siva Tau

RIGHT: Australia's James Tedesco skips away from Samoa's Chanel Harris-Tavita on the way to scoring

RUGBY LEAGUE MEN'S WORLD CUP
ENGLAND 2021

RUGBY LEAGUE WOMEN'S WORLD CUP
ENGLAND 2021

...stralia won their third World Cup on a row, ...lly dominating with a 54-4 win over ...w Zealand in the final at Old Trafford. ...t was a far cry from the pool match ...tween the two teams, in which New ...aland put in a great effort before going ...wn to a narrow 10-8 defeat.

...li Brigginshaw was the player of the ...tch, her second successive player of the ...tch award in a World Cup Final. But the ...aroos were athletic and skilful across ...e board, testament to the professional ...tional Rugby League Women's ...mpetition down under.

...Sydney Roosters' centres Isabelle Kelly ...d Jessica Sergis both finished with ...-doubles as did Parramatta's Kennedy ...errington. Brisbane winger Julia Robinson's try after ...t less than half an hour was the pick of the scores, ...h Brigginshaw's perfectly timed kick finding the ...nger to race in.

...he sixth staging of the tournament saw the ...rgeoning women's game soar in profile, with every game broadcast live.

A record eight nations participated in two groups - England, France, Australia, New Zealand, Cook Islands, Papua New Guinea, Canada and Brazil, with England, Papua New Guinea, Australia and New Zealand qualifying for the semi-finals.

Canada and Brazil added an exotic touch to the tournament and their group clash at Headingley was a highlight, Canada edging it 22-16 with a converted try in the last minute.

England were knocked out in the semis by the Kiwi Ferns by 20-6 in the second game of a double header at York's LNER Stadium, in front of a crowd of over 7,000. They had marched through their group and won a host of admirers but their amateur status told in the end. Australia had already hammered PNG 82-0.

England's improvement led to a number of their stars being lured down under on professional contracts.

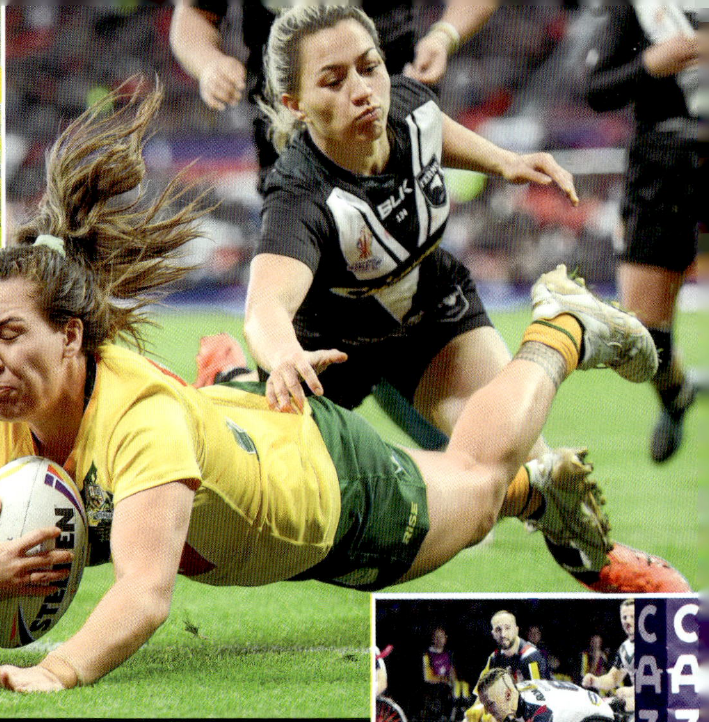

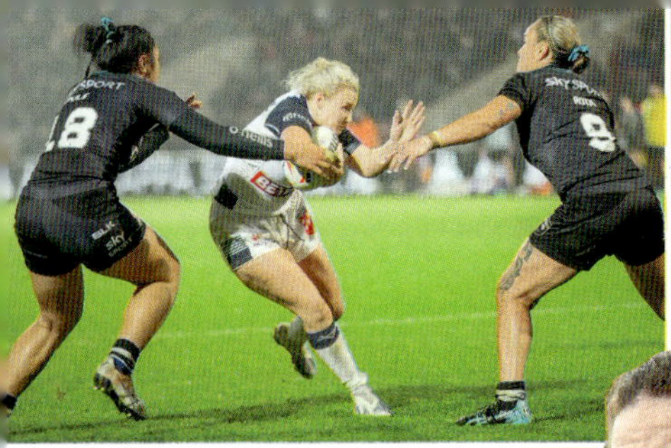

ABOVE: Georgia Roche takes on Otesa Pule and Krystal Rota as England suffer semi-final defeat to New Zealand

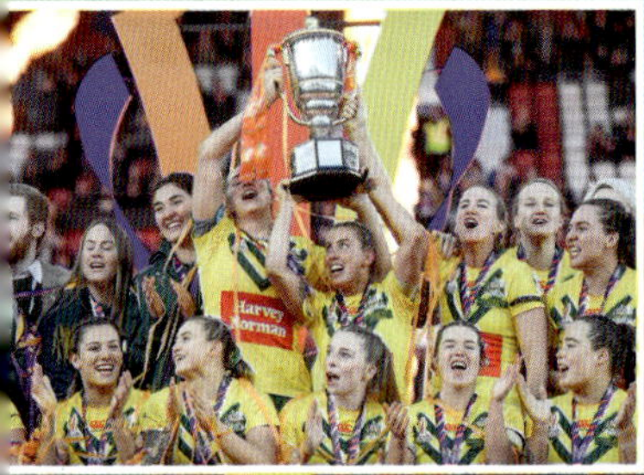

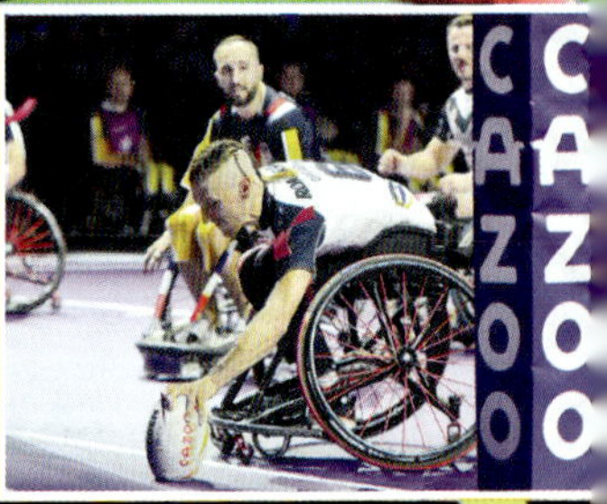

ABOVE: Australia's Evania Pelite dives over against New Zealand during the Women's World Cup Final

LEFT: The Jillaroos savour the moment

ABOVE: Jack Brown stretches out to score

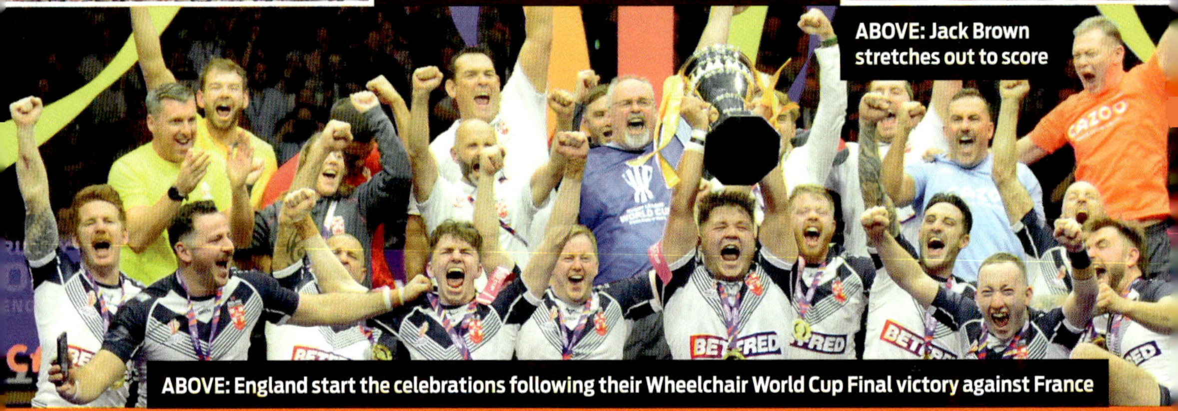

ABOVE: England start the celebrations following their Wheelchair World Cup Final victory against France

The 2021 Wheelchair Rugby League World Cup was the fourth staging of the Wheelchair Rugby League World Cup. But for the first time it ran concurrently with the men's and women's tournaments.

England won the title, defeating holders France in a thrilling final, Tom Halliwell getting over the line to secure a 28-24 victory for the home nation, which led to ecstatic scenes in the Manchester Central venue.

The England captain scored two tries in a player-of-the-match performance to deliver his country their first wheelchair title since the inaugural competition in 2008.

A record eight nations participated in two groups - England, France, Australia, Wales, Spain, Scotland, Ireland, replacing Norway who withdrew before the tournament because of Covid-related issues, and the United States.

From the very first pool game, the sport became a major attraction because of its skill, speed and bravery. England and Australia qualified from Group A and France and Wales from Group B.

The final, played the night before the men's and the women's, drew a huge TV audience and proved a spectacular event.

WORLD CUP 2021
Statistical review

WORLD CUP 2021
Men

World Cup 2021 - Statistical review

GROUP A

Saturday 15th October 2022

ENGLAND 60 SAMOA 6

ENGLAND: Sam Tomkins (C); Dominic Young; Kallum Watkins; Herbie Farnworth; Tommy Makinson; Jack Welsby; George Williams; Tom Burgess; Michael McIlorum; Chris Hill; Elliott Whitehead; Mike McMeeken; Victor Radley. Subs (all used): Mike Cooper; Morgan Knowles; Matty Lees; Luke Thompson. 18th man (not used): Kai Pearce-Paul.
Tries: Welsby (19), Young (25, 30), Watkins (49), Farnworth (65), Whitehead (69, 71), Makinson (73), Williams (77), Burgess (80);
Goals: Makinson 10/12.
SAMOA: Joseph Sua'ali'i; Brian To'o; Stephen Crichton; Izack Tago; Hamiso Tabuai-Fidow; Jarome Luai; Anthony Milford; Josh Papalii; Danny Levi; Junior Paulo (C); Josh Aloiai; Jaydn Su'A; Braden Hamlin-Uele. Subs (all used): Tyrone May; Kelma Tuilagi; Spencer Leniu; Martin Taupau. 18th man (not used): Chanel Harris-Tavita.
Try: Tago (34); **Goals:** Crichton 1/1.
Sin bin: Milford (63) - shoulder charge on Tomkins.
Rugby Leaguer & League Express Men of the Match:
England: George Williams; *Samoa:* Junior Paulo.
Penalty count: 6-3; **Half-time:** 18-6; **Referee:** Ashley Klein;
Attendance: 43,119 *(at St James' Park, Newcastle).*

Monday 17th October 2022

FRANCE 34 GREECE 12

FRANCE: Morgan Escare; Arthur Romano; Samisoni Langi; Matthieu Laguerre; Fouad Yaha; Arthur Mourgue; Tony Gigot; Jordan Dezaria; Alrix Da Costa; Lambert Belmas; Benjamin Jullien; Paul Seguier; Benjamin Garcia (C). Subs (all used): Eloi Pelissier; Justin Sangare; Corentin Le Cam; Mickael Goudemand. 18th man (not used): Cesar Rouge.
Tries: Dezaria (9), Gigot (30), Jullien (35, 74), Mourgue (47);
Goals: Mourgue 7/7.
GREECE: Chaise Robinson; Siteni Taukamo; Terry Constantinou; Nick Mougios; John Mitsias; Lachlan Ilias; Jordan Meads (C); Rob Tuliatu; Peter Mamouzelos; Sebastian Sell; Mitchell Zampetides; Nick Flocas; Billy Magoulias. Subs (all used): Jake Kambos; Myles Gal; Theodoros Nianiakas; Aris Dardamanis. 18th man (not used): Liam Sue-Tin.
Tries: Taukamo (56), Mougios (79); **Goals:** Ilias 2/2.
Rugby Leaguer & League Express Men of the Match:
France: Arthur Mourgue; *Greece:* Billy Magoulias.
Penalty count: 8-7; **Half-time:** 20-0; **Referee:** Adam Gee;
Attendance: 4,182 *(at Eco-Power Stadium, Doncaster).*

Saturday 22nd October 2022

ENGLAND 42 FRANCE 18

ENGLAND: Sam Tomkins (C); Dominic Young; Kallum Watkins; Herbie Farnworth; Ryan Hall; Marc Sneyd; George Williams; Tom Burgess; Michael McIlorum; Chris Hill; Elliott Whitehead; John Bateman; Victor Radley. Subs (all used): Jack Welsby; Mikolaj Oledzki; Luke Thompson; Andy Ackers. 18th man (not used): Joe Batchelor.
Tries: Hall (6, 11), Thompson (24), Whitehead (45), Radley (49), Young (56, 66); **Goals:** Sneyd 7/7.
Sin bin: Burgess (80) - fighting.
FRANCE: Morgan Escare; Arthur Romano; Benjamin Jullien; Samisoni Langi; Matthieu Laguerre; Arthur Mourgue; Tony Gigot; Jordan Dezaria; Alrix Da Costa; Lambert Belmas; Mickael Goudemand; Paul Seguier; Benjamin Garcia (C). Subs (all used): Eloi Pelissier; Justin Sangare; Gadwin Springer; Corentin Le Cam. 18th man (not used): Cesar Rouge.
Tries: Mourgue (29), Pelissier (33), Romano (76); **Goals:** Mourgue 3/3.
Rugby Leaguer & League Express Men of the Match:
England: Victor Radley; *France:* Arthur Mourgue.
Penalty count: 1-3; **Half-time:** 18-12; **Referee:** Gerard Sutton;
Attendance: 23,648 *(at University of Bolton Stadium).*

Sunday 23rd October 2022

SAMOA 72 GREECE 4

SAMOA: Joseph Sua'ali'i; Brian To'o; Stephen Crichton; Tim Lafai; Mathew Feagai; Jarome Luai; Chanel Harris-Tavita; Josh Papalii; Danny Levi; Junior Paulo (C); Ligi Sao; Jaydn Su'A; Josh Aloiai. Subs (all used): Royce Hunt; Martin Taupau; Fa'amanu Brown; Oregon Kaufusi. 18th man (not used): Ken Sio.
Tries: To'o (2), Paulo (5), Levi (16, 69), Harris-Tavita (21, 60), Hunt (30), Luai (33), Lafai (36, 79), Brown (52), Crichton (55), Feagai (63);
Goals: Crichton 10/13.
Sin bin: Su'A (73) - high tackle on Mitsias.
GREECE: Chaise Robinson; Siteni Taukamo; Terry Constantinou (C); Nick Mougios; John Mitsias; Billy Magoulias; Lachlan Ilias; Nick Flocas; Peter Mamouzelos; Stefanos Bastas; Jake Kambos; Adam Vrahnos; Sebastian Sell. Subs (all used): Myles Gal; Theodoros Nianiakas; Liam Sue-Tin; Nikolaos Bosmos. 18th man (not used): Rob Tuliatu.
Try: Ilias (48); **Goals:** Ilias 0/1.
Rugby Leaguer & League Express Men of the Match:
Samoa: Jarome Luai; *Greece:* John Mitsias.
Penalty count: 2-2; **Half-time:** 42-0; **Referee:** James Child;
Attendance: 4,415 *(at Eco-Power Stadium, Doncaster).*

Saturday 29th October 2022

ENGLAND 94 GREECE 4

ENGLAND: Tommy Makinson; Dominic Young; Kai Pearce-Paul; Jack Welsby; Ryan Hall; Marc Sneyd; George Williams (C); Mike Cooper; Andy Ackers; Matty Lees; Joe Batchelor; John Bateman; Victor Radley. Subs (all used): Morgan Knowles; Mike McMeeken; Tom Burgess; Chris Hill. 18th man (not used): Mikolaj Oledzki.
Tries: Lees (3), Young (13, 26, 35, 37), Hall (28, 59), Burgess (33, 53), Williams (40), Makinson (42), Sneyd (49), Batchelor (63), Ackers (67, 75), Pearce-Paul (73), McMeeken (77); **Goals:** Sneyd 13/17.
GREECE: Siteni Taukamo; John Mitsias; Terry Constantinou; Adam Vrahnos; Nick Mougios; Lachlan Ilias; Jordan Meads (C); Rob Tuliatu; Peter Mamouzelos; Ioannis Rousoglou; Mitchell Zampetides; Jake Kambos; Nick Flocas. Subs (all used): Ionnis Nake; Sebastian Sell; Konstantinos Katsidonis; Theodoros Nianiakas. 18th man (not used): Liam Sue-Tin.
Try: Taukamo (18); **Goals:** Ilias 0/1.
Rugby Leaguer & League Express Men of the Match:
England: Tom Burgess; *Greece:* Terry Constantinou.
Penalty count: 2-1; **Half-time:** 44-4; **Referee:** Belinda Sharpe;
Attendance: 18,760 *(at Bramall Lane, Sheffield).*

Sunday 30th October 2022

SAMOA 62 FRANCE 4

SAMOA: Joseph Sua'ali'i; Brian To'o; Stephen Crichton; Tim Lafai; Taylan May; Jarome Luai; Anthony Milford; Royce Hunt; Danny Levi; Junior Paulo (C); Ligi Sao; Jaydn Su'A; Oregon Kaufusi. Subs (all used): Josh Papalii; Spencer Leniu; Martin Taupau; Chanel Harris-Tavita. 18th man (not used): Ken Sio.
Tries: Lafai (3, 66), To'o (17, 46), Taylan May (20, 34, 40, 43), Milford (63, 73), Harris-Tavita (69); **Goals:** Crichton 9/11.
FRANCE: Arthur Mourgue; Arthur Romano; Matthieu Laguerre; Samisoni Langi; Fouad Yaha; Cesar Rouge; Tony Gigot; Jordan Dezaria; Alrix Da Costa; Gadwin Springer; Benjamin Jullien; Paul Seguier; Benjamin Garcia (C). Subs (all used): Eloi Pelissier; Justin Sangare; Mickael Goudemand; Maxime Puech. 18th man (not used): Louis Jouffret.
Try: Yaha (53); **Goals:** Mourgue 0/1.
Rugby Leaguer & League Express Men of the Match:
Samoa: Anthony Milford; *France:* Tony Gigot.
Penalty count: 3-6; **Half-time:** 28-0; **Referee:** Todd Smith;
Attendance: 6,756 *(at Halliwell Jones Stadium, Warrington).*

GROUP A - FINAL STANDINGS

	P	W	D	L	F	A	D	Pts
England	3	3	0	0	196	28	168	6
Samoa	3	2	0	1	140	68	72	4
France	3	1	0	2	56	116	-60	2
Greece	3	0	0	3	20	200	-180	0

World Cup 2021 - Statistical review

GROUP B

Saturday 15th October 2022

AUSTRALIA 42 FIJI 8

AUSTRALIA: James Tedesco (C); Josh Addo-Carr; Valentine Holmes; Latrell Mitchell; Murray Taulagi; Cameron Munster; Daly Cherry-Evans; Jake Trbojevic; Ben Hunt; Tino Fa'asuamaleaui; Angus Crichton; Jeremiah Nanai; Cameron Murray. Subs (all used): Jack Wighton; Patrick Carrigan; Reuben Cotter; Harry Grant. 18th man (not used): Matt Burton.
Tries: Nanai (15), Addo-Carr (23, 67), Crichton (34), Mitchell (43), Grant (54), Tedesco (60); **Goals:** Holmes 7/7.
FIJI: Sunia Turuva; Maika Sivo; Kevin Naiqama (C); Semi Valemei; Mitieli Vulikijapani; Sitiveni Moceidreke; Brandon Wakeham; Tui Kamikamica; Api Koroisau; King Vuniyayawa; Viliame Kikau; Siua Wong; Lamar Manuel-Liolevave. Subs (all used): Ben Nakubuwai; Taniela Sadrugu; Penioni Tagituimua; Jowasa Drodrolagi. 18th man (not used): Netane Masima.
Tries: Valemei (3), Turuva (75); **Goals:** Wakeham 0/2.
Rugby Leaguer & League Express Men of the Match:
Australia: Harry Grant; *Fiji:* Semi Valemei.
Penalty count: 3-5; **Half-time:** 18-4; **Referee:** Chris Kendall; **Attendance:** 13,366 *(at Headingley, Leeds).*

Sunday 16th October 2022

SCOTLAND 4 ITALY 28

SCOTLAND: Ryan Brierley; Lachlan Walmsley; Bayley Liu; Kieran Buchanan; Matty Russell; Bailey Hayward; Calum Gahan; Sam Luckley; Liam Hood; Logan Bayliss-Brow; Euan Aitken; Kane Linnett; James Bell. Subs (all used): Ben Hellewell; Luke Bain; Kyle Schneider; Dale Ferguson (C). 18th man (not used): Jack Teanby.
Try: Walmsley (78); **Goals:** Brierley 0/1.
Sin bin: Ferguson (36) - stamp on Atkinson.
ITALY: Luke Polselli; Richard Lepori; Ethan Natoli; Daniel Atkinson; Jake Maizen; Jack Campagnolo; Radean Robinson; Luca Moretti; Dean Parata; Anton Iaria; Brenden Santi; Ryan King; Nathan Brown (C). Subs (all used): Joey Tramontana; Luke Hodge; Gioele Celerino; Jack Colovatti. 18th man (not used): Kyle Pickering.
Tries: Polselli (10), Parata (24), Maizen (44, 48, 73); **Goals:** Campagnolo 4/5.
Rugby Leaguer & League Express Men of the Match:
Scotland: Euan Aitken; *Italy:* Luke Polselli.
Penalty count: 9-5; **Half-time:** 0-12; **Referee:** Todd Smith; **Attendance:** 6,206 *(at Kingston Park, Newcastle).*

Friday 21st October 2022

AUSTRALIA 84 SCOTLAND 0

AUSTRALIA: James Tedesco (C); Campbell Graham; Jack Wighton; Matt Burton; Josh Addo-Carr; Cameron Munster; Nathan Cleary; Reagan Campbell-Gillard; Harry Grant; Patrick Carrigan; Angus Crichton; Liam Martin; Isaah Yeo. Subs (all used): Ben Hunt; Lindsay Collins; Valentine Holmes; Jake Trbojevic. 18th man (not used): Daly Cherry-Evans.
Tries: Addo-Carr (6, 31, 49, 79), Wighton (11, 35), Crichton (15), Graham (20, 59, 74), Cleary (28), Tedesco (41), Hunt (43), Burton (66), Yeo (77); **Goals:** Cleary 12/15.
SCOTLAND: Alex Walker; Lachlan Walmsley; Ben Hellewell; Kieran Buchanan; Matty Russell; Calum Gahan; Bailey Hayward; Logan Bayliss-Brow; Liam Hood; Jack Teanby; Euan Aitken; Kane Linnett; James Bell. Subs (all used): Kyle Schneider; Luke Bain; Guy Graham; Dale Ferguson (C). 18th man (not used): Davey Dixon.
Sin bin: Linnett (59) - professional foul.
Rugby Leaguer & League Express Men of the Match:
Australia: Josh Addo-Carr; *Scotland:* James Bell.
Penalty count: 2-1; **Half-time:** 40-0; **Referee:** Grant Atkins; **Attendance:** 10,276 *(at Coventry Building Society Arena).*

Saturday 22nd October 2022

FIJI 60 ITALY 4

FIJI: Sunia Turuva; Vuate Karawalevu; Kevin Naiqama (C); Semi Valemei; Maika Sivo; Api Koroisau; Brandon Wakeham; Tui Kamikamica; Penioni Tagituimua; King Vuniyayawa; Viliame Kikau; Siua Wong; Korbin Sims. Subs (all used): Ben Nakubuwai; Taniela Sadrugu; Lamar Manuel-Liolevave; Henry Raiwalui. 18th man (not used): Netane Masima.
Tries: Kikau (9, 23), Naiqama (11), Tagituimua (15, 46), Koroisau (37), Nakubuwai (50), Sivo (53, 64), Sadrugu (79); **Goals:** Wakeham 7/7, Koroisau 2/2, Raiwalui 1/1.
ITALY: Luke Polselli; Richard Lepori; Ethan Natoli; Daniel Atkinson; Jake Maizen; Jack Campagnolo; Radean Robinson; Alec Susino; Dean Parata; Anton Iaria; Brenden Santi; Ryan King; Nathan Brown (C). Subs (all used): Joey Tramontana; Luca Moretti; Luke Hodge; Jack Colovatti. 18th man (not used): Kyle Pickering.
Try: Maizen (56); **Goals:** Campagnolo 0/1.
Rugby Leaguer & League Express Men of the Match:
Fiji: Viliame Kikau; *Italy:* Jake Maizen.
Penalty count: 3-4; **Half-time:** 30-0; **Referee:** Jack Smith; **Attendance:** 3,675 *(at Kingston Park, Newcastle).*

Saturday 29th October 2022

FIJI 30 SCOTLAND 14

FIJI: Sunia Turuva; Maika Sivo; Kevin Naiqama (C); Semi Valemei; Vuate Karawalevu; Henry Raiwalui; Brandon Wakeham; King Vuniyayawa; Api Koroisau; Korbin Sims; Viliame Kikau; Siua Wong; Taniela Sadrugu. Subs (all used): Joseph Ratuvakacereivalu; Penioni Tagituimua; Tevita Toloi; Lamar Manuel-Liolevave. 18th man (not used): Netane Masima.
Tries: Sadrugu (4), Kikau (14), Raiwalui (35), Sivo (45), Sims (67); **Goals:** Wakeham 5/5.
Sin bin: Kikau (66) - fighting.
SCOTLAND: Davey Dixon; Lachlan Walmsley; Bayley Liu; Kieran Buchanan; Matty Russell; James Bell; Calum Gahan; Jack Teanby; Kyle Schneider; Sam Luckley; Ben Hellewell; Kane Linnett; Luke Bain. Subs (all used): Logan Bayliss-Brow; Guy Graham; Charlie Emslie; Dale Ferguson (C). 18th man (not used): Ryan Brierley.
Tries: Walmsley (20), Hellewell (40), Liu (51);
Goals: Walmsley 0/2, Schneider 1/1.
Sin bin: Bain (41) - high tackle on Turuva; Walmsley (66) - fighting.
Rugby Leaguer & League Express Men of the Match:
Fiji: Henry Raiwalui; *Scotland:* Bayley Liu.
Penalty count: 8-5; **Half-time:** 18-8; **Referee:** Tom Grant; **Attendance:** 6,736 *(at Kingston Park, Newcastle).*

AUSTRALIA 66 ITALY 6

AUSTRALIA: James Tedesco (C); Campbell Graham; Valentine Holmes; Latrell Mitchell; Murray Taulagi; Daly Cherry-Evans; Nathan Cleary; Lindsay Collins; Ben Hunt; Reuben Cotter; Liam Martin; Jeremiah Nanai; Cameron Murray. Subs (all used): Isaah Yeo; Tino Fa'asuamaleaui; Reagan Campbell-Gillard; Matt Burton. 18th man (not used): Jack Wighton.
Tries: Holmes (7), Taulagi (11, 40), Tedesco (19), Graham (28, 68), Mitchell (36), Yeo (46), Martin (51), Murray (58), Nanai (74), Collins (80); **Goals:** Cleary 9/12.
ITALY: Luke Polselli; Kyle Pickering; Daniel Atkinson; Ethan Natoli; Jake Maizen; Jack Campagnolo; Radean Robinson; Alec Susino; Dean Parata; Anton Iaria; Luca Moretti; Brenden Santi; Nathan Brown (C). Subs (all used): Joey Tramontana; Ronny Palumbo; Jack Colovatti; Gioele Celerino. 18th man (not used): Luke Hodge.
Try: Palumbo (54); **Goals:** Campagnolo 1/1.
Rugby Leaguer & League Express Men of the Match:
Australia: Latrell Mitchell; *Italy:* Luke Polselli.
Penalty count: 5-3; **Half-time:** 30-0; **Referee:** Liam Moore; **Attendance:** 5,586 *(at Totally Wicked Stadium, St Helens).*

GROUP B - FINAL STANDINGS

	P	W	D	L	F	A	D	Pts
Australia	3	3	0	0	192	14	178	6
Fiji	3	2	0	1	98	60	38	4
Italy	3	1	0	2	38	130	-92	2
Scotland	3	0	0	3	18	142	-124	0

World Cup 2021 - Statistical review

GROUP C

Sunday 16th October 2022

JAMAICA 2 IRELAND 48

JAMAICA: Ben Jones-Bishop; Mo Agoro; Greg Johnson; Jacob Ogden; Alex Young; James Woodburn-Hall; Kieran Rush; Jordan Andrade; Ashton Golding (C); Michael Lawrence; AJ Wallace; Chevaughn Bailey; Joe Brown. Subs (all used): Keenen Tomlinson; Aaron Jones-Bishop; Bradley Ho; Ross Peltier. 18th man (not used): Andrew Simpson.
Goals: Rush 1/1.
IRELAND: Richie Myler; Louis Senior; Ed Chamberlain; Toby King; Innes Senior; Luke Keary; Joe Keyes; Liam Byrne; Brendan O'Hagan; Jaimin Jolliffe; James Bentley; Frankie Halton; George King (C). Subs (all used): Josh Cook; James McDonnell; Harry Rushton; James Hasson. 18th man (not used): Ronan Michael.
Tries: L Senior (13, 64), G King (16), O'Hagan (20), Chamberlain (37), I Senior (52), T King (57), McDonnell (72), Bentley (77), Halton (80);
Goals: Chamberlain 1/4, Keyes 3/6.
Rugby Leaguer & League Express Men of the Match:
Jamaica: Ashton Golding; *Ireland:* Luke Keary.
Penalty count: 4-4; **Half-time:** 2-18; **Referee:** Benjamin Casty;
Attendance: 6,320 *(at Headingley, Leeds).*

NEW ZEALAND 34 LEBANON 12

NEW ZEALAND: Joseph Manu; Ronaldo Mulitalo; Peta Hiku; Charnze Nicoll-Klokstad; Jordan Rapana; Dylan Brown; Kieran Foran; Jesse Bromwich (C); Brandon Smith; James Fisher-Harris; Isaiah Papali'i; Kenny Bromwich; Joseph Tapine. Subs (all used): Marata Niukore; Nelson Asofa-Solomona; Briton Nikora; Jeremy Marshall-King. 18th man (not used): Scott Sorensen.
Tries: K Bromwich (5), Asofa-Solomona (24), Hiku (29), Brown (54), Manu (56), Rapana (60); **Goals:** Rapana 5/6.
LEBANON: Jacob Kiraz; Josh Mansour; Brad Morkos; Reece Robinson; Abbas Miski; Adam Doueihi; Mitchell Moses (C); Kayne Kalache; Andrew Kazzi; Khalil Rahme; Elie El-Zakhem; Charbel Tasipale; James Roumanos. Subs (all used): Michael Tannous; Hanna El-Nachar; Jalal Bazzaz; Joshua Maree. 18th man (not used): Anthony Layoun.
Tries: Mansour (1), Miski (45); **Goals:** Moses 2/2.
Dismissal: Doueihi (59) - dissent.
Rugby Leaguer & League Express Men of the Match:
New Zealand: Joseph Manu; *Lebanon:* Mitchell Moses.
Penalty count: 8-7; **Half-time:** 18-6; **Referee:** Grant Atkins;
Attendance: 5,435 *(at Halliwell Jones Stadium, Warrington).*

Saturday 22nd October 2022

NEW ZEALAND 68 JAMAICA 6

NEW ZEALAND: Charnze Nicoll-Klokstad; Sebastian Kris; Marata Niukore; Peta Hiku; Dallin Watene-Zelezniak; Joseph Manu; Kieran Foran; Moses Leota; Brandon Smith; James Fisher-Harris (C); Briton Nikora; Kenny Bromwich; Isaac Liu. Subs (all used): Isaiah Papali'i; Nelson Asofa-Solomona; Jeremy Marshall-King; Scott Sorensen. 18th man (not used): Jesse Bromwich.
Tries: Watene-Zelezniak (4, 14, 18, 58), Hiku (10), Niukore (29), Kris (37), Marshall-King (39, 56), Nicoll-Klokstad (43), Nikora (53), Smith (66, 72);
Goals: Foran 6/10, Watene-Zelezniak 2/3.
JAMAICA: Ben Jones-Bishop; Mo Agoro; Greg Johnson; Jacob Ogden; Andrew Simpson; James Woodburn-Hall; Kieran Rush; Michael Lawrence; Ashton Golding (C); Keenen Tomlinson; AJ Wallace; Joel Farrell; Joe Brown. Subs (all used): Bradley Ho; Marvin Thompson; Jordan Andrade; Chevaughn Bailey. 18th man (not used): Alex Young.
Try: B Jones-Bishop (75); **Goals:** Rush 1/1.
Rugby Leaguer & League Express Men of the Match:
New Zealand: Dallin Watene-Zelezniak; *Jamaica:* Ben Jones-Bishop.
Penalty count: 3-5; **Half-time:** 34-0; **Referee:** Marcus Griffiths;
Attendance: 6,850 *(at MKM Stadium, Hull).*

Sunday 23rd October 2022

LEBANON 32 IRELAND 14

LEBANON: Jacob Kiraz; Josh Mansour; Brad Morkos; Reece Robinson; Abbas Miski; Khaled Rajab; Mitchell Moses (C); Kayne Kalache; Andrew Kazzi; Khalil Rahme; Elie El-Zakhem; Charbel Tasipale; James Roumanos. Subs (all used): Bilaal Maarbani; Anthony Layoun; Jalal Bazzaz; Jaxson Rahme. 18th man (not used): Michael Tannous.
Tries: Robinson (21), Kiraz (25), Morkos (31), El-Zakhem (52), Miski (58);
Goals: Moses 6/7.
Sin bin: Bazzaz (40) - fighting.
IRELAND: Richie Myler; Louis Senior; Ed Chamberlain; Toby King; Innes Senior; Luke Keary; Joe Keyes; Liam Byrne; Brendan O'Hagan; Jaimin Jolliffe; James Bentley; Frankie Halton; George King (C). Subs (all used): Josh Cook; Harry Rushton; Robbie Mulhern; James Hasson. 18th man (not used): Ronan Michael.
Tries: L Senior (37, 48), Chamberlain (78); **Goals:** Chamberlain 1/3.
Sin bin: Mulhern (40) - fighting; Byrne (70) - late challenge on Moses.
Rugby Leaguer & League Express Men of the Match:
Lebanon: Mitchell Moses; *Ireland:* Jaimin Jolliffe.
Penalty count: 11-5; **Half-time:** 20-4; **Referee:** Adam Gee;
Attendance: 6,057 *(at Leigh Sports Village).*

Friday 28th October 2022

NEW ZEALAND 48 IRELAND 10

NEW ZEALAND: Joseph Manu; Jordan Rapana; Peta Hiku; Briton Nikora; Ronaldo Mulitalo; Dylan Brown; Jahrome Hughes; Jesse Bromwich (C); Brandon Smith; James Fisher-Harris; Kenny Bromwich; Nelson Asofa-Solomona; Joseph Tapine. Subs (all used): Isaiah Papali'i; Kieran Foran; Jared Waerea-Hargreaves; Isaac Liu. 18th man (not used): Charnze Nicoll-Klokstad.
Tries: Hughes (15, 59), Rapana (20, 48), Hiku (27, 33), Mulitalo (38), Fisher-Harris (54), K Bromwich (62), Manu (78);
Goals: Rapana 2/4, Brown 2/6.
Sin bin: Waerea-Hargreaves (37) - high tackle.
IRELAND: Richie Myler; Louis Senior; Ed Chamberlain; Toby King; Innes Senior; Luke Keary; Joe Keyes; James Hasson; Josh Cook; George King (C); James Bentley; Frankie Halton; Ronan Michael. Subs (all used): Brendan O'Hagan; Harry Rushton; Dan Norman; Henry O'Kane. 18th man (not used): James McDonnell.
Tries: L Senior (30, 66); **Goals:** Chamberlain 1/3.
Rugby Leaguer & League Express Men of the Match:
New Zealand: Jahrome Hughes; *Ireland:* Louis Senior.
Penalty count: 8-3; **Half-time:** 24-6; **Referee:** Robert Hicks;
Attendance: 14,044 *(at Headingley, Leeds).*

Sunday 30th October 2022

LEBANON 74 JAMAICA 12

LEBANON: Adam Doueihi; Josh Mansour; Brad Morkos; Reece Robinson; Abbas Miski; Mitchell Moses (C); Khaled Rajab; Michael Tannous; James Roumanos; Khalil Rahme; Elie El-Zakhem; Charbel Tasipale; Andrew Kazzi. Subs (all used): Anthony Layoun; Jalal Bazzaz; Jaxson Rahme; Tony Maroun. 18th man (not used): Bilaal Maarbani.
Tries: Tannous (6), Miski (8, 80), El-Zakhem (12), Robinson (14), Rajab (23), Tasipale (27, 56), Mansour (32, 61, 71), Doueihi (45), Maroun (59); **Goals:** Moses 7/7, Doueihi 4/6.
Sin bin: J Rahme (39) - late challenge.
JAMAICA: Ben Jones-Bishop; Mo Agoro; Alex Young; Jacob Ogden; Abevia McDonald; James Woodburn-Hall; Kieran Rush; Khamisi McKain; Jy-mel Coleman; Michael Lawrence; Keenen Tomlinson; Joel Farrell; Ashton Golding (C). Subs (all used): Joe Brown; AJ Wallace; Chevaughn Bailey; Jordan Andrade. 18th man (not used): Greg Johnson.
Tries: Agoro (50), Andrade (66); **Goals:** Woodburn-Hall 1/1, Rush 1/1.
Sin bin: Lawrence (57) - holding down.
Rugby Leaguer & League Express Men of the Match:
Lebanon: Adam Doueihi; *Jamaica:* Ashton Golding.
Penalty count: 8-8; **Half-time:** 42-0; **Referee:** Paki Parkinson;
Attendance: 5,006 *(at Leigh Sports Village).*

GROUP C - FINAL STANDINGS

	P	W	D	L	F	A	D	Pts
New Zealand	3	3	0	0	150	28	122	6
Lebanon	3	2	0	1	118	60	58	4
Ireland	3	1	0	2	72	82	-10	2
Jamaica	3	0	0	3	20	190	-170	0

World Cup 2021 - Statistical review
GROUP D

Tuesday 18th October 2022

TONGA 24 PAPUA NEW GUINEA 18

TONGA: Tolutau Koula; Daniel Tupou; Will Penisini; Moses Suli; Sione Katoa; Isaiya Katoa; Tui Lolohea; Addin Fonua-Blake; Keaon Koloamatangi; Tevita Tatola; Felise Kaufusi; Haumole Olakau'atu; Sio Siua Taukeiaho (C). Subs (all used): Siosifa Talakai; Soni Luke; Moeaki Fotuaika; David Fifita. 18th man (not used): Talatau Amone.
Tries: Penisini (13), Fotuaika (34), I Katoa (36), Koloamatangi (77); **Goals:** I Katoa 4/5.
PAPUA NEW GUINEA: Alex Johnston; Rodrick Tai; Nene Macdonald; Justin Olam; Dan Russell; Kyle Laybutt; Lachlan Lam; Wellington Albert; Edwin Ipape; Sylvester Namo; Nixon Putt; Rhyse Martin (C); Jacob Alick. Subs (all used): McKenzie Yei; Emmanuel Waine; Keven Appo; Watson Boas. 18th man (not used): Sherwin Tanabi.
Tries: Martin (5), Lam (41), Russell (67); **Goals:** Martin 3/3.
Rugby Leaguer & League Express Men of the Match:
Tonga: Keaon Koloamatangi; *Papua New Guinea:* Edwin Ipape.
Penalty count: 5-4; **Half-time:** 18-6; **Referee:** Liam Moore;
Attendance: 10,409 *(at Totally Wicked Stadium, St Helens).*

Wednesday 19th October 2022

WALES 12 COOK ISLANDS 18

WALES: Caleb Aekins; Mike Butt; Will Evans; Elliot Kear (C); Rhys Williams; Ollie Olds; Josh Ralph; Anthony Walker; Matty Fozard; Dan Fleming; Rhodri Lloyd; Bailey Antrobus; Joe Burke. Subs (all used): Chester Butler; Ben Evans; Curtis Davies; Connor Davies. 18th man (not used): Tom Hopkins.
Tries: Lloyd (14), O Olds (30); **Goals:** Fozard 2/2.
COOK ISLANDS: Kayal Iro; Steven Marsters; Anthony Gelling; Reubenn Rennie; Paul Ulberg; Esan Marsters; Johnathon Ford; Pride Petterson-Robati; Aaron Teroi; Vincent Rennie; Dominique Peyroux; Reuben Porter; Zane Tetevano. Subs (all used): Makahesi Makatoa; Davvy Moale; Rua Ngatikaura; Brad Takairangi (C). 18th man (not used): Moses Noovao-McGreal.
Tries: Gelling (25), Moale (60), S Marsters (64); **Goals:** S Marsters 3/4.
Rugby Leaguer & League Express Men of the Match:
Wales: Matty Fozard; *Cook Islands:* Johnathon Ford.
Penalty count: 4-4; **Half-time:** 12-8; **Referee:** Robert Hicks;
Attendance: 6,188 *(at Leigh Sports Village).*

Monday 24th October 2022

TONGA 32 WALES 6

TONGA: Tesi Niu; Sione Katoa; Konrad Hurrell; Siosifa Talakai; Daniel Tupou; Talatau Amone; Tui Lolohea; Addin Fonua-Blake; Soni Luke; Moeaki Fotuaika; Felise Kaufusi; Keaon Koloamatangi; Sio Siua Taukeiaho (C). Subs (all used): Tolutau Koula; Tevita Tatola; David Fifita; Ben Murdoch-Masila. 18th man (not used): Haumole Olakau'atu.
Tries: Tupou (20, 59, 71), Fifita (37), Koloamatangi (40), Niu (47); **Goals:** Taukeiaho 3/4, Lolohea 3/4, Talakai 1/1.
WALES: Caleb Aekins; Kyle Evans; Dalton Grant; Elliot Kear (C); Rhys Williams; Ollie Olds; Josh Ralph; Anthony Walker; Matty Fozard; Gavin Bennion; Chester Butler; Bailey Antrobus; Joe Burke. Subs (all used): Dan Fleming; Curtis Davies; Connor Davies; Tom Hopkins. 18th man (not used): James Olds.
Try: K Evans (16); **Goals:** Fozard 1/1.
Rugby Leaguer & League Express Men of the Match:
Tonga: Daniel Tupou; *Wales:* Kyle Evans.
Penalty count: 3-4; **Half-time:** 16-6; **Referee:** Kasey Badger;
Attendance: 7,752 *(at Totally Wicked Stadium, St Helens).*

Tuesday 25th October 2022

PAPUA NEW GUINEA 32 COOK ISLANDS 16

PAPUA NEW GUINEA: Alex Johnston; Rodrick Tai; Nene Macdonald; Justin Olam; Jimmy Ngutlik; Kyle Laybutt; Lachlan Lam; Wellington Albert; Edwin Ipape; Sylvester Namo; Nixon Putt; Rhyse Martin (C); Jacob Alick. Subs (all used): Dan Russell; McKenzie Yei; Keven Appo; Watson Boas. 18th man (not used): Jeremiah Simbiken.
Tries: Tai (14, 46), Laybutt (23), Martin (41), Lam (56), Olam (68); **Goals:** Martin 4/6.
Sin bin: Yei (27) - dangerous challenge.
COOK ISLANDS: Kayal Iro; Steven Marsters; Anthony Gelling; Reubenn Rennie; Paul Ulberg; Brad Takairangi (C); Esan Marsters; Tepai Moeroa; Aaron Teroi; Vincent Rennie; Dominique Peyroux; Brendan Piakura; Zane Tetevano. Subs (all used): Makahesi Makatoa; Rua Ngatikaura; Moses Noovao-McGreal; Davvy Moale. 18th man (not used): Tevin Arona.
Tries: Ulberg (34), Gelling (60), Iro (77); **Goals:** S Marsters 2/4.
Sin bin: R Rennie (66) - dangerous challenge.
Rugby Leaguer & League Express Men of the Match:
Papua New Guinea: Rhyse Martin; *Cook Islands:* Kayal Iro.
Penalty count: 7-8; **Half-time:** 10-8; **Referee:** Chris Kendall;
Attendance: 6,273 *(at Halliwell Jones Stadium, Warrington).*

Sunday 30th October 2022

TONGA 92 COOK ISLANDS 10

TONGA: Tesi Niu; Daniel Tupou; Moses Suli; Will Penisini; Sione Katoa; Isaiya Katoa; Tui Lolohea; Addin Fonua-Blake; Soni Luke; Moeaki Fotuaika; Felise Kaufusi; Keaon Koloamatangi; Jason Taumalolo (C). Subs (all used): Talatau Amone; Tevita Tatola; David Fifita; Ben Murdoch-Masila. 18th man (not used): Konrad Hurrell.
Tries: Tupou (2, 64), Taumalolo (14, 20), Niu (23, 30, 49), Penisini (26, 32, 61, 75), Lolohea (35, 58), Kaufusi (40), I Katoa (44), Amone (77); **Goals:** I Katoa 14/16.
COOK ISLANDS: Kayal Iro; Steven Marsters; Esan Marsters; Geoff Daniela; Paul Ulberg; Brad Takairangi (C); Johnathon Ford; Makahesi Makatoa; Aaron Teroi; Tepai Moeroa; Dominique Peyroux; Brendan Piakura; Zane Tetevano. Subs (all used): Tevin Arona; Tinirau Arona; Davvy Moale; Dylan Napa. 18th man (not used): Pride Petterson-Robati.
Tries: S Marsters (70), Tinirau Arona (80);
Goals: S Marsters 0/1, Tinirau Arona 1/1.
Rugby Leaguer & League Express Men of the Match:
Tonga: Jason Taumalolo; *Cook Islands:* Kayal Iro.
Penalty count: 5-4; **Half-time:** 52-0; **Referee:** Ashley Klein;
Attendance: 8,342 *(at Riverside Stadium, Middlesbrough).*

Monday 31st October 2022

PAPUA NEW GUINEA 36 WALES 0

PAPUA NEW GUINEA: Alex Johnston; Rodrick Tai; Nene Macdonald; Justin Olam; Jimmy Ngutlik; Kyle Laybutt; Lachlan Lam; Wellington Albert; Edwin Ipape; Emmanuel Waine; Nixon Putt; Rhyse Martin (C); Jacob Alick. Subs (all used): Wesser Tenza; Dan Russell; Sherwin Tanabi; Jeremiah Simbiken. 18th man (not used): Zev John.
Tries: Laybutt (8), Putt (12, 47), Ngutlik (25, 77), Russell (30);
Goals: Martin 6/6.
WALES: Caleb Aekins; Kyle Evans; Will Evans; Elliot Kear (C); Rhys Williams; Ollie Olds; Josh Ralph; Anthony Walker; Matty Fozard; Gavin Bennion; Rhodri Lloyd; Bailey Antrobus; Joe Burke. Subs (all used): Dan Fleming; Chester Butler; Curtis Davies; Connor Davies. 18th man (not used): Mike Butt.
Rugby Leaguer & League Express Men of the Match:
Papua New Guinea: Nixon Putt; *Wales:* Kyle Evans.
Penalty count: 6-5; **Half-time:** 24-0; **Referee:** Gerard Sutton;
Attendance: 6,968 *(at Eco-Power Stadium, Doncaster).*

GROUP D - FINAL STANDINGS

	P	W	D	L	F	A	D	Pts
Tonga	3	3	0	0	148	34	114	6
Papua New Guinea	3	2	0	1	86	40	46	4
Cook Islands	3	1	0	2	44	136	-92	2
Wales	3	0	0	3	18	86	-68	0

World Cup 2021 - Statistical review

QUARTER FINALS

Friday 4th November 2022

AUSTRALIA 48 LEBANON 4

AUSTRALIA: James Tedesco (C); Valentine Holmes; Jack Wighton; Latrell Mitchell; Josh Addo-Carr; Cameron Munster; Nathan Cleary; Jake Trbojevic; Harry Grant; Tino Fa'asuamaleaui; Angus Crichton; Liam Martin; Isaah Yeo. Subs (all used): Daly Cherry-Evans; Patrick Carrigan; Cameron Murray; Lindsay Collins. 18th man (not used): Campbell Graham.
Tries: Addo-Carr (5, 16, 19, 44, 59), Mitchell (24), Murray (30, 33), Martin (69); **Goals:** Cleary 6/9.
LEBANON: Jacob Kiraz; Josh Mansour; Brad Morkos; Reece Robinson; Abbas Miski; Adam Doueihi; Mitchell Moses (C); James Roumanos; Anthony Layoun; Khalil Rahme; Elie El-Zakherm; Charbel Tasipale; Andrew Kazzi. Subs (all used): Michael Tannous; Khaled Rajab; Jalal Bazzaz; Jaxson Rahme. 18th man (not used): Bilaal Maarbani.
Try: Mansour (52); **Goals:** Moses 0/1.
Rugby Leaguer & League Express Men of the Match:
Australia: Josh Addo-Carr; *Lebanon:* Michael Tannous.
Penalty count: 4-2; **Half-time:** 30-0; **Referee:** Chris Kendall;
Attendance: 8,206 *(at John Smith's Stadium, Huddersfield).*

Saturday 5th November 2022

ENGLAND 46 PAPUA NEW GUINEA 6

ENGLAND: Sam Tomkins (C); Dominic Young; Kallum Watkins; Herbie Farnworth; Tommy Makinson; Jack Welsby; George Williams; Tom Burgess; Michael McIlorum; Chris Hill; Elliott Whitehead; John Bateman; Victor Radley. Subs (all used): Morgan Knowles; Matty Lees; Mike Cooper; Mike McMeeken. 18th man (not used): Kai Pearce-Paul.
Tries: Burgess (5), Makinson (9, 18, 27, 58, 75), Young (15), Williams (21), Watkins (24); **Goals:** Makinson 5/9.
PAPUA NEW GUINEA: Alex Johnston; Rodrick Tai; Nene Macdonald; Justin Olam; Jimmy Ngutlik; Kyle Laybutt; Lachlan Lam; Wellington Albert; Edwin Ipape; Sylvester Namo; Nixon Putt; Rhyse Martin (C); Jacob Alick. Subs (all used): Watson Boas; Dan Russell; McKenzie Yei; Jeremiah Simbiken. 18th man (not used): Keven Appo.
Try: Ngutlik (70); **Goals:** Martin 1/1.
Rugby Leaguer & League Express Men of the Match:
England: Tommy Makinson; *Papua New Guinea:* Jimmy Ngutlik.
Penalty count: 4-3; **Half-time:** 38-0; **Referee:** Liam Moore;
Attendance: 23,179 *(at DW Stadium, Wigan).*

NEW ZEALAND 24 FIJI 18

NEW ZEALAND: Joseph Manu; Jordan Rapana; Peta Hiku; Charnze Nicoll-Klokstad; Ronaldo Mulitalo; Dylan Brown; Jahrome Hughes; Jesse Bromwich (C); Brandon Smith; James Fisher-Harris; Kenny Bromwich; Nelson Asofa-Solomona; Joseph Tapine. Subs (all used): Isaiah Papali'i; Kieran Foran; Briton Nikora; Isaac Liu. 18th man (not used): Scott Sorensen.
Tries: Mulitalo (27), Nikora (48), Manu (63), Rapana (80);
Goals: Rapana 4/5.
FIJI: Sunia Turuva; Vuate Karawalevu; Kevin Naiqama (C); Semi Valemei; Maika Sivo; Api Koroisau; Brandon Wakeham; Korbin Sims; Penioni Tagituimua; Tui Kamikamica; Siua Wong; Viliame Kikau; Taniela Sadrugu. Subs (all used): Ben Nakubuwai; King Vuniyayawa; Lamar Manuel-Liolevave; Henry Raiwalui. 18th man (not used): Mitieli Vulikijapani.
Tries: Sivo (12), Naiqama (19, 43); **Goals:** Wakeham 3/3.
Rugby Leaguer & League Express Men of the Match:
New Zealand: Joseph Manu; *Fiji:* Sunia Turuva.
Penalty count: 5-4; **Half-time:** 6-12; **Referee:** Gerard Sutton;
Attendance: 7,080 *(at MKM Stadium, Hull).*

Sunday 6th November 2022

TONGA 18 SAMOA 20

TONGA: Will Hopoate; Sione Katoa; Will Penisini; Moses Suli; Daniel Tupou; Isaiya Katoa; Tui Lolohea; Addin Fonua-Blake; Siliva Havili; Moeaki Fotuaika; Felise Kaufusi; Keaon Koloamatangi; Jason Taumalolo (C). Subs (all used): Sio Siua Taukeiaho; Soni Luke; David Fifita; Ben Murdoch-Masila. 18th man (not used): Talatau Amone.
Tries: Tupou (9), Taukeiaho (33), S Katoa (72); **Goals:** I Katoa 3/4.
SAMOA: Joseph Sua'ali'i; Brian To'o; Stephen Crichton; Tim Lafai; Taylan May; Jarome Luai; Anthony Milford; Royce Hunt; Junior Paulo (C); Ligi Sao; Jaydn Su'A; Oregon Kaufusi; Kelma Tuilagi. 18th man (not used): Fa'amanu Brown.
Tries: Su'A (5), Luai (18), To'o (59); **Goals:** Crichton 4/4.
Rugby Leaguer & League Express Men of the Match:
Tonga: Jason Taumalolo; *Samoa:* Junior Paulo.
Penalty count: 6-5; **Half-time:** 10-12; **Referee:** Ashley Klein;
Attendance: 12,674 *(at Halliwell Jones Stadium, Warrington).*

SEMI-FINALS

Friday 11th November 2022

AUSTRALIA 16 NEW ZEALAND 14

AUSTRALIA: James Tedesco (C); Valentine Holmes; Jack Wighton; Latrell Mitchell; Josh Addo-Carr; Cameron Munster; Nathan Cleary; Jake Trbojevic; Ben Hunt; Reagan Campbell-Gillard; Angus Crichton; Liam Martin; Isaah Yeo. Subs (all used): Harry Grant; Patrick Carrigan; Cameron Murray; Tino Fa'asuamaleaui. 18th man (not used): Daly Cherry-Evans.
Tries: Addo-Carr (16), Holmes (30), Murray (54); **Goals:** Cleary 2/3.
NEW ZEALAND: Joseph Manu; Jordan Rapana; Peta Hiku; Charnze Nicoll-Klokstad; Ronaldo Mulitalo; Dylan Brown; Jahrome Hughes; Jesse Bromwich (C); Brandon Smith; James Fisher-Harris; Isaiah Papali'i; Briton Nikora; Joseph Tapine. Subs (all used): Kieran Foran; Moses Leota; Nelson Asofa-Solomona; Isaac Liu. 18th man (not used): Kenny Bromwich.
Tries: Hughes (11), Brown (37); **Goals:** Rapana 3/3.
Rugby Leaguer & League Express Men of the Match:
Australia: Liam Martin; *New Zealand:* Joseph Tapine.
Penalty count: 3-4; **Half-time:** 10-14; **Referee:** Ashley Klein;
Attendance: 28,113 *(at Elland Road, Leeds).*

Saturday 12th November 2022

ENGLAND 26 SAMOA 27
(after golden point extra-time)

ENGLAND: Sam Tomkins (C); Dominic Young; Kallum Watkins; Herbie Farnworth; Tommy Makinson; Jack Welsby; George Williams; Tom Burgess; Michael McIlorum; Chris Hill; Elliott Whitehead; John Bateman; Victor Radley. Subs (all used): Mike McMeeken; Morgan Knowles; Luke Thompson; Mike Cooper. 18th man (not used): Kai Pearce-Paul.
Tries: Whitehead (25), Bateman (45), Farnworth (64, 78);
Goals: Makinson 5/5.
SAMOA: Joseph Sua'ali'i; Brian To'o; Stephen Crichton; Tim Lafai; Taylan May; Jarome Luai; Anthony Milford; Royce Hunt; Fa'amanu Brown; Junior Paulo (C); Ligi Sao; Jaydn Su'A; Oregon Kaufusi. Subs (all used): Chanel Harris-Tavita; Josh Papalii; Spencer Leniu; Kelma Tuilagi. 18th man (not used): Ken Sio.
Tries: Lafai (6, 57), Sao (31), Crichton (48, 73); **Goals:** Crichton 3/5;
Field goal: Crichton (83).
Sin bin: Paulo (13) - dangerous challenge on Burgess.
Rugby Leaguer & League Express Men of the Match:
England: John Bateman; *Samoa:* Jarome Luai.
Penalty count: 8-5; **Half-time:** 6-10; **Referee:** Gerard Sutton;
Attendance: 40,489 *(at Emirates Stadium, London).*

FINAL

Saturday 19th November 2022

AUSTRALIA 30 SAMOA 10

AUSTRALIA: James Tedesco (C); Valentine Holmes; Jack Wighton; Latrell Mitchell; Josh Addo-Carr; Cameron Munster; Nathan Cleary; Jake Trbojevic; Ben Hunt; Reagan Campbell-Gillard; Liam Martin; Angus Crichton; Isaah Yeo. Subs (all used): Harry Grant; Patrick Carrigan; Cameron Murray; Tino Fa'asuamaleaui. 18th man (not used): Daly Cherry-Evans.
Tries: Mitchell (14, 80), Tedesco (18, 68), Martin (30), Murray (53);
Goals: Cleary 3/5, Addo-Carr 0/1.
Sin bin: Crichton (47) - use of the elbow on Harris-Tavita.
SAMOA: Joseph Sua'ali'i; Brian To'o; Stephen Crichton; Tim Lafai; Taylan May; Jarome Luai; Anthony Milford; Royce Hunt; Chanel Harris-Tavita; Junior Paulo (C); Ligi Sao; Jaydn Su'A; Oregon Kaufusi. Subs (all used): Kelma Tuilagi; Josh Papalii; Spencer Leniu; Martin Taupau. 18th man (not used): Ken Sio.
Tries: To'o (61), Crichton (71); **Goals:** Crichton 1/2.
Rugby Leaguer & League Express Men of the Match:
Australia: James Tedesco; *Samoa:* Stephen Crichton.
Penalty count: 1-3; **Half-time:** 14-0; **Referee:** Ashley Klein;
Attendance: 67,502 *(at Old Trafford, Manchester).*

AUSTRALIA

NO.	PLAYER	CLUB	APPS	SUBS	TRIES	GOALS	FG	PTS
9	Josh Addo-Carr	Canterbury Bulldogs	5	0	12	0	0	48
12	Matt Burton	Canterbury Bulldogs	2	1	1	0	0	4
6	Reagan Campbell-Gillard	Parramatta Eels	3	1	0	0	0	0
13	Patrick Carrigan	Brisbane Broncos	1	4	0	0	0	0
2	Daly Cherry-Evans	Manly Sea Eagles	2	0	1	0	0	4
14	Nathan Cleary	Penrith Panthers	5	0	1	32	0	68
15	Lindsay Collins	Sydney Roosters	1	2	0	0	0	0
16	Reuben Cotter	North Queensland Cowboys	5	0	1	0	0	4
17	Angus Crichton	Sydney Roosters	4	1	2	0	0	8
18	Tino Fa'asuamaleaui	Gold Coast Titans	4	1	0	0	0	0
19	Campbell Graham	South Sydney Rabbitohs	5	0	5	0	0	20
20	Harry Grant	Melbourne Storm	2	3	2	0	0	8
4	Valentine Holmes	North Queensland Cowboys	5	0	1	0	0	4
3	Ben Hunt	St George Illawarra Dragons	4	1	5	1	0	22
21	Liam Martin	Penrith Panthers	5	0	3	0	0	12
8	Latrell Mitchell	South Sydney Rabbitohs	5	0	5	0	0	20
7	Cameron Munster	Melbourne Storm	5	0	5	0	0	20
11	Cameron Murray	South Sydney Rabbitohs	2	3	0	0	0	0
22	Jeremiah Nanai	North Queensland Cowboys	2	0	2	0	0	8
23	Murray Taulagi	North Queensland Cowboys	2	0	1	0	0	4
1	James Tedesco	Sydney Roosters	6	0	5	0	0	20
5	Jake Trbojevic	Manly Sea Eagles	4	1	0	0	0	0
10	Jack Wighton	Canberra Raiders	4	1	2	0	0	8
24	Isaah Yeo	Penrith Panthers	4	1	2	0	0	8

COOK ISLANDS

NO.	PLAYER	CLUB	APPS	SUBS	TRIES	GOALS	FG	PTS
14	Tevin Arona	Auckland Vulcans	0	1	0	0	0	0
15	Tinirau Arona	Wakefield Trinity	1	0	0	0	0	0
22	Geoff Daniela	St Mary's Saints	1	1	0	0	0	0
7	Johnathon Ford	Featherstone Rovers	2	0	1	3	0	10
3	Anthony Gelling	Unattached	2	0	2	0	0	8
1	Kayal Iro	Cronulla Sharks	2	0	0	0	0	0
8	Makahesi Makatoa	Parramatta Eels	1	2	1	0	0	4
4	Esan Marsters	Gold Coast Titans	3	0	4	1	0	18
5	Steven Marsters	Thirroul Butchers	3	0	1	0	0	4
20	Davvy Moale	South Sydney Rabbitohs	0	3	0	0	0	0
10	Tepai Moeroa	Melbourne Storm	3	0	5	0	0	20
24	Dylan Napa	Catalans Dragons	1	0	1	0	0	4
17	Rua Ngatikaura	Wests Tigers	2	0	2	0	0	8
18	Moses Noovao-McGreal	Norths Devils	3	0	0	0	0	0
19	Pride Petterson-Robati	New Zealand Warriors	1	2	0	0	0	0
11	Dominique Peyroux	Toulouse Olympique	3	0	0	0	0	0
12	Brendan Piakura	Brisbane Broncos	0	2	0	0	0	0
23	Reuben Porter	Tweed Heads Seagulls	1	1	0	0	0	0
16	Reubenn Rennie	Newtown Jets	0	2	0	0	0	0
21	Vincent Rennie	Newtown Jets	1	1	1	0	0	4
6	Brad Takairangi	Hull Kingston Rovers	2	0	1	0	0	4
9	Aaron Teroi	Central Queensland Capras	3	0	0	0	0	0
13	Zane Tetevano	Leeds Rhinos	3	0	0	0	0	0
2	Paul Ulberg	London Broncos	3	0	1	0	0	4

ENGLAND

NO.	PLAYER	CLUB	APPS	SUBS	TRIES	GOALS	FG	PTS
19	Andy Ackers	Salford Red Devils	1	2	2	0	0	8
22	Joe Batchelor	St Helens	1	0	0	0	0	0
12	John Bateman	Wigan Warriors	4	0	1	0	0	4
8	Tom Burgess	South Sydney Rabbitohs	0	4	0	0	0	0
17	Mike Cooper	Wigan Warriors	0	3	0	0	0	0
4	Herbie Farnworth	Brisbane Broncos	4	0	3	0	0	12
21	Ryan Hall	Hull Kingston Rovers	4	0	4	0	0	16
18	Chris Hill	Huddersfield Giants	0	4	0	0	0	0
15	Morgan Knowles	St Helens	4	0	3	0	0	12
16	Matty Lees	St Helens	0	4	0	0	0	0
9	Tommy Makinson	St Helens	4	0	7	20	0	68
20	Mike McMeeken	Catalans Dragons	1	3	0	0	0	0
13	Mikolaj Oledzki	Leeds Rhinos	0	4	0	0	0	0
24	Kai Pearce-Paul	Wigan Warriors	0	1	0	0	0	0
23	Victor Radley	Sydney Roosters	5	0	0	0	0	0
2	Marc Sneyd	Salford Red Devils	2	0	1	20	0	44
10	Luke Thompson	Catalans Dragons	4	0	1	0	0	4
21	Sam Tomkins	Catalans Dragons	4	0	0	0	0	0
3	Kallum Watkins	Salford Red Devils	4	0	2	0	0	8
6	Jack Welsby	St Helens	4	0	2	0	0	8
11	Elliott Whitehead	Canberra Raiders	4	0	4	0	0	16
7	George Williams	Warrington Wolves	5	0	3	0	0	12
14	Dominic Young	Newcastle Knights	5	0	9	0	0	36

FIJI

NO.	PLAYER	CLUB	APPS	SUBS	TRIES	GOALS	FG	PTS
23	Jowasa Drodrolagi	Carcassonne	0	1	0	0	0	0
13	Tui Kamikamica	Melbourne Storm	3	0	0	0	0	0
24	Vuate Karawalevu	Sydney Roosters	3	0	1	0	0	4
9	Viliame Kikau	Penrith Panthers	4	0	2	0	0	8
4	Api Koroisau	Penrith Panthers	4	0	3	0	0	12
16	Isaac Lumelume	Canterbury Bulldogs	1	3	0	0	0	0
18	Lamar Manuel-Liolevave	Tweed Heads Seagulls	0	1	0	0	0	0
6	Netane Masima	Western Suburbs Magpies	0	1	0	0	0	0
3	Sitiveni Moceidreke	London Broncos	4	0	2	0	0	8
20	Kevin Naiqama	Sydney Roosters	4	0	3	0	0	12
10	Ben Nakubuwai	Leigh Centurions	0	3	0	0	0	0
8	Joseph Ratuvakacerelvalu	Wentworthville Magpies	0	2	0	0	0	0
11	Taniela Sadrugu	Redcliffe Dolphins	2	2	2	0	0	8
14	Korbin Sims	North Queensland Cowboys	3	1	0	0	0	0
2	Maika Sivo	Parramatta Eels	4	0	4	0	0	16
15	Penioni Tagitiurmua	Canterbury Bulldogs	0	2	0	0	0	0
1	Tevita Toloi	Canterbury Bulldogs	4	0	2	0	0	8
19	Sunia Turuva	Newcastle Knights	4	0	1	0	0	4
5	Semi Valemei	Penrith Panthers	4	0	1	0	0	4
17	Mitieli Vulikijapani	Canberra Raiders	1	3	1	0	0	4
7	King Vuniyayawa	Salford Red Devils	3	1	0	15	0	30
22	Brandon Wakeham	Canterbury Bulldogs	4	0	1	0	0	4
	Siua Wong	Sydney Roosters	4	0	0	0	0	0

153

FRANCE

NO.	PLAYER	CLUB	APPS	SUBS	TRIES	GOALS	FG	PTS
10	Lambert Belmas	Toulouse Olympique	2	0	0	0	0	0
9	Afrix Da Costa	Catalans Dragons	3	0	1	0	0	4
8	Jordan Dezaria	Catalans Dragons	2	0	0	0	0	0
1	Morgan Escare	Salford Red Devils	2	0	1	0	0	4
13	Benjamin Garcia	Catalans Dragons	3	0	0	0	0	0
7	Tony Gigot	Toulouse Olympique	3	0	1	0	0	4
17	Mickael Goudemand	Catalans Dragons	1	2	0	0	0	0
24	Louis Jouffret	Halifax Panthers	3	0	2	0	0	8
11	Benjamin Jullien	Catalans Dragons	3	0	0	0	0	0
4	Matthieu Laguerre	Catalans Dragons	3	0	0	0	0	0
3	Samisoni Langi	Catalans Dragons	3	0	0	0	0	0
19	Corentin Le Cam	Catalans Dragons	0	2	0	0	0	0
22	Paul Marcon	Toulouse Olympique	3	0	1	0	0	4
18	Anthony Marion	Toulouse Olympique	0	3	2	10	0	28
6	Arthur Mourgue	Toulouse Olympique	3	0	1	0	0	4
14	Eloi Pelissier	Albi	0	3	0	0	0	0
21	Maxime Puech	Catalans Dragons	0	1	1	0	0	4
2	Arthur Romano	Catalans Dragons	3	0	0	0	0	0
23	Cesar Rouge	Catalans Dragons	2	0	0	0	0	0
15	Justin Sangare	Toulouse Olympique	0	3	0	0	0	0
12	Paul Seguier	Catalans Dragons	3	0	0	0	0	0
16	Gadwin Springer	Featherstone Rovers	1	2	0	0	0	0
20	Maxime Stefani	Toulouse Olympique	0	0	0	0	0	0
5	Fouad Yaha	Catalans Dragons	2	0	1	0	0	4

IRELAND

NO.	PLAYER	CLUB	APPS	SUBS	TRIES	GOALS	FG	PTS
11	James Bentley	Leeds Rhinos	3	0	1	0	0	4
2	Keanan Brand	Leigh Centurions	2	0	0	0	0	0
8	Liam Byrne	Wigan Warriors	3	0	0	0	0	0
3	Ed Chamberlain	Leigh Centurions	3	0	2	3	0	14
9	Josh Cook	Canterbury Bulldogs	1	2	0	0	0	0
12	Frankie Hatton	Hull Kingston Rovers	3	2	1	0	0	4
22	James Hasson	South Sydney Rabbitohs	1	2	0	0	0	0
10	Jaimin Jolliffe	Gold Coast Titans	2	0	0	0	0	0
6	Luke Keary	Sydney Roosters	3	0	1	1	0	6
7	Joe Keyes	Halifax Panthers	3	0	0	3	0	6
13	George King	Hull Kingston Rovers	3	0	1	0	0	4
4	Toby King	Huddersfield Giants	3	0	0	0	0	0
24	Ben Mathiou	Featherstone Rovers	3	0	1	0	0	4
14	James McDonnell	Wigan Warriors	1	0	0	0	0	0
21	Ronan Michael	York City Knights	3	0	1	0	0	4
19	Robbie Mulhern	Warrington Wolves	0	3	0	0	0	0
1	Richie Myler	Leeds Rhinos	3	0	0	0	0	0
17	Dan Norman	St Helens	0	1	0	0	0	0
16	Brendan O'Hagan	York City Knights	2	1	1	0	0	4
18	Henry O'Kane	Wests Tigers	0	1	0	0	0	0
15	Harry Rushton	Canberra Raiders	0	3	0	0	0	0
5	Innes Senior	Huddersfield Giants	3	0	1	0	0	4
20	Louis Senior	Huddersfield Giants	3	0	6	0	0	24
23	Michael Ward	Batley Bulldogs	0	0	0	0	0	0

GREECE

NO.	PLAYER	CLUB	APPS	SUBS	TRIES	GOALS	FG	PTS
10	Stefanos Bastas	Midlands Hurricanes	0	1	0	0	0	0
23	Nikolaos Bosmos	Rhodes Knights	0	1	0	0	0	0
3	Terry Constantinou	Sunbury Tigers	0	1	0	0	0	0
18	Aris Dardamanis	Aris Eagles	0	2	0	0	0	0
12	Nick Flocas	Ipswich Jets	3	0	1	0	0	4
15	Myles Gal	Central Queensland Capras	0	2	0	0	0	0
6	Lachlan Illas	South Sydney Rabbitohs	3	0	0	0	0	0
14	Jake Kambos	Western Suburbs Magpies	2	0	1	0	0	4
21	Konstantinos Katsidonis	Rhodes Knights	0	1	0	0	0	0
24	Greg Koutsimporgiorgos	Aris Eagles	0	0	0	0	0	0
13	Billy Magoulias	Newtown Jets	3	0	0	0	0	0
9	Peter Mamouzelos	South Sydney Rabbitohs	3	0	0	0	0	0
7	Jordan Meads	Beerwah Bulldogs	2	0	2	0	0	8
5	John Mitsias	Western Suburbs Magpies	3	0	0	0	0	0
4	Nick Mougios	South Sydney Rabbitohs	3	0	1	0	0	4
20	Ionnis Nake	Attica Rhinos	0	3	0	0	0	0
17	Theodoros Nianiakas	Woolston Rovers	0	0	0	0	0	0
1	Chaise Robinson	South Sydney Rabbitohs	2	0	1	0	0	4
22	Ioannis Rousoglou	Aris Eagles	2	0	0	0	0	0
16	Sebastian Sell	Mittagong Lions	0	0	0	0	0	0
19	Liam Sue-Tin	Unattached	3	0	0	0	0	0
2	Siteni Taukamo	Cronulla Sharks	3	0	2	0	0	8
8	Rob Tuliatu	London Broncos	2	0	0	0	0	0
25	Adam Vranos	London Broncos	2	0	0	0	0	0
11	Mitchell Zampetides	Western Suburbs Magpies	2	0	0	0	0	0

ITALY

NO.	PLAYER	CLUB	APPS	SUBS	TRIES	GOALS	FG	PTS
24	Giordano Arena	Catania Bulls	3	0	0	0	0	0
3	Daniel Atkinson	Sunshine Coast Falcons	3	0	0	0	0	0
22	Simone Boscolo	Salon	3	0	0	0	0	0
13	Nathan Brown	South Sydney Rabbitohs	3	0	0	0	0	0
6	Jack Campagnolo	Saint-Gaudens Bears	0	2	0	0	0	0
16	Gioele Celerino	Parramatta Eels	3	0	0	5	0	10
20	Jack Colovatti	Blacktown Workers Sea Eagles	0	3	0	0	0	0
19	Luke Hodge	Barrow Raiders	0	2	0	0	0	0
10	Anton Iaria	Whitehaven	2	0	0	0	0	0
11	Ryan King	Swinton Lions	2	0	0	0	0	0
2	Richard Lepori	Sunshine Coast Falcons	2	1	4	0	0	16
5	Jake Maizen	Parramatta Eels	2	1	0	0	0	0
15	Luca Moretti	Newtown Jets	3	0	0	0	0	0
4	Ethan Natoli	Lignano Sharks	3	0	0	0	0	0
23	Ippolito Occhialini	London Broncos	0	3	1	0	0	4
17	Ronny Palumbo	London Broncos	0	0	1	0	0	4
9	Dean Parata	Cronulla Sharks	3	0	0	0	0	0
18	Kyle Pickering	Sunshine Coast Falcons	3	0	1	0	0	4
1	Luke Polselli	Central Queensland Capras	3	0	0	0	0	0
7	Radean Robinson	Keighley Cougars	3	0	0	0	0	0
12	Brenden Santi	Penrith Panthers	2	0	0	0	0	0
8	Alec Susino	Wentworthville Magpies	2	0	0	0	0	0
21	Nicholas Tilburg	Blacktown Workers Sea Eagles	0	3	0	0	0	0
14	Joey Tramontana							

JAMAICA

NO.	PLAYER	CLUB	APPS	SUBS	TRIES	GOALS	FG	PTS
2	Mo Agoro	Keighley Cougars	3	0	1	0	0	4
15	Jordan Andrade	Unattached	1	2	0	0	0	0
22	Chevaughn Bailey	Duhaney Park Red Sharks	2	2	0	0	0	0
3	Joe Brown	Workington Town	2	1	2	0	0	8
9	Jy-mel Coleman	Unattached	1	1	1	0	0	4
12	Joel Farrell	Sheffield Eagles	2	1	0	0	0	0
13	Ashton Golding	Huddersfield Giants	2	0	0	0	0	0
19	Bradley Ho	Keighley Cougars	0	2	3	0	0	12
20	Greg Johnson	Batley Bulldogs	2	0	0	0	0	0
17	Aaron Jones-Bishop	Cornwall	3	0	1	0	0	4
1	Ben Jones-Bishop	Sheffield Eagles	3	0	0	0	0	0
10	Michael Lawrence	Huddersfield Giants	3	0	0	0	0	0
18	Alevia McDonald	London Skolars	1	2	1	0	0	4
8	Khamis McKain	Duhaney Park Red Sharks	2	1	0	0	0	0
4	Jacob Ogden	York City Knights	3	0	1	0	0	4
21	Ross Peltier	Hunslet	0	3	0	0	0	0
7	Kieran Rush	Rochdale Hornets	3	0	0	0	0	0
24	Andrew Simpson	Duhaney Park Red Sharks	1	0	0	0	0	0
14	Marvin Thompson	Duhaney Park Red Sharks	0	2	0	0	0	0
16	Keenen Tomlinson	Dewsbury Rams	0	2	0	0	0	0
23	Renaldo Wade	Duhaney Park Red Sharks	0	1	0	0	0	0
11	AJ Wallace	Bradford Bulls	2	1	0	0	0	0
6	James Woodburn-Hall	Halifax Panthers	3	0	0	0	2	2
5	Alex Young	Workington Town	2	0	0	0	0	0

LEBANON

NO.	PLAYER	CLUB	APPS	SUBS	TRIES	GOALS	FG	PTS
17	Jalal Bazzaz	Western Suburbs Red Devils	0	4	0	0	0	0
6	Adam Doueihi	Wests Tigers	3	0	1	4	0	12
24	Toufic El Haji	American University of Beirut	3	0	0	0	0	0
10	Hanna El-Nachar	Penrith Panthers	0	1	0	0	0	0
23	Elie El-Zakhem	Parramatta Eels	0	2	0	0	0	0
8	Robin Hachache	Tripoli	4	0	2	0	0	8
15	Kayne Kalache	Newtown Jets	2	0	0	0	0	0
1	Andrew Kazzi	Western Suburbs Magpies	3	0	0	0	0	0
14	Jacob Kiraz	Canterbury Bulldogs	3	1	6	0	0	24
3	Anthony Layoun	St Marys Saints	1	2	1	0	0	4
2	Bilaal Maarbani	Blacktown Workers Sea Eagles	4	0	1	0	0	4
9	Josh Mansour	South Sydney Rabbitohs	4	0	5	0	0	20
21	Joshua Maree	Wentworthville Magpies	0	1	0	0	0	0
22	Tony Maroun	Ryde-Eastwood Hawks	0	1	0	0	0	0
5	Abbas Miski	Wigan Warriors	4	0	3	0	0	12
4	Brad Morkos	Canberra Raiders	4	0	4	0	0	16
7	Mitchell Moses	Parramatta Eels	4	0	1	15	0	30
20	Jaxson Rahme	South Sydney Rabbitohs	0	3	1	0	0	4
19	Khalil Rahme	Mount Pritchard Mounties	4	0	1	0	0	4
18	Khaled Rajab	Canterbury Bulldogs	4	0	0	0	0	0
16	Reece Robinson	Unattached	4	0	2	0	0	8
13	James Roumanos	Manly Sea Eagles	4	0	1	0	0	4
9	Michael Tannous	Wests Tigers	1	2	2	0	0	8
12	Charbel Tasipale	Newtown Jets	4	0	4	0	0	16

NEW ZEALAND

NO.	PLAYER	CLUB	APPS	SUBS	TRIES	GOALS	FG	PTS
2	Nelson Asofa-Solomona	Melbourne Storm	2	3	1	0	0	4
16	Jesse Bromwich	Melbourne Storm	4	0	2	0	0	8
12	Kenny Bromwich	Melbourne Storm	4	0	2	0	0	8
6	Dylan Brown	Parramatta Eels	4	0	1	0	0	4
10	James Fisher-Harris	Penrith Panthers	5	0	0	0	0	0
14	Kieran Foran	Manly Sea Eagles	3	0	1	0	0	4
7	Peta Hiku	North Queensland Cowboys	5	0	3	0	0	12
4	Jahrome Hughes	Melbourne Storm	4	0	4	0	0	16
24	Sebastian Kris	Canberra Raiders	3	0	3	0	0	12
15	Moses Leota	Penrith Panthers	1	3	0	0	0	0
20	Isaac Liu	Gold Coast Titans	3	1	0	0	0	0
1	Joseph Manu	Sydney Roosters	5	0	3	0	0	12
22	Jeremy Marshall-King	Canterbury Bulldogs	0	3	2	0	0	8
21	Ronaldo Mulitalo	Cronulla Sharks	4	0	2	0	0	8
2	Chanze Nicoll-Klokstad	Canberra Raiders	3	0	1	0	0	4
17	Briton Nikora	Cronulla Sharks	3	2	1	0	0	4
3	Marata Niukore	Parramatta Eels	3	1	0	0	0	0
11	Isaiah Papali'i	Parramatta Eels	5	0	2	0	0	8
5	Jordan Rapana	Canberra Raiders	4	0	4	14	0	44
8	Brandon Smith	Melbourne Storm	4	1	2	0	0	8
23	Scott Sorensen	Penrith Panthers	5	0	1	0	0	4
13	Joseph Tapine	Canberra Raiders	4	1	0	0	0	0
18	Jared Waerea-Hargreaves	Sydney Roosters	4	0	0	0	0	0
19	Dallin Watene-Zelezniak	New Zealand Warriors	1	0	0	0	0	0

PAPUA NEW GUINEA

NO.	PLAYER	CLUB	APPS	SUBS	TRIES	GOALS	FG	PTS
8	Wellington Albert	London Broncos	4	0	0	0	0	0
13	Jacob Alick	Gold Coast Titans	4	0	2	0	0	8
18	Keven Appo	PNG Hunters	4	0	1	0	0	4
23	Watson Boas	Doncaster	0	3	0	0	0	0
5	Xavier Coates	Melbourne Storm	4	0	9	0	0	36
9	Edene Gebbie	Townsville Blackhawks	4	0	1	0	0	4
24	Edwin Ipape	Leigh Centurions	4	0	2	0	0	8
7	Zev John	Central Queensland Capras	0	2	0	0	0	0
6	Alex Johnston	South Sydney Rabbitohs	4	0	2	0	0	8
3	Lachlan Lam	Leigh Centurions	4	0	3	0	0	12
20	Kyle Laybutt	Townsville Blackhawks	4	0	2	14	0	36
12	Nene Macdonald	Leigh Centurions	4	0	2	0	0	8
10	Rhyse Martin	Leeds Rhinos	4	0	3	0	0	12
19	Sylvester Namo	PNG Hunters	3	1	0	0	0	0
4	Jimmy Ngutlik	Western Suburbs Magpies	4	0	3	0	0	12
11	Justin Olam	Melbourne Storm	4	0	1	0	0	4
15	Nixon Putt	Central Queensland Capras	4	0	2	0	0	8
22	Dan Russell	Brisbane Tigers	0	2	0	0	0	0
2	Jeremiah Simbiken	Redcliffe Dolphins	4	0	2	0	0	8
21	Rodrick Tai	PNG Hunters	0	3	0	0	0	0
14	Sherwin Tanabi	PNG Hunters	4	0	0	0	0	0
1	Wesser Tenza	PNG Hunters	4	0	3	0	0	12
17	Emmanuel Waine	PNG Hunters	1	0	0	0	0	0
16	McKenzie Yei	Central Queensland Capras	0	3	0	0	0	0

SAMOA

NO.	PLAYER	CLUB	APPS	SUBS	TRIES	GOALS	FG	PTS
13	Josh Aloiai	Manly Sea Eagles	2	0	0	0	0	0
21	Fa'amanu Brown	Wests Tigers	1	0	1	0	0	4
4	Stephen Crichton	Penrith Panthers	6	0	4	28	1	73
19	Mathew Feagai	St George Illawarra Dragons	1	0	1	0	0	4
24	Braden Hamlin-Uele	Cronulla Sharks	2	2	0	0	0	0
20	Chanel Harris-Tavita	New Zealand Warriors	2	3	3	0	0	12
15	Royce Hunt	Cronulla Sharks	4	1	0	0	0	0
23	Oregon Kaufusi	Parramatta Eels	4	4	0	0	0	0
25	Tim Lafai	Salford Red Devils	5	0	6	0	0	24
27	Connelly Lemuelu	North Queensland Cowboys	0	4	0	0	0	0
16	Spencer Leniu	Penrith Panthers	0	4	0	0	0	0
9	Danny Levi	Huddersfield Giants	6	0	2	0	0	8
6	Jarome Luai	Penrith Panthers	4	0	4	0	0	16
14	Taylan May	Penrith Panthers	4	0	0	0	0	0
7	Tyrone May	Catalans Dragons	5	0	2	0	0	8
8	Anthony Milford	Newcastle Knights	0	1	0	0	0	0
10	Josh Papalii	Canberra Raiders	4	0	1	0	0	4
11	Junior Paulo	Parramatta Eels	6	0	1	0	0	4
26	Ligi Sao	Hull FC	5	0	0	0	0	0
2	Ken Sio	Salford Red Devils	6	0	5	0	0	20
12	Jaydn Su'A	St George Illawarra Dragons	6	0	0	0	0	0
1	Joseph Sua'ali'i	Sydney Roosters	6	0	1	0	0	4
18	Hamiso Tabuai-Fidow	North Queensland Cowboys	1	0	0	0	0	0
3	Izack Tago	Penrith Panthers	6	0	1	0	0	4
17	Martin Taupau	Manly Sea Eagles	6	5	0	0	0	0
5	Brian To'o	Penrith Panthers	6	0	5	0	0	20
22	Kelma Tuilagi	Wests Tigers	0	4	0	0	0	0

TONGA

NO.	PLAYER	CLUB	APPS	SUBS	TRIES	GOALS	FG	PTS
6	Talatau Amone	St George Illawarra Dragons	1	1	1	0	0	4
18	David Fifita	Gold Coast Titans	0	4	1	0	0	4
8	Addin Fonua-Blake	New Zealand Warriors	4	0	1	0	0	4
17	Moeaki Fotuaika	Gold Coast Titans	3	1	0	0	0	0
9	Siliva Havili	Cronulla Sharks	1	1	0	0	0	0
1	Will Hopoate	St Helens	1	0	0	0	0	0
23	Konrad Hurrell	South Sydney Rabbitohs	1	0	0	0	0	0
24	Isaiya Katoa	St Helens	1	0	2	21	0	50
5	Sione Katoa	Penrith Panthers	4	0	1	0	0	4
11	Felise Kaufusi	Melbourne Storm	4	0	2	0	0	8
12	Keaon Koloamatangi	South Sydney Rabbitohs	4	1	0	0	0	0
20	Tolutau Koula	Manly Sea Eagles	1	0	2	0	0	8
7	Tui Lolohea	Huddersfield Giants	4	2	0	1	0	14
14	Soni Luke	Penrith Panthers	2	2	0	0	0	0
21	Ben Murdoch-Masila	New Zealand Warriors	0	3	4	0	0	16
22	Tesi Niu	Brisbane Broncos	1	0	0	0	0	0
15	Haumole Olakau'atu	Manly Sea Eagles	3	0	5	0	0	0
4	Will Penisini	Parramatta Eels	1	0	5	0	0	20
19	Moses Suli	St George Illawarra Dragons	1	0	0	0	0	0
3	Siosifa Talakai	Cronulla Sharks	0	2	0	1	0	2
16	Tevita Tatola	South Sydney Rabbitohs	1	2	2	0	0	0
10	Sio Siua Taukeiaho	Sydney Roosters	2	0	2	0	0	4
13	Jason Taumalolo	North Queensland Cowboys	2	0	6	0	0	8
2	Daniel Tupou	Sydney Roosters	4	0	6	0	0	24

SCOTLAND

NO.	PLAYER	CLUB	APPS	SUBS	TRIES	GOALS	FG	PTS
11	Euan Aitken	New Zealand Warriors	2	0	0	0	0	0
15	Luke Bain	Parramatta Eels	1	2	0	0	0	0
8	Logan Bayliss-Brow	Brisbane Broncos	3	1	0	0	0	0
13	James Bell	St Helens	3	0	0	0	0	0
7	Ryan Brierley	Salford Red Devils	3	0	0	0	0	0
4	Kieran Buchanan	Batley Bulldogs	0	1	0	0	0	0
1	Lewis Clarke	Edinburgh Eagles	3	0	0	0	0	0
20	Davey Dixon	Dewsbury Rams	0	1	1	0	0	4
17	Charlie Emslie	Barrow Raiders	0	3	0	0	0	0
24	Dale Ferguson	Dewsbury Rams	3	0	0	0	0	0
19	Calum Gahan	London Broncos	0	2	0	0	0	0
16	Guy Graham	Whitehaven	3	2	0	0	0	0
6	Bailey Hayward	Canterbury Bulldogs	2	0	1	0	0	4
3	Ben Hellewell	Featherstone Rovers	2	0	0	0	0	0
9	Liam Hood	Wakefield Trinity	2	2	0	0	0	0
12	Kane Linnett	Hull Kingston Rovers	3	0	1	0	0	4
23	Bayley Liu	Sheffield Eagles	2	2	0	0	0	0
10	Sam Luckley	Salford Red Devils	3	0	0	0	0	0
2	Matty Russell	Toulouse Olympique	3	1	0	0	0	0
14	Kyle Schneider	Mackay Cutters	1	2	0	0	0	0
18	Jack Teanby	York City Knights	0	3	0	0	0	0
21	Shane Toal	Barrow Raiders	1	0	0	0	0	0
22	Alex Walker	London Broncos	3	0	2	0	0	8
5	Lachlan Walmsley	Halifax Panthers	3	0	0	0	0	0

WALES

NO.	PLAYER	CLUB	APPS	SUBS	TRIES	GOALS	FG	PTS
1	Caleb Aekins	Leigh Centurions	3	0	0	0	0	0
17	Bailey Antrobus	York City Knights	3	0	0	0	0	0
24	Gavin Bennion	Rochdale Hornets	3	0	0	0	0	0
16	Joe Burke	West Wales Raiders	1	2	0	0	0	0
12	Chester Butler	Bradford Bulls	2	0	0	0	0	0
19	Mike Butt	Swinton Lions	3	0	1	0	0	4
18	Connor Davies	Dewsbury Rams	0	3	0	0	0	0
15	Curtis Davies	Whitehaven	3	0	0	0	0	0
13	Ben Evans	Bradford Bulls	2	0	0	0	0	0
22	Kyle Evans	Wakefield Trinity	0	1	1	0	0	4
3	Rhys Evans	Bradford Bulls	3	0	0	0	0	0
4	Will Evans	Whitehaven	2	0	0	0	0	0
10	Dan Fleming	Featherstone Rovers	2	1	0	0	0	0
9	Matty Fozard	Widnes Vikings	3	0	1	3	0	10
14	Dalton Grant	London Broncos	1	0	0	0	0	0
21	Tom Hopkins	Barrow Raiders	2	1	0	0	0	0
6	Elliot Kear	Bradford Bulls	3	0	0	0	0	0
11	Rhodri Lloyd	Swinton Lions	3	0	1	0	0	4
23	James Olds	Valley Diehards	2	2	0	0	0	0
14	Ollie Olds	Valley Diehards	3	0	1	0	0	4
7	Josh Ralph	Mount Pritchard Mounties	3	0	0	0	0	0
20	Luis Roberts	Widnes Vikings	0	0	0	0	0	0
25	Luke Thomas	Warrington Wolves	3	0	0	0	0	0
8	Anthony Walker	Bradford Bulls	3	0	0	0	0	0
2	Rhys Williams	Salford Red Devils	3	0	0	0	0	0

WORLD CUP 2021
Women

World Cup 2021 - Statistical review

GROUP A

Tuesday 1st November 2022

ENGLAND 72 BRAZIL 4

ENGLAND: Fran Goldthorp; Caitlin Beevers; Tara Jane Stanley; Amy Hardcastle; Leah Burke; Georgia Roche; Courtney Winfield-Hill; Shona Hoyle; Tara Jones; Olivia Wood; Vicky Molyneux; Emily Rudge (C); Jodie Cunningham. Subs (all used): Zoe Harris; Hollie Dodd; Vicky Whitfield; Grace Field. 18th woman (not used): Keara Bennett.
Tries: Beevers (2), Stanley (6, 40), Winfield-Hill (16, 22, 73), Field (28), Hardcastle (37, 49, 67), Goldthorp (44), Jones (64), Burke (70), Wood (80); **Goals:** Stanley 8/14.
BRAZIL: Natalia Momberg; Edna Santini; Leticia Medeiros; Adriana Felix; Tati Fernandes; Giovanna Moura; Maria Graf (C); Franciny Amaral; Patricia Bodeman; Franciele Barros; Patricia Oliveria; Amanda Welter; Barbara Leal. Subs (all used): Giovanna Barth; Paula Casemiro; Brena Prioste; Ana Loschi de Quadros. 18th woman (not used): Pamella Silva.
Try: Momberg (59); **Goals:** Oliveria 0/1.
Rugby Leaguer & League Express Women of the Match:
England: Courtney Winfield-Hill; *Brazil:* Patricia Oliveria.
Penalty count: 4-2; **Half-time:** 34-0; **Referee:** Rochelle Tamarua.

PAPUA NEW GUINEA 34 CANADA 12

PAPUA NEW GUINEA: Martha Molowia; Lisa-Marie Alu; Shellie Long; Belinda Gwasamun; Anika Butler; Sera Koroi; Lila Malabag; Elsie Albert (C); Therese Aiton; Gloria Kaupa; Emily Veivers; Essay Banu; Ua Ravu. Subs (all used): Jessikah Reeves; Bertshiba Awoi; Michelle John; Talitha Kunjil. 18th woman (not used): Tara Moxon.
Tries: Long (25), Molowia (39, 41), Ravu (47), Banu (63), Gwasamun (76), Butler (78); **Goals:** Veivers 2/5, Malabag 1/2.
CANADA: Karina Gauto; Lauren Mueller; Ferris Sandboe; Petra Woods; Dani Franada; Laura Mariu; Sabrina McDaid; Kristy Sargent; Alanna Fittes; Liz Steele; Gabrielle Hindley (C); Maddy Aberg; Megan Pakulis. Subs (all used): Natalie Tam; Sarah Maguire; Ada Jane Okonkwo; Jade Menin. 18th woman (not used): Brittany Douglas.
Tries: Woods (30), Pakulis (60); **Goals:** Franada 2/2.
Rugby Leaguer & League Express Women of the Match:
Papua New Guinea: Martha Molowia; *Canada:* Petra Woods.
Penalty count: 2-6; **Half-time:** 8-6; **Referee:** Geoffrey Plumes.

Attendance: 8,621 *(at Headingley, Leeds).*

Saturday 5th November 2022

ENGLAND 54 CANADA 4

ENGLAND: Fran Goldthorp; Georgia Wilson; Tara Jane Stanley; Carrie Roberts; Leah Burke; Georgia Roche; Courtney Winfield-Hill; Shona Hoyle; Keara Bennett; Paige Travis; Hollie Dodd; Emily Rudge (C); Vicky Molyneux. Subs (all used): Vicky Whitfield; Beth Stott; Zoe Hornby; Dannielle Anderson. 18th woman (not used): Olivia Wood.
Tries: Burke (1, 68), Dodd (17, 26), Wilson (20), Goldthorp (32), Roche (37), Stanley (41, 44, 60), Roberts (52); **Goals:** Stanley 5/11.
CANADA: Karina Gauto; Brittany Jones; Maddy Aberg; Petra Woods; Lauren Mueller; Laura Mariu; Sabrina McDaid; Kristy Sargent; Natalie Tam; Ada Jane Okonkwo; Gabrielle Hindley (C); Rachel Chaboter; Megan Pakulis. Subs (all used): Alix Evans; Liz Steele; Brittany Douglas; Zoey Siciliano. 18th woman (not used): Natasha Naismith.
Try: Woods (47); **Goals:** Aberg 0/1.
Rugby Leaguer & League Express Women of the Match:
England: Tara Jane Stanley; *Canada:* Sabrina McDaid.
Penalty count: 3-2; **Half-time:** 30-0; **Referee:** Paki Parkinson;
Attendance: 23,179 *(at DW Stadium, Wigan)*
(double header with England v Papua New Guinea Men's Quarter Final).

PAPUA NEW GUINEA 70 BRAZIL 0

PAPUA NEW GUINEA: Martha Molowia; Tara Moxon; Shae-Yvonne De La Cruz; Belinda Gwasamun; Anika Butler; Sera Koroi; Lila Malabag; Elsie Albert (C); Shirley Joe; Bertshiba Awoi; Essay Banu; Carol Humeu; Jessikah Reeves. Subs (all used): Therese Aiton; Gloria Kaupa; Ua Ravu; Veronica Waula. 18th woman (not used): Talitha Kunjil.
Tries: Gwasamun (4, 27, 52, 61), Moxon (12, 55), Butler (16), Albert (43), Reeves (46), Koroi (49), Joe (66), Molowia (70), Malabag (73), Aiton (76);
Goals: Malabag 7/14.
BRAZIL: Adriana Felix; Edna Santini; Leticia Medeiros; Amanda Welter; Natalia Momberg; Giovanna Moura (C); Bryanca Santa Rita; Franciny Amaral; Patricia Bodeman; Paula Casemiro; Patricia Oliveria; Ana Loschi de Quadros; Brena Prioste. Subs (all used): Giovanna Barth; Franciele Barros; Pamella Silva; Ellen Trindade. 18th woman (not used): Daniele Soares.
Rugby Leaguer & League Express Women of the Match:
Papua New Guinea: Belinda Gwasamun; *Brazil:* Patricia Bodeman.
Penalty count: 5-3; **Half-time:** 18-0; **Referee:** Benjamin Casty;
Attendance: 7,080 *(at MKM Stadium, Hull)*
(double header with New Zealand v Fiji Men's Quarter Final).

Wednesday 9th November 2022

CANADA 22 BRAZIL 16

CANADA: Petra Woods; Ferris Sandboe; Dani Franada; Nina Bui; Lauren Mueller; Laura Mariu; Sabrina McDaid; Ada Jane Okonkwo; Alanna Fittes; Liz Steele; Gabrielle Hindley (C); Maddy Aberg; Megan Pakulis. Subs (all used): Natasha Naismith; Kristy Sargent; Sarah Maguire; Jade Menin. 18th woman (not used): Rachel Chaboter.
Tries: Sandboe (25), Maguire (30), Pakulis (59), Fittes (79);
Goals: Franada 3/4.
BRAZIL: Natalia Momberg; Edna Santini; Leticia Medeiros; Amanda Welter; Daniele Soares; Giovanna Moura; Maria Graf (C); Franciny Amaral; Patricia Bodeman; Paula Casemiro; Patricia Oliveria; Ana Loschi de Quadros; Brena Prioste. Subs (all used): Tati Fernandes; Barbara Leal; Franciele Barros; Natalia Jonck. 18th woman (not used): Pamella Silva.
Tries: Amaral (7), Santini (44), Bodeman (73); **Goals:** Graf 2/3.
Rugby Leaguer & League Express Women of the Match:
Canada: Megan Pakulis; *Brazil:* Patricia Bodeman.
Penalty count: 4-4; **Half-time:** 10-6; **Referee:** Michael Smaill.

ENGLAND 42 PAPUA NEW GUINEA 4

ENGLAND: Fran Goldthorp; Caitlin Beevers; Tara Jane Stanley; Amy Hardcastle; Leah Burke; Georgia Roche; Courtney Winfield-Hill; Shona Hoyle; Tara Jones; Olivia Wood; Hollie Dodd; Emily Rudge (C); Jodie Cunningham. Subs (all used): Vicky Whitfield; Keara Bennett; Paige Travis; Grace Field. 18th woman (not used): Zoe Harris.
Tries: Burke (25, 45, 64), Hardcastle (27, 78), Stanley (37), Whitfield (52), Beevers (75); **Goals:** Stanley 5/8.
PAPUA NEW GUINEA: Martha Molowia; Lisa-Marie Alu; Shellie Long; Belinda Gwasamun; Anika Butler; Sera Koroi; Lila Malabag; Elsie Albert (C); Shirley Joe; Gloria Kaupa; Emily Veivers; Essay Banu; Jessikah Reeves. Subs (all used): Ua Ravu; Carol Humeu; Michelle John; Shae-Yvonne De La Cruz. 18th woman (not used): Talitha Kunjil.
Try: Molowia (4); **Goals:** Veivers 0/1.
Sin bin: Humeu (63) - high tackle.
Rugby Leaguer & League Express Women of the Match:
England: Vicky Whitfield; *Papua New Guinea:* Belinda Gwasamun.
Penalty count: 8-1; **Half-time:** 14-4; **Referee:** Benjamin Casty.

Attendance: 5,471 *(at Headingley, Leeds).*

GROUP A - FINAL STANDINGS

	P	W	D	L	F	A	D	Pts
England	3	3	0	0	168	12	156	6
Papua New Guinea	3	2	0	1	108	54	54	4
Canada	3	1	0	2	38	104	-66	2
Brazil	3	0	0	3	20	164	-144	0

World Cup 2021 - Statistical review

GROUP B

Wednesday 2nd November 2022

NEW ZEALAND 46 FRANCE 0

NEW ZEALAND: Apii Nicholls; Katelyn Vaha'akolo; Shanice Parker; Page McGregor; Madison Bartlett; Autumn-Rain Stephens-Daly; Raecene McGregor; Mya Hill-Moana; Krystal Rota (C); Annetta-Claudia Nu'uausala; Roxy Murdoch-Masila; Amber Hall; Georgia Hale. Subs (all used): Nita Maynard; Charlotte Scanlan; Otesa Pule; Brianna Clark. 18th woman (not used): Crystal Tamarua.
Tries: Bartlett (24), Nicholls (29), Hall (33), Murdoch-Masila (39, 76), Vaha'akolo (42, 56), P McGregor (50), Parker (78);
Goals: Clark 4/7, Nicholls 1/2.
FRANCE: Manon Samarra; Margot Canal; Laureane Biville; Zoe Pastre-Courtine; Cristina Song-Puche; Elisa Ciria; Alice Varela (C); Cyndia Mansard; Fanny Ramos; Gaelle Alverhne; Elisa Akpa; Perrine Monsarrat; Leila Bessahli. Subs (all used): Elodie Pacull; Mailys Borak; Tallis Kuresa; Dorine Samarra. 18th woman (not used): Anais Fourcroy.
Rugby Leaguer & League Express Women of the Match:
New Zealand: Roxy Murdoch-Masila; *France:* Laureane Biville.
Penalty count: 4-2; **Half-time:** 20-0; **Referee:** Ben Thaler.

AUSTRALIA 74 COOK ISLANDS 0

AUSTRALIA: Sammy Bremner (C); Julia Robinson; Shenae Ciesiolka; Isabelle Kelly; Evania Pelite; Tarryn Aiken; Ali Brigginshaw; Shannon Mato; Lauren Brown; Caitlan Johnston; Kezie Apps; Olivia Kernick; Simaima Taufa. Subs (all used): Taliah Fuimaono; Holli Wheeler; Kennedy Cherrington; Yasmin Clydsdale. 18th woman (not used): Emma Tonegato.
Tries: Pelite (3, 25, 70), Johnston (9), Aiken (14, 78), Bremner (21, 44, 60, 63), Ciesiolka (30), Robinson (33, 57), Fuimaono (54);
Goals: Brown 6/9, Brigginshaw 0/2, Wheeler 3/3.
COOK ISLANDS: Mackenzie Wiki; Beniamina Koitau; Kerehitina Matua; Kiana Takairangi; Daimzel Rongokea; Kimiora Breayley-Nati (C); Chantay Kiria-Ratu; Karol-Ann Tanevesi; Tetuanui Dean; April Ngatupuna; Lavinia Kitai; Alekermay Tuaana; Anekka Stephens. Subs (all used): Jazmon Tupou-Witchman; Toka Natua; Charlize Tumu-Makara; Tehinnah-Leal Tatuava. 18th woman (not used): Mireka Dean.
Rugby Leaguer & League Express Women of the Match:
Australia: Sammy Bremner; *Cook Islands:* Kerehitina Matua.
Penalty count: 2-1; **Half-time:** 36-0; **Referee:** Michael Smaill.

Attendance: 3,091 *(at LNER Community Stadium, York).*

Sunday 6th November 2022

NEW ZEALAND 34 COOK ISLANDS 4

NEW ZEALAND: Shanice Parker; Mele Hufanga; Hailee-Jay Ormond-Maunsell; Page McGregor; Madison Bartlett; Laishon Albert-Jones; Raecene McGregor; Mya Hill-Moana; Krystal Rota (C); Annetta-Claudia Nu'uausala; Otesa Pule; Amber Hall; Charlotte Scanlan. Subs (all used): Nita Maynard; Christyl Stowers; Crystal Tamarua; Brianna Clark. 18th woman (not used): Karli Hansen.
Tries: R McGregor (10, 55), Rota (15), Hall (31), Hufanga (59, 72), Nu'uausala (80); **Goals:** Albert-Jones 0/4, Clark 3/3.
COOK ISLANDS: Alekermay Tuaana; Tehinnah-Leal Tatuava; Charlize Tumu-Makara; Daimzel Rongokea; Mackenzie Wiki; Kimiora Breayley-Nati (C); Kerehitina Matua; Karol-Ann Tanevesi; Annekka Stephens; April Ngatupuna; Lavinia Kitai; Jazmon Tupou-Witchman; Elianna Walton. Subs (all used): Kennedy Harrison-Vahua; Moniqca Mo'ale; Maleyna Hunapo; Terehia Matua. 18th woman (not used): Mireka Dean.
Try: Wiki (67); **Goals:** K Matua 0/1.
Sin bin: Hunapo (64) - professional foul.
Rugby Leaguer & League Express Women of the Match:
New Zealand: Raecene McGregor; *Cook Islands:* April Ngatupuna.
Penalty count: 4-4; **Half-time:** 14-0; **Referee:** Michael Smaill.

AUSTRALIA 92 FRANCE 0

AUSTRALIA: Emma Tonegato; Julia Robinson; Jessica Sergis; Jaime Chapman; Shenae Ciesiolka; Taliah Fuimaono; Tarryn Aiken; Tallisha Harden (C); Lauren Brown; Kennedy Cherrington; Yasmin Clydsdale; Shaylee Bent; Keilee Joseph. Subs (all used): Shannon Mato; Holli Wheeler; Olivia Kernick; Evania Pelite. 18th woman (not used): Ali Brigginshaw.
Tries: Ciesiolka (2), Chapman (5, 11, 62), Sergis (9, 16, 36, 41), Tonegato (20), Harden (26), Pelite (34, 78), Robinson (45, 66, 73), Kernick (54); **Goals:** Brown 10/13, Aiken 1/2, Wheeler 1/2.
FRANCE: Manon Samarra; Margot Canal; Anais Fourcroy; Laureane Biville; Chloe Guillerot; Elisa Ciria; Alice Varela (C); Cyndia Mansard; Fanny Ramos; Jeanne Bernard; Elisa Akpa; Perrine Monsarrat; Dorine Samarra. Subs (all used): Lise Michel; Elodie Pacull; Mailys Borak; Tallis Kuresa. 18th woman (not used): Cristina Song-Puche.
Rugby Leaguer & League Express Women of the Match:
Australia: Jessica Sergis; *France:* Laureane Biville.
Penalty count: 6-1; **Half-time:** 58-0; **Referee:** Rochelle Tamarua.

Attendance: 3,006 *(at LNER Community Stadium, York).*

Thursday 10th November 2022

FRANCE 18 COOK ISLANDS 26

FRANCE: Chloe Guillerot; Cristina Song-Puche; Melanie Bianchini; Laureane Biville; Anaelle Meunier; Elisa Ciria; Alice Varela (C); Gaelle Alverhne; Fanny Ramos; Cyndia Mansard; Elisa Akpa; Perrine Monsarrat; Dorine Samarra. Subs (all used): Jeanne Bernard; Mailys Borak; Zoe Pastre-Courtine; Manon Samarra. 18th woman (not used): Anais Fourcroy.
Tries: Bianchini (25), Ciria (48, 76), Song-Puche (65); **Goals:** Ciria 1/4.
COOK ISLANDS: Alekermay Tuaana; Mackenzie Wiki; Jazmon Tupou-Witchman; Charlize Tumu-Makara; Daimzel Rongokea; Kerehitina Matua; Anekka Stephens; Karol-Ann Tanevesi; Tetuanui Dean; April Ngatupuna; Moniqca Mo'ale; Lavinia Kitai; Elianna Walton (C). Subs (all used): Kennedy Harrison-Vahua; Mireka Dean; Erikana Dean; Terehia Matua. 18th woman (not used): Beniamina Koitau.
Tries: Ngatupuna (17), T Matua (27), Wiki (41), Tuaana (60), T Dean (72); **Goals:** K Matua 3/5.
Rugby Leaguer & League Express Women of the Match:
France: Elisa Ciria; *Cook Islands:* Kerehitina Matua.
Penalty count: 7-6; **Half-time:** 4-12; **Referee:** Ben Thaler.

AUSTRALIA 10 NEW ZEALAND 8

AUSTRALIA: Sammy Bremner; Julia Robinson; Jessica Surgis; Isabelle Kelly; Jaime Chapman; Tarryn Aiken; Ali Brigginshaw (C); Shannon Mato; Keeley Davis; Caitlan Johnston; Kezie Apps; Yasmin Clydsdale; Simaima Taufa. Subs (all used): Kennedy Cherrington; Shaylee Bent; Lauren Brown; Emma Tonegato. 18th woman (not used): Keilee Joseph.
Tries: Aiken (20), Robinson (62); **Goals:** Brigginshaw 1/1, Brown 0/1.
NEW ZEALAND: Apii Nicholls; Autumn-Rain Stephens-Daly; Mele Hufanga; Page McGregor; Katelyn Vaha'akolo; Abigail Roache; Raecene McGregor; Brianna Clark; Krystal Rota (C); Annetta-Claudia Nu'uausala; Roxy Murdoch-Masila; Amber Hall; Georgia Hale. Subs (all used): Nita Maynard; Mya Hill-Moana; Otesa Pule; Christyl Stowers. 18th woman (not used): Karli Hansen.
Tries: Nicholls (30), Stephens-Daly (55); **Goals:** Clark 0/2.
Rugby Leaguer & League Express Women of the Match:
Australia: Tarryn Aiken; *New Zealand:* Amber Hall.
Penalty count: 4-7; **Half-time:** 6-4; **Referee:** Todd Smith.

Attendance: 3,370 *(at LNER Community Stadium, York).*

GROUP B - FINAL STANDINGS

	P	W	D	L	F	A	D	Pts
Australia	3	3	0	0	176	8	168	6
New Zealand	3	2	0	1	88	14	74	4
Cook Islands	3	1	0	2	30	126	-96	2
France	3	0	0	3	18	164	-146	0

World Cup 2021 - Statistical review

SEMI-FINALS

Monday 14th November 2022

AUSTRALIA 82 PAPUA NEW GUINEA 0

AUSTRALIA: Emma Tonegato; Evania Pelite; Isabelle Kelly; Jaime Chapman; Shenae Ciesiolka; Taliah Fuimaono; Lauren Brown; Holli Wheeler; Keeley Davis; Tallisha Harden; Shaylee Bent; Olivia Kernick; Ali Brigginshaw (C). Subs (all used): Jessica Sergis; Yasmin Clydsdale; Sammy Bremner; Keilee Joseph. 18th woman (not used): Tarryn Aiken.
Tries: Davis (9), Kelly (15, 17, 37), Bent (19), Pelite (25), Ciesiolka (27, 45), Kernick (34), Sergis (42), Harden (49), Tonegato (52, 57, 75), Chapman (66); **Goals:** Brown 9/13, Brigginshaw 2/2.
PAPUA NEW GUINEA: Shae-Yvonne De La Cruz; Anika Butler; Shellie Long; Belinda Gwasamun; Martha Molowia; Sera Koroi; Lila Malabag; Elsie Albert (C); Therese Aiton; Gloria Kaupa; Bertshiba Awoi; Essay Banu; Jessikah Reeves. Subs (all used): Talitha Kunjil; Emily Veivers; Michelle John; Carol Humeu. 18th woman (not used): Shirley Joe.
Rugby Leaguer & League Express Women of the Match:
Australia: Emma Tonegato; *Papua New Guinea:* Elsie Albert.
Penalty count: 3-3; **Half-time:** 40-0; **Referee:** Belinda Sharpe.

ENGLAND 6 NEW ZEALAND 20

ENGLAND: Fran Goldthorp; Caitlin Beevers; Tara Jane Stanley; Amy Hardcastle; Leah Burke; Georgia Roche; Courtney Winfield-Hill; Shona Hoyle; Tara Jones; Olivia Wood; Vicky Molyneux; Emily Rudge (C); Jodie Cunningham. Subs (all used): Keara Bennett; Hollie Dodd; Grace Field; Vicky Whitfield. 18th woman (not used): Paige Travis.
Try: Goldthorp (5); **Goals:** Stanley 1/1.
NEW ZEALAND: Apii Nicholls; Katelyn Vaha'akolo; Mele Hufanga; Page McGregor; Madison Bartlett; Abigail Roache; Raecene McGregor; Brianna Clark; Krystal Rota (C); Annetta-Claudia Nu'uausala; Roxy Murdoch-Masila; Amber Hall; Georgia Hale. Subs (all used): Nita Maynard; Mya Hill-Moana; Otesa Pule; Charlotte Scanlan. 18th woman (not used): Christyl Stowers.
Tries: Hufanga (16), R McGregor (29), Pule (47), Clark (52);
Goals: Clark 0/1, Nicholls 2/3.
Rugby Leaguer & League Express Women of the Match:
England: Fran Goldthorp; *New Zealand:* Mele Hufanga.
Penalty count: 3-3; **Half-time:** 6-8; **Referee:** Kasey Badger.

Attendance: 7,139 *(at LNER Community Stadium, York).*

FINAL

Saturday 19th November 2022

AUSTRALIA 54 NEW ZEALAND 4

AUSTRALIA: Sammy Bremner; Julia Robinson; Jessica Sergis; Isabelle Kelly; Evania Pelite; Tarryn Aiken; Ali Brigginshaw; Shannon Mato; Keeley Davis; Kennedy Cherrington; Yasmin Clydsdale; Kezie Apps (C); Simaima Taufa. Subs (all used): Lauren Brown; Emma Tonegato; Shaylee Bent; Caitlan Johnston. 18th woman (not used): Holli Wheeler.
Tries: Sergis (5, 52), Kelly (15, 36), Robinson (27), Tonegato (49), Aiken (57), Cherrington (67, 70), Pelite (73); **Goals:** Brigginshaw 2/5, Brown 5/5.
NEW ZEALAND: Apii Nicholls; Autumn-Rain Stephens-Daly; Mele Hufanga; Page McGregor; Madison Bartlett; Abigail Roache; Raecene McGregor; Brianna Clark; Krystal Rota (C); Annetta-Claudia Nu'uausala; Roxy Murdoch-Masila; Amber Hall; Georgia Hale. Subs (all used): Nita Maynard; Mya Hill-Moana; Otesa Pule; Christyl Stowers. 18th woman (not used): Charlotte Scanlan.
Try: Bartlett (64); **Goals:** R McGregor 0/1.
Rugby Leaguer & League Express Women of the Match:
Australia: Ali Brigginshaw; *New Zealand:* Raecene McGregor.
Penalty count: 1-4; **Half-time:** 20-0; **Referee:** Belinda Sharpe;
Attendance: 67,502 *(at Old Trafford, Manchester)*
(double header with Australia v Samoa Men's Final).

AUSTRALIA

NO.	PLAYER	CLUB	APPS	SUBS	TRIES	GOALS	FG	PTS
12	Tarryn Aiken	Brisbane Broncos	4	0	5	1	0	22
1	Kezie Apps	St George Illawarra Dragons	3	2	1	0	0	4
13	Shaylee Bent	St George Illawarra Dragons	2	2	0	0	0	0
2	Sammy Bremner	Sydney Roosters	2	1	4	0	0	16
3	Ali Brigginshaw	Brisbane Broncos	4	0	4	0	0	16
14	Lauren Brown	Gold Coast Titans	3	2	2	5	0	18
15	Jaime Chapman	Brisbane Broncos	4	0	4	0	0	16
16	Kennedy Cherrington	Parramatta Eels	0	3	0	0	0	0
17	Shenae Ciesiolka	Brisbane Broncos	3	0	4	0	0	16
18	Yasmin Clydsdale	Newcastle Knights	3	0	0	0	0	0
8	Keeley Davis	St George Illawarra Dragons	3	2	0	0	0	0
19	Taliah Fuimaono	Brisbane Broncos	2	1	1	0	0	4
7	Tallisha Harden	St George Illawarra Dragons	2	0	2	0	0	8
20	Caitlan Johnston	Newcastle Knights	2	1	1	0	0	4
5	Isabelle Kelly	Sydney Roosters	4	0	5	0	0	20
21	Kellee Joseph	Sydney Roosters	1	1	0	0	0	0
22	Olivia Kernick	Sydney Roosters	4	0	2	0	0	8
23	Shannon Mato	Gold Coast Titans	3	1	0	0	0	0
24	Evania Pelite	Gold Coast Titans	3	0	7	0	0	28
10	Julia Robinson	Brisbane Broncos	4	0	7	0	0	28
11	Jessica Sergis	Sydney Roosters	3	1	1	0	0	4
4	Simaima Taufa	Parramatta Eels	3	2	0	0	0	0
6	Emma Tonegato	St George Illawarra Dragons	2	2	5	0	0	20
9	Holli Wheeler	St George Illawarra Dragons	1	2	2	0	0	8

BRAZIL

NO.	PLAYER	CLUB	APPS	SUBS	TRIES	GOALS	FG	PTS
8	Franciny Amaral	Melina	3	0	1	0	0	4
15	Franciele Barros	Melina	1	2	0	0	0	0
14	Giovanna Barth	Maringa Hawks	0	2	0	0	0	0
9	Patricia Bodeman	Melina	3	0	0	0	0	0
10	Paula Casemiro	Vitoria Rhinos	3	0	1	0	0	4
1	Adriana Felix	Vitoria Rhinos	2	0	0	0	0	0
2	Tati Fernandes	Vitoria Rhinos	2	1	0	0	0	0
7	Maria Graf	Urutau	1	1	0	0	0	0
23	Natalia Jonck	Melina	2	0	2	0	0	0
13	Barbara Leal	Vitoria Rhinos	0	1	0	0	0	0
17	Ana Loschi de Quadros	Vitoria Rhinos	3	2	1	0	0	4
3	Leticia Medeiros	Melina	3	0	0	0	0	0
18	Natalia Momberg	Vitoria Rhinos	3	0	1	0	0	4
6	Giovanna Moura	Maringa Hawks	3	0	0	0	0	0
11	Patricia Oliveria	Melina	2	1	0	0	0	0
16	Brena Prioste	Urutau	2	1	0	0	0	0
5	Suzana Rodrigues	Vitoria Rhinos	0	1	0	0	0	0
19	Bryanca Santa Rita	Melina	3	0	0	0	0	0
22	Edna Santini	Melina	1	1	1	0	0	4
20	Pamella Silva	Vitoria Rhinos	3	0	0	0	0	0
4	Daniele Soares	Maringa Hawks	2	1	0	0	0	0
21	Ellen Trindade	Melina	0	1	0	0	0	0
12	Amanda Welter	Maringa Hawks	3	0	0	0	0	0

CANADA

NO.	PLAYER	CLUB	APPS	SUBS	TRIES	GOALS	FG	PTS
14	Maddy Aberg	British Columbia	3	0	0	0	0	0
15	Nina Bui	Ontario	1	0	0	0	0	0
16	Rachel Chaboter	British Columbia	0	1	0	0	0	0
17	Brittany Douglas	Ontario	0	1	0	0	0	0
18	Alix Evans	Alberta	2	0	0	0	0	0
6	Alanna Fittes	Alberta	2	0	1	0	0	4
1	Dani Franada	Alberta	3	0	0	0	0	0
4	Karina Gauto	Alberta	2	0	0	0	0	0
11	Gabrielle Hindley	British Columbia	3	0	0	0	0	0
5	Brittany Jones	Alberta	1	0	0	0	0	0
12	Sarah Maguire	Alberta	3	0	0	0	0	0
10	Laura Mariu	Richmond Rovers	3	0	0	0	0	0
19	Sabrina McDaid	Alberta	3	0	1	0	0	4
20	Jade Menin	Ontario	3	0	0	0	0	0
20	Lauren Mueller	London Broncos	2	1	0	0	0	0
22	Natasha Naismith	Ontario	2	0	0	0	0	0
13	Ada Jane Okonkwo	British Columbia	2	0	2	0	0	8
3	Megan Pakulis	Ontario	3	0	2	0	0	8
4	Ferris Sandboe	Alberta	3	0	1	0	0	4
8	Kristy Sargent	Alberta	2	1	0	0	0	0
2	Zoey Siciliano	Ontario	3	0	0	0	0	0
9	Liz Steele	Ontario	2	1	0	0	0	0
7	Natalie Tam	Ontario	1	0	0	0	0	0
3	Petra Woods	Ontario	3	0	2	0	0	8

COOK ISLANDS

NO.	PLAYER	CLUB	APPS	SUBS	TRIES	GOALS	FG	PTS
6	Kimiora Brearley-Nati	Gold Coast Titans	2	0	0	0	0	0
6	Erikana Dean	Oakley Bears	2	0	0	0	0	0
24	Mireka Dean	Toowoomba Clydesdales	0	1	0	0	0	0
20	Tetuanui Dean	Campbelltown Collegians	0	1	0	0	0	0
9	Kennedy Harrison-Vahua	Wynnum Manly Seagulls	3	0	1	0	0	4
12	Maleyna Hunapo	Truganina Rabbitohs	0	2	0	0	0	0
22	Chantay Kiria-Ratu	Tweed Heads Seagulls	0	1	0	0	0	0
7	Lavinia Kitai	Brisbane Tigers	3	0	2	0	0	8
17	Beniamina Koitau	Unattached	3	0	1	0	0	4
2	Kerehitina Matua	Manurewa Marlins	0	3	0	0	0	0
23	Terehia Matua	South Sydney Rabbitohs	3	0	0	0	0	0
15	Monica Mo'ale	Waikato	3	0	0	0	0	0
10	Toka Natua	Gold Coast Titans	3	0	1	0	0	4
21	April Ngatupuna	Otago	3	0	0	0	0	0
5	Daimzel Rongokea	Joondalup Giants	2	1	0	0	0	0
8	Aneika Stephens	Newcastle Knights	3	0	0	0	0	0
19	Kiana Takairangi	Mount Pritchard Mounties	3	0	1	0	0	4
16	Karol-Ann Taneyesi	Titikaveka Bulldogs	1	2	0	0	0	0
4	Tehinnah-Leal Tatuava	Souths Union	3	0	0	0	0	0
18	Alekermay Tuaana	Richmond Rovers	2	1	0	0	0	0
14	Charlize Turnu-Makara	Wynnum Manly Seagulls	2	0	0	0	0	0
13	Jazmon Tupou-Witchman	Mount Pritchard Mounties	0	1	0	0	0	0
11	Eliianna Walton	Manukau Counties	3	0	2	0	0	8
1	Mackenzie Wiki							

161

ENGLAND

NO.	PLAYER	CLUB	APPS	SUBS	TRIES	GOALS	FG	PTS
10	Dannielle Anderson	Leeds Rhinos	3	1	0	0	0	0
2	Caitlin Beevers	Leeds Rhinos	3	0	2	0	0	8
21	Keara Bennett	Leeds Rhinos	3	2	0	0	0	0
5	Leah Burke	St Helens	4	0	6	0	0	24
13	Jodie Cunningham	St Helens	3	0	0	0	0	0
12	Hollie Dodd	York City Knights	2	2	2	0	0	8
11	Grace Field	York City Knights	0	3	1	0	0	4
22	Fran Goldthorp	Leeds Rhinos	4	0	3	0	0	12
8	Amy Hardcastle	St Helens	4	0	5	0	0	20
24	Zoe Harris	St Helens	0	1	0	0	0	0
22	Zoe Hornby	Leeds Rhinos	4	0	0	0	0	0
17	Shona Hoyle	St Helens	4	0	0	0	0	0
9	Tara Jones	St Helens	3	0	1	0	0	4
14	Vicky Molyneux	Wigan Warriors	3	0	0	0	0	0
23	Carrie Roberts	St Helens	1	0	1	0	0	4
6	Georgia Roche	Leeds Rhinos	4	0	1	0	0	4
12	Emily Rudge	St Helens	4	0	0	0	0	0
1	Tara Jane Stanley	York City Knights	4	0	6	19	0	62
16	Beth Stott	St Helens	4	0	1	0	0	4
19	Paige Travis	St Helens	1	0	0	0	0	0
15	Vicky Whitfield	St Helens	0	4	1	0	0	4
20	Georgia Wilson	Wigan Warriors	4	0	3	0	0	12
7	Courtney Winfield-Hill	Leeds Rhinos	4	0	0	0	0	0
18	Olivia Wood	York City Knights	3	0	1	0	0	4

FRANCE

NO.	PLAYER	CLUB	APPS	SUBS	TRIES	GOALS	FG	PTS
1	Elisa Akpa	Saint-Esteve Catalan	2	0	0	0	0	0
10	Gaelle Alverhne	Lescure Arthes	2	0	0	0	0	0
8	Jeanne Bernard	Lescure Arthes	1	0	0	0	0	0
13	Leila Bessahli	Saint-Esteve Catalan	1	0	1	0	0	4
3	Melanie Bianchini	Saint-Esteve Catalan	1	0	0	0	0	0
4	Laureane Biville	Lescure Arthes	3	0	0	0	0	0
17	Mailys Borak	Saint-Esteve Catalan	2	0	0	0	0	0
23	Margot Canal	Saint-Esteve Catalan	1	3	0	0	0	0
6	Elisa Ciria	Lescure Arthes	2	0	2	1	0	10
20	Anais Fourcroy	Saint-Esteve Catalan	1	0	0	0	0	0
15	Chloe Guillerot	Lescure Arthes	2	0	0	0	0	0
11	Tallis Kuresa	Begles Bordeaux	2	2	0	0	0	0
9	Cyndia Mansard	Toulouse Ovalie	3	0	1	0	0	4
-	Sarah Menaa	Saint-Esteve Catalan	1	0	0	0	0	0
18	Anaelle Meunier	Begles Bordeaux	1	0	0	0	0	0
24	Lise Michel	Ayguesvives	0	1	0	0	0	0
12	Perrine Monsarrat	Lescure Arthes	3	0	1	0	0	4
16	Elodie Pacull	Saint-Esteve Catalan	2	0	0	0	0	0
19	Zoe Pastre-Courtine	Saint-Esteve Catalan	1	1	1	0	0	4
14	Fanny Ramos	Saint-Esteve Catalan	3	0	0	0	0	0
21	Dorine Samarra	Lescure Arthes	2	1	0	0	0	0
5	Manon Samarra	Lescure Arthes	2	0	1	0	0	4
2	Cristina Song-Puche	Saint-Esteve Catalan	2	0	3	0	0	12
-	Louisa Tooman	Lescure Arthes	0	0	1	0	0	4
7	Alice Varela	Toulouse Ovalie	3	0	0	0	0	0

NEW ZEALAND

NO.	PLAYER	CLUB	APPS	SUBS	TRIES	GOALS	FG	PTS
6	Laishon Albert-Jones	Point Chevalier Pirates	4	1	2	0	0	8
5	Madison Bartlett	Gold Coast Titans	5	0	2	0	0	8
23	Brianna Clark	Brisbane Broncos	3	2	1	7	0	18
13	Georgia Hale	Gold Coast Titans	4	0	0	0	0	0
12	Amber Hall	Brisbane Broncos	5	0	2	0	0	8
22	Karli Hansen	Tweed Heads Seagulls	2	3	2	0	0	8
8	Mya Hill-Moana	Sydney Roosters	2	3	0	0	0	0
24	Mele Hufanga	Ponsonby Ponies	4	0	3	0	0	12
14	Nita Maynard	Brisbane Broncos	5	0	1	0	0	4
4	Page McGregor	St George Illawarra Dragons	5	0	0	0	0	0
7	Raecene McGregor	Sydney Roosters	5	0	3	0	0	12
11	Roxy Murdoch-Masila	Gold Coast Titans	4	0	2	0	0	8
1	Apii Nicholls	Gold Coast Titans	5	0	3	1	0	14
10	Annetta-Claudia Nu'uausala	Brisbane Broncos	1	4	0	0	0	0
19	Hallee-Jay Ormond-Maunsell	Newcastle Knights	2	2	1	0	0	4
21	Shanice Parker	Sydney Roosters	1	0	1	0	0	4
18	Otesa Pule	Richmond Rovers	1	4	0	0	0	0
15	Abigail Roache	Manurewa Marlins	3	0	0	0	0	0
9	Krystal Rota	Point Chevalier Pirates	5	0	1	0	0	4
16	Charlotte Scanlan	Newcastle Knights	1	2	0	0	0	0
3	Autumn-Rain Stephens-Daly	Manurewa Marlins	4	0	1	0	0	4
17	Christyl Stowers	Brisbane Broncos	3	1	0	0	0	0
20	Crystal Tamarua	Point Chevalier Pirates	0	3	0	0	0	0
2	Katelyn Vaha'akolo	Manurewa Marlins	3	0	2	0	0	8
-	Kararaina Wira-Kohu	Manurewa Marlins	0	0	0	0	0	0

PAPUA NEW GUINEA

NO.	PLAYER	CLUB	APPS	SUBS	TRIES	GOALS	FG	PTS
9	Therese Aiton	South Sydney Rabbitohs	2	1	1	0	0	4
8	Elsie Albert	St George Illawarra Dragons	2	0	0	0	0	0
23	Lisa-Marie Alu	PNG Highlands Confederate	2	0	0	0	0	0
15	Bertshiba Awoi	PNG Southern Confederate	4	0	0	0	0	0
12	Essay Banu	Wynnum Manly Seagulls	1	0	1	0	0	4
2	Anika Butler	Newcastle Knights	4	0	0	0	0	0
5	Shae-Yvonne De La Cruz	Souths Logan Magpies	3	0	2	0	0	8
3	Belinda Gwasamun	PNG Highlands Confederate	4	0	5	0	0	20
21	Carol Humeu	PNG Southern Confederate	1	2	0	0	0	0
22	Shirley Joe	PNG Southern Confederate	2	0	1	0	0	4
16	Michelle John	PNG Southern Confederate	3	0	0	0	0	0
-	Elizabeth Kapa	PNG Southern Confederate	0	3	1	0	0	4
9	Roswita Kapo	PNG Highlands Confederate	3	1	0	0	0	0
10	Gloria Kaupa	PNG Southern Confederate	3	0	1	0	0	4
6	Sera Koroi	Souths Logan Magpies	0	1	0	0	0	0
19	Talitha Kunjil	PNG Highlands Confederate	4	0	0	0	0	0
-	Joanne Lagona	PNG Southern Confederate	3	0	1	0	0	4
4	Shellie Long	Brisbane Tigers	3	0	0	0	0	0
7	Lila Malabag	PNG Southern Confederate	4	0	1	8	0	20
17	Martha Molowia	PNG Southern Confederate	2	1	4	0	0	16
1	Tara Moxon	Leeds Rhinos	1	0	2	0	0	8
14	Ua Ravu	Riverina Bulls	2	1	1	0	0	4
13	Jessikah Reeves	Souths Logan Magpies	3	2	1	0	0	4
11	Emily Veivers	Brisbane Tigers	2	0	0	2	0	4
18	Veronica Waula	PNG Southern Confederate	0	1	0	0	0	0

WORLD CUP 2021
Wheelchair

World Cup 2021 - Statistical review

GROUP A

Thursday 3rd November 2022

SPAIN 55 IRELAND 32

SPAIN: Joel Lacombe; Raphael Monedero; Yannick Martin (C); Theo Gonzalez; David Berty. Subs (all used): Eric Perez; David Raymond; Jonathan Palomo; Wilfrid Seron; Pascal Ambrosino.
Tries: Martin (4, 61), Lacombe (7), Berty (9, 26, 44), Gonzalez (23, 67), Monedero (58); **Goals:** Gonzalez 8/8, Seron 1/1; **Field goal:** Gonzalez (70).
IRELAND: Toby Burton-Carter; Peter Johnston (C); Rick Rodgers; Phil Roberts; Tom Martin. Subs (all used): Paddy Forbes; Oran Spain; Kenneth Maloney; Stephen Campbell; James McCarthy.
Tries: Roberts (2), Johnston (30, 47, 49, 77), McCarthy (65);
Goals: Johnston 4/6.
Rugby Leaguer & League Express Players of the Match:
Spain: Theo Gonzalez; *Ireland:* Peter Johnston.
Penalty count: 7-10; **Half-time:** 30-10; **Referee:** Laurent Abrial.

ENGLAND 38 AUSTRALIA 8

ENGLAND: Rob Hawkins; Joe Coyd; Seb Bechara; Lewis King; Tom Halliwell (C). Subs: Nathan Collins; Jack Brown; Adam Rigby (not used); Declan Roberts (not used); Wayne Boardman (not used).
Tries: Coyd (19, 22), Brown (25, 35), Collins (32, 71), King (46);
Goals: Hawkins 1/3, Collins 4/5.
AUSTRALIA: Peter Arbuckle; Cory Cannane; Brad Grove (C); Diab Karim; Zac Schumacher. Subs (all used): Craig Cannane; James Hill; Liam Luff; Bayley McKenna; Adam Tannock.
Try: Karim (8); **Goals:** Karim 1/1, McKenna 1/1.
Rugby Leaguer & League Express Players of the Match:
England: Jack Brown; *Australia:* Bayley McKenna.
Penalty count: 6-10; **Half-time:** 26-6; **Referee:** Ollie Cruickshank.

Attendance: 3,033 *(at Copper Box Arena, London).*

Sunday 6th November 2022

ENGLAND 104 SPAIN 12

ENGLAND: Lewis King; Jack Brown; Tom Halliwell (C); Wayne Boardman; James Simpson. Subs (all used): Nathan Collins; Rob Hawkins; Joe Coyd; Adam Rigby; Declan Roberts.
Tries: Brown (1, 5), Simpson (12), Boardman (14, 32), Halliwell (21), Hawkins (30, 36, 38, 70, 76), Roberts (41, 46, 73), King (49), Coyd (56, 61), Rigby (66); **Goals:** Boardman 3/5, Collins 7/7, Roberts 6/6.
SPAIN: Joel Lacombe; Raphael Monedero; Yannick Martin (C); Theo Gonzalez; David Berty. Subs: Eric Perez (not used); David Raymond; Jonathan Palomo; Wilfrid Seron; Pascal Ambrosino (not used).
Tries: Gonzalez (2), Monedero (8); **Goals:** Gonzalez 2/3.
Rugby Leaguer & League Express Players of the Match:
England: Rob Hawkins; *Spain:* Yannick Martin.
Penalty count: 3-2; **Half-time:** 50-10; **Referee:** Kim Abel.

AUSTRALIA 76 IRELAND 18

AUSTRALIA: Peter Arbuckle; Brad Grove (C); Diab Karim; Bayley McKenna; Adam Tannock. Subs (all used): Craig Cannane; Zac Schumacher; James Hill; Liam Luff; Shaun Harre.
Tries: Tannock (6), Karim (8, 71), McKenna (15, 36, 68), Grove (27, 35, 56), Arbuckle (38), Hill (44), Luff (59, 61); **Goals:** McKenna 10/10, Karim 2/3.
IRELAND: Toby Burton-Carter; Peter Johnston (C); Phil Roberts; Tom Martin; James McCarthy. Subs: Rick Rodgers; Paddy Forbes; Oran Spain (not used); Kenneth Maloney; Scott Robertson.
Tries: Roberts (19), McCarthy (21, 65); **Goals:** Johnston 3/3.
Rugby Leaguer & League Express Players of the Match:
Australia: Bayley McKenna; *Ireland:* Tom Martin.
Penalty count: 3-3; **Half-time:** 42-12; **Referee:** Matthew Ball.

Attendance: 3,268 *(at Copper Box Arena, London).*

Wednesday 9th November 2022

AUSTRALIA 52 SPAIN 32

AUSTRALIA: Peter Arbuckle; Brad Grove (C); Adam Tannock; Bayley McKenna; Diab Karim. Subs (all used): Liam Luff; James Hill; Cory Cannane; Zac Schumacher; Craig Cannane.
Tries: Arbuckle (4), Karim (7, 17), Hill (27, 31, 33, 46), Cory Cannane (60), Grove (70); **Goals:** McKenna 3/4, Karim 3/6, Craig Cannane 2/2.
SPAIN: Joel Lacombe; Raphael Monedero; Yannick Martin (C); Theo Gonzalez; David Berty. Subs: Eric Perez (not used); David Raymond; Jonathan Palomo; Wilfrid Seron; Pascal Ambrosino (not used).
Tries: Gonzalez (14, 43), Monedero (23, 75), Lacombe (48), Martin (52);
Goals: Gonzalez 3/5, Seron 1/1.
Rugby Leaguer & League Express Players of the Match:
Australia: Diab Karim; *Spain:* Theo Gonzalez.
Penalty count: 14-7; **Half-time:** 32-10; **Referee:** David Butler.

ENGLAND 121 IRELAND 0

ENGLAND: Joe Coyd; Seb Bechara; Lewis King; Tom Halliwell (C); James Simpson. Subs (all used): Nathan Collins; Jack Brown; Adam Rigby; Declan Roberts; Wayne Boardman.
Tries: Bechara (2, 14), Coyd (6, 17, 27, 78), Halliwell (8, 23), Simpson (12, 19, 76, 80), Brown (31, 38, 47), Collins (34, 55, 60), King (63), Rigby (65, 71); **Goals:** Coyd 4/7, Collins 8/8, Roberts 6/6;
Field goal: Roberts (80).
IRELAND: Toby Burton-Carter; Tom Martin; Phil Roberts; Peter Johnston (C); James McCarthy. Subs: Rick Rodgers; Paddy Forbes (not used); Stephen Campbell; Oran Spain; Scott Robertson.
Goals: Johnston 0/1.
Rugby Leaguer & League Express Players of the Match:
England: Seb Bechara; *Ireland:* Peter Johnston.
Penalty count: 3-2; **Half-time:** 66-0; **Referee:** Ollie Cruickshank.

Attendance: 3,847 *(at Copper Box Arena, London).*

GROUP A - FINAL STANDINGS

	P	W	D	L	F	A	D	Pts
England	3	3	0	0	263	20	243	6
Australia	3	2	0	1	136	88	48	4
Spain	3	1	0	2	99	188	-89	2
Ireland	3	0	0	3	50	252	-202	0

GROUP B

Friday 4th November 2022

FRANCE 154 WALES 6

FRANCE: Lionel Alazard; Gilles Clausells (C); Florian Guttadoro; Jeremy Bourson; Julien Penella. Subs (all used, only four named): Mostefa Abassi; Guillaume Mautz; Arno Vargas; Jonathan Hivernat.
Tries: Alazard (1, 3, 14, 21, 25, 52), G Clausells (5, 53), Bourson (10, 18, 23, 34, 45), Guttadoro (16, 74), Penella (19, 36, 48), Abassi (35, 42, 55, 70, 78), Vargas (38, 72), Hivernat (40, 67);
Goals: Alazard 13/14, Guttadoro 4/6, Penella 6/7.
WALES: Stephen Halsey; Scott Trigg-Turner; Gary Preece; Jodie Boyd-Ward; Stuart Williams (C). Subs (all used): Lucie Roberts; Martin Lane; Harry Jones; Andrew Higgins; Mark Williams.
Try: Jones (27); **Goals:** Halsey 1/1.
Rugby Leaguer & League Express Players of the Match:
France: Lionel Alazard; *Wales:* Stuart Williams.
Penalty count: 3-4; **Half-time:** 96-6; **Referee:** David Butler.

SCOTLAND 41 USA 62

SCOTLAND: Conor Blackmore; Dan Grant; Mike Mellon (C); John Willans; Callum Young. Subs: Gregor Anderson (not used); Paul Hartley (not used); Peter Lauder (not used); Graeme Stewart; Cayden Thompson.
Tries: Young (6, 13, 17, 67), Grant (22, 51), Blackmore (25), Willans (43);
Goals: Grant 0/2, Willans 4/5, Mellon 0/1; Field goal: Grant (53).
USA: Mackenzie Johnson; William Johnstone; Micah Stewart; Jeff Townsend (C); Matt Wooloff. Subs: Jesse Lind; Andy Kingsley; Jensen Blaine (not used); Freddie Smith (not used); Jabrier Lee (not used).
Tries: Johnson (1, 4, 28, 45), Wooloff (20, 31), Lind (34, 40), Townsend (47, 55, 66, 70); **Goals:** Johnstone 5/8, Stewart 1/2, Townsend 1/2.
Rugby Leaguer & League Express Players of the Match:
Scotland: Callum Young; *USA:* Mackenzie Johnson.
Penalty count: 5-5; **Half-time:** 24-38; **Referee:** Grant Jackson.

Attendance: 1,129 *(at English Institute of Sport, Sheffield).*

World Cup 2021 - Statistical review

Monday 7th November 2022

FRANCE 80 SCOTLAND 15

FRANCE: Nicolas Clausells; Florian Guttadoro; Guillaume Mautz (C); Arno Vargas; Yann Verdi. Subs: Mostefa Abassi; Jeremy Bourson (not used); Gilles Clausells; Thomas Duhalde; Julien Penella.
Tries: N Clausells (1, 6, 30, 40), Mautz (16, 45), Verdi (19, 55), Vargas (22, 67), Abassi (26, 59), Guttadoro (29), Penella (53);
Goals: N Clausells 7/9, Duhalde 5/5.
SCOTLAND: Callum Young; Mike Mellon (C); Dan Grant; John Willans; Conor Blackmore. Subs (all used): Dave Anderson; Gregor Anderson; Dave Birtles; Peter Lauder; Cayden Thompson.
Tries: Young (13), Mellon (63), Grant (76); **Goals:** Grant 1/2, Mellon 0/2;
Field goal: Grant (50).
Rugby Leaguer & League Express Players of the Match:
France: Nicolas Clausells; *Scotland:* Mike Mellon.
Penalty count: 2-11; **Half-time:** 50-6; **Referee:** Steve Hewson.

WALES 50 USA 32

WALES: Stephen Halsey; Gary Preece; Jodie Boyd-Ward; Stuart Williams (C); Martin Lane. Subs (all used): Alan Caron; Harry Jones; Andrew Higgins; Mark Williams; Scott Trigg-Turner.
Tries: Preece (12, 58), S Williams (25, 29, 39), Halsey (31), Jones (46), Higgins (61), Trigg-Turner (68); **Goals:** Halsey 5/6, Higgins 2/3.
USA: Mackenzie Johnson; Jeff Townsend (C); Micah Stewart; William Johnstone; Matt Wooloff. Subs: Tony Leboutillier (not used); Jesse Lind; Andy Kingsley; Gabi Cha (not used); Jensen Blaine (not used).
Tries: Townsend (8, 18, 54, 72), Johnson (10), Wooloff (36);
Goals: Johnstone 3/4, Stewart 1/2.
Rugby Leaguer & League Express Players of the Match:
Wales: Stuart Williams; *USA:* Jeff Townsend.
Penalty count: 8-5; **Half-time:** 30-22; **Referee:** David Roig.

Attendance: 1,214 *(at English Institute of Sport, Sheffield).*

Thursday 10th November 2022

FRANCE 116 USA 6

FRANCE: Lionel Alazard; Mostefa Abassi; Jeremy Bourson; Nicolas Clausells; Jonathan Hivernat. Subs (all used): Gilles Clausells (C); Thomas Duhalde; Julien Penella; Arno Vargas; Guillaume Mautz.
Tries: Bourson (2, 7, 9, 16, 37), Hivernat (11, 20, 23), Abassi (12, 18, 63, 75, 78), Duhalde (33, 60), G Clausells (41, 45, 51), Mautz (56), N Clausells (57), Alazard (65); **Goals:** Alazard 9/11, G Clausells 3/4, Duhalde 4/6.
USA: Jeff Townsend (C); Mackenzie Johnson; Matt Wooloff; Micah Stewart; William Johnstone. Subs (all used): Jensen Blaine; Gabi Cha; Andy Kingsley; Jabrier Lee; Jesse Lind.
Try: Johnson (71); **Goals:** Stewart 1/1.
Rugby Leaguer & League Express Players of the Match:
France: Jeremy Bourson; *USA:* Mackenzie Johnson.
Penalty count: 6-3; **Half-time:** 64-0; **Referee:** Matthew Ball.

WALES 70 SCOTLAND 36

WALES: Scott Trigg-Turner; Gary Preece; Jodie Boyd-Ward; Andrew Higgins; Stuart Williams (C). Subs (all used): Martin Lane; Harry Jones; Lucie Roberts; Mark Williams; Alan Caron.
Tries: Trigg-Turner (2, 12, 53), Preece (5), Higgins (17, 46, 48, 73), Lane (33, 77), Jones (35, 42); **Goals:** Higgins 9/11, M Williams 2/2.
SCOTLAND: Conor Blackmore; Dan Grant; Mike Mellon (C); John Willans; Callum Young. Subs: Dave Anderson (not used); Dave Birtles; Paul Hartley; Peter Lauder (not used); Cayden Thompson.
Tries: Grant (8, 38, 70, 80), Willans (22), Mellon (25, 56);
Goals: Willans 1/3, Grant 3/4.
Rugby Leaguer & League Express Players of the Match:
Wales: Andrew Higgins; *Scotland:* Mike Mellon.
Penalty count: 9-8; **Half-time:** 36-20; **Referee:** Laurent Abrial.

Attendance: 1,129 *(at English Institute of Sport, Sheffield).*

GROUP B - FINAL STANDINGS

	P	W	D	L	F	A	D	Pts
France	3	3	0	0	350	27	323	6
Wales	3	2	0	1	126	222	-96	4
USA	3	1	0	2	100	207	-107	2
Scotland	3	0	0	3	92	212	-120	0

SEMI-FINALS

Sunday 13th November 2022

FRANCE 84 AUSTRALIA 40

FRANCE: Lionel Alazard; Mostefa Abassi; Jeremy Bourson; Florian Guttadoro; Nicolas Clausells. Subs (all used): Gilles Clausells (C); Julien Penella; Guillaume Mautz; Arno Vargas; Thomas Duhalde.
Tries: Guttadoro (1, 45, 60), Bourson (6, 8, 17, 21, 26), N Clausells (29, 78), Abassi (31, 35, 39, 52), Duhalde (75);
Goals: Alazard 7/8, G Clausells 5/7, N Clausells 0/1.
AUSTRALIA: Peter Arbuckle; Brad Grove (C); Diab Karim; Zac Schumacher; Bayley McKenna. Subs (all used): Cory Cannane; Craig Cannane; James Hill; Liam Luff; Shaun Harre.
Tries: Grove (3, 69), Schumacher (13, 58), Karim (41), Luff (62), Craig Cannane (73); **Goals:** McKenna 4/5, Karim 2/2.
Rugby Leaguer & League Express Players of the Match:
France: Jeremy Bourson; *Australia:* Zac Schumacher.
Penalty count: 4-9; **Half-time:** 54-10; **Referee:** Ollie Cruickshank.

ENGLAND 125 WALES 22

ENGLAND: Rob Hawkins; Joe Coyd; Seb Bechara; Lewis King; Tom Halliwell (C). Subs (all used): Nathan Collins; Jack Brown; Declan Roberts; Wayne Boardman; James Simpson.
Tries: Bechara (2, 4, 7, 32), Coyd (11, 20, 23, 43), Brown (26, 30, 34, 36, 41, 50, 57, 59), Hawkins (28, 77), King (46), Collins (53), Roberts (68), Simpson (75);
Goals: Hawkins 7/8, Collins 10/11, Roberts 1/3; **Field goal:** Roberts (70).
WALES: Andrew Higgins; Martin Lane; Gary Preece; Scott Trigg-Turner; Stuart Williams (C). Subs (all used): Harry Jones; Lucie Roberts; Alan Caron; Jodie Boyd-Ward; Stephen Halsey.
Tries: Trigg-Turner (17), Preece (49), S Williams (55), Caron (65);
Goals: Preece 1/2, Higgins 2/2.
Sin bin: Preece (75) - dissent.
Rugby Leaguer & League Express Players of the Match:
England: Jack Brown; *Wales:* Andrew Higgins.
Penalty count: 5-6; **Half-time:** 70-6; **Referee:** Laurent Abrial.

Attendance: 1,318 *(at English Institute of Sport, Sheffield).*

FINAL

Friday 18th November 2022

FRANCE 24 ENGLAND 28

FRANCE: Mostefa Abassi; Lionel Alazard; Jeremy Bourson; Julien Penella; Nicolas Clausells. Subs: Florian Guttadoro; Jonathan Hivernat; Guillaume Mautz (not used); Gilles Clausells (C); Arno Vargas.
Tries: Alazard (9), Abassi (29), G Clausells (58);
Goals: Alazard 1/1, N Clausells 5/6.
ENGLAND: Tom Halliwell (C); Rob Hawkins; Joe Coyd; Seb Bechara; Lewis King. Subs: Nathan Collins; Jack Brown; Declan Roberts (not used); Wayne Boardman (not used); James Simpson (not used).
Tries: Halliwell (20, 78), Brown (40, 54), King (42);
Goals: Hawkins 1/1, Collins 3/5.
Rugby Leaguer & League Express Players of the Match:
France: Nicolas Clausells; *England:* Tom Halliwell.
Penalty count: 9-13; **Half-time:** 14-12; **Referee:** Ollie Cruickshank;
Attendance: 4,526 *(at Manchester Central).*

AUSTRALIA

NO.	PLAYER	CLUB	APPS	SUBS	TRIES	GOALS	FG	PTS
1	Peter Arbuckle	Queensland	4	1	2	0	0	8
5	Cory Cannane	New South Wales	2	2	1	0	0	4
10	Craig Cannane	New South Wales	4	4	2	0	0	8
7	Richard Engles	New South Wales	0	0	0	2	0	4
6	Brad Grove	New South Wales	4	0	6	4	0	38
3	Shaun Harre	Queensland	0	0	0	0	0	0
4	James Hill	New South Wales	0	2	0	0	0	0
12	Diab Karim	New South Wales	4	0	5	0	0	20
2	Liam Luff	New South Wales	4	4	6	8	0	40
11	Bayley McKenna	Queensland	0	4	3	0	0	12
8	Zac Schumacher	Queensland	2	2	3	18	0	48
9	Adam Tannock	Queensland	2	1	2	0	0	8

ENGLAND

NO.	PLAYER	CLUB	APPS	SUBS	TRIES	GOALS	FG	PTS
4	Seb Bechara	Catalans Dragons	4	0	6	0	0	24
10	Wayne Boardman	Halifax Panthers	1	4	2	3	0	14
6	Jack Brown	Halifax Panthers	4	4	17	0	0	68
1	Nathan Collins	Leeds Rhinos	0	5	6	32	0	88
7	Joe Coyd	London Roosters	4	0	12	4	0	56
3	Tom Halliwell	Leeds Rhinos	5	1	5	0	0	20
2	Rob Hawkins	Halifax Panthers	5	0	7	9	0	46
5	Lewis King	London Roosters	5	1	5	0	0	20
8	Adam Rigby	Wigan Warriors	0	3	3	0	0	12
9	Declan Roberts	Wigan Warriors	0	1	4	13	2	44
11	James Simpson	Leeds Rhinos	2	1	6	0	0	24

FRANCE

NO.	PLAYER	CLUB	APPS	SUBS	TRIES	GOALS	FG	PTS
3	Mostefa Abassi	Saint-Jory	4	2	17	0	0	68
1	Lionel Alazard	Montauban	4	0	8	30	0	92
4	Jeremy Bourson	Catalans Dragons	4	4	15	0	0	60
2	Gilles Clausells	Catalans Dragons	1	4	6	8	0	40
8	Nicolas Clausells	Catalans Dragons	4	0	7	12	0	52
5	Thomas Duhalde	Euskadi	4	3	2	6	0	30
10	Florian Guttadoro	Avignon	3	1	6	4	0	32
11	Jonathan Hivernat	Catalans Dragons	3	3	5	0	0	20
12	Guillaume Mautz	Avignon	1	3	3	0	0	12
6	Julien Penella	Euskadi	2	2	4	6	0	28
7	Arno Vargas	Catalans Dragons	4	4	4	0	0	16
9	Yann Verdi	Avignon	1	0	2	0	0	8

IRELAND

NO.	PLAYER	CLUB	APPS	SUBS	TRIES	GOALS	FG	PTS
1	Toby Burton-Carter	Warrington Wolves	3	0	0	0	0	0
9	Stephen Campbell	Sheffield Eagles	0	2	0	0	0	0
5	Paddy Forbes	Unattached	0	0	0	0	0	0
–	Nash Jennings	Unattached	0	0	4	7	0	30
8	Peter Johnston	The Argonauts	3	0	0	0	0	0
18	Kenneth Maloney	Gravesend Dynamites	3	2	0	0	0	0
2	Tom Martin	Halifax Panthers	3	0	3	0	0	12
10	James McCarthy	Unattached	2	1	2	0	0	8
16	Phil Roberts	Wigan Warriors	3	0	0	0	0	0
–	Scott Robertson	Unattached	0	2	0	0	0	0
3	Rick Rodgers	The Argonauts	1	2	0	0	0	0
11	Oran Spain	Unattached	0	2	0	0	0	0

SCOTLAND

NO.	PLAYER	CLUB	APPS	SUBS	TRIES	GOALS	FG	PTS
3	Dave Anderson	West Wales Raiders	0	1	0	0	0	0
4	Gregor Anderson	Dundee Dragons	0	1	0	0	0	0
10	Dave Birtles	Dundee Dragons	3	0	1	0	0	4
9	Conor Blackmore	Dundee Dragons	3	0	7	4	0	38
6	Dan Grant	Gravesend Dynamites	3	0	0	2	0	4
8	Paul Hartley	Glasgow	0	1	0	0	0	0
12	Peter Lauder	Unattached	3	0	0	0	0	0
7	Mike Mellon	Dundee Dragons	3	1	3	0	0	12
5	Graeme Stewart	Glasgow	0	0	0	0	0	0
2	Cayden Thompson	Dundee Dragons	3	3	2	5	0	18
11	John Willans	Dundee Dragons	3	0	5	0	0	20
1	Callum Young	Warrington Wolves	3	0	0	0	0	0

SPAIN

NO.	PLAYER	CLUB	APPS	SUBS	TRIES	GOALS	FG	PTS
10	Pascal Ambrosino	Toulon	3	1	0	0	0	0
11	David Berty	St Toulousain	3	0	3	0	0	12
–	Jorge Gelade-Panzo	Catalans Dragons	3	0	5	13	0	47
7	Theo Gonzalez	Handisport Roannais	3	0	2	0	0	8
–	Joel Lacombe	Catalans Dragons	3	0	3	0	0	12
3	Yannick Martin	Montauban	3	0	4	0	0	16
–	Fabien Moisdon	Catalans Dragons	0	0	0	0	0	0
2	Raphael Monedero	Catalans Dragons	3	3	4	0	0	16
–	Jonathan Palomo	Biganos	0	1	0	0	0	0
5	Eric Perez	Biganos	3	0	0	0	0	0
4	David Raymond	Biganos	3	3	0	0	0	0
8	Wilfrid Seron	St Toulousain	0	0	0	2	0	4

USA

NO.	PLAYER	CLUB	APPS	SUBS	TRIES	GOALS	FG	PTS
3	Jensen Blaine	Unattached	0	1	0	0	0	0
4	Gabi Cha	Unattached	3	0	6	0	0	24
5	Mackenzie Johnson	Unattached	3	0	0	8	0	16
11	William Johnstone	Unattached	3	0	0	0	0	0
1	Andy Kingsley	Unattached	3	3	0	0	0	0
8	Tony Leboutillier	Unattached	3	0	2	0	0	8
2	Jabrier Lee	Unattached	0	0	2	0	0	8
4	Jesse Lind	Unattached	0	3	0	0	0	0
7	Freddie Smith	Unattached	0	0	0	3	0	6
–	Micah Stewart	Unattached	0	0	8	1	0	34
6	Jeff Townsend	Unattached	3	0	3	0	0	12
–	Matt Wooloff	Wigan Warriors	3	0	0	0	0	0

WALES

NO.	PLAYER	CLUB	APPS	SUBS	TRIES	GOALS	FG	PTS
4	Mason Baker	North Wales Crusaders	3	0	0	0	0	0
9	Jodie Boyd-Ward	Leeds Rhinos	0	1	1	0	0	4
5	Alan Caron	Hereford Harriers	3	3	1	6	0	16
12	Stephen Halsey	North Wales Crusaders	2	1	5	13	0	46
6	Andrew Higgins	Hereford Harriers	2	2	4	0	0	16
11	Harry Jones	Hereford Harriers	4	2	2	0	0	8
2	Martin Lane	North Wales Crusaders	3	0	4	1	0	18
8	Gary Preece	Hereford Harriers	4	3	0	0	0	0
1	Lucie Roberts	North Wales Crusaders	4	0	5	0	0	20
10	Scott Trigg-Turner	North Wales Crusaders	0	3	1	0	0	4
3	Mark Williams	Wigan Warriors	3	0	0	2	0	4
7	Stuart Williams	North Wales Crusaders	4	0	4	0	0	16

WORLD CUP 2021
Leading scorers

MEN

TRIES

1	Josh Addo-Carr	Australia	12
2	Dominic Young	England	9
3	Tommy Makinson	England	7
4	Louis Senior	Ireland	6
	Tim Lafai	Samoa	6
	Daniel Tupou	Tonga	6
7	Campbell Graham	Australia	5
	Latrell Mitchell	Australia	5
	Cameron Murray	Australia	5
	James Tedesco	Australia	5
	Josh Mansour	Lebanon	5
	Brian To'o	Samoa	5
	Will Penisini	Tonga	5

GOALS

1	Nathan Cleary	Australia	32
2	Stephen Crichton	Samoa	28
3	Isaiya Katoa	Tonga	21
4	Tommy Makinson	England	20
	Marc Sneyd	England	20
6	Mitchell Moses	Lebanon	15
	Brandon Wakeham	Fiji	15
8	Rhyse Martin	Papua New Guinea	14
	Jordan Rapana	New Zealand	14
10	Arthur Mourgue	France	10

POINTS

			T	G	FG	PTS
1	Stephen Crichton	Samoa	4	28	1	73
2	Nathan Cleary	Australia	1	32	0	68
	Tommy Makinson	England	7	20	0	68
4	Isaiya Katoa	Tonga	2	21	0	50
5	Josh Addo-Carr	Australia	12	0	0	48
6	Jordan Rapana	New Zealand	4	14	0	44
	Marc Sneyd	England	1	20	0	44
8	Rhyse Martin	Papua New Guinea	2	14	0	36
	Dominic Young	England	9	0	0	36
10	Mitchell Moses	Lebanon	0	15	0	30
	Brandon Wakeham	Fiji	0	15	0	30

WOMEN

TRIES

1	Evania Pelite	Australia	7
	Julia Robinson	Australia	7
	Jessica Sergis	Australia	7
4	Leah Burke	England	6
	Tara Jane Stanley	England	6
6	Tarryn Aiken	Australia	5
	Isabelle Kelly	Australia	5
	Emma Tonegato	Australia	5
	Amy Hardcastle	England	5
	Belinda Gwasamun	Papua New Guinea	5

GOALS

1	Lauren Brown	Australia	30
2	Tara Jane Stanley	England	19
3	Lila Malabag	Papua New Guinea	8
4	Brianna Clark	New Zealand	7
5	Ali Brigginshaw	Australia	5
	Dani Franada	Canada	5
7	Holli Wheeler	Australia	4
8	Kerehitina Matua	Cook Islands	3
	Apii Nicholls	New Zealand	3
10	Maria Graf	Brazil	2
	Emily Veivers	Papua New Guinea	2

POINTS

			T	G	FG	PTS
1	Tara Jane Stanley	England	6	19	0	62
2	Lauren Brown	Australia	0	30	0	60
3	Evania Pelite	Australia	7	0	0	28
	Julia Robinson	Australia	7	0	0	28
	Jessica Sergis	Australia	7	0	0	28
6	Leah Burke	England	6	0	0	24
7	Tarryn Aiken	Australia	5	1	0	22
8	Belinda Gwasamun	Papua New Guinea	5	0	0	20
	Amy Hardcastle	England	5	0	0	20
	Isabelle Kelly	Australia	5	0	0	20
	Lila Malabag	Papua New Guinea	1	8	0	20
	Emma Tonegato	Australia	5	0	0	20

WHEELCHAIR

TRIES

1	Jack Brown	England	17
	Mostefa Abassi	France	17
3	Jeremy Bourson	France	15
4	Joe Coyd	England	12
5	Lionel Alazard	France	8
	Jeff Townsend	USA	8
7	Rob Hawkins	England	7
	Nicolas Clausells	France	7
	Dan Grant	Scotland	7
10	Brad Grove	Australia	6
	Diab Karim	Australia	6
	Seb Bechara	England	6
	Nathan Collins	England	6
	James Simpson	England	6
	Gilles Clausells	France	6
	Florian Guttadoro	France	6
	Mackenzie Johnson	USA	6

GOALS

1	Nathan Collins	England	32
2	Lionel Alazard	France	30
3	Bayley McKenna	Australia	18
4	Theo Gonzalez	Spain	13
	Andrew Higgins	Wales	13
	Declan Roberts	England	13
7	Nicolas Clausells	France	12
8	Thomas Duhalde	France	9
	Rob Hawkins	England	9
10	Gilles Clausells	France	8
	William Johnstone	USA	8
	Diab Karim	Australia	8

POINTS

			T	G	FG	PTS
1	Lionel Alazard	France	8	30	0	92
2	Nathan Collins	England	6	32	0	88
3	Mostefa Abassi	France	17	0	0	68
	Jack Brown	England	17	0	0	68
5	Jeremy Bourson	France	15	0	0	60
6	Joe Coyd	England	12	4	0	56
7	Nicolas Clausells	France	7	12	0	52
8	Bayley McKenna	Australia	3	18	0	48
9	Theo Gonzalez	Spain	5	13	1	47
10	Rob Hawkins	England	7	9	0	46
	Andrew Higgins	Wales	5	13	0	46

5
SEASON DOWN UNDER

NRL
Treble-top Panthers

Nathan Cleary produced a stunning individual performance in the last quarter of the 2023 NRL Grand Final to carry Penrith to their third consecutive Premiership.

It was true drama. Brisbane Broncos led 24-8 with little more than 17 minutes remaining before Cleary picked up his teammates and carried the men in black to a historic three-peat.

Cleary sparked the late rally by scything through the right centre in the 63rd minute and finding prop Moses Leota on his inside for a try. Then he booted an inspirational 40/20 to increase the momentum.

Five minutes later, the star halfback threw the final pass for Stephen Crichton's muscular four-pointer before completing the comeback with a stunning individual try, skipping inside and past four Broncos' defenders and converting easily to clinch a 26-24 victory.

Cleary deserved the Clive Churchill Medal, becoming just the third player (after Bradley Clyde in 1989 and 1991 then Billy Slater in 2009 and 2017) to earn the award twice.

Earlier in the second half, rookie Broncos stand-off Ezra Mam scored three speedy tries in 12 blistering minutes to place one hand on the trophy.

Brisbane did superbly to repel Penrith in a lopsided first half, until Thomas Flegler's score in the shadow of half-time gave them a huge psychological boost heading into the break.

But Cleary's late heroics ensured the Provan-Summons Trophy remained at the foot of the Blue Mountains for another 12 months.

Ivan Cleary's squad were the first club since Parramatta in 1981, '82 and '83 to claim three Premierships on the bounce.

And their backs-against-the-wall effort against Brisbane easily ranked as the best Grand Final triumph of the three. Leota was immense and Crichton marked his last game in a black jumper before joining Canterbury with a massive performance.

While nine members of Ivan Cleary's line-up suited up for their fourth consecutive decider (Dylan Edwards, Crichton, Brian To'o, Jarome Luai, Cleary, Leota, James Fisher-Harris, Liam Martin and Isaah Yeo), Broncos coach Kevin Walters only had two men with Grand Final experience: South Sydney title winner Adam Reynolds and ex-Panther Kurt Capewell.

The Panthers took the lead after a sloppy Kotoni Staggs play-the-ball invited Penrith to camp in Brisbane's red zone, before a short Reynolds goal-line drop-out ended in disaster. Herbie Farnworth elected to bat down the ball rather than catch it and hooker Mitch Kenny gleefully accepted for the game's opening score.

Kenny's cheeky kick pinned fullback Reece Walsh in his own in-goal and the Broncos botched that drop-out too. This time, Reynolds' kick sailed out on the full and failed to travel 10 metres, handing Cleary another two points with the kicking tee.

The Panthers' famously stingy defence refused to give the Broncos an inch, starving Walsh and his teammates of meaningful opportunities. At half-time, Brisbane had completed just 13 of 21 sets, compared to Penrith's 18 of 19.

But the one penalty they coughed up left the door ajar for the underdogs. With their opponents finally on the back foot, Jordan Riki and Farnworth both threatened to break through before dummy-half Tyson Smoothy sent Flegler crashing over beneath the posts.

Despite being battered all half, the resilient Broncos headed to the sheds trailing by only two points. Then, straight after the restart, Mam cracked the contest wide open.

NRL

Penrith Panthers start the party after their third successive NRL Grand Final win

Spotting forward Lindsay Smith in front of him, the 20-year-old stand-off burned his slower opponent, palmed off Izack Tago and outpaced fullback Dylan Edwards into the left corner.

Next, Payne Haas's offload fractured Penrith's line and Mam left Cleary and Yeo grasping at shadows as he sprinted 30 metres to the stripe.

Then from the restart, Cleary tried to rush up on Walsh - but the speedster raced past him and fended off Tago to send Mam wheeling around Sunia Turuva for try number three.

As if trailing by 16 with a quarter of the game left didn't look bleak enough for Penrith, Luai re-aggravated a troublesome shoulder injury and forwards Yeo and Scott Sorensen departed for head-injury assessments.

With the responsibility entirely on his back, Cleary stepped up with a legacy-defining display that was capped when he burned his opposite number Reynolds and left Billy Walters, Riki and Walsh in his wake to score under the uprights. The simple conversion was a formality and a fitting way for an epic battle to be decided.

It was one of the best finales to a season in which crowds smashed previous records. The average attendance was up 22.6 per cent on the previous year in a season in which the NRL expanded to 17 clubs with the successful entry of a second Brisbane based club in the Dolphins.

And that was amid an almost season-long dispute between the NRL and the Rugby League Players Association. The fall out over a new Collective Bargaining Agreement, which saw a media boycott by players for part of the season, was only resolved in August.

Here's how it went for all 17 clubs:

PENRITH PANTHERS (Premiers/Minor Premiers)
Top pointscorer: Nathan Cleary (216); Top tryscorer: Brian To'o (21)

Back-to-back Premierships have been very rare since the formation of the NRL in 1998. Three in a row was unknown. Until Penrith Panthers achieved the feat in 2023.

NRL

Nathan Cleary collected his second Clive Churchill Medal in the Grand Final, producing an amazing display in the last 20 minutes at a stage when all looked lost. He may have not won the Dally M Medal (Newcastle Knights' Kalyn Ponga did) but he was 2023's most influential player.

A disappointing start to the year, which saw them slip to a shock defeat to St Helens in the World Club Challenge before losing two of their opening four NRL matches, had many believing the Panthers had lost their pre-eminence.

It fitted in with the narrative after salary cap pressures saw the departures of Api Koroisau and Viliame Kikau at the end of the 2022 season. Then they lost boom winger Taylan May to a season-ending injury in the World Club Challenge. But the Panthers silenced their doubters with an eight-match winning streak towards the end of the regular season that secured the Minor Premiership.

The final 20 minutes of their season against Brisbane were the stuff of legend. It was the biggest comeback in NRL grand final history.

May was hardly missed as Fijian Sunia Turuva filled in and bagged the Dally M Rookie of the Year award. On the other wing Brian To'o scored 16 tries in his final 12 matches. Centre Stephen Crichton had a brilliant year on the back of his World Cup heroics with Samoa. Isaah Yeo was huge and Moses Leota and James Fisher-Harris were a fearsome middle.

Crichton, to Canterbury, and Roosters-bound backrower Spencer Leniu are off but three good players in Brad Schneider (Hull KR), Daine Laurie (Wests Tigers) and Paul Alamoti (Bulldogs) have been recruited.

BRISBANE BRONCOS (Runners-up/3rd in table)
Top pointscorer: Adam Reynolds (212); Top tryscorer: Selwyn Cobbo (20)

The Broncos were close in 2023, but not close enough. After 63 minutes of the Grand Final they looked like they had won their first Premiership since 2006 thanks to a brilliant Ezra Mam hat-trick that gave them a 24-8 lead over the Panthers. If it hadn't been for Nathan Cleary they probably would have won.

Despite the heartbreak, 2023 was a great year for the Broncos who were wooden spooners in 2000 and finished in 14th spot the year after, in Kevin Walters' first season as head coach. In 2022 they finished outside the play-offs in ninth.

Halfback Adam Reynolds copped some criticism for the Grand Final collapse but he was the ship-steadier for some inexperienced if brilliant players around him as Brisbane came home with a wet sail.

In the play-offs, they played Melbourne off the park with a 26-0 win at Suncorp Stadium. After earning a week off, they got off to a shaky start in their grand final qualifier against the Warriors but ran away to a 42-12 win.

Mam, Reynolds, Reece Walsh, Payne Haas, Selwyn Cobbo and Patrick Carrigan were stand-outs in an outstanding team.

New recruit Walsh in the fullback role was incredible. He also shone in State of Origin, forcing his way into the Maroons side and taunting NSW in the first two games.

The loss of prop Thomas Flegler and England centre Herbie Farnworth to the Dolphins will weaken them, but the Broncos still look well-set for the future.

MELBOURNE STORM (2nd)
Top pointscorer: Nick Meaney (222); Top tryscorer: Will Warbrick (17)

The once pre-eminent Storm didn't have a perfect year but second place in the table was an improvement on 2022 when they finished outside the top four for the first time since 2014 and were eliminated in the first week of the finals.

2023 was much better and they overcame plenty of hiccups to make the Preliminary Final, when they made an exit to the brilliant Panthers.

Ryan Papenhuyzen has had some tough luck with injury in recent seasons but 2023 was probably the worst. He returned only in round 26 after over a year's rehabilitation for a shattered kneecap. Two weeks later he was carted off Suncorp Stadium with a fractured ankle with seven minutes to play in the Storm's 26-0 qualifying-final defeat by the Broncos.

The exit at the end of 2022 of Kenny and Jesse Bromwich and Felise Kaufusi, all to the Dolphins, and Brandon Smith to the Roosters left a big hole in terms of experience in the pack. In their absence, Nelson Asofa-Solomona and Josh King played big roles in the middle and signing from the Warriors Eliesa Katoa had a good first season.

Winger Will Warbrick had a boom year with 17 tries, topped off by his last minute effort to snatch the win over the Roosters in week two of the finals.

Their star spine of Cameron Munster, Jahrome Hughes and Harry Grant were always a threat and the Storm expertly navigated the Origin period with Munster, Grant, and Xavier Coates all receiving call-ups as they moved into the top-four midway through the season.

Papenhuyzen's injury was bad, but not as bad as first thought and his pace and anticipation will make for a better Storm, although Nick Meaney proved an excellent replacement

Legendary coach Craig Bellamy, who changed his mind mid-season to stay in the job for another year, is never happy to not win the competition. Melbourne of 2023 might not have but they did show they remain amongst the competition's elite sides.

NEW ZEALAND WARRIORS (4th)

Top pointscorer: Shaun Johnson (176); Top tryscorer: Dallin Watene-Zelezniak (24)

It's fair to say the Covid years disrupted the NZ Warriors more than any other club in the NRL. Their 15th-place finish of 2022 was at the end of a season in which they started the season still based at Redcliffe but 2023 was the year they returned permanently to their home in Auckland.

It certainly showed as rookie head coach Andrew Webster woke up the sleeping giant and captured the hearts of the people of New Zealand.

The Warriors' season ended at the penultimate stage when they lost 42-12 at Brisbane, a week after a passionate and powerful win over the in-form Knights in Auckland.

Shaun Johnson, 33 years-old, had a dream year at halfback, Tohu Harris led the side brilliantly, Addin Fonua-Blake and Wayde Egan terrorising defences around the ruck. Charnze Nicoll-Klokstad was great at the back and winger Dallin Watene-Zelezniak scored 24 tries out of 20 games.

They suffered a three-game losing streak from round 8 onwards, to the Storm, Roosters and Panthers. But after a 28-6 loss to South Sydney on home soil in round 18, the Warriors went on a seven-game winning run to secure a finish in the top four.

Mid-season there was an off-field blip when Jason Paris, boss of the Warriors' naming-rights sponsor OneNZ, was forced to apologise, after threats of legal action, for describing decisions against the club as 'cheating of the highest order'.

Dally M Coach of the Year Webster took the accolades for the new Warriors mentality though it will be a hard season to follow. Two of the club's favourite sons make returns, as former skipper and Dally M Medal winner Roger Tuivasa-Sheck and Chanel Harris-Tavita re-join the Warriors.

NEWCASTLE KNIGHTS (5th)

Top pointscorer: Kalyn Ponga (128); Top tryscorer: Dominic Young (25)

The Knights were a good news story in 2023 and a fifth-placed finish, meaning a first home finals tie in 15 years, 12 months after they finished ten places below that, was just reward.

Expectations were low in Newcastle following 2022 and for the first half of the season that mood didn't change. But then the Knights turned their season on its head with an unbeaten run to finish in fifth spot.

NRL

Midway through the season head coach Adam O'Brien looked to be in a shaky position. The Knights started with a defeat at the Warriors, scraped past Wests Tigers and then got hammered at home to the Dolphins.

The experiment of Kalyn Ponga at five-eighth, with 2024 Leeds recruit Lachlan Miller taking over at fullback, resulted in some bad head knocks to the Knights' marquee player.

A round 18, 66-0 hammering of Canterbury turned the corner. The Knights didn't taste defeat again for over two months. Ponga's reversion to fullback proved a masterstroke. In a ten-game winning run, Ponga crossed for five tries and won himself the Dally M Medal.

After the thrilling comeback play-off win over the Raiders on home soil, the Knights' season came to an end at the Warriors in the semi-finals.

England winger Dom Young broke the club's all-time try-scoring record with 25 in as many games (Greg Marzhew on the other wing scored 22) but he is leaving (for the Roosters), as are Super League-bound Lachlan Fitzgibbon and Miller.

The arrival of Kai Pearce-Paul and Will Pryce in the other direction will add interest to their season. But the fitness of Ponga is key to Newcastle's chances in 2024.

CRONULLA SHARKS (6th)
Top pointscorer: Nicho Hynes (187); Top tryscorer: Ronaldo Mulitalo (21)

The Sharks managed to make the finals but as in recent years they couldn't progress any further.

They had a home eliminator with the Roosters, admittedly an in-form Roosters, in the bag this year but somehow managed to lose the game to a Sam Walker field goal. It was their sixth straight finals defeat.

The Sharks recorded only three victories over top eight teams, despite having a brilliant attack orchestrated by Nicho Hynes and two superb finishers in wingers Sione Katoa and Ronaldo Mulitalo. They scored 34 tries between them and fullback William Kennedy also had a fine year with 14 tries. His hamstring injury in the defeat by Penrith at the end of July badly hampered Cronulla's play-off chances.

Early in the season, convincing wins over the Dragons, Roosters, Bulldogs and Cowboys had the Sharks in second position. But coach Craig Fitzgibbon wouldn't have been satisfied with the Sharks defence which conceded 20 points per game during the season, compared to 15 in 2022. A 54-10 hammering by Melbourne Storm in round 15 was the low point.

2022 Dally M winner Hynes was the man who made the Sharks tick but halves partner Matt Moylan fell out of favour and was linked with a move to Super League early in the summer. His future was unknown but they'll definitely miss retiring backrower Wade Graham. Apart from his huge absence, the Sharks will be largely unchanged for 2024.

SYDNEY ROOSTERS (7th)
Top pointscorer: Joseph Suaalii (124); Top tryscorer: James Tedesco (11)

Many people's pre-season premiership favourites, the Roosters struggled for large parts of the year.

Sitting in 14th spot with two months remaining in the regular season, coach Trent Robinson and several of his biggest stars were under pressure given the high expectations at Bondi.

But a stunning run home into the finals saw them win their last five games, booking their play-off spot with an impressive victory over rivals South Sydney.

With injuries piling up, the Roosters pulled off a 13-12 finals win over the Sharks on the road, before falling agonisingly short to a last-minute Will Warbrick try at Melbourne a week later to end their season.

Halfback Sam Walker was axed before the half-way mark of the season and ultimately suffered a long-term injury, while the likes of big-signing for 2023 Brandon Smith and Victor Radley spent extended periods on the sidelines.

Joseph Suaalii's much publicised defection to rugby union was another distraction, although his agent was reportedly looking for a way out after the union world cup.

But there were also positives - Luke Keary played every game and was a stand-out. Their late-season performances also saw the likes of Siua Wong and Sandon Smith perform admirably, while the return to form of Walker, Radley and Brandon Smith was a boost.

Nat Butcher was one of the Roosters' most reliable players, missing just one game all year and locking down the left-edge spot while front-rowers Lindsay Collins and Terrell May were both good at the back-end of the season.

The additions of Spencer Leniu and Dom Young will bolster two important positions and the arrival of Wakefield winger Lewis Murphy will be a story to follow.

CANBERRA RAIDERS (8th)
Top pointscorer: Jarrod Croker (130); Top tryscorer: Jordan Rapana (11)

Same again for the Raiders, who emulated their eight-placed finish of 2022. Canberra were workmanlike if unspectacular but they earned their play-off place by their ability to win close matches.

By Round 5 the Raiders looked like wooden spoon contenders but they kick-started their season, defeating a full-strength and up-to-then undefeated Broncos side in Brisbane.

Tight victories over the Dragons, Dolphins, Bulldogs and Eels put them seventh in the standings. Another good period between rounds 17 and 19 winning three on the trot elevated them into fourth spot.

But the Raiders dropped off towards the end of the season, only picking up wins against the lowly Tigers and Bulldogs, although a last-round win over the Sharks gave them a shot at the eliminators. Their 30-28 extra-time defeat at Newcastle displayed their never-say-die spirit.

Prop Pasami Saulo and Danny Levi from Huddersfield were the Raiders' only two signings for 2023. Saulo was a sound addition to what was an already good forward pack. Levi was expected to emerge as the Raiders' leader at hooker but had wretched luck with injuries, featuring in only four games.

The departure of megastar Jack Wighton was the headline story for the Raiders as early as April as the one-club man signed a long-term deal with South Sydney. He's almost impossible to replace and coach Ricky Stuart will plough on with his current squad, Newcastle centre Simi Sasagi, Manly fullback Kaeo Weekes, both with limited NRL experience, and Wigan's Morgan Smithies the only additions.

SOUTH SYDNEY RABBITOHS (9th)
Top pointscorer: Latrell Mitchell (143); Top tryscorer: Alex Johnston (21)

2023 was the first time the Rabbitohs missed the finals since 2017.

A season of two halves saw them top the ladder after 11 rounds - and then go on to miss the play-offs as they won only four of their next 13 games. And in a final humiliation they were dumped out of the finals in the last round by the Roosters.

It all started going wrong after star fullback Latrell Mitchell aggravated a calf injury in the Blues' Origin camp following Round 12.

Mitchell returned from his calf injury in round 22 and the Bunnies won two of their next three games, but a brain explosion saw him suspended for the crunch clash against the Roosters. Mitchell picked up a season-ending ban when he elbowed former NSW teammate Tyson Frizell in the back of the head at Newcastle and missed the 'decider' with the Roosters.

The losing run-in was made worse by Rabbitohs legend Sam Burgess walking out on the club - where he was working as an assistant coach - before their final game, accusing head coach Jason Demetriou of not holding Mitchell and fellow superstar Cody Walker to the same standards as the rest of the team.

In 2024, Canberra's Jack Wighton will be a great addition to one of the best backlines in the NRL and in Tongan backrower Keaon Koloamatangi they already have one of the best forwards. A more stable back room will make them Premiership contenders once more.

NRL

PARRAMATTA EELS (10th)
Top pointscorer: Mitchell Moses (169); Top tryscorer: Maika Sivo (20)

Following up a runners-up finish in 2022 with a tenth-placed finish has got to be seen as a failure for the Eels.

Parramatta sat in 15th place after five rounds and although they recovered, their form faltered again towards the end of the season.

Injuries and suspensions contributed to a poor season. The keystone arrivals of J'maine Hopgood and Josh Hodgson for 2023 produced mixed results after the losses of key figures in Reed Mahoney, Marata Niukore, and Isaiah Papali'i at the end of 2022.

England hooker Hodgson had to retire due to injury after 13 rounds. Hopgood was a real workhorse but most of the rest of the forward pack was uninspiring, though Reagan Campbell-Gillard gave his all up front.

Halves Mitchell Moses and Dylan Brown were a mix of brilliant and low key. And Brown was suspended by the NRL for seven games in July after his arrest for 'sexual touching' in a Sydney bar, to which he pleaded guilty. It added to a hugely disappointing year for Eels fans as results tailed off towards the end of the season.

Brown was missing during the Origin period after the Blues call-up for Moses left a massive hole that the Eels could not fill. Then an eye socket injury ruled Moses out for the final three weeks.

Bryce Cartwright was a shining light on the edge with his offloads and the Eels fought off plenty of interest to sign him up for two more years. And club Rookie of the Year prop Wiremu Greig was contracted for another three years.

Brad Arthur will enter his tenth season as head coach without only two headline additions in Manly pair centre Morgan Harper and Samoa forward Kelma Tuilagi but there is enough talent at Parramatta to contend again.

NORTH QUEENSLAND COWBOYS (11th)
Top pointscorer: Valentine Holmes (170); Top tryscorer: Scott Drinkwater (11)

The Cowboys were the surprise packets of 2022, coming within an inch of making the Grand Final.

But in 2023 the brilliant youngsters who had got them there couldn't reproduce their form to back up. The Cowboy lost eight of their first 13 games and were playing catch-up in the second half of the season, although they won seven of their next ten games. They hammered both the Storm and Rabbitohs in that period and conceded just 30 points in a four-match streak which included wins over Souths, Manly and Parramatta.

In their last five games of the campaign they won just once. Their finals hopes came down to the last round of the regular season, needing to win a daunting challenge at Penrith. They lost 44-12, meaning an eleventh place finish.

The suspension of strike centre Valentine Holmes for a high shot on young Titan Jayden Campbell in round 23 effectively sealed their fate. They won just one game without him - against the Dolphins.

Fullback Scott Drinkwater was their standout. Hooker Reece Robson won an NSW call-up off the back of his consistent form, while halfback Tom Dearden shone.

And the Cowboys have some of the most promising forwards in the competition in Jeremiah Nanai, Heilum Luki, Luciano Leilua and Kulikefu Finefeuiaki.

They will certainly miss, through retirement, Jason Taumalolo, their biggest strike threat over the years. But in 16 games in 2023 he didn't score one single try

2022 Coach of the Year Todd Payten has brought in former halfback Jake Clifford after his year at Hull FC. Young Warriors centre Viliami Vailea has also been recruited.

MANLY SEA EAGLES (12th)

Top pointscorer: Reuben Garrick (174); Top tryscorer: Jason Saab (14)

The Sea Eagles were inconsistent all season after the massive shake up at Brookvale at the end of 2022 in the wake of the Rainbow shirt bust-up.

Anthony Seibold took over the coaching reins from Des Hasler but results were mixed. In April they battled to an 18-8 home win over the Storm, only to bomb at Brookvale to the Titans two weeks after. A 58-18 win over the Dolphins was followed by a 34-4 loss to the Eels.

The Sea Eagles' hopes of featuring in the finals had disappeared as early as June. After bagging wins over the Sharks and Dragons as the home straight came into view, Manly then lost three games in a row for the first time in the season to slide out of contention for the top eight.

The big hiccup? Another injury to Tom Trbojevic, this time a season-ending pectoral tear three minutes into Origin 2 at Suncorp. Manly lost just four of 11 games with Turbo in the team, but won just four of 12 without him.

Manly's best two spells were at the start and end of the campaign with Seibold's reign starting with a bang when they posted 31 points against Canterbury. They then edged Parramatta in a high-scoring affair which saw Josh Schuster and Tom Trbojevic tear apart the Eels.

Then with the pressure relieved as the chance of the finals footy disappeared, Manly put 42 points on the Bulldogs and 54 points on the Tigers to provide a bit of late entertainment.

Halfback and captain Daly Cherry-Evans was the rock alongside Jake Trbojevic. Back-rower Haumole Olakau'atu came of age, playing every game, scoring 10 tries and creating many more. Winger Jason Saab scored 14 tries from 19 games.

Halfback Luke Brooks arrives from Wests Tigers, as Schuster finally displayed he wasn't an answer at halfback. How they need an injury-free run from Turbo Tom.

DOLPHINS (13th)

Top pointscorer: Jamayne Isaako (244); Top tryscorer: Jamayne Isaako (24)

Strongly predicted to be wooden spoonists in their first season as a new franchise, the Dolphins made a staggering entry into the NRL in 2023.

Recruiting mastercoach Wayne Bennett to head up the recruitment and playing operation was their smartest move. Bennett's unfancied troops defied all expectations to start the season with a bang before trailing off and winning only two of their final 12 matches during their inaugural campaign.

The Dolphins recorded victories over the Roosters and Raiders to start the year and tasted defeat, a narrow one at that, for the first time in round four against the Broncos. And they reached their first bye in round 11 having won six of their first 10 matches to put themselves firmly in the charge for the play-offs.

A run of four losses and then another run of seven consecutive losses in the run-in brought a reality check.

Tom Gilbert, one of Bennett's early signings from North Queensland, had set the standards from the start but he picked up a season-ending shoulder injury in Origin I and the side won just two matches in his absence.

Fullback Hamiso Tabuai-Fidow, signed from the Cowboys, was a sensation. The Hammer scored eight tries in his first six matches to earn cult hero status at Redcliffe.

The feel-good factor around the club translated off the field as well with 30,000 people signing up for membership, placing the Dolphins in the top three for membership numbers in the NRL after just one season.

Bennett has recruited some gems for next year with Herbie Farnworth and Thomas Flegler from the Broncos sure to help them improve through the middle and with their ability to post points. Jake Averillo is also an astute purchase, offering glimpses of his huge potential during a trying time with the Bulldogs.

NRL

GOLD COAST TITANS (14th)
Top pointscorer: Tanah Boyd (147); Top tryscorer: Alofiana Khan-Pereira (20)

Another year of non-achievement for the Titans in 2023.

Former St Helens coach Justin Holbrook got the push in June and contract negotiations with their two big stars, Tino Fa'asuamaleaui and David Fifita, led to an unhappy season at Robina.

The Titans fell from 9th to 13th, gaining just two more wins after Holbrook's departure.

Fifita re-signed early in the season but Fa'asuamaleaui was tipped to move on after Holbrook's sacking. He was eventually tied up on a decade-long deal worth an estimated $12 million.

The Titans of 2023 showed flashes of excellence but had a knack of throwing away first-half leads. Their defeat in round eight against the Dolphins saw them lose 28-26 after leading 26-6 at half-time, equalling the biggest ever comeback victory in the NRL.

The signings of Kieran Foran and Sam Verrills were supposed to fix the shortfall they had in 2022 at halfback and at hooker. They were both solid but both had problems with injury - Verrills played only eleven games. The Titans' biggest problem was the lack of a class number seven to go alongside Foran.

Hooker Kruise Leeming appeared in only ten games and was set to return to Super League with Wigan for 2024.

Captain Fa'asuamaleaui was again their best - they won only one game without their star prop and just weren't able to compete in the middle without his presence.

Des Hasler came in as coach for 2024 but a lack of strength in depth could make his job a tough gig.

CANTERBURY BULLDOGS (15th)
Top pointscorer: Matt Burton (138); Top tryscorer: Jake Averillo (12)

It was supposed to be they year that the long-term plan designed by Phil Gould would start to bear fruit for the Bulldogs.

With a new coach in Cameron Ciraldo and high-profile recruits in Reed Mahoney from the Eels and Viliame Kikau from premiers Penrith, many expected the Bulldogs to secure a finals spot.

It started well. After a disappointing loss on the road against Manly, they secured an impressive 26-12 victory over the Storm in round two. They beat the Tigers in round three, lost by only two points at the Warriors and then edged the Cowboys thanks to a late try by Josh Addo-Carr.

Fortunes turned as losses to the Rabbitohs and Eels ended a promising start to their campaign.

The season run-in was a wash-out. After defeat at the Sharks, the Bulldogs conceded 328 points in just eight matches, with only two wins during that period, even when the side were close to full strength. The Bulldogs' points difference was the worst in the NRL, conceding more than 30 points in 16 games. The late-season suspension for a hip drop of boom rookie backrower Jacob Preston didn't help.

And by the time of the run-in, the Dogs were in turmoil following a training drama, which saw one un-named player walk out after a punishment for turning up late for training, being forced to wrestle at least 12 teammates. That was followed by reports that several players were unhappy with the training load under Ciraldo.

The recruitment of Stephen Crichton from Penrith should more than compensate for the losses of Dolphins-bound Jake Averillo but results need to improve to satisfy frustrated Bulldogs fans.

ST GEORGE ILLAWARRA DRAGONS (16th)
Top pointscorer: Zac Lomax (142); Top tryscorer: Mikaele Ravalawa (21)

In what was the worst season in their history as a joint venture, the Dragons recored only five wins and avoided the wooden spoon by a single league win.

It was though a case of what might have been, with ten of their defeats during the season coming by ten points or fewer.

At the end of 2022, the Dragons were in a state of turmoil with pundits expecting head coach Anthony Griffin to be pushed out, with player morale at an all-time low after the club's Mad Monday was cancelled by the coach.

When boom halfback Junior Amone was arrested on assault charges at the start of pre-season, it was clear that the drama was far from over.

On the field, the Dragons' season never got going and the 42-22 round 11 defeat at the Cowboys was a sixth-straight loss.

A few days after, Griffin was axed as head coach. Dragons skipper Ben Hunt promptly dropped a bombshell by asking for a transfer, reportedly willing to pay $150,000 of his own money to leave the club.

Thankfully for St George Illawarra fans, Hunt has since insisted he would remain at the Dragons in 2024, the influence of incoming boss Shane Flanagan pivotal.

With young half Jayden Sullivan already off to Wests Tigers for 2024, losing Hunt would have left the Dragons in disarray.

Interim coach Ryan Carr, the former Featherstone coach, managed to steady the ship in the month that followed Griffin's exit, defeating the Roosters 24-22 in a nail-biting clash at Kogarah, before beating the Rabbitohs 36-30 during the State of Origin period.

After that initial honeymoon period under Carr's leadership, the Saints produced just one victory - a narrow triumph over the Tigers, which ultimately saw them avoid the wooden spoon.

Hunt was the Dragons' star man and Fijian winger Mikaele Ravalawa was prolific, scoring 21 tries in 20 games.

WESTS TIGERS (17th)
Top pointscorer: Brandon Wakeham (62); Top tryscorer: Starford To'a (7)

The Wests Tigers' five-year plan did not go smoothly. A second consecutive wooden spoon says it all.

Tim Sheens was brought in as head coach at the end of the 2022 season with a view to club legend Benji Marshall taking over the coaching role after two seasons.

But the club confirmed in early August that Sheens would be leaving at the end of the season after concerns were raised by key stakeholders over the direction of the club.

After the end of the season, those majority shareholders brought in a former NRL executive to scrutinise the club's structure.

Supporters blamed CEO Justin Pascoe, in particular, with banners inside stadiums during the final weeks of a dismal season.

The past two seasons have been a washout but there has been a longer-term malaise, the Tigers having failed to make the NRL finals for 12 straight seasons.

The Tigers lost the first six games in 2023, got their first points courtesy of the bye, stunned a near full-strength Penrith side 12-8 in treacherous conditions at Bathurst in round 9 and four rounds later hammered the Cowboys 66-18 at Leichhardt. But six weeks after, the result was reversed in Townsville, losing by a record 74-0.

Marshall will become head coach 12 months earlier than planned and his rookie status will be put to the test as a few Tigers stalwarts have made their way out of the exit door.

Luke Brooks heads to Manly Sea Eagles, Daine Laurie to the Panthers, Ken Maumalo to Gold Coast Titans and Joe Ofahengaue to the Eels. Alex Twaal was also being offered around.

Still, Api Koroisau and John Bateman remain and they will be joined by halfbacks Aidan Sezer, Latu Fainu and Dragon Jayden Sullivan. Prop Stefano Utoikamanu, who made Origin, and sensational rookie fullback Jahream Bula also remain.

NRL ROUND-UP

NRL PREMIERSHIP FINALS SERIES

QUALIFYING FINALS
Friday 8th September 2023
Brisbane Broncos 26 .... Melbourne Storm 0
Saturday 9th September 2023
Penrith Panthers 32 .... New Zealand Warriors 6

ELIMINATION FINALS
Saturday 9th September 2023
Cronulla Sharks 12 .... Sydney Roosters 13
Sunday 10th September 2023
Newcastle Knights 30 .... Canberra Raiders 28

SEMI-FINALS
Friday 15th September 2023
Melbourne Storm 18 .... Sydney Roosters 13
Saturday 16th September 2023
New Zealand Warriors 40 .... Newcastle Knights 10

PRELIMINARY FINALS
Friday 22nd September 2023
Penrith Panthers 32 .... Melbourne Storm 4
(at Accor Stadium, Sydney)
Saturday 23rd September 2023
Brisbane Broncos 42 .... New Zealand Warriors 12

NRL GRAND FINAL

Sunday 1st October 2023

BRISBANE BRONCOS 24 PENRITH PANTHERS 26

BRONCOS: 1 Reece Walsh; 2 Jesse Arthars; 3 Kotoni Staggs; 4 Herbie Farnworth; 5 Selwyn Cobbo; 6 Ezra Mam; 7 Adam Reynolds (C); 8 Thomas Flegler; 9 Billy Walters; 10 Payne Haas; 11 Kurt Capewell; 12 Jordan Riki; 13 Patrick Carrigan. Subs (all used): 14 Tyson Smoothy; 15 Brendan Piakura; 16 Kobe Hetherington; 17 Keenan Palasia.
Tries: Flegler (39), Mam (45, 53, 55); **Goals:** Reynolds 4/4.
PANTHERS: 1 Dylan Edwards; 2 Sunia Turuva; 3 Izack Tago; 4 Stephen Crichton; 5 Brian To'o; 6 Jarome Luai; 7 Nathan Cleary (C); 8 Moses Leota; 9 Mitch Kenny; 10 James Fisher-Harris; 11 Scott Sorensen; 12 Liam Martin; 13 Isaah Yeo. Subs (all used): 14 Jack Cogger; 15 Lindsay Smith; 16 Spencer Leniu; 17 Luke Garner.
Tries: Kenny (18), Leota (63), Crichton (68), Cleary (77);
Goals: Cleary 4/4, Crichton 1/1.
Rugby Leaguer & League Express Men of the Match:
Broncos: Ezra Mam; *Panthers:* Nathan Cleary.
Penalty count: 3-2; **Half-time:** 6-8; **Referee:** Adam Gee;
Attendance: 81,947 *(at Accor Stadium, Sydney).*

NRL PREMIERSHIP - FINAL TABLE

	P	W	D	L	B	F	A	D	Pts
Penrith Panthers	24	18	0	6	3	645	312	333	42
Brisbane Broncos	24	18	0	6	3	639	425	214	42
Melbourne Storm	24	16	0	8	3	627	459	168	38
New Zealand Warriors	24	16	0	8	3	572	448	124	38
Newcastle Knights	24	14	1	9	3	626	451	175	35
Cronulla Sharks	24	14	0	10	3	619	497	122	34
Sydney Roosters	24	13	0	11	3	472	496	-24	32
Canberra Raiders	24	13	0	11	3	486	623	-137	32
South Sydney Rabbitohs	24	12	0	12	3	564	505	59	30
Parramatta Eels	24	12	0	12	3	587	574	13	30
North Queensland Cowboys	24	12	0	12	3	546	542	4	30
Manly Sea Eagles	24	11	1	12	3	545	539	6	29
Dolphins	24	9	0	15	3	520	631	-111	24
Gold Coast Titans	24	8	0	16	3	527	653	-126	22
Canterbury Bulldogs	24	7	0	17	3	438	769	-331	20
St George Illawarra Dragons	24	5	0	19	3	474	673	-199	16
Wests Tigers	24	4	0	20	3	385	675	-290	14

* Additional two competition points awarded for each team's bye fixture

LEADING POINTSCORERS

Jamayne Isaako	Dolphins	244
Nick Meaney	Melbourne Storm	222
Nathan Cleary	Penrith Panthers	216
Adam Reynolds	Brisbane Broncos	212
Nicho Hynes	Cronulla Sharks	187

TOP TRYSCORERS

Dominic Young	Newcastle Knights	25
Jamayne Isaako	Dolphins	24
Dallin Watene-Zelezniak	New Zealand Warriors	24
Greg Marzhew	Newcastle Knights	22
Alex Johnston	South Sydney Rabbitohs	21
Ronaldo Mulitalo	Cronulla Sharks	21
Mikaele Ravalawa	St George Illawarra Dragons	21
Brian To'o	Penrith Panthers	21

DALLY M AWARDS

Dally M Medal (Player of the Year): Kalyn Ponga (Newcastle Knights)
Provan Summons Medal (People's choice):
Nicho Hynes (Cronulla Sharks)
Coach of the Year: Andrew Webster (New Zealand Warriors)
Captain of the Year: Adam Reynolds (Brisbane Broncos)
Rookie of the Year: Sunia Turuva (Penrith Panthers)

STATE CHAMPIONSHIP *(winners of NSW and Queensland Cups)*
Sunday 1st October 2023
Brisbane Tigers 22 .... South Sydney Rabbitohs 42
(at Accor Stadium, Sydney)

NRLW GRAND FINAL *(Women's Premiership)*
Sunday 1st October 2023
Gold Coast Titans 18 .... Newcastle Knights 24
(at Accor Stadium, Sydney)

STATE OF ORIGIN
That Queensland spirit

Queensland wrapped up the 2023 State of Origin series after the first two games, recording a stunning comeback win in Adelaide before putting the cleaners through the Blues in game two in front of a passionate crowd in Brisbane.

New South Wales avoided the whitewash back in Sydney for game three but it didn't ease the pressure on coach Brad Fittler in the wake of the Blues' second-straight series loss to Queensland. He resigned at the end of September.

The history of State of Origin is littered with against-the-odds Queensland comebacks.

Game One of the 2023 series will go down as one of the greatest.

Trailing by two points with seven minutes remaining, down to 12 men due to a contentious Thomas Flegler sin-binning and already without injured trio Tom Gilbert, Selwyn Cobbo and Murray Taulagi, the Maroons shocked the Blues with two tries in three minutes to snatch a 26-18 victory.

The Queenslanders hit the front thanks to two-try hero Hamiso Tabuai-Fidow, before hulking prop Lindsay Collins sprinted past a slew of tired Blues, out-leaping his club captain James Tedesco to reel in a Daly Cherry-Evans kick and hand Cameron Munster the match-sealing score.

The Maroons had charged to an early 10-0 lead before the Blues eventually converted a mountain of possession into an 18-16 lead.

And Brad Fittler's men looked certain to win once Flegler was dispatched for a supposed shoulder charge on Tom Trbojevic in the 69th minute, which resulted in a failed head-injury assessment for the star centre. But Queensland somehow clawed their way to victory.

Three years after Rugby League's greatest rivalry hit the Adelaide Oval for the first time in the COVID-affected 2020 series, 48,613 fans packed the scenic and historic venue.

Gutsy Cowboys prop Reuben Cotter claimed man-of-the-match honours for his Herculean 80-minute effort, covering for the injured Gilbert and churning out 48 desperate tackles - nine more than anyone else on the park.

Queensland coach Billy Slater wasn't afraid to tinker with the line-up that claimed the previous year's series, notably dumping fullback Kalyn Ponga for debutant Reece Walsh and Origin stalwart Dane Gagai for Dolphins rookie Tabuai-Fidow, as well as snubbing reliable second-rower Kurt Capewell despite suspensions sidelining back-row pair Jeremiah Nanai and Felise Kaufusi.

STATE OF ORIGIN - GAME I

Wednesday 31st May 2023

NEW SOUTH WALES 18 QUEENSLAND 26

NEW SOUTH WALES: 1 James Tedesco (Sydney Roosters) (C); 2 Brian To'o (Penrith Panthers); 3 Stephen Crichton (Penrith Panthers); 4 Tom Trbojevic (Manly Sea Eagles); 5 Josh Addo-Carr (Canterbury Bulldogs); 6 Jarome Luai (Penrith Panthers); 7 Nathan Cleary (Penrith Panthers); 8 Tevita Pangai (Canterbury Bulldogs); 9 Api Koroisau (Wests Tigers); 10 Payne Haas (Brisbane Broncos); 11 Tyson Frizell (Newcastle Knights); 12 Hudson Young (Canberra Raiders); 13 Isaah Yeo (Penrith Panthers). Subs (all used): 14 Junior Paulo (Parramatta Eels); 15 Cameron Murray (South Sydney Rabbitohs); 16 Liam Martin (Penrith Panthers); 17 Nicho Hynes (Cronulla Sharks).
Tries: Martin (32), Koroisau (44), Crichton (67); **Goals:** Cleary 3/3.
QUEENSLAND: 1 Reece Walsh (Brisbane Broncos); 2 Selwyn Cobbo (Brisbane Broncos); 3 Valentine Holmes (North Queensland Cowboys); 4 Hamiso Tabuai-Fidow (Dolphins); 5 Murray Taulagi (North Queensland Cowboys); 6 Cameron Munster (Melbourne Storm); 7 Daly Cherry-Evans (Manly Sea Eagles) (C); 8 Tino Fa'asuamaleaui (Gold Coast Titans); 9 Ben Hunt (St George Illawarra Dragons); 16 Reuben Cotter (North Queensland Cowboys); 11 David Fifita (Gold Coast Titans); 12 Tom Gilbert (Dolphins); 13 Patrick Carrigan (Brisbane Broncos). Subs (all used): 8 Thomas Flegler (Brisbane Broncos); 10 Lindsay Collins (Sydney Roosters); 14 Harry Grant (Melbourne Storm); 17 Jai Arrow (South Sydney Rabbitohs).
Tries: Tabuai-Fidow (8, 74), Cobbo (11, 57), Munster (77); **Goals:** Holmes 3/5.
Sin bin: Flegler (69) - dangerous challenge on Trbojevic.
Rugby Leaguer & League Express Men of the Match:
New South Wales: Liam Martin; *Queensland:* Reuben Cotter.
Penalty count: 8-6; **Half-time:** 6-10; **Referee:** Ashley Klein; **Attendance:** 48,613 *(at Adelaide Oval).*

State of Origin

Fittler also reshuffled his deck in a bid to reclaim the shield, calling up first-gamers Tevita Pangai Junior, Hudson Young and Nicho Hynes, plus recalling Josh Addo-Carr, Tyson Frizell and the fit-again Tom Trbojevic.

Strike centre Latrell Mitchell was NSW's most notable omission after suffering a calf complaint at training on the Sunday, replaced by Penrith's Stephen Crichton. But halfback Nathan Cleary managed to overcome an infected tooth to take the field.

Another bizarre chapter in the build-up was the back and forth over NSW's uncharacteristic navy-blue jumper, rejecting the NRL's request for them to don their traditional sky-blue kit.

The Maroons wrapped up their second straight Origin crown with a ruthless 32-6 dismantling of New South Wales in Brisbane.

Valentine Holmes scored a try in each half lining up against hooker Damien Cook, who Brad Fittler deployed in the centres after Tom Trbojevic went off with a torn pectoral muscle in the third minute.

The Blues dominated the first half but failed to penetrate the disciplined defence of the hosts, who turned on the style late.

While heart-and-soul prop Lindsay Collins won the official man-of-the-match gong, Maroons skipper Daly Cherry-Evans was the most influential player on the field and rookie Reece Walsh was electric at the back.

The dual dismissals of Walsh and Jarome Luai for head-butting each other in the 80th minute, plus Josh Addo-Carr's sin-binning for a punch in the same scuffle, added a fiery footnote to a bitter night for the Blues.

It was Queensland's biggest win since their 52-6 demolition job in the 2015 deciders.

Cook's display was the talking point of the evening, caught out for five of Queensland's six tries. But he was hung out to dry by his coach, who should have chosen a more suitable replacement for Trbojevic out wide. The obvious option was agile backrower Cameron Murray, who instead sat on the bench until the 48th minute, replacing debutant Stefano Utoikamanu after a bafflingly short 12-minute stint.

Fittler's bizarre in-game management was only one piece of a lifeless performance by his side, which looked bereft of ideas and basic organisation.

In fairness, injury ripped major holes through NSW's team sheet, after halfback Nathan Cleary tore his hamstring and hooker Api Koroisau broke his jaw on club duties. Latrell Mitchell was also named to make his return from the calf complaint that ruled him out of the first clash, but failed to recover in time to line up.

On top of his casualty list, Fittler dropped debutants Tevita Pangai Junior and Nicho Hynes after a tough Game One.

Cowboys dummy-half Reece Robson made a surprising Origin debut at hooker, toiling for 80 minutes with his intended replacement Cook used out of position.

Eels playmaker Mitchell Moses controversially leapfrogged Hynes to Cleary's vacant number seven jersey, while Tigers forward Stefano Utoikamanu also made his bow from the interchange.

Rampaging Maroons backrower David Fifita challenged Moses all night in defence. While

STATE OF ORIGIN - GAME II
Wednesday 21st June 2023

QUEENSLAND 32 NEW SOUTH WALES 6

QUEENSLAND: 1 Reece Walsh (Brisbane Broncos); 2 Xavier Coates (Melbourne Storm); 3 Valentine Holmes (North Queensland Cowboys); 4 Hamiso Tabuai-Fidow (Dolphins); 5 Murray Taulagi (North Queensland Cowboys); 6 Cameron Munster (Melbourne Storm); 7 Daly Cherry-Evans (Manly Sea Eagles) (C); 10 Tino Fa'asuamaleaui (Gold Coast Titans); 9 Ben Hunt (St George Illawarra Dragons); 15 Thomas Flegler (Brisbane Broncos); 11 David Fifita (Gold Coast Titans); 16 Reuben Cotter (North Queensland Cowboys); 13 Patrick Carrigan (Brisbane Broncos). Subs (all used): 8 Lindsay Collins (Sydney Roosters); 12 Jeremiah Nanai (North Queensland Cowboys); 14 Harry Grant (Melbourne Storm); 17 Moeaki Fotuaika (Gold Coast Titans).
Tries: Holmes (9, 43), Taulagi (34), Tabuai-Fidow (51), Coates (65), Nanai (74); **Goals:** Holmes 4/6.
Dismissal: Walsh (80) - headbutt on Luai.
NEW SOUTH WALES: 1 James Tedesco (Sydney Roosters) (C); 2 Brian To'o (Penrith Panthers); 3 Stephen Crichton (Penrith Panthers); 4 Tom Trbojevic (Manly Sea Eagles); 5 Josh Addo-Carr (Canterbury Bulldogs); 6 Jarome Luai (Penrith Panthers); 7 Mitchell Moses (Parramatta Eels); 8 Junior Paulo (Parramatta Eels); 17 Reece Robson (North Queensland Cowboys); 10 Payne Haas (Brisbane Broncos); 11 Tyson Frizell (Newcastle Knights); 12 Hudson Young (Canberra Raiders); 13 Isaah Yeo (Penrith Panthers). Subs (all used): 9 Damien Cook (South Sydney Rabbitohs); 14 Stefano Utoikamanu (Wests Tigers); 15 Cameron Murray (South Sydney Rabbitohs); 16 Liam Martin (Penrith Panthers).
Try: Cook (58); **Goals:** Crichton 1/1.
Dismissal: Luai (80) - headbutt on Walsh.
Sin bin: Addo-Carr (80) - punching.
Rugby Leaguer & League Express Men of the Match:
Queensland: Daly Cherry-Evans; *New South Wales:* Payne Haas.
Penalty count: 2-8; **Half-time:** 10-0; **Referee:** Ashley Klein; **Attendance:** 52,433 *(at Suncorp Stadium, Brisbane).*

the Parramatta halfback stood up well physically, he struggled to make an impact alongside disappointing stand-off Luai.

For Queensland, winger Selwyn Cobbo (hip), backrower Tom Gilbert (shoulder) and bench forward Jai Arrow (ankle) all dropped out of the 17 that claimed the series opener, replaced by Xavier Coates, Jeremiah Nanai and Moeaki Fotuaika.

The Maroons scored six tries on the night but it was their defence in their own '20' that was the foundation, the Blues having the wealth of possession for the vast majority of the match. Queensland led 10-0 at half-time despite only having 42 per cent of the ball. But they still had more energy in the second half, adding four more tries to finish off the rout.

Walsh, making just his second Origin appearance, was inspirational for Queensland; superb under the high ball and decisive on attack as he played major roles in two of the hosts' tries.

Valentine Holmes scored two tries, while Murray Taulagi, Hamiso Tabuai-Fidow, Xavier Coates and Nanai also crossed. Cook crossed for the Blues' only try in the 57th minute of a disjointed performance.

New South Wales avoided the whitewash with a 24-10 win at the Accor Stadium (Homebush).

Barnstorming 21-year-old on-debut Newcastle centre Bradman Best scored a try in each half, teaming up with Cody Walker and Josh Addo-Carr to torment the Maroons down the Blues' left edge.

Coach Fittler attracted plenty of heat for selecting Best over Penrith's Izack Tago or Parramatta's Will Penisini - one of seven changes to his team sheet for the dead rubber. But Best vindicated Fittler's faith with a memorable Origin bow.

Fellow Game Three call-up Walker earned man-of-the-match honours for his dazzling display, while maligned captain James Tedesco also shone.

The Blues scored three tries in a ten-minute patch midway through the first half and kept Queensland at arm's length for the remainder of the contest as the vast majority of the impressive 75,342 crowd in Sydney got the result they were hoping for.

Reuben Cotter was awarded the Wally Lewis Medal for player of the series following another industrious display.

Victorious Queensland coach Billy Slater only made two enforced changes, swapping suspended fullback Reece Walsh and injured forward Thomas Flegler with dependable Titan AJ Brimson and firebrand Raider Corey Horsburgh.

Fittler, on the other hand, looked like he was throwing darts at the selection table ... but he was vindicated in the end. Hudson Young, Jarome Luai, Junior Paulo, Stefano Utoikamanu, Tyson Frizell and injured pair Payne Haas (ankle) and Tom Trbojevic (pectoral) exited the side that lost Game Two in Brisbane, replaced by debutants Best and Keaon Koloamatangi plus Walker, Jake Trbojevic, Reagan Campbell-Gillard, Jacob Saifiti and Clint Gutherson.

Queensland opened the scoring through David Fifita in the 12th minute but Walker turned the game on its head in a ten-minute spell midway through the first half.

First, NSW released Josh Addo-Carr down the left and while the lightning-quick winger was brought down after a 50-metre break, the Blues quickly shifted right for Brian To'o to touch down.

STATE OF ORIGIN - GAME III

Wednesday 12th July 2023

NEW SOUTH WALES 24 QUEENSLAND 10

NEW SOUTH WALES: 1 James Tedesco (Sydney Roosters) (C); 2 Brian To'o (Penrith Panthers); 3 Stephen Crichton (Penrith Panthers); 4 Bradman Best (Newcastle Knights); 5 Josh Addo-Carr (Canterbury Bulldogs); 6 Cody Walker (South Sydney Rabbitohs); 7 Mitchell Moses (Parramatta Eels); 8 Jake Trbojevic (Manly Sea Eagles); 9 Damien Cook (South Sydney Rabbitohs); 10 Reagan Campbell-Gillard (Parramatta Eels); 11 Liam Martin (Penrith Panthers); 12 Keaon Koloamatangi (South Sydney Rabbitohs); 13 Cameron Murray (South Sydney Rabbitohs). Subs (all used): 14 Isaah Yeo (Penrith Panthers); 15 Jacob Saifiti (Newcastle Knights); 16 Reece Robson (North Queensland Cowboys); 17 Clint Gutherson (Parramatta Eels).
Tries: To'o (15), Addo-Carr (21), Best (24, 65); **Goals:** Crichton 4/6.
QUEENSLAND: 1 AJ Brimson (Gold Coast Titans); 2 Xavier Coates (Melbourne Storm); 3 Valentine Holmes (North Queensland Cowboys); 4 Hamiso Tabuai-Fidow (Dolphins); 5 Murray Taulagi (North Queensland Cowboys); 6 Cameron Munster (Melbourne Storm); 7 Daly Cherry-Evans (Manly Sea Eagles) (C); 8 Reuben Cotter (North Queensland Cowboys); 9 Harry Grant (Melbourne Storm); 10 Tino Fa'asuamaleaui (Gold Coast Titans); 11 David Fifita (Gold Coast Titans); 12 Jeremiah Nanai (North Queensland Cowboys); 13 Patrick Carrigan (Brisbane Broncos). Subs (all used): 14 Ben Hunt (St George Illawarra Dragons); 15 Lindsay Collins (Sydney Roosters); 16 Moeaki Fotuaika (Gold Coast Titans); 17 Corey Horsburgh (Canberra Raiders).
Tries: Fifita (12), Tabuai-Fidow (36); **Goals:** Holmes 1/2.
Rugby Leaguer & League Express Men of the Match:
New South Wales: Cody Walker; *Queensland:* Reuben Cotter.
Penalty count: 6-5; **Half-time:** 18-10; **Referee:** Ashley Klein; **Attendance:** 75,342 *(at Accor Stadium, Sydney)*.

Wally Lewis Medal (Man of the Series): Reuben Cotter (Queensland).

State of Origin

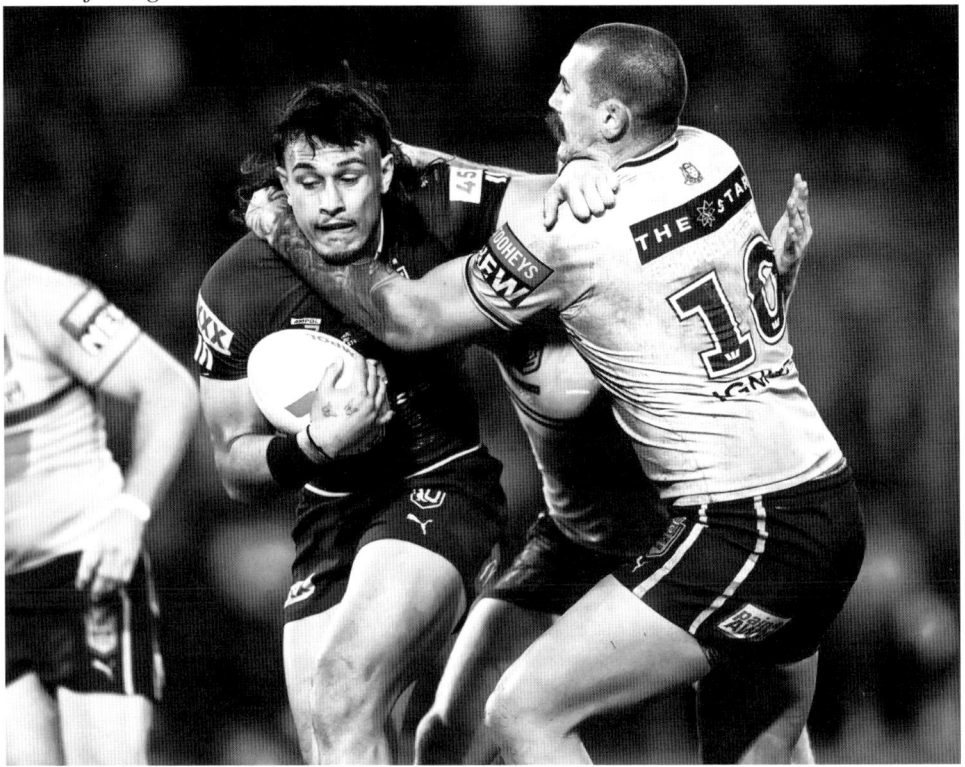

Queensland's Tino Fa'asuamaleaui collared by New South Wales' Reagan Campbell-Gillard during Origin III

Walker went back to that same edge soon after, spreading the ball wide to Best, who tipped onto Addo-Carr. The Canterbury winger was inside his own 40 metres but dashed down field, chipped over Queensland fullback AJ Brimson and regathered to score a sensational try. Walker then sent Best over by delaying a pass that tricked the Queensland defence.

Stephen Crichton added two penalties for the Blues but missed two of his three first-half conversions to keep the Maroons in the contest.

Queensland were sloppy and struggled for territory but a try courtesy of Hamiso Tabuai-Fidow before the half-time break brought them to within eight points at the interval.

As the second half wore on, Queensland looked bereft of ideas and resorted to kicking high bombs.

The NSW back three handled that with ease and then went up the other end to put the game beyond doubt as Best profited from a vintage Tedesco break.

6
INTERNATIONAL YEAR

INTERNATIONALS
England tough it out

The end of the domestic seasons on both sides of the world saw a flurry of international activity.

In May, the French Federation XIII announced that it would be unable as planned to host the 2025 World Cup for financial reasons which meant the eight-team European Championships scheduled for the end of 2023, which was to act as a World Cup qualifier, were cancelled, so Ireland, Scotland, Wales and Spain didn't get in a single game that year.

The on-going stalemate between the NRL and its players and clubs over a collective bargaining agreement which wasn't settled until August also meant a delay in finalising an international calendar. Tonga's three-match Test series in England, a piece of history as the first tour by a Pacific nation, did take place, with the players taking the option to play in England rather than compete in a possible Four Nations tournament down under.

And once the CBA was agreed, a Pacific Rugby League Championship involving six men's teams and seven women's teams was announced.

England won the series against Tonga 3-0 after three close-fought games.

With so many players proving their international class in the absence of some of England's first-choice stars, the series on the whole was a success ahead of subsequent planned challenges - though Samoa's planned tour in 2024 was cancelled - a tour to Australia in 2025 and the next World Cup in the southern hemisphere in 2026 were still in the calendar.

The first Test in St Helens saw Shaun Wane's side emerge with a 22-18 victory over Tonga, despite having only a week's preparation time after the previous week's Grand Final.

It was 12-12 at half-time, England then stretching the lead to 22-12, before Tonga came back with a late converted try to threaten victory.

Without captain George Williams, suspended for the first two games from the domestic season, St Helens prodigy Jack Welsby was given the captain's role for England at the age of 22

Wane selected four players from the NRL in his starting line-up, with Tom Burgess, John Bateman, Elliott Whitehead and Victor Radley all selected in the forwards, only Daryl Clark and Mike McMeeken from Super League.

But his seven starting backs were all Super League players, with Hull KR's Mikey Lewis replacing Williams, while a serious sinus infection for Dominic Young meant an easy selection on the wings, with St Helens' Tommy Makinson and Catalans' Tom Johnstone earning the spots, with a centre combination of Harry Newman and Toby King.

Johnstone scored two great tries - the first one coming from a brilliant long Welsby pass that put the winger in at the corner and the second when he intercepted Will Hopoate's pass, which was effectively the game breaking moment.

Lewis was sensational, scoring a try and setting up another with two superb pieces of individual play in the first half.

He needed only eight minutes to make his first highlight on the international stage, setting the opening try of the series in motion with a step inside that beat Tyson Frizell and saw him break clean through the line. He rounded the fullback, Will Hopoate, and was only finally tackled close to the try-line by covering right winger Starford Toa.

But the damage had been done, with Tonga now lacking numbers on that side and Clark

Tommy Makinson brought down by the challenge of Tui Lolohea

quickly moved the ball left to Radley, who passed wide to King, one of several players queuing up to score the try.

But two Tongan tries in nine minutes turned things around, the first scored by Toa, off Hopoate's delayed pass, and the second by Frizell, from Tui Lolohea's perfect grubber. Isaiah Katoa kicked Tonga into a 10-6 lead but the crowd soon had something to cheer again thanks to Lewis.

The halfback received the ball on the right side with Toluta'u Koula rapidly advancing on him from the wing. Lewis dummied to see off that threat and then stepped around Moses Suli to clear the path to his first international try.

Harry Smith's conversion nudged England back ahead at 12-10 but they couldn't hold onto that lead for the final eight minutes of the first half as Katoa knocked over a penalty after Bateman was punished for interference.

Tonga could even have led if Katoa had landed from over 40 metres with the final kick of the half after a penalty for a Lewis ball steal but his effort flew short and wide as the teams returned to the changing rooms at 12-12.

The crucial try came in the 54th minute. Welsby, on home soil in St Helens, created it with a brilliant assist, perfectly arrowing his over-the-top pass to miss out Will Penisini and land in the hands of Johnstone.

The winger could only score from there, and the same could be said of his second try 13 minutes later, which this time came from poor Tongan handling rather than good English play.

Hopoate's pass from fullback was fumbled by both Penisini and then Toa, with Johnstone the man to pouch the ball and gallop away for a try which, allied with a third Smith goal of the day, put England 22-12 ahead.

An excellent tackle over the line by Haumole Olakau'atu prevented Tom Burgess touching down. It was a lifeline Tonga made use of with three minutes to go. Welsby fumbled a Radley pass

FIRST TEST

Sunday 22nd October 2023

ENGLAND 22 TONGA 18

ENGLAND: 1 Jack Welsby (St Helens) (C); 2 Tommy Makinson (St Helens); 3 Harry Newman (Leeds Rhinos); 4 Toby King (Wigan Warriors); 5 Tom Johnstone (Catalans Dragons); 6 Mikey Lewis (Hull KR); 7 Harry Smith (Wigan Warriors); 8 Tom Burgess (South Sydney Rabbitohs); 9 Daryl Clark (Warrington Wolves); 10 Matty Lees (St Helens); 11 John Bateman (Wests Tigers); 12 Elliott Whitehead (Canberra Raiders); 13 Victor Radley (Sydney Roosters). Subs (all used): 14 Danny Walker (Warrington Wolves); 15 Morgan Knowles (St Helens); 16 Chris Hill (Huddersfield Giants); 17 Mike McMeeken (Catalans Dragons).
Tries: King (8), Lewis (30), Johnstone (54, 67); **Goals:** Smith 3/4.
TONGA: 1 Will Hopoate (St Helens); 2 Starford Toa (Wests Tigers); 3 Will Penisini (Parramatta Eels); 4 Moses Suli (St George Illawarra Dragons); 5 Tolutau Koula (Manly Sea Eagles); 6 Tui Lolohea (Huddersfield Giants); 7 Isaiya Katoa (Dolphins); 8 Addin Fonua-Blake (New Zealand Warriors) (C); 9 Silvia Havili (South Sydney Rabbitohs); 10 Moeaki Fotuaika (Gold Coast Titans); 11 Tyson Frizell (Newcastle Knights); 12 Keaon Koloamatangi (South Sydney Rabbitohs); 13 Felise Kaufusi (Dolphins). Subs (all used): 14 Dion Teaupa (South Sydney Rabbitohs); 15 Tevita Tatola (South Sydney Rabbitohs); 16 Haumole Olakau'atu (Manly Sea Eagles); 17 Hame Sele (South Sydney Rabbitohs).
Tries: Toa (15), Frizell (24), Koula (78); **Goals:** I Katoa 3/5.
Rugby Leaguer & League Express Men of the Match:
England: Mikey Lewis; *Tonga:* Addin Fonua-Blake.
Penalty count: 4-4; **Half-time:** 12-12; **Referee:** Liam Moore; **Attendance:** 12,898 *(at Totally Wicked Stadium, St Helens).*

Internationals

in attack and England were soon on the back foot, watching Koula go into the left corner from quick passes by Hopoate and Suli. Katoa converted from the touchline. It was a nervy final two minutes but England navigated through.

Tonga coach Kristian Woolf was returning to his old stomping ground of St Helens, where he won three Super League titles and after the game he was critical of the differing refereeing interpretations in Super League that allowed slowing down the play the ball. Wane used the comment as motivation for the rest of the series.

England secured the series with a 14-4 win in Huddersfield the following Saturday after a tough battle against a strong Tongan side struggling in wet conditions.

Both teams made two changes to their line-ups from the first Test. But while Tonga's were by choice, calling up Junior Tupou and Eliesa Katoa, England's were both enforced.

St Helens players Tommy Makinson and Morgan Knowles were out with wrist and thumb injuries respectively and were replaced by Matty Ashton and Liam Farrell.

The game was decided by two first-half Ashton tries. Warrington winger Ashton wasted little time in making an impact, with his first try coming just seven minutes into his second England appearance.

After Felise Kaufusi gifted England attacking position with an off-the-ball hit on Jack Welsby, Victor Radley and Harry Smith combined nicely to find Harry Newman, whose smartly-timed pass gave Ashton enough space to race into the corner.

Smith continued his superb recent kicking record from the tee with a touchline conversion and England were 6-0 ahead.

Tonga certainly had their chances to respond, but couldn't take them. Tupou was excellently tackled into touch by Ashton, while Toluta'u Koula - listed on the wing but playing at fullback - dashed straight through the defensive line from a scrum, bisecting Newman and Ashton, only to inexplicably drop the ball over the sideline.

Smith took the chance to extend the score to 8-0 with a penalty awarded for a ball-steal and England continued to defend their advantage well.

Isaiah Katoa was held out just short after a dummy and the subsequent, and last, play was smothered by Daryl Clark, forcing a Tui Lolohea error on his home Huddersfield turf.

That proved a costly moment, as England marched down the pitch and Mikey

Mikey Lewis and Tom Burgess celebrate victory

SECOND TEST

Saturday 28th October 2023

ENGLAND 14 TONGA 4

ENGLAND: 1 Jack Welsby (St Helens) (C); 2 Matty Ashton (Warrington Wolves); 3 Harry Newman (Leeds Rhinos); 4 Toby King (Wigan Warriors); 5 Tom Johnstone (Catalans Dragons); 6 Mikey Lewis (Hull KR); 7 Harry Smith (Wigan Warriors); 8 Tom Burgess (South Sydney Rabbitohs); 9 Daryl Clark (Warrington Wolves); 10 Matty Lees (St Helens); 11 John Bateman (Wests Tigers); 12 Elliott Whitehead (Canberra Raiders); 13 Victor Radley (Sydney Roosters). Subs (all used): 14 Danny Walker (Warrington Wolves); 15 Liam Farrell (Wigan Warriors); 16 Chris Hill (Huddersfield Giants); 17 Mike McMeeken (Catalans Dragons).
Tries: Ashton (7, 36); **Goals:** Smith 3/4.
TONGA: 1 Will Hopoate (St Helens); 2 Junior Tupou (Wests Tigers); 3 Will Penisini (Parramatta Eels); 4 Moses Suli (St George Illawarra Dragons); 5 Tolutau Koula (Manly Sea Eagles); 6 Tui Lolohea (Huddersfield Giants); 7 Isaiya Katoa (Dolphins); 8 Addin Fonua-Blake (New Zealand Warriors) (C); 9 Siliva Havili (South Sydney Rabbitohs); 10 Tevita Tatola (South Sydney Rabbitohs); 11 Tyson Frizell (Newcastle Knights); 12 Haumole Olakau'atu (Manly Sea Eagles); 13 Felise Kaufusi (Dolphins). Subs (all used): 14 Dion Teaupa (South Sydney Rabbitohs); 15 Moeaki Fotuaika (Gold Coast Titans); 16 Keaon Koloamatangi (South Sydney Rabbitohs); 17 Eliesa Katoa (Melbourne Storm).
Try: Koula (56); **Goals:** I Katoa 0/1.
Rugby Leaguer & League Express Men of the Match:
England: Mike McMeeken; *Tonga:* Felise Kaufusi.
Penalty count: 7-5; **Half-time:** 12-0; **Referee:** Jack Smith; **Attendance:** 11,210 *(at John Smith's Stadium, Huddersfield).*

Lewis placed a perfectly-weighted kick that sat at the end of the in-goal. Ashton was sharper than Will Hopoate, touching down for a 12-0 half-time lead.

His two scores proved the only England tries of the game, with their second-half performance failing to match the first.

That said, opposing winger - and the two-try hero of the first Test - Tom Johnstone should have got them another, when Mike McMeeken defied his front-row position with a perfect low kick out wide. But Johnstone mis-judged the low bounce and knocked on inches from the line.

It proved a rare chance for England, whose only second-half points instead came from the boot of Smith with another penalty, given for a Tyson Frizell ball-steal.

Tonga enjoyed their best spell. Katoa made a break but Dion Teaupa was subsequently tackled in front of the posts, while a deflected kick allowed Frizell to run in behind and pick out Koula, only for Johnstone to come across in heroic fashion and make the tackle.

But after back-to-back penalties, Tonga finally found a way to score as Hopoate's sharp, cut-out pass allowed Koula to this time go over.

Katoa couldn't add the conversion and it would remain at 14-4 for the rest of the match. The only moment of excitement in the final quarter came from England. Tom Burgess's offload released Lewis down middle and he almost went all the way to add to his burgeoning international highlight reel, but the Hull KR man was denied at the last by Katoa.

England saved their best performance of the series for the dry track of Headingley where they thoroughly outplayed Tonga in a 26-4 win and a 3-0 series whitewash.

Making his final appearance before international retirement, Elliot Whitehead was one of the try-scorers (and was very close to scoring another) and among the best performers. John Bateman and Tom Burgess also shone in the pack to defuse the Tongan power.

George Williams made a seamless return to the team after England's captain missed the first two games through suspension, providing a fine balance in the halves alongside Harry Smith, who again controlled proceedings and was afterwards named Player of the Series, earning the Nan Halafihi Medal, named after the Tongan player who came to England in the 1950s and played for Hull FC in the 1960 Challenge Cup Final.

In the outside backs, Tom Johnstone was again a threat in a dangerous left-edge combination with Ben Currie who, alongside Robbie Mulhern and Tyler Dupree, made a first appearance of the series, and marked it with a try.

On the other flank, both Matty Ashton and Harry Newman also registered tries, the latter giving another standout performance in front of his home Headingley crowd.

England quickly backed up a much-publicised pre-match determination to seal a whitewash and twice could have scored in the opening minutes.

First Ashton, whose try double won the second Test, chased a Williams kick to the right corner and, when Toluta'u Koula slipped and missed the ball, was agonisingly close to touching down over the line. Instead England settled for a drop-out and after an error apiece were back on the attack with Currie the next to go close, held up by Koula and Haumole Olakau'atu over the line after a nice move on the last play.

They broke the deadlock after 14

THIRD TEST

Saturday 4th November 2023

ENGLAND 26 TONGA 4

ENGLAND: 1 Jack Welsby (St Helens); 2 Matty Ashton (Warrington Wolves); 3 Harry Newman (Leeds Rhinos); 4 Ben Currie (Warrington Wolves); 5 Tom Johnstone (Catalans Dragons); 6 George Williams (Warrington Wolves) (C); 7 Harry Smith (Wigan Warriors); 8 Tom Burgess (South Sydney Rabbitohs); 9 Daryl Clark (Warrington Wolves); 10 Matty Lees (St Helens); 11 John Bateman (Wests Tigers); 12 Elliott Whitehead (Canberra Raiders); 13 Robbie Mulhern (Leigh Leopards). Subs (all used): 14 Danny Walker (Warrington Wolves); 15 Tyler Dupree (Wigan Warriors); 16 Chris Hill (Huddersfield Giants); 17 Mike McMeeken (Catalans Dragons).
Tries: Currie (14), Ashton (25), Whitehead (45), Newman (65);
Goals: Smith 5/5.
Sin bin: Lees (35) - hair pull on Olakau'atu.
TONGA: 1 Will Hopoate (St Helens) (C); 2 Will Penisini (Parramatta Eels); 3 Konrad Hurrell (St Helens); 4 Moses Suli (St George Illawarra Dragons); 5 Tolutau Koula (Manly Sea Eagles); 6 Tui Lolohea (Huddersfield Giants); 7 Isaiya Katoa (Dolphins); 8 Hame Sele (South Sydney Rabbitohs); 9 Siliva Havili (South Sydney Rabbitohs); 17 Felise Kaufusi (Dolphins); 11 Tyson Frizell (Newcastle Knights); 12 Haumole Olakau'atu (Manly Sea Eagles); 13 Keaon Koloamatangi (South Sydney Rabbitohs). Subs (all used): 14 Latu Fainu (Wests Tigers); 15 Moeaki Fotuaika (Gold Coast Titans); 16 Eliesa Katoa (Melbourne Storm); 18 Siua Wong (Sydney Roosters).
Try: E Katoa (68); **Goals:** I Katoa 0/1.
Sin bin: Koloamatangi (35) - fighting; Hurrell (57) - punching McMeeken.
Rugby Leaguer & League Express Men of the Match:
England: Elliott Whitehead; *Tonga:* Haumole Olakau'atu.
Penalty count: 6-6; **Half-time:** 14-0; **Referee:** Chris Kendall;
Attendance: 15,477 *(at Headingley, Leeds).*

Internationals

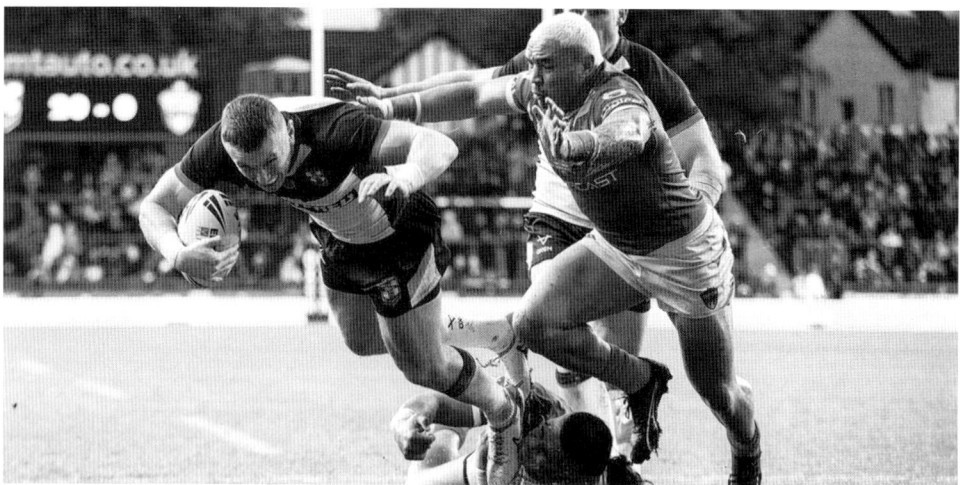

Harry Newman crashes over the Tonga tryline

minutes, with Currie getting his try this time after an exceptional play down the middle involving Newman and Burgess before Harry Smith sent in Currie, with Smith converting.

England comfortably saw out the first assault on their try-line midway through the half, and then immediately switched focus to attack, with Bateman offloading superbly for Newman to send in Ashton with a brilliant backflick.

Smith converted from the sideline and added a penalty - awarded for a Latu Fainu tip tackle on Burgess - to make the score 14-0 with seven minutes of the first half to go.

Tonga's response from the restart was extra physicality and it brought the biggest on-field flashpoint of a tense series. Matty Lees suffered a big Siua Wong hit from the kick-off and Haumole Olakau'atu stayed down on the prop, who showed his frustration by pulling the lengthy hair of his opponent (Newman also committed the same bizarre offence in the second half, on the similarly long-locked Moses Suli). Lees and the in-running Keaon Koloamatangi were both shown yellow cards by Chris Kendall for their part.

Tonga got hooker Siliva Havili back at the start of the second half following a HIA but the game was put beyond them for certain within five minutes of the restart.

Jack Welsby sparked the move with a fine cut-out pass for Johnstone, who hared down the left wing with plenty of support on the inside. He found Currie, who slipped in Whitehead for a fitting try, converted by Smith for 20-0.

Tonga now needed to regain some respect. Instead, Konrad Hurrell mindlessly had several swings at Mike McMeeken in a tackle and the yellow card given was the very least he deserved on his only appearance of the series.

The one-man advantage gave England extra impetus to play. Whitehead was unfortunate not to have a second try when he dived onto a Danny Walker grubber, video-referee Tom Grant deciding he hadn't quite grounded. But they were soon celebrating the try of the series anyway.

Again it came from a Johnstone sprint down the left touchline, with the ball subsequently kept alive through several hands before being launched to the other side of the field by a booming flat Smith kick.

Newman juggled the catch, then handed off one defender and made for the line. Tyson Frizell tried to stop him in time but the centre slid over and the try was approved.

Tonga got a consolation try on 68 minutes as Eliesa Katoa crashed onto a ball from unrelated namesake Isaiya to give the always-smiling Tongan contingent in the crowd something to applaud.

But England's rearguard was back in evidence at the very end, as a charging Will Hopoate was halted and then, with the final play of the game, Koula went for the corner, only for Newman and Welsby to race in and intervene with a tackle that was celebrated like a try.

Internationals

Newly appointed England captain George Williams led a youthful England side to a resounding 64-0 victory over France in the mid-season international held at Warrington in April.

With 13 players earning first caps, England ran in eleven tries in a high-quality performance. Of the new boys, Leeds winger Ash Handley made the most notable impression, scoring a hat-trick of tries amid a top all-round display. Matty Ashton was just as hard-working on the opposite wing, while Tyler Dupree and James Harrison were strong off the bench, along with starting prop Tom Holroyd.

Toby King, who played for Ireland at the previous year's World Cup, was also among a diverse group of debutants, along with the lively Jez Litten, solid Morgan Smithies and teenager Matty Nicholson.

Ethan Havard and Danny Walker also touched down on their international bow, as two of ten players wearing an England shirt for the very first time.

Other debutants Handley, Jake Wardle and Harry Smith had all appeared in non-Test games, which left only four in the team with previous caps - Jack Welsby, Kai Pearce-Paul, Ben Currie and the new captain Williams.

Williams' appointment by coach Shaun Wane brought few grumbles after a brilliant start to the season with Warrington and he produced a vintage display.

Wane said the Jez Litten break that led to Ash Handley's hat-trick try reminded him of Rob Burrow, on a day when England wore special jerseys to raise funds for motor neurone disease.

INTERNATIONAL

Saturday 29th April 2023

ENGLAND 64 FRANCE 0

ENGLAND: 1 Jack Welsby (St Helens); 2 Ash Handley (Leeds Rhinos); 3 Toby King (Wigan Warriors); 4 Jake Wardle (Wigan Warriors); 5 Matty Ashton (Warrington Wolves); 6 George Williams (Warrington Wolves) (C); 7 Harry Smith (Wigan Warriors); 8 Ethan Havard (Wigan Warriors); 9 Danny Walker (Warrington Wolves); 10 Tom Holroyd (Leeds Rhinos); 11 Kai Pearce-Paul (Wigan Warriors); 12 Matty Nicholson (Warrington Wolves); 13 Morgan Smithies (Wigan Warriors). Subs (all used): 14 Jez Litten (Hull KR); 15 James Harrison (Warrington Wolves); 16 Ben Currie (Warrington Wolves); 17 Tyler Dupree (Salford Red Devils).
Tries: Handley (4, 40, 60), Smith (20), Havard (24), Wardle (32), Williams (35, 53, 66), Pearce-Paul (64), Walker (80);
Goals: Smith 9/10, Williams 1/1.
FRANCE: 1 Tanguy Zenon (Catalans Dragons); 2 Arthur Romano (Catalans Dragons); 3 Samisoni Langi (Wakefield Trinity); 4 Matthieu Laguerre (Catalans Dragons); 5 Paul Marcon (Toulouse Olympique); 6 Arthur Mourgue (Catalans Dragons); 7 Cesar Rouge (Catalans Dragons); 8 Tiaki Chan (Catalans Dragons); 9 Anthony Marion (Toulouse Olympique); 10 Florian Vailhen (Pia); 11 Benjamin Jullien (Pia); 12 Mathieu Cozza (Featherstone Rovers); 13 Mickael Goudemand (Catalans Dragons) (C). Subs (all used): 14 Ugo Tison (Catalans Dragons); 15 Justin Sangare (Leeds Rhinos); 16 Bastien Scimone (Catalans Dragons); 17 Louis Jouffret (Halifax Panthers).
Rugby Leaguer & League Express Men of the Match:
England: George Williams; *France:* Justin Sangare.
Penalty count: 5-1; **Half-time:** 36-0; **Referee:** Liam Moore;
Attendance: 8,422 *(at Halliwell Jones Stadium, Warrington).*

England's Jez Litten dragged down by France's Louis Jouffret

Internationals

England Women had two internationals in the year that both ended in lopsided scorelines.

In April they beat France 64-0, St Helens winger Leah Burke profiting with four tries. New coach Stuart Barrow named both York's Hollie-Mae Dodd and Leeds' Georgia Roche. Both headed to Australia shortly after to play in the NRLW. They both impressed, with Dodd taking two well taken tries and Roche leading from the halves.

In November, England put in a dominant second-half performance to finally put Wales to the sword for the third time in as many years.

When the sides had met for the first time in 2021, England raced away to a 60-0 win at the Halliwell Jones Stadium but twelve months later a marked improvement was seen as England played out a 32-6 victory on Welsh soil at Cross Keys.

With Wales, the week before, putting in strong performance in a narrow 14-4 defeat in France, and then restricting England to a 20-0 lead at the break, it looked as though more improvement had been made. But Tara Jane Stanley's first try within minutes of the restart kick-started England's second half-dominance as Roche returned from the NRLW to lead England to another 60-0 victory.

Pacific Championship

New Zealand stunned Australia to win the revived Pacific Championship, recording a record 30-0 victory over their old foes in the final in Hamilton. And Papua New Guinea won the Pacific Bowl, beating Fiji in Port Moresby in the final by 32-12.

The tournament - which was to receive significant funding from the Australian Federal Government over the first two years - was divided into two divisions of three teams based on IRL rankings, while the seventh team, in 2023 Tonga, toured England. A seven-team women's competition was also played.

In the men's final, New Zealand inflicted Australia's heaviest defeat in its history, only a week after defeating the Kiwis 36-18 in Melbourne in a round-robin game, for their first win over the Kangaroos since 2018.

Winger Jamayne Isaako scored a double either side of half-time, Charnze Nicoll-Klokstad claimed man-of-the-match honours for his dominant display at fullback (despite playing with a broken rib) and halves Dylan Brown and Jahrome Hughes pulled the strings as New Zealand re-wrote the record books.

Winger Ronaldo Mulitalo was on fire throughout the first half - starting and finishing a sensational length-of-the-field movement by the Kiwis in the 14th minute - one of the highlights a crunching ball-and-all tackle on a breaking Valentine Holmes. The Kiwis pack was just as ferocious, led by Canberra's Joseph Tapine.

The Kiwis led 12-0 at the break and didn't give the green-and-gold any sniff of a comeback, adding three more tries in the second half, centre Matthew Timoko and prop Griffin Neame finishing off the scoring.

World Cup finalists Samoa were the other team in the group and both the Kiwis and Kangaroos disposed them with relative ease.

In the opening game Townsville, Australia debutant Hamiso Tabuai-Fidow crossed twice against the side he represented in the World Cup in a 38-12 victory over Samoa, who were fielding nine debutants.

With Payne Haas and Tino Fa'asuamaleaui providing the platform, veteran captain James Tedesco answered his critics with an excellent performance at the back, while experienced Queensland playmakers Cameron Munster, Daly Cherry-Evans and Ben Hunt called the shots.

Despite the entire threequarter line of Dylan Edwards, Tabuai-Fidow, Kotoni Staggs and Selwyn Cobbo making their Kangaroos bow, plus the absence of Nathan Cleary and Latrell Mitchell, Mal Meninga's side looked every inch the world champions.

The week after, former Samoa internationals Jamayne Isaako and Ronaldo Mulitalo both bagged braces against their old teammates as the Kiwis ran in a 50-0 win in Auckland.

Isaako crossed twice in the first half and Mulitalo grabbed a late double as the hosts steamrolled an undermanned Toa Samoa, who were missing their star playmaker Jarome Luai with a shoulder issue.

In week three, Australia came out 36-18 winners in Melbourne, Roosters prop Lindsay Collins scoring an unlikely double as the Kangaroos downed the Kiwis. Collins crossed 24 seconds after coming off the bench, grabbing his second nine minutes later.

In the three-nation Pacific Bowl hosted by PNG, the Kumuls beat Fiji 32-12 in the final, a week after being thrashed by the Bati by 43-16 in a group game.

Cowboys rookie Robert Derby struck twice in five minutes as the Kumuls established an unassailable 26-nil lead at half-time, with Leigh hooker Edwin Ipape leading the charge from dummy-half.

With a stiff breeze at their back in the second half, Fiji threatened a comeback courtesy of Waqa Blake's brace. But a stormy clash fizzled out, with referee Grant Atkins sending rival big men Epel Kapinias and Taane Milne to the sin bin in separate incidents, with Kapinias crossing for a try within seconds of his return to secure PNG's silverware.

The third nation, Cook Islands had been beaten 46-10 by PNG and 22-18 by Fiji, thanks to a last-minute try from Dally M Rookie of the Year, Penrith's Sunia Turuva.

New Zealand Ferns mirrored the fortunes of the men's side by upsetting the odds in their final game with a 12-6 win over the Jillaroos in Melbourne.

Winger Leianne Tufugu's 63rd-minute try sealed New Zealand's first win against their trans-Tasman rivals since 2016.

A brutal defensive battle was locked at six points apiece until Tufuga chose the perfect moment to score her first international try, snapping New Zealand's seven-game losing streak against Australia. Raecene McGregor drilled the sideline conversion to give the Ferns a six-point edge, which they defended valiantly. It was fully deserved. Fullback Apii Nicholls was dangerous with ball in hand and stoic in defence, while lock forward Georgia Hale churned through a mountain of work.

The two had met in the first game of the series, with Australia edging a tight affair in Townsville by 16-10. Two weeks after winning the Karyn Murphy Medal for helping Newcastle Knights to their second straight NRLW crown and claiming the Dally M Medal as the NRLW's premier player, Tamika Upton crossed twice in the first half of a dream international bow.

New Zealand also beat Tonga in a one-off match by 28-20 in week two. Samoa beat Fiji 26-12 and PNG edged Cook Islands 28-20.

AMERICAS CHAMPIONSHIP

Saturday 23rd September 2023
Jamaica 8 USA 78
Monday 25th September 2023
USA 4 Canada 30
Wednesday 27th September 2023
Jamaica 2 Canada 58
(all played at Mona Bowl, University of West Indies, Kingston)

OTHER INTERNATIONALS

Saturday 13th May 2023
Greece 6 Serbia 40
(at Nea Smyrni Stadium, Athens)
Saturday 27th May 2023
Italy 4 Serbia 52
(at Rugby Club Pasian di Prato, Udine)
Saturday 22nd July 2023
Philippines 14 South Africa 72
(at Tugun RLFC, Gold Coast)
Saturday 26th August 2023
Czech Republic 16 Serbia 28
(at Městský Stadion, Krupka, Czechia)
Saturday 16th September 2023
Montenegro 10 Malta 34
(at Marsa Rugby Ground, Marsa, Malta)
Poland 28 Czech Republic 36
(at Majkowski Wembley, Kalisz, Poland)
Sunday 24th September 2023
Serbia 10 France 78
(at Stadion FK Obilić, Belgrade, Serbia)

Saturday 30th September 2023
Netherlands 58 Norway 22
(at RC The Bassets, Sassenheim, South Holland)
Saturday 7th October 2023
Netherlands 58 Albania 18
(at Zaandijk RC, North Holland)
Malta 12 Italy 38
(at Lidcombe Oval, Sydney)
Saturday 14th October 2023
Netherlands 40 Serbia 10
(at RC Zwolle, Netherlands)
Saturday 21st October 2023
Germany 18 Netherlands 44
(at Althoff-Stadion, Hattingen, Germany)
North Macedonia 8 Poland 40
Malta 30 Chile 22
(both at Foreshore Park, Sylvania Waters, NSW)
Saturday 28th October 2023
Malta 46 Philippines 22
(at New Era Stadium, Cabramatta, NSW)
Czech Republic 2 Netherlands 26
(at Harta RC, Vrchlabí, Czechia)
Greece 24 Ukraine 38
(at Gkorytsa Stadium, Aspropygos, Greece)
Italy 50 South Africa 20
(at Lidcombe Oval, Sydney)
Sunday 29th October 2023
Greece 12 Ukraine 22
(at Goudi Municipal Stadium, Athens)
Saturday 4th November 2023
Germany 54 Poland 10
(at RK03 Berlin)
Norway 6 Greece 36
(at Øster Hus Arena, Sandes, Norway)

WOMEN

Saturday 3rd June 2023
Italy 34 Serbia 14
(at RC Pasian di Prato, Udine, Italy)
Saturday 28th October 2023
Malta 0 Philippines 42
(at New Era Stadium, Cabramatta, NSW)
Sunday 29th October 2023
France 14 Wales 4
(at Stade Albert Domec, Carcassonne)
Friday 3rd November 2023
Nigeria 40 Ghana 4
Sunday 5th November 2023
Nigeria 14 Ghana 6
(both at Teslim Balogun Stadium, Lagos)
England 60 Wales 0
(at Headingley, Leeds)

WHEELCHAIR

Celtic Cup - Sunday 18th June 2023
Scotland 24 Ireland 58
Ireland 30 Wales 30
Scotland 30 Wales 76
(all at Oriam, Scotland's Performance Sports Centre, Edinburgh)
Sunday 5th November 2023
England 34 France 43
(at First Direct Arena, Leeds)

7
STATISTICAL REVIEW

SUPER LEAGUE PLAYERS
1996-2023

Super League Players 1996-2023

PLAYER	CLUB	YEAR	APP	TRIES	GOALS	FG	PTS
Jordan Abdull	Hull KR	2020-23	44(6)	11	60	4	168
	London	2019	25(2)	10	1	0	42
	Hull	2014-16, 2018	32(20)	9	7	0	50
Carl Ablett	Leeds	2004, 2006-18	238(37)	63	0	0	252
	London	2005	3(2)	0	0	0	0
Darren Abram	Oldham	1996-97	25(2)	11	0	0	44
Mitch Achurch	Leeds	2013-16	25(50)	14	0	0	56
Andy Ackers	Salford	2020-23	62(10)	9	0	0	36
	Toronto	2020	5	1	0	0	4
Jamie Acton	Leigh	2017	11(4)	4	0	0	16
Brad Adams	Bradford	2014	1(1)	0	0	0	0
Darren Adams	Paris	1996	9(1)	1	0	0	4
Guy Adams	Huddersfield	1998	1(2)	0	0	0	0
Luke Adamson	Salford	2006-07, 2009-12	73(39)	11	1	0	46
Matt Adamson	Leeds	2002-04	54(8)	9	0	0	36
Phil Adamson	St Helens	1999	(1)	0	0	0	0
Toby Adamson	Salford	2010	(1)	0	0	0	0
Danny Addy	Salford	2021-23	19(20)	0	0	0	0
	Hull KR	2019	9(10)	2	0	0	8
	Bradford	2010-14	49(42)	13	7	0	66
Ade Adebisi	London	2004	(1)	0	0	0	0
Sadiq Adebiyi	Wakefield	2022	1(2)	0	0	0	0
	London	2019	6(7)	3	0	0	12
Patrick Ah Van	Widnes	2012-18	99	73	56	0	404
	Bradford	2011	26	9	87	0	210
Jamie Ainscough	Wigan	2002-03	30(2)	18	0	0	72
Shaun Ainscough	Bradford	2011-12	27	15	0	0	60
	Wigan	2009-10	12	13	0	0	52
	Castleford	2010	7	4	0	0	16
Glen Air	London	1998-2001	57(13)	27	0	1	109
Paul Aiton	Catalans	2016-18	30(11)	3	0	0	12
	Leeds	2014-15	36(6)	2	0	0	8
	Wakefield	2012-13	43(2)	7	0	0	28
Makali Aizue	Hull KR	2007-09	18(32)	4	0	0	16
Sitaleki Akauola	Salford	2022	12(7)	2	0	0	8
	Warrington	2018-21	12(48)	6	0	0	24
Darren Albert	St Helens	2002-05	105	77	0	0	308
Lucas Albert	Toulouse	2022	16(5)	1	0	0	4
	Catalans	2015-20	35(10)	7	23	0	74
Wellington Albert	Leeds	2019	2(2)	0	0	0	0
	Widnes	2018	(11)	2	0	0	8
Paul Alcock	Widnes	2003, 2005	1(7)	1	0	0	4
Neil Alexander	Salford	1998	(1)	0	0	0	0
Malcolm Alker	Salford	1997-2002, 2004-07, 2009-10	271(2)	40	0	1	161
Danny Allan	Leeds	2008-09	2(5)	0	0	0	0
Chris Allen	Castleford	1996	(1)	0	0	0	0
Dave Allen	Widnes	2012-14	50(13)	5	0	0	20
	Wigan	2003, 2005	6(15)	2	0	0	8
Gavin Allen	London	1996	10	0	0	0	0
John Allen	Workington	1996	20(1)	6	0	0	24
Ray Allen	London	1996	5(3)	3	0	0	12
Mitch Allgood	Wakefield	2017	6(2)	0	0	0	0
	Hull KR	2015-16	27(5)	5	0	0	20
Richard Allwood	Gateshead	1999	(4)	0	0	0	0
Sean Allwood	Gateshead	1999	3(17)	1	0	0	4
David Alstead	Warrington	2000-02	23(10)	3	0	0	12
Daniel Alvaro	Toulouse	2022	14(1)	1	0	0	4
Luke Ambler	Harlequins	2011	5(17)	1	0	0	4
	Leeds	2010	1(8)	1	0	0	4
Asa Amone	Halifax	1996-97	32(7)	10	0	0	40
Tom Amone	Leigh	2023	27(1)	6	0	0	24
Kyle Amor	Warrington	2022	1(3)	0	0	0	0
	St Helens	2014-22	103(87)	18	0	0	72
	Wakefield	2011-13	51(23)	9	0	0	36
	Leeds	2010	(3)	0	0	0	0
Thibaut Ancely	Catalans	2011	(2)	0	0	0	0
Grant Anderson	Castleford	1996-97	15(6)	3	0	0	12
Louis Anderson	Catalans	2012-18	86(41)	32	0	0	128
	Warrington	2008-11	92	18	0	0	72
Paul Anderson	St Helens	2005-06	48(5)	7	1	0	30
	Bradford	1997-2004	74(104)	30	0	0	120
	Halifax	1996	5(1)	1	0	0	4
Paul Anderson	Sheffield	1999	3(7)	1	0	0	4
	St Helens	1996-98	2(28)	4	1	0	18
Scott Anderson	Wakefield	2014-16	25(18)	2	0	0	8
Vinnie Anderson	Salford	2011-12	33(3)	14	0	0	56
	Warrington	2007-10	57(19)	22	0	0	88
	St Helens	2005-06	28(14)	17	0	0	68
Phil Anderton	St Helens	2004	1	0	0	0	0
Chris Annakin	Wakefield	2013-19	7(62)	1	0	0	4
Eric Anselme	Leeds	2008	2(2)	2	0	0	8
	Halifax	1997	(2)	0	0	0	0
Mark Applegarth	Wakefield	2004-07	20(5)	3	0	0	12
Graham Appo	Warrington	2002-05	60(13)	35	80	0	300
	Huddersfield	2001	7	4	0	0	16
Ellis Archer	St Helens	2022	1	0	0	0	0
Guy Armitage	Toulouse	2022	15	7	0	0	28
	London	2019	(2)	0	0	0	0
Anthony Armour	London	2005	11(7)	1	0	0	4
Colin Armstrong	Workington	1996	11(2)	1	0	0	4
Tom Armstrong	Widnes	2017	11	1	0	0	4
	St Helens	2009-11	10(5)	9	0	0	36
Richard Armswood	Workington	1996	5(1)	1	0	0	4
Danny Arnold	Salford	2001-02	26(13)	13	0	0	52
	Huddersfield	1998-2000	55(7)	26	0	0	104
	Castleford	2000	(4)	0	0	0	0
	St Helens	1996-97	40(1)	33	0	0	132
Tinirau Arona	Wakefield	2016-22	110(43)	8	0	0	32
Joe Arundel	Wakefield	2015-21	88(10)	22	4	0	96
	Bradford	2014	9(3)	5	0	0	20
	Hull	2013-14	16	7	1	0	30
	Castleford	2008, 2010-12	35(4)	14	2	0	60
Craig Ashall	St Helens	2006	1	1	0	0	4
Olly Ashall-Bott	Toulouse	2022	24	6	0	0	24
	Huddersfield	2021-22	8(2)	3	0	0	12
	Wakefield	2021	2	1	0	0	4
	Salford	2020	3	1	0	0	4
	Widnes	2018	5	1	0	0	4
Nathan Ashe	St Helens	2011-13	6(4)	0	0	0	0
Chris Ashton	Wigan	2005-07	44(2)	25	2	0	104
Matty Ashton	Warrington	2020-23	59(7)	44	0	0	176
Matty Ashurst	Wakefield	2015-23	177(5)	33	0	0	132
	Salford	2012-14	65(7)	11	0	0	44
	St Helens	2009-11	12(39)	8	0	0	32
Jack Ashworth	Huddersfield	2021-23	7(19)	0	0	0	0
	Leigh	2021	1(4)	0	0	0	0
	St Helens	2015-16, 2018-20	6(37)	4	0	0	16
John Asiata	Leigh	2023	23(1)	1	0	0	4
Roy Asotasi	Warrington	2014-15	16(37)	5	1	0	22
Connor Aspey	Salford	2020-21	(2)	0	0	0	0
Peter Aspinall	Huddersfield	2013	1(1)	0	0	0	0
Martin Aspinwall	Hull	2012	12(15)	0	0	0	0
	Castleford	2011	12(6)	2	0	0	8
	Huddersfield	2006-10	72(8)	22	0	0	88
	Wigan	2001-05	85(13)	27	0	0	108
Logan Astley	Wigan	2022	2	0	0	0	0
Cory Aston	Castleford	2019	8	3	0	0	12
Mark Aston	Sheffield	1996-99	67(6)	6	243	6	516
Paul Atcheson	Widnes	2002-06	16(35)	4	0	0	16
	St Helens	1998-2000	58(4)	18	0	0	72
	Oldham	1996-97	40	21	0	0	84
Chris Atkin	Salford	2020-23	37(38)	14	4	1	65
	Hull KR	2018-19	28(19)	7	1	3	33
David Atkins	Huddersfield	2001	26(1)	4	0	0	16
Jordan Atkins	London	2014	13(1)	4	0	0	16
Ryan Atkins	Wakefield	2006-09, 2019-23	90(2)	47	0	0	188
	Warrington	2010-19	235(2)	139	0	0	556
Josh Atkinson	Castleford	2012	2	0	0	0	0
Renouf Atoni	Wakefield	2023	10(11)	1	0	0	4
Brad Attwood	Halifax	2003	(3)	0	0	0	0
Blake Austin	Castleford	2023	5	0	1	1	3
	Leeds	2022-23	39(1)	5	0	1	21
	Warrington	2019-21	57(2)	30	0	6	126
Yusuf Aydin	Hull KR	2023	1(4)	0	0	0	0
	Wakefield	2020-22	6(18)	2	0	0	8
	Leeds	2022	(1)	0	0	0	0
Warren Ayres	Salford	1999	2(9)	1	2	0	8
Jerome Azema	Paris	1997	(1)	0	0	0	0
Marcus Bai	Bradford	2006	24	9	0	0	36
	Leeds	2004-05	57	42	0	0	168
David Baildon	Hull	1998-99	26(2)	4	0	0	16
Jean-Philippe Baile	Catalans	2008-14	62(16)	23	0	0	92
Andy Bailey	Hull	2004-05	2(8)	1	0	0	4
Chris Bailey	Huddersfield	2014-15	17(17)	5	0	0	20
	London	2012-13	41	14	0	0	56
	Harlequins	2011	24	3	0	0	12
Connor Bailey	Wakefield	2020	3(2)	0	0	0	0
Julian Bailey	Huddersfield	2003-04	47	13	0	0	52
Phil Bailey	Wigan	2007-10	84(4)	13	0	0	52
Ricky Bailey	St Helens	2015, 2017	2	0	0	0	0
Ryan Bailey	Warrington	2016	1(11)	0	0	0	0
	Castleford	2015	3(2)	0	0	0	0
	Hull KR	2015	(1)	1	0	0	4
	Leeds	2002-14	171(102)	17	0	0	68

198

Super League Players 1996-2023

PLAYER	CLUB	YEAR	APP	TRIES	GOALS	FG	PTS
Jason Baitieri	Catalans	2011-21	136(89)	20	0	0	80
Simon Baldwin	Salford	2004-06	20(29)	3	0	0	12
	Sheffield	1999	7(15)	2	0	0	8
	Halifax	1996-98	41(15)	16	0	1	65
Jordan Baldwinson	Wakefield	2018	(4)	0	0	0	0
	Leeds	2013, 2016-17	4(9)	1	0	0	4
	Bradford	2014	2(4)	0	0	0	0
Rob Ball	Wigan	1998-2000	3(4)	0	0	0	0
Paul Ballard	Celtic	2009	2	0	0	0	0
	Widnes	2005	3(1)	2	0	0	8
Denive Balmforth	Hull	2022	(4)	1	0	0	4
Darren Bamford	Salford	2005	2(1)	0	0	0	0
Michael Banks	Bradford	1998	(1)	0	0	0	0
Steve Bannister	Harlequins	2007	(6)	0	0	0	0
	St Helens	2006-07	(3)	0	0	0	0
Frederic Banquet	Paris	1996	16(2)	7	4	0	36
Ben Barba	St Helens	2017-18	31	31	0	0	124
Lee Bardauskas	Castleford	1996-97	(2)	0	0	0	0
Harry Bardle	Hull KR	2019	(1)	0	0	0	0
Craig Barker	Workington	1996	(2)	0	0	0	0
Dwayne Barker	Harlequins	2008	5(5)	1	0	0	4
	London	2004	3	1	0	0	4
	Hull	2003	(1)	0	0	0	0
Connor Barley	Hull KR	2022-23	2(2)	1	0	0	4
Mark Barlow	Wakefield	2002	(1)	0	0	0	0
Danny Barnes	Halifax	1999	2	0	0	0	0
Richie Barnett	Salford	2007	7	4	0	0	16
	Warrington	2006-07	26(10)	15	0	0	60
	Hull	2004-05	21(5)	21	0	0	84
	Widnes	2005	4	2	0	0	8
Richie Barnett	Hull	2003-04	31(1)	17	0	0	68
	London	2001-02	31(4)	13	0	0	52
David Barnhill	Leeds	2000	20(8)	5	0	0	20
Trent Barrett	Wigan	2007-08	53(1)	22	0	4	92
Harvey Barron	Hull	2022-23	6(1)	4	0	0	16
Paul Barrow	Warrington	1996-97	1(10)	1	0	0	4
Scott Barrow	St Helens	1997-2000	9(13)	1	0	0	4
Steve Barrow	London	2000	2	0	0	0	0
	Hull	1998-99	4(17)	1	0	0	4
	Wigan	1996	(8)	3	0	0	12
William Barthau	Catalans	2010, 2012-14	13(3)	2	15	0	38
Ben Barton	Huddersfield	1998	1(6)	1	0	0	4
Danny Barton	Salford	2001	1	0	0	0	0
Wayne Bartrim	Castleford	2002-03	41(2)	9	157	0	350
Greg Barwick	London	1996-97	30(4)	21	110	2	306
David Bastian	Halifax	1996	(2)	0	0	0	0
James Batchelor	Hull KR	2023	22	7	0	0	28
	Wakefield	2016-22	60(30)	13	13	0	78
Joe Batchelor	St Helens	2019-23	53(15)	17	0	0	68
Ashley Bateman	Celtic	2009	1	0	0	0	0
John Bateman	Wigan	2014-18, 2021-22	143(11)	35	0	0	140
	Bradford	2011-13	25(5)	7	0	0	28
David Bates	Castleford	2001-02	(4)	0	0	0	0
	Warrington	2001	1(2)	0	0	0	0
Sam Bates	Bradford	2014	(2)	0	0	0	0
Nathan Batty	Wakefield	2001	1(1)	0	0	0	0
Eddie Battye	Wakefield	2020-23	21(52)	1	0	0	4
	London	2019	19(10)	3	0	0	12
Andreas Bauer	Hull	2007	10(2)	5	0	0	20
Russell Bawden	London	1996-97, 2002-04	50(49)	15	0	0	60
Lewis Baxter	St Helens	2022-23	(3)	0	0	0	0
Neil Baxter	Salford	2001	1	0	0	0	0
Neil Baynes	Salford	1999-2002, 2004	84(19)	10	0	0	40
	Wigan	1996-98	(10)	1	0	0	4
Chris Beasley	Celtic	2009	15(5)	2	0	0	8
Chris Beattie	Catalans	2006	22(5)	3	0	0	12
Richard Beaumont	Hull KR	2011-13	1(16)	1	0	0	4
Robbie Beazley	London	1997-99	48(15)	13	0	0	52
Robbie Beckett	Halifax	2002	27	15	0	0	60
Matty Beharrell	Hull KR	2013	1	0	0	0	0
Dean Bell	Leeds	1996	1	1	0	0	4
Ian Bell	Hull	2003	(1)	0	0	0	0
James Bell	St Helens	2022-23	27(17)	4	0	0	16
	Leigh	2021	16(2)	1	0	0	4
Mark Bell	Wigan	1998	22	12	0	0	48
Paul Bell	Leeds	2000	1	0	0	0	0
Steven Bell	Catalans	2009-10	43	14	0	0	56
Troy Bellamy	Paris	1997	5(10)	0	0	0	0
Adrian Belle	Huddersfield	1998	10(2)	0	0	0	0
	Oldham	1996	19	8	0	0	32
Lambert Belmas	Toulouse	2022	2(10)	1	0	0	4
	Catalans	2017-21	3(13)	0	0	0	0
Jamie Benn	Castleford	1998, 2000	3(8)	1	15	0	34
Andy Bennett	Warrington	1996	6(5)	1	0	0	4
Mike Bennett	St Helens	2000-08	74(70)	15	0	0	60
Gavin Bennion	Salford	2018	1(1)	0	0	0	0
Jonathan Bennison	St Helens	2021-23	37(1)	14	6	0	68
Andrew Bentley	Catalans	2007-10	9(15)	1	0	0	4
James Bentley	Leeds	2022-23	33(5)	10	0	0	40
	St Helens	2018-21	32(13)	9	0	0	36
John Bentley	Huddersfield	1999	13(4)	3	0	0	12
	Halifax	1996, 1998	22(3)	24	0	0	96
Kane Bentley	Catalans	2007-10	11(19)	5	0	0	20
Ilias Bergal	Toulouse	2022	8	3	0	0	12
Phil Bergman	Paris	1997	20(1)	14	0	0	56
Shaun Berrigan	Hull	2008-10	60(8)	12	0	0	48
Joe Berry	Huddersfield	1998-99	25(14)	3	0	0	12
David Berthezene	Salford	2007	9(1)	0	0	0	0
	Catalans	2006-07	5(14)	0	0	0	0
Colin Best	Hull	2003-04	57	34	0	0	136
Roger Best	London	1997-98	1(5)	1	0	0	4
Bob Beswick	Wigan	2004-05	5(14)	2	0	0	8
Monty Betham	Wakefield	2006	26	2	0	0	8
Mike Bethwaite	Workington	1996	17(3)	1	0	0	4
Denis Betts	Wigan	1998-2001	82(24)	33	0	0	132
Cliff Beverley	Salford	2004-05	47(1)	14	0	0	56
Kyle Bibb	Wakefield	2008-10	1(24)	0	0	0	0
	Harlequins	2010	(2)	0	0	0	0
	Hull KR	2009	(2)	0	0	0	0
Jack Bibby	Wigan	2022	(1)	1	0	0	4
Jake Bibby	Huddersfield	2023	17	4	0	0	16
	Wigan	2020-22	67	26	0	0	104
	Salford	2016-19	65(3)	32	0	0	128
Adam Bibey	Widnes	2004	(1)	0	0	0	0
Ricky Bibey	Wakefield	2007-09	32(25)	1	0	0	4
	St Helens	2004	4(14)	0	0	0	0
	Wigan	2001-03	5(29)	0	0	0	0
Lewis Bienek	Castleford	2021	1(5)	0	0	0	0
	Hull	2018, 2020	(8)	0	0	0	0
Chris Birchall	Halifax	2002-03	24(22)	4	0	0	16
	Bradford	2000	(1)	0	0	0	0
Deon Bird	Castleford	2006	17(6)	5	0	0	20
	Widnes	2003-04	39(6)	9	0	0	36
	Wakefield	2002	10(1)	1	0	0	4
	Hull	2000-02	37(22)	20	0	0	80
	Gateshead	1999	19(3)	13	0	0	52
	Paris	1996-97	30	12	2	0	52
Greg Bird	Catalans	2009, 2017-19	68(6)	11	3	0	50
Mike Bishay	London	2013-14	7(11)	2	2	0	12
Nathan Blacklock	Hull	2005-06	44(3)	33	0	0	132
Ben Blackmore	Huddersfield	2013-14	3	4	0	0	16
	Castleford	2012	1	0	0	0	0
Richie Blackmore	Leeds	1997-2000	63	25	0	0	100
Anthony Blackwood	Crusaders	2010	1	0	0	0	0
	Celtic	2009	25	5	0	0	20
Jack Blagbrough	Huddersfield	2013	(1)	0	0	0	0
Cheyse Blair	Castleford	2019-22	45(6)	10	0	0	40
Maurice Blair	Hull KR	2015-16, 2018	62(3)	10	1	0	42
Luke Blake	Wakefield	2009	(2)	0	0	0	0
Matthew Blake	Wakefield	2003-04	1(5)	0	0	0	0
Steve Blakeley	Salford	1997-2002	103(5)	26	241	2	588
	Warrington	2000	4(3)	1	9	0	22
Richard Blakeway	Castleford	2002-04	1(14)	0	0	0	0
Damien Blanch	Catalans	2011-13	70	42	0	0	168
	Wakefield	2008-10	44(3)	31	0	0	124
	Castleford	2006	3(2)	0	0	0	0
Matt Blaymire	Wakefield	2007-11	96(3)	26	0	1	105
Ian Blease	Salford	1997	(1)	0	0	0	0
Jamie Bloem	Huddersfield	2003	18(4)	3	11	0	34
	Halifax	1998-2002	82(25)	25	100	2	302
Vea Bloomfield	Paris	1996	4(14)	3	0	0	12
Matty Blythe	Warrington	2007-12, 2017	30(28)	12	0	0	48
	Bradford	2013-14	24(6)	8	0	0	32
Ben Bolger	London	2012	2(7)	1	0	0	4
	Harlequins	2010-11	4(15)	0	0	0	0
Pascal Bomati	Paris	1996	17(1)	10	0	0	40
Simon Booth	Hull	1998-99	15(9)	2	0	0	8
	St Helens	1996-97	10(4)	1	0	0	4
Steve Booth	Huddersfield	1998-99	16(4)	2	3	0	14
Alan Boothroyd	Halifax	1997	2(3)	0	0	0	0
Thomas Bosc	Catalans	2006-17	199(21)	48	483	12	1170
John Boslem	Paris	1996	(5)	0	0	0	0
Liam Bostock	St Helens	2004	1	0	0	0	0
Liam Botham	Wigan	2005	5	0	0	0	0
	Leeds	2003-05	2(11)	4	0	0	16
	London	2004	6(2)	3	7	0	26
Frano Botica	Castleford	1996	21	5	84	2	190

Super League Players 1996-2023

PLAYER	CLUB	YEAR	APP	TRIES	GOALS	FG	PTS
Matthew Bottom	Leigh	2005	(1)	0	0	0	0
Hadj Boudebza	Paris	1996	(2)	0	0	0	0
John Boudebza	Hull KR	2015-16	13(17)	2	0	0	8
David Boughton	Huddersfield	1999	26(1)	4	0	0	16
Amir Bourouh	Salford	2022-23	8(10)	0	0	0	0
	Wigan	2019-21	1(8)	0	0	0	0
Julian Bousquet	Catalans	2012-23	108(122)	25	0	0	100
David Bouveng	Halifax	1997-99	66(2)	19	0	0	76
Josh Bowden	Wakefield	2022-23	14(9)	0	0	0	0
	Hull	2012-22	65(100)	13	0	0	52
Matt Bowen	Wigan	2014-15	43	21	31	0	146
Harry Bowes	Wakefield	2020-23	10(16)	0	0	0	0
Tony Bowes	Huddersfield	1998	3(2)	0	0	0	0
Radney Bowker	London	2004	3	1	0	0	4
	St Helens	2001	(1)	0	0	0	0
David Boyle	Bradford	1999-2000	36(13)	15	0	1	61
Ryan Boyle	Castleford	2006, 2008-09, 2013-16	12(60)	5	0	0	20
	Salford	2010-14	57(14)	3	0	0	12
Andy Bracek	Crusaders	2011	(2)	0	0	0	0
	Warrington	2005-08	7(49)	7	0	0	28
	St Helens	2004	(1)	0	0	0	0
David Bradbury	Hudds-Sheff	2000	21(2)	1	0	0	4
	Salford	1997-99	23(10)	6	0	0	24
	Oldham	1996-97	19(6)	9	0	0	36
John Braddish	St Helens	2001-02	1(1)	0	3	0	6
Graeme Bradley	Bradford	1996-98	62(1)	29	0	0	116
Nick Bradley-Qalilawa							
	Harlequins	2006	27	6	0	0	24
	London	2005	28	19	0	0	76
Darren Bradstreet	London	1999-2000	1(3)	0	0	0	0
Dominic Brambani	Castleford	2004	2(2)	0	0	0	0
Keanan Brand	Leigh	2021	12	1	0	0	4
	Warrington	2020	3	0	0	0	0
	Widnes	2018	1	0	0	0	0
Joe Bretherton	Toulouse	2022	16(2)	3	0	0	12
	Wigan	2016-17	2(13)	1	0	0	4
Liam Bretherton	Wigan	1999	(5)	2	0	0	8
	Warrington	1997	(2)	0	0	0	0
Johnny Brewer	Halifax	1996	4(2)	2	0	0	8
Chris Bridge	Widnes	2016-17	28(1)	4	11	0	38
	Warrington	2005-15	186(17)	89	248	1	853
	Bradford	2003-04	2(14)	4	6	0	28
Danny Bridge	Bradford	2014	4(4)	0	0	0	0
	Warrington	2013	(2)	0	0	0	0
Ryan Brierley	Salford	2022-23	50(1)	21	9	0	102
	Leigh	2021	17	10	29	0	98
	Hull KR	2020	10	3	8	0	28
	Huddersfield	2016-17	19(1)	6	2	0	28
Lee Briers	Warrington	1997-2013	365(12)	130	810	70	2210
	St Helens	1997	3	0	11	0	22
Carl Briggs	Salford	1999	8(5)	3	0	1	13
	Halifax	1996	5(3)	1	0	0	4
Kyle Briggs	Bradford	2011	6	4	0	0	16
	Harlequins	2011	3	0	0	0	0
Mike Briggs	Widnes	2002	1(2)	1	0	0	4
Kriss Brining	Salford	2017	2(20)	4	0	0	16
Luke Briscoe	Leeds	2014, 2016, 2018-21	47(9)	15	0	0	60
	Wakefield	2014	2	0	0	0	0
Shaun Briscoe	Widnes	2012-13	11(2)	4	0	0	16
	Hull KR	2008-11	92	27	0	0	108
	Hull	2004-07	83(9)	50	0	0	200
	Wigan	2002-03	23(5)	11	0	0	44
Tom Briscoe	Leigh	2023	28	14	0	0	56
	Leeds	2014-22	172(2)	66	0	0	264
	Hull	2008-13	131(3)	83	0	0	332
Darren Britt	St Helens	2002-03	41	3	0	0	12
Gary Broadbent	Salford	1997-2002	117(2)	22	0	0	88
Jack Broadbent	Castleford	2023	24(1)	6	0	0	24
	Leeds	2020-22	20(1)	9	0	0	36
Paul Broadbent	Wakefield	2002	16(5)	0	0	0	0
	Hull	2000-01	40(9)	3	0	0	12
	Halifax	1999	26(1)	2	0	0	8
	Sheffield	1996-98	63(1)	6	0	0	24
Robin Brochon	Catalans	2018-19, 2021	2(1)	0	0	0	0
Andrew Brocklehurst							
	Salford	2004-07	34(23)	5	0	0	20
	London	2004	12(6)	2	0	0	8
	Halifax	2001-03	37(8)	2	0	0	8
Justin Brooker	Wakefield	2001	25	9	0	0	36
	Bradford	2000	17(4)	11	0	0	44
Sam Brooks	Widnes	2016-17	1(3)	1	0	0	4
Danny Brough	Wakefield	2008-10, 2019-20	74(1)	16	247	9	567
	Huddersfield	2010-18	220(4)	45	721	20	1642
	Castleford	2006	10	1	31	2	68
	Hull	2005-06	25(12)	3	85	1	183
Jodie Broughton	Catalans	2016-19	48	34	0	0	136
	Huddersfield	2014-15	30	16	0	0	64
	Salford	2010-13	93	53	0	0	212
	Hull	2008-09	9(3)	6	0	0	24
Alex Brown	Hull KR	2013	16	9	0	0	36
	Huddersfield	2009	1	0	0	0	0
Darren Brown	Salford	1999-2001	47(9)	11	6	0	56
Gavin Brown	Leeds	1996-97	5(2)	1	2	0	8
Jack Brown	Hull	2019-23	10(48)	5	0	0	20
Kevin Brown	Salford	2020-21	18	6	1	0	26
	Warrington	2017-18	41(1)	9	0	0	36
	Widnes	2013-16	80	37	1	1	151
	Huddersfield	2006-12	156	43	0	1	173
	Wigan	2003-06	46(18)	27	0	0	108
Lee Brown	Hull	1999	(1)	0	0	0	0
Michael Brown	Huddersfield	2008	(1)	0	0	0	0
Michael Brown	London	1996	(2)	0	0	0	0
Mitch Brown	Warrington	2018	10(1)	2	0	0	8
	Leigh	2017	21	4	0	0	16
Todd Brown	Paris	1996	8(1)	2	0	0	8
Adrian Brunker	Wakefield	1999	17	6	0	0	24
Lamont Bryan	Harlequins	2008-11	9(22)	2	0	0	8
Justin Bryant	Paris	1996	4(1)	0	0	0	0
	London	1996	7(8)	1	0	0	4
Mark Bryant	London	2012-13	16(36)	3	1	0	14
	Crusaders	2010-11	42(8)	1	0	0	4
	Celtic	2009	23(3)	0	0	0	0
Austin Buchanan	Wakefield	2005-06	6	2	0	0	8
	London	2003	3(1)	2	0	0	8
Jack Buchanan	Widnes	2016-17	29(2)	2	0	0	8
Kieran Buchanan	Hull	2019-20	10(3)	3	0	0	12
McKenzie Buckley	St Helens	2022	(1)	0	0	0	0
Owen Buckley	Widnes	2018	4	3	0	0	12
Danny Buderus	Leeds	2009-11	57(14)	14	0	0	56
Neil Budworth	Celtic	2009	8(19)	0	0	0	0
	Harlequins	2006	2(19)	0	0	0	0
	London	2002-05	59(11)	4	1	0	18
Joe Bullock	Warrington	2022-23	9(30)	0	0	0	0
	Wigan	2019-21	27(27)	4	0	0	16
James Bunyan	Huddersfield	1998-99	8(7)	2	0	0	8
Andy Burgess	Salford	1997	3(12)	0	0	0	0
George Burgess	Wigan	2020	2(6)	1	0	0	4
Joe Burgess	Salford	2021-23	51	21	0	0	84
	Wigan	2013-15, 2017-20	115	91	0	0	364
Luke Burgess	Salford	2018	3(8)	0	0	0	0
	Catalans	2017	3(2)	0	0	0	0
	Leeds	2008-11	10(63)	6	0	0	24
	Harlequins	2007	(3)	0	0	0	0
Sam Burgess	Bradford	2006-09	46(34)	14	5	0	66
Tom Burgess	Bradford	2011-12	1(41)	3	0	0	12
Greg Burke	Salford	2018-22	34(38)	2	0	0	8
	Widnes	2016-18	22(12)	1	0	0	4
	Wigan	2013-14, 2016	13(26)	1	0	0	4
	Hull KR	2015	9(5)	0	0	0	0
	Bradford	2014	(1)	0	0	0	0
Joe Burke	Crusaders	2011	(1)	0	0	0	0
Mike Burnett	Harlequins	2011	16(4)	1	0	0	4
	Hull	2008-10	13(21)	3	0	0	12
Darren Burns	Warrington	2002-04	66(6)	19	0	0	76
Gary Burns	Oldham	1996	6	1	0	0	4
Paul Burns	Workington	1996	5(2)	1	0	0	4
Travis Burns	St Helens	2015-16	27(2)	4	28	0	72
	Hull KR	2013-14	46	8	81	2	196
Lachlan Burr	Leigh	2017	5(14)	1	0	0	4
Aidan Burrell	Hull	2021	(1)	0	0	0	0
Luther Burrell	Warrington	2019-20	2(6)	0	0	0	0
Rob Burrow	Leeds	2001-17	313(116)	168	131	5	939
Dean Busby	Warrington	1999-2002	34(34)	7	0	0	28
	Hull	1998	8(6)	0	0	0	0
	St Helens	1996-98	1(7)	0	0	0	0
Tom Bush	Leeds	2010	3(1)	1	0	0	4
Chester Butler	Huddersfield	2019	(1)	0	0	0	0
Rob Butler	Wakefield	2022-23	1(11)	0	0	0	0
	Warrington	2021-22	(5)	0	0	0	0
	Leigh	2021	3(3)	0	0	0	0
	London	2019	17(7)	2	0	0	8
Ikram Butt	London	1996	5(1)	1	0	0	4
Reiss Butterworth	Huddersfield	2020	1(1)	0	0	0	0
Robbie Butterworth	Wakefield	2023	1	0	0	0	0

Super League Players 1996-2023

PLAYER	CLUB	YEAR	APP	TRIES	GOALS	FG	PTS
Liam Byrne	Wigan	2019-23	46(48)	2	0	0	8
Shane Byrne	Huddersfield	1998-99	1(5)	0	0	0	0
Todd Byrne	Hull	2008-09	20	4	0	0	16
Didier Cabestany	Paris	1996-97	20(6)	2	0	0	8
Hep Cahill	Widnes	2012-18	106(13)	4	0	0	16
	Crusaders	2011	16	2	0	0	8
Joel Caine	Salford	2004	24	8	13	0	58
	London	2003	6	4	1	0	18
Mark Calderwood	Harlequins	2011	13	2	0	0	8
	Hull	2009-10	23	6	0	0	24
	Wigan	2006-08	64	23	0	0	92
	Leeds	2001-05	117(9)	88	0	0	352
Mike Callan	Warrington	2002	(4)	0	0	0	0
Matt Calland	Huddersfield	2003	2	0	0	0	0
	Hull	1999	1	0	0	0	0
	Bradford	1996-98	44(5)	24	0	0	96
Dean Callaway	London	1999-2000	26(24)	12	0	0	48
Laurent Cambres	Paris	1996	(1)	0	0	0	0
Chris Campbell	Warrington	2000	7(1)	2	0	0	8
Liam Campbell	Wakefield	2005	(1)	0	0	0	0
Logan Campbell	Hull	1998-99, 2001	70(13)	14	0	0	56
	Castleford	2000	14(2)	3	0	0	12
	Workington	1996	7(1)	1	0	0	4
Terry Campese	Hull KR	2015-16	19(1)	2	4	0	16
Blake Cannova	Widnes	2002	(1)	0	0	0	0
Phil Cantillon	Widnes	2002-03	27(21)	18	0	0	72
	Leeds	1997	(1)	0	0	0	0
Liam Carberry	Widnes	2014-15	2(5)	0	0	0	0
Damien Cardace	Catalans	2012, 2014-15	23	14	0	0	56
Daryl Cardiss	Warrington	2003-04	23(2)	3	4	0	20
	Halifax	1999-2003	91(8)	39	4	0	164
	Wigan	1996-98	12(6)	4	0	0	16
Dale Cardoza	Warrington	2002	5	1	0	0	4
	Halifax	2001	3	1	0	0	4
	Huddersfield	2000-01	20(9)	11	0	0	44
	Sheffield	1998-99	11(7)	3	0	0	12
Paul Carige	Salford	1999	24(1)	7	0	0	28
Dane Carlaw	Catalans	2008-10	58(15)	9	0	0	36
Keal Carlile	Hull KR	2012-15	6(28)	1	0	0	4
	Huddersfield	2009, 2011	2(1)	1	0	0	4
	Bradford	2008	(1)	0	0	0	0
Jim Carlton	Huddersfield	1999	3(11)	2	0	0	8
George Carmont	Wigan	2008-12	136	71	0	0	284
Brian Carney	Warrington	2009	4	2	0	0	8
	Wigan	2001-05	91(10)	42	1	0	170
	Hull	2000	13(3)	7	0	0	28
	Gateshead	1999	3(2)	2	0	0	8
Justin Carney	Hull KR	2018	14	3	0	0	12
	Salford	2016-17	28	12	0	0	48
	Castleford	2013-15	58	56	0	0	224
Martin Carney	Warrington	1997	(1)	0	0	0	0
Todd Carney	Hull KR	2018	(1)	0	0	0	0
	Salford	2017	9(5)	0	7	0	14
	Catalans	2015-16	32	9	4	1	45
Omari Caro	Hull KR	2013-14	21	20	0	0	80
	London	2012	11	4	0	0	16
Paul Carr	Sheffield	1996-98	45(5)	15	0	0	60
Bernard Carroll	London	1996	2(1)	1	0	0	4
Mark Carroll	London	1998	15(3)	1	0	0	4
Tonie Carroll	Leeds	2001-02	42(2)	30	0	0	120
Darren Carter	Workington	1996	10(3)	0	1	0	2
Steve Carter	Widnes	2002	14(7)	4	0	0	16
John Cartwright	Salford	1997	9	0	0	0	0
Garreth Carvell	Castleford	2014	1(4)	1	0	0	4
	Hull	2001-08, 2014	75(84)	22	0	0	88
	Warrington	2009-13	77(40)	13	0	0	52
	Leeds	1997-2000	(4)	0	0	0	0
	Gateshead	1999	4(4)	1	0	0	4
Garen Casey	Salford	1999	13(5)	3	23	0	58
Ray Cashmere	Salford	2009-11	63(3)	5	0	0	20
Mick Cassidy	Widnes	2005	24	0	0	0	0
	Wigan	1996-2004	184(36)	30	0	0	120
Loan Castano	Catalans	2022	(1)	0	0	0	0
Remi Casty	Catalans	2006-13, 2015-20	207(97)	26	0	0	104
Ned Catic	Castleford	2008	7(7)	3	0	0	12
	Wakefield	2006-07	17(29)	4	0	0	16
Mason Caton-Brown	Wakefield	2017-19	34	27	0	0	108
	Salford	2014-16	28	10	0	0	40
	London	2013-14	19	15	0	0	60
Joe Cator	Hull	2020-23	37(12)	1	0	0	4
	Hull KR	2016, 2018	2(3)	0	0	0	0
Chris Causey	Warrington	1997-99	(18)	1	0	0	4
Charlie Cavanaugh	Hull KR	2022	(1)	0	0	0	0
Jason Cayless	St Helens	2006-09	62(9)	7	0	0	28
Arnaud Cervello	Paris	1996	4	4	0	0	16
Marshall Chalk	Celtic	2009	13	4	0	0	16
Ed Chamberlain	Leigh	2023	13(1)	4	0	0	16
	Salford	2018-20	10(1)	3	21	0	54
	Widnes	2016-18	16(1)	2	7	0	22
Gary Chambers	Warrington	1996-2000	65(28)	2	0	0	8
Pierre Chamorin	Paris	1996-97	27(3)	8	3	0	38
Alex Chan	Catalans	2006-08	59(19)	11	0	0	44
Jason Chan	Hull KR	2014	5(1)	3	0	0	12
	Huddersfield	2012-14	46(12)	9	0	0	36
	Crusaders	2010-11	48(1)	10	0	0	40
	Celtic	2009	17(6)	3	0	0	12
Joe Chan	Catalans	2021-22	10(16)	9	0	0	36
Tiaki Chan	Catalans	2022-23	1(15)	1	0	0	4
Joe Chandler	Leeds	2008	(1)	0	0	0	0
Michael Channing	Castleford	2013-15	27(2)	8	0	0	32
	London	2012-13	15(3)	2	0	0	8
Jay Chapelhow	Widnes	2016-18	23(15)	4	0	0	16
Ted Chapelhow	Widnes	2016-18	7(13)	0	0	0	0
Chris Chapman	Leeds	1999	(1)	0	0	0	0
Damien Chapman	London	1998	6(2)	3	4	1	21
David Chapman	Castleford	1996-98	24(6)	8	0	0	32
Jaymes Chapman	Halifax	2002-03	5(8)	1	0	0	4
Richard Chapman	Sheffield	1996	1	2	0	0	8
Chris Charles	Salford	2004-06	59(16)	6	140	0	304
	Castleford	2001	1(4)	1	0	0	4
Olivier Charles	Catalans	2007	2	2	0	0	8
Josh Charnley	Leigh	2023	26	27	0	0	108
	Warrington	2018-22	94	57	0	0	228
	Wigan	2010-16	151(2)	141	77	0	718
	Hull KR	2010	5	5	0	0	20
Lewis Charnock	St Helens	2013, 2015	4(1)	2	6	0	20
Rangi Chase	Widnes	2017	6	0	0	0	0
	Castleford	2009-13, 2016-17	122(12)	39	0	3	159
	Salford	2014-15	37	10	13	2	68
Andy Cheetham	Huddersfield	1998-99	30	11	0	0	44
Kris Chesney	London	1998	1(2)	0	0	0	0
Chris Chester	Hull KR	2007-08	28(6)	4	0	0	16
	Hull	2002-06	67(25)	13	0	0	52
	Wigan	1999-2001	21(22)	5	0	0	20
	Halifax	1996-99	47(14)	16	15	1	95
Lee Chilton	Workington	1996	10(3)	6	0	0	24
Dane Chisholm	Hull KR	2015	1	0	0	0	0
Gary Christie	Bradford	1996-97	4(7)	1	0	0	4
James Clare	Castleford	2012-15, 2018-22	100(1)	50	0	0	200
Daryl Clark	Warrington	2015-23	184(30)	47	0	0	188
	Castleford	2011-14	34(51)	31	0	0	124
Dean Clark	Leeds	1996	11(2)	3	0	0	12
Des Clark	St Helens	1999	4	0	0	0	0
	Halifax	1998-99	35(13)	6	0	0	24
Jason Clark	Warrington	2019-22	32(45)	2	1	0	10
Mitch Clark	Wigan	2020-21	(16)	2	0	0	8
	Castleford	2018-19	(24)	3	0	0	12
Greg Clarke	Halifax	1997	1(1)	0	0	0	0
John Clarke	Oldham	1996-97	27(4)	5	0	0	20
Jon Clarke	Widnes	2012-14	59(1)	5	0	0	20
	Warrington	2001-11	217(25)	56	2	0	228
	London	2000-01	19(11)	2	0	0	8
	Wigan	1997-99	13(10)	3	0	0	12
Chris Clarkson	Castleford	2019	11(8)	4	0	0	16
	Hull KR	2016, 2018	38(2)	4	0	0	16
	Widnes	2015	17(1)	4	0	0	16
	Leeds	2010-14	61(39)	9	0	0	36
Adam Clay	Salford	2011	2	3	0	0	12
Ryan Clayton	Castleford	2004, 2008-10	36(24)	5	0	0	20
	Salford	2006	3(8)	2	0	0	8
	Huddersfield	2005	4(6)	0	0	0	0
	Halifax	2000, 2002-03	28(12)	6	0	0	24
Jake Clifford	Hull	2023	25	5	50	0	124
Gavin Clinch	Salford	2004	21(1)	1	0	1	5
	Halifax	1998-99, 2001-02	88(2)	26	45	5	199
	Hudds-Sheff	2000	18(2)	5	0	1	21
	Wigan	1999	10(2)	4	12	0	40
Joel Clinton	Hull KR	2010-12	42(14)	2	0	0	8
John Clough	Salford	2004-06	1(16)	0	0	0	0
Paul Clough	Huddersfield	2017-20	35(43)	3	0	0	12
	Widnes	2014	4(8)	1	0	0	4
	St Helens	2005-13	53(113)	16	0	0	64

201

Super League Players 1996-2023

PLAYER	CLUB	YEAR	APP	TRIES	GOALS	FG	PTS
Tony Clubb	Wigan	2014-21	81(72)	20	0	0	80
	London	2012-13	24(8)	7	0	0	28
	Harlequins	2006-11	100(11)	29	0	0	116
Bradley Clyde	Leeds	2001	7(5)	1	0	0	4
Michael Coady	Leeds	2010	1	0	0	0	0
Evan Cochrane	London	1996	5(1)	1	0	0	4
Ben Cockayne	Hull KR	2007-11, 2014-16	125(30)	38	18	0	188
	Wakefield	2012-13	54	28	2	0	116
Jack Cogger	Huddersfield	2021-22	21(2)	1	0	1	5
Liam Colbon	Hull	2014	8	1	0	0	4
	London	2012-13	22	5	0	0	20
	Hull KR	2009-11	51	20	0	0	80
	Wigan	2004-05, 2007-08	37(14)	15	0	0	60
Anthony Colella	Huddersfield	2003	5(1)	2	0	0	8
Liam Coleman	Leigh	2005	1(4)	0	0	0	0
Andy Coley	Wigan	2008-11	100(10)	8	0	0	32
	Salford	2001-02, 2004-07	112(34)	34	0	0	136
Richard Colley	Bradford	2004	1	0	0	0	0
Steve Collins	Hull	2000	28	17	0	0	68
	Gateshead	1999	20(4)	13	0	0	52
Wayne Collins	Leeds	1997	21	3	0	0	12
Dean Collis	Wakefield	2012-15	64	28	0	0	112
Aurelien Cologni	Catalans	2006	4(1)	3	0	0	12
Gary Connolly	Widnes	2005	20	4	1	0	18
	Wigan	1996-2002, 2004	168(10)	70	5	0	290
	Leeds	2003-04	27	6	0	0	24
Jake Connor	Huddersfield	2013-16, 2023	67(2)	23	31	2	156
	Hull	2017-22	114(13)	34	92	4	324
Nathan Conroy	Bradford	2013-14	(4)	0	0	0	0
Matt Cook	Castleford	2008, 2015-20	22(88)	13	0	0	52
	London	2012-14	50(7)	8	0	0	32
	Hull KR	2010-11	9(16)	7	0	0	28
	Bradford	2005-09	11(52)	4	0	0	16
Mick Cook	Sheffield	1996	9(10)	2	0	0	8
Paul Cook	Huddersfield	1998-99	11(6)	2	13	0	34
	Bradford	1996-97	14(8)	7	38	1	105
Peter Cook	St Helens	2004	(1)	0	0	0	0
Paul Cooke	Wakefield	2010	16(1)	3	36	1	85
	Hull KR	2007-10	54(5)	8	76	2	186
	Hull	1999-2007	177(27)	32	333	4	798
Joseph Coope-Franklin	Salford	2022	1	0	0	0	0
Ben Cooper	Leigh	2005	25(1)	5	0	0	20
	Huddersfield	2000-01, 2003-04	28(12)	3	0	0	12
Mike Cooper	Wigan	2022-23	10(5)	1	0	0	4
	Warrington	2006-13, 2017-22	146(89)	18	0	0	72
	Castleford	2010	1(5)	2	0	0	8
Lachlan Coote	Hull KR	2022-23	26	11	53	1	151
	St Helens	2019-21	58	31	256	1	637
Ged Corcoran	Halifax	2003	1(11)	0	0	0	0
Wayne Corcoran	Halifax	2003	4(2)	0	0	0	0
Jamie Cording	Huddersfield	2011-13	4(21)	5	0	0	20
Josh Cordoba	Hull	2009	8	1	0	0	4
Rio-Osayomwanbo Corkill	St Helens	2022	(1)	0	0	0	0
Mark Corvo	Salford	2002	7(5)	0	0	0	0
Matthew Costello	Salford	2021-23	20(3)	6	0	0	24
	St Helens	2018-20	22(2)	6	0	0	24
Neville Costigan	Hull KR	2014	24	3	0	0	12
Brandon Costin	Huddersfield	2001, 2003-04	69	42	93	3	357
	Bradford	2002	20(1)	8	0	0	32
Wes Cotton	London	1997-98	12	3	0	0	12
Phil Coussons	Salford	1997	7(2)	3	0	0	12
Alex Couttet	Paris	1997	1	0	0	0	0
Nick Couttet	Paris	1997	1	0	0	0	0
Jamie Coventry	Castleford	1996	1	0	0	0	0
Jimmy Cowan	Oldham	1996-97	2(8)	0	0	0	0
Will Cowell	Warrington	1998-2000	6(8)	1	0	0	4
Neil Cowie	Wigan	1996-2001	116(27)	10	0	1	41
Danny Cowling	Wakefield	2012-13	2	0	0	0	0
Jordan Cox	Warrington	2016	(16)	0	0	0	0
	Hull KR	2011-15	17(44)	4	0	0	16
	Huddersfield	2015	(2)	0	0	0	0
Mark Cox	London	2003	(3)	0	0	0	0
James Coyle	Wigan	2005	2(3)	1	0	0	4
Thomas Coyle	Wigan	2008	2(1)	0	0	0	0
Mathieu Cozza	Catalans	2021-22	3(7)	0	0	0	0
Earl Crabtree	Huddersfield	2001, 2003-16	180(167)	52	0	0	208
Andy Craig	Halifax	1999	13(7)	1	3	0	10
	Wigan	1996	5(5)	2	0	0	8
Owen Craigie	Widnes	2005	15	7	0	2	30
Scott Cram	London	1999-2002	65(7)	4	0	0	16
Danny Craven	Widnes	2012-15, 2017-18	53(17)	13	6	3	67
Steve Craven	Hull	1998-2003	53(42)	4	0	0	16
Nicky Crellin	Workington	1996	(2)	0	0	0	0
Jason Critchley	Wakefield	2000	7(1)	4	0	0	16
	Castleford	1997-98	27(3)	11	0	0	44
Brodie Croft	Salford	2022-23	32	12	0	0	48
Jack Croft	Wakefield	2019-20, 2022-23	25	2	0	0	8
Jason Croker	Catalans	2007-09	56(2)	11	0	1	45
Martin Crompton	Salford	1998-2000	30(6)	11	6	2	58
	Oldham	1996-97	36(1)	16	0	3	67
Paul Crook	Widnes	2005	2(2)	0	5	1	11
Paul Crook	Oldham	1996	4(9)	0	3	0	6
Jason Crookes	Hull	2013-14	15(1)	5	0	0	20
	Bradford	2009-12	25(1)	7	0	0	28
Ben Crooks	Hull KR	2018-22	69(1)	35	15	0	170
	Leigh	2017	19	6	0	0	24
	Castleford	2016	24(2)	5	1	0	22
	Hull	2012-14	42(3)	30	23	0	166
Lee Crooks	Castleford	1996-97	27(2)	2	14	0	36
Dominic Crosby	Leeds	2018	(2)	0	0	0	0
	Warrington	2017-18	(16)	0	0	0	0
	Wigan	2012-16	57(35)	6	0	0	24
Alan Cross	St Helens	1997	(2)	0	0	0	0
Ben Cross	Widnes	2012-13	27(1)	2	0	0	8
	Wigan	2011	(4)	0	0	0	0
	Leeds	2011	1(9)	0	0	0	0
Deon Cross	Salford	2022-23	54(1)	18	0	0	72
Steve Crossley	Castleford	2015	(6)	0	0	0	0
	Bradford	2010-11	(9)	1	0	0	4
Garret Crossman	Hull KR	2008	8(18)	0	0	0	0
Steve Crouch	Castleford	2004	4(1)	2	0	0	8
Kevin Crouthers	Warrington	2001-03	12(1)	4	0	0	16
	London	2000	6(4)	1	0	0	4
	Wakefield	1999	4(4)	1	0	0	4
	Bradford	1997-98	3(9)	2	0	0	8
Jordan Crowther	Warrington	2023	5(3)	0	0	0	0
	Wakefield	2014-23	55(33)	4	0	0	16
Matt Crowther	Hull	2001-03	48	20	166	0	412
	Hudds-Sheff	2000	10(4)	5	22	0	64
	Sheffield	1996-99	43(4)	22	10	0	108
Heath Cruckshank	Halifax	2003	19(1)	0	0	0	0
	St Helens	2001	1(12)	0	0	0	0
Leroy Cudjoe	Huddersfield	2008-23	322(3)	116	57	1	579
Paul Cullen	Warrington	1996	19	3	0	0	12
Francis Cummins	Leeds	1996-2005	217(13)	120	26	2	534
James Cunningham	Toulouse	2022	7(5)	1	0	0	4
	Huddersfield	2021	8(1)	0	0	0	0
	Toronto	2020	2(1)	0	0	0	0
	London	2014, 2019	34(8)	3	0	0	12
	Hull	2012, 2014-15	(9)	0	0	0	0
Keiron Cunningham	St Helens	1996-2010	357(24)	138	0	0	552
Liam Cunningham	Hull	2010	1(1)	0	0	0	0
Ben Currie	Warrington	2012-23	197(32)	77	0	0	308
Andy Currier	Warrington	1996-97	(2)	1	0	0	4
Peter Cusack	Hull	2008-10	34(22)	3	0	0	12
Cade Cust	Wigan	2022-23	27(8)	5	0	0	20
Adam Cuthbertson	Leeds	2015-20	91(39)	30	0	0	120
Alrix Da Costa	Catalans	2016-23	45(49)	4	0	0	16
Will Dagger	Wakefield	2023	14(2)	1	27	1	59
	Hull KR	2018-23	41(4)	3	26	1	65
	Warrington	2017	3	0	0	0	0
Joe Dakuitoga	Sheffield	1996	6(3)	0	0	0	0
Matty Dale	Hull	2006, 2008	(7)	1	0	0	4
	Wakefield	2008	1(1)	0	0	0	0
Brett Dallas	Wigan	2000-06	156	89	0	0	356
Mark Dalle Cort	Celtic	2009	23	4	0	0	16
Myles Dalton-Harrop	Salford	2022	1	1	0	0	4
Paul Darbyshire	Warrington	1997	(6)	0	0	0	0
James Davey	Wakefield	2009-11	3(14)	1	0	0	4
Maea David	Hull	1998	1	0	0	0	0
Alex Davidson	Salford	2011, 2013	(3)	0	0	0	0
Paul Davidson	Halifax	2001-03	22(30)	10	0	0	40
	London	2000	6(10)	1	0	0	4
	St Helens	1998-99	27(16)	7	0	0	28
	Oldham	1996-97	17(18)	14	0	1	57

Super League Players 1996-2023

PLAYER	CLUB	YEAR	APP	TRIES	GOALS	FG	PTS
Ben Davies	St Helens	2020-23	26(1)	10	1	0	42
	Salford	2021	2(1)	1	0	0	4
Ben Davies	Castleford	2011, 2013	3(4)	2	0	0	8
	Widnes	2012-13	10(15)	3	0	0	12
	Wigan	2010	(5)	0	0	0	0
Gareth Davies	Warrington	1996-97	1(6)	0	0	0	0
Geraint Davies	Celtic	2009	(7)	0	0	0	0
Henry Davies	Salford	2022	(1)	0	0	0	0
John Davies	Castleford	2010-12	1(6)	1	0	0	4
Jordan Davies	Salford	2013	2(3)	0	0	0	0
Macauley Davies	Wigan	2016	(1)	0	0	0	0
Matthew Davies	London	2019	(1)	0	0	0	0
Olly Davies	St Helens	2016	(1)	0	0	0	0
Tom Davies	Catalans	2020-23	78	48	0	0	192
	Wigan	2017-19	57	27	0	0	108
Wes Davies	Wigan	1998-2001	22(22)	11	0	0	44
Brad Davis	Castleford	1997-2000, 2004, 2006	102(3)	31	43	10	220
	Wakefield	2001-03	51(12)	15	22	5	109
Matt Davis	Leigh	2023	6(20)	1	0	0	4
	Warrington	2019-22	21(32)	5	0	0	20
	London	2019	4	0	0	0	0
Sam Davis	London	2019	2(1)	0	0	0	0
Matty Dawson-Jones	Hull	2019	1	1	0	0	4
	Leigh	2017	23	12	0	0	48
	St Helens	2014-16	46(1)	15	0	0	60
	Huddersfield	2012-13	4	0	0	0	0
Brad Day	Castleford	2014	(1)	0	0	0	0
Matt Daylight	Hull	2000	17(1)	7	0	0	28
	Gateshead	1999	30	25	0	0	100
Michael De Vere	Huddersfield	2005-06	36	6	74	0	172
Paul Deacon	Wigan	2010-11	32(11)	4	14	0	44
	Bradford	1998-2009	258(43)	72	1029	23	2369
	Oldham	1997	(2)	0	0	0	0
Chris Dean	Widnes	2012-18	115(6)	23	0	0	92
	Wakefield	2011	20	8	0	0	32
	St Helens	2007-10	18(3)	9	0	0	36
Craig Dean	Halifax	1996-97	25(11)	12	1	1	51
Gareth Dean	London	2002	(4)	0	0	0	0
Riley Dean	Castleford	2023	4	0	0	2	4
	Warrington	2019-23	8(2)	3	5	0	22
Yacine Dekkiche	Hudds-Sheff	2000	11(3)	3	0	0	12
Brett Delaney	Leeds	2010-18	151(30)	23	0	0	92
George Delaney	St Helens	2022-23	6(14)	0	0	0	0
Jason Demetriou	Wakefield	2004-10	174(3)	50	2	0	204
	Widnes	2002-03	47(1)	15	1	0	62
Martin Dermott	Warrington	1997	1	0	0	0	0
David Despin	Paris	1996	(1)	0	0	0	0
Fabien Devecchi	Paris	1996-97	17(10)	2	0	0	8
Paul Devlin	Widnes	2002-04	32	16	0	0	64
Jordan Dezaria	Catalans	2016-17, 2021-23	14(32)	1	0	0	4
Stuart Dickens	Salford	2005	4(5)	0	4	0	8
Tyler Dickinson	Huddersfield	2016-18	(17)	1	0	0	4
Matt Diskin	Bradford	2011-14	64(16)	11	0	0	44
	Leeds	2001-10	195(37)	40	0	0	160
Andrew Dixon	Salford	2013-14, 2023	35(6)	8	0	0	32
	Toulouse	2022	14	0	0	0	0
	Toronto	2020	1(1)	0	0	0	0
	St Helens	2009-12	19(41)	12	0	0	48
Kieran Dixon	London	2012-14, 2019	76(1)	42	77	0	322
	Hull KR	2015-16	23(4)	21	9	0	102
Kirk Dixon	Castleford	2008-14	143(2)	63	267	0	786
	Hull	2004-06	13(4)	7	4	0	36
Paul Dixon	Sheffield	1996-97	5(9)	1	0	0	4
Nabil Djalout	Catalans	2017	1	0	0	0	0
Gareth Dobson	Castleford	1998-2000	(10)	0	0	0	0
Michael Dobson	Salford	2015-17	58(1)	14	77	1	211
	Hull KR	2008-13	142	51	500	11	1215
	Wigan	2006	14	5	61	0	142
	Catalans	2006	10	4	31	1	79
Michael Docherty	Hull	2000-01	(6)	0	0	0	0
Lewis Dodd	St Helens	2020-23	50(9)	20	12	1	105
Mitchell Dodds	Warrington	2016	(2)	0	0	0	0
Erjon Dollapi	London	2013-14	(18)	4	0	0	16
Sid Domic	Hull	2006-07	39(4)	15	0	0	60
	Wakefield	2004-05	48	30	0	0	120
	Warrington	2002-03	41(4)	17	0	0	68
Scott Donald	Leeds	2006-10	131	77	0	0	308
James Donaldson	Leeds	2019-23	22(77)	8	0	0	32
	Hull KR	2015-16, 2018	12(30)	4	0	0	16
	Bradford	2009-14	38(35)	4	0	0	16
Glen Donkin	Hull	2002-03	(10)	1	0	0	4
Stuart Donlan	Castleford	2008	2	0	0	0	0
	Huddersfield	2004-06	59(3)	15	0	0	60
	Halifax	2001-03	65(2)	22	0	0	88
Jason Donohue	Bradford	1996	(4)	0	0	0	0
Jeremy Donougher	Bradford	1996-99	40(21)	13	0	0	52
Justin Dooley	London	2000-01	37(18)	2	0	0	8
Dane Dorahy	Halifax	2003	20	7	45	0	118
	Wakefield	2000-01	16(2)	4	19	1	55
Jamie Doran	Wigan	2014	(2)	0	0	0	0
Luke Dorn	Castleford	2008, 2014-16	78(2)	60	0	0	240
	London Harlequins	2005, 2012-13 2006,	58(8)	42	0	0	168
		2009-11	83(1)	57	0	0	228
	Salford	2007	19(8)	11	0	0	44
Eribe Doro	Warrington	2020-21	1(3)	1	0	0	4
Brandon Douglas	Castleford	2016	(1)	0	0	0	0
Luke Douglas	St Helens	2017-18	23(32)	5	0	0	20
Ewan Dowes	Hull	2003-11	169(51)	10	0	0	40
	Leeds	2001-03	1(9)	0	0	0	0
Jack Downs	Hull	2015-18	5(15)	1	0	0	4
Adam Doyle	Warrington	1998	9(3)	4	0	0	16
Rod Doyle	Sheffield	1997-99	52(10)	10	0	0	40
Brad Drew	Huddersfield	2005-07, 2010	78(13)	18	13	1	99
	Wakefield	2008-09	27(9)	7	14	1	57
Josh Drinkwater	Warrington	2023	24	2	0	0	8
	Catalans	2018, 2020-22	75	15	60	0	180
	Hull KR	2019	29	4	6	0	28
	Leigh	2017	19	1	12	1	29
	London	2014	23(1)	5	54	0	128
Damien Driscoll	Salford	2001	23(1)	1	0	0	4
James Duckworth	London	2014	3	0	0	0	0
	Leeds	2013	2	1	0	0	4
Gil Dudson	Warrington	2023	8(6)	0	0	0	0
	Catalans	2021-22	25(10)	5	0	0	20
	Salford	2019-20	39(2)	2	0	0	8
	Widnes	2015-18	57(11)	1	0	0	4
	Wigan	2012-14	26(16)	2	0	0	8
	Crusaders	2011	3(7)	0	0	0	0
	Celtic	2009	(1)	0	0	0	0
Jason Duffy	Leigh	2005	3(1)	0	0	0	0
John Duffy	Leigh	2005	21	6	0	0	24
	Salford	2000	3(11)	0	1	1	3
	Warrington	1997-99	12(12)	0	0	0	0
Matt Dufty	Warrington	2022-23	32(2)	18	0	0	72
Tony Duggan	Celtic	2009	4	3	0	0	12
Andrew Duncan	London	1997	2(4)	2	0	0	8
	Warrington	1997	(1)	0	0	0	0
Andrew Dunemann	Salford	2006	25	1	0	2	6
	Leeds	2003-05	76(4)	11	0	2	46
	Halifax	1999-2002	68	19	0	1	77
Matt Dunford	London	1997-98	18(20)	3	0	1	13
Vincent Duport	Catalans	2007-09, 2011-18	156(16)	75	0	0	300
Tyler Dupree	Wigan	2023	6(3)	1	0	0	4
	Salford	2022-23	18(15)	3	0	0	12
Jamie Durbin	Widnes	2005	1	0	0	0	0
	Warrington	2003	(1)	0	0	0	0
Scott Dureau	Catalans	2011-15	88(1)	29	315	10	756
James Durkin	Paris	1997	(5)	0	0	0	0
Bernard Dwyer	Bradford	1996-2000	65(10)	14	0	0	56
Brad Dwyer	Hull	2023	7(17)	2	0	0	8
	Leeds	2018-22	51(55)	29	0	1	117
	Warrington	2012-17	12(63)	11	0	0	44
	Huddersfield	2013	(6)	0	0	0	0
Luke Dyer	Crusaders	2010	23(1)	5	0	0	20
	Celtic	2009	21	6	0	0	24
	Hull KR	2007	26	13	0	0	52
	Castleford	2006	17(2)	5	0	0	20
Adam Dykes	Hull	2008	12	1	0	2	6
Jim Dymock	London	2001-04	94(1)	15	0	1	61
Leo Dynevor	London	1996	8(11)	5	7	0	34
Jason Eade	Paris	1997	9	4	0	0	16
Michael Eagar	Hull	2004-05	12	4	0	0	16
	Castleford	1999-2003	130(2)	60	0	0	240
	Warrington	1998	21	6	0	0	24
Kyle Eastmond	Leeds	2021	2	0	0	0	0
	St Helens	2007-11	46(20)	35	117	3	377
Greg Eastwood	Leeds	2010	5(12)	1	0	0	4
Barry Eaton	Widnes	2002	25	2	49	4	110
	Castleford	2000	1(4)	0	3	0	6
Josh Eaves	St Helens	2019-21	1(3)	1	0	0	4
	Leigh	2021	4(1)	0	0	0	0
	Wakefield	2021	(3)	0	0	0	0
Greg Ebrill	Salford	2002	15(6)	1	0	0	4
Cliff Eccles	Salford	1997-98	30(5)	1	0	0	4

203

Super League Players 1996-2023

PLAYER	CLUB	YEAR	APP	TRIES	GOALS	FG	PTS
Chris Eckersley	Warrington	1996	1	0	0	0	0
Zach Eckersley	Wigan	2022	(1)	0	0	0	0
Greg Eden	Castleford	2011, 2017-23	116(1)	105	0	0	420
	Hull KR	2013-14	37	23	0	0	92
	Salford	2014	4	1	0	0	4
	Huddersfield	2012	24	8	0	0	32
Alfie Edgell	Leeds	2023	(1)	0	0	0	0
Steve Edmed	Sheffield	1997	15(1)	0	0	0	0
Mark Edmondson	Salford	2007	10(2)	0	0	0	0
	St Helens	1999-2005	27(75)	10	0	0	40
Diccon Edwards	Castleford	1996-97	10(5)	1	0	0	4
Grant Edwards	Castleford	2006	(2)	0	0	0	0
Kenny Edwards	Castleford	2022-23	44(4)	5	0	0	20
	Huddersfield	2020-21	19(7)	2	0	0	8
	Catalans	2018-19	14(18)	10	0	0	40
Max Edwards	Harlequins	2010	1	0	0	0	0
Peter Edwards	Salford	1997-98	35(2)	4	0	0	16
Shaun Edwards	London	1997-2000	32(8)	16	1	0	66
	Bradford	1998	8(2)	4	0	0	16
	Wigan	1996	17(3)	12	1	0	50
Tuoyo Egodo	Castleford	2017-19	10(4)	11	0	0	44
Danny Ekis	Halifax	2001	(1)	0	0	0	0
Abi Ekoku	Bradford	1997-98	21(4)	6	0	0	24
	Halifax	1996	15(1)	5	0	0	20
Shane Elford	Huddersfield	2007-08	26(1)	7	0	0	28
Olivier Elima	Catalans	2008-10, 2013-16	99(35)	34	0	0	136
	Bradford	2011-12	37(3)	12	0	0	48
	Wakefield	2003-07	40(47)	13	0	0	52
	Castleford	2002	(1)	1	0	0	4
Abderazak Elkhalouki	Paris	1997	(1)	0	0	0	0
Brendan Elliot	Leigh	2021	10(1)	3	0	0	12
George Elliott	Leeds	2011	1	0	0	0	0
Andy Ellis	Wakefield	2012	10	0	0	0	0
	Harlequins	2010-11	26(11)	8	0	0	32
Gareth Ellis	Hull	2013-17, 2019-20	96(16)	19	0	0	76
	Leeds	2005-08	109	24	1	0	98
	Wakefield	1999-2004	86(17)	21	2	0	88
Jamie Ellis	Leigh	2021	4(4)	1	1	0	6
	Hull KR	2020	7	1	18	0	40
	Castleford	2012-14, 2018-19	58(8)	12	150	2	350
	Huddersfield	2015-16	37(3)	14	31	3	121
	Hull	2012	4(5)	1	0	0	4
	St Helens	2009	1(2)	0	1	0	2
Kaide Ellis	Wigan	2022-23	25(18)	2	0	0	8
Lennie Ellis	Hull KR	2023	(1)	0	0	0	0
Danny Ellison	Castleford	1998-99	7(16)	6	0	0	24
	Wigan	1996-97	15(1)	13	0	0	52
Andrew Emelio	Widnes	2005	22(2)	8	0	0	32
Jake Emmitt	Salford	2013	5(10)	0	0	0	0
	Castleford	2011-13	32(17)	0	0	0	0
	St Helens	2008-10	1(16)	1	0	0	4
Anthony England	Wakefield	2016-19	68(11)	2	0	0	8
	Warrington	2014-15	12(21)	3	0	0	12
Matty English	Huddersfield	2017-23	46(57)	8	0	0	32
Patrick Entat	Paris	1996	22	2	0	0	8
Jason Erba	Sheffield	1997	1(4)	0	0	0	0
Morgan Escare	Salford	2021-22	16(3)	6	3	0	30
	Wakefield	2019, 2022	7	2	0	0	8
	Wigan	2017-19	23(22)	14	39	2	136
	Catalans	2013-16	83	58	1	2	236
Ryan Esders	Harlequins	2009-10	9(11)	3	0	0	12
	Hull KR	2009	(1)	0	0	0	0
Sam Eseh	Wakefield	2023	(14)	0	0	0	0
Sonny Esslemont	Hull KR	2014-15	(5)	0	0	0	0
Niall Evalds	Castleford	2021-23	32	8	0	0	32
	Salford	2013-20	119(11)	88	0	0	352
Ben Evans	Warrington	2014-15	3(16)	2	0	0	8
	Bradford	2013	3(12)	1	0	0	4
James Evans	Castleford	2009-10	26(1)	13	0	0	52
	Bradford	2007-08	43(5)	20	0	0	80
	Wakefield	2006	6	3	0	0	12
	Huddersfield	2004-06	51	22	0	0	88
Kane Evans	Hull	2022-23	14(8)	1	0	0	4
Kyle Evans	Wakefield	2022	3	1	0	0	4
Paul Evans	Paris	1997	18	8	0	0	32
Rhys Evans	Leeds	2020	4(1)	1	0	0	4
	Warrington	2010-17	87(7)	37	0	0	148
Wayne Evans	London	2002	11(6)	2	0	0	8
Toby Everett	London	2014	(2)	0	0	0	0
Richie Eyres	Warrington	1997	2(5)	0	0	0	0
	Sheffield	1997	2(3)	0	0	0	0
Henry Fa'afili	Warrington	2004-07	90(1)	70	0	0	280
David Fa'alogo	Huddersfield	2010-12	38(16)	13	0	0	52
Sala Fa'alogo	Widnes	2004-05	8(15)	2	0	0	8
Richard Fa'aoso	Castleford	2006	10(15)	5	0	0	20
Maurie Fa'asavalu	St Helens	2004-10	5(137)	29	0	0	116
Bolouagi Fagborun	Huddersfield	2004-06	4(2)	1	0	0	4
Theo Fages	Huddersfield	2022-23	21(1)	3	0	0	12
	St Helens	2016-21	101(25)	34	0	2	138
	Salford	2013-15	57(5)	18	4	0	80
Esene Faimalo	Salford	1997-99	23(25)	2	0	0	8
	Leeds	1996	3(3)	0	0	0	0
Joe Faimalo	Salford	1998-2000	23(47)	7	0	0	28
	Oldham	1996-97	37(5)	7	0	0	28
Jacob Fairbank	Huddersfield	2011-15	12(3)	0	0	0	0
	Wakefield	2014	1(3)	0	0	0	0
	London	2013	4(1)	1	0	0	4
	Bradford	2013	(2)	0	0	0	0
Karl Fairbank	Bradford	1996	17(2)	4	0	0	16
David Fairleigh	St Helens	2001	26(1)	8	0	0	32
David Faiumu	Huddersfield	2008-14	38(108)	13	0	0	52
Jamal Fakir	Bradford	2014	5(8)	1	0	0	4
	Catalans	2006-14	55(100)	13	0	0	52
Jim Fallon	Leeds	1996	10	5	0	0	20
Beau Falloon	Leeds	2016	8(2)	0	0	0	0
Bureta Faraimo	Castleford	2022-23	32(1)	15	0	0	60
	Hull	2018-21	78(1)	37	4	0	156
Owen Farnworth	Widnes	2017-18	1(4)	0	0	0	0
Ben Farrar	London	2014	22	1	0	0	4
	Catalans	2011	13	3	0	0	12
Danny Farrer	Warrington	1998-2000	76	13	0	0	52
Andy Farrell	Wigan	1996-2004	230	77	1026	16	2376
Anthony Farrell	Widnes	2002-03	24(22)	4	1	0	18
	Leeds	1997-2001	99(23)	18	0	0	72
	Sheffield	1996	14(5)	5	0	0	20
Connor Farrell	Widnes	2016	3(9)	3	0	0	12
	Wigan	2014-15	1(8)	1	0	0	4
Craig Farrell	Hull	2000-01	1(3)	0	0	0	0
Izaac Farrell	Huddersfield	2019	2	0	4	0	8
Liam Farrell	Wigan	2010-23	261(50)	124	0	0	496
Brad Fash	Hull	2015, 2017-23	54(94)	6	0	0	24
Abraham Fatnowna	London	1997-98	7(2)	2	0	0	8
	Workington	1996	5	2	0	0	8
Sione Faumuina	Castleford	2009	18	1	0	0	4
	Hull	2005	3	1	0	0	4
Vince Fawcett	Wakefield	1999	13(1)	2	0	0	8
	Warrington	1998	4(7)	1	0	0	4
	Oldham	1997	5	3	0	0	12
Danny Fearon	Huddersfield	2001	(1)	0	0	0	0
	Halifax	1999-2000	5(6)	0	0	0	0
Chris Feather	Castleford	2009	1(23)	0	0	0	0
	Bradford	2007-08	7(20)	1	0	0	4
	Leeds	2003-04, 2006	16(35)	6	0	0	24
	Wakefield	2001-02, 2004-05	29(32)	9	0	0	36
Dom Feaunati	Leigh	2005	4	1	0	0	4
	St Helens	2004	10(7)	7	0	0	28
Sosaia Feki	Castleford	2022	(1)	0	0	0	0
Adel Fellous	Hull	2008	1(2)	0	0	0	0
	Catalans	2006-07	16(22)	4	0	0	16
Luke Felsch	Hull	2000-01	46(6)	7	0	0	28
	Gateshead	1999	28(1)	2	0	0	8
Leon Felton	Warrington	2002	4(2)	0	0	0	0
	St Helens	2001	1(1)	0	0	0	0
Dale Ferguson	Huddersfield	2011-13, 2017-19	61(23)	16	0	0	64
	Bradford	2014	3(3)	0	0	0	0
	Hull KR	2013	3(1)	1	0	0	4
	Wakefield	2007-08	40(14)	12	0	0	48
Brett Ferres	Leeds	2016-20	52(16)	11	0	0	44
	Huddersfield	2012-15	72	27	0	0	108
	Castleford	2009-12	78(5)	26	0	0	104
	Wakefield	2007-08	36(2)	6	5	0	34
	Bradford	2005-06	18(17)	11	2	0	48
David Ferriol	Catalans	2007-12	72(55)	8	0	0	32
Jason Ferris	Leigh	2005	4	1	0	0	4
Callum Field	Wigan	2017-18	(8)	0	0	0	0
Jai Field	Wigan	2021-23	52(1)	38	4	0	160
Jamie Field	Wakefield	1999-2006	133(59)	19	0	0	76
	Huddersfield	1998	15(5)	0	0	0	0
	Leeds	1996-97	3(11)	0	0	0	0
Mark Field	Wakefield	2003-07	28(7)	3	0	0	12
Jamie Fielden	London	2003	(1)	0	0	0	0
	Huddersfield	1998-2000	4(8)	0	0	0	0
Stuart Fielden	Huddersfield	2013	8(1)	0	0	0	0
	Wigan	2006-12	105(24)	2	0	0	8
	Bradford	1998-2006	142(78)	41	0	0	164

Super League Players 1996-2023

PLAYER	CLUB	YEAR	APP	TRIES	GOALS	FG	PTS
David Fifita	Wakefield	2016-23	66(79)	25	2	0	104
Lafaele Filipo	Workington	1996	15(4)	3	0	0	12
Salesi Finau	Warrington	1996-97	16(15)	8	0	0	32
Brett Finch	Wigan	2011-12	49(3)	16	0	0	64
Vinny Finigan	Bradford	2010	4(1)	4	0	0	16
Liam Finn	Widnes	2018	1	0	0	0	0
	Wakefield	2004, 2016-18	71(4)	5	220	0	460
	Castleford	2014-15	45(2)	8	5	2	44
	Halifax	2002-03	16(5)	2	30	1	69
Lee Finnerty	Halifax	2003	18(2)	5	2	0	24
Phil Finney	Warrington	1998	1	0	0	0	0
Simon Finnigan	Widnes	2003-05, 2012	56(24)	21	0	0	84
	Huddersfield	2009-10	22(5)	6	0	0	24
	Bradford	2008	14(13)	8	0	0	32
	Salford	2006-07	50	17	0	0	68
Matt Firth	Halifax	2000-01	12(2)	0	0	0	0
Andy Fisher	Wakefield	1999-2000	31(8)	4	0	0	16
Ben Fisher	London	2013	8(12)	1	0	0	4
	Catalans	2012	9(5)	1	0	0	4
	Hull KR	2007-11	78(46)	18	0	0	72
Zach Fishwick	Hull KR	2022	1(6)	1	0	0	4
Craig Fitzgibbon	Hull	2010-11	42(1)	9	8	0	52
Daniel Fitzhenry	Hull KR	2008-09	36(11)	14	0	0	56
Karl Fitzpatrick	Salford	2004-07, 2009-10	89(11)	33	2	0	136
Conor Fitzsimmons	Castleford	2016	(2)	0	0	0	0
Mark Flanagan	Salford	2016-20	62(27)	8	0	0	32
	St Helens	2012-15	40(39)	9	0	0	36
	Wigan	2009	3(7)	1	0	0	4
Chris Flannery	St Helens	2007-12	108(11)	32	0	0	128
Darren Fleary	Leigh	2005	24	1	0	0	4
	Huddersfield	2003-04	43(8)	4	0	0	16
	Leeds	1997-2002	98(9)	3	0	0	12
Dan Fleming	Castleford	2013-14, 2020	(16)	1	0	0	4
Greg Fleming	London	1999-2001	64(1)	40	2	0	164
Matty Fleming	London	2019	12(1)	6	0	0	24
	Leigh	2017	5	1	0	0	4
	St Helens	2015-17	17	7	0	0	28
Adam Fletcher	Castleford	2006, 2008	16(7)	11	0	0	44
Bryan Fletcher	Wigan	2006-07	47(2)	14	0	0	56
Richard Fletcher	Castleford	2006	13(5)	3	4	0	20
	Hull	1999-2004	11(56)	5	0	0	20
Greg Florimo	Halifax	2000	26	4	4	0	32
	Wigan	1999	18(2)	7	1	0	30
Ben Flower	Leigh	2021	2(2)	0	0	0	0
	Wigan	2012-20	131(37)	21	0	0	84
	Crusaders	2010-11	10(23)	2	0	0	8
	Celtic	2009	2(15)	0	0	0	0
Jason Flowers	Salford	2004	6(1)	0	0	0	0
	Halifax	2002	24(4)	4	0	0	16
	Castleford	1996-2001	119(19)	33	0	1	133
Stuart Flowers	Castleford	1996	(3)	0	0	0	0
Adrian Flynn	Castleford	1996-97	19(2)	10	0	0	40
Paddy Flynn	Castleford	2016	9(1)	6	0	0	24
	Widnes	2012-15	72	41	0	0	164
Wayne Flynn	Sheffield	1997	3(5)	0	0	0	0
Adam Fogerty	Warrington	1998	4	0	0	0	0
	St Helens	1996	13	1	0	0	4
Israel Folau	Catalans	2020	13	5	0	0	20
Mahe Fonua	Castleford	2022-23	35(1)	5	0	0	20
	Hull	2016-17, 2020-21	78(5)	39	0	0	156
Liam Foran	Salford	2013	10(3)	1	0	0	4
Carl Forber	Leigh	2005	4	1	0	0	4
	St Helens	2004	1(1)	0	6	0	12
Paul Forber	Salford	1997-98	19(12)	4	0	0	16
Tom Forber	Wakefield	2023	(2)	0	0	0	0
	Wigan	2022	(1)	0	0	0	0
Byron Ford	Hull KR	2007	13	6	0	0	24
James Ford	Castleford	2009	3(5)	1	0	0	4
Mike Ford	Castleford	1997-98	25(12)	5	0	3	23
	Warrington	1996	3	0	0	0	0
Jim Forshaw	Salford	1999	(1)	0	0	0	0
Mike Forshaw	Warrington	2004	20(1)	5	0	0	20
	Bradford	1997-2003	162(7)	32	0	0	128
	Leeds	1996	11(3)	5	0	0	20
Carl Forster	Salford	2015-16	5(7)	1	0	0	4
	St Helens	2011-12, 2014	(4)	0	0	0	0
	London	2014	2(3)	0	0	0	0
Mark Forster	Warrington	1996-2000	102(1)	40	0	0	160
Liam Forsyth	Wigan	2017-18	11(2)	3	0	0	12
Alex Foster	Castleford	2017-21, 2023	41(23)	12	0	0	48
	London	2014	20	3	0	0	12
	Leeds	2013	(8)	1	0	0	4
David Foster	Halifax	2000-01	4(9)	0	0	0	0
Jamie Foster	Huddersfield	2016	3	2	5	0	18
	Bradford	2013-14	32	12	111	0	270
	Hull	2012	9	5	45	0	110
	St Helens	2010-12	44(3)	30	201	0	522
Matthew Foster	Leigh	2021	4(2)	0	0	0	0
	St Helens	2020	(1)	0	0	0	0
Peter Fox	Wakefield	2007, 2012-14	85	44	0	0	176
	Hull KR	2008-11	95	52	0	0	208
Matty Fozard	London	2019	7(16)	3	0	0	12
	St Helens	2014	1	0	0	0	0
Nick Fozzard	Castleford	2011	7(10)	0	0	0	0
	St Helens	2004-08, 2010	100(25)	7	0	0	28
	Hull KR	2009	18(4)	1	0	0	4
	Warrington	2002-03	43(11)	2	0	0	8
	Huddersfield	1998-2000	24(8)	2	0	0	8
	Leeds	1996-97	6(16)	3	0	0	12
David Fraisse	Workington	1996	8	0	0	0	0
Daniel Frame	Widnes	2002-05	100(6)	24	0	0	96
Romain Franco	Wakefield	2023	4	2	0	0	8
	Catalans	2021-22	6(1)	1	0	0	4
Paul Franze	Castleford	2006	2(1)	0	0	0	0
Matt Frawley	Huddersfield	2019	19(2)	4	0	0	16
Laurent Frayssinous	Catalans	2006	14(2)	3	32	0	76
Bevan French	Wigan	2019-23	75(6)	72	0	0	288
Andrew Frew	Halifax	2003	17	5	0	0	20
	Wakefield	2002	21	8	0	0	32
	Huddersfield	2001	26	15	0	0	60
Dale Fritz	Castleford	1999-2003	120(4)	9	0	0	36
Gareth Frodsham	St Helens	2008-09	1(9)	0	0	0	0
Liam Fulton	Huddersfield	2009	12(3)	4	0	0	16
David Furner	Leeds	2003-04	45	8	23	0	78
	Wigan	2001-02	51(2)	21	13	0	110
David Furness	Castleford	1996	(1)	0	0	0	0
David Fusitu'a	Leeds	2022-23	31	15	0	0	60
Matt Gafa	Harlequins	2006-09	81	26	16	0	136
Luke Gale	Wakefield	2023	10	1	2	1	9
	Hull	2022	19	2	38	1	85
	Leeds	2020-21	26	8	16	4	68
	Castleford	2015-18	100	32	402	15	947
	Bradford	2012-14	56(2)	13	108	4	272
	Harlequins	2009-11	56(12)	18	86	3	247
Ben Galea	Hull	2013	12(2)	3	0	0	12
	Hull KR	2008-12	115(2)	33	0	0	132
Danny Galea	Widnes	2014-15	38(4)	5	0	0	20
Tommy Gallagher	Hull KR	2007	1(7)	0	0	0	0
	Widnes	2004	(6)	0	0	0	0
	London	2003	1(9)	1	0	0	4
Keith Galloway	Leeds	2016-17	28(4)	1	0	0	4
Mark Gamson	Sheffield	1996	3	0	0	0	0
Jim Gannon	Hull KR	2007	7(16)	1	0	0	4
	Huddersfield	2003-06	79(14)	11	0	0	44
	Halifax	1999-2002	83(4)	14	0	0	56
Morgan Gannon	Leeds	2021-23	25(21)	7	0	0	28
Josh Ganson	Wigan	2017-18	1(6)	2	0	0	8
Mitch Garbutt	Toulouse	2022	3(5)	1	0	0	4
	Hull KR	2019-20	5(22)	5	0	0	20
	Leeds	2015-18	36(25)	7	0	0	28
Steve Garces	Salford	2001	(1)	0	0	0	0
Benjamin Garcia	Catalans	2013-23	147(47)	33	0	0	132
Jean-Marc Garcia	Sheffield	1996-97	35(3)	22	0	0	88
Will Gardiner	Hull	2022-23	2(6)	1	0	0	4
Ade Gardner	Hull KR	2014	18	7	0	0	28
	St Helens	2002-13	236(12)	146	0	0	584
Matt Gardner	Harlequins	2009	6(3)	2	0	0	8
	Huddersfield	2006-07	22(3)	7	0	0	28
	Castleford	2004	1	1	0	0	4
Tom Garratt	Hull KR	2022	3(2)	0	0	0	0
Steve Gartland	Oldham	1996	1(1)	0	1	0	2
Daniel Gartner	Bradford	2001-03	74(1)	26	0	0	104
Dean Gaskell	Warrington	2002-05	58(1)	10	0	0	40
Lee Gaskell	Wakefield	2022-23	22	3	2	0	16
	Huddersfield	2017-21	89(1)	24	30	1	157
	Bradford	2014	21	5	0	0	20
	Salford	2013	17	8	2	0	36
	St Helens	2010-13	33(9)	14	12	1	81
George Gatis	Huddersfield	2008	5(5)	1	0	0	4
James Gavet	Huddersfield	2020-21	12(12)	4	0	0	16
Richard Gay	Castleford	1996-2002	94(16)	39	0	0	156
Andrew Gee	Warrington	2000	33(1)	4	0	0	16
Matty Gee	Leigh	2021	9(5)	4	0	0	16
	Hull KR	2020	6(5)	0	0	0	0
	London	2019	14(8)	5	0	0	20
	Salford	2015	(2)	0	0	0	0

205

Super League Players 1996-2023

PLAYER	CLUB	YEAR	APP	TRIES	GOALS	FG	PTS
Anthony Gelling	Leigh	2021	6	2	0	0	8
	Warrington	2020	11	6	0	0	24
	Wigan	2012-17	101(1)	52	0	0	208
Stanley Gene	Hull KR	2007-09	37(17)	9	0	0	36
	Bradford	2006	5(16)	8	0	0	32
	Huddersfield	2001, 2003-05	70(6)	27	0	0	108
	Hull	2000-01	5(23)	6	0	0	24
Steve Georgallis	Warrington	2001	5(1)	2	0	0	8
Luke George	Bradford	2014	9(1)	3	0	0	12
	Huddersfield	2012-13	28(2)	18	0	0	72
	Hull KR	2013	4	2	0	0	8
	Wakefield	2007-11	38(3)	24	0	0	96
Shaun Geritas	Warrington	1997	(5)	1	0	0	4
Alex Gerrard	Salford	2022-23	16(13)	2	0	0	8
	Leigh	2021	5(9)	0	0	0	0
	Widnes	2012-18	48(40)	4	0	0	16
Anthony Gibbons	Leeds	1996	9(4)	2	0	1	9
David Gibbons	Leeds	1996	3(4)	2	0	0	8
Scott Gibbs	St Helens	1996	9	3	0	0	12
Ashley Gibson	Wakefield	2016-17	9	4	0	0	16
	Castleford	2014-15	27	9	0	0	36
	Salford	2010-13	77(4)	41	0	0	164
	Leeds	2005-09	25(7)	13	9	0	70
Damian Gibson	Castleford	2003-04	40(3)	5	0	0	20
	Salford	2002	28	3	0	0	12
	Halifax	1998-2001	104(1)	39	0	0	156
	Leeds	1997	18	3	0	0	12
Kurt Gidley	Warrington	2016-17	44	11	97	0	238
Matt Gidley	St Helens	2007-10	105	40	6	0	172
Tony Gigot	Toulouse	2022	19	2	1	2	12
	Wakefield	2020	6(1)	1	6	0	16
	Toronto	2020	2(1)	0	0	0	0
	Catalans	2010-11, 2015-19	117(13)	43	51	12	286
	London	2014	2	0	4	0	8
Ian Gildart	Oldham	1996-97	31(7)	0	0	0	0
Oliver Gildart	Leeds	2023	8	1	0	0	4
	Wigan	2015-21	128(2)	58	0	0	232
	Salford	2015	3	1	0	0	4
Chris Giles	Widnes	2003-04	35	12	0	0	48
	St Helens	2002	(1)	0	0	0	0
Keane Gilford	St Helens	2022	1	0	0	0	0
Kieran Gill	Castleford	2017-18	4	4	0	0	16
Peter Gill	London	1996-99	75(6)	20	0	0	80
Carl Gillespie	Halifax	1996-99	47(36)	13	0	0	52
Michael Gillett	London	2001-02	23(21)	12	2	0	52
Simon Gillies	Warrington	1999	28	6	0	0	24
Tom Gilmore	Salford	2020	2	1	0	0	4
	Widnes	2012-18	38(1)	11	51	3	149
Lee Gilmour	Wakefield	2014	10(3)	2	0	0	8
	Castleford	2013	10(2)	0	0	0	0
	Huddersfield	2010-12	71(1)	17	0	0	68
	St Helens	2004-09	149(3)	41	0	0	164
	Bradford	2001-03	44(31)	20	0	0	80
	Wigan	1997-2000	44(39)	22	0	0	88
Marc Glanville	Leeds	1998-99	43(3)	5	0	0	20
Eddie Glaze	Castleford	1996	1	0	0	0	0
Paul Gleadhill	Leeds	1996	4	0	0	0	0
Ben Gledhill	Salford	2012-13	3(10)	1	0	0	4
	Wakefield	2010-11	(16)	0	0	0	0
Mark Gleeson	Warrington	2000-08	38(102)	12	0	0	48
Martin Gleeson	Salford	2013-14	26(1)	4	0	0	16
	Hull	2011	6	4	0	0	16
	Wigan	2009-11	46(1)	19	0	0	76
	Warrington	2005-09	110(1)	44	0	0	176
	St Helens	2002-04	56(1)	25	0	0	100
	Huddersfield	1999-2001	47(9)	18	0	0	72
Sean Gleeson	Hull KR	2013	6	0	0	0	0
	Salford	2011-12	35	14	0	0	56
	Wakefield	2007-10	67(6)	20	0	0	80
	Wigan	2005-06	3(3)	0	0	0	0
Jon Goddard	Hull KR	2007	20	2	0	0	8
	Castleford	2000-01	(2)	0	0	0	0
Richard Goddard	Castleford	1996-97	11(3)	2	10	0	28
Brad Godden	Leeds	1998-99	47	15	0	0	60
Pita Godinet	Wakefield	2014-15	18(19)	10	0	0	40
Wayne Godwin	Salford	2011-13, 2015	43(8)	6	0	0	24
	Bradford	2008-10	16(44)	9	0	0	36
	Hull	2007	3(13)	1	0	0	4
	Wigan	2005-06	9(38)	6	0	0	24
	Castleford	2001-04	30(33)	18	56	0	184
Jason Golden	London	2012	7(2)	1	0	0	4
	Harlequins	2009-11	34(12)	3	0	0	12
	Wakefield	2007-08	26(5)	1	0	0	4
Marvin Golden	Widnes	2003	4	1	0	0	4
	London	2001	17(2)	1	0	0	4
	Halifax	2000	20(2)	5	0	0	20
	Leeds	1996-99	43(11)	19	0	0	76
Ashton Golding	Huddersfield	2020-23	33(14)	8	0	0	32
	Leeds	2014-18	42(9)	5	14	0	48
Brett Goldspink	Halifax	2000-02	64(5)	2	0	0	8
	Wigan	1999	6(16)	1	0	0	4
	St Helens	1998	19(4)	2	0	0	8
	Oldham	1997	13(2)	0	0	0	0
Lee Gomersall	Hull KR	2008	1	0	0	0	0
Bryson Goodwin	Warrington	2018-19	52	20	29	0	138
Luke Goodwin	London	1998	9(2)	3	1	1	15
	Oldham	1997	16(4)	10	17	2	76
Grant Gore	Widnes	2012-15	6(11)	1	0	0	4
Louix Gorman	Hull KR	2023	1	0	0	0	0
Aaron Gorrell	Catalans	2007-08	23	6	14	0	52
Andy Gorski	Salford	2001-02	(2)	0	0	0	0
Cyrille Gossard	Catalans	2006-12	54(30)	5	0	0	20
Mickael Goudemand	Catalans	2018-23	26(68)	9	0	0	36
Bobbie Goulding	Salford	2001-02	31(1)	2	56	4	124
	Wakefield	2000	12	3	25	3	65
	Huddersfield	1998-99	27(1)	3	65	4	146
	St Helens	1996-98	42(2)	9	210	4	460
Bobbie Goulding (Jnr)	Wakefield	2013	1(2)	0	1	0	2
Darrell Goulding	Hull KR	2015	8	1	0	0	4
	Wigan	2005-14	129(24)	68	0	0	272
	Salford	2009	9	5	0	0	20
Mick Govin	Leigh	2005	5(6)	4	0	0	16
Craig Gower	London	2012-13	40	7	24	0	76
David Gower	Salford	2006-07	(16)	0	0	0	0
Regan Grace	St Helens	2017-22	128	75	0	0	300
Shane Grady	London	2013	5(4)	1	2	0	8
Brad Graham	Castleford	2020-21	3	1	0	0	4
James Graham	St Helens	2003-11, 2020	143(63)	48	0	0	192
Nathan Graham	Bradford	1996-98	17(28)	4	0	1	17
Nick Graham	Wigan	2003	13(1)	2	0	0	8
Dalton Grant	Crusaders	2011	(1)	0	0	0	0
Jon Grayshon	Harlequins	2007-09	10(32)	4	0	0	16
	Huddersfield	2003-06	7(43)	5	0	0	20
Blake Green	Wigan	2013-14	42(1)	15	0	0	60
	Hull KR	2011-12	35	14	0	0	56
Brett Green	Gateshead	1999	10(2)	0	0	0	0
Chris Green	Wakefield	2019-21	8(19)	1	0	0	4
	Hull	2012-19	33(92)	7	0	0	28
James Green	Castleford	2018	1(3)	0	0	0	0
	Leigh	2017	4(5)	0	0	0	0
	Hull KR	2012-16	8(64)	3	0	0	12
Lucas Green	Warrington	2023	(4)	0	0	0	0
Toby Green	Huddersfield	2001	3(1)	1	0	0	4
Craig Greenhill	Castleford	2004	21(4)	1	0	0	4
	Hull	2002-03	56	3	2	0	16
Clint Greenshields	Catalans	2007-12	137	81	0	0	324
Ollie Greensmith	Wakefield	2021	1	0	0	0	0
Brandon Greenwood	Halifax	1996	1	0	0	0	0
Gareth Greenwood	Huddersfield	2003	(1)	0	0	0	0
	Halifax	2002	1	0	0	0	0
James Greenwood	Salford	2015, 2020-23	16(4)	3	0	0	12
	Hull KR	2015-16, 2018-23	29(23)	7	0	0	28
	Wigan	2013, 2015	(2)	0	0	0	0
	London	2014	10(5)	3	0	0	12
Joe Greenwood	Huddersfield	2021-23	22(35)	4	0	0	16
	Wigan	2018-20	23(16)	12	0	0	48
	St Helens	2012-17	40(28)	26	0	0	104
Lee Greenwood	Huddersfield	2005	7	3	0	0	12
	London	2004-05	30(2)	19	0	0	76
	Halifax	2000-03	38(2)	17	0	0	68
	Sheffield	1999	1(1)	0	0	0	0
Nick Gregson	Wigan	2016-17	5(9)	1	0	0	4
James Grehan	Castleford	2012	2(2)	0	0	0	0
Maxime Greseque	Wakefield	2007	2(1)	0	0	0	0
Mathieu Griffi	Catalans	2006-08	1(25)	0	0	0	0
Darrell Griffin	Salford	2013-15	31(27)	1	0	0	4
	Leeds	2012	8(19)	2	0	0	8
	Huddersfield	2007-11	65(60)	13	0	0	52
	Wakefield	2003-06	55(37)	9	3	0	42
George Griffin	Castleford	2020-23	60(12)	5	0	0	20
	Salford	2015-19	69(22)	16	0	0	64
	Wakefield	2015	5	0	0	0	0
	London	2014	(19)	1	0	0	4
	Hull KR	2012-13	11(7)	0	0	0	0

Super League Players 1996-2023

PLAYER	CLUB	YEAR	APP	TRIES	GOALS	FG	PTS
Josh Griffin	Wakefield	2011, 2023	23	7	21	0	70
	Hull	2017-23	119(8)	38	4	0	160
	Salford	2014-16	42	23	77	0	246
	Castleford	2012	20	13	1	0	54
	Huddersfield	2009	2	0	0	0	0
Jonathan Griffiths	Paris	1996	(4)	1	0	0	4
Andrew Grima	Workington	1996	2(9)	2	0	0	8
Tony Grimaldi	Hull	2000-01	56(1)	14	0	0	56
	Gateshead	1999	27(2)	10	0	0	40
Danny Grimley	Sheffield	1996	4(1)	1	0	0	4
Scott Grix	Huddersfield	2010-16, 2019	141(11)	53	32	0	276
	Wakefield	2008-09, 2017-18	81(3)	32	0	0	128
Simon Grix	Warrington	2006-14	133(25)	42	0	0	168
	Halifax	2003	2(4)	0	0	0	0
Brett Grogan	Gateshead	1999	14(7)	3	0	0	12
Brent Grose	Warrington	2003-07	134(1)	55	0	0	220
David Guasch	Catalans	2010	1	0	0	0	0
Joan Guasch	Catalans	2014-15	(6)	0	0	0	0
Renaud Guigue	Catalans	2006	14(4)	3	0	0	12
Jerome Guisset	Catalans	2006-10	102(23)	9	0	0	36
	Wigan	2005	20(2)	3	0	0	12
	Warrington	2000-04	59(65)	21	0	0	84
Awen Guttenbeil	Castleford	2008	19	0	0	0	0
Reece Guy	Oldham	1996	3(4)	0	0	0	0
Josh Guzdek	Hull KR	2013, 2015	2	1	0	0	4
Titus Gwaze	Wakefield	2019-20	(5)	0	0	0	0
Tom Haberecht	Castleford	2008	2(2)	1	0	0	4
Dean Hadley	Hull KR	2019-23	54(15)	4	0	0	16
	Hull	2013-16, 2018-19	55(26)	10	0	0	40
	Wakefield	2017	14(7)	2	0	0	8
Gareth Haggerty	Harlequins	2008-09	8(28)	6	0	0	24
	Salford	2004-07	1(93)	15	0	0	60
	Widnes	2002	1(2)	1	0	0	4
Kurt Haggerty	Widnes	2012	6(8)	2	0	0	8
Andy Haigh	St Helens	1996-98	20(16)	11	0	0	44
Scott Hale	Hull KR	2011	(3)	1	0	0	4
Michael Haley	Leeds	2008	(1)	0	0	0	0
Carl Hall	Leeds	1996	7(2)	3	0	0	12
Corey Hall	Hull KR	2023	8	2	0	0	8
	Wakefield	2022-23	27(1)	8	0	0	32
	Leeds	2020-21	1(2)	0	0	0	0
Craig Hall	Hull KR	2011-14, 2018-19	102(3)	51	65	2	336
	Wakefield	2015-16	35	14	30	0	116
	Hull	2007-10	59(9)	39	11	0	178
Glenn Hall	Bradford	2010	7(18)	2	0	0	8
Martin Hall	Halifax	1998	2(10)	1	0	0	4
	Hull	1999	7	0	0	0	0
	Castleford	1998	4	0	0	0	0
	Wigan	1996-97	31(5)	7	6	0	40
Ryan Hall	Hull KR	2021-23	68	44	0	0	176
	Leeds	2007-18	278(3)	196	0	0	784
Sam Hall	Castleford	2020-23	4(17)	1	0	0	4
Steve Hall	Widnes	2004	1	0	0	0	0
	London	2002-03	35(3)	10	0	0	40
	St Helens	1999-2001	36(22)	19	0	0	76
Graeme Hallas	Huddersfield	2001	1	0	0	0	0
	Hull	1998-99	30(10)	6	39	1	103
	Halifax	1996	11(4)	5	0	0	20
Sam Hallas	Leeds	2016	(2)	0	0	0	0
Macauley Hallett	Hull KR	2014	2	3	0	0	12
Dave Halley	Bradford	2007-10	63(12)	20	0	0	80
	Wakefield	2009	5	4	0	0	16
Danny Halliwell	Salford	2007	2(3)	0	0	0	0
	Leigh	2005	5	3	0	0	12
	Halifax	2000-03	17(8)	4	0	0	16
	Warrington	2002	9(1)	8	0	0	32
	Wakefield	2002	3	0	0	0	0
Colum Halpenny	Wakefield	2003-06	103(1)	36	0	0	144
	Halifax	2002	22	12	0	0	48
Sam Halsall	Huddersfield	2023	16	9	0	0	36
	Wigan	2020-22	15(1)	7	0	0	28
Frankie Halton	Leigh	2023	(3)	0	0	0	0
	Hull KR	2022-23	20(5)	6	0	0	24
Jon Hamer	Bradford	1996	(1)	0	0	0	0
Andrew Hamilton	London	1997, 2003	1(20)	3	0	0	12
John Hamilton	St Helens	1998	3	0	0	0	0
Gabe Hamlin	Wigan	2018-19	6(18)	3	0	0	12
Karle Hammond	Halifax	2002	10(2)	2	14	0	36
	Salford	2001	2(3)	1	0	0	4
	London	1999-2000	47	23	2	3	99
	St Helens	1996-98	58(8)	28	0	4	116
Ryan Hampshire	Wigan	2013-15, 2023	21(6)	8	27	0	86
	Castleford	2016, 2022	24(2)	10	0	0	40
	Wakefield	2018-21	75(6)	27	122	3	355
	Leigh	2017	12(1)	3	0	0	12
Rhys Hanbury	Widnes	2012-18	153	71	99	1	483
	Crusaders	2010-11	26(1)	14	0	0	56
Anthony Hancock	Paris	1997	8(6)	1	0	0	4
Michael Hancock	Salford	2001-02	12(24)	7	0	0	28
Jordan Hand	Wakefield	2015	(2)	0	0	0	0
	St Helens	2013-14	(3)	0	0	0	0
Gareth Handford	Castleford	2001	7(2)	0	0	0	0
	Bradford	2000	1(1)	0	0	0	0
Paul Handforth	Castleford	2006	2(15)	2	1	0	10
	Wakefield	2000-04	17(44)	10	13	0	66
Ash Handley	Leeds	2014-23	173(3)	101	2	0	408
Paddy Handley	Leeds	1996	1(1)	2	0	0	8
Dean Hanger	Warrington	1999	7(11)	3	0	0	12
	Huddersfield	1998	20(1)	5	0	0	20
Chris Hankinson	Toulouse	2022	25	5	64	0	148
	Wigan	2018-20	18(4)	4	19	0	54
Umyla Hanley	Leigh	2023	1	0	0	0	0
	Wigan	2020-22	10	4	0	0	16
Josh Hannay	Celtic	2009	17	2	24	0	56
Harrison Hansen	Toulouse	2022	1(19)	1	0	0	4
	Widnes	2018	1	1	0	0	4
	Leigh	2017	19(2)	1	0	0	4
	Salford	2014-15	41(2)	7	0	0	28
	Wigan	2004-13	155(62)	39	0	0	156
Lee Hansen	Wigan	1997	10(5)	0	0	0	0
Shontayne Hape	Bradford	2003-08	123(2)	79	0	0	316
Lionel Harbin	Wakefield	2001	(1)	0	0	0	0
Zak Hardaker	Leigh	2023	23	3	14	0	40
	Leeds	2011-16, 2022	153	59	55	1	347
	Wigan	2019-22	70(1)	22	195	2	480
	Castleford	2017	28	12	1	0	50
Ian Hardman	Hull KR	2007	18	4	0	0	16
	St Helens	2003-07	32(11)	9	5	0	46
Jeff Hardy	Hudds-Sheff	2000	20(5)	6	0	1	25
	Sheffield	1999	22(4)	7	0	0	28
Spencer Hargrave	Castleford	1996-99	(6)	0	0	0	0
Bryn Hargreaves	Bradford	2011-12	45(5)	1	0	0	4
	St Helens	2007-10	53(44)	7	0	0	28
	Wigan	2004-06	16(12)	1	0	0	4
Lee Harland	Castleford	1996-2004	148(35)	20	0	0	80
Neil Harmon	Halifax	2003	13(3)	0	0	0	0
	Salford	2001	6(5)	0	0	0	0
	Bradford	1998-2000	15(13)	2	0	0	8
	Huddersfield	1998	12	1	0	0	4
	Leeds	1996	10	1	0	0	4
Ben Harris	Bradford	2005-07	70(4)	24	0	0	96
Iestyn Harris	Bradford	2004-08	109(11)	35	87	2	316
	Leeds	1997-2001	111(7)	57	490	6	1214
	Warrington	1996	16	4	63	2	144
Liam Harris	Hull	2018	9(2)	3	0	0	12
Ben Harrison	Wakefield	2016	3	0	0	0	0
	Warrington	2007-15	125(59)	14	0	0	56
James Harrison	Warrington	2022-23	25(5)	5	0	0	20
	Leeds	2020	2(2)	0	0	0	0
Karl Harrison	Hull	1999	26	2	0	0	8
	Halifax	1996-98	60(2)	2	0	0	8
Owen Harrison	Hull KR	2019-20	3(6)	0	0	0	0
Andrew Hart	London	2004	12(1)	2	0	0	8
Tim Hartley	Harlequins	2006	2	1	0	0	4
	Salford	2004-05	6(7)	5	0	0	20
Carlos Hassan	Bradford	1996	6(4)	2	0	0	8
Phil Hassan	Wakefield	2002	9(1)	0	0	0	0
	Halifax	2000-01	25(4)	3	0	0	12
	Salford	1998	15	2	0	0	8
	Leeds	1996-97	38(4)	12	0	0	48
James Hasson	Wakefield	2017	(4)	0	0	0	0
	Salford	2017	4(1)	0	0	0	0
Jackson Hastings	Wigan	2020-21	42	13	1	3	57
	Salford	2018-19	34	11	4	0	52
Tom Haughey	Castleford	2006	1(3)	1	0	0	4
	London	2003-04	10(8)	1	0	0	4
	Salford	2001-02	5(11)	0	0	0	0
Simon Haughton	Wigan	1996-2002	63(46)	32	0	0	128
Solomon Haumono	Harlequins	2006	10(9)	6	0	0	24
	London	2005	24(5)	8	0	0	32
Weller Hauraki	Hull KR	2019-20	34(4)	5	0	0	20
	Widnes	2018	7	0	0	0	0
	Salford	2015-18	45(12)	8	0	0	32
	Castleford	2013-14	50(2)	9	0	0	36
	Leeds	2011-12	18(17)	6	0	0	24
	Crusaders	2010	26(1)	11	0	0	44

Super League Players 1996-2023

PLAYER	CLUB	YEAR	APP	TRIES	GOALS	FG	PTS
Ethan Havard	Wigan	2019-23	23(44)	7	0	0	28
Richie Hawkyard	Bradford	2007	1(2)	1	0	0	4
Andy Hay	Widnes	2003-04	50(2)	7	0	0	28
	Leeds	1997-2002	112(27)	43	0	0	172
	Sheffield	1996-97	17(3)	5	0	0	20
Adam Hayes	Hudds-Sheff	2000	2(1)	0	0	0	0
Joey Hayes	Salford	1999	9	2	0	0	8
	St Helens	1996-98	11(6)	7	0	0	28
Leon Hayes	Warrington	2022-23	2(1)	0	6	0	12
James Haynes	Hull KR	2009	1	0	0	0	0
Callum Hazzard	St Helens	2019	(1)	0	0	0	0
Mathew Head	Hull	2007	9(1)	1	0	1	5
Mitch Healey	Castleford	2001-03	68(1)	10	16	0	72
Daniel Heckenberg	Harlequins	2006-09	31(39)	4	0	0	16
Andrew Heffernan	Hull KR	2018	7	2	0	0	8
Chris Heil	Hull KR	2012-13	4	2	0	0	8
Ben Hellewell	Salford	2022-23	6(13)	4	0	0	16
	Leigh	2021	22	4	0	0	16
	London	2019	2	0	0	0	0
Ricky Helliwell	Salford	1997-99	(2)	0	0	0	0
Tom Hemingway	Huddersfield	2005-09	7(7)	1	17	0	38
Bryan Henare	St Helens	2000-01	4(12)	1	0	0	4
Richard Henare	Warrington	1996-97	28(2)	24	0	0	96
Andrew Henderson	Castleford	2006, 2008	44(11)	4	0	0	16
Ian Henderson	Catalans	2011-15	118(9)	12	0	0	48
	Bradford	2005-07	33(37)	13	0	0	52
Kevin Henderson	Wakefield	2005-11	52(68)	9	0	0	36
	Leigh	2005	(1)	0	0	0	0
Adam Henry	Bradford	2014	23(1)	5	0	0	20
Mark Henry	Salford	2009-11	67	22	0	0	88
Brad Hepi	Castleford	1999, 2001	9(21)	3	0	0	12
	Salford	2000	3(5)	0	0	0	0
	Hull	1998	15(1)	3	0	0	12
Tyla Hepi	Castleford	2020-22	5(17)	0	0	0	0
	Hull KR	2013	(4)	0	0	0	0
Jon Hepworth	Castleford	2003-04	19(23)	7	8	0	44
	Leeds	2003	(1)	0	0	0	0
	London	2002	(2)	0	0	0	0
Marc Herbert	Bradford	2011	20	4	2	0	20
Aaron Heremaia	Widnes	2015-18	44(41)	7	0	0	28
	Hull	2012-14	27(37)	12	0	0	48
Maxime Herold	London	2014	(2)	0	0	0	0
Ian Herron	Hull	2000	9	1	17	0	38
	Gateshead	1999	25	4	105	0	226
Jason Hetherington	London	2001-02	37	9	0	0	36
Gareth Hewitt	Salford	1999	2(1)	0	0	0	0
Sam Hewitt	Huddersfield	2018-23	21(38)	5	0	0	20
	Wakefield	2023	6(1)	0	0	0	0
Andrew Hick	Hull	2000	9(9)	1	0	0	4
	Gateshead	1999	12(5)	2	0	0	8
Jarrad Hickey	Wakefield	2011	(8)	2	0	0	8
Chris Hicks	Warrington	2008-10	72	56	119	0	462
Paul Hicks	Wakefield	1999	(1)	0	0	0	0
Darren Higgins	London	1998	5(6)	2	0	0	8
Iain Higgins	London	1997-98	1(7)	2	0	0	8
Liam Higgins	Wakefield	2011	4(12)	0	0	0	0
	Castleford	2008-10	42(32)	2	0	0	8
	Hull	2003-06	1(34)	0	0	0	0
Jack Higginson	Wigan	2016	2(1)	1	0	0	4
Micky Higham	Leigh	2017	11(1)	2	0	0	8
	Warrington	2009-15	73(78)	34	0	0	136
	Wigan	2006-08	61(28)	13	0	0	52
	St Helens	2001-05	43(56)	32	0	0	128
Chris Highton	Warrington	1997	1(1)	0	0	0	0
David Highton	London	2004-05	21(24)	2	0	0	8
	Salford	2002	4(5)	2	0	0	8
	Warrington	1998-2001	18(14)	2	0	0	8
Paul Highton	Salford	1998-2002, 2004-07	114(80)	14	0	0	56
	Halifax	1996-97	12(18)	2	0	0	8
Adam Higson	Leigh	2017	13	2	0	0	8
Peta Hiku	Warrington	2017	4	1	0	0	4
Andy Hill	Huddersfield	1999	(4)	0	0	0	0
	Castleford	1999	4(4)	0	0	0	0
Chris Hill	Huddersfield	2022-23	39	1	0	0	4
	Warrington	2012-21	245(10)	28	0	0	112
	Leigh	2005	(1)	0	0	0	0
Daniel Hill	St Helens	2022	2	0	0	0	0
Danny Hill	Wigan	2006-07	1(10)	0	0	0	0
	Hull KR	2007	2	0	0	0	0
	Hull	2004-06	4(6)	0	0	0	0
Harvie Hill	Wigan	2022-23	(14)	0	0	0	0
Howard Hill	Oldham	1996-97	22(12)	4	0	0	16
John Hill	St Helens	2003	(1)	0	0	0	0
	Halifax	2003	1(2)	0	0	0	0
	Warrington	2001-02	(4)	0	0	0	0
Scott Hill	Harlequins	2007-08	41(2)	13	0	0	52
Mark Hilton	Warrington	1996-2000, 2002-06	141(40)	7	0	0	28
Ryan Hinchcliffe	Huddersfield	2016-18	70(11)	11	0	0	44
Daniel Hindmarsh	London	2019	(6)	0	0	0	0
Ian Hindmarsh	Catalans	2006	25	3	0	0	12
Ata Hingano	Salford	2021	3(2)	1	0	0	4
Keegan Hirst	Wakefield	2017-19	17(44)	1	0	0	4
Jy Hitchcox	Castleford	2016-18	25(1)	21	0	0	84
Brendan Hlad	Castleford	2008	(3)	0	0	0	0
Andy Hobson	Widnes	2004	5(13)	0	0	0	0
	Halifax	1998-2003	51(85)	8	0	0	32
Gareth Hock	Leigh	2017	12(1)	3	0	0	12
	Salford	2014-15	15(1)	4	0	0	16
	Widnes	2013	15(2)	9	1	0	38
	Wigan	2003-09, 2011-12	126(43)	38	0	0	152
Tommy Hodgkinson	St Helens	2006	(1)	0	0	0	0
Andy Hodgson	Wakefield	1999	14(2)	2	1	0	10
	Bradford	1997-98	8(2)	4	0	0	16
Bailey Hodgson	Castleford	2020	1	0	0	0	0
Brett Hodgson	Warrington	2011-13	66	33	268	1	669
	Huddersfield	2009-10	45	13	166	0	384
David Hodgson	Hull KR	2012-14	51	31	0	0	124
	Huddersfield	2008-11	84	59	0	0	236
	Salford	2005-07	81	30	47	0	214
	Wigan	2000-04	90(19)	43	0	0	172
	Halifax	1999	10(3)	5	0	0	20
Elliot Hodgson	Huddersfield	2009	1	0	0	0	0
Josh Hodgson	Hull KR	2010-14	98(29)	35	0	0	140
	Hull	2009	(2)	0	0	0	0
Ryan Hoffman	Wigan	2011	28(1)	11	0	0	44
Darren Hogg	London	1996	(1)	0	0	0	0
Michael Hogue	Paris	1997	5(7)	0	0	0	0
Lance Hohaia	St Helens	2012-15	67(9)	21	0	1	85
Chris Holden	Warrington	1996-97	2(1)	0	0	0	0
Daniel Holdsworth	Hull	2013	19	2	28	2	66
	Salford	2010-12	71	18	183	1	439
Stephen Holgate	Halifax	2000	1(10)	0	0	0	0
	Hull	1999	1	0	0	0	0
	Wigan	1997-98	11(26)	2	0	0	8
	Workington	1996	19	3	0	0	12
Stephen Holker	Hull KR	2015-16	(4)	0	0	0	0
Martyn Holland	Wakefield	2000-03	52(3)	6	0	0	24
Oliver Holmes	Leigh	2023	14(5)	2	0	0	8
	Warrington	2022	21(2)	3	0	0	12
	Castleford	2010-21	176(35)	42	0	0	168
Tim Holmes	Widnes	2004-05	15(4)	0	0	0	0
Tom Holmes	Huddersfield	2019-20	12(5)	0	0	0	0
	Castleford	2015-17	7(8)	3	0	0	12
Adam Holroyd	Warrington	2022-23	3(4)	0	0	0	0
Graham Holroyd	Huddersfield	2003	3(5)	0	0	0	0
	Salford	2000-02	40(11)	8	75	5	187
	Halifax	1999	24(2)	3	74	5	165
	Leeds	1996-98	40(26)	22	101	8	298
Tom Holroyd	Leeds	2018-21, 2023	21(29)	6	0	0	24
Dallas Hood	Wakefield	2003-04	18(9)	1	0	0	4
Liam Hood	Wakefield	2022-23	37(2)	8	0	0	32
	Leigh	2017, 2021	24(8)	7	0	0	28
	Salford	2015	2(15)	0	0	0	0
	Leeds	2012	1(4)	3	0	0	12
Jacob Hookem	Hull	2021-22	1(4)	0	0	0	0
Luke Hooley	Leeds	2023	8	4	0	0	16
Jason Hooper	St Helens	2003-07	89(6)	35	30	0	200
Will Hope	Salford	2013	1(2)	0	0	0	0
Lee Hopkins	Harlequins	2006-07	44(3)	11	0	0	44
	London	2005	29	6	0	0	24
Sam Hopkins	Leigh	2017	3(17)	6	0	0	24
Will Hopoate	St Helens	2022-23	27	5	0	0	20
Sean Hoppe	St Helens	1999-2002	69(16)	32	0	0	128
Graeme Horne	Hull KR	2012-16	81(18)	21	0	0	84
	Huddersfield	2010-11	23(17)	11	0	0	44
	Hull	2003-09	49(74)	24	0	0	96
Liam Horne	Castleford	2023	4(1)	0	0	0	0
Richard Horne	Hull	1999-2014	341(16)	115	12	6	490
Justin Horo	Wakefield	2018-19	22(14)	6	0	0	24
	Catalans	2016-17	34(1)	12	0	0	48
John Hough	Warrington	1996-97	9	2	0	0	8
Danny Houghton	Hull	2007-23	339(57)	49	0	0	196
Sylvain Houles	Wakefield	2003, 2005	8(1)	1	0	0	4
	London	2001-02	17(10)	11	0	0	44
	Hudds-Sheff	2000	5(2)	1	0	0	4

208

Super League Players 1996-2023

PLAYER	CLUB	YEAR	APP	TRIES	GOALS	FG	PTS
Chris Houston	Widnes	2016-18	58(1)	5	0	0	20
Harvey Howard	Wigan	2001-02	25(27)	1	0	0	4
	Bradford	1998	4(2)	1	0	0	4
	Leeds	1996	8	0	0	0	0
Kim Howard	London	1997	4(5)	0	0	0	0
Stuart Howarth	Wakefield	2011, 2015-16	30(5)	4	0	0	16
	Hull	2015	2(3)	0	0	0	0
	Salford	2012-14	25(12)	1	0	0	4
	St Helens	2013	14(1)	0	0	0	0
Stuart Howarth	Workington	1996	(2)	0	0	0	0
David Howell	London	2012-13	24	5	0	0	20
	Harlequins	2008-11	76	26	0	0	104
Phil Howlett	Bradford	1999	5(1)	2	0	0	8
Tex Hoy	Hull	2023	14(1)	2	2	0	12
Craig Huby	Wakefield	2017-19	25(26)	3	0	0	12
	Huddersfield	2015-16	37(2)	2	0	0	8
	Castleford	2003-04, 2006, 2008-14	130(57)	27	41	0	190
Ryan Hudson	Castleford	2002-04, 2009-12	138(12)	31	0	0	124
	Huddersfield	1998-99, 2007-08	51(22)	10	0	0	40
	Wakefield	2000-01	42(9)	11	0	1	45
Adam Hughes	Widnes	2002-05	89(2)	45	51	0	282
	Halifax	2001	8(8)	8	0	0	32
	Wakefield	1999-2000	43(3)	21	34	0	152
	Leeds	1996-97	4(5)	4	0	0	16
Ian Hughes	Sheffield	1996	9(8)	4	0	0	16
Jack Hughes	Leigh	2023	10(5)	2	0	0	8
	Warrington	2016-22	141(2)	19	0	0	76
	Huddersfield	2015	30(1)	5	0	0	20
	Wigan	2011-14	31(33)	9	0	0	36
Mark Hughes	Catalans	2006	23	9	0	0	36
Steffan Hughes	London	1999-2001	1(13)	1	0	0	4
David Hulme	Salford	1997-99	53(1)	5	0	0	20
	Leeds	1996	8(1)	2	0	0	8
Declan Hulme	Widnes	2013-15	5	2	0	0	8
Paul Hulme	Warrington	1996-97	23(1)	2	0	0	8
Gary Hulse	Widnes	2005	12(5)	2	0	0	8
	Warrington	2001-04	20(28)	8	0	1	33
Alan Hunte	Salford	2002	19(2)	9	0	0	36
	Warrington	1999-2001	83	49	0	0	196
	Hull	1998	21	7	0	0	28
	St Helens	1996-97	30(2)	28	0	0	112
Konrad Hurrell	St Helens	2022-23	42	16	0	0	64
	Leeds	2019-21	47(5)	23	0	0	92
Alex Hurst	London	2013	8(2)	2	0	0	8
Kieran Hyde	Wakefield	2010-11	11	4	4	0	24
Nick Hyde	Paris	1997	5(5)	1	0	0	4
Chaz I'Anson	Hull KR	2007-10	17(13)	3	0	0	12
Sebastine Ikahihifo	Huddersfield	2016-19, 2022-23	48(51)	2	0	0	8
	Salford	2020-21	11(16)	0	0	0	0
Matt Ikuvalu	Catalans	2023	13	5	0	0	20
Ryan Ince	Widnes	2016-18	19	11	0	0	44
Greg Inglis	Warrington	2021	2	2	0	0	8
Krisnan Inu	Salford	2019-21	43(3)	20	167	1	415
	Widnes	2018	14	6	21	0	66
	Catalans	2015-17	39	11	3	0	50
Mark Ioane	Leigh	2021	10(5)	2	0	0	8
	London	2019	1(14)	1	0	0	4
Edwin Ipape	Leigh	2023	20(5)	8	0	0	32
Andy Ireland	Hull	1998-99	22(15)	0	0	0	0
	Bradford	1996	1	0	0	0	0
Kevin Iro	St Helens	1999-2001	76	39	0	0	156
	Leeds	1996	16	9	0	0	36
Willie Isa	Wigan	2016-23	162(21)	14	0	0	56
	Widnes	2012-15	44(33)	3	0	0	12
	Castleford	2011	7(2)	6	0	0	24
Andrew Isherwood	Wigan	1998-99	(5)	0	0	0	0
Olu Iwenofu	London	2000-01	2(1)	0	0	0	0
Chico Jackson	Hull	1999	(4)	0	0	0	0
Lee Jackson	Hull	2001-02	37(9)	12	1	0	50
	Leeds	1999-2000	28(24)	7	0	0	28
Michael Jackson	Sheffield	1998-99	17(17)	2	0	0	8
	Halifax	1996-97	27(6)	11	0	0	44
Paul Jackson	Castleford	2003-04, 2010-12	44(30)	5	0	0	20
	Huddersfield	1998, 2005-09	50(73)	4	0	0	16
	Wakefield	1999-2002	57(42)	2	0	0	8
Rob Jackson	Leigh	2005	20(3)	5	0	0	20
	London	2002-04	26(14)	9	0	0	36
Wayne Jackson	Halifax	1996-97	17(5)	2	0	0	8
Aled James	Crusaders	2011	1	0	0	0	0
	Celtic	2009	3(3)	0	0	0	0
	Widnes	2003	3	0	0	0	0
Andy James	Halifax	1996	(4)	0	0	0	0
Jordan James	Wigan	2006, 2014	3(18)	4	0	0	16
	Salford	2012-13	1(40)	6	0	0	24
	Crusaders	2010-11	5(24)	3	0	0	12
	Celtic	2009	17(4)	1	0	0	4
Matt James	Wakefield	2012	(4)	0	0	0	0
	Harlequins	2010	(2)	0	0	0	0
	Bradford	2006-09	1(23)	0	0	0	0
Pascal Jampy	Catalans	2006	4(7)	0	0	0	0
	Paris	1996-97	3(2)	0	0	0	0
Adam Janowski	Harlequins	2008	(1)	0	0	0	0
Zach Jebson	Hull	2023	(1)	0	0	0	0
Ben Jeffries	Bradford	2008-09, 2011-12	76(3)	20	0	0	80
	Wakefield	2003-07, 2010-11	151(10)	70	20	6	326
Mick Jenkins	Hull	2000	24	2	0	0	8
	Gateshead	1999	16	3	0	0	12
Ed Jennings	London	1998-99	1(2)	0	0	0	0
Rod Jensen	Huddersfield	2007-08	26(3)	13	0	0	52
Anthony Jerram	Warrington	2007	(2)	0	0	0	0
Lee Jewitt	Hull KR	2018-19	10(2)	0	0	0	0
	Castleford	2014-16	22(12)	0	0	0	0
	Salford	2007, 2009-13	32(62)	4	0	0	16
	Wigan	2005	(2)	0	0	0	0
Maxime Jobe	Catalans	2022	1	0	0	0	0
Isaac John	Wakefield	2012	13	1	19	0	42
Andrew Johns	Warrington	2005	3	1	12	1	29
Matthew Johns	Wigan	2001	24	3	0	1	13
Andy Johnson	Salford	2004-05	8(26)	7	0	0	28
	Castleford	2002-03	32(16)	11	0	0	44
	London	2000-01	24(21)	12	0	0	48
	Huddersfield	1999	5	1	0	0	4
	Wigan	1996-99	24(20)	19	0	0	76
Bruce Johnson	Widnes	2004-05	(4)	0	0	0	0
Corey Johnson	Leeds	2019, 2021-23	6(18)	1	0	0	4
Dallas Johnson	Catalans	2010	26	1	0	0	4
Greg Johnson	Salford	2014-19	86	36	1	0	146
	Wakefield	2011	11	2	0	0	8
Jack Johnson	Warrington	2015-17, 2019	17	5	0	0	20
	Widnes	2017	3	1	0	0	4
Jason Johnson	St Helens	1997-99	2	0	0	0	0
Josh Johnson	Salford	2019-22	11(16)	1	0	0	4
	Hull KR	2018	2(2)	0	0	0	0
	Huddersfield	2013-16	14(17)	0	0	0	0
Luis Johnson	Castleford	2023	(3)	0	0	0	0
	Hull KR	2019, 2021-23	27(5)	2	0	0	8
	Warrington	2018-20	1(8)	0	0	0	0
Mark Johnson	Salford	1999-2000	22(9)	16	0	0	64
	Hull	1998	10(1)	4	0	0	16
	Workington	1996	12	4	0	0	16
Nick Johnson	Hull KR	2012	1	0	0	0	0
Nick Johnson	London	2003	(1)	0	0	0	0
Paul Johnson	Crusaders	2011	6(4)	0	0	0	0
	Wakefield	2010	12(3)	4	0	0	16
	Warrington	2007-09	37(9)	17	0	0	68
	Bradford	2004-06	46(8)	19	0	0	76
	Wigan	1996-2003	74(46)	54	0	0	216
Paul Johnson	Wakefield	2014	5(11)	0	0	0	0
	Hull	2013	3(16)	0	0	0	0
	Wakefield	2011-12	25(21)	6	0	0	24
	St Helens	2010	(2)	0	0	0	0
Richard Johnson	Bradford	2008	(2)	0	0	0	0
Ben Johnston	Castleford	2012	2	0	0	0	0
Jordan Johnstone	Leigh	2023	5(3)	0	0	0	0
	Hull	2020-22	23(27)	1	0	0	4
	Widnes	2016-18	17(13)	1	0	0	4
Tom Johnstone	Catalans	2023	28	27	0	0	108
	Wakefield	2015-22	106	81	0	0	324
Ben Jones	Harlequins	2010	(2)	0	0	0	0
Chris Jones	Leigh	2005	1(1)	0	0	0	0
Connor Jones	Salford	2020	7	1	0	0	4
Danny Jones	Halifax	2003	1	0	0	0	0
David Jones	Oldham	1997	14(1)	5	0	0	20
Josh Jones	Huddersfield	2021-23	45(1)	8	0	0	32
	Hull	2020	7	0	0	0	0
	Salford	2016-19	92(4)	17	0	0	68
	St Helens	2012-16	88(9)	22	0	0	88
Mark Jones	Warrington	1996	8(11)	2	0	0	8
Phil Jones	Leigh	2005	16	8	31	0	94
	Wigan	1999-2001	14(7)	6	25	0	74
Stacey Jones	Catalans	2006-07	39	11	43	3	133

Super League Players 1996-2023

PLAYER	CLUB	YEAR	APP	TRIES	GOALS	FG	PTS
Stephen Jones	Huddersfield	2005	(1)	0	0	0	0
Stuart Jones	Castleford	2009-12	69(27)	14	0	0	56
	Huddersfield	2004-08	96(22)	17	0	0	68
	St Helens	2003	(18)	2	0	0	8
	Wigan	2002	5(3)	1	0	0	4
Ben Jones-Bishop	Wakefield	2016-20	110	61	0	0	244
	Salford	2015	17	12	0	0	48
	Leeds	2008-09, 2011-14	70(2)	46	0	0	184
	Harlequins	2010	17	10	0	0	40
Jamie Jones-Buchanan	Leeds	1999-2019	293(73)	70	1	0	282
Tim Jonkers	Wigan	2006	3(1)	0	0	0	0
	Salford	2004-06	5(11)	0	0	0	0
	St Helens	1999-2004	41(64)	12	0	0	48
Caelum Jordan	Castleford	2021	1	0	0	0	0
Darren Jordan	Wakefield	2003	(1)	0	0	0	0
Josh Jordan-Roberts	Leeds	2017	(1)	0	0	0	0
Phil Joseph	Salford	2016	(12)	0	0	0	0
	Widnes	2013-15	11(38)	1	0	0	4
	Bradford	2012	(6)	0	0	0	0
	Huddersfield	2004	7(6)	0	0	0	0
Max Jowitt	Wakefield	2014-23	104(2)	32	33	0	194
Warren Jowitt	Hull	2003	(2)	0	0	0	0
	Salford	2001-02	17(4)	2	0	0	8
	Wakefield	2000	19(3)	8	0	0	32
	Bradford	1996-99	13(25)	5	0	0	20
Chris Joynt	St Helens	1996-2004	201(14)	68	0	0	272
Benjamin Jullien	Catalans	2018-22	66(12)	16	0	0	64
	Warrington	2016-17	19(7)	4	0	0	16
Mathieu Jussaume	Toulouse	2022	12	2	0	0	8
Gregory Kacala	Paris	1996	7	1	0	0	4
Andy Kain	Castleford	2004, 2006	9(7)	3	10	0	32
Sam Kasiano	Warrington	2023	6(18)	3	0	0	12
	Catalans	2019-22	3(73)	12	0	0	48
Antonio Kaufusi	Huddersfield	2014	15(2)	1	0	0	4
	Bradford	2014	4	0	0	0	0
	London	2012-13	44(5)	5	0	0	20
Mal Kaufusi	London	2004	1(3)	0	0	0	0
Ben Kavanagh	Hull KR	2018	13(8)	0	0	0	0
	Wakefield	2015	6(3)	0	0	0	0
	Widnes	2012-15	18(33)	0	0	0	0
Liam Kay	Wakefield	2012-13, 2020-23	45(21)	18	0	0	72
	Toronto	2020	6	1	0	0	4
Ben Kaye	Harlequins	2009-10	2(13)	0	0	0	0
	Leeds	2008	2(2)	1	0	0	4
Elliot Kear	Salford	2020-21	12(1)	1	0	0	4
	London	2019	26	3	0	0	12
	Bradford	2012-14	53(2)	17	0	0	68
	Crusaders	2010-11	16(1)	4	0	0	16
	Celtic	2009	3	0	0	0	0
Brett Kearney	Bradford	2010-14	107	55	0	0	220
Stephen Kearney	Hull	2005	22(2)	5	0	0	20
Damon Keating	Wakefield	2002	7(17)	1	0	0	4
Kris Keating	Hull KR	2014	23	5	0	0	20
Shaun Keating	London	1996	1(3)	0	0	0	0
Mark Keenan	Workington	1996	3(4)	1	0	0	4
Adam Keighran	Catalans	2023	25	13	73	0	198
Jimmy Keinhorst	Hull KR	2019-23	42(21)	13	0	0	52
	Castleford	2021	(2)	1	0	0	4
	Leeds	2012-18	46(23)	25	0	0	100
	Widnes	2018	3	1	0	0	4
	Wakefield	2014	7	1	0	0	4
Albert Kelly	Hull	2017-20	63(2)	39	0	1	157
	Hull KR	2015-16	37	21	3	0	90
Tony Kemp	Wakefield	1999-2000	15(5)	2	0	1	9
	Leeds	1996-98	23(2)	5	0	2	22
Damien Kennedy	London	2003	5(11)	1	0	0	4
Rhys Kennedy	Hull KR	2023	16(6)	1	0	0	4
Ian Kenny	St Helens	2004	(1)	0	0	0	0
Sean Kenny	Salford	2016	(4)	0	0	0	0
Shaun Kenny-Dowall	Hull KR	2020-23	83	19	0	0	76
Jason Kent	Leigh	2005	23	1	0	0	4
Liam Kent	Hull	2012-13	1(5)	0	0	0	0
Shane Kenward	Wakefield	1999	28	6	0	0	24
	Salford	1998	1	0	0	0	0
Jason Keough	Paris	1997	2	1	0	0	4
Keiran Kerr	Widnes	2005	6	2	0	0	8
Lee Kershaw	Wakefield	2019-23	48	17	0	0	68
Martin Ketteridge	Halifax	1996	7(5)	0	0	0	0
Ronnie Kettlewell	Warrington	1996	(1)	0	0	0	0
Joe Keyes	Hull KR	2020-21	5(1)	1	6	0	16
	London	2014	7	5	0	0	20
Younes Khattabi	Catalans	2006-08	24(4)	10	0	0	40
Samy Kibula	Warrington	2020	(2)	0	0	0	0
	Wigan	2018	(1)	0	0	0	0
David Kidwell	Warrington	2001-02	14(12)	9	0	0	36
Ben Kilner	Wigan	2020	(1)	0	0	0	0
Andrew King	London	2003	23(1)	15	0	0	60
Dave King	Huddersfield	1998-99	11(17)	2	0	0	8
George King	Hull KR	2020-23	68(8)	3	0	0	12
	Wakefield	2019-20	8(19)	0	0	0	0
	Warrington	2014-18	12(68)	1	0	0	4
James King	Leigh	2005	5(7)	0	0	0	0
Kevin King	Wakefield	2005	8(1)	2	0	0	8
	Castleford	2004	(1)	0	0	0	0
Matt King	Warrington	2008-11	91	58	0	0	232
Paul King	Wakefield	2010-11	10(19)	0	0	1	1
	Hull	1999-2009	136(93)	20	0	1	81
Toby King	Wigan	2023	28	11	0	0	44
	Huddersfield	2022	12	2	0	0	8
	Warrington	2014-22	117(7)	44	0	0	176
Jon Luke Kirby	Huddersfield	2019	(3)	0	0	0	0
Andy Kirk	Wakefield	2005	6(3)	1	0	0	4
	Salford	2004	20	5	0	0	20
	Leeds	2001-02	4(4)	0	0	0	0
Ian Kirke	Wakefield	2015	2(2)	1	0	0	4
	Leeds	2006-14	52(132)	10	0	0	40
John Kirkpatrick	London	2004-05	18(1)	5	0	0	20
	St Helens	2001-03	10(11)	0	0	0	40
	Halifax	2003	4	1	0	0	4
Danny Kirmond	Wakefield	2010, 2012-20	147(15)	42	0	0	168
	Huddersfield	2008-11	18(31)	9	0	0	36
Wayne Kitchin	Workington	1996	11(6)	3	17	1	47
Sione Kite	Widnes	2012	6(8)	1	0	0	4
Ian Knott	Leigh	2005	8(1)	2	0	0	8
	Wakefield	2002-03	34(5)	7	79	0	186
	Warrington	1996-2001	68(41)	24	18	0	132
Matt Knowles	Wigan	1996	(3)	0	0	0	0
Michael Knowles	Castleford	2006	(1)	0	0	0	0
Morgan Knowles	St Helens	2016-23	132(48)	26	0	0	104
Phil Knowles	Salford	1997	1	0	0	0	0
Simon Knox	Halifax	1999	(6)	0	0	0	0
	Salford	1998	1(1)	0	0	0	0
	Bradford	1996-98	9(19)	7	0	0	28
Toa Kohe-Love	Warrington	1996-2001, 2005-06	166(3)	90	0	0	360
	Bradford	2004	1(1)	0	0	0	0
	Hull	2002-03	42	19	0	0	76
Paul Koloi	Wigan	1997	1(2)	1	0	0	4
Craig Kopczak	Wakefield	2019-20	25(15)	3	0	0	12
	Salford	2016-18	39(27)	11	0	0	44
	Huddersfield	2013-15	48(37)	6	0	0	24
	Bradford	2006-12	32(83)	10	0	0	40
Michael Korkidas	Wakefield	2003-06, 2009-11	133(36)	15	0	0	60
	Huddersfield	2009	4(1)	1	0	0	4
	Castleford	2008	15(6)	1	0	0	4
	Salford	2007	26(1)	1	0	0	4
Nick Kouparitsas	Harlequins	2011	2(13)	1	0	0	4
Olsi Krasniqi	London	2012-14, 2019	36(35)	3	0	0	12
	Salford	2015-17	8(29)	1	0	0	4
	Harlequins	2010-11	3(20)	1	0	0	4
David Krause	London	1996-97	22(1)	7	0	0	28
Ben Kusto	Huddersfield	2001	21(4)	9	0	1	37
Tim Lafai	Salford	2022-23	43	11	0	0	44
Anthony Laffranchi	St Helens	2012-14	50(18)	19	0	0	76
Ben Laguerre	Toulouse	2022	1	0	0	0	0
Matthieu Laguerre	Catalans	2021-23	27(1)	16	0	0	64
Matty Laidlaw	Hull	2022	(8)	0	0	0	0
James Laithwaite	Warrington	2013-15	23(22)	1	0	0	4
	Hull KR	2012	1(2)	1	0	0	4
Adrian Lam	Wigan	2001-04	105(2)	40	1	9	171
Lachlan Lam	Leigh	2023	28	9	0	0	36
Brock Lamb	London	2019	6	3	0	1	13
Callum Lancaster	Hull	2014-16	7	9	0	0	36
Ben Lane	St Helens	2022	2	0	1	0	2
Jordan Lane	Hull	2018-23	81(31)	14	0	0	56
Mark Lane	Paris	1996	(2)	0	0	0	0
Allan Langer	Warrington	2000-01	47	13	4	0	60
Kevin Langer	London	1996	12(4)	2	0	0	8
Junior Langi	Salford	2005-06	27(7)	7	0	0	28
Samisoni Langi	Wakefield	2023	8	2	0	0	8
	Catalans	2018-22	98(1)	27	0	0	108
	Leigh	2017	3	1	0	0	4
Chris Langley	Huddersfield	2000-01	18(1)	3	0	0	12
Gareth Langley	St Helens	2006	1	1	3	0	10

Super League Players 1996-2023

PLAYER	CLUB	YEAR	APP	TRIES	GOALS	FG	PTS
Jamie Langley	Hull KR	2014	6(5)	1	0	0	4
	Bradford	2002-13	182(57)	36	0	0	144
Ryan Lannon	Salford	2015-22	52(39)	6	0	0	24
	Hull KR	2019	1(5)	1	0	0	4
Kevin Larroyer	Castleford	2017	2(4)	0	0	0	0
	Hull KR	2014-16	34(13)	9	0	0	36
	Catalans	2012-13	9(10)	6	0	0	24
Andy Last	Hull	1999-2005	16(10)	4	0	0	16
Leilani Latu	Warrington	2020	3	1	0	0	4
Sam Latus	Hull KR	2010-13	34(3)	13	0	0	52
Epalahame Lauaki	Wigan	2012-13	14(16)	2	0	0	8
	Hull	2009-11	3(50)	4	0	0	16
Dale Laughton	Warrington	2002	15(1)	0	0	0	0
	Huddersfield	2000-01	36(2)	4	0	0	16
	Sheffield	1996-99	48(22)	5	0	0	20
Ali Lauitiiti	Wakefield	2012-15	46(31)	16	0	0	64
	Leeds	2004-11	64(117)	58	0	0	232
Phoenix Laulu-Togaga'e	Hull KR	2022-23	4(4)	0	0	0	0
Quentin Laulu-Togaga'e	Castleford	2018	8(1)	6	0	0	24
Jason Laurence	Salford	1997	1	0	0	0	0
Leo Laurent	Catalans	2022	1	0	0	0	0
Graham Law	Wakefield	1999-2002	34(30)	6	40	0	104
Joe Law	Wakefield	2023	(1)	0	0	0	0
Neil Law	Wakefield	1999-2002	83	39	0	0	156
	Sheffield	1998	1(1)	1	0	0	4
Dean Lawford	Widnes	2003-04	17(1)	5	2	4	28
	Halifax	2001	1(1)	0	0	0	0
	Leeds	1997-2000	15(8)	2	3	0	14
	Huddersfield	1999	6(1)	0	6	1	13
	Sheffield	1996	9(5)	2	1	1	11
George Lawler	Castleford	2022-23	33(8)	1	0	0	4
	Hull KR	2016, 2018-21	62(11)	5	0	0	20
Johnny Lawless	Halifax	2001-03	73(1)	10	0	0	40
	Hudds-Sheff	2000	19(6)	3	0	0	12
	Sheffield	1996-99	76(4)	11	0	0	44
Michael Lawrence	Huddersfield	2007-22	235(60)	47	0	0	188
Adam Lawton	Salford	2019	1(1)	0	0	0	0
	Widnes	2013-14	2(10)	5	0	0	20
Corentin Le Cam	Catalans	2021-22	5(6)	0	0	0	0
Charlie Leaeno	Wakefield	2010	7(3)	2	0	0	8
Mark Leafa	Castleford	2008	5(9)	1	0	0	4
	Leigh	2005	28	2	0	0	8
Leroy Leapai	London	1996	2	0	0	0	0
Jim Leatham	Hull	1998-99	20(18)	4	0	0	16
	Leeds	1997	(1)	0	0	0	0
Andy Leathem	Warrington	1999	2(8)	0	0	0	0
	St Helens	1996-98	20(1)	1	0	0	4
Danny Lee	Gateshead	1999	16(2)	0	0	0	0
Jason Lee	Halifax	2001	10(1)	2	0	0	8
Mark Lee	Salford	1997-2000	25(11)	1	0	4	8
Robert Lee	Hull	1999	4(3)	0	0	0	0
Tommy Lee	Hull KR	2018-19	24(6)	2	0	0	8
	St Helens	2017	9(9)	0	0	0	0
	Salford	2014-16	37(5)	4	0	0	16
	London	2013	16(4)	2	0	0	8
	Huddersfield	2012	11(7)	3	0	0	12
	Wakefield	2011	25	6	0	0	24
	Crusaders	2010	3(9)	0	0	0	0
	Hull	2005-09	44(27)	6	0	0	24
Kruise Leeming	Leeds	2020-23	51(9)	16	0	2	66
	Huddersfield	2013-19	49(67)	15	0	0	60
Matty Lees	St Helens	2017-23	85(41)	5	0	0	20
Matthew Leigh	Salford	2000	(6)	0	0	0	0
Chris Leikvoll	Warrington	2004-07	72(18)	4	0	0	16
Jim Lenihan	Huddersfield	1999	19(1)	10	0	0	40
Mark Lennon	Celtic	2009	10(3)	1	8	0	20
	Hull KR	2007	11(4)	5	7	0	34
	Castleford	2001-03	30(21)	10	21	0	82
Tevita Leo-Latu	Wakefield	2006-10	28(49)	10	0	0	40
Gary Lester	Hull	1998-99	46	17	0	0	68
Stuart Lester	Wigan	1997	1(3)	0	0	0	0
Heath L'Estrange	Bradford	2010-13	56(35)	7	0	0	28
Afi Leuila	Oldham	1996-97	17(3)	2	0	0	8
Kylie Leuluai	Leeds	2007-15	182(45)	20	0	0	80
Macgraff Leuluai	Widnes	2012-18	52(64)	5	0	0	20
Phil Leuluai	Salford	2007, 2009-10	7(47)	3	0	0	12
Thomas Leuluai	Wigan	2007-12, 2017-22	290(3)	64	0	1	257
	Harlequins	2006	15(2)	6	0	0	24
	London	2005	20	13	0	0	52
Ricky Leutele	Leigh	2023	19	3	0	0	12
	Huddersfield	2021-22	32	17	0	0	68
	Toronto	2020	6	0	0	0	0
Danny Levi	Huddersfield	2022	19(7)	4	0	0	16
Mikey Lewis	Hull KR	2019-23	60(2)	30	10	0	140
Simon Lewis	Castleford	2001	4	3	0	0	12
Paul Leyland	St Helens	2006	1	0	0	0	0
Jon Liddell	Leeds	2001	1	0	0	0	0
Jason Lidden	Castleford	1997	15(1)	7	0	0	28
Jordan Lilley	Leeds	2015-18	21(11)	2	42	0	92
Danny Lima	Wakefield	2007	(3)	0	0	0	0
	Salford	2006	7(2)	0	0	0	0
	Warrington	2004-06	15(47)	9	0	0	36
Jeff Lima	Catalans	2014-15	37(7)	3	1	0	14
	Wigan	2011-12	24(29)	4	0	0	16
Tom Lineham	Wakefield	2022-23	19	3	0	0	12
	Warrington	2016-21	115	70	0	0	280
	Hull	2012-15	61(1)	50	0	0	200
Kane Linnett	Hull KR	2019-23	96(1)	35	0	0	140
Mason Lino	Wakefield	2021-23	67	7	132	2	294
Sam Lisone	Leeds	2023	5(18)	4	0	0	16
Davy Litten	Hull	2022-23	17(2)	3	0	0	12
Jez Litten	Hull KR	2019-23	35(49)	7	0	0	28
	Hull	2017-19	(17)	1	0	0	4
Harry Little	London	2013	2	0	0	0	0
Jack Littlejohn	Salford	2018	15(3)	3	1	0	14
Craig Littler	St Helens	2006	1	1	0	0	4
Stuart Littler	Salford	1998-2002, 2004-07, 2009-10	217(30)	65	0	0	260
Harvey Livett	Huddersfield	2023	8	1	0	0	4
	Salford	2021-22	26(1)	8	13	0	58
	Hull KR	2019-20	8(5)	3	0	0	12
	Warrington	2017-19	23(14)	13	21	0	94
Peter Livett	Workington	1996	3(1)	0	0	0	0
Leo Llong	Catalans	2022	(1)	0	0	0	0
Rhodri Lloyd	Wigan	2012-13, 2015	3(4)	0	0	0	0
	Widnes	2014	(4)	0	0	0	0
	London	2013	2	0	0	0	0
Garry Lo	Castleford	2018	1	1	0	0	4
Kevin Locke	Wakefield	2015	3	0	0	0	0
	Salford	2014-15	13	6	11	0	46
Jack Logan	Leigh	2021	5	0	0	0	0
	Hull	2014-16, 2018-19, 2021	37(2)	16	0	0	64
Scott Logan	Wigan	2006	10(1)	0	0	0	0
	Hull	2001-03	27(20)	5	0	0	20
Jamahl Lolesi	Huddersfield	2007-10	75(9)	27	0	0	108
Filimone Lolohea	Harlequins	2006	3(6)	1	0	0	4
	London	2005	8(15)	0	0	0	0
Tui Lolohea	Huddersfield	2022-23	47(3)	11	13	0	70
	Salford	2019-21	50	17	29	1	127
	Leeds	2019	15	2	19	0	46
David Lomax	Huddersfield	2000-01	45(9)	4	0	0	16
	Paris	1997	19(2)	1	0	0	4
Jonny Lomax	St Helens	2009-23	293(2)	123	92	3	679
Dave Long	London	1999	(1)	0	0	0	0
Karl Long	London	2003	(1)	0	0	0	0
	Widnes	2002	4	1	0	0	4
Sean Long	Hull	2010-11	22	6	0	0	24
	St Helens	1997-2009	263(8)	126	826	20	2176
	Wigan	1996-97	1(5)	0	0	0	0
Davide Longo	Bradford	1996	1(3)	0	0	0	0
Ellis Longstaff	Salford	2023	2(3)	2	0	0	8
	Hull	2022	9(1)	6	0	0	24
	Warrington	2020-22	5(9)	0	0	0	0
Gary Lord	Oldham	1996-97	28(12)	3	0	0	12
Paul Loughlin	Huddersfield	1998-99	34(2)	4	4	0	24
	Bradford	1996-97	34(2)	15	8	0	76
Rhys Lovegrove	Hull KR	2007-14	75(74)	19	0	0	76
Karl Lovell	Hudds-Sheff	2000	14	5	0	0	20
	Sheffield	1999	22(4)	8	0	0	32
Will Lovell	London	2012-14, 2019	26(23)	5	0	0	20
Joe Lovodua	Hull	2022-23	26(16)	6	0	0	24
James Lowes	Bradford	1996-2003	205	84	2	2	342
Laurent Lucchese	Paris	1996	13(5)	2	0	0	8
Sam Luckley	Hull KR	2023	4(23)	1	0	0	4
	Salford	2021-22	2(25)	1	0	0	4
Robert Lui	Leeds	2019-21	34	11	0	1	45
	Salford	2016-19	84(3)	26	33	0	170
Zebastian Luisi	Harlequins	2006-07	23(2)	4	0	0	16
	London	2004-05	21(1)	7	0	0	28
Keith Lulia	Bradford	2012-13	50	19	0	0	76
Shaun Lunt	Leeds	2012, 2019	15(10)	7	0	0	28
	Hull KR	2015-16, 2018-19	25(18)	11	0	0	44
	Huddersfield	2009-15	73(39)	60	0	0	240

211

Super League Players 1996-2023

PLAYER	CLUB	YEAR	APP	TRIES	GOALS	FG	PTS
Peter Lupton	Crusaders	2010-11	37(9)	10	0	0	40
	Celtic	2009	16(4)	4	0	0	16
	Castleford	2006, 2008	40	11	0	0	44
	Hull	2003-06	19(26)	10	3	0	46
	London	2000-02	10(15)	2	2	0	12
Darcy Lussick	Salford	2021	(4)	1	0	0	4
Joey Lussick	St Helens	2022-23	9(36)	7	6	0	40
	Salford	2019-20	27(21)	15	4	0	68
Andy Lynch	Castleford	1999-2004, 2014-17	157(54)	17	0	0	68
	Hull	2012-13	39(14)	3	0	0	12
	Bradford	2005-11	159(29)	46	0	0	184
Josh Lynch	Warrington	2022	1	1	0	0	4
Reece Lyne	Wakefield	2013-23	213(1)	60	0	0	240
	Hull	2010-11	11(1)	2	0	0	8
Jamie Lyon	St Helens	2005-06	54(1)	39	172	0	500
Iliess Macani	London	2013-14	12(3)	4	0	0	16
Nene Macdonald	Leeds	2023	19	2	0	0	8
Duncan MacGillivray	Wakefield	2004-08	75(18)	6	0	0	24
Brad Mackay	Bradford	2000	24(2)	8	0	0	32
Graham Mackay	Hull	2002	27	18	24	0	120
	Bradford	2001	16(3)	12	1	0	50
	Leeds	2000	12(8)	10	2	0	44
Keiron Maddocks	Leigh	2005	1(3)	0	0	0	0
Steve Maden	Leigh	2005	23	9	0	0	36
	Warrington	2002	3	0	0	0	0
Mateaki Mafi	Warrington	1996-97	7(8)	7	0	0	28
Nathan Magee	Castleford	2021	(1)	0	0	0	0
Shaun Magennis	St Helens	2010-12	7(19)	3	0	0	12
Brendan Magnus	London	2000	3	1	0	0	4
Patrick Mago	Wigan	2022-23	1(51)	3	0	0	12
Billy Magoulias	Warrington	2022	5(2)	0	0	0	0
Mark Maguire	London	1996-97	11(4)	7	13	0	54
Adam Maher	Hull	2000-03	88(4)	24	0	0	96
	Gateshead	1999	21(5)	3	0	0	12
Lee Maher	Leeds	1996	4(1)	0	0	0	0
Will Maher	Hull KR	2020-22	21(22)	0	0	0	0
	Castleford	2014-19	5(30)	1	0	0	4
Shaun Mahony	Paris	1997	5	0	0	0	0
Hutch Maiava	Hull	2007	(19)	1	0	0	4
David Maiden	Hull	2000-01	32(10)	11	0	0	44
	Gateshead	1999	5(16)	8	0	0	32
Craig Makin	Salford	1999-2001	24(20)	2	0	0	8
Tommy Makinson	St Helens	2011-23	279(5)	177	235	1	1179
Brady Malam	Wigan	2000	5(20)	1	0	0	4
Dominic Maloney	Hull	2009	(7)	0	0	0	0
Francis Maloney	Castleford	1998-99, 2003-04	71(7)	24	33	3	165
	Salford	2001-02	45(1)	26	5	0	114
	Wakefield	2000	11	1	1	0	6
	Oldham	1996-97	39(2)	12	91	2	232
James Maloney	Catalans	2020-21	38	7	169	5	371
Jake Mamo	Castleford	2022-23	17(3)	10	0	0	40
	Warrington	2019-21	42(6)	27	0	0	108
	Huddersfield	2017-18	23	17	0	0	68
Dom Manfredi	Wigan	2013-16, 2018-21	73	55	0	0	220
	Salford	2014	1	2	0	0	8
George Mann	Warrington	1997	14(5)	1	0	0	4
	Leeds	1996	11(4)	2	0	0	8
Dane Manning	Leeds	2009	(1)	0	0	0	0
Josh Mantellato	Hull KR	2015-16	26	16	88	0	240
Misali Manu	Widnes	2005	1	0	0	0	0
Sika Manu	Hull	2016-19	90(4)	10	0	0	40
Willie Manu	St Helens	2013-14	35(11)	9	0	0	36
	Hull	2007-12	133(18)	33	0	0	132
	Castleford	2006	19(4)	9	0	0	36
Manase Manuokafoa	Widnes	2015-17	3(54)	3	0	0	12
	Bradford	2012-14	49(21)	3	0	0	12
Darren Mapp	Celtic	2009	9(2)	1	0	0	4
David March	Wakefield	1999-2007	164(23)	34	126	0	388
Paul March	Wakefield	1999-2001, 2007	42(31)	17	23	0	114
	Huddersfield	2003-06	71(19)	17	36	1	141
Paul Marcon	Toulouse	2022	16	5	0	0	20
Nick Mardon	London	1997-98	14	2	0	0	8
Thibaut Margalet	Catalans	2013-18	1(22)	0	0	0	0
Remy Marginet	Catalans	2011	2	0	9	0	18
Antoni Maria	Catalans	2012-16, 2018-20	10(57)	0	0	0	0
	Hull KR	2019	2(3)	0	0	0	0
	Leigh	2017	2(6)	0	0	0	0
Frankie Mariano	Castleford	2014-16	14(21)	8	0	0	32
	Wakefield	2011-13	41(12)	20	0	0	80
	Hull KR	2010	(3)	0	0	0	0
Anthony Marion	Toulouse	2022	17(3)	1	2	0	8
Oliver Marns	Halifax	1996-2002	54(19)	23	0	0	92
Paul Marquet	Warrington	2002	23(2)	0	0	0	0
Callum Marriott	Salford	2011	(1)	0	0	0	0
Iain Marsh	Salford	1998-2001	1(4)	0	0	0	0
Lee Marsh	Salford	2001-02	3(4)	0	0	0	0
Matty Marsh	Hull KR	2015-16, 2018	18(4)	3	0	0	12
Stefan Marsh	Widnes	2012-18	122	56	21	0	266
	Wigan	2010-11	12	3	0	0	12
Liam Marshall	Wigan	2017-23	138	111	5	0	454
Richard Marshall	Leigh	2005	4(16)	0	0	0	0
	London	2002-03	33(11)	1	0	0	4
	Huddersfield	2000-01	35(14)	1	0	0	4
	Halifax	1996-99	38(34)	2	0	0	8
Esan Marsters	Huddersfield	2023	21	3	0	0	12
Brad Martin	Castleford	2020-23	6(22)	1	0	0	4
Charlie Martin	Castleford	2013	(6)	0	0	0	0
Jason Martin	Paris	1997	15(2)	3	0	0	12
Lewis Martin	Hull	2023	1	1	0	0	4
Rhyse Martin	Leeds	2019-23	95(3)	26	329	0	762
Scott Martin	Salford	1997-99	32(18)	8	0	0	32
Tony Martin	Hull	2012	10	1	0	0	4
	Crusaders	2010-11	40(1)	14	1	0	58
	Wakefield	2008-09	33	10	33	0	106
	London	1996-97, 2001-03	97(1)	36	170	1	485
Ugo Martin	Catalans	2018	1	0	0	0	0
Mick Martindale	Halifax	1996	(4)	0	0	0	0
Sebastien Martins	Catalans	2006, 2009-11	(21)	2	0	0	8
Shay Martyn	St Helens	2021-22	2	0	4	0	8
Tommy Martyn	St Helens	1996-2003	125(20)	87	63	12	486
Dean Marwood	Workington	1996	9(6)	0	22	0	44
Martin Masella	Warrington	2001	10(14)	5	0	0	20
	Wakefield	2000	14(8)	4	0	0	16
	Leeds	1997-1999	59(5)	1	0	0	4
Colin Maskill	Castleford	1996	8	1	1	0	6
Mose Masoe	Hull KR	2018-19	28(18)	6	0	0	24
	St Helens	2014-15	17(39)	10	0	0	40
Keith Mason	Castleford	2006, 2013	11(6)	0	0	0	0
	Huddersfield	2006-12	118(14)	4	0	0	16
	St Helens	2003-05	33(23)	4	0	0	16
	Wakefield	2000-01	5(17)	0	0	0	0
Nathan Mason	Wakefield	2023	1	0	0	0	0
	Huddersfield	2013, 2015-17, 2022	4(32)	3	0	0	12
	Leigh	2021	4(4)	1	0	0	4
	London	2019	5(10)	1	0	0	4
Willie Mason	Catalans	2016	6(8)	1	0	0	4
	Hull KR	2011	6	1	0	0	4
Samy Masselot	Wakefield	2011	(1)	0	0	0	0
Nathan Massey	Castleford	2008-23	197(81)	10	0	0	40
Suaia Matagi	Castleford	2021-23	12(35)	3	0	0	12
	Huddersfield	2018-20	39(9)	3	0	0	12
Nesiasi Mataitonga	London	2014	11(1)	1	0	0	4
Peter Mata'utia	Warrington	2022-23	50(2)	6	8	0	40
	Castleford	2018-21	63	11	58	1	161
Sione Mata'utia	St Helens	2021-23	46(8)	12	0	0	48
Vila Matautia	St Helens	1996-2001	31(68)	9	0	0	36
Feleti Mateo	London	2005	4(10)	1	0	0	4
Barrie-Jon Mather	Castleford	1998, 2000-02	50(12)	21	0	0	84
Richard Mathers	Wakefield	2012-14	71	24	0	0	96
	Castleford	2011	21(1)	7	0	0	28
	Warrington	2002, 2009-10	42(3)	11	0	0	44
	Wigan	2008-09	23(1)	2	0	0	8
	Leeds	2002-06	85(2)	26	0	0	104
Jamie Mathiou	Leeds	1997-2001	31(82)	3	0	0	12
Masi Matongo	Hull	2015, 2017-20	16(38)	3	0	0	12
Terry Matterson	London	1996-98	46	15	90	6	246
Manu Ma'u	Catalans	2023	4(14)	3	0	0	12
	Hull	2020-22	40	5	0	0	20
Vic Mauro	Salford	2013	1(7)	1	0	0	4
Luke May	Harlequins	2009-10	(3)	0	0	0	0
Tyrone May	Catalans	2022-23	36(7)	6	2	0	28
Casey Mayberry	Halifax	2000	1(1)	0	0	0	0
Chris Maye	Halifax	2003	3(4)	1	0	0	4
Judah Mazive	Wakefield	2016	2	1	0	0	4
Joe Mbu	Harlequins	2006-09	33(20)	3	0	0	12
	London	2003-05	29(19)	4	0	0	16
Moses Mbye	St Helens	2023	(11)	2	0	0	8
Danny McAllister	Gateshead	1999	3(3)	1	0	0	4
	Sheffield	1996-97	33(7)	10	0	0	40
John McAtee	St Helens	1996	2(1)	0	0	0	0

Super League Players 1996-2023

PLAYER	CLUB	YEAR	APP	TRIES	GOALS	FG	PTS
Nathan McAvoy	Bradford	1998-2002, 2007	83(31)	46	0	0	184
	Wigan	2006	15(2)	5	0	0	20
	Salford	1997-98, 2004-05	57(4)	18	0	0	72
Tyrone McCarthy	Leigh	2021	8(3)	0	0	0	0
	Salford	2017-20	41(20)	8	2	0	36
	Hull KR	2015	20(1)	4	0	0	16
	Warrington	2009-13	12(24)	2	0	0	8
	Wakefield	2011	2(5)	1	0	0	4
Louie McCarthy-Scarsbrook	St Helens	2011-23	150(189)	59	0	0	236
	Harlequins	2006-10	41(50)	17	0	0	68
Dave McConnell	London	2003	(4)	0	0	0	0
	St Helens	2001-02	3(2)	4	0	0	16
Loui McConnell	Leeds	2020	(2)	0	0	0	0
Robbie McCormack	Wigan	1998	24	2	0	0	8
Josh McCrone	Toronto	2020	6	1	0	0	4
Steve McCurrie	Leigh	2005	7(3)	1	0	0	4
	Widnes	2002-04	55(22)	10	0	0	40
	Warrington	1998-2001	69(26)	31	0	0	124
Barrie McDermott	Leeds	1996-2005	163(69)	28	0	0	112
Brian McDermott	Bradford	1996-2002	138(32)	33	0	0	132
Ryan McDonald	Widnes	2002-03	6(4)	0	0	0	0
Wayne McDonald	Huddersfield	2005-06	11(23)	1	0	0	4
	Wigan	2005	(4)	0	0	0	0
	Leeds	2002-05	34(47)	14	0	0	56
	St Helens	2001	7(11)	4	0	0	16
	Hull	2000	5(8)	4	0	0	16
	Wakefield	1999	9(17)	8	0	0	32
James McDonnell	Leeds	2023	23	4	0	0	16
	Wigan	2020-22	5(1)	2	0	0	8
Shannon McDonnell	St Helens	2014-16	28	15	0	0	60
	Hull	2013	19	2	0	0	8
	Hull KR	2012	21	6	0	0	24
Craig McDowell	Huddersfield	2003	(1)	0	0	0	0
	Warrington	2002	(1)	0	0	0	0
	Bradford	2000	(1)	0	0	0	0
Wes McGibbon	Halifax	1999	1	0	0	0	0
Jermaine McGillvary	Huddersfield	2010-23	287(1)	196	0	0	784
Dean McGilvray	Salford	2009-10	14	4	0	0	16
	St Helens	2006-08	5(1)	1	0	0	4
Billy McGinty	Workington	1996	1	0	0	0	0
Ryan McGoldrick	Salford	2013	19(1)	3	0	1	13
	Hull	2012	8	1	0	0	4
	Castleford	2006, 2008-12	129(5)	24	11	0	118
Kevin McGuinness	Salford	2004-07	63(3)	11	0	0	44
Casey McGuire	Catalans	2007-10	87(4)	27	0	0	108
Danny McGuire	Hull KR	2018-19	36	9	1	3	41
	Leeds	2001-17	331(39)	238	0	6	958
Josh McGuire	Warrington	2023	6	1	0	0	4
Gary McGuirk	Workington	1996	(4)	0	0	0	0
Michael McIlorum	Catalans	2018-23	106(2)	7	0	0	28
	Wigan	2007-17	156(54)	22	0	0	88
Darnell McIntosh	Hull	2022-23	41(1)	22	8	0	104
	Huddersfield	2017-21	91(1)	43	12	0	196
Richard McKell	Castleford	1997-98	22(7)	2	0	0	8
Chris McKenna	Bradford	2006-07	40(7)	7	0	0	28
	Leeds	2003-05	65(4)	18	0	0	72
Phil McKenzie	Workington	1996	4	0	0	0	0
Chris McKinney	Oldham	1996-97	4(9)	2	0	0	8
Wade McKinnon	Hull	2012	10	4	0	0	16
Callum McLelland	Leeds	2019-21	10(3)	1	0	0	4
Mark McLinden	Harlequins	2006-08	46(1)	20	0	1	81
	London	2005	22(3)	8	0	0	32
Mike McMeeken	Catalans	2021-23	61	15	0	0	60
	Castleford	2015-20	118(13)	30	0	0	120
	London	2012-14	25(9)	5	0	0	20
Shayne McMenemy	Hull	2003-07	80(8)	12	0	0	48
	Halifax	2001-03	63	11	0	0	44
Andy McNally	London	2004	5(3)	0	0	0	0
	Castleford	2001, 2003	2(5)	1	0	0	4
Gregg McNally	Leigh	2017	9	3	0	0	12
	Huddersfield	2011	1	0	6	0	12
Ben McNamara	Hull	2020-23	22(9)	2	16	0	40
Steve McNamara	Huddersfield	2001, 2003	41(9)	3	134	1	281
	Wakefield	2000	15(2)	2	32	0	72
	Bradford	1996-99	90(3)	14	348	7	759
Paul McNicholas	Hull	2004-05	28(12)	4	0	0	16
Neil McPherson	Salford	1997	(1)	0	0	0	0
Shannan McPherson	Salford	2012-14	20(11)	0	0	0	0
Chris McQueen	Huddersfield	2020-23	73(5)	33	0	0	132
Duncan McRae	London	1996	11(2)	3	0	1	13
Paul McShane	Castleford	2015-23	174(24)	24	63	1	223
	Wakefield	2014-15	39(4)	5	0	0	20
	Leeds	2009-13	17(38)	12	0	0	48
	Widnes	2012	6(5)	3	4	0	20
	Hull	2010	(4)	0	0	0	0
Derek McVey	St Helens	1996-97	28(4)	6	1	0	26
Dallas Mead	Warrington	1997	2	0	0	0	0
David Mead	Catalans	2018-20	51	23	0	0	92
James Meadows	London	2019	1	0	0	0	0
Robbie Mears	Leigh	2005	8(6)	0	0	0	0
	Leeds	2001	23	6	0	0	24
Paul Medley	Bradford	1996-98	6(35)	9	0	0	36
Francis Meli	Salford	2014	16	11	0	0	44
	St Helens	2006-13	194(1)	122	0	0	488
Vince Mellars	Wakefield	2012-13	21(5)	4	0	0	16
	Crusaders	2010-11	46	17	0	0	68
Chris Melling	London	2012-13	25(12)	5	2	0	24
	Harlequins	2007-11	100(11)	33	6	0	144
	Wigan	2004-06	8(2)	1	3	0	10
Alex Mellor	Castleford	2022-23	35(1)	6	0	0	24
	Leeds	2020-22	27(3)	4	0	0	16
	Huddersfield	2017-19	65(10)	19	0	0	76
	Bradford	2013-14	(10)	0	0	0	0
Joe Mellor	Leigh	2021, 2023	21(16)	6	0	0	24
	Toronto	2020	2	0	0	0	0
	Widnes	2012-18	134(1)	46	0	1	185
	Wigan	2012	1(1)	1	0	0	4
	Harlequins	2011	(1)	0	0	0	0
Paul Mellor	Castleford	2003-04	36(3)	18	0	0	72
James Mendeika	London	2013	4(2)	2	0	0	8
Craig Menkins	Paris	1997	4(5)	1	0	0	4
Luke Menzies	Hull KR	2008	(1)	0	0	0	0
Steve Menzies	Catalans	2011-13	61(6)	30	0	0	120
	Bradford	2009-10	52(1)	24	1	0	98
Gary Mercer	Castleford	2002	(1)	0	0	0	0
	Leeds	1996-97, 2001	40(2)	9	0	0	36
	Warrington	2001	18	2	0	0	8
	Halifax	1998-2001	73(2)	16	0	0	64
Trent Merrin	Leeds	2019	27	4	0	0	16
Tony Mestrov	London	1996-97, 2001	59(8)	4	0	0	16
	Wigan	1998-2000	39(39)	3	0	0	12
Keiran Meyer	London	1996	4	1	0	0	4
Brad Meyers	Bradford	2005-06	40(11)	13	0	0	52
Ronan Michael	Huddersfield	2020	(1)	0	0	0	0
Steve Michaels	Hull	2015-19	68(1)	26	0	0	104
Gary Middlehurst	Widnes	2004	(2)	0	0	0	0
Simon Middleton	Castleford	1996-97	19(3)	8	0	0	32
Constantine Mika	Hull KR	2012-13	45(4)	9	0	0	36
Thomas Mikaele	Warrington	2022-23	13(12)	4	0	0	16
Daryl Millard	Catalans	2011-14	91	38	1	0	154
	Wakefield	2010-11	21(1)	11	0	0	44
Shane Millard	Wigan	2007	19(6)	3	0	0	12
	Leeds	2006	6(21)	3	0	0	12
	Widnes	2003-05	69	23	0	0	92
	London	1998-2001	72(14)	11	1	0	46
Jack Miller	Huddersfield	2013	1	0	1	0	2
Jacob Miller	Castleford	2023	26	3	0	1	13
	Wakefield	2015-22	177(3)	55	17	9	263
	Hull	2013-14	26	6	9	0	42
Grant Millington	Castleford	2012-21	155(75)	33	0	0	132
David Mills	Harlequins	2006-07, 2010	25(32)	2	0	0	8
	Hull KR	2008-09	20(11)	1	0	0	4
	Widnes	2002-05	17(77)	8	0	0	32
Lewis Mills	Celtic	2009	(4)	0	0	0	0
Adam Milner	Huddersfield	2023	11(2)	1	0	0	4
	Castleford	2010-23	177(104)	37	1	0	150
Lee Milner	Halifax	1999	(1)	0	0	0	0
Rowan Milnes	Hull KR	2020-23	40(3)	6	37	0	98
	Wakefield	2023	1	0	0	0	0
Hakim Miloudi	Toronto	2020	5(1)	1	0	0	4
	Hull	2018-19	13(2)	5	1	0	22
Elliot Minchella	Hull KR	2020-23	52(12)	11	0	0	44
	Leeds	2013-14	(6)	1	0	0	4
Mark Minichiello	Hull	2015-19	118(4)	20	0	0	80
Greg Minikin	Warrington	2022-23	14(6)	2	0	0	8
	Hull KR	2020-21	23	10	0	0	40
	Castleford	2016-19	89(2)	39	0	0	156

Super League Players 1996-2023

PLAYER	CLUB	YEAR	APP	TRIES	GOALS	FG	PTS
Thomas Minns	Wakefield	2022	4	1	0	0	4
	Hull KR	2016, 2018	24(1)	14	0	0	56
	London	2014	23	6	0	0	24
	Leeds	2013	2(1)	1	0	0	4
John Minto	London	1996	13	4	0	0	16
Abbas Miski	Wigan	2022-23	32	36	0	0	144
Lee Mitchell	Castleford	2012	13(10)	2	0	0	8
	Warrington	2007-11	8(27)	4	0	0	16
	Harlequins	2011	11(1)	1	0	0	4
Sam Moa	Catalans	2017-20	68(6)	6	0	0	24
	Hull	2009-12	29(44)	6	0	0	24
Martin Moana	Salford	2004	6(3)	1	0	0	4
	Halifax	1996-2001, 2003	126(22)	62	0	1	249
	Wakefield	2002	19(2)	10	0	0	40
	Huddersfield	2001	3(3)	2	0	0	8
Adam Mogg	Catalans	2007-10	74	19	0	1	77
Jon Molloy	Wakefield	2013-16	25(18)	5	0	0	20
	Huddersfield	2011-12	2(1)	0	0	0	0
Steve Molloy	Huddersfield	2000-01	26(20)	3	0	0	12
	Sheffield	1998-99	32(17)	3	0	0	12
Chris Molyneux	Huddersfield	2000-01	1(18)	0	0	0	0
	Sheffield	1999	1(2)	0	0	0	0
Joel Monaghan	Castleford	2016-17	29(3)	13	0	0	52
	Warrington	2011-15	127	125	2	0	504
Michael Monaghan	Warrington	2008-14	143(28)	31	0	4	128
Joel Moon	Leeds	2013-18	136(1)	61	0	0	244
	Salford	2012	17	9	0	0	36
Adrian Moore	Huddersfield	1998-99	1(4)	0	0	0	0
Brandon Moore	Huddersfield	2020	4	0	0	0	0
Connor Moore	Hull KR	2022	(3)	0	0	0	0
Danny Moore	London	2000	7	0	0	0	0
	Wigan	1998-99	49(3)	18	0	0	72
Gareth Moore	Wakefield	2011	5	1	14	1	33
Jason Moore	Workington	1996	(5)	0	0	0	0
Richard Moore	Wakefield	2007-10, 2014	52(57)	10	0	0	40
	Leeds	2012-13	3(27)	1	0	0	4
	Crusaders	2011	11(10)	1	0	0	4
	Leigh	2005	2(5)	0	0	0	0
	Bradford	2002-04	1(26)	0	0	0	0
	London	2002, 2004	5(9)	2	0	0	8
Scott Moore	Wakefield	2015-16	12(2)	0	0	0	0
	Castleford	2008, 2015	24(6)	2	0	0	8
	London	2014	26	3	0	0	12
	Huddersfield	2009, 2012	29(7)	9	0	0	36
	Widnes	2012	3(3)	0	0	0	0
	St Helens	2004-07, 2010-11	29(37)	9	0	0	36
Junior Moors	Castleford	2015-20	46(63)	18	0	0	72
Dennis Moran	Wigan	2005-06	39	17	1	1	71
	London	2001-04	107(2)	74	2	5	305
Kieran Moran	Hull KR	2016	(5)	0	0	0	0
Pat Moran	Warrington	2019	(1)	0	0	0	0
Ryan Morgan	London	2019	21	5	0	0	20
	St Helens	2017-18	46	22	0	0	88
Willie Morganson	Sheffield	1997-98	18(12)	5	3	0	26
Paul Moriarty	Halifax	1996	3(2)	0	0	0	0
Adrian Morley	Salford	2014-15	31(14)	2	0	0	8
	Warrington	2007-13	135(21)	8	0	0	32
	Bradford	2005	2(4)	0	0	0	0
	Leeds	1996-2000	95(14)	25	0	0	100
Chris Morley	Salford	1999	3(5)	0	0	0	0
	Warrington	1998	2(8)	0	0	0	0
	St Helens	1996-97	21(16)	4	0	0	16
Frazer Morris	Wakefield	2016	(1)	0	0	0	0
Glenn Morrison	Wakefield	2010-11	43(1)	9	0	0	36
	Bradford	2007-09	48(2)	19	0	0	76
Iain Morrison	Hull KR	2007	5(6)	1	0	0	4
	Huddersfield	2003-05	11(23)	0	0	0	0
	London	2001	(1)	0	0	0	0
Daniel Mortimer	Leigh	2017	3	0	0	0	0
Dale Morton	Wakefield	2009-11	22(3)	8	5	0	42
Gareth Morton	Hull KR	2007	7(4)	3	23	0	58
	Leeds	2001-02	1(1)	0	0	0	0
Daniel Moss	St Helens	2022	2	0	0	0	0
Kieren Moss	Hull KR	2018	2(1)	4	0	0	16
Lee Mossop	Salford	2017-21	68(3)	6	0	0	24
	Wigan	2008-13, 2015-16	80(65)	11	0	0	44
	Huddersfield	2009	1(4)	1	0	0	4
Aaron Moule	Salford	2006-07	45	17	0	0	68
	Widnes	2004-05	29	12	0	0	48
Bradley Moules	Wakefield	2016	(1)	0	0	0	0
Wilfried Moulinec	Paris	1996	1	0	0	0	0
Gregory Mounis	Catalans	2006-16	149(105)	27	19	0	146
Arthur Mourgue	Catalans	2018-23	41(26)	17	83	0	234
Mark Moxon	Huddersfield	1998-2001	20(5)	1	0	1	5
Robbie Mulhern	Leigh	2023	26(1)	4	0	0	16
	Warrington	2021-22	20(23)	1	0	0	4
	Hull KR	2016, 2018-20	43(27)	4	0	0	16
	Leeds	2014-15	(5)	0	0	0	0
Anthony Mullally	Toronto	2020	2(4)	0	0	0	0
	Leeds	2016-18	10(48)	9	0	0	36
	Wakefield	2015	(2)	0	0	0	0
	Huddersfield	2013-15	12(24)	5	0	0	20
	Bradford	2014	1(5)	0	0	0	0
	Widnes	2012	(9)	0	0	0	0
Jake Mullaney	Salford	2014	12	2	24	0	56
Craig Mullen	Leigh	2021	9(4)	1	13	0	30
	Wigan	2018	1(1)	0	0	0	0
Brett Mullins	Leeds	2001	5(3)	1	0	0	4
Damian Munro	Widnes	2002	8(2)	1	0	0	4
	Halifax	1996-97	9(6)	8	0	0	32
Matt Munro	Oldham	1996-97	26(5)	8	0	0	32
Ben Murdoch-Masila	Warrington	2018-20	23(35)	13	0	0	52
	Salford	2016-17	46(1)	15	0	0	60
Craig Murdock	Salford	2000	(2)	0	0	0	0
	Hull	1998-99	21(6)	8	0	2	34
	Wigan	1996-98	18(17)	14	0	0	56
Aaron Murphy	Huddersfield	2012-20	169(6)	71	0	0	284
	Wakefield	2008-11	57(2)	12	0	0	48
Jack Murphy	Wigan	2012, 2014	3	1	0	0	4
	Salford	2013	10	3	1	0	14
Jamie Murphy	Crusaders	2011	(2)	0	0	0	0
Jobe Murphy	Bradford	2013	(4)	0	0	0	0
Justin Murphy	Catalans	2006-08	59	49	0	0	196
	Widnes	2004	5	1	0	0	4
Lewis Murphy	Wakefield	2022-23	22	17	0	0	68
Daniel Murray	Hull KR	2019-20	15(8)	0	0	0	0
	Salford	2017-19	14(14)	2	0	0	8
Doc Murray	Warrington	1997	(2)	0	0	0	0
	Wigan	1997	6(2)	0	0	0	0
Scott Murrell	Hull KR	2007-12	114(24)	24	26	1	149
	Leeds	2005	(1)	0	0	0	0
	London	2004	3(3)	2	0	0	8
Muizz Mustapha	Castleford	2023	3(12)	0	0	0	0
	Leeds	2020, 2022	(8)	1	0	0	4
	Hull KR	2021	1(9)	0	0	0	0
David Mycoe	Sheffield	1996-97	12(13)	1	0	0	4
Richie Myler	Leeds	2018-23	113(5)	43	6	1	185
	Catalans	2016-17	40	21	2	0	88
	Warrington	2010-15	127(4)	69	1	1	279
	Salford	2009	18	11	0	0	44
Rob Myler	Oldham	1996-97	19(2)	6	0	0	24
Stephen Myler	Salford	2006	4(8)	1	15	0	34
	Widnes	2003-05	35(14)	8	74	0	180
Vinny Myler	Salford	2004	(4)	0	0	0	0
	Bradford	2003	(1)	0	0	0	0
Matt Nable	London	1997	2(2)	1	0	0	4
Kevin Naiqama	Huddersfield	2023	24	14	0	0	56
	St Helens	2019-21	67	36	0	0	144
Brad Nairn	Workington	1996	14	4	0	0	16
Ben Nakubuwai	Leigh	2023	2(17)	1	0	0	4
	Salford	2018-19	7(28)	2	0	0	8
Dylan Napa	Catalans	2022	18	0	0	0	0
Frank Napoli	London	2000	14(6)	2	0	0	8
Carlo Napolitano	Salford	2000	(3)	1	0	0	4
Stephen Nash	Castleford	2012	3(4)	0	0	0	0
	Salford	2007, 2009	2(18)	1	0	0	4
	Widnes	2005	4(1)	0	0	0	0
Curtis Naughton	Leigh	2017	5	3	0	0	12
	Hull	2015-16	26	13	1	0	54
	Bradford	2013	1	0	0	0	0
Ratu Naulago	Hull	2019-20	30	20	0	0	80
Romain Navarrete	Catalans	2016-17, 2023	21(17)	1	0	0	4
	Toulouse	2022	23	2	0	0	8
	Wakefield	2020	3(7)	0	0	0	0
	Wigan	2017-19	36(20)	0	0	0	0
Jim Naylor	Halifax	2000	7(6)	2	0	0	8
Scott Naylor	Salford	1997-98, 2004	30(1)	9	0	0	36
	Bradford	1999-2003	127(1)	51	0	0	204
Adam Neal	Salford	2010-13	17(28)	0	0	0	0
Mike Neal	Salford	1998	(1)	0	0	0	0
	Oldham	1996-97	6(4)	3	0	0	12
Jonathan Neill	Huddersfield	1998-99	20(11)	0	0	0	0
	St Helens	1996	1	0	0	0	0
Chris Nero	Salford	2011-13	31(16)	7	0	0	28
	Bradford	2008-10	65(5)	24	0	0	96
	Huddersfield	2004-07	97(8)	38	0	0	152

Super League Players 1996-2023

PLAYER	CLUB	YEAR	APP	TRIES	GOALS	FG	PTS
Jason Netherton	Hull KR	2007-14	60(74)	4	0	0	16
	London	2003-04	6	0	0	0	0
	Halifax	2002	2(3)	0	0	0	0
	Leeds	2001	(3)	0	0	0	0
Kirk Netherton	Castleford	2009-10	5(23)	3	0	0	12
	Hull KR	2007-08	9(15)	2	0	0	8
Paul Newlove	Castleford	2004	5	1	0	0	4
	St Helens	1996-2003	162	106	0	0	424
Richard Newlove	Wakefield	2003	17(5)	8	0	0	32
Harry Newman	Leeds	2017-23	69(3)	19	2	0	80
Clint Newton	Hull KR	2008-11	90(3)	37	0	0	148
Terry Newton	Wakefield	2010	(2)	0	0	0	0
	Bradford	2006-09	83(6)	26	0	0	104
	Wigan	2000-05	157(9)	62	0	0	248
	Leeds	1996-1999	55(14)	4	0	0	16
Gene Ngamu	Huddersfield	1999-2000	29(2)	9	67	0	170
Matty Nicholson	Warrington	2022-23	25	7	0	0	28
	Wigan	2022	(1)	2	0	0	8
Tom Nicholson-Watton	Leeds	2023	(1)	0	0	0	0
Danny Nicklas	Hull	2010, 2012	2(8)	0	0	0	0
Sonny Nickle	St Helens	1999-2002	86(18)	14	0	0	56
	Bradford	1996-98	25(16)	9	0	0	36
Jason Nicol	Salford	2000-02	52(7)	11	0	0	44
Tawera Nikau	Warrington	2000-01	51	7	0	0	28
Tom Nisbet	Leigh	2021, 2023	3(1)	0	0	0	0
	St Helens	2020	1	0	0	0	0
Rob Nolan	Hull	1998-99	20(11)	6	0	0	24
Paul Noone	Harlequins	2006	5(2)	0	0	0	0
	Warrington	2000-06	60(59)	12	20	0	88
Chris Norman	Halifax	2003	13(3)	2	0	0	8
Corey Norman	Toulouse	2022	11	1	0	0	4
Dan Norman	St Helens	2021-23	2(16)	2	0	0	8
	Leigh	2023	(3)	0	0	0	0
	Salford	2021	(3)	1	0	0	4
	Widnes	2018	(1)	0	0	0	0
Paul Norman	Oldham	1996	(1)	0	0	0	0
Andy Northey	St Helens	1996-97	8(17)	2	0	0	8
Junior Nsemba	Wigan	2022-23	2(13)	0	0	0	0
Danny Nutley	Castleford	2006	28	3	0	0	12
	Warrington	1998-2001	94(1)	3	0	0	12
Tony Nuttall	Oldham	1996-97	1(7)	0	0	0	0
Frank-Paul Nuuausala	Wigan	2016-18	34(8)	2	0	0	8
Levy Nzoungou	Hull	2019	(1)	0	0	0	0
	Salford	2018	(3)	0	0	0	0
Will Oakes	Hull KR	2016, 2018-19	12	5	0	0	20
Adam O'Brien	Huddersfield	2017-23	61(50)	19	0	0	76
	Bradford	2011-14	12(29)	6	0	0	24
Clinton O'Brien	Wakefield	2003	(2)	0	0	0	0
Gareth O'Brien	Leigh	2023	27	4	0	3	19
	Castleford	2013, 2020-22	37	6	52	3	131
	Toronto	2020	4	1	2	0	8
	Salford	2016-18	49(3)	12	105	2	260
	Warrington	2011-15	48(3)	16	69	3	205
	St Helens	2013	7	0	25	0	50
	Widnes	2012	4	0	15	0	30
Sam Obst	Hull	2011	17(6)	6	0	0	24
	Wakefield	2005-11	100(28)	40	7	0	174
Jamie O'Callaghan	London	2012-14	44(2)	4	0	0	16
	Harlequins	2008-11	54(3)	12	0	0	48
Eamon O'Carroll	Widnes	2012-17	58(11)	3	0	0	12
	Hull	2012	1(9)	0	0	0	0
	Wigan	2006-11	2(59)	3	0	0	12
Jarrod O'Connor	Leeds	2020-23	46(20)	4	2	0	20
Matt O'Connor	Paris	1997	11(4)	1	26	2	58
Terry O'Connor	Widnes	2005	25	2	0	0	8
	Wigan	1996-2004	177(45)	9	0	0	36
Jarrod O'Doherty	Huddersfield	2003	26	3	0	0	12
David O'Donnell	Paris	1997	21	3	0	0	12
Kai O'Donnell	Leigh	2023	20(2)	3	0	0	12
Luke O'Donnell	Huddersfield	2011-13	22(2)	2	0	0	8
Martin Offiah	Salford	2000-01	41	20	0	2	82
	London	1996-99	29(3)	21	0	0	84
	Wigan	1996	8	7	0	0	28
Jacob Ogden	London	2019	2	0	0	0	0
Mark O'Halloran	London	2004-05	34(3)	10	0	0	40
Ryan O'Hara	Hull KR	2012	8(7)	1	0	4	4
	Crusaders	2010-11	41(8)	3	0	0	12
	Celtic	2009	27	3	0	0	12
Hefin O'Hare	Huddersfield	2001, 2003-05	72(10)	27	0	0	108
Edwin Okanga-Ajwang	Salford	2013	2	0	0	0	0
Ben O'Keefe	Wigan	2022	1	1	4	0	12
Hitro Okesene	Hull	1998	21(1)	0	0	0	0
Anderson Okiwe	Sheffield	1997	1	0	0	0	0
Tom Olbison	Toronto	2020	3(3)	0	0	0	0
	Widnes	2017-18	18(22)	4	0	0	16
	Bradford	2009-14	55(26)	11	0	0	44
Michael Oldfield	Catalans	2014-15	41	28	0	0	112
Mikolaj Oledzki	Leeds	2017-23	87(35)	12	0	0	48
Jamie Olejnik	Paris	1997	11	8	0	0	32
Aaron Ollett	Hull KR	2013-15	5(16)	1	0	0	4
Kevin O'Loughlin	Halifax	1997-98	2(4)	0	0	0	0
	St Helens	1997	(3)	0	0	0	0
Sean O'Loughlin	Wigan	2002-20	371(32)	71	3	2	292
Derrell Olpherts	Leeds	2023	12(1)	4	0	0	16
	Castleford	2020-22	59(1)	34	0	0	136
	Salford	2018-19	35	11	0	0	44
Mark O'Meley	Hull	2010-13	70(13)	13	0	0	52
Brad O'Neill	Wigan	2021-23	23(20)	1	0	0	4
Jacques O'Neill	Castleford	2019-21	2(25)	3	0	0	12
Jules O'Neill	Widnes	2003-05	57(3)	14	158	7	379
	Wakefield	2005	10(2)	2	4	0	16
	Wigan	2002-03	29(1)	12	72	0	192
Julian O'Neill	Widnes	2002-05	57(39)	3	0	0	12
	Wakefield	2001	24(1)	2	0	0	8
	St Helens	1997-2000	95(8)	5	0	0	20
Mark O'Neill	Hull KR	2007	17	5	0	0	20
	Leeds	2006	1(8)	0	0	0	0
Steve O'Neill	Gateshead	1999	1(1)	0	0	0	0
Tom Opacic	Hull KR	2023	26	9	0	0	36
Tom O'Reilly	Warrington	2001-02	8(6)	1	0	0	4
Matt Orford	Bradford	2010	12	3	31	2	76
Jack Ormondroyd	Salford	2020-23	45(26)	6	0	0	24
	Leeds	2017-18	3(9)	0	0	0	0
Gene Ormsby	Huddersfield	2016-17	8	4	0	0	16
	Warrington	2014-16	37	26	0	0	104
Chris Orr	Huddersfield	1998	19(3)	2	0	0	8
Danny Orr	Castleford	1997-2003, 2011-12	197(23)	75	308	3	919
	Harlequins	2007-10	90(4)	13	96	0	244
	Wigan	2004-06	66(2)	18	12	0	96
Gareth Owen	Salford	2010, 2012-13	4(32)	6	0	0	24
Nick Owen	Leigh	2005	8(1)	1	11	0	26
Richard Owen	Wakefield	2014-15	29(1)	9	0	0	36
	Castleford	2008-14	109(3)	57	0	0	228
Jack Owens	St Helens	2016-17	31	8	14	0	60
	Widnes	2012-15	53(1)	26	103	0	310
Agnatius Paasi	St Helens	2021-23	10(45)	3	0	0	12
Lopini Paea	Wakefield	2015	1(3)	0	0	0	0
	Catalans	2011-14	41(41)	9	0	0	36
Mickey Paea	Hull	2014-15, 2018-19	78(18)	9	0	0	36
	Hull KR	2012-13	34(17)	5	0	0	20
Liam Paisley	Wigan	2018-19	6(2)	2	0	0	8
Mathias Pala	Catalans	2011-15	28(1)	4	0	0	16
Iafeta Palea'aesina	Hull	2014-16	(47)	1	0	0	4
	Salford	2011-12	4(37)	3	0	0	12
	Wigan	2006-10	55(77)	16	0	0	64
Jason Palmada	Workington	1996	12	2	0	0	8
Junior Paramore	Castleford	1996	5(5)	3	0	0	12
Matt Parcell	Hull KR	2019-23	67(17)	21	0	0	84
	Leeds	2017-19	50(16)	27	0	0	108
Mike Parenti	Catalans	2022	1	0	0	0	0
Paul Parker	Hull	1999-2002	23(18)	9	0	0	36
Rob Parker	Castleford	2011	4(2)	2	0	0	8
	Salford	2009-11	23(14)	4	0	0	16
	Warrington	2006-08	10(56)	6	0	0	24
	Bradford	2000, 2002-05	19(76)	14	0	0	56
	London	2001	9	1	0	0	4
Wayne Parker	Halifax	1996-97	12(1)	0	0	0	0
Ian Parry	Warrington	2001	(1)	0	0	0	0
Jules Parry	Paris	1996	10(2)	0	0	0	0
Oliver Partington	Salford	2023	20	0	0	0	0
	Wigan	2018-22	56(30)	5	0	0	20
Regis Pastre-Courtine	Paris	1996	4(3)	4	0	0	16
Cory Paterson	Leigh	2017	13	2	0	0	8
	Salford	2015	14(1)	7	6	0	40
	Hull KR	2013	15	7	0	0	28
Andrew Patmore	Oldham	1996	8(5)	3	0	0	12
Larne Patrick	Castleford	2016-17	14(7)	1	0	0	4
	Huddersfield	2009-14, 2016	30(107)	30	0	0	120
	Wigan	2015	7(20)	4	0	0	16
Luke Patten	Salford	2011-12	53	16	0	0	64
Dec Patton	Salford	2021	6(4)	1	3	0	10
	Warrington	2015-20	69(19)	11	105	6	260

215

Super League Players 1996-2023

PLAYER	CLUB	YEAR	APP	TRIES	GOALS	FG	PTS
Henry Paul	Harlequins	2006-08	60(1)	8	94	2	222
	Bradford	1999-2001	81(5)	29	350	6	822
	Wigan	1996-98	60	37	23	0	194
Junior Paul	London	1996	3	1	0	0	4
Robbie Paul	Salford	2009	2(24)	2	0	0	8
	Huddersfield	2006-07	44(8)	7	0	0	28
	Bradford	1996-2005	198(31)	121	3	0	490
Pauli Pauli	Salford	2019-21	9(21)	4	0	0	16
	Wakefield	2018-19	14(30)	10	0	0	40
Joseph Paulo	Toulouse	2022	8(4)	0	0	0	0
	St Helens	2019-20	6(25)	1	0	0	4
Jason Payne	Castleford	2006	1(1)	0	0	0	0
Lewis Peachey	Castleford	2019-21	1(10)	0	0	0	0
Danny Peacock	Bradford	1997-99	32(2)	15	0	0	60
Jamie Peacock	Leeds	2006-15	234(16)	24	0	0	96
	Bradford	1999-2005	163(25)	38	0	0	152
Mitchell Pearce	Catalans	2022-23	39	14	0	0	56
Kai Pearce-Paul	Wigan	2020-23	46(13)	7	0	0	28
Martin Pearson	Wakefield	2001	21(1)	3	60	3	135
	Halifax	1997-98, 2000	55(6)	24	181	0	458
	Sheffield	1999	17(6)	9	36	2	110
Nathan Peats	Huddersfield	2021, 2023	27(10)	1	0	0	4
	Toulouse	2022	13	2	0	0	8
	Leigh	2021	2(8)	0	0	0	0
Jacques Pech	Paris	1996	16	0	0	0	0
Mike Pechey	Warrington	1998	6(3)	2	0	0	8
Bill Peden	London	2003	21(3)	7	0	0	28
Adam Peek	Crusaders	2010-11	5(22)	1	0	0	4
	Celtic	2009	5(12)	3	0	0	12
Eloi Pelissier	Toulouse	2022	2(17)	3	0	1	13
	London	2019	7(6)	1	0	0	4
	Leigh	2017	4(16)	0	0	0	0
	Catalans	2011-16	38(104)	23	0	1	93
Dimitri Pelo	Catalans	2007-10	79	37	0	0	148
Taylor Pemberton	St Helens	2022	(1)	0	0	0	0
Sean Penkywicz	Huddersfield	2004-05	21(11)	7	0	0	28
	Halifax	2000-03	29(27)	8	0	0	32
Julian Penni	Salford	1998-99	4	0	0	0	0
Kevin Penny	Warrington	2006-09, 2014-17	83(1)	52	0	0	208
	Wakefield	2011	5	1	0	0	4
	Harlequins	2010	5	3	0	0	12
Lee Penny	Warrington	1996-2003	140(5)	54	0	0	216
Paul Penrice	Workington	1996	11(2)	2	0	0	8
Chris Percival	Widnes	2002-03	26	6	0	0	24
Mark Percival	St Helens	2013-23	198(2)	102	284	0	976
Apollo Perelini	St Helens	1996-2000	103(16)	27	0	0	108
Ugo Perez	Catalans	2015, 2017-18	2(5)	0	0	0	0
Mark Perrett	Halifax	1996-97	15(4)	4	0	0	16
Josh Perry	St Helens	2011-13	32(9)	2	0	0	8
Shane Perry	Catalans	2009	8(8)	1	0	0	4
Adam Peters	Paris	1997	16(3)	0	0	0	0
Dominic Peters	London	1998-2003	58(11)	12	0	0	48
Mike Peters	Warrington	2000	2(12)	1	0	0	4
	Halifax	2000	1	0	0	0	0
Willie Peters	Widnes	2004	9	3	0	2	14
	Wigan	2000	29	15	5	6	76
	Gateshead	1999	27	11	1	6	52
Dave Petersen	Hull KR	2012	2(2)	1	0	0	4
Matt Petersen	Wakefield	2008-09	14	3	0	0	12
Nathaniel Peteru	Huddersfield	2021	(12)	3	0	0	12
	Leigh	2021	2(8)	0	0	0	0
	Hull KR	2020	5(3)	0	0	0	0
	Leeds	2018-19	15(6)	0	0	0	0
Adrian Petrie	Workington	1996	(1)	0	0	0	0
Eddy Pettybourne	Wigan	2014	1(15)	0	0	0	0
Dominique Peyroux	Toulouse	2022	15(1)	2	0	0	8
	St Helens	2016-20	88(25)	16	0	0	64
Hugo Pezet	Toulouse	2022	2(1)	0	0	0	0
Cameron Phelps	Widnes	2012-15	66(1)	23	2	0	96
	Hull	2011	19	2	0	0	8
	Wigan	2008-10	43(1)	14	4	0	64
Joe Philbin	Warrington	2014-23	42(126)	12	0	0	48
Rowland Phillips	Workington	1996	22	1	0	0	4
Nathan Picchi	Leeds	1996	(1)	0	0	0	0
Ian Pickavance	Hull	1999	4(2)	2	0	0	8
	Huddersfield	1999	3(14)	0	0	0	0
	St Helens	1996-98	12(44)	6	0	0	24
James Pickering	Castleford	1999	1(19)	0	0	0	0
Steve Pickersgill	Widnes	2012-13	27(8)	1	0	0	4
	Warrington	2005-09	1(36)	0	0	0	0
Nick Pinkney	Salford	2000-02	64	29	0	0	116
	Halifax	1999	26(2)	13	0	0	52
	Sheffield	1997-98	33	10	0	0	40
Mikhail Piskunov	Paris	1996	1(1)	1	0	0	4
Darryl Pitt	London	1996	2(16)	4	0	1	17
Jay Pitts	Wakefield	2008-09, 2020-23	85(9)	11	0	0	44
	London	2019	27	7	0	0	28
	Bradford	2014	15(1)	3	0	0	12
	Hull	2012-14	18(30)	1	0	0	4
	Leeds	2009-12	10(15)	2	0	0	8
Andy Platt	Salford	1997-98	20(3)	1	0	0	4
Michael Platt	Salford	2001-02, 2014	4(1)	1	0	0	4
	Bradford	2007-13	121(6)	44	0	0	176
	Castleford	2006	26	7	0	0	28
Willie Poching	Leeds	2002-06	58(73)	44	0	0	176
	Wakefield	1999-2001	65(4)	20	0	0	80
Ben Pomeroy	Warrington	2017-18	3(7)	1	0	0	4
	Catalans	2014-15	44	10	0	0	40
Quentin Pongia	Wigan	2003-04	15(10)	0	0	0	0
Justin Poore	Hull KR	2014	7	0	0	0	0
	Wakefield	2013	23	1	0	0	4
Dan Potter	Widnes	2002-03	34(2)	6	0	0	24
	London	2001	1(3)	1	0	0	4
Craig Poucher	Hull	1999-2002	31(5)	5	0	0	20
Andy Powell	Wigan	2013	2(3)	1	0	0	4
Bryn Powell	Salford	2004	1(1)	0	0	0	0
Daio Powell	Sheffield	1999	13(1)	2	0	0	8
	Halifax	1997-98	30(3)	17	0	0	68
Daryl Powell	Leeds	1998-2000	49(30)	12	0	2	50
Sam Powell	Wigan	2012-23	193(57)	40	4	4	172
Karl Pratt	Bradford	2003-05	35(19)	18	0	0	72
	Leeds	1999-2002	62(12)	33	0	0	132
Oliver Pratt	Wakefield	2023	1	0	0	0	0
Paul Prescott	Wigan	2004-13	49(75)	4	0	0	16
Steve Prescott	Hull	1998-99, 2001-03	99	46	191	3	569
	Wakefield	2000	22(1)	3	13	0	38
	St Helens	1996-97	32	15	17	0	94
Lee Prest	Workington	1996	(1)	0	0	0	0
Gareth Price	Salford	2002	(2)	0	0	0	0
	London	2002	2(2)	3	0	0	12
	St Helens	1999	(11)	2	0	0	8
Gary Price	Wakefield	1999-2001	55(13)	11	0	0	44
Richard Price	Sheffield	1996	1(2)	0	0	0	0
Tony Priddle	Paris	1997	11	3	0	0	12
Matt Prior	Leeds	2020-22	52(6)	7	0	0	28
Frank Pritchard	Hull	2016	10(13)	4	0	0	16
Kevin Proctor	Wakefield	2023	12(8)	1	0	0	4
Karl Pryce	Bradford	2003-06, 2012	47(19)	46	1	0	186
	Harlequins	2011	11(7)	12	0	0	48
	Wigan	2009-10	11(2)	12	0	0	48
Leon Pryce	Hull	2015-16	32(2)	8	0	0	32
	Catalans	2012-14	72(2)	15	0	0	60
	St Helens	2006-11	133(3)	64	0	0	256
	Bradford	1998-2005	159(29)	86	0	0	344
Waine Pryce	Wakefield	2007	10(2)	4	0	0	16
	Castleford	2000-06	97(12)	49	0	0	196
Will Pryce	Huddersfield	2021-23	38(6)	17	62	0	192
Maxime Puech	Toulouse	2022	8(9)	0	0	0	0
Tony Puletua	Hull KR	2015	7	0	0	0	0
	Salford	2014	16(9)	3	0	0	12
	St Helens	2009-13	108(18)	39	0	0	156
Andrew Purcell	Castleford	2000	15(5)	3	0	0	12
	Hull	1999	27	4	0	0	16
Rob Purdham	Harlequins	2006-11	112(3)	18	131	1	335
	London	2002-05	53(15)	16	2	1	69
Adrian Purtell	Bradford	2012-14	45(1)	16	0	0	64
Jason Qareqare	Castleford	2021-23	16(5)	14	0	0	56
Luke Quigley	Catalans	2007	16(1)	1	0	0	4
Adam Quinlan	Hull KR	2018-21	47	24	0	0	96
	St Helens	2015	11	6	0	0	24
Damien Quinn	Celtic	2009	20(1)	4	12	0	40
Scott Quinnell	Wigan	1996	6(3)	1	0	0	4
Florian Quintilla	Catalans	2008-09	1(4)	0	0	0	0
Lee Radford	Hull	1998, 2006-12	138(30)	23	1	0	94
	Bradford	1999-2005	79(65)	18	12	0	96
Kris Radlinski	Wigan	1996-2006	236(1)	134	1	0	538
Sebastien Raguin	Catalans	2007-12	103(22)	28	0	0	112
Adrian Rainey	Castleford	2002	4(7)	1	0	0	4
Andy Raleigh	Wakefield	2012-14	42(21)	9	0	0	36
	Huddersfield	2006-11	74(46)	13	0	0	52
Jean-Luc Ramondou	Paris	1996	1	1	0	0	4
Chad Randall	London	2012-13	29(9)	4	0	0	16
	Harlequins	2006-11	141(2)	37	0	1	149

Super League Players 1996-2023

PLAYER	CLUB	YEAR	APP	TRIES	GOALS	FG	PTS
Craig Randall	Halifax	1999	8(11)	4	0	0	16
	Salford	1997-98	12(18)	4	0	0	16
Tyler Randell	Wakefield	2017-19	37(8)	9	1	0	38
Jordan Rankin	Castleford	2019-20	29(2)	10	19	0	78
	Huddersfield	2017-18	39	3	9	0	30
	Hull	2014-15	41(6)	20	43	0	166
Scott Ranson	Oldham	1996-97	19(2)	7	0	0	28
Aaron Raper	Castleford	1999-2001	48(4)	4	2	1	21
Sam Rapira	Huddersfield	2016-17	29(19)	3	0	0	12
Steve Rapira	Salford	2014	5(13)	0	0	0	0
Stefan Ratchford	Warrington	2012-23	281(11)	79	562	2	1442
	Salford	2007, 2009-11	65(5)	23	20	0	132
Mike Ratu	Hull KR	2010	5	1	0	0	4
	Leeds	2007, 2009	1(5)	1	0	0	4
Paul Rauhihi	Warrington	2006-09	67(20)	10	0	0	40
Ben Rauter	Wakefield	2001	15(6)	4	0	0	16
Nick Rawsthorne	Hull KR	2020	5	0	0	0	0
	Leigh	2017	1	1	0	0	4
	Hull	2017	3	2	2	0	12
Gareth Raynor	Bradford	2011	18	4	0	0	16
	Crusaders	2010	7	4	0	0	16
	Hull	2001-09	186	102	0	0	408
	Leeds	2000	(3)	0	0	0	0
Tony Rea	London	1996	22	4	0	0	16
Stuart Reardon	Crusaders	2011	25	11	0	0	44
	Bradford	2003-05, 2010	78(11)	37	0	0	148
	Warrington	2006-08	48	12	0	0	48
	Salford	2002	7(1)	3	0	0	12
Mark Reber	Wigan	1999-2000	9(9)	5	0	0	20
Alan Reddicliffe	Warrington	2001	1	0	0	0	0
Tahi Reihana	Bradford	1997-98	17(21)	0	0	0	0
Paul Reilly	Wakefield	2008	5(2)	1	0	0	4
	Huddersfield	1999-2001, 2003-07	150(8)	35	1	0	142
Robert Relf	Widnes	2002-04	68(2)	5	0	0	20
Steve Renouf	Wigan	2000-01	55	40	0	0	160
Steele Retchless	London	1998-2004	177(6)	13	0	0	52
Ben Reynolds	Leigh	2017, 2021, 2023	50	14	135	0	326
	Wakefield	2019	5	1	0	0	4
	Castleford	2013-14	1(3)	0	0	0	0
Josh Reynolds	Hull	2021-22	22	7	0	0	28
Scott Rhodes	Hull	2000	2	0	0	0	0
Lucas Ribas	Catalans	2022	(1)	0	0	0	0
Phillipe Ricard	Paris	1996-97	2	0	0	0	0
Andy Rice	Huddersfield	2000-01	2(13)	1	0	0	4
Basil Richards	Huddersfield	1998-99	28(17)	1	0	0	4
Craig Richards	Oldham	1996	1	0	0	0	0
Greg Richards	Hull KR	2022	(13)	0	0	0	0
	London	2019	5(15)	0	0	0	0
	Leigh	2017	(1)	0	0	0	0
	St Helens	2013-17	19(49)	1	0	0	4
Pat Richards	Catalans	2016	19	9	69	0	174
	Wigan	2006-13	199	147	759	4	2110
Andy Richardson	Hudds-Sheff	2000	(2)	0	0	0	0
Danny Richardson	Castleford	2020-22	43	5	131	7	289
	St Helens	2017-19	52(2)	9	158	8	360
Sean Richardson	Widnes	2002	2(18)	1	0	0	4
	Wakefield	1999	5(1)	0	0	0	0
	Castleford	1996-97	3(8)	1	0	0	4
Mark Riddell	Wigan	2009-10	45(11)	5	2	0	24
Martyn Ridyard	Huddersfield	2017	7	1	26	0	56
	Leigh	2017	4	0	2	0	4
Neil Rigby	St Helens	2006	(1)	0	0	0	0
Shane Rigon	Bradford	2001	14(11)	12	0	0	48
Craig Rika	Halifax	1996	2	0	0	0	0
Chris Riley	Wakefield	2014-15	44	16	0	0	64
	Warrington	2005-14	146(10)	102	0	0	408
	Harlequins	2011	3	2	0	0	8
Glenn Riley	Warrington	2013-14	(15)	0	0	0	0
Peter Riley	Workington	1996	7(5)	0	0	0	0
Julien Rinaldi	London	2012	4(16)	1	0	0	4
	Wakefield	2002, 2010-11	27(9)	6	0	0	24
	Bradford	2009	(7)	1	0	0	4
	Harlequins	2007-08	4(43)	9	0	0	36
	Catalans	2006	16(6)	3	1	0	14
Dean Ripley	Castleford	2004	3(4)	1	0	0	4
Tee Ritson	St Helens	2023	12(1)	3	0	0	12
Leroy Rivett	Warrington	2002	9	1	0	0	4
	Hudds-Sheff	2000	5(1)	1	0	0	4
	Leeds	1996-2000	39(15)	21	0	0	84
Nico Rizzelli	St Helens	2020	1	0	0	0	0
Jason Roach	Warrington	1998-99	29(7)	15	0	0	60
	Castleford	1997	7	4	0	0	16
Ben Roarty	Castleford	2006	11(6)	2	0	0	8
	Huddersfield	2003-05	52	5	0	0	20
Cain Robb	Castleford	2021-23	2(11)	0	0	0	0
Amos Roberts	Wigan	2009-11	47(2)	27	5	0	118
Ben Roberts	Castleford	2015-19	60(15)	20	0	2	82
Luis Roberts	Leeds	2023	7(2)	1	0	0	4
	Salford	2020	2	0	0	0	0
Mark Roberts	Wigan	2003	(3)	0	0	0	0
Oliver Roberts	Huddersfield	2016-19, 2022	43(43)	13	0	0	52
	Salford	2020-21	13(7)	1	0	0	4
	Bradford	2013-14	(5)	0	0	0	0
Robert Roberts	Huddersfield	2001	(1)	0	0	0	0
	Halifax	2000	(3)	0	0	0	0
	Hull	1999	24(2)	4	13	4	46
Tyrone Roberts	Warrington	2018	28	5	32	1	85
Michael Robertson	London	2012-13	35	17	0	0	68
Stan Robin	Catalans	2015-16	5(2)	1	0	0	4
Chad Robinson	Harlequins	2009	13(1)	2	0	0	8
Connor Robinson	Hull KR	2014-15	(2)	0	0	0	0
Craig Robinson	Wakefield	2005	(1)	0	0	0	0
Jason Robinson	Wigan	1996-2000	126(1)	87	0	1	349
Jeremy Robinson	Paris	1997	10(3)	1	21	0	46
John Robinson	Widnes	2003-04	7	1	0	0	4
Luke Robinson	Huddersfield	2008-15	191(18)	45	4	0	188
	Salford	2005-07	79	28	10	2	134
	Wigan	2002-04	17(25)	9	6	1	49
	Castleford	2004	9	4	3	0	22
Will Robinson	Hull	2000	22	4	0	0	16
	Gateshead	1999	28	9	0	0	36
Ash Robson	Castleford	2015	3	1	0	0	4
Ellis Robson	Toulouse	2022	(2)	0	0	0	0
	Salford	2021	4(3)	1	0	0	4
	Warrington	2020-21	2(3)	0	0	0	0
James Roby	St Helens	2004-23	368(127)	105	1	1	423
Mike Roby	St Helens	2004	(1)	0	0	0	0
Colton Roche	Huddersfield	2018-19	1(7)	0	0	0	0
Carl Roden	Warrington	1997	1	0	0	0	0
Shane Rodney	London	2012-13	28	3	12	0	36
Matt Rodwell	Warrington	2002	10	3	0	0	12
Nathan Roebuck	Warrington	2020	1	1	0	0	4
Darren Rogers	Castleford	1999-2004	162(1)	81	0	0	324
	Salford	1997-98	42	16	0	0	64
Fenton Rogers	Huddersfield	2023	(1)	0	0	0	0
Arthur Romano	Catalans	2017, 2019-20, 2022-23	48(2)	11	0	0	44
Adam Rooks	Hull KR	2019	(4)	0	0	0	0
Fletcher Rooney	Castleford	2023	1	0	0	0	0
Jamie Rooney	Wakefield	2003-09	113(7)	60	321	21	903
	Castleford	2001	2(1)	0	6	0	12
Jonathan Roper	Castleford	2001	13	7	12	0	52
	Salford	2000	1(4)	1	3	0	10
	London	2000	4	0	0	0	0
	Warrington	1996-2000	75(8)	33	71	0	274
Scott Roskell	London	1996-97	30(2)	16	0	0	64
Steve Rosolen	London	1996-98	25(9)	10	0	0	40
Adam Ross	London	1996	(1)	0	0	0	0
Cesar Rouge	Hull KR	2023	1	0	0	0	0
	Catalans	2021-23	10(2)	2	0	0	8
Paul Round	Castleford	1996	(3)	0	0	0	0
Josh Rourke	Salford	2022	1	0	0	0	0
Steve Rowlands	Widnes	2004-05	18(3)	2	15	0	38
	St Helens	2003	(1)	0	0	0	0
Paul Rowley	Leigh	2005	15(7)	3	0	0	12
	Huddersfield	2001	24	3	0	0	12
	Halifax	1996-2000	107(3)	27	1	3	113
Nigel Roy	London	2001-04	100	39	0	0	156
Nicky Royle	Widnes	2004	13	7	0	0	28
Sam Royle	St Helens	2021-23	11(9)	0	0	0	0
	Hull KR	2022	2(1)	1	0	0	4
Shad Royston	Bradford	2011	17(1)	10	0	0	40
Leon Ruan	Leeds	2023	(5)	1	0	0	4
Chris Rudd	Warrington	1996-98	31(17)	10	16	0	72
Sean Rudder	Catalans	2006	22(1)	6	0	0	24
	Castleford	2004	9(3)	2	0	0	8
Charly Runciman	Widnes	2016-18	68	9	0	0	36
Kieran Rush	Huddersfield	2023	1	0	0	0	0
James Rushforth	Halifax	1997	(4)	0	0	0	0
Harry Rushton	Huddersfield	2023	1(10)	0	0	0	0
	Wigan	2020	1	0	0	0	0
Adam Rusling	Castleford	2021	(1)	0	0	0	0
Danny Russell	Huddersfield	1998-2000	50(13)	8	0	0	32
	Oldham	1997	1(3)	1	0	0	4
Ian Russell	Paris	1996	3	0	0	0	0

Super League Players 1996-2023

PLAYER	CLUB	YEAR	APP	TRIES	GOALS	FG	PTS
Matty Russell	Warrington	2014-18, 2023	89(6)	25	0	0	100
	Toulouse	2022	21	13	0	0	52
	Leigh	2021	12(1)	4	0	0	16
	Toronto	2020	6	2	0	0	8
	Hull	2012	6	0	0	0	0
	Wigan	2012	2	3	0	0	12
Oliver Russell	Huddersfield	2018-23	73(6)	5	162	5	349
Richard Russell	Castleford	1996-98	37(4)	2	0	0	8
Robert Russell	Salford	1998-99	2(1)	0	1	0	2
Sean Rutgerson	Salford	2004-06	60(9)	4	0	0	16
Chris Ryan	London	1998-99	44(3)	17	10	0	88
Ethan Ryan	Hull KR	2020-23	35	17	0	0	68
Matt Ryan	Wakefield	2014-15	28(12)	7	0	0	28
Sean Ryan	Castleford	2004	11(5)	2	0	0	8
	Hull	2002-03	53	8	0	0	32
Justin Ryder	Wakefield	2004	19(3)	11	0	0	44
Jason Ryles	Catalans	2009	19(2)	2	0	0	8
Setaimata Sa	Widnes	2016	7(5)	3	0	0	12
	Hull	2014-15	18(6)	6	0	0	24
	Catalans	2010-12	58(5)	21	0	0	84
Teddy Sadaoui	Catalans	2006	7	0	0	0	0
Jack Sadler	Castleford	2021	1	0	0	0	0
Hugo Salabio	Wakefield	2023	(3)	0	0	0	0
	Catalans	2022	(1)	0	0	0	0
Liam Salter	Hull KR	2012-16, 2018	83(3)	17	0	0	68
Matt Salter	London	1997-99	14(34)	0	0	0	0
Jumah Sambou	St Helens	2022	1	1	0	0	4
Ben Sammut	Hull	2000	20	4	67	0	150
	Gateshead	1999	26(2)	6	17	0	58
Jarrod Sammut	Wigan	2019	6(6)	2	0	0	8
	Wakefield	2014-15	19(1)	9	52	0	140
	Bradford	2012-13	35(3)	28	47	1	207
	Crusaders	2010-11	17(16)	17	0	0	68
Dean Sampson	Castleford	1996-2003	124(28)	24	0	0	96
Paul Sampson	London	2004	1(2)	1	0	0	4
	Wakefield	2000	17	8	0	0	32
Jack Sanderson	Castleford	2020	3	1	0	0	4
Lee Sanderson	London	2004	1(5)	1	7	0	18
Chris Sandow	Warrington	2015-16	27(1)	11	26	1	97
Jason Sands	Paris	1996-97	28	0	0	0	0
Justin Sangare	Leeds	2023	(17)	1	0	0	4
	Toulouse	2022	5(18)	0	0	0	0
Ligi Sao	Hull	2020-23	64(10)	3	0	0	12
Mitchell Sargent	Castleford	2008-10	37(21)	6	0	0	24
Dan Sarginson	Salford	2020-22	25(1)	4	0	0	16
	Wigan	2014-16, 2018-19	112(2)	30	0	0	120
	London	2012-13	35(1)	10	0	0	40
	Harlequins	2011	8	5	0	0	20
Matt Sarsfield	Salford	2016	2(2)	1	0	0	4
Tevita Satae	Hull	2019-23	36(52)	14	0	0	56
Junior Sa'u	Leigh	2021	15(1)	3	0	0	12
	Salford	2014-19	115	46	0	0	184
	Wakefield	2019	3	0	0	0	0
Andre Savelio	Hull	2019-23	46(11)	15	0	0	60
	Warrington	2017	3(14)	4	0	0	16
	Castleford	2016	6(1)	1	0	0	4
	St Helens	2014-16	12(25)	2	0	0	8
Lokeni Savelio	Halifax	2000	2(11)	0	0	0	0
	Salford	1997-98	18(20)	0	0	0	0
Tom Saxton	Salford	2007	5	0	0	0	0
	Wakefield	2006	9(6)	2	0	0	8
	Hull	2005	19(8)	3	0	0	12
	Castleford	2002-04	37(12)	11	0	0	44
Jonathan Scales	Halifax	2000	1	0	0	0	0
	Bradford	1996-98	46(4)	24	0	0	96
Latrell Schaumkel	Toulouse	2022	10	4	0	0	16
Andrew Schick	Castleford	1996-98	45(13)	10	0	0	40
Clinton Schifcofske	Crusaders	2010-11	44	5	115	0	250
Brad Schneider	Hull KR	2023	10	3	35	1	83
Garry Schofield	Huddersfield	1998	(2)	0	0	0	0
Jordan Schofield	Wakefield	2023	(1)	0	0	0	0
Gary Schubert	Workington	1996	(1)	0	0	0	0
Matt Schultz	Hull	1998-99	23(9)	2	0	0	8
	Leeds	1996	2(4)	0	0	0	0
John Schuster	Halifax	1996-97	31	9	127	3	293
Bastien Scimone	Catalans	2022-23	1(2)	0	0	0	0
Cameron Scott	Hull	2018-23	50(7)	11	0	0	44
Nick Scruton	Hull KR	2018	7(10)	0	0	0	0
	Wakefield	2014-16	62(3)	9	0	0	36
	Bradford	2009-14	70(27)	5	0	0	20
	Leeds	2002, 2004-08	11(53)	3	0	0	12
	Hull	2004	2(16)	3	0	0	12
Danny Sculthorpe	Huddersfield	2009	5(8)	0	0	0	0
	Wakefield	2007-09	14(28)	1	0	0	4
	Castleford	2006	18(1)	4	0	1	17
	Wigan	2002-05	13(49)	7	0	0	28
Paul Sculthorpe	St Helens	1998-2008	223(4)	94	356	7	1095
	Warrington	1996-97	40	6	0	0	24
Mick Seaby	London	1997	3(2)	1	0	0	4
Danny Seal	Halifax	1996-99	8(17)	3	0	0	12
Matt Seers	Wakefield	2003	11(1)	2	0	0	8
James Segeyaro	Leeds	2016	3	1	0	0	4
Paul Seguier	Catalans	2016-17, 2020-23	36(34)	6	0	0	24
Anthony Seibold	London	1999-2000	33(19)	5	0	0	20
Jesse Sene-Lefao	Castleford	2017-21	72(30)	15	0	0	60
Innes Senior	Wakefield	2020-21, 2023	30	15	0	0	60
	Huddersfield	2018-19, 2022-23	53	20	0	0	80
Keith Senior	Leeds	1999-2011	319(2)	159	0	0	636
	Sheffield	1996-99	90(2)	40	0	0	160
Louis Senior	Hull KR	2023	15	7	0	0	28
	Huddersfield	2018-23	40	25	0	0	100
Fili Seru	Hull	1998-99	37(1)	13	0	0	52
Ava Seumanufagai	Leigh	2023	1(14)	1	0	0	4
	Leeds	2019-20	26(2)	3	0	0	12
Anthony Seuseu	Halifax	2003	1(11)	1	0	0	4
Jerry Seuseu	Wigan	2005-06	29(9)	1	0	0	4
Charlie Severs	Hull	2022	(2)	0	0	0	0
Brett Seymour	Hull	2012-13	26(1)	7	0	0	28
Aidan Sezer	Leeds	2022-23	35	3	4	0	20
	Huddersfield	2020-21	22(1)	9	60	2	158
Will Sharp	Hull	2011-12	27(8)	10	0	0	40
	Harlequins	2008-10	65(1)	19	0	0	76
Jamie Shaul	Hull	2013-23	180(3)	88	0	1	353
	Wakefield	2022	5	1	0	0	4
Darren Shaw	Salford	2002	5(9)	1	0	0	4
	London	1996, 2002	22(8)	3	0	0	12
	Castleford	2000-01	50(6)	1	0	0	4
	Sheffield	1998-99	51	3	0	1	13
Isaac Shaw	Hull KR	2023	(1)	0	0	0	0
	Wakefield	2022-23	(6)	0	0	0	0
Mick Shaw	Halifax	1999	5	1	0	0	4
	Leeds	1996	12(2)	7	0	0	28
Ryan Shaw	Hull KR	2016, 2018-19	44(1)	19	125	0	326
	London	2013	2	1	2	0	8
Phil Shead	Paris	1996	3(2)	0	0	0	0
Richard Sheil	St Helens	1997	(1)	0	0	0	0
Kelly Shelford	Warrington	1996-97	25(3)	4	0	2	18
Kyle Shelford	Warrington	2020	(1)	0	0	0	0
	Wigan	2016	(1)	0	0	0	0
Michael Shenton	Castleford	2004, 2006, 2008-10, 2013-21	276(2)	111	0	0	444
	St Helens	2011-12	51	15	0	0	60
Ryan Sheridan	Castleford	2004	2	0	0	0	0
	Widnes	2003	14(3)	2	0	0	8
	Leeds	1997-2002	123(7)	46	0	1	185
	Sheffield	1996	9(3)	5	0	1	21
Louis Sheriff	Hull KR	2011-12	8	3	0	0	12
Rikki Sheriffe	Bradford	2009-10	51	14	0	0	56
	Harlequins	2006-08	35(1)	16	0	0	64
	Halifax	2003	6(1)	3	0	0	12
Ian Sherratt	Oldham	1996	5(3)	1	0	0	4
Brent Sherwin	Catalans	2010	12	1	0	1	5
	Castleford	2008-10	48(1)	4	0	3	19
Peter Shiels	St Helens	2001-02	44(3)	11	0	0	44
Gary Shillabeer	Huddersfield	1999	(2)	0	0	0	0
Mark Shipway	Salford	2004-05	30(12)	3	0	0	12
Jake Shorrocks	Wigan	2016-17, 2019-20	9(19)	2	8	0	24
	Salford	2018	10	0	1	0	2
Joe Shorrocks	Wigan	2019-23	25(40)	3	0	0	12
	Leigh	2023	4	1	0	0	4
Ian Sibbit	Bradford	2011-12	11(7)	0	0	0	0
	Salford	2005-07, 2009-10	64(17)	11	0	0	44
	Warrington	1999-2001, 2003-04	63(18)	24	0	0	96
Mark Sibson	Huddersfield	1999	2	2	0	0	8
Adam Sidlow	Salford	2009-12, 2023	36(54)	14	0	0	56
	Leigh	2021	10(1)	6	0	0	24
	Toronto	2020	3(3)	0	0	0	0
	Bradford	2013-14	20(2)	8	0	0	32
Harry Siejka	Wakefield	2014	6(3)	1	0	0	4
Jordan Sigismeau	Catalans	2015-16	11	3	0	0	12

Super League Players 1996-2023

PLAYER	CLUB	YEAR	APP	TRIES	GOALS	FG	PTS
Josh Simm	St Helens	2019-22	18	7	0	0	28
	Hull	2022	5	2	0	0	8
	Leigh	2021	1	0	0	0	0
Jon Simms	St Helens	2002	(1)	0	0	0	0
Craig Simon	Hull	2000	23(2)	8	0	0	32
	Gateshead	1999	25(4)	6	0	0	24
Mickael Simon	Catalans	2010-14, 2017-20	55(76)	3	0	0	12
	Wakefield	2015-16	15(22)	3	0	0	12
Darren Simpson	Huddersfield	1998-99	17(1)	5	0	0	20
Jamie Simpson	Huddersfield	2011	8(1)	0	0	0	0
Jared Simpson	Huddersfield	2015-18	12	4	0	0	16
Max Simpson	Leeds	2022	4	0	0	0	0
Robbie Simpson	London	1999	6(7)	0	0	0	0
Ashton Sims	Warrington	2015-17	69(11)	5	0	0	20
Korbin Sims	Hull KR	2021-22	12(17)	1	0	0	4
Jack Sinfield	Leeds	2022-23	9(2)	1	0	0	4
Kevin Sinfield	Leeds	1997-2015	425(29)	70	1566	31	3443
Matt Sing	Hull	2007-08	41	14	0	0	56
Wayne Sing	Paris	1997	18(1)	2	0	0	8
Brad Singleton	Salford	2023	6	0	0	0	0
	Wigan	2020-23	51(8)	5	0	0	20
	Toronto	2020	3(1)	1	0	0	4
	Leeds	2011-19	92(61)	17	0	0	68
	Wakefield	2013	(1)	0	0	0	0
Fata Sini	Salford	1997	22	7	0	0	28
Ken Sio	Salford	2019-23	100(1)	78	13	0	338
	Hull KR	2015-16	42	23	13	0	118
Michael Sio	Wakefield	2015-17	25(14)	6	0	0	24
Curtis Sironen	St Helens	2022-23	31(5)	5	0	0	20
John Skandalis	Huddersfield	2007-08	37(5)	4	0	0	16
Dylan Skee	Harlequins	2008-09	(3)	0	0	0	0
Ben Skerrett	Castleford	2003	(1)	0	0	0	0
Kelvin Skerrett	Halifax	1997-99	31(6)	2	0	0	8
	Wigan	1996	1(8)	0	0	0	0
Troy Slattery	Wakefield	2002-03	33(5)	4	0	0	16
	Huddersfield	1999	3	1	0	0	4
Mick Slicker	Huddersfield	2001, 2003-05	17(48)	2	0	0	8
	Sheffield	1999	(3)	1	0	0	4
	Halifax	1997	2(5)	0	0	0	0
Nick Slyney	London	2014	20(4)	3	0	0	12
Ian Smales	Castleford	1996-97	10(8)	5	0	0	20
Aaron Smith	Leigh	2023	1	0	0	0	0
	St Helens	2018-21	13(24)	9	0	0	36
	Hull KR	2018	3(1)	0	0	0	0
Aaron Smith	Castleford	2006	(2)	0	0	0	0
	Bradford	2003-04	12(1)	3	0	0	12
Andy Smith	Harlequins	2007	6(3)	3	0	0	12
	Bradford	2004-06	9(9)	4	0	0	16
	Salford	2005	4	1	0	0	4
Byron Smith	Castleford	2004	(9)	0	0	0	0
	Halifax	2003	6(1)	0	0	0	0
Cameron Smith	Leeds	2016-23	65(52)	16	1	0	66
Chris Smith	Hull	2001-02	12	3	0	0	12
	St Helens	1998-2000	62(9)	26	0	0	104
	Castleford	1996-97	36(1)	12	0	0	48
Craig Smith	Wigan	2002-04	77(3)	10	0	0	40
Damien Smith	St Helens	1998	21(1)	8	0	0	32
Daniel Smith	Castleford	2019-23	29(41)	4	0	0	16
	Huddersfield	2015-18	9(38)	5	0	0	20
	Wakefield	2014-15	21(15)	6	0	0	24
Danny Smith	Paris	1996	10(2)	1	15	0	34
	London	1996	2(1)	1	0	0	4
Darren Smith	St Helens	2003	25(1)	14	0	0	56
Gary Smith	Castleford	2001	(1)	0	0	0	0
Harry Smith	Wigan	2019-23	79(14)	16	219	6	508
Harvey Smith	Wakefield	2023	(1)	0	0	0	0
Hudson Smith	Bradford	2000	8(22)	2	0	0	8
	Salford	1999	23(2)	5	0	0	20
James Smith	Salford	2000	23(3)	6	0	0	24
Jamie Smith	Hull	1998-99	24(6)	6	12	0	48
	Workington	1996	5(3)	0	1	0	2
Jason Smith	Hull	2001-04	61(3)	17	0	1	69
Jeremy Smith	Wakefield	2011	9(1)	1	0	0	4
	Salford	2009-10	27(17)	2	0	0	8
Kris Smith	London	2001	(1)	0	0	0	0
	Halifax	2001	(1)	0	0	0	0
Lee Smith	Wakefield	2012-13, 2015	30(4)	16	54	2	174
	Leeds	2005-12	125(10)	60	34	1	309
Leigh Smith	Workington	1996	9	4	0	0	16
Mark Smith	Widnes	2005	12(15)	4	0	0	16
	Wigan	1999-2004	35(77)	8	0	0	32
Martyn Smith	Harlequins	2010	(2)	0	0	0	0
Matty Smith	Warrington	2019	4(1)	0	0	0	0
	Catalans	2019	16	0	0	1	1
	St Helens	2006-08, 2010, 2017-19	38(9)	5	10	4	44
	Wigan	2012-16	122(3)	17	279	25	651
	Salford	2010-12	67(4)	13	6	1	65
	Celtic	2009	15(1)	3	2	1	17
Michael Smith	Hull KR	2007	(3)	1	0	0	4
	Castleford	1998, 2001-04	86(33)	32	0	0	128
	Hull	1999	12(6)	3	0	0	12
Morgan Smith	Wakefield	2023	11(2)	2	0	0	8
	London	2019	15(1)	1	1	2	8
	Warrington	2016-18	(18)	1	1	0	6
Paul Smith	Huddersfield	2004-06	52(17)	13	0	0	52
Paul Smith	Warrington	2001	(1)	0	0	0	0
	Castleford	1997-2000	6(37)	3	0	0	12
Paul Smith	London	1997	7(1)	2	0	0	8
Peter Smith	Oldham	1996	2	0	0	0	0
Richard Smith	Wakefield	2001	8(1)	1	0	0	4
	Salford	1997	(1)	1	0	0	4
Tim Smith	Wakefield	2012-15	79	11	0	0	44
	Salford	2014	12	2	7	0	22
	Wigan	2008-09	13(8)	2	0	0	8
Tony Smith	Hull	2001-03	43(5)	26	0	0	104
	Wigan	1997-2000	66(5)	46	0	0	184
	Castleford	1996-97	18(2)	10	0	0	40
Tony Smith	Workington	1996	9	1	0	0	4
Tyrone Smith	Harlequins	2006-07	49(3)	13	0	0	52
	London	2005	20(4)	11	0	0	44
Will Smith	Hull	2022	7	2	0	0	8
Morgan Smithies	Wigan	2019-23	76(29)	2	0	0	8
Rob Smyth	Leigh	2005	15(1)	4	0	0	16
	Warrington	2000-03	65	35	20	0	180
	London	1998-2000	32(2)	9	15	0	66
	Wigan	1996	11(5)	16	0	0	64
Marc Sneyd	Salford	2010-13, 2022-23	85(12)	11	250	9	553
	Hull	2015-21	161	19	558	33	1225
	Castleford	2014	25(1)	6	100	2	226
Steve Snitch	Castleford	2010-12	38(18)	10	0	0	40
	Wakefield	2002-05, 2009	33(55)	9	0	0	36
	Huddersfield	2006-08	24(35)	12	0	0	48
Bright Sodje	Wakefield	2000	15	4	0	0	16
	Sheffield	1996-99	54	34	0	0	136
Iosia Soliola	St Helens	2010-14	83(24)	27	0	0	108
David Solomona	Warrington	2010-12	8(49)	16	1	0	66
	Bradford	2007-09	44(9)	19	0	0	76
	Wakefield	2004-06	73(3)	26	0	0	104
Denny Solomona	Castleford	2015-16	42	58	0	0	232
	London	2014	19(1)	8	0	0	32
Alfred Songoro	Wakefield	1999	8(5)	4	0	0	16
Romain Sort	Paris	1997	(1)	0	0	0	0
Paul Southern	Salford	1997-2002	79(33)	6	13	0	50
	St Helens	2002	1(1)	0	0	0	0
Steve Southern	Wakefield	2012	7(8)	3	0	0	12
Cain Southernwood	Bradford	2010	2	0	0	0	0
Roy Southernwood	Wakefield	1999	1	0	0	0	0
	Halifax	1996	2	0	0	0	0
Jason Southwell	Huddersfield	2004	(1)	0	0	0	0
Waisale Sovatabua	Wakefield	2001-03	44(3)	19	0	0	76
	Hudds-Sheff	2000	23(1)	8	0	0	32
	Sheffield	1996-99	56(17)	19	0	1	77
Jamie Soward	London	2013	6(1)	4	21	0	58
Yusef Sozi	London	2000-01	(5)	0	0	0	0
Scott Spaven	Hull KR	2010	(2)	0	0	0	0
Andy Speak	Castleford	2001	4(4)	0	0	0	0
	Wakefield	2000	6(5)	2	0	0	8
	Leeds	1999	4	1	0	0	4
Dom Speakman	St Helens	2013	(1)	0	0	0	0
Tim Spears	Castleford	2003	(3)	0	0	0	0
Jake Spedding	St Helens	2016-18	3(1)	0	0	0	0
Ady Spencer	London	1996-99	8(36)	5	0	0	20
Jack Spencer	Salford	2009-11	(7)	0	0	0	0
Tom Spencer	Leigh	2021	(1)	0	0	0	0
	Wigan	2012-13	(7)	0	0	0	0
Daniel Spencer-Tonks	Salford	2022	(1)	0	0	0	0
Rob Spicer	Wakefield	2002-05	28(18)	4	0	0	16
Russ Spiers	Wakefield	2011	(2)	0	0	0	0
Gadwin Springer	Toulouse	2022	(5)	0	0	0	0
	Toronto	2020	4(1)	0	0	0	0
	Castleford	2015-18	15(41)	3	0	0	12
	Catalans	2014-15	1	1	0	0	4

219

Super League Players 1996-2023

PLAYER	CLUB	YEAR	APP	TRIES	GOALS	FG	PTS
Stuart Spruce	Widnes	2002-03	45(4)	19	0	0	76
	Bradford	1996-2001	107(2)	57	0	0	228
Lee St Hilaire	Castleford	1997	4(2)	0	0	0	0
Marcus St Hilaire	Bradford	2006-07	34(1)	12	0	0	48
	Huddersfield	2003-05	72(2)	30	0	0	120
	Leeds	1996-2002	59(33)	31	0	0	124
Cyril Stacul	Catalans	2007-12	61(1)	18	0	0	72
Dylan Stainton	Workington	1996	2(3)	0	0	0	0
Mark Stamper	Workington	1996	(1)	0	0	0	0
John Stankevitch	Widnes	2005	17(5)	0	0	0	0
	St Helens	2000-04	74(40)	25	0	0	100
Gareth Stanley	Bradford	2000	1	1	0	0	4
Craig Stapleton	Salford	2009	24	2	0	0	8
	Leigh	2005	27(1)	4	0	0	16
Nick Staveley	Hull	2023	(2)	0	0	0	0
Graham Steadman	Castleford	1996-97	11(17)	5	0	0	20
Jon Steel	Hull KR	2007-08	18	6	0	0	24
Maxime Stefani	Toulouse	2022	13	2	0	0	8
Jamie Stenhouse	Warrington	2000-01	9(3)	3	0	0	12
Gareth Stephens	Sheffield	1997-99	23(6)	2	0	0	8
David Stephenson	Hull	1998	11(7)	3	0	0	12
	Oldham	1997	10(8)	2	0	0	8
Francis Stephenson	London	2002-05	42(34)	5	0	0	20
	Wigan	2001	2(9)	0	0	0	0
	Wakefield	1999-2000	50(1)	6	0	0	24
Paul Sterling	Leeds	1997-2000	79(12)	50	0	0	200
Jack Stevens	Salford	2022	(1)	0	0	0	0
Paul Stevens	Oldham	1996	2(1)	0	0	0	0
	London	1996	(1)	0	0	0	0
Robson Stevens	Huddersfield	2021	(2)	0	0	0	0
Warren Stevens	Leigh	2005	4(14)	1	0	0	4
	Warrington	1996-99, 2002-05	17(66)	1	0	0	4
	Salford	2001	(8)	0	0	0	0
Anthony Stewart	Harlequins	2006	4	0	0	0	0
	Salford	2004-06	51(2)	15	0	0	60
	St Helens	1997-2003	93(23)	44	0	0	176
Glenn Stewart	Leigh	2017	15	0	0	0	0
	Catalans	2016	28	3	0	0	12
Sam Stone	Salford	2023	22(1)	6	0	0	24
	Leigh	2021	5	2	0	0	8
Troy Stone	Widnes	2002	18(6)	1	0	0	4
	Huddersfield	2001	12(1)	1	0	0	4
Matty Storton	Hull KR	2020-23	31(41)	7	0	0	28
James Stosic	Wakefield	2009	8(10)	1	0	0	4
Lynton Stott	Wakefield	1999	21	4	6	1	29
	Sheffield	1996-98	40(4)	15	0	0	60
Mitchell Stringer	Salford	2005-06	12(4)	0	0	0	0
	London	2004-05	10(19)	0	0	0	0
Graham Strutton	London	1996	9(1)	2	0	0	8
Matt Sturm	Leigh	2005	8(19)	3	0	0	12
	Warrington	2002-04	1(18)	0	0	0	0
	Huddersfield	1998-99	46	8	0	0	32
Sauaso Sue	Hull KR	2023	6(9)	1	0	0	4
Anthony Sullivan	St Helens	1996-2001	137(5)	105	0	0	420
Michael Sullivan	Warrington	2006-07	21(16)	8	1	0	34
Phil Sumner	Warrington	1996	(5)	0	0	0	0
Alex Sutcliffe	Castleford	2022-23	16(5)	2	0	0	8
	Leeds	2017, 2019-21	10(5)	2	0	0	8
Liam Sutcliffe	Hull	2023	19	6	10	0	44
	Leeds	2013-22	160(32)	62	168	3	587
	Bradford	2014	3(1)	1	0	0	4
Alex Sutton	Wigan	2022	1	0	0	0	0
Ryan Sutton	Wigan	2014-18	38(65)	10	0	0	40
Simon Svabic	Salford	1998-2000	13(5)	3	19	0	50
Luke Swain	Salford	2009-10	54	3	0	0	12
Richard Swain	Hull	2004-07	89	5	0	0	20
Anthony Swann	Warrington	2001	3	1	0	0	4
Logan Swann	Warrington	2005-06	49(1)	17	0	0	68
	Bradford	2004	25	6	0	0	24
Willie Swann	Warrington	1996-97	25(2)	6	0	0	24
Jake Sweeting	Castleford	2021	(1)	1	0	0	4
Adam Swift	Hull	2020-23	58	42	0	0	168
	St Helens	2012-19	120	80	0	0	320
Nathan Sykes	Castleford	1996-2004	158(52)	3	0	0	12
Paul Sykes	Wakefield	2012-14	59(1)	12	135	6	324
	Bradford	1999-2002, 2008-12	99(4)	35	64	2	270
	Harlequins	2006-07	31(2)	15	47	1	155
	London	2001-05	95(1)	26	219	3	545
Wayne Sykes	London	1999	(2)	0	0	0	0
Tom Symonds	Huddersfield	2016-18	6(1)	3	0	0	12
Ukuma Ta'ai	Huddersfield	2013-20	118(63)	43	0	0	172
Semi Tadulala	Wakefield	2004-07, 2011	92	37	0	0	148
	Bradford	2008-09	49	30	0	0	120
Whetu Taewa	Sheffield	1997-98	33(7)	8	0	0	32
Zeb Taia	St Helens	2017-20	96(3)	22	0	0	88
	Catalans	2013-15	75	35	0	0	140
Alan Tait	Leeds	1996	3(3)	1	0	0	4
Brad Takairangi	Hull KR	2021-22	24	4	0	0	16
Fetuli Talanoa	Hull	2014-18	115(1)	54	0	0	216
Willie Talau	Salford	2009-10	22	4	0	0	16
	St Helens	2003-08	130(1)	50	0	0	200
Ian Talbot	Wakefield	1999	9(5)	2	31	0	70
	Wigan	1997	3	1	0	0	4
Albert Talipeau	Wakefield	2004	2(3)	0	0	0	0
Gael Tallec	Halifax	2000	5(19)	3	0	0	12
	Castleford	1998-99	19(21)	3	0	0	12
	Wigan	1996-97	8(12)	3	0	0	12
Joe Tamani	Bradford	1996	11(3)	4	0	0	16
Ryan Tandy	Hull KR	2007	8(4)	2	0	0	8
Adam Tangata	Wakefield	2019-21	2(15)	1	0	0	4
Andrew Tangata-Toa	Huddersfield	1999	15	2	0	0	8
David Tangata-Toa	Celtic	2009	1(18)	4	0	0	16
	Hull KR	2007	(17)	3	0	0	12
Kelepi Tanginoa	Wakefield	2019-23	64(18)	21	0	0	84
Jordan Tansey	Huddersfield	2016	2	1	1	0	6
	Wakefield	2015	4	1	0	0	4
	Castleford	2013-15	44(1)	15	0	0	60
	Crusaders	2011	14(4)	5	0	0	20
	Hull	2009-10	30	9	0	0	36
	Leeds	2006-08	18(32)	19	3	0	82
Lama Tasi	Warrington	2019	9(8)	0	0	0	0
	Salford	2014-15, 2017-18	55(26)	4	0	0	16
	St Helens	2016	9(8)	0	0	0	0
Charbel Tasipale	Castleford	2023	4	1	0	0	4
Kris Tassell	Wakefield	2002	24	10	0	0	40
	Salford	2000-01	35(10)	12	0	0	48
Will Tate	Castleford	2023	5(1)	2	0	0	8
	Hull KR	2020-22	11(5)	4	0	0	16
Shem Tatupu	Wigan	1996	(3)	0	0	0	0
Tony Tatupu	Wakefield	2000-01	20	2	0	0	8
	Warrington	1997	21(1)	6	0	0	24
Jorge Taufua	Wakefield	2022-23	13	1	0	0	4
Sio Siua Taukeiaho	Catalans	2023	3(6)	1	0	0	4
Taulima Tautai	Wigan	2015-19	7(111)	4	0	0	16
	Wakefield	2013-14	6(19)	2	0	0	8
Dave Taylor	Catalans	2016	20(4)	8	0	0	32
Elijah Taylor	Salford	2021-22	34(5)	1	0	0	4
James Taylor	Leigh	2005	(4)	0	0	0	0
Joe Taylor	Paris	1997	9(5)	2	0	0	8
Lawrence Taylor	Sheffield	1996	(1)	0	0	0	0
Scott Taylor	Hull	2016-23	134(31)	20	1	0	82
	Salford	2015	23	5	0	0	20
	Wigan	2013-14	18(29)	6	0	0	24
	Hull KR	2009-12	21(29)	8	0	0	32
Frederic Teixido	Sheffield	1999	(4)	0	0	0	0
	Paris	1996-97	2(3)	1	0	0	4
Lionel Teixido	Catalans	2006-07	11(13)	3	0	0	12
Karl Temata	London	2005, 2012	1(8)	1	0	0	4
	Harlequins	2006-11	94(22)	7	0	0	28
Jason Temu	Hull	1998	13(2)	1	0	0	4
	Oldham	1996-97	25(3)	1	0	0	4
Leo Tennison	Hull KR	2023	(1)	0	0	0	0
Paul Terry	London	1997	(1)	0	0	0	0
Zane Tetevano	Leeds	2021-23	40(6)	3	0	0	12
Anthony Thackeray	Castleford	2008	3(6)	0	0	0	0
	Hull	2007	2	0	0	0	0
Jamie Thackray	Crusaders	2010	1(16)	2	0	0	8
	Hull	2005-06, 2008-09	37(45)	6	0	0	24
	Leeds	2006-07	5(27)	7	0	0	28
	Castleford	2003-04	7(11)	3	0	0	12
	Halifax	2000-02	10(38)	3	0	0	12
Adam Thaler	Castleford	2002	(1)	0	0	0	0
Josh Thewlis	Warrington	2019-23	55(3)	22	2	0	92
Gareth Thomas	Crusaders	2010-11	27(1)	6	0	0	24
Giles Thomas	London	1997-99	1(2)	0	0	0	0
Luke Thomas	Hull KR	2023	(1)	0	0	0	0
	Warrington	2022-23	(6)	1	0	0	4
Oscar Thomas	London	2014	4(2)	0	1	0	2
Rob Thomas	Harlequins	2011	(2)	0	0	0	0
Steve Thomas	London	2004	4(2)	0	0	0	0
	Warrington	2001	2	0	0	0	0
Alex Thompson	Warrington	2009	(1)	1	0	0	4
Alex Thompson	Sheffield	1997	4(11)	0	0	0	0
Bobby Thompson	Salford	1999	28	5	2	0	24

Super League Players 1996-2023

PLAYER	CLUB	YEAR	APP	TRIES	GOALS	FG	PTS
Bodene Thompson	Leeds	2020-22	31(17)	4	0	0	16
	Toronto	2020	4(1)	1	0	0	4
	Warrington	2018	7	0	0	0	0
Corey Thompson	Widnes	2016-17	48	36	9	0	162
David Thompson	Leigh	2017	1	0	0	0	0
	Hull KR	2016	1	0	0	0	0
Joel Thompson	St Helens	2021	13(2)	1	0	0	4
Jordan Thompson	Leigh	2021	13(5)	1	0	0	4
	Hull	2014-17, 2019	27(81)	12	0	0	48
	Leeds	2018	1	0	0	0	0
	Castleford	2009-13	47(24)	25	0	0	100
Luke Thompson	St Helens	2013-20	100(54)	28	0	0	112
Sam Thompson	Harlequins	2009	(2)	0	0	0	0
	St Helens	2008	(5)	0	0	0	0
Chris Thorman	Hull	2009	19(2)	1	0	0	4
	Huddersfield	2000-01, 2005-08	126(20)	51	320	3	847
	London	2003	26(1)	7	81	1	191
	Sheffield	1999	5(13)	2	8	1	25
Tony Thorniley	Warrington	1997	(5)	0	0	0	0
Andy Thornley	Salford	2009	(1)	1	0	0	4
Iain Thornley	Wigan	2012-14, 2022-23	50	30	0	0	120
	Leigh	2021	19	3	0	0	12
	Catalans	2017-18	31(1)	7	0	0	28
	Hull KR	2016	21	10	0	0	40
Danny Tickle	Hull KR	2018	14(3)	4	20	0	56
	Leigh	2017	10(13)	4	0	0	16
	Castleford	2016	6(3)	0	1	0	2
	Widnes	2014-15	33(1)	3	88	0	188
	Hull	2007-13	159(5)	45	528	1	1237
	Wigan	2002-06	94(36)	34	200	2	538
	Halifax	2000-02	25(17)	10	91	2	224
Kris Tickle	Warrington	2001	(1)	0	0	0	0
Lewis Tierney	Leigh	2021	8	2	0	0	8
	Catalans	2017-20	52	15	0	0	60
	Wigan	2013-17	35	17	0	0	68
James Tilley	St Helens	2013-14	(3)	0	0	0	0
Dane Tilse	Hull KR	2015-16	29(1)	1	0	0	4
John Timu	London	1998-2000	57(3)	11	0	0	44
Liam Tindall	Leeds	2020-23	16(5)	2	0	0	8
Ugo Tison	Catalans	2022-23	1(2)	0	0	0	0
Kerrod Toby	Hull	1997	2(2)	0	0	0	0
Tulsen Tollett	London	1996-2001	105(5)	38	49	1	251
Joel Tomkins	Catalans	2020-21	17(6)	5	0	0	20
	Hull KR	2018-19	27	7	0	0	28
	Wigan	2005-11, 2014-18	161(51)	60	0	0	240
Logan Tomkins	Salford	2014-19	85(31)	6	0	0	24
	Wigan	2012-15	9(32)	1	0	0	4
Sam Tomkins	Catalans	2019-23	93(3)	32	135	5	403
	Wigan	2009-13, 2016-18	177(6)	129	125	7	773
Glen Tomlinson	Wakefield	1999-2000	41(5)	8	0	0	32
	Hull	1998	5	1	0	0	4
	Bradford	1996-97	27(13)	12	0	0	48
Willie Tonga	Leigh	2017	3	0	0	0	0
	Catalans	2015	18	6	0	0	24
Ryan Tongia	Wakefield	2011	4	2	0	0	8
Ian Tonks	Castleford	1996-2001	32(50)	11	13	0	70
Tony Tonks	Huddersfield	2012	(1)	0	0	0	0
Motu Tony	Wakefield	2011-12	7(3)	1	0	0	4
	Hull	2005-09	76(20)	25	0	0	100
	Castleford	2004	8(1)	1	0	0	4
Mark Tookey	Harlequins	2006	12(14)	1	0	0	4
	London	2005	13(14)	5	0	0	20
	Castleford	2004	2(8)	1	0	0	4
Clinton Toopi	Leeds	2006-08	40(3)	9	0	0	36
David Tootill	Harlequins	2008	(4)	0	0	0	0
Paul Topping	Oldham	1996-97	23(10)	1	19	0	42
Patrick Torreilles	Paris	1996	9(1)	1	25	0	54
Albert Torrens	Huddersfield	2006	7	5	0	0	20
Mat Toshack	London	1998-2004	120(21)	24	0	0	96
Julien Touxagas	Catalans	2006-11	14(45)	4	0	0	16
Darren Treacy	Salford	2002	24(1)	6	1	0	26
Dean Treister	Hull	2003	16(1)	3	0	0	12
Rocky Trimarchi	Crusaders	2010	16(8)	0	0	0	0
Steve Trindall	London	2003-05	40(20)	3	0	0	12
Shane Tronc	Wakefield	2010	8(3)	2	0	0	8
Kyle Trout	Hull KR	2019-20	1(14)	0	0	0	0
	Wakefield	2012-15	6(17)	3	0	0	12
Owen Trout	Huddersfield	2020-23	27(23)	9	0	0	36
	Leeds	2019	1(1)	0	0	0	0
George Truelove	Wakefield	2002	2	1	0	0	4
	London	2000	5	1	0	0	4
Jake Trueman	Hull	2023	12(1)	2	0	0	8
	Castleford	2017-22	93(2)	28	0	1	113
Billy Tsikrikas	Castleford	2023	(4)	0	0	0	0
Va'aiga Tuigamala	Wigan	1996	21	10	3	0	46
Fereti Tuilagi	St Helens	1999-2000	43(15)	21	0	0	84
	Halifax	1996-98	55(3)	27	0	0	108
Carlos Tuimavave	Hull	2016-23	144(6)	48	0	0	192
Evarn Tuimavave	Hull KR	2013	11(12)	2	0	0	8
Sateki Tuipulotu	Leeds	1996	6(3)	1	2	0	8
Anthony Tupou	Wakefield	2016	12(9)	4	0	0	16
Bill Tupou	Wakefield	2015-21	109(3)	38	0	0	152
Tame Tupou	Bradford	2007-08	10(7)	8	0	0	32
Jansin Turgut	Salford	2019	8(2)	1	0	0	4
	Hull	2015-18	10(18)	3	0	0	12
Neil Turley	Leigh	2005	6(3)	2	20	1	49
Calum Turner	Castleford	2018-20	7(6)	4	10	0	36
Darren Turner	Huddersfield	2000-01, 2003-04	42(13)	13	0	0	52
	Sheffield	1996-99	41(19)	15	0	0	60
Ian Turner	Paris	1996	1(1)	1	0	0	4
Jordan Turner	Castleford	2021-23	39(4)	17	0	1	69
	Huddersfield	2017-20	66(2)	10	0	1	41
	St Helens	2013-16	106(4)	44	13	3	205
	Hull	2010-12	62(5)	28	0	0	112
	Salford	2006-07, 2009	22(10)	4	1	0	18
Chris Tuson	Hull	2014	10(1)	0	0	0	0
	Wigan	2008, 2010-13	24(49)	13	0	0	52
	Castleford	2010	3(5)	0	0	0	0
Gregory Tutard	Paris	1996	1(1)	0	0	0	0
Brendon Tuuta	Warrington	1998	18(2)	4	0	0	16
	Castleford	1996-97	41(1)	3	0	0	12
Steve Tyrer	Salford	2010	20	6	9	0	42
	Celtic	2009	8	2	5	0	18
	St Helens	2006-08	17(3)	12	42	0	132
Bobby Tyson-Wilson	Hull	2015	(1)	0	0	0	0
Harry Tyson-Wilson	Hull	2014	(1)	0	0	0	0
Akuila Uate	Huddersfield	2019	12	5	0	0	20
Wayne Ulugia	Hull KR	2014	3	1	0	0	4
Mike Umaga	Halifax	1996-98	38(1)	16	5	0	74
Kava Utoikamanu	Paris	1996	6(3)	0	0	0	0
Frederic Vaccari	Catalans	2010-11, 2013-14	50	26	0	0	104
David Vaealiki	Wigan	2005-07	67(1)	17	0	0	68
Joe Vagana	Bradford	2001-08	176(44)	17	0	0	68
Nigel Vagana	Warrington	1997	20	17	0	0	68
Tevita Vaikona	Bradford	1998-2004	145(2)	89	0	0	356
Lesley Vainikolo	Bradford	2002-07	132(4)	136	1	0	546
Junior Vaivai	Toulouse	2022	5	2	0	0	8
	Hull KR	2018-19	22(1)	8	0	0	32
Eric Van Brussell	Paris	1996	2	0	0	0	0
Jace Van Dijk	Celtic	2009	19	1	1	0	6
Richard Varkulis	Warrington	2004	4(1)	3	0	0	12
Marcus Vassilakopoulos	Sheffield	1997-99	15(11)	3	10	2	34
	Leeds	1996-97	1(3)	0	0	0	0
Manu Vatuvei	Salford	2017	7	5	0	0	20
Paul Vaughan	Warrington	2023	25	6	0	0	24
Atelea Vea	Leigh	2017	19(1)	5	0	0	20
	St Helens	2015-16	19(17)	10	0	0	40
	London	2014	19(3)	2	0	0	8
Josh Veivers	Salford	2012	5	2	0	0	8
	Wakefield	2011	10(2)	2	22	0	52
Phil Veivers	Huddersfield	1998	7(6)	1	0	0	4
	St Helens	1996	(1)	1	0	0	4
Michael Vella	Hull KR	2007-11	111(5)	13	0	0	52
Bruno Verges	Catalans	2006	25	6	0	0	24
Eric Vergniol	Paris	1996	14(1)	6	0	0	24
Albert Vete	Castleford	2023	3(3)	0	0	0	0
	Hull KR	2021-22	11(20)	7	0	0	28
Gray Viane	Salford	2007	9	2	0	0	8
	Castleford	2006	20(7)	14	0	0	56
	Widnes	2005	20	13	0	0	52
	St Helens	2004	4	1	0	0	4
Joe Vickery	Leeds	2013	9	1	0	0	4
Daniel Vidot	Salford	2016	5(1)	5	0	0	20
Adrian Vowles	Castleford	1997-2001, 2003	125(1)	29	1	1	119
	Wakefield	2002-03	24(3)	6	1	0	26
	Leeds	2002	14(2)	2	0	0	8
Mitieli Vulikijapani	Hull	2021-23	17(5)	7	0	0	28
King Vuniyayawa	Salford	2022-23	24(17)	4	0	0	16
	Leeds	2021	3(12)	1	0	0	4

Super League Players 1996-2023

PLAYER	CLUB	YEAR	APP	TRIES	GOALS	FG	PTS
Michael Wainwright	Castleford	2008-10	70	22	0	0	88
	Wakefield	2004-05	21(10)	8	0	0	32
Mike Wainwright	Salford	2000-02, 2007	75(3)	9	0	0	36
	Warrington	1996-99, 2003-07	168(14)	23	0	0	92
Shannon Wakeman	Huddersfield	2017-18	16(13)	3	0	0	12
Adam Walker	Salford	2019	9(14)	4	0	0	16
	Wakefield	2017	5(1)	0	0	0	0
	St Helens	2017	(9)	1	0	0	4
	Hull KR	2013-16	60(27)	6	0	0	24
	Huddersfield	2010-12	1(5)	0	0	0	0
Alex Walker	Wakefield	2020-21	8	1	0	0	4
	London	2014, 2019	28	6	0	0	24
Anthony Walker	Wakefield	2015-17	1(11)	1	0	0	4
	St Helens	2013-14	9(7)	2	0	0	8
Ben Walker	Leeds	2002	23(1)	8	100	0	232
Brad Walker	Wakefield	2020-22	17(8)	0	3	0	6
	Widnes	2016-18	3(5)	0	0	0	0
Chev Walker	Bradford	2011-14	44(22)	5	0	0	20
	Hull KR	2008-09	24(7)	5	0	0	20
	Leeds	1999-2006	142(19)	77	0	0	308
Chris Walker	Catalans	2010	11	6	2	0	28
Danny Walker	Warrington	2019-23	38(52)	11	0	0	44
	Widnes	2017-18	3(16)	2	0	0	8
Jack Walker	Hull KR	2023	10	5	0	0	20
	Hull	2022	6	2	0	0	8
	Leeds	2017-20, 2022	60(4)	18	0	0	72
Jonathan Walker	Hull KR	2014	2(6)	0	0	0	0
	Castleford	2010-13	17(31)	4	0	0	16
Jonny Walker	Wigan	2010	(1)	0	0	0	0
Marcus Walker	Hull	2021	1	0	0	0	0
Matt Walker	Huddersfield	2001	3(6)	0	0	0	0
Anthony Wall	Paris	1997	9	3	3	0	18
Blake Wallace	Leigh	2021	2	0	0	0	0
	Toronto	2020	5(1)	0	7	0	14
Jon Wallace	London	2014	4(12)	0	0	0	0
Mark Wallace	Workington	1996	14(1)	3	0	0	12
Elliot Wallis	Castleford	2023	13	4	0	0	16
	Hull KR	2018	4	2	0	0	8
Alex Walmsley	St Helens	2013-23	168(77)	48	0	0	192
Adam Walne	Huddersfield	2018-20	4(9)	0	0	0	0
	Salford	2012-17	15(50)	2	0	0	8
Jordan Walne	Hull KR	2018	(6)	0	0	0	0
	Salford	2013-17	20(32)	3	0	0	12
Joe Walsh	Huddersfield	2009	1(1)	1	0	0	4
	Harlequins	2007-08	1(4)	0	0	0	0
Liam Walsh	Widnes	2017	(1)	0	0	0	0
Luke Walsh	Catalans	2017-18	23	2	71	4	154
	St Helens	2014-16	56(2)	14	188	9	441
Lucas Walshaw	Wakefield	2011-14	15(6)	3	0	0	12
Josh Walters	Leeds	2014-18	15(36)	9	0	0	36
Kerrod Walters	Gateshead	1999	10(12)	2	1	0	10
Kevin Walters	Warrington	2001	1	0	0	0	0
Sam Walters	Leeds	2020-23	24(17)	9	0	0	36
Jason Walton	Wakefield	2016	7(8)	0	0	0	0
	Salford	2009, 2014-15	7(19)	1	0	0	4
Barry Ward	St Helens	2002-03	20(30)	4	0	0	16
Danny Ward	Harlequins	2008-11	89(7)	4	0	0	16
	Hull KR	2007	11(9)	0	0	0	0
	Castleford	2006	18(7)	2	0	0	8
	Leeds	1999-2005	70(48)	9	0	1	37
Robbie Ward	Leeds	2014-15	5(3)	1	0	0	4
Stevie Ward	Leeds	2012-20	86(29)	19	0	0	76
Joe Wardill	Hull KR	2016, 2018	6(2)	1	0	0	4
Jake Wardle	Wigan	2023	28	15	0	0	60
	Warrington	2022	11	6	0	0	24
	Huddersfield	2018-22	62	22	6	0	100
Joe Wardle	Leigh	2023	5(6)	1	0	0	4
	Huddersfield	2011-16, 2019-21	152(1)	65	0	0	260
	Castleford	2018	15(2)	1	0	0	4
	Bradford	2010	1(1)	0	0	0	0
Phil Waring	Salford	1997-99	6(8)	2	0	0	8
Brett Warton	London	1999-2001	49(7)	14	133	0	322
Kyle Warren	Castleford	2002	13(14)	3	0	0	12
Danny Washbrook	Hull	2005-11, 2016-19	136(71)	19	0	0	76
	Wakefield	2012-15	93(8)	12	0	0	48
Adam Watene	Wakefield	2006-08	45(8)	5	0	0	20
	Bradford	2006	(4)	0	0	0	0
Frank Watene	Wakefield	1999-2001	24(37)	6	0	0	24
Trent Waterhouse	Warrington	2012-14	65(5)	15	0	0	60
Luke Waterworth	Wigan	2016	1	0	0	0	0
Kallum Watkins	Salford	2020-23	54(1)	18	0	0	72
	Leeds	2008-19	215(7)	110	85	0	610
Dave Watson	Sheffield	1998-99	41(4)	4	0	0	16
Ian Watson	Salford	1997, 2002	24(17)	8	3	5	43
	Workington	1996	4(1)	1	15	0	34
Kris Watson	Warrington	1996	11(2)	2	0	0	8
Anthony Watts	Widnes	2012	(1)	0	0	0	0
Brad Watts	Widnes	2005	6	3	0	0	12
Liam Watts	Castleford	2018-23	86(29)	9	0	0	36
	Hull	2012-18	116(19)	9	0	0	36
	Hull KR	2008, 2010-12	31(26)	6	0	0	24
Michael Watts	Warrington	2002	3	0	0	0	0
Brent Webb	Catalans	2013-14	10	2	0	0	8
	Leeds	2007-12	137(1)	73	0	0	292
Jason Webber	Salford	2000	25(1)	10	0	0	40
Ian Webster	St Helens	2006	1	0	0	0	0
Jake Webster	Castleford	2013-18	103(12)	45	0	0	180
	Hull KR	2008-12	95(1)	34	7	0	150
James Webster	Hull	2008	1	0	0	0	0
	Hull KR	2007-08	36	2	0	2	10
Pat Weisner	Hull KR	2007	(2)	0	0	0	0
	Harlequins	2006	10(6)	3	0	0	12
Taylor Welch	Warrington	2008	1	0	0	0	0
Kris Welham	Salford	2017-20	85(1)	27	0	0	108
	Hull KR	2007-15	164(2)	90	1	0	362
Paul Wellens	St Helens	1998-2015	399(40)	199	34	1	865
Calvin Wellington	St Helens	2016	1	0	0	0	0
Jack Wells	Salford	2021-22	6(6)	1	0	0	4
	Wigan	2016-17, 2020	5(12)	1	0	0	4
	Toronto	2020	(2)	1	0	0	4
Jon Wells	Harlequins	2006-09	66	10	0	0	40
	London	2004-05	42(2)	19	0	0	76
	Wakefield	2003	22(1)	1	0	0	4
	Castleford	1996-2002	114(14)	49	0	0	196
Jack Welsby	St Helens	2018-23	95(9)	49	0	3	199
Dwayne West	St Helens	2000-02	8(16)	6	0	0	24
	Wigan	1999	1(1)	0	0	0	0
Joe Westerman	Castleford	2008-10, 2022-23	117(7)	31	151	0	426
	Wakefield	2020-21	31	6	0	0	24
	Hull	2011-15, 2018-19	135(13)	36	52	1	249
	Warrington	2016-17	45(1)	12	0	0	48
Craig Weston	Widnes	2002, 2004	23(9)	2	1	2	12
	Huddersfield	1998-99	46(1)	15	15	0	90
Dayne Weston	Leigh	2017	6(5)	1	0	0	4
Ben Westwood	Warrington	2002-19	363(29)	112	64	0	576
	Wakefield	1999-2002	31(7)	8	1	0	34
Michael Weyman	Hull KR	2014	22(1)	7	0	0	28
Andrew Whalley	Workington	1996	(2)	0	0	0	0
Dean Whare	Catalans	2021-22	36	6	0	0	24
Paul Whatuira	Huddersfield	2008-10	59	23	0	0	92
Scott Wheeldon	Castleford	2014-15	14(23)	5	0	0	20
	London	2012-13	27(4)	3	0	0	12
	Hull KR	2009-12	30(42)	4	0	0	16
	Hull	2006-09	2(60)	4	0	0	16
Gary Wheeler	Toronto	2020	(2)	2	0	0	8
	Warrington	2015-16	6(4)	4	0	0	16
	St Helens	2008-14	48(17)	17	13	0	94
Matt Whitaker	Castleford	2006	8(2)	0	0	0	0
	Widnes	2004-05	10(20)	9	0	0	36
	Huddersfield	2003-04	3(14)	1	0	0	4
Jai Whitbread	Wakefield	2022-23	29(8)	4	0	0	16
	Leigh	2021	2(2)	1	0	0	4
Ben White	Leeds	2014	1	0	0	0	0
David White	Wakefield	2000	(1)	0	0	0	0
Josh White	Salford	1998	18(3)	5	5	1	31
	London	1997	14(2)	8	0	1	33
Lloyd White	Toulouse	2022	5	0	0	0	0
	Widnes	2012-18	72(43)	27	24	1	157
	Crusaders	2010-11	13(11)	8	0	0	32
	Celtic	2009	6	1	0	0	4
Paul White	Salford	2009	1	1	0	0	4
	Wakefield	2006-07	24(12)	12	0	0	48
	Huddersfield	2003-05	11(32)	17	16	0	100
Elliott Whitehead	Catalans	2013-15	64(1)	30	0	0	120
	Bradford	2009-13	90(10)	30	0	0	120
Tom Whitehead	Warrington	2022-23	1(2)	0	0	0	0
Harvey Whiteley	Leeds	2017, 2020	(3)	0	0	0	0
Richard Whiting	Hull	2004-15	163(72)	69	19	2	316
Matt Whitley	Catalans	2019-23	93(4)	31	0	0	124
	Widnes	2015-18	50(27)	13	0	0	52
Emmerson Whittel	Bradford	2014	(1)	0	0	0	0

Super League Players 1996-2023

PLAYER	CLUB	YEAR	APP	TRIES	GOALS	FG	PTS
Danny Whittle	Warrington	1998	(2)	0	0	0	0
David Whittle	St Helens	2002	1(2)	0	0	0	0
	Warrington	2001	1(2)	0	0	0	0
Jon Whittle	Wakefield	2006	8(2)	3	0	0	12
	Widnes	2005	13	2	0	0	8
	Wigan	2003	1	0	0	0	0
Joel Wicks	London	2013-14	3(10)	0	0	0	0
Dean Widders	Castleford	2009-11	25(32)	23	0	0	92
Gareth Widdop	Castleford	2023	21	1	37	1	79
	Warrington	2020-22	45	20	36	1	153
Stephen Wild	Salford	2011-13	71	4	0	0	16
	Huddersfield	2006-10	116(2)	33	0	0	132
	Wigan	2001-05	67(20)	24	0	0	96
Nathan Wilde	Leigh	2023	(8)	0	0	0	0
Sam Wilde	Widnes	2017-18	14(7)	2	0	0	8
	Warrington	2015-17	3(15)	1	0	0	4
Matty Wildie	Leigh	2021	2(9)	0	0	0	0
	Wakefield	2010-14	13(26)	3	0	0	12
Brayden Wiliame	Catalans	2017-19	64	25	0	0	100
Oliver Wilkes	Wakefield	2008-09, 2012-13	55(47)	10	0	0	40
	Harlequins	2010-11	39(13)	4	0	0	16
	Wigan	2006	1(5)	0	0	0	0
	Leigh	2005	13(1)	1	0	0	4
	Huddersfield	2000-01	1(6)	0	0	0	0
	Sheffield	1998	(1)	0	0	0	0
Jon Wilkin	Toronto	2020	5	1	0	0	4
	St Helens	2003-18	350(30)	78	0	2	314
Alex Wilkinson	Hull	2003-04	11(4)	1	0	0	4
	Huddersfield	2003	8	4	0	0	16
	London	2002	5(1)	0	0	0	0
	Bradford	2000-01	3(3)	1	0	0	4
Bart Williams	London	1998	5(3)	1	0	0	4
Connor Williams	Salford	2016	(1)	0	0	0	0
Daley Williams	Salford	2006-07	9(2)	4	0	0	16
Danny Williams	Harlequins	2006	9(13)	4	0	0	16
	London	2005	1(16)	0	0	0	0
Danny Williams	Bradford	2014	7	2	0	0	8
	Salford	2011-14	54	31	0	0	124
	Leeds	2006, 2008	13(2)	7	0	0	28
	Hull	2008	3	0	0	0	0
Dave Williams	Harlequins	2008-11	1(17)	1	0	0	4
Desi Williams	Wigan	2004	2	0	0	0	0
George Williams	Warrington	2021-23	53	22	0	4	92
	Wigan	2013-19	149(13)	55	56	1	333
Jonny Williams	London	2004	(4)	0	0	0	0
Lee Williams	Crusaders	2011	1(7)	0	0	0	0
Rhys Williams	Salford	2013, 2020-23	55	18	0	0	72
	London	2019	29	13	0	0	52
	Warrington	2010-13	23(1)	15	0	0	60
	Castleford	2012	8	4	0	0	16
	Crusaders	2011	6	3	0	0	12
Sam Williams	Wakefield	2017	17(5)	4	26	0	68
	Catalans	2014	11(1)	4	21	0	58
Sonny Bill Williams	Toronto	2020	4(1)	0	0	0	0
Luke Williamson	Harlequins	2009-10	39	6	0	0	24
Aaron Willis	Castleford	2023	(1)	0	0	0	0
John Wilshere	Salford	2006-07, 2009	72(2)	32	142	0	412
	Leigh	2005	26	8	6	0	44
	Warrington	2004	5	2	0	0	8
Craig Wilson	Hull	2000	2(16)	1	0	1	5
	Gateshead	1999	17(11)	5	0	1	21
George Wilson	Paris	1996	7(2)	3	0	0	12
John Wilson	Catalans	2006-08	69	23	0	0	92
Oliver Wilson	Huddersfield	2019-23	38(30)	0	0	0	0
Richard Wilson	Hull	1998-99	(13)	0	0	0	0
Scott Wilson	Warrington	1998-99	23(2)	6	0	0	24
Johan Windley	Hull	1999	2(2)	1	0	0	4
Jake Wingfield	St Helens	2020-23	7(28)	0	0	0	0
Paul Wingfield	Warrington	1997	5(3)	6	1	0	26
Frank Winterstein	Widnes	2012-13	37(9)	16	0	0	64
	Crusaders	2010-11	26(19)	4	0	0	16
	Wakefield	2009	(5)	0	0	0	0
Lincoln Withers	Hull KR	2012-13	18(22)	10	0	0	40
	Crusaders	2010-11	47	4	0	0	16
	Celtic	2009	21	6	0	0	24
Michael Withers	Wigan	2007	6(1)	1	0	0	4
	Bradford	1999-2006	156(6)	94	15	4	410
Michael Witt	London	2012-13	37	10	89	1	219
	Crusaders	2010-11	39	13	47	4	150
Jeff Wittenberg	Huddersfield	1998	18(1)	1	0	0	4
	Bradford	1997	8(9)	4	0	0	16
Josh Wood	Wakefield	2020-21	7(6)	1	0	0	4
	Salford	2015-19	19(17)	2	0	0	8
Kyle Wood	Wakefield	2012-13, 2017-21	62(93)	26	0	0	104
	Huddersfield	2011, 2013-16	39(33)	7	0	0	28
	Castleford	2010	1(4)	0	0	0	0
Martin Wood	Sheffield	1997-98	24(11)	4	18	2	54
Mikey Wood	Huddersfield	2016-17	1(1)	0	0	0	0
Nathan Wood	Warrington	2002-05	90	38	0	3	155
	Wakefield	2002	11	2	0	0	8
Paul Wood	Warrington	2000-14	138(171)	40	0	0	160
Phil Wood	Widnes	2004	2(1)	0	0	0	0
Sam Wood	Bradford	2013-14	7(1)	0	0	0	0
Sam Wood	Hull KR	2022-23	26(4)	8	2	0	36
	Huddersfield	2016-18, 2020-21	39(9)	13	4	0	60
James Woodburn-Hall	London	2013-14	9(4)	2	0	0	8
Darren Woods	Widnes	2005	(1)	0	0	0	0
David Woods	Halifax	2002	18(2)	8	0	0	32
Josh Woods	Wigan	2017-18	10(1)	1	4	1	13
Simon Worrall	Leeds	2008-09	5(16)	1	0	0	4
Michael Worrincy	Bradford	2009-10	12(34)	12	0	0	48
	Harlequins	2006-08	20(12)	10	0	0	40
Rob Worrincy	Castleford	2004	1	0	0	0	0
Greg Worthington	Toronto	2020	(1)	0	0	0	0
James Worthington							
	Wigan	2017	1	2	0	0	8
Troy Wozniak	Widnes	2004	13(7)	1	0	0	4
Matthew Wray	Wakefield	2002-03	13(3)	2	0	0	8
Connor Wrench	Warrington	2020-23	26(2)	12	0	0	48
David Wrench	Wakefield	2002-06	28(52)	6	0	0	24
	Leeds	1999-2001	7(17)	0	0	0	0
Callum Wright	Wigan	2014	(2)	0	0	0	0
Craig Wright	Castleford	2000	1(9)	0	0	0	0
Nigel Wright	Huddersfield	1999	4(6)	1	0	0	4
	Wigan	1996-97	5(5)	2	0	1	9
Ricky Wright	Sheffield	1997-99	2(13)	0	0	0	0
Shane Wright	Salford	2022-23	12(12)	6	0	0	24
Vincent Wulf	Paris	1996	13(4)	4	0	0	16
Connor Wynne	Hull	2019-22	29(4)	11	0	0	44
Andrew Wynyard	London	1999-2000	34(6)	4	0	0	16
Bagdad Yaha	Paris	1996	4(4)	2	4	0	16
Fouad Yaha	Catalans	2015-23	131	88	0	0	352
	Hull KR	2023	2	0	0	0	0
Malakai Yasa	Sheffield	1996	1(3)	0	0	0	0
Andy Yates	Wakefield	2016	(7)	0	0	0	0
	Leeds	2015	(9)	1	0	0	4
Luke Yates	Huddersfield	2021-23	63(3)	9	0	0	36
	Salford	2020	12(5)	3	0	0	12
	London	2019	28	2	0	0	8
Kirk Yeaman	Hull	2001-16, 2018	322(18)	159	0	0	636
Dominic Young	Huddersfield	2019-20	2	0	0	0	0
Grant Young	London	1998-99	22(2)	2	0	0	8
Nick Youngquest	Castleford	2011-12	37	28	0	0	112
	Crusaders	2010	26(1)	9	0	0	36
Ronel Zenon	Paris	1996	(4)	2	0	0	8
Tanguy Zenon	Hull KR	2023	2	0	0	0	0
	Catalans	2022-23	2(2)	1	0	0	4
Nick Zisti	Bradford	1999	6(1)	0	0	0	0
Freddie Zitter	Catalans	2006	1	0	0	0	0

All totals in 'Super League Players 1996-2023' include play-off games & Super League Super 8s from 2015-2018. Super 8s (Qualifiers) not included.

Toronto Wolfpack games from 2020 season also included.

Super League Players 1996-2023

NEW FACES - Players making their Super League debuts in 2023

PLAYER	CLUB	DEBUT vs	ROUND	DATE
Tom Amone	Leigh	Salford (h)	1	17/2/23
(club debut: Whitehaven (h), Ch1, 30/1/22)				
John Asiata	Leigh	Salford (h)	1	17/2/23
(club debut: Whitehaven (h), Ch1, 30/1/22)				
Renouf Atoni	Wakefield	Catalans (h)	1	17/2/23
Robbie Butterworth	Wakefield	Hull KR (h)	6	24/3/23
Jake Clifford	Hull FC	Castleford (h)	1	19/2/23
Alfie Edgell	Leeds	Castleford (h)	27	22/9/23
Lennie Ellis	Hull KR	Wigan (h)	21	4/8/23
Sam Eseh	Wakefield	Huddersfield (h)	3	3/3/23
Louix Gorman	Hull KR	Wigan (a)	21	4/8/23
Lucas Green	Warrington	Wigan (h)	9	14/4/23
Luke Hooley	Leeds	Hull KR (a)	7	31/3/23
Liam Horne	Castleford	Huddersfield (h)	21	4/8/23
Tex Hoy	Hull FC	Castleford (h)	1	19/2/23
Matt Ikuvalu	Catalans	St Helens (h)	11	5/5/23
Edwin Ipape	Leigh	Salford (h)	1	17/2/23
(club debut: York (a), Ch4, 20/2/22)				
Zach Jebson	Hull FC	St Helens (h)	27	22/9/23
Adam Keighran	Catalans	Wakefield (a)	1	17/2/23
Rhys Kennedy	Hull KR	Wigan (h)	1	18/2/23
Lachlan Lam	Leigh	Salford (h)	1	17/2/23
(club debut: Featherstone (SB), Ch21, 30/7/22)				
Joe Law	Wakefield	Leeds (h)	15	11/6/23
Sam Lisone	Leeds	Warrington (a)	1	16/2/23
Nene Macdonald	Leeds	Hull KR (h)	2	24/2/23
Esan Marsters	Huddersfield	Warrington (h)	2	24/2/23
Lewis Martin	Hull FC	St Helens (a)	27	22/9/23
Moses Mbye	St Helens	Leeds (h)	20	28/7/23
Josh McGuire	Warrington	Catalans (a)	8	8/4/23
Tom Nicholson-Watton	Leeds	Castleford (h)	27	22/9/23
Kai O'Donnell	Leigh	Salford (h)	1	17/2/23
(club debut: Widnes (a), Ch8, 15/4/22)				
Tom Opacic	Hull KR	Wigan (h)	1	18/2/23
Oliver Pratt	Wakefield	Hull KR (h)	27	22/9/23
(club debut: Leigh (h), CC6, 19/5/23)				
Kevin Proctor	Wakefield	Catalans (h)	1	17/2/23
Tee Ritson	St Helens	Castleford (a)	2	26/2/23
Fenton Rogers	Huddersfield	Wigan (a)	17	30/6/23
Fletcher Rooney	Castleford	Leeds (a)	27	22/9/23
Leon Ruan	Leeds	Wakefield (a)	15	11/6/23
Kieran Rush	Huddersfield	Leigh (h)	12	12/5/23
Brad Schneider	Hull KR	Leeds (a)	19	14/7/23
Jordan Schofield	Wakefield	Hull KR (h)	27	22/9/23
Harvey Smith	Wakefield	Hull KR (h)	27	22/9/23
Nick Staveley	Hull FC	Castleford (a)	25	8/9/23
(club debut: Castleford (a), CC6, 21/5/23)				
Sauaso Sue	Hull KR	Wigan (h)	1	18/2/23
Charbel Tasipale	Castleford	Huddersfield (h)	21	4/8/23
Sio Siua Taukeiaho	Catalans	Hull FC (h)	3	3/3/23
Leo Tennison	Hull KR	Wigan (a)	21	4/8/23
Billy Tsikrikas	Castleford	Hull KR (a)	20	28/7/23
Paul Vaughan	Warrington	Leeds (h)	1	16/2/23
Nathan Wilde	Leigh	Wakefield (a)	9	14/4/23
Aaron Willis	Castleford	Salford (h)	15	9/6/23

Players making their club debuts in other competitions in 2023

PLAYER	CLUB	DEBUT vs	ROUND	DATE
Jacob Hookem	Castleford	Hull FC (h)	CC6	21/5/23
Dane Windrow	Wakefield	Leigh (h)	CC6	19/5/23

OLD FACES - Players making their Super League debuts for new clubs in 2023

PLAYER	CLUB	DEBUT vs	ROUND	DATE
Blake Austin	Castleford	Wakefield (a)	22	18/8/23
Yusuf Aydin	Hull KR	Catalans (a)	15	10/6/23
(club debut: Batley (h), CC6, 19/5/23)				
James Batchelor	Hull KR	Wigan (h)	1	18/2/23
Jake Bibby	Huddersfield	Wakefield (a)	3	3/3/23
Tom Briscoe	Leigh	Salford (h)	1	17/2/23
Jack Broadbent	Castleford	Hull FC (a)	1	19/2/23
Ed Chamberlain	Leigh	Salford (h)	1	17/2/23
(club debut: Whitehaven (h), Ch1, 30/1/22)				
Josh Charnley	Leigh	Salford (h)	1	17/2/23
(club debut: Workington (a), Ch18, 10/7/22)				
Jake Connor	Huddersfield	St Helens (h) (D2)	6	23/3/23
Jack Croft	Wakefield	Catalans (a) (D2)	13	26/5/23
Jordan Crowther	Warrington	Catalans (h)	21	4/8/23
Will Dagger	Wakefield	St Helens (a)	7	31/3/23
Matt Davis	Leigh	Salford (h)	1	17/2/23
Riley Dean	Castleford	St Helens (a)	17	30/6/23
Andrew Dixon	Salford	Huddersfield (h) (D2)	7	2/4/23
Josh Drinkwater	Warrington	Leeds (h)	1	16/2/23
Gil Dudson	Warrington	Castleford (a)	6	24/3/23
Tyler Dupree	Wigan	Leigh (h)	20	29/7/23
Brad Dwyer	Hull FC	Castleford (h)	1	19/2/23
David Fifita	Wakefield	Leigh (MW) (D2)	14	4/6/23
Tom Forber	Wakefield	Hull KR (h)	6	24/3/23
Alex Foster	Castleford	Hull KR (a) (D2)	20	28/7/23
Romain Franco	Wakefield	Leeds (h)	15	11/6/23
Luke Gale	Wakefield	Hull KR (a)	16	23/6/23
Oliver Gildart	Leigh	Leeds (a)	21	6/8/23
Josh Griffin	Wakefield	Castleford (h) (D3)	22	18/8/23
Corey Hall	Hull KR	St Helens (a)	9	14/4/23
Sam Halsall	Huddersfield	St Helens (h)	6	23/3/23
Frankie Halton	Leigh	Warrington (a)	13	26/5/23
Ryan Hampshire	Wigan	Hull KR (a)	13	25/5/23
Umyla Hanley	Leigh	Catalans (a)	16	24/6/23
(club debut: York (a), CCQF, 18/6/23)				
Zak Hardaker	Leigh	Salford (h)	1	17/2/23
Ben Hellewell	Salford	Huddersfield (h) (D2)	7	2/4/23
Sam Hewitt	Wakefield	Salford (a)	5	19/3/23
Oliver Holmes	Leigh	Salford (h)	1	17/2/23
Jack Hughes	Leigh	Salford (h) (D2)	1	17/2/23
Luis Johnson	Castleford	Wakefield (a)	8	6/4/23
Jordan Johnstone	Castleford	Leigh (h)	18	7/7/23
Tom Johnstone	Catalans	Wakefield (a)	1	17/2/23
Sam Kasiano	Warrington	Leeds (h)	1	16/2/23
Toby King	Wigan	Hull KR (a)	1	18/2/23
Samisoni Langi	Wakefield	Catalans (h)	1	17/2/23
Ricky Leutele	Leigh	Salford (h)	1	17/2/23
Harvey Livett	Huddersfield	St Helens (h)	6	23/3/23
Ellis Longstaff	Salford	Warrington (a)	3	2/3/23
Sam Luckley	Hull KR	Salford (a)	2	23/2/23
Nathan Mason	Wakefield	Castleford (a)	8	6/4/23
Manu Ma'u	Catalans	Wakefield (a)	1	17/2/23
James McDonnell	Leeds	St Helens (a)	3	3/3/23
Thomas Mikaele	Warrington	Catalans (h) (D2)	21	4/8/23
Jacob Miller	Castleford	Hull FC (a)	1	19/2/23
Adam Milner	Huddersfield	St Helens (MW)	14	4/6/23
Rowan Milnes	Wakefield	Wigan (a)	10	23/4/23
Robbie Mulhern	Leigh	Salford (h)	1	17/2/23
Muizz Mustapha	Castleford	St Helens (h)	2	26/2/23
Kevin Naiqama	Huddersfield	Warrington (h)	2	24/2/23
Ben Nakubuwai	Leigh	Salford (h)	1	17/2/23
(club debut: Sheffield (h), 1895CSF, 8/5/22)				
Romain Navarrete	Catalans	Wakefield (a) (D2)	1	17/2/23
Dan Norman	Leigh	Hull FC (h) (D2)	15	9/6/23
Gareth O'Brien	Leigh	Salford (h)	1	17/2/23
Derrell Olpherts	Leeds	Warrington (a)	1	16/2/23
Oliver Partington	Salford	Leigh (a)	1	17/2/23
Nathan Peats	Huddersfield	Warrington (h) (D2)	2	24/2/23
Luis Roberts	Leeds	Warrington (a)	1	16/2/23
Cesar Rouge	Hull KR	Wigan (a)	21	4/8/23
Harry Rushton	Huddersfield	Wigan (h)	5	17/3/23
Matty Russell	Warrington	Castleford (a) (D2)	6	24/3/23
Hugo Salabio	Wakefield	Leeds (h)	15	11/6/23
Justin Sangare	Leeds	Warrington (a)	1	16/2/23
Innes Senior	Wakefield	St Helens (a) (D3)	7	31/3/23
	Wakefield	Warrington (h) (D4)	20	30/7/23
Louis Senior	Hull KR	Warrington (h)	4	10/3/23
Ava Seumanufagai	Leigh	Catalans (a)	2	25/2/23
Isaac Shaw	Hull KR	Wigan (a)	21	4/8/23
Isaac Shaw	Wakefield	Hull KR (a) (D2)	16	23/6/23
Joe Shorrocks	Leigh	Hull KR (a)	3	3/3/23
Adam Sidlow	Salford	Warrington (a) (D2)	3	2/3/23
Brad Singleton	Salford	St Helens (h)	21	6/8/23
Aaron Smith	Leigh	Catalans (a)	2	25/2/23
(club debut: Toulouse (h), Ch1, 3/2/19)				
Morgan Smith	Wakefield	Catalans (h)	1	17/2/23
Sam Stone	Salford	Leigh (a)	1	17/2/23
Liam Sutcliffe	Hull FC	Castleford (h)	1	19/2/23
Will Tate	Castleford	Hull KR (h)	10	21/4/23
Luke Thomas	Hull KR	Wigan (a)	21	4/8/23
Jake Trueman	Hull FC	Wigan (h)	11	4/5/23
Albert Vete	Castleford	St Helens (h)	2	26/2/23
Jack Walker	Hull KR	Catalans (a)	15	10/6/23
Elliot Wallis	Castleford	Leigh (a)	11	5/5/23
Jake Wardle	Wigan	Hull KR (a)	1	18/2/23
Joe Wardle	Leigh	Salford (h)	1	17/2/23
(club debut: Featherstone (h), Ch2, 7/2/22)				
Gareth Widdop	Castleford	Hull FC (h)	1	19/2/23
Fouad Yaha	Hull KR	Wakefield (h)	16	23/6/23
Tanguy Zenon	Hull KR	Wakefield (h)	16	23/6/23
(club debut: Salford (h), CCQF, 17/6/23)				

SUPER LEAGUE XXVIII
Club by Club

Super League XXVIII - Club by Club

KEY DATES

2nd December 2022 - utility back Jack Broadbent signs from Leeds on two-year contract.

6th December 2022 - former Hull FC halfback Jacob Hookem signs one-year deal with option of further year.

13th December 2022 - young forwards Ilikaya Mafi, Hull FC and Bailey Dawson, Hull KR, sign one-year contracts, with club option for further year.

20th January 2023 - young forward Kieran Hudson suffers pre-season Achilles injury.

19th February 2023 - 32-30 round-one defeat at Hull FC after trailing 32-6.

26th February 2023 - 24-6 home defeat to St Helens. Jake Mamo injures back.

3rd March 2023 - Paul McShane suffers back spasm in first minute of 200th Tigers appearance in 36-0 home hammering by Wigan. Niall Evalds (shoulder) and Bureta Faraimo (hip) also injured.

6th March 2023 - head coach Lee Radford leaves by mutual agreement. Assistant Andy Last takes over on interim basis.

10th March 2023 - 36-6 defeat at Huddersfield.

15th March 2023 - Jake Mamo retires with immediate effect.

16th March 2023 - 14-8 round-5 home victory over Leeds marks first win.

24th March 2023 - 38-0 home hammering by league leaders Warrington.

1st April 2023 - battling 22-18 defeat at Catalans.

2nd April 2023 - former scholarship backrower Luis Johnson joins from Hull KR on season-loan. Prop Albert Vete joins Featherstone on loan.

6th April 2023 - 16-4 home win over winless Wakefield takes Tigers four points clear of bottom.

9th April 2023 - winger Will Tate signs from Hull KR on two-and-a-half year contract.

13th April 2023 - 14-6 defeat at Salford.

19th April 2023 - interim coach Andy Last appointed head coach on two-and-a-half year contract.

20th April 2023 - hooker Jacques O'Neill re-signs on initial contract until end of 2023.

21st April 2023 - 12-7 home defeat to Hull KR.

3rd May 2023 - prop Daniel Smith goes to Featherstone on loan.

5th May 2023 - 30-6 defeat at Leigh after 6-6 half-time scoreline.

9th May 2023 - Batley coach Craig Lingard appointed assistant.

12th May 2023 - 46-22 home defeat to Catalans is fourth straight loss. Liam Watts and Bureta Fairamo banned for one game for dangerous contact.

21st May 2023 - 32-8 home Challenge Cup exit to Hull FC.

25th May 2023 - utility forward Adam Milner signs for Huddersfield on loan deal to be made permanent at end of season.

26th May 2023 - 20-4 defeat at Huddersfield.

3rd June 2023 - Joe Westerman makes 400th career appearance as Gareth Widdop kicks late touchline conversion to secure 26-24 Magic Weekend win over Leeds.

9th June 2023 - Paul McShane breaks arm in 42-10 home defeat to Salford.

13th June 2023 - Warrington halfback Riley Dean signs on loan until end of season.

21st June 2023 - halfback Callum McLelland leaves after agreement on early termination of contract.

24th June 2023 - 23-14 home win over Warrington moves Tigers six points from bottom.

30th June 2023 - 22-0 defeat at St Helens.

4th July 2023 - Widnes hooker Jordan Johnstone signs on loan to end of season.

4th July 2023 - Liam Watts dangerous contact charge revoked on appeal.

7th July 2023 - 34-16 home defeat to Leigh.

15th July 2023 - 36-18 defeat at Hull FC.

20th July 2023 - Canterbury prop Billy Tsikrikas and Alex Foster join on loan to end of season.

24th July 2023 - PNG international Liam Horne joins on one-and-a-half year deal, with option of further year.

25th July 2023 - Lebanon international back-rower Charbel Tasipale joins on immediate deal from Newtown Jets. Wingers Bureta Faraimo and Mahe Fonua both leave the club.

28th July 2023 - 34-16 defeat at Hull KR.

3rd August 2023 - halfback Blake Austin joins on loan from Leeds.

4th August 2023 - head coach Andy Last sacked after 28-0 home defeat by Huddersfield.

9th August 2023 - former London Broncos coach Danny Ward appointed head coach on contract until end of season. Dane Dorahy joins as assistant.

18th August 2023 - Greg Eden scores hat-trick in 28-12 win at Wakefield.

25th August 2023 - 34-4 home defeat by St Helens. Liam Watts (one game) and Liam Horne (two) get bans.

2nd September 2023 - 66-12 defeat at Warrington.

8th September 2023 - Jason Qareqare scores try-double as 29-12 home win over Hull FC stretches lead over Wakefield to four points.

12th September 2023 - prop Nathan Massey to leave at end of season.

15th September 2023 - 48-6 defeat at Wigan as Wakefield also lose to be relegated.

19th September 2023 - Greg Eden and Matagi released at end of season. Kenny Edwards to retire.

22nd September 2023 - 46-0 final round defeat at Leeds.

29th September 2023 - Papuan second row Nixon Putt and Lebanese forward Elie El-Zakhem join on two-year contracts. Joe Westerman signs new two-year contract.

1st October 2023 - Papua New Guinea international Sylvester Namo joins on two-year deal. Prop Liam Watts signs 12-month contract.

3rd October 2023 - centre Josh Hodson signs from Batley Bulldogs on two-year deal. Ex-St Helens centre Josh Simm signs from Wynnum-Manly Seagulls on two-year deal

4th October 2023 - utility-back Sam Wood signs from Hull KR on three-year contract.

5th October 2023 - Leeds Rhinos fullback Luke Hooley signs on two-year contract.

7th October 2023 - Hull KR halfback Rowan Milnes signs on two-year contract.

9th October 2023 - forward George Lawler signs two-year contract extension. Prop Muizz Mustapha signs new one-year contract.

11th October 2023 - winger Elliot Wallis signs for Huddersfield, Giants winger Innes Senior joins on season loan.

17th October 2023 - Craig Lingard appointed head coach on two-year deal, with Danny McGuire joining as assistant.

18th October 2023 - Gareth Widdop leaves by mutual consent and retires.

20th October 2023 - prop Samy Kibula signs from Batley on one-year deal, with option for further year.

CLUB RECORDS

Highest score:
106-0 v Rochdale, 9/9/2007
Highest score against:
12-76 v Leeds, 14/8/2009
Record attendance:
25,449 v Hunslet, 9/3/35

MATCH RECORDS

Tries:
5 Derek Foster v Hunslet, 10/11/72
John Joyner v Millom, 16/9/73
Steve Fenton v Dewsbury, 27/1/78
Ian French v Hunslet, 9/2/86
St John Ellis v Whitehaven, 10/12/89
Greg Eden v Warrington, 11/6/2017
Goals: 17 Sammy Lloyd v Millom, 16/9/73
Points: 43 Sammy Lloyd v Millom, 16/9/73

SEASON RECORDS

Tries: 42 Denny Solomona 2016
Goals: 158 Sammy Lloyd 1976-77
Points: 355 Luke Gale 2017

CAREER RECORDS

Tries: 206 Alan Hardisty 1958-71
Goals: 875 Albert Lunn 1951-63
Points: 1,870 Albert Lunn 1951-63
Appearances: 613 John Joyner 1973-92

Super League XXVIII - Club by Club

CASTLEFORD TIGERS

DATE	FIXTURE	RESULT	SCORERS	LGE	ATT
19/2/23	Hull FC (a)	L32-30	t:Faraimo(2),Edwards,Miller,Mamo g:Widdop(5)	8th	15,383
26/2/23	St Helens (h)	L6-24	t:Broadbent g:Widdop	10th	10,042
3/3/23	Wigan (h)	L0-36		11th	7,565
10/3/23	Huddersfield (a)	L36-6	t:Lawler g:Widdop	11th	4,071
16/3/23	Leeds (h)	W14-8	t:Faraimo(2) g:Widdop(3)	11th	7,458
24/3/23	Warrington (h)	L0-38		11th	7,348
1/4/23	Catalans Dragons (a)	L22-18	t:Broadbent(2),Turner g:McShane(3)	11th	8,109
6/4/23	Wakefield (h)	W16-4	t:McShane,Eden(2) g:McShane(2)	10th	8,075
13/4/23	Salford (a)	L14-6	t:Eden g:Widdop	10th	4,468
21/4/23	Hull KR (h)	L7-12	t:Miller g:McShane fg:Miller	11th	7,110
5/5/23	Leigh (a)	L30-6	t:Westerman g:Widdop	11th	5,423
12/5/23	Catalans Dragons (h)	L22-46	t:Mellor(2),Faraimo(2) g:Widdop,McShane(2)	11th	5,788
21/5/23	Hull FC (h) (CCR6)	L8-32	t:Fonua,Tate	N/A	4,249
26/5/23	Huddersfield (a)	L20-4	t:Mellor	11th	4,206
3/6/23	Leeds (MW) ●	W26-24	t:Miller,Wallis,Mellor(2),Qareqare g:Widdop(3)	11th	N/A
9/6/23	Salford (h)	L10-42	t:Qareqare,Edwards g:Widdop	11th	6,354
23/6/23	Warrington (h)	W23-14	t:Tate,Qareqare,Broadbent g:Widdop(5) fg:Widdop	11th	6,066
30/6/23	St Helens (a)	L22-0		11th	11,488
7/7/23	Leigh (h)	L16-34	t:Widdop,Wallis(2) g:Widdop(2)	11th	6,344
15/7/23	Hull FC (a)	L36-18	t:Wallis,Broadbent,Faraimo g:Widdop(3)	11th	12,352
28/7/23	Hull KR (a)	L34-16	t:Tate,Broadbent,Eden g:Dean(2)	11th	8,636
4/8/23	Huddersfield (h)	L0-28		11th	6,452
18/8/23	Wakefield (a)	W12-28	t:Tasipale,Eden(3),Foster g:Widdop(4)	11th	4,710
25/8/23	St Helens (h)	L4-34	t:Turner	11th	6,868
2/9/23	Warrington (a)	L66-12	t:Hall,Eden g:Widdop(2)	11th	9,103
8/9/23	Hull FC (h)	W29-12	t:Qareqare(2),Eden,Foster,Turner g:Widdop(4) fg:Austin	11th	7,947
15/9/23	Wigan (a)	L48-6	t:Qareqare g:Austin	11th	13,109
22/9/23	Leeds (a)	L46-0		11th	15,109

● Played at St James' Park, Newcastle

		APP		TRIES		GOALS		FG		PTS	
	D.O.B.	ALL	SL	ALL	SL	ALL	SL	ALL	SL	ALL	SL
Blake Austin	1/2/91	5	5	0	0	1	1	1	1	3	3
Jack Broadbent	1/11/01	25(1)	24(1)	6	6	0	0	0	0	24	24
Riley Dean	10/8/01	4	4	0	0	2	2	0	0	4	4
Greg Eden	14/11/90	15	15	9	9	0	0	0	0	36	36
Kenny Edwards	13/9/89	22(3)	22(3)	2	2	0	0	0	0	8	8
Niall Evalds	26/8/93	7	7	0	0	0	0	0	0	0	0
Bureta Faraimo	16/7/90	14	14	7	7	0	0	0	0	28	28
Mahe Fonua	24/12/92	10	9	1	0	0	0	0	0	4	0
Alex Foster	25/9/93	1(5)	1(5)	2	2	0	0	0	0	8	8
George Griffin	26/6/92	12(10)	12(9)	0	0	0	0	0	0	0	0
Sam Hall	8/5/02	4(12)	3(12)	1	1	0	0	0	0	4	4
Jacob Hookem	4/10/02	(1)		0	0	0	0	0	0	0	0
Liam Horne	3/2/97	4(1)	4(1)	0	0	0	0	0	0	0	0
Luis Johnson	20/2/99	(3)	(3)	0	0	0	0	0	0	0	0
Jordan Johnstone	24/5/97	5(3)	5(3)	0	0	0	0	0	0	0	0
George Lawler	1/9/95	17(3)	16(3)	1	1	0	0	0	0	4	4
Jake Mamo	6/6/94	2	2	1	1	0	0	0	0	4	4
Brad Martin	6/2/01	2(7)	1(7)	0	0	0	0	0	0	0	0
Nathan Massey	11/7/89	13(7)	12(7)	0	0	0	0	0	0	0	0
Suaia Matagi	23/3/88	8(7)	7(7)	0	0	0	0	0	0	0	0
Paul McShane	19/11/89	15	14	1	1	8	8	0	0	20	20
Alex Mellor	24/9/94	25(1)	24(1)	5	5	0	0	0	0	20	20
Jacob Miller	22/8/92	26	26	3	3	0	0	1	1	13	13
Adam Milner	19/12/91	6(3)	6(3)	0	0	0	0	0	0	0	0
Muizz Mustapha	3/4/00	3(13)	3(12)	0	0	0	0	0	0	0	0
Jason Qareqare	26/1/04	10	10	6	6	0	0	0	0	24	24
Cain Robb	5/1/03	(8)	(7)	0	0	0	0	0	0	0	0
Fletcher Rooney	12/1/06	1	1	0	0	0	0	0	0	0	0
Daniel Smith	20/3/93	1(4)	1(4)	0	0	0	0	0	0	0	0
Alex Sutcliffe	21/1/99	5(2)	4(2)	0	0	0	0	0	0	0	0
Charbel Tasipale	24/2/00	4	4	1	1	0	0	0	0	4	4
Will Tate	20/12/01	6(1)	5(1)	3	2	0	0	0	0	12	8
Billy Tsikrikas	11/5/95	(4)	(4)	0	0	0	0	0	0	0	0
Jordan Turner	9/1/89	21	20	3	3	0	0	0	0	12	12
Albert Vete	24/1/93	3(3)	3(3)	0	0	0	0	0	0	0	0
Elliot Wallis	10/5/00	13	13	4	4	0	0	0	0	16	16
Liam Watts	8/7/90	11(9)	11(9)	0	0	0	0	0	0	0	0
Joe Westerman	15/11/89	23	22	1	1	0	0	0	0	4	4
Gareth Widdop	12/3/89	21	21	1	1	37	37	1	1	79	79
Aaron Willis	11/12/03	(1)	(1)	0	0	0	0	0	0	0	0

'SL' totals include Super League games only; 'All' totals also include Challenge Cup

Jack Broadbent

LEAGUE RECORD
P27-W6-D0-L21
(11th)
F323, A774, Diff-451
12 points.

CHALLENGE CUP
Round Six

ATTENDANCES
Best - v St Helens (SL - 10,042)
Worst - v Hull FC (CC - 4,249)
Total (SL only) - 93,417
Average (SL only) - 7,186
(Down by 322 on 2022)

Super League XXVIII - Club by Club

11th November 2022 - prop Romain Navarrete returns on two-year deal.

18th November 2022 - Josh Drinkwater released to join Warrington.

20th November 2022 - Sydney Roosters centre Adam Keighran signs one-year deal.

3rd December 2022 - Samisoni Langi signs for Wakefield.

9th December 2022 - prop Dylan Napa released from contract.

5th January 2023 - Fouad Yaha dislocates shoulder in training.

6th January 2023 - Tiaki Chan signs one-year deal.

6th January 2023 - Dragons fined £25,000, half suspended until end of 2023 season, for supporter misbehaviour after play-off defeat by Leeds.

31st January 2023 - winger Fouad Yaha out for long spell after undergoing shoulder surgery.

17th February 2023 - Tom Johnstone scores hat-trick on debut in 38-24 round-one win at Wakefield.

25th February 2023 - hard-fought 14-6 home win over Leigh.

4th March 2023 - 38-6 home win over unbeaten Hull FC.

9th March 2023 - Manu Ma'u scores two tries in 18-10 win at Wigan.

10th March 2023 - Sam Tomkins to retire at end of season.

18th March 2023 - Tom Johnstone scores hat-trick in 26-12 home win over Hull KR.

25th March 2023 - 32-22 round-6 defeat at Leeds ends 100 per cent start, after leading 22-8 at half-time.

29th March 2023 - prop Julian Bousquet signs contract extension to end of 2025.

1st April 2023 - hard-fought 22-18 home win over Castleford.

5th April 2023 - hooker Ugo Tison and fullback/winger Tanguy Zenon sign two-year professional contracts.

8th April 2023 - 20-14 defeat at home to leaders Warrington features eleven home-grown players. Tanguy Zenon makes debut at fullback.

14th April 2023 - 26-14 defeat at Huddersfield.

20th April 2023 - Cronulla centre Matt Ikuvalu signs to end of season, with option for another year.

23rd April 2023 - 16-14 defeat at Salford.

5th May 2023 - Matt Ikuvalu makes try-scoring debut in 24-12 home win over St Helens.

12th May 2023 - 46-22 win at Castleford after leading 34-6 at half-time.

17th May 2023 - fullback Arthur Mourgue signs two-year contract extension to end of 2025.

KEY DATES

20th May 2023 - Matty Ashton try for Warrington two minutes from time means home 16-14 exit from Challenge Cup.

24th May 2023 - centre Arthur Romano signs new two-year contract.

26th May 2023 - Tom Johnstone scores twice in 36-6 home win over Wakefield.

31st May 2023 - Hull FC prop Tevita Satae signs two-year contract from 2024.

3rd June 2023 - Tom Johnstone scores hat-trick in 46-22 Magic Weekend win over Wigan as Dragons top table.

10th June 2023 - 38-4 home win over Hull KR. Mitchell Pearce gets three-game penalty notice for late high tackle. Matt Whitley one game.

13th June 2023 - Tanguy Zenon joins Hull KR on loan.

18th June 2023 - Fouad Yaha joins Hull KR on loan.

24th June 2023 - 38-30 home victory over Leigh moves Dragons two points clear at top of table.

27th June 2023 - prop Mickael Goudemand to join Leeds at end of season.

1st July 2023 - Tom Davies scores double as 28-18 win at Hull FC moves Dragons four points clear at top of table.

3rd July 2023 - Romain Navarrete suspended for one game for dangerous contact.

8th July 2023 - seven-game winning league run ends with 22-14 home defeat to Huddersfield. Arthur Mourgue injures ankle.

13th July 2023 - 14-12 win at St Helens.

16th July 2023 - Adam Keighran and Tiaki Chan to join Wigan at end of season.

20th July 2023 - Michael McIlorum signs one-year contract extension.

29th July 2023 - 42-0 home win over Salford re-opens four-point gap at top of table.

4th August 2023 - 30-10 win at Warrington maintains four-point lead in table.

7th August 2023 - prop Sio Siua Taukeiaho to be released from remainder of contract at end of season for family reasons.

11th August 2023 - halfback Theo Fages signs from Huddersfield on two-year contract.

15th August 2023 - Tyrone May to join Hull KR at end of season.

19th August 2023 - 30-14 win at Leigh maintains four-point lead at top of table.

21st August 2023 - Michael McIlorum appeal against one-game ban for late contact successful.

26th August 2023 - 34-0 home defeat to Wigan cuts lead to two points.

1st September 2023 - 26-18 defeat at Hull KR puts Catalans second on points difference.

8th September 2023 - 18-10 win at Wakefield after back-to-back defeats keeps League Leaders' Shield hopes alive.

11th September 2023 - halfback Mitchell Pearce to retire at season end.

16th September 2023 - Adam Keighran scores hat-trick, Tom Johnstone and Tom Davies doubles in 61-0 home win over Leeds.

22nd September 2023 - 19-8 win at Salford secures second spot.

29th September 2023 - prop Tariq Sims and halfback Jayden Nikorima sign from Melbourne on two-year contracts.

2nd October 2023 - Sam Moa to leave to return to Australia. Andy Last appointed assistant coach.

5th October 2023 - backrower Bayley Sironen signs from New Zealand Warriors on two-year contract.

6th October 2023 - Sam Tomkins try 80 seconds from time secures 12-6 home semi-final win over champions St Helens.

13th October 2023 - 10-2 Grand Final defeat by Wigan.

18th October 2023 - back-rower Matt Whitley signs for St Helens.

CLUB RECORDS

Highest score: 92-8 v York, 12/5/2013
Highest score against:
0-62 v Hull FC, 12/5/2017
Record attendance: 31,555 v Wigan, 18/5/2019 *(Barcelona)*
11,856 v Wigan, 2/7/2016
(Stade Gilbert Brutus)

MATCH RECORDS

Tries:
4 Justin Murphy v Warrington, 13/9/2008
Damien Cardace v Widnes, 31/3/2012
Kevin Larroyer v York, 12/5/2013
Jodie Broughton v St Helens, 14/4/2016
Fouad Yaha v Salford, 21/7/2018
David Mead v Huddersfield, 29/9/2018
Fouad Yaha v Leeds, 23/3/2019
Brayden Wiliame v Doncaster, 11/5/2019
Goals:
11 Thomas Bosc v Featherstone, 31/3/2007
Thomas Bosc v Batley, 29/5/2010
Scott Dureau v Widnes, 31/3/2012
Points:
30 Adam Keighran v Leeds, 16/9/2023

SEASON RECORDS

Tries: 29 Morgan Escare 2014
Goals: 134 Scott Dureau 2012
Points: 319 Scott Dureau 2012

CAREER RECORDS

Tries: 101 Fouad Yaha 2015-2023
Goals:
579 *(inc 14fg)* Thomas Bosc 2006-2017
Points: 1,380 Thomas Bosc 2006-2017
Appearances:
337 Remi Casty 2006-2013; 2015-2020

Super League XXVIII - Club by Club

CATALANS DRAGONS

DATE	FIXTURE	RESULT	SCORERS	LGE	ATT
17/2/23	Wakefield (a)	W24-38	t:Laguerre,Johnstone(3),Davies(2),Rouge g:Keighran(5)	2nd	4,076
25/2/23	Leigh (h)	W14-6	t:Johnstone,Goudemand g:Mourgue(3)	3rd	7,862
3/3/23	Hull FC (h)	W38-6	t:Johnstone,Seguier,Goudemand,Taukeiaho,Keighran,Garcia g:Keighran(7)	2nd	6,933
9/3/23	Wigan (a)	W10-18	t:Ma'u(2),Romano g:Keighran(3)	2nd	11,451
18/3/23	Hull KR (h)	W26-12	t:Johnstone(3),Davies,Bousquet g:Keighran,Mourgue(2)	2nd	7,682
25/3/23	Leeds (a)	L32-22	t:Davies,Keighran,Pearce,Seguier g:Keighran(3)	2nd	14,321
1/4/23	Castleford (h)	W22-18	t:Seguier,Johnstone,Mourgue,McMeeken g:Keighran(2),Mourgue	2nd	8,109
8/4/23	Warrington (a)	L14-20	t:McMeeken,Keighran,Romano g:Keighran	3rd	10,786
14/4/23	Huddersfield (a)	L26-14	t:Johnstone,Laguerre g:Keighran(3)	4th	4,685
23/4/23	Salford (a)	L16-14	t:Johnstone,Seguier,Keighran g:Keighran	4th	3,974
5/5/23	St Helens (h)	W24-12	t:Mourgue,Ikuvalu,Davies(2) g:Keighran(4)	4th	10,763
12/5/23	Castleford (a)	W22-46	t:Dezaria,Keighran(2),Ikuvalu,Johnstone,Garcia,Whitley,Tomkins g:Keighran(5),Mourgue(2)	4th	5,788
20/5/23	Warrington (h) (CCR6)	L14-16	t:Romano,Johnstone,Ikuvalu g:Mourgue	N/A	5,014
26/5/23	Wakefield (h)	W36-6	t:Johnstone(2),Rouge,McMeeken,Mourgue,Zenon g:Mourgue(6)	3rd	8,120
3/6/23	Wigan (MW) ●	W46-22	t:Tomkins,Johnstone(3),Whitley(2),Mourgue,Romano g:Mourgue(7)	1st	N/A
10/6/23	Hull KR (h)	W38-4	t:Whitley(2),May,McMeeken,Johnstone,Mourgue g:Mourgue(6),Keighran	1st	9,450
24/6/23	Leigh (h)	W38-30	t:Mourgue,Garcia(2),Johnstone(2),Romano g:Mourgue(7)	1st	9,636
1/7/23	Hull FC (a)	W18-28	t:Johnstone,Davies,Romano,Bousquet g:Mourgue(4)	1st	13,480
8/7/23	Huddersfield (h)	L14-22	t:Davies(2) g:Mourgue(3)	1st	9,189
13/7/23	St Helens (a)	W12-14	t:Johnstone,Ikuvalu g:Keighran(3)	1st	12,193
29/7/23	Salford (h)	W42-0	t:Keighran(2),Johnstone(2),May,Chan,Tomkins g:Keighran(4),Tomkins(3)	1st	9,503
4/8/23	Warrington (a)	W10-30	t:Keighran,Davies,Pearce,Whitley,Ikuvalu g:Keighran(5)	1st	10,312
19/8/23	Leigh (a)	W14-30	t:Pearce,Seguier,Davies,May,Ma'u g:Keighran(5)	1st	8,602
26/8/23	Wigan (h)	L0-34		1st	10,614
1/9/23	Hull KR (a)	L26-18	t:Navarrete,Garcia,Yaha g:Keighran(3)	2nd	9,102
8/9/23	Wakefield (a)	W10-18	t:Johnstone,Keighran,Davies g:Keighran(3)	2nd	3,348
16/9/23	Leeds (h)	W61-0	t:Keighran(3),Garcia,Davies(2),Johnstone(2),Pearce,Ikuvalu g:Keighran(9),Tomkins fg:Tomkins	2nd	9,162
22/9/23	Salford (a)	W8-19	t:Whitley,Bousquet,Tomkins g:Tomkins(3) fg:Tomkins	2nd	4,212
6/10/23	St Helens (h) (SF)	W12-6	t:Tomkins g:Keighran(4)	N/A	11,530
14/10/23	Wigan (GF) ●●	L2-10	g:Keighran	N/A	58,137

● Played at St James' Park, Newcastle
●● Played at Old Trafford, Manchester

		APP		TRIES		GOALS		FG		PTS	
	D.O.B.	ALL	SL	ALL	SL	ALL	SL	ALL	SL	ALL	SL
Julian Bousquet	18/7/91	15(14)	15(13)	3	3	0	0	0	0	12	12
Tiaki Chan	15/6/00	(13)	(13)	1	1	0	0	0	0	4	4
Alrix Da Costa	2/10/97	3(8)	3(8)	0	0	0	0	0	0	0	0
Tom Davies	11/1/97	25	25	15	15	0	0	0	0	60	60
Jordan Dezaria	6/11/96	4(19)	3(19)	1	1	0	0	0	0	4	4
Benjamin Garcia	5/4/93	30	29	6	6	0	0	0	0	24	24
Mickael Goudemand	9/3/96	1(16)	1(16)	2	2	0	0	0	0	8	8
Matt Ikuvalu	9/11/93	14	13	6	5	0	0	0	0	24	20
Tom Johnstone	13/8/95	29	28	28	27	0	0	0	0	112	108
Adam Keighran	24/4/97	25	25	13	13	73	73	0	0	198	198
Matthieu Laguerre	3/2/99	6	6	2	2	0	0	0	0	8	8
Manu Ma'u	24/8/88	5(14)	4(14)	3	3	0	0	0	0	12	12
Tyrone May	21/6/96	19(1)	19(1)	3	3	0	0	0	0	12	12
Michael McIlorum	10/1/88	25	24	0	0	0	0	0	0	0	0
Mike McMeeken	10/5/94	27	26	4	4	0	0	0	0	16	16
Arthur Mourgue	2/5/99	20(4)	19(4)	6	6	42	41	0	0	108	106
Romain Navarrete	30/6/94	20(6)	20(5)	1	1	0	0	0	0	4	4
Mitchell Pearce	7/4/89	18	17	4	4	0	0	0	0	16	16
Arthur Romano	17/8/97	21(1)	20(1)	6	5	0	0	0	0	24	20
Cesar Rouge	3/10/02	7	7	2	2	0	0	0	0	8	8
Bastien Scimone	2/11/98	(2)	(2)	0	0	0	0	0	0	0	0
Paul Seguier	8/9/97	25(2)	24(2)	5	5	0	0	0	0	20	20
Sio Siua Taukeiaho	3/1/92	3(7)	3(6)	1	1	0	0	0	0	4	4
Ugo Tison	7/7/01	(2)	(2)	0	0	0	0	0	0	0	0
Sam Tomkins	23/3/89	19(3)	18(3)	5	5	7	7	2	2	36	36
Matt Whitley	20/1/96	25	24	7	7	0	0	0	0	28	28
Fouad Yaha	19/8/96	3	3	1	1	0	0	0	0	4	4
Tanguy Zenon	8/5/02	1(2)	1(2)	1	1	0	0	0	0	4	4

'SL' totals include regular season & play-offs; 'All' totals also include Challenge Cup

Tom Johnstone

LEAGUE RECORD
P27-W20-D0-L7
(2nd/Grand Final Runners-up)
F722, A420, Diff+302
40 points.

CHALLENGE CUP
Round Six

ATTENDANCES
Best - v St Helens (SL-SF - 11,530)
Worst - v Warrington (CC - 5,014)
Total (SL, inc play-offs) - 129,339
Average (SL, inc play-offs) - 9,239
(Up by 1,067 on 2022)

Super League XXVIII - Club by Club

KEY DATES

14th November 2022 - youngsters Fenton Rogers and George Roby join Bradford Bulls on season-loan.

17th November 2022 - Michael Lawrence leaves for Bradford after 16 years at Giants.

4th December 2022 - 19-year-old Will Pryce to join Newcastle Knights at end of 2023 season.

6th December 2022 - young fullback Aidan McGowan to join Batley Bulldogs on season-long loan.

21st December 2022 - young halfback George Flanagan Jr signs from Bradford for undisclosed fee and will play 2023 at Bulls.

17th February 2023 - round-one game with St Helens postponed to accommodate World Club Challenge.

24th February 2023 - 26-16 home defeat to Warrington.

3rd March 2023 - Joe Greenwood scores only try in 8-0 win at Wakefield.

10th March 2023 - prop Matty English signs new three-year contract.

10th March 2023 - Chris McQueen scores two tries in 36-6 home win over Castleford.

11th March 2023 - prop Sam Hewitt goes to Wakefield on loan.

17th March 2023 - 14-12 home defeat to Wigan.

23rd March 2023 - Jake Connor makes second club debut in 14-12 home defeat to St Helens.

29th March 2023 - Innes Senior joins Wakefield on loan.

2nd April 2023 - Owen Trout scores two tries in 26-16 win at Salford. Ash Golding suffers hamstring injury.

3rd April 2023 - Nathan Mason joins Wakefield on loan.

9th April 2023 - Chris McQueen scores two tries in 18-17 Easter Sunday defeat at Leeds. Olly Russell misses game with torn hamstring suffered in training.

13th April 2023 - hooker George Roby goes to Swinton on season loan.

14th April 2023 - Sam Halsall scores try-double in 26-14 home win over Catalans.

23rd April 2023 - 20-14 defeat at Hull FC.

5th May 2023 - 28-0 defeat at Hull KR.

12th May 2023 - 30-4 home defeat to Leigh. Nathan Peats gets one-match ban for dangerous contact.

19th May 2023 - prop Chris Hill signs new contract to end of 2025.

20th May 2023 - Luke Yates scores hat-trick in 42-40 Challenge Cup sixth round defeat at Salford, after trailing 24-0 and 42-22.

25th May 2023 - utility forward Adam Milner signs from Castleford on loan deal to be made permanent at end of season.

26th May 2023 - 20-4 home win over Castleford ends three-match losing league run.

4th June 2023 - 48-6 Magic Weekend defeat by St Helens.

10th June 2023 - 30-26 defeat at Warrington.

23rd June 2023 - 54-0 defeat at Leeds.

30th June 2023 - 22-6 defeat at Wigan.

9th July 2023 - Chris McQueen scores try double in 22-14 win at Catalans.

14th July 2023 - Tui Lolohea gets try double in 34-6 home win over Wakefield.

21st July 2023 - Academy halfback Kieran Rush signs new three-year deal

27th July 2023 - 19-12 home victory over Hull FC is third on a row.

4th August 2023 - 28-0 win at Castleford.

11th August 2023 - half-back Theo Fages to leave for Catalans with year left on contract.

14th August 2023 - 32-18 defeat at St Helens after Joe Greenwood sent off in 28th minute.

15th August 2023 - Joe Greenwood fined for retaliation on St Helens prop Matty Lees, who is banned for two games.

18th August 2023 - 32-8 home defeat by Salford.

27th August 2023 - Will Pryce kicks two penalty goals in try-less second half to secure 21-12 home win over Leeds.

28th August 2023 - second-rower Jack Murchie signs from Parramatta Eels on three-year contract from 2024.

1st September 2023 - game at Leigh abandoned, Leigh leading 16-12, after 48 minutes due to floodlight failure.

3rd September 2023 - final 32 minutes played with 34-16 final scoreline defeat.

8th September 2023 - 26-18 home defeat by Hull KR ends play-off chances.

11th September 2023 - backrower Josh Jones leaves the club after concussion issues.

16th September 2023 - Kevin Naiqama scores hat-trick and Jermaine McGillvary double in 52-20 win at Hull FC.

17th September 2023 - Chris McQueen to retire at end of season.

19th September 2023 - Jermaine McGillvary to be released at end of season.

22nd September 2023 - 20-8 final-round home defeat to Warrington means ninth place finish.

24th September 2023 - winger Adam Swift signs from Hull FC on three-year contract.

28th September 2023 - Oldham-born hooker Thomas Deakin joins on two-year contract from Sydney Roosters.

29th September 2023 - Leroy Cudjoe signs one-year contract extension.

4th October 2023 - backrower Andre Savelio signs from Hull FC on two-year contract. Forward Jack Ashworth joins Hull FC.

10th October 2023 - Castleford winger Elliot Wallis signs on four-year deal, Innes Senior goes other way on loan.

11th October 2023 - former Wakefield trialist prop Hugo Salabio signs three-year deal.

14th October 2023 - Owen Trout signs for Leigh.

23rd October 2023 - utility Ashton Golding signs new three-year contract.

23rd October 2023 - Newcastle Knights scrum-half Adam Clune joins on three-year deal.

CLUB RECORDS

Highest score:
142-4 v Blackpool, 26/11/94
Highest score against:
12-94 v Castleford, 18/9/88
Record attendance:
32,912 v Wigan, 4/3/50 *(Fartown)*
15,629 v Leeds, 10/2/2008
*(McAlpine/Galpharm/
John Smith's Stadium)*

MATCH RECORDS

Tries:
10 Lionel Cooper v Keighley, 17/11/51
Goals: 18 Major Holland
v Swinton Park, 28/2/1914
Points: 39 Major Holland
v Swinton Park, 28/2/1914

SEASON RECORDS

Tries: 80 Albert Rosenfeld 1913-14
Goals: 156 *(inc 2fg)* Danny Brough 2013
Points: 346 Danny Brough 2013

CAREER RECORDS

Tries: 420 Lionel Cooper 1947-55
Goals: 958 Frank Dyson 1949-63
Points: 2,072 Frank Dyson 1949-63
Appearances: 485 Douglas Clark 1909-29

Super League XXVIII - Club by Club

HUDDERSFIELD GIANTS

DATE	FIXTURE	RESULT	SCORERS	LGE	ATT
24/2/23	Warrington (h)	L16-26	t:Greenwood,Pryce,Naiqama g:Pryce(2)	8th	7,731
3/3/23	Wakefield (a)	W0-8	t:Greenwood g:Lolohea(2)	7th	4,155
10/3/23	Castleford (h)	W36-6	t:McQueen(2),Pryce,Bibby,Lolohea,Cudjoe g:Russell(6)	4th	4,071
17/3/23	Wigan (h)	L12-14	t:Naiqama g:Russell(4)	5th	5,777
23/3/23	St Helens (h)	L12-14	t:Golding,Senior g:Russell(2)	9th	4,684
2/4/23	Salford (a)	W16-26	t:Golding,Trout(2),McQueen g:Russell(5)	6th	4,764
9/4/23	Leeds (a)	L18-17	t:McGillvary,McQueen(2) g:Connor(2) fg:Connor	8th	13,234
14/4/23	Catalans Dragons (h)	W26-14	t:Halsall(2),Livett,Naiqama g:Connor(5)	7th	4,685
23/4/23	Hull FC (a)	L20-14	t:McQueen,Marsters g:Connor(3)	9th	10,856
5/5/23	Hull KR (a)	L28-0		9th	8,490
12/5/23	Leigh (h)	L4-30	t:Naiqama	10th	4,977
20/5/23	Salford (a) (CCR6)	L42-40	t:Hewitt,Yates(3),Bibby,Lolohea,Naiqama g:Connor(6)	N/A	2,872
26/5/23	Castleford (h)	W20-4	t:Marsters,Senior,Naiqama g:Connor(4)	9th	4,206
4/6/23	St Helens (MW) ●	L6-48	t:Naiqama g:Connor	10th	N/A
10/6/23	Warrington (a)	L30-26	t:Bibby,Cudjoe,Naiqama,Fages,Lolohea g:Russell(3)	10th	9,007
23/6/23	Leeds (a)	L54-0		10th	14,590
30/6/23	Wigan (a)	L22-6	t:Bibby g:Connor	10th	13,464
8/7/23	Catalans Dragons (a)	W14-22	t:Naiqama,McQueen(2) g:Russell(5)	10th	9,189
14/7/23	Wakefield (h)	W34-6	t:McQueen,Naiqama,Halsall,McGillvary,Lolohea(2) g:Russell(5)	10th	5,872
27/7/23	Hull FC (h)	W19-12	t:McGillvary,Lolohea,McQueen g:Russell(3) fg:Russell	10th	4,579
4/8/23	Castleford (a)	W0-28	t:Halsall(3),Cudjoe,McQueen,Milner g:Russell(2)	10th	6,452
13/8/23	St Helens (a)	L32-18	t:English,Golding,Naiqama g:Russell,Connor(2)	10th	12,028
18/8/23	Salford (h)	L8-32	t:Bibby g:Russell(2)	10th	4,685
27/8/23	Leeds (h)	W21-12	t:Halsall,Naiqama,Lolohea g:Russell(2),Pryce(2) fg:Connor	9th	6,621
1/9/23	Leigh (h) ●●	L34-16	t:Connor(2),Halsall g:Pryce(2)	9th	6,064
8/9/23	Hull KR (h)	L18-26	t:Pryce,McGillvary,Halsall g:Connor(3)	9th	4,628
16/9/23	Hull FC (a)	W20-52	t:McGillvary(2),Marsters,Ikahihifo,Naiqama(3),Pryce(2) g:Connor(8)	9th	10,451
22/9/23	Warrington (h)	L8-20	t:McQueen,Pryce	9th	5,656

● Played at St James' Park, Newcastle
●● Abandoned due to floodlight failure after 48 minutes, remaining 32 played 3/9/23

		APP		TRIES		GOALS		FG		PTS	
	D.O.B.	ALL	SL	ALL	SL	ALL	SL	ALL	SL	ALL	SL
Jack Ashworth	3/7/95	2(8)	2(8)	0	0	0	0	0	0	0	0
Jake Bibby	17/6/96	18	17	5	4	0	0	0	0	20	16
Jake Connor	18/10/94	21(1)	20(1)	2	2	35	29	2	2	80	68
Leroy Cudjoe	7/4/88	19(2)	18(2)	3	3	0	0	0	0	12	12
Matty English	14/11/97	10(9)	10(9)	1	1	0	0	0	0	4	4
Theo Fages	23/8/94	8	7	1	1	0	0	0	0	4	4
Ashton Golding	4/9/96	5(3)	5(3)	3	3	0	0	0	0	12	12
Joe Greenwood	2/4/93	3(12)	3(11)	2	2	0	0	0	0	8	8
Sam Halsall	18/8/01	17	16	9	9	0	0	0	0	36	36
Sam Hewitt	29/4/99	6(9)	5(9)	1	0	0	0	0	0	4	0
Chris Hill	3/11/87	25	24	0	0	0	0	0	0	0	0
Sebastine Ikahihifo	27/1/91	3(19)	3(18)	1	1	0	0	0	0	4	4
Josh Jones	12/5/93	4	4	0	0	0	0	0	0	0	0
Harvey Livett	4/1/97	8	8	1	1	0	0	0	0	4	4
Tui Lolohea	23/1/95	23(4)	23(3)	7	6	2	2	0	0	32	28
Esan Marsters	17/8/96	22	21	3	3	0	0	0	0	12	12
Jermaine McGillvary	16/5/88	13	13	6	6	0	0	0	0	24	24
Chris McQueen	8/3/87	25(2)	25(2)	12	12	0	0	0	0	48	48
Adam Milner	19/12/91	11(2)	11(2)	1	1	0	0	0	0	4	4
Kevin Naiqama	4/2/89	25	24	15	14	0	0	0	0	60	56
Adam O'Brien	11/7/93	2(7)	1(7)	0	0	0	0	0	0	0	0
Nathan Peats	5/10/90	15(10)	15(10)	0	0	0	0	0	0	0	0
Will Pryce	5/12/02	16(2)	15(2)	6	6	6	6	0	0	36	36
Fenton Rogers	4/8/03	(1)	(1)	0	0	0	0	0	0	0	0
Kieran Rush	3/9/02	1	1	0	0	0	0	0	0	0	0
Harry Rushton	13/11/01	2(10)	1(10)	0	0	0	0	0	0	0	0
Oliver Russell	21/9/98	14	14	0	0	40	40	1	1	81	81
Innes Senior	30/5/00	6	6	2	2	0	0	0	0	8	8
Owen Trout	15/10/99	1(4)	1(4)	2	2	0	0	0	0	8	8
Oliver Wilson	22/3/99	15(6)	14(6)	0	0	0	0	0	0	0	0
Luke Yates	6/3/95	24(1)	24	3	3	0	0	0	0	12	0

'SL' totals include Super League games only; 'All' totals also include Challenge Cup

Kevin Naiqama

LEAGUE RECORD
P27-W11-D0-L16
(9th)
F473, A552, Diff-79
22 points.

CHALLENGE CUP
Round Six

ATTENDANCES
Best - v Warrington (SL - 7,731)
Worst - v Castleford (SL - 4,071)
Total (SL only) - 68,172
Average (SL only) - 5,244
(Up by 11 on 2022)

Super League XXVIII - Club by Club

KEY DATES

3rd November 2022 - Stanley Gene appointed assistant coach.

7th November 2022 - Harvey Barron, Will Gardiner, Matty Laidlaw, Lewis Martin, and Manoa Wacokecoke sign first-team contracts.

19th January 2023 - Carlos Tuimavave appointed first-team captain.

3rd February 2023 - young hooker Denive Balmforth joins Newcastle Thunder on loan.

19th February 2023 - 32-30 home round-one win over Castleford after leading 32-6, in front of biggest opening round attendance since 2005.

24th February 2023 - late Scott Taylor try seals 22-18 win at Leeds. Taylor gets one-match ban for dangerous contact.

3rd March 2023 - 38-6 defeat at Catalans ends winning start.

11th March 2023 - 60-14 home hammering by Salford.

14th March 2023 - Connor Wynne goes to Newcastle Thunder on loan.

17th March 2023 - 20-12 defeat at St Helens.

25th March 2023 - Ligi Sao sin-binned twice in 24-16 home defeat to Leigh. Captain Carlos Tuimavave returns. Ligi Sao suspended for one game.

1st April 2023 - 34-6 defeat at leaders Warrington after trailing 28-0 in first half.

7th April 2023 - 40-0 home Good Friday defeat by Hull KR. Jake Clifford and Jamie Shaul injured in first half. Mitieli Vulikijapani (dangerous throw) and Kane Evans (dangerous contact) both banned for one game.

14th April 2023 - rain-soaked 34-10 defeat at Leeds.

23rd April 2023 - Liam Sutcliffe scores two tries in 20-14 home win over Huddersfield as losing run ends at seven games.

27th April 2023 - prop Ligi Sao signs new contract to end of 2025 season.

3rd May 2023 - prop Brad Fash signs three-year contract extension until end of 2026 season.

4th May 2023 - 14-10 home win over current leaders Wigan.

10th May 2023 - one-year contract extensions for centre Cameron Scott, prop Jack Brown and utility forward Joe Cator.

11th May 2023 - 26-6 win at Wakefield. Scott Taylor gets one-match ban for dangerous contact.

16th May 2023 - prop Kane Evans released from contract to return to Australia for personal reasons.

21st May 2023 - Adam Swift scores hat-trick in 32-8 Challenge Cup sixth round win at Castleford.

28th May 2023 - 29-22 defeat at Salford.

31st May 2023 - prop Tevita Satae, to Catalans, and hooker Brad Dwyer, Warrington, to leave at end of season.

4th June 2023 - Josh Griffin scores hat-trick in 30-18 comeback win over Warrington at Magic Weekend.

4th June 2023 - threequarter Mitieli Vulikijapani (knee) and young forward Charlie Severs (shoulder) out for rest of 2023 after surgery.

9th June 2023 - 28-16 defeat at Leigh.

17th June 2023 - Josh Griffin sent off for dissent at half-time of 32-18 Challenge Cup quarter-final home defeat by St Helens.

20th June 2023 - Josh Griffin banned for seven matches for questioning integrity of match official.

22nd June 2023 - Jake Clifford shines in 34-6 home league win over St Helens.

1st July 2023 - 28-18 home defeat to Catalans.

9th July 2023 - Adam Swift second-half double seals 16-6 win at Hull KR.

10th July 2023 - Josh Griffin released from contract to end of season and joins Wakefield.

15th July 2023 - Adam Swift and Cameron Scott both score doubles in 36-18 home win over Castleford.

27th July 2023 - 19-12 defeat at Huddersfield dents play-of hopes.

2nd August 2023 - halfback Jake Clifford to return to North Queensland Cowboys at end of season.

4th August 2023 - Canterbury Bulldogs prop Franklin Pele signs two-year contract from 2024 season.

6th August 2023 - 42-4 home win over Wakefield.

14th August 2023 - NRL Dolphins prop Herman Ese'ese signs for 2024 Super League season on three-year deal.

16th August 2023 - winger Adam Swift and forward Andre Savelio to leave for Huddersfield at end of season.

18th August 2023 - Harry Smith golden-point field goal means 13-12 defeat at Wigan.

25th August 2023 - Canterbury Bulldogs backrower Jayden Okunbor signs two-year deal from 2024 season.

26th August 2023 - Jake Trueman ruptures Achilles in 18-4 home defeat by Warrington.

1st September 2023 - Scott Taylor to retire at end of season.

2nd September 2023 - 28-12 home defeat by Leeds ends play-off chances.

8th September 2023 - 29-12 defeat at Castleford.

14th September 2023 - hooker Danny Houghton signs new one-year deal for 2024 season. Fullback Jamie Shaul to retire at end of season.

15th September 2023 - Connor Wynne, Joe Lovodua and Ben McNamara to depart at end of season.

16th September 2023 - 52-20 home defeat by Huddersfield after second-half collapse.

21st September 2023 - fullback Jack Walker signs on two-year contract.

22nd September 2023 - 30-12 defeat at St Helens means tenth-place finish. Lewis Martin scores on debut.

1st October 2023 - Leeds Rhinos winger Liam Tindall signs on two-year contract.

4th October 2023 - forward Jack Ashworth signs from Huddersfield on two-year contract.

6th October 2023 - half-back Morgan Smith signs from relegated Wakefield on two-year contract.

13th October 2023 - Newcastle Knights halfback Fa'amanu Brown signs on one-year contract.

16th October 2023 - Ben McNamara signs for Leigh.

CLUB RECORDS

Highest score: 88-0 v Sheffield, 2/3/2003
Highest score against:
10-80 v Warrington, 30/8/2018
Record attendance:
28,798 v Leeds, 7/3/36 (The Boulevard)
23,004 v Hull KR, 2/9/2007
(KC/KCOM/MKM Stadium)

MATCH RECORDS

Tries: 7 Clive Sullivan v Doncaster, 15/4/68
Goals:
14 Jim Kennedy v Rochdale, 7/4/1921
Sammy Lloyd v Oldham, 10/9/78
Matt Crowther v Sheffield, 2/3/2003
Points:
36 Jim Kennedy v Keighley, 29/1/1921

SEASON RECORDS

Tries: 52 Jack Harrison 1914-15
Goals: 170 Sammy Lloyd 1978-79
Points: 369 Sammy Lloyd 1978-79

CAREER RECORDS

Tries: 250 Clive Sullivan 1961-74; 1981-85
Goals: 687 Joe Oliver 1928-37; 1943-45
Points: 1,842 Joe Oliver 1928-37; 1943-45
Appearances: 500 Edward Rogers 1906-25

Super League XXVIII - Club by Club

HULL F.C.

DATE	FIXTURE	RESULT	SCORERS	LGE	ATT
19/2/23	Castleford (h)	W32-30	t:McIntosh(2),Sutcliffe,Swift(2),Houghton g:Clifford(4)	5th	15,383
24/2/23	Leeds (a)	W18-22	t:Scott,Sutcliffe,Swift,Taylor g:Clifford(3)	4th	16,140
3/3/23	Catalans Dragons (a)	L38-6	t:Savelio g:Clifford	5th	6,933
11/3/23	Salford (h)	L14-60	t:Clifford,Swift,Fash g:Clifford	9th	11,323
17/3/23	St Helens (a)	L20-12	t:Taylor,Clifford g:Clifford(2)	10th	10,350
25/3/23	Leigh (h)	L16-24	t:Litten,Clifford,Sutcliffe g:Clifford(2)	10th	10,952
1/4/23	Warrington (a)	L34-6	t:Dwyer g:Clifford	10th	10,797
7/4/23	Hull KR (h)	L0-40		11th	20,985
14/4/23	Leeds (a)	L34-10	t:Tuimavave,Litten g:McNamara	11th	12,644
23/4/23	Huddersfield (h)	W20-14	t:Sutcliffe(2),Satae g:Clifford(4)	10th	10,856
4/5/23	Wigan (h)	W14-10	t:McIntosh,Clifford g:Clifford(3)	10th	10,251
11/5/23	Wakefield (a)	W6-26	t:Swift,Tuimavave,Sutcliffe,Taylor g:Clifford(5)	9th	3,976
21/5/23	Castleford (a) (CCR6)	W8-32	t:Griffin,Swift(3),Brown,Lane g:Clifford(4)	N/A	4,249
28/5/23	Salford (a)	L29-22	t:Clifford,Trueman,McIntosh,Griffin g:Clifford(3)	10th	4,569
4/6/23	Warrington (MW) ●	W30-18	t:Houghton,Swift,Griffin(3),Hoy g:Clifford(3)	9th	N/A
9/6/23	Leigh (a)	L28-16	t:Swift,McIntosh,Griffin g:Sutcliffe(2)	9th	6,006
17/6/23	St Helens (h) (CCQF)	L18-32	t:Griffin,Savelio,Trueman g:Sutcliffe(3)	N/A	8,127
22/6/23	St Helens (h)	W34-6	t:Clifford,Tuimavave,Trueman,Satae,Scott,McIntosh g:Clifford(5)	9th	9,937
1/7/23	Catalans Dragons (h)	L18-28	t:Satae,McIntosh,Swift g:Clifford(3)	9th	13,480
9/7/23	Hull KR (a)	W6-16	t:Swift(2),Sao g:Clifford(2)	9th	10,050
15/7/23	Castleford (h)	W36-18	t:Swift(2),Tuimavave,Satae,Litten,Scott(2) g:Clifford(4)	9th	12,352
27/7/23	Huddersfield (a)	L19-12	t:Swift,Fash g:Sutcliffe(2)	9th	4,579
6/8/23	Wakefield (h)	W42-4	t:Swift,Tuimavave,Scott,Lane,McIntosh(2),Lovodua g:Clifford(7)	8th	11,956
18/8/23	Wigan (a)	L13-12 (aet)	t:Swift,Dwyer g:Sutcliffe(2)	9th	12,107
26/8/23	Warrington (h)	L4-18	t:Swift	10th	11,624
2/9/23	Leeds (h)	L12-28	t:Swift,Barron,Scott	10th	11,064
8/9/23	Castleford (a)	L29-12	t:Swift(2) g:McIntosh(2)	10th	7,947
16/9/23	Huddersfield (h)	L20-52	t:Hoy,McIntosh,Savelio,Taylor g:Clifford,Taylor	10th	10,451
22/9/23	St Helens (a)	L30-12	t:Martin,Scott g:Hoy(2)	10th	14,036

● Played at St James' Park, Newcastle

	D.O.B.	APP ALL	APP SL	TRIES ALL	TRIES SL	GOALS ALL	GOALS SL	FG ALL	FG SL	PTS ALL	PTS SL
Harvey Barron	13/5/03	3	3	1	1	0	0	0	0	4	4
Jack Brown	25/6/00	3(16)	3(15)	1	0	0	0	0	0	4	0
Joe Cator	15/6/98	21(5)	19(5)	0	0	0	0	0	0	0	0
Jake Clifford	2/1/98	26	25	6	6	54	50	0	0	132	124
Brad Dwyer	28/4/93	7(19)	7(17)	2	2	0	0	0	0	8	8
Kane Evans	9/1/92	1(5)	1(5)	0	0	0	0	0	0	0	0
Brad Fash	24/1/96	27	25	2	2	0	0	0	0	8	8
Will Gardiner	21/5/01	(6)	(5)	0	0	0	0	0	0	0	0
Josh Griffin	9/5/90	17	15	7	5	0	0	0	0	28	20
Danny Houghton	25/9/88	22(2)	20(2)	2	2	0	0	0	0	8	8
Tex Hoy	4/11/99	16(1)	14(1)	2	2	2	2	0	0	12	12
Zach Jebson	9/5/04	(1)	(1)	0	0	0	0	0	0	0	0
Jordan Lane	20/10/97	21(7)	20(6)	2	1	0	0	0	0	8	4
Davy Litten	3/5/03	16	15	3	3	0	0	0	0	12	12
Joe Lovodua	18/3/98	11(8)	11(8)	1	1	0	0	0	0	4	4
Lewis Martin	19/8/04	1	1	1	1	0	0	0	0	4	4
Darnell McIntosh	5/7/97	21(1)	20(1)	10	10	2	2	0	0	44	44
Ben McNamara	18/12/01	7(2)	7(2)	0	0	1	1	0	0	2	2
Ligi Sao	11/10/92	12(6)	12(5)	1	1	0	0	0	0	4	4
Tevita Satae	22/10/92	11(17)	10(16)	4	4	0	0	0	0	16	16
Andre Savelio	21/3/95	15(3)	14(3)	3	2	0	0	0	0	12	8
Cameron Scott	7/10/99	23(1)	22(1)	7	7	0	0	0	0	28	28
Jamie Shaul	1/7/92	4(1)	4(1)	0	0	0	0	0	0	0	0
Nick Staveley	19/1/04	(3)	(2)	0	0	0	0	0	0	0	0
Liam Sutcliffe	25/11/94	21	19	6	6	13	10	0	0	50	44
Adam Swift	20/2/93	26	24	22	19	0	0	0	0	88	76
Scott Taylor	27/2/91	13(10)	12(10)	4	4	1	1	0	0	18	18
Jake Trueman	16/2/99	14(1)	12(1)	3	2	0	0	0	0	12	8
Carlos Tuimavave	10/1/92	18	16	5	5	0	0	0	0	20	20
Mitieli Vulikijapani	27/6/94	(1)	(1)	0	0	0	0	0	0	0	0

'SL' totals include Super League games only; 'All' totals also include Challenge Cup

Adam Swift

LEAGUE RECORD
P27-W10-D0-L17
(10th)
F476, A654, Diff-178
20 points.

CHALLENGE CUP
Quarter Finalists

ATTENDANCES
Best - v Hull KR (SL - 20,985)
Worst - v St Helens (CC - 8,127)
Total (SL only) - 160,614
Average (SL only) - 12,355
(Up by 1,592 on 2022)

Super League XXVIII - Club by Club

KEY DATES

7th November 2022 - young forwards Connor Moore and Dan Okoro join Newcastle Thunder on season loan.

6th January 2023 - Phoenix Laulu-Togaga'e signs new two-year extension to end of 2025 season.

18th February 2023 - Shaun Kenny-Dowall scores hat-trick in 27-18 home round-one win over Wigan.

23rd February 2023 - Jordan Abdull stars in 24-10 win at Salford. Lachlan Coote misses game with hamstring injury.

3rd March 2023 - last-minute converted try from Josh Charnley means 30-25 home defeat to Leigh. Kane Linnett suffers knee injury.

7th March 2023 - Shaun Kenny-Dowall gets four-match suspension for unnecessary contact with injured opponent.

10th March 2023 - 18-10 home defeat to unbeaten Warrington.

18th March 2023 - Jordan Abdull, Frankie Halton and Dean Hadley all fail HIAs in 26-12 defeat at Catalans.

24th March 2023 - 34-6 win at Wakefield ends three-match losing run.

27th March 2023 - Ryan Hall signs new one-year contract extension to end of 2024.

28th March 2023 - Wakefield centre Corey Hall, 20, signs with immediate effect, until end of 2025 season. Will Dagger leaves in other direction.

31st March 2023 - 20-12 home win over Leeds.

2nd April 2023 - backrower Luis Johnson joins Castleford on season loan.

5th April 2023 - prop Yusuf Aydin joins Featherstone on short-term loan.

7th April 2023 - Shaun Kenny-Dowall back and Ryan Hall scores hat-trick in 40-0 Good Friday away hammering of Hull FC. Sauaso Sue gets two-match penalty notice for dangerous throw; James Batchelor one match for dangerous contact.

9th April 2023 - utility-back Will Tate signs for Castleford with immediate effect.

13th April 2023 - backrower Dean Hadley signs new two-year contract extension to end of 2025 season.

14th April 2023 - Corey Hall makes impressive debut in 26-14 home win over St Helens.

18th April 2023 - halfback Rowan Milnes joins Wakefield on two-week loan.

21st April 2023 - 12-7 win at Castleford is fifth on a row.

5th May 2023 - Ryan Hall and Joe Batchelor score doubles in 28-0 home win over Huddersfield. Rowan Milnes breaks hand. Jordan Abdull sidelined by thigh injury in training.

10th May 2023 - Lachlan Coote to retire at season end.

12th May 2023 - 21-14 defeat at Warrington after leading 12-0 ends winning run at six. Sauaso Sue gets one-match ban for dangerous contact.

13th May 2023 - Bradford backrower AJ Wallace signs for 2024 on two-year contract.

17th May 2023 - backrower Frankie Halton released to join Leigh with immediate effect.

17th May 2023 - backrower Kane Linnett signs one-year contract extension to end of 2024 season.

19th May 2023 - Ethan Ryan scores hat-trick in 50-0 home Challenge Cup sixth round win over Batley.

21st May 2023 - New Zealand international centre Peta Hiku to join for 2024 on three-year contract.

23rd May 2023 - Shaun Kenny-Dowall to retire at end of season and join Robins coaching staff.

25th May 2023 - 26-22 home defeat to Wigan after leading 22-14 with ten minutes left. Stand-in fullback Ethan Ryan breaks jaw.

1st June 2023 - England centre Oliver Gildart signs three-year deal from 2024 when contract with NRL Dolphins contract expires.

2nd June 2023 - fullback Jack Walker signs from Bradford Bulls until end of 2023.

3rd June 2023 - Sauaso Sue (hamstring) and Joe Batchelor (head) injured in 26-16 Magic Weekend defeat to Salford.

8th June 2023 - halfback Jordan Abdull extends contract to end of 2026.

10th June 2023 - Jordan Abdull injures hamstring and Jack Walker suffers head knock on debut in 38-4 defeat at Catalans.

13th June 2023 - fullback Tanguy Zenon joins on two-week loan from Catalans.

17th June 2023 - Tanguy Zenon scores try on debut in 28-10 home Challenge Cup quarter-final win over Salford.

18th June 2023 - winger Fouad Yaha joins on two-week loan from Catalans.

21st June 2023 - fullback Lachlan Coote retires with immediate effect on medical advice after series of concussions.

23rd June 2023 - 28-12 home win over Wakefield ends four-match losing run.

30th June 2023 - 34-4 defeat at Leigh.

6th July 2023 - Canberra Raiders halfback Brad Schneider signs until end of season.

9th July 2023 - 16-6 home defeat to Hull FC.

13th July 2023 - prop George King signs new contract to end of 2027.

14th July 2023 - on-debut Brad Schneider kicks golden-point field goal to secure 19-18 win at Leeds. James Batchelor returns from injury.

21st July 2023 - James Batchelor signs two-year contract extension to end of 2026.

23rd July 2023 - Brad Schneider kicks golden-point field goal to secure 11-10 Challenge Cup semi-final win over Wigan at Leeds.

28th July 2023 - 34-16 home win over Castleford.

4th August 2023 - weakened side suffers 64-6 defeat at Wigan.

12th August 2023 - Lachlan Lam slots golden-point field goal to secure 17-16 defeat by Leigh at Wembley. Elliot Minchella sin-binned and gets one game for late hit on kicker.

15th August 2023 - Catalans Dragons halfback Tyrone May signs two-year contract from 2024 season.

18th August 2023 - 28-6 defeat at St Helens.

23rd August 2023 - Castleford Tigers fullback Niall Evalds signs two-year contract from 2024 season.

25th August 2023 - Mikey Lewis and Ryan Hall score doubles in 52-10 home hammering of Leigh.

1st September 2023 - 26-18 home win over Catalans.

8th September 2023 - 26-18 win at Huddersfield.

16th September 2023 - 12-0 home win over Salford secures play-off place.

22nd September 2023 - 56-12 win at relegated Wakefield secures fourth spot and home play-off.

29th September 2023 - 20-6 home victory over Leigh in first eliminator.

4th October 2023 - England hooker Jez Litten signs new four-year contract to end of 2027 season. Sam Wood joins Castleford.

6th October 2023 - halfback Rowan Milnes leaves for Castleford.

7th October 2023 - 42-12 semi-final defeat at Wigan.

8th October 2023 - centre Tom Opacic extends contract to end of 2025 season.

9th October 2023 - prop Jai Whitbread signs from Wakefield on three-year deal. Rhys Kennedy released.

18th October 2023 - hooker Reiss Butterworth signs from Dewsbury on one-season contract with option for another year.

30th October 2023 - Danny Ward joins as assistant coach.

CLUB RECORDS

Highest score:
100-6 v Nottingham City, 19/8/90
Highest score against:
6-84 v Wigan, 1/4/2013
Record attendance:
27,670 v Hull FC, 3/4/53 *(Boothferry Park)*
12,100 v Hull FC, 1/2/2019 *(Craven Park)*

MATCH RECORDS

Tries: 11 George West
v Brooklands Rovers, 4/3/1905
Goals:
14 Alf Carmichael v Merthyr, 8/10/1910
Mike Fletcher v Whitehaven, 18/3/97
Colin Armstrong v Nottingham City, 19/8/90
Damien Couturier v Halifax, 23/4/2006
Points: 53 George West
v Brooklands Rovers, 4/3/1905

SEASON RECORDS

Tries: 45 Gary Prohm 1984-85
Goals: 199 Mike Fletcher 1989-90
Points: 450 Mike Fletcher 1989-90

CAREER RECORDS

Tries: 207 Roger Millward 1966-80
Goals: 1,268 Mike Fletcher 1987-98
Points: 2,760 Mike Fletcher 1987-98
Appearances: 489 Mike Smith 1975-91

Super League XXVIII - Club by Club

HULL KR

DATE	FIXTURE	RESULT	SCORERS	LGE	ATT
18/2/23	Wigan (h)	W27-18	t:R Hall,Kenny-Dowall(3),Linnett g:Coote(3) fg:Abdull	4th	10,029
23/2/23	Salford (a)	W10-24	t:Ryan,Halton,Wood(2) g:Dagger(4)	2nd	5,565
3/3/23	Leigh (h)	L25-30	t:Kenny-Dowall,Lewis,Batchelor,Abdull g:Dagger(4) fg:Abdull	4th	8,448
10/3/23	Warrington (h)	L10-18	t:Halton(2) g:Coote	6th	8,082
18/3/23	Catalans Dragons (a)	L26-12	t:Milnes,R Hall g:Lewis(2)	7th	7,682
24/3/23	Wakefield (a)	W6-34	t:Wood,Senior,Opacic(2),Linnett,Lewis,Minchella g:Coote(3)	4th	4,705
31/3/23	Leeds (h)	W20-12	t:Senior,Sue,Linnett g:Coote(4)	5th	8,512
7/4/23	Hull FC (a)	W0-40	t:R Hall(3),Opacic,Batchelor,Coote,Lewis g:Coote(6)	4th	20,985
14/4/23	St Helens (h)	W26-14	t:Lewis(2),Coote,Litten g:Coote(5)	3rd	8,540
21/4/23	Castleford (a)	W7-12	t:C Hall,Parcell g:Coote(2)	3rd	7,110
5/5/23	Huddersfield (h)	W28-0	t:R Hall(2),Batchelor(2),Opacic g:Milnes(4)	3rd	8,490
12/5/23	Warrington (a)	L21-14	t:Ryan,Linnett g:Lewis(3)	3rd	10,179
19/5/23	Batley (h) (CCR6)	W50-0	t:Linnett(2),Ryan(3),Kenny-Dowall(2),Lewis,Luckley g:Lewis(5),Wood(2)	N/A	5,143
25/5/23	Wigan (h)	L22-26 (aet)	t:R Hall,Parcell,Batchelor,Johnson g:Lewis(3)	4th	8,068
3/6/23	Salford (MW) ●	L16-26	t:Minchella,King,R Hall g:Coote(2)	7th	N/A
10/6/23	Catalans Dragons (a)	L38-4	t:C Hall	7th	9,450
17/6/23	Salford (h) (CCQF)	W28-10	t:R Hall,Zenon,Linnett,Kenny-Dowall,Hadley g:Milnes(4)	N/A	6,289
23/6/23	Wakefield (h)	W28-12	t:Opacic(2),Senior(2),Lewis g:Milnes(4)	7th	8,185
30/6/23	Leigh (a)	L34-4	t:Lewis	7th	6,012
9/7/23	Hull FC (h)	L6-16	t:Walker g:Milnes	8th	10,050
14/7/23	Leeds (a)	W18-19 (aet)	t:Schneider,Opacic,Senior g:Milnes(3) fg:Schneider	6th	13,728
23/7/23	Wigan (CCSF) ●●	W11-10 (aet)	t:Senior,Ryan g:Schneider fg:Schneider	N/A	10,926
28/7/23	Castleford (h)	W34-16	t:Opacic,Kennedy,Linnett,Minchella,Batchelor,Ryan g:Milnes(5)	5th	8,636
4/8/23	Wigan (a)	L64-6	t:Walker g:Milnes	6th	11,464
12/8/23	Leigh (CCF) ●●●	L16-17 (aet)	t:Litten,Parcell g:Schneider(4)	N/A	58,213
18/8/23	St Helens (a)	L28-6	t:Lewis g:Schneider	7th	11,258
25/8/23	Leigh (h)	W52-10	t:Kenny-Dowall,Minchella,R Hall(2),Senior,Lewis(2),Linnett,Litten g:Schneider(8)	7th	8,013
1/9/23	Catalans Dragons (h)	W26-18	t:Kenny-Dowall,Linnett,Walker,Lewis g:Schneider(5)	6th	9,102
8/9/23	Huddersfield (a)	W18-26	t:Kenny-Dowall,Abdull,Linnett,Senior g:Schneider(5)	5th	4,628
16/9/23	Salford (h)	W12-0	t:Batchelor,R Hall g:Schneider(2)	5th	9,848
22/9/23	Wakefield (a)	W12-56	t:Walker,Lewis,Storton(2),Schneider(2),Opacic,R Hall,Litten(2) g:Schneider(8)	4th	4,710
29/9/23	Leigh (h) (E)	W20-6	t:Walker,R Hall,Luckley g:Schneider(4)	N/A	9,305
7/10/23	Wigan (a) (SF)	L42-12	t:Minchella,Litten g:Schneider(2)	N/A	15,162

● *Played at St James' Park, Newcastle* ●● *Played at Headingley, Leeds* ●●● *Played at Wembley Stadium*

		APP		TRIES		GOALS		FG		PTS	
	D.O.B.	ALL	SL	ALL	SL	ALL	SL	ALL	SL	ALL	SL
Jordan Abdull	5/2/96	9(5)	9(5)	2	2	0	0	2	2	10	10
Yusuf Aydin	13/9/00	1(6)	1(4)	0	0	0	0	0	0	0	0
Connor Barley	16/9/04	1	1	0	0	0	0	0	0	0	0
James Batchelor	9/4/98	25	22	7	7	0	0	0	0	28	28
Lachlan Coote	6/4/90	10	10	2	2	26	26	0	0	60	60
Will Dagger	21/2/99	2(1)	2(1)	0	0	8	8	0	0	16	16
Lennie Ellis	8/7/05	(1)	(1)	0	0	0	0	0	0	0	0
Louix Gorman	25/4/05	1	1	0	0	0	0	0	0	0	0
Dean Hadley	5/8/92	18(8)	16(7)	1	0	0	0	0	0	4	0
Corey Hall	7/8/02	8	8	2	2	0	0	0	0	8	8
Ryan Hall	27/11/87	28	25	15	14	0	0	0	0	60	56
Frankie Halton	18/6/96	3(3)	3(3)	3	3	0	0	0	0	12	12
Luis Johnson	20/2/99	2(3)	2(3)	1	1	0	0	0	0	4	4
Jimmy Keinhorst	14/7/90	4(4)	4(2)	0	0	0	0	0	0	0	0
Rhys Kennedy	11/10/94	19(7)	16(6)	1	1	0	0	0	0	4	4
Shaun Kenny-Dowall	23/1/88	28	24	10	7	0	0	0	0	40	28
George King	24/2/95	27(3)	24(3)	1	1	0	0	0	0	4	4
Phoenix Laulu-Togaga'e	16/4/03	2	1	0	0	0	0	0	0	0	0
Mikey Lewis	4/7/01	31	27	13	12	13	8	0	0	78	64
Kane Linnett	11/1/89	28	24	11	8	0	0	0	0	44	32
Jez Litten	10/3/98	15(16)	11(16)	6	5	0	0	0	0	24	20
Sam Luckley	29/11/95	5(26)	4(23)	2	1	0	0	0	0	8	4
Rowan Milnes	1/9/97	13(1)	10(1)	1	1	22	18	0	0	48	40
Elliot Minchella	28/1/96	26(1)	22(1)	5	5	0	0	0	0	20	20
Tom Opacic	7/9/94	30	26	9	9	0	0	0	0	36	36
Matt Parcell	30/10/92	20(10)	20(7)	3	2	0	0	0	0	12	8
Cesar Rouge	3/10/02	1	1	0	0	0	0	0	0	0	0
Ethan Ryan	12/5/96	12	9	7	3	0	0	0	0	28	12
Brad Schneider	15/1/01	12	10	3	3	40	35	2	1	94	83
Louis Senior	30/5/00	17	15	8	7	0	0	0	0	32	28
Isaac Shaw	11/9/02	(1)	(1)	0	0	0	0	0	0	0	0
Matty Storton	10/3/99	2(23)	2(19)	2	2	0	0	0	0	8	8
Sauaso Sue	20/4/92	6(9)	6(9)	1	1	0	0	0	0	4	4
Leo Tennison	31/5/04	(1)	(1)	0	0	0	0	0	0	0	0
Luke Thomas	19/10/02	(1)	(1)	0	0	0	0	0	0	0	0
Jack Walker	8/8/99	10	10	5	5	0	0	0	0	20	20
Sam Wood	11/6/97	8(3)	7(3)	3	3	2	2	0	0	16	12
Fouad Yaha	19/8/96	2	2	0	0	0	0	0	0	0	0
Tanguy Zenon	8/5/02	3	2	1	0	0	0	0	0	4	0

'SL' totals include regular season & play-offs; 'All' totals also include Challenge Cup

Mikey Lewis

LEAGUE RECORD
P27-W16-D0-L11
(4th/Semi-Final)
F589, A498, Diff+91
32 points.

CHALLENGE CUP
Runners-up

ATTENDANCES
Best - v Hull FC (SL - 10,050)
Worst - v Batley (CC - 5,143)
Total (SL, inc play-offs) - 123,308
Average (SL, inc play-offs) - 8,808
(Up by 1,019 on 2022)

Super League XXVIII - Club by Club

KEY DATES

25th November 2022 - Matt Cook appointed new general manager.

30th November 2022 - Cameron Smith signs new contract to end of 2026 season.

1st December 2022 - PNG centre Nene Macdonald signs from Leigh on two-year contract.

26th December 2022 - young side suffers 38-20 defeat to Wakefield in Wetherby Whaler Challenge.

8th February 2023 - 19-year-old centre Levi Edwards leaves for York.

16th February 2023 - 42-10 round-one defeat at Warrington.

24th February 2023 - Nene Macdonald makes debut in 22-18 home defeat to Hull FC.

3rd March 2023 - Blake Austin kicks late field goal to secure 25-24 round-three win at St Helens. James McDonnell makes debut. Kruise Leeming suffers ankle injury.

6th March 2023 - Sam Walters charged with shoulder charge and cops fine instead of ban under new regulations.

10th March 2023 - Harry Newman and James Bentley make first appearances of 2023 in 26-0 home win over Wakefield. Ash Handley injures ankle.

16th March 2023 - hooker Kruise Leeming granted permission to seek contract elsewhere.

16th March 2023 - 14-8 defeat at Castleford. James Bentley suspended for one game for dangerous contact.

25th March 2023 - 32-22 round-6 home win ends Catalans 100 per cent start, after trailing 22-8 at half-time.

1st April 2023 - 20-12 defeat at Hull KR. Mikolaj Oledzki back for first game since England World Cup win over France. Winger David Fusitu'a suffers ankle injury.

9th April 2023 - Richie Myler, Nene Macdonald and Ash Handley return for Easter Sunday 18-17 home win over Huddersfield.

14th April 2023 - 34-10 home win over Hull FC.

21st April 2023 - Aidan Sezer injures quad muscle in 20-6 defeat at Leigh.

5th May 2023 - 22-12 home defeat by Salford.

12th May 2023 - second-half comeback ends in 40-18 win at Wigan despite 37th minute dismissal of Zane Tetevano. Tetevano banned for two games.

20th May 2023 - 18-14 home Challenge Cup exit to Wigan after leading 14-0.

26th May 2023 - James McDonnell sent off at end of normal time as Lewis Dodd golden-point field goal means 13-12 home defeat to St Helens.

30th May 2023 - James McDonnell banned for two games, but overturned on appeal.

3rd June 2023 - 26-24 Magic Weekend defeat to Castleford.

9th June 2023 - halfback Jack Sinfield signs new contract to end of 2026.

11th June 2023 - 24-14 defeat at previously winless Wakefield.

14th June 2023 - winger Ash Handley extends contract to end of 2026 season.

14th June 2023 - prop Zane Tetevano to have heart surgery after suffering stroke in training.

23rd June 2023 - utility forward Jarrod O'Connor signs new three-year contract to end of 2026 season.

23rd June 2023 - Aidan Sezer returns as Rhyse Martin scores 26 points in 54-0 home win over Huddersfield.

25th June 2023 - prop Sam Lisone extends contract to end of 2025 season.

27th June 2023 - Catalans Dragons prop Mickael Goudemand signs two-year deal from 2024 season.

29th June 2023 - Ash Handley scores try-double in 22-6 win at Warrington.

5th July 2023 - centre Nene Macdonald extends contract to end of 2027 season. Prop Justin Sangaré extends to end of 2025 season.

9th July 2023 - late Rhyse Martin penalty goal seals 16-14 win at Salford.

14th July 2023 - Ash Handley plays 200th career game in 19-18 home golden point defeat to Hull KR.

28th July 2023 - 22-18 defeat at St Helens.

3rd August 2023 - halfback Blake Austin joins Castleford on loan.

6th August 2023 - 13-6 home defeat to Leigh.

20th August 2023 - 24-22 home win over Warrington.

23rd August 2023 - Newcastle Knights fullback Lachlan Miller signs three-year contract from 2024 season.

20th August 2023 - James Donaldson signs one-year contract extension for 2024 season.

27th August 2023 - 21-12 defeat at Huddersfield.

2nd September 2023 - prop Sam Lisone scores hat-trick as 28-12 win at Hull FC leaves Rhinos four points off play-offs with three games to go.

5th September 2023 - Canberra Raiders halfback Matt Frawley signs two-year deal from 2024. Prop Zane Tetevano released to return to New Zealand.

7th September 2023 - backrower James Bentley (two years) and winger David Fusitu'a (one) extend contracts.

9th September 2023 - Injury-hit side falls to 50-0 home defeat to Wigan.

16th September 2023 - 61-0 defeat at Catalans.

22nd September 2023 - David Fusitu'a scores hat-trick in 46-0 home final round win over Castleford.

4th October 2023 - Nene Macdonald leaves club by mutual consent. Halfback Aidan Sezer joins Wests Tigers.

6th October 2023 - fullback Luke Hooley leaves for Castleford.

7th October 2023 - centre Paul Momirovski signs from Sydney Roosters on two-year contract.

14th October 2023 - Nene MacDonald signs for Salford.

18th October 2023 - halfback Brodie Croft and hooker Andy Ackers sign from Salford on three-year contracts.

CLUB RECORDS

Highest score:
106-10 v Swinton, 11/2/2001
Highest score against:
6-74 v Wigan, 20/5/92
Record attendance:
40,175 v Bradford, 21/5/47

MATCH RECORDS

Tries:
8 Fred Webster v Coventry, 12/4/1913
Eric Harris v Bradford, 14/9/31
Goals:
17 Iestyn Harris v Swinton, 11/2/2001
Points:
42 Iestyn Harris v Huddersfield, 16/7/99

SEASON RECORDS

Tries: 63 Eric Harris 1935-36
Goals: 173 *(inc 5fg)* Kevin Sinfield 2012
Points: 431 Lewis Jones 1956-57

CAREER RECORDS

Tries: 391 Eric Harris 1930-39
Goals:
1,831 *(inc 39fg)* Kevin Sinfield 1997-2015
Points: 3,967 Kevin Sinfield 1997-2015
Appearances: 625 John Holmes 1968-89

LEEDS RHINOS

Super League XXVIII - Club by Club

DATE	FIXTURE	RESULT	SCORERS	LGE	ATT
16/2/23	Warrington (a)	L42-10	t:Olpherts,Sangare g:Martin	12th	11,082
24/2/23	Hull FC (h)	L18-22	t:Smith,Leeming,Fusitu'a g:Martin(3)	11th	16,140
3/3/23	St Helens (a)	W24-25	t:Handley,Martin(2),Smith g:Martin(4) fg:Austin	10th	15,148
10/3/23	Wakefield (h)	W26-0	t:Fusitu'a(2),Newman,Holroyd,Macdonald g:Martin(2),Sezer	8th	11,717
16/3/23	Castleford (a)	L14-8	t:Myler g:Martin(2)	8th	7,458
25/3/23	Catalans Dragons (h)	W32-22	t:Newman(2),Martin,Myler,O'Connor,Olpherts,Holroyd g:Martin,Sezer	7th	14,321
31/3/23	Hull KR (a)	L20-12	t:Roberts,McDonnell g:Martin(2)	8th	8,512
9/4/23	Huddersfield (h)	W18-17	t:Handley,McDonnell,Martin,Smith g:Martin	7th	13,234
14/4/23	Hull FC (h)	W34-10	t:McDonnell,Handley(2),Holroyd,Oledzki,Martin g:Martin(5)	6th	12,644
21/4/23	Leigh (a)	L20-6	t:Bentley g:Martin	8th	6,686
5/5/23	Salford (h)	L12-22	t:Myler,Bentley g:Martin(2)	8th	13,007
12/5/23	Wigan (a)	W18-40	t:Newman(2),Holroyd,Myler,Martin,Smith,Tindall g:Martin(6)	8th	12,167
20/5/23	Wigan (h) (CCR6)	L14-18	t:Holroyd,Newman g:Martin(3)	N/A	7,103
26/5/23	St Helens (h)	L12-13 (aet)	t:Handley,Smith g:Martin(2)	8th	14,161
3/6/23	Castleford (MW) ●	L26-24	t:Olpherts,Bentley,Martin,Oledzki g:Martin(4)	8th	N/A
11/6/23	Wakefield (a)	L24-14	t:Smith,Ruan,Austin g:Martin	8th	4,710
23/6/23	Huddersfield (h)	W54-0	t:Walters(2),Myler,Handley,Fusitu'a(2),McDonnell,Martin(2) g:Martin(9)	8th	14,590
29/6/23	Warrington (a)	W6-22	t:Walters,Handley(2),Myler g:Martin(3)	8th	8,981
9/7/23	Salford (a)	W14-16	t:Smith,Handley g:Martin(4)	7th	5,157
14/7/23	Hull KR (h)	L18-19 (aet)	t:O'Connor,Johnson,Handley g:Martin(3)	8th	13,728
28/7/23	St Helens (a)	L22-18	t:Martin,Walters,Macdonald g:Martin(3)	8th	12,108
6/8/23	Leigh (h)	L6-13	t:O'Connor g:Martin	9th	12,785
20/8/23	Warrington (h)	W24-22	t:Walters,Fusitu'a,Hooley,Bentley g:Martin(4)	8th	15,166
27/8/23	Huddersfield (a)	L21-12	t:Hooley,Handley g:Martin(2)	8th	6,621
2/9/23	Hull FC (a)	W12-28	t:Hooley,Lisone(3),Fusitu'a g:Martin(4)	8th	11,064
9/9/23	Wigan (h)	L0-50		8th	12,861
16/9/23	Catalans Dragons (a)	L61-0		8th	9,162
22/9/23	Castleford (h)	W46-0	t:Hooley,Fusitu'a(3),Olpherts,Sinfield,Lisone,Walters g:Martin(7)	8th	15,109

● *Played at St James' Park, Newcastle*

		APP		TRIES		GOALS		FG		PTS	
	D.O.B.	ALL	SL	ALL	SL	ALL	SL	ALL	SL	ALL	SL
Blake Austin	1/2/91	18	18	1	1	0	0	1	1	5	5
James Bentley	19/10/97	13(4)	13(4)	4	4	0	0	0	0	16	16
James Donaldson	14/9/91	2(16)	2(15)	0	0	0	0	0	0	0	0
Alfie Edgell	25/7/04	(1)	(1)	0	0	0	0	0	0	0	0
David Fusitu'a	16/10/94	17	17	10	10	0	0	0	0	40	40
Morgan Gannon	2/12/03	7(4)	6(4)	0	0	0	0	0	0	0	0
Ash Handley	16/2/96	23	23	11	11	0	0	0	0	44	44
Tom Holroyd	9/2/01	15(9)	14(9)	5	4	0	0	0	0	20	16
Luke Hooley	1/8/98	8	8	4	4	0	0	0	0	16	16
Corey Johnson	16/11/00	3(15)	3(14)	1	1	0	0	0	0	4	4
Kruise Leeming	7/9/95	2(1)	2(1)	1	1	0	0	0	0	4	4
Sam Lisone	19/2/94	5(19)	5(18)	4	4	0	0	0	0	16	16
Nene Macdonald	11/5/94	20	19	2	2	0	0	0	0	8	8
Rhyse Martin	1/3/93	28	27	10	10	80	77	0	0	200	194
James McDonnell	12/1/00	24	23	4	4	0	0	0	0	16	16
Richie Myler	21/5/90	20	19	6	6	0	0	0	0	24	24
Harry Newman	19/2/00	15(2)	14(2)	6	5	0	0	0	0	24	20
Tom Nicholson-Watton	13/12/02	(1)	(1)	0	0	0	0	0	0	0	0
Jarrod O'Connor	20/7/01	26(2)	25(2)	3	3	0	0	0	0	12	12
Mikolaj Oledzki	8/11/98	20(2)	19(2)	2	2	0	0	0	0	8	8
Derrell Olpherts	7/1/92	13(1)	12(1)	4	4	0	0	0	0	16	16
Luis Roberts	24/3/02	7(2)	7(2)	1	1	0	0	0	0	4	4
Leon Ruan	14/5/03	(5)	(5)	1	1	0	0	0	0	4	4
Justin Sangare	7/3/98	(18)	(17)	1	1	0	0	0	0	4	4
Aidan Sezer	24/6/91	20	19	0	0	2	2	0	0	4	4
Jack Sinfield	21/9/04	5(1)	5(1)	1	1	0	0	0	0	4	4
Cameron Smith	7/11/98	26(1)	25(1)	7	7	0	0	0	0	28	28
Zane Tetevano	4/11/90	10(1)	10(1)	0	0	0	0	0	0	0	0
Liam Tindall	27/9/01	3(3)	2(3)	1	1	0	0	0	0	4	4
Sam Walters	25/12/00	14(3)	14(3)	6	6	0	0	0	0	24	24

'SL' totals include Super League games only; 'All' totals also include Challenge Cup

Rhyse Martin

LEAGUE RECORD
P27-W12-D0-L15
(8th)
F535, A534, Diff+1
24 points.

CHALLENGE CUP
Round Six

ATTENDANCES
Best - v Hull FC (SL - 16,140)
Worst - v Wigan (CC - 7,103)
Total (SL only) - 179,463
Average (SL only) - 13,805
(Up by 864 on 2022)

Super League XXVIII - Club by Club

KEY DATES

20th October 2022 - Centurions nickname is dropped in rebrand as Leopards.

20th October 2022 - Gareth O'Brien (Castleford), Tom Briscoe and Zak Hardaker (both Leeds) and Ricky Leutele (Huddersfield) announced as signings on two-year contracts. Oliver Holmes, Jack Hughes, Rob Mulhern, Matt Davis and Jacob Gannon all join from Warrington on two-year deals. Nathan Wilde signs from Newcastle Thunder on one-year contract.

20th October 2022 - Adam Sidlow (Salford Red Devils), Luis Roberts (Leeds Rhinos), Krisnan Inu (retired), Caleb Aekins (released), Sam Stone (Salford Red Devils), Mark Ioane (Keighley Cougars), Ata Hingano (York Knights), Kieran Dixon (Widnes Vikings), Jy Hitchcox (retired) all leave.

1st December 2022 - Nene Macdonald signs for Leeds.

2nd December 2022 - Blake Ferguson released on compassionate grounds to return to Australia.

23rd January 2023 - former Leeds prop Ava Seumanufagai signs on one-year contract.

17th February 2023 - 20-10 home round-one defeat to Salford.

25th February 2023 - 14-6 defeat at Catalans.

3rd March 2023 - Josh Charnley scores last-minute try to secure 30-25 win at Hull KR.

7th March 2023 - Ben Reynolds gets two-match ban for late hit on passer.

10th March 2023 - 20-12 home win over St Helens after trailing 12-0.

17th March 2023 - 38-20 defeat at leaders Warrington.

25th March 2023 - Josh Charnley scores hat-trick in 24-16 win at Hull FC.

30th March 2023 - 34-6 home defeat by Wigan.

8th April 2023 - 22-20 home defeat by Salford. Josh Charnley scores try-double. Jack Hughes suffers calf injury.

17th April 2023 - Josh Charnley scores try-double in 32-0 win at Wakefield.

21st April 2023 - Edwin Ipape scores try-double in 20-6 home win over Leeds.

5th May 2023 - 30-6 home win over Castleford moves Leopards into sixth.

12th May 2023 - 30-4 win at Huddersfield is fourth in a row.

17th May 2023 - Hull KR second row Frankie Halton joins on two-and-a-half-year contract with immediate effect.

19th May 2023 - 40-12 Challenge Cup sixth round win at Wakefield.

26th May 2023 - Gareth O'Brien scores double in 30-12 home win over table toppers Warrington. Frankie Halton tears pectoral on debut.

4th June 2023 - Ben Reynolds sent off in first half for punching in 30-4 Magic Weekend victory over Wakefield, for seventh win in a row. Tom Nisbet sin-binned for dangerous contact.

5th June 2023 - Ben Reynolds gets two-match penalty notice. Tom Nisbet gets one match.

9th June 2023 - 28-16 home win over Hull FC moves Leopards into third.

18th June 2023 - Kai O'Donnell sent off for dangerous tackle early in 34-14 Challenge Cup quarter-final win at York.

20th June 2023 - Kai O'Donnell suspended for six games. Zak Hardaker gets one game for dangerous throw. Appeal fails.

24th June 2023 - 38-30 defeat at Catalans.

30th June 2023 - 34-4 home win over Hull KR moves Leopards second in table.

7th July 2023 - Lachlan Lam and Josh Charnley score doubles in 34-16 win at Castleford.

16th July 2023 - late Ben Reynolds penalty secures 24-22 win at Salford after trailing 22-10.

22nd July 2023 - 12-10 Challenge Cup semi-final win over St Helens at Warrington.

29th July 2023 - 44-18 defeat at Wigan.

1st August 2023 - former England centre Oliver Gildart signs from NRL Dolphins until end of 2023 season.

2nd August 2023 - halfback Lachlan Lam extends contract to end of 2025 season.

6th August 2023 - late Gareth O'Brien field goal seals 13-6 win at Leeds.

8th August 2023 - Australian backrower Kai O'Donnell signs two-year contract extension to end of 2025 season.

12th August 2023 - first Challenge Cup for 52 years as Lachlan Lam slots golden-point field goal to secure 17-16 Wembley win over Hull KR. Lam wins Lance Todd Trophy.

19th August 2023 - 30-14 home defeat by table-toppers Catalans.

25th August 2023 - 52-10 defeat at Hull KR.

1st September 2023 - home game against Huddersfield abandoned, Leigh leading 16-12, after 48 minutes due to floodlight failure.

3rd September 2023 - final 32 minutes played with 34-16 final scoreline.

8th September 2023 - 22-12 defeat at St Helens.

15th September 2023 - Gareth O'Brien field goal secures 20-19 home golden-point win over Wakefield.

22nd September 2023 - 10-6 home defeat to Wigan means fifth-place finish.

24th September 2023 - Tom Amone gets one-match ban for dangerous contact, overturned on appeal.

25th September 2023 - Josh Charnley, Lachlan Lam, Tom Amone, John Asiata and Edwin Ipape all named in Dream Team.

29th September 2023 - 20-6 defeat at Hull KR in eliminator.

14th October 2023 - Owen Trout signs from Huddersfield on three-year contract. Fellow forwards Louis Brogan from Swinton and St Helens' Dan Norman sign two-year contracts. Lewis Baxter from St Helens joins on one-year deal.

16th October 2023 - Ben McNamara, 21, signs two-year deal from Hull FC. Kavan Rothwell, Wigan, and Jack Darbyshire, Warrington, sign one-year contracts.

CLUB RECORDS

Highest score: 100-4 v York, 21/8/2022
Highest score against:
4-94 v Workington, 26/2/95
Record attendance:
31,326 v St Helens, 14/3/53 *(Hilton Park)*
10,556 v Batley, 17/9/2016
(Leigh Sports Village)

MATCH RECORDS

Tries: 6 Jack Wood v York, 4/10/47
Neil Turley v Workington, 31/1/2001
Goals: 16 Krisnan Inu v York, 21/8/2022
Points: 42 Neil Turley v Chorley, 4/4/2004

SEASON RECORDS

Tries: 55 Neil Turley 2001
Goals: 187 Neil Turley 2004
Points: 468 Neil Turley 2004

CAREER RECORDS

Tries: 189 Mick Martyn 1954-67
Goals: 1,043 Jimmy Ledgard 1948-58
Points:
2,492 John Woods 1976-85; 1990-92
Appearances: 503 Albert Worrall 1920-38

Super League XXVIII - Club by Club

LEIGH LEOPARDS

DATE	FIXTURE	RESULT	SCORERS	LGE	ATT
17/2/23	Salford (h)	L10-20	t:Charnley,Hughes g:Hardaker	10th	8,589
25/2/23	Catalans Dragons (a)	L14-6	t:Wardle g:Reynolds	9th	7,862
3/3/23	Hull KR (a)	W25-30	t:Amone,Briscoe(2),Charnley(2) g:Reynolds(5)	8th	8,448
10/3/23	St Helens (h)	W20-12	t:Charnley,Briscoe,Hardaker,Shorrocks g:Hardaker(2)	7th	7,734
17/3/23	Warrington (a)	L38-20	t:Briscoe,Charnley,Amone,Hardaker g:Hardaker(2)	9th	12,073
25/3/23	Hull FC (a)	W16-24	t:O'Donnell,Charnley(3) g:Reynolds(4)	8th	10,952
30/3/23	Wigan (h)	L6-34	t:Briscoe g:Reynolds	9th	9,189
8/4/23	Salford (h)	L20-22	t:Charnley(2),Briscoe,Reynolds g:Reynolds(2)	9th	6,002
16/4/23	Wakefield (a)	W0-32	t:O'Brien,Reynolds,Lam,Charnley(2),Mellor g:Reynolds(4)	9th	4,710
21/4/23	Leeds (h)	W20-6	t:Ipape(2),O'Donnell g:Reynolds(4)	7th	6,686
5/5/23	Castleford (h)	W30-6	t:Reynolds,O'Donnell,Seumanufagai,Leutele,Davis g:Reynolds(5)	6th	5,423
12/5/23	Huddersfield (a)	W4-30	t:Reynolds,Charnley(2),Lam,Mellor g:Reynolds(5)	5th	4,977
19/5/23	Wakefield (a) (CCR6)	W12-40	t:Briscoe(2),Asiata,O'Donnell(2),Leutele,Charnley g:Reynolds(6)	N/A	1,568
26/5/23	Warrington (h)	W30-12	t:O'Brien(2),Briscoe,Charnley,Reynolds g:Reynolds(5)	5th	8,120
4/6/23	Wakefield (MW) ●	W30-4	t:Lam(2),Mulhern,Ipape,Charnley g:Reynolds,Hardaker(4)	4th	N/A
9/6/23	Hull FC (h)	W28-16	t:O'Brien,Briscoe,Charnley(2),Mellor g:Hardaker(4)	3rd	6,006
18/6/23	York (h) (CCQF)	W14-34	t:Mellor,Amone,Charnley(2),Briscoe(2) g:O'Brien(2),Hardaker(3)	N/A	2,412
24/6/23	Catalans Dragons (a)	L38-30	t:Chamberlain(2),Charnley,Ipape,Briscoe g:Reynolds(5)	4th	9,636
30/6/23	Hull KR (h)	W34-4	t:Briscoe,Ipape,Chamberlain,Charnley,Leutele,Mulhern g:Reynolds(5)	2nd	6,012
7/7/23	Castleford (a)	W16-34	t:Amone,Lam(2),Briscoe,Charnley(2) g:Reynolds(5)	2nd	6,344
16/7/23	Salford (a)	W22-24	t:Chamberlain,Leutele,Lam,Hardaker g:Reynolds(4)	2nd	6,892
22/7/23	St Helens (CCSF) ●●	W12-10	t:Holmes,Hardaker g:Reynolds(2)	N/A	12,113
29/7/23	Wigan (a)	L44-18	t:Amone,Briscoe,Mulhern g:Reynolds(3)	3rd	15,377
6/8/23	Leeds (a)	W6-13	t:Ipape,Amone g:Reynolds(2) fg:O'Brien	3rd	12,785
12/8/23	Hull KR (CCF) ●●●	W16-17 (aet)	t:Lam,Briscoe g:Reynolds(4) fg:Lam	N/A	58,213
19/8/23	Catalans Dragons (h)	L14-30	t:Amone,Nakubuwai g:Reynolds(3)	4th	8,602
25/8/23	Hull KR (a)	L52-10	t:Charnley,Ipape g:Hardaker	4th	8,013
1/9/23	Huddersfield (h) ●●●●	W34-16	t:Charnley(2),Briscoe,Ipape,Asiata,Lam g:Reynolds(5)	4th	6,064
8/9/23	St Helens (a)	L22-12	t:Gildart,Mulhern g:Reynolds(2)	4th	13,428
15/9/23	Wakefield (h)	W20-19 (aet)	t:Briscoe,Charnley,Hughes g:Reynolds(3) fg:O'Brien(2)	4th	5,565
22/9/23	Wigan (h)	L6-10	t:Lam g:Reynolds	5th	10,308
29/9/23	Hull KR (a) (E)	L20-6	t:Charnley g:Reynolds	N/A	9,305

● Played at St James' Park, Newcastle
●● Played at Halliwell Jones Stadium, Warrington
●●● Played at Wembley Stadium
●●●● Abandoned due to floodlight failure after 48 minutes, remaining 32 played 3/9/23

		APP		TRIES		GOALS		FG		PTS	
	D.O.B.	ALL	SL	ALL	SL	ALL	SL	ALL	SL	ALL	SL
Tom Amone	19/12/96	31(1)	27(1)	7	6	0	0	0	0	28	24
John Asiata	19/4/93	27(1)	23(1)	2	1	0	0	0	0	8	4
Tom Briscoe	19/3/90	32	28	19	14	0	0	0	0	76	56
Ed Chamberlain	8/2/96	15(2)	13(1)	4	4	0	0	0	0	16	16
Josh Charnley	26/6/91	30	26	30	27	0	0	0	0	120	108
Matt Davis	5/7/96	7(23)	6(20)	1	1	0	0	0	0	4	4
Oliver Gildart	6/8/96	8	8	1	1	0	0	0	0	4	4
Frankie Halton	18/6/96	(3)	(3)	0	0	0	0	0	0	0	0
Umyla Hanley	5/3/02	2	1	0	0	0	0	0	0	0	0
Zak Hardaker	17/10/91	27	23	4	3	17	14	0	0	50	40
Oliver Holmes	7/8/92	16(6)	14(5)	1	0	0	0	0	0	4	0
Jack Hughes	4/1/92	12(5)	10(5)	2	2	0	0	0	0	8	8
Edwin Ipape	2/2/99	23(5)	20(5)	8	8	0	0	0	0	32	32
Lachlan Lam	25/3/98	32	28	10	9	0	0	1	0	41	36
Ricky Leutele	10/4/90	20	19	4	3	0	0	0	0	16	12
Joe Mellor	28/11/90	7(19)	6(16)	4	3	0	0	0	0	16	12
Robbie Mulhern	18/10/94	30(1)	26(1)	4	4	0	0	0	0	16	16
Ben Nakubuwai	15/3/96	2(19)	2(17)	1	1	0	0	0	0	4	4
Tom Nisbet	8/10/99	3(1)	2(1)	0	0	0	0	0	0	0	0
Dan Norman	8/9/97	(3)	(3)	0	0	0	0	0	0	0	0
Gareth O'Brien	31/10/91	31	27	4	4	2	0	3	3	23	19
Kai O'Donnell	21/2/99	23(2)	20(2)	5	3	0	0	0	0	20	12
Ben Reynolds	15/1/94	27	24	5	5	88	76	0	0	196	172
Ava Seumanufagai	4/6/91	1(16)	1(14)	1	1	0	0	0	0	4	4
Joe Shorrocks	25/11/99	4	4	1	1	0	0	0	0	4	4
Aaron Smith	12/10/96	1(1)	1	0	0	0	0	0	0	0	0
Joe Wardle	22/9/91	5(6)	5(6)	1	1	0	0	0	0	4	4
Nathan Wilde	29/12/99	(10)	(8)	0	0	0	0	0	0	0	0

'SL' totals include regular season & play-offs; 'All' totals also include Challenge Cup

Josh Charnley

LEAGUE RECORD
P27-W16-D0-L11
(5th/Eliminator)
F585, A508, Diff+77
32 points.

CHALLENGE CUP
Winners

ATTENDANCES
Best - v Wigan (SL - 10,308)
Worst - v Castleford (SL - 5,423)
Total (SL only) - 94,300
Average (SL only) - 7,254
(Up by 4,010 on 2022, Championship)

Super League XXVIII - Club by Club

KEY DATES

4th November 2022 - Krisnan Inu returns to take up assistant coach role.

7th November 2022 - backrower Sam Stone signs from Leigh on two-year contract.

14th November 2022 - backrower Ellis Longstaff joins from Warrington on one-year loan.

2nd December 2022 - centre Tim Lafai signs new three-year deal to end of 2025. Morgan Escaré joins Carcassonne.

16th December 2022 - prop Tyler Dupree signs new three-year contract to end of 2025.

16th January 2023 - Kallum Watkins named team captain.

17th January 2023 - utility Ben Hellewell joins from Featherstone on one-year deal.

5th February 2023 - 32-4 defeat at Wigan in pre-season warm-up.

7th February 2023 - Man of Steel Brodie Croft signs new contract until 2030.

13th February 2023 - prop Jack Ormondroyd signs three-year contract to end of 2025 season.

15th February 2023 - hooker Andy Ackers signs new four-year contract to end of 2026.

17th February 2023 - 20-10 round-one win at Leigh.

21st February 2023 - winger Joe Burgess signs three-year contract to end of 2025.

22nd February 2023 - captain Kallum Watkins signs new three-year contract to end of 2025.

24th February 2023 - 24-10 home defeat by Hull KR. Alex Gerrard suffers knee injury.

3rd March 2023 - 36-20 defeat at Warrington after leading 20-6 at half-time. Adam Sidlow makes second debut. Oliver Partington (knee) and Joe Burgess (shoulder) suffer injuries.

11th March 2023 - 60-14 win at Hull FC.

14th March 2023 - former England centre Dan Sarginson retires at the age of 29.

19th March 2023 - golden-point Marc Sneyd field goal earns 14-13 home win over Wakefield.

25th March 2023 - 20-16 defeat Wigan.

2nd April 2023 - 26-16 home defeat to Huddersfield.

3rd April 2023 - prop Ryan Lannon joins Halifax for undisclosed transfer fee.

8th April 2023 - 22-20 Easter Saturday win at Leigh.

13th April 2023 - Oliver Partington returns from knee injury in 14-6 home win over Castleford.

23rd April 2023 - Joe Burgess makes 150th Super League appearance in 16-14 home win over Catalans.

3rd May 2023 - Ken Sio suffers ankle injury in training.

5th May 2023 - 22-12 win at Leeds is fourth in a row.

13th May 2023 - 26-12 defeat at St Helens after leading 12-6 at half-time.

20th May 2023 - 42-40 home Challenge Cup sixth round win over Huddersfield, after leading 24-0 and 42-22.

22nd May 2023 - transfer request from prop Tyler Dupree turned down.

24th May 2023 - halfback Chris Atkin signs two-year contract extension.

28th May 2023 - 29-22 home win over Hull FC.

3rd June 2023 - Marc Sneyd makes 300th career appearance in 26-16 Magic Weekend win over Hull KR.

9th June 2023 - wingers Rhys Williams and Ken Sio score doubles in 42-10 win at Castleford.

17th June 2023 - 28-10 Challenge Cup quarter-final exit at Hull KR.

25th June 2023 - Brodie Croft and Andy Ackers miss 26-6 home defeat by Wigan. Ryan Brierley fails HIA.

30th June 2023 - Brodie Croft, Ryan Brierley missing with injury for 32-6 defeat at Wakefield.

9th July 2023 - late Rhyse Martin penalty goal means 16-14 home defeat to Leeds.

16th July 2023 - late Ben Reynolds penalty goal means 24-22 home defeat to Leigh.

26th July 2023 - England prop Tyler Dupree signs for Wigan for undisclosed fee. Brad Singleton joins Salford.

29th July 2023 - 42-0 defeat at Catalans.

3rd August 2023 - backrower Shane Wright signs new three-year contract.

6th August 2023 - 18-15 home defeat by St Helens.

18th August 2023 - Sam Stone scores try double as six-match losing run ends with 32-8 win at Huddersfield.

25th August 2023 - Ryan Brierley scores try-double in 20-0 home win over Wakefield.

1st September 2023 - 26-8 defeat at Wigan leaves Red Devils seventh.

4th September 2023 - prop King Vuniyayawa signs new two-year contract.

10th September 2023 - Sam Stone scores golden-point try to keep top-six hopes alive with 24-20 home win over Warrington.

16th September 2023 - 12-0 defeat at Hull KR leaves play-off place in balance.

22nd September 2023 - 19-8 home defeat to Catalans means seventh place finish.

28th September 2023 - centre Deon Cross signs new two-year contract, with option of further year.

6th October 2023 - winger Ken Sio signs one-year contract extension with option for further 12 months.

8th October 2023 - hooker Amir Bourouh signs one-year contract extension.

14th October 2023 - PNG threequarter Nene MacDonald signs from Leeds on four-year deal to end of 2027.

18th October 2023 - halfback Brodie Croft and hooker Andy Ackers sign for Leeds.

30th October 2023 - former Hull KR winger Ethan Ryan signs on three-year contract. Utility Ben Hellewell signs one-year contract extension. Released St Helens back-rower Matty Foster joins one one-year contract.

31st October 2023 - fullback Ryan Brierley signs new three-year contract. Danny Addy released.

CLUB RECORDS

Highest score:
100-12 v Gateshead, 23/3/2003
Highest score against:
16-96 v Bradford, 25/6/2000
Record attendance:
26,470 v Warrington, 13/2/37
(The Willows)
7,854 v Wigan, 25/6/2023
(AJ Bell Stadium)

MATCH RECORDS

Tries:
6 Frank Miles v Lees, 5/3/1898
Ernest Bone v Goole, 29/3/1902
Jack Hilton v Leigh, 7/10/39
Goals:
14 Steve Blakeley v Gateshead, 23/3/2003
Points:
39 Jim Lomas v Liverpool City, 2/2/1907

SEASON RECORDS

Tries: 46 Keith Fielding 1973-74
Goals: 221 David Watkins 1972-73
Points: 493 David Watkins 1972-73

CAREER RECORDS

Tries: 297 Maurice Richards 1969-83
Goals: 1,241 David Watkins 1967-79
Points: 2,907 David Watkins 1967-79
Appearances:
498 Maurice Richards 1969-83

Super League XXVIII - Club by Club

SALFORD RED DEVILS

DATE	FIXTURE	RESULT	SCORERS	LGE	ATT
17/2/23	Leigh (a)	W10-20	t:Watkins,Ackers,Brierley g:Sneyd(4)	3rd	8,589
23/2/23	Hull KR (h)	L10-24	t:Sio,Cross g:Sneyd	7th	5,565
2/3/23	Warrington (a)	L36-20	t:Longstaff,Brierley,Sneyd g:Sneyd(4)	9th	9,616
11/3/23	Hull FC (a)	W14-60	t:Cross(2),Wright(2),Brierley,Dupree,Watkins,Sneyd,Lafai(2) g:Sneyd(10)	5th	11,323
19/3/23	Wakefield (h)	W14-13 (aet)	t:Costello,Atkin g:Sneyd(2) fg:Sneyd(2)	4th	4,757
24/3/23	Wigan (a)	L20-16	t:Sio(2) g:Sneyd(4)	5th	11,497
2/4/23	Huddersfield (h)	L16-26	t:Wright,Costello,Watkins g:Sneyd(2)	7th	4,764
8/4/23	Leigh (a)	W20-22	t:Sio,Stone,Croft,Dupree g:Sneyd(3)	6th	6,002
13/4/23	Castleford (h)	W14-6	t:Croft,Wright g:Sneyd(3)	5th	4,468
23/4/23	Catalans Dragons (h)	W16-14	t:Vuniyayawa,Burgess g:Sneyd(4)	5th	3,974
5/5/23	Leeds (a)	W12-22	t:Williams,Stone,Longstaff g:Sneyd(5)	5th	13,007
13/5/23	St Helens (a)	L26-12	t:Croft,Brierley g:Sneyd(2)	6th	11,881
20/5/23	Huddersfield (h) (CCR6)	W42-40	t:Costello,Gerrard,Watkins,Williams(2),Burgess,Sneyd g:Sneyd(7)	N/A	2,872
28/5/23	Hull FC (h)	W29-22	t:Dupree,Cross,Brierley,Sneyd,Sio g:Sneyd(4) fg:Sneyd	6th	4,569
3/6/23	Hull KR (MW) ●	W16-26	t:Burgess,Sio,Atkin g:Sneyd(7)	5th	N/A
9/6/23	Castleford (a)	W10-42	t:Williams(2),Atkin,Cross,Sio(2),Lafai,Stone g:Sneyd(5)	4th	6,354
17/6/23	Hull KR (a) (CCQF)	L28-10	t:Lafai,Burgess g:Sneyd	N/A	6,289
25/6/23	Wigan (h)	L6-26	t:Hellewell g:Sneyd	5th	7,854
30/6/23	Wakefield (a)	L32-6	t:Gerrard g:Sneyd	6th	3,854
9/7/23	Leeds (h)	L14-16	t:Lafai(2),Sio g:Brierley	6th	5,157
16/7/23	Leigh (h)	L22-24	t:Sio,Vuniyayawa,Ackers,Hellewell g:Sneyd(3)	7th	6,892
29/7/23	Catalans Dragons (a)	L42-0		7th	9,503
6/8/23	St Helens (h)	L15-18	t:Watkins,Brierley g:Sneyd(3) fg:Sneyd	7th	6,515
18/8/23	Huddersfield (a)	W8-32	t:Brierley,Stone(2),Sio,Atkin g:Sneyd(6)	6th	4,685
25/8/23	Wakefield (h)	W20-0	t:Brierley(2),Ackers g:Sneyd(4)	6th	3,836
1/9/23	Wigan (a)	L26-8	t:Sio g:Brierley(2)	7th	12,905
10/9/23	Warrington (h)	W24-20 (aet)	t:Hellewell,Croft(2),Stone g:Sneyd(4)	7th	6,252
16/9/23	Hull KR (a)	L12-0		7th	9,848
22/9/23	Catalans Dragons (h)	L8-19	t:Hellewell g:Sneyd(2)	7th	4,212

● Played at St James' Park, Newcastle

Marc Sneyd

		APP		TRIES		GOALS		FG		PTS	
	D.O.B.	ALL	SL	ALL	SL	ALL	SL	ALL	SL	ALL	SL
Andy Ackers	25/12/93	19(1)	19(1)	3	3	0	0	0	0	12	12
Danny Addy	15/1/91	9(7)	9(6)	0	0	0	0	0	0	0	0
Chris Atkin	7/2/93	12(17)	10(17)	4	4	0	0	0	0	16	16
Amir Bourouh	5/1/01	5(7)	5(6)	0	0	0	0	0	0	0	0
Ryan Brierley	12/3/92	28	26	9	9	3	3	0	0	42	42
Joe Burgess	14/10/94	25	23	4	2	0	0	0	0	16	8
Matthew Costello	9/4/98	8(1)	7(1)	3	2	0	0	0	0	12	8
Brodie Croft	14/7/97	27	25	5	5	0	0	0	0	20	20
Deon Cross	30/7/96	29	27	5	5	0	0	0	0	20	20
Andrew Dixon	28/2/90	1(4)	1(4)	0	0	0	0	0	0	0	0
Tyler Dupree	8/2/00	15(6)	14(5)	3	3	0	0	0	0	12	12
Alex Gerrard	5/11/91	3(4)	2(4)	2	1	0	0	0	0	8	4
James Greenwood	17/6/91	(1)	(1)	0	0	0	0	0	0	0	0
Ben Hellewell	30/7/92	6(13)	5(12)	4	4	0	0	0	0	16	16
Tim Lafai	27/5/91	20	19	6	5	0	0	0	0	24	20
Ellis Longstaff	5/7/02	2(4)	2(3)	2	2	0	0	0	0	8	8
Jack Ormondroyd	7/11/91	11(12)	11(11)	0	0	0	0	0	0	0	0
Oliver Partington	3/9/98	21(1)	20	0	0	0	0	0	0	0	0
Adam Sidlow	25/10/87	2(11)	2(10)	0	0	0	0	0	0	0	0
Brad Singleton	29/10/92	6	6	0	0	0	0	0	0	0	0
Ken Sio	29/10/90	25	24	12	12	0	0	0	0	48	48
Marc Sneyd	9/2/91	28	26	4	3	92	84	4	4	204	184
Sam Stone	4/8/97	24(1)	22(1)	6	6	0	0	0	0	24	24
King Vuniyayawa	13/3/95	15(12)	13(12)	2	2	0	0	0	0	8	8
Kallum Watkins	12/3/91	25	23	5	4	0	0	0	0	20	16
Rhys Williams	8/12/89	9	8	5	3	0	0	0	0	20	12
Shane Wright	13/3/96	2(10)	2(10)	4	4	0	0	0	0	16	16

'SL' totals include Super League games only; 'All' totals also include Challenge Cup

LEAGUE RECORD
P27-W13-D0-L14
(7th)
F494, A512, Diff-18
26 points.

CHALLENGE CUP
Quarter Finalists

ATTENDANCES
Best - v Wigan (SL - 7,854)
Worst - v Huddersfield (CC - 2,872)
Total (SL only) - 68,815
Average (SL only) - 5,293
(Up by 654 on 2022)

Super League XXVIII - Club by Club

KEY DATES

24th October 2022 - Taylor Pemberton, Matty Foster, and Jumah Sambou sign new one-year contracts. McKenzie Buckley (one year) and Ben Lane (two) sign first full-time contracts.

8th November 2022 - Barrow winger Tee Ritson joins on season-long loan with option for permanent deal.

9th November 2022 - outside back Wesley Bruines joins on one-year deal.

27th January 2023 - Lewis Dodd makes comeback in 16-12 home win over Widnes in Mark Percival Testimonial.

3rd February 2023 - France coach Laurent Frayssinous joins as assistant.

11th February 2023 - 30-18 win at St George Illawarra in World Club Challenge warm-up.

18th February 2023 - Lewis Dodd kicks golden-point field goal as 13-12 win at Penrith Panthers secures World Club title.

26th February 2023 - winger Tee Ritson scores first Super League try on debut in 24-6 opening win at Castleford.

3rd March 2023 - late Blake Austin field goal means 25-24 home defeat to Leeds. Konrad Hurrell red-carded, Sione Mata'utia and Curtis Sironen get yellows all for late tackles.

6th March 2023 - Konrad Hurrell gets two matches, Sione Mata'utia and Curtis Sironen one each.

10th March 2023 - shock 20-12 defeat at Leigh after leading 12-0.

17th March 2023 - tough 20-12 home win over Hull FC. Morgan Knowles gets one-match penalty notice for dangerous contact. Appeal fails.

23rd March 2023 - hard-fought 14-12 win at Huddersfield.

31st March 2023 - Jonny Lomax makes 300th Saints appearance in 38-0 home win over Wakefield.

7th April 2023 - 14-6 Good Friday defeat at Wigan.

11th April 2023 - Morgan Knowles cops five-game ban for hip-drop tackle.

14th April 2023 - rain-soaked 26-14 defeat at Hull KR.

20th April 2023 - Joe Batchelor back for first game of season in dominant 28-6 home win over Warrington.

5th May 2023 - 24-12 defeat at Catalans after leading 12-0.

13th May 2023 - James Roby becomes record club appearance maker with 532 in 26-12 win over Salford. Curtis Sironen gets one-game ban for late challenge on Brodie Croft.

16th May 2023 - Matty Lees banned for two games after pleading guilty to off-the-ball strike during victory over Salford.

19th May 2023 - Morgan Knowles sent off near end of 26-6 Challenge Cup sixth round win at Halifax.

22nd May 2023 - Morgan Knowles banned for two games.

26th May 2023 - Lewis Dodd golden-point field goal edges 13-12 win at Leeds.

1st June 2023 - forward James Bell signs new contract to end of 2025 season.

4th June 2023 - Tommy Makinson scores four tries in 48-6 Magic Weekend win over Huddersfield.

9th June 2023 - James Roby stars in 34-16 home win over Wigan.

12th June 2023 - backrower Curtis Sironen signs new deal to end of 2025 campaign.

14th June 2023 - forward Jake Wingfield likely to miss rest of season after shoulder surgery.

17th June 2023 - 32-18 Challenge Cup quarter-final win at Hull FC. Tommy Makinson suffers hamstring injury.

22nd June 2023 - 34-6 defeat at Hull FC after trailing 22-0 at half-time.

29th June 2023 - centre Konrad Hurrell extends contract until end of 2024 season.

30th June 2023 - rain-soaked 22-0 home win over Castleford.

7th July 2023 - comeback from 20-12 deficit in last 20 minutes secures 24-20 win at Warrington.

13th July 2023 - James Roby and Mark Percival both fail HIAs in 14-12 home defeat to Catalans.

22nd July 2023 - 12-10 Challenge Cup semi-final defeat by Leigh at Warrington.

22nd July 2023 - hooker Joey Lussick signs for Parramatta with immediate effect for undisclosed fee.

23rd July 2023 - utility/hooker Moses Mbye signs two-and-a-half-year contract from St George Illawarra Dragons.

26th July 2023 - hooker Daryl Clark signs for 2024 from Warrington on three-year contract.

28th July 2023 - Jack Welsby scores two tries in 22-18 home win over Leeds.

6th August 2023 - 18-15 win at Salford.

11th August 2023 - teenage prop George Delaney signs contract to end of 2026 season.

14th August 2023 - Tommy Makinson scores hat-trick in 32-18 home win over Huddersfield.

15th August 2023 - Matty Lees banned for two games for high tackle. Appeal fails.

19th August 2023 - Tommy Makinson scores try-double and kicks seven goals in 28-6 home win over Hull KR.

25th August 2023 - Tommy Makinson scores try-double in 34-4 win at Castleford.

3rd September 2023 - Tommy Makinson scores try-double in 32-16 win at Wakefield.

4th September 2023 - backrower Sione Mata'utia signs new 12-month deal for 2024.

7th September 2023 - centre Wesley Bruines signs for Warrington.

8th September 2023 - Tommy Makinson scores try-double in 22-12 home win over Leigh.

15th September 2023 - 18-6 win at Warrington makes it eight wins on the bounce.

20th September 2023 - prop Louie McCarthy-Scarsbrook to retire at end of season.

22nd September 2023 - 30-12 home win over Hull FC is ninth on a row in league meaning third-place finish.

30th September 2023 - 16-8 home win over Warrington in eliminator.

1st October 2023 - forward Jake Wingfield signs two-year contract extension to end of 2025 season.

6th October 2023 - Sam Tomkins try 80 seconds from time means 12-6 semi-final defeat at Catalans.

14th October 2023 - Dan Norman signs for Leigh.

18th October 2023 - winger Tee Ritson, on loan from Barrow, signs permanent two-year contract.

18th October 2023 - back-rower Matt Whitley signs from Catalans on two-year contract.

CLUB RECORDS

Highest score:
112-0 v Carlisle, 14/9/86
Highest score against:
6-78 v Warrington, 12/4/1909
Record attendance:
35,695 v Wigan, 26/12/49 *(Knowsley Road)*
17,980 v Wigan, 6/4/2012
v Wigan, 18/4/2014
v South Sydney, 22/2/2015
v Wigan, 30/3/2018
v Wigan, 15/4/2022
(Langtree Park/Totally Wicked Stadium)

MATCH RECORDS

Tries: 6 Alf Ellaby v Barrow, 5/3/32
Steve Llewellyn v Castleford, 3/3/56
Steve Llewellyn v Liverpool, 20/8/56
Tom van Vollenhoven v Wakefield, 21/12/57
Tom van Vollenhoven v Blackpool, 23/4/62
Frank Myler v Maryport, 1/9/69
Shane Cooper v Hull, 17/2/88
Goals: 16 Paul Loughlin v Carlisle, 14/9/86
Points:
40 Paul Loughlin v Carlisle, 14/9/86

SEASON RECORDS

Tries: 62 Tom van Vollenhoven 1958-59
Goals: 214 Kel Coslett 1971-72
Points: 452 Kel Coslett 1971-72

CAREER RECORDS

Tries: 392 Tom van Vollenhoven 1957-68
Goals: 1,639 Kel Coslett 1962-76
Points: 3,413 Kel Coslett 1962-76
Appearances: 551 James Roby 2004-2023

ST HELENS

DATE	FIXTURE	RESULT	SCORERS	LGE	ATT
18/2/23	Penrith Panthers (a) (WCC)	W12-13 (aet)	t:Welsby,Hurrell g:Makinson,Percival fg:Dodd	N/A	13,873
26/2/23	Castleford (a)	W6-24	t:Welsby,Ritson,Walmsley(2) g:Percival(3),Lomax	6th	10,042
3/3/23	Leeds (h)	L24-25	t:Lussick,Dodd(2),Percival g:Makinson(4)	6th	15,148
10/3/23	Leigh (a)	L20-12	t:Lomax,Bennison g:Makinson(2)	10th	7,734
17/3/23	Hull FC (h)	W20-12	t:Davies,Bennison(2),Welsby g:Lussick(2)	6th	10,350
23/3/23	Huddersfield (a)	W12-14	t:Hurrell,Makinson g:Makinson(3)	6th	4,684
31/3/23	Wakefield (h)	W38-0	t:Percival,Hopoate,Makinson,Dodd,Hurrell(2),Lomax g:Percival(5)	4th	10,304
7/4/23	Wigan (a)	L14-6	t:Lomax g:Percival	5th	24,275
14/4/23	Hull KR (a)	L26-14	t:Lomax,Lussick g:Percival(3)	8th	8,540
20/4/23	Warrington (h)	W28-6	t:Hurrell,Lomax,Hopoate,Bennison,Ritson g:Bennison(2),Lussick(2)	6th	14,866
5/5/23	Catalans Dragons (a)	L24-12	t:Walmsley,Welsby g:Makinson(2)	7th	10,763
13/5/23	Salford (h)	W26-12	t:Bell,Sironen,Lomax,Makinson,Batchelor g:Makinson(3)	7th	11,881
19/5/23	Halifax (a) (CCR6)	W6-26	t:Lussick(2),Wingfield,Makinson,Welsby g:Makinson(3)	N/A	4,693
26/5/23	Leeds (a)	W12-13 (aet)	t:Makinson,Sironen g:Makinson(2) fg:Dodd	7th	14,161
4/6/23	Huddersfield (MW) ●	W6-48	t:Hurrell(2),Percival,Makinson(4),McCarthy-Scarsbrook,Lussick g:Makinson(6)	6th	N/A
9/6/23	Wigan (h)	W34-16	t:Batchelor,Makinson(2),Welsby(2),Paasi g:Makinson(5)	5th	17,088
17/6/23	Hull FC (a) (CCQF)	W18-32	t:Batchelor,Hurrell,Sironen,Dodd,Bell g:Makinson(2),Lussick(2)	N/A	8,127
22/6/23	Hull FC (a)	L34-6	t:Bell g:Bennison	6th	9,937
30/6/23	Castleford (h)	W22-0	t:Mata'utia,Welsby,Bennison,Percival g:Percival(3)	5th	11,488
7/7/23	Warrington (a)	W20-24	t:Percival,Bell,Lomax,Dodd g:Percival(4)	3rd	12,385
13/7/23	Catalans Dragons (h)	L12-14	t:Percival,Dodd g:Percival,Lussick	4th	12,193
22/7/23	Leigh (CCSF) ●●	L12-10	t:Lussick,Lomax g:Makinson	N/A	12,113
28/7/23	Leeds (h)	W22-18	t:Hopoate,Ritson,Welsby(2) g:Makinson(2),Dodd	4th	12,108
6/8/23	Salford (a)	W15-18	t:Lees,Makinson,Welsby g:Percival(3)	4th	6,515
13/8/23	Huddersfield (h)	W32-18	t:Makinson(3),Dodd,Welsby g:Percival(6)	3rd	12,028
18/8/23	Hull KR (h)	W28-6	t:Mata'utia,Makinson(2),Mbye,Davies g:Percival(4)	3rd	11,258
25/8/23	Castleford (a)	W4-34	t:Percival,Makinson(2),Bennison,Batchelor,Lomax g:Percival(5)	3rd	6,868
3/9/23	Wakefield (a)	W16-32	t:Lomax,Makinson(2),Roby,Bennison,Dodd g:Percival(4)	3rd	4,544
8/9/23	Leigh (h)	W22-12	t:Makinson(2),Lomax,Batchelor g:Percival(3)	3rd	13,428
15/9/23	Warrington (a)	W6-18	t:Sironen,Percival,Mbye g:Percival(3)	3rd	12,855
22/9/23	Hull FC (h)	W30-12	t:Percival,Dodd,Lomax,Welsby(2) g:Percival(5)	3rd	14,036
30/9/23	Warrington (h) (E)	W16-8	t:Dodd,Makinson g:Percival(4)	N/A	13,801
6/10/23	Catalans Dragons (a) (SF)	L12-6	t:Hopoate g:Percival	N/A	11,530

● Played at St James' Park, Newcastle
●● Played at Halliwell Jones Stadium, Warrington

		APP		TRIES		GOALS		FG		PTS	
	D.O.B.	ALL	SL	ALL	SL	ALL	SL	ALL	SL	ALL	SL
Joe Batchelor	28/10/94	16(1)	14(1)	5	4	0	0	0	0	20	16
Lewis Baxter	1/6/02	(1)	(1)	0	0	0	0	0	0	0	0
James Bell	2/5/94	22(9)	20(7)	4	3	0	0	0	0	16	12
Jonathan Bennison	1/12/02	18(2)	18(1)	7	7	3	3	0	0	34	34
Ben Davies	21/4/00	10(1)	9(1)	2	2	0	0	0	0	8	8
George Delaney	4/2/04	6(14)	6(12)	0	0	0	0	0	0	0	0
Lewis Dodd	27/1/02	33	29	10	9	1	1	2	1	44	39
Will Hopoate	9/5/92	19	16	4	4	0	0	0	0	16	16
Konrad Hurrell	5/8/91	21	18	8	6	0	0	0	0	32	24
Morgan Knowles	5/11/96	25	21	0	0	0	0	0	0	0	0
Matty Lees	4/2/98	29	26	1	1	0	0	0	0	4	4
Jonny Lomax	4/9/90	33	29	12	11	1	1	0	0	50	46
Joey Lussick	28/12/95	4(16)	2(14)	6	3	7	5	0	0	38	22
Tommy Makinson	10/10/91	27	23	24	23	36	29	0	0	168	150
Sione Mata'utia	25/6/96	19(5)	16(4)	2	2	0	0	0	0	8	8
Moses Mbye	13/8/93	(11)	(11)	2	2	0	0	0	0	8	8
Louie McCarthy-Scarsbrook	14/1/86	5(23)	5(21)	1	1	0	0	0	0	4	4
Dan Norman	8/9/97	(7)	(7)	0	0	0	0	0	0	0	0
Agnatius Paasi	30/11/91	2(13)	2(9)	1	1	0	0	0	0	4	4
Mark Percival	29/5/94	23	21	9	9	59	58	0	0	154	152
Tee Ritson	7/1/96	15(1)	12(1)	3	3	0	0	0	0	12	12
James Roby	22/11/85	28(1)	26(1)	1	1	0	0	0	0	4	4
Sam Royle	12/2/00	7(7)	7(7)	0	0	0	0	0	0	0	0
Curtis Sironen	31/7/93	16(1)	14(1)	4	3	0	0	0	0	16	12
Alex Walmsley	10/4/90	18(4)	14(4)	3	3	0	0	0	0	12	12
Jack Welsby	17/3/01	33	29	15	12	0	0	0	0	60	48
Jake Wingfield	1/8/01	(10)	(8)	1	0	0	0	0	0	4	0

'SL' totals include regular season & play-offs; 'All' totals also include Challenge Cup & World Club Challenge

James Roby

LEAGUE RECORD
P27-W20-D0-L7
(3rd/Semi-Final)
F613, A366, Diff+247
40 points.

CHALLENGE CUP
Semi-Finalists

ATTENDANCES
Best - v Wigan (SL - 17,088)
Worst - v Wakefield (SL - 10,304)
Total (SL, inc play-offs) - 179,977
Average (SL, inc play-offs) - 12,856
(Up by 960 on 2022)

Super League XXVIII - Club by Club

KEY DATES

30th November 2022 - prop Renouf Atoni signs from Sydney Roosters on one-year deal, with club option for further year.

3rd December 2022 - utility back Samisoni Langi signs from Catalans on two-year deal.

23rd December 2022 - 18-year-old utility back Oliver Pratt signs three-year contract.

26th December 2022 - 38-20 win at Leeds in Wetherby Whaler Challenge.

1st January 2023 - hooker Liam Hood extends contract to end of 2024.

17th February 2023 - 38-24 home round-one defeat by Catalans.

23rd February 2023 - Max Jowitt suffers long-term ankle injury in training.

24th February 2023 - 60-0 hammering at Wigan.

1st March 2023 - new hybrid pitch inspected and passed to stage next game with Huddersfield.

3rd March 2023 - Lewis Murphy injures knee in 8-0 home defeat to Huddersfield.

6th March 2023 - Lewis Murphy out for season with ACL injury.

9th March 2023 - CEO Michael Carter to step down before end of season.

10th March 2023 - 26-0 defeat at Leeds after 0-0 half-time scoreline. Lee Gaskell suffers pectoral injury.

11th March 2023 - forward Sam Hewitt joins from Huddersfield on initial two-week loan deal.

19th March 2023 - Marc Sneyd golden-point field goal means 14-13 defeat at Salford.

21st March 2023 - young Wigan hooker Tom Forber joins on loan.

24th March 2023 - 34-6 home defeat by Hull KR.

28th March 2023 - Will Dagger joins from Hull KR with immediate effect to end of 2024. Corey Hall goes in opposite direction.

29th March 2023 - Huddersfield winger Innes Senior joins on loan.

31st March 2023 - 38-0 defeat at St Helens.

3rd April 2023 - Huddersfield prop Nathan Mason joins on loan.

6th April 2023 - 16-4 Easter Thursday defeat at Castleford leaves Trinity four points adrift at bottom of table.

16th April 2023 - 32-0 home defeat by Leigh.

18th April 2023 - halfback Rowan Milnes joins from Hull KR on two-week loan. Hooker Liam Hood suspended for two games for two late contact offences.

23rd April 2023 - 22-6 defeat at Wigan.

27th April 2023 - winger Lewis Murphy to join Sydney Roosters at end of 2023 season.

1st May 2023 - halfback Luke Gale signs from Keighley until end of 2024.

5th May 2023 - Kevin Proctor sent off for high tackle early in second half of 32-18 defeat at Warrington, after 12-12 half-time scoreline.

11th May 2023 - 26-6 home defeat to Hull FC. Kelepi Tanginoa gets one-match ban for dangerous contact.

18th May 2023 - halfback Mason Lino signs new contract until end of 2026 season.

19th May 2023 - Oliver Pratt and Dane Windrow make debuts in 40-12 home Challenge Cup sixth round defeat by Leigh.

20th May 2023 - fullback Max Jowitt signs new two-year contract to end of 2025.

23rd May 2023 - centre Jack Croft signs until end of season after brief spell with Wynnum Manly Seagulls.

26th May 2023 - Kelepi Tanginoa breaks arm in 36-6 defeat at Catalans.

31st May 2023 - David Fifita re-signs until end of 2023 season. Isaac Shaw returns from Villeneuve, Sam Hewitt returns on loan from Huddersfield. French forward Hugo Salabio and centre Romain Franco arrive on 28-day trial.

4th June 2023 - David Fifita makes second debut in 30-4 Magic Weekend defeat by Leigh.

11th June 2023 - 24-14 home win over Leeds is first of season. Hugo Salabio sent off in 45th minute for spear tackle on Richie Myler.

13th June 2023 - Hugo Salabio banned for seven matches. Sam Eseh gets one game for dangerous contact. Sam Hewitt one game for trip.

16th June 2023 - Lee Gaskell released and joins Bradford.

21st June 2023 - winger Jorge Taufua released and joins Bradford.

22nd June 2023 - utility Liam Kay, two years, and back-rower Jay Pitts, one, sign contract extensions.

23rd June 2023 - 28-12 defeat at Hull KR leaves Trinity four points adrift at bottom. Luke Gale makes debut.

30th June 2023 - Will Dagger kicks eight goals and scores try in 32-6 home win over Salford.

7th July 2023 - Will Dagger kicks golden-point field goal to secure 27-26 home win over Wigan.

10th July 2023 - Josh Griffin, in middle of seven-game ban, signs from Hull FC.

14th July 2023 - 34-6 defeat at Huddersfield.

19th July 2023 - Matty Ashurst agrees further one-year deal to end of 2024.

19th July 2023 - Jordan Crowther released from contract and joins Warrington.

24th July 2023 - Huddersfield winger Innes Senior joins on loan, for fourth time, to end of season.

25th July 2023 - Catalans hooker Ugo Tison joins on initial month deal.

30th July 2023 - Innes Senior scores four tries in 42-6 home thrashing of Warrington.

6th August 2023 - 42-4 defeat at Hull FC.

9th August 2023 - Sean Long, sacked by Featherstone, appointed assistant coach until end of 2024 season.

18th August 2023 - Josh Griffin scores two tries in 28-12 home defeat by Castleford.

25th August 2023 - Reece Lyne suffers season-ending hamstring injury in 20-0 defeat at Salford.

3rd September 2023 - Will Dagger breaks collar bone in 32-16 home defeat by St Helens.

8th September 2023 - 18-10 home defeat by Catalans, in David Fifita's last game, leaves Trinity four points adrift at bottom of table with two games to go.

15th September 2023 - 20-19 golden-point defeat at Leigh means relegation from Super League after 25 seasons.

22nd September 2023 - 56-12 home final-round defeat to Hull KR.

28th September 2023 - takeover by Matt Ellis agreed with Daryl Powell appointed coach on four-year contract.

CLUB RECORDS

Highest score:
90-12 v Highfield, 27/10/92
Highest score against:
0-86 v Castleford, 17/4/95
Record attendance:
30,676 v Huddersfield, 26/2/1921

MATCH RECORDS

Tries:
7 Fred Smith v Keighley, 25/4/59
Keith Slater v Hunslet, 6/2/71
Goals:
13 Mark Conway v Highfield, 27/10/92
Points:
36 Jamie Rooney v Chorley, 27/2/2004

SEASON RECORDS

Tries: 38 Fred Smith 1959-60
David Smith 1973-74
Goals: 163 Neil Fox 1961-62
Points: 407 Neil Fox 1961-62

CAREER RECORDS

Tries: 272 Neil Fox 1956-74
Goals: 1,836 Neil Fox 1956-74
Points: 4,488 Neil Fox 1956-74
Appearances:
605 Harry Wilkinson 1930-49

Super League XXVIII - Club by Club

WAKEFIELD TRINITY

DATE	FIXTURE	RESULT	SCORERS	LGE	ATT
17/2/23	Catalans Dragons (h)	L24-38	t:Jowitt,Hall,Ashurst,Gaskell g:Lino(4)	11th	4,076
24/2/23	Wigan (a)	L60-0		12th	12,306
3/3/23	Huddersfield (h)	L0-8		12th	4,155
10/3/23	Leeds (a)	L26-0		12th	11,717
19/3/23	Salford (a)	L14-13 (aet)	t:Hall,Lyne g:Lino fg:Lino	12th	4,757
24/3/23	Hull KR (h)	L6-34	t:Whitbread g:Lino	12th	4,705
31/3/23	St Helens (a)	L38-0		12th	10,304
6/4/23	Castleford (a)	L16-4	t:Langi	12th	8,075
16/4/23	Leigh (h)	L0-32		12th	4,710
23/4/23	Wigan (a)	L22-6	t:Pitts g:Lino	12th	12,240
5/5/23	Warrington (a)	L32-18	t:M Smith,Tanginoa,Ashurst g:Dagger(3)	12th	10,209
11/5/23	Hull FC (h)	L6-26	t:Ashurst g:Dagger	12th	3,976
19/5/23	Leigh (h) (CCR6)	L12-40	t:Pitts,Dagger g:Dagger(2)	N/A	1,568
26/5/23	Catalans Dragons (a)	L36-6	t:Kay g:Dagger	12th	8,120
4/6/23	Leigh (MW) ●	L30-4	t:Jowitt	12th	N/A
11/6/23	Leeds (h)	W24-14	t:Croft,Franco,Ashurst,M Smith g:Dagger(4)	12th	4,710
23/6/23	Hull KR (a)	L28-12	t:Franco,Gale g:Dagger(2)	12th	8,185
30/6/23	Salford (h)	W32-6	t:Kay,Dagger,Lyne,Kershaw g:Dagger(8)	12th	3,854
7/7/23	Wigan (h)	W27-26 (aet)	t:Lineham,Kershaw,Atoni,Whitbread g:Dagger(5) fg:Dagger	12th	4,185
14/7/23	Huddersfield (a)	L34-6	t:Langi g:Jowitt	12th	5,872
30/7/23	Warrington (h)	W42-6	t:Senior(4),Proctor,Lineham,Hood,Jowitt g:Gale(2),Jowitt(3)	12th	4,470
6/8/23	Hull FC (a)	L42-4	t:Senior	12th	11,956
18/8/23	Castleford (h)	L12-28	t:Jowitt,Griffin(2)	12th	4,710
25/8/23	Salford (a)	L20-0		12th	3,836
3/9/23	St Helens (h)	L16-32	t:Ashurst,Kershaw(2) g:Dagger,Lino	12th	4,544
8/9/23	Catalans Dragons (h)	L10-18	t:Tanginoa,Kershaw g:Jowitt	12th	3,348
15/9/23	Leigh (a)	L20-19 (aet)	t:Hood,Kershaw(2) g:Lino(3) fg:Gale	12th	5,565
22/9/23	Hull KR (h)	L12-56	t:Tanginoa,Kay g:Dagger(2)	12th	4,710

● Played at St James' Park, Newcastle

		APP		TRIES		GOALS		FG		PTS	
	D.O.B.	ALL	SL	ALL	SL	ALL	SL	ALL	SL	ALL	SL
Matty Ashurst	1/11/89	27	27	5	5	0	0	0	0	20	20
Renouf Atoni	26/6/95	11(11)	10(11)	1	1	0	0	0	0	4	4
Eddie Battye	24/7/91	8(17)	8(16)	0	0	0	0	0	0	0	0
Josh Bowden	14/1/92	13(4)	12(4)	0	0	0	0	0	0	0	0
Harry Bowes	7/9/01	5(9)	4(9)	0	0	0	0	0	0	0	0
Rob Butler	15/5/98	1(3)	1(3)	0	0	0	0	0	0	0	0
Robbie Butterworth	7/6/02	1		0	0	0	0	0	0	0	0
Jack Croft	21/12/00	9	9	1	1	0	0	0	0	4	4
Jordan Crowther	19/2/97	6(3)	5(3)	0	0	0	0	0	0	0	0
Will Dagger	21/2/99	15(2)	14(2)	2	1	29	27	1	1	67	59
Sam Eseh	30/6/03	(15)	(14)	0	0	0	0	0	0	0	0
David Fifita	28/6/89	(12)	(12)	0	0	0	0	0	0	0	0
Tom Forber	22/5/03	(2)	(2)	0	0	0	0	0	0	0	0
Romain Franco	5/6/98	4	4	2	2	0	0	0	0	8	8
Luke Gale	22/6/88	10	10	1	1	2	2	1	1	9	9
Lee Gaskell	28/10/90	7	6	1	1	0	0	0	0	4	4
Josh Griffin	9/5/90	5	5	2	2	0	0	0	0	8	8
Corey Hall	7/8/02	3(1)	3(1)	2	2	0	0	0	0	8	8
Sam Hewitt	29/4/99	6(1)	6(1)	0	0	0	0	0	0	0	0
Liam Hood	6/1/92	19(3)	19(2)	2	2	0	0	0	0	8	8
Max Jowitt	6/5/97	15	15	4	4	5	5	0	0	26	26
Liam Kay	17/12/91	17(8)	17(8)	3	3	0	0	0	0	12	12
Lee Kershaw	2/5/99	17	17	7	7	0	0	0	0	28	28
Samisoni Langi	11/6/93	14	14	2	2	0	0	0	0	8	8
Joe Law	18/2/04	(1)	(1)	0	0	0	0	0	0	0	0
Tom Lineham	21/9/91	13	12	2	2	0	0	0	0	8	8
Mason Lino	4/2/94	23	22	0	0	12	12	1	1	25	25
Reece Lyne	2/12/92	15	15	2	2	0	0	0	0	8	8
Nathan Mason	8/9/93	1	1	0	0	0	0	0	0	0	0
Rowan Milnes	1/9/97	1	1	0	0	0	0	0	0	0	0
Lewis Murphy	24/3/02	3	3	0	0	0	0	0	0	0	0
Jay Pitts	9/12/89	28	27	2	1	0	0	0	0	8	4
Oliver Pratt	4/9/04	2	1	0	0	0	0	0	0	0	0
Kevin Proctor	28/2/89	13(8)	12(8)	1	1	0	0	0	0	4	4
Hugo Salabio	27/7/00	(3)	(3)	0	0	0	0	0	0	0	0
Jordan Schofield	23/9/00	(1)	(1)	0	0	0	0	0	0	0	0
Innes Senior	30/5/00	8	8	5	5	0	0	0	0	20	20
Isaac Shaw	11/9/02	(1)	(1)	0	0	0	0	0	0	0	0
Harvey Smith	16/1/06	(1)	(1)	0	0	0	0	0	0	0	0
Morgan Smith	30/4/98	12(2)	11(2)	2	2	0	0	0	0	8	8
Kelepi Tanginoa	1/3/94	4(3)	4(3)	3	3	0	0	0	0	12	12
Jorge Taufua	23/10/91	12	11	0	0	0	0	0	0	0	0
Jai Whitbread	16/1/98	16	16	2	2	0	0	0	0	8	8
Dane Windrow	9/6/02	(1)	0	0	0	0	0	0	0	0	0

'SL' totals include Super League games only; 'All' totals also include Challenge Cup

Matty Ashurst

LEAGUE RECORD
P27-W4-D0-L23
(12th)
F303, A742, Diff-439
8 points.

CHALLENGE CUP
Round Six

ATTENDANCES
Best - v Leigh/Leeds/Castleford/
Hull KR (SL - 4,710)
Worst - v Leigh (CC - 1,568)
Total (SL only) - 56,153
Average (SL only) - 4,319
(Down by 315 on 2022)

Super League XXVIII - Club by Club

KEY DATES

14th November 2022 - Ellis Longstaff joins Salford on season loan.

23rd November 2022 - halfback Josh Drinkwater signs from Catalans on two-year contract.

24th November 2022 - winger Matty Russell returns on one-year contract. Halfback Riley Dean goes to Featherstone on season loan.

6th December 2022 - prop James Harrison signs three-year contract extension to end of 2025 season.

25th January 2023 - Stefan Ratchford appointed club captain.

4th February 2023 - 22-10 home win over Leigh in Ben Currie testimonial. New prop Gil Dudson suffers hand injury.

15th February 2023 - new prop Josh McGuire banned for seven-games for use of discriminatory language in Leigh friendly.

16th February 2023 - new prop Paul Vaughan stars in 42-10 home hammering of Leeds.

24th February 2023 - Matty Ashton scores try-double in 26-16 round-two win at Huddersfield.

2nd March 2023 - 36-20 home win over Salford after trailing 20-6 at half-time.

10th March 2023 - late Paul Vaughan try seals hard-fought 18-10 win at Hull KR.

17th March 2023 - Matty Ashton scores eight-minute hat-trick in 38-20 home win over Leigh. Joe Philbin returns from ACL injury.

26th March 2023 - Matty Russell scores two tries on second club debut in 38-0 win at Castleford.

31st March 2023 - prop Thomas Mikaele joins Gold Coast Titans with immediate effect for undisclosed transfer fee.

1st April 2023 - Thomas Mikaele plays final game in 34-6 win over Hull FC after leading 28-0 at half-time.

8th April 2023 - Josh Thewlis try seals 20-14 win at Catalans. Josh McGuire makes debut after suspension. Gil Dudson sent off on 66 minutes.

12th April 2023 - Gil Dudson banned for five games for punching. Joe Philbin two matches for dangerous contact.

12th April 2023 - George Williams signs new long-term deal until November 2026. Prop Paul Vaughan extends to end of 2025.

14th April 2023 - 13-6 defeat to Wigan ends eight-game winning start in front of record HJ Stadium attendance. Paul Vaughan suspended for one game for dangerous contact.

20th April 2023 - 28-6 defeat at St Helens.

3rd May 2023 - Matty Ashton extends contract to end of 2026 season.

5th May 2023 - Josh Thewlis and Matty Ashton score doubles in 32-18 home win over Wakefield.

10th May 2023 - hooker Danny Walker signs new deal to end of 2026 season.

12th May 2023 - 21-14 home win over Hull KR after trailing 12-0.

20th May 2023 - Matty Ashton try two minutes from time earns 16-14 Challenge Cup sixth round win at Catalans.

26th May 2023 - 30-12 defeat at Leigh.

4th June 2023 - 30-18 defeat by Hull FC at Magic Weekend.

6th June 2023 - Josh McGuire given 12-match ban for using unacceptable language during defeat by Leigh.

10th June 2023 - 30-26 home win over Huddersfield.

14th June 2023 - backrower Ben Currie signs new three-year contract to end of 2026 season.

18th June 2023 - 14-12 Challenge Cup home quarter-final exit to 12-man Wigan.

19th June 2023 - prop Josh McGuire's contract terminated by mutual agreement.

24th June 2023 - 23-14 defeat at Castleford.

25th June 2023 - James Harrison gets two-game ban for dangerous contact.

29th June 2023 - 22-6 home defeat by Leeds.

6th July 2023 - Newcastle Knights back-rower Lachlan Fitzgibbon signs three-year contract from 2024 season.

7th July 2023 - Matty Ashton scores try-double in 24-20 home defeat by St Helens.

14th July 2023 - 26-12 defeat at Wigan after 12-12 half-time scoreline.

19th July 2023 - Wakefield backrower Jordan Crowther signs to end of season.

26th July 2023 - hooker Daryl Clark to join St Helens at end of season.

30th July 2023 - coach Daryl Powell leaves after 42-6 thrashing at Wakefield.

2nd August 2023 - prop Thomas Mikaele rejoins from Gold Coast Titans until end of season, four months after returning to Australia on compassionate grounds.

4th August 2023 - 30-10 home defeat to Catalans, in interim Gary Cambers first game in charge.

7th August 2023 - Sam Burgess to take over as head coach from 2024 season on two-year contract. Interim coach Gary Chambers to take up director of rugby role.

20th August 2023 - 24-22 defeat at Leeds is seventh in a row.

26th August 2023 - Eight-game losing run ends with 18-4 win at Hull FC.

2nd September 2023 - 66-12 home rout of Castleford.

1st September 2023 - Papua New Guinea international Rodrick Tai signs 12-month contract for 2024, with club option for further year.

7th September 2023 - St Helens centre Wesley Bruines signs one-year contract for 2024.

10th September 2023 - Sam Stone golden-point try means 24-20 defeat at Salford.

13th September 2023 - centre Toby King, on loan at Wigan, to return at end of season.

14th September 2023 - prop Thomas Mikaele and centre Peter Mata'utia to leave at end of season.

15th September 2023 - 18-6 defeat at St Helens.

19th September 2023 - Paul Vaughan banned for four games for attempting to lift injured Sione Mata'utia.

20th September 2023 - former centre Martin Gleeson joins as a first-team coach on two-year deal.

22nd September 2023 - 20-8 final round win at Huddersfield secures sixth place play-off spot.

29th September 2023 - Jordan Crowther signs two-year contract.

30th September 2023 - 16-8 defeat at St Helens means eliminator exit.

2nd October 2023 - George Williams banned for one game for shoulder charge.

5th October 2023 - prop Zane Musgrove signs from St George Illawarra on two-year contract.

11th October 2023 - George Williams ban doubled to two matches after frivolous appeal. Further appeal fails.

24th October 2023 - hooker Brad Dwyer re-signs from Hull FC on two-year contract.

CLUB RECORDS

Highest score:
112-0 v Swinton, 20/5/2011
Highest score against:
12-84 v Bradford, 9/9/2001
Record attendance:
34,404 v Wigan, 22/1/49 *(Wilderspool)*
15,026 v Wigan, 14/4/2023
(Halliwell Jones Stadium)

MATCH RECORDS

Tries:
7 Brian Bevan v Leigh, 29/3/48
Brian Bevan v Bramley, 22/4/53
Goals:
16 Lee Briers v Swinton, 20/5/2011
Points:
44 Lee Briers v Swinton, 20/5/2011

SEASON RECORDS

Tries: 66 Brian Bevan 1952-53
Goals: 170 Steve Hesford 1978-79
Points: 363 Harry Bath 1952-53

CAREER RECORDS

Tries: 740 Brian Bevan 1945-62
Goals: 1,159 Steve Hesford 1975-85
Points: 2,586 Lee Briers 1997-2013
Appearances: 620 Brian Bevan 1945-62

Super League XXVIII - Club by Club

WARRINGTON WOLVES

DATE	FIXTURE	RESULT	SCORERS	LGE	ATT
16/2/23	Leeds (h)	W42-10	t:Dufty,Clark,Thewlis,Walker,Kasiano,Harrison,Minikin g:Ratchford(7)	1st	11,082
24/2/23	Huddersfield (a)	W16-26	t:Mata'utia,Harrison,Ashton(2) g:Ratchford(5)	1st	7,731
2/3/23	Salford (h)	W36-20	t:Currie,Ashton,Mikaele,Thewlis,Williams,Dufty g:Ratchford(6)	1st	9,616
10/3/23	Hull KR (a)	W10-18	t:Mikaele,Nicholson,Vaughan g:Ratchford(3)	1st	8,082
17/3/23	Leigh (h)	W38-20	t:Drinkwater,Vaughan,Ratchford,Dufty,Ashton(3) g:Ratchford(5)	1st	12,073
24/3/23	Castleford (a)	W0-38	t:Kasiano,Russell(2),Mikaele,Vaughan,Williams,Dufty g:Ratchford(5)	1st	7,348
1/4/23	Hull FC (h)	W34-6	t:Ashton,Mata'utia,Currie,Dufty,Drinkwater,Nicholson g:Ratchford(5)	1st	10,797
8/4/23	Catalans Dragons (a)	W14-20	t:Thewlis(2),Dufty,Williams g:Ratchford,Thewlis	1st	10,786
14/4/23	Wigan (h)	L6-13	t:Nicholson g:Ratchford	1st	15,026
20/4/23	St Helens (a)	L28-6	t:Russell g:Ratchford	2nd	14,866
5/5/23	Wakefield (h)	W32-18	t:Thewlis(2),Ashton(2),Williams g:Ratchford(6)	1st	10,209
12/5/23	Hull KR (h)	W21-14	t:McGuire,Currie,Ashton g:Ratchford(4) fg:Williams	1st	10,179
20/5/23	Catalans Dragons (a) (CCR6)	W14-16	t:Ashton(2),Dufty g:Ratchford(2)	N/A	5,014
26/5/23	Leigh (a)	L30-12	t:Williams,Philbin g:Ratchford(2)	1st	8,120
4/6/23	Hull FC (MW) ●	L30-18	t:Wrench(2),Williams g:Ratchford(3)	2nd	N/A
10/6/23	Huddersfield (h)	W30-26	t:Kasiano,Thewlis,Williams,Walker,Dufty g:Ratchford(5)	2nd	9,007
18/6/23	Wigan (a) (CCQF)	L14-12	t:Bullock,Thewlis g:Ratchford(2)	N/A	9,302
23/6/23	Castleford (a)	L23-14	t:Ashton(2),Wrench g:Mata'utia	2nd	6,066
29/6/23	Leeds (h)	L6-22	t:Ashton g:Ratchford	4th	8,981
7/7/23	St Helens (a)	L20-24	t:Ashton(2),Dufty g:Ratchford(4)	5th	12,385
14/7/23	Wigan (a)	L26-12	t:Harrison,Clark g:Ratchford(2)	5th	13,105
30/7/23	Wakefield (a)	L42-6	t:Vaughan g:Ratchford	6th	4,470
4/8/23	Catalans Dragons (h)	L10-30	t:Currie,Thewlis g:Ratchford	5th	10,312
20/8/23	Leeds (a)	L24-22	t:Dufty,Ashton,Ratchford,Nicholson g:Ratchford(3)	5th	15,166
26/8/23	Hull FC (a)	W4-18	t:Williams,Dufty,Ashton g:Ratchford(3)	5th	11,624
2/9/23	Castleford (a)	W66-12	t:Vaughan(2),Dufty(2),Currie,Clark,Nicholson,Ashton,Williams(2),Harrison g:Ratchford(11)	5th	9,103
10/9/23	Salford (a)	L24-20 (aet)	t:Nicholson,Currie,Williams g:Ratchford(4)	6th	6,252
15/9/23	St Helens (h)	L6-18	t:Clark g:Ratchford	6th	12,855
22/9/23	Huddersfield (a)	W8-20	t:Dufty,Harrison g:Ratchford(6)	6th	5,656
30/9/23	St Helens (a) (E)	L16-8	t:Wrench g:Ratchford(2)	N/A	13,801

● Played at St James' Park, Newcastle

		APP		TRIES		GOALS		FG		PTS	
	D.O.B.	ALL	SL	ALL	SL	ALL	SL	ALL	SL	ALL	SL
Matty Ashton	28/7/98	27	25	20	18	0	0	0	0	80	72
Joe Bullock	27/11/92	3(14)	2(13)	1	0	0	0	0	0	4	0
Daryl Clark	10/2/93	15(12)	14(11)	4	4	0	0	0	0	16	16
Jordan Crowther	19/2/97	5(3)	5(3)	0	0	0	0	0	0	0	0
Ben Currie	15/7/94	30	28	6	6	0	0	0	0	24	24
Riley Dean	10/8/01	1	1	0	0	0	0	0	0	0	0
Josh Drinkwater	15/6/92	25	24	2	2	0	0	0	0	8	8
Gil Dudson	16/6/90	9(7)	8(6)	0	0	0	0	0	0	0	0
Matt Dufty	10/1/96	28(2)	26(2)	14	13	0	0	0	0	56	52
Lucas Green	11/9/04	(5)	(4)	0	0	0	0	0	0	0	0
James Harrison	15/6/96	18(2)	16(2)	5	5	0	0	0	0	20	20
Leon Hayes	4/3/04	1	1	0	0	0	0	0	0	0	0
Adam Holroyd	5/9/04	2(3)	2(3)	0	0	0	0	0	0	0	0
Sam Kasiano	21/9/90	7(19)	6(18)	3	3	0	0	0	0	12	12
Peter Mata'utia	2/11/90	26(2)	24(2)	2	2	1	1	0	0	10	10
Josh McGuire	2/3/90	7	6	1	1	0	0	0	0	4	4
Thomas Mikaele	11/1/98	13(1)	13(1)	3	3	0	0	0	0	12	12
Greg Minikin	29/3/95	8(6)	8(6)	1	1	0	0	0	0	4	4
Matty Nicholson	18/7/03	18	18	6	6	0	0	0	0	24	24
Joe Philbin	16/11/94	5(17)	5(15)	1	1	0	0	0	0	4	4
Stefan Ratchford	19/7/88	30	28	2	2	102	98	0	0	212	204
Matty Russell	6/6/93	12(2)	12(2)	3	3	0	0	0	0	12	12
Josh Thewlis	30/4/02	21(2)	19(2)	9	8	1	1	0	0	38	34
Luke Thomas	19/10/02	(3)	(3)	0	0	0	0	0	0	0	0
Paul Vaughan	23/4/91	27	25	6	6	0	0	0	0	24	24
Danny Walker	29/6/99	18(12)	17(11)	2	2	0	0	0	0	8	8
Tom Whitehead	7/11/02	1(1)	1(1)	0	0	0	0	0	0	0	0
George Williams	31/10/94	25	23	11	11	0	0	1	1	45	45
Connor Wrench	4/10/01	8(1)	7(1)	4	4	0	0	0	0	16	16

'SL' totals include regular season & play-offs; 'All' totals also include Challenge Cup

Matty Ashton

LEAGUE RECORD
P27-W14-D0-L13
(6th/Eliminator)
F597, A512, Diff+85
28 points.

CHALLENGE CUP
Quarter Finalists

ATTENDANCES
Best - v Wigan (SL - 15,026)
Worst - v Leeds (SL - 8,981)
Total (SL only) - 141,625
Average (SL only) - 10,894
(Up by 2,173 on 2022)

Super League XXVIII - Club by Club

KEY DATES

5th December 2022 - Kai Pearce-Paul to leave at end of 2023 season to join Newcastle Knights.

20th December 2022 - Liam Farrell named new club captain.

23rd December 2022 - John Bateman leaves with immediate effect to sign for Wests Tigers.

27th January 2023 - utility back Ryan Hampshire re-joins on one-year contract, with option for two more years.

5th February 2023 - 32-4 home win over Salford in Sam Powell testimonial.

18th February 2023 - 27-18 opening-round defeat at Hull KR.

24th February 2023 - Liam Marshall gets four tries in 60-0 home hammering of Wakefield.

3rd March 2023 - Liam Marshall gets hat-trick in 36-0 win at Castleford.

9th March 2023 - 18-10 home defeat to Catalans in icy conditions.

17th March 2023 - Bevan French scores try-double in tough 14-12 win at Huddersfield.

24th March 2023 - Bevan French scores double in 20-16 home, comeback win over Salford.

30th March 2023 - winger Abbas Miski scores try-double in 34-6 win at Leigh. Willie Isa plays 300th career game. Jai Field out for two months with hamstring injury.

7th April 2023 - 14-6 home Good Friday win over St Helens in front of sell-out crowd. Mike Cooper suffers season-ending knee injury.

10th April 2023 - Morgan Smithies gets one-match ban for dangerous contact.

14th April 2023 - 13-6 win at undefeated Warrington. Brad Singleton suffers calf injury.

23rd April 2023 - 22-6 home win over Wakefield.

4th May 2023 - 14-10 defeat at Hull FC ends six-match winning run.

12th May 2023 - 40-18 home defeat by Leeds after leading 14-6 at half-time.

20th May 2023 - 18-14 Challenge Cup sixth round win at Leeds after trailing 14-0. Ryan Hampshire makes second debut.

25th May 2023 - Liam Farrell scores hat-trick try in golden point to secure 26-22 win at Hull KR after trailing 22-14 with ten minutes left.

3rd June 2023 - 46-22 Magic Weekend defeat by Catalans.

9th June 2023 - 34-16 defeat at St Helens.

18th June 2023 - Kaide Ellis sent off early for head butt in 14-12 Challenge Cup quarter-final win at Warrington.

19th June 2023 - prop Ethan Havard signs new four-year contract.

25th June 2023 - Liam Farrell scores two tries as 26-6 win at Salford moves Warriors into third spot.

25th June 2023 - ex-Leeds Rhinos hooker Kruise Leeming signs from Gold Coast Titans on four-year contract from 2024.

25th June 2023 - Leeds Rhinos forward Sam Walters and Catalans prop Tiaki Chan sign for 2024 season on three-year contracts.

30th June 2023 - Abbas Miski scores try double in 22-6 home win over Huddersfield.

1st July 2023 - Warriors take up option to extend winger Abbas Miski's contract until end of 2024 season.

7th July 2023 - 27-26 golden-point defeat at Wakefield.

12th July 2023 - hooker Brad O'Neill signs new four-year deal to end of 2027.

14th July 2023 - Kai Pearce-Paul returns from hamstring injury in 26-12 home win over Warrington.

15th July 2023 - chairman Ian Lenagan to step down at end of season as club bought by Mike Danson.

16th July 2023 - Adam Keighran signs from Catalans on two-year deal from 2024.

18th July 2023 - prop Kaide Ellis extends contract by three years to end of 2026 season.

23rd July 2023 - Brad Schneider golden-point field goal means 11-10 Challenge Cup semi-final defeat to Hull KR at Leeds.

26th July 2023 - prop Tyler Dupree joins on immediate four-year deal from Salford for undisclosed fee. Brad Singleton joins Salford.

29th July 2023 - Abbas Miski scores hat-trick in 44-18 home win over Leigh.

4th August 2023 - Abbas Miski scores four tries and Jai Field a hat-trick in 64-6 home defeat of Cup finalists Hull KR.

18th August 2023 - Harry Smith kicks golden-point field goal to secure 13-12 home win over Hull FC.

26th August 2023 - Abbas Miski scores hat-trick in 34-0 win at leaders Catalans.

1st September 2023 - 26-8 home win over Salford moves Warriors top of table on points difference.

9th September 2023 - Jake Wardle scores hat-trick in 50-0 win at Leeds.

13th September 2023 - head coach Matt Peet signs new four-year contract until end of 2027 season.

13th September 2023 - on-loan centre Toby King to return to parent club Warrington at end of season.

14th September 2023 - veteran Willie Isa and prop Mike Cooper sign one-year deals for 2024 season.

15th September 2023 - Abbas Miski scores five tries in 48-6 home win over Castleford.

22nd September 2023 - 10-6 win at Leigh secures League Leaders Shield.

25th September 2023 - Bevan French (contact with match official), Kaide Ellis (high tackle). and Harvie Hill (striking) all get one-match penalty notice. Following weekend's Reserve Final allows them to serve suspension.

4th October 2023 - prop Luke Thompson signs from Canterbury Bulldogs on four-year contract.

7th October 2023 - Liam Marshall scores hat-trick in 42-12 home semi-final win over Hull KR.

9th October 2023 - Bevan French named 2023 Steve Prescott MBE Man of Steel.

13th October 2023 - Jake Wardle wins Harry Sunderland Trophy in 10-2 Grand Final win over Catalans.

22nd October 2023 - 19-year-old forward Junior Nsemba signs new four-year contract.

23rd October 2023 - 20-year-old forward Sam Eseh signs from Wakefield on two-year contract.

25th October 2023 - halfback Cade Cust leaves the club. Iain Thornley joins relegated Wakefield.

30th October 2023 - loose forward Morgan Smithies released to join Canberra Raiders.

CLUB RECORDS

Highest score:
116-0 v Flimby & Fothergill, 14/2/25
Highest score against:
0-75 v St Helens, 26/6/2005
Record attendance:
47,747 v St Helens, 27/3/59 (Central Park)
25,004 v St Helens, 25/3/2005
(JJB/DW Stadium)

MATCH RECORDS

Tries: 10 Martin Offiah v Leeds, 10/5/92
Shaun Edwards v Swinton, 29/9/92
Goals: 22 Jim Sullivan
v Flimby & Fothergill, 14/2/25
Points: 44 Jim Sullivan
v Flimby & Fothergill, 14/2/25

SEASON RECORDS

Tries: 62 Johnny Ring 1925-26
Goals: 186 Frano Botica 1994-95
Points: 462 Pat Richards 2010

CAREER RECORDS

Tries: 478 Billy Boston 1953-68
Goals: 2,317 Jim Sullivan 1921-46
Points: 4,883 Jim Sullivan 1921-46
Appearances: 774 Jim Sullivan 1921-46

Super League XXVIII - Club by Club

WIGAN WARRIORS

DATE	FIXTURE	RESULT	SCORERS	LGE	ATT
18/2/23	Hull KR (a)	L27-18	t:Marshall,Field,Pearce-Paul,Wardle g:Smith	9th	10,029
24/2/23	Wakefield (h)	W60-0	t:French(2),Marshall(4),Farrell,Field,Powell,Smith,Cust g:Smith(8)	5th	12,306
3/3/23	Castleford (a)	W0-36	t:Marshall(3),Havard,King,Field g:Smith(6)	3rd	7,565
9/3/23	Catalans Dragons (h)	L10-18	t:Smith g:Smith(3)	3rd	11,451
17/3/23	Huddersfield (a)	W12-14	t:French(2),Wardle g:Smith	3rd	5,777
24/3/23	Salford (h)	W20-16	t:French(2),King g:Smith(4)	3rd	11,497
30/3/23	Leigh (a)	W6-34	t:French,Field(2),Wardle,Miski(2),King g:Smith(3)	3rd	9,189
7/4/23	St Helens (h)	W14-6	t:Smith,King g:Smith(3)	2nd	24,275
14/4/23	Warrington (a)	W6-13	t:Wardle,O'Neill g:Smith(2) fg:Smith	2nd	15,026
23/4/23	Wakefield (h)	W22-6	t:Marshall,Miski,Havard,French g:Smith(3)	1st	12,240
4/5/23	Hull FC (a)	L14-10	t:Thornley(2) g:Smith	2nd	10,251
12/5/23	Leeds (h)	L18-40	t:Miski,French,Thornley g:Smith(3)	2nd	12,167
20/5/23	Leeds (a) (CCR6)	W14-18	t:French(2),Nsemba,Wardle g:Smith	N/A	7,103
25/5/23	Hull KR (a)	W22-26 (aet)	t:Farrell(3),Marshall(2),Miski g:Smith	2nd	8,068
3/6/23	Catalans Dragons (MW) ●	L46-22	t:Wardle,French,Miski,Marshall,Smithies g:Smith	3rd	N/A
9/6/23	St Helens (a)	L34-16	t:Field,French,Miski g:Smith(2)	6th	17,088
18/6/23	Warrington (h) (CCQF)	W14-12	t:King,Miski g:Smith(3)	N/A	9,302
25/6/23	Salford (a)	W6-26	t:Shorrocks,Farrell(2),Miski,Marshall g:Smith(3)	3rd	7,854
30/6/23	Huddersfield (h)	W22-6	t:Miski(2),Field,Marshall g:Smith(3)	3rd	13,464
7/7/23	Wakefield (a)	L27-26 (aet)	t:Field(2),French,Marshall,King g:Smith(3)	4th	4,185
14/7/23	Warrington (h)	W26-12	t:Marshall,French,Wardle,Farrell g:Smith(5)	3rd	13,105
23/7/23	Hull KR (CCSF) ●●	L11-10 (aet)	t:Field g:Smith(3)	N/A	10,926
29/7/23	Leigh (h)	W44-18	t:French(2),King,Dupree,Miski(3),Marshall g:Smith(6)	2nd	15,377
4/8/23	Hull KR (h)	W64-6	t:Miski(4),Wardle,King,Smith,Mago,Field(3),Marshall g:Smith(8)	2nd	11,464
18/8/23	Hull FC (h)	W13-12 (aet)	t:Marshall,King,Wardle fg:Smith	2nd	12,107
26/8/23	Catalans Dragons (a)	W0-34	t:Miski(3),King,French,Wardle g:Smith(5)	2nd	10,614
1/9/23	Salford (h)	W26-8	t:Farrell,Miski,Wardle,Field,King g:Smith(3)	1st	12,905
9/9/23	Leeds (a)	W0-50	t:Wardle(3),Field,Marshall,Pearce-Paul,Miski,Farrell,Mago g:Smith(7)	1st	12,861
15/9/23	Castleford (h)	W48-6	t:Miski(5),Wardle,Powell,Pearce-Paul,Field,French g:Smith,Hampshire(3)	1st	13,109
22/9/23	Leigh (a)	W6-10	t:Field,Wardle g:Smith	1st	10,308
7/10/23	Hull KR (h) (SF)	W42-12	t:Marshall(3),Field(2),King,Miski g:Smith(7)	N/A	15,162
14/10/23	Catalans Dragons (GF) ●●●	W2-10	t:Marshall g:Smith(3)	N/A	58,137

● Played at St James' Park, Newcastle   ●● Played at Headingley, Leeds   ●●● Played at Old Trafford, Manchester

		APP		TRIES		GOALS		FG		PTS	
	D.O.B.	ALL	SL	ALL	SL	ALL	SL	ALL	SL	ALL	SL
Liam Byrne	18/8/99	23(1)	20(1)	0	0	0	0	0	0	0	0
Mike Cooper	15/9/88	7(1)	7(1)	0	0	0	0	0	0	0	0
Cade Cust	14/9/98	6(9)	6(8)	1	1	0	0	0	0	4	4
Tyler Dupree	8/2/00	6(3)	6(3)	1	1	0	0	0	0	4	4
Kaide Ellis	4/8/96	16(9)	14(8)	0	0	0	0	0	0	0	0
Liam Farrell	2/7/90	30	27	9	9	0	0	0	0	36	36
Jai Field	6/9/97	25	23	19	18	0	0	0	0	76	72
Bevan French	4/1/96	32	29	19	17	0	0	0	0	76	68
Ryan Hampshire	29/12/94	2(1)	1(1)	0	0	3	3	0	0	6	6
Ethan Havard	26/10/00	9(9)	7(9)	2	2	0	0	0	0	8	8
Harvie Hill	3/9/03	(14)	(13)	0	0	0	0	0	0	0	0
Willie Isa	1/1/89	9(2)	8(2)	0	0	0	0	0	0	0	0
Toby King	9/7/96	31	28	12	11	0	0	0	0	48	44
Patrick Mago	4/12/94	(27)	(25)	2	2	0	0	0	0	8	8
Liam Marshall	9/5/96	29	26	24	24	0	0	0	0	96	96
Abbas Miski	25/7/95	26	23	29	28	0	0	0	0	116	112
Junior Nsemba	27/6/04	1(14)	1(13)	1	0	0	0	0	0	4	0
Brad O'Neill	22/7/02	16(11)	14(10)	1	1	0	0	0	0	4	4
Kai Pearce-Paul	19/2/01	16(7)	16(6)	3	3	0	0	0	0	12	12
Sam Powell	3/7/92	16(7)	15(7)	2	2	0	0	0	0	8	8
Joe Shorrocks	25/11/99	14(4)	12(3)	1	1	0	0	0	0	4	4
Brad Singleton	29/10/92	5(7)	5(6)	0	0	0	0	0	0	0	0
Harry Smith	25/1/00	32	29	4	4	104	97	2	2	226	212
Morgan Smithies	7/11/00	30(1)	28	1	1	0	0	0	0	4	4
Iain Thornley	11/9/91	4	4	3	3	0	0	0	0	12	12
Jake Wardle	18/11/98	31	28	16	15	0	0	0	0	64	60

'SL' totals include regular season & play-offs; 'All' totals also include Challenge Cup

Harry Smith

LEAGUE RECORD
P27-W20-D0-L7
(1st/Grand Final Winners, Champions)
F722, A360, Diff+362
40 points.

CHALLENGE CUP
Semi-Finalists

ATTENDANCES
Best - v St Helens (SL - 24,275)
Worst - v Warrington (CC - 9,302)
Total (SL, inc play-offs) - 190,629
Average (SL, inc play-offs) - 13,616
(Up by 1,302 on 2022)

ROUND 1

Thursday 16th February 2023

WARRINGTON WOLVES 42 LEEDS RHINOS 10

WOLVES: 1 Matt Dufty; 2 Josh Thewlis; 3 Peter Mata'utia; 4 Stefan Ratchford (C); 5 Matty Ashton; 6 George Williams; 7 Josh Drinkwater (D); 18 Thomas Mikaele; 9 Daryl Clark; 10 Paul Vaughan (D); 11 Ben Currie; 12 Matty Nicholson; 8 James Harrison. Subs (all used): 14 Sam Kasiano (D); 16 Danny Walker; 19 Joe Bullock; 21 Greg Minikin.
Tries: Dufty (4), Clark (17), Thewlis (22), Walker (30), Kasiano (39), Harrison (62), Minikin (67);
Goals: Ratchford 7/8.
RHINOS: 1 Richie Myler; 24 Luis Roberts (D); 2 David Fusitu'a; 5 Ash Handley; 16 Derrell Olpherts (D); 6 Blake Austin; 7 Aidan Sezer; 18 Tom Holroyd; 9 Kruise Leeming (C); 15 Sam Lisone (D); 20 Morgan Gannon; 12 Rhyse Martin; 10 Zane Tetevano. Subs (all used): 13 Cameron Smith; 14 Jarrod O'Connor; 17 Justin Sangare (D); 25 James Donaldson.
Tries: Olpherts (60), Sangare (72); **Goals:** Martin 1/2.
Rugby Leaguer & League Express Men of the Match: *Wolves:* Paul Vaughan; *Rhinos:* Justin Sangare.
Penalty count: 5-3; **Half-time:** 30-0;
Referee: Liam Moore; **Attendance:** 11,082.

Friday 17th February 2023

WAKEFIELD TRINITY 24 CATALANS DRAGONS 38

TRINITY: 1 Max Jowitt; 5 Tom Lineham; 4 Reece Lyne; 21 Samisoni Langi (D); 23 Lewis Murphy; 6 Lee Gaskell; 7 Mason Lino; 10 Jai Whitbread; 20 Morgan Smith (D); 17 Renouf Atoni (D); 13 Jay Pitts; 11 Matty Ashurst (C); 19 Kevin Proctor (D). Subs (all used): 3 Corey Hall; 8 Eddie Battye; 15 Liam Kay; 22 Rob Butler.
Tries: Jowitt (10), Hall (28), Ashurst (51), Gaskell (70);
Goals: Lino 4/4.
DRAGONS: 1 Arthur Mourgue; 2 Tom Davies; 11 Matt Whitley; 4 Matthieu Laguerre; 24 Tom Johnstone (D); 3 Adam Keighran (D); 17 Cesar Rouge; 16 Romain Navarrete (D2); 9 Michael McIlorum; 10 Julian Bousquet; 26 Manu Ma'u (D); 12 Paul Seguier; 13 Benjamin Garcia (C). Subs: 15 Mickael Goudemand; 18 Tiaki Chan; 23 Jordan Dezaria; 31 Tanguy Zenon (not used).
Tries: Laguerre (22), Johnstone (24, 34, 44), Davies (63, 68), Rouge (80); **Goals:** Keighran 5/7.
Rugby Leaguer & League Express Men of the Match: *Trinity:* Max Jowitt; *Dragons:* Adam Keighran.
Penalty count: 3-3; **Half-time:** 12-16;
Referee: Tom Grant; **Attendance:** 4,076.

LEIGH LEOPARDS 10 SALFORD RED DEVILS 20

LEOPARDS: 1 Zak Hardaker (D); 5 Josh Charnley; 3 Ed Chamberlain; 4 Ricky Leutele (D); 2 Tom Briscoe (D); 17 Gareth O'Brien (D); 7 Lachlan Lam; 8 Tom Amone; 18 Matt Davis (D); 10 Robbie Mulhern (D); 11 Joe Wardle; 16 Oliver Holmes (D); 13 Josh Asiata (C). Subs (all used): 14 Ben Nakubuwai; 12 Jack Hughes (D2); 24 Kai O'Donnell; 9 Edwin Ipape.
Tries: Charnley (21), Hughes (59, pen); **Goals:** Hardaker 1/2.
Sin bin: Amone (80) - dangerous challenge.
RED DEVILS: 1 Ryan Brierley; 2 Ken Sio; 28 Deon Cross; 4 Tim Lafai; 22 Rhys Williams; 6 Brodie Croft; 7 Marc Sneyd; 16 Tyler Dupree; 9 Andy Ackers; 10 King Vuniyayawa; 3 Kallum Watkins (C); 12 Sam Stone (D); 13 Oliver Partington (D). Subs (all used): 8 Jack Ormondroyd; 14 Chris Atkin; 17 Shane Wright; 18 Alex Gerrard.
Tries: Watkins (34), Ackers (39), Brierley (50);
Goals: Sneyd 4/4.
Sin bin: Sneyd (56) - professional foul.
Rugby Leaguer & League Express Men of the Match: *Leopards:* Josh Charnley; *Red Devils:* Ryan Brierley.
Penalty count: 6-2; **Half-time:** 4-12;
Referee: Jack Smith; **Attendance:** 8,589.

Saturday 18th February 2023

HULL KR 27 WIGAN WARRIORS 18

HULL KR: 1 Lachlan Coote; 2 Ethan Ryan; 3 Tom Opacic (D); 4 Shaun Kenny-Dowall (C); 5 Ryan Hall; 20 Mikey Lewis; 7 Jordan Abdull; 8 Sauaso Sue (D); 9 Matt Parcell; 15 Rhys Kennedy (D); 16 James Batchelor (D); 12 Kane Linnett; 13 Elliot Minchella. Subs (all used): 10 George King; 14 Jez Litten; 17 Matty Storton; 22 Dean Hadley.
Tries: R Hall (4), Kenny-Dowall (29, 63, 75), Linnett (48);
Goals: Coote 3/4, Lewis 0/2; Field goal: Abdull (40).
WARRIORS: 1 Jai Field; 2 Bevan French; 3 Toby King (D); 4 Jake Wardle (D); 5 Liam Marshall; 6 Cade Cust; 7 Harry Smith; 16 Ethan Havard; 9 Sam Powell; 14 Mike Cooper; 17 Kai Pearce-Paul; 12 Liam Farrell (C); 13 Morgan Smithies. Subs (all used): 8 Brad Singleton; 10 Liam Byrne; 15 Kaide Ellis; 22 Brad O'Neill.
Tries: Marshall (10), Field (15), Pearce-Paul (22), Wardle (69); **Goals:** Smith 1/4.
Sin bin: Smithies (57) - shoulder charge on Lewis.
Rugby Leaguer & League Express Men of the Match: *Hull KR:* Shaun Kenny-Dowall; *Warriors:* Jai Field.
Penalty count: 6-2; **Half-time:** 13-12;
Referee: Chris Kendall; **Attendance:** 10,029.

Sunday 19th February 2023

HULL FC 32 CASTLEFORD TIGERS 30

HULL FC: 1 Tex Hoy (D); 2 Adam Swift; 4 Liam Sutcliffe (D); 17 Cameron Scott; 5 Darnell McIntosh; 7 Jake Clifford (D); 19 Ben McNamara; 10 Tevita Satae; 33 Brad Dwyer (D); 30 Scott Taylor; 12 Jordan Lane; 23 Josh Griffin (C); 13 Brad Fash. Subs (all used): 9 Danny Houghton; 14 Joe Lovodua; 15 Joe Cator; 16 Kane Evans.
Tries: McIntosh (8, 15), Sutcliffe (10), Swift (28, 34), Houghton (47); **Goals:** Clifford 4/6.
TIGERS: 1 Niall Evalds; 5 Bureta Faraimo; 4 Mahe Fonua; 3 Jordan Turner; 21 Jake Mamo; 6 Gareth Widdop (D); 7 Jacob Miller (D); 32 Liam Watts; 9 Paul McShane (C); 14 Nathan Massey; 11 Kenny Edwards; 12 Alex Mellor; 13 Joe Westerman. Subs (all used): 8 George Lawler; 10 George Griffin; 17 Jack Broadbent (D); 23 Suaia Matagi.
Tries: Faraimo (21, 67), Edwards (60), Miller (62), Mamo (75); **Goals:** Widdop 5/5.
Rugby Leaguer & League Express Men of the Match: *Hull FC:* Tex Hoy; *Tigers:* Jacob Miller.
Penalty count: 6-5; **Half-time:** 26-6;
Referee: Marcus Griffiths; **Attendance:** 15,383.

ROUND 2

Thursday 23rd February 2023

SALFORD RED DEVILS 10 HULL KR 24

RED DEVILS: 1 Ryan Brierley; 2 Ken Sio; 28 Deon Cross; 4 Tim Lafai; 5 Joe Burgess; 6 Brodie Croft; 7 Marc Sneyd; 8 Jack Ormondroyd; 9 Andy Ackers; 16 Tyler Dupree; 3 Kallum Watkins (C); 12 Sam Stone; 13 Oliver Partington. Subs (all used): 10 King Vuniyayawa; 14 Chris Atkin; 17 Shane Wright; 18 Alex Gerrard.
Tries: Sio (10), Cross (54); **Goals:** Sneyd 1/2.
HULL KR: 19 Will Dagger; 2 Ethan Ryan; 4 Shaun Kenny-Dowall (C); 3 Tom Opacic; 24 Sam Wood; 20 Mikey Lewis; 7 Jordan Abdull; 8 Sauaso Sue; 9 Matt Parcell; 10 George King; 16 James Batchelor; 12 Kane Linnett; 13 Elliot Minchella. Subs (all used): 11 Frankie Halton; 14 Jez Litten; 22 Dean Hadley; 26 Sam Luckley (D).
Tries: Ryan (45), Halton (51), Wood (57, 73);
Goals: Dagger 4/4.
Rugby Leaguer & League Express Men of the Match: *Red Devils:* Tim Lafai; *Hull KR:* Jordan Abdull.
Penalty count: 1-4; **Half-time:** 4-0;
Referee: Marcus Griffiths; **Attendance:** 5,565.

Friday 24th February 2023

HUDDERSFIELD GIANTS 16
WARRINGTON WOLVES 26

GIANTS: 6 Tui Lolohea; 2 Jermaine McGillvary; 4 Kevin Naiqama (D); 3 Esan Marsters (D); 21 Leroy Cudjoe; 32 Will Pryce; 7 Theo Fages; 8 Chris Hill; 9 Nathan Peats (D2); 20 Oliver Wilson; 11 Josh Jones; 12 Chris McQueen; 13 Luke Yates (C). Subs (all used): 10 Joe Greenwood; 14 Ashton Golding; 15 Matty English; 17 Owen Trout.
Tries: Greenwood (51), Pryce (75), Naiqama (79);
Goals: Pryce 2/3.
WOLVES: 1 Matt Dufty; 5 Matty Ashton; 4 Stefan Ratchford (C); 3 Peter Mata'utia; 2 Josh Thewlis; 6 George Williams; 7 Josh Drinkwater; 18 Thomas Mikaele; 9 Daryl Clark; 10 Paul Vaughan; 11 Ben Currie; 26 Adam Holroyd; 8 James Harrison. Subs (all used): 14 Sam Kasiano; 16 Danny Walker; 19 Joe Bullock; 21 Greg Minikin.
Tries: Mata'utia (8), Harrison (42), Ashton (62, 68);
Goals: Ratchford 5/5.
Rugby Leaguer & League Express Men of the Match: *Giants:* Matty English; *Wolves:* James Harrison.
Penalty count: 3-4; **Half-time:** 0-8;
Referee: Chris Kendall; **Attendance:** 7,731.

LEEDS RHINOS 18 HULL FC 22

RHINOS: 1 Richie Myler; 2 David Fusitu'a; 4 Nene Macdonald (D); 5 Ash Handley (C); 16 Derrell Olpherts; 6 Blake Austin; 7 Aidan Sezer; 10 Zane Tetevano; 9 Kruise Leeming; 18 Tom Holroyd; 20 Morgan Gannon; 12 Rhyse Martin; 13 Cameron Smith. Subs (all used): 15 Sam Lisone; 25 James Donaldson; 17 Justin Sangare; 14 Jarrod O'Connor.
Tries: Smith (19), Leeming (56), Fusitu'a (69);
Goals: Martin 3/3.
HULL FC: 1 Tex Hoy; 2 Adam Swift; 4 Liam Sutcliffe; 17 Cameron Scott; 5 Darnell McIntosh; 19 Ben McNamara; 7 Jake Clifford; 13 Brad Fash; 33 Brad Dwyer; 30 Scott Taylor; 12 Jordan Lane; 23 Josh Griffin (C); 14 Joe Lovodua. Subs (all used): 9 Danny Houghton; 10 Tevita Satae; 16 Kane Evans; 15 Joe Cator.
Tries: Scott (12), Sutcliffe (26), Swift (48), Taylor (74);
Goals: Clifford 3/4.
Rugby Leaguer & League Express Men of the Match: *Rhinos:* Cameron Smith; *Hull FC:* Cameron Scott.
Penalty count: 5-4; **Half time:** 6-10;
Referee: Jack Smith; **Attendance:** 16,140.

WIGAN WARRIORS 60 WAKEFIELD TRINITY 0

WARRIORS: 1 Jai Field; 2 Bevan French; 3 Toby King; 4 Jake Wardle; 5 Liam Marshall; 6 Cade Cust; 7 Harry Smith; 8 Brad Singleton; 9 Sam Powell; 14 Mike Cooper; 11 Willie Isa; 12 Liam Farrell (C); 13 Morgan Smithies. Subs (all used): 15 Kaide Ellis; 16 Ethan Havard; 20 Patrick Mago; 22 Brad O'Neill.
Tries: French (8, 16), Marshall (11, 22, 43, 53), Farrell (26), Field (36), Powell (65), Smith (70), Cust (74);
Goals: Smith 8/11.
TRINITY: 6 Lee Gaskell; 5 Tom Lineham; 3 Corey Hall; 2 Jorge Taufua; 23 Lewis Murphy; 21 Samisoni Langi; 7 Mason Lino; 10 Jai Whitbread; 20 Morgan Smith; 22 Rob Butler; 13 Jay Pitts; 11 Matty Ashurst (C); 19 Kevin Proctor. Subs (all used): 8 Eddie Battye; 12 Kelepi Tanginoa; 15 Liam Kay; 17 Renouf Atoni.
Rugby Leaguer & League Express Men of the Match: *Warriors:* Harry Smith; *Trinity:* Lewis Murphy.
Penalty count: 3-3; **Half-time:** 34-0;
Referee: Aaron Moore; **Attendance:** 12,306.

Saturday 25th February 2023

CATALANS DRAGONS 14 LEIGH LEOPARDS 6

DRAGONS: 1 Arthur Mourgue; 2 Tom Davies; 19 Arthur Romano; 4 Matthieu Laguerre; 24 Tom Johnstone; 17 Cesar Rouge; 29 Sam Tomkins; 16 Romain Navarrete; 9 Michael McIlorum; 10 Julian Bousquet; 15 Mickael Goudemand; 12 Paul Seguier; 13 Benjamin Garcia (C). Subs: 18 Tiaki Chan; 23 Jordan Dezaria; 25 Bastien Scimone; 31 Tanguy Zenon (not used).
Tries: Johnstone (35), Goudemand (65);
Goals: Mourgue 3/3.
LEOPARDS: 17 Gareth O'Brien; 2 Tom Briscoe; 1 Zak Hardaker; 4 Ricky Leutele; 5 Josh Charnley; 15 Ben Reynolds; 7 Lachlan Lam; 8 Tom Amone; 19 Aaron Smith; 10 Robbie Mulhern; 11 Joe Wardle; 3 Ed Chamberlain; 13 John Asiata (C). Subs (all used): 14 Ben Nakubuwai; 18 Matt Davis; 24 Kai O'Donnell; 27 Ava Seumanufagai (D).
Try: Wardle (45); **Goals:** Reynolds 1/1.
Rugby Leaguer & League Express Men of the Match: *Dragons:* Sam Tomkins; *Leopards:* Lachlan Lam.
Penalty count: 6-4; **Half-time:** 8-0;
Referee: Tom Grant; **Attendance:** 7,862.

Sunday 26th February 2023

CASTLEFORD TIGERS 6 ST HELENS 24

TIGERS: 1 Niall Evalds; 21 Jake Mamo; 3 Jordan Turner; 17 Jack Broadbent; 5 Bureta Faraimo; 6 Gareth Widdop; 7 Jacob Miller; 10 George Griffin; 9 Paul McShane (C); 19 Albert Vete (D); 11 Kenny Edwards; 12 Alex Mellor; 8 George Lawler. Subs (all used): 16 Adam Milner; 20 Muizz Mustapha (D); 24 Cain Robb; 32 Liam Watts.
Try: Broadbent (50, pen); **Goals:** Widdop 1/1.
SAINTS: 1 Jack Welsby; 25 Tee Ritson (D); 23 Konrad Hurrell; 4 Mark Percival; 5 Jonathan Bennison; 6 Jonny Lomax (C); 7 Lewis Dodd; 8 Alex Walmsley; 14 Joey Lussick; 10 Matty Lees; 11 Sione Mata'utia; 19 James Bell; 13 Morgan Knowles. Subs (all used): 15 Louie McCarthy-Scarsbrook; 18 Jake Wingfield; 20 Dan Norman; 22 Sam Royle.
Tries: Welsby (24), Ritson (46), Walmsley (64, 72);
Goals: Percival 3/3, Lomax 1/1.
Rugby Leaguer & League Express Men of the Match: *Tigers:* Jack Broadbent; *Saints:* Alex Walmsley.
Penalty count: 6-2; **Half-time:** 0-6;
Referee: Liam Moore; **Attendance:** 10,042.

ROUND 3

Thursday 2nd March 2023

WARRINGTON WOLVES 36 SALFORD RED DEVILS 20

WOLVES: 1 Matt Dufty; 2 Josh Thewlis; 21 Greg Minikin; 4 Stefan Ratchford (C); 5 Matty Ashton; 6 George Williams; 7 Josh Drinkwater; 18 Thomas Mikaele; 9 Daryl Clark; 10 Paul Vaughan; 11 Ben Currie; 3 Peter Mata'utia; 8 James Harrison. Subs: 14 Sam Kasiano; 16 Danny Walker; 19 Joe Bullock; 23 Tom Whitehead (not used).

Tries: Currie (8), Ashton (43), Mikaele (60), Thewlis (64), Williams (69), Dufty (76); **Goals:** Ratchford 6/8.
RED DEVILS: 1 Ryan Brierley; 2 Ken Sio; 28 Deon Cross; 4 Tim Lafai; 5 Joe Burgess; 6 Brodie Croft; 7 Marc Sneyd; 8 Jack Ormondroyd; 9 Andy Ackers; 16 Tyler Dupree; 3 Kallum Watkins (C); 20 Ellis Longstaff (D); 13 Oliver Partington. Subs (all used): 19 Adam Sidlow (D2); 10 King Vuniyayawa; 14 Chris Atkin; 17 Shane Wright.
Tries: Longstaff (11), Brierley (22), Sneyd (26);
Goals: Sneyd 4/5.
Sin bin: Brierley (59) - professional foul.
Rugby Leaguer & League Express Men of the Match:
Wolves: Daryl Clark; *Red Devils:* Oliver Partington.
Penalty count: 8-5; **Half-time:** 6-20;
Referee: Jack Smith; **Attendance:** 9,616.

Friday 3rd March 2023

CATALANS DRAGONS 38 HULL FC 6

DRAGONS: 1 Arthur Mourgue; 2 Tom Davies; 3 Adam Keighran; 19 Arthur Romano; 24 Tom Johnstone; 6 Tyrone May; 17 Cesar Rouge; 16 Romain Navarrete; 9 Michael Mcllorum; 10 Julian Bousquet; 8 Mike McMeeken; 12 Paul Seguier; 13 Benjamin Garcia (C). Subs (all used): 15 Mickael Goudemand; 18 Tiaki Chan; 22 Sio Siua Taukeiaho (D); 23 Jordan Dezaria.
Tries: Johnstone (20), Seguier (23), Goudemand (44), Taukeiaho (48), Keighran (57), Garcia (78);
Goals: Keighran 7/8.
HULL FC: 1 Tex Hoy; 2 Adam Swift; 4 Liam Sutcliffe; 17 Cameron Scott; 5 Darnell McIntosh; 19 Ben McNamara; 7 Jake Clifford; 16 Kane Evans; 33 Brad Dwyer; 10 Tevita Satae; 23 Josh Griffin (C); 12 Jordan Lane; 13 Brad Fash. Subs (all used): 8 Ligi Sao; 11 Andre Savelio; 14 Joe Lovodua; 20 Jack Brown.
Try: Savelio (74); **Goals:** Clifford 1/1.
Rugby Leaguer & League Express Men of the Match:
Dragons: Adam Keighran; *Hull FC:* Jake Clifford.
Penalty count: 6-5; **Half-time:** 14-0;
Referee: Marcus Griffiths; **Attendance:** 6,933.

WAKEFIELD TRINITY 0 HUDDERSFIELD GIANTS 8

TRINITY: 15 Liam Kay; 18 Lee Kershaw; 21 Samisoni Langi; 2 Jorge Taufua; 23 Lewis Murphy; 6 Lee Gaskell; 7 Mason Lino; 10 Jai Whitbread; 9 Liam Hood; 17 Renouf Atoni; 13 Jay Pitts; 11 Matty Ashurst (C); 14 Jordan Crowther. Subs (all used): 8 Eddie Battye; 19 Kevin Proctor; 20 Morgan Smith; 25 Sam Eseh (D).
GIANTS: 6 Tui Lolohea; 2 Jermaine McGillvary; 3 Esan Marsters; 5 Jake Bibby (D); 21 Leroy Cudjoe; 32 Will Pryce; 7 Theo Fages; 8 Chris Hill; 9 Nathan Peats; 20 Oliver Wilson; 12 Chris McQueen; 11 Josh Jones; 13 Luke Yates (C). Subs (all used): 10 Joe Greenwood; 14 Ashton Golding; 15 Matty English; 17 Owen Trout.
Try: Greenwood (58); **Goals:** Lolohea 2/2.
Rugby Leaguer & League Express Men of the Match:
Trinity: Liam Kay; *Giants:* Joe Greenwood.
Penalty count: 4-3; **Half-time:** 0-0;
Referee: Aaron Moore; **Attendance:** 4,155.

CASTLEFORD TIGERS 0 WIGAN WARRIORS 36

TIGERS: 1 Niall Evalds; 2 Greg Eden; 4 Mahe Fonua; 17 Jack Broadbent; 5 Bureta Faraimo; 6 Gareth Widdop; 7 Jacob Miller; 19 Albert Vete; 9 Paul McShane (C); 8 George Lawler; 11 Kenny Edwards; 12 Alex Mellor; 13 Joe Westerman. Subs (all used): 14 Nathan Massey; 16 Adam Milner; 23 Suaia Matagi; 32 Liam Watts.
WARRIORS: 1 Jai Field; 2 Bevan French; 3 Toby King; 4 Jake Wardle; 5 Liam Marshall; 6 Cade Cust; 7 Harry Smith; 8 Brad Singleton; 9 Sam Powell; 14 Mike Cooper; 11 Willie Isa; 12 Liam Farrell (C); 13 Morgan Smithies. Subs (all used): 15 Kaide Ellis; 16 Ethan Havard; 17 Kai Pearce-Paul; 20 Patrick Mago.
Tries: Marshall (38, 56, 80), Havard (44), King (74), Field (78); **Goals:** Smith 6/8.
Rugby Leaguer & League Express Men of the Match:
Tigers: Mahe Fonua; *Warriors:* Liam Marshall.
Penalty count: 7-6; **Half-time:** 0-6;
Referee: Tom Grant; **Attendance:** 7,565.

HULL KR 25 LEIGH LEOPARDS 30

HULL KR: 19 Will Dagger; 2 Ethan Ryan; 3 Tom Opacic; 4 Shaun Kenny-Dowall (C); 5 Ryan Hall; 20 Mikey Lewis; 7 Jordan Abdull; 8 Sauaso Sue; 14 Jez Litten; 15 Rhys Kennedy; 16 James Batchelor; 12 Kane Linnett; 13 Elliot Minchella. Subs (all used): 9 Matt Parcell; 10 George King; 11 Frankie Halton; 26 Sam Luckley.
Tries: Kenny-Dowall (4), Lewis (14), Batchelor (37), Abdull (58); **Goals:** Dagger 4/4; **Field goal:** Abdull (40).
LEOPARDS: 17 Gareth O'Brien; 2 Tom Briscoe; 1 Zak Hardaker; 4 Ricky Leutele; 5 Josh Charnley; 15 Ben Reynolds; 7 Lachlan Lam; 8 Tom Amone; 18 Matt Davis; 10 Robbie Mulhern; 28 Joe Shorrocks (D); 24 Kai O'Donnell; 13 John Asiata (C). Subs: 3 Ed Chamberlain (not used); 9 Edwin Ipape; 14 Ben Nakubuwai; 27 Ava Seumanufagai.
Tries: Amone (10), Briscoe (24, 73), Charnley (47, 80);
Goals: Reynolds 5/5.
Rugby Leaguer & League Express Men of the Match:
Hull KR: Jordan Abdull; *Leopards:* Lachlan Lam.
Penalty count: 3-5; **Half-time:** 19-12;
Referee: Liam Moore; **Attendance:** 8,448.

ST HELENS 24 LEEDS RHINOS 25

SAINTS: 1 Jack Welsby; 2 Tommy Makinson; 23 Konrad Hurrell; 4 Mark Percival; 5 Jonathan Bennison; 6 Jonny Lomax (C); 7 Lewis Dodd; 8 Alex Walmsley; 14 Joey Lussick; 10 Matty Lees; 11 Sione Mata'utia; 16 Curtis Sironen; 13 Morgan Knowles. Subs: 15 Louie McCarthy-Scarsbrook; 18 Jake Wingfield; 19 James Bell; 22 Sam Royle (not used).
Tries: Lussick (16), Dodd (20, 28), Percival (45, pen);
Goals: Makinson 4/5.
Dismissal: Hurrell (78) - late challenge on Myler.
Sin bin: Mata'utia (7) - late challenge on Sezer; Sironen (57) - late challenge on Myler.
RHINOS: 1 Richie Myler; 2 David Fusitu'a; 4 Nene Macdonald; 5 Ash Handley; 16 Derrell Olpherts; 6 Blake Austin; 7 Aidan Sezer; 18 Tom Holroyd; 14 Jarrod O'Connor; 10 Zane Tetevano; 19 James McDonnell (D); 12 Rhyse Martin; 13 Cameron Smith. Subs (all used): 9 Kruise Leeming (C); 17 Justin Sangare; 22 Sam Walters; 25 James Donaldson.
Tries: Handley (11), Martin (24, 70), Smith (60);
Goals: Martin 4/4; **Field goal:** Austin (80).
Rugby Leaguer & League Express Men of the Match:
Saints: Lewis Dodd; *Rhinos:* Nene Macdonald.
Penalty count: 4-8; **Half-time:** 18-12;
Referee: Chris Kendall; **Attendance:** 15,148.

ROUND 4

Thursday 9th March 2023

WIGAN WARRIORS 10 CATALANS DRAGONS 18

WARRIORS: 1 Jai Field; 2 Bevan French; 3 Toby King; 4 Jake Wardle; 5 Liam Marshall; 6 Cade Cust; 7 Harry Smith; 8 Brad Singleton; 9 Sam Powell; 14 Mike Cooper; 11 Willie Isa; 12 Liam Farrell (C); 13 Morgan Smithies. Subs (all used): 15 Kaide Ellis; 16 Ethan Havard; 17 Kai Pearce-Paul; 20 Patrick Mago.
Try: Smith (44); **Goals:** Smith 3/3.
DRAGONS: 1 Arthur Mourgue; 2 Tom Davies; 19 Arthur Romano; 4 Matthieu Laguerre; 24 Tom Johnstone; 6 Tyrone May; 3 Adam Keighran; 8 Mike McMeeken; 9 Michael Mcllorum; 10 Julian Bousquet; 26 Manu Ma'u; 12 Paul Seguier; 13 Benjamin Garcia (C). Subs (all used): 15 Mickael Goudemand; 18 Tiaki Chan; 23 Jordan Dezaria; 28 Ugo Tison.
Tries: Ma'u (6, 63), Romano (34); **Goals:** Keighran 3/4.
Sin bin: Ma'u (39) - late challenge on Cust.
Rugby Leaguer & League Express Men of the Match:
Warriors: Harry Smith; *Dragons:* Tyrone May.
Penalty count: 9-6; **Half-time:** 2-12;
Referee: Marcus Griffiths; **Attendance:** 11,451.

Friday 10th March 2023

HUDDERSFIELD GIANTS 36 CASTLEFORD TIGERS 6

GIANTS: 6 Tui Lolohea; 14 Ashton Golding; 5 Jake Bibby; 3 Esan Marsters; 21 Leroy Cudjoe; 23 Oliver Russell; 7 Theo Fages; 8 Chris Hill; 9 Nathan Peats; 20 Oliver Wilson; 11 Josh Jones; 12 Chris McQueen; 13 Luke Yates (C). Subs (all used): 10 Joe Greenwood; 27 Jack Ashworth; 15 Matty English; 32 Will Pryce.
Tries: McQueen (15, 44), Pryce (30), Bibby (36), Lolohea (53), Cudjoe (64); **Goals:** Russell 6/9.
TIGERS: 17 Jack Broadbent; 2 Greg Eden; 15 Alex Sutcliffe; 4 Mahe Fonua; 31 Jason Qareqare; 6 Gareth Widdop; 7 Jacob Miller; 23 Suaia Matagi; 8 George Lawler; 14 Nathan Massey; 12 Alex Mellor (C); 11 Kenny Edwards; 13 Joe Westerman. Subs (all used): 16 Adam Milner; 32 Liam Watts; 22 Daniel Smith; 20 Muizz Mustapha.
Try: Lawler (8); **Goals:** Widdop 1/1.
Rugby Leaguer & League Express Men of the Match:
Giants: Oliver Russell; *Tigers:* Alex Mellor.
Penalty count: 7-4; **Half-time:** 20-6;
Referee: Tom Grant; **Attendance:** 4,071.

HULL KR 10 WARRINGTON WOLVES 18

HULL KR: 1 Lachlan Coote; 23 Louis Senior (D); 3 Tom Opacic; 24 Sam Wood; 5 Ryan Hall; 20 Mikey Lewis; 21 Rowan Milnes; 26 Sam Luckley; 9 Matt Parcell (C); 10 George King; 11 Frankie Halton; 16 James Batchelor; 22 Dean Hadley. Subs (all used): 8 Sauaso Sue; 14 Jez Litten; 15 Rhys Kennedy; 17 Matty Storton.
Tries: Halton (8, 46); **Goals:** Coote 1/3.
WOLVES: 1 Matt Dufty; 2 Josh Thewlis; 3 Peter Mata'utia; 4 Stefan Ratchford (C); 5 Matty Ashton; 6 George Williams; 7 Josh Drinkwater; 18 Thomas Mikaele; 9 Daryl Clark; 10 Paul Vaughan; 11 Ben Currie; 12 Matty Nicholson; 14 Sam Kasiano. Subs: 19 Joe Bullock; 16 Danny Walker; 23 Tom Whitehead; 21 Greg Minikin (not used).
Tries: Mikaele (17), Nicholson (31), Vaughan (79);
Goals: Ratchford 3/3.
Rugby Leaguer & League Express Men of the Match:
Hull KR: Frankie Halton; *Wolves:* George Williams.
Penalty count: 4-4; **Half-time:** 6-12;
Referee: Jack Smith; **Attendance:** 8,082.

LEEDS RHINOS 26 WAKEFIELD TRINITY 0

RHINOS: 1 Richie Myler; 16 Derrell Olpherts; 4 Nene Macdonald; 5 Ash Handley (C); 2 David Fusitu'a; 6 Blake Austin; 7 Aidan Sezer; 18 Tom Holroyd; 14 Jarrod O'Connor; 10 Zane Tetevano; 19 James McDonnell; 12 Rhyse Martin; 13 Cameron Smith. Subs (all used): 11 James Bentley; 22 Sam Walters; 15 Sam Lisone; 3 Harry Newman.
Tries: Fusitu'a (44, 66), Newman (58), Holroyd (62), Macdonald (73); **Goals:** Martin 2/4, Sezer 1/1.
TRINITY: 15 Liam Kay; 18 Lee Kershaw; 4 Reece Lyne; 21 Samisoni Langi; 2 Jorge Taufua; 6 Lee Gaskell; 7 Mason Lino; 17 Renouf Atoni; 9 Liam Hood; 10 Jai Whitbread; 13 Jay Pitts; 11 Matty Ashurst (C); 14 Jordan Crowther. Subs (all used): 8 Eddie Battye; 19 Kevin Proctor; 20 Morgan Smith; 25 Sam Eseh.
Rugby Leaguer & League Express Men of the Match:
Rhinos: Jarrod O'Connor; *Trinity:* Jai Whitbread.
Penalty count: 13-3; **Half time:** 0-0;
Referee: Ben Thaler; **Attendance:** 11,717.

LEIGH LEOPARDS 20 ST HELENS 12

LEOPARDS: 17 Gareth O'Brien; 2 Tom Briscoe; 1 Zak Hardaker; 4 Ricky Leutele; 5 Josh Charnley; 6 Joe Mellor; 7 Lachlan Lam; 8 Tom Amone; 18 Matt Davis; 10 Robbie Mulhern; 28 Joe Shorrocks; 24 Kai O'Donnell; 13 John Asiata (C). Subs: 3 Ed Chamberlain (not used); 9 Edwin Ipape; 14 Ben Nakubuwai; 27 Ava Seumanufagai.
Tries: Charnley (57), Briscoe (68), Hardaker (74), Shorrocks (77); **Goals:** Hardaker 2/4.
SAINTS: 1 Jack Welsby; 2 Tommy Makinson; 21 Ben Davies; 4 Mark Percival; 5 Jonathan Bennison; 6 Jonny Lomax; 7 Lewis Dodd; 17 Agnatius Paasi; 9 James Roby (C); 10 Matty Lees; 22 Sam Royle; 19 James Bell; 13 Morgan Knowles. Subs (all used): 8 Alex Walmsley; 14 Joey Lussick; 15 Louie McCarthy-Scarsbrook; 18 Jake Wingfield.
Tries: Lomax (9), Bennison (19); **Goals:** Makinson 2/3.
Sin bin: Lees (67) - high tackle on O'Brien.
Rugby Leaguer & League Express Men of the Match:
Leopards: John Asiata; *Saints:* James Roby.
Penalty count: 6-4; **Half-time:** 0-12;
Referee: Aaron Moore; **Attendance:** 7,734.

Saturday 11th March 2023

HULL FC 14 SALFORD RED DEVILS 60

HULL FC: 1 Tex Hoy; 2 Adam Swift; 23 Josh Griffin (C); 17 Cameron Scott; 5 Darnell McIntosh; 14 Joe Lovodua; 7 Jake Clifford; 30 Scott Taylor; 9 Danny Houghton; 13 Brad Fash; 8 Ligi Sao; 11 Andre Savelio; 12 Jordan Lane. Subs (all used): 10 Tevita Satae; 16 Kane Evans; 20 Jack Brown; 33 Brad Dwyer.
Tries: Clifford (3), Swift (63), Fash (75); **Goals:** Clifford 1/3.
RED DEVILS: 1 Ryan Brierley; 2 Ken Sio; 28 Deon Cross; 4 Tim Lafai; 22 Rhys Williams; 6 Brodie Croft; 7 Marc Sneyd; 8 Jack Ormondroyd; 9 Andy Ackers; 10 King Vuniyayawa; 3 Kallum Watkins (C); 17 Shane Wright; 14 Chris Atkin. Subs (all used): 16 Tyler Dupree; 19 Adam Sidlow; 20 Ellis Longstaff; 21 Amir Bourouh.
Tries: Cross (7, 41), Wright (12, 34), Brierley (17), Dupree (23), Watkins (45), Sneyd (49), Lafai (55, 79);
Goals: Sneyd 10/12.
Rugby Leaguer & League Express Men of the Match:
Hull FC: Josh Griffin; *Red Devils:* Brodie Croft.
Penalty count: 7-4; **Half-time:** 4-30;
Referee: Chris Kendall; **Attendance:** 11,323.

ROUND 5

Thursday 16th March 2023

CASTLEFORD TIGERS 14 LEEDS RHINOS 8

TIGERS: 2 Greg Eden; 5 Bureta Faraimo; 17 Jack Broadbent; 4 Mahe Fonua; 31 Jason Qareqare; 6 Gareth Widdop; 7 Jacob Miller; 20 Muizz Mustapha; 9 Paul McShane (C); 14 Nathan Massey; 16 Adam Milner; 12 Alex Mellor; 13 Joe Westerman. Subs (all used): 11 Kenny Edwards; 22 Daniel Smith; 23 Suaia Matagi; 32 Liam Watts.
Tries: Faraimo (17, 57); **Goals:** Widdop 3/5.

RHINOS: 1 Richie Myler; 16 Derrell Olpherts; 4 Nene Macdonald; 3 Harry Newman; 2 David Fusitu'a; 6 Blake Austin; 7 Aidan Sezer; 18 Tom Holroyd; 14 Jarrod O'Connor; 10 Zane Tetevano; 19 James McDonnell; 12 Rhyse Martin; 13 Cameron Smith (C). Subs (all used): 11 James Bentley; 15 Sam Lisone; 17 Justin Sangare; 24 Luis Roberts.
Try: Myler (27); **Goals:** Martin 2/2.
Rugby Leaguer & League Express Men of the Match: *Tigers:* Paul McShane; *Rhinos:* Tom Holroyd.
Penalty count: 9-6; **Half-time:** 6-8;
Referee: Aaron Moore; **Attendance:** 7,458.

Friday 17th March 2023

HUDDERSFIELD GIANTS 12 WIGAN WARRIORS 14

GIANTS: 6 Tui Lolohea; 5 Jake Bibby; 4 Kevin Naiqama; 3 Esan Marsters; 21 Leroy Cudjoe; 23 Oliver Russell; 32 Will Pryce; 8 Chris Hill; 9 Nathan Peats; 20 Oliver Wilson; 11 Josh Jones; 12 Chris McQueen; 13 Luke Yates (C). Subs (all used): 14 Ashton Golding; 16 Harry Rushton (D); 18 Sebastine Ikahihifo; 27 Jack Ashworth.
Try: Naiqama (46); **Goals:** Russell 4/4.
WARRIORS: 1 Jai Field; 2 Bevan French; 3 Toby King; 4 Jake Wardle; 5 Liam Marshall; 6 Cade Cust; 7 Harry Smith; 14 Mike Cooper; 9 Sam Powell; 10 Liam Byrne; 11 Willie Isa; 12 Liam Farrell (C); 13 Morgan Smithies. Subs (all used): 15 Kaide Ellis; 16 Ethan Havard; 17 Kai Pearce-Paul; 20 Patrick Mago.
Tries: French (16, 61), Wardle (25); **Goals:** Smith 1/3.
Rugby Leaguer & League Express Men of the Match: *Giants:* Sebastine Ikahihifo; *Warriors:* Bevan French.
Penalty count: 6-3; **Half-time:** 6-8;
Referee: Jack Smith; **Attendance:** 5,777.

ST HELENS 20 HULL FC 12

SAINTS: 1 Jack Welsby; 25 Tee Ritson; 21 Ben Davies; 2 Tommy Makinson; 5 Jonathan Bennison; 6 Jonny Lomax; 7 Lewis Dodd; 8 Alex Walmsley; 9 James Roby (C); 10 Matty Lees; 19 James Bell; 16 Curtis Sironen; 13 Morgan Knowles. Subs (all used): 14 Joey Lussick; 15 Louie McCarthy-Scarsbrook; 17 Agnatius Paasi; 18 Jake Wingfield.
Tries: Davies (39), Bennison (55, 78), Welsby (61);
Goals: Makinson 0/1, Lussick 2/2, Dodd 0/1.
HULL FC: 1 Tex Hoy; 25 Davy Litten; 17 Cameron Scott; 23 Josh Griffin (C); 2 Adam Swift; 14 Joe Lovodua; 7 Jake Clifford; 20 Jack Brown; 9 Danny Houghton; 10 Tevita Satae; 11 Andre Savelio; 8 Ligi Sao; 13 Brad Fash. Subs (all used): 12 Jordan Lane; 15 Joe Cator; 30 Scott Taylor; 33 Brad Dwyer.
Tries: Taylor (48), Clifford (64); **Goals:** Clifford 2/2.
Rugby Leaguer & League Express Men of the Match: *Saints:* Lewis Dodd; *Hull FC:* Josh Griffin.
Penalty count: 4-3; **Half-time:** 4-0;
Referee: Liam Moore; **Attendance:** 10,350.

WARRINGTON WOLVES 38 LEIGH LEOPARDS 20

WOLVES: 1 Matt Dufty; 2 Josh Thewlis; 3 Peter Mata'utia; 4 Stefan Ratchford (C); 5 Matty Ashton; 6 George Williams; 7 Josh Drinkwater; 18 Thomas Mikaele; 9 Daryl Clark; 10 Paul Vaughan; 11 Ben Currie; 12 Matty Nicholson; 14 Sam Kasiano. Subs (all used): 15 Joe Philbin; 16 Danny Walker; 21 Greg Minikin; 24 Luke Thomas.
Tries: Drinkwater (1), Vaughan (8), Ratchford (22), Dufty (35), Ashton (42, 47, 52); **Goals:** Ratchford 5/8.
Sin bin: Kasiano (69) - high tackle on Ipape.
LEOPARDS: 17 Gareth O'Brien; 2 Tom Briscoe; 1 Zak Hardaker; 4 Ricky Leutele; 5 Josh Charnley; 6 Joe Mellor; 7 Lachlan Lam; 8 Tom Amone; 18 Matt Davis; 10 Robbie Mulhern; 28 Joe Shorrocks; 24 Kai O'Donnell; 13 John Asiata (C). Subs (all used): 9 Edwin Ipape; 12 Jack Hughes; 14 Ben Nakubuwai; 27 Ava Seumanufagai.
Tries: Briscoe (15), Charnley (38), Amone (73), Hardaker (75); **Goals:** Hardaker 2/4.
Sin bin: Ipape (51) - dangerous challenge on Clark.
Rugby Leaguer & League Express Men of the Match: *Wolves:* Josh Drinkwater; *Leopards:* John Asiata.
Penalty count: 7-7; **Half-time:** 22-8;
Referee: Ben Thaler; **Attendance:** 12,073.

Saturday 18th March 2023

CATALANS DRAGONS 26 HULL KR 12

DRAGONS: 1 Arthur Mourgue; 2 Tom Davies; 3 Adam Keighran; 19 Arthur Romano; 24 Tom Johnstone; 6 Tyrone May; 17 Cesar Rouge; 8 Mike McMeeken; 9 Michael McIlorum; 10 Julian Bousquet; 26 Manu Ma'u; 12 Paul Seguier; 13 Benjamin Garcia (C). Subs (all used): 14 Alrix Da Costa; 15 Mickael Goudemand; 18 Tiaki Chan; 23 Jordan Dezaria.
Tries: Johnstone (3, 50, 64), Davies (18), Bousquet (67);
Goals: Keighran 1/2, Mourgue 2/4.
Sin bin: Chan (77) - high tackle.

HULL KR: 1 Lachlan Coote; 23 Louis Senior; 3 Tom Opacic; 24 Sam Wood; 5 Ryan Hall; 20 Mikey Lewis; 7 Jordan Abdull (C); 15 Rhys Kennedy; 14 Jez Litten; 10 George King; 11 Frankie Halton; 16 James Batchelor; 22 Dean Hadley. Subs (all used): 8 Sauaso Sue; 13 Elliot Minchella; 21 Rowan Milnes; 26 Sam Luckley. 18th man (used): 19 Will Dagger.
Tries: Milnes (53), R Hall (79); **Goals:** Lewis 2/2.
Rugby Leaguer & League Express Men of the Match: *Dragons:* Tom Johnstone; *Hull KR:* Mikey Lewis.
Penalty count: 8-6; **Half-time:** 10-0;
Referee: Chris Kendall; **Attendance:** 7,682.

Sunday 19th March 2023

SALFORD RED DEVILS 14 WAKEFIELD TRINITY 13
(after golden point extra-time)

RED DEVILS: 1 Ryan Brierley; 2 Ken Sio; 28 Deon Cross; 24 Matthew Costello; 22 Rhys Williams; 6 Brodie Croft; 7 Marc Sneyd; 8 Jack Ormondroyd; 9 Andy Ackers; 10 King Vuniyayawa; 17 Shane Wright; 3 Kallum Watkins (C); 14 Chris Atkin. Subs (all used): 12 Sam Stone; 15 Danny Addy; 16 Tyler Dupree; 19 Adam Sidlow.
Tries: Costello (5), Atkin (38); **Goals:** Sneyd 2/2;
Field goals: Sneyd (74, 85).
TRINITY: 15 Liam Kay; 18 Lee Kershaw; 4 Reece Lyne; 3 Corey Hall; 2 Jorge Taufua; 20 Morgan Smith; 7 Mason Lino; 17 Renouf Atoni; 9 Liam Hood; 10 Jai Whitbread; 11 Matty Ashurst (C); 13 Jay Pitts; 14 Jordan Crowther. Subs (all used): 8 Eddie Battye; 24 Harry Bowes; 25 Sam Eseh; 31 Sam Hewitt (D).
Tries: Hall (10), Lyne (24); **Goals:** Lino 2/3;
Field goal: Lino (76).
Rugby Leaguer & League Express Men of the Match: *Red Devils:* Marc Sneyd; *Trinity:* Jai Whitbread.
Penalty count: 4-3; **Half-time:** 12-10;
Referee: Marcus Griffiths; **Attendance:** 4,757.

ROUND 6

Thursday 23rd March 2023

HUDDERSFIELD GIANTS 12 ST HELENS 14

GIANTS: 32 Will Pryce; 14 Ashton Golding; 4 Kevin Naiqama; 24 Sam Halsall (D); 25 Innes Senior; 23 Oliver Russell; 3 Esan Marsters; 8 Chris Hill; 9 Nathan Peats; 17 Owen Trout; 22 Harvey Livett (D); 12 Chris McQueen; 13 Luke Yates (C). Subs (all used): 1 Jake Connor (D2); 16 Harry Rushton; 18 Sebastine Ikahihifo; 27 Jack Ashworth.
Tries: Golding (38), Senior (65); **Goals:** Russell 2/2.
SAINTS: 1 Jack Welsby; 2 Tommy Makinson; 23 Konrad Hurrell; 3 Will Hopoate; 5 Jonathan Bennison; 6 Jonny Lomax; 7 Lewis Dodd; 8 Alex Walmsley; 9 James Roby (C); 10 Matty Lees; 11 Sione Mata'utia; 16 Curtis Sironen; 19 James Bell. Subs (all used): 14 Joey Lussick; 15 Louie McCarthy-Scarsbrook; 17 Agnatius Paasi; 22 Sam Royle.
Tries: Hurrell (28), Makinson (31); **Goals:** Makinson 3/3.
Rugby Leaguer & League Express Men of the Match: *Giants:* Ashton Golding; *Saints:* Matty Lees.
Penalty count: 4-5; **Half-time:** 6-12;
Referee: Jack Smith; **Attendance:** 4,684.

Friday 24th March 2023

CASTLEFORD TIGERS 0 WARRINGTON WOLVES 38

TIGERS: 2 Greg Eden; 5 Bureta Faraimo; 17 Jack Broadbent; 3 Jordan Turner; 31 Jason Qareqare; 6 Gareth Widdop; 7 Jacob Miller; 14 Nathan Massey; 9 Paul McShane (C); 22 Daniel Smith; 16 Adam Milner; 12 Alex Mellor; 13 Joe Westerman. Subs (all used): 10 George Griffin; 11 Kenny Edwards; 19 Albert Vete; 32 Liam Watts.
WOLVES: 1 Matt Dufty; 34 Matty Russell (D2); 21 Greg Minikin; 4 Stefan Ratchford (C); 5 Matty Ashton; 6 George Williams; 3 Peter Mata'utia; 10 Paul Vaughan; 9 Daryl Clark; 18 Thomas Mikaele; 11 Ben Currie; 12 Matty Nicholson; 14 Sam Kasiano. Subs (all used): 15 Joe Philbin; 16 Danny Walker; 17 Gil Dudson (D); 24 Luke Thomas.
Tries: Kasiano (8), Russell (19, 35), Mikaele (21), Vaughan (52), Williams (58), Dufty (62);
Goals: Ratchford 5/7.
Rugby Leaguer & League Express Men of the Match: *Tigers:* Paul McShane; *Wolves:* George Williams.
Penalty count: 7-3; **Half-time:** 0-24;
Referee: Marcus Griffiths; **Attendance:** 7,348.

WAKEFIELD TRINITY 6 HULL KR 34

TRINITY: 27 Robbie Butterworth (D); 18 Lee Kershaw; 4 Reece Lyne; 3 Corey Hall; 2 Jorge Taufua; 21 Samisoni Langi; 7 Mason Lino; 17 Renouf Atoni; 15 Liam Kay; 10 Jai Whitbread; 31 Sam Hewitt; 11 Matty Ashurst (C); 13 Jay Pitts. Subs (all used): 8 Eddie Battye; 22 Rob Butler; 25 Sam Eseh; 32 Tom Forber (D).
Try: Whitbread (60); **Goals:** Lino 1/2.
Sin bin: Hewitt (36) - dangerous contact on Lewis.

HULL KR: 1 Lachlan Coote; 23 Louis Senior; 3 Tom Opacic; 24 Sam Wood; 5 Ryan Hall; 20 Mikey Lewis; 21 Rowan Milnes; 15 Rhys Kennedy; 9 Matt Parcell; 10 George King; 16 James Batchelor; 12 Kane Linnett (C); 13 Elliot Minchella. Subs (all used): 8 Sauaso Sue; 14 Jez Litten; 17 Matty Storton; 26 Sam Luckley.
Tries: Wood (13), Senior (19), Opacic (23, 73), Linnett (37), Lewis (48), Minchella (54);
Goals: Lewis 0/3, Coote 3/4.
Rugby Leaguer & League Express Men of the Match: *Trinity:* Jai Whitbread; *Hull KR:* Tom Opacic.
Penalty count: 4-6; **Half-time:** 0-18;
Referee: Aaron Moore; **Attendance:** 4,705.

WIGAN WARRIORS 20 SALFORD RED DEVILS 16

WARRIORS: 1 Jai Field; 2 Bevan French; 3 Toby King; 4 Jake Wardle; 5 Liam Marshall; 6 Cade Cust; 7 Harry Smith; 8 Brad Singleton; 9 Sam Powell; 10 Liam Byrne; 17 Kai Pearce-Paul; 12 Liam Farrell (C); 13 Morgan Smithies. Subs (all used): 14 Mike Cooper; 15 Kaide Ellis; 16 Ethan Havard; 22 Brad O'Neill.
Tries: French (29, 68), King (73); **Goals:** Smith 4/4.
RED DEVILS: 1 Ryan Brierley; 2 Ken Sio; 28 Deon Cross; 4 Tim Lafai; 5 Joe Burgess; 6 Brodie Croft; 7 Marc Sneyd; 16 Tyler Dupree; 21 Amir Bourouh; 19 Adam Sidlow; 3 Kallum Watkins (C); 12 Sam Stone; 15 Danny Addy. Subs (all used): 8 Jack Ormondroyd; 10 King Vuniyayawa; 14 Chris Atkin; 17 Shane Wright.
Tries: Sio (15, 47); **Goals:** Sneyd 4/4.
Rugby Leaguer & League Express Men of the Match: *Warriors:* Liam Farrell; *Red Devils:* Marc Sneyd.
Penalty count: 6-3; **Half-time:** 8-8;
Referee: Chris Kendall; **Attendance:** 11,497.

Saturday 25th March 2023

LEEDS RHINOS 32 CATALANS DRAGONS 22

RHINOS: 1 Richie Myler; 2 David Fusitu'a; 3 Harry Newman; 12 Rhyse Martin; 4 Nene Macdonald; 6 Blake Austin; 7 Aidan Sezer; 22 Sam Walters; 14 Jarrod O'Connor; 18 Tom Holroyd; 19 James McDonnell; 10 Zane Tetevano; 13 Cameron Smith (C). Subs (all used): 15 Sam Lisone; 16 Derrell Olpherts; 17 Justin Sangare; 26 Corey Johnson.
Tries: Newman (9, 74), Martin (12), Myler (49), O'Connor (53), Olpherts (60), Holroyd (66);
Goals: Martin 1/6, Sezer 1/1.
Sin bin: Newman (45) - dissent.
DRAGONS: 1 Arthur Mourgue; 2 Tom Davies; 3 Adam Keighran; 19 Arthur Romano; 24 Tom Johnstone; 6 Tyrone May; 7 Mitchell Pearce; 8 Mike McMeeken; 9 Michael McIlorum; 10 Julian Bousquet; 26 Manu Ma'u; 11 Matt Whitley; 13 Benjamin Garcia (C). Subs (all used): 12 Paul Seguier; 14 Alrix Da Costa; 15 Mickael Goudemand; 23 Jordan Dezaria.
Tries: Davies (3), Keighran (22), Pearce (27), Seguier (36);
Goals: Keighran 3/4.
Rugby Leaguer & League Express Men of the Match: *Rhinos:* Blake Austin; *Dragons:* Mitchell Pearce.
Penalty count: 1-4; **Half time:** 8-22;
Referee: Liam Moore; **Attendance:** 14,321.

HULL FC 16 LEIGH LEOPARDS 24

HULL FC: 1 Tex Hoy; 2 Adam Swift; 3 Carlos Tuimavave (C); 4 Liam Sutcliffe; 25 Davy Litten; 14 Joe Lovodua; 7 Jake Clifford; 20 Jack Brown; 33 Brad Dwyer; 10 Tevita Satae; 11 Andre Savelio; 23 Josh Griffin; 13 Brad Fash. Subs (all used): 8 Ligi Sao; 15 Joe Cator; 17 Cameron Scott; 30 Scott Taylor.
Tries: Litten (26), Clifford (62), Sutcliffe (71);
Goals: Clifford 2/3.
Sin bin: Sao (40) - high tackle on O'Donnell, (56) - off the ball challenge.
LEOPARDS: 17 Gareth O'Brien; 5 Josh Charnley; 4 Ricky Leutele; 1 Zak Hardaker; 2 Tom Briscoe; 15 Ben Reynolds; 7 Lachlan Lam; 8 Tom Amone; 9 Edwin Ipape; 10 Robbie Mulhern; 24 Kai O'Donnell; 28 Joe Shorrocks; 13 John Asiata (C). Subs (all used): 14 Ben Nakubuwai; 16 Oliver Holmes; 18 Matt Davis; 27 Ava Seumanufagai.
Tries: O'Donnell (4), Charnley (6, 12, 56);
Goals: Reynolds 4/7.
Rugby Leaguer & League Express Men of the Match: *Hull FC:* Jake Clifford; *Leopards:* Edwin Ipape.
Penalty count: 5-11; **Half-time:** 6-16;
Referee: Ben Thaler; **Attendance:** 10,952.

ROUND 7

Thursday 30th March 2023

LEIGH LEOPARDS 6 WIGAN WARRIORS 34

LEOPARDS: 17 Gareth O'Brien; 5 Josh Charnley; 4 Ricky Leutele; 1 Zak Hardaker; 2 Tom Briscoe; 15 Ben Reynolds;

7 Lachlan Lam; 8 Tom Amone; 9 Edwin Ipape; 10 Robbie Mulhern; 24 Kai O'Donnell; 16 Oliver Holmes; 13 John Asiata (C). Subs (all used): 14 Ben Nakubuwai; 27 Ava Seumanufagai; 18 Matt Davis; 3 Ed Chamberlain.
Try: Briscoe (7); **Goals:** Reynolds 1/1.
WARRIORS: 2 Bevan French; 3 Toby King; 17 Kai Pearce-Paul; 4 Jake Wardle; 23 Abbas Miski; 1 Jai Field; 7 Harry Smith; 14 Mike Cooper; 9 Sam Powell; 10 Liam Byrne; 11 Willie Isa; 12 Liam Farrell (C); 13 Morgan Smithies. Subs (all used): 15 Kaide Ellis; 16 Ethan Havard; 22 Brad O'Neill; 19 Joe Shorrocks.
Tries: French (12), Field (21, 58), Wardle (45), Miski (54, 80), King (78); **Goals:** Smith 3/7.
Sin bin: Wardle (8) - late challenge on O'Brien.
Rugby Leaguer & League Express Men of the Match: *Leopards:* Tom Briscoe; *Warriors:* Bevan French.
Penalty count: 5-4; **Half-time:** 6-10;
Referee: Liam Moore; **Attendance:** 9,189.

Friday 31st March 2023

HULL KR 20 LEEDS RHINOS 12

HULL KR: 1 Lachlan Coote; 23 Louis Senior; 16 James Batchelor; 24 Sam Wood; 5 Ryan Hall; 20 Mikey Lewis; 7 Jordan Abdull; 15 Rhys Kennedy; 9 Matt Parcell (C); 10 George King; 11 Frankie Halton; 12 Kane Linnett; 13 Elliot Minchella. Subs (all used): 8 Sauaso Sue; 14 Jez Litten; 22 Dean Hadley; 26 Sam Luckley.
Tries: Senior (24), Sue (29), Linnett (41); **Goals:** Coote 4/5.
RHINOS: 21 Luke Hooley (D); 2 David Fusitu'a; 3 Harry Newman; 12 Rhyse Martin (C); 16 Derrell Olpherts; 6 Blake Austin; 7 Aidan Sezer; 18 Tom Holroyd; 14 Jarrod O'Connor; 10 Zane Tetevano; 11 James Bentley; 19 James McDonnell; 13 Cameron Smith. Subs (all used): 8 Mikolaj Oledzki; 15 Sam Lisone; 17 Justin Sangare; 24 Luis Roberts.
Tries: Roberts (43), McDonnell (74); **Goals:** Martin 2/2.
Rugby Leaguer & League Express Men of the Match: *Hull KR:* Jordan Abdull; *Rhinos:* Rhyse Martin.
Penalty count: 6-5; **Half-time:** 14-0;
Referee: Marcus Griffiths; **Attendance:** 8,512.

ST HELENS 38 WAKEFIELD TRINITY 0

SAINTS: 1 Jack Welsby; 2 Tommy Makinson; 23 Konrad Hurrell; 4 Mark Percival; 3 Will Hopoate; 6 Jonny Lomax; 7 Lewis Dodd; 8 Alex Walmsley; 9 James Roby (C); 10 Matty Lees; 16 Curtis Sironen; 19 James Bell; 13 Morgan Knowles. Subs (all used): 14 Joey Lussick; 15 Louie McCarthy-Scarsbrook; 22 Sam Royle; 30 George Delaney.
Tries: Percival (7), Hopoate (32), Makinson (37), Dodd (57), Hurrell (63, 74), Lomax (69);
Goals: Makinson 0/2, Percival 5/6.
TRINITY: 33 Will Dagger (D); 18 Lee Kershaw; 4 Reece Lyne; 21 Samisoni Langi; 34 Innes Senior (D3); 20 Morgan Smith; 7 Mason Lino; 8 Eddie Battye; 15 Liam Kay; 10 Jai Whitbread; 11 Matty Ashurst (C); 13 Jay Pitts; 14 Jordan Crowther. Subs (all used): 22 Rob Butler; 24 Harry Bowes; 25 Sam Eseh; 32 Tom Forber.
Rugby Leaguer & League Express Men of the Match: *Saints:* Konrad Hurrell; *Trinity:* Morgan Smith.
Penalty count: 4-3; **Half-time:** 12-0;
Referee: Chris Kendall; **Attendance:** 10,304.

Saturday 1st April 2023

WARRINGTON WOLVES 34 HULL FC 6

WOLVES: 1 Matt Dufty; 34 Matty Russell; 21 Greg Minikin; 4 Stefan Ratchford (C); 5 Matty Ashton; 6 George Williams; 7 Josh Drinkwater; 18 Thomas Mikaele; 16 Danny Walker; 10 Paul Vaughan; 11 Ben Currie; 12 Matty Nicholson; 3 Peter Mata'utia. Subs (all used): 2 Josh Thewlis; 15 Joe Philbin; 17 Gil Dudson; 24 Luke Thomas.
Tries: Ashton (6), Mata'utia (12), Currie (20), Dufty (30), Drinkwater (38), Nicholson (71); **Goals:** Ratchford 5/6.
HULL FC: 1 Tex Hoy; 25 Davy Litten; 3 Carlos Tuimavave (C); 4 Liam Sutcliffe; 2 Adam Swift; 14 Joe Lovodua; 7 Jake Clifford; 30 Scott Taylor; 9 Danny Houghton; 10 Tevita Satae; 11 Andre Savelio; 23 Josh Griffin; 13 Brad Fash. Subs (all used): 12 Jordan Lane; 15 Joe Cator; 16 Kane Evans; 33 Brad Dwyer.
Try: Dwyer (62); **Goals:** Clifford 1/1.
Rugby Leaguer & League Express Men of the Match: *Wolves:* George Williams; *Hull FC:* Davy Litten.
Penalty count: 3-2; **Half-time:** 28-0;
Referee: Aaron Moore; **Attendance:** 10,797.

CATALANS DRAGONS 22 CASTLEFORD TIGERS 18

DRAGONS: 1 Arthur Mourgue; 2 Tom Davies; 3 Adam Keighran; 4 Matthieu Laguerre; 24 Tom Johnstone; 17 Cesar Rouge; 7 Mitchell Pearce; 8 Mike McMeeken; 14 Alrix Da Costa; 10 Julian Bousquet; 11 Matt Whitley; 12 Paul Seguier; 13 Benjamin Garcia (C). Subs (all used): 16 Romain Navarrete; 18 Tiaki Chan; 23 Jordan Dezaria; 29 Sam Tomkins.
Tries: Seguier (3), Johnstone (24), Mourgue (41), McMeeken (76); **Goals:** Keighran 2/4, Mourgue 1/1.
TIGERS: 2 Greg Eden; 5 Bureta Faraimo; 11 Kenny Edwards; 3 Jordan Turner; 4 Mahe Fonua; 17 Jack Broadbent; 7 Jacob Miller; 14 Nathan Massey; 9 Paul McShane (C); 23 Suaia Matagi; 10 George Griffin; 12 Alex Mellor; 13 Joe Westerman. Subs (all used): 8 George Lawler; 20 Muizz Mustapha; 19 Albert Vete; 22 Daniel Smith.
Tries: Broadbent (10, 69), Turner (58); **Goals:** McShane 3/3.
Rugby Leaguer & League Express Men of the Match: *Dragons:* Arthur Mourgue; *Tigers:* Paul McShane.
Penalty count: 9-2; **Half-time:** 12-6;
Referee: Jack Smith; **Attendance:** 8,109.

Sunday 2nd April 2023

SALFORD RED DEVILS 16 HUDDERSFIELD GIANTS 26

RED DEVILS: 1 Ryan Brierley; 2 Ken Sio; 28 Deon Cross; 24 Matthew Costello; 5 Joe Burgess; 6 Brodie Croft; 7 Marc Sneyd; 16 Tyler Dupree; 14 Chris Atkin; 8 Jack Ormondroyd; 3 Kallum Watkins (C); 12 Sam Stone; 15 Danny Addy. Subs (all used): 10 King Vuniyayawa; 11 Andrew Dixon (D2); 17 Shane Wright; 25 Ben Hellewell (D2).
Tries: Wright (33), Costello (48), Watkins (79);
Goals: Sneyd 2/3.
GIANTS: 32 Will Pryce; 14 Ashton Golding; 3 Esan Marsters; 4 Kevin Naiqama; 24 Sam Halsall; 1 Jake Connor; 23 Oliver Russell; 8 Chris Hill; 9 Nathan Peats; 15 Matty English; 12 Chris McQueen; 16 Harry Rushton; 13 Luke Yates (C). Subs (all used): 6 Tui Lolohea; 17 Owen Trout; 18 Sebastine Ikahihifo; 27 Jack Ashworth.
Tries: Golding (11), Trout (36, 65), McQueen (76);
Goals: Russell 5/6.
Rugby Leaguer & League Express Men of the Match: *Red Devils:* King Vuniyayawa; *Giants:* Matty English.
Penalty count: 6-10; **Half-time:** 6-14;
Referee: Ben Thaler; **Attendance:** 4,764.

ROUND 8

Thursday 6th April 2023

CASTLEFORD TIGERS 16 WAKEFIELD TRINITY 4

TIGERS: 1 Niall Evalds; 5 Bureta Faraimo; 4 Mahe Fonua; 3 Jordan Turner; 2 Greg Eden; 17 Jack Broadbent; 7 Jacob Miller; 14 Nathan Massey; 9 Paul McShane (C); 23 Suaia Matagi; 10 George Griffin; 12 Alex Mellor; 13 Joe Westerman. Subs (all used): 8 George Lawler; 11 Kenny Edwards; 20 Muizz Mustapha; 38 Luis Johnson (D).
Tries: McShane (3), Eden (33, 69); **Goals:** McShane 2/3.
Sin bin: Westerman (61) - trip on Pitts.
TRINITY: 33 Will Dagger; 18 Lee Kershaw; 4 Reece Lyne; 21 Samisoni Langi; 34 Innes Senior; 20 Morgan Smith; 7 Mason Lino; 35 Nathan Mason (D); 9 Liam Hood; 10 Jai Whitbread; 11 Matty Ashurst (C); 31 Sam Hewitt; 13 Jay Pitts. Subs (all used): 14 Jordan Crowther; 15 Liam Kay; 17 Renouf Atoni; 19 Kevin Proctor.
Try: Langi (48); **Goals:** Lino 0/1.
Rugby Leaguer & League Express Men of the Match: *Tigers:* Paul McShane; *Trinity:* Sam Hewitt.
Penalty count: 4-3; **Half-time:** 12-0;
Referee: Marcus Griffiths; **Attendance:** 8,075.

Friday 7th April 2023

HULL FC 0 HULL KR 40

HULL FC: 29 Jamie Shaul; 2 Adam Swift; 4 Liam Sutcliffe; 3 Carlos Tuimavave (C); 5 Darnell McIntosh; 19 Ben McNamara; 7 Jake Clifford; 13 Brad Fash; 33 Brad Dwyer; 10 Tevita Satae; 12 Jordan Lane; 23 Josh Griffin; 15 Joe Cator. Subs (all used): 8 Ligi Sao; 16 Kane Evans; 22 Mitieli Vulikijapani; 30 Scott Taylor.
HULL KR: 1 Lachlan Coote; 24 Sam Wood; 3 Tom Opacic; 4 Shaun Kenny-Dowall (C); 5 Ryan Hall; 20 Mikey Lewis; 7 Jordan Abdull; 15 Rhys Kennedy; 9 Matt Parcell; 10 George King; 16 James Batchelor; 12 Kane Linnett; 13 Elliot Minchella. Subs (all used): 8 Sauaso Sue; 14 Jez Litten; 22 Dean Hadley; 26 Sam Luckley.
Tries: R Hall (9, 57, 73), Opacic (17), Batchelor (48), Coote (51), Lewis (60); **Goals:** Coote 6/8.
Sin bin: Batchelor (33) - dangerous challenge on Clifford.
Rugby Leaguer & League Express Men of the Match: *Hull FC:* Josh Griffin; *Hull KR:* Jordan Abdull.
Penalty count: 8-3; **Half-time:** 0-14;
Referee: Jack Smith; **Attendance:** 20,985.

WIGAN WARRIORS 14 ST HELENS 6

WARRIORS: 2 Bevan French; 23 Abbas Miski; 3 Toby King; 4 Jake Wardle; 5 Liam Marshall; 19 Joe Shorrocks; 7 Harry Smith; 14 Mike Cooper; 9 Sam Powell; 10 Liam Byrne; 17 Kai Pearce-Paul; 12 Liam Farrell (C); 13 Morgan Smithies. Subs (all used): 8 Brad Singleton; 15 Kaide Ellis; 16 Ethan Havard; 22 Brad O'Neill.
Tries: Smith (10), King (51); **Goals:** Smith 3/3.
SAINTS: 1 Jack Welsby; 2 Tommy Makinson; 23 Konrad Hurrell; 4 Mark Percival; 3 Will Hopoate; 6 Jonny Lomax; 7 Lewis Dodd; 17 Agnatius Paasi; 9 James Roby (C); 10 Matty Lees; 16 Curtis Sironen; 11 Sione Mata'utia; 13 Morgan Knowles. Subs (all used): 14 Joey Lussick; 15 Louie McCarthy-Scarsbrook; 19 James Bell; 30 George Delaney.
Try: Lomax (61); **Goals:** Percival 1/1.
Rugby Leaguer & League Express Men of the Match: *Warriors:* Joe Shorrocks; *Saints:* Konrad Hurrell.
Penalty count: 7-2; **Half-time:** 8-0;
Referee: Liam Moore; **Attendance:** 24,275.

Saturday 8th April 2023

LEIGH LEOPARDS 20 SALFORD RED DEVILS 22

LEOPARDS: 1 Zak Hardaker; 2 Tom Briscoe; 4 Ricky Leutele; 3 Ed Chamberlain; 5 Josh Charnley; 15 Ben Reynolds; 7 Lachlan Lam; 8 Tom Amone; 9 Edwin Ipape; 10 Robbie Mulhern; 16 Oliver Holmes; 24 Kai O'Donnell; 13 John Asiata (C). Subs (all used): 12 Jack Hughes; 27 Ava Seumanufagai; 22 Tom Nisbet; 18 Matt Davis.
Tries: Charnley (6, 64), Briscoe (52), Reynolds (80);
Goals: Reynolds 2/5.
RED DEVILS: 1 Ryan Brierley; 2 Ken Sio; 28 Deon Cross; 24 Matthew Costello; 5 Joe Burgess; 6 Brodie Croft; 7 Marc Sneyd; 16 Tyler Dupree; 9 Andy Ackers; 10 King Vuniyayawa; 3 Kallum Watkins (C); 12 Sam Stone; 15 Danny Addy. Subs (all used): 11 Andrew Dixon; 14 Chris Atkin; 17 Shane Wright; 25 Ben Hellewell.
Tries: Sio (16), Stone (23), Croft (25), Dupree (58);
Goals: Sneyd 3/4.
Sin bin: Brierley (48) - professional foul.
Rugby Leaguer & League Express Men of the Match: *Leopards:* Edwin Ipape; *Red Devils:* Tyler Dupree.
Penalty count: 5-5; **Half-time:** 6-16;
Referee: Aaron Moore; **Attendance:** 6,002.

CATALANS DRAGONS 14 WARRINGTON WOLVES 20

DRAGONS: 31 Tanguy Zenon; 2 Tom Davies; 19 Arthur Romano; 11 Matt Whitley; 24 Tom Johnstone; 3 Adam Keighran; 1 Arthur Mourgue; 16 Romain Navarrete; 14 Alrix Da Costa; 10 Julian Bousquet; 8 Mike McMeeken; 12 Paul Seguier; 13 Benjamin Garcia (C). Subs (all used): 15 Mickael Goudemand; 22 Sio Siua Taukeiaho; 23 Jordan Dezaria; 28 Ugo Tison.
Tries: McMeeken (25), Keighran (29, pen), Romano (59);
Goals: Keighran 1/3.
WOLVES: 1 Matt Dufty; 2 Josh Thewlis; 3 Peter Mata'utia; 4 Stefan Ratchford (C); 5 Matty Ashton; 6 George Williams; 7 Josh Drinkwater; 17 Gil Dudson; 16 Danny Walker; 10 Paul Vaughan; 11 Ben Currie; 12 Matty Nicholson; 13 Josh McGuire (D). Subs: 14 Sam Kasiano; 15 Joe Philbin; 21 Greg Minikin; 35 Lucas Green (not used).
Tries: Thewlis (7, 72), Dufty (32), Williams (46);
Goals: Ratchford 1/3, Thewlis 1/1.
Dismissal: Dudson (66) - punching Johnstone.
Rugby Leaguer & League Express Men of the Match: *Dragons:* Benjamin Garcia; *Wolves:* George Williams.
Penalty count: 2-5; **Half-time:** 10-8;
Referee: Chris Kendall; **Attendance:** 10,786.

Sunday 9th April 2023

LEEDS RHINOS 18 HUDDERSFIELD GIANTS 17

RHINOS: 1 Richie Myler; 4 Nene Macdonald; 3 Harry Newman; 12 Rhyse Martin; 5 Ash Handley; 6 Blake Austin; 7 Aidan Sezer; 8 Mikolaj Oledzki; 14 Jarrod O'Connor; 18 Tom Holroyd; 11 James Bentley; 19 James McDonnell; 13 Cameron Smith (C). Subs (all used): 10 Zane Tetevano; 15 Sam Lisone; 17 Justin Sangare; 26 Corey Johnson.
Tries: Handley (34), McDonnell (47), Martin (55), Smith (59); **Goals:** Martin 1/3, Sezer 0/1.
Sin bin: Myler (15) - trip on McGillvary.
GIANTS: 32 Will Pryce; 2 Jermaine McGillvary; 3 Esan Marsters; 4 Kevin Naiqama; 24 Sam Halsall; 1 Jake Connor; 6 Tui Lolohea; 8 Chris Hill; 9 Nathan Peats; 15 Matty English; 12 Chris McQueen; 22 Harvey Livett; 13 Luke Yates (C). Subs (all used): 16 Harry Rushton; 18 Sebastine Ikahihifo; 19 Adam O'Brien; 27 Jack Ashworth.
Tries: McGillvary (4), McQueen (7, 69); **Goals:** Connor 2/4;
Field goal: Connor (40).
Rugby Leaguer & League Express Men of the Match: *Rhinos:* Blake Austin; *Giants:* Tui Lolohea.
Penalty count: 3-5; **Half-time:** 4-13;
Referee: Ben Thaler; **Attendance:** 13,234.

ROUND 9

Thursday 13th April 2023

SALFORD RED DEVILS 14 CASTLEFORD TIGERS 6

RED DEVILS: 1 Ryan Brierley; 2 Ken Sio; 28 Deon Cross;

Super League XXVIII - Round by Round

24 Matthew Costello; 5 Joe Burgess; 6 Brodie Croft; 7 Marc Sneyd; 16 Tyler Dupree; 9 Andy Ackers; 10 King Vuniyayawa; 3 Kallum Watkins (C); 12 Sam Stone; 13 Oliver Partington. Subs (all used): 8 Jack Ormondroyd; 14 Chris Atkin; 15 Danny Addy; 17 Shane Wright.
Tries: Croft (37), Wright (57); **Goals:** Sneyd 3/3.
TIGERS: 1 Niall Evalds; 2 Greg Eden; 3 Jordan Turner; 17 Jack Broadbent; 5 Bureta Faraimo; 6 Gareth Widdop; 7 Jacob Miller; 14 Nathan Massey; 9 Paul McShane (C); 8 George Lawler; 11 Kenny Edwards; 12 Alex Mellor; 16 Adam Milner. Subs (all used): 10 George Griffin; 22 Daniel Smith; 28 Sam Hall; 38 Luis Johnson.
Try: Eden (3); **Goals:** Widdop 1/1.
Rugby Leaguer & League Express Men of the Match:
Red Devils: Ryan Brierley; *Tigers:* Adam Milner.
Penalty count: 5-3; **Half-time:** 6-6;
Referee: Aaron Moore; **Attendance:** 4,468.

Friday 14th April 2023

HUDDERSFIELD GIANTS 26 CATALANS DRAGONS 14

GIANTS: 32 Will Pryce; 2 Jermaine McGillvary; 4 Kevin Naiqama; 3 Esan Marsters; 24 Sam Halsall; 1 Jake Connor; 6 Tui Lolohea; 8 Chris Hill; 9 Nathan Peats; 15 Matty English; 22 Harvey Livett; 12 Chris McQueen; 13 Luke Yates (C). Subs (all used): 16 Harry Rushton; 18 Sebastine Ikahihifo; 19 Adam O'Brien; 27 Jack Ashworth.
Tries: Halsall (20, 36), Livett (46), Naiqama (69);
Goals: Connor 5/6.
DRAGONS: 1 Arthur Mourgue; 2 Tom Davies; 19 Arthur Romano; 4 Matthieu Laguerre; 21 Tom Johnstone; 17 Cesar Rouge; 3 Adam Keighran; 10 Julian Bousquet; 13 Benjamin Garcia (C); 16 Romain Navarrete; 11 Matt Whitley; 12 Paul Seguier; 8 Mike McMeeken. Subs (all used): 15 Mickael Goudemand; 18 Tiaki Chan; 23 Jordan Dezaria; 29 Sam Tomkins.
Tries: Johnstone (10), Laguerre (52); **Goals:** Keighran 3/3.
Rugby Leaguer & League Express Men of the Match:
Giants: Harvey Livett; *Dragons:* Adam Keighran.
Penalty count: 3-4; **Half-time:** 10-8;
Referee: Liam Moore; **Attendance:** 4,685.

HULL KR 26 ST HELENS 14

HULL KR: 1 Lachlan Coote; 4 Shaun Kenny-Dowall (C); 3 Tom Opacic; 33 Corey Hall (D); 5 Ryan Hall; 20 Mikey Lewis; 7 Jordan Abdull; 15 Rhys Kennedy; 9 Matt Parcell; 10 George King; 22 Dean Hadley; 12 Kane Linnett; 13 Elliot Minchella. Subs (all used): 11 Frankie Halton; 14 Jez Litten; 17 Matty Storton; 26 Sam Luckley.
Tries: Lewis (25, 48), Coote (60), Litten (66);
Goals: Coote 5/5.
SAINTS: 1 Jack Welsby; 2 Tommy Makinson; 23 Konrad Hurrell; 3 Will Hopoate; 5 Jonathan Bennison; 6 Jonny Lomax; 7 Lewis Dodd; 10 Matty Lees; 9 James Roby (C); 15 Louie McCarthy-Scarsbrook; 4 Mark Percival; 22 Sam Royle; 19 James Bell. Subs (all used): 14 Joey Lussick; 18 Jake Wingfield; 25 Tee Ritson; 30 George Delaney.
Tries: Lomax (15), Lussick (70); **Goals:** Percival 3/3.
Sin bin: Lees (38) - late challenge on Luckley.
Rugby Leaguer & League Express Men of the Match:
Hull KR: Lachlan Coote; *Saints:* Jonny Lomax.
Penalty count: 8-10; **Half-time:** 8-8;
Referee: Ben Thaler; **Attendance:** 8,540.

LEEDS RHINOS 34 HULL FC 10

RHINOS: 1 Richie Myler; 4 Nene Macdonald; 3 Harry Newman; 12 Rhyse Martin; 5 Ash Handley; 6 Blake Austin; 7 Aidan Sezer; 8 Mikolaj Oledzki; 14 Jarrod O'Connor; 15 Sam Lisone; 19 James McDonnell; 10 Zane Tetevano; 13 Cameron Smith (C). Subs (all used): 17 Justin Sangare; 18 Tom Holroyd; 23 Liam Tindall; 26 Corey Johnson.
Tries: McDonnell (22), Handley (31, 47), Holroyd (34), Oledzki (60), Martin (71); **Goals:** Martin 5/6.
HULL FC: 25 Davy Litten; 5 Darnell McIntosh; 3 Carlos Tuimavave (C); 4 Liam Sutcliffe; 2 Adam Swift; 14 Joe Lovodua; 19 Ben McNamara; 8 Ligi Sao; 9 Danny Houghton; 13 Brad Fash; 12 Jordan Lane; 23 Josh Griffin; 15 Joe Cator. Subs (all used): 10 Tevita Satae; 20 Jack Brown; 27 Will Gardiner; 33 Brad Dwyer.
Tries: Tuimavave (54), Litten (65); **Goals:** McNamara 1/2.
Rugby Leaguer & League Express Men of the Match:
Rhinos: Ash Handley; *Hull FC:* Tevita Satae.
Penalty count: 6-5; **Half time:** 18-0;
Referee: Jack Smith; **Attendance:** 12,644.

WARRINGTON WOLVES 6 WIGAN WARRIORS 13

WOLVES: 1 Matt Dufty; 2 Josh Thewlis; 3 Peter Mata'utia; 4 Stefan Ratchford (C); 5 Matty Ashton; 6 George Williams; 7 Josh Drinkwater; 14 Sam Kasiano; 16 Danny Walker; 10 Paul Vaughan; 11 Ben Currie; 12 Matty Nicholson; 13 Josh McGuire. Subs (all used): 9 Daryl Clark; 21 Greg Minikin; 34 Matty Russell; 35 Lucas Green (D).
Try: Nicholson (37); **Goals:** Ratchford 1/1.

Hull KR's Elliot Minchella offloads as Castleford's Paul McShane closes in

WARRIORS: 2 Bevan French; 23 Abbas Miski; 3 Toby King; 4 Jake Wardle; 5 Liam Marshall; 19 Joe Shorrocks; 7 Harry Smith; 8 Brad Singleton; 9 Sam Powell; 10 Liam Byrne; 11 Willie Isa; 12 Liam Farrell (C); 15 Kaide Ellis. Subs (all used): 16 Ethan Havard; 17 Kai Pearce-Paul; 20 Patrick Mago; 22 Brad O'Neill.
Tries: Wardle (7), O'Neill (27); **Goals:** Smith 2/3;
Field goal: Smith (64).
Rugby Leaguer & League Express Men of the Match:
Wolves: Matty Nicholson; *Warriors:* Harry Smith.
Penalty count: 5-4; **Half-time:** 6-10;
Referee: Chris Kendall; **Attendance:** 15,026.

Sunday 16th April 2023

WAKEFIELD TRINITY 0 LEIGH LEOPARDS 32

TRINITY: 33 Will Dagger; 18 Lee Kershaw; 4 Reece Lyne; 21 Samisoni Langi; 2 Jorge Taufua; 20 Morgan Smith; Mason Lino; 10 Jai Whitbread; 9 Liam Hood; 17 Renouf Atoni; 31 Sam Hewitt; 11 Matty Ashurst (C); 13 Jay Pitts. Subs (all used): 8 Eddie Battye; 15 Liam Kay; 16 Josh Bowden; 19 Kevin Proctor.
LEOPARDS: 17 Gareth O'Brien; 2 Tom Briscoe; 4 Ricky Leutele; 1 Zak Hardaker; 5 Josh Charnley; 15 Ben Reynolds; 7 Lachlan Lam; 27 Ava Seumanufagai; 9 Edwin Ipape; 8 Tom Amone; 16 Oliver Holmes; 24 Kai O'Donnell; 13 John Asiata (C). Subs (all used): 6 Joe Mellor; 10 Robbie Mulhern; 18 Matt Davis; 25 Nathan Wilde (D).
Tries: O'Brien (25), Reynolds (30), Lam (46), Charnley (55, 68), Mellor (71); **Goals:** Reynolds 4/6.
Rugby Leaguer & League Express Men of the Match:
Trinity: Jai Whitbread; *Leopards:* Lachlan Lam.
Penalty count: 5-8; **Half-time:** 0-10;
Referee: Marcus Griffiths; **Attendance:** 4,710.

ROUND 10

Thursday 20th April 2023

ST HELENS 28 WARRINGTON WOLVES 6

SAINTS: 1 Jack Welsby; 25 Tee Ritson; 23 Konrad Hurrell; 3 Will Hopoate; 5 Jonathan Bennison; 6 Jonny Lomax; 7 Lewis Dodd; 15 Louie McCarthy-Scarsbrook; 9 James Roby (C); 10 Matty Lees; 22 Sam Royle; 12 Joe Batchelor; 19 James Bell. Subs: 14 Joey Lussick; 24 Lewis Baxter (not used); 30 George Delaney; 34 Wesley Bruines (not used).

Tries: Hurrell (10), Lomax (14), Hopoate (19), Bennison (43), Ritson (80); **Goals:** Bennison 2/4, Lussick 2/2.
WOLVES: 1 Matt Dufty; 34 Matty Russell; 21 Greg Minikin; 4 Stefan Ratchford (C); 5 Matty Ashton; 6 George Williams; 7 Josh Drinkwater; 8 James Harrison; 16 Danny Walker; 13 Josh McGuire; 11 Ben Currie; 12 Matty Nicholson; 9 Daryl Clark. Subs (all used): 2 Josh Thewlis; 3 Peter Mata'utia; 14 Sam Kasiano; 35 Lucas Green.
Try: Russell (25); **Goals:** Ratchford 1/1.
Rugby Leaguer & League Express Men of the Match:
Saints: Jonny Lomax; *Wolves:* Matty Russell.
Penalty count: 6-4; **Half-time:** 16-6;
Referee: Jack Smith; **Attendance:** 14,866.

Friday 21st April 2023

CASTLEFORD TIGERS 7 HULL KR 12

TIGERS: 2 Greg Eden; 5 Bureta Faraimo; 12 Alex Mellor; 3 Jordan Turner; 4 Mahe Fonua; 17 Jack Broadbent; 7 Jacob Miller; 8 George Lawler; 9 Paul McShane (C); 10 George Griffin; 16 Adam Milner; 11 Kenny Edwards; 13 Joe Westerman. Subs (all used): 23 Suaia Matagi; 28 Sam Hall; 32 Liam Watts; 39 Will Tate (D).
Try: Miller (10); **Goals:** McShane 1/1; **Field goal:** Miller (58).
Sin bin: Watts (27) - late challenge on Abdull.
HULL KR: 1 Lachlan Coote; 4 Shaun Kenny-Dowall (C); 3 Tom Opacic; 33 Corey Hall; 5 Ryan Hall; 20 Mikey Lewis; 7 Jordan Abdull; 15 Rhys Kennedy; 9 Matt Parcell; 10 George King; 16 James Batchelor; 12 Kane Linnett; 13 Elliot Minchella. Subs (all used): 14 Jez Litten; 17 Matty Storton; 22 Dean Hadley; 26 Sam Luckley.
Tries: C Hall (48), Parcell (60); **Goals:** Coote 2/2.
Rugby Leaguer & League Express Men of the Match:
Tigers: Jacob Miller; *Hull KR:* Matt Parcell.
Penalty count: 6-5; **Half-time:** 6-0;
Referee: Marcus Griffiths; **Attendance:** 7,110.

LEIGH LEOPARDS 20 LEEDS RHINOS 6

LEOPARDS: 17 Gareth O'Brien; 2 Tom Briscoe; 4 Ricky Leutele; 1 Zak Hardaker; 5 Josh Charnley; 15 Ben Reynolds; 7 Lachlan Lam; 8 Tom Amone; 9 Edwin Ipape; 10 Robbie Mulhern; 16 Oliver Holmes; 24 Kai O'Donnell; 13 John Asiata (C). Subs (all used): 6 Joe Mellor; 18 Matt Davis; 25 Nathan Wilde; 27 Ava Seumanufagai.
Tries: Ipape (2, 18), O'Donnell (9); **Goals:** Reynolds 4/5.

RHINOS: 1 Richie Myler; 4 Nene Macdonald; 3 Harry Newman; 12 Rhyse Martin; 5 Ash Handley; 6 Blake Austin; 7 Aidan Sezer; 8 Mikolaj Oledzki; 14 Jarrod O'Connor; 15 Sam Lisone; 19 James McDonnell; 10 Zane Tetevano; 13 Cameron Smith (C). Subs (all used): 11 James Bentley; 17 Justin Sangare; 18 Tom Holroyd; 23 Liam Tindall.
Try: Bentley (39); **Goals:** Martin 1/1.
Rugby Leaguer & League Express Men of the Match: *Leopards:* Edwin Ipape; *Rhinos:* Cameron Smith.
Penalty count: 6-2; **Half-time:** 16-6;
Referee: Ben Thaler; **Attendance:** 6,686.

Sunday 23rd April 2023

HULL FC 20 HUDDERSFIELD GIANTS 14

HULL FC: 25 Davy Litten; 17 Cameron Scott; 3 Carlos Tuimavave (C); 4 Liam Sutcliffe; 2 Adam Swift; 7 Jake Clifford; 19 Ben McNamara; 13 Brad Fash; 9 Danny Houghton; 8 Ligi Sao; 23 Josh Griffin; 12 Jordan Lane; 15 Joe Cator. Subs (all used): 10 Tevita Satae; 27 Will Gardiner; 30 Scott Taylor; 33 Brad Dwyer.
Tries: Sutcliffe (7, 56), Satae (43); **Goals:** Clifford 4/4.
GIANTS: 32 Will Pryce; 2 Jermaine McGillvary; 3 Esan Marsters; 4 Kevin Naiqama; 24 Sam Halsall; 1 Jake Connor; 6 Tui Lolohea; 8 Chris Hill; 9 Nathan Peats; 15 Matty English; 12 Chris McQueen; 22 Harvey Livett; 13 Luke Yates (C). Subs (all used): 16 Harry Rushton; 18 Sebastine Ikahihifo; 19 Adam O'Brien; 20 Oliver Wilson.
Tries: McQueen (24), Marsters (75); **Goals:** Connor 3/3.
Rugby Leaguer & League Express Men of the Match: *Hull FC:* Danny Houghton; *Giants:* Luke Yates.
Penalty count: 5-5; **Half-time:** 8-8;
Referee: Liam Moore; **Attendance:** 10,856.

SALFORD RED DEVILS 16 CATALANS DRAGONS 14

RED DEVILS: 1 Ryan Brierley; 22 Rhys Williams; 24 Matthew Costello; 28 Deon Cross; 5 Joe Burgess; 6 Brodie Croft; 7 Marc Sneyd; 16 Tyler Dupree; 9 Andy Ackers; 10 King Vuniyayawa; 3 Kallum Watkins (C); 12 Sam Stone; 13 Oliver Partington. Subs (all used): 8 Jack Ormondroyd; 14 Chris Atkin; 17 Shane Wright; 20 Ellis Longstaff.
Tries: Vuniyayawa (13), Burgess (39); **Goals:** Sneyd 4/4.
DRAGONS: 1 Arthur Mourgue; 2 Tom Davies; 19 Arthur Romano; 4 Matthieu Laguerre; 24 Tom Johnstone; 3 Adam Keighran; 29 Sam Tomkins; 8 Mike McMeeken; 9 Michael McIlorum; 16 Romain Navarrete; 11 Matt Whitley; 12 Paul Seguier; 13 Benjamin Garcia (C). Subs (all used): 15 Mickael Goudemand; 22 Sio Siua Taukeiaho; 23 Jordan Dezaria; 31 Tanguy Zenon.
Tries: Johnstone (27), Seguier (50), Keighran (78);
Goals: Keighran 1/3.
Rugby Leaguer & League Express Men of the Match: *Red Devils:* Marc Sneyd; *Dragons:* Sam Tomkins.
Penalty count: 4-5; **Half-time:** 14-4;
Referee: Chris Kendall; **Attendance:** 3,974.

WIGAN WARRIORS 22 WAKEFIELD TRINITY 6

WARRIORS: 2 Bevan French; 23 Abbas Miski; 3 Toby King; 4 Jake Wardle; 5 Liam Marshall; 19 Joe Shorrocks; 7 Harry Smith; 10 Liam Byrne; 9 Sam Powell (C); 16 Ethan Havard; 11 Willie Isa; 17 Kai Pearce-Paul; 13 Morgan Smithies. Subs (all used): 20 Patrick Mago; 22 Brad O'Neill; 26 Harvie Hill; 27 Junior Nsemba.
Tries: Marshall (7), Miski (20), Havard (29), French (68);
Goals: Smith 3/4.
Sin bin: Isa (52) - dangerous challenge on Bowes.
TRINITY: 15 Liam Kay; 18 Lee Kershaw; 4 Reece Lyne; 21 Samisoni Langi; 2 Jorge Taufua; 36 Rowan Milnes (D); 7 Mason Lino; 10 Jai Whitbread; 24 Harry Bowes; 19 Kevin Proctor; 31 Sam Hewitt; 11 Matty Ashurst (C); 13 Jay Pitts. Subs (all used): 8 Eddie Battye; 16 Josh Bowden; 17 Renouf Atoni; 25 Sam Eseh.
Try: Pitts (60); **Goals:** Lino 1/1.
Rugby Leaguer & League Express Men of the Match: *Warriors:* Bevan French; *Trinity:* Jay Pitts.
Penalty count: 7-3; **Half-time:** 18-0;
Referee: Aaron Moore; **Attendance:** 12,240.

ROUND 11

Thursday 4th May 2023

HULL FC 14 WIGAN WARRIORS 10

HULL FC: 25 Davy Litten; 17 Cameron Scott; 3 Carlos Tuimavave (C); 4 Liam Sutcliffe; 5 Darnell McIntosh; 7 Jake Clifford; 19 Ben McNamara; 13 Brad Fash; 9 Danny Houghton; 8 Ligi Sao; 23 Josh Griffin; 12 Jordan Lane; 15 Joe Cator. Subs (all used): 6 Jake Trueman (D); 10 Tevita Satae; 30 Scott Taylor; 33 Brad Dwyer.
Tries: McIntosh (5), Clifford (16); **Goals:** Clifford 3/3.
Sin bin: Trueman (80) - professional foul.
WARRIORS: 2 Bevan French; 23 Abbas Miski; 4 Jake Wardle; 3 Toby King; 21 Iain Thornley; 19 Joe Shorrocks; 7 Harry Smith; 16 Ethan Havard; 9 Sam Powell; 10 Liam Byrne; 17 Kai Pearce-Paul; 12 Liam Farrell (C); 13 Morgan Smithies. Subs (all used): 20 Patrick Mago; 22 Brad O'Neill; 26 Harvie Hill; 27 Junior Nsemba.
Tries: Thornley (39, 45); **Goals:** Smith 1/2.
Rugby Leaguer & League Express Men of the Match: *Hull FC:* Jake Clifford; *Warriors:* Morgan Smithies.
Penalty count: 5-4; **Half-time:** 14-6;
Referee: Ben Thaler; **Attendance:** 10,251.

Friday 5th May 2023

CATALANS DRAGONS 24 ST HELENS 12

DRAGONS: 1 Arthur Mourgue; 2 Tom Davies; 3 Adam Keighran; 21 Matt Ikuvalu (D); 24 Tom Johnstone; 7 Mitchell Pearce; 29 Sam Tomkins; 23 Jordan Dezaria; 13 Benjamin Garcia (C); 10 Julian Bousquet; 11 Matt Whitley; 12 Paul Seguier; 8 Mike McMeeken. Subs: 16 Romain Navarrete; 18 Tiaki Chan (not used); 22 Sio Siua Taukeiaho; 26 Manu Ma'u.
Tries: Mourgue (29), Ikuvalu (37), Davies (50, 60);
Goals: Keighran 4/5.
Sin bin: Taukeiaho (39) - high tackle on Welsby.
SAINTS: 1 Jack Welsby; 25 Tee Ritson; 23 Konrad Hurrell; 3 Will Hopoate; 2 Tommy Makinson; 6 Jonny Lomax; 7 Lewis Dodd; 8 Alex Walmsley; 9 James Roby (C); 10 Matty Lees; 22 Sam Royle; 12 Joe Batchelor; 19 James Bell. Subs (all used): 14 Joey Lussick; 15 Louie McCarthy-Scarsbrook; 18 Jake Wingfield; 30 George Delaney.
Tries: Walmsley (12), Welsby (22); **Goals:** Makinson 2/2.
Sin bin: Hurrell (36) - dissent.
Rugby Leaguer & League Express Men of the Match: *Dragons:* Benjamin Garcia; *Saints:* James Roby.
Penalty count: 3-4; **Half-time:** 12-12;
Referee: Liam Moore; **Attendance:** 10,763.

HULL KR 28 HUDDERSFIELD GIANTS 0

HULL KR: 1 Lachlan Coote; 4 Shaun Kenny-Dowall (C); 3 Tom Opacic; 33 Corey Hall; 5 Ryan Hall; 21 Rowan Milnes; 20 Mikey Lewis; 22 Dean Hadley; 9 Matt Parcell; 10 George King; 16 James Batchelor; 12 Kane Linnett; 13 Elliot Minchella. Subs (all used): 8 Sauaso Sue; 14 Jez Litten; 15 Rhys Kennedy; 26 Sam Luckley.
Tries: R Hall (14, 22), Batchelor (45, 75), Opacic (69);
Goals: Milnes 4/7.
GIANTS: 32 Will Pryce; 21 Leroy Cudjoe; 4 Kevin Naiqama; 3 Esan Marsters; 25 Innes Senior; 1 Jake Connor; 6 Tui Lolohea; 8 Chris Hill; 9 Nathan Peats; 20 Oliver Wilson; 12 Chris McQueen; 29 Sam Hewitt; 13 Luke Yates (C). Subs (all used): 16 Harry Rushton; 17 Owen Trout; 27 Jack Ashworth; 19 Adam O'Brien.
Rugby Leaguer & League Express Men of the Match: *Hull KR:* Jez Litten; *Giants:* Tui Lolohea.
Penalty count: 5-5; **Half-time:** 14-0;
Referee: Chris Kendall; **Attendance:** 8,490.

LEEDS RHINOS 12 SALFORD RED DEVILS 22

RHINOS: 1 Richie Myler; 4 Nene Macdonald; 3 Harry Newman; 12 Rhyse Martin; 5 Ash Handley (C); 6 Blake Austin; 29 Jack Sinfield; 8 Mikolaj Oledzki; 14 Jarrod O'Connor; 15 Sam Lisone; 19 James McDonnell; 11 James Bentley; 13 Cameron Smith. Subs (all used): 18 Tom Holroyd; 22 Sam Walters; 20 Morgan Gannon; 26 Corey Johnson.
Tries: Myler (39), Bentley (65); **Goals:** Martin 2/2.
Sin bin: Austin (17) - obstruction.
RED DEVILS: 1 Ryan Brierley; 22 Rhys Williams; 28 Deon Cross; 20 Ellis Longstaff; 5 Joe Burgess; 6 Brodie Croft; 7 Marc Sneyd; 16 Tyler Dupree; 9 Andy Ackers; 10 King Vuniyayawa; 12 Sam Stone; 3 Kallum Watkins (C); 13 Oliver Partington. Subs (all used): 17 Shane Wright; 8 Jack Ormondroyd; 14 Chris Atkin; 11 Andrew Dixon.
Tries: Williams (18), Stone (23), Longstaff (56);
Goals: Sneyd 5/5.
Rugby Leaguer & League Express Men of the Match: *Rhinos:* Harry Newman; *Red Devils:* Brodie Croft.
Penalty count: 3-10; **Half time:** 6-12;
Referee: Jack Smith; **Attendance:** 13,007.

LEIGH LEOPARDS 30 CASTLEFORD TIGERS 6

LEOPARDS: 17 Gareth O'Brien; 2 Tom Briscoe; 4 Ricky Leutele; 1 Zak Hardaker; 5 Josh Charnley; 15 Ben Reynolds; 7 Lachlan Lam; 8 Tom Amone; 9 Edwin Ipape; 10 Robbie Mulhern; 16 Oliver Holmes; 24 Kai O'Donnell; 13 John Asiata (C). Subs (all used): 6 Joe Mellor; 18 Matt Davis; 25 Nathan Wilde; 27 Ava Seumanufagai.
Tries: Reynolds (18), O'Donnell (49), Seumanufagai (54), Leutele (62), Davis (75); **Goals:** Reynolds 5/5.
TIGERS: 1 Niall Evalds; 5 Bureta Faraimo; 17 Jack Broadbent; 3 Jordan Turner; 26 Elliot Wallis (D); 6 Gareth Widdop; 7 Jacob Miller; 8 George Lawler; 9 Paul McShane (C); 14 Nathan Massey; 11 Kenny Edwards; 16 Adam Milner; 13 Joe Westerman. Subs (all used): 10 George Griffin; 12 Alex Mellor; 24 Cain Robb; 28 Sam Hall.
Try: Westerman (14); **Goals:** Widdop 1/1.
Rugby Leaguer & League Express Men of the Match: *Leopards:* Lachlan Lam; *Tigers:* Cain Robb.
Penalty count: 1-1; **Half-time:** 6-6;
Referee: Aaron Moore; **Attendance:** 5,423.

WARRINGTON WOLVES 32 WAKEFIELD TRINITY 18

WOLVES: 2 Josh Thewlis; 34 Matty Russell; 3 Peter Mata'utia; 4 Stefan Ratchford (C); 5 Matty Ashton; 6 George Williams; 7 Josh Drinkwater; 8 James Harrison; 16 Danny Walker; 10 Paul Vaughan; 11 Ben Currie; 12 Matty Nicholson; 13 Josh McGuire. Subs (all used): 1 Matt Dufty; 14 Sam Kasiano; 15 Joe Philbin; 19 Joe Bullock.
Tries: Thewlis (9, 12), Ashton (60, 78), Williams (70);
Goals: Ratchford 6/6.
TRINITY: 33 Will Dagger; 15 Liam Kay; 6 Lee Gaskell; 13 Jay Pitts; 2 Jorge Taufua; 20 Morgan Smith; 7 Mason Lino; 10 Jai Whitbread; 24 Harry Bowes; 19 Kevin Proctor; 11 Matty Ashurst (C); 12 Kelepi Tanginoa; 14 Jordan Crowther. Subs (all used): 9 Liam Hood; 16 Josh Bowden; 17 Renouf Atoni; 25 Sam Eseh.
Tries: M Smith (17), Tanginoa (24), Ashurst (75);
Goals: Dagger 3/3.
Dismissal: Proctor (53) - high tackle on Josh Thewlis.
Rugby Leaguer & League Express Men of the Match: *Wolves:* Josh Thewlis; *Trinity:* Jai Whitbread.
Penalty count: 4-3; **Half-time:** 12-12;
Referee: Marcus Griffiths; **Attendance:** 10,209.

ROUND 12

Thursday 11th May 2023

WAKEFIELD TRINITY 6 HULL FC 26

TRINITY: 33 Will Dagger; 5 Tom Lineham; 6 Lee Gaskell; 21 Samisoni Langi; 2 Jorge Taufua; 20 Morgan Smith; 7 Mason Lino; 10 Jai Whitbread; 24 Harry Bowes; 19 Kevin Proctor; 12 Kelepi Tanginoa; 11 Matty Ashurst (C); 13 Jay Pitts. Subs (all used): 8 Eddie Battye; 9 Liam Hood; 16 Josh Bowden; 25 Sam Eseh.
Try: Ashurst (68); **Goals:** Dagger 1/1.
HULL FC: 25 Davy Litten; 2 Adam Swift; 4 Liam Sutcliffe; 3 Carlos Tuimavave (C); 17 Cameron Scott; 6 Jake Trueman; 7 Jake Clifford; 30 Scott Taylor; 9 Danny Houghton; 8 Ligi Sao; 23 Josh Griffin; 12 Jordan Lane; 14 Joe Lovodua. Subs (all used): 5 Darnell McIntosh; 10 Tevita Satae; 20 Jack Brown; 33 Brad Dwyer.
Tries: Swift (19), Tuimavave (48), Sutcliffe (63), Taylor (78);
Goals: Clifford 5/5.
Rugby Leaguer & League Express Men of the Match: *Trinity:* Matty Ashurst; *Hull FC:* Scott Taylor.
Penalty count: 4-8; **Half-time:** 0-6;
Referee: Jack Smith; **Attendance:** 3,976.

Friday 12th May 2023

HUDDERSFIELD GIANTS 4 LEIGH LEOPARDS 30

GIANTS: 6 Tui Lolohea; 5 Jake Bibby; 4 Kevin Naiqama; 3 Esan Marsters; 21 Leroy Cudjoe; 1 Jake Connor; 33 Kieran Rush (D); 8 Chris Hill; 19 Adam O'Brien; 20 Oliver Wilson; 29 Sam Hewitt; 12 Chris McQueen; 13 Luke Yates (C). Subs (all used): 9 Nathan Peats; 15 Matty English; 16 Harry Rushton; 18 Sebastine Ikahihifo.
Try: Naiqama (78); **Goals:** Connor 0/1.
LEOPARDS: 17 Gareth O'Brien; 2 Tom Briscoe; 4 Ricky Leutele; 1 Zak Hardaker; 5 Josh Charnley; 15 Ben Reynolds; 7 Lachlan Lam; 8 Tom Amone; 9 Edwin Ipape; 10 Robbie Mulhern; 16 Oliver Holmes; 24 Kai O'Donnell; 13 John Asiata (C). Subs (all used): 6 Joe Mellor; 14 Ben Nakubuwai; 18 Matt Davis; 27 Ava Seumanufagai.
Tries: Reynolds (8), Charnley (34, 47), Lam (59), Mellor (65); **Goals:** Reynolds 5/5.
Rugby Leaguer & League Express Men of the Match: *Giants:* Luke Yates; *Leopards:* Ben Reynolds.
Penalty count: 2-3; **Half-time:** 0-12;
Referee: Marcus Griffiths; **Attendance:** 4,977.

CASTLEFORD TIGERS 22 CATALANS DRAGONS 46

TIGERS: 1 Niall Evalds; 5 Bureta Faraimo; 17 Jack Broadbent; 12 Alex Mellor; 26 Elliot Wallis; 6 Gareth Widdop; 7 Jacob Miller; 8 George Lawler; 9 Paul McShane (C); 14 Nathan Massey; 16 Adam Milner; 10 George Griffin; 13 Joe Westerman. Subs (all used): 23 Suaia Matagi; 28 Sam Hall; 32 Liam Watts; 38 Luis Johnson.
Tries: Mellor (25, 70), Faraimo (52, 67);
Goals: Widdop 1/1, McShane 2/3.
DRAGONS: 1 Arthur Mourgue; 19 Arthur Romano; 21 Matt Ikuvalu; 3 Adam Keighran; 24 Tom Johnstone; 29 Sam Tomkins; 7 Mitchell Pearce; 23 Jordan Dezaria; 9 Michael McIlorum; 8 Mike McMeeken; 11 Matt Whitley; 12 Paul

Seguier; 13 Benjamin Garcia (C). Subs (all used): 10 Julian Bousquet; 15 Mickael Goudemand; 16 Romain Navarrete; 26 Manu Ma'u.
Tries: Dezaria (8), Keighran (13, 34), Ikuvalu (17), Johnstone (29), Garcia (38), Whitley (45), Tomkins (60);
Goals: Keighran 5/6, Mourgue 2/2.
Rugby Leaguer & League Express Men of the Match: *Tigers:* Bureta Faraimo; *Dragons:* Adam Keighran.
Penalty count: 6-3; **Half-time:** 6-34;
Referee: Aaron Moore; **Attendance:** 5,788.

WARRINGTON WOLVES 21 HULL KR 14

WOLVES: 2 Josh Thewlis; 34 Matty Russell; 3 Peter Mata'utia; 4 Stefan Ratchford (C); 5 Matty Ashton; 6 George Williams; 7 Josh Drinkwater; 19 Joe Bullock; 16 Danny Walker; 10 Paul Vaughan; 11 Ben Currie; 13 Josh McGuire; 8 James Harrison. Subs (all used): 1 Matt Dufty; 9 Daryl Clark; 14 Sam Kasiano; 15 Joe Philbin.
Tries: McGuire (34), Currie (45), Ashton (72);
Goals: Ratchford 4/5; **Field goal:** Williams (75).
HULL KR: 2 Ethan Ryan; 4 Shaun Kenny-Dowall (C); 3 Tom Opacic; 33 Corey Hall; 5 Ryan Hall; 14 Jez Litten; 20 Mikey Lewis; 22 Dean Hadley; 9 Matt Parcell; 10 George King; 16 James Batchelor; 12 Kane Linnett; 13 Elliot Minchella. Subs (all used): 8 Sauaso Sue; 15 Rhys Kennedy; 24 Sam Wood; 26 Sam Luckley.
Tries: Ryan (16), Linnett (21); **Goals:** Lewis 3/3.
Rugby Leaguer & League Express Men of the Match: *Wolves:* Joe Philbin; *Hull KR:* Mikey Lewis.
Penalty count: 11-6; **Half-time:** 6-12;
Referee: Ben Thaler; **Attendance:** 10,179.

WIGAN WARRIORS 18 LEEDS RHINOS 40

WARRIORS: 2 Bevan French; 23 Abbas Miski; 3 Toby King; 4 Jake Wardle; 21 Iain Thornley; 19 Joe Shorrocks; 7 Harry Smith; 16 Ethan Havard; 9 Sam Powell; 10 Liam Byrne; 11 Willie Isa; 12 Liam Farrell (C); 13 Morgan Smithies. Subs (all used): 6 Cade Cust; 17 Kai Pearce-Paul; 20 Patrick Mago; 22 Brad O'Neill.
Tries: Miski (16), French (26), Thornley (57);
Goals: Smith 3/4.
Sin bin: French (77) - professional foul.
RHINOS: 5 Ash Handley (C); 4 Nene Macdonald; 3 Harry Newman; 12 Rhyse Martin; 23 Liam Tindall; 6 Blake Austin; 1 Richie Myler; 8 Mikolaj Oledzki; 14 Jarrod O'Connor; 15 Sam Lisone; 10 Zane Tetevano; 11 James Bentley; 13 Cameron Smith. Subs (all used): 17 Justin Sangare; 18 Tom Holroyd; 20 Morgan Gannon; 25 James Donaldson.
Tries: Newman (35, 62), Holroyd (46), Myler (50), Martin (66), Smith (70), Tindall (80); **Goals:** Martin 6/7.
Dismissal: Tetevano (38) - high tackle on Smith.
Rugby Leaguer & League Express Men of the Match: *Warriors:* Bevan French; *Rhinos:* Rhyse Martin.
Penalty count: 7-4; **Half-time:** 14-6;
Referee: Liam Moore; **Attendance:** 12,167.

Saturday 13th May 2023

ST HELENS 26 SALFORD RED DEVILS 12

SAINTS: 1 Jack Welsby; 2 Tommy Makinson; 3 Will Hopoate; 21 Ben Davies; 25 Tee Ritson; 6 Jonny Lomax; 7 Lewis Dodd; 8 Alex Walmsley; 9 James Roby (C); 10 Matty Lees; 16 Curtis Sironen; 12 Joe Batchelor; 19 James Bell. Subs (all used): 5 Jonathan Bennison; 15 Louie McCarthy-Scarsbrook; 18 Jake Wingfield; 30 George Delaney.
Tries: Bell (32), Sironen (43), Lomax (46), Makinson (50), Batchelor (55); **Goals:** Makinson 3/5.
RED DEVILS: 1 Ryan Brierley; 22 Rhys Williams; 24 Matthew Costello; 28 Deon Cross; 5 Joe Burgess; 6 Brodie Croft; 7 Marc Sneyd; 16 Tyler Dupree; 9 Andy Ackers; 10 King Vuniyayawa; 12 Sam Stone; 3 Kallum Watkins (C); 13 Oliver Partington. Subs: 14 Chris Atkin; 17 Shane Wright; 18 Alex Gerrard; 20 Ellis Longstaff (not used).
Tries: Croft (5), Brierley (18); **Goals:** Sneyd 2/2.
Rugby Leaguer & League Express Men of the Match: *Saints:* Curtis Sironen; *Red Devils:* Ryan Brierley.
Penalty count: 6-3; **Half-time:** 6-12;
Referee: Chris Kendall; **Attendance:** 11,881.

ROUND 13

Thursday 25th May 2023

HULL KR 22 WIGAN WARRIORS 26
(after golden point extra-time)

HULL KR: 2 Ethan Ryan; 33 Corey Hall; 3 Tom Opacic; 4 Shaun Kenny-Dowall (C); 5 Ryan Hall; 20 Mikey Lewis; 14 Jez Litten; 22 Dean Hadley; 9 Matt Parcell; 8 Sauaso Sue; 16 James Batchelor; 12 Kane Linnett; 13 Elliot Minchella. Subs (all used): 17 Matty Storton; 24 Sam Wood; 25 Luis Johnson; 26 Sam Luckley.
Tries: R Hall (22), Parcell (48), Batchelor (60), Johnson (69); **Goals:** Lewis 3/4.
Sin bin: R Hall (55) - professional foul.
WARRIORS: 2 Bevan French; 23 Abbas Miski; 3 Toby King; 4 Jake Wardle; 5 Liam Marshall; 32 Ryan Hampshire; 7 Harry Smith; 15 Kaide Ellis; 9 Sam Powell; 10 Liam Byrne; 12 Liam Farrell (C); 13 Morgan Smithies; 19 Joe Shorrocks. Subs (all used): 20 Patrick Mago; 26 Harvie Hill; 22 Brad O'Neill; 27 Junior Nsemba.
Tries: Farrell (12, 35, 85), Marshall (44, 73), Miski (80);
Goals: Smith 1/5 *(last conversion attempt not taken).*
Rugby Leaguer & League Express Men of the Match: *Hull KR:* James Batchelor; *Warriors:* Liam Farrell.
Penalty count: 7-4; **Half-time:** 4-10;
Referee: Jack Smith; **Attendance:** 8,068.

Friday 26th May 2023

CATALANS DRAGONS 36 WAKEFIELD TRINITY 6

DRAGONS: 1 Arthur Mourgue; 5 Fouad Yaha; 19 Arthur Romano; 21 Matt Ikuvalu; 24 Tom Johnstone; 6 Tyrone May; 17 Cesar Rouge; 16 Romain Navarrete; 9 Michael McIlorum; 10 Julian Bousquet; 11 Matt Whitley; 8 Mike McMeeken; 13 Benjamin Garcia (C). Subs (all used): 15 Mickael Goudemand; 22 Sio Siua Taukeiaho; 23 Jordan Dezaria; 31 Tanguy Zenon.
Tries: Johnstone (23, 54), Rouge (27), McMeeken (33), Mourgue (72), Zenon (78); **Goals:** Mourgue 6/7.
TRINITY: 1 Max Jowitt; 15 Liam Kay; 38 Jack Croft (D2); 33 Will Dagger; 2 Jorge Taufua; 20 Morgan Smith; 7 Mason Lino; 19 Kevin Proctor; 9 Liam Hood; 16 Josh Bowden; 11 Matty Ashurst (C); 12 Kelepi Tanginoa; 13 Jay Pitts. Subs (all used): 8 Eddie Battye; 14 Jordan Crowther; 24 Harry Bowes; 25 Sam Eseh.
Try: Kay (52); **Goals:** Dagger 1/1.
Rugby Leaguer & League Express Men of the Match: *Dragons:* Arthur Mourgue; *Trinity:* Mason Lino.
Penalty count: 4-5; **Half-time:** 18-0;
Referee: Ben Thaler; **Attendance:** 8,120.

HUDDERSFIELD GIANTS 20 CASTLEFORD TIGERS 4

GIANTS: 6 Tui Lolohea; 5 Jake Bibby; 4 Kevin Naiqama; 3 Esan Marsters; 25 Innes Senior; 1 Jake Connor; 7 Theo Fages; 8 Chris Hill; 9 Nathan Peats; 15 Matty English; 21 Leroy Cudjoe; 12 Chris McQueen; 13 Luke Yates (C). Subs (all used): 19 Adam O'Brien; 10 Joe Greenwood; 16 Harry Rushton; 18 Sebastine Ikahihifo.
Tries: Marsters (3), Senior (48), Naiqama (55);
Goals: Connor 4/5.
TIGERS: 6 Gareth Widdop; 5 Bureta Faraimo; 12 Alex Mellor; 3 Jordan Turner; 26 Elliot Wallis; 17 Jack Broadbent; 7 Jacob Miller; 23 Suaia Matagi; 9 Paul McShane (C); 14 Nathan Massey; 11 Kenny Edwards; 8 George Lawler; 13 Joe Westerman. Subs (all used): 20 Muizz Mustapha; 25 Brad Martin; 28 Sam Hall; 32 Liam Watts.
Try: Mellor (28); **Goals:** Widdop 0/1.
Rugby Leaguer & League Express Men of the Match: *Giants:* Theo Fages; *Tigers:* Elliot Wallis.
Penalty count: 7-4; **Half-time:** 10-4;
Referee: Aaron Moore; **Attendance:** 4,206.

LEEDS RHINOS 12 ST HELENS 13
(after golden point extra-time)

RHINOS: 1 Richie Myler; 5 Ash Handley; 3 Harry Newman; 4 Nene Macdonald; 16 Derrell Olpherts; 20 Morgan Gannon; 7 Aidan Sezer; 22 Sam Walters; 14 Jarrod O'Connor; 18 Tom Holroyd; 19 James McDonnell; 12 Rhyse Martin; 13 Cameron Smith (C). Subs (all used): 8 Mikolaj Oledzki; 17 Justin Sangare; 25 James Donaldson; 26 Corey Johnson.
Tries: Handley (4), Smith (21); **Goals:** Martin 2/2.
Dismissal: McDonnell (76) - fighting.
SAINTS: 1 Jack Welsby; 2 Tommy Makinson; 23 Konrad Hurrell; 3 Will Hopoate; 25 Tee Ritson; 6 Jonny Lomax; 7 Lewis Dodd; 8 Alex Walmsley; 9 James Roby (C); 15 Louie McCarthy-Scarsbrook; 16 Curtis Sironen; 12 Joe Batchelor; 19 James Bell. Subs (all used): 11 Sione Mata'utia; 14 Joey Lussick; 17 Agnatius Paasi; 18 Jake Wingfield.
Tries: Makinson (11), Sironen (44); **Goals:** Makinson 2/3;
Field goal: Dodd (89).
Sin bin: Mata'utia (84) - dangerous challenge.
Rugby Leaguer & League Express Men of the Match: *Rhinos:* Tom Holroyd; *Saints:* Alex Walmsley.
Penalty count: 6-6; **Half time:** 12-4;
Referee: Liam Moore; **Attendance:** 14,161.

LEIGH LEOPARDS 30 WARRINGTON WOLVES 12

LEOPARDS: 17 Gareth O'Brien; 2 Tom Briscoe; 1 Zak Hardaker; 4 Ricky Leutele; 5 Josh Charnley; 15 Ben Reynolds; 7 Lachlan Lam; 8 Tom Amone; 39 Edwin Ipape; 10 Robbie Mulhern; 16 Oliver Holmes; 24 Kai O'Donnell; 13 John Asiata (C). Subs (all used): 6 Joe Mellor; 18 Matt Davis; 27 Ava Seumanufagai; 29 Frankie Halton (D).
Tries: O'Brien (7, 33), Briscoe (20), Charnley (64), Reynolds (76); **Goals:** Reynolds 5/6.
WOLVES: 1 Matt Dufty; 34 Matty Russell; 3 Peter Mata'utia; 4 Stefan Ratchford (C); 5 Matty Ashton; 6 George Williams; 22 Riley Dean; 8 James Harrison; 16 Danny Walker; 10 Paul Vaughan; 11 Ben Currie; 13 Josh McGuire; 9 Daryl Clark. Subs (all used): 14 Sam Kasiano; 15 Joe Philbin; 17 Gil Dudson; 21 Greg Minikin.
Tries: Williams (27), Philbin (39); **Goals:** Ratchford 2/2.
Rugby Leaguer & League Express Men of the Match: *Leopards:* Tom Amone; *Wolves:* George Williams.
Penalty count: 6-7; **Half-time:** 20-12;
Referee: Chris Kendall; **Attendance:** 8,120.

Sunday 28th May 2023

SALFORD RED DEVILS 29 HULL FC 22

RED DEVILS: 1 Ryan Brierley; 2 Ken Sio; 28 Deon Cross; 4 Tim Lafai; 5 Joe Burgess; 6 Brodie Croft; 7 Marc Sneyd; 16 Tyler Dupree; 9 Andy Ackers; 10 King Vuniyayawa; 3 Kallum Watkins (C); 12 Sam Stone; 13 Oliver Partington. Subs (all used): 14 Chris Atkin; 8 Jack Ormondroyd; 19 Adam Sidlow; 25 Ben Hellewell.
Tries: Dupree (18), Cross (34), Brierley (38), Sneyd (52), Sio (73); **Goals:** Sneyd 4/6; **Field goal:** Sneyd (76).
Sin bin: Sneyd (80) - interference.
HULL FC: 1 Tex Hoy; 5 Darnell McIntosh; 17 Cameron Scott; 4 Liam Sutcliffe; 2 Adam Swift; 6 Jake Trueman; 7 Jake Clifford; 8 Ligi Sao; 9 Danny Houghton; 13 Brad Fash; 23 Josh Griffin (C); 12 Jordan Lane; 15 Joe Cator. Subs (all used): 10 Tevita Satae; 20 Jack Brown; 30 Scott Taylor; 33 Brad Dwyer.
Tries: Clifford (9), Trueman (22), McIntosh (42), Griffin (59);
Goals: Clifford 3/5.
Rugby Leaguer & League Express Men of the Match: *Red Devils:* Marc Sneyd; *Hull FC:* Jake Clifford.
Penalty count: 9-10; **Half-time:** 18-10;
Referee: Marcus Griffiths; **Attendance:** 4,569.

ROUND 14 - MAGIC WEEKEND

Saturday 3rd June 2023

HULL KR 16 SALFORD RED DEVILS 26

HULL KR: 1 Lachlan Coote; 4 Shaun Kenny-Dowall (C); 3 Tom Opacic; 33 Corey Hall; 5 Ryan Hall; 14 Jez Litten; 20 Mikey Lewis; 8 Sauaso Sue; 9 Matt Parcell; 22 Dean Hadley; 16 James Batchelor; 12 Kane Linnett; 13 Elliot Minchella. Subs (all used): 10 George King; 17 Matty Storton; 24 Sam Wood; 26 Sam Luckley.
Tries: Minchella (12), King (36), R Hall (66);
Goals: Coote 2/2, Lewis 0/1.
Sin bin: Hadley (62) - high tackle on Sneyd.
RED DEVILS: 1 Ryan Brierley; 2 Ken Sio; 28 Deon Cross; 4 Tim Lafai; 5 Joe Burgess; 6 Brodie Croft; 7 Marc Sneyd; 16 Tyler Dupree; 14 Chris Atkin; 10 King Vuniyayawa; 3 Kallum Watkins (C); 12 Sam Stone; 13 Oliver Partington. Subs (all used): 8 Jack Ormondroyd; 19 Adam Sidlow; 21 Amir Bourouh; 25 Ben Hellewell.
Tries: Burgess (20), Sio (69), Atkin (74); **Goals:** Sneyd 7/7.
Sin bin: Cross (64) - high tackle on Coote.
Rugby Leaguer & League Express Men of the Match: *Hull KR:* Elliot Minchella; *Red Devils:* Ryan Brierley.
Penalty count: 8-9; **Half-time:** 12-10;
Referee: Chris Kendall.

CATALANS DRAGONS 46 WIGAN WARRIORS 22

DRAGONS: 1 Arthur Mourgue; 24 Tom Johnstone; 21 Matt Ikuvalu; 19 Arthur Romano; 5 Fouad Yaha; 7 Mitchell Pearce; 29 Sam Tomkins; 22 Sio Siua Taukeiaho; 9 Michael McIlorum; 16 Romain Navarrete; 11 Matt Whitley; 8 Mike McMeeken; 13 Benjamin Garcia (C). Subs (all used): 6 Tyrone May; 10 Julian Bousquet; 12 Paul Seguier; 23 Jordan Dezaria.
Tries: Tomkins (14), Johnstone (18, 42, 59), Whitley (24, 50), Mourgue (28), Romano (55); **Goals:** Mourgue 7/9.
WARRIORS: 2 Bevan French; 23 Abbas Miski; 3 Toby King; 4 Jake Wardle; 5 Liam Marshall; 1 Jai Field; 7 Harry Smith; 15 Kaide Ellis; 9 Sam Powell; 10 Liam Byrne; 13 Morgan Smithies; 12 Liam Farrell (C); 19 Joe Shorrocks. Subs (all used): 6 Cade Cust; 20 Patrick Mago; 26 Harvie Hill; 27 Junior Nsemba.
Tries: Wardle (9), French (34), Miski (65), Marshall (76), Smithies (80); **Goals:** Smith 1/5, Field 0/1.
Rugby Leaguer & League Express Men of the Match: *Dragons:* Tom Johnstone; *Warriors:* Liam Farrell.
Penalty count: 4-7; **Half-time:** 24-8; **Referee:** Liam Moore.

CASTLEFORD TIGERS 26 LEEDS RHINOS 24

TIGERS: 6 Gareth Widdop; 31 Jason Qareqare; 12 Alex Mellor; 3 Jordan Turner; 26 Elliot Wallis; 17 Jack Broadbent; 7 Jacob Miller; 32 Liam Watts; 9 Paul McShane (C); 23 Suaia Matagi; 11 Kenny Edwards; 8 George Lawler;

Super League XXVIII - Round by Round

13 Joe Westerman. Subs (all used): 10 George Griffin; 20 Muizz Mustapha; 25 Brad Martin; 28 Sam Hall.
Tries: Miller (11), Wallis (13), Mellor (48, 69), Qareqare (72); **Goals:** Widdop 3/5.
RHINOS: 5 Ash Handley (C); 4 Nene Macdonald; 24 Luis Roberts; 12 Rhyse Martin; 16 Derrell Olpherts; 6 Blake Austin; 1 Richie Myler; 8 Mikolaj Oledzki; 14 Jarrod O'Connor; 22 Sam Walters; 19 James McDonnell; 25 James Donaldson; 13 Cameron Smith. Subs (all used): 11 James Bentley; 17 Justin Sangare; 23 Liam Tindall; 26 Corey Johnson.
Tries: Olpherts (5), Bentley (36), Martin (43), Oledzki (62); **Goals:** Martin 4/4.
Rugby Leaguer & League Express Men of the Match:
Tigers: Joe Westerman; *Rhinos:* James McDonnell.
Penalty count: 4-7; **Half-time:** 10-12; **Referee:** Ben Thaler.

Attendance: 36,943 *(at St James' Park, Newcastle)*.

Sunday 4th June 2023

LEIGH LEOPARDS 30 WAKEFIELD TRINITY 4

LEOPARDS: 17 Gareth O'Brien; 2 Tom Briscoe; 1 Zak Hardaker; 4 Ricky Leutele; 5 Josh Charnley; 15 Ben Reynolds; 7 Lachlan Lam; 8 Tom Amone; 9 Edwin Ipape; 10 Robbie Mulhern; 22 Tom Nisbet; 16 Oliver Holmes; 13 John Asiata (C). Subs (all used): 6 Joe Mellor; 18 Matt Davis; 25 Nathan Wilde; 27 Ava Seumanufagai.
Tries: Lam (7, 67), Mulhern (14), Ipape (47), Charnley (59); **Goals:** Reynolds 1/2, Hardaker 4/4.
Dismissal: Reynolds (27) - punching Fifita.
Sin bin: Nisbet (29) - dangerous challenge.
TRINITY: 1 Max Jowitt; 2 Jorge Taufua; 15 Liam Kay; 38 Jack Croft; 5 Tom Lineham; 33 Will Dagger; 7 Mason Lino; 16 Josh Bowden; 9 Liam Hood; 19 Kevin Proctor; 11 Matty Ashurst (C); 31 Sam Hewitt; 13 Jay Pitts. Subs (all used): 8 Eddie Battye; 14 Jordan Crowther; 24 Harry Bowes; 40 David Fifita (D2).
Try: Jowitt (71); **Goals:** Dagger 0/1.
Rugby Leaguer & League Express Men of the Match:
Leopards: Lachlan Lam; *Trinity:* Mason Lino.
Penalty count: 5-4; **Half-time:** 10-0;
Referee: Aaron Moore.

HUDDERSFIELD GIANTS 6 ST HELENS 48

GIANTS: 6 Tui Lolohea; 5 Jake Bibby; 4 Kevin Naiqama; 3 Esan Marsters; 25 Innes Senior; 1 Jake Connor; 7 Theo Fages; 8 Chris Hill; 9 Nathan Peats; 15 Matty English; 21 Leroy Cudjoe; 12 Chris McQueen; 13 Luke Yates (C). Subs (all used): 35 Adam Milner (D); 10 Joe Greenwood; 16 Harry Rushton; 18 Sebastine Ikahihifo.
Try: Naiqama (7); **Goals:** Connor 1/1.
Sin bin: Yates (24) - dangerous challenge.
SAINTS: 1 Jack Welsby; 2 Tommy Makinson; 23 Konrad Hurrell; 4 Mark Percival; 25 Tee Ritson; 6 Jonny Lomax; 7 Lewis Dodd; 8 Alex Walmsley; 9 James Roby (C); 10 Matty Lees; 16 Curtis Sironen; 12 Joe Batchelor; 19 James Bell. Subs (all used): 11 Sione Mata'utia; 14 Joey Lussick; 15 Louie McCarthy-Scarsbrook; 17 Agnatius Paasi.
Tries: Hurrell (10, 51), Percival (19), Makinson (33, 47, 57, 65), McCarthy-Scarsbrook (42), Lussick (74); **Goals:** Makinson 6/9.
Rugby Leaguer & League Express Men of the Match:
Giants: Kevin Naiqama; *Saints:* Tommy Makinson.
Penalty count: 1-6; **Half-time:** 6-16;
Referee: Marcus Griffiths.

HULL FC 30 WARRINGTON WOLVES 18

HULL FC: 1 Tex Hoy; 5 Darnell McIntosh; 17 Cameron Scott; 4 Liam Sutcliffe; 2 Adam Swift; 6 Jake Trueman; 7 Jake Clifford; 8 Brad Fash; 9 Danny Houghton; 30 Scott Taylor; 23 Josh Griffin (C); 12 Jordan Lane; 15 Joe Cator. Subs (all used): 8 Ligi Sao; 10 Tevita Satae; 11 Andre Savelio; 33 Brad Dwyer.
Tries: Houghton (16), Swift (44), Griffin (47, 51, 65), Hoy (74); **Goals:** Clifford 3/6.
WOLVES: 1 Matt Dufty; 20 Connor Wrench; 21 Greg Minikin; 4 Stefan Ratchford (C); 5 Matty Ashton; 6 George Williams; 7 Josh Drinkwater; 17 Gil Dudson; 9 Daryl Clark; 10 Paul Vaughan; 11 Ben Currie; 8 James Harrison; 3 Peter Mata'utia. Subs: 15 Joe Philbin; 16 Danny Walker; 19 Joe Bullock; 35 Lucas Green (not used).
Tries: Wrench (4, 57), Williams (13); **Goals:** Ratchford 3/3.
Rugby Leaguer & League Express Men of the Match:
Hull FC: Josh Griffin; *Wolves:* Daryl Clark.
Penalty count: 4-7; **Half-time:** 6-12; **Referee:** Jack Smith.

Attendance: 26,326 *(at St James' Park, Newcastle)*.

ROUND 15

Friday 9th June 2023

CASTLEFORD TIGERS 10 SALFORD RED DEVILS 42

TIGERS: 6 Gareth Widdop; 31 Jason Qareqare; 4 Mahe Fonua; 3 Jordan Turner; 39 Will Tate; 17 Jack Broadbent;

Wakefield's Eddie Battye takes on Leeds' Mikolaj Oledzki and Sam Walters

7 Jacob Miller; 25 Brad Martin; 9 Paul McShane (C); 10 George Griffin; 11 Kenny Edwards; 15 Alex Sutcliffe; 13 Joe Westerman. Subs (all used): 14 Nathan Massey; 20 Muizz Mustapha; 24 Cain Robb; 33 Aaron Willis (D).
Tries: Qareqare (13), Edwards (40); **Goals:** Widdop 1/2.
RED DEVILS: 1 Ryan Brierley; 2 Ken Sio; 28 Deon Cross; 4 Tim Lafai; 22 Rhys Williams; 6 Brodie Croft; 7 Marc Sneyd; 16 Tyler Dupree; 14 Chris Atkin; 10 King Vuniyayawa; 3 Kallum Watkins (C); 12 Sam Stone; 13 Oliver Partington. Subs (all used): 8 Jack Ormondroyd; 19 Adam Sidlow; 21 Amir Bourouh; 25 Ben Hellewell.
Tries: Williams (11, 48), Atkin (18), Cross (21), Sio (25, 51), Lafai (53), Stone (72); **Goals:** Sneyd 5/8.
Rugby Leaguer & League Express Men of the Match:
Tigers: Joe Westerman; *Red Devils:* Tim Lafai.
Penalty count: 10-3; **Half-time:** 10-24;
Referee: Jack Smith; **Attendance:** 6,354.

LEIGH LEOPARDS 28 HULL FC 16

LEOPARDS: 17 Gareth O'Brien; 2 Tom Briscoe; 1 Zak Hardaker; 4 Ricky Leutele; 5 Josh Charnley; 6 Joe Mellor; 7 Lachlan Lam; 8 Tom Amone; 9 Edwin Ipape; 10 Robbie Mulhern; 16 Oliver Holmes; 24 Kai O'Donnell; 13 John Asiata (C). Subs: 25 Nathan Wilde (not used); 27 Ava Seumanufagai; 30 Dan Norman (D2); 18 Matt Davis.
Tries: O'Brien (12), Briscoe (20), Charnley (30, 54), Mellor (78); **Goals:** Hardaker 4/7.
HULL FC: 1 Tex Hoy; 2 Adam Swift; 4 Liam Sutcliffe; 3 Carlos Tuimavave (C); 5 Darnell McIntosh; 6 Jake Trueman; 7 Jake Clifford; 13 Brad Fash; 9 Danny Houghton; 30 Scott Taylor; 23 Josh Griffin; 12 Jordan Lane; 15 Joe Cator. Subs (all used): 8 Ligi Sao; 20 Jack Brown; 11 Andre Savelio; 33 Brad Dwyer.
Tries: Swift (25), McIntosh (34), Griffin (58); **Goals:** Clifford 0/1, Sutcliffe 2/2.
Rugby Leaguer & League Express Men of the Match:
Leopards: Gareth O'Brien; *Hull FC:* Adam Swift.
Penalty count: 11-8; **Half-time:** 16-10;
Referee: Ben Thaler; **Attendance:** 6,006.

ST HELENS 34 WIGAN WARRIORS 16

SAINTS: 1 Jack Welsby; 2 Tommy Makinson; 23 Konrad Hurrell; 4 Mark Percival; 25 Tee Ritson; 6 Jonny Lomax; 7 Lewis Dodd; 8 Alex Walmsley; 9 James Roby (C); 10 Matty Lees; 16 Curtis Sironen; 12 Joe Batchelor; 13 Morgan Knowles. Subs (all used): 11 Sione Mata'utia; 14 Joey Lussick; 17 Agnatius Paasi; 19 James Bell.

Tries: Batchelor (3), Makinson (22, 63), Welsby (39, 52), Paasi (48); **Goals:** Makinson 5/8.
WARRIORS: 1 Jai Field; 23 Abbas Miski; 21 Iain Thornley; 4 Jake Wardle; 5 Liam Marshall; 2 Bevan French; 7 Harry Smith; 15 Kaide Ellis; 22 Brad O'Neill; 10 Liam Byrne; 19 Joe Shorrocks; 12 Liam Farrell (C); 13 Morgan Smithies. Subs (all used): 6 Cade Cust; 8 Brad Singleton; 20 Patrick Mago; 26 Harvie Hill.
Tries: Field (12), French (29), Miski (79); **Goals:** Smith 2/3.
Rugby Leaguer & League Express Men of the Match:
Saints: James Roby; *Warriors:* Morgan Smithies.
Penalty count: 5-6; **Half-time:** 18-10;
Referee: Chris Kendall; **Attendance:** 17,088.

Saturday 10th June 2023

WARRINGTON WOLVES 30 HUDDERSFIELD GIANTS 26

WOLVES: 1 Matt Dufty; 2 Josh Thewlis; 20 Connor Wrench; 4 Stefan Ratchford (C); 5 Matty Ashton; 3 Peter Mata'utia; 6 George Williams; 17 Gil Dudson; 16 Danny Walker; 10 Paul Vaughan; 11 Ben Currie; 8 James Harrison; 14 Sam Kasiano. Subs: 9 Daryl Clark; 19 Joe Bullock; 34 Matty Russell (not used); 35 Lucas Green.
Tries: Kasiano (4), Thewlis (18), Williams (24), Walker (43), Dufty (62); **Goals:** Ratchford 5/5.
GIANTS: 32 Will Pryce; 25 Innes Senior; 3 Esan Marsters; 4 Kevin Naiqama; 5 Jake Bibby; 23 Oliver Russell; 7 Theo Fages; 8 Chris Hill; 9 Nathan Peats; 20 Oliver Wilson; 21 Leroy Cudjoe; 12 Chris McQueen; 13 Luke Yates (C). Subs (all used): 6 Tui Lolohea; 16 Harry Rushton; 18 Sebastine Ikahihifo; 35 Adam Milner.
Tries: Bibby (11), Cudjoe (28), Naiqama (52), Fages (56), Lolohea (76); **Goals:** Russell 3/5.
Rugby Leaguer & League Express Men of the Match:
Wolves: Danny Walker; *Giants:* Kevin Naiqama.
Penalty count: 4-2; **Half-time:** 18-10;
Referee: Liam Moore; **Attendance:** 9,007.

CATALANS DRAGONS 38 HULL KR 4

DRAGONS: 1 Arthur Mourgue; 21 Matt Ikuvalu; 3 Adam Keighran; 19 Arthur Romano; 24 Tom Johnstone; 6 Tyrone May; 7 Mitchell Pearce; 8 Mike McMeeken; 9 Michael McIlorum; 10 Paul Seguier; 13 Benjamin Garcia (C). Subs (all used): 10 Julian Bousquet; 15 Mickael Goudemand; 23 Jordan Dezaria; 29 Sam Tomkins.

Tries: Whitley (24, 39), May (31), McMeeken (52), Johnstone (63), Mourgue (69);
Goals: Mourgue 6/7, Keighran 1/1.
Sin bin: Bousquet (36) - dangerous challenge on Walker; Goudemand (60) - dangerous contact.
HULL KR: 34 Jack Walker (D); 24 Sam Wood; 33 Corey Hall; 4 Shaun Kenny-Dowall (C); 5 Ryan Hall; 20 Mikey Lewis; 7 Jordan Abdull; 15 Rhys Kennedy; 9 Matt Parcell; 10 George King; 25 Luis Johnson; 12 Kane Linnett; 13 Elliot Minchella. Subs (all used): 14 Jez Litten; 17 Matty Storton; 26 Sam Luckley; 27 Yusuf Aydin.
Try: C Hall (72); **Goals:** Lewis 0/1.
Rugby Leaguer & League Express Men of the Match:
Dragons: Arthur Mourgue; *Hull KR:* Rhys Kennedy.
Penalty count: 2-10; **Half-time:** 20-0;
Referee: Marcus Griffiths; **Attendance:** 9,450.

Sunday 11th June 2023

WAKEFIELD TRINITY 24 LEEDS RHINOS 14

TRINITY: 1 Max Jowitt; 18 Lee Kershaw; 38 Jack Croft; 15 Liam Kay; 41 Romain Franco (D); 33 Will Dagger; 20 Morgan Smith; 19 Kevin Proctor; 24 Harry Bowes; 8 Eddie Battye; 31 Sam Hewitt; 11 Matty Ashurst (C); 13 Jay Pitts. Subs (all used): 25 Sam Eseh; 29 Joe Law (D); 40 David Fifita; 42 Hugo Salabio (D).
Tries: Croft (12), Franco (21), Ashurst (62), M Smith (65);
Goals: Dagger 4/6.
Dismissal: Salabio (45) - dangerous challenge on Myler.
RHINOS: 5 Ash Handley (C); 4 Nene Macdonald; 24 Luis Roberts; 12 Rhyse Martin; 23 Liam Tindall; 6 Blake Austin; 1 Richie Myler; 8 Mikolaj Oledzki; 14 Jarrod O'Connor; 22 Sam Walters; 19 James McDonnell; 11 James Bentley; 13 Cameron Smith. Subs (all used): 17 Justin Sangare; 25 James Donaldson; 26 Corey Johnson; 31 Leon Ruan (D).
Tries: Smith (33), Ruan (35), Austin (56); **Goals:** Martin 1/3.
Sin bin: Handley (61) - trip on Franco.
Rugby Leaguer & League Express Men of the Match:
Trinity: Morgan Smith; *Rhinos:* Blake Austin.
Penalty count: 7-1; **Half-time:** 10-10;
Referee: Aaron Moore; **Attendance:** 4,710.

ROUND 16

Thursday 22nd June 2023

HULL FC 34 ST HELENS 6

HULL FC: 29 Jamie Shaul; 25 Davy Litten; 17 Cameron Scott; 3 Carlos Tuimavave (C); 5 Darnell McIntosh; 6 Jake Trueman; 7 Jake Clifford; 13 Brad Fash; 9 Danny Houghton; 8 Ligi Sao; 14 Joe Lovodua; 11 Andre Savelio; 15 Joe Cator. Subs (all used): 10 Tevita Satae; 12 Jordan Lane; 19 Ben McNamara; 20 Jack Brown.
Tries: Clifford (6), Tuimavave (16), Trueman (22), Satae (36), Scott (48), McIntosh (77); **Goals:** Clifford 5/6.
SAINTS: 1 Jack Welsby; 25 Tee Ritson; 23 Konrad Hurrell; 3 Will Hopoate; 5 Jonathan Bennison; 6 Jonny Lomax; 7 Lewis Dodd; 8 Alex Walmsley; 13 Morgan Knowles; 10 Matty Lees; 16 Curtis Sironen; 12 Joe Batchelor; 15 Louie McCarthy-Scarsbrook. Subs (all used): 9 James Roby (C); 11 Sione Mata'utia; 17 Agnatius Paasi; 19 James Bell.
Try: Bell (44); **Goals:** Bennison 1/1.
Rugby Leaguer & League Express Men of the Match:
Hull FC: Jake Clifford; *Saints:* Konrad Hurrell.
Penalty count: 3-7; **Half-time:** 22-0;
Referee: Jack Smith; **Attendance:** 9,937.

Friday 23rd June 2023

CASTLEFORD TIGERS 23 WARRINGTON WOLVES 14

TIGERS: 6 Gareth Widdop; 39 Will Tate; 12 Alex Mellor (C); 3 Jordan Turner; 31 Jason Qareqare; 17 Jack Broadbent; 7 Jacob Miller; 32 Liam Watts; 14 Nathan Massey; 10 George Griffin; 11 Kenny Edwards; 15 Alex Sutcliffe; 13 Joe Westerman. Subs (all used): 20 Muizz Mustapha; 24 Cain Robb; 25 Brad Martin; 28 Sam Hall.
Tries: Tate (7), Qareqare (33), Broadbent (78);
Goals: Widdop 5/7; **Field goal:** Widdop (74).
WOLVES: 1 Matt Dufty; 2 Josh Thewlis; 20 Connor Wrench; 21 Greg Minikin; 5 Matty Ashton; 3 Peter Mata'utia; 4 Stefan Ratchford (C); 17 Gil Dudson; 16 Danny Walker; 10 Paul Vaughan; 11 Ben Currie; 8 James Harrison; 15 Joe Philbin. Subs (all used): 9 Daryl Clark; 14 Sam Kasiano; 19 Joe Bullock; 34 Matty Russell.
Tries: Ashton (46, 62), Wrench (68);
Goals: Ratchford 0/1, Mata'utia 1/2.
Sin bin: Harrison (4) - dangerous challenge on Massey.
Rugby Leaguer & League Express Men of the Match:
Tigers: Gareth Widdop; *Wolves:* Paul Vaughan.
Penalty count: 10-10; **Half-time:** 14-0;
Referee: Marcus Griffiths; **Attendance:** 6,066.

HULL KR 28 WAKEFIELD TRINITY 12

HULL KR: 35 Tanguy Zenon; 36 Fouad Yaha (D); 3 Tom Opacic; 4 Shaun Kenny-Dowall (C); 23 Louis Senior; 21 Rowan Milnes; 20 Mikey Lewis; 26 Sam Luckley; 14 Jez Litten; 10 George King; 22 Dean Hadley; 12 Kane Linnett; 13 Elliot Minchella. Subs (all used): 9 Matt Parcell; 15 Rhys Kennedy; 17 Matty Storton; 27 Yusuf Aydin.
Tries: Opacic (7, 33), Senior (12, 24), Lewis (72);
Goals: Milnes 4/5.
Sin bin: Yaha (32) - dangerous challenge on Jowitt.
TRINITY: 1 Max Jowitt; 18 Lee Kershaw; 38 Jack Croft; 33 Will Dagger; 41 Romain Franco; 20 Morgan Smith; 37 Luke Gale (D); 8 Eddie Battye; 9 Liam Hood; 16 Josh Bowden; 11 Matty Ashurst (C); 13 Jay Pitts; 15 Liam Kay. Subs (all used): 17 Renouf Atoni; 24 Harry Bowes; 40 David Fifita; 39 Isaac Shaw (D2).
Tries: Franco (37), Gale (57); **Goals:** Dagger 2/2.
Sin bin: Fifita (69) - dangerous challenge on Senior.
Rugby Leaguer & League Express Men of the Match:
Hull KR: Rowan Milnes; *Trinity:* Renouf Atoni.
Penalty count: 6-4; **Half-time:** 22-6;
Referee: Chris Kendall; **Attendance:** 8,185.

LEEDS RHINOS 54 HUDDERSFIELD GIANTS 0

RHINOS: 1 Richie Myler; 2 David Fusitu'a; 12 Rhyse Martin; 24 Luis Roberts; 5 Ash Handley; 6 Blake Austin; 7 Aidan Sezer; 22 Sam Walters; 14 Jarrod O'Connor; 8 Mikolaj Oledzki; 19 James McDonnell; 11 James Bentley; 13 Cameron Smith (C). Subs (all used): 15 Sam Lisone; 17 Justin Sangare; 25 James Donaldson; 26 Corey Johnson.
Tries: Walters (9, 60), Myler (16), Handley (21), Fusitu'a (35, 68), McDonnell (43), Martin (63, 76);
Goals: Martin 9/10.
GIANTS: 32 Will Pryce; 2 Jermaine McGillvary; 4 Kevin Naiqama; 5 Jake Bibby; 25 Innes Senior; 23 Oliver Russell; 7 Theo Fages; 8 Chris Hill; 9 Nathan Peats; 10 Joe Greenwood; 21 Leroy Cudjoe; 12 Chris McQueen; 13 Luke Yates (C). Subs (all used): 18 Sebastine Ikahihifo; 6 Tui Lolohea; 27 Jack Ashworth; 20 Oliver Wilson.
Sin bin: Senior (57) - professional foul.
Rugby Leaguer & League Express Men of the Match:
Rhinos: Blake Austin; *Giants:* Luke Yates.
Penalty count: 10-5; **Half time:** 22-0;
Referee: Ben Thaler; **Attendance:** 14,590.

Saturday 24th June 2023

CATALANS DRAGONS 38 LEIGH LEOPARDS 30

DRAGONS: 1 Arthur Mourgue; 2 Tom Davies; 3 Adam Keighran; 19 Arthur Romano; 24 Tom Johnstone; 6 Tyrone May; 29 Sam Tomkins; 16 Romain Navarrete; 9 Michael McIlorum; 10 Julian Bousquet; 8 Mike McMeeken; 12 Paul Seguier; 13 Benjamin Garcia (C). Subs: 15 Mickael Goudemand; 21 Matt Ikuvalu (not used); 23 Jordan Dezaria; 26 Manu Ma'u.
Tries: Mourgue (2), Garcia (5, 69), Johnstone (17, 74), Romano (42); **Goals:** Mourgue 7/7.
LEOPARDS: 17 Gareth O'Brien; 2 Tom Briscoe; 26 Umyla Hanley; 4 Ricky Leutele; 5 Josh Charnley; 15 Ben Reynolds; 7 Lachlan Lam; 8 Tom Amone; 9 Edwin Ipape; 10 Robbie Mulhern; 3 Ed Chamberlain; 16 Oliver Holmes; 13 John Asiata (C). Subs (all used): 6 Joe Mellor; 18 Matt Davis; 25 Nathan Wilde; 30 Dan Norman.
Tries: Chamberlain (27, 34), Charnley (38), Ipape (55), Briscoe (57); **Goals:** Reynolds 5/5.
Rugby Leaguer & League Express Men of the Match:
Dragons: Benjamin Garcia; *Leopards:* Edwin Ipape.
Penalty count: 5-5; **Half-time:** 20-18;
Referee: Liam Moore; **Attendance:** 9,636.

Sunday 25th June 2023

SALFORD RED DEVILS 6 WIGAN WARRIORS 26

RED DEVILS: 1 Ryan Brierley; 2 Ken Sio; 28 Deon Cross; 4 Tim Lafai; 5 Joe Burgess; 14 Chris Atkin; 7 Marc Sneyd; 10 King Vuniyayawa; 21 Amir Bourouh; 19 Adam Sidlow; 12 Sam Stone; 3 Kallum Watkins (C); 13 Oliver Partington. Subs (all used): 15 Danny Addy; 16 Tyler Dupree; 24 Matthew Costello; 25 Ben Hellewell.
Try: Hellewell (31); **Goals:** Sneyd 1/1.
WARRIORS: 1 Jai Field; 23 Abbas Miski; 3 Toby King; 4 Jake Wardle; 5 Liam Marshall; 2 Bevan French; 7 Harry Smith; 16 Ethan Havard; 22 Brad O'Neill; 10 Liam Byrne; 19 Joe Shorrocks; 12 Liam Farrell (C); 13 Morgan Smithies. Subs (all used): 6 Cade Cust; 8 Brad Singleton; 20 Patrick Mago; 26 Harvie Hill.
Tries: Shorrocks (22), Farrell (39, 58), Miski (47), Marshall (73); **Goals:** Smith 3/5.
Rugby Leaguer & League Express Men of the Match:
Red Devils: Ken Sio; *Warriors:* Brad O'Neill.
Penalty count: 3-7; **Half-time:** 6-8;
Referee: Aaron Moore; **Attendance:** 7,854.

ROUND 17

Thursday 29th June 2023

WARRINGTON WOLVES 6 LEEDS RHINOS 22

WOLVES: 2 Josh Thewlis; 34 Matty Russell; 3 Peter Mata'utia; 4 Stefan Ratchford (C); 5 Matty Ashton; 1 Matt Dufty; 7 Josh Drinkwater; 17 Gil Dudson; 9 Daryl Clark; 10 Paul Vaughan; 11 Ben Currie; 26 Adam Holroyd; 15 Joe Philbin. Subs (all used): 14 Sam Kasiano; 16 Danny Walker; 19 Joe Bullock; 20 Connor Wrench.
Try: Ashton (63); **Goals:** Ratchford 1/1.
Sin bin: Kasiano (22) - shoulder charge on Handley.
RHINOS: 1 Richie Myler; 5 Ash Handley; 12 Rhyse Martin; 4 Nene Macdonald; 2 David Fusitu'a; 6 Blake Austin; 7 Aidan Sezer; 8 Mikolaj Oledzki; 14 Jarrod O'Connor; 22 Sam Walters; 11 James Bentley; 19 James McDonnell; 13 Cameron Smith (C). Subs (all used): 15 Sam Lisone; 18 Tom Holroyd; 25 James Donaldson; 26 Corey Johnson.
Tries: Walters (6), Handley (11, 15), Myler (70);
Goals: Martin 3/4.
Rugby Leaguer & League Express Men of the Match:
Wolves: Joe Bullock; *Rhinos:* Blake Austin.
Penalty count: 10-10; **Half-time:** 0-16;
Referee: Chris Kendall; **Attendance:** 8,981.

Friday 30th June 2023

WAKEFIELD TRINITY 32 SALFORD RED DEVILS 6

TRINITY: 1 Max Jowitt; 5 Tom Lineham; 4 Reece Lyne; 38 Jack Croft; 18 Lee Kershaw; 33 Will Dagger; 37 Luke Gale; 16 Josh Bowden; 9 Liam Hood; 8 Eddie Battye; 13 Jay Pitts; 11 Matty Ashurst (C); 15 Liam Kay. Subs (all used): 24 Harry Bowes; 25 Sam Eseh; 17 Renouf Atoni; 40 David Fifita.
Tries: Kay (3), Dagger (26), Lyne (37), Kershaw (48);
Goals: Dagger 8/8.
RED DEVILS: 14 Chris Atkin; 22 Rhys Williams; 2 Ken Sio; 4 Tim Lafai; 5 Joe Burgess; 3 Kallum Watkins (C); 7 Marc Sneyd; 25 Ben Hellewell; 21 Amir Bourouh; 10 King Vuniyayawa; 11 Andrew Dixon; 28 Deon Cross; 13 Oliver Partington. Subs (all used): 16 Tyler Dupree; 18 Alex Gerrard; 19 Adam Sidlow; 20 Ellis Longstaff.
Try: Gerrard (63); **Goals:** Sneyd 1/1.
Rugby Leaguer & League Express Men of the Match:
Trinity: Will Dagger; *Red Devils:* Ken Sio.
Penalty count: 12-3; **Half-time:** 22-0;
Referee: Ben Thaler; **Attendance:** 3,854.

LEIGH LEOPARDS 34 HULL KR 4

LEOPARDS: 17 Gareth O'Brien; 2 Tom Briscoe; 1 Zak Hardaker; 4 Ricky Leutele; 5 Josh Charnley; 15 Ben Reynolds; 7 Lachlan Lam; 8 Tom Amone; 9 Edwin Ipape; 10 Robbie Mulhern; 16 Oliver Holmes; 3 Ed Chamberlain; 13 John Asiata (C). Subs (all used): 6 Joe Mellor; 12 Jack Hughes; 14 Ben Nakubuwai; 30 Dan Norman.
Tries: Briscoe (9), Ipape (12), Chamberlain (17), Charnley (36), Leutele (50, pen), Mulhern (65);
Goals: Reynolds 5/7.
HULL KR: 35 Tanguy Zenon; 36 Fouad Yaha; 3 Tom Opacic; 4 Shaun Kenny-Dowall (C); 5 Ryan Hall; 20 Mikey Lewis; 21 Rowan Milnes; 26 Sam Luckley; 14 Jez Litten; 10 George King; 22 Dean Hadley; 12 Kane Linnett; 13 Elliot Minchella. Subs (all used): 9 Matt Parcell; 15 Rhys Kennedy; 17 Matty Storton; 27 Yusuf Aydin.
Try: Lewis (71); **Goals:** Milnes 0/1.
Sin bin: Lewis (3) - trip on Briscoe.
Rugby Leaguer & League Express Men of the Match:
Leopards: Robbie Mulhern; *Hull KR:* Jez Litten.
Penalty count: 5-7; **Half-time:** 22-0;
Referee: Marcus Griffiths; **Attendance:** 6,012.

ST HELENS 22 CASTLEFORD TIGERS 0

SAINTS: 1 Jack Welsby; 3 Will Hopoate; 23 Konrad Hurrell; 4 Mark Percival; 5 Jonathan Bennison; 6 Jonny Lomax; 7 Lewis Dodd; 8 Alex Walmsley; 9 James Roby (C); 10 Matty Lees; 11 Sione Mata'utia; 19 James Bell; 13 Morgan Knowles. Subs (all used): 14 Joey Lussick; 15 Louie McCarthy-Scarsbrook; 17 Agnatius Paasi; 30 George Delaney.
Tries: Mata'utia (18), Welsby (36), Bennison (57), Percival (75); **Goals:** Percival 3/4.
TIGERS: 6 Gareth Widdop; 39 Will Tate; 12 Alex Mellor (C); 3 Jordan Turner; 31 Jason Qareqare; 40 Riley Dean (D); 7 Jacob Miller; 10 George Griffin; 17 Jack Broadbent; 32 Liam Watts; 15 Alex Sutcliffe; 11 Kenny Edwards; 28 Sam Hall. Subs (all used): 19 Albert Vete; 20 Muizz Mustapha; 24 Cain Robb; 25 Brad Martin.
Rugby Leaguer & League Express Men of the Match:
Saints: Jonathan Bennison; *Tigers:* Riley Dean.
Penalty count: 4-5; **Half-time:** 10-0;
Referee: Aaron Moore; **Attendance:** 11,488.

WIGAN WARRIORS 22 HUDDERSFIELD GIANTS 6

WARRIORS: 1 Jai Field; 23 Abbas Miski; 3 Toby King; 4 Jake Wardle; 5 Liam Marshall; 2 Bevan French; 7 Harry Smith; 16 Ethan Havard; 22 Brad O'Neill; 10 Liam Byrne; 19 Joe Shorrocks; 12 Liam Farrell (C); 13 Morgan Smithies. Subs (all used): 6 Cade Cust; 8 Brad Singleton; 20 Patrick Mago; 26 Harvie Hill.
Tries: Miski (9, 37), Field (45), Marshall (65);
Goals: Smith 3/4.
Sin bin: Havard (61) - shoulder charge on Wilson.
GIANTS: 1 Jake Connor; 21 Leroy Cudjoe; 5 Jake Bibby; 4 Kevin Naiqama; 2 Jermaine McGillvary; 23 Oliver Russell; 6 Tui Lolohea; 8 Chris Hill; 35 Adam Milner; 20 Oliver Wilson; 22 Harvey Livett; 12 Chris McQueen; 13 Luke Yates (C). Subs (all used): 9 Nathan Peats; 18 Sebastine Ikahihifo; 29 Sam Hewitt; 30 Fenton Rogers (D).
Try: Bibby (76); **Goals:** Connor 1/1.
Rugby Leaguer & League Express Men of the Match:
Warriors: Abbas Miski; *Giants:* Sebastine Ikahihifo.
Penalty count: 8-4; **Half-time:** 10-0;
Referee: Jack Smith; **Attendance:** 13,464.

Saturday 1st July 2023

HULL FC 18 CATALANS DRAGONS 28

HULL FC: 29 Jamie Shaul; 2 Adam Swift; 17 Cameron Scott; 3 Carlos Tuimavave (C); 5 Darnell McIntosh; 6 Jake Trueman; 7 Jake Clifford; 13 Brad Fash; 9 Danny Houghton; 8 Ligi Sao; 14 Joe Lovodua; 11 Andre Savelio; 15 Joe Cator. Subs (all used): 10 Tevita Satae; 12 Jordan Lane; 19 Ben McNamara; 20 Jack Brown.
Tries: Satae (27), McIntosh (37), Swift (40);
Goals: Clifford 3/3.
DRAGONS: 1 Arthur Mourgue; 24 Tom Johnstone; 19 Arthur Romano; 3 Adam Keighran; 2 Tom Davies; 6 Tyrone May; 29 Sam Tomkins; 8 Mike McMeeken; 9 Michael McIlorum; 16 Romain Navarrete; 11 Matt Whitley; 12 Paul Seguier; 13 Benjamin Garcia (C). Subs (all used): 10 Julian Bousquet; 14 Alrix Da Costa; 23 Jordan Dezaria; 26 Manu Ma'u.
Tries: Johnstone (5), Davies (18, 63), Romano (31), Bousquet (34); **Goals:** Mourgue 4/5.
Rugby Leaguer & League Express Men of the Match:
Hull FC: Danny Houghton; *Dragons:* Tom Davies.
Penalty count: 3-4; **Half-time:** 18-22;
Referee: Liam Moore; **Attendance:** 13,480.

ROUND 18

Friday 7th July 2023

WAKEFIELD TRINITY 27 WIGAN WARRIORS 26
(after golden point extra-time)

TRINITY: 1 Max Jowitt; 5 Tom Lineham; 4 Reece Lyne; 21 Samisoni Langi; 18 Lee Kershaw; 33 Will Dagger; 15 Liam Kay; 16 Josh Bowden; 9 Liam Hood; 10 Jai Whitbread; 13 Jay Pitts; 11 Matty Ashurst (C); 8 Eddie Battye. Subs (all used): 17 Renouf Atoni; 24 Harry Bowes; 19 Kevin Proctor; 40 David Fifita.
Tries: Lineham (14), Kershaw (36), Atoni (55), Whitbread (60); **Goals:** Dagger 5/5;
Field goal: Dagger (83).
WARRIORS: 1 Jai Field; 23 Abbas Miski; 3 Toby King; 21 Iain Thornley; 5 Liam Marshall; 2 Bevan French; 7 Harry Smith; 16 Ethan Havard; 22 Brad O'Neill; 10 Liam Byrne; 19 Joe Shorrocks; 12 Liam Farrell (C); 13 Morgan Smithies. Subs (all used): 6 Cade Cust; 8 Brad Singleton; 20 Patrick Mago; 27 Junior Nsemba.
Tries: Field (23, 43), French (30), Marshall (53), King (67);
Goals: Smith 3/5.
Rugby Leaguer & League Express Men of the Match:
Trinity: Will Dagger; *Warriors:* Abbas Miski.
Penalty count: 2-3; **Half-time:** 12-12;
Referee: Marcus Griffiths; **Attendance:** 4,185.

CASTLEFORD TIGERS 16 LEIGH LEOPARDS 34

TIGERS: 6 Gareth Widdop; 5 Bureta Faraimo; 17 Jack Broadbent; 3 Jordan Turner; 26 Elliot Wallis; 40 Riley Dean; 7 Jacob Miller; 32 Liam Watts; 41 Jordan Johnstone (D); 10 George Griffin; 11 Kenny Edwards; 12 Alex Mellor (C); 13 Joe Westerman. Subs (all used): 15 Alex Sutcliffe; 20 Muizz Mustapha; 24 Cain Robb; 28 Sam Hall.
Tries: Widdop (31), Wallis (39, 46); **Goals:** Widdop 2/3.
LEOPARDS: 17 Gareth O'Brien; 5 Josh Charnley; 4 Ricky Leutele; 1 Zak Hardaker; 2 Tom Briscoe; 15 Ben Reynolds; 7 Lachlan Lam; 8 Tom Amone; 9 Edwin Ipape; 14 Ben Nakubuwai; 3 Ed Chamberlain; 16 Oliver Holmes; 13 John Asiata (C). Subs (all used): 6 Joe Mellor; 12 Jack Hughes; 18 Matt Davis; 25 Nathan Wilde.
Tries: Amone (16), Lam (19, 67), Briscoe (24), Charnley (42, 61); **Goals:** Reynolds 5/6.
Rugby Leaguer & League Express Men of the Match:
Tigers: Elliot Wallis; *Leopards:* Tom Amone.
Penalty count: 7-7; **Half-time:** 12-18;
Referee: Liam Moore; **Attendance:** 6,344.

WARRINGTON WOLVES 20 ST HELENS 24

WOLVES: 1 Matt Dufty; 34 Matty Russell; 21 Greg Minikin; 4 Stefan Ratchford (C); 5 Matty Ashton; 3 Peter Mata'utia; 7 Josh Drinkwater; 10 Paul Vaughan; 9 Daryl Clark; 17 Gil Dudson; 11 Ben Currie; 23 Tom Whitehead; 15 Joe Philbin. Subs (all used): 35 Lucas Green; 16 Danny Walker; 19 Joe Bullock; 26 Adam Holroyd.
Tries: Ashton (25, 45), Dufty (55); **Goals:** Ratchford 4/5.
SAINTS: 1 Jack Welsby; 3 Will Hopoate; 23 Konrad Hurrell; 4 Mark Percival; 5 Jonathan Bennison; 6 Jonny Lomax; 7 Lewis Dodd; 8 Alex Walmsley; 9 James Roby (C); 10 Matty Lees; 11 Sione Mata'utia; 19 James Bell; 13 Morgan Knowles. Subs (all used): 14 Joey Lussick; 15 Louie McCarthy-Scarsbrook; 17 Agnatius Paasi; 30 George Delaney.
Tries: Percival (15), Bell (29), Lomax (60), Dodd (67);
Goals: Percival 4/4.
Rugby Leaguer & League Express Men of the Match:
Wolves: Matty Ashton; *Saints:* Jonny Lomax.
Penalty count: 6-5; **Half-time:** 6-12;
Referee: Jack Smith; **Attendance:** 12,385.

Saturday 8th July 2023

CATALANS DRAGONS 14 HUDDERSFIELD GIANTS 22

DRAGONS: 1 Arthur Mourgue; 2 Tom Davies; 21 Matt Ikuvalu; 19 Arthur Romano; 24 Tom Johnstone; 6 Tyrone May; 3 Adam Keighran; 8 Mike McMeeken; 9 Michael McIlorum; 10 Julian Bousquet; 11 Matt Whitley; 12 Paul Seguier; 13 Benjamin Garcia (C). Subs (all used): 14 Alrix Da Costa; 15 Mickael Goudemand; 23 Jordan Dezaria; 26 Manu Ma'u.
Tries: Davies (12, 33); **Goals:** Mourgue 3/3.
GIANTS: 1 Jake Connor; 24 Sam Halsall; 5 Jake Bibby; 4 Kevin Naiqama; 2 Jermaine McGillvary; 23 Oliver Russell; 6 Tui Lolohea; 8 Chris Hill; 35 Adam Milner; 20 Oliver Wilson; 22 Harvey Livett; 12 Chris McQueen; 13 Luke Yates (C). Subs (all used): 9 Nathan Peats; 15 Matty English; 18 Sebastine Ikahihifo; 29 Sam Hewitt.
Tries: Naiqama (8), McQueen (27, 61); **Goals:** Russell 5/5.
Rugby Leaguer & League Express Men of the Match:
Dragons: Tom Davies; *Giants:* Oliver Russell.
Penalty count: 4-6; **Half-time:** 12-14;
Referee: Chris Kendall; **Attendance:** 9,189.

Sunday 9th July 2023

HULL KR 6 HULL FC 16

HULL KR: 34 Jack Walker; 2 Ethan Ryan; 3 Tom Opacic; 4 Shaun Kenny-Dowall (C); 5 Ryan Hall; 21 Rowan Milnes; 20 Mikey Lewis; 15 Rhys Kennedy; 14 Jez Litten; 10 George King; 18 Jimmy Keinhorst; 12 Kane Linnett; 22 Dean Hadley. Subs (all used): 9 Matt Parcell; 17 Matty Storton; 25 Luis Johnson; 26 Sam Luckley.
Try: Walker (5); **Goals:** Milnes 1/2.
Sin bin: Kenny-Dowall (60) - high tackle on Clifford.
HULL FC: 1 Tex Hoy; 2 Adam Swift; 17 Cameron Scott; 3 Carlos Tuimavave (C); 5 Darnell McIntosh; 6 Jake Trueman; 7 Jake Clifford; 30 Scott Taylor; 9 Danny Houghton; 8 Ligi Sao; 13 Brad Fash; 12 Jordan Lane; 15 Joe Cator. Subs (all used): 10 Tevita Satae; 20 Jack Brown; 27 Will Gardiner; 33 Brad Dwyer.
Tries: Swift (45, 77), Sao (65); **Goals:** Clifford 2/3.
Rugby Leaguer & League Express Men of the Match:
Hull KR: Rowan Milnes; *Hull FC:* Jake Clifford.
Penalty count: 6-4; **Half-time:** 6-0;
Referee: Ben Thaler; **Attendance:** 10,050.

SALFORD RED DEVILS 14 LEEDS RHINOS 16

RED DEVILS: 1 Ryan Brierley; 2 Ken Sio; 28 Deon Cross; 4 Tim Lafai; 5 Joe Burgess; 6 Brodie Croft; 7 Marc Sneyd (C); 8 Jack Ormondroyd; 9 Andy Ackers; 18 Alex Gerrard; 15 Danny Addy; 25 Ben Hellewell; 13 Oliver Partington. Subs: 10 King Vuniyayawa; 14 Chris Atkin; 16 Tyler Dupree; 24 Matthew Costello (not used).
Tries: Lafai (20, 42), Sio (48); **Goals:** Sneyd 0/1, Brierley 1/2.
Sin bin: Atkin (65) - fighting.
RHINOS: 1 Richie Myler; 5 Ash Handley; 12 Rhyse Martin; 4 Nene Macdonald; 2 David Fusitu'a; 26 Corey Johnson; 7 Aidan Sezer; 8 Mikolaj Oledzki; 14 Jarrod O'Connor; 22 Sam Walters; 11 James Bentley; 19 James McDonnell; 13 Cameron Smith (C). Subs: 15 Sam Lisone; 18 Tom Holroyd; 24 Luis Roberts (not used); 25 James Donaldson.
Tries: Smith (5), Handley (31); **Goals:** Martin 4/5.
Sin bin: Oledzki (65) - fighting.
Rugby Leaguer & League Express Men of the Match:
Red Devils: Tim Lafai; *Rhinos:* Aidan Sezer.
Penalty count: 5-10; **Half-time:** 4-12;
Referee: Aaron Moore; **Attendance:** 5,157.

ROUND 19

Thursday 13th July 2023

ST HELENS 12 CATALANS DRAGONS 14

SAINTS: 1 Jack Welsby; 3 Will Hopoate; 23 Konrad Hurrell; 4 Mark Percival; 5 Jonathan Bennison; 6 Jonny Lomax; 7 Lewis Dodd; 8 Alex Walmsley; 9 James Roby (C); 10 Matty Lees; 11 Sione Mata'utia; 19 James Bell; 13 Morgan Knowles. Subs (all used): 14 Joey Lussick; 15 Louie McCarthy-Scarsbrook; 17 Agnatius Paasi; 30 George Delaney.
Tries: Percival (34), Dodd (74);
Goals: Percival 1/1, Lussick 1/1.
DRAGONS: 29 Sam Tomkins; 2 Tom Davies; 21 Matt Ikuvalu; 3 Adam Keighran; 24 Tom Johnstone; 6 Tyrone May; 7 Mitchell Pearce; 8 Mike McMeeken; 9 Michael McIlorum; 16 Romain Navarrete; 11 Matt Whitley; 12 Paul Seguier; 13 Benjamin Garcia (C). Subs (all used): 10 Julian Bousquet; 18 Tiaki Chan; 23 Jordan Dezaria; 26 Manu Ma'u.
Tries: Johnstone (21), Ikuvalu (45); **Goals:** Keighran 3/3.
Rugby Leaguer & League Express Men of the Match:
Saints: Sione Mata'utia; *Dragons:* Michael McIlorum.
Penalty count: 9-6; **Half-time:** 6-8;
Referee: Liam Moore; **Attendance:** 12,193.

Friday 14th July 2023

HUDDERSFIELD GIANTS 34 WAKEFIELD TRINITY 6

GIANTS: 1 Jake Connor; 2 Jermaine McGillvary; 4 Kevin Naiqama; 5 Jake Bibby; 24 Sam Halsall; 23 Oliver Russell; 6 Tui Lolohea; 8 Chris Hill; 35 Adam Milner; 20 Oliver Wilson; 21 Leroy Cudjoe; 12 Chris McQueen; 13 Luke Yates (C). Subs (all used): 9 Nathan Peats; 10 Joe Greenwood; 15 Matty English; 29 Sam Hewitt.
Tries: McQueen (4), Naiqama (33), Halsall (40), McGillvary (42), Lolohea (47, 75); **Goals:** Russell 5/6.
TRINITY: 1 Max Jowitt; 5 Tom Lineham; 4 Reece Lyne; 21 Samisoni Langi; 18 Lee Kershaw; 33 Will Dagger; 7 Mason Lino; 16 Josh Bowden; 9 Liam Hood; 8 Eddie Battye; 11 Matty Ashurst (C); 13 Jay Pitts; 15 Liam Kay. Subs (all used): 24 Harry Bowes; 19 Kevin Proctor; 17 Renouf Atoni; 40 David Fifita.
Try: Langi (61); **Goals:** Jowitt 1/1.
Rugby Leaguer & League Express Men of the Match:
Giants: Chris McQueen; *Trinity:* David Fifita.
Penalty count: 4-3; **Half-time:** 16-0;
Referee: Aaron Moore; **Attendance:** 5,872.

LEEDS RHINOS 18 HULL KR 19
(after golden point extra-time)

RHINOS: 1 Richie Myler; 2 David Fusitu'a; 12 Rhyse Martin; 4 Nene Macdonald; 5 Ash Handley; 6 Blake Austin; 7 Aidan Sezer; 8 Mikolaj Oledzki; 14 Jarrod O'Connor; 22 Sam Walters; 19 James McDonnell; 11 James Bentley; 13 Cameron Smith (C). Subs (all used): 15 Sam Lisone; 17 Justin Sangare; 18 Tom Holroyd; 26 Corey Johnson.
Tries: O'Connor (11), Johnson (34), Handley (52);
Goals: Martin 3/3.
HULL KR: 2 Ethan Ryan; 23 Louis Senior; 3 Tom Opacic; 4 Shaun Kenny-Dowall (C); 5 Ryan Hall; 21 Rowan Milnes; 37 Brad Schneider (D); 15 Rhys Kennedy; 14 Jez Litten; 10 George King; 16 James Batchelor; 18 Jimmy Keinhorst; 22 Dean Hadley. Subs (all used): 9 Matt Parcell; 17 Matty Storton; 25 Luis Johnson; 26 Sam Luckley.
Tries: Schneider (6), Opacic (16), Senior (29);
Goals: Milnes 3/4; **Field goal:** Schneider (83).
Rugby Leaguer & League Express Men of the Match:
Rhinos: Jarrod O'Connor; *Hull KR:* Tom Opacic.
Penalty count: 5-3; **Half-time:** 12-18;
Referee: Tom Grant; **Attendance:** 13,728.

WIGAN WARRIORS 26 WARRINGTON WOLVES 12

WARRIORS: 1 Jai Field; 23 Abbas Miski; 3 Toby King; 4 Jake Wardle; 5 Liam Marshall; 2 Bevan French; 7 Harry Smith; 15 Kaide Ellis; 22 Brad O'Neill; 10 Liam Byrne; 19 Joe Shorrocks; 12 Liam Farrell (C); 13 Morgan Smithies. Subs (all used): 17 Kai Pearce-Paul; 20 Patrick Mago; 26 Harvie Hill; 27 Junior Nsemba.
Tries: Marshall (29), French (39), Wardle (48), Farrell (71);
Goals: Smith 5/5.
WOLVES: 1 Matt Dufty; 34 Matty Russell; 3 Peter Mata'utia; 4 Stefan Ratchford (C); 21 Greg Minikin; 16 Danny Walker; 7 Josh Drinkwater; 10 Paul Vaughan; 9 Daryl Clark; 17 Gil Dudson; 11 Ben Currie; 8 James Harrison; 15 Joe Philbin. Subs: 14 Sam Kasiano; 19 Joe Bullock; 23 Tom Whitehead (not used); 26 Adam Holroyd.
Tries: Harrison (7), Clark (34); **Goals:** Ratchford 2/2.
Rugby Leaguer & League Express Men of the Match:
Warriors: Kai Pearce-Paul; *Wolves:* Daryl Clark.
Penalty count: 6-5; **Half-time:** 12-12;
Referee: Chris Kendall; **Attendance:** 13,105.

Saturday 15th July 2023

HULL FC 36 CASTLEFORD TIGERS 18

HULL FC: 25 Davy Litten; 2 Adam Swift; 4 Liam Sutcliffe; 3 Carlos Tuimavave (C); 26 Harvey Barron; 6 Jake Trueman; 7 Jake Clifford; 13 Brad Fash; 9 Danny Houghton; 8 Ligi Sao; 17 Cameron Scott; 11 Andre Savelio; 15 Joe Cator. Subs (all used): 10 Tevita Satae; 12 Jordan Lane; 30 Scott Taylor; 33 Brad Dwyer.
Tries: Swift (7, 45), Tuimavave (20), Satae (43), Litten (54), Scott (57, 66); **Goals:** Clifford 0/2, Sutcliffe 4/5.
TIGERS: 6 Gareth Widdop; 5 Bureta Faraimo; 4 Mahe Fonua; 17 Jack Broadbent; 26 Elliot Wallis; 40 Riley Dean; 7 Jacob Miller; 32 Liam Watts; 41 Jordan Johnstone; 19 Albert Vete; 12 Alex Mellor (C); 11 Kenny Edwards; 13 Joe Westerman. Subs (all used): 10 George Griffin; 15 Alex Sutcliffe; 20 Muizz Mustapha; 28 Sam Hall.
Tries: Wallis (12), Broadbent (51), Faraimo (70); **Goals:** Widdop 3/4.
Rugby Leaguer & League Express Men of the Match: *Hull FC:* Tevita Satae; *Tigers:* Joe Westerman.
Penalty count: 5-4; **Half-time:** 8-8;
Referee: Marcus Griffiths; **Attendance:** 12,352.

Sunday 16th July 2023

SALFORD RED DEVILS 22 LEIGH LEOPARDS 24

RED DEVILS: 1 Ryan Brierley; 2 Ken Sio; 28 Deon Cross; 4 Tim Lafai; 5 Joe Burgess; 6 Brodie Croft; 7 Marc Sneyd (C); 8 Jack Ormondroyd; 9 Andy Ackers; 16 Tyler Dupree; 15 Danny Addy; 12 Sam Stone; 14 Chris Atkin. Subs (all used): 10 King Vuniyayawa; 19 Adam Sidlow; 21 Amir Bourouh; 25 Ben Hellewell.
Tries: Sio (11), Vuniyayawa (30), Ackers (38), Hellewell (46); **Goals:** Sneyd 3/4.
LEOPARDS: 17 Gareth O'Brien; 5 Josh Charnley; 4 Ricky Leutele; 1 Zak Hardaker; 2 Tom Briscoe; 15 Ben Reynolds; 7 Lachlan Lam; 8 Tom Amone; 6 Joe Mellor; 10 Robbie Mulhern; 3 Ed Chamberlain; 12 Jack Hughes; 13 John Asiata (C). Subs (all used): 14 Ben Nakubuwai; 16 Oliver Holmes; 18 Matt Davis; 25 Nathan Wilde.
Tries: Chamberlain (16), Leutele (21), Lam (50), Hardaker (65); **Goals:** Reynolds 4/5.
Rugby Leaguer & League Express Men of the Match: *Red Devils:* Chris Atkin; *Leopards:* John Asiata.
Penalty count: 3-10; **Half-time:** 16-10;
Referee: Ben Thaler; **Attendance:** 6,892.

ROUND 20

Thursday 27th July 2023

HUDDERSFIELD GIANTS 19 HULL FC 12

GIANTS: 1 Jake Connor; 2 Jermaine McGillvary; 4 Kevin Naiqama; 5 Jake Bibby; 24 Sam Halsall; 23 Oliver Russell; 6 Tui Lolohea; 8 Chris Hill; 35 Adam Milner; 20 Oliver Wilson; 21 Leroy Cudjoe; 12 Chris McQueen; 13 Luke Yates (C). Subs (all used): 9 Nathan Peats; 10 Joe Greenwood; 15 Matty English; 29 Sam Hewitt.
Tries: McGillvary (12), Lolohea (27), McQueen (69); **Goals:** Russell 3/3; **Field goal:** Russell (73).
HULL FC: 25 Davy Litten; 2 Adam Swift; 4 Liam Sutcliffe; 17 Cameron Scott; 5 Darnell McIntosh; 6 Jake Trueman; 7 Jake Clifford; 13 Brad Fash; 9 Danny Houghton (C); 8 Ligi Sao; 12 Jordan Lane; 11 Andre Savelio; 15 Joe Cator. Subs (all used): 10 Tevita Satae; 14 Joe Lovodua; 30 Scott Taylor; 33 Brad Dwyer.
Tries: Swift (18), Fash (23); **Goals:** Sutcliffe 2/2.
Rugby Leaguer & League Express Men of the Match: *Giants:* Chris Hill; *Hull FC:* Jake Clifford.
Penalty count: 5-3; **Half-time:** 12-12;
Referee: Aaron Moore; **Attendance:** 4,579.

Friday 28th July 2023

HULL KR 34 CASTLEFORD TIGERS 16

HULL KR: 20 Mikey Lewis; 2 Ethan Ryan; 3 Tom Opacic; 4 Shaun Kenny-Dowall (C); 23 Louis Senior; 21 Rowan Milnes; 37 Brad Schneider; 15 Rhys Kennedy; 14 Jez Litten; 10 George King; 16 James Batchelor; 12 Kane Linnett; 13 Elliot Minchella. Subs (all used): 9 Matt Parcell; 17 Matty Storton; 18 Jimmy Keinhorst; 26 Sam Luckley.
Tries: Opacic (15), Kennedy (17), Linnett (23), Minchella (43), Batchelor (53), Ryan (62); **Goals:** Milnes 5/7.
TIGERS: 17 Jack Broadbent; 26 Elliot Wallis; 12 Alex Mellor (C); 39 Will Tate; 2 Greg Eden; 40 Riley Dean; 7 Jacob Miller; 32 Liam Watts; 41 Jordan Johnstone; 10 George Griffin; 11 Kenny Edwards; 8 George Lawler; 13 Joe Westerman. Subs (all used): 14 Nathan Massey; 23 Suaia Matagi; 42 Alex Foster (D2); 43 Billy Tsikrikas (D).
Tries: Tate (29), Broadbent (38), Eden (72); **Goals:** Dean 2/3.
Sin bin: Broadbent (55) - interference.
Rugby Leaguer & League Express Men of the Match: *Hull KR:* Rhys Kennedy; *Tigers:* Riley Dean.
Penalty count: 4-4; **Half-time:** 16-10;
Referee: Chris Kendall; **Attendance:** 8,636.

ST HELENS 22 LEEDS RHINOS 18

SAINTS: 1 Jack Welsby; 2 Tommy Makinson; 23 Konrad Hurrell; 3 Will Hopoate; 25 Tee Ritson; 6 Jonny Lomax; 7 Lewis Dodd; 10 Matty Lees; 9 James Roby (C); 30 George Delaney; 19 James Bell; 22 Sam Royle; 13 Morgan Knowles. Subs (all used): 20 Dan Norman; 21 Ben Davies; 24 Lewis Baxter; 35 Moses Mbye (D).
Tries: Hopoate (3), Ritson (39), Welsby (44, 66); **Goals:** Makinson 2/4, Dodd 1/1.
RHINOS: 1 Richie Myler; 2 David Fusitu'a; 12 Rhyse Martin; 4 Nene Macdonald; 5 Ash Handley; 6 Blake Austin; 7 Aidan Sezer; 8 Mikolaj Oledzki; 14 Jarrod O'Connor; 22 Sam Walters; 11 James Bentley; 19 James McDonnell; 13 Cameron Smith (C). Subs (all used): 18 Tom Holroyd; 15 Sam Lisone; 17 Justin Sangare; 26 Corey Johnson.
Tries: Martin (22), Walters (29), Macdonald (63); **Goals:** Martin 3/3.
Rugby Leaguer & League Express Men of the Match: *Saints:* Jack Welsby; *Rhinos:* Nene Macdonald.
Penalty count: 9-5; **Half-time:** 12-12;
Referee: Liam Moore; **Attendance:** 12,108.

Saturday 29th July 2023

WIGAN WARRIORS 44 LEIGH LEOPARDS 18

WARRIORS: 1 Jai Field; 23 Abbas Miski; 3 Toby King; 4 Jake Wardle; 5 Liam Marshall; 2 Bevan French; 7 Harry Smith; 15 Kaide Ellis; 22 Brad O'Neill; 10 Liam Byrne; 17 Kai Pearce-Paul; 12 Liam Farrell (C); 13 Morgan Smithies. Subs (all used): 6 Cade Cust; 20 Patrick Mago; 27 Junior Nsemba; 34 Tyler Dupree (D).
Tries: French (17, 40), King (37), Dupree (47), Miski (52, 60, 71), Marshall (62); **Goals:** Smith 6/8.
LEOPARDS: 17 Gareth O'Brien; 2 Tom Briscoe; 1 Zak Hardaker; 3 Ed Chamberlain; 5 Josh Charnley; 15 Ben Reynolds; 7 Lachlan Lam; 8 Tom Amone; 6 Joe Mellor; 10 Robbie Mulhern; 12 Jack Hughes; 16 Oliver Holmes; 13 John Asiata (C). Subs (all used): 11 Joe Wardle; 14 Ben Nakubuwai; 18 Matt Davis; 25 Nathan Wilde.
Tries: Amone (12), Briscoe (68), Mulhern (79); **Goals:** Reynolds 3/3.
Rugby Leaguer & League Express Men of the Match: *Warriors:* Tyler Dupree; *Leopards:* Tom Amone.
Penalty count: 1-3; **Half-time:** 16-6;
Referee: Jack Smith; **Attendance:** 15,377.

CATALANS DRAGONS 42 SALFORD RED DEVILS 0

DRAGONS: 29 Sam Tomkins; 2 Tom Davies; 3 Adam Keighran; 21 Matt Ikuvalu; 24 Tom Johnstone; 6 Tyrone May; 7 Mitchell Pearce; 8 Mike McMeeken; 9 Michael McIlorum; 16 Romain Navarrete; 11 Matt Whitley; 12 Paul Seguier; 13 Benjamin Garcia (C). Subs (all used): 10 Julian Bousquet; 14 Alrix Da Costa; 18 Tiaki Chan; 23 Jordan Dezaria.
Tries: Keighran (19, 28), Johnstone (36, 45), May (40), Chan (55), Tomkins (74); **Goals:** Keighran 4/6, Tomkins 3/3.
Sin bin: Davies (60) - holding down.
RED DEVILS: 1 Ryan Brierley (C); 2 Ken Sio; 28 Deon Cross; 24 Matthew Costello; 5 Joe Burgess; 6 Brodie Croft; 14 Chris Atkin; 8 Jack Ormondroyd; 21 Amir Bourouh; 18 Alex Gerrard; 25 Ben Hellewell; 12 Sam Stone; 13 Oliver Partington. Subs (all used): 9 Andy Ackers; 11 Andrew Dixon; 19 Adam Sidlow; 26 James Greenwood.
Rugby Leaguer & League Express Men of the Match: *Dragons:* Adam Keighran; *Red Devils:* Ryan Brierley.
Penalty count: 8-2; **Half-time:** 22-0;
Referee: Marcus Griffiths; **Attendance:** 9,503.

Sunday 30th July 2023

WAKEFIELD TRINITY 42 WARRINGTON WOLVES 6

TRINITY: 1 Max Jowitt; 5 Tom Lineham; 4 Reece Lyne; 21 Samisoni Langi; 34 Innes Senior (D4); 7 Mason Lino; 37 Luke Gale; 16 Josh Bowden; 9 Liam Hood; 19 Kevin Proctor; 13 Jay Pitts; 11 Matty Ashurst (C); 17 Renouf Atoni. Subs (all used): 25 Sam Eseh; 8 Eddie Battye; 24 Harry Bowes; 40 David Fifita.
Tries: Senior (9, 18, 30, 76), Proctor (14), Lineham (53), Hood (56), Jowitt (78); **Goals:** Gale 2/4, Jowitt 3/5.
WOLVES: 1 Matt Dufty; 2 Josh Thewlis; 3 Peter Mata'utia; 4 Stefan Ratchford (C); 5 Matty Ashton; 6 George Williams; 7 Josh Drinkwater; 19 Joe Bullock; 9 Daryl Clark; 10 Paul Vaughan; 11 Ben Currie; 12 Matty Nicholson; 15 Joe Philbin. Subs (all used): 14 Sam Kasiano; 26 Adam Holroyd; 16 Danny Walker; 17 Gil Dudson.
Try: Vaughan (46); **Goals:** Ratchford 1/1.
Rugby Leaguer & League Express Men of the Match: *Trinity:* Luke Gale; *Wolves:* Matty Nicholson.
Penalty count: 4-3; **Half-time:** 22-0;
Referee: Tom Grant; **Attendance:** 4,470.

ROUND 21

Friday 4th August 2023

CASTLEFORD TIGERS 0 HUDDERSFIELD GIANTS 28

TIGERS: 6 Gareth Widdop; 26 Elliot Wallis; 44 Charbel Tasipale (D); 12 Alex Mellor (C); 2 Greg Eden; 17 Jack Broadbent; 7 Jacob Miller; 23 Suaia Matagi; 41 Jordan Johnstone; 8 George Lawler; 11 Kenny Edwards; 42 Alex Foster; 13 Joe Westerman. Subs (all used): 14 Nathan Massey; 28 Sam Hall; 43 Billy Tsikrikas; 45 Liam Horne (D).
GIANTS: 1 Jake Connor; 24 Sam Halsall; 5 Jake Bibby; 3 Esan Marsters; 14 Ashton Golding; 23 Oliver Russell; 6 Tui Lolohea; 8 Chris Hill; 35 Adam Milner; 20 Oliver Wilson; 21 Leroy Cudjoe (C); 12 Chris McQueen; 15 Matty English. Subs (all used): 9 Nathan Peats; 10 Joe Greenwood; 18 Sebastine Ikahihifo; 29 Sam Hewitt.
Tries: Halsall (7, 54, 73), Cudjoe (16), McQueen (38), Milner (77); **Goals:** Russell 2/6.
Rugby Leaguer & League Express Men of the Match: *Tigers:* Joe Westerman; *Giants:* Leroy Cudjoe.
Penalty count: 6-4; **Half-time:** 0-14;
Referee: Tom Grant; **Attendance:** 6,452.

WARRINGTON WOLVES 10 CATALANS DRAGONS 30

WOLVES: 1 Matt Dufty; 2 Josh Thewlis; 3 Peter Mata'utia; 4 Stefan Ratchford (C); 20 Connor Wrench; 6 George Williams; 7 Josh Drinkwater; 17 Gil Dudson; 16 Danny Walker; 10 Paul Vaughan; 11 Ben Currie; 12 Matty Nicholson; 36 Jordan Crowther (D). Subs (all used): 9 Daryl Clark; 14 Sam Kasiano; 15 Joe Philbin; 18 Thomas Mikaele (D2).
Tries: Currie (37), Thewlis (77); **Goals:** Ratchford 1/1, Thewlis 0/1.
DRAGONS: 29 Sam Tomkins; 2 Tom Davies; 3 Adam Keighran; 21 Matt Ikuvalu; 24 Tom Johnstone; 6 Tyrone May; 7 Mitchell Pearce; 16 Romain Navarrete; 14 Alrix Da Costa; 10 Julian Bousquet; 11 Matt Whitley; 12 Paul Seguier; 13 Benjamin Garcia (C). Subs (all used): 18 Tiaki Chan; 15 Mickael Goudemand; 19 Arthur Romano; 25 Bastien Scimone.
Tries: Keighran (13), Davies (18), Pearce (29), Whitley (54), Ikuvalu (67); **Goals:** Keighran 5/6.
Rugby Leaguer & League Express Men of the Match: *Wolves:* Jordan Crowther; *Dragons:* Benjamin Garcia.
Penalty count: 7-4; **Half-time:** 6-18;
Referee: Liam Moore; **Attendance:** 10,312.

WIGAN WARRIORS 64 HULL KR 6

WARRIORS: 1 Jai Field; 23 Abbas Miski; 3 Toby King; 4 Jake Wardle; 5 Liam Marshall; 2 Bevan French; 7 Harry Smith; 34 Tyler Dupree; 22 Brad O'Neill; 15 Kaide Ellis; 17 Kai Pearce-Paul; 12 Liam Farrell (C); 13 Morgan Smithies. Subs (all used): 6 Cade Cust; 20 Patrick Mago; 26 Harvie Hill; 27 Junior Nsemba.
Tries: Miski (11, 22, 30, 49), Wardle (27), King (34), Smith (46), Mago (65), Field (68, 70, 73), Marshall (78); **Goals:** Smith 8/12.
HULL KR: 34 Jack Walker; 32 Connor Barley; 33 Corey Hall; 40 Louix Gorman (D); 23 Louis Senior; 29 Phoenix Laulu-Togaga'e; 21 Rowan Milnes; 17 Matty Storton; 41 Cesar Rouge (D); 27 Yusuf Aydin; 25 Luis Johnson; 18 Jimmy Keinhorst; 22 Dean Hadley (C). Subs (all used): 38 Lennie Ellis (D); 39 Leo Tennison (D); 42 Isaac Shaw (D); 43 Luke Thomas (D).
Try: Walker (40); **Goals:** Milnes 1/1.
Rugby Leaguer & League Express Men of the Match: *Warriors:* Jai Field; *Hull KR:* Dean Hadley.
Penalty count: 1-2; **Half-time:** 26-6;
Referee: Aaron Moore; **Attendance:** 11,464.

Sunday 6th August 2023

HULL FC 42 WAKEFIELD TRINITY 4

HULL FC: 25 Davy Litten; 5 Darnell McIntosh; 3 Carlos Tuimavave (C); 17 Cameron Scott; 2 Adam Swift; 6 Jake Trueman; 7 Jake Clifford; 13 Brad Fash; 9 Danny Houghton; 30 Scott Taylor; 12 Jordan Lane; 11 Andre Savelio; 15 Joe Cator. Subs (all used): 10 Tevita Satae; 14 Joe Lovodua; 20 Jack Brown; 33 Brad Dwyer.
Tries: Swift (10), Tuimavave (29), Scott (46), Lane (49), McIntosh (63, 74), Lovodua (80); **Goals:** Clifford 7/7.
TRINITY: 1 Max Jowitt; 5 Tom Lineham; 4 Reece Lyne; 21 Samisoni Langi; 34 Innes Senior; 37 Luke Gale; 7 Mason Lino; 16 Josh Bowden; 9 Liam Hood; 19 Kevin Proctor; 13 Jay Pitts; 11 Matty Ashurst (C); 15 Liam Kay. Subs (all used): 8 Eddie Battye; 17 Renouf Atoni; 33 Will Dagger; 40 David Fifita.
Try: Senior (53); **Goals:** Dagger 0/1.
Rugby Leaguer & League Express Men of the Match: *Hull FC:* Jake Clifford; *Trinity:* Liam Hood.
Penalty count: 5-8; **Half-time:** 12-0;
Referee: Chris Kendall; **Attendance:** 11,956.

LEEDS RHINOS 6 LEIGH LEOPARDS 13

RHINOS: 21 Luke Hooley; 4 Nene Macdonald; 24 Luis Roberts; 12 Rhyse Martin; 5 Ash Handley; 26 Corey Johnson; 7 Aidan Sezer; 18 Tom Holroyd; 14 Jarrod O'Connor; 8 Mikolaj Oledzki; 19 James McDonnell; 11 James Bentley; 13 Cameron Smith (C). Subs (all used): 15 Sam Lisone; 17 Justin Sangare; 25 James Donaldson; 29 Jack Sinfield.
Try: O'Connor (33); **Goals:** Martin 1/1.
Sin bin: Lisone (51) - trip on Briscoe.
LEOPARDS: 17 Gareth O'Brien; 2 Tom Briscoe; 3 Ed Chamberlain; 31 Oliver Gildart (D); 22 Tom Nisbet; 15 Ben Reynolds; 7 Lachlan Lam; 8 Tom Amone; 9 Edwin Ipape; 10 Robbie Mulhern; 24 Kai O'Donnell; 12 Jack Hughes; 13 John Asiata (C). Subs (all used): 18 Matt Davis; 11 Joe Wardle; 27 Ava Seumanufagai; 6 Joe Mellor.
Tries: Ipape (22), Amone (46); **Goals:** Reynolds 2/3;
Field goal: O'Brien (74).
Rugby Leaguer & League Express Men of the Match:
Rhinos: James Bentley; *Leopards:* Ben Reynolds.
Penalty count: 6-5; **Half-time:** 6-4;
Referee: Marcus Griffiths; **Attendance:** 12,785.

SALFORD RED DEVILS 15 ST HELENS 18

RED DEVILS: 1 Ryan Brierley; 2 Ken Sio; 28 Deon Cross; 4 Tim Lafai; 5 Joe Burgess; 6 Brodie Croft; 7 Marc Sneyd; 38 Brad Singleton (D); 9 Andy Ackers; 13 Oliver Partington; 3 Kallum Watkins (C); 12 Sam Stone; 15 Danny Addy. Subs: 8 Jack Ormondroyd (not used); 10 King Vuniyayawa; 14 Chris Atkin; 25 Ben Hellewell.
Tries: Watkins (9), Brierley (15); **Goals:** Sneyd 3/3;
Field goal: Sneyd (40).
Sin bin: Cross (47) - obstruction.
SAINTS: 1 Jack Welsby; 2 Tommy Makinson; 4 Mark Percival; 21 Ben Davies; 25 Tee Ritson; 6 Jonny Lomax; 7 Lewis Dodd; 10 Matty Lees; 9 James Roby (C); 30 George Delaney; 22 Sam Royle; 19 James Bell; 13 Morgan Knowles. Subs: 16 Curtis Sironen; 20 Dan Norman; 24 Lewis Baxter (not used); 35 Moses Mbye.
Tries: Lees (49), Makinson (61), Welsby (70);
Goals: Percival 3/4.
Rugby Leaguer & League Express Men of the Match:
Red Devils: Marc Sneyd; *Saints:* Jack Welsby.
Penalty count: 6-11; **Half-time:** 15-2;
Referee: Jack Smith; **Attendance:** 6,515.

ROUND 1

Sunday 13th August 2023

ST HELENS 32 HUDDERSFIELD GIANTS 18

SAINTS: 1 Jack Welsby; 2 Tommy Makinson; 4 Mark Percival; 21 Ben Davies; 25 Tee Ritson; 6 Jonny Lomax; 7 Lewis Dodd; 30 George Delaney; 9 James Roby (C); 10 Matty Lees; 22 Sam Royle; 11 Sione Mata'utia; 13 Morgan Knowles. Subs (all used): 12 Joe Batchelor; 15 Louie McCarthy-Scarsbrook; 20 Dan Norman; 35 Moses Mbye.
Tries: Makinson (4, 8, 39), Dodd (75), Welsby (79);
Goals: Percival 6/7.
GIANTS: 1 Jake Connor; 14 Ashton Golding; 4 Kevin Naiqama; 5 Jake Bibby; 24 Sam Halsall; 6 Tui Lolohea; 23 Oliver Russell; 8 Chris Hill; 35 Adam Milner; 20 Oliver Wilson; 21 Leroy Cudjoe; 12 Chris McQueen (C); 15 Matty English. Subs (all used): 9 Nathan Peats; 10 Joe Greenwood; 18 Sebastine Ikahihifo; 29 Sam Hewitt.
Tries: English (35), Golding (62), Naiqama (68);
Goals: Russell 1/1, Connor 2/2.
Dismissal: Greenwood (27) - use of the elbow.
Sin bin: English (17) - dangerous challenge.
Rugby Leaguer & League Express Men of the Match:
Saints: Jack Welsby; *Giants:* Jake Connor.
Penalty count: 6-4; **Half-time:** 18-6;
Referee: Ben Thaler; **Attendance:** 12,028.

ROUND 22

Friday 18th August 2023

HUDDERSFIELD GIANTS 8 SALFORD RED DEVILS 32

GIANTS: 1 Jake Connor; 3 Esan Marsters; 4 Kevin Naiqama; 5 Jake Bibby; 24 Sam Halsall; 23 Oliver Russell; 6 Tui Lolohea; 8 Chris Hill; 35 Adam Milner; 20 Oliver Wilson; 21 Leroy Cudjoe; 12 Chris McQueen; 13 Luke Yates (C). Subs (all used): 9 Nathan Peats; 18 Sebastine Ikahihifo; 15 Matty English; 29 Sam Hewitt.
Try: Bibby (17); **Goals:** Russell 2/2.
RED DEVILS: 1 Ryan Brierley; 2 Ken Sio; 28 Deon Cross; 4 Tim Lafai; 5 Joe Burgess; 6 Brodie Croft; 7 Marc Sneyd; 38 Brad Singleton; 9 Andy Ackers; 13 Oliver Partington; 3 Kallum Watkins (C); 12 Sam Stone; 15 Danny Addy. Subs (all used): 8 Jack Ormondroyd; 10 King Vuniyayawa; 14 Chris Atkin; 25 Ben Hellewell.
Tries: Brierley (21), Stone (33, 52), Sio (58), Atkin (73);
Goals: Sneyd 6/6.
Rugby Leaguer & League Express Men of the Match:
Giants: Oliver Russell; *Red Devils:* Marc Sneyd.
Penalty count: 6-6; **Half-time:** 8-12;
Referee: Liam Moore; **Attendance:** 4,685.

ST HELENS 28 HULL KR 6

SAINTS: 1 Jack Welsby; 2 Tommy Makinson; 4 Mark Percival; 21 Ben Davies; 5 Jonathan Bennison; 6 Jonny Lomax; 7 Lewis Dodd; 13 Morgan Knowles; 30 George Delaney; 9 James Roby (C); 11 Sione Mata'utia; 12 Joe Batchelor; 19 James Bell. Subs (all used): 15 Louie McCarthy-Scarsbrook; 20 Dan Norman; 22 Sam Royle; 35 Moses Mbye.
Tries: Mata'utia (36), Makinson (44, 54), Mbye (47), Davies (76); **Goals:** Percival 4/6, Makinson 0/1.
HULL KR: 20 Mikey Lewis; 2 Ethan Ryan; 3 Tom Opacic; 4 Shaun Kenny-Dowall (C); 5 Ryan Hall; 21 Rowan Milnes; 37 Brad Schneider; 15 Rhys Kennedy; 14 Jez Litten; 10 George King; 16 James Batchelor; 12 Kane Linnett; 22 Dean Hadley. Subs (all used): 9 Matt Parcell; 17 Matty Storton; 18 Jimmy Keinhorst; 26 Sam Luckley.
Try: Lewis (62); **Goals:** Schneider 1/1.
Rugby Leaguer & League Express Men of the Match:
Saints: James Bell; *Hull KR:* George King.
Penalty count: 5-4; **Half-time:** 6-0;
Referee: Tom Grant; **Attendance:** 11,258.

WAKEFIELD TRINITY 12 CASTLEFORD TIGERS 28

TRINITY: 1 Max Jowitt; 34 Innes Senior; 43 Josh Griffin (D3); 4 Reece Lyne; 5 Tom Lineham; 7 Mason Lino; 37 Luke Gale; 16 Josh Bowden; 9 Liam Hood; 10 Jai Whitbread; 11 Matty Ashurst (C); 13 Jay Pitts; 19 Kevin Proctor. Subs (all used): 8 Eddie Battye; 15 Liam Kay; 17 Renouf Atoni; 40 David Fifita.
Tries: Jowitt (27), Griffin (31, 53); **Goals:** Jowitt 0/2, Gale 0/1.
TIGERS: 6 Gareth Widdop; 26 Elliot Wallis; 17 Jack Broadbent; 3 Jordan Turner; 2 Greg Eden; 46 Blake Austin (D); 7 Jacob Miller; 32 Liam Watts (C); 45 Liam Horne; 8 George Lawler; 11 Kenny Edwards; 44 Charbel Tasipale; 13 Joe Westerman. Subs (all used): 10 George Griffin; 14 Nathan Massey; 23 Suaia Matagi; 42 Alex Foster.
Tries: Tasipale (8), Eden (36, 40, 80), Foster (48);
Goals: Widdop 4/6.
Rugby Leaguer & League Express Men of the Match:
Trinity: David Fifita; *Tigers:* Charbel Tasipale.
Penalty count: 6-7; **Half-time:** 8-16;
Referee: Chris Kendall; **Attendance:** 4,710.

WIGAN WARRIORS 13 HULL FC 12
(after golden point extra-time)

WARRIORS: 1 Jai Field; 23 Abbas Miski; 3 Toby King; 4 Jake Wardle; 5 Liam Marshall; 2 Bevan French; 7 Harry Smith; 34 Tyler Dupree; 22 Brad O'Neill; 10 Liam Byrne; 17 Kai Pearce-Paul; 12 Liam Farrell (C); 13 Morgan Smithies. Subs (all used): 9 Sam Powell; 20 Patrick Mago; 26 Harvie Hill; 27 Junior Nsemba.
Tries: Marshall (31), King (60), Wardle (77);
Goals: Smith 0/3; **Field goal:** Smith (88).
HULL FC: 25 Davy Litten; 5 Darnell McIntosh; 3 Carlos Tuimavave (C); 4 Liam Sutcliffe; 2 Adam Swift; 6 Jake Trueman; 7 Jake Clifford; 30 Scott Taylor; 9 Danny Houghton; 20 Jack Brown; 17 Cameron Scott; 11 Andre Savelio; 15 Joe Cator. Subs (all used): 10 Tevita Satae; 12 Jordan Lane; 14 Joe Lovodua; 33 Brad Dwyer.
Tries: Swift (40), Dwyer (54); **Goals:** Sutcliffe 2/3.
Sin bin: Tuimavave (76) - dangerous challenge on Wardle.
Rugby Leaguer & League Express Men of the Match:
Warriors: Jake Wardle; *Hull FC:* Jake Clifford.
Penalty count: 9-5; **Half-time:** 4-6;
Referee: Aaron Moore; **Attendance:** 12,107.

Saturday 19th August 2023

LEIGH LEOPARDS 14 CATALANS DRAGONS 30

LEOPARDS: 17 Gareth O'Brien; 5 Josh Charnley; 31 Oliver Gildart; 1 Zak Hardaker; 2 Tom Briscoe; 15 Ben Reynolds; 7 Lachlan Lam; 8 Tom Amone; 6 Joe Mellor; 10 Robbie Mulhern; 12 Jack Hughes; 24 Kai O'Donnell; 11 Joe Wardle. Subs (all used): 9 Edwin Ipape; 13 John Asiata (C); 14 Ben Nakubuwai; 18 Matt Davis.
Tries: Amone (20), Nakubuwai (40); **Goals:** Reynolds 3/3.
DRAGONS: 29 Sam Tomkins; 2 Tom Davies; 3 Adam Keighran; 19 Arthur Romano; 24 Tom Johnstone; 6 Tyrone May; 7 Mitchell Pearce; 8 Mike McMeeken; 9 Michael McIlorum; 16 Romain Navarrete; 11 Matt Whitley; 12 Paul Seguier; 13 Benjamin Garcia (C). Subs (all used): 1 Arthur Mourgue; 10 Julian Bousquet; 15 Mickael Goudemand; 26 Manu Ma'u.
Tries: Pearce (25), Seguier (29), Davies (49), May (56), Ma'u (62); **Goals:** Keighran 5/5.
Sin bin: McMeeken (15) - shoulder charge on Asiata; McIlorum (38) - high tackle on Asiata.
Rugby Leaguer & League Express Men of the Match:
Leopards: Robbie Mulhern; *Dragons:* Mitchell Pearce.
Penalty count: 7-3; **Half-time:** 14-12;
Referee: Jack Smith; **Attendance:** 8,602.

Sunday 20th August 2023

LEEDS RHINOS 24 WARRINGTON WOLVES 22

RHINOS: 21 Luke Hooley; 2 David Fusitu'a; 12 Rhyse Martin; 4 Nene Macdonald; 5 Ash Handley; 26 Corey Johnson; 7 Aidan Sezer; 22 Sam Walters; 14 Jarrod O'Connor; 8 Mikolaj Oledzki; 19 James McDonnell; 11 James Bentley; 13 Cameron Smith (C). Subs (all used): 3 Harry Newman; 15 Sam Lisone; 18 Tom Holroyd; 25 James Donaldson.
Tries: Walters (22), Fusitu'a (49), Hooley (61), Bentley (69);
Goals: Martin 4/4.
WOLVES: 1 Matt Dufty; 2 Josh Thewlis; 3 Peter Mata'utia; 4 Stefan Ratchford (C); 5 Matty Ashton; 6 George Williams; 7 Josh Drinkwater; 18 Thomas Mikaele; 16 Danny Walker; 10 Paul Vaughan; 11 Ben Currie; 12 Matty Nicholson; 36 Jordan Crowther. Subs (all used): 8 James Harrison; 15 Joe Philbin; 9 Daryl Clark; 17 Gil Dudson.
Tries: Dufty (2), Ashton (24), Ratchford (54), Nicholson (72); **Goals:** Ratchford 3/5.
Rugby Leaguer & League Express Men of the Match:
Rhinos: Cameron Smith; *Wolves:* George Williams.
Penalty count: 5-3; **Half-time:** 6-10;
Referee: Ben Thaler; **Attendance:** 15,166.

ROUND 23

Friday 25th August 2023

SALFORD RED DEVILS 20 WAKEFIELD TRINITY 0

RED DEVILS: 1 Ryan Brierley; 2 Ken Sio; 28 Deon Cross; 4 Tim Lafai; 5 Joe Burgess; 6 Brodie Croft; 7 Marc Sneyd; 38 Brad Singleton; 9 Andy Ackers; 13 Oliver Partington; 3 Kallum Watkins (C); 12 Sam Stone; 15 Danny Addy. Subs (all used): 8 Jack Ormondroyd; 10 King Vuniyayawa; 14 Chris Atkin; 25 Ben Hellewell.
Tries: Brierley (4, 78), Ackers (49); **Goals:** Sneyd 4/4.
TRINITY: 1 Max Jowitt; 34 Innes Senior; 43 Josh Griffin; 4 Reece Lyne; 5 Tom Lineham; 7 Mason Lino; 37 Luke Gale; 16 Josh Bowden; 9 Liam Hood; 10 Jai Whitbread; 11 Matty Ashurst (C); 13 Jay Pitts; 15 Liam Kay. Subs (all used): 19 Kevin Proctor; 33 Will Dagger; 17 Renouf Atoni; 40 David Fifita.
Rugby Leaguer & League Express Men of the Match:
Red Devils: Ken Sio; *Trinity:* Matty Ashurst.
Penalty count: 4-7; **Half-time:** 8-0;
Referee: Tom Grant; **Attendance:** 3,836.

CASTLEFORD TIGERS 4 ST HELENS 34

TIGERS: 6 Gareth Widdop; 26 Elliot Wallis; 44 Charbel Tasipale; 3 Jordan Turner; 39 Will Tate; 13 Joe Westerman (C); 7 Jacob Miller; 32 Liam Watts; 45 Liam Horne; 10 George Griffin; 11 Kenny Edwards; 12 Alex Mellor; 8 George Lawler. Subs (all used): 28 Sam Hall; 41 Jordan Johnstone; 42 Alex Foster; 43 Billy Tsikrikas.
Try: Turner (61); **Goals:** Widdop 0/1.
SAINTS: 1 Jack Welsby; 2 Tommy Makinson; 21 Ben Davies; 4 Mark Percival; 5 Jonathan Bennison; 6 Jonny Lomax; 7 Lewis Dodd; 13 Morgan Knowles; 9 James Roby (C); 30 George Delaney; 11 Sione Mata'utia; 12 Joe Batchelor; 19 James Bell. Subs (all used): 15 Louie McCarthy-Scarsbrook; 20 Dan Norman; 22 Sam Royle; 35 Moses Mbye.
Tries: Percival (11), Makinson (18, 36), Bennison (24), Batchelor (27), Lomax (45); **Goals:** Percival 5/6.
Sin bin: Royle (71) - professional foul.
Rugby Leaguer & League Express Men of the Match:
Tigers: Liam Watts; *Saints:* Tommy Makinson.
Penalty count: 4-3; **Half-time:** 0-30;
Referee: Aaron Moore; **Attendance:** 6,868.

HULL KR 52 LEIGH LEOPARDS 10

HULL KR: 34 Jack Walker; 23 Louis Senior; 3 Tom Opacic; 4 Shaun Kenny-Dowall (C); 5 Ryan Hall; 20 Mikey Lewis; 37 Brad Schneider; 15 Rhys Kennedy; 9 Matt Parcell; 10 George King; 16 James Batchelor; 12 Kane Linnett; 13 Elliot Minchella. Subs (all used): 14 Jez Litten; 17 Matty Storton; 22 Dean Hadley; 26 Sam Luckley.
Tries: Kenny-Dowall (11), Minchella (14), R Hall (20, 60), Senior (27), Lewis (38, 41), Linnett (71), Litten (76);
Goals: Schneider 8/11.
LEOPARDS: 17 Gareth O'Brien; 2 Tom Briscoe; 1 Zak Hardaker; 31 Oliver Gildart; 5 Josh Charnley; 15 Ben Reynolds; 7 Lachlan Lam; 14 Ben Nakubuwai; 9 Edwin Ipape; 10 Robbie Mulhern; 24 Kai O'Donnell; 12 Jack Hughes; 13 John Asiata (C). Subs (all used): 6 Joe Mellor; 8 Tom Amone; 11 Joe Wardle; 18 Matt Davis.

Super League XXVIII - Round by Round

Tries: Charnley (54), Ipape (79); **Goals:** Hardaker 1/2.
Rugby Leaguer & League Express Men of the Match:
Hull KR: Elliot Minchella; *Leopards:* Edwin Ipape.
Penalty count: 8-2; **Half-time:** 30-0;
Referee: Jack Smith; **Attendance:** 8,013.

Saturday 26th August 2023

HULL FC 4 WARRINGTON WOLVES 18

HULL FC: 25 Davy Litten; 5 Darnell McIntosh; 17 Cameron Scott; 4 Liam Sutcliffe; 2 Adam Swift; 6 Jake Trueman; 7 Jake Clifford (C); 13 Brad Fash; 33 Brad Dwyer; 10 Tevita Satae; 12 Jordan Lane; 11 Andre Savelio; 15 Joe Cator. Subs (all used): 14 Joe Lovodua; 20 Jack Brown; 27 Will Gardiner; 29 Jamie Shaul.
Try: Swift (15); **Goals:** Sutcliffe 0/1.
WOLVES: 1 Matt Dufty; 2 Josh Thewlis; 3 Peter Mata'utia; 4 Stefan Ratchford (C); 5 Matty Ashton; 6 George Williams; 7 Josh Drinkwater; 18 Thomas Mikaele; 16 Danny Walker; 10 Paul Vaughan; 11 Ben Currie; 12 Matty Nicholson; 8 James Harrison. Subs (all used): 9 Daryl Clark; 14 Sam Kasiano; 15 Joe Philbin; 36 Jordan Crowther.
Tries: Williams (22), Dufty (34), Ashton (56);
Goals: Ratchford 3/3.
Rugby Leaguer & League Express Men of the Match:
Hull FC: Jake Clifford; *Wolves:* Danny Walker.
Penalty count: 6-5; **Half-time:** 4-12;
Referee: Chris Kendall; **Attendance:** 11,624.

CATALANS DRAGONS 0 WIGAN WARRIORS 34

DRAGONS: 29 Sam Tomkins; 2 Tom Davies; 3 Adam Keighran; 19 Arthur Romano; 24 Tom Johnstone; 6 Tyrone May; 7 Mitchell Pearce; 8 Mike McMeeken; 9 Michael McIlorum; 16 Romain Navarrete; 11 Matt Whitley; 12 Paul Seguier; 13 Benjamin Garcia (C). Subs (all used): 1 Arthur Mourgue; 10 Julian Bousquet; 22 Siu Siua Taukeiaho; 26 Manu Ma'u.
WARRIORS: 1 Jai Field; 23 Abbas Miski; 3 Toby King; 4 Jake Wardle; 5 Liam Marshall; 2 Bevan French; 7 Harry Smith; 15 Kaide Ellis; 22 Brad O'Neill; 10 Liam Byrne; 17 Kai Pearce-Paul; 12 Liam Farrell (C); 13 Morgan Smithies. Subs (all used): 9 Sam Powell; 20 Patrick Mago; 27 Junior Nsemba; 34 Tyler Dupree.
Tries: Miski (9, 39, 48), King (22), French (36), Wardle (73);
Goals: Smith 5/7.
Rugby Leaguer & League Express Men of the Match:
Dragons: Adam Keighran; *Warriors:* Bevan French.
Penalty count: 6-6; **Half-time:** 0-22;
Referee: Liam Moore; **Attendance:** 10,614.

Sunday 27th August 2023

HUDDERSFIELD GIANTS 21 LEEDS RHINOS 12

GIANTS: 1 Jake Connor; 3 Esan Marsters; 4 Kevin Naiqama; 5 Jake Bibby; 24 Sam Halsall; 23 Oliver Russell; 6 Tui Lolohea; 8 Chris Hill; 35 Adam Milner; 27 Jack Ashworth; 21 Leroy Cudjoe; 12 Chris McQueen; 13 Luke Yates (C). Subs (all used): 10 Joe Greenwood; 18 Sebastine Ikahihifo; 29 Sam Hewitt; 32 Will Pryce.
Tries: Halsall (10), Naiqama (15), Lolohea (20);
Goals: Russell 2/3, Pryce 2/2. **Field goal:** Connor (75).
Sin bin: Hewitt (37) - professional foul.
RHINOS: 21 Luke Hooley; 16 Derrell Olpherts; 24 Luis Roberts; 3 Harry Newman; 5 Ash Handley; 12 Rhyse Martin; 7 Aidan Sezer; 8 Mikolaj Oledzki; 14 Jarrod O'Connor; 18 Tom Holroyd; 11 James Bentley; 22 Sam Walters; 13 Cameron Smith (C). Subs (all used): 20 Morgan Gannon; 15 Sam Lisone; 25 James Donaldson; 31 Leon Ruan.
Tries: Hooley (32), Handley (54); **Goals:** Martin 2/2.
Rugby Leaguer & League Express Men of the Match:
Giants: Chris Hill; *Rhinos:* Sam Lisone.
Penalty count: 5-7; **Half-time:** 16-12;
Referee: Marcus Griffiths; **Attendance:** 6,621.

ROUND 24

Friday 1st September 2023

HULL KR 26 CATALANS DRAGONS 18

HULL KR: 34 Jack Walker; 23 Louis Senior; 3 Tom Opacic; 4 Shaun Kenny-Dowall (C); 5 Ryan Hall; 20 Mikey Lewis; 37 Brad Schneider; 15 Rhys Kennedy; 9 Matt Parcell; 10 George King; 16 James Batchelor; 12 Kane Linnett; 18 Elliot Minchella. Subs (all used): 14 Jez Litten; 17 Matty Storton; 22 Dean Hadley; 26 Sam Luckley.
Tries: Kenny-Dowall (13), Linnett (37), Walker (42), Lewis (63); **Goals:** Schneider 5/5.
DRAGONS: 29 Sam Tomkins; 2 Tom Davies; 3 Adam Keighran; 19 Arthur Romano; 5 Fouad Yaha; 6 Tyrone May; 7 Mitchell Pearce; 10 Julian Bousquet; 9 Michael McIlorum; 16 Romain Navarrete; 8 Mike McMeeken; 11 Matt Whitley; 13 Benjamin Garcia (C). Subs (all used): 1 Arthur Mourgue; 15 Mickael Goudemand; 23 Jordan Dezaria; 26 Manu Ma'u.

Warrington's Matt Dufty tries to escape the clutches of Hull FC's Jake Clifford

Tries: Navarrete (5), Garcia (28), Yaha (52);
Goals: Keighran 3/4.
Sin bin: Ma'u (62) - high tackle on Opacic.
Rugby Leaguer & League Express Men of the Match:
Hull KR: Jack Walker; *Dragons:* Julian Bousquet.
Penalty count: 8-4; **Half-time:** 12-14;
Referee: Ben Thaler; **Attendance:** 9,102.

LEIGH LEOPARDS 34 HUDDERSFIELD GIANTS 16

(abandoned due to floodlight failure after 48 minutes, remaining 32 played Sunday 3rd September)

LEOPARDS: 17 Gareth O'Brien; 2 Tom Briscoe; 1 Zak Hardaker; 31 Oliver Gildart; 5 Josh Charnley; 15 Ben Reynolds; 7 Lachlan Lam; 10 Robbie Mulhern; 9 Edwin Ipape; 8 Tom Amone; 12 Jack Hughes; 24 Kai O'Donnell; 13 John Asiata (C). Subs (all used): 6 Joe Mellor; 14 Ben Nakubuwai; 29 Frankie Halton; 11 Joe Wardle.
Tries: Charnley (7, 19), Briscoe (33), Ipape (57), Asiata (75), Lam (77); **Goals:** Reynolds 5/6.
GIANTS: 32 Will Pryce; 24 Sam Halsall; 5 Jake Bibby; 4 Kevin Naiqama; 3 Esan Marsters; 1 Jake Connor; 6 Tui Lolohea; 8 Chris Hill; 35 Adam Milner; 15 Matty English; 21 Leroy Cudjoe; 12 Chris McQueen; 13 Luke Yates (C). Subs (all used): 9 Nathan Peats; 20 Oliver Wilson; 29 Sam Hewitt; 18 Sebastine Ikahihifo.
Tries: Connor (14, 43), Halsall (69);
Goals: Pryce 2/2, Connor 0/1.
Rugby Leaguer & League Express Men of the Match:
Leopards: John Asiata; *Giants:* Will Pryce.
Penalty count: 8-2; **Half-time:** 16-6;
Referee: Liam Moore; **Attendance:** 6,064.

WIGAN WARRIORS 26 SALFORD RED DEVILS 8

WARRIORS: 1 Jai Field; 23 Abbas Miski; 3 Toby King; 4 Jake Wardle; 5 Liam Marshall; 2 Bevan French; 7 Harry Smith; 15 Kaide Ellis; 22 Brad O'Neill; 10 Liam Byrne; 17 Kai Pearce-Paul; 12 Liam Farrell (C); 13 Morgan Smithies. Subs (all used): 9 Sam Powell; 19 Joe Shorrocks; 20 Patrick Mago; 27 Junior Nsemba.
Tries: Farrell (21), Miski (33), Wardle (36), Field (40), King (50); **Goals:** Smith 3/5.
RED DEVILS: 1 Ryan Brierley; 2 Ken Sio; 28 Deon Cross; 4 Tim Lafai; 5 Joe Burgess; 6 Brodie Croft; 7 Marc Sneyd; 38 Brad Singleton; 9 Andy Ackers; 13 Oliver Partington; 3 Kallum Watkins (C); 12 Sam Stone; 15 Danny Addy. Subs (all used): 8 Jack Ormondroyd; 10 King Vuniyayawa; 14 Chris Atkin; 25 Ben Hellewell.
Try: Sio (70); **Goals:** Brierley 2/2, Sneyd 0/1.
Sin bin: Vuniyayawa (45) - high tackle on French.
Rugby Leaguer & League Express Men of the Match:
Warriors: Bevan French; *Red Devils:* Brodie Croft.
Penalty count: 6-5; **Half-time:** 20-4;
Referee: Chris Kendall; **Attendance:** 12,905.

Saturday 2nd September 2023

HULL FC 12 LEEDS RHINOS 28

HULL FC: 29 Jamie Shaul; 2 Adam Swift; 4 Liam Sutcliffe; 17 Cameron Scott; 26 Harvey Barron; 14 Joe Lovodua; 7 Jake Clifford; 13 Brad Fash; 9 Danny Houghton (C); 30 Scott Taylor; 12 Jordan Lane; 11 Andre Savelio; 15 Joe Cator. Subs (all used): 1 Tex Hoy; 10 Tevita Satae; 20 Jack Brown; 33 Brad Dwyer.
Tries: Swift (19), Barron (51), Scott (59); **Goals:** Clifford 0/3.
RHINOS: 21 Luke Hooley; 2 David Fusitu'a; 3 Harry Newman; 24 Luis Roberts; 16 Derrell Olpherts; 12 Rhyse Martin; 29 Jack Sinfield; 18 Tom Holroyd; 14 Jarrod O'Connor; 8 Mikolaj Oledzki; 19 James McDonnell; 22 Sam Walters; 13 Cameron Smith (C). Subs (all used): 15 Sam Lisone; 20 Morgan Gannon; 25 James Donaldson; 31 Leon Ruan.
Tries: Hooley (10), Lisone (29, 37, 73), Fusitu'a (42);
Goals: Martin 4/6.
Rugby Leaguer & League Express Men of the Match:
Hull FC: Tevita Satae; *Rhinos:* Sam Lisone.
Penalty count: 4-2; **Half-time:** 4-18;
Referee: Tom Grant; **Attendance:** 11,064.

WARRINGTON WOLVES 66 CASTLEFORD TIGERS 12

WOLVES: 1 Matt Dufty; 2 Josh Thewlis; 3 Peter Mata'utia; 4 Stefan Ratchford (C); 5 Matty Ashton; 6 George Williams; 7 Josh Drinkwater; 18 Thomas Mikaele; 16 Danny Walker; 10 Paul Vaughan; 11 Ben Currie; 12 Matty Nicholson; 8 James Harrison. Subs (all used): 9 Daryl Clark; 14 Sam Kasiano; 15 Joe Philbin; 36 Jordan Crowther.
Tries: Vaughan (16, 76), Dufty (22, 52), Currie (25), Clark (54), Nicholson (58), Ashton (61), Williams (66, 77), Harrison (71); **Goals:** Ratchford 11/11.

263

Super League XXVIII - Round by Round

TIGERS: 6 Gareth Widdop; 26 Elliot Wallis; 44 Charbel Tasipale; 3 Jordan Turner; 2 Greg Eden; 46 Blake Austin; 7 Jacob Miller; 28 Sam Hall; 8 George Lawler; 10 George Griffin; 11 Kenny Edwards; 12 Alex Mellor; 13 Joe Westerman (C). Subs (all used): 25 Brad Martin; 41 Jordan Johnstone; 42 Billy Tsikrikas; 43 Alex Foster.
Tries: Hall (4), Eden (48); **Goals:** Widdop 2/2.
Sin bin: Miller (51) - dangerous challenge.
Rugby Leaguer & League Express Men of the Match:
Wolves: George Williams; *Tigers:* Joe Westerman.
Penalty count: 3-4; **Half-time:** 18-6;
Referee: Jack Smith; **Attendance:** 9,103.

Sunday 3rd September 2023

WAKEFIELD TRINITY 16 ST HELENS 32

TRINITY: 33 Will Dagger; 34 Innes Senior; 41 Romain Franco; 38 Jack Croft; 18 Lee Kershaw; 7 Mason Lino; 37 Luke Gale; 16 Josh Bowden; 9 Liam Hood; 17 Renouf Atoni; 11 Matty Ashurst (C); 43 Josh Griffin; 13 Jay Pitts. Subs (all used): 15 Liam Kay; 40 David Fifita; 8 Eddie Battye; 25 Sam Eseh.
Tries: Ashurst (8), Kershaw (46, 78);
Goals: Dagger 1/1, Lino 1/2.
SAINTS: 1 Jack Welsby; 2 Tommy Makinson; 23 Konrad Hurrell; 4 Mark Percival; 5 Jonathan Bennison; 6 Jonny Lomax; 7 Lewis Dodd; 10 Matty Lees; 9 James Roby (C); 30 George Delaney; 11 Sione Mata'utia; 12 Joe Batchelor; 19 James Bell. Subs (all used): 15 Louie McCarthy-Scarsbrook; 20 Dan Norman; 22 Sam Royle; 35 Moses Mbye.
Tries: Lomax (3), Makinson (18, 50), Roby (34), Bennison (38), Dodd (57); **Goals:** Percival 4/6.
Rugby Leaguer & League Express Men of the Match:
Trinity: David Fifita; *Saints:* Tommy Makinson.
Penalty count: 3-5; **Half-time:** 6-20;
Referee: Marcus Griffiths; **Attendance:** 4,544.

ROUND 25

Friday 8th September 2023

WAKEFIELD TRINITY 10 CATALANS DRAGONS 18

TRINITY: 1 Max Jowitt; 34 Innes Senior; 43 Josh Griffin; 38 Jack Croft; 18 Lee Kershaw; 7 Mason Lino; 37 Luke Gale; 17 Renouf Atoni; 9 Liam Hood; 8 Eddie Battye; 19 Kevin Proctor; 11 Matty Ashurst; 13 Jay Pitts. Subs (all used): 15 Liam Kay; 12 Kelepi Tanginoa; 40 David Fifita (C); 25 Sam Eseh.
Tries: Tanginoa (75), Kershaw (79);
Goals: Lino 0/1, Jowitt 1/1.
Sin bin: Eseh (29) - dangerous challenge.
DRAGONS: 1 Arthur Mourgue; 2 Tom Davies; 3 Adam Keighran; 11 Arthur Romano; 24 Tom Johnstone; 29 Sam Tomkins; 7 Mitchell Pearce; 8 Mike McMeeken; 9 Michael McIlorum; 16 Romain Navarrete; 11 Matt Whitley; 12 Paul Seguier; 13 Benjamin Garcia (C). Subs (all used): 10 Julian Bousquet; 14 Alrix Da Costa; 18 Tiaki Chan; 26 Manu Ma'u.
Tries: Johnstone (7), Keighran (17), Davies (61);
Goals: Keighran 3/4.
Rugby Leaguer & League Express Men of the Match:
Trinity: Kelepi Tanginoa; *Dragons:* Sam Tomkins.
Penalty count: 5-8; **Half-time:** 0-12;
Referee: Aaron Moore; **Attendance:** 3,348.

HUDDERSFIELD GIANTS 18 HULL KR 26

GIANTS: 32 Will Pryce; 24 Sam Halsall; 3 Esan Marsters; 4 Kevin Naiqama; 2 Jermaine McGillvary; 1 Jake Connor; 6 Tui Lolohea; 18 Sebastine Ikahihifo; 9 Nathan Peats; 27 Jack Ashworth; 29 Sam Hewitt; 22 Harvey Livett; 13 Luke Yates (C). Subs (all used): 10 Joe Greenwood; 12 Chris McQueen; 19 Adam O'Brien; 20 Oliver Wilson.
Tries: Pryce (6), McGillvary (57), Halsall (74);
Goals: Connor 3/4.
Sin bin: Connor (40) - fighting;
Ashworth (60) - high tackle on Abdull.
HULL KR: 34 Jack Walker; 23 Louis Senior; 3 Tom Opacic; 4 Shaun Kenny-Dowall; 5 Ryan Hall; 20 Mikey Lewis; 37 Brad Schneider; 29 Sam Kenny; 9 Matt Parcell; 10 George King; 18 Jimmy Keinhorst; 12 Kane Linnett; 22 Dean Hadley. Subs (all used): 7 Jordan Abdull; 14 Jez Litten; 17 Matty Storton; 26 Sam Luckley.
Tries: Kenny-Dowall (23), Abdull (33), Linnett (52), Senior (72); **Goals:** Schneider 5/6.
Sin bin: Senior (40) - fighting.
Rugby Leaguer & League Express Men of the Match:
Giants: Jermaine McGillvary; *Hull KR:* Jordan Abdull.
Penalty count: 5-9; **Half-time:** 6-14;
Referee: Tom Grant; **Attendance:** 4,628.

CASTLEFORD TIGERS 29 HULL FC 12

TIGERS: 6 Gareth Widdop; 31 Jason Qareqare; 3 Jordan Turner; 17 Jack Broadbent; 26 Elliot Wallis; 2 Greg Eden; 46 Blake Austin; 32 Liam Watts; 41 Jordan Johnstone; 20 Muizz Mustapha; 11 Kenny Edwards; 12 Alex Mellor; 13 Joe Westerman. Subs (all used): 10 George Griffin; 14 Nathan Massey (C); 24 Cain Robb; 42 Alex Foster.
Tries: Qareqare (3, 25), Eden (33), Foster (67), Turner (75); **Goals:** Widdop 4/6; **Field goal:** Austin (65).
HULL FC: 25 Davy Litten; 2 Adam Swift; 17 Cameron Scott; 3 Carlos Tuimavave (C); 5 Darnell McIntosh; 14 Joe Lovodua; 1 Tex Hoy; 13 Brad Fash; 9 Danny Houghton; 10 Tevita Satae; 12 Jordan Lane; 11 Andre Savelio; 15 Joe Cator. Subs (all used): 20 Jack Brown; 30 Scott Taylor; 31 Nick Staveley; 33 Brad Dwyer.
Tries: Swift (11, 72); **Goals:** McIntosh 2/2.
Sin bin: Litten (58) - high tackle on Qareqare.
Rugby Leaguer & League Express Men of the Match:
Tigers: Jason Qareqare; *Hull FC:* Adam Swift.
Penalty count: 4-3; **Half-time:** 18-6;
Referee: Ben Thaler; **Attendance:** 7,947.

ST HELENS 22 LEIGH LEOPARDS 12

SAINTS: 1 Jack Welsby; 2 Tommy Makinson; 4 Mark Percival; 21 Ben Davies; 5 Jonathan Bennison; 6 Jonny Lomax; 7 Lewis Dodd; 10 Matty Lees; 9 James Roby (C); 30 George Delaney; 11 Sione Mata'utia; 12 Joe Batchelor; 19 James Bell. Subs: 15 Louie McCarthy-Scarsbrook; 22 Sam Royle (not used); 30 George Delaney; 35 Moses Mbye.
Tries: Makinson (18, 51), Lomax (58), Batchelor (77);
Goals: Percival 3/4.
LEOPARDS: 17 Gareth O'Brien; 2 Tom Briscoe; 3 Ed Chamberlain; 1 Zak Hardaker; 31 Oliver Gildart; 15 Ben Reynolds; 7 Lachlan Lam; 8 Tom Amone; 9 Edwin Ipape; 10 Robbie Mulhern; 24 Kai O'Donnell; 12 Jack Hughes (C); 18 Matt Davis. Subs (all used): 6 Joe Mellor; 29 Frankie Halton; 14 Ben Nakubuwai; 11 Joe Wardle.
Tries: Gildart (9), Mulhern (64); **Goals:** Reynolds 2/2.
Rugby Leaguer & League Express Men of the Match:
Saints: James Bell; *Leopards:* Edwin Ipape.
Penalty count: 2-4; **Half-time:** 6-6;
Referee: Chris Kendall; **Attendance:** 13,428.

Wigan's Abbas Miski breaks past Leeds' Sam Lisone

Saturday 9th September 2023

LEEDS RHINOS 0 WIGAN WARRIORS 50

RHINOS: 21 Luke Hooley; 2 David Fusitu'a; 3 Harry Newman; 12 Rhyse Martin; 5 Ash Handley; 20 Morgan Gannon; 29 Jack Sinfield; 8 Mikolaj Oledzki; 14 Jarrod O'Connor; 18 Tom Holroyd; 19 James McDonnell; 22 Sam Walters; 13 Cameron Smith (C). Subs (all used): 15 Sam Lisone; 25 James Donaldson; 26 Corey Johnson; 31 Leon Ruan.
WARRIORS: 1 Jai Field; 23 Abbas Miski; 3 Toby King; 4 Jake Wardle; 5 Liam Marshall; 2 Bevan French; 7 Harry Smith; 15 Kaide Ellis; 22 Brad O'Neill; 10 Liam Byrne; 17 Kai Pearce-Paul; 12 Liam Farrell (C); 13 Morgan Smithies. Subs (all used): 9 Sam Powell; 20 Patrick Mago; 27 Junior Nsemba; 34 Tyler Dupree.
Tries: Wardle (15, 38, 62), Field (22), Marshall (33), Pearce-Paul (42), Miski (70), Farrell (75), Mago (79);
Goals: Smith 7/9.
Rugby Leaguer & League Express Men of the Match:
Rhinos: Ash Handley; *Warriors:* Jake Wardle.
Penalty count: 6-5; **Half-time:** 0-22;
Referee: Jack Smith; **Attendance:** 12,861.

Sunday 10th September 2023

SALFORD RED DEVILS 24 WARRINGTON WOLVES 20
(after golden point extra-time)

RED DEVILS: 1 Ryan Brierley; 2 Ken Sio; 28 Deon Cross; 4 Tim Lafai; 5 Joe Burgess; 6 Brodie Croft; 7 Marc Sneyd (C); 38 Brad Singleton; 9 Andy Ackers; 8 Jack Ormondroyd; 25 Ben Hellewell; 12 Sam Stone; 14 Chris Atkin. Subs: 10 King Vuniyayawa; 11 Andrew Dixon (not used); 15 Danny Addy; 21 Amir Bourouh.
Tries: Hellewell (23), Croft (31, 65), Stone (84);
Goals: Sneyd 4/4 *(last conversion attempt not taken)*.
WOLVES: 1 Matt Dufty; 2 Josh Thewlis; 3 Peter Mata'utia; 4 Stefan Ratchford (C); 5 Matty Ashton; 6 George Williams; 7 Gareth Widdop; 18 Thomas Mikaele; 16 Danny Walker; 10 Paul Vaughan; 11 Ben Currie; 12 Matty Nicholson; 8 James Harrison. Subs (all used): 9 Daryl Clark; 14 Sam Kasiano; 17 Gil Dudson; 36 Jordan Crowther.

Tries: Nicholson (3), Currie (43), Williams (70);
Goals: Ratchford 4/4.
Rugby Leaguer & League Express Men of the Match: *Red Devils:* Brodie Croft; *Wolves:* Ben Currie.
Penalty count: 3-7; **Half-time:** 12-6;
Referee: Liam Moore; **Attendance:** 6,252.

ROUND 26

Friday 15th September 2023

LEIGH LEOPARDS 20 WAKEFIELD TRINITY 19
(after golden point extra-time)

LEOPARDS: 17 Gareth O'Brien; 2 Tom Briscoe; 31 Oliver Gildart; 3 Ed Chamberlain; 5 Josh Charnley; 15 Ben Reynolds; 7 Lachlan Lam; 8 Tom Amone; 9 Edwin Ipape; 10 Robbie Mulhern; 12 Jack Hughes (C); 24 Kai O'Donnell; 18 Matt Davis. Subs (all used): 6 Joe Mellor; 11 Joe Wardle; 14 Ben Nakubuwai; 16 Oliver Holmes.
Tries: Briscoe (3), Charnley (21), Hughes (43);
Goals: Reynolds 3/4; **Field goals:** O'Brien (76, 89).
TRINITY: 1 Max Jowitt; 18 Lee Kershaw; 38 Jack Croft; 41 Romain Franco; 5 Tom Lineham; 37 Luke Gale; 7 Mason Lino; 8 Eddie Battye; 9 Liam Hood; 10 Jai Whitbread; 11 Matty Ashurst (C); 43 Josh Griffin; 13 Jay Pitts. Subs (all used): 12 Kelepi Tanginoa; 15 Liam Kay; 19 Kevin Proctor; 42 Hugo Salabio.
Tries: Hood (9), Kershaw (46, 51); **Goals:** Lino 3/4;
Field goal: Gale (79).
Sin bin: Proctor (37) - late challenge.
Rugby Leaguer & League Express Men of the Match: *Leopards:* Tom Amone; *Trinity:* Lee Kershaw.
Penalty count: 8-1; **Half-time:** 12-6;
Referee: Tom Grant; **Attendance:** 5,565.

WARRINGTON WOLVES 6 ST HELENS 18

WOLVES: 1 Matt Dufty; 34 Matty Russell; 20 Connor Wrench; 4 Stefan Ratchford; 5 Matty Ashton; 25 Leon Hayes; 7 Josh Drinkwater; 18 Thomas Mikaele; 9 Daryl Clark (C); 10 Paul Vaughan; 11 Ben Currie; 12 Matty Nicholson; 36 Jordan Crowther. Subs (all used): 8 James Harrison; 14 Sam Kasiano; 15 Joe Philbin; 16 Danny Walker.
Try: Clark (56); **Goals:** Ratchford 1/1.
SAINTS: 1 Jack Welsby; 2 Tommy Makinson; 4 Mark Percival; 21 Ben Davies; 5 Jonathan Bennison; 6 Jonny Lomax; 7 Lewis Dodd; 10 Matty Lees; 9 James Roby (C); 11 Sione Mata'utia; 16 Curtis Sironen; 12 Joe Batchelor; 13 Morgan Knowles. Subs (all used): 15 Louie McCarthy-Scarsbrook; 19 James Bell; 22 Sam Royle; 35 Moses Mbye.
Tries: Sironen (12), Percival (20), Mbye (79);
Goals: Percival 3/3.
Sin bin: Bennison (76) - obstruction.
Rugby Leaguer & League Express Men of the Match: *Wolves:* Daryl Clark; *Saints:* Jack Welsby.
Penalty count: 9-4; **Half-time:** 0-12;
Referee: Jack Smith; **Attendance:** 12,855.

WIGAN WARRIORS 48 CASTLEFORD TIGERS 6

WARRIORS: 1 Jai Field; 23 Abbas Miski; 3 Toby King; 4 Jake Wardle; 5 Liam Marshall; 2 Bevan French; 7 Harry Smith; 15 Kaide Ellis; 9 Sam Powell (C); 34 Tyler Dupree; 17 Kai Pearce-Paul; 27 Junior Nsemba; 13 Morgan Smithies. Subs (all used): 19 Joe Shorrocks; 20 Patrick Mago; 26 Harvie Hill; 32 Ryan Hampshire.
Tries: Miski (6, 10, 32, 39, 77), Wardle (17), Powell (42), Pearce-Paul (45), Field (58), French (71);
Goals: Smith 1/5, Hampshire 3/5.
TIGERS: 2 Greg Eden; 31 Jason Qareqare; 3 Jordan Turner; 17 Jack Broadbent; 26 Elliot Wallis; 46 Blake Austin; 7 Jacob Miller; 32 Liam Watts; 45 Liam Horne; 20 Muizz Mustapha; 12 Alex Mellor; 8 George Lawler; 28 Sam Hall. Subs (all used): 10 George Griffin; 14 Nathan Massey (C); 25 Brad Martin; 41 Jordan Johnstone.
Try: Qareqare (22); **Goals:** Austin 1/1.
Sin bin: Austin (56) - dangerous challenge.
Rugby Leaguer & League Express Men of the Match: *Warriors:* Bevan French; *Tigers:* Greg Eden.
Penalty count: 4-2; **Half-time:** 22-6;
Referee: Chris Kendall; **Attendance:** 13,109.

Saturday 16th September 2023

HULL FC 20 HUDDERSFIELD GIANTS 52

HULL FC: 5 Darnell McIntosh; 2 Adam Swift; 17 Cameron Scott; 4 Liam Sutcliffe; 26 Harvey Barron; 1 Tex Hoy; 7 Jake Clifford; 13 Brad Fash; 9 Danny Houghton (C); 10 Tevita Satae; 12 Jordan Lane; 11 Andre Savelio; 15 Joe Cator. Subs (all used): 14 Joe Lovodua; 20 Jack Brown; 30 Scott Taylor; 31 Nick Staveley.
Tries: Hoy (9), McIntosh (17), Savelio (45), Taylor (80);
Goals: Clifford 1/3, Taylor 1/1.
GIANTS: 32 Will Pryce; 24 Sam Halsall; 3 Esan Marsters; 4 Kevin Naiqama; 2 Jermaine McGillvary; 1 Jake Connor; 6 Tui Lolohea; 18 Sebastine Ikahihifo; 35 Adam Milner; 10 Joe Greenwood; 29 Sam Hewitt; 22 Harvey Livett; 15 Matty English. Subs (all used): 12 Chris McQueen (C); 19 Adam O'Brien; 20 Oliver Wilson; 21 Leroy Cudjoe.
Tries: McGillvary (4, 76), Marsters (25), Ikahihifo (29), Naiqama (48, 52, 68), Pryce (57, 62); **Goals:** Connor 8/9.
Rugby Leaguer & League Express Men of the Match: *Hull FC:* Cameron Scott; *Giants:* Tui Lolohea.
Penalty count: 4-1; **Half-time:** 10-16;
Referee: James Vella; **Attendance:** 10,451.

CATALANS DRAGONS 61 LEEDS RHINOS 0

DRAGONS: 29 Sam Tomkins; 2 Tom Davies; 3 Adam Keighran; 21 Matt Ikuvalu; 24 Tom Johnstone; 6 Tyrone May; 7 Mitchell Pearce; 8 Mike McMeeken; 9 Michael McIlorum; 16 Romain Navarrete; 11 Matt Whitley; 12 Paul Seguier; 13 Benjamin Garcia (C). Subs (all used): 10 Julian Bousquet; 14 Alrix Da Costa; 18 Tiaki Chan; 26 Manu Ma'u.
Tries: Keighran (3, 54, 78), Garcia (12), Davies (16, 36), Johnstone (28, 48), Pearce (44), Ikuvalu (66);
Goals: Keighran 9/10, Tomkins 1/1; **Field goal:** Tomkins (73).
RHINOS: 21 Luke Hooley; 2 David Fusitu'a; 3 Harry Newman; 5 Ash Handley; 16 Derrell Olpherts; 12 Rhyse Martin; 29 Jack Sinfield; 8 Mikolaj Oledzki; 14 Jarrod O'Connor; 18 Tom Holroyd; 19 James McDonnell; 20 Morgan Gannon; 13 Cameron Smith (C). Subs (all used): 15 Sam Lisone; 25 James Donaldson; 26 Corey Johnson; 31 Leon Ruan.
Sin bin: Newman (75) - holding down;
Lisone (80) - late challenge on Pearce.
Rugby Leaguer & League Express Men of the Match: *Dragons:* Adam Keighran; *Rhinos:* Cameron Smith.
Penalty count: 5-3; **Half-time:** 28-0;
Referee: Ben Thaler; **Attendance:** 9,162.

HULL KR 12 SALFORD RED DEVILS 0

HULL KR: 34 Jack Walker; 23 Louis Senior; 3 Tom Opacic; 4 Shaun Kenny-Dowall (C); 5 Ryan Hall; 20 Mikey Lewis; 37 Brad Schneider; 22 Dean Hadley; 9 Matt Parcell; 10 George King; 16 James Batchelor; 12 Kane Linnett; 13 Elliot Minchella. Subs (all used): 7 Jordan Abdull; 8 Sauaso Sue; 15 Rhys Kennedy; 26 Sam Luckley.
Tries: Batchelor (22), R Hall (72); **Goals:** Schneider 2/3.
RED DEVILS: 1 Ryan Brierley; 2 Ken Sio; 28 Deon Cross; 4 Tim Lafai; 5 Joe Burgess; 6 Brodie Croft; 7 Marc Sneyd; 25 Ben Hellewell; 9 Andy Ackers; 8 Jack Ormondroyd; 3 Kallum Watkins (C); 12 Sam Stone; 13 Oliver Partington. Subs (all used): 10 King Vuniyayawa; 14 Chris Atkin; 15 Danny Addy; 21 Amir Bourouh.
Sin bin: Vuniyayawa (39) - late challenge on Walker.
Rugby Leaguer & League Express Men of the Match: *Hull KR:* Ryan Hall; *Red Devils:* Ryan Brierley.
Penalty count: 4-4; **Half-time:** 6-0;
Referee: Liam Moore; **Attendance:** 9,848.

ROUND 27

Friday 22nd September 2023

HUDDERSFIELD GIANTS 8 WARRINGTON WOLVES 20

GIANTS: 32 Will Pryce; 24 Sam Halsall; 3 Esan Marsters; 4 Kevin Naiqama; 2 Jermaine McGillvary; 1 Jake Connor; 6 Tui Lolohea; 18 Sebastine Ikahihifo; 35 Adam Milner; 10 Joe Greenwood; 29 Sam Hewitt; 12 Chris McQueen; 13 Luke Yates (C). Subs (all used): 9 Nathan Peats; 15 Matty English; 20 Oliver Wilson; 21 Leroy Cudjoe.
Tries: McQueen (38), Pryce (55); **Goals:** Connor 0/2.
WOLVES: 1 Matt Dufty; 2 Josh Thewlis; 20 Connor Wrench; 4 Stefan Ratchford (C); 34 Matty Russell; 6 George Williams; 7 Josh Drinkwater; 18 Thomas Mikaele; 16 Danny Walker; 8 James Harrison; 11 Ben Currie; 12 Matty Nicholson; 36 Jordan Crowther. Subs (all used): 9 Daryl Clark; 14 Sam Kasiano; 15 Joe Philbin; 19 Joe Bullock.
Tries: Dufty (5), Harrison (10); **Goals:** Ratchford 6/6.
Rugby Leaguer & League Express Men of the Match: *Giants:* Chris McQueen; *Wolves:* Stefan Ratchford.
Penalty count: 5-4; **Half-time:** 4-12;
Referee: Tom Grant; **Attendance:** 5,656.

LEEDS RHINOS 46 CASTLEFORD TIGERS 0

RHINOS: 21 Luke Hooley; 2 David Fusitu'a; 3 Harry Newman; 5 Ash Handley (C); 16 Derrell Olpherts; 12 Rhyse Martin; 29 Jack Sinfield; 22 Sam Walters; 14 Jarrod O'Connor; 8 Mikolaj Oledzki; 19 James McDonnell; 20 Morgan Gannon; 25 James Donaldson. Subs (all used): 15 Sam Lisone; 26 Corey Johnson; 34 Alfie Edgell (D); 36 Tom Nicholson-Watton (D).
Tries: Hooley (11), Fusitu'a (19, 42, 46), Olpherts (29), Sinfield (36), Lisone (58), Walters (68); **Goals:** Martin 7/8.
Sin bin: Lisone (45) - retaliation.
TIGERS: 47 Fletcher Rooney (D); 31 Jason Qareqare; 17 Jack Broadbent; 3 Jordan Turner; 2 Greg Eden; 46 Blake Austin; 7 Jacob Miller; 23 Suaia Matagi; 45 Liam Horne; 14 Nathan Massey (C); 11 Kenny Edwards; 12 Alex Mellor; 8 George Lawler. Subs (all used): 28 Sam Hall; 32 Liam Watts; 20 Muizz Mustapha; 25 Brad Martin.
Sin bin: Watts (45) - late challenge on Sinfield.
Rugby Leaguer & League Express Men of the Match: *Rhinos:* David Fusitu'a; *Tigers:* Liam Horne.
Penalty count: 6-7; **Half-time:** 22-0;
Referee: James Vella; **Attendance:** 15,109.

LEIGH LEOPARDS 6 WIGAN WARRIORS 10

LEOPARDS: 17 Gareth O'Brien; 5 Josh Charnley; 31 Oliver Gildart; 3 Ed Chamberlain; 2 Tom Briscoe; 15 Ben Reynolds; 7 Lachlan Lam (C); 10 Robbie Mulhern; 9 Edwin Ipape; 8 Tom Amone; 24 Kai O'Donnell; 12 Jack Hughes; 11 Joe Wardle. Subs (all used): 6 Joe Mellor; 18 Matt Davis; 14 Ben Nakubuwai; 16 Oliver Holmes.
Try: Lam (36); **Goals:** Reynolds 1/1.
WARRIORS: 1 Jai Field; 23 Abbas Miski; 3 Toby King; 4 Jake Wardle; 5 Liam Marshall; 2 Bevan French; 7 Harry Smith; 34 Tyler Dupree; 22 Brad O'Neill; 15 Kaide Ellis; 17 Kai Pearce-Paul; 12 Liam Farrell (C); 13 Morgan Smithies. Subs (all used): 9 Sam Powell; 20 Patrick Mago; 26 Harvie Hill; 27 Junior Nsemba.
Tries: Field (18), Wardle (28); **Goals:** Smith 1/2.
Rugby Leaguer & League Express Men of the Match: *Leopards:* Edwin Ipape; *Warriors:* Jai Field.
Penalty count: 2-2; **Half-time:** 6-10;
Referee: Liam Moore; **Attendance:** 10,308.

SALFORD RED DEVILS 8 CATALANS DRAGONS 19

RED DEVILS: 1 Ryan Brierley; 2 Ken Sio; 28 Deon Cross; 4 Tim Lafai; 5 Joe Burgess; 6 Brodie Croft; 7 Marc Sneyd; 8 Jack Ormondroyd; 21 Amir Bourouh; 38 Brad Singleton; 3 Kallum Watkins (C); 12 Sam Stone; 13 Oliver Partington. Subs (all used): 14 Chris Atkin; 15 Danny Addy; 19 Adam Sidlow; 25 Ben Hellewell.
Try: Hellewell (57); **Goals:** Sneyd 2/2.
Sin bin: Bourouh (36) - fighting.
DRAGONS: 29 Sam Tomkins; 2 Tom Davies; 19 Arthur Romano; 21 Matt Ikuvalu; 24 Tom Johnstone; 6 Tyrone May; 7 Mitchell Pearce; 16 Romain Navarrete; 9 Michael McIlorum; 23 Jordan Dezaria; 11 Matt Whitley; 8 Mike McMeeken; 13 Benjamin Garcia (C). Subs (all used): 14 Alrix Da Costa; 10 Julian Bousquet; 18 Tiaki Chan; 26 Manu Ma'u.
Tries: Whitley (10), Bousquet (70), Tomkins (74);
Goals: Tomkins 3/4; **Field goal:** Tomkins (67).
Sin bin: Tomkins (36) - fighting; May (39) - delaying restart.
Rugby Leaguer & League Express Men of the Match: *Red Devils:* Marc Sneyd; *Dragons:* Sam Tomkins.
Penalty count: 5-6; **Half-time:** 2-8;
Referee: Jack Smith; **Attendance:** 4,212.

ST HELENS 30 HULL FC 12

SAINTS: 1 Jack Welsby; 2 Tommy Makinson; 23 Konrad Hurrell; 4 Mark Percival; 3 Will Hopoate; 6 Jonny Lomax; 7 Lewis Dodd; 10 Matty Lees; 9 James Roby (C); 11 Sione Mata'utia; 12 Joe Batchelor; 16 Curtis Sironen; 13 Morgan Knowles. Subs (all used): 8 Alex Walmsley; 15 Louie McCarthy-Scarsbrook; 30 George Delaney; 35 Moses Mbye.
Tries: Percival (19), Dodd (42), Lomax (65), Welsby (67, 80);
Goals: Percival 5/5, Dodd 0/1.
HULL FC: 25 Davy Litten; 35 Lewis Martin (D); 3 Carlos Tuimavave (C); 17 Cameron Scott; 5 Darnell McIntosh; 1 Tex Hoy; 7 Jake Clifford; 10 Tevita Satae; 33 Brad Dwyer; 30 Scott Taylor; 12 Jordan Lane; 13 Brad Fash; 15 Joe Cator. Subs (all used): 14 Joe Lovodua; 20 Jack Brown; 27 Will Gardiner; 37 Zach Jebson (D).
Tries: Martin (51), Scott (70); **Goals:** Hoy 2/2.
Rugby Leaguer & League Express Men of the Match: *Saints:* Mark Percival; *Hull FC:* Lewis Martin.
Penalty count: 4-5; **Half-time:** 8-0;
Referee: Ben Thaler; **Attendance:** 14,036.

WAKEFIELD TRINITY 12 HULL KR 56

TRINITY: 1 Max Jowitt; 15 Liam Kay; 30 Oliver Pratt; 38 Jack Croft; 18 Lee Kershaw; 33 Will Dagger; 37 Luke Gale; 17 Renouf Atoni; 9 Liam Hood; 16 Josh Bowden; 11 Matty Ashurst (C); 12 Kelepi Tanginoa; 13 Jay Pitts. Subs (all used): 8 Eddie Battye; 42 Hugo Salabio; 44 Harvey Smith (D); 45 Jordan Schofield (D).
Tries: Tanginoa (28), Kay (46); **Goals:** Dagger 2/2.
Sin bin: Jowitt (58) - professional foul.
HULL KR: 34 Jack Walker; 23 Louis Senior; 3 Tom Opacic; 4 Shaun Kenny-Dowall (C); 5 Ryan Hall; 20 Mikey Lewis; 37 Brad Schneider; 26 Sam Luckley; 9 Matt Parcell; 10 George King; 16 James Batchelor; 17 Matty Storton; 13 Elliot Minchella. Subs (all used): 7 Jordan Abdull; 8 Sauaso Sue; 14 Jez Litten; 27 Yusuf Aydin.
Tries: Walker (5), Lewis (9), Storton (34, 65), Schneider (54, 63), Opacic (60), R Hall (73), Litten (75, 79);
Goals: Schneider 8/11.
Rugby Leaguer & League Express Men of the Match: *Trinity:* Oliver Pratt; *Hull KR:* Mikey Lewis.
Penalty count: 3-8; **Half-time:** 6-18;
Referee: Chris Kendall; **Attendance:** 4,710.

Super League XXVIII - Round by Round

Tommy Makinson touches down in St Helens' play-off victory against Warrington

THE ELIMINATORS

Friday 29th September 2023

HULL KR 20 LEIGH LEOPARDS 6

HULL KR: 34 Jack Walker; 23 Louis Senior; 3 Tom Opacic; 4 Shaun Kenny-Dowall (C); 5 Ryan Hall; 20 Mikey Lewis; 37 Brad Schneider; 8 Sauaso Sue; 9 Matt Parcell; 10 George King; 16 James Batchelor; 12 Kane Linnett; 13 Elliot Minchella. Subs (all used): 7 Jordan Abdull; 14 Jez Litten; 17 Matty Storton; 26 Sam Luckley.
Tries: Walker (33), R Hall (38), Luckley (42);
Goals: Schneider 4/5.
LEOPARDS: 17 Gareth O'Brien; 2 Tom Briscoe; 31 Oliver Gildart; 3 Ed Chamberlain; 5 Josh Charnley; 15 Ben Reynolds; 7 Lachlan Lam (C); 8 Tom Amone; 9 Edwin Ipape; 10 Robbie Mulhern; 12 Jack Hughes; 24 Kai O'Donnell; 11 Joe Wardle. Subs (all used): 6 Joe Mellor; 14 Ben Nakubuwai; 16 Oliver Holmes; 18 Matt Davis.
Try: Charnley (57); **Goals:** Reynolds 1/2.
Rugby Leaguer & League Express Men of the Match: *Hull KR:* Matt Parcell; *Leopards:* Josh Charnley.
Penalty count: 6-4; **Half-time:** 14-2;
Referee: Jack Smith; **Attendance:** 9,305.

Saturday 30th September 2023

ST HELENS 16 WARRINGTON WOLVES 8

SAINTS: 1 Jack Welsby; 2 Tommy Makinson; 4 Mark Percival; 3 Will Hopoate; 5 Jonathan Bennison; 6 Jonny Lomax; 7 Lewis Dodd; 10 Matty Lees; 9 James Roby (C); 11 Sione Mata'utia; 12 Joe Batchelor; 16 Curtis Sironen; 13 Morgan Knowles. Subs (all used): 8 Alex Walmsley; 15 Louie McCarthy-Scarsbrook; 19 James Bell; 35 Moses Mbye.
Tries: Dodd (25), Makinson (57); **Goals:** Percival 4/4.
Sin bin: Walmsley (46) - high tackle on Crowther.
WOLVES: 1 Matt Dufty; 34 Matty Russell; 20 Connor Wrench; 4 Stefan Ratchford (C); 5 Matty Ashton; 6 George Williams; 7 Josh Drinkwater; 8 James Harrison; 16 Danny Walker; 14 Sam Kasiano; 11 Ben Currie; 12 Matty Nicholson; 36 Jordan Crowther. Subs (all used): 3 Peter Mata'utia; 9 Daryl Clark; 15 Joe Philbin; 19 Joe Bullock.
Try: Wrench (43); **Goals:** Ratchford 2/2.
Sin bin: Bullock (60) - high tackle on Lees.
Rugby Leaguer & League Express Men of the Match: *Saints:* Jack Welsby; *Wolves:* Stefan Ratchford.
Penalty count: 6-7; **Half-time:** 8-0;
Referee: Ben Thaler; **Attendance:** 13,801.

SEMI-FINALS

Friday 6th October 2023

CATALANS DRAGONS 12 ST HELENS 6

DRAGONS: 29 Sam Tomkins; 2 Tom Davies; 3 Adam Keighran; 21 Matt Ikuvalu; 24 Tom Johnstone; 6 Tyrone May; 7 Mitchell Pearce; 8 Mike McMeeken; 9 Michael McIlorum; 22 Sio Siua Taukeiaho; 11 Matt Whitley; 12 Paul Seguier; 13 Benjamin Garcia (C). Subs: 1 Arthur Mourgue (not used); 10 Julian Bousquet; 16 Romain Navarrete; 26 Manu Ma'u.
Try: Tomkins (79); **Goals:** Keighran 4/4.
SAINTS: 1 Jack Welsby; 2 Tommy Makinson; 4 Mark Percival; 3 Will Hopoate; 5 Jonathan Bennison; 6 Jonny Lomax; 7 Lewis Dodd; 15 Louie McCarthy-Scarsbrook; 9 James Roby (C); 10 Matty Lees; 11 Sione Mata'utia; 16 Curtis Sironen; 13 Morgan Knowles. Subs (all used): 8 Alex Walmsley; 19 James Bell; 30 George Delaney; 35 Moses Mbye.
Try: Hopoate (50); **Goals:** Percival 1/1.
Sin bin: Lees (72) - holding down.
Rugby Leaguer & League Express Men of the Match: *Dragons:* Sam Tomkins; *Saints:* Jack Welsby.
Penalty count: 7-2; **Half-time:** 2-0;
Referee: Chris Kendall; **Attendance:** 11,530.

Saturday 7th October 2023

WIGAN WARRIORS 42 HULL KR 12

WARRIORS: 1 Jai Field; 23 Abbas Miski; 3 Toby King; 4 Jake Wardle; 5 Liam Marshall; 2 Bevan French; 7 Harry Smith; 34 Tyler Dupree; 22 Brad O'Neill; 15 Kaide Ellis; 17 Kai Pearce-Paul; 12 Liam Farrell (C); 13 Morgan Smithies. Subs (all used): 9 Sam Powell; 11 Willie Isa; 20 Patrick Mago; 26 Harvie Hill.
Tries: Marshall (3, 12, 43), Field (6, 54), King (48), Miski (56); **Goals:** Smith 7/7.
HULL KR: 34 Jack Walker; 23 Louis Senior; 3 Tom Opacic; 4 Shaun Kenny-Dowall (C); 5 Ryan Hall; 20 Mikey Lewis; 37 Brad Schneider; 22 Dean Hadley; 9 Matt Parcell; 10 George King; 16 James Batchelor; 12 Kane Linnett; 13 Elliot Minchella. Subs (all used): 7 Jordan Abdull; 14 Jez Litten; 17 Matty Storton; 26 Sam Luckley.
Tries: Minchella (24), Litten (77); **Goals:** Schneider 2/2.
Rugby Leaguer & League Express Men of the Match: *Warriors:* Jai Field; *Hull KR:* Elliot Minchella.
Penalty count: 4-4; **Half-time:** 18-6;
Referee: Liam Moore; **Attendance:** 15,162.

GRAND FINAL

Saturday 14th October 2023

CATALANS DRAGONS 2 WIGAN WARRIORS 10

DRAGONS: 29 Sam Tomkins; 2 Tom Davies; 21 Matt Ikuvalu; 3 Adam Keighran; 24 Tom Johnstone; 6 Tyrone May; 7 Mitchell Pearce; 8 Mike McMeeken; 9 Michael McIlorum; 22 Sio Siua Taukeiaho; 11 Matt Whitley; 12 Paul Seguier; 13 Benjamin Garcia (C). Subs (all used): 1 Arthur Mourgue; 10 Julian Bousquet; 16 Romain Navarrete; 26 Manu Ma'u.
Goals: Keighran 1/1.
Sin bin:
Keighran (20) - dangerous challenge on Pearce-Paul; Davies (43) - obstructing Marshall.
WARRIORS: 1 Jai Field; 23 Abbas Miski; 3 Toby King; 4 Jake Wardle; 5 Liam Marshall; 2 Bevan French; 7 Harry Smith; 34 Tyler Dupree; 22 Brad O'Neill; 15 Kaide Ellis; 12 Liam Farrell (C); 17 Kai Pearce-Paul; 13 Morgan Smithies. Subs (all used): 9 Sam Powell; 11 Willie Isa; 16 Ethan Havard; 20 Patrick Mago.
Try: Marshall (52); **Goals:** Smith 3/3.
Rugby Leaguer & League Express Men of the Match: *Dragons:* Tom Johnstone; *Warriors:* Harry Smith.
Penalty count: 4-6; **Half-time:** 2-2;
Referee: Liam Moore; **Attendance:** 58,137
(at Old Trafford, Manchester).

Wigan's Jai Field races away from Catalans' Paul Seguier and Michael McIlorum during the Super League Grand Final

SUPER LEAGUE RECORDS *1996-2023*

PLAYER RECORDS

COMPETITION
Includes play-off games & Super League Super 8s (2015-2018)

TRIES
Danny McGuire (Hull Kingston Rovers/Leeds Rhinos) (2001-2019) 247

GOALS
Kevin Sinfield (Leeds Rhinos) (1997-2015) 1,566

FIELD GOALS
Lee Briers (Warrington Wolves/St Helens) (1997-2013) 70

POINTS
Kevin Sinfield (Leeds Rhinos) (1997-2015) 3,443

APPEARANCES
James Roby (St Helens) (2004-2023) 495

SEASON
Includes play-off games & Super League Super 8s (2015-2018)
(Play-offs in brackets)

TRIES
Denny Solomona (Castleford Tigers) (2016) 40 (-)

GOALS
Henry Paul (Bradford Bulls) (2001) 178 (13)

FIELD GOALS
Lee Briers (Warrington Wolves) (2002) 11 (-)

POINTS
Pat Richards (Wigan Warriors) (2010) 434 (46)

MATCH RECORDS
Includes play-off games & Super League Super 8s (2015-2018)

TRIES
Bevan French (Wigan Warriors) 7
(v Hull FC (h), 15/7/22)

GOALS
Henry Paul (Bradford Bulls) 14
(v Salford City Reds (h), 25/6/00)

FIELD GOALS
Lee Briers (Warrington Wolves) 5
(v Halifax Blue Sox (a), 25/5/02)

POINTS
Iestyn Harris (Leeds Rhinos) 42
(v Huddersfield Giants (h), 16/7/99)

TEAM RECORDS
Includes play-off games & Super League Super 8s (2015-2018)

HIGHEST SCORE
Bradford Bulls 96 Salford City Reds 16 (25/6/00)

WIDEST MARGIN
Leeds Rhinos 86 Huddersfield Giants 6 (16/7/99)
Bradford Bulls 96 Salford City Reds 16 (25/6/00)
Warrington Wolves 80 Wakefield Trinity Wildcats 0 (11/4/15)

ATTENDANCE RECORDS

GRAND FINAL
73,512 Leeds Rhinos v Wigan Warriors (10/10/15)

PLAY-OFFS
21,790 Wigan Warriors v St Helens (3/10/03)

REGULAR SEASON *(includes Super League Super 8s (2015-2018)*
31,555 Catalans Dragons v Wigan Warriors (18/5/19)
(at Camp Nou, Barcelona)

CHAMPIONSHIP 2023
Club by Club

Championship 2023 - Club by Club

BARROW RAIDERS

DATE	FIXTURE	RESULT	SCORERS	LGE	ATT
4/2/23	Toulouse (h)	L4-24	t:Shaw	13th	2,177
12/2/23	Sheffield (h)	L16-36	t:Gillam,Sammut,Toal g:Shaw(2)	13th	2,094
19/2/23	Swinton (a)	L20-18	t:Toal,Worthington,Johnston g:Shaw(3)	13th	1,139
26/2/23	York (a)	L28-14	t:Bourouh,Toal(2) g:Sammut	14th	1,525
5/3/23	Newcastle (h)	D18-18	t:Stack(2),J Carter g:Shaw(3)	14th	1,752
12/3/23	Swinton (h) (CCR3)	W32-14	t:Langtree,Shaw,Johnston,Evans,Broadbent g:Shaw(6)	N/A	1,161
20/3/23	Batley (a) ●	L24-12	t:Burke,Sammut g:Shaw(2)	14th	1,187
26/3/23	Halifax (h)	W16-12	t:Stack,Thornley,Sammut g:Sammut(2)	13th	1,879
2/4/23	Halifax (a) (CCR4)	L24-18	t:Langtree(2),Corkill g:Sammut(3)	N/A	1,474
7/4/23	Whitehaven (h)	L14-16	t:Johnston,Stack g:Sammut(3)	13th	3,136
16/4/23	Widnes (a)	L23-14	t:Broadbent,Wood g:Shaw(3)	13th	2,772
7/5/23	Bradford (h)	W46-12	t:Broadbent(2),Cresswell(3),Corkill,Toal,Sammut g:Shaw(7)	13th	2,440
13/5/23	London Broncos (a)	L30-16	t:Broadbent,Shaw,Langtree g:Shaw(2)	13th	806
27/5/23	Whitehaven (SB) ●●	W32-16	t:Toal,Cresswell,Sammut,Langtree,Iaria g:Shaw(6)	12th	N/A
4/6/23	Featherstone (a)	L64-6	t:Broadbent g:Archer	13th	2,756
11/6/23	Keighley (h)	W18-16	t:Iaria,Broadbent,Sammut g:Shaw(3)	12th	2,250
18/6/23	Widnes (h)	W26-18	t:Iaria(2),Emslie,Toal g:Shaw(5)	10th	2,150
25/6/23	Halifax (a)	L48-20	t:Gillam,Shaw,Bulman,Johnston g:Shaw(2)	11th	1,744
2/7/23	Batley (h)	L6-12	t:Broadbent g:Shaw	13th	2,096
9/7/23	Sheffield (a)	L36-18	t:Johnston,Burke,Cresswell g:Shaw(3)	13th	1,011
16/7/23	Featherstone (h)	L10-20	t:Shaw,Bulman g:Shaw	13th	2,361
31/7/23	Bradford (a)	W10-14	t:Shaw g:Shaw(5)	11th	2,862
6/8/23	London Broncos (h)	L6-26	t:Corkill g:Shaw	12th	1,786
21/8/23	Whitehaven (a)	W22-23	t:Stack,Bulman,Wilkinson,Evans g:Shaw(3) fg:Johnston	11th	1,176
26/8/23	Toulouse (a) ●●●	L34-10	t:Bulman(2) g:Shaw	11th	2,487
3/9/23	Keighley (a)	L26-20	t:Bulman(2),Wood g:Shaw(4)	12th	1,828
10/9/23	Swinton (h)	W32-14	t:Broadbent(2),Brand(2),Bulman,Shaw g:Shaw(4)	10th	2,117
16/9/23	Newcastle (a)	L36-24	t:Bulman(2),Broadbent,Jackson g:Shaw(4)	10th	904
24/9/23	York (h)	L18-31	t:Johnston,Bulman,Wilkinson g:Shaw(3)	11th	2,292

● Played at FLAIR Stadium, Dewsbury
●● Played at LNER Community Stadium, York
●●● Played at Stade Mazicou, Albi

		APP		TRIES		GOALS		FG		PTS	
	D.O.B.	ALL	Ch	ALL	Ch	ALL	Ch	ALL	Ch	ALL	Ch
Ellis Archer	21/4/04	3(2)	3(2)	0	0	1	1	0	0	2	2
Jack Billington	24/10/04	1(6)	1(6)	0	0	0	0	0	0	0	0
Amir Bourouh	5/1/01	2	2	1	1	0	0	0	0	4	4
Keanan Brand	8/1/99	7	7	2	2	0	0	0	0	8	8
Luke Broadbent	17/12/02	23	22	11	10	0	0	0	0	44	40
Sam Brooks	29/9/93	4(10)	4(8)	0	0	0	0	0	0	0	0
Andrew Bulman	4/10/99	22	21	11	11	0	0	0	0	44	44
Greg Burke	12/2/93	9(14)	8(14)	2	2	0	0	0	0	8	8
Brett Carter	9/7/88	5(4)	5(4)	0	0	0	0	0	0	0	0
Jake Carter	24/11/98	2(7)	1(6)	1	1	0	0	0	0	4	4
Rio-Osayomwanbo Corkill	29/9/02	8(5)	6(5)	3	2	0	0	0	0	12	8
Luke Cresswell	5/5/95	16(7)	15(7)	5	5	0	0	0	0	20	20
Hanley Dawson	25/5/96	(2)	(1)	0	0	0	0	0	0	0	0
Zach Eckersley	10/11/03	3	3	0	0	0	0	0	0	0	0
Charlie Emslie	30/10/00	10(11)	10(10)	1	1	0	0	0	0	4	4
Ben Evans	30/10/92	6(16)	6(14)	2	1	0	0	0	0	8	4
Ellis Gillam	6/10/97	13(4)	12(3)	2	2	0	0	0	0	8	8
James Greenwood	17/6/91	1	1	0	0	0	0	0	0	0	0
Tom Hopkins	21/12/92	2(1)	1(1)	0	0	0	0	0	0	0	0
Anton Iaria	24/1/96	17(1)	15(1)	4	4	0	0	0	0	16	16
Adam Jackson	11/12/92	5(1)	5(1)	1	1	0	0	0	0	4	4
Ryan Johnston	16/3/98	27	26	6	5	0	0	1	1	25	21
Danny Langtree	18/2/91	21	19	5	2	0	0	0	0	20	8
Harvey Makin	17/11/03	4(1)	4(1)	0	0	0	0	0	0	0	0
Nathan Mossop	21/2/88	1(7)	1(7)	0	0	0	0	0	0	0	0
Kavan Rothwell	1/2/03	(3)	(3)	0	0	0	0	0	0	0	0
Jarrod Sammut	15/2/87	22(1)	20(1)	6	6	9	6	0	0	42	36
Connor Saunders	31/5/97	2(6)	1(6)	0	0	0	0	0	0	0	0
Ryan Shaw	27/2/92	24	23	7	6	74	68	0	0	176	160
Jarrad Stack	13/2/88	24	23	5	5	0	0	0	0	20	20
Iain Thornley	11/9/91	1	1	1	1	0	0	0	0	4	4
Shane Toal	11/11/95	28	26	7	7	0	0	0	0	28	28
Jack Wells	21/9/97	15	13	0	0	0	0	0	0	0	0
Tom Wilkinson	19/4/96	7(3)	7(3)	2	2	0	0	0	0	8	8
Josh Wood	15/11/95	24	23	2	2	0	0	0	0	8	8
Greg Worthington	17/7/90	18(4)	16(4)	1	1	0	0	0	0	4	4

'Ch' totals include Championship games only; 'All' totals also include Challenge Cup

Luke Broadbent

LEAGUE RECORD
P27-W8-D1-L18 (11th)
F471, A672, Diff-201, 17 points.

CHALLENGE CUP
Round Four

ATTENDANCES
Best - v Whitehaven (Ch - 3,136)
Worst - v Swinton (CC - 1,161)
Total (excluding Challenge Cup - 28,530
Average (excluding
Challenge Cup) - 2,195
(Down by 129 on 2022)

CLUB RECORDS	
	Highest score: 138-0 v Nottingham City, 27/11/94 Highest score against: 0-90 v Leeds, 11/2/90 Record attendance: 21,651 v Salford, 15/4/38
MATCH RECORDS	Tries: 7 Theerapol Ritson v West Wales, 11/9/2021 Goals: 17 Darren Carter v Nottingham City, 27/11/94 Points: 42 Darren Carter v Nottingham City, 27/11/94
SEASON RECORDS	Tries: 50 Jim Lewthwaite 1956-57 Goals: 135 Joe Ball 1956-57 Points: 323 Jamie Rooney 2010
CAREER RECORDS	Tries: 352 Jim Lewthwaite 1943-57 Goals: 1,099 (inc 63fg) Darren Holt 1998-2002; 2004-2009; 2012
	Points: 2,403 Darren Holt 1998-2002; 2004-2009; 2012 Appearances: 500 Jim Lewthwaite 1943-57

Championship 2023 - Club by Club

BATLEY BULLDOGS

DATE	FIXTURE	RESULT	SCORERS	LGE	ATT
5/2/23	London Broncos (a)	W20-30	t:Leak,Buchanan(2),Hodson,Flynn g:Morton,Woods,Meadows(2),White	5th	1,849
12/2/23	Swinton (h)	L16-30	t:Walshaw,Manning,Buchanan g:Meadows(2)	8th	1,551
17/2/23	Sheffield (a)	L36-0		11th	878
26/2/23	Keighley (h)	W28-23	t:Meadows,Kibula,Buchanan(2),Morton g:Meadows(4)	8th	1,624
5/3/23	Halifax (a)	L20-16	t:Morton,McGowan,Kibula g:Meadows(2)	9th	1,703
12/3/23	Wath Brow (h) (CCR3)	W60-0	t:Gledhill,Kaye,Morton(2),Hodson(4),White,Buchanan,Burton g:Meadows(7),Morton	N/A	493
20/3/23	Barrow (h) ●	W24-12	t:Hodson,Kibula,Meadows,Morton g:Meadows(4)	8th	1,187
26/3/23	Whitehaven (a)	W16-18	t:Leak,Kear,Walshaw g:Meadows(3)	7th	1,006
2/4/23	Hunslet ARLFC (a) (CCR4) ●●	W6-80	t:McGowan(2),White(2),Hodson(4),Morton(3),Flynn,Meadows(2),Woods g:Meadows(10)	N/A	579
7/4/23	Featherstone (h)	L18-26	t:Hodson,Gledhill,McGowan g:Meadows(3)	8th	2,309
16/4/23	Bradford (h)	W16-21	t:Walshaw,Hodson g:Hooley(6) fg:Woods	7th	3,330
23/4/23	Keighley (h) (CCR5)	W34-16	t:Walshaw(2),Hodson,Morton,McGowan(2),Meadows g:Meadows(3)	N/A	923
8/5/23	Widnes (h)	W11-4	t:Walshaw g:Hooley(3) fg:Woods	6th	923
13/5/23	Toulouse (h)	W17-16	t:Kear,McGowan(2) g:Hooley(2) fg:Woods	5th	1,331
19/5/23	Hull KR (a) (CCR6)	L50-0		N/A	5,143
28/5/23	Halifax (SB) ●●●	W20-12	t:Kear,Manning,Woods,Meadows g:Meadows(2)	3rd	N/A
4/6/23	York (h)	W14-8	t:Kear,Buchanan,Morton g:Meadows	3rd	2,003
11/6/23	Newcastle (h)	W12-26	t:Morton(2),McGowan,Meadows,Hodson g:Meadows(3)	3rd	694
18/6/23	Swinton (a)	W6-48	t:Meadows,Buchanan,Brown,Hodson,Morton,Gledhill,Manning,Hirst g:Meadows(8)	2nd	1,009
25/6/23	London Broncos (h)	L18-20	t:Morton(2),Hodson g:Meadows(3)	4th	1,372
2/7/23	Barrow (a)	W6-12	t:Meadows,Hodson g:Meadows(2)	3rd	2,096
9/7/23	Halifax (h)	W42-0	t:Hooley(3),Manning(2),Senior,Hodson g:Hooley(7)	2nd	2,014
15/7/23	Toulouse (a)	L34-12	t:Reilly,Meadows g:Hooley(2)	3rd	3,557
23/7/23	York (a) (1895CSF)	W8-22	t:Hodson,Gledhill,Leak g:Hooley(5)	N/A	1,646
29/7/23	Featherstone (a)	L28-8	t:McGowan,Morton	4th	3,145
6/8/23	Bradford (a)	L6-42	t:McGowan g:Meadows	4th	2,780
12/8/23	Halifax (1895CF) ●●●●	L10-12	t:Morton,Kear g:Hooley	N/A	N/A
20/8/23	Keighley (a)	L26-20	t:McGowan(2),Morton,Meadows g:Meadows(2)	5th	1,468
25/8/23	Sheffield (h)	L6-49	t:Meadows g:Morton	6th	1,209
3/9/23	Widnes (h)	L12-4	t:McGowan	7th	3,219
10/9/23	Whitehaven (h)	W25-12	t:Meadows(2),Morton(2) g:Morton(4) fg:Woods	6th	1,172
18/9/23	York (a)	L15-14	t:Walshaw,Meadows,Morton g:Morton	8th	2,377
23/9/23	Newcastle (h)	W32-18	t:Leak,Meadows(2),Manning,Kear,Campbell g:Morton(4)	7th	1,070

● *Played at FLAIR Stadium, Dewsbury* ●● *Played at Fox's Biscuits Stadium* ●●● *Played at LNER Community Stadium, York* ●●●● *Played at Wembley Stadium*

		APP		TRIES		GOALS		FG		PTS	
	D.O.B.	ALL	Ch	ALL	Ch	ALL	Ch	ALL	Ch	ALL	Ch
Luke Blake	10/8/89	11(4)	11(3)	0	0	0	0	0	0	0	0
James Brown	6/5/88	20	16	1	1	0	0	0	0	4	4
Kieran Buchanan	26/1/98	33	27	8	7	0	0	0	0	32	28
Oli Burton	15/3/02	(5)	(4)	1	0	0	0	0	0	4	0
Johnny Campbell	17/7/87	9(2)	6(2)	1	1	0	0	0	0	4	4
Nyle Flynn	27/7/97	5(26)	3(22)	2	1	0	0	0	0	8	4
Adam Gledhill	15/2/93	18(8)	13(7)	4	2	0	0	0	0	16	8
Keegan Hirst	13/12/88	4(4)	4(3)	1	1	0	0	0	0	4	4
Josh Hodson	15/6/00	29	23	19	9	0	0	0	0	76	36
Luke Hooley	1/8/98	10	8	3	3	28	22	0	0	68	56
Greg Johnson	20/2/90	4(1)	3(1)	0	0	0	0	0	0	0	0
Ben Kaye	19/12/88	13	10	1	0	0	0	0	0	4	0
Elliot Kear	29/11/88	25	21	6	5	0	0	0	0	24	20
Samy Kibula	7/8/99	4(15)	4(11)	3	3	0	0	0	0	12	12
Alistair Leak	5/4/92	7(15)	6(13)	4	3	0	0	0	0	16	12
Tom Lillycrop	29/11/91	11(3)	9(1)	0	0	0	0	0	0	0	0
Dane Manning	15/4/89	30	26	6	6	0	0	0	0	24	24
Aidan McGowan	12/3/02	28	22	14	10	0	0	0	0	56	40
James Meadows	15/6/99	24(7)	20(5)	17	14	60	40	0	0	188	136
Dale Morton	31/10/90	28	23	21	14	12	11	0	0	108	78
Martyn Reilly	5/1/96	28(3)	22(3)	1	1	0	0	0	0	4	4
Toby Richardson	5/6/96	(1)		0	0	0	0	0	0	0	0
George Senior	29/8/99	9(4)	9(4)	1	1	0	0	0	0	4	4
Lucas Walshaw	4/8/92	22(1)	18(1)	7	5	0	0	0	0	28	20
Michael Ward	10/2/91	(29)	(25)	0	0	0	0	0	0	0	0
Ben White	27/10/94	33	27	3	0	1	1	0	0	14	2
Josh Woods	13/12/97	24(3)	20(2)	2	1	1	1	4	4	14	10

'Ch' totals include Championship games only; 'All' totals also include Challenge Cup & 1895 Cup

James Meadows

LEAGUE RECORD
P27-W15-D0-L12 (7th)
F506, A519, Diff-13, 30 points.

CHALLENGE CUP
Round Six

1895 CUP
Runners-up

ATTENDANCES
Best - v Bradford (Ch - 2,780)
Worst - v Wath Brow (CC - 493)
Total (excluding Challenge Cup) - 20,545
Average (excluding Challenge Cup) - 1,580
(Up by 250 on 2022)

CLUB RECORDS
MATCH RECORDS Highest score: 100-4 v Gateshead, 17/3/2010 Highest score against: 9-78 v Wakefield, 26/8/67 Record attendance: 23,989 v Leeds, 14/3/25
Tries: 5 Joe Oakland v Bramley, 19/12/1908; Tommy Brannan v Swinton, 17/1/1920; Jim Wale v Bramley, 4/12/26; Jim Wale v Cottingham, 12/2/27; Tommy Oldroyd v Highfield, 6/3/94; Ben Feehan v Halifax, 10/8/2008; Jermaine McGillvary v Whitehaven, 24/5/2009
Goals: 16 Gareth Moore v Gateshead, 17/3/2010 Points: 40 Gareth Moore v Gateshead, 17/3/2010
SEASON RECORDS Tries: 30 Johnny Campbell 2010 Goals: 144 Barry Eaton 2004 Points: 308 Richard Price 1997
CAREER RECORDS Tries: 142 Craig Lingard 1998-2008 Goals: 463 Wharton 'Wattie' Davies 1897-1912 Points: 1,297 Wharton 'Wattie' Davies 1897-1912
Appearances: 421 Wharton 'Wattie' Davies 1897-1912

Championship 2023 - Club by Club

BRADFORD BULLS

DATE	FIXTURE	RESULT	SCORERS	LGE	ATT
5/2/23	Whitehaven (h)	W24-8	t:C Butler,Gill(2),Flanagan g:Patton(4)	3rd	4,878
13/2/23	York (a)	L32-16	t:Foggin-Johnston,Thompson,Lilley g:Patton(2)	7th	2,381
19/2/23	Widnes (h)	W14-12	t:Foggin-Johnston,Blackmore,Holmes g:Patton	6th	4,827
25/2/23	Toulouse (h)	W28-18	t:Flanagan,Arundel,Tindall,Wallace g:Patton(6)	5th	2,798
6/3/23	Featherstone (a)	L26-12	t:Holmes,Gill,Arundel	6th	4,809
12/3/23	York Acorn (h) (CCR3)	W62-6	t:Foster,Flanagan Jr,Gill(3),Scurr(2),Lawford,Appo,Myers,Patton g:Patton(5),Flanagan Jr(4)	N/A	1,143
19/3/23	Sheffield (h)	W32-18	t:Arundel,Flanagan,Holmes(2),Tindall g:Patton(6)	4th	3,004
26/3/23	Keighley (a)	L34-6	t:Tindall g:Patton	6th	4,793
2/4/23	Midlands Hurricanes (a) (CCR4) ●	W18-66	t:Holmes(2),C Butler(3),Arundel,Jowitt(2),Lawford,Rogers,Appo g:Lawford(11)	N/A	1,003
10/4/23	Halifax (a)	W22-26	t:Walters,Baldwinson,Gill,Holmes g:Patton(5)	5th	3,053
16/4/23	Batley (h)	L16-21	t:Jowitt,Foggin-Johnston,Holmes g:Patton,Lilley	6th	3,330
22/4/23	Halifax (a) (CCR5)	L26-0		N/A	2,146
7/5/23	Barrow (a)	L46-12	t:Roberts,Walker g:Patton,Lilley	8th	2,440
14/5/23	Swinton (h)	W44-38	t:Gill,England,Mason(2),Foggin-Johnston(2),Appo g:Patton(8)	7th	2,935
28/5/23	Keighley (SB) ●●	W42-18	t:Blackmore(2),Gill(2),Walker(2),Appo,Foggin-Johnston g:Patton(5)	7th	N/A
2/6/23	Newcastle (h)	W12-28	t:Foggin-Johnston,Holmes,Baldwinson,Appo,Gill g:Patton(4)	5th	2,465
11/6/23	London Broncos (h)	W32-16	t:Blackmore,Holmes(2),Gill(2) g:Patton(6)	5th	3,482
18/6/23	Halifax (h)	D22-22	t:Arundel,Rogers,England g:Patton(5)	5th	4,717
24/6/23	Toulouse (a)	L52-14	t:Blackmore,Gaskell,Gill g:Patton	6th	4,211
2/7/23	Keighley (h)	W74-12	t:Blackmore(2),Wallace(2),Taufua(3),Scurr,Wynne(2),Gill(3) g:Patton(9),Thompson(2)	5th	4,879
10/7/23	Widnes (a)	L31-14	t:C Butler,Gill g:Patton(3)	5th	2,561
16/7/23	Whitehaven (a)	W18-44	t:Segeyaro,Blackmore,Appo,Gill,Matongo,C Butler,Wallace,Patton g:Patton(6)	5th	1,257
31/7/23	Barrow (h)	L10-14	t:Myers,Blackmore g:Gaskell	5th	2,862
6/8/23	Batley (a)	W6-42	t:Taufua,Blackmore(2),Wallace(2),Appo,Scurr,Lawrence g:Lilley(5)	5th	2,780
20/8/23	Newcastle (h)	W36-8	t:Flanagan(2),Holmes,Arundel,Lilley,Gill g:Lilley(6)	3rd	2,685
27/8/23	Swinton (a)	W26-42	t:Gill,Scurr,Appo,Lilley,Myers,Foggin-Johnston(2),Rogers g:Lilley(5)	3rd	1,073
3/9/23	Featherstone (h)	L8-16	t:Myers,England	3rd	4,567
10/9/23	York (h)	L10-20	t:Wynne g:Lilley(3)	5th	3,603
17/9/23	London Broncos (a)	W10-12	t:Myers(2) g:Lilley(2)	4th	1,158
24/9/23	Sheffield (a)	W16-17	t:Arundel,Tindall,Lilley g:Lilley(2) fg:Lilley	3rd	1,976
1/10/23	York (h) (E)	W22-8	t:Rogers,Appo,Holmes g:Lilley(5)	N/A	2,738
7/10/23	Toulouse (a) (SF)	L38-20	t:Taufua,Arundel,Appo g:Lilley(4)	N/A	4,352

● Played at Odsal Stadium ●● Played at LNER Community Stadium, York

Jordan Lilley

	D.O.B.	APP ALL	Ch	TRIES ALL	Ch	GOALS ALL	Ch	FG ALL	Ch	PTS ALL	Ch
Keven Appo	9/1/99	8(21)	5(21)	10	8	0	0	0	0	40	32
Joe Arundel	22/8/91	26	24	8	7	0	0	0	0	32	28
Jason Baitieri	2/7/89	10(1)	10(1)	0	0	0	0	0	0	0	0
Jordan Baldwinson	10/11/94	15(3)	14(2)	2	2	0	0	0	0	8	8
Jack Bibby	14/10/01	2(1)	2(1)	0	0	0	0	0	0	0	0
Ben Blackmore	19/2/93	25	23	11	11	0	0	0	0	44	44
Chester Butler	10/3/95	22(1)	19(1)	6	3	0	0	0	0	24	12
Rob Butler	15/5/98	(2)	(1)	0	0	0	0	0	0	0	0
James Donaldson	14/9/91	1	1	0	0	0	0	0	0	0	0
Eribe Doro	26/3/01	4(4)	4(4)	0	0	0	0	0	0	0	0
Brad England	20/11/94	7(6)	7(6)	3	3	0	0	0	0	12	12
George Flanagan	8/10/86	19(3)	18(3)	5	5	0	0	0	0	20	20
George Flanagan Jr	24/12/04	1	0	1	0	4	0	0	0	12	0
David Foggin-Johnston	19/8/96	17	15	9	9	0	0	0	0	36	36
Brad Foster	28/8/95	5(4)	3(3)	1	0	0	0	0	0	4	0
Lee Gaskell	28/10/90	13	13	1	1	1	1	0	0	6	6
Kieran Gill	4/12/95	31	29	21	18	0	0	0	0	84	72
Marcus Green	27/3/03	(1)	0	0	0	0	0	0	0	0	0
Tom Holmes	2/3/96	25	23	13	11	0	0	0	0	52	44
Corey Johnson	16/11/00	(1)	(1)	0	0	0	0	0	0	0	0
Josh Johnson	25/7/94	3(8)	2(6)	0	0	0	0	0	0	0	0
Billy Jowitt	7/4/01	5(11)	4(10)	3	1	0	0	0	0	12	4
Myles Lawford	9/9/03	2	0	2	0	11	0	0	0	30	0
Michael Lawrence	12/4/90	19	19	1	1	0	0	0	0	4	4
Jordan Lilley	4/9/96	29(2)	27(2)	4	4	34	34	1	1	85	85
Nathan Mason	8/9/93	(2)	(2)	2	2	0	0	0	0	8	8
Masi Matongo	15/5/96	6(3)	6(3)	1	1	0	0	0	0	4	4
Jayden Myers	13/4/03	12	9	6	5	0	0	0	0	24	20
Daniel Okoro	18/4/03	(2)	(2)	0	0	0	0	0	0	0	0
Dec Patton	23/5/95	22	20	2	1	79	74	0	0	166	152
Jason Qareqare	26/1/04	2	1	0	0	0	0	0	0	0	0
Luis Roberts	24/3/02	3	3	1	1	0	0	0	0	4	4
George Roby	3/5/02	(5)	(5)	0	0	0	0	0	0	0	0
Fenton Rogers	4/8/03	15(1)	14(9)	4	3	0	0	0	0	16	12
Leon Ruan	14/5/03	2	2	0	0	0	0	0	0	0	0
Ebon Scurr	11/5/00	3(22)	3(21)	5	3	0	0	0	0	20	12
James Segeyaro	11/7/90	1(6)	1(6)	1	1	0	0	0	0	4	4
Jorge Taufua	23/10/91	7	7	5	5	0	0	0	0	20	20
Bodene Thompson	1/8/88	13	12	1	1	2	2	0	0	8	8
Liam Tindall	27/9/01	7	7	4	4	0	0	0	0	16	16
Jansin Turgut	8/3/96	(2)	(1)	0	0	0	0	0	0	0	0
Jack Walker	8/8/99	7	6	3	3	0	0	0	0	12	12
AJ Wallace	31/3/03	21(3)	20(3)	6	6	0	0	0	0	24	24
Sam Walters	25/12/00	1	1	1	1	0	0	0	0	4	4
Connor Wynne	15/1/01	5(2)	5(2)	3	3	0	0	0	0	12	12

'Ch' totals include regular season & play-offs; 'All' totals also include Challenge Cup

LEAGUE RECORD
P27-W16-D1-L10 (3rd/Semi-Final)
F677, A572, Diff+105, 33 points.

CHALLENGE CUP
Round Five

ATTENDANCES
Best - v Keighley (Ch - 4,879)
Worst - v Midlands Hurricanes (CC - 1,003)
Total (excluding Challenge Cup) - 51,305
Average (excluding Challenge Cup) - 3,665
(Up by 174 on 2022)

CLUB RECORDS / MATCH RECORDS
Highest score: 124-0 v West Wales, 6/5/2018 Highest score against: 6-84 v Wigan, 21/4/2014 Record attendance: 69,429 v Huddersfield, 14/3/53
Tries: 6 Eric Batten v Leeds, 15/9/45; Trevor Foster v Wakefield, 10/4/48; Steve McGowan v Barrow, 8/11/92; Lesley Vainikolo v Hull, 2/9/2005
Goals: 20 Dane Chisholm v West Wales, 6/5/2018 Points: 48 Dane Chisholm v West Wales, 6/5/2018

SEASON RECORDS / CAREER RECORDS
Tries: 63 Jack McLean 1951-52 Goals: 213 (inc 5fg) Henry Paul 2001 Points: 457 Henry Paul 2001
Tries: 261 Jack McLean 1950-56 Goals: 1,165 (inc 25fg) Paul Deacon 1998-2009 Points: 2,605 Paul Deacon 1998-2009
Appearances: 588 Keith Mumby 1973-90; 1992-93

Championship 2023 - Club by Club

FEATHERSTONE ROVERS

DATE	FIXTURE	RESULT	SCORERS	LGE	ATT
6/2/23	Keighley (a)	W0-50	t:Gale(2),Dean(2),Day,Lockwood,Yei,Hardcastle,Aekins g:Hankinson(7)	1st	2,443
12/2/23	Halifax (h)	W46-22	t:Hankinson(2),Springer,Wildie,Aekins,Dean,Jones,Gale g:Hankinson(7)	2nd	3,794
19/2/23	Whitehaven (h)	W76-4	t:Leilua(2),Lacans,Kopczak,Davies,Yei,Dean,Gale(3),Bussey,Jones,Aekins,Briscoe g:Hall(10)	1st	2,248
26/2/23	Newcastle (h)	W56-6	t:Hardcastle(2),Day,Bussey(2),Yei,Jones,Leilua(2),Briscoe g:Dean(8)	1st	2,489
6/3/23	Bradford (h)	W26-12	t:Dean,Briscoe,Gale,Davies,Ford g:Dean(3)	1st	4,809
12/3/23	Halifax (h) (CCR3)	L18-22	t:Hardcastle,Lacans,Springer g:Hall(3)	N/A	1,487
19/3/23	Swinton (a)	W6-34	t:Gale,Evans(2),Hardcastle,Lacans,Jones,Aekins g:Dean(3)	1st	1,090
26/3/23	York (h)	W46-4	t:Cozza,Taylor,Evans,Jones,Gale(3),Leilua g:Hall(7)	1st	2,892
7/4/23	Batley (a)	W18-26	t:Hardcastle(2),Briscoe,Leilua,Jones g:Hall(3)	1st	2,309
16/4/23	London Broncos (a)	W10-40	t:Aekins(2),Day(2),Jones(3) g:Dean(6)	1st	977
7/5/23	Sheffield (h)	W28-20	t:Hardcastle,Briscoe,Bussey,Aekins g:Dean(3),Bussey	1st	3,187
14/5/23	Widnes (a)	W0-30	t:Gale(3),Bussey,Hall,Jones g:Hall(3)	1st	2,832
27/5/23	York (SB) ●	W46-16	t:Gale(4),Springer,Yei,Jones,Ford,Lacans g:Smith,Bussey(4)	1st	N/A
4/6/23	Barrow (h)	W64-6	t:Hall,Briscoe,Aekins,Gale,Yei,Hankinson,Hau,Bussey,Jones(2),Lacans g:Hall(10)	1st	2,756
10/6/23	Toulouse (h)	L18-36	t:Hall,Briscoe,Davies,Hankinson g:Hall	1st	3,489
18/6/23	London Broncos (h)	W50-6	t:Aekins(2),Wildie,Leilua,Lacans,Jones,Day,Kheirallah,Gale g:Kheirallah(7)	1st	2,255
25/6/23	York (a)	W8-24	t:Leilua(2),Kheirallah,Jones g:Kheirallah(4)	1st	2,554
2/7/23	Whitehaven (a)	W0-60	t:Jones,Springer,Cozza(2),Aekins(2),Hau,Kheirallah(2),Briscoe,Leilua g:Kheirallah(8)	1st	841
9/7/23	Swinton (h)	W52-6	t:Hau(2),Kheirallah,Briscoe,Hall(2),Jones,Springer,Lacans g:Kheirallah(8)	1st	2,845
16/7/23	Barrow (a)	W10-20	t:Gale,Hall,Briscoe,Hau g:Kheirallah(2)	1st	2,361
29/7/23	Batley (h)	W28-8	t:Taylor,Wildie,Smith,Hau(2) g:Hankinson(4)	1st	3,145
6/8/23	Halifax (a)	L25-22	t:Springer,Kheirallah,Kopczak,Briscoe g:Kheirallah(3)	1st	1,609
18/8/23	Sheffield (a)	W10-38	t:Hau(2),Aekins,Moors,Hankinson,Chisholm,Gale g:Kheirallah(5)	1st	1,709
27/8/23	Keighley (h)	W36-6	t:Kheirallah(2),Gale(2),Jones(2),Leilua g:Kheirallah(4)	1st	3,235
3/9/23	Bradford (a)	W8-16	t:Smith,Gale,Aekins g:Kheirallah(2)	1st	4,567
8/9/23	Newcastle (a)	W22-56	t:Gale(3),Cozza,Hall(2),Taylor,Day,Longstaff,Wildie g:Hall(8)	1st	747
16/9/23	Toulouse (a) ●●	W16-29	t:Lacans,Kheirallah,Taylor,Hall,Jones g:Kheirallah(4) fg:Lacans	1st	2,603
23/9/23	Widnes (h)	W62-10	t:Lacans,Hall,Moors,Gale(2),Aekins(2),Hankinson,Leilua(2),Jones g:Kheirallah(9)	1st	3,874
8/10/23	London Broncos (h) (SF)	L26-36	t:Hankinson(2),Leilua(2),Briscoe g:Kheirallah(3)	N/A	-

● Played at LNER Community Stadium, York
●● Played at Stade des Minimes

		APP		TRIES		GOALS		FG		PTS	
	D.O.B.	ALL	Ch	ALL	Ch	ALL	Ch	ALL	Ch	ALL	Ch
Caleb Aekins	21/11/97	26	26	16	16	0	0	0	0	64	64
Logan Astley	18/5/03	2(1)	2(1)	0	0	0	0	0	0	0	0
Yusuf Aydin	13/9/00	(2)	(2)	0	0	0	0	0	0	0	0
Luke Briscoe	11/3/94	23	22	13	13	0	0	0	0	52	52
Jack Bussey	17/8/92	13(4)	12(4)	6	6	5	5	0	0	34	34
Dane Chisholm	4/7/90	6	6	1	1	0	0	0	0	4	4
Luke Cooper	28/7/94	(1)	(1)	0	0	0	0	0	0	0	0
Mathieu Cozza	12/4/00	17(5)	16(5)	4	4	0	0	0	0	16	16
John Davies	8/1/91	1(23)	1(22)	3	3	0	0	0	0	12	12
Brad Day	23/9/94	20	19	6	6	0	0	0	0	24	24
Riley Dean	10/8/01	11	11	5	5	23	23	0	0	66	66
Kyle Evans	11/9/90	2	2	3	3	0	0	0	0	12	12
Dan Fleming	8/7/92	(2)	(1)	0	0	0	0	0	0	0	0
Johnathon Ford	17/8/89	9(1)	9(1)	2	2	0	0	0	0	8	8
Gareth Gale	5/6/93	29	28	30	30	0	0	0	0	120	120
Craig Hall	21/2/88	13(1)	12(1)	10	10	45	42	0	0	130	124
Chris Hankinson	30/11/93	18	18	8	8	18	18	0	0	68	68
Josh Hardcastle	28/8/92	12(1)	11(1)	8	7	0	0	0	0	32	28
Arama Hau	27/8/04	8(2)	8(2)	9	9	0	0	0	0	36	36
Connor Jones	26/1/96	5(24)	4(24)	21	21	0	0	0	0	84	84
Mark Kheirallah	15/2/90	12	12	9	9	59	59	0	0	154	154
Craig Kopczak	20/12/86	6(9)	6(9)	2	2	0	0	0	0	8	8
Thomas Lacans	7/12/00	15(1)	14(1)	9	8	0	0	1	1	37	33
Joey Leilua	12/12/91	20	19	15	15	0	0	0	0	60	60
James Lockwood	21/3/86	24	24	1	1	0	0	0	0	4	4
Ellis Longstaff	5/7/02	3(1)	3(1)	1	1	0	0	0	0	4	4
Junior Moors	30/7/86	3(11)	3(10)	2	2	0	0	0	0	8	8
Brandon Pickersgill	29/3/97	1	1	0	0	0	0	0	0	0	0
Daniel Smith	20/3/93	14(4)	14(4)	2	2	1	1	0	0	10	10
Gadwin Springer	4/4/93	17(2)	16(2)	6	5	0	0	0	0	24	20
Elijah Taylor	27/2/90	18(1)	17(1)	4	4	0	0	0	0	16	16
Albert Vete	24/1/93	(2)	(2)	0	0	0	0	0	0	0	0
Matty Wildie	25/10/90	27	26	4	4	0	0	0	0	16	16
McKenzie Yei	3/6/97	2(17)	2(16)	5	5	0	0	0	0	20	20

'Ch' totals include regular season & play-offs; 'All' totals also include Challenge Cup

Gareth Gale

LEAGUE RECORD
P27-W25-D0-L2 (1st/Semi-Final)
F1079, A295, Diff+784, 50 points.

CHALLENGE CUP
Round Three

ATTENDANCES
Best - v Bradford (Ch - 4,809)
Worst - v Halifax (CC - 1,487)
Total (excluding Challenge Cup) - 41,018
Average (excluding Challenge Cup) - 3,155
(Up by 104 on 2022)

● Attendance figures do not include Semi-Final v London Broncos (total not given by club)

CLUB RECORDS
MATCH RECORDS Highest score: 96-0 v Castleford Lock Lane, 8/2/2004 Highest score against: 14-80 v Bradford, 3/4/2005 Record attendance: 17,531 v St Helens, 21/3/59
Tries: 6 Mike Smith v Doncaster, 13/4/68; Chris Bibb v Keighley, 17/9/89; Brad Dwyer v Rochdale, 1/7/2018; Gareth Gale v Newcastle, 26/6/2021
Goals: 13 Mark Knapper v Keighley, 17/9/89; Liam Finn v Hunslet Old Boys, 25/3/2012; Liam Finn v Swinton, 12/8/2012
Points: 40 Martin Pearson v Whitehaven, 26/11/95

SEASON RECORDS Tries: 48 Paul Newlove 1992-93 Goals: 183 (inc 2fg) Liam Finn 2012 Points: 436 Liam Finn 2012
CAREER RECORDS Tries: 162 Don Fox 1953-66 Goals: 1,210 Steve Quinn 1975-88 Points: 2,654 Steve Quinn 1975-88 Appearances: 440 Jim Denton 1921-34

Championship 2023 - Club by Club

HALIFAX PANTHERS

DATE	FIXTURE	RESULT	SCORERS	LGE	ATT
5/2/23	Sheffield (h)	W26-18	t:Saltonstall,Walmsley,Maizen(2) g:Keyes(5)	6th	2,101
12/2/23	Featherstone (a)	L46-22	t:Walmsley(2),Woodburn-Hall(2) g:Keyes(3)	10th	3,794
19/2/23	London Broncos (h)	W26-18	t:Jouffret,Saltonstall(2),Walmsley,Doro g:Keyes(3)	7th	1,950
27/2/23	Widnes (a)	L42-14	t:Walmsley(2),Gee g:Jouffret	9th	3,187
5/3/23	Batley (h)	W20-16	t:Walmsley(2),Woodburn-Hall,Saltonstall g:Jouffret(2)	7th	1,703
12/3/23	Featherstone (a) (CCR3)	W18-22	t:Gee,Walmsley,Inman,Jouffret g:Jouffret(3)	N/A	1,487
19/3/23	Keighley (h)	W34-10	t:Saltonstall,Keyes,Kavanagh,Walmsley(2),Inman g:Keyes(5)	5th	2,123
26/3/23	Barrow (a)	L16-12	t:Jouffret,Pickersgill g:Keyes(2)	5th	1,879
2/4/23	Barrow (h) (CCR4)	W24-18	t:Saltonstall(2),Maizen,Jouffret,Doro g:Keyes(2)	N/A	1,474
10/4/23	Bradford (a)	L22-26	t:Moore,Walmsley,Maizen(2) g:Keyes(3)	7th	3,053
16/4/23	York (h)	W16-6	t:Walmsley(2),Fairbank g:Keyes,Jouffret	5th	1,454
22/4/23	Bradford (h) (CCR5)	W26-0	t:Jouffret(2),Saltonstall(2),Maizen g:Keyes(3)	N/A	2,146
7/5/23	Newcastle (a)	W16-36	t:Keyes(2),Walmsley,Woodburn-Hall,McComb,Inman g:Keyes(6)	5th	1,067
14/5/23	Whitehaven (h)	W60-0	t:Walmsley(4),Saltonstall,Woodburn-Hall,Kavanagh,Doro(2),Fairbank g:Keyes(8)	4th	1,998
19/5/23	St Helens (h) (CCR6)	L6-26	t:Fairbank g:Jouffret	N/A	4,693
28/5/23	Batley (SB) ●	L20-12	t:Moore,Woodburn-Hall g:Jouffret(2)	5th	N/A
3/6/23	Toulouse (a)	L28-22	t:McComb,Wood,Moore,Walmsley g:Jouffret(3)	6th	4,806
11/6/23	Swinton (a)	W8-46	t:Tibbs,Walmsley(4),Tangata,Kavanagh,Woodburn-Hall,Moore g:Jouffret(5)	6th	1,109
18/6/23	Bradford (a)	D22-22	t:Gee,Saltonstall,Jouffret,Walmsley g:Jouffret(3)	6th	4,717
25/6/23	Barrow (h)	W48-22	t:Walmsley(4),O'Brien,Kavanagh(2),Fleming,Woodburn-Hall g:Jouffret(6)	5th	1,744
2/7/23	York (a)	L28-18	t:Woodburn-Hall,Saltonstall(2) g:Jouffret(3)	6th	1,823
9/7/23	Batley (a)	L42-0		6th	2,014
16/7/23	Newcastle (h)	W50-12	t:Crooks,Walmsley(2),Gee,Murray,McComb,Kavanagh,Moore g:Jouffret(7)	6th	1,453
22/7/23	London Broncos (a) (1895CSF) ●●	W6-10	t:Walmsley g:Jouffret(3)	N/A	417
28/7/23	Sheffield (h)	L32-30	t:Woodburn-Hall,Fairbank(2),Jouffret,Lannon g:Jouffret(5)	6th	1,327
6/8/23	Featherstone (h)	W25-22	t:Woodburn-Hall(2),Gee,Maizen g:Jouffret(4) fg:Woodburn-Hall	6th	1,609
12/8/23	Batley (1895CF) ●●●	W10-12	t:Moore g:Jouffret(4)	N/A	N/A
20/8/23	London Broncos (a)	L26-12	t:Maizen,Walmsley g:Jouffret(2)	7th	859
27/8/23	Widnes (h)	L26-28	t:Crooks(2),Tangata,Saltonstall g:Jouffret(5)	8th	1,685
3/9/23	Whitehaven (a)	W8-30	t:Woodburn-Hall,Jouffret(2),Kavanagh,Gee g:Jouffret(5)	8th	1,056
9/9/23	Toulouse (h)	W26-18	t:Saltonstall,Woodburn-Hall,Kavanagh,Walmsley g:Jouffret(5)	7th	1,437
17/9/23	Keighley (a)	W22-23	t:Walmsley(2),Sutcliffe,Woodburn-Hall g:Jouffret(3) fg:Jouffret	6th	2,367
24/9/23	Swinton (h)	L12-22	t:Crooks,Walmsley(2)	8th	2,122

● Played at LNER Community Stadium, York ●● Played at The Rock, Roehampton ●●● Played at Wembley Stadium

		APP		TRIES		GOALS		FG		PTS	
	D.O.B.	ALL	Ch	ALL	Ch	ALL	Ch	ALL	Ch	ALL	Ch
Will Calcott	16/12/97	25(6)	21(4)	0	0	0	0	0	0	0	0
Ben Crooks	15/6/93	13	13	4	4	0	0	0	0	16	16
Eribe Doro	26/3/01	(8)	(5)	4	3	0	0	0	0	16	12
Jacob Fairbank	4/3/90	23(2)	18(2)	5	4	0	0	0	0	20	16
Dan Fleming	8/7/92	(8)	(8)	1	1	0	0	0	0	4	4
Mahe Fonua	24/12/92	1	1	0	0	0	0	0	0	0	0
Jacob Gannon	18/3/02	(2)	(2)	0	0	0	0	0	0	0	0
Matty Gee	12/12/94	31(2)	25(2)	7	6	0	0	0	0	28	24
Tom Inman	24/12/02	2(18)	2(14)	3	2	0	0	0	0	12	8
Louis Jouffret	24/5/95	32	26	10	6	73	62	1	1	187	149
Ben Kavanagh	4/3/88	31	26	8	8	0	0	0	0	32	32
Joe Keyes	17/9/95	19	15	3	0	41	36	0	0	94	84
Ryan King	28/6/97	2	2	0	0	0	0	0	0	0	0
Ryan Lannon	11/1/96	1(21)	(18)	1	1	0	0	0	0	4	4
Kevin Larroyer	19/6/89	9(9)	9(6)	0	0	0	0	0	0	0	0
Will Maher	4/11/95	7(1)	5(1)	0	0	0	0	0	0	0	0
Jake Maizen	4/1/97	19	14	8	6	0	0	0	0	32	24
Suaia Matagi	23/3/88	(1)	(1)	0	0	0	0	0	0	0	0
Zack McComb	9/9/95	24(5)	19(4)	3	3	0	0	0	0	12	12
Brandon Moore	27/7/96	25(3)	20(2)	6	5	0	0	0	0	24	20
Dan Murray	21/3/96	26(2)	20(2)	1	1	0	0	0	0	4	4
Adam O'Brien	11/7/93	6(7)	5(6)	1	1	0	0	0	0	4	4
Cole Oakley	25/10/00	(1)	0	0	0	0	0	0	0	0	0
Brandon Pickersgill	29/3/97	9(1)	7(1)	1	1	0	0	0	0	4	4
James Saltonstall	27/9/93	28	22	15	11	0	0	0	0	60	44
Daniel Smith	20/3/93	(1)	(1)	0	0	0	0	0	0	0	0
Alex Sutcliffe	21/1/99	2(5)	2(5)	1	1	0	0	0	0	4	4
Adam Tangata	17/3/91	9(23)	8(18)	2	2	0	0	0	0	8	8
Ben Tibbs	3/11/00	15	12	1	1	0	0	0	0	4	4
Lachlan Walmsley	12/6/98	31	26	38	36	0	0	0	0	152	144
Kyle Wood	18/6/89	9(5)	9(5)	1	1	0	0	0	0	4	4
James Woodburn-Hall	2/2/95	30	24	16	16	0	0	1	1	65	65

'Ch' totals include Championship games only; 'All' totals also include Challenge Cup & 1895 Cup

Lachlan Walmsley

LEAGUE RECORD
P27-W14-D1-L12 (8th)
F690, A572, Diff+118, 29 points.

CHALLENGE CUP
Round Six

1895 CUP
Winners

ATTENDANCES
Best - v St Helens (CC - 4,693)
Worst - v Toulouse (Ch - 1,437)
Total (excluding Challenge Cup) - 24,432
Average (excluding Challenge Cup) - 1,879
(Up by 78 on 2022)

CLUB RECORDS

MATCH RECORDS Highest score: 94-4 v Myton, 25/3/2012 Highest score against: 6-88 v Hull KR, 23/4/2006
Record attendance: 29,153 v Wigan, 21/3/59 *(Thrum Hall)*; 9,827 v Bradford, 12/3/2000 *(The Shay)*
Tries: 8 Keith Williams v Dewsbury, 9/11/57 Goals: 14 Bruce Burton v Hunslet, 27/8/72 Points: 34 Joe Keyes v Workington, 17/7/2022

SEASON RECORDS Tries: 48 Johnny Freeman 1956-57 Goals: 156 Graham Holroyd 2008 Points: 362 John Schuster 1994-95

CAREER RECORDS Tries: 290 Johnny Freeman 1954-67 Goals: 1,028 Ronnie James 1961-71 Points: 2,191 Ronnie James 1961-71 Appearances: 482 Stan Kielty 1946-58

Championship 2023 - Club by Club

KEIGHLEY COUGARS

DATE	FIXTURE	RESULT	SCORERS	LGE	ATT
6/2/23	Featherstone (h)	L0-50		14th	2,443
12/2/23	Widnes (a)	L26-18	t:Gale(2),Storey g:Chisholm(3)	14th	3,449
19/2/23	Newcastle (h)	W44-24	t:Graham,Tomlinson,Roebuck(2),Walker,Storey(2),Agoro g:Chisholm(6)	10th	1,658
26/2/23	Batley (a)	L28-23	t:Storey,Graham,Young g:Chisholm(5) fg:Chisholm	11th	1,624
5/3/23	London Broncos (h)	W33-22	t:Agoro,Graham(2),Santi,Storey,Tomlinson g:Chisholm(4) fg:Chisholm	8th	1,693
12/3/23	Hunslet (a) (CCR3)	W14-16	t:Stephenson,Storey,Levy g:Young(2)	N/A	519
19/3/23	Halifax (a)	L34-10	t:Storey(2) g:Gale	10th	2,123
26/3/23	Bradford (h)	W34-6	t:Stephenson,Chisholm,Gibbons,Gale,Graham,Storey g:Chisholm(4),Gale	10th	4,793
1/4/23	North Wales (h) (CCR4)	W36-14	t:Dyer-Dixon(2),Agoro(2),Gaylor,Doyle,Young g:Parker(2),Spence(2)	N/A	862
7/4/23	York (h)	W10-22	t:Chisholm,Crooks,Keinhorst,Ioane g:Gale(3)	6th	2,218
15/4/23	Toulouse (h)	L6-34	t:Levy g:Chisholm	8th	1,739
23/4/23	Batley (a) (CCR5)	L34-16	t:Storey,Ioane,Parker g:Gale(2)	N/A	923
7/5/23	Whitehaven (a)	W24-32	t:Doyle,Ioane,Crooks(3) g:Chisholm(6)	7th	1,065
14/5/23	Sheffield (h)	L18-46	t:Robson,Stephenson,Ioane g:Chisholm(3)	9th	1,347
28/5/23	Bradford (SB) ●	L42-18	t:Crooks(2),Stephenson g:Spence(3)	10th	N/A
4/6/23	Swinton (h)	L28-32	t:Ioane,Spence,Doyle,Lynam,Agoro g:Spence(4)	10th	1,138
11/6/23	Barrow (a)	L18-16	t:Lynam,Stephenson(2) g:Chisholm(2)	10th	2,250
18/6/23	Newcastle (a)	L18-16	t:Storey,Rush,Graham g:Rush,Chisholm	11th	684
25/6/23	Whitehaven (h)	W28-18	t:Stephenson,Agoro,Roby,Robson,Gaylor g:Walker(4)	9th	2,106
2/7/23	Bradford (a)	L74-12	t:Levy,Graham g:Spence(2)	11th	4,879
9/7/23	York (h)	L10-50	t:Stephenson(2) g:Walker	11th	1,654
16/7/23	Widnes (h)	L22-38	t:Sa'u,Roby,Robson,Graham g:Walker(3)	11th	1,267
29/7/23	Toulouse (a)	L64-0		12th	3,250
6/8/23	Swinton (a)	L18-10	t:Young,Robson g:Thomas	13th	1,179
20/8/23	Batley (h)	W26-20	t:Kesik,Robson,Agoro(2) g:Thomas(5)	12th	1,468
27/8/23	Featherstone (a)	L36-6	t:Adebiyi g:Thomas	12th	3,235
3/9/23	Barrow (h)	W26-20	t:Graham,Sa'u,Young,Parker,Bibby g:Spence,Rush(2)	10th	1,828
8/9/23	Sheffield (a)	L38-10	t:Young(2) g:Spence	12th	932
17/9/23	Halifax (h)	L22-23	t:Agoro(2),Graham,Ioane g:Thomas(3)	12th	2,367
24/9/23	London Broncos (a)	L24-16	t:Parker,Ioane g:Thomas(4)	13th	1,269

● Played at LNER Community Stadium, York

		APP		TRIES		GOALS		FG		PTS	
	D.O.B.	ALL	Ch	ALL	Ch	ALL	Ch	ALL	Ch	ALL	Ch
Sadiq Adebiyi	8/1/97	18(7)	17(6)	1	1	0	0	0	0	4	4
Mo Agoro	29/1/93	23	21	10	8	0	0	0	0	40	32
Luca Atkinson	18/9/02	(3)	(3)	0	0	0	0	0	0	0	0
Jack Bibby	14/10/01	6(7)	6(7)	1	1	0	0	0	0	4	4
Dane Chisholm	4/7/90	12	12	2	2	35	35	2	2	80	80
Ben Crooks	15/6/93	8	7	6	6	0	0	0	0	24	24
Thomas Doyle	29/6/99	19(4)	16(4)	3	2	0	0	0	0	12	8
Keenan Dyer-Dixon	17/4/03	4	2	2	0	0	0	0	0	8	0
Toby Everett	22/12/95	6(9)	6(6)	0	0	0	0	0	0	0	0
Luke Gale	22/6/88	9	8	3	3	7	5	0	0	26	22
Billy Gaylor	30/4/97	8(8)	6(8)	2	1	0	0	0	0	8	4
Joe Gibbons	5/12/02	6	5	1	1	0	0	0	0	4	4
Charlie Graham	14/5/00	26	24	10	10	0	0	0	0	40	40
Joe Hird	8/2/03	2(4)	2(4)	0	0	0	0	0	0	0	0
Mark Ioane	3/2/90	20(3)	17(3)	7	6	0	0	0	0	28	24
Jimmy Keinhorst	14/7/90	2	2	1	1	0	0	0	0	4	4
Kyle Kesik	3/6/89	13(6)	12(4)	1	1	0	0	0	0	4	4
Matty Laidlaw	22/1/04	3(1)	3(1)	0	0	0	0	0	0	0	0
Phoenix Laulu-Togaga'e	16/4/03	4	4	0	0	0	0	0	0	0	0
Aaron Levy	19/12/95	8(9)	6(8)	3	2	0	0	0	0	12	8
Josh Lynam	16/2/93	1(8)	1(8)	2	2	0	0	0	0	8	8
Tom Nicholson-Watton	13/12/02	2(4)	2(4)	0	0	0	0	0	0	0	0
Cole Oakley	25/10/00	2(1)	2(1)	0	0	0	0	0	0	0	0
Dan Parker	11/3/93	6(17)	4(16)	3	2	2	0	0	0	16	8
Ellis Robson	14/9/98	21(1)	21	5	5	0	0	0	0	20	20
Lloyd Roby	3/1/99	12(4)	11(4)	2	2	0	0	0	0	8	8
Nathan Roebuck	2/10/99	3(1)	3	2	2	0	0	0	0	8	8
Kieran Rush	3/9/02	5(1)	5(1)	1	1	3	3	0	0	10	10
Brenden Santi	5/8/93	11(4)	8(4)	1	1	0	0	0	0	4	4
Junior Sa'u	18/4/87	9	9	2	2	0	0	0	0	8	8
Aidan Scully	16/5/92	(1)	(1)	0	0	0	0	0	0	0	0
Harvey Spence	14/9/00	14(8)	12(7)	1	1	13	11	0	0	30	26
Alix Stephenson	19/4/99	17	14	9	8	0	0	0	0	36	32
Robbie Storey	21/10/99	27	24	11	9	0	0	0	0	44	36
Jake Sweeting	15/12/99	1	1	0	0	0	0	0	0	0	0
Oscar Thomas	3/1/94	5(2)	5(2)	0	0	14	14	0	0	28	28
Keenen Tomlinson	22/5/97	8(1)	7(1)	2	2	0	0	0	0	8	8
Kyle Trout	1/3/91	9(2)	9(2)	0	0	0	0	0	0	0	0
Brad Walker	30/1/98	18(4)	18(3)	1	1	8	8	0	0	20	20
Jake Webster	29/10/83	1	1	0	0	0	0	0	0	0	0
Lewis Young	1/7/95	21	18	6	5	2	0	0	0	28	20

'Ch' totals include Championship games only; 'All' totals also include Challenge Cup

Mark Ioane

LEAGUE RECORD
P27-W8-D0-L19 (13th)
F506, A837, Diff-331, 16 points.

CHALLENGE CUP
Round Five

ATTENDANCES
Best - v Bradford (Ch - 4,793)
Worst - v North Wales (CC - 862)
Total (excluding Challenge Cup) - 25,501
Average (excluding Challenge Cup) - 1,962
(Up by 310 on 2022, League One)

CLUB RECORDS
MATCH RECORDS
Highest score: 112-6 v West Wales, 15/9/2018 Highest score against: 2-92 v Leigh, 30/4/86 Record attendance: 14,500 v Halifax, 3/3/51
Tries: 6 Jason Critchley v Widnes, 18/8/96
Goals: 15 John Wasyliw v Nottingham City, 1/11/92; Martyn Wood v Lancashire Lynx, 1/5/2000 Points: 36 John Wasyliw v Nottingham City, 1/11/92
SEASON RECORDS
Tries: 45 Nick Pinkney 1994-95 Goals: 187 John Wasyliw 1992-93 Points: 490 John Wasyliw 1992-93
CAREER RECORDS
Tries: 155 Sam Stacey 1904-20 Goals: 967 Brian Jefferson 1965-77 Points: 2,116 Brian Jefferson 1965-77
Appearances: 372 Hartley Tempest 1902-15; David McGoun 1925-38

Championship 2023 - Club by Club

LONDON BRONCOS

DATE	FIXTURE	RESULT	SCORERS	LGE	ATT
5/2/23	Batley (h)	L20-30	t:Grant,B Leyland,Walker,Ulberg g:O Leyland(2)	10th	1,849
12/2/23	Whitehaven (a)	W16-20	t:Ulberg(2),B Leyland,Bassett g:O Leyland(2)	9th	750
19/2/23	Halifax (a)	L26-18	t:Eckersley,Parata,B Leyland g:O Leyland(3)	8th	1,950
26/2/23	Sheffield (h)	L20-21	t:Ulberg,Lovell,B Leyland g:O Leyland(4)	10th	1,175
5/3/23	Keighley (a)	L33-22	t:Ulberg,Miski,Walker,Bassett g:O Leyland(3)	12th	1,693
11/3/23	Whitehaven (h) (CCR3)	W32-10	t:Bassett(3),B Leyland,Stock,Horsman g:O Leyland(4)	N/A	347
18/3/23	Newcastle (a)	W6-36	t:Natoli,B Leyland,Walker(3),Bassett,Waine g:O Leyland(4)	9th	978
26/3/23	Swinton (h)	W16-14	t:Parata,Ulberg,Bassett g:O Leyland(2)	8th	657
1/4/23	Doncaster (h) (CCR4) ●	W66-16	t:B Leyland,O Leyland(2),Ulberg(2),Grant,Macani,Waine,Horsman,Parata,Silva,Albert g:O Leyland(9)	N/A	428
7/4/23	Toulouse (a)	L52-0		10th	3,358
16/4/23	Featherstone (h)	L10-40	t:Macani,Bassett g:O Leyland	11th	977
23/4/23	Dewsbury (h) (CCR5) ●	W36-16	t:Macani(2),B Leyland,Bienek,Albert,Stock,Bassett g:O Leyland(4)	N/A	353
7/5/23	York (a)	L30-28	t:Natoli,Williams,Albert,Stock,Macani g:O Leyland(4)	11th	1,802
13/5/23	Barrow (h)	W30-16	t:Natoli,B Leyland,Macani,O Leyland,Bassett g:O Leyland(5)	10th	806
21/5/23	York (a) (CCR6)	L36-12	t:Walker,Bassett g:O Leyland(2)	N/A	951
27/5/23	Toulouse (SB) ●●	W14-10	t:Whare,Lovell g:O Leyland(3)	8th	N/A
4/6/23	Widnes (a)	W18-26	t:Macani(2),Raiwalui,Ulberg,Whare g:O Leyland(3)	8th	2,547
11/6/23	Bradford (a)	L32-16	t:Macani(2),Whare g:O Leyland(2)	8th	3,482
18/6/23	Featherstone (a)	L50-6	t:O Leyland g:O Leyland	8th	2,255
25/6/23	Batley (a)	W18-20	t:Parata,Macani,B Leyland g:O Leyland(4)	8th	1,372
2/7/23	Newcastle (h) ●●●	W56-10	t:B Leyland,Butler(2),Ulberg,Walker(2),Gannon,O Leyland,Raiwalui,Williams g:O Leyland(8)	7th	1,208
8/7/23	Toulouse (h) ●●●	W22-6	t:Walker(2),Ulberg,O Leyland g:O Leyland(3)	7th	1,089
16/7/23	Swinton (a)	W6-12	t:Macani(2) g:O Leyland(2)	7th	940
22/7/23	Halifax (h) (1895CSF) ●	L6-10	t:Stock g:O Leyland	N/A	417
30/7/23	York (h)	L10-24	t:Parata,Ulberg g:Norman	8th	957
6/8/23	Barrow (a)	W6-26	t:Norman,Whare(2),Bienek,Grant g:Norman(3)	8th	1,786
20/8/23	Halifax (h)	W26-12	t:Bienek,Walker,Macani(2) g:Norman(2),O Leyland	6th	859
27/8/23	Whitehaven (h)	W34-18	t:O Leyland,B Leyland,Whare,Bassett(2),Grant(2) g:Norman(2),O Leyland	5th	786
3/9/23	Sheffield (a)	W18-26	t:Bassett,Walker(2),Parata,Macani g:Norman(3)	5th	910
10/9/23	Widnes (h)	W52-12	t:Albert,Stock,Whare(2),Williams,Walker,Bassett,Raiwalui,O Leyland g:Norman(8)	4th	1,062
17/9/23	Bradford (h)	L10-12	t:Raiwalui,Walker g:Norman	5th	1,158
24/9/23	Keighley (h)	W24-16	t:Whare(2),Macani(2),B Leyland g:Norman(2)	5th	1,269
1/10/23	Sheffield (a) (E)	W0-42	t:Grant(2),Bassett(2),Williams,Walker,Lovell g:Norman(7)	N/A	648
8/10/23	Featherstone (a) (SF)	W26-36	t:Walker(2),Whare,Macani,Grant,Raiwalui g:Norman(6)	N/A	-
15/10/23	Toulouse (a) (GF)	W14-18	t:Whare,Walker,Macani(2) g:Norman	N/A	3,974

● Played at The Rock, Roehampton
●● Played at LNER Community Stadium, York
●●● Played at Kuflink Stadium, Ebsfleet

		APP		TRIES		GOALS		FG		PTS	
	D.O.B.	ALL	Ch	ALL	Ch	ALL	Ch	ALL	Ch	ALL	Ch
Wellington Albert	3/9/93	13(13)	11(12)	4	2	0	0	0	0	16	8
Max Allen	5/10/02	(3)	(2)	0	0	0	0	0	0	0	0
Jarred Bassett	23/11/91	32	27	17	12	0	0	0	0	68	48
Lewis Bienek	11/4/98	21(4)	18(3)	3	2	0	0	0	0	12	8
Rob Butler	15/5/98	15(2)	15(2)	2	2	0	0	0	0	8	8
Matthew Davies	9/4/98	(7)	(6)	0	0	0	0	0	0	0	0
Sam Davis	11/11/98	26(3)	22(3)	0	0	0	0	0	0	0	0
Zach Eckersley	10/11/03	4	4	1	1	0	0	0	0	4	4
Kyle Evans	11/9/90	1	1	0	0	0	0	0	0	0	0
Jacob Gannon	18/3/02	5(1)	4(1)	1	1	0	0	0	0	4	4
Dalton Grant	21/4/90	16	14	8	7	0	0	0	0	32	28
Harvie Hill	3/9/03	1(3)	1(3)	0	0	0	0	0	0	0	0
Rian Horsman	4/4/01	4(4)	2(3)	2	2	0	0	0	0	8	8
Daniel Hoyes	12/12/03	4(3)	2(3)	0	0	0	0	0	0	0	0
Jacob Jones	15/2/99	4	4	0	0	0	0	0	0	0	0
Bill Leyland	3/2/03	8(24)	7(20)	13	10	0	0	0	0	52	40
Oliver Leyland	17/5/01	30(2)	25(2)	8	6	78	58	0	0	188	140
Will Lovell	10/5/93	31	27	3	3	0	0	0	0	12	12
Iliess Macani	6/12/93	30	26	21	18	0	0	0	0	84	72
Harvey Makin	17/11/03	(1)	(1)	0	0	0	0	0	0	0	0
Abbas Miski	25/7/95	1	1	1	1	0	0	0	0	4	4
Jenson Monk	31/12/03	(3)	(2)	0	0	0	0	0	0	0	0
Ethan Natoli	5/4/95	31(1)	27(1)	3	3	0	0	0	0	12	12
Corey Norman	3/2/91	15	14	1	1	36	36	0	0	76	76
Dean Parata	4/10/91	33(1)	28(1)	6	5	0	0	0	0	24	20
Euan Parke	19/3/04	(5)	(3)	0	0	0	0	0	0	0	0
Henry Raiwalui	24/2/89	22(1)	19(1)	5	5	0	0	0	0	20	20
Ramon Silva	7/11/01	(11)	(10)	1	0	0	0	0	0	4	0
Harry Stevens	27/5/05	1	1	0	0	0	0	0	0	0	0
Marcus Stock	1/5/96	20(13)	16(12)	5	2	0	0	0	0	20	8
Kieran Tyrer	24/10/02	1	1	0	0	0	0	0	0	0	0
Paul Ulberg	14/11/95	25	20	12	10	0	0	0	0	48	40
Emmanuel Waine	6/10/96	5(9)	4(7)	2	1	0	0	0	0	8	4
Alex Walker	4/9/95	33	28	20	19	0	0	0	0	80	76
Dean Whare	22/1/90	12(1)	12	12	12	0	0	0	0	48	48
Jordan Williams	4/6/97	11(22)	9(19)	4	4	0	0	0	0	16	16

'Ch' totals include regular season & play-offs; 'All' totals also include Challenge Cup & 1895 Cup

Iliess Macani

LEAGUE RECORD
P27-W16-D0-L11 (5th/Grand Final Winners, Champions)
F600, A552, Diff+48, 32 points.

CHALLENGE CUP
Round Six

1895 CUP
Semi-Finalists

ATTENDANCES
Best - v Batley (Ch - 1,849)
Worst - v Whitehaven (CC - 347)
Total (excluding Challenge Cup) - 14,269
Average (excluding Challenge Cup) - 1,019
(Up by 84 on 2022)

CLUB RECORDS Highest score: 82-0 v Highfield, 12/11/95; 82-2 v Barrow, 20/5/2006 Highest score against: 6-82 v Warrington, 20/3/2011; 10-82 v Warrington, 8/6/2013
Record attendance: 15,013 v Wakefield, 15/2/81 *(Craven Cottage)*; 2,182 v Widnes, 30/1/2022 *(Cherry Red Records Stadium)*
MATCH RECORDS Tries: 5 Martin Offiah v Whitehaven, 14/3/99; Sean Morris v Batley, 13/9/2015
Goals: 13 Rob Purdham v Barrow, 20/5/2006 Points: 34 Rob Purdham v Barrow, 20/5/2006; Jarrod Sammut v Sheffield, 13/5/2018
SEASON RECORDS Tries: 43 Mark Johnson 1993-94 Goals: 159 John Gallagher 1993-94 Points: 384 John Gallagher 1993-94
CAREER RECORDS Tries: 109 Luke Dorn 2005-2006; 2009-2013 Goals: 309 Steve Diamond 1981-84 Points: 772 Paul Sykes 2001-2007
Appearances: 202 Steele Retchless 1998-2004

Championship 2023 - Club by Club

NEWCASTLE THUNDER

DATE	FIXTURE	RESULT	SCORERS	LGE	ATT
5/2/23	Swinton (a)	W6-18	t:Young(2),Williams g:Williams(3)	4th	877
11/2/23	Toulouse (a)	L58-0		11th	3,047
19/2/23	Keighley (a)	L44-24	t:Lawther,Johnson(2),Clegg g:Williams(4)	12th	1,658
26/2/23	Featherstone (a)	L56-6	t:Clegg g:Williams	13th	2,489
5/3/23	Barrow (a)	D18-18	t:Foster,Walker,Williams g:Williams(3)	11th	1,752
12/3/23	Stanningley (a) (CCR3)	W16-58	t:Moore,Foster,Clegg(3),Johnson(2),Bailey,Miller,Lawther,Flanagan g:Williams(2),Miller(5)	N/A	-
18/3/23	London Broncos (h)	L6-36	t:Miller g:Williams	13th	978
26/3/23	Widnes (a)	L24-16	t:J Chapelhow,Clark,Foster g:Williams(2)	14th	2,743
1/4/23	Rochdale Mayfield (a) (CCR4)	W12-22	t:Johnson,Young,T Chapelhow,Moore g:Miller(3)	N/A	-
7/4/23	Sheffield (h)	L20-44	t:T Chapelhow,Young(2),Donaghy g:Williams(2)	14th	817
16/4/23	Whitehaven (a)	L31-6	t:Donaghy g:Williams	14th	987
21/4/23	York (a) (CCR5)	L22-18	t:Walker,Miller,Walsh g:Williams(3)	N/A	1,100
7/5/23	Halifax (h)	L16-36	t:Balmforth,Clegg,J Chapelhow g:Williams(2)	14th	1,067
14/5/23	York (a)	L26-22	t:T Chapelhow,Boafo,Clark,Donaghy g:Williams(3)	14th	2,276
28/5/23	Sheffield (SB) ●	L32-38	t:Boafo,Bailey,Windrow,Balmforth(2),Clegg g:Williams(4)	14th	N/A
2/6/23	Bradford (h)	L12-28	t:Staveley,Balmforth g:Williams(2)	14th	2,465
11/6/23	Batley (h)	L12-26	t:J Chapelhow,Donaghy g:Williams(2)	14th	694
18/6/23	Keighley (h)	W18-16	t:Davies,T Chapelhow,Clegg,Gallagher g:Williams	14th	684
23/6/23	Sheffield (a)	L40-0		14th	879
2/7/23	London Broncos (a) ●●	L56-10	t:J Chapelhow,Bailey g:Miller	14th	1,208
9/7/23	Whitehaven (h)	W30-12	t:J Chapelhow(2),T Chapelhow,Boafo,Clark g:Miller(5)	14th	1,284
16/7/23	Halifax (a)	L50-12	t:J Chapelhow(2) g:Miller(2)	14th	1,453
30/7/23	Swinton (h)	W25-19	t:Boafo(2),Moore,Bailey g:Miller(4) fg:Williams	14th	889
5/8/23	Widnes (h)	L6-50	t:Balmforth g:Donaghy	14th	2,206
20/8/23	Bradford (a)	L36-8	t:Tuliatu,Clegg	14th	2,685
25/8/23	York (h)	L6-20	t:Boafo g:Williams	14th	788
2/9/23	Toulouse (h)	L16-36	t:Johnson(2),Boafo g:Williams(2)	14th	639
8/9/23	Featherstone (h)	L22-56	t:Balmforth,Boafo(2),Williams g:Williams(3)	14th	747
16/9/23	Barrow (h)	W36-24	t:Boafo(2),Donaghy(2),Clegg,Bailey,Burns g:Williams(4)	14th	904
23/9/23	Batley (a)	L32-18	t:T Chapelhow,Johnson,Williams g:Williams(3)	14th	1,070

● Played at LNER Community Stadium, York
●● Played at Kuflink Stadium, Ebsfleet

		APP		TRIES		GOALS		FG		PTS	
	D.O.B.	ALL	Ch	ALL	Ch	ALL	Ch	ALL	Ch	ALL	Ch
Jake Anderson	21/11/02	2(1)	2	0	0	0	0	0	0	0	0
Connor Bailey	10/10/00	29(1)	26(1)	5	4	0	0	0	0	20	16
Denive Balmforth	1/10/03	8(18)	8(18)	6	6	0	0	0	0	24	24
Harvey Barron	13/5/03	1	1	0	0	0	0	0	0	0	0
Gideon Boafo	10/2/99	18	18	11	11	0	0	0	0	44	44
Paddy Burns	15/3/98	2(1)	2(1)	1	1	0	0	0	0	4	4
Jay Chapelhow	21/9/95	24(4)	22(3)	8	8	0	0	0	0	32	32
Ted Chapelhow	21/9/95	14(11)	13(9)	6	5	0	0	0	0	24	20
Mitch Clark	13/3/93	16(9)	15(8)	3	3	0	0	0	0	12	12
Rhys Clarke	12/3/91	3(6)	1(5)	0	0	0	0	0	0	0	0
Alex Clegg	9/7/99	27	24	10	7	0	0	0	0	40	28
Curtis Davies	17/1/97	29(1)	26(1)	1	1	0	0	0	0	4	4
Alex Donaghy	22/9/01	26	24	6	6	1	1	0	0	26	26
Max Flanagan	20/6/01	1(2)	0	1	0	0	0	0	0	4	0
Alex Foster	25/9/93	15	14	3	2	0	0	0	0	12	8
Brad Gallagher	28/2/00	17	15	1	1	0	0	0	0	4	4
Jack Johnson	25/4/96	18	15	8	5	0	0	0	0	32	20
Matty Laidlaw	22/1/04	1(4)	1(4)	0	0	0	0	0	0	0	0
Evan Lawther	14/8/03	3(1)	2(1)	2	1	0	0	0	0	8	4
Jake Lightowler	22/2/99	(11)	(10)	0	0	0	0	0	0	0	0
Jack Miller	28/11/94	20(1)	17(1)	3	1	20	12	0	0	52	28
Connor Moore	8/7/03	9(10)	7(9)	3	1	0	0	0	0	12	4
Daniel Okoro	18/4/03	(7)	(6)	0	0	0	0	0	0	0	0
Nathan Rushworth	16/10/02	(2)	(2)	0	0	0	0	0	0	0	0
Evan Simons	11/10/91	(12)	(12)	0	0	0	0	0	0	0	0
Nick Staveley	19/1/04	12(1)	12(1)	1	1	0	0	0	0	4	4
Oscar Thomas	3/1/94	2	2	0	0	0	0	0	0	0	0
Rob Tuliatu	11/10/95	15(10)	13(9)	1	1	0	0	0	0	4	4
Marcus Walker	12/8/02	23	21	2	1	0	0	0	0	8	4
Mac Walsh	23/12/03	9	8	1	0	0	0	0	0	4	0
Tyler Walton	20/12/00	1(7)	1(7)	0	0	0	0	0	0	0	0
Nikau Williams	11/11/99	25	23	4	4	49	44	1	1	115	105
Dane Windrow	9/6/02	3	3	1	1	0	0	0	0	4	4
Connor Wynne	15/1/01	3	3	0	0	0	0	0	0	0	0
Alex Young	6/4/99	14	12	5	4	0	0	0	0	20	16

'Ch' totals include Championship games only; 'All' totals also include Challenge Cup

Gideon Boafo

LEAGUE RECORD
P27-W5-D1-L21 (14th)
F415, A918, Diff-503, 11 points.

CHALLENGE CUP
Round Five

ATTENDANCES
Best - v Bradford (Ch - 2,465)
Worst - v Toulouse (Ch - 639)
Total (all home games included) - 14,162
Average (all home games included) - 1,089
(Up by 24 on 2022)

CLUB RECORDS
MATCH RECORDS Highest score: 98-6 v West Wales, 23/9/2018 Highest score against: 0-132 v Blackpool Panthers, 16/5/2010
Record attendance: 6,631 v Bradford, 16/5/99 *(Gateshead International Stadium)*; 4,137 v Bradford, 18/5/2018 *(Kingston Park)*
Tries: 5 Andy Walker v London Skolars, 22/6/2003 Goals: 12 Rhys Clarke v Coventry, 18/8/2019 Points: 28 Benn Hardcastle v Oxford, 18/6/2017
SEASON RECORDS Tries: 28 Kieran Gill 2019 Goals: 129 *(inc 1fg)* Dan Russell 2008 Points: 293 Dan Russell 2008
CAREER RECORDS Tries: 74 Kevin Neighbour 2001-2006; 2008-2010 Goals: 283 *(inc 8fg)* Benn Hardcastle 2013-2017 Points: 682 Benn Hardcastle 2013-2017
Appearances: 234 Joe Brown 2005-2006; 2010-2021

Championship 2023 - Club by Club

SHEFFIELD EAGLES

DATE	FIXTURE	RESULT	SCORERS	LGE	ATT
5/2/23	Halifax (a)	L26-18	t:Murphy,Liu(2) g:Hansen(3)	9th	2,101
12/2/23	Barrow (a)	W16-36	t:Welham(2),Dawson-Jones,Oakes(2),Liu,Thackeray g:Aston(4)	4th	2,094
17/2/23	Batley (h)	W36-0	t:Thackeray,Halafihi,Sene-Lefao,Oakes,Jones-Bishop,Murphy g:Aston(6)	3rd	878
26/2/23	London Broncos (a)	W20-21	t:Jones-Bishop(2),Oakes,Gwaze g:Aston(2) fg:Thackeray	3rd	1,175
5/3/23	Widnes (h)	W42-12	t:Dawson-Jones(2),Jones-Bishop,Gwaze,Douglas,Chrimes,Aston g:Aston(7)	3rd	1,319
12/3/23	Siddal (a) (CCR3)	W12-34	t:Johnson,Peachey,Bass(3),Hansen g:Aston(5)	N/A	-
19/3/23	Bradford (a)	L32-18	t:Sene-Lefao(2),Dawson-Jones g:Aston(3)	3rd	3,004
25/3/23	Toulouse (h)	W32-4	t:Sene-Lefao,Halafihi,Thackeray,Jones-Bishop,Bass,Roberts g:Aston(4)	3rd	959
2/4/23	York (a) (CCR4)	L24-22	t:Welham,Aston,Bass,Chrimes g:Aston(3)	N/A	832
7/4/23	Newcastle (a)	W20-44	t:Thackeray(3),Laulu-Togaga'e(2),Dickinson,Douglas,Chrimes g:Aston(6)	3rd	817
17/4/23	Swinton (h)	W16-6	t:Laulu-Togaga'e,Aston,Jones-Bishop g:Aston(2)	3rd	1,179
7/5/23	Featherstone (a)	L28-20	t:Liu,Dawson-Jones(2),Jones-Bishop g:Aston(2)	3rd	3,187
14/5/23	Keighley (a)	W18-46	t:Welham(2),Liu,Jones-Bishop(2),Aston,Dawson-Jones,Halafihi g:Aston(7)	2nd	1,347
28/5/23	Newcastle (SB) ●	W32-38	t:Liu(2),Jones-Bishop(2),Welham,Douglas g:Hansen(6),I Farrell	2nd	N/A
4/6/23	Whitehaven (a)	L26-40	t:Liu(2),Jones-Bishop(2),I Farrell g:Aston(3)	2nd	1,179
9/6/23	York (h)	W40-10	t:Jones-Bishop,Dawson-Jones,Welham(3),Thackeray,Laulu-Togaga'e g:Aston(6)	2nd	1,051
17/6/23	Toulouse (a)	L48-10	t:Sene-Lefao,Liu g:Aston	4th	3,344
23/6/23	Newcastle (h)	W40-0	t:Gwaze,Hansen,Aston(2),Halafihi,Wood,Dawson-Jones g:Aston(6)	3rd	879
2/7/23	Swinton (a)	L30-22	t:Dickinson,Dawson-Jones(2),Thackeray g:Aston(3)	4th	1,094
9/7/23	Barrow (h)	W36-18	t:J Farrell,Dawson-Jones,Thackeray(2),Sene-Lefao(2),Oakes g:Aston(4)	4th	1,011
16/7/23	York (a)	L23-18	t:Jones-Bishop,Dawson-Jones,Sene-Lefao g:Aston(3)	4th	2,266
28/7/23	Halifax (h)	W32-30	t:Dawson-Jones(2),Hansen,Aston,Douglas,Jones-Bishop g:Aston(4)	3rd	1,327
6/8/23	Whitehaven (a)	L32-20	t:Thackeray,Hansen,Dawson-Jones,Liu g:Aston(2)	3rd	720
18/8/23	Featherstone (h)	L10-28	t:Jones-Bishop,Dawson-Jones g:Aston	4th	1,709
25/8/23	Batley (a)	W6-49	t:Liu,Oakes(2),Jones-Bishop(2),Thackeray(3) g:Aston(6),Hansen(2) fg:Thackeray	4th	1,209
3/9/23	London Broncos (h)	L18-26	t:Laulu-Togaga'e,Glover(2) g:Aston(3)	4th	910
8/9/23	Keighley (h)	W38-10	t:Aston,Oakes,Glover,Sene-Lefao,Jones-Bishop,Murphy,Laulu-Togaga'e g:Aston(3),I Farrell(2)	3rd	932
17/9/23	Widnes (a)	W18-38	t:Murphy(2),Aston,Hansen,Thackeray,Hodgson g:Aston(7)	3rd	2,961
24/9/23	Bradford (h)	L16-17	t:Laulu-Togaga'e,Jones-Bishop,Dawson-Jones g:Aston,Hansen	4th	1,976
1/10/23	London Broncos (h) (E)	L0-42		N/A	648

● Played at LNER Community Stadium, York

Ben Jones-Bishop

	D.O.B.	APP ALL	Ch	TRIES ALL	Ch	GOALS ALL	Ch	FG ALL	Ch	PTS ALL	Ch
Cory Aston	1/3/95	28	26	9	8	104	96	0	0	244	224
Jason Bass	10/5/96	6	4	5	1	0	0	0	0	20	4
Connor Bower	18/1/97	9(1)	8(1)	0	0	0	0	0	0	0	0
Blake Broadbent	11/12/98	1(21)	(21)	0	0	0	0	0	0	0	0
Matty Chrimes	2/11/97	7	5	3	2	0	0	0	0	12	8
Matty Dawson-Jones	2/10/90	25	25	18	18	0	0	0	0	72	72
Tyler Dickinson	18/8/96	24(2)	22(2)	2	2	0	0	0	0	8	8
Brandon Douglas	17/8/97	18(6)	17(6)	4	4	0	0	0	0	16	16
Izaac Farrell	30/1/98	2(3)	2(3)	1	1	3	3	0	0	10	10
Joel Farrell	15/3/94	12(7)	12(6)	1	1	0	0	0	0	4	4
James Glover	2/12/93	10	10	3	3	0	0	0	0	12	12
Josh Guzdek	22/4/95	2	1	0	0	0	0	0	0	0	0
Titus Gwaze	8/6/99	16(6)	14(6)	3	3	0	0	0	0	12	12
Vila Halafihi	24/1/94	24(1)	23(1)	4	4	0	0	0	0	16	16
Jack Hansen	12/1/97	12(8)	11(8)	5	4	12	12	0	0	44	40
Joe Hird	8/2/03	(2)	(1)	0	0	0	0	0	0	0	0
Evan Hodgson	14/9/98	14(11)	13(10)	1	1	0	0	0	0	4	4
Ryan Johnson	3/8/00	1	0	1	0	0	0	0	0	4	0
Ben Jones-Bishop	24/8/88	29	28	21	21	0	0	0	0	84	84
Liam Kirk	26/3/97	12(5)	12(5)	0	0	0	0	0	0	0	0
Quentin Laulu-Togaga'e	1/12/84	21	21	7	7	0	0	0	0	28	28
Bayley Liu	3/8/96	17(9)	16(8)	12	12	0	0	0	0	48	48
Aaron Murphy	26/11/88	13(1)	13(1)	5	5	0	0	0	0	20	20
Ross Oakes	12/10/96	15(3)	14(2)	8	8	0	0	0	0	32	32
Lewis Peachey	25/3/01	(3)	(2)	1	0	0	0	0	0	4	0
Oliver Roberts	24/12/94	5(6)	4(5)	1	1	0	0	0	0	4	4
Jesse Sene-Lefao	8/12/89	19(8)	17(8)	9	9	0	0	0	0	36	36
Anthony Thackeray	19/2/86	22(1)	21(1)	15	15	0	0	2	2	62	62
Kris Welham	12/5/87	20	19	9	8	0	0	0	0	36	32
Mikey Wood	18/4/96	6(15)	6(14)	1	1	0	0	0	0	4	4

'Ch' totals include regular season & play-offs; 'All' totals also include Challenge Cup

LEAGUE RECORD
P27-W16-D0-L11 (4th/Eliminator)
F780, A560, Diff+220, 32 points.

CHALLENGE CUP
Round Four

ATTENDANCES
Best - v Bradford (Ch - 1,976)
Worst - v London Broncos (Ch-E - 648)
Total (all home games included) - 15,957
Average (all home games included) - 1,140
(Up by 471 on 2022)

CLUB RECORDS	
	Highest score: 112-6 v Leigh East, 7/4/2013 **Highest score against:** 0-88 v Hull, 2/3/2003
	Record attendance: 10,603 v Bradford, 16/8/97 (Don Valley Stadium); 1,976 v Bradford, 24/9/2023 (Olympic Legacy Park)
MATCH RECORDS	**Tries:** 5 Daryl Powell v Mansfield, 2/1/89; Menzie Yere v Leigh East, 7/4/2013; Quentin Laulu-Togaga'e v Rochdale, 7/9/2014; Garry Lo v Rochdale, 4/6/2017
	Goals: 14 Dominic Brambani v Leigh East, 7/4/2013 **Points:** 32 Roy Rafferty v Fulham, 21/9/86
SEASON RECORDS	**Tries:** 46 Menzie Yere 2013 **Goals:** 169 (inc 1fg) Dominic Brambani 2013 **Points:** 361 Dominic Brambani 2013
CAREER RECORDS	**Tries:** 196 Menzie Yere 2009-2020 **Goals:** 986 Mark Aston 1986-2004 **Points:** 2,142 Mark Aston 1986-2004 **Appearances:** 389 Mark Aston 1986-2004

Championship 2023 - Club by Club

SWINTON LIONS

DATE	FIXTURE	RESULT	SCORERS	LGE	ATT
5/2/23	Newcastle (h)	L6-18	t:Badrock g:Gregson	11th	877
12/2/23	Batley (a)	W16-30	t:Butt,Eaves,Badrock,Abram,Olds g:Abram(5)	6th	1,551
19/2/23	Barrow (h)	W20-18	t:Hatton,Badrock,Eaves,Gibson g:Abram(2)	5th	1,139
26/2/23	Whitehaven (a)	L20-4	t:Badrock	6th	891
5/3/23	York (h)	L0-40		10th	1,029
12/3/23	Barrow (a) (CCR3)	L32-14	t:Lloyd(2),Baker g:Abram	N/A	1,161
19/3/23	Featherstone (h)	L6-34	t:Greenwood g:Abram	11th	1,090
26/3/23	London Broncos (a)	L16-14	t:Eaves,Brogan g:Gregson(3)	11th	657
7/4/23	Widnes (h)	L16-48	t:Gibson,Eaves,Badrock g:Abram(2)	12th	1,403
17/4/23	Sheffield (a)	L16-6	t:Rodden g:Abram	12th	1,179
6/5/23	Toulouse (h)	W19-12	t:Spedding,Brogan g:Davies(5) fg:Gibson	12th	957
14/5/23	Bradford (a)	L44-38	t:Hatton,Bourouh,Lloyd(2),Bruines,Badrock g:Abram(7)	12th	2,935
27/5/23	Widnes (SB) ●	L6-38	t:Royle g:Abram	13th	N/A
4/6/23	Keighley (a)	W28-32	t:Romeo(4),Spedding g:Abram(6)	12th	1,138
11/6/23	Halifax (h)	L8-46	t:Eaves g:Abram(2)	13th	1,109
18/6/23	Batley (h)	L6-48	t:Brogan g:Gregson	13th	1,009
25/6/23	Widnes (a)	W18-25	t:Ellis,Roby,Lloyd,Hatton g:Roberts(3),Davies fg:Ellis	13th	2,833
2/7/23	Sheffield (h)	W30-22	t:Roby(2),Butt,Gregson,Romeo g:Gregson(4),Gibson(1)	12th	1,094
9/7/23	Featherstone (a)	L52-6	t:Hatton g:Gibson	12th	2,845
16/7/23	London Broncos (h)	L6-12	t:Baker g:Abram	12th	940
30/7/23	Newcastle (a)	L25-19	t:Eaves,Hall,Butt g:Gibson(3) fg:Gibson	13th	889
6/8/23	Keighley (h)	W18-10	t:Foster,Abram,Butterworth g:Abram(3)	11th	1,179
19/8/23	Toulouse (a) ●●	L26-6	t:Abram g:Abram	13th	2,430
27/8/23	Bradford (h)	L26-42	t:Hatton,Lepori,Butt,Spedding,Rodden g:Abram(3)	13th	1,073
3/9/23	York (a)	L26-22	t:Abram,Lowe,Roby,Brogan g:Abram(3)	13th	2,114
10/9/23	Barrow (a)	L32-14	t:Abram,Badrock g:Abram(3)	13th	2,117
17/9/23	Whitehaven (h)	W21-20	t:Gibson(2),Baker g:Abram(4) fg:Gibson	13th	1,315
24/9/23	Halifax (a)	W12-22	t:Cox(2),Gregson,Lloyd g:Abram(3)	10th	2,122

● Played at LNER Community Stadium, York
●● Played at Stade Albert Domec, Carcassonne

		APP		TRIES		GOALS		FG		PTS	
	D.O.B.	ALL	Ch	ALL	Ch	ALL	Ch	ALL	Ch	ALL	Ch
Dan Abram	11/11/95	20(1)	19(1)	5	5	49	48	0	0	118	116
Andy Badrock	25/10/00	25	24	7	7	0	0	0	0	28	28
Kenny Baker	1/3/92	12(13)	11(13)	3	2	0	0	0	0	12	8
Lewis Baxter	1/6/02	2(3)	2(3)	0	0	0	0	0	0	0	0
Gavin Bennion	31/12/93	16(1)	16(1)	0	0	0	0	0	0	0	0
Amir Bourouh	5/1/01	1(1)	1(1)	1	1	0	0	0	0	4	4
Louis Brogan	6/5/00	21(4)	20(4)	4	4	0	0	0	0	16	16
Wesley Bruines	25/6/03	6	6	1	1	0	0	0	0	4	4
Morgan Burgess	7/1/02	(3)	(2)	0	0	0	0	0	0	0	0
Mike Butt	6/5/95	17	17	4	4	0	0	0	0	16	16
Robbie Butterworth	7/6/02	5	5	1	1	0	0	0	0	4	4
Jordan Case	10/4/93	5(19)	4(19)	0	0	0	0	0	0	0	0
Liam Cooper	28/7/94	4(6)	3(6)	0	0	0	0	0	0	0	0
Mitch Cox	15/11/93	16(4)	15(4)	2	2	0	0	0	0	8	8
Ben Davies	21/4/00	3	3	0	0	6	6	0	0	12	12
George Delaney	4/2/04	5(1)	5(1)	0	0	0	0	0	0	0	0
Josh Eaves	20/10/97	12(7)	12(7)	6	6	0	0	0	0	24	24
Jamie Ellis	4/10/89	2	2	1	1	0	0	1	1	5	5
Matthew Foster	25/6/01	7(1)	7(1)	1	1	0	0	0	0	4	4
Jordy Gibson	11/6/92	26	25	4	4	8	8	3	3	35	35
James Greenwood	17/6/91	3	3	1	1	0	0	0	0	4	4
Nick Gregson	17/12/95	19	18	2	2	6	6	0	0	20	20
Lewis Hall	2/9/94	10(8)	10(7)	1	1	0	0	0	0	4	4
Jayden Hatton	23/9/99	18	17	5	5	0	0	0	0	20	20
Daniel Hill	15/7/02	1	1	0	0	0	0	0	0	0	0
Callum Hughes	28/2/95	1	0	0	0	0	0	0	0	0	0
Ryan Lannon	11/1/96	2	2	0	0	0	0	0	0	0	0
Richard Lepori	22/10/91	4	4	1	1	0	0	0	0	4	4
Rhodri Lloyd	22/7/93	22(1)	21(1)	6	4	0	0	0	0	24	16
Joe Lowe	24/4/01	7(1)	6(1)	1	1	0	0	0	0	4	4
Dan Norman	8/9/97	1(3)	1(3)	0	0	0	0	0	0	0	0
Ollie Olds	14/8/93	7(1)	7(1)	1	1	0	0	0	0	4	4
Scott Parnaby	27/1/04	(4)	(3)	0	0	0	0	0	0	0	0
Cain Robb	5/1/03	1(2)	1(2)	0	0	0	0	0	0	0	0
Will Roberts	24/2/05	3	3	0	0	3	3	0	0	6	6
George Roby	3/5/02	7(9)	7(9)	4	4	0	0	0	0	16	16
Gav Rodden	20/12/96	12(6)	12(6)	2	2	0	0	0	0	8	8
Joey Romeo	28/9/99	16(3)	16(3)	5	5	0	0	0	0	20	20
Sam Royle	12/2/00	1	1	1	1	0	0	0	0	4	4
Jumah Sambou	21/11/01	1	1	0	0	0	0	0	0	0	0
Jake Spedding	26/9/96	20(1)	20(1)	3	3	0	0	0	0	12	12
Luke Thomas	19/10/02	(1)	(1)	0	0	0	0	0	0	0	0
Luke Waterworth	20/6/96	3(3)	3(2)	0	0	0	0	0	0	0	0
Tom Whitehead	7/11/02	(1)	(1)	0	0	0	0	0	0	0	0
Dane Windrow	9/6/02	(1)	(1)	0	0	0	0	0	0	0	0

'Ch' totals include Championship games only; 'All' totals also include Challenge Cup

Joey Romeo

LEAGUE RECORD
P27-W9-D0-L18 (10th)
F426, A739, Diff-313, 18 points.

CHALLENGE CUP
Round Three

ATTENDANCES
Best - v Widnes (Ch - 1,403)
Worst - v Newcastle (Ch - 877)
Total (all home games included) - 14,214
Average (all home games included) - 1,093
(Up by 201 on 2022, League One)

CLUB RECORDS
MATCH RECORDS Highest score: 96-4 v Oxford, 12/7/2015; 96-0 v West Wales, 30/1/2022 Highest score against: 0-112 v Warrington, 20/5/2011
Record attendance: 26,891 v Wigan, 12/2/64 (Station Road); 2,155 v Toulouse, 28/4/2018 (Heywood Road)
Tries: 6 Mark Riley v Prescot, 11/8/96 Goals: 15 Dan Abram v West Wales, 13/8/2022 Points: 48 Ian Mort v Oxford, 12/7/2015
SEASON RECORDS Tries: 42 John Stopford 1963-64 Goals: 154 Dan Abram 2022 Points: 352 Dan Abram 2022
CAREER RECORDS Tries: 197 Frank Evans 1921-31 Goals: 970 Ken Gowers 1954-73 Points: 2,105 Ken Gowers 1954-73 Appearances: 601 Ken Gowers 1954-73

Championship 2023 - Club by Club

TOULOUSE OLYMPIQUE

DATE	FIXTURE	RESULT	SCORERS	LGE	ATT
4/2/23	Barrow (a)	W4-24	t:Ashall-Bott,Rennie,B Laguerre(2),Peyroux,Ralph	2nd	2,177
11/2/23	Newcastle (h)	W58-0	t:Armitage(2),Shorrocks,Marcon,Richards,Peyroux,Brochon,Rennie,Ralph, Hansen,Marion g:Shorrocks(3),Brochon(4)	1st	3,047
18/2/23	York (h)	W36-0	t:Armitage(4),Rennie,Ashall-Bott,Jussaume g:Shorrocks(3),Marion	2nd	2,761
25/2/23	Bradford (a)	L28-18	t:Marion,Marcon,Belmas g:Shorrocks(3)	2nd	2,798
4/3/23	Whitehaven (h)	W72-10	t:Rennie,Lima(3),Ashall-Bott,Marcon,Richards,Shorrocks(3), Maxime Stefani,Jussaume g:Shorrocks(12)	2nd	2,558
18/3/23	Widnes (a)	W12-14	t:Bretherton,Rennie,Marcon g:Shorrocks	2nd	3,093
25/3/23	Sheffield (h)	L32-4	t:Jussaume	2nd	959
7/4/23	London Broncos (h)	W52-0	t:Brochon,Ralph(2),Armitage(2),Rennie(2),Pelissier(2) g:Shorrocks(8)	2nd	3,358
15/4/23	Keighley (a)	W6-34	t:Marion,Ralph(2),Rennie,Maxime Stefani,Armitage g:Shorrocks(5)	2nd	1,739
6/5/23	Swinton (a)	L19-12	t:Akauola,Peyroux g:Shorrocks(2)	3rd	957
13/5/23	Batley (a)	L17-16	t:Jussaume,Brochon,Ralph g:Brochon(2)	4th	1,331
27/5/23	London Broncos (SB) ●	L14-10	t:Marion(2) g:Shorrocks	4th	N/A
3/6/23	Halifax (h)	W28-22	t:Marion,Armitage(2),Lima,Maxime Stefani g:Shorrocks(4)	4th	4,806
10/6/23	Featherstone (a)	W18-36	t:Armitage(2),Lima,Peyroux(2),Marcon g:Shorrocks(6)	4th	3,489
17/6/23	Sheffield (h)	W48-10	t:Belmas,Maxime Stefani(2),Armitage(2),Richards(2),Jussaume,Ralph g:Shorrocks(6)	3rd	3,344
24/6/23	Bradford (h)	W52-14	t:B Laguerre(2),Ralph(3),Armitage(2),Brochon,Maxime Stefani g:Shorrocks(8)	2nd	4,211
1/7/23	Widnes (h)	W40-28	t:Biscarro(2),Gahan,Maxime Stefani,Marcon,Jussaume,Armitage g:Shorrocks(6)	2nd	3,870
8/7/23	London Broncos (a) ●●	L22-6	t:Santo g:Shorrocks	3rd	1,089
15/7/23	Batley (h)	W34-12	t:Ralph,Marion,B Laguerre,Maxime Stefani,Santo(2) g:Shorrocks(5)	2nd	3,557
29/7/23	Keighley (h)	W64-0	t:Marion(2),Ralph,Maxime Stefani(3),B Laguerre,Bretherton,Armitage(2),Marcon g:Shorrocks(10)	2nd	3,250
5/8/23	York (a)	W14-18	t:Armitage,Richards,Marion g:Shorrocks(3)	2nd	1,483
19/8/23	Swinton (h) ●●●	W26-6	t:Brochon,Bretherton,Marion,Akauola g:Brochon(3)	2nd	2,430
26/8/23	Barrow (h) ●●●●	W34-10	t:B Laguerre,Richards,Marion,Pelissier(2),Santo g:Shorrocks(4),Brochon	2nd	2,487
2/9/23	Newcastle (a)	W16-36	t:Marion,Silva,Santo(2),Maxime Stefani,Richards g:Shorrocks(6)	2nd	639
9/9/23	Halifax (a)	L26-18	t:Brochon,Lima,Santo g:Shorrocks(3)	2nd	1,437
16/9/23	Featherstone (h) ●●●●●	L16-29	t:B Laguerre,Brochon,Akauola g:Shorrocks(2)	2nd	2,603
23/9/23	Whitehaven (a)	W16-26	t:Biscarro,Ashall-Bott,Santo(2),Gahan g:Santo(3)	2nd	997
7/10/23	Bradford (h) (SF)	W38-20	t:Santo,Maxime Stefani,Armitage,B Laguerre(2),Ralph,Marcon g:Santo,Brochon(4)	N/A	4,352
15/10/23	London Broncos (h) (GF)	L14-18	t:Jussaume,Ralph g:Shorrocks(3)	N/A	3,974

● Played at LNER Community Stadium, York ●● Played at Kuflink Stadium, Ebsfleet
●●● Played at Stade Albert Domec, Carcassonne ●●●● Played at Stade Mazicou, Albi ●●●●● Played at Stade des Minimes

	D.O.B.	APP ALL	Ch	TRIES ALL	Ch	GOALS ALL	Ch	FG ALL	Ch	PTS ALL	Ch
Sitaleki Akauola	7/4/92	(16)	(16)	3	3	0	0	0	0	12	12
Guy Armitage	29/11/91	22	22	22	22	0	0	0	0	88	88
Olly Ashall-Bott	24/11/97	6	6	4	4	0	0	0	0	16	16
Lambert Belmas	11/8/97	19(1)	19(1)	2	2	0	0	0	0	8	8
Dimitri Biscarro	11/7/01	11(6)	11(6)	3	3	0	0	0	0	12	12
Joe Bretherton	5/10/95	11(11)	11(11)	3	3	0	0	0	0	12	12
Robin Brochon	21/9/00	18(2)	18(2)	8	8	14	14	0	0	60	60
Loan Castano	24/2/02	(1)	(1)	0	0	0	0	0	0	0	0
Tiaki Chan	15/6/00	(4)	(4)	0	0	0	0	0	0	0	0
Calum Gahan	23/4/97	20	20	2	2	0	0	0	0	8	8
Anthony Guidez	11/1/01	1	1	0	0	0	0	0	0	0	0
Stephane Guillon	22/8/02	(2)	(2)	0	0	0	0	0	0	0	0
Harrison Hansen	26/10/85	24(1)	24(1)	1	1	0	0	0	0	4	4
Harvie Hill	3/9/03	(2)	(2)	0	0	0	0	0	0	0	0
Mathieu Jussaume	17/5/99	22	22	7	7	0	0	0	0	28	28
Benjamin Laguerre	13/9/01	15	15	10	10	0	0	0	0	40	40
Matthieu Laguerre	3/2/99	8	8	0	0	0	0	0	0	0	0
Pierre-Jean Lima	13/10/00	16(4)	16(4)	6	6	0	0	0	0	24	24
Paul Marcon	10/7/95	29	29	8	8	0	0	0	0	32	32
Anthony Marion	12/1/94	29	29	13	13	1	1	0	0	54	54
Eloi Pelissier	18/6/91	5(16)	5(16)	4	4	0	0	0	0	16	16
Dominique Peyroux	21/1/89	10(4)	10(4)	5	5	0	0	0	0	20	20
Hugo Pezet	20/10/00	(10)	(10)	0	0	0	0	0	0	0	0
Josh Ralph	21/7/97	23	23	15	15	0	0	0	0	60	60
Reubenn Rennie	22/10/95	13	13	8	8	0	0	0	0	32	32
Greg Richards	12/7/95	8(17)	8(17)	7	7	0	0	0	0	28	28
Zac Santo	8/4/93	12	12	10	10	4	4	0	0	48	48
Latrell Schaumkel	22/7/94	1(1)	1(1)	0	0	0	0	0	0	0	0
Bastien Scimone	2/11/98	(3)	(3)	0	0	0	0	0	0	0	0
Jake Shorrocks	26/10/95	25	25	4	4	105	105	0	0	226	226
Ramon Silva	7/11/01	(8)	(8)	1	1	0	0	0	0	4	4
Wail Skoundri	25/5/02	(3)	(3)	0	0	0	0	0	0	0	0
Matteo Stefani	29/6/04	1	1	0	0	0	0	0	0	0	0
Maxime Stefani	10/3/98	27	27	13	13	0	0	0	0	52	52
Ugo Tison	7/7/01	(2)	(2)	0	0	0	0	0	0	0	0
Justin Tropis	31/5/03	1(1)	1(1)	0	0	0	0	0	0	0	0

'Ch' totals include regular season & play-offs

Anthony Marion

LEAGUE RECORD
P27-W19-D0-L8
(2nd/Grand Final Runners-up)
F832, A385, Diff+447, 38 points.

CHALLENGE CUP
Not entered

ATTENDANCES
Best - v Halifax (Ch - 4,806)
Worst - v Swinton (Ch - 2,430)
Total (all home games included) - 50,608
Average (all home games included) - 3,374
(Down by 1,594 on 2022, Super League)

CLUB RECORDS
MATCH RECORDS Highest score: 84-6 v Keighley, 18/6/2016 Highest score against: 10-90 v Featherstone, 3/7/2011 Record attendance: 9,235 v Featherstone, 10/10/2021
Tries: 6 Ilias Bergal v Rochdale, 13/7/2019 Goals: 12 Mark Kheirallah v Keighley, 18/6/2016; Jake Shorrocks v Whitehaven, 4/3/2023
Points: 40 Mark Kheirallah v Keighley, 18/6/2016
SEASON RECORDS Tries: 36 Kuni Minga 2016 Goals: 171 Mark Kheirallah 2016 Points: 466 Mark Kheirallah 2016
CAREER RECORDS Tries: 98 Mark Kheirallah 2016-2021 Goals: 650 (inc 1fg) Mark Kheirallah 2016-2021
Points: 1,691 Mark Kheirallah 2016-2021 Appearances: 177 Anthony Marion 2016-2019; 2021-2023

● *Records only include seasons when the club competed in the British game (2009-2011 & 2016-2023)*

Championship 2023 - Club by Club

WHITEHAVEN

DATE	FIXTURE	RESULT	SCORERS	LGE	ATT
5/2/23	Bradford (a)	L24-8	t:Eccleston g:Freeman(2)	12th	4,878
12/2/23	London Broncos (h)	L16-20	t:Douglas(2),Nsemba g:Rourke(2)	12th	750
19/2/23	Featherstone (a)	L76-4	t:Rourke	14th	2,248
26/2/23	Swinton (h)	W20-4	t:Taylor,Freeman(2) g:Freeman(4)	12th	891
4/3/23	Toulouse (a)	L72-10	t:Rourke,Teare g:Freeman	13th	2,558
11/3/23	London Broncos (a) (CCR3)	L32-10	t:Teare,Taylor g:Freeman	N/A	347
19/3/23	York (a)	W12-14	t:Spencer-Tonks(2),Teare g:Freeman	12th	1,614
26/3/23	Batley (h)	L16-18	t:O'Brien,Newton,Teare g:Freeman(2)	12th	1,006
7/4/23	Barrow (a)	W14-16	t:King,Dixon,Aiye g:Rourke(2)	11th	3,136
16/4/23	Newcastle (h)	W31-6	t:Dixon,Bishop,Walker,Singleton,Rourke g:Rourke(5) fg:J Doran	9th	987
7/5/23	Keighley (h)	L24-32	t:Graham(2),Eccleston,Teare g:Rourke(4)	10th	1,065
14/5/23	Halifax (a)	L60-0		11th	1,998
27/5/23	Barrow (SB) ●	L32-16	t:Teare(2),Rourke g:Rourke(2)	11th	N/A
4/6/23	Sheffield (a)	W26-40	t:Teare,Taylor,Spencer-Tonks,Rourke(2),King g:Rourke(8)	11th	1,179
11/6/23	Widnes (h)	W36-12	t:Rourke,Newton,Taylor(2),Tabu,King g:Rourke(6)	9th	960
25/6/23	Keighley (a)	L28-18	t:Eccleston,King,Rourke g:Rourke(3)	10th	2,106
28/6/23	York (h)	W26-24	t:King,Aiye,Rourke,Teare,O Doran g:Rourke(3)	9th	951
2/7/23	Featherstone (h)	L0-60		9th	841
9/7/23	Newcastle (a)	L30-12	t:Hill,Carter g:Rourke(2)	10th	1,284
16/7/23	Bradford (h)	L18-44	t:Holliday,Aiye,King g:Rourke(3)	10th	1,257
30/7/23	Widnes (a)	L36-28	t:Castle,Eccleston(2),King,Graham g:Rourke(4)	10th	2,785
6/8/23	Sheffield (h)	W32-20	t:Teare,Rourke,Eccleston,O Doran,Spencer-Tonks,King g:Rourke(4)	10th	720
21/8/23	Barrow (h)	L22-23	t:O Doran,Holliday,Carter,King g:Rourke(3)	10th	1,176
27/8/23	London Broncos (a)	L34-18	t:Eccleston,Lanskey,Rourke g:Rourke(3)	10th	786
3/9/23	Halifax (h)	L8-30	t:Spencer-Tonks,O Doran	11th	1,056
10/9/23	Batley (a)	L25-12	t:Eccleston,Aiye g:Rourke(2)	11th	1,172
17/9/23	Swinton (a)	L21-20	t:Taylor,Teare,Aiye,Eccleston g:Rourke(2)	11th	1,315
23/9/23	Toulouse (h)	L16-26	t:J Doran,Teare,Dixon g:Rourke(2)	12th	997

● Played at LNER Community Stadium, York

		APP		TRIES		GOALS		FG		PTS	
	D.O.B.	ALL	Ch	ALL	Ch	ALL	Ch	ALL	Ch	ALL	Ch
Ross Ainley	17/1/97	13(9)	13(8)	0	0	0	0	0	0	0	0
Dion Aiye	6/11/87	7(19)	7(18)	5	5	0	0	0	0	20	20
Alex Bishop	18/1/94	6	6	1	1	0	0	0	0	4	4
Jake Bradley	29/4/01	(3)	(2)	0	0	0	0	0	0	0	0
Jake Carter	24/11/98	11(1)	11(1)	2	2	0	0	0	0	8	8
Lucas Castle	7/9/99	26(2)	25(2)	1	1	0	0	0	0	4	4
Bailey Dawson	18/5/03	1	1	0	0	0	0	0	0	0	0
Karl Dixon	13/9/93	7	7	3	3	0	0	0	0	12	12
Jamie Doran	8/12/94	27	26	1	1	0	0	1	1	5	5
Oscar Doran	17/10/04	11	11	4	4	0	0	0	0	16	16
Jacob Douglas	17/8/97	3	3	2	2	0	0	0	0	8	8
Dave Eccleston	12/9/96	27	26	9	9	0	0	0	0	36	36
Tom Forber	22/5/03	(2)	(2)	0	0	0	0	0	0	0	0
Sam Freeman	3/4/99	7	6	2	2	11	10	0	0	30	28
Guy Graham	29/8/98	11(2)	10(2)	3	3	0	0	0	0	12	12
Will Groves	9/4/04	1(1)	1(1)	0	0	0	0	0	0	0	0
Sam Haynes	24/6/04	2	2	0	0	0	0	0	0	0	0
George Hill	29/7/04	4(6)	4(6)	1	1	0	0	0	0	4	4
Connor Holliday	9/6/95	24(1)	23(1)	2	2	0	0	0	0	8	8
Brad Holroyd	15/4/00	2	2	0	0	0	0	0	0	0	0
Ryan King	28/6/97	15	15	9	9	0	0	0	0	36	36
Lachlan Lanskey	29/5/97	22(2)	21(2)	1	1	0	0	0	0	4	4
Liam McAvoy	24/9/93	7(1)	6(1)	0	0	0	0	0	0	0	0
James Newton	20/12/91	22(2)	21(2)	2	2	0	0	0	0	8	8
Junior Nsemba	27/6/04	3	3	1	1	0	0	0	0	4	4
Marcus O'Brien	13/7/93	6(3)	6(2)	1	1	0	0	0	0	4	4
Callum Phillips	19/2/92	(3)	(3)	0	0	0	0	0	0	0	0
Josh Rourke	27/10/99	28	27	11	11	60	60	0	0	164	164
Connor Saunders	31/5/97	(1)	(1)	0	0	0	0	0	0	0	0
Perry Singleton	5/1/94	3(21)	2(21)	1	1	0	0	0	0	4	4
Daniel Spencer-Tonks	18/1/95	3(15)	3(15)	5	5	0	0	0	0	20	20
Lasarusa Tabu	8/8/89	9(10)	9(10)	1	1	0	0	0	0	4	4
Chris Taylor	25/10/93	23	22	6	5	0	0	0	0	24	20
Curtis Teare	13/2/99	28	27	12	11	0	0	0	0	48	44
Tom Walker	25/12/94	5(5)	5(5)	1	1	0	0	0	0	4	4

'Ch' totals include Championship games only; 'All' totals also include Challenge Cup

Josh Rourke

LEAGUE RECORD
P27-W8-D0-L19 (12th)
F481, A809, Diff-328, 16 points.

CHALLENGE CUP
Round Three

ATTENDANCES
Best - v Bradford (Ch - 1,257)
Worst - v Sheffield (Ch - 720)
Total (all home games included) - 12,657
Average (all home games included) - 974
(Down by 112 on 2022)

CLUB RECORDS
MATCH RECORDS Highest score: 86-6 v Highfield, 25/1/95 Highest score against: 8-106 v Wigan, 12/5/2008 Record attendance: 18,500 v Wakefield, 19/3/60
Tries: 6 Vince Gribbin v Doncaster, 18/11/84; Andrew Bulman v Wigan St Patricks, 10/3/2019
Goals: 13 Lee Anderson v Highfield, 25/1/95 Points: 32 Mick Nanyn v Batley, 22/8/2004
SEASON RECORDS Tries: 34 Mike Pechey 1994-95 Goals: 141 John McKeown 1956-57 Points: 398 Mick Nanyn 2004
CAREER RECORDS Tries: 239 Craig Calvert 2004-2017 Goals: 1,050 John McKeown 1948-61 Points: 2,133 John McKeown 1948-61 Appearances: 417 John McKeown 1948-61

Championship 2023 - Club by Club

WIDNES VIKINGS

DATE	FIXTURE	RESULT	SCORERS	LGE	ATT
5/2/23	York (a)	W12-19	t:Millar,Grady,Walker g:Gilmore,Owens(2) fg:Gilmore	7th	1,895
12/2/23	Keighley (h)	W26-18	t:Craven,Millar(3),Owens g:Owens(3)	3rd	3,449
19/2/23	Bradford (a)	L14-12	t:Grady,Lawton g:K Dixon(2)	4th	4,827
27/2/23	Halifax (h)	W42-14	t:K Dixon(2),Grady(2),Millar,Craven,Owens,Edge g:K Dixon(5)	4th	3,187
5/3/23	Sheffield (a)	L42-12	t:Ince,Craven g:Owens(2)	5th	1,319
11/3/23	Wests Warriors (a) (CCR3) ●	W4-80	t:Edge(2),Holroyd(2),Brookes(2),Field,Brown(2),Davies,Fleming(2),Ince(2),Walker g:Edge(10)	N/A	843
18/3/23	Toulouse (h)	L12-14	t:Ince,K Dixon,Edge	7th	3,093
26/3/23	Newcastle (h)	W24-16	t:Owens,K Dixon,Wilde,Lyons g:Edge(4)	4th	2,743
2/4/23	Dewsbury (a) (CCR4)	L32-12	t:Fozard,Lawton g:Owens(2)	N/A	802
7/4/23	Swinton (a)	W16-48	t:Fleming,Owens,Craven,Eckersley(3),Lawton(2),K Dixon g:Owens(6)	4th	1,403
16/4/23	Barrow (h)	W23-14	t:Lawton,Eckersley,Craven,Ince g:Owens(3) fg:Owens	4th	2,772
8/5/23	Batley (a)	L11-4	t:Eckersley	4th	923
14/5/23	Featherstone (h)	L0-30		6th	2,832
27/5/23	Swinton (SB) ●●	W6-38	t:Ince,Lyons,K Dixon(2),Owens(2) g:Edge,Gilmore(4)	6th	N/A
4/6/23	London Broncos (h)	L18-26	t:Wilde(2),K Dixon g:Gilmore(3)	7th	2,547
11/6/23	Whitehaven (a)	L36-12	t:Roberts,Wilde g:Gilmore(2)	7th	960
18/6/23	Barrow (a)	L26-18	t:Wilde,Lyons,Brown g:Gilmore(3)	7th	2,150
25/6/23	Swinton (h)	L18-25	t:Walker,Davies,Lawton g:Gilmore(3)	7th	2,833
1/7/23	Toulouse (a)	L40-28	t:Millar(2),Grady,K Dixon(2),Wilde g:Edge(2)	8th	3,870
10/7/23	Bradford (h)	W31-14	t:Fozard,K Dixon(2),Lawton,Brookes g:Gilmore,Edge(4) fg:Gilmore	8th	2,561
16/7/23	Keighley (a)	W22-38	t:Lawton,Fozard,Lyons,Gilmore,Roberts(2),Wilde g:K Dixon(5)	8th	1,267
30/7/23	Whitehaven (h)	W36-28	t:Edge(2),Brookes,Farnworth,Grady,Davies g:K Dixon(6)	7th	2,785
5/8/23	Newcastle (a)	W6-50	t:Roberts(2),Lyons,Wilde(2),K Dixon,Gilmore,Field,Brookes,Fleming g:K Dixon(5)	7th	2,206
20/8/23	York (h)	L30-40	t:Wilde,Brookes,Farnworth,Edge,K Dixon g:K Dixon(4),Gilmore	8th	3,008
27/8/23	Halifax (a)	W26-28	t:Ince(3),Craven,Owens g:K Dixon(4)	7th	1,685
3/9/23	Batley (h)	W12-4	t:Field,Owens g:K Dixon(2)	6th	3,219
10/9/23	London Broncos (a)	L52-12	t:Davies,K Dixon g:K Dixon(2)	8th	1,062
17/9/23	Sheffield (h)	L18-38	t:Lawton,K Dixon(2) g:K Dixon(3)	9th	2,961
23/9/23	Featherstone (a)	L62-10	t:Lyons,Ince g:K Dixon	9th	3,874

● Played at DCBL Stadium
●● Played at LNER Community Stadium, York

	D.O.B.	APP ALL	APP Ch	TRIES ALL	TRIES Ch	GOALS ALL	GOALS Ch	FG ALL	FG Ch	PTS ALL	PTS Ch
Kyle Amor	26/5/87	8(2)	8(1)	0	0	0	0	0	0	0	0
Liam Bent	11/10/97	7(1)	6(1)	0	0	0	0	0	0	0	0
Ollie Brookes	19/6/01	7(1)	6	6	4	0	0	0	0	24	16
Aaron Brown	27/7/92	11(8)	10(7)	3	1	0	0	0	0	12	4
Danny Craven	21/11/91	13	12	6	6	0	0	0	0	24	24
Olly Davies	30/11/95	11(15)	10(15)	4	3	0	0	0	0	16	12
Andrew Dixon	28/2/90	1	1	0	0	0	0	0	0	0	0
Kieran Dixon	22/8/92	27	26	17	17	39	39	0	0	146	146
Zach Eckersley	10/11/03	7(1)	7(1)	5	5	0	0	0	0	20	20
Joe Edge	22/2/00	28	26	7	5	21	11	0	0	70	42
Owen Farnworth	11/2/99	10(7)	10(6)	2	2	0	0	0	0	8	8
Callum Field	7/10/97	18(6)	16(6)	3	2	0	0	0	0	12	8
Matty Fleming	13/1/96	25	23	4	2	0	0	0	0	16	8
Tom Forber	22/5/03	(8)	(8)	0	0	0	0	0	0	0	0
Matty Fozard	3/3/95	25(4)	24(3)	3	2	0	0	0	0	12	8
Tom Gilmore	2/2/94	17	17	2	2	18	18	2	2	46	46
Shane Grady	13/12/89	21(1)	20(1)	6	6	0	0	0	0	24	24
Lewis Hatton	14/1/97	(16)	(16)	0	0	0	0	0	0	0	0
Brad Holroyd	15/4/00	1	0	2	0	0	0	0	0	8	0
Ryan Ince	16/9/96	18	16	11	9	0	0	0	0	44	36
Jordan Johnstone	24/5/97	11(2)	10(2)	0	0	0	0	0	0	0	0
Jacob Jones	15/2/99	5(2)	5(2)	0	0	0	0	0	0	0	0
Adam Lawton	13/6/93	17(8)	15(8)	9	8	0	0	0	0	36	32
Joe Lyons	16/10/97	23	21	6	6	0	0	0	0	24	24
Ryan Millar	12/5/94	8	8	7	7	0	0	0	0	28	28
Jack Owens	3/6/94	20(1)	19(1)	8	8	18	16	1	1	69	65
Max Roberts	8/9/00	9(5)	9(5)	5	5	0	0	0	0	20	20
Will Tilleke	18/11/99	1(3)	(3)	0	0	0	0	0	0	0	0
Anthony Walker	28/12/91	6(16)	5(15)	3	2	0	0	0	0	12	8
Sam Wilde	8/9/95	22(5)	21(4)	10	10	0	0	0	0	40	40
Huw Worthington	28/10/94	(3)	(3)	0	0	0	0	0	0	0	0

'Ch' totals include Championship games only; 'All' totals also include Challenge Cup

Kieran Dixon

LEAGUE RECORD
P27-W13-D0-L14 (9th)
F619, A652, Diff-33, 26 points.

CHALLENGE CUP
Round Four

ATTENDANCES
Best - v Keighley (Ch - 3,449)
Worst - v Wests Warriors (CC - 843)
Total (excluding Challenge Cup) - 37,990
Average (excluding Challenge Cup) - 2,922
(Up by 62 on 2022)

CLUB RECORDS Highest score: 90-4 v Doncaster, 10/6/2007; 90-0 v Coventry, 21/4/2018 Highest score against: 6-76 v Catalans Dragons, 31/3/2012
Record attendance: 24,205 v St Helens, 16/2/61
MATCH RECORDS Tries: 7 Phil Cantillon v York, 18/2/2001 Goals: 14 Mark Hewitt v Oldham, 25/7/97; Tim Hartley v Saddleworth, 7/3/2009
Points: 38 Gavin Dodd v Doncaster, 10/6/2007
SEASON RECORDS Tries: 58 Martin Offiah 1988-89 Goals: 161 Mick Nanyn 2007 Points: 434 Mick Nanyn 2007
CAREER RECORDS Tries: 234 Mal Aspey 1964-80 Goals: 1,083 Ray Dutton 1966-78 Points: 2,195 Ray Dutton 1966-78 Appearances: 591 Keith Elwell 1970-86

Championship 2023 - Club by Club

YORK KNIGHTS

DATE	FIXTURE	RESULT	SCORERS	LGE	ATT
5/2/23	Widnes (h)	L12-19	t:Kirmond,Brown g:Glover(2)	8th	1,895
13/2/23	Bradford (h)	W32-16	t:Jubb,Kirby,Michael,Daley g:Glover(8)	5th	2,381
18/2/23	Toulouse (a)	L36-0		9th	2,761
26/2/23	Barrow (h)	W28-14	t:Harrison,Dee,Kirby,Hingano,Brown g:Glover(4)	7th	1,525
5/3/23	Swinton (a)	W0-40	t:Towse(2),Hingano,Harrison(2),Brown(2),Daley g:Glover(4)	4th	1,029
12/3/23	West Bowling (h) (CCR3)	W52-12	t:Harris(2),Towse,Marsh,Ward(2),Brown,Antrobus(2),Kirmond g:Harris(6)	N/A	1,040
19/3/23	Whitehaven (h)	L12-14	t:Marsh,Towse g:Glover(2)	6th	1,614
26/3/23	Featherstone (a)	L46-4	t:Glover	9th	2,892
2/4/23	Sheffield (h) (CCR4)	W24-22	t:Harrison,Kirmond(2),Fitzsimmons,Towse g:Glover(2)	N/A	832
7/4/23	Keighley (h)	L10-22	t:Antrobus,Harris g:Glover	9th	2,218
16/4/23	Halifax (a)	L16-6	t:Glover g:Glover	10th	1,454
21/4/23	Newcastle (h) (CCR5)	W22-18	t:Brown,Towse,Marsh,Harris g:Glover(3)	N/A	1,100
7/5/23	London Broncos (h)	W30-28	t:Towse(3),Clarkson,Ta'ai g:Glover(5)	9th	1,802
14/5/23	Newcastle (a)	W26-22	t:Towse,Brown,Field(2),Glover,Pratt g:Glover	8th	2,276
21/5/23	London Broncos (h) (CCR6)	W36-12	t:Butterworth(3),Daley,Brown,Thompson,Dee g:Glover(4)	N/A	951
27/5/23	Featherstone (SB) ●	L46-16	t:Dee,Brown,Daley g:Glover(2)	9th	N/A
4/6/23	Batley (a)	L14-8	t:Glover,Dee	9th	2,003
9/6/23	Sheffield (a)	L40-10	t:Clarkson,Fitzsimmons g:Brown	11th	1,051
18/6/23	Leigh (h) (CCQF)	L14-34	t:Brown,Harrison g:Harrison(3)	N/A	2,412
25/6/23	Featherstone (h)	L8-24	t:Hingano,Towse	12th	2,554
28/6/23	Whitehaven (a)	L26-24	t:Towse(2),Kirmond,Santi,Pratt g:Harrison(2)	12th	951
2/7/23	Halifax (h)	W28-18	t:Cunningham,Dee,Harrison(2),Towse g:Harrison(4)	10th	1,823
9/7/23	Keighley (a)	W10-50	t:Dee(3),Field,Fitzsimmons,Brown(2),Towse g:Harrison(9)	9th	1,654
16/7/23	Sheffield (h)	W23-18	t:Harris,Bass,Thompson,Dee g:Harris(3) fg:Harris	9th	2,266
23/7/23	Batley (a) (1895CSF)	L8-22	t:Towse,Harris	N/A	1,646
30/7/23	London Broncos (a)	W10-24	t:Field,Fitzsimmons,Bass,Jubb g:Harris(4)	9th	957
5/8/23	Toulouse (h)	L14-18	t:Bass(2),Santi g:Harris	9th	1,483
20/8/23	Widnes (a)	W30-40	t:Dee,Pemberton,Pratt,Field(2),Towse,Fitzsimmons g:Harris(6)	9th	3,008
25/8/23	Newcastle (a)	W6-20	t:Jubb,Harrison(2) g:Harris(4)	9th	788
3/9/23	Swinton (h)	W26-22	t:Thompson,Jubb,Pratt(2) g:Harris(5)	9th	2,114
10/9/23	Bradford (a)	W10-20	t:Harrison,Towse,Fitzsimmons g:Harris(4)	9th	3,603
18/9/23	Batley (h)	W15-14	t:Pratt,Towse,Brown g:Harris fg:Harris	7th	2,377
24/9/23	Barrow (a)	W18-31	t:Field,Michael,Towse,Ta'ai,Santi g:Harris(5) fg:Harris	6th	2,292
1/10/23	Bradford (a) (E)	L22-8	t:Dee g:Harris(2)	N/A	2,738

● Played at LNER Community Stadium

		APP		TRIES		GOALS		FG		PTS	
	D.O.B.	ALL	Ch	ALL	Ch	ALL	Ch	ALL	Ch	ALL	Ch
Bailey Antrobus	18/2/00	16	12	3	1	0	0	0	0	12	4
Connor Barley	16/9/04	4(1)	3(1)	0	0	0	0	0	0	0	0
Ben Barnard	4/8/02	2(3)	1(3)	0	0	0	0	0	0	0	0
Jason Bass	10/5/96	9(1)	8(1)	4	4	0	0	0	0	16	16
Joe Brown	14/1/99	32	26	13	9	1	1	0	0	54	38
Olly Butterworth	12/1/98	3	2	3	0	0	0	0	0	12	0
Chris Clarkson	7/4/90	25	20	2	2	0	0	0	0	8	8
James Cunningham	3/4/94	15(1)	11(1)	1	1	0	0	0	0	4	4
Josh Daley	28/11/95	13(11)	10(9)	4	3	0	0	0	0	16	12
Jesse Dee	25/10/94	23	20	11	10	0	0	0	0	44	40
Levi Edwards	25/12/03	4	4	0	0	0	0	0	0	0	0
Oli Field	3/9/02	25(1)	20(1)	7	7	0	0	0	0	28	28
Conor Fitzsimmons	7/5/98	24(4)	21(4)	6	5	0	0	0	0	24	20
James Glover	2/12/93	16	13	4	4	39	30	0	0	94	76
Liam Harris	20/4/97	25	21	6	2	41	35	3	3	109	81
Myles Harrison	11/8/03	20(4)	17(3)	10	8	18	15	0	0	76	62
Ata Hingano	11/3/97	11(2)	10(1)	3	3	0	0	0	0	12	12
Adam Jones	11/1/03	1(1)	(1)	0	0	0	0	0	0	0	0
Will Jubb	17/9/96	29(2)	24(1)	4	4	0	0	0	0	16	16
Jon Luke Kirby	23/9/98	9(6)	8(4)	2	2	0	0	0	0	8	8
Danny Kirmond	11/11/85	19(2)	16(1)	5	2	0	0	0	0	20	8
Matty Marsh	21/4/95	10	7	3	1	0	0	0	0	12	4
Ronan Michael	3/7/00	8(21)	6(18)	2	2	0	0	0	0	8	8
Pauli Pauli	4/8/94	(5)	(5)	0	0	0	0	0	0	0	0
Taylor Pemberton	17/4/98	(7)	(7)	1	1	0	0	0	0	4	4
Oliver Pratt	4/9/04	10(1)	10(1)	6	6	0	0	0	0	24	24
Harry Price	8/11/03	(4)	(3)	0	0	0	0	0	0	0	0
Brenden Santi	5/8/93	11(3)	11(3)	3	3	0	0	0	0	12	12
Reagan Sumner	23/2/04	(1)	0	0	0	0	0	0	0	0	0
Ukuma Ta'ai	17/1/87	12(14)	9(11)	2	2	0	0	0	0	8	8
Jack Teanby	14/5/96	(25)	(19)	0	0	0	0	0	0	0	0
Jordan Thompson	4/9/91	26(2)	22(2)	3	2	0	0	0	0	12	8
AJ Towse	19/8/03	34	28	20	16	0	0	0	0	80	64
Brad Ward	4/6/03	6(1)	4(1)	2	0	0	0	0	0	8	0
Toby Warren	5/9/03	(3)	(3)	0	0	0	0	0	0	0	0

'Ch' totals include regular season & play-offs; 'All' totals also include Challenge Cup & 1895 Cup

AJ Towse

LEAGUE RECORD
P27-W15-D0-L12 (6th/Eliminator)
F557, A557, Diff 0, 30 points.

CHALLENGE CUP
Quarter Finalists

1895 CUP
Semi-Finalists

ATTENDANCES
Best - v Featherstone (Ch - 2,554)
Worst - v Sheffield (CC - 832)
Total (excluding Challenge Cup) - 27,974
Average (excluding Challenge Cup) - 1,998
(Up by 14 on 2022)

CLUB RECORDS	Highest score: 144-0 v West Wales, 29/4/2018 Highest score against: 4-100 v Leigh, 21/8/2022
	Record attendance: 14,689 v Swinton, 10/2/34 *(Clarence Street)*; 3,602 v Featherstone, 31/1/2022 *(LNER Community Stadium)*
MATCH RECORDS	Tries: 7 Brad Davis v Highfield, 17/9/95; Kieren Moss v West Wales, 29/4/2018
	Goals: 21 Connor Robinson v West Wales, 11/8/2018 Points: 56 Chris Thorman v Northumbria University, 6/3/2011
SEASON RECORDS	Tries: 35 John Crossley 1980-81 Goals: 186 *(inc 4fg)* Connor Robinson 2018 Points: 420 Connor Robinson 2018
CAREER RECORDS	Tries: 167 Peter Foster 1955-67 Goals: 1,060 Vic Yorke 1954-67 Points: 2,159 Vic Yorke 1954-67 Appearances: 449 Willie Hargreaves 1952-65

CHAMPIONSHIP 2023
Round by Round

Championship 2023 - Round by Round

ROUND 1

Saturday 4th February 2023

BARROW RAIDERS 4 TOULOUSE OLYMPIQUE 24

RAIDERS: 1 Luke Cresswell; 2 Shane Toal; 4 Greg Worthington; 3 Rio-Osayomwanbo Corkill; 5 Ryan Shaw; 6 Jarrod Sammut; 7 Ryan Johnston; 16 Sam Brooks; 22 Josh Wood; 15 Ellis Gillam; 11 Danny Langtree; 12 Jarrad Stack; 13 Jack Wells. Subs (all used): 8 Greg Burke; 10 Anton Iaria; 14 Jake Carter; 20 Ben Evans.
Try: Shaw (22); **Goals:** Shaw 0/1.
OLYMPIQUE: 1 Olly Ashall-Bott; 5 Paul Marcon; 4 Mathieu Jussaume; 3 Reubenn Rennie; 19 Benjamin Laguerre; 6 Josh Ralph; 7 Jake Shorrocks; 8 Lambert Belmas; 14 Eloi Pelissier; 10 Harrison Hansen; 12 Dominique Peyroux; 11 Maxime Stefani; 13 Anthony Marion. Subs (all used): 16 Joe Bretherton; 17 Hugo Pezet; 20 Greg Richards; 24 Pierre-Jean Lima.
Tries: Ashall-Bott (4), Rennie (7), B Laguerre (12, 48), Peyroux (33), Ralph (66); **Goals:** Marcon 0/3, Shorrocks 0/3.
Rugby Leaguer & League Express Men of the Match: *Raiders:* Anton Iaria; *Olympique:* Jake Shorrocks.
Penalty count: 7-3; **Half-time:** 4-16;
Referee: Cameron Worsley; **Attendance:** 2,177.

Sunday 5th February 2023

BRADFORD BULLS 24 WHITEHAVEN 8

BULLS: 31 Jack Walker; 2 Ben Blackmore; 3 Joe Arundel; 4 Kieran Gill; 5 David Foggin-Johnston; 1 Tom Holmes; 6 Dec Patton; 10 Michael Lawrence; 7 Jordan Lilley; 16 Brad Foster; 12 Chester Butler; 15 AJ Wallace; 13 Bodene Thompson. Subs (all used): 9 George Flanagan; 8 Jordan Baldwinson; 21 Fenton Rogers; 11 Brad England.
Tries: C Butler (27), Gill (49, 51), Flanagan (77);
Goals: Patton 4/4.
WHITEHAVEN: 1 Sam Freeman; 2 Dave Eccleston; 23 Josh Rourke; 18 Perry Singleton; 4 Curtis Teare; 14 Jamie Doran; 7 Alex Bishop; 22 Lucas Castle; 21 Marcus O'Brien; 10 Tom Walker; 11 Connor Holliday; 12 Lachlan Lanskey; 8 Liam McAvoy. Subs (all used): 28 Ross Ainley; 13 Dion Aiye; 20 Jake Bradley; 16 Lasarusa Tabu.
Try: Eccleston (64); **Goals:** Freeman 2/2.
Rugby Leaguer & League Express Men of the Match: *Bulls:* Tom Holmes; *Whitehaven:* Sam Freeman.
Penalty count: 8-7; **Half-time:** 6-2;
Referee: Nick Bennett; **Attendance:** 4,878.

HALIFAX PANTHERS 26 SHEFFIELD EAGLES 18

PANTHERS: 1 James Woodburn-Hall; 2 Lachlan Walmsley; 22 Jake Maizen; 3 Zack McComb; 5 James Saltonstall; 6 Louis Jouffret; 7 Joe Keyes; 16 Will Calcott; 9 Brandon Moore; 10 Dan Murray; 11 Ben Kavanagh; 12 Matty Gee; 8 Adam Tangata. Subs (all used): 13 Jacob Fairbank; 15 Will Maher; 20 Tom Inman; 31 Kevin Larroyer.
Tries: Saltonstall (5), Walmsley (21), Maizen (27, 79);
Goals: Keyes 5/6.
EAGLES: 5 Jason Bass; 2 Ben Jones-Bishop; 3 Kris Welham; 4 Ross Oakes; 28 Matty Dawson-Jones; 32 Cory Aston; 19 Jack Hansen; 17 Liam Kirk; 9 Vila Halafihi; 10 Tyler Dickinson; 18 Aaron Murphy; 12 Joel Farrell; 14 Titus Gwaze. Subs (all used): 8 Brandon Douglas; 15 Mikey Wood; 16 Blake Broadbent; 23 Bayley Liu.
Tries: Murphy (36), Liu (56, 72); **Goals:** Hansen 3/3.
Sin bin: Douglas (26) - dissent.
Rugby Leaguer & League Express Men of the Match: *Panthers:* Jake Maizen; *Eagles:* Bayley Liu.
Penalty count: 7-3; **Half-time:** 16-6;
Referee: Liam Rush; **Attendance:** 2,101.

LONDON BRONCOS 20 BATLEY BULLDOGS 30

BRONCOS: 1 Alex Walker; 2 Paul Ulberg; 3 Jarred Bassett; 4 Dalton Grant; 5 Iliess Macani; 6 Oliver Leyland; 7 Rian Horsman; 15 Lewis Bienek; 9 Sam Davis; 10 Jordan Williams; 11 Will Lovell; 16 Ethan Natoli; 13 Dean Parata. Subs (all used): 14 Bill Leyland; 8 Wellington Albert; 12 Marcus Stock; 27 Ramon Silva.
Tries: Grant (18), B Leyland (28), Walker (41), Ulberg (75);
Goals: O Leyland 2/4.
BULLDOGS: 21 Aidan McGowan; 22 Dale Morton; 4 Josh Hodson; 3 Kieran Buchanan; 5 Johnny Campbell; 6 Ben White; 7 Josh Woods; 8 Adam Gledhill; 9 Alistair Leak; 10 Keegan Hirst; 11 Dane Manning; 12 Lucas Walshaw; 17 Luke Blake. Subs (all used): 14 James Meadows; 26 Nyle Flynn; 16 Michael Ward; 30 Martyn Reilly.
Tries: Leak (3), Buchanan (38, 60), Hodson (50), Flynn (70); **Goals:** Morton 1/1, Woods 1/2, Meadows 2/3, White 1/1.
Rugby Leaguer & League Express Men of the Match: *Broncos:* Alex Walker; *Bulldogs:* Josh Woods.
Penalty count: 7-7; **Half-time:** 10-10;
Referee: Aaron Moore; **Attendance:** 1,849.

SWINTON LIONS 6 NEWCASTLE THUNDER 18

LIONS: 26 Joey Romeo; 3 Jake Spedding; 22 Andy Badrock; 11 Rhodri Lloyd; 2 Mike Butt; 6 Nick Gregson; 7 Jordy Gibson; 8 Gavin Bennion; 14 Josh Eaves; 10 Kenny Baker; 12 Mitch Cox; 16 Gav Rodden; 13 Louis Brogan. Subs (all used): 9 Luke Waterworth; 15 Jordan Case; 18 Liam Cooper; 19 Ollie Olds.
Try: Badrock (38); **Goals:** Gregson 1/2.
THUNDER: 1 Jack Johnson; 5 Alex Clegg; 3 Marcus Walker; 26 Mac Walsh; 2 Alex Young; 6 Alex Donaghy; 7 Nikau Williams; 8 Jay Chapelhow; 9 Curtis Davies; 10 Mitch Clark; 11 Alex Foster; 12 Brad Gallagher; 13 Connor Bailey. Subs (all used): 14 Denive Balmforth; 15 Ted Chapelhow; 16 Rhys Clarke; 23 Connor Moore.
Tries: Young (56, 75), Williams (79); **Goals:** Williams 3/3.
Rugby Leaguer & League Express Men of the Match: *Lions:* Andy Badrock; *Thunder:* Nikau Williams.
Penalty count: 6-6; **Half-time:** 4-0;
Referee: Ryan Cox; **Attendance:** 877.

YORK KNIGHTS 12 WIDNES VIKINGS 19

KNIGHTS: 1 Matty Marsh; 2 Joe Brown; 3 James Glover; 15 Myles Harrison; 5 AJ Towse; 14 James Cunningham; 7 Liam Harris; 8 Jon Luke Kirby; 9 Will Jubb; 10 Conor Fitzsimmons; 16 Bailey Antrobus; 12 Danny Kirmond; 13 Jordan Thompson. Subs: 17 Ronan Michael; 19 Josh Daley; 20 Jack Teanby; 24 Ben Barnard (not used).
Tries: Kirmond (29), Brown (56); **Goals:** Glover 2/2.
VIKINGS: 1 Jack Owens; 28 Ryan Millar; 3 Matty Fleming; 20 Joe Edge; 5 Kieran Dixon; 18 Joe Lyons; 7 Tom Gilmore; 12 Adam Lawton; 14 Jordan Johnstone; 10 Kyle Amor; 19 Olly Davies; 17 Shane Grady; 13 Liam Bent. Subs (all used): 9 Matty Fozard; 16 Callum Field; 21 Lewis Hatton; 27 Anthony Walker.
Tries: Millar (9), Grady (47), Walker (69);
Goals: Gilmore 1/3, Owens 2/2; **Field goal:** Gilmore (78).
Rugby Leaguer & League Express Men of the Match: *Knights:* Bailey Antrobus; *Vikings:* Ryan Millar.
Penalty count: 3-4; **Half-time:** 6-4;
Referee: Michael Smaill; **Attendance:** 1,895.

Monday 6th February 2023

KEIGHLEY COUGARS 0 FEATHERSTONE ROVERS 50

COUGARS: 1 Lewis Young; 3 Charlie Graham; 25 Ben Crooks; 23 Robbie Storey; 5 Mo Agoro; 22 Dane Chisholm; 31 Luke Gale; 15 Brenden Santi; 13 Kyle Kesik; 11 Kyle Trout; 19 Ellis Robson; 12 Aaron Levy; 27 Sadiq Adebiyi. Subs (all used): 9 Billy Gaylor; 8 Dan Parker; 10 Toby Everett; 14 Harvey Spence.
Sin bin: Everett (50) - high tackle.
ROVERS: 23 Caleb Aekins; 2 Luke Briscoe; 3 Chris Hankinson; 18 Josh Hardcastle; 5 Gareth Gale; 6 Johnathon Ford; 7 Riley Dean; 10 James Lockwood; 14 Matty Wildie; 17 Gadwin Springer; 11 Brad Day; 12 Elijah Taylor; 24 Mathieu Cozza. Subs (all used): 9 Connor Jones; 8 Craig Kopczak; 27 McKenzie Yei; 19 Luke Cooper.
Tries: Gale (12, 43), Dean (17, 32), Day (25), Lockwood (29), Yei (53), Hardcastle (57), Aekins (63);
Goals: Hankinson 7/9.
Rugby Leaguer & League Express Men of the Match: *Cougars:* Sadiq Adebiyi; *Rovers:* Riley Dean.
Penalty count: 3-7; **Half-time:** 0-28;
Referee: Tom Grant; **Attendance:** 2,443.

ROUND 2

Saturday 11th February 2023

TOULOUSE OLYMPIQUE 58 NEWCASTLE THUNDER 0

OLYMPIQUE: 25 Robin Brochon; 5 Paul Marcon; 4 Mathieu Jussaume; 3 Reubenn Rennie; 18 Guy Armitage; 6 Josh Ralph; 7 Jake Shorrocks; 8 Lambert Belmas; 13 Anthony Marion; 16 Joe Bretherton; 12 Dominique Peyroux; 11 Maxime Stefani; 10 Harrison Hansen. Subs (all used): 14 Eloi Pelissier; 15 Sitaleki Akauola; 17 Hugo Pezet; 20 Greg Richards.
Tries: Armitage (2, 28), Shorrocks (7), Marcon (12), Richards (32), Peyroux (50), Brochon (56), Rennie (63), Ralph (69), Hansen (73), Marion (77);
Goals: Shorrocks 3/7, Brochon 4/4.
THUNDER: 1 Jack Johnson; 5 Alex Clegg; 3 Marcus Walker; 26 Mac Walsh; 2 Alex Young; 6 Alex Donaghy; 7 Nikau Williams; 8 Jay Chapelhow; 9 Curtis Davies; 10 Mitch Clark; 11 Alex Foster; 22 Jake Anderson; 13 Connor Bailey. Subs (all used): 14 Denive Balmforth; 15 Ted Chapelhow; 16 Rhys Clarke; 17 Rob Tuliatu.
Sin bin: Foster (39) - dangerous challenge.
Rugby Leaguer & League Express Men of the Match: *Olympique:* Jake Shorrocks; *Thunder:* Alex Donaghy.
Penalty count: 8-3; **Half-time:** 24-0;
Referee: Marcus Griffiths; **Attendance:** 3,047.

Sunday 12th February 2023

BARROW RAIDERS 16 SHEFFIELD EAGLES 36

RAIDERS: 1 Luke Cresswell; 27 Andrew Bulman; 4 Greg Worthington; 5 Ryan Shaw; 2 Shane Toal; 6 Jarrod Sammut; 7 Ryan Johnston; 10 Anton Iaria; 22 Josh Wood; 15 Ellis Gillam; 11 Danny Langtree; 12 Jarrad Stack; 13 Jack Wells. Subs (all used): 14 Jake Carter; 17 Charlie Emslie; 20 Ben Evans; 8 Greg Burke.
Tries: Gillam (11), Sammut (37), Toal (52); **Goals:** Shaw 2/3.
Sin bin: Johnston (77) - fighting.
EAGLES: 2 Ben Jones-Bishop; 5 Jason Bass; 3 Kris Welham; 4 Ross Oakes; 28 Matty Dawson-Jones; 32 Cory Aston; 7 Anthony Thackeray; 17 Liam Kirk; 9 Vila Halafihi; 10 Tyler Dickinson; 18 Aaron Murphy; 12 Joel Farrell; 14 Titus Gwaze. Subs (all used): 23 Bayley Liu; 15 Mikey Wood; 27 Jesse Sene-Lefao; 8 Brandon Douglas.
Tries: Welham (3, 20), Dawson-Jones (24), Oakes (34, 42), Liu (48), Thackeray (59); **Goals:** Aston 4/7.
Sin bin: Welham (66) - interference; J Farrell (77) - fighting.
Rugby Leaguer & League Express Men of the Match: *Raiders:* Anton Iaria; *Eagles:* Anthony Thackeray.
Penalty count: 5-5; **Half-time:** 12-22;
Referee: Ben Thaler; **Attendance:** 2,094.

BATLEY BULLDOGS 16 SWINTON LIONS 30

BULLDOGS: 14 James Meadows; 29 Greg Johnson; 12 Lucas Walshaw; 3 Kieran Buchanan; 5 Johnny Campbell; 6 Ben White; 7 Josh Woods; 10 Keegan Hirst; 24 Ben Kaye; 8 Adam Gledhill; 26 Nyle Flynn; 11 Dane Manning; 17 Luke Blake. Subs (all used): 9 Alistair Leak; 16 Michael Ward; 19 Tom Lillycrop; 30 Martyn Reilly.
Tries: Walshaw (25), Manning (32), Buchanan (47);
Goals: Meadows 2/3.
LIONS: 1 Dan Abram; 2 Mike Butt; 11 Rhodri Lloyd; 22 Andy Badrock; 4 Jayden Hatton; 19 Ollie Olds; 7 Jordy Gibson; 10 Kenny Baker; 9 Luke Waterworth; 34 George Delaney; 12 Mitch Cox; 16 Gav Rodden; 13 Louis Brogan. Subs (all used): 14 Josh Eaves; 15 Jordan Case; 18 Liam Cooper; 20 Morgan Burgess.
Tries: Butt (16), Eaves (59), Badrock (62), Abram (70), Olds (78); **Goals:** Abram 5/6.
Rugby Leaguer & League Express Men of the Match: *Bulldogs:* Nyle Flynn; *Lions:* Gav Rodden.
Penalty count: 8-4; **Half-time:** 10-6;
Referee: Aaron Moore; **Attendance:** 1,551.

WHITEHAVEN 16 LONDON BRONCOS 20

WHITEHAVEN: 23 Josh Rourke; 2 Dave Eccleston; 3 Chris Taylor; 4 Curtis Teare; 19 Jacob Douglas; 14 Jamie Doran; 13 Dion Aiye; 10 Tom Walker; 21 Marcus O'Brien; 8 Liam McAvoy; 29 Junior Nsemba; 12 Lachlan Lanskey; 16 Lasarusa Tabu. Subs (all used): 11 Connor Holliday; 18 Perry Singleton; 22 Lucas Castle; 28 Ross Ainley.
Tries: Douglas (35, 54), Nsemba (67); **Goals:** Rourke 2/3.
Sin bin: Tabu (72) - use of the knee.
BRONCOS: 1 Alex Walker; 2 Paul Ulberg; 3 Jarred Bassett; 29 Zach Eckersley; 5 Iliess Macani; 6 Oliver Leyland; 13 Dean Parata; 15 Lewis Bienek; 9 Sam Davis; 10 Jordan Williams; 11 Will Lovell; 16 Ethan Natoli; 12 Marcus Stock. Subs (all used): 8 Wellington Albert; 14 Bill Leyland; 27 Ramon Silva; 28 Harvie Hill.
Tries: Ulberg (9, 15), B Leyland (62), Bassett (73);
Goals: O Leyland 2/4.
Rugby Leaguer & League Express Men of the Match: *Whitehaven:* Junior Nsemba; *Broncos:* Sam Davis.
Penalty count: 4-4; **Half-time:** 6-10;
Referee: Tom Grant; **Attendance:** 750.

WIDNES VIKINGS 26 KEIGHLEY COUGARS 18

VIKINGS: 1 Jack Owens; 28 Ryan Millar; 3 Matty Fleming; 20 Joe Edge; 5 Kieran Dixon; 6 Danny Craven; 18 Joe Lyons; 27 Anthony Walker; 9 Matty Fozard; 10 Kyle Amor; 17 Shane Grady; 19 Olly Davies; 13 Liam Bent. Subs (all used): 22 Aaron Brown; 11 Sam Wilde; 16 Callum Field; 21 Lewis Hatton.
Tries: Craven (15), Millar (28, 70, 79), Owens (48);
Goals: Owens 3/6.
COUGARS: 1 Lewis Young; 5 Mo Agoro; 23 Robbie Storey; 25 Ben Crooks; 3 Charlie Graham; 22 Dane Chisholm; 31 Luke Gale; 24 Mark Ioane; 9 Billy Gaylor; 12 Aaron Levy; 19 Ellis Robson; 27 Sadiq Adebiyi; 20 Brad Walker. Subs (all used): 13 Kyle Kesik; 15 Brenden Santi; 10 Toby Everett; 28 Keenen Tomlinson.
Tries: Gale (22, 59), Storey (61); **Goals:** Chisholm 3/3.
Rugby Leaguer & League Express Men of the Match: *Vikings:* Joe Lyons; *Cougars:* Lewis Young.
Penalty count: 5-5; **Half-time:** 12-6;
Referee: Liam Moore; **Attendance:** 3,449.

Championship 2023 - Round by Round

FEATHERSTONE ROVERS 46 HALIFAX PANTHERS 22

ROVERS: 23 Caleb Aekins; 2 Luke Briscoe; 3 Chris Hankinson; 18 Josh Hardcastle; 5 Gareth Gale; 6 Johnathon Ford; 7 Riley Dean; 10 James Lockwood; 14 Matty Wildie; 17 Gadwin Springer; 11 Brad Day; 12 Elijah Taylor; 24 Mathieu Cozza. Subs (all used): 8 Craig Kopczak; 9 Connor Jones; 13 Jack Bussey; 27 McKenzie Yei.
Tries: Hankinson (7, 47), Springer (10), Wildie (24), Aekins (34), Dean (54), Jones (66), Gale (75);
Goals: Hankinson 7/9.
Sin bin: Yei (36) - high tackle on Woodburn-Hall.
PANTHERS: 1 James Woodburn-Hall; 2 Lachlan Walmsley; 3 Zack McComb; 22 Jake Maizen; 5 James Saltonstall; 6 Louis Jouffret; 7 Joe Keyes; 31 Kevin Larroyer; 9 Brandon Moore; 13 Jacob Fairbank; 11 Ben Kavanagh; 17 Ryan King; 8 Adam Tangata. Subs (all used): 10 Dan Murray; 12 Matty Gee; 14 Kyle Wood; 16 Will Calcott.
Tries: Walmsley (37, 57), Woodburn-Hall (73, 79);
Goals: Keyes 3/4.
Rugby Leaguer & League Express Men of the Match:
Rovers: Chris Hankinson; *Panthers:* James Woodburn-Hall.
Penalty count: 8-5; **Half-time:** 24-4;
Referee: Chris Kendall; **Attendance:** 3,794.

Monday 13th February 2023

YORK KNIGHTS 32 BRADFORD BULLS 16

KNIGHTS: 2 Joe Brown; 5 AJ Towse; 28 Levi Edwards; 3 James Glover; 15 Myles Harrison; 1 Matty Marsh; 7 Liam Harris; 16 Bailey Antrobus; 9 Will Jubb; 10 Conor Fitzsimmons; 4 Jesse Dee; 12 Danny Kirmond; 13 Jordan Thompson. Subs (all used): 8 Jon Luke Kirby; 17 Ronan Michael; 19 Josh Daley; 20 Jack Teanby.
Tries: Jubb (25), Kirby (32), Michael (36), Daley (74);
Goals: Glover 8/8.
BULLS: 1 Tom Holmes; 2 Ben Blackmore; 3 Joe Arundel; 4 Kieran Gill; 5 David Foggin-Johnston; 7 Jordan Lilley; 6 Dec Patton; 10 Michael Lawrence; 9 George Flanagan; 16 Brad Foster; 11 Brad England; 15 AJ Wallace; 13 Bodene Thompson. Subs (all used): 8 Jordan Baldwinson; 12 Chester Butler; 21 Fenton Rogers; 22 George Roby.
Tries: Foggin-Johnston (19), Thompson (29), Lilley (80);
Goals: Patton 2/3.
Rugby Leaguer & League Express Men of the Match:
Knights: Jesse Dee; *Bulls:* David Foggin-Johnston.
Penalty count: 6-4; **Half-time:** 18-10;
Referee: Jack Smith; **Attendance:** 2,381.

ROUND 3

Friday 17th February 2023

SHEFFIELD EAGLES 36 BATLEY BULLDOGS 0

EAGLES: 29 Quentin Laulu-Togaga'e; 2 Ben Jones-Bishop; 3 Kris Welham; 4 Ross Oakes; 28 Matty Dawson-Jones; 32 Cory Aston; 7 Anthony Thackeray; 8 Brandon Douglas; 9 Vila Halafihi; 10 Tyler Dickinson; 18 Aaron Murphy; 12 Joel Farrell; 14 Titus Gwaze. Subs (all used): 15 Mikey Wood; 20 Lewis Peachey; 23 Bayley Liu; 27 Jesse Sene-Lefao.
Tries: Thackeray (3), Halafihi (11), Sene-Lefao (56), Oakes (65), Jones-Bishop (71), Murphy (76);
Goals: Aston 6/6.
BULLDOGS: 21 Aidan McGowan; 29 Greg Johnson; 3 Kieran Buchanan; 15 Elliot Kear; 22 Dale Morton; 6 Ben White; 7 Josh Woods; 19 Tom Lillycrop; 24 Ben Kaye; 10 Keegan Hirst; 11 Dane Manning; 12 Lucas Walshaw; 17 Luke Blake. Subs (all used): 9 Alistair Leak; 14 James Meadows; 16 Michael Ward; 30 Martyn Reilly.
Rugby Leaguer & League Express Men of the Match:
Eagles: Brandon Douglas; *Bulldogs:* Aidan McGowan.
Penalty count: 4-2; **Half-time:** 12-0;
Referee: James Vella; **Attendance:** 878.

Saturday 18th February 2023

TOULOUSE OLYMPIQUE 36 YORK KNIGHTS 0

OLYMPIQUE: 1 Olly Ashall-Bott; 5 Paul Marcon; 4 Mathieu Jussaume; 3 Reubenn Rennie; 18 Guy Armitage; 6 Josh Ralph; 7 Jake Shorrocks; 8 Lambert Belmas; 13 Anthony Marion; 16 Joe Bretherton; 12 Dominique Peyroux; 11 Maxime Stefani; 10 Harrison Hansen. Subs (all used): 14 Eloi Pelissier; 15 Sitaleki Akauola; 17 Hugo Pezet; 20 Greg Richards.
Tries: Armitage (4, 8, 35, 79), Rennie (45), Ashall-Bott (65), Jussaume (71); **Goals:** Shorrocks 3/7, Marion 1/1.
KNIGHTS: 2 Joe Brown; 15 Myles Harrison; 25 Brad Ward; 28 Levi Edwards; 5 AJ Towse; 4 Jesse Dee; 7 Liam Harris; 8 Jon Luke Kirby; 9 Will Jubb; 10 Conor Fitzsimmons; 16 Bailey Antrobus; 12 Danny Kirmond; 24 Ben Barnard. Subs: 11 Chris Clarkson (not used); 17 Ronan Michael; 20 Jack Teanby; 27 Harry Price.
Rugby Leaguer & League Express Men of the Match:
Olympique: Guy Armitage; *Knights:* Bailey Antrobus.
Penalty count: 6-1; **Half-time:** 18-0;
Referee: Aaron Moore; **Attendance:** 2,761.

Sunday 19th February 2023

BRADFORD BULLS 14 WIDNES VIKINGS 12

BULLS: 1 Tom Holmes; 2 Ben Blackmore; 3 Joe Arundel; 4 Kieran Gill; 5 David Foggin-Johnston; 6 Dec Patton; 7 Jordan Lilley; 8 Jordan Baldwinson; 9 George Flanagan; 21 Fenton Rogers; 11 Brad England; 12 Chester Butler; 13 Bodene Thompson. Subs (all used): 18 Keven Appo; 22 George Roby; 15 AJ Wallace; - Masi Matongo.
Tries: Foggin-Johnston (27), Blackmore (53), Holmes (79);
Goals: Patton 1/3.
Sin bin: Holmes (32) - fighting.
VIKINGS: 1 Jack Owens; 28 Ryan Millar; 3 Matty Fleming; 20 Joe Edge; 5 Kieran Dixon; 6 Danny Craven; 18 Joe Lyons; 27 Anthony Walker; 9 Matty Fozard; 10 Kyle Amor; 17 Shane Grady; 19 Olly Davies; 13 Liam Bent. Subs (all used): 22 Aaron Brown; 16 Callum Field; 21 Lewis Hatton; 12 Adam Lawton.
Tries: Grady (34), Lawton (60); **Goals:** K Dixon 2/3.
Rugby Leaguer & League Express Men of the Match:
Bulls: Dec Patton; *Vikings:* Adam Lawton.
Penalty count: 3-8; **Half-time:** 4-6;
Referee: Ben Thaler; **Attendance:** 4,827.

FEATHERSTONE ROVERS 76 WHITEHAVEN 4

ROVERS: 23 Caleb Aekins; 2 Luke Briscoe; 21 Joey Leilua; 4 Craig Hall; 5 Gareth Gale; 25 Thomas Lacans; 7 Riley Dean; 8 Craig Kopczak; 14 Matty Wildie; 17 Gadwin Springer; 13 Jack Bussey; 18 Josh Hardcastle; 24 Mathieu Cozza. Subs (all used): 9 Connor Jones; 12 Elijah Taylor; 15 John Davies; 27 McKenzie Yei.
Tries: Leilua (3, 71), Lacans (11), Kopczak (13), Davies (32), Yei (35), Dean (38), Gale (45, 68, 77), Bussey (51), Jones (57), Aekins (61), Briscoe (64); **Goals:** Hall 10/14.
WHITEHAVEN: 23 Josh Rourke; 2 Dave Eccleston; 3 Chris Taylor; 4 Curtis Teare; 19 Jacob Douglas; 13 Dion Aiye; 14 Jamie Doran; 22 Lucas Castle; 21 Marcus O'Brien; 24 Daniel Spencer-Tonks; 29 Junior Nsemba; 12 Lachlan Lanskey; 8 Liam McAvoy. Subs (all used): 16 Lasarusa Tabu; 18 Perry Singleton; 26 Tom Forber; 28 Ross Ainley.
Try: Rourke (16); **Goals:** Rourke 0/1.
Rugby Leaguer & League Express Men of the Match:
Rovers: Matty Wildie; *Whitehaven:* Liam McAvoy.
Penalty count: 3-2; **Half-time:** 36-4;
Referee: Michael Smaill; **Attendance:** 2,248.

HALIFAX PANTHERS 26 LONDON BRONCOS 18

PANTHERS: 1 James Woodburn-Hall; 2 Lachlan Walmsley; 4 Ben Tibbs; 3 Zack McComb; 5 James Saltonstall; 6 Louis Jouffret; 7 Joe Keyes; 31 Kevin Larroyer; 9 Brandon Moore; 15 Will Maher; 11 Ben Kavanagh; 12 Matty Gee; 8 Adam Tangata. Subs (all used): 14 Kyle Wood; 27 Daniel Smith; 10 Dan Murray; 21 Eribe Doro.
Tries: Jouffret (16), Saltonstall (30, 57), Walmsley (46), Doro (50); **Goals:** Keyes 3/6.
Sin bin: Murray (71) - professional foul.
BRONCOS: 1 Alex Walker; 2 Paul Ulberg; 3 Jarred Bassett; 29 Zach Eckersley; 5 Iliess Macani; 6 Oliver Leyland; 13 Dean Parata; 15 Lewis Bienek; 9 Sam Davis; 28 Harvie Hill; 11 Will Lovell; 16 Ethan Natoli; 12 Marcus Stock. Subs (all used): 14 Bill Leyland; 10 Jordan Williams; 8 Wellington Albert; 27 Ramon Silva.
Tries: Eckersley (37), Parata (64), B Leyland (68);
Goals: O Leyland 3/3.
Rugby Leaguer & League Express Men of the Match:
Panthers: James Saltonstall; *Broncos:* Dean Parata.
Penalty count: 5-8; **Half-time:** 10-6;
Referee: Cameron Worsley; **Attendance:** 1,950.

KEIGHLEY COUGARS 44 NEWCASTLE THUNDER 24

COUGARS: 1 Lewis Young; 5 Mo Agoro; 23 Robbie Storey; 4 Nathan Roebuck; 3 Charlie Graham; 22 Dane Chisholm; 31 Luke Gale; 12 Aaron Levy; 26 Thomas Doyle; 24 Mark Ioane; 28 Keenen Tomlinson; 27 Sadiq Adebiyi; 20 Brad Walker. Subs (all used): 8 Dan Parker; 10 Toby Everett; 13 Kyle Kesik; 15 Brenden Santi.
Tries: Graham (6), Tomlinson (9), Roebuck (12, 70), Walker (26), Storey (35, 48), Agoro (76);
Goals: Chisholm 6/8.
THUNDER: 1 Jack Johnson; 5 Alex Clegg; 3 Marcus Walker; 21 Evan Lawther; 2 Alex Young; 6 Alex Donaghy; 7 Nikau Williams; 8 Jay Chapelhow; 9 Curtis Davies; 10 Mitch Clark; 11 Alex Foster; 12 Brad Gallagher; 13 Connor Bailey. Subs (all used): 14 Denive Balmforth; 15 Ted Chapelhow; 16 Rhys Clarke; 23 Connor Moore.
Tries: Lawther (18), Johnson (30, 80), Clegg (59);
Goals: Williams 4/4.
Sin bin: Moore (40) - professional foul.
Rugby Leaguer & League Express Men of the Match:
Cougars: Dane Chisholm; *Thunder:* Evan Lawther.
Penalty count: 8-5; **Half-time:** 28-12;
Referee: Nick Bennett; **Attendance:** 1,658.

SWINTON LIONS 20 BARROW RAIDERS 18

LIONS: 1 Dan Abram; 32 Jumah Sambou; 2 Mike Butt; 22 Andy Badrock; 4 Jayden Hatton; 19 Ollie Olds; 7 Jordy Gibson; 10 Kenny Baker; 9 Luke Waterworth; 34 George Delaney; 11 Rhodri Lloyd; 12 Mitch Cox; 13 Louis Brogan. Subs (all used): 14 Josh Eaves; 15 Jordan Case; 18 Liam Cooper; 3 Jake Spedding.
Tries: Hatton (41), Badrock (62), Eaves (73), Gibson (79);
Goals: Abram 2/5.
Sin bin: Olds (14) - dissent;
Waterworth (66) - holding down.
RAIDERS: 1 Luke Cresswell; 27 Andrew Bulman; 4 Greg Worthington; 5 Ryan Shaw; 2 Shane Toal; 6 Jarrod Sammut; 7 Ryan Johnston; 15 Ellis Gillam; 23 Connor Saunders; 10 Anton Iaria; 11 Danny Langtree; 12 Jarrad Stack; 13 Jack Wells. Subs (all used): 14 Jake Carter; 17 Charlie Emslie; 20 Ben Evans; 8 Greg Burke.
Tries: Toal (38), Worthington (51), Johnston (67);
Goals: Shaw 3/4.
Rugby Leaguer & League Express Men of the Match:
Lions: Jordy Gibson; *Raiders:* Luke Cresswell.
Penalty count: 7-5; **Half-time:** 2-6;
Referee: Liam Rush; **Attendance:** 1,139.

ROUND 4

Saturday 25th February 2023

BRADFORD BULLS 28 TOULOUSE OLYMPIQUE 18

BULLS: 1 Tom Holmes; 2 Ben Blackmore; 3 Joe Arundel; 4 Kieran Gill; 38 Liam Tindall; 6 Dec Patton; 7 Jordan Lilley; 8 Jordan Baldwinson; 9 George Flanagan; 21 Fenton Rogers; 15 AJ Wallace; 11 Brad England; 10 Michael Lawrence. Subs (all used): 22 George Roby; 18 Keven Appo; 17 Josh Johnson; 16 Brad Foster.
Tries: Flanagan (10), Arundel (56), Tindall (60), Wallace (67); **Goals:** Patton 6/6.
Sin bin: Appo (48) - dangerous challenge;
Lilley (54) - fighting.
OLYMPIQUE: 1 Olly Ashall-Bott; 5 Paul Marcon; 4 Mathieu Jussaume; 3 Reubenn Rennie; 18 Guy Armitage; 6 Josh Ralph; 7 Jake Shorrocks; 8 Lambert Belmas; 14 Eloi Pelissier; 16 Joe Bretherton; 12 Dominique Peyroux; 11 Maxime Stefani; 13 Anthony Marion. Subs (all used): 25 Robin Brochon; 27 Dimitri Biscarro; 17 Hugo Pezet; 24 Pierre-Jean Lima.
Tries: Marion (17), Marcon (36), Belmas (49);
Goals: Shorrocks 3/4.
Sin bin: Maxime Stefani (54) - fighting;
Bretherton (68) - dangerous challenge; Belmas (72) - trip.
Rugby Leaguer & League Express Men of the Match:
Bulls: Dec Patton; *Olympique:* Eloi Pelissier.
Penalty count: 12-7; **Half-time:** 8-12;
Referee: Michael Smaill; **Attendance:** 2,798.

Sunday 26th February 2023

BATLEY BULLDOGS 28 KEIGHLEY COUGARS 23

BULLDOGS: 21 Aidan McGowan; 22 Dale Morton; 15 Elliot Kear; 3 Kieran Buchanan; 5 Johnny Campbell; 6 Ben White; 14 James Meadows; 8 Adam Gledhill; 9 Alistair Leak; 13 James Brown; 11 Dane Manning; 12 Lucas Walshaw; 30 Martyn Reilly. Subs: 16 Michael Ward; 20 Samy Kibula; 26 Nyle Flynn; 28 Oli Burton (not used).
Tries: Meadows (15), Kibula (52), Buchanan (65, 69), Morton (80); **Goals:** Meadows 4/6.
Sin bin: Walshaw (74) - dissent.
COUGARS: 1 Lewis Young; 5 Mo Agoro; 23 Robbie Storey; 4 Nathan Roebuck; 3 Charlie Graham; 22 Dane Chisholm; 31 Luke Gale; 12 Aaron Levy; 26 Thomas Doyle; 10 Toby Everett; 28 Keenen Tomlinson; 27 Sadiq Adebiyi; 20 Brad Walker. Subs (all used): 8 Dan Parker; 13 Kyle Kesik; 15 Brenden Santi; 24 Mark Ioane.
Tries: Storey (24), Graham (36), Young (45);
Goals: Chisholm 5/5; **Field goal:** Chisholm (75).
Sin bin: Gale (62) - off the ball challenge.
Rugby Leaguer & League Express Men of the Match:
Bulldogs: James Brown; *Cougars:* Lewis Young.
Penalty count: 7-8; **Half-time:** 8-14;
Referee: Liam Rush; **Attendance:** 1,624.

FEATHERSTONE ROVERS 56
NEWCASTLE THUNDER 6

ROVERS: 23 Caleb Aekins; 2 Luke Briscoe; 21 Joey Leilua; 18 Josh Hardcastle; 5 Gareth Gale; 6 Johnathon Ford; 7 Riley Dean; 24 Mathieu Cozza; 14 Matty Wildie; 10 James Lockwood; 11 Brad Day; 13 Jack Bussey; 12 Elijah Taylor. Subs (all used): 9 Connor Jones; 27 McKenzie Yei; 22 Dan Fleming; 15 John Davies.
Tries: Hardcastle (10, 20), Day (17), Bussey (25, 76), Yei (46), Jones (62), Leilua (69, 80), Briscoe (74);
Goals: Dean 8/10.
Sin bin: Fleming (65) - retaliation.

Championship 2023 - Round by Round

THUNDER: 1 Jack Johnson; 5 Alex Clegg; 3 Marcus Walker; 21 Evan Lawther; 2 Alex Young; 27 Jack Miller; 7 Nikau Williams; 15 Ted Chapelhow; 14 Denive Balmforth; 23 Connor Moore; 29 Nick Staveley; 13 Connor Bailey; 16 Rhys Clarke. Subs (all used): 9 Curtis Davies; 10 Mitch Clark; 17 Rob Tuliatu; 28 Matty Laidlaw.
Try: Clegg (30); **Goals:** Williams 1/1.
Dismissal: Laidlaw (65) - high tackle on Briscoe.
Sin bin: Clark (61) - use of the elbow.
Rugby Leaguer & League Express Men of the Match: *Rovers:* Josh Hardcastle; *Thunder:* Jack Johnson.
Penalty count: 6-6; **Half-time:** 22-6;
Referee: Cameron Worsley; **Attendance:** 2,489.

LONDON BRONCOS 20 SHEFFIELD EAGLES 21

BRONCOS: 1 Alex Walker; 2 Paul Ulberg; 3 Jarred Bassett; 29 Zach Eckersley; 5 Iliess Macani; 6 Oliver Leyland; 13 Dean Parata; 8 Wellington Albert; 9 Sam Davis; 10 Jordan Williams; 11 Will Lovell; 16 Ethan Natoli; 12 Marcus Stock. Subs (all used): 7 Rian Horsman; 14 Bill Leyland; 28 Harvie Hill; 27 Ramon Silva.
Tries: Ulberg (19), Lovell (30), B Leyland (37);
Goals: O Leyland 4/6.
EAGLES: 1 Josh Guzdek; 2 Ben Jones-Bishop; 3 Kris Welham; 4 Ross Oakes; 28 Matty Dawson-Jones; 32 Cory Aston; 7 Anthony Thackeray; 8 Brandon Douglas; 9 Vila Halafihi; 10 Tyler Dickinson; 11 Connor Bower; 12 Joel Farrell; 13 Evan Hodgson. Subs (all used): 14 Titus Gwaze; 16 Blake Broadbent; 23 Bayley Liu; 27 Jesse Sene-Lefao.
Tries: Jones-Bishop (1, 27), Oakes (52), Gwaze (72);
Goals: Aston 2/4; **Field goal:** Thackeray (76).
Rugby Leaguer & League Express Men of the Match: *Broncos:* Alex Walker; *Eagles:* Ross Oakes.
Penalty count: 8-2; **Half-time:** 16-10;
Referee: James Vella; **Attendance:** 1,175.

WHITEHAVEN 20 SWINTON LIONS 4

WHITEHAVEN: 23 Josh Rourke; 2 Dave Eccleston; 3 Chris Taylor; 4 Curtis Teare; 19 Jacob Douglas; 1 Sam Freeman; 14 Jamie Doran; 22 Lucas Castle; 15 James Newton; 8 Liam McAvoy; 29 Junior Nsemba; 11 Connor Holliday; 13 Dion Aiye. Subs (all used): 18 Perry Singleton; 21 Marcus O'Brien; 24 Daniel Spencer-Tonks; 26 Tom Forber.
Tries: Taylor (34), Freeman (43, 68); **Goals:** Freeman 4/4.
LIONS: 1 Dan Abram; 3 Jake Spedding; 22 Andy Badrock; 11 Rhodri Lloyd; 2 Mike Butt; 6 Nick Gregson; 7 Jordy Gibson; 10 Kenny Baker; 9 Luke Waterworth; 34 George Delaney; 12 Mitch Cox; 16 Gav Rodden; 13 Louis Brogan. Subs: 14 Josh Eaves; 15 Jordan Case; 18 Liam Cooper; 26 Joey Romeo (not used).
Try: Badrock (16); **Goals:** Abram 0/1.
Rugby Leaguer & League Express Men of the Match: *Whitehaven:* Sam Freeman; *Lions:* Louis Brogan.
Penalty count: 5-5; **Half-time:** 6-4;
Referee: Nick Bennett; **Attendance:** 891.

YORK KNIGHTS 28 BARROW RAIDERS 14

KNIGHTS: 2 Joe Brown; 5 AJ Towse; 28 Levi Edwards; 3 James Glover; 15 Myles Harrison; 6 Ata Hingano; 7 Liam Harris; 16 Bailey Antrobus; 9 Will Jubb; 10 Conor Fitzsimmons; 4 Jesse Dee; 12 Danny Kirmond; 13 Jordan Thompson. Subs (all used): 8 Jon Luke Kirby; 19 Josh Daley; 20 Jack Teanby; 24 Ben Barnard.
Tries: Harrison (2), Dee (28), Kirby (51), Hingano (55), Brown (75); **Goals:** Glover 4/5.
Sin bin: Kirby (39) - fighting.
RAIDERS: 1 Luke Cresswell; 27 Andrew Bulman; 4 Greg Worthington; 3 Rio-Osayomwanbo Corkill; 2 Shane Toal; 6 Jarrod Sammut; 7 Ryan Johnston; 13 Jack Wells; 25 Amir Bourouh; 10 Anton Iaria; 11 Danny Langtree; 32 James Greenwood; 12 Jarrad Stack. Subs (all used): 8 Greg Burke; 15 Ellis Gillam; 20 Ben Evans; 28 Ellis Archer.
Tries: Bourouh (14), Toal (40, 64); **Goals:** Sammut 1/3.
Rugby Leaguer & League Express Men of the Match: *Knights:* Ata Hingano; *Raiders:* Jarrod Sammut.
Penalty count: 2-2; **Half-time:** 10-10;
Referee: Scott Mikalauskas; **Attendance:** 1,525.

Monday 27th February 2023

WIDNES VIKINGS 42 HALIFAX PANTHERS 14

VIKINGS: 1 Jack Owens; 28 Ryan Millar; 3 Matty Fleming; 20 Joe Edge; 5 Kieran Dixon; 6 Danny Craven; 18 Joe Lyons; 12 Adam Lawton; 9 Matty Fozard; 10 Kyle Amor; 17 Shane Grady; 11 Sam Wilde; 13 Liam Bent. Subs (all used): 16 Callum Field; 19 Olly Davies; 21 Lewis Hatton; 27 Anthony Walker.
Tries: K Dixon (16, 33), Grady (19, 55), Millar (26), Craven (35), Owens (49), Edge (77); **Goals:** K Dixon 5/8.
PANTHERS: 1 James Woodburn-Hall; 5 James Saltonstall; 4 Ben Tibbs; 22 Jake Maizen; 2 Lachlan Walmsley; 6 Louis Jouffret; 7 Joe Keyes; 16 Will Calcott; 9 Brandon Moore; 15 Will Maher; 11 Ben Kavanagh; 12 Matty Gee; 8 Adam Tangata. Subs (all used): 13 Jacob Fairbank; 14 Kyle Wood; 21 Eribe Doro; - Suaia Matagi.
Tries: Walmsley (9, 71), Gee (77);
Goals: Keyes 0/1, Jouffret 1/2.
Rugby Leaguer & League Express Men of the Match: *Vikings:* Danny Craven; *Panthers:* Jacob Fairbank.
Penalty count: 6-3; **Half-time:** 28-4;
Referee: Ben Thaler; **Attendance:** 3,187.

ROUND 5

Saturday 4th March 2023

TOULOUSE OLYMPIQUE 72 WHITEHAVEN 10

OLYMPIQUE: 1 Olly Ashall-Bott; 5 Paul Marcon; 4 Mathieu Jussaume; 3 Reubenn Rennie; 2 Latrell Schaumkel; 6 Josh Ralph; 7 Jake Shorrocks; 8 Lambert Belmas; 14 Eloi Pelissier; 16 Joe Bretherton; 24 Pierre-Jean Lima; 11 Maxime Stefani; 13 Anthony Marion. Subs (all used): 26 Stephane Guillon; 10 Harrison Hansen; 17 Hugo Pezet; 20 Greg Richards.
Tries: Rennie (2), Lima (8, 29, 62), Ashall-Bott (16), Marcon (19), Richards (37), Shorrocks (42, 60, 72), Maxime Stefani (51), Jussaume (53); **Goals:** Shorrocks 12/12.
WHITEHAVEN: 23 Josh Rourke; 2 Dave Eccleston; 3 Chris Taylor; 18 Perry Singleton; 4 Curtis Teare; 1 Sam Freeman; 14 Jamie Doran; 22 Lucas Castle; 15 James Newton; 24 Daniel Spencer-Tonks; 11 Connor Holliday; 12 Lachlan Lanskey; 8 Liam McAvoy. Subs (all used): 28 Ross Ainley; 17 Guy Graham; 21 Marcus O'Brien; 16 Lasarusa Tabu.
Tries: Rourke (26), Teare (48); **Goals:** Freeman 1/2.
Rugby Leaguer & League Express Men of the Match: *Olympique:* Jake Shorrocks; *Whitehaven:* Perry Singleton.
Penalty count: 5-2; **Half-time:** 36-4;
Referee: Ben Thaler; **Attendance:** 2,558.

Sunday 5th March 2023

BARROW RAIDERS 18 NEWCASTLE THUNDER 18

RAIDERS: 24 Luke Broadbent; 27 Andrew Bulman; 4 Greg Worthington; 5 Ryan Shaw; 2 Shane Toal; 6 Jarrod Sammut; 7 Ryan Johnston; 16 Sam Brooks; 25 Amir Bourouh; 10 Anton Iaria; 21 Tom Hopkins; 12 Jarrad Stack; 13 Jack Wells. Subs (all used): 8 Greg Burke; 14 Jake Carter; 15 Ellis Gillam; 20 Ben Evans.
Tries: Stack (16, 55), J Carter (41); **Goals:** Shaw 3/3.
THUNDER: 1 Jack Johnson; 5 Alex Clegg; 11 Alex Foster; 3 Marcus Walker; 2 Alex Young; 27 Jack Miller; 7 Nikau Williams; 8 Jay Chapelhow; 9 Curtis Davies; 23 Connor Moore; 13 Connor Bailey; 29 Nick Staveley; 10 Mitch Clark. Subs (all used): 14 Denive Balmforth; 15 Ted Chapelhow; 16 Rhys Clarke; 17 Rob Tuliatu.
Tries: Foster (31), Walker (34), Williams (45);
Goals: Williams 3/4.
Rugby Leaguer & League Express Men of Match: *Raiders:* Jarrad Stack; *Thunder:* Nikau Williams.
Penalty count: 3-7; **Half-time:** 6-10;
Referee: Michael Smaill; **Attendance:** 1,752.

HALIFAX PANTHERS 20 BATLEY BULLDOGS 16

PANTHERS: 1 James Woodburn-Hall; 2 Lachlan Walmsley; 22 Jake Maizen; 3 Zack McComb; 5 James Saltonstall; 6 Louis Jouffret; 14 Kyle Wood; 16 Will Calcott; 9 Brandon Moore; 10 Dan Murray; 11 Ben Kavanagh; 17 Ryan King; 13 Jacob Fairbank. Subs (all used): 20 Tom Inman; 8 Adam Tangata; 12 Matty Gee; 21 Eribe Doro.
Tries: Walmsley (4, 44), Woodburn-Hall (39), Saltonstall (65); **Goals:** Jouffret 2/4.
BULLDOGS: 21 Aidan McGowan; 22 Dale Morton; 15 Elliot Kear; 3 Kieran Buchanan; 5 Johnny Campbell; 14 James Meadows; 6 Ben White; 8 Adam Gledhill; 24 Ben Kaye; 13 James Brown; 11 Dane Manning; 12 Lucas Walshaw; 30 Martyn Reilly. Subs (all used): 9 Alistair Leak; 26 Nyle Flynn; 16 Michael Ward; 20 Samy Kibula.
Tries: Morton (15), McGowan (23), Kibula (33);
Goals: Meadows 2/3.
Rugby Leaguer & League Express Men of the Match: *Panthers:* James Woodburn-Hall; *Bulldogs:* Aidan McGowan.
Penalty count: 4-6; **Half-time:** 8-16;
Referee: Scott Mikalauskas; **Attendance:** 1,703.

KEIGHLEY COUGARS 33 LONDON BRONCOS 22

COUGARS: 1 Lewis Young; 5 Mo Agoro; 23 Robbie Storey; 4 Nathan Roebuck; 3 Charlie Graham; 22 Dane Chisholm; 9 Billy Gaylor; 27 Sadiq Adebiyi; 26 Thomas Doyle; 13 Kyle Kesik; 28 Keenen Tomlinson; 8 Dan Parker; 20 Brad Walker. Subs (all used): 12 Aaron Levy; 14 Harvey Spence; 15 Brenden Santi; 24 Mark Ioane.
Tries: Agoro (26), Graham (42, 76), Santi (47), Storey (50), Tomlinson (80); **Goals:** Chisholm 4/7;
Field goal: Chisholm (73).
BRONCOS: 1 Alex Walker; 2 Paul Ulberg; 3 Jarred Bassett; 29 Zach Eckersley; 30 Abbas Miski; 6 Oliver Leyland; 7 Rian Horsman; 10 Jordan Williams; 9 Sam Davis; 12 Marcus Stock; 11 Will Lovell; 16 Ethan Natoli; 13 Dean Parata. Subs: 8 Wellington Albert; 14 Bill Leyland; 24 Jenson Monk (not used); 28 Harvie Hill.
Tries: Ulberg (3), Miski (13), Walker (36), Bassett (66);
Goals: O Leyland 3/4.
Sin bin: Davis (74) - professional foul; Natoli (78) - trip on Chisholm.
Rugby Leaguer & League Express Men of the Match: *Cougars:* Brenden Santi; *Broncos:* Oliver Leyland.
Penalty count: 7-3; **Half-time:** 4-16;
Referee: Nick Bennett; **Attendance:** 1,693.

SHEFFIELD EAGLES 42 WIDNES VIKINGS 12

EAGLES: 22 Matty Chrimes; 2 Ben Jones-Bishop; 3 Kris Welham; 23 Bayley Liu; 28 Matty Dawson-Jones; 32 Cory Aston; 7 Anthony Thackeray; 8 Brandon Douglas; 9 Vila Halafihi; 10 Tyler Dickinson; 18 Aaron Murphy; 12 Joel Farrell; 14 Titus Gwaze. Subs (all used): 13 Evan Hodgson; 15 Mikey Wood; 16 Blake Broadbent; 27 Jesse Sene-Lefao.
Tries: Dawson-Jones (8, 26), Jones-Bishop (15), Gwaze (17), Douglas (66), Chrimes (70), Aston (75);
Goals: Aston 7/8.
Sin bin: J Farrell (55) - dangerous challenge.
VIKINGS: 1 Jack Owens; 28 Ryan Millar; 3 Matty Fleming; 20 Joe Edge; 2 Ryan Ince; 6 Danny Craven; 18 Joe Lyons; 12 Adam Lawton; 9 Matty Fozard; 10 Kyle Amor; 17 Shane Grady; 11 Sam Wilde; 13 Liam Bent. Subs (all used): 16 Callum Field; 19 Olly Davies; 21 Lewis Hatton; 27 Anthony Walker.
Tries: Ince (40), Craven (46); **Goals:** Owens 2/2.
Sin bin: Craven (52) - professional foul.
Rugby Leaguer & League Express Men of the Match: *Eagles:* Titus Gwaze; *Vikings:* Shane Grady.
Penalty count: 7-7; **Half-time:** 24-6;
Referee: Liam Rush; **Attendance:** 1,319.

SWINTON LIONS 0 YORK KNIGHTS 40

LIONS: 1 Dan Abram; 2 Mike Butt; 32 Daniel Hill; 22 Andy Badrock; 3 Jake Spedding; 23 Joe Lowe; 7 Jordy Gibson; 18 Liam Cooper; 6 Nick Gregson; 34 George Delaney; 11 Rhodri Lloyd; 12 Mitch Cox; 13 Louis Brogan. Subs (all used): 10 Kenny Baker; 20 Morgan Burgess; 26 Joey Romeo; - Lewis Baxter.
KNIGHTS: 2 Joe Brown; 15 Myles Harrison; 3 James Glover; 28 Levi Edwards; 5 AJ Towse; 6 Ata Hingano; 7 Liam Harris; 16 Bailey Antrobus; 9 Will Jubb; 10 Conor Fitzsimmons; 4 Jesse Dee; 11 Chris Clarkson; 13 Jordan Thompson. Subs (all used): 8 Jon Luke Kirby; 17 Ronan Michael; 19 Josh Daley; 20 Jack Teanby.
Tries: Towse (2, 57), Hingano (6), Harrison (15, 74), Brown (28, 38), Daley (45); **Goals:** Glover 4/7, Harris 0/1.
Rugby Leaguer & League Express Men of the Match: *Lions:* George Delaney; *Knights:* Joe Brown.
Penalty count: 8-5; **Half-time:** 0-26;
Referee: Cameron Worsley; **Attendance:** 1,029.

Monday 6th March 2023

FEATHERSTONE ROVERS 26 BRADFORD BULLS 12

ROVERS: 1 Brandon Pickersgill; 2 Luke Briscoe; 21 Joey Leilua; 18 Josh Hardcastle; 5 Gareth Gale; 6 Johnathon Ford; 7 Riley Dean; 10 James Lockwood; 14 Matty Wildie; 24 Mathieu Cozza; 11 Brad Day; 13 Jack Bussey; 12 Elijah Taylor. Subs (all used): 8 Craig Kopczak; 9 Connor Jones; 15 John Davies; 27 McKenzie Yei.
Tries: Dean (9), Briscoe (26), Gale (36), Davies (49), Ford (76); **Goals:** Dean 3/5.
BULLS: 1 Tom Holmes; 2 Ben Blackmore; 3 Joe Arundel; 4 Kieran Gill; 38 Liam Tindall; 6 Dec Patton; 7 Jordan Lilley; 8 Jordan Baldwinson; 9 George Flanagan; 21 Fenton Rogers; 15 AJ Wallace; 13 Bodene Thompson; 10 Michael Lawrence. Subs (all used): 16 Brad Foster; 17 Josh Johnson; 18 Keven Appo; 22 George Roby.
Tries: Holmes (18), Gill (22), Arundel (62);
Goals: Patton 0/4.
Sin bin: Roby (32) - off the ball challenge.
Rugby Leaguer & League Express Men of the Match: *Rovers:* Riley Dean; *Bulls:* Kieran Gill.
Penalty count: 8-6; **Half-time:** 14-8;
Referee: James Vella; **Attendance:** 4,809.

ROUND 6

Saturday 18th March 2023

NEWCASTLE THUNDER 6 LONDON BRONCOS 36

THUNDER: 1 Jack Johnson; 2 Alex Young; 11 Alex Foster; 4 Connor Wynne; 5 Alex Clegg; 27 Jack Miller; 7 Nikau Williams; 8 Jay Chapelhow; 9 Curtis Davies; 10 Mitch Clark; 29 Nick Staveley; 12 Brad Gallagher; 13 Connor

Championship 2023 - Round by Round

Bailey. Subs (all used): 14 Denive Balmforth; 15 Ted Chapelhow; 23 Connor Moore; 28 Matty Laidlaw.
Try: Miller (55); **Goals:** Williams 1/1.
BRONCOS: 1 Alex Walker; 2 Paul Ulberg; 3 Jarred Bassett; 16 Ethan Natoli; 4 Dalton Grant; 6 Oliver Leyland; 13 Dean Parata; 15 Lewis Bienek; 9 Sam Davis; 10 Jordan Williams; 11 Will Lovell; 32 Jacob Jones; 12 Marcus Stock. Subs (all used): 8 Wellington Albert; 14 Bill Leyland; 17 Henry Raiwalui; 18 Emmanuel Waine.
Tries: Natoli (21), B Leyland (31), Walker (33, 69, 75), Bassett (39), Waine (79); **Goals:** O Leyland 4/7.
Rugby Leaguer & League Express Men of the Match: *Thunder:* Matty Laidlaw; *Broncos:* Alex Walker.
Penalty count: 7-2; **Half-time:** 0-18;
Referee: Nick Bennett; **Attendance:** 978.

WIDNES VIKINGS 12 TOULOUSE OLYMPIQUE 14

VIKINGS: 1 Jack Owens; 2 Ryan Ince; 3 Matty Fleming; 20 Joe Edge; 5 Kieran Dixon; 6 Danny Craven; 18 Joe Lyons; 16 Callum Field; 9 Matty Fozard; 10 Kyle Amor; 17 Shane Grady; 19 Olly Davies; 22 Aaron Brown. Subs (all used): 11 Sam Wilde; 14 Jordan Johnstone; 21 Lewis Hatton; 27 Anthony Walker.
Tries: Ince (14), K Dixon (56), Edge (66);
Goals: K Dixon 0/3, Owens 0/1.
Sin bin: Craven (76) - late challenge on Bretherton.
OLYMPIQUE: 1 Olly Ashall-Bott; 5 Paul Marcon; 4 Mathieu Jussaume; 18 Guy Armitage; 25 Robin Brochon; 6 Josh Ralph; 7 Jake Shorrocks; 8 Lambert Belmas; 13 Anthony Marion; 20 Greg Richards; 16 Joe Bretherton; 3 Reubenn Rennie; 10 Harrison Hansen. Subs (all used): 2 Latrell Schaumkel; 14 Eloi Pelissier; 17 Hugo Pezet; 27 Dimitri Biscarro.
Tries: Bretherton (21), Rennie (27), Marcon (77);
Goals: Shorrocks 1/3.
Sin bin: Ralph (11) - high tackle on Ince.
Rugby Leaguer & League Express Men of the Match: *Vikings:* Jack Owens; *Olympique:* Joe Bretherton.
Penalty count: 5-6; **Half-time:** 4-10;
Referee: James Vella; **Attendance:** 3,093.

Sunday 19th March 2023

BRADFORD BULLS 32 SHEFFIELD EAGLES 18

BULLS: 1 Tom Holmes; 38 Liam Tindall; 3 Joe Arundel; 4 Kieran Gill; 5 David Foggin-Johnston; 7 Jordan Lilley; 6 Dec Patton; 8 Jordan Baldwinson; 9 George Flanagan; 21 Fenton Rogers; 15 AJ Wallace; 42 Leon Ruan; 12 Chester Butler. Subs (all used): 14 Ebon Scurr; 16 Brad Foster; 18 Keven Appo; 43 Corey Johnson.
Tries: Arundel (2), Flanagan (7), Holmes (16, 73), Tindall (36); **Goals:** Patton 6/7.
EAGLES: 2 Ben Jones-Bishop; 5 Jason Bass; 3 Kris Welham; 4 Ross Oakes; 28 Matty Dawson-Jones; 32 Cory Aston; 7 Anthony Thackeray; 8 Brandon Douglas; 9 Vila Halafihi; 10 Tyler Dickinson; 18 Aaron Murphy; 12 Joel Farrell; 14 Titus Gwaze. Subs (all used): 13 Evan Hodgson; 16 Blake Broadbent; 24 Oliver Roberts; 27 Jesse Sene-Lefao.
Tries: Sene-Lefao (23, 54), Dawson-Jones (32);
Goals: Aston 3/3.
Rugby Leaguer & League Express Men of the Match: *Bulls:* Tom Holmes; *Eagles:* Jesse Sene-Lefao.
Penalty count: 9-6; **Half-time:** 24-12;
Referee: Marcus Griffiths; **Attendance:** 3,004.

HALIFAX PANTHERS 34 KEIGHLEY COUGARS 10

PANTHERS: 1 James Woodburn-Hall; 2 Lachlan Walmsley; 22 Jake Maizen; 3 Zack McComb; 5 James Saltonstall; 6 Louis Jouffret; 7 Joe Keyes; 15 Will Maher; 14 Kyle Wood; 10 Dan Murray; 11 Ben Kavanagh; 12 Matty Gee; 13 Jacob Fairbank. Subs (all used): 8 Adam Tangata; 16 Will Calcott; 20 Tom Inman; 29 Jacob Gannon.
Tries: Saltonstall (5), Keyes (23), Kavanagh (29), Walmsley (37, 71), Inman (40); **Goals:** Keyes 5/6.
Sin bin: Maizen (42) - off the ball challenge on Storey; Fairbank (68) - dangerous contact on Parker.
COUGARS: 1 Lewis Young; 3 Charlie Graham; 23 Robbie Storey; 2 Alix Stephenson; 17 Keenan Dyer-Dixon; 31 Luke Gale; 9 Billy Gaylor; 15 Brenden Santi; 13 Kyle Kesik; 8 Dan Parker; 28 Keenen Tomlinson; 12 Aaron Levy; 14 Harvey Spence. Subs (all used): 20 Brad Walker; 24 Mark Ioane; 26 Thomas Doyle; 27 Sadiq Adebiyi.
Tries: Storey (14, 42); **Goals:** Gale 1/2.
Sin bin: Santi (20) - late challenge on Jouffret.
Rugby Leaguer & League Express Men of the Match: *Panthers:* Ben Kavanagh; *Cougars:* Charlie Graham.
Penalty count: 9-8; **Half-time:** 28-4;
Referee: Liam Rush; **Attendance:** 2,123.

SWINTON LIONS 6 FEATHERSTONE ROVERS 34

LIONS: 1 Dan Abram; 32 Wesley Bruines; 2 Mike Butt; 22 Andy Badrock; 4 Jayden Hatton; 23 Joe Lowe; 7 Jordy Gibson; 33 George Delaney; 14 Josh Eaves; 10 Kenny Baker; 34 Ryan Lannon; 36 James Greenwood; 13 Louis Brogan. Subs (all used): 15 Jordan Case; 18 Liam Cooper; 35 Lewis Hall; - Dan Norman.
Try: Greenwood (22); **Goals:** Abram 1/1.
Sin bin: Abram (77) - holding down.
ROVERS: 23 Caleb Aekins; 28 Kyle Evans; 21 Joey Leilua; 18 Josh Hardcastle; 5 Gareth Gale; 25 Thomas Lacans; 7 Riley Dean; 17 Gadwin Springer; 14 Matty Wildie; 10 James Lockwood; 11 Brad Day; 12 Elijah Taylor; 24 Mathieu Cozza. Subs (all used): 8 Craig Kopczak; 9 Connor Jones; 15 John Davies; 27 McKenzie Yei.
Tries: Gale (4), Evans (13, 75), Hardcastle (38), Lacans (50), Jones (65), Aekins (78); **Goals:** Dean 3/8.
Sin bin: Leilua (46) - obstruction;
Cozza (62) - high tackle on Brogan.
Rugby Leaguer & League Express Men of the Match: *Lions:* George Delaney; *Rovers:* Matty Wildie.
Penalty count: 8-7; **Half-time:** 6-16;
Referee: Michael Smaill; **Attendance:** 1,090.

YORK KNIGHTS 12 WHITEHAVEN 14

KNIGHTS: 1 Matty Marsh; 2 Joe Brown; 3 James Glover; 15 Myles Harrison; 5 AJ Towse; 6 Ata Hingano; 7 Liam Harris; 16 Bailey Antrobus; 9 Will Jubb; 10 Conor Fitzsimmons; 13 Jordan Thompson; 12 Danny Kirmond; 17 Ronan Michael. Subs (all used): 19 Josh Daley; 20 Jack Teanby; 21 Ukuma Ta'ai; 29 Connor Barley.
Tries: Marsh (37), Towse (39); **Goals:** Glover 2/2.
WHITEHAVEN: 23 Josh Rourke; 2 Dave Eccleston; 3 Chris Taylor; 6 Karl Dixon; 4 Curtis Teare; 1 Sam Freeman; 14 Jamie Doran; 22 Lucas Castle; 15 James Newton; 16 Lasarusa Tabu; 12 Lachlan Lanskey; 11 Connor Holliday; 21 Marcus O'Brien. Subs: 13 Dion Aiye; 18 Perry Singleton (not used); 24 Daniel Spencer-Tonks; 28 Ross Ainley.
Tries: Spencer-Tonks (10, 15), Teare (70);
Goals: Freeman 1/3.
Rugby Leaguer & League Express Men of the Match: *Knights:* Conor Fitzsimmons;
Whitehaven: Daniel Spencer-Tonks.
Penalty count: 3-3; **Half-time:** 12-10;
Referee: Scott Mikalauskas; **Attendance:** 1,614.

Monday 20th March 2023

BATLEY BULLDOGS 24 BARROW RAIDERS 12

BULLDOGS: 21 Aidan McGowan; 22 Dale Morton; 4 Josh Hodson; 3 Kieran Buchanan; 15 Elliot Kear; 14 James Meadows; 6 Ben White; 19 Tom Lillycrop; 9 Alistair Leak; 13 James Brown; 11 Dane Manning; 12 Lucas Walshaw; 30 Martyn Reilly. Subs (all used): 5 Johnny Campbell; 16 Michael Ward; 20 Samy Kibula; 26 Nyle Flynn.
Tries: Hodson (4), Kibula (41), Meadows (53), Morton (70);
Goals: Meadows 4/5.
Sin bin: Meadows (22) - interference.
RAIDERS: 1 Luke Cresswell; 27 Andrew Bulman; 24 Luke Broadbent; 5 Ryan Shaw; 2 Shane Toal; 6 Jarrod Sammut; 14 Jake Carter; 8 Greg Burke; 22 Josh Wood; 10 Anton Iaria; 11 Danny Langtree; 12 Jarrad Stack; 13 Jack Wells. Subs (all used): 15 Ellis Gillam; 16 Sam Brooks; 20 Ben Evans; 26 Hanley Dawson.
Tries: Burke (77), Sammut (80); **Goals:** Shaw 2/2.
Rugby Leaguer & League Express Men of the Match: *Bulldogs:* James Meadows; *Raiders:* Jarrad Stack.
Penalty count: 5-4; **Half-time:** 8-0;
Referee: Cameron Worsley; **Attendance:** 1,187
(at FLAIR Stadium, Dewsbury).

ROUND 7

Saturday 25th March 2023

SHEFFIELD EAGLES 32 TOULOUSE OLYMPIQUE 4

EAGLES: 2 Ben Jones-Bishop; 22 Matty Chrimes; 3 Kris Welham; 4 Ross Oakes; 5 Jason Bass; 32 Cory Aston; 7 Anthony Thackeray; 8 Brandon Douglas; 9 Vila Halafihi; 10 Tyler Dickinson; 18 Aaron Murphy; 27 Jesse Sene-Lefao; 14 Titus Gwaze. Subs (all used): 13 Evan Hodgson; 15 Mikey Wood; 23 Bayley Liu; 24 Oliver Roberts.
Tries: Sene-Lefao (4), Halafihi (19), Thackeray (24), Jones-Bishop (26), Bass (39), Roberts (69);
Goals: Aston 4/6.
Sin bin: Douglas (58) - late challenge.
OLYMPIQUE: 25 Robin Brochon; 5 Paul Marcon; 4 Mathieu Jussaume; 3 Reubenn Rennie; 26 Anthony Guidez; 6 Josh Ralph; 7 Jake Shorrocks; 8 Lambert Belmas; 13 Anthony Marion; 20 Greg Richards; 16 Joe Bretherton; 11 Maxime Stefani; 10 Harrison Hansen. Subs (all used): 14 Eloi Pelissier; 17 Hugo Pezet; 27 Dimitri Biscarro; 28 Harvie Hill.
Try: Jussaume (56); **Goals:** Shorrocks 0/1.
Rugby Leaguer & League Express Men of the Match: *Eagles:* Jesse Sene-Lefao; *Olympique:* Reubenn Rennie.
Penalty count: 4-4; **Half-time:** 26-0;
Referee: Tom Grant; **Attendance:** 959.

Sunday 26th March 2023

BARROW RAIDERS 16 HALIFAX PANTHERS 12

RAIDERS: 24 Luke Broadbent; 27 Andrew Bulman; 4 Greg Worthington; 30 Iain Thornley; 2 Shane Toal; 6 Jarrod Sammut; 7 Ryan Johnston; 15 Ellis Gillam; 22 Josh Wood; 10 Anton Iaria; 11 Danny Langtree; 12 Jarrad Stack; 13 Jack Wells. Subs (all used): 14 Jake Carter; 20 Ben Evans; 8 Greg Burke; 16 Sam Brooks.
Tries: Stack (5), Thornley (35), Sammut (56);
Goals: Sammut 2/4.
PANTHERS: 18 Brandon Pickersgill; 4 Ben Tibbs; 22 Jake Maizen; 3 Zack McComb; 5 James Saltonstall; 6 Louis Jouffret; 7 Joe Keyes; 15 Will Maher; 9 Brandon Moore; 10 Dan Murray; 11 Ben Kavanagh; 12 Matty Gee; 13 Jacob Fairbank. Subs (all used): 20 Tom Inman; 8 Adam Tangata; 16 Will Calcott; 33 Jacob Gannon.
Tries: Jouffret (12), Pickersgill (24); **Goals:** Keyes 2/3.
Rugby Leaguer & League Express Men of the Match: *Raiders:* Jarrod Sammut; *Panthers:* Joe Keyes.
Penalty count: 5-3; **Half-time:** 10-10;
Referee: James Vella; **Attendance:** 1,879.

FEATHERSTONE ROVERS 46 YORK KNIGHTS 4

ROVERS: 23 Caleb Aekins; 28 Kyle Evans; 21 Joey Leilua; 4 Craig Hall; 5 Gareth Gale; 12 Elijah Taylor; 7 Riley Dean; 8 Craig Kopczak; 14 Matty Wildie; 10 James Lockwood; 11 Brad Day; 13 Jack Bussey; 24 Mathieu Cozza. Subs (all used): 9 Connor Jones; 15 John Davies; 16 Junior Moors; 27 McKenzie Yei.
Tries: Cozza (14), Taylor (22), Evans (44), Jones (47), Gale (51, 53, 70), Leilua (74); **Goals:** Hall 7/9.
KNIGHTS: 2 Joe Brown; 25 Brad Ward; 3 James Glover; 29 Connor Barley; 5 AJ Towse; 1 Matty Marsh; 7 Liam Harris; 16 Bailey Antrobus; 9 Will Jubb; 10 Conor Fitzsimmons; 4 Jesse Dee; 12 Danny Kirmond; 13 Jordan Thompson. Subs (all used): 17 Ronan Michael; 19 Josh Daley; 20 Jack Teanby; 21 Ukuma Ta'ai.
Try: Glover (58); **Goals:** Glover 0/1.
Rugby Leaguer & League Express Men of the Match: *Rovers:* Riley Dean; *Knights:* Bailey Antrobus.
Penalty count: 2-3; **Half-time:** 14-0;
Referee: Liam Rush; **Attendance:** 2,892.

KEIGHLEY COUGARS 34 BRADFORD BULLS 6

COUGARS: 1 Lewis Young; 3 Charlie Graham; 33 Jake Webster; 23 Robbie Storey; 2 Alix Stephenson; 22 Dane Chisholm; 31 Luke Gale; 15 Brenden Santi; 26 Thomas Doyle; 24 Mark Ioane; 30 Jimmy Keinhorst; 29 Joe Gibbons; 20 Brad Walker. Subs (all used): 14 Harvey Spence; 27 Sadiq Adebiyi; 8 Dan Parker; 9 Billy Gaylor.
Tries: Stephenson (24), Chisholm (30), Gibbons (32), Gale (34), Graham (62), Storey (79);
Goals: Chisholm 4/6, Gale 1/1.
BULLS: 1 Tom Holmes; 44 Luis Roberts; 3 Joe Arundel; 4 Kieran Gill; 38 Liam Tindall; 6 Dec Patton; 7 Jordan Lilley; 8 Jordan Baldwinson; 9 George Flanagan; 21 Fenton Rogers; 42 Leon Ruan; 15 AJ Wallace; 12 Chester Butler. Subs (all used): 14 Ebon Scurr; 18 Keven Appo; 22 George Roby; 17 Josh Johnson.
Try: Tindall (76); **Goals:** Patton 1/1.
Sin bin: Rogers (13) - high tackle on Walker.
Rugby Leaguer & League Express Men of the Match: *Cougars:* Dane Chisholm; *Bulls:* Joe Arundel.
Penalty count: 7-6; **Half-time:** 24-0;
Referee: Scott Mikalauskas; **Attendance:** 4,793.

LONDON BRONCOS 16 SWINTON LIONS 14

BRONCOS: 1 Alex Walker; 2 Paul Ulberg; 3 Jarred Bassett; 16 Ethan Natoli; 4 Dalton Grant; 6 Oliver Leyland; 17 Henry Raiwalui; 12 Marcus Stock; 9 Sam Davis; 10 Jordan Williams; 18 Emmanuel Waine; 32 Jacob Jones; 13 Dean Parata. Subs: 14 Bill Leyland; 8 Wellington Albert; 27 Ramon Silva; 7 Rian Horsman (not used).
Tries: Parata (14), Ulberg (48), Bassett (61);
Goals: O Leyland 2/3.
Sin bin: Albert (45) - interference.
LIONS: 2 Mike Butt; 3 Jake Spedding; 22 Andy Badrock; 16 Gav Rodden; 32 Wesley Bruines; 6 Nick Gregson; 7 Jordy Gibson; 10 Kenny Baker; 14 Josh Eaves; 35 Lewis Hall; 34 Ryan Lannon; 36 James Greenwood; 13 Louis Brogan. Subs (all used): 9 Luke Waterworth; 15 Jordan Case; 18 Liam Cooper; 12 Mitch Cox.
Tries: Eaves (2), Brogan (65); **Goals:** Gregson 3/4.
Rugby Leaguer & League Express Men of the Match: *Broncos:* Jarred Bassett; *Lions:* Mike Butt.
Penalty count: 6-11; **Half-time:** 6-8;
Referee: Nick Bennett; **Attendance:** 657.

Championship 2023 - Round by Round

WHITEHAVEN 16 BATLEY BULLDOGS 18

WHITEHAVEN: 23 Josh Rourke; 3 Chris Taylor; 11 Connor Holliday; 6 Karl Dixon; 4 Curtis Teare; 1 Sam Freeman; 14 Jamie Doran; 22 Lucas Castle; 21 Marcus O'Brien; 16 Lasarusa Tabu; 12 Lachlan Lanskey; 19 Ryan King; 8 Liam McAvoy. Subs (all used): 10 Tom Walker; 13 Dion Aiye; 15 James Newton; 18 Perry Singleton.
Tries: O'Brien (7), Newton (54), Teare (72);
Goals: Freeman 2/2, Rourke 0/1.
Sin bin: Walker (60) - high tackle on Kear.
BULLDOGS: 21 Aidan McGowan; 22 Dale Morton; 4 Josh Hodson; 3 Kieran Buchanan; 15 Elliot Kear; 14 James Meadows; 6 Ben White; 19 Tom Lillycrop; 9 Alistair Leak; 13 James Brown; 11 Dane Manning; 12 Lucas Walshaw; 30 Martyn Reilly. Subs (all used): 7 Josh Woods; 26 Nyle Flynn; 16 Michael Ward; 20 Samy Kibula.
Tries: Leak (17), Kear (31), Walshaw (50);
Goals: Meadows 3/3.
Sin bin: Hodson (80) - late challenge.
Rugby Leaguer & League Express Men of the Match: *Whitehaven:* Tom Walker; *Bulldogs:* James Brown.
Penalty count: 6-5; **Half-time:** 6-12;
Referee: Michael Smaill; **Attendance:** 1,006.

WIDNES VIKINGS 24 NEWCASTLE THUNDER 16

VIKINGS: 1 Jack Owens; 2 Ryan Ince; 3 Matty Fleming; 20 Joe Edge; 5 Kieran Dixon; 6 Danny Craven; 18 Joe Lyons; 16 Callum Field; 9 Matty Fozard; 10 Kyle Amor; 17 Shane Grady; 11 Sam Wilde; 22 Aaron Brown. Subs (all used): 12 Adam Lawton; 13 Liam Bent; 19 Olly Davies; 27 Anthony Walker.
Tries: Owens (19), K Dixon (37), Wilde (53), Lyons (66);
Goals: Edge 4/5.
Sin bin: Craven (74) - professional foul.
THUNDER: 6 Alex Donaghy; 2 Alex Young; 11 Alex Foster; 4 Connor Wynne; 1 Jack Johnson; 27 Jack Miller; 7 Nikau Williams; 8 Jay Chapelhow; 9 Curtis Davies; 10 Mitch Clark; 29 Nick Staveley; 12 Brad Gallagher; 28 Matty Laidlaw. Subs (all used): 14 Denive Balmforth; 15 Ted Chapelhow; 13 Connor Bailey; 23 Connor Moore.
Tries: J Chapelhow (74), Clark (79), Foster (80);
Goals: Williams 2/3.
Sin bin: Gallagher (27) - dangerous challenge on Grady; T Chapelhow (52) - high tackle on Dixon.
Rugby Leaguer & League Express Men of the Match: *Vikings:* Kieran Dixon; *Thunder:* Nikau Williams.
Penalty count: 5-7; **Half-time:** 14-0;
Referee: Cameron Worsley; **Attendance:** 2,743.

ROUND 8

Friday 7th April 2023

BARROW RAIDERS 14 WHITEHAVEN 16

RAIDERS: 24 Luke Broadbent; 27 Andrew Bulman; 4 Greg Worthington; 3 Rio-Osayomwanbo Corkill; 2 Shane Toal; 6 Jarrod Sammut; 7 Ryan Johnston; 15 Ellis Gillam; 22 Josh Wood; 10 Anton Iaria; 11 Danny Langtree; 12 Jarrad Stack; 13 Jack Wells. Subs (all used): 14 Jake Carter; 16 Sam Brooks; 20 Ben Evans; 8 Greg Burke.
Tries: Johnston (35), Stack (55); **Goals:** Sammut 3/4.
Sin bin: Wells (24) - punching.
WHITEHAVEN: 1 Sam Freeman; 2 Dave Eccleston; 23 Josh Rourke; 6 Karl Dixon; 4 Curtis Teare; 14 Jamie Doran; 7 Alex Bishop; 22 Lucas Castle; 21 Marcus O'Brien; 16 Lasarusa Tabu; 19 Ryan King; 12 Lachlan Lanskey; 17 Guy Graham. Subs (all used): 13 Dion Aiye; 15 James Newton; 18 Perry Singleton; 10 Tom Walker.
Tries: King (24), Dixon (32), Aiye (51);
Goals: Freeman 0/2, Rourke 2/2.
Rugby Leaguer & League Express Men of the Match: *Raiders:* Danny Langtree; *Whitehaven:* Dion Aiye.
Penalty count: 6-8; **Half-time:** 6-8;
Referee: Cameron Worsley; **Attendance:** 3,136.

NEWCASTLE THUNDER 20 SHEFFIELD EAGLES 44

THUNDER: 6 Alex Donaghy; 2 Alex Young; 3 Marcus Walker; 4 Connor Wynne; 1 Jack Johnson; 27 Jack Miller; 7 Nikau Williams; 8 Jay Chapelhow; 9 Curtis Davies; 10 Mitch Clark; 29 Nick Staveley; 11 Alex Foster; 13 Connor Bailey. Subs (all used): 14 Denive Balmforth; 15 Ted Chapelhow; 17 Rob Tuliatu; 28 Matty Laidlaw.
Tries: T Chapelhow (31), Young (35, 49), Donaghy (55);
Goals: Williams 2/4.
Sin bin: Foster (39) - late challenge on Aston.
EAGLES: 29 Quentin Laulu-Togaga'e; 2 Ben Jones-Bishop; 3 Kris Welham; 23 Bayley Liu; 22 Matty Chrimes; 32 Cory Aston; 7 Anthony Thackeray; 8 Brandon Douglas; 9 Vila Halafihi; 17 Liam Kirk; 24 Oliver Roberts; 12 Joel Farrell; 14 Titus Gwaze. Subs (all used): 10 Tyler Dickinson; 13 Evan Hodgson; 16 Blake Broadbent; 27 Jesse Sene-Lefao.
Tries: Thackeray (5, 20, 46), Laulu-Togaga'e (15, 61), Dickinson (40), Douglas (70), Chrimes (75);
Goals: Aston 6/8.
Rugby Leaguer & League Express Men of the Match: *Thunder:* Alex Donaghy; *Eagles:* Quentin Laulu-Togaga'e.
Penalty count: 5-6; **Half-time:** 10-24;
Referee: Brad Milligan; **Attendance:** 817.

SWINTON LIONS 16 WIDNES VIKINGS 48

LIONS: 1 Dan Abram; 2 Mike Butt; 22 Andy Badrock; 11 Rhodri Lloyd; 4 Jayden Hatton; 19 Ollie Olds; 7 Jordy Gibson; 18 Liam Cooper; 14 Josh Eaves; 13 Louis Brogan; 12 Mitch Cox; 36 James Greenwood; 6 Nick Gregson. Subs (all used): 10 Kenny Baker; 15 Jordan Case; 16 Gav Rodden; 35 Lewis Hall.
Tries: Gibson (31), Eaves (43), Badrock (60);
Goals: Abram 2/3.
Sin bin: Olds (69) - dissent.
VIKINGS: 3 Matty Fleming; 2 Ryan Ince; 29 Zach Eckersley; 20 Joe Edge; 5 Kieran Dixon; 6 Danny Craven; 1 Jack Owens; 16 Callum Field; 9 Matty Fozard; 10 Kyle Amor; 12 Adam Lawton; 17 Shane Grady; 13 Liam Bent. Subs (all used): 11 Sam Wilde; 14 Jordan Johnstone; 21 Lewis Hatton; 27 Anthony Walker.
Tries: Fleming (14), Owens (18), Craven (20), Eckersley (22, 64, 80), Lawton (67, 71), K Dixon (75);
Goals: Owens 6/10.
Rugby Leaguer & League Express Men of the Match: *Lions:* Jordy Gibson; *Vikings:* Zach Eckersley.
Penalty count: 6-4; **Half-time:** 6-24;
Referee: Scott Mikalauskas; **Attendance:** 1,403.

BATLEY BULLDOGS 18 FEATHERSTONE ROVERS 26

BULLDOGS: 32 Luke Hooley; 21 Aidan McGowan; 4 Josh Hodson; 3 Kieran Buchanan; 15 Elliot Kear; 14 James Meadows; 6 Ben White; 19 Tom Lillycrop; 9 Alistair Leak; 13 James Brown; 11 Dane Manning; 12 Lucas Walshaw; 30 Martyn Reilly. Subs (all used): 7 Josh Woods; 20 Samy Kibula; 26 Nyle Flynn; 8 Adam Gledhill.
Tries: Hodson (47), Gledhill (58), McGowan (75);
Goals: Meadows 3/4.
Sin bin: Manning (72) - dangerous contact.
ROVERS: 23 Caleb Aekins; 2 Luke Briscoe; 21 Joey Leilua; 18 Josh Hardcastle; 5 Gareth Gale; 4 Craig Hall; 7 Riley Dean; 27 McKenzie Yei; 14 Matty Wildie; 10 James Lockwood; 11 Brad Day; 13 Jack Bussey; 24 Mathieu Cozza. Subs (all used): 9 Connor Jones; 15 John Davies; 30 Albert Vete; 29 Yusuf Aydin.
Tries: Hardcastle (7, 16), Briscoe (21), Leilua (24), Jones (49); **Goals:** Hall 3/5.
Sin bin: Day (75) - repeated team offences.
Rugby Leaguer & League Express Men of the Match: *Bulldogs:* Adam Gledhill; *Rovers:* Josh Hardcastle.
Penalty count: 10-5; **Half-time:** 2-20;
Referee: James Vella; **Attendance:** 2,309.

TOULOUSE OLYMPIQUE 52 LONDON BRONCOS 0

OLYMPIQUE: 23 Robin Brochon; 5 Paul Marcon; 4 Mathieu Jussaume; 3 Reubenn Rennie; 18 Guy Armitage; 6 Josh Ralph; 7 Jake Shorrocks; 20 Greg Richards; 14 Eloi Pelissier; 10 Harrison Hansen; 24 Pierre-Jean Lima; 11 Maxime Stefani; 13 Anthony Marion. Subs (all used): 17 Hugo Pezet; 28 Harvie Hill; 27 Dimitri Biscarro; 26 Stephane Guillon.
Tries: Brochon (10), Ralph (25, 79), Armitage (31, 42), Rennie (51, 65), Pelissier (70, 75); **Goals:** Shorrocks 8/9.
Sin bin: Maxime Stefani (35) - dangerous challenge.
BRONCOS: 1 Alex Walker; 2 Paul Ulberg; 3 Jarred Bassett; 4 Dalton Grant; 5 Iliess Macani; 6 Oliver Leyland; 13 Dean Parata; 15 Lewis Bienek; 14 Bill Leyland; 10 Jordan Williams; 32 Jacob Jones; 16 Ethan Natoli; 12 Marcus Stock. Subs (all used): 24 Jenson Monk; 27 Ramon Silva; 22 Max Allen; 26 Euan Parke.
Rugby Leaguer & League Express Men of the Match: *Olympique:* Josh Ralph; *Broncos:* Oliver Leyland.
Penalty count: 4-3; **Half-time:** 18-0;
Referee: Michael Smaill; **Attendance:** 3,358.

YORK KNIGHTS 10 KEIGHLEY COUGARS 22

KNIGHTS: 2 Joe Brown; 5 AJ Towse; 3 James Glover; 29 Connor Barley; 15 Myles Harrison; 1 Matty Marsh; 7 Liam Harris; 16 Bailey Antrobus; 9 Will Jubb; 10 Conor Fitzsimmons; 32 Oli Field; 12 Danny Kirmond; 13 Jordan Thompson. Subs (all used): 8 Jon Luke Kirby; 19 Josh Daley; 20 Jack Teanby; 21 Ukuma Ta'ai.
Tries: Antrobus (6), Harris (62); **Goals:** Glover 1/2.
COUGARS: 1 Lewis Young; 5 Mo Agoro; 23 Robbie Storey; 30 Jimmy Keinhorst; 25 Ben Crooks; 22 Dane Chisholm; 31 Luke Gale; 15 Brenden Santi; 26 Thomas Doyle; 24 Mark Ioane; 29 Joe Gibbons; 19 Ellis Robson; 14 Harvey Spence. Subs (all used): 21 Lloyd Roby; 10 Toby Everett; 8 Dan Parker; 12 Aaron Levy.
Tries: Chisholm (21), Crooks (25), Keinhorst (49), Ioane (53); **Goals:** Gale 3/4.
Rugby Leaguer & League Express Men of the Match: *Knights:* Will Jubb; *Cougars:* Dane Chisholm.
Penalty count: 3-3; **Half-time:** 6-10;
Referee: Nick Bennett; **Attendance:** 2,218.

Monday 10th April 2023

HALIFAX PANTHERS 22 BRADFORD BULLS 26

PANTHERS: 1 James Woodburn-Hall; 2 Lachlan Walmsley; 22 Jake Maizen; 3 Zack McComb; 5 James Saltonstall; 6 Louis Jouffret; 7 Joe Keyes; 15 Will Maher; 9 Brandon Moore; 10 Dan Murray; 11 Ben Kavanagh; 12 Matty Gee; 8 Adam Tangata. Subs (all used): 16 Will Calcott; 19 Ryan Lannon; 20 Tom Inman; 21 Eribe Doro.
Tries: Moore (11), Walmsley (30), Maizen (63, 75);
Goals: Keyes 3/4.
Sin bin: Kavanagh (58) - dangerous challenge.
BULLS: 1 Tom Holmes; 2 Ben Blackmore; 3 Joe Arundel; 4 Kieran Gill; 44 Luis Roberts; 6 Dec Patton; 7 Jordan Lilley; 8 Jordan Baldwinson; 9 George Flanagan; 36 Sam Walters; 46 James Donaldson; 18 Keven Appo; 13 Bodene Thompson. Subs (all used): 14 Ebon Scurr; 15 AJ Wallace; 20 Billy Jowitt; 35 Jack Bibby.
Tries: Walters (5), Baldwinson (26), Gill (40), Holmes (68);
Goals: Patton 5/5.
Rugby Leaguer & League Express Men of the Match: *Panthers:* Brandon Moore; *Bulls:* James Donaldson.
Penalty count: 3-8; **Half-time:** 12-20;
Referee: Tom Grant; **Attendance:** 3,053.

ROUND 9

Saturday 15th April 2023

KEIGHLEY COUGARS 6 TOULOUSE OLYMPIQUE 34

COUGARS: 1 Lewis Young; 25 Ben Crooks; 2 Alix Stephenson; 23 Robbie Storey; 5 Mo Agoro; 22 Dane Chisholm; 31 Luke Gale; 15 Brenden Santi; 26 Thomas Doyle; 24 Mark Ioane; 28 Keenen Tomlinson; 20 Brad Walker; 14 Harvey Spence. Subs (all used): 10 Toby Everett; 12 Aaron Levy; 21 Lloyd Roby; 27 Sadiq Adebiyi.
Try: Levy (65); **Goals:** Chisholm 1/1.
OLYMPIQUE: 23 Robin Brochon; 5 Paul Marcon; 4 Mathieu Jussaume; 3 Reubenn Rennie; 18 Guy Armitage; 6 Josh Ralph; 7 Jake Shorrocks; 20 Greg Richards; 14 Eloi Pelissier; 10 Harrison Hansen; 24 Pierre-Jean Lima; 11 Maxime Stefani; 13 Anthony Marion. Subs (all used): 15 Sitaleki Akauola; 17 Hugo Pezet; 27 Dimitri Biscarro; 28 Bastien Scimone.
Tries: Marion (11), Ralph (27, 62), Rennie (58), Maxime Stefani (71), Armitage (79); **Goals:** Shorrocks 5/6.
Rugby Leaguer & League Express Men of the Match: *Cougars:* Lewis Young; *Olympique:* Anthony Marion.
Penalty count: 5-3; **Half-time:** 0-10;
Referee: Tom Grant; **Attendance:** 1,739.

Sunday 16th April 2023

BRADFORD BULLS 16 BATLEY BULLDOGS 21

BULLS: 1 Tom Holmes; 2 Ben Blackmore; 30 Jayden Myers; 4 Kieran Gill; 5 David Foggin-Johnston; 6 Dec Patton; 7 Jordan Lilley; 8 Jordan Baldwinson; 9 George Flanagan; 14 Ebon Scurr; 18 Keven Appo; 13 Bodene Thompson; 35 Jack Bibby. Subs (all used): 17 Josh Johnson; 15 AJ Wallace; 20 Billy Jowitt; 29 Rob Butler.
Tries: Jowitt (39), Foggin-Johnston (55), Holmes (79);
Goals: Patton 1/2, Lilley 1/1.
Sin bin: Patton (50) - fighting.
BULLDOGS: 32 Luke Hooley; 21 Aidan McGowan; 4 Josh Hodson; 3 Kieran Buchanan; 15 Elliot Kear; 6 Ben White; 7 Josh Woods; 19 Tom Lillycrop; 24 Ben Kaye; 13 James Brown; 12 Lucas Walshaw; 11 Dane Manning; 30 Martyn Reilly. Subs (all used): 14 James Meadows; 8 Adam Gledhill; 26 Nyle Flynn; 20 Samy Kibula.
Tries: Walshaw (15), Hodson (61); **Goals:** Hooley 6/6;
Field goal: Woods (72).
Rugby Leaguer & League Express Men of the Match: *Bulls:* Tom Holmes; *Bulldogs:* Luke Hooley.
Penalty count: 6-13; **Half-time:** 6-8;
Referee: Liam Rush; **Attendance:** 3,330.

HALIFAX PANTHERS 16 YORK KNIGHTS 6

PANTHERS: 1 James Woodburn-Hall; 2 Lachlan Walmsley; 22 Jake Maizen; 4 Ben Tibbs; 3 Zack McComb; 6 Louis Jouffret; 7 Joe Keyes; 16 Will Calcott; 9 Brandon Moore; 10 Dan Murray; 11 Ben Kavanagh; 12 Matty Gee; 13 Jacob Fairbank. Subs (all used): 8 Adam Tangata; 18 Brandon Pickersgill; 19 Ryan Lannon; 20 Tom Inman.
Tries: Walmsley (16, 26), Fairbank (49);
Goals: Keyes 1/2, Jouffret 1/1.
KNIGHTS: 2 Joe Brown; 29 Connor Barley; 3 James Glover; 15 Myles Harrison; 5 AJ Towse; 32 Oli Field; 14 James Cunningham; 8 Jon Luke Kirby; 9 Will Jubb; 21

Championship 2023 - Round by Round

Ukuma Ta'ai; 11 Chris Clarkson; 16 Bailey Antrobus; 13 Jordan Thompson. Subs (all used): 17 Ronan Michael; 19 Josh Daley; 20 Jack Teanby; 25 Brad Ward.
Try: Glover (77); **Goals:** Glover 1/1.
Sin bin: Cunningham (32) - high tackle on Keyes.
Rugby Leaguer & League Express Men of the Match: *Panthers:* Lachlan Walmsley; *Knights:* James Glover.
Penalty count: 3-1; **Half-time:** 10-0;
Referee: James Vella; **Attendance:** 1,454.

LONDON BRONCOS 10 FEATHERSTONE ROVERS 40

BRONCOS: 1 Alex Walker; 2 Paul Ulberg; 3 Jarred Bassett; 16 Ethan Natoli; 5 Iliess Macani; 6 Oliver Leyland; 17 Henry Raiwalui; 8 Wellington Albert; 13 Dean Parata; 15 Lewis Bienek; 32 Jacob Jones; 18 Emmanuel Waine; 12 Marcus Stock. Subs (all used): 14 Bill Leyland; 10 Jordan Williams; 27 Ramon Silva; 23 Daniel Hoyes.
Tries: Macani (58), Bassett (75); **Goals:** O Leyland 1/2.
ROVERS: 23 Caleb Aekins; 2 Luke Briscoe; 21 Joey Leilua; 18 Josh Hardcastle; 5 Gareth Gale; 14 Matty Wildie; 7 Riley Dean; 27 McKenzie Yei; 9 Connor Jones; 10 James Lockwood; 11 Brad Day; 15 John Davies; 24 Mathieu Cozza. Subs (all used): 4 Craig Hall; 30 Albert Vete; 8 Craig Kopczak; 29 Yusuf Aydin.
Tries: Aekins (8, 18), Day (30, 69), Jones (38, 46, 54);
Goals: Dean 6/7.
Rugby Leaguer & League Express Men of the Match: *Broncos:* Henry Raiwalui; *Rovers:* Caleb Aekins.
Penalty count: 4-2; **Half-time:** 0-22;
Referee: Michael Smaill; **Attendance:** 977.

WHITEHAVEN 31 NEWCASTLE THUNDER 6

WHITEHAVEN: 23 Josh Rourke; 2 Dave Eccleston; 11 Connor Holliday; 6 Karl Dixon; 4 Curtis Teare; 14 Jamie Doran; 7 Alex Bishop; 22 Lucas Castle; 15 James Newton; 28 Ross Ainley; 12 Lachlan Lanskey; 19 Ryan King; 17 Guy Graham. Subs (all used): 10 Tom Walker; 13 Dion Aiye; 18 Perry Singleton; 26 Connor Saunders.
Tries: Dixon (17), Bishop (49), Walker (58), Singleton (63), Rourke (67); **Goals:** Rourke 5/6; **Field goal:** J Doran (79).
Sin bin: King (70) - punching.
THUNDER: 6 Alex Donaghy; 1 Jack Johnson; 3 Marcus Walker; 11 Alex Foster; 5 Alex Clegg; 27 Jack Miller; 7 Nikau Williams; 8 Jay Chapelhow; 9 Curtis Davies; 10 Mitch Clark; 29 Nick Staveley; 14 Denive Balmforth; 13 Connor Bailey. Subs (all used): 15 Ted Chapelhow; 28 Matty Laidlaw; 17 Rob Tuliatu; 16 Rhys Clarke.
Try: Donaghy (71); **Goals:** Williams 1/1.
Sin bin: J Chapelhow (77) - high tackle on Aiye.
Rugby Leaguer & League Express Men of the Match: *Whitehaven:* Tom Walker; *Thunder:* Nick Staveley.
Penalty count: 13-7; **Half-time:** 8-0;
Referee: Cameron Worsley; **Attendance:** 987.

WIDNES VIKINGS 23 BARROW RAIDERS 14

VIKINGS: 3 Matty Fleming; 20 Joe Edge; 2 Ryan Ince; 29 Zach Eckersley; 5 Kieran Dixon; 6 Danny Craven; 1 Jack Owens; 16 Callum Field; 9 Matty Fozard; 8 Owen Farnworth; 12 Adam Lawton; 11 Sam Wilde; 14 Jordan Johnstone. Subs: 18 Joe Lyons (not used); 27 Anthony Walker; 21 Lewis Hatton; 19 Olly Davies.
Tries: Lawton (18), Eckersley (22), Craven (60), Ince (72);
Goals: Owens 3/4; **Field goal:** Owens (40).
RAIDERS: 1 Luke Cresswell; 5 Ryan Shaw; 18 Brett Carter; 2 Shane Toal; 24 Luke Broadbent; 6 Jarrod Sammut; 7 Ryan Johnston; 15 Ellis Gillam; 22 Josh Wood; 10 Anton Iaria; 11 Danny Langtree; 12 Jarrad Stack; 13 Jack Wells. Subs (all used): 9 Nathan Mossop; 21 Tom Hopkins; 8 Greg Burke; 17 Charlie Emslie.
Tries: Broadbent (53), Wood (79); **Goals:** Shaw 3/3.
Rugby Leaguer & League Express Men of the Match: *Vikings:* Jack Owens; *Raiders:* Jarrod Sammut.
Penalty count: 3-5; **Half-time:** 13-2;
Referee: Scott Mikalauskas; **Attendance:** 2,772.

Monday 17th April 2023

SHEFFIELD EAGLES 16 SWINTON LIONS 6

EAGLES: 29 Quentin Laulu-Togaga'e; 2 Ben Jones-Bishop; 3 Kris Welham; 23 Bayley Liu; 22 Matty Chrimes; 11 Connor Bower; 32 Cory Aston; 8 Brandon Douglas; 9 Vila Halafihi; 17 Liam Kirk; 24 Oliver Roberts; 12 Joel Farrell; 10 Tyler Dickinson. Subs (all used): 13 Evan Hodgson; 15 Mikey Wood; 16 Blake Broadbent; 27 Jesse Sene-Lefao.
Tries: Laulu-Togaga'e (15), Aston (20), Jones-Bishop (77);
Goals: Aston 2/3.
LIONS: 1 Dan Abram; 26 Joey Romeo; 11 Rhodri Lloyd; 22 Andy Badrock; 3 Jake Spedding; 19 Ollie Olds; 7 Jordy Gibson; 18 Liam Cooper; 14 Josh Eaves; 15 Jordan Case; 10 Kenny Baker; 16 Gav Rodden; 6 Nick Gregson. Subs: 13 Louis Brogan; 25 Scott Parnaby (not used); 31 George Roby; 35 Lewis Hall.
Try: Rodden (48); **Goals:** Abram 1/1.
Rugby Leaguer & League Express Men of the Match: *Eagles:* Tyler Dickinson; *Lions:* Gav Rodden.
Penalty count: 5-8; **Half-time:** 10-0;
Referee: Nick Bennett; **Attendance:** 1,179.

ROUND 10

Saturday 6th May 2023

SWINTON LIONS 19 TOULOUSE OLYMPIQUE 12

LIONS: 23 Joe Lowe; 3 Jake Spedding; 36 Ben Davies; 11 Rhodri Lloyd; 26 Joey Romeo; 19 Ollie Olds; 7 Jordy Gibson; 10 Kenny Baker; 14 Josh Eaves; 15 Jordan Case; 16 Gav Rodden; 22 Andy Badrock; 6 Nick Gregson. Subs (all used): 13 Louis Brogan; 31 George Roby; 34 Luke Thomas; 35 Lewis Hall.
Tries: Spedding (21), Brogan (47); **Goals:** Davies 5/5;
Field goal: Gibson (63).
OLYMPIQUE: 23 Robin Brochon; 5 Paul Marcon; 4 Mathieu Jussaume; 25 Matthieu Laguerre; 18 Guy Armitage; 6 Josh Ralph; 7 Jake Shorrocks; 20 Greg Richards; 9 Calum Gahan; 10 Harrison Hansen; 12 Dominique Peyroux; 16 Joe Bretherton; 13 Anthony Marion. Subs (all used): 15 Sitaleki Akauola; 17 Hugo Pezet; 22 Ugo Tison; 27 Dimitri Biscarro.
Tries: Akauola (65), Peyroux (75); **Goals:** Shorrocks 2/2.
Sin bin: Akauola (20) - dissent, (54) - holding down.
Rugby Leaguer & League Express Men of the Match: *Lions:* Louis Brogan; *Olympique:* Robin Brochon.
Penalty count: 6-8; **Half-time:** 8-0;
Referee: Brad Milligan; **Attendance:** 957.

Sunday 7th May 2023

NEWCASTLE THUNDER 16 HALIFAX PANTHERS 36

THUNDER: 6 Alex Donaghy; 20 Gideon Boafo; 29 Nick Staveley; 11 Alex Foster; 5 Alex Clegg; 27 Jack Miller; 7 Nikau Williams; 8 Jay Chapelhow; 9 Curtis Davies; 23 Connor Moore; 12 Brad Gallagher; 17 Rob Tuliatu; 13 Connor Bailey. Subs (all used): 10 Mitch Clark; 14 Denive Balmforth; 15 Ted Chapelhow; 24 Daniel Okoro.
Tries: Balmforth (60), Clegg (70), J Chapelhow (74);
Goals: Williams 2/3.
PANTHERS: 18 Brandon Pickersgill; 2 Lachlan Walmsley; 22 Jake Maizen; 4 Ben Tibbs; 3 Zack McComb; 1 James Woodburn-Hall; 7 Joe Keyes; 16 Will Calcott; 14 Kyle Wood; 10 Dan Murray; 11 Ben Kavanagh; 12 Matty Gee; 13 Jacob Fairbank. Subs (all used): 8 Adam Tangata; 19 Ryan Lannon; 20 Tom Inman; 31 Kevin Larroyer.
Tries: Keyes (17, 78), Walmsley (34), Woodburn-Hall (45), McComb (48), Inman (57); **Goals:** Keyes 6/7.
Rugby Leaguer & League Express Men of the Match: *Thunder:* Denive Balmforth; *Panthers:* Joe Keyes.
Penalty count: 2-5; **Half-time:** 0-12;
Referee: Scott Mikalauskas; **Attendance:** 1,067.

BARROW RAIDERS 46 BRADFORD BULLS 12

RAIDERS: 1 Luke Cresswell; 5 Ryan Shaw; 3 Rio-Osayomwanbo Corkill; 2 Shane Toal; 24 Luke Broadbent; 6 Jarrod Sammut; 7 Ryan Johnston; 15 Ellis Gillam; 9 Nathan Mossop; 10 Anton Iaria; 11 Danny Langtree; 12 Jarrad Stack; 13 Jack Wells. Subs (all used): 23 Connor Saunders; 16 Sam Brooks; 8 Greg Burke; 17 Charlie Emslie.
Tries: Broadbent (14, 54), Cresswell (44, 49, 75), Corkill (61), Toal (65), Sammut (78); **Goals:** Shaw 7/8.
BULLS: 31 Jack Walker; 37 Jason Qareqare; 30 Jayden Myers; 4 Kieran Gill; 44 Luis Roberts; 6 Dec Patton; 7 Jordan Lilley; 8 Jordan Baldwinson; 9 George Flanagan; 21 Fenton Rogers; 15 AJ Wallace; 12 Chester Butler; 35 Jack Bibby. Subs (all used): 20 Billy Jowitt; 39 Jansin Turgut; 14 Ebon Scurr; 17 Josh Johnson.
Tries: Roberts (27), Walker (59); **Goals:** Patton 1/4, Lilley 1/1.
Sin bin: Roberts (11) - delaying restart.
Rugby Leaguer & League Express Men of the Match: *Raiders:* Luke Cresswell; *Bulls:* Jayden Myers.
Penalty count: 4-3; **Half-time:** 4-6;
Referee: James Vella; **Attendance:** 2,440.

FEATHERSTONE ROVERS 28 SHEFFIELD EAGLES 20

ROVERS: 23 Caleb Aekins; 2 Luke Briscoe; 21 Joey Leilua; 18 Josh Hardcastle; 5 Gareth Gale; 25 Thomas Lacans; 7 Riley Dean; 17 Gadwin Springer; 14 Matty Wildie; 10 James Lockwood; 11 Brad Day; 13 Jack Bussey; 32 Daniel Smith. Subs (all used): 8 Craig Kopczak; 9 Connor Jones; 15 John Davies; 16 Junior Moors.
Tries: Hardcastle (5), Briscoe (18, 68), Bussey (62), Aekins (80); **Goals:** Dean 3/4, Bussey 1/1.
Sin bin: Dean (66) - fighting.
EAGLES: 29 Quentin Laulu-Togaga'e; 2 Ben Jones-Bishop; 3 Kris Welham; 23 Bayley Liu; 28 Matty Dawson-Jones; 32 Cory Aston; 7 Anthony Thackeray; 8 Brandon Douglas; 9 Vila Halafihi; 17 Liam Kirk; 24 Oliver Roberts; 27 Jesse Sene-Lefao; 12 Joel Farrell. Subs (all used): 11 Connor Bower; 13 Evan Hodgson; 15 Mikey Wood; 16 Blake Broadbent.
Tries: Liu (25), Dawson-Jones (35, 55), Jones-Bishop (74);
Goals: Aston 2/3, J Farrell 0/1.
Sin bin: Halafihi (62) - dangerous contact; Aston (66) - fighting; Sene-Lefao (66) - dissent.
Rugby Leaguer & League Express Men of the Match: *Rovers:* Jack Bussey; *Eagles:* Jesse Sene-Lefao.
Penalty count: 7-6; **Half-time:** 10-10;
Referee: Tom Grant; **Attendance:** 3,187.

WHITEHAVEN 24 KEIGHLEY COUGARS 32

WHITEHAVEN: 23 Josh Rourke; 2 Dave Eccleston; 27 Sam Haynes; 26 Oscar Doran; 4 Curtis Teare; 14 Jamie Doran; 7 Alex Bishop; 22 Lucas Castle; 15 James Newton; 28 Ross Ainley; 12 Lachlan Lanskey; 19 Ryan King; 17 Guy Graham. Subs (all used): 10 Tom Walker; 13 Dion Aiye; 18 Perry Singleton; 20 Jake Bradley.
Tries: Graham (14, 75), Eccleston (29), Teare (47);
Goals: Rourke 4/4.
COUGARS: 1 Lewis Young; 5 Mo Agoro; 23 Robbie Storey; 25 Ben Crooks; 3 Charlie Graham; 21 Lloyd Roby; 22 Dane Chisholm; 15 Brenden Santi; 26 Thomas Doyle; 24 Mark Ioane; 29 Joe Gibbons; 19 Ellis Robson; 20 Brad Walker. Subs (all used): 14 Harvey Spence; 27 Sadiq Adebiyi; 8 Dan Parker; 16 Josh Lynam.
Tries: Doyle (7), Ioane (21), Crooks (25, 35, 39);
Goals: Chisholm 6/7.
Rugby Leaguer & League Express Men of the Match: *Whitehaven:* Tom Walker; *Cougars:* Dane Chisholm.
Penalty count: 4-3; **Half-time:** 12-28;
Referee: Liam Rush; **Attendance:** 1,065.

YORK KNIGHTS 30 LONDON BRONCOS 28

KNIGHTS: 1 Matty Marsh; 2 Joe Brown; 33 Oliver Pratt; 3 James Glover; 5 AJ Towse; 6 Ata Hingano; 19 Josh Daley; 8 Jon Luke Kirby; 9 Will Jubb; 21 Ukuma Ta'ai; 11 Chris Clarkson; 32 Oli Field; 13 Jordan Thompson. Subs: 15 Myles Harrison (not used); 17 Ronan Michael; 20 Jack Teanby; 24 Ben Barnard (not used).
Tries: Towse (18, 38, 71), Clarkson (25), Ta'ai (56);
Goals: Glover 5/6.
BRONCOS: 1 Alex Walker; 2 Paul Ulberg; 3 Jarred Bassett; 18 Emmanuel Waine; 5 Iliess Macani; 6 Oliver Leyland; 17 Henry Raiwalui; 15 Lewis Bienek; 9 Sam Davis; 12 Marcus Stock; 11 Will Lovell; 16 Ethan Natoli; 13 Dean Parata. Subs (all used): 14 Bill Leyland; 8 Wellington Albert; 10 Jordan Williams; 27 Ramon Silva.
Tries: Natoli (12), Williams (43), Albert (47), Stock (67), Macani (75); **Goals:** O Leyland 4/5.
Rugby Leaguer & League Express Men of the Match: *Knights:* AJ Towse; *Broncos:* Jarred Bassett.
Penalty count: 4-5; **Half-time:** 16-4;
Referee: Cameron Worsley; **Attendance:** 1,802.

Monday 8th May 2023

BATLEY BULLDOGS 11 WIDNES VIKINGS 4

BULLDOGS: 32 Luke Hooley; 22 Dale Morton; 4 Josh Hodson; 15 Elliot Kear; 21 Aidan McGowan; 6 Ben White; 7 Josh Woods; 8 Adam Gledhill; 24 Ben Kaye; 19 Tom Lillycrop; 3 Kieran Buchanan; 12 Lucas Walshaw; 30 Martyn Reilly. Subs (all used): 16 Michael Ward; 10 Keegan Hirst; 26 Nyle Flynn; 28 Oli Burton.
Try: Walshaw (15); **Goals:** Hooley 3/3;
Field goal: Woods (77).
VIKINGS: 3 Matty Fleming; 2 Ryan Ince; 29 Zach Eckersley; 20 Joe Edge; 5 Kieran Dixon; 6 Danny Craven; 1 Jack Owens; 8 Owen Farnworth; 9 Matty Fozard; 16 Callum Field; 11 Sam Wilde; 12 Adam Lawton; 14 Jordan Johnstone. Subs (all used): 10 Kyle Amor; 21 Lewis Hatton; 27 Anthony Walker; 30 Jacob Jones.
Try: Eckersley (74); **Goals:** Owens 0/1.
Rugby Leaguer & League Express Men of the Match: *Bulldogs:* Josh Woods; *Vikings:* Zach Eckersley.
Penalty count: 4-3; **Half-time:** 8-0;
Referee: Michael Smaill; **Attendance:** 923.

ROUND 11

Saturday 13th May 2023

LONDON BRONCOS 30 BARROW RAIDERS 16

BRONCOS: 1 Alex Walker; 2 Paul Ulberg; 3 Jarred Bassett; 18 Emmanuel Waine; 5 Iliess Macani; 6 Oliver Leyland; 17 Henry Raiwalui; 15 Lewis Bienek; 9 Sam Davis; 8 Wellington Albert; 11 Will Lovell; 16 Ethan Natoli; 12 Marcus Stock. Subs (all used): 14 Bill Leyland; 13 Dean Parata; 10 Jordan Williams; 27 Ramon Silva.
Tries: Natoli (24), B Leyland (33), Macani (36), O Leyland (55), Bassett (62); **Goals:** O Leyland 5/6.
Sin bin: Lovell (79) - delaying restart.
RAIDERS: 1 Luke Cresswell; 5 Ryan Shaw; 25 Keanan Brand; 2 Shane Toal; 24 Luke Broadbent; 6 Jarrod

Championship 2023 - Round by Round

Featherstone's Gareth Gale fends off Widnes' Jordan Johnstone

Sammut; 7 Ryan Johnston; 16 Sam Brooks; 22 Josh Wood; 10 Anton Iaria; 11 Danny Langtree; 12 Jarrad Stack; 13 Jack Wells. Subs (all used): 9 Nathan Mossop; 4 Greg Worthington; 17 Charlie Emslie; 20 Ben Evans.
Tries: Broadbent (12), Shaw (42), Langtree (69);
Goals: Shaw 2/3.
Sin bin: Johnston (50) - interference.
Rugby Leaguer & League Express Men of the Match:
Broncos: Emmanuel Waine; *Raiders:* Ryan Shaw.
Penalty count: 9-7; **Half-time:** 16-6;
Referee: Michael Smaill; **Attendance:** 806.

BATLEY BULLDOGS 17 TOULOUSE OLYMPIQUE 16

BULLDOGS: 32 Luke Hooley; 21 Aidan McGowan; 4 Josh Hodson; 3 Kieran Buchanan; 15 Elliot Kear; 6 Ben White; 7 Josh Woods; 13 James Brown; 17 Luke Blake; 19 Tom Lillycrop; 11 Dane Manning; 12 Lucas Walshaw; 30 Martyn Reilly. Subs (all used): 8 Adam Gledhill; 16 Michael Ward; 26 Nyle Flynn; 28 Oli Burton.
Tries: Kear (19), McGowan (24, 57); **Goals:** Hooley 2/3;
Field goal: Woods (75).
OLYMPIQUE: 23 Robin Brochon; 5 Paul Marcon; 4 Mathieu Jussaume; 3 Reubenn Rennie; 18 Guy Armitage; 6 Josh Ralph; 13 Anthony Marion; 20 Greg Richards; 9 Calum Gahan; 27 Dimitri Biscarro; 24 Pierre-Jean Lima; 11 Maxime Stefani; 10 Harrison Hansen. Subs (all used): 15 Sitaleki Akauola; 16 Joe Bretherton; 22 Ugo Tison; 26 Bastien Scimone.
Tries: Jussaume (34), Brochon (37), Ralph (45);
Goals: Brochon 2/3.
Rugby Leaguer & League Express Men of the Match:
Bulldogs: Luke Hooley; *Olympique:* Robin Brochon.
Penalty count: 3-1; **Half-time:** 10-12;
Referee: Tom Grant; **Attendance:** 1,331.

Sunday 14th May 2023

BRADFORD BULLS 44 SWINTON LIONS 38

BULLS: 31 Jack Walker; 2 Ben Blackmore; 12 Chester Butler; 4 Kieran Gill; 5 David Foggin-Johnston; 20 Billy Jowitt; 6 Dec Patton; 8 Jordan Baldwinson; 7 Jordan Lilley; 21 Fenton Rogers; 11 Brad England; 15 AJ Wallace; 17 Josh Johnson. Subs (all used): 9 George Flanagan; 14 Ebon Scurr; 18 Keven Appo; 40 Nathan Mason.
Tries: Gill (7), England (11), Mason (31, 57), Foggin-Johnston (36, 57), Appo (61); **Goals:** Patton 8/8.
LIONS: 2 Mike Butt; 4 Jayden Hatton; 3 Jake Spedding; 32 Wesley Bruines; 26 Joey Romeo; 19 Ollie Olds; 7 Jordy Gibson; 36 Lewis Baxter; 14 Josh Eaves; 34 Dan Norman; 22 Andy Badrock; 11 Rhodri Lloyd; 15 Jordan Case.
Subs (all used): 33 Amir Bourouh; 1 Dan Abram; - Tom Whitehead; 25 Scott Parnaby.
Tries: Hatton (28), Bourouh (43), Lloyd (47, 51), Bruines (75), Badrock (78); **Goals:** Abram 7/7.
Rugby Leaguer & League Express Men of the Match:
Bulls: Billy Jowitt; *Lions:* Dan Abram.
Penalty count: 13-14; **Half-time:** 26-8;
Referee: Cameron Worsley; **Attendance:** 2,935.

HALIFAX PANTHERS 60 WHITEHAVEN 0

PANTHERS: 1 James Woodburn-Hall; 2 Lachlan Walmsley; 4 Ben Tibbs; 3 Zack McComb; 5 James Saltonstall; 6 Louis Jouffret; 7 Joe Keyes; 16 Will Calcott; 9 Brandon Moore; 10 Dan Murray; 11 Ben Kavanagh; 12 Matty Gee; 13 Jacob Fairbank. Subs (all used): 14 Kyle Wood; 8 Adam Tangata; 21 Eribe Doro; 29 Dan Fleming.
Tries: Walmsley (4, 12, 43, 74), Saltonstall (14), Woodburn-Hall (35, 38), Kavanagh (49), Doro (56, 66), Fairbank (60); **Goals:** Keyes 8/11.
WHITEHAVEN: 23 Josh Rourke; 7 Dave Eccleston; 27 Sam Haynes; 4 Curtis Teare; 26 Oscar Doran; 14 Jamie Doran; 7 Alex Bishop; 22 Lucas Castle; 15 James Newton; 28 Ross Ainley; 11 Connor Holliday; 12 Lachlan Lanskey; 17 Guy Graham. Subs (all used): 13 Dion Aiye; 18 Perry Singleton; 16 Lasarusa Tabu; 10 Tom Walker.
Sin bin: Singleton (80) - professional foul.
Rugby Leaguer & League Express Men of the Match:
Panthers: Joe Keyes; *Whitehaven:* Tom Walker.
Penalty count: 3-4; **Half-time:** 26-0;
Referee: Nick Bennett; **Attendance:** 1,998.

KEIGHLEY COUGARS 18 SHEFFIELD EAGLES 46

COUGARS: 35 Phoenix Laulu-Togaga'e; 3 Charlie Graham; 25 Ben Crooks; 23 Robbie Storey; 5 Mo Agoro; 2 Alix Stephenson; 22 Dane Chisholm; 15 Brenden Santi; 26 Thomas Doyle; 24 Mark Ioane; 19 Ellis Robson; 29 Joe Gibbons; 20 Brad Walker. Subs (all used): 14 Harvey Spence; 27 Sadiq Adebiyi; 8 Dan Parker; 16 Josh Lynam.
Tries: Robson (9), Stephenson (50), Ioane (52);
Goals: Chisholm 3/3.
EAGLES: 29 Quentin Laulu-Togaga'e; 2 Ben Jones-Bishop; 3 Kris Welham; 23 Bayley Liu; 28 Matty Dawson-Jones; 32 Cory Aston; 7 Anthony Thackeray; 8 Brandon Douglas; 9 Vila Halafihi; 17 Liam Kirk; 24 Oliver Roberts; 27 Jesse Sene-Lefao; 13 Evan Hodgson. Subs (all used): 10 Tyler Dickinson; 12 Joel Farrell; 16 Blake Broadbent; 19 Jack Hansen.
Tries: Welham (21, 40), Liu (25), Jones-Bishop (28, 32), Aston (37), Dawson-Jones (46), Halafihi (66);
Goals: Aston 7/8.
Rugby Leaguer & League Express Men of the Match:
Cougars: Mark Ioane; *Eagles:* Kris Welham.
Penalty count: 3-3; **Half-time:** 6-34;
Referee: James Vella; **Attendance:** 1,347.

WIDNES VIKINGS 0 FEATHERSTONE ROVERS 30

VIKINGS: 3 Matty Fleming; 2 Ryan Ince; 29 Zach Eckersley; 20 Joe Edge; 5 Kieran Dixon; 18 Joe Lyons; 1 Jack Owens; 8 Owen Farnworth; 9 Matty Fozard; 16 Callum Field; 30 Jacob Jones; 11 Sam Wilde; 14 Jordan Johnstone. Subs (all used): 19 Olly Davies; 21 Lewis Hatton; 26 Max Roberts; 27 Anthony Walker. 18th man (used): 23 Will Tilleke.
ROVERS: 23 Caleb Aekins; 2 Luke Briscoe; 18 Josh Hardcastle; 4 Craig Hall; 5 Gareth Gale; 25 Thomas Lacans; 7 Riley Dean; 17 Gadwin Springer; 14 Matty Wildie; 10 James Lockwood; 11 Brad Day; 13 Jack Bussey; 32 Daniel Smith. Subs (all used): 9 Connor Jones; 15 John Davies; 27 McKenzie Yei; 31 Arama Hau.
Tries: Gale (11, 25, 36), Bussey (16), Hall (53), Jones (76);
Goals: Hall 3/6.
Sin bin: Bussey (60) - high tackle on Ince.
Rugby Leaguer & League Express Men of the Match:
Vikings: Matty Fozard; *Rovers:* Gareth Gale.
Penalty count: 7-7; **Half-time:** 0-22;
Referee: Liam Rush; **Attendance:** 2,832.

YORK KNIGHTS 26 NEWCASTLE THUNDER 22

KNIGHTS: 1 Matty Marsh; 5 AJ Towse; 3 James Glover; 33 Oliver Pratt; 2 Joe Brown; 6 Ata Hingano; 19 Josh Daley; 8 Jon Luke Kirby; 9 Will Jubb; 21 Ukuma Ta'ai; 11 Chris Clarkson; 32 Oli Field; 13 Jordan Thompson. Subs (all used): 12 Danny Kirmond; 14 James Cunningham; 17 Ronan Michael; 20 Jack Teanby.
Tries: Towse (1), Brown (27), Field (34, 50), Glover (64), Pratt (75); **Goals:** Glover 1/6.
THUNDER: 6 Alex Donaghy; 20 Gideon Boafo; 4 Oscar Thomas; 3 Marcus Walker; 5 Alex Clegg; 7 Nikau Williams; 27 Jack Miller; 15 Ted Chapelhow; 9 Curtis Davies; 23 Connor Moore; 28 Dane Windrow; 29 Nick Staveley; 13 Connor Bailey. Subs (all used): 10 Mitch Clark; 14 Denive Balmforth; 17 Rob Tuliatu; 24 Daniel Okoro.
Tries: T Chapelhow (3), Boafo (14), Clark (22), Donaghy (39); **Goals:** Williams 3/4.

Championship 2023 - Round by Round

Rugby Leaguer & League Express Men of the Match: *Knights:* Oli Field; *Thunder:* Alex Donaghy.
Penalty count: 4-3; **Half-time:** 14-22;
Referee: Scott Mikalauskas; **Attendance:** 2,276.

ROUND 12 - SUMMER BASH

Saturday 27th May 2023

SWINTON LIONS 6 WIDNES VIKINGS 38

LIONS: 1 Dan Abram; 2 Mike Butt; 36 Ben Davies; 3 Jake Spedding; 4 Jayden Hatton; 14 Josh Eaves; 7 Jordy Gibson; 15 Jordan Case; 33 Amir Bourouh; 32 Sam Royle; 22 Andy Badrock; 11 Rhodri Lloyd; 6 Nick Gregson. Subs (all used): 8 Gavin Bennion; 13 Louis Brogan; 26 Joey Romeo; - Dan Norman.
Try: Royle (51); **Goals:** Abram 1/1.
Sin bin: Lloyd (68) - dissent;
Butt (71) - repeated team offences.
VIKINGS: 1 Jack Owens; 2 Ryan Ince; 3 Matty Fleming; 20 Joe Edge; 5 Kieran Dixon; 18 Joe Lyons; 7 Tom Gilmore; 8 Owen Farnworth; 9 Matty Fozard; 30 Jacob Jones; 31 Andrew Dixon; 17 Shane Grady; 14 Jordan Johnstone. Subs (all used): 11 Sam Wilde; 12 Adam Lawton; 19 Olly Davies; 22 Aaron Brown.
Tries: Ince (27, 65), Lyons (36), K Dixon (39, 75), Owens (58, 80); **Goals:** Edge 1/4, Gilmore 4/4.
Rugby Leaguer & League Express Men of the Match: *Lions:* Ben Davies; *Vikings:* Jack Owens.
Penalty count: 2-11; **Half-time:** 0-14;
Referee: Cameron Worsley.

BARROW RAIDERS 32 WHITEHAVEN 16

RAIDERS: 1 Luke Cresswell; 5 Ryan Shaw; 25 Keanan Brand; 2 Shane Toal; 24 Luke Broadbent; 6 Jarrod Sammut; 7 Ryan Johnston; 15 Ellis Gillam; 22 Josh Wood; 10 Anton Iaria; 11 Danny Langtree; 12 Jarrad Stack; 13 Jack Wells. Subs (all used): 9 Nathan Mossop; 4 Greg Worthington; 17 Charlie Emslie; 16 Sam Brooks.
Tries: Toal (16), Cresswell (23), Sammut (36), Langtree (65), Iaria (75); **Goals:** Shaw 6/6.
WHITEHAVEN: 23 Josh Rourke; 2 Dave Eccleston; 3 Chris Taylor; 11 Connor Holliday; 4 Curtis Teare; 14 Jamie Doran; 7 Alex Bishop; 22 Lucas Castle; 15 James Newton; 10 Tom Walker; 12 Lachlan Lanskey; 19 Ryan King; 17 Guy Graham. Subs (all used): 13 Dion Aiye; 16 Lasarusa Tabu; 24 Daniel Spencer-Tonks; 28 Ross Ainley.
Tries: Teare (12, 51), Rourke (78); **Goals:** Rourke 2/5.
Rugby Leaguer & League Express Men of the Match: *Raiders:* Luke Cresswell; *Whitehaven:* Dion Aiye.
Penalty count: 7-8; **Half-time:** 18-6;
Referee: Michael Smaill.

LONDON BRONCOS 14 TOULOUSE OLYMPIQUE 10

BRONCOS: 1 Alex Walker; 2 Paul Ulberg; 3 Jarred Bassett; 19 Dean Whare; 5 Iliess Macani; 6 Oliver Leyland; 17 Henry Raiwalui; 8 Wellington Albert; 9 Sam Davis; 15 Lewis Bienek; 11 Will Lovell; 16 Ethan Natoli; 13 Dean Parata. Subs: 14 Bill Leyland; 10 Jordan Williams; 27 Ramon Silva; 7 Rian Horsman (not used).
Tries: Whare (23), Lovell (32); **Goals:** O Leyland 3/4.
Sin bin: B Leyland (42) - interference;
Walker (71) - professional foul.
OLYMPIQUE: 5 Paul Marcon; 25 Matthieu Laguerre; 4 Mathieu Jussaume; 3 Reubenn Rennie; 31 Matteo Stefani; 6 Josh Ralph; 7 Jake Shorrocks; 27 Dimitri Biscarro; 9 Calum Gahan; 20 Greg Richards; 11 Maxime Stefani; 10 Harrison Hansen; 13 Anthony Marion. Subs: 26 Bastien Scimone; 22 Loan Castano; 30 Tiaki Chan; 16 Joe Bretherton (not used).
Tries: Marion (69, 73); **Goals:** Shorrocks 1/2.
Sin bin: Castano (10) - professional foul.
Rugby Leaguer & League Express Men of the Match: *Broncos:* Will Lovell; *Olympique:* Anthony Marion.
Penalty count: 3-7; **Half-time:** 12-0; **Referee:** Liam Rush.

FEATHERSTONE ROVERS 46 YORK KNIGHTS 16

ROVERS: 23 Caleb Aekins; 2 Luke Briscoe; 18 Josh Hardcastle; 3 Chris Hankinson; 5 Gareth Gale; 6 Johnathon Ford; 25 Thomas Lacans; 17 Gadwin Springer; 14 Matty Wildie; 8 Craig Kopczak; 11 Brad Day; 13 Jack Bussey; 32 Daniel Smith. Subs (all used): 9 Connor Jones; 15 John Davies; 16 Junior Moors; 27 McKenzie Yei.
Tries: Gale (12, 47, 60, 79), Springer (19), Yei (36), Jones (63), Ford (67), Lacans (74);
Goals: Smith 1/2, Bussey 4/7.
KNIGHTS: 2 Joe Brown; 23 Olly Butterworth; 4 Jesse Dee; 3 James Glover; 5 AJ Towse; 14 James Cunningham; 19 Josh Daley; 8 Jon Luke Kirby; 9 Will Jubb; 10 Conor Fitzsimmons; 11 Chris Clarkson; 32 Oli Field; 17 Ronan Michael. Subs (all used): 15 Myles Harrison; 20 Jack Teanby; 21 Ukuma Ta'ai; 24 Ben Barnard.
Tries: Dee (26), Brown (70), Daley (77); **Goals:** Glover 2/3.
Sin bin: Fitzsimmons (18) - interference.
Rugby Leaguer & League Express Men of the Match: *Rovers:* Gareth Gale; *Knights:* Josh Daley.
Penalty count: 4-2; **Half-time:** 16-4;
Referee: Scott Mikalauskas.

Attendance: 3,793 *(at LNER Community Stadium, York).*

Sunday 28th May 2023

NEWCASTLE THUNDER 32 SHEFFIELD EAGLES 38

THUNDER: 6 Alex Donaghy; 5 Alex Clegg; 29 Nick Staveley; 4 Oscar Thomas; 20 Gideon Boafo; 27 Jack Miller; 7 Nikau Williams; 15 Ted Chapelhow; 9 Curtis Davies; 17 Rob Tuliatu; 12 Brad Gallagher; 28 Dane Windrow; 13 Connor Bailey. Subs (all used): 8 Jay Chapelhow; 10 Mitch Clark; 14 Denive Balmforth; 24 Daniel Okoro.
Tries: Boafo (15), Bailey (46), Windrow (58), Balmforth (62, 77), Clegg (78);
Goals: Williams 4/5, Miller 0/1.
Sin bin: J Chapelhow (40) - fighting.
EAGLES: 29 Quentin Laulu-Togaga'e; 2 Ben Jones-Bishop; 3 Kris Welham; 23 Bayley Liu; 28 Matty Dawson-Jones; 19 Jack Hansen; 7 Anthony Thackeray; 8 Brandon Douglas; 9 Vila Halafihi; 10 Tyler Dickinson; 11 Connor Bower; 12 Joel Farrell; 13 Evan Hodgson. Subs (all used): 6 Izaac Farrell; 15 Mikey Wood; 16 Blake Broadbent; 17 Liam Kirk.
Tries: Liu (7, 50), Jones-Bishop (10, 54), Welham (26), Douglas (34); **Goals:** Hansen 6/6, I Farrell 1/1.
Sin bin: I Farrell (40) - fighting, (74) - fighting.
Rugby Leaguer & League Express Men of the Match: *Thunder:* Denive Balmforth; *Eagles:* Kris Welham.
Penalty count: 7-3; **Half-time:** 6-24;
Referee: Nick Bennett.

BATLEY BULLDOGS 20 HALIFAX PANTHERS 12

BULLDOGS: 21 Aidan McGowan; 22 Dale Morton; 4 Josh Hodson; 3 Kieran Buchanan; 15 Elliot Kear; 6 Ben White; 7 Josh Woods; 8 Adam Gledhill; 17 Luke Blake; 19 Tom Lillycrop; 11 Dane Manning; 12 Lucas Walshaw; 30 Martyn Reilly. Subs (all used): 14 James Meadows; 26 Nyle Flynn; 16 Michael Ward; 18 George Senior.
Tries: Kear (32), Manning (45), Woods (54), Meadows (78);
Goals: Meadows 2/4.
PANTHERS: 1 James Woodburn-Hall; 2 Lachlan Walmsley; 3 Zack McComb; 4 Ben Tibbs; 22 Jake Maizen; 6 Louis Jouffret; 20 Tom Inman; 16 Will Calcott; 9 Brandon Moore; 10 Dan Murray; 11 Ben Kavanagh; 12 Matty Gee; 13 Jacob Fairbank. Subs (all used): 14 Kyle Wood; 8 Adam Tangata; 31 Kevin Larroyer; 19 Ryan Lannon.
Tries: Moore (2), Woodburn-Hall (22); **Goals:** Jouffret 2/2.
Rugby Leaguer & League Express Men of the Match: *Bulldogs:* Kieran Buchanan; *Panthers:* Kyle Wood.
Penalty count: 3-5; **Half-time:** 4-12; **Referee:** James Vella.

BRADFORD BULLS 42 KEIGHLEY COUGARS 18

BULLS: 31 Jack Walker; 2 Ben Blackmore; 12 Chester Butler; 4 Kieran Gill; 5 David Foggin-Johnston; 1 Tom Holmes; 6 Dec Patton; 8 Jordan Baldwinson; 7 Jordan Lilley; 21 Fenton Rogers; 11 Brad England; 13 Bodene Thompson; 17 Josh Johnson. Subs (all used): 14 Ebon Scurr; 18 Keven Appo; 20 Billy Jowitt; 40 Nathan Mason.
Tries: Blackmore (20, 68), Gill (24, 53), Walker (38, 46), Appo (59), Foggin-Johnston (64); **Goals:** Patton 5/8.
Sin bin: Appo (77) - high tackle.
COUGARS: 2 Alix Stephenson; 3 Charlie Graham; 25 Ben Crooks; 23 Robbie Storey; 5 Mo Agoro; 14 Harvey Spence; 21 Lloyd Roby; 24 Mark Ioane; 13 Kyle Kesik; 15 Brenden Santi; 19 Ellis Robson; 28 Keenen Tomlinson; 20 Brad Walker. Subs (all used): 8 Dan Parker; 16 Josh Lynam; 26 Thomas Doyle; 27 Sadiq Adebiyi.
Tries: Crooks (2, 32), Stephenson (9); **Goals:** Spence 3/3.
Rugby Leaguer & League Express Men of the Match: *Bulls:* Jack Walker; *Cougars:* Ben Crooks.
Penalty count: 10-6; **Half-time:** 14-18;
Referee: Tom Grant.

Attendance: 2,948 *(at LNER Community Stadium, York).*

ROUND 13

Friday 2nd June 2023

NEWCASTLE THUNDER 12 BRADFORD BULLS 28

THUNDER: 6 Alex Donaghy; 5 Alex Clegg; 29 Nick Staveley; 11 Alex Foster; 20 Gideon Boafo; 7 Nikau Williams; 27 Jack Miller; 17 Rob Tuliatu; 9 Curtis Davies; 15 Ted Chapelhow; 12 Brad Gallagher; 28 Dane Windrow; 13 Connor Bailey. Subs (all used): 8 Jay Chapelhow; 10 Mitch Clark; 14 Denive Balmforth; 24 Daniel Okoro.
Tries: Staveley (42), Balmforth (53); **Goals:** Williams 2/2.
Sin bin: Clark (80) - dissent.
BULLS: 31 Jack Walker; 2 Ben Blackmore; 3 Joe Arundel; 4 Kieran Gill; 5 David Foggin-Johnston; 1 Tom Holmes; 6 Dec Patton; 8 Jordan Baldwinson; 7 Jordan Lilley; 21 Fenton Rogers; 13 Bodene Thompson; 11 Brad England; 12 Chester Butler. Subs (all used): 14 Ebon Scurr; 17 Josh Johnson; 18 Keven Appo; 20 Billy Jowitt.
Tries: Foggin-Johnston (6), Holmes (17), Baldwinson (20), Appo (47), Gill (72); **Goals:** Patton 4/5.
Rugby Leaguer & League Express Men of the Match: *Thunder:* Alex Donaghy; *Bulls:* Fenton Rogers.
Penalty count: 4-9; **Half-time:** 0-16;
Referee: Michael Smaill; **Attendance:** 2,465.

Saturday 3rd June 2023

TOULOUSE OLYMPIQUE 28 HALIFAX PANTHERS 22

OLYMPIQUE: 23 Robin Brochon; 5 Paul Marcon; 4 Mathieu Jussaume; 3 Reubenn Rennie; 18 Guy Armitage; 6 Josh Ralph; 7 Jake Shorrocks; 27 Dimitri Biscarro; 9 Calum Gahan; 10 Harrison Hansen; 24 Pierre-Jean Lima; 11 Maxime Stefani; 13 Anthony Marion. Subs (all used): 20 Greg Richards; 26 Ramon Silva; 30 Tiaki Chan; 16 Joe Bretherton.
Tries: Marion (5), Armitage (8, 67), Lima (51), Maxime Stefani (54); **Goals:** Shorrocks 4/6.
PANTHERS: 1 James Woodburn-Hall; 3 Zack McComb; 22 Jake Maizen; 4 Ben Tibbs; 2 Lachlan Walmsley; 6 Louis Jouffret; 14 Kyle Wood; 16 Will Calcott; 9 Brandon Moore; 10 Dan Murray; 28 Alex Sutcliffe; 12 Matty Gee; 8 Adam Tangata. Subs: 18 Brandon Pickersgill (not used); 19 Ryan Lannon; 20 Tom Inman; 31 Kevin Larroyer.
Tries: McComb (12), Wood (26), Moore (33), Walmsley (59);
Goals: Jouffret 3/4.
Rugby Leaguer & League Express Men of the Match: *Olympique:* Guy Armitage; *Panthers:* Louis Jouffret.
Penalty count: 6-4; **Half-time:** 10-18;
Referee: James Vella; **Attendance:** 4,806.

Sunday 4th June 2023

BATLEY BULLDOGS 14 YORK KNIGHTS 8

BULLDOGS: 21 Aidan McGowan; 22 Dale Morton; 4 Josh Hodson; 3 Kieran Buchanan; 15 Elliot Kear; 6 Ben White; 7 Josh Woods; 8 Adam Gledhill; 24 Ben Kaye; 26 Nyle Flynn; 11 Dane Manning; 12 Lucas Walshaw; 30 Martyn Reilly. Subs (all used): 18 George Senior; 16 Michael Ward; 14 James Meadows; 17 Luke Blake.
Tries: Kear (38), Buchanan (49), Morton (79);
Goals: Meadows 1/4.
KNIGHTS: 2 Joe Brown; 15 Myles Harrison; 33 Oliver Pratt; 3 James Glover; 5 AJ Towse; 4 Jesse Dee; 19 Josh Daley; 8 Jon Luke Kirby; 9 Will Jubb; 10 Conor Fitzsimmons; 11 Chris Clarkson; 32 Oli Field; 14 James Cunningham. Subs: 20 Jack Teanby; 17 Ronan Michael; 21 Ukuma Ta'ai; 24 Ben Barnard (not used).
Tries: Glover (20), Dee (60); **Goals:** Glover 0/1, Dee 0/1.
Rugby Leaguer & League Express Men of the Match: *Bulldogs:* Aidan McGowan; *Knights:* James Cunningham.
Penalty count: 4-3; **Half-time:** 4-4;
Referee: Matt Rossleigh; **Attendance:** 2,003.

FEATHERSTONE ROVERS 64 BARROW RAIDERS 6

ROVERS: 23 Caleb Aekins; 2 Luke Briscoe; 4 Craig Hall; 3 Chris Hankinson; 5 Gareth Gale; 6 Johnathon Ford; 25 Thomas Lacans; 16 Junior Moors; 14 Matty Wildie; 10 James Lockwood; 31 Arama Hau; 13 Jack Bussey; 24 Mathieu Cozza. Subs (all used): 9 Connor Jones; 15 John Davies; 27 McKenzie Yei; 32 Daniel Smith.
Tries: Hall (12), Briscoe (15), Aekins (31), Gale (35), Yei (38), Hankinson (54), Hau (57), Bussey (61), Jones (65, 80), Lacans (77); **Goals:** Hall 10/11.
RAIDERS: 1 Luke Cresswell; 27 Andrew Bulman; 3 Rio Osayomwanbo-Corkill; 2 Shane Toal; 24 Luke Broadbent; 28 Ellis Archer; 7 Ryan Johnston; 15 Ellis Gillam; 22 Josh Wood; 10 Anton Iaria; 11 Danny Langtree; 12 Jarrad Stack; 13 Jack Wells. Subs (all used): 4 Greg Worthington; 16 Sam Brooks; 17 Charlie Emslie; 23 Connor Saunders.
Try: Broadbent (51); **Goals:** Archer 1/1.
Rugby Leaguer & League Express Men of the Match: *Rovers:* Craig Hall; *Raiders:* Ellis Archer.
Penalty count: 5-4; **Half-time:** 30-0;
Referee: Nick Bennett; **Attendance:** 2,756.

KEIGHLEY COUGARS 28 SWINTON LIONS 32

COUGARS: 2 Alix Stephenson; 17 Keenan Dyer-Dixon; 28 Keenen Tomlinson; 23 Robbie Storey; 5 Mo Agoro; 14 Harvey Spence; 21 Lloyd Roby; 24 Mark Ioane; 26 Thomas Doyle; 8 Dan Parker; 19 Ellis Robson; 27 Sadiq Adebiyi; 20 Brad Walker. Subs (all used): 10 Toby Everett; 9 Billy Gaylor; 12 Aaron Levy; 16 Josh Lynam.
Tries: Ioane (12), Spence (39), Doyle (60), Lynam (69), Agoro (77); **Goals:** Spence 4/5.

Championship 2023 - Round by Round

LIONS: 22 Andy Badrock; 26 Joey Romeo; 32 Wesley Bruines; 3 Jake Spedding; 4 Jayden Hatton; 1 Dan Abram; 7 Jordy Gibson; 8 Gavin Bennion; 14 Josh Eaves; 13 Louis Brogan; 11 Rhodri Lloyd; 10 Kenny Baker; 6 Nick Gregson. Subs (all used): 15 Jordan Case; 30 George Roby; 34 Dan Norman; 36 Lewis Baxter.
Tries: Romeo (2, 24, 33, 42), Spedding (21);
Goals: Abram 6/7.
Rugby Leaguer & League Express Men of the Match: *Cougars:* Sadiq Adebiyi; *Lions:* Jake Spedding.
Penalty count: 9-6; **Half-time:** 12-24;
Referee: Brad Milligan; **Attendance:** 1,138.

SHEFFIELD EAGLES 26 WHITEHAVEN 40

EAGLES: 2 Ben Jones-Bishop; 22 Matty Chrimes; 3 Kris Welham; 23 Bayley Liu; 28 Matty Dawson-Jones; 32 Cory Aston; 19 Jack Hansen; 8 Brandon Douglas; 9 Vila Halafihi; 10 Tyler Dickinson; 11 Connor Bower; 27 Jesse Sene-Lefao; 13 Evan Hodgson. Subs (all used): 6 Izaac Farrell; 15 Mikey Wood; 16 Blake Broadbent; 20 Lewis Peachey.
Tries: Liu (4, 60), Jones-Bishop (19, 21), I Farrell (69);
Goals: Aston 3/5.
Sin bin: Wood (51) - late challenge.
WHITEHAVEN: 23 Josh Rourke; 2 Dave Eccleston; 3 Chris Taylor; 4 Curtis Teare; 27 Oscar Doran; 19 Ryan King; 14 Jamie Doran; 22 Lucas Castle; 15 James Newton; 10 Tom Walker; 11 Connor Holliday; 12 Lachlan Lanskey; 16 Lasarusa Tabu. Subs (all used): 13 Dion Aiye; 18 Perry Singleton; 24 Daniel Spencer-Tonks; 28 Ross Ainley.
Tries: Teare (11), Taylor (15), Spencer-Tonks (34), Rourke (37, 54), King (75); **Goals:** Rourke 8/8.
Rugby Leaguer & League Express Men of the Match: *Eagles:* Bayley Liu; *Whitehaven:* Josh Rourke.
Penalty count: 4-8; **Half-time:** 14-24;
Referee: Kevin Moore; **Attendance:** 1,179.

WIDNES VIKINGS 18 LONDON BRONCOS 26

VIKINGS: 1 Jack Owens; 2 Ryan Ince; 3 Matty Fleming; 20 Joe Edge; 5 Kieran Dixon; 18 Joe Lyons; 7 Tom Gilmore; 8 Owen Farnworth; 9 Matty Fozard; 30 Jacob Jones; 11 Sam Wilde; 19 Olly Davies; 14 Jordan Johnstone. Subs (all used): 29 Zach Eckersley; 21 Lewis Hatton; 12 Adam Lawton; 22 Aaron Brown.
Tries: Wilde (7, 42), K Dixon (58); **Goals:** Gilmore 3/4.
BRONCOS: 1 Alex Walker; 2 Paul Ulberg; 3 Jarred Bassett; 19 Dean Whare; 5 Iliess Macani; 6 Oliver Leyland; 17 Henry Raiwalui; 15 Lewis Bienek; 9 Sam Davis; 8 Wellington Albert; 11 Will Lovell; 16 Ethan Natoli; 13 Dean Parata. Subs (all used): 7 Rian Horsman; 33 Rob Butler; 10 Jordan Williams; 18 Emmanuel Waine.
Tries: Macani (22, 67), Raiwalui (33), Ulberg (52), Whare (76); **Goals:** O Leyland 3/5.
Sin bin: Horsman (38) - dangerous challenge on Lawton.
Rugby Leaguer & League Express Men of the Match: *Vikings:* Sam Wilde; *Broncos:* Dean Parata.
Penalty count: 6-4; **Half-time:** 8-12;
Referee: Andy Sweet; **Attendance:** 2,547.

ROUND 14

Friday 9th June 2023

SHEFFIELD EAGLES 40 YORK KNIGHTS 10

EAGLES: 29 Quentin Laulu-Togaga'e; 2 Ben Jones-Bishop; 3 Kris Welham; 4 Ross Oakes; 28 Matty Dawson-Jones; 32 Cory Aston; 7 Anthony Thackeray; 17 Liam Kirk; 9 Vila Halafihi; 10 Tyler Dickinson; 23 Bayley Liu; 27 Jesse Sene-Lefao; 13 Evan Hodgson. Subs (all used): 8 Brandon Douglas; 15 Mikey Wood; 16 Blake Broadbent; 19 Jack Hansen.
Tries: Jones-Bishop (7), Dawson-Jones (22), Welham (34, 56, 75), Thackeray (36), Laulu-Togaga'e (72);
Goals: Aston 6/7.
KNIGHTS: 2 Joe Brown; 23 Olly Butterworth; 4 Jesse Dee; 3 James Glover; 5 AJ Towse; 14 James Cunningham; 19 Josh Daley; 8 Jon Luke Kirby; 9 Will Jubb; 10 Conor Fitzsimmons; 11 Chris Clarkson; 32 Oli Field; 17 Ronan Michael. Subs (all used): 15 Myles Harrison; 20 Jack Teanby; 21 Ukuma Ta'ai; 24 Ben Barnard.
Tries: Clarkson (30), Fitzsimmons (64); **Goals:** Brown 1/2.
Rugby Leaguer & League Express Men of the Match: *Eagles:* Kris Welham; *Knights:* Josh Daley.
Penalty count: 6-4; **Half-time:** 22-6;
Referee: Michael Smaill; **Attendance:** 1,051.

Saturday 10th June 2023

FEATHERSTONE ROVERS 18 TOULOUSE OLYMPIQUE 36

ROVERS: 23 Caleb Aekins; 2 Luke Briscoe; 4 Craig Hall; 3 Chris Hankinson; 5 Gareth Gale; 6 Johnathon Ford; 25 Thomas Lacans; 17 Gadwin Springer; 14 Matty Wildie; 10 James Lockwood; 11 Brad Day; 13 Jack Bussey; 24 Mathieu Cozza. Subs (all used): 9 Connor Jones; 15 John Davies; 27 McKenzie Yei; 32 Daniel Smith.
Tries: Hall (26), Briscoe (40), Davies (48), Hankinson (55);
Goals: Hall 1/4.
OLYMPIQUE: 23 Robin Brochon; 18 Guy Armitage; 3 Reubenn Rennie; 4 Mathieu Jussaume; 5 Paul Marcon; 6 Josh Ralph; 7 Jake Shorrocks; 27 Dimitri Biscarro; 9 Calum Gahan; 10 Harrison Hansen; 11 Maxime Stefani; 24 Pierre-Jean Lima; 13 Anthony Marion. Subs (all used): 20 Greg Richards; 30 Tiaki Chan; 8 Lambert Belmas; 12 Dominique Peyroux.
Tries: Armitage (10, 74), Lima (28), Peyroux (44, 67), Marcon (62); **Goals:** Shorrocks 6/6.
Sin bin: Chan (36) - headbutt.
Rugby Leaguer & League Express Men of the Match: *Rovers:* John Davies; *Olympique:* Dominique Peyroux.
Penalty count: 11-1; **Half-time:** 8-12;
Referee: Tom Grant; **Attendance:** 3,489.

Sunday 11th June 2023

BARROW RAIDERS 18 KEIGHLEY COUGARS 16

RAIDERS: 1 Luke Cresswell; 5 Ryan Shaw; 25 Keanan Brand; 2 Shane Toal; 24 Luke Broadbent; 6 Jarrod Sammut; 7 Ryan Johnston; 15 Ellis Gillam; 22 Josh Wood; 20 Ben Evans; 11 Danny Langtree; 12 Jarrad Stack; 10 Anton Iaria. Subs (all used): 9 Nathan Mossop; 4 Greg Worthington; 17 Charlie Emslie; 8 Greg Burke.
Tries: Iaria (9), Broadbent (53), Sammut (70);
Goals: Shaw 3/3.
COUGARS: 22 Dane Chisholm; 2 Alix Stephenson; 3 Charlie Graham; 23 Robbie Storey; 5 Mo Agoro; 21 Lloyd Roby; 14 Harvey Spence; 10 Toby Everett; 26 Thomas Doyle; 24 Mark Ioane; 19 Ellis Robson; 27 Sadiq Adebiyi; 20 Brad Walker. Subs (all used): 9 Billy Gaylor; 16 Josh Lynam; 8 Dan Parker; 38 Joe Hird.
Tries: Lynam (30), Stephenson (32, 56);
Goals: Chisholm 2/3.
Rugby Leaguer & League Express Men of the Match: *Raiders:* Luke Broadbent; *Cougars:* Dane Chisholm.
Penalty count: 7-2; **Half-time:** 6-10;
Referee: Nick Bennett; **Attendance:** 2,250.

BRADFORD BULLS 32 LONDON BRONCOS 16

BULLS: 1 Tom Holmes; 2 Ben Blackmore; 3 Joe Arundel; 4 Kieran Gill; 5 David Foggin-Johnston; 20 Billy Jowitt; 6 Dec Patton; 8 Jordan Baldwinson; 7 Jordan Lilley; 21 Fenton Rogers; 13 Bodene Thompson; 12 Chester Butler; 18 Keven Appo. Subs (all used): 11 Brad England; 14 Ebon Scurr; 24 Masi Matongo; 23 James Segeyaro.
Tries: Blackmore (4), Holmes (24, 33), Gill (54, 68);
Goals: Patton 6/6.
BRONCOS: 3 Jarred Bassett; 2 Paul Ulberg; 16 Ethan Natoli; 19 Dean Whare; 5 Iliess Macani; 6 Oliver Leyland; 17 Henry Raiwalui; 8 Wellington Albert; 9 Sam Davis; 15 Lewis Bienek; 11 Will Lovell; 12 Marcus Stock; 13 Dean Parata. Subs (all used): 10 Jordan Williams; 23 Daniel Hoyes; 26 Euan Parke; 33 Rob Butler.
Tries: Macani (57, 78), Whare (76); **Goals:** O Leyland 2/3.
Rugby Leaguer & League Express Men of the Match: *Bulls:* Tom Holmes; *Broncos:* Jarred Bassett.
Penalty count: 5-8; **Half-time:** 18-0;
Referee: James Vella; **Attendance:** 3,482.

NEWCASTLE THUNDER 12 BATLEY BULLDOGS 26

THUNDER: 6 Alex Donaghy; 5 Alex Clegg; 4 Harvey Barron; 11 Alex Foster; 20 Gideon Boafo; 13 Connor Bailey; 7 Nikau Williams; 15 Ted Chapelhow; 9 Curtis Davies; 17 Rob Tuliatu; 12 Brad Gallagher; 29 Nick Staveley; 23 Connor Moore. Subs (all used): 8 Jay Chapelhow; 14 Denive Balmforth; 24 Daniel Okoro; 40 Evan Simons.
Tries: J Chapelhow (33), Donaghy (51); **Goals:** Williams 2/2.
Sin bin: Williams (77) - dissent.
BULLDOGS: 21 Aidan McGowan; 22 Dale Morton; 4 Josh Hodson; 18 George Senior; 15 Elliot Kear; 14 James Meadows; 7 Josh Woods; 30 Martyn Reilly; 24 Ben Kaye; 13 James Brown; 11 Dane Manning; 3 Kieran Buchanan; 6 Ben White. Subs (all used): 8 Adam Gledhill; 16 Michael Ward; 17 Luke Blake; 26 Nyle Flynn.
Tries: Morton (12, 71), McGowan (25), Meadows (57), Hodson (67); **Goals:** Meadows 3/6.
Rugby Leaguer & League Express Men of the Match: *Thunder:* Daniel Okoro; *Bulldogs:* James Meadows.
Penalty count: 5-10; **Half-time:** 6-10;
Referee: Cameron Worsley; **Attendance:** 694.

SWINTON LIONS 8 HALIFAX PANTHERS 46

LIONS: 22 Andy Badrock; 26 Joey Romeo; 3 Jake Spedding; 32 Wesley Bruines; 4 Jayden Hatton; 1 Dan Abram; 7 Jordy Gibson; 8 Gavin Bennion; 14 Josh Eaves; 13 Louis Brogan; 11 Rhodri Lloyd; 10 Kenny Baker; 6 Nick Gregson. Subs (all used): 12 Mitch Cox; 15 Jordan Case; 30 George Roby; 34 Lewis Baxter.
Try: Eaves (20); **Goals:** Abram 2/2.
PANTHERS: 1 James Woodburn-Hall; 5 James Saltonstall; 3 Zack McComb; 4 Ben Tibbs; 2 Lachlan Walmsley; 6 Louis Jouffret; 14 Kyle Wood; 16 Will Calcott; 9 Brandon Moore; 10 Dan Murray; 11 Ben Kavanagh; 12 Matty Gee; 31 Kevin Larroyer. Subs (all used): 8 Adam Tangata; 19 Ryan Lannon; 29 Dan Fleming; 34 Adam O'Brien.
Tries: Tibbs (5), Walmsley (25, 46, 58, 63), Tangata (41), Kavanagh (60), Woodburn-Hall (66), Moore (71);
Goals: Jouffret 5/9.
Sin bin: McComb (50) - dangerous contact; Fleming (79) - high tackle on Hatton.
Rugby Leaguer & League Express Men of the Match: *Lions:* Nick Gregson; *Panthers:* Kyle Wood.
Penalty count: 10-6; **Half-time:** 8-8;
Referee: Matt Rossleigh; **Attendance:** 1,109.

WHITEHAVEN 36 WIDNES VIKINGS 12

WHITEHAVEN: 23 Josh Rourke; 2 Dave Eccleston; 3 Chris Taylor; 4 Curtis Teare; 27 Oscar Doran; 19 Ryan King; 14 Jamie Doran; 22 Lucas Castle; 15 James Newton; 10 Tom Walker; 11 Connor Holliday; 12 Lachlan Lanskey; 16 Lasarusa Tabu. Subs (all used): 24 Daniel Spencer-Tonks; 13 Dion Aiye; 18 Perry Singleton; 28 Ross Ainley.
Tries: Rourke (28), Newton (36), Taylor (40, 75), Tabu (60), King (64); **Goals:** Rourke 6/7.
VIKINGS: 5 Kieran Dixon; 2 Ryan Ince; 29 Zach Eckersley; 26 Max Roberts; 20 Joe Edge; 18 Joe Lyons; 7 Tom Gilmore; 8 Owen Farnworth; 9 Matty Fozard; 12 Adam Lawton; 17 Shane Grady; 11 Sam Wilde; 14 Jordan Johnstone. Subs (all used): 22 Aaron Brown; 19 Olly Davies; 21 Lewis Hatton; 27 Anthony Walker.
Tries: Roberts (4), Wilde (72); **Goals:** Gilmore 2/2.
Sin bin: Fozard (27) - professional foul; K Dixon (60) - late challenge.
Rugby Leaguer & League Express Men of the Match: *Whitehaven:* Ryan King; *Vikings:* Matty Fozard.
Penalty count: 5-4; **Half-time:** 18-6;
Referee: Liam Rush; **Attendance:** 960.

ROUND 15

Saturday 17th June 2023

TOULOUSE OLYMPIQUE 48 SHEFFIELD EAGLES 10

OLYMPIQUE: 23 Robin Brochon; 5 Paul Marcon; 4 Mathieu Jussaume; 18 Guy Armitage; 25 Matthieu Laguerre; 6 Josh Ralph; 7 Jake Shorrocks; 8 Lambert Belmas; 9 Calum Gahan; 10 Harrison Hansen; 12 Dominique Peyroux; 11 Maxime Stefani; 13 Anthony Marion. Subs (all used): 20 Greg Richards; 30 Tiaki Chan; 15 Sitaleki Akauola; 24 Pierre-Jean Lima.
Tries: Belmas (15), Maxime Stefani (18, 62), Armitage (24, 45), Richards (34, 59), Jussaume (47), Ralph (78); **Goals:** Shorrocks 6/9.
Dismissal: Akauola (73) - dangerous challenge on Kirk.
EAGLES: 29 Quentin Laulu-Togaga'e; 2 Ben Jones-Bishop; 3 Kris Welham; 23 Bayley Liu; 28 Matty Dawson-Jones; 32 Cory Aston; 6 Izaac Farrell; 17 Liam Kirk; 9 Vila Halafihi; 10 Tyler Dickinson; 15 Mikey Wood; 27 Jesse Sene-Lefao; 13 Evan Hodgson. Subs (all used): 19 Jack Hansen; 16 Blake Broadbent; 12 Joel Farrell; 8 Brandon Douglas.
Tries: Sene-Lefao (3), Liu (66); **Goals:** Aston 1/2.
Rugby Leaguer & League Express Men of the Match: *Olympique:* Maxime Stefani; *Eagles:* Bayley Liu.
Penalty count: 6-2; **Half-time:** 20-6;
Referee: Aaron Moore; **Attendance:** 3,344.

Sunday 18th June 2023

BARROW RAIDERS 26 WIDNES VIKINGS 18

RAIDERS: 24 Luke Broadbent; 5 Ryan Shaw; 25 Keanan Brand; 2 Shane Toal; 27 Andrew Bulman; 6 Jarrod Sammut; 7 Ryan Johnston; 15 Ellis Gillam; 22 Josh Wood; 20 Ben Evans; 11 Danny Langtree; 12 Jarrad Stack; 10 Anton Iaria. Subs (all used): 9 Nathan Mossop; 17 Charlie Emslie; 16 Sam Brooks; 8 Greg Burke.
Tries: Iaria (5, 34), Emslie (25), Toal (79); **Goals:** Shaw 5/5.
VIKINGS: 1 Jack Owens; 2 Ryan Ince; 29 Zach Eckersley; 20 Joe Edge; 5 Kieran Dixon; 18 Joe Lyons; 7 Tom Gilmore; 8 Owen Farnworth; 9 Matty Fozard; 12 Adam Lawton; 11 Sam Wilde; 17 Shane Grady; 14 Jordan Johnstone. Subs (all used): 22 Aaron Brown; 26 Max Roberts; 21 Lewis Hatton; 19 Olly Davies.
Tries: Wilde (44), Lyons (46), Brown (57);
Goals: Gilmore 3/4.
Rugby Leaguer & League Express Men of the Match: *Raiders:* Anton Iaria; *Vikings:* Sam Wilde.
Penalty count: 3-3; **Half-time:** 18-0;
Referee: James Vella; **Attendance:** 2,150.

Championship 2023 - Round by Round

BRADFORD BULLS 22 HALIFAX PANTHERS 22

BULLS: 1 Tom Holmes; 2 Ben Blackmore; 3 Joe Arundel; 4 Kieran Gill; 5 David Foggin-Johnston; 6 Dec Patton; 7 Jordan Lilley; 8 Jordan Baldwinson; 9 George Flanagan; 10 Michael Lawrence; 12 Chester Butler; 13 Bodene Thompson; 18 Keven Appo. Subs (all used): 11 Brad England; 14 Ebon Scurr; 21 Fenton Rogers; 23 James Segeyaro.
Tries: Arundel (11), Rogers (47), England (71);
Goals: Patton 5/5.
PANTHERS: 1 James Woodburn-Hall; 2 Lachlan Walmsley; 35 Ben Crooks; 4 Ben Tibbs; 5 James Saltonstall; 6 Louis Jouffret; 14 Kyle Wood; 16 Will Calcott; 9 Brandon Moore; 10 Dan Murray; 11 Ben Kavanagh; 12 Matty Gee; 31 Kevin Larroyer. Subs (all used): 34 Adam O'Brien; 8 Adam Tangata; 19 Ryan Lannon; 3 Zack McComb.
Tries: Gee (27), Saltonstall (37), Jouffret (57), Walmsley (65); **Goals:** Jouffret 3/4.
Rugby Leaguer & League Express Men of the Match:
Bulls: James Segeyaro; *Panthers:* Adam O'Brien.
Penalty count: 5-9; **Half-time:** 8-12;
Referee: Tom Grant; **Attendance:** 4,717.

FEATHERSTONE ROVERS 50 LONDON BRONCOS 6

ROVERS: 20 Mark Kheirallah; 2 Luke Briscoe; 21 Joey Leilua; 3 Chris Hankinson; 5 Gareth Gale; 23 Caleb Aekins; 25 Thomas Lacans; 10 James Lockwood; 14 Matty Wildie; 17 Gadwin Springer; 11 Brad Day; 13 Jack Bussey; 32 Daniel Smith. Subs (all used): 9 Connor Jones; 15 John Davies; 27 McKenzie Yei; 31 Arama Hau.
Tries: Aekins (7, 36), Wildie (15), Leilua (26), Lacans (29), Jones (56), Day (61), Kheirallah (70), Gale (73);
Goals: Kheirallah 7/8, Bussey 0/1.
Sin bin: Kheirallah (47) - delaying restart.
BRONCOS: 1 Alex Walker; 2 Paul Ulberg; 3 Jarred Bassett; 23 Daniel Hoyes; 5 Iliess Macani; 6 Oliver Leyland; 17 Henry Raiwalui; 8 Wellington Albert; 9 Sam Davis; 10 Jordan Williams; 11 Will Lovell; 16 Ethan Natoli; 12 Marcus Stock. Subs (all used): 14 Bill Leyland; 15 Lewis Bienek; 22 Max Allen; 26 Euan Parke.
Try: O Leyland (80); **Goals:** O Leyland 1/1.
Rugby Leaguer & League Express Men of the Match:
Rovers: Caleb Aekins; *Broncos:* Will Lovell.
Penalty count: 4-6; **Half-time:** 30-0;
Referee: Liam Rush; **Attendance:** 2,255.

NEWCASTLE THUNDER 18 KEIGHLEY COUGARS 16

THUNDER: 6 Alex Donaghy; 5 Alex Clegg; 3 Marcus Walker; 11 Alex Foster; 20 Gideon Boafo; 27 Jack Miller; 7 Nikau Williams; 8 Jay Chapelhow; 9 Curtis Davies; 15 Ted Chapelhow; 12 Brad Gallagher; 29 Nick Staveley; 13 Connor Bailey. Subs (all used): 14 Denive Balmforth; 24 Daniel Okoro; 10 Mitch Clark; 17 Rob Tuliatu.
Tries: Davies (6), T Chapelhow (20), Clegg (47), Gallagher (58); **Goals:** Williams 1/4.
COUGARS: 21 Lloyd Roby; 2 Alix Stephenson; 3 Charlie Graham; 23 Robbie Storey; 5 Mo Agoro; 22 Dane Chisholm; 40 Kieran Rush; 32 Jack Bibby; 9 Billy Gaylor; 8 Dan Parker; 19 Ellis Robson; 36 Cole Oakley; 20 Brad Walker. Subs (all used): 14 Harvey Spence; 12 Aaron Levy; 38 Joe Hird; 37 Luca Atkinson.
Tries: Storey (17), Rush (28), Graham (69);
Goals: Rush 1/2, Chisholm 1/2.
Rugby Leaguer & League Express Men of the Match:
Thunder: Ted Chapelhow; *Cougars:* Kieran Rush.
Penalty count: 4-4; **Half-time:** 10-12;
Referee: Matt Rossleigh; **Attendance:** 684.

SWINTON LIONS 6 BATLEY BULLDOGS 48

LIONS: 1 Dan Abram; 4 Jayden Hatton; 22 Andy Badrock; 11 Rhodri Lloyd; 3 Jake Spedding; 31 Will Roberts; 36 Jamie Ellis; 8 Gavin Bennion; 14 Josh Eaves; 34 Lewis Baxter; 16 Gav Rodden; 10 Kenny Baker; 6 Nick Gregson. Subs (all used): 13 Louis Brogan; 26 Joey Romeo; 30 George Roby; 35 Lewis Hall.
Try: Brogan (43); **Goals:** Gregson 1/1.
BULLDOGS: 21 Aidan McGowan; 22 Dale Morton; 4 Josh Hodson; 18 George Senior; 15 Elliot Kear; 14 James Meadows; 7 Josh Woods; 13 James Brown; 17 Luke Blake; 30 Martyn Reilly; 11 Dane Manning; 3 Kieran Buchanan; 6 Ben White. Subs (all used): 8 Adam Gledhill; 10 Keegan Hirst; 16 Michael Ward; 26 Nyle Flynn.
Tries: Meadows (2), Buchanan (7), Brown (13), Hodson (17), Morton (27), Gledhill (35), Manning (71), Hirst (80);
Goals: Meadows 8/9.
Rugby Leaguer & League Express Men of the Match:
Lions: Lewis Hall; *Bulldogs:* James Meadows.
Penalty count: 4-7; **Half-time:** 0-36;
Referee: Michael Smaill; **Attendance:** 1,009.

ROUND 16

Friday 23rd June 2023

SHEFFIELD EAGLES 40 NEWCASTLE THUNDER 0

EAGLES: 29 Quentin Laulu-Togaga'e; 2 Ben Jones-Bishop; 3 Kris Welham; 23 Bayley Liu; 28 Matty Dawson-Jones; 32 Cory Aston; 19 Jack Hansen; 8 Brandon Douglas; 9 Vila Halafihi; 10 Tyler Dickinson; 18 Aaron Murphy; 27 Jesse Sene-Lefao; 14 Titus Gwaze. Subs (all used): 12 Joel Farrell; 13 Evan Hodgson; 15 Mikey Wood; 24 Oliver Roberts.
Tries: Gwaze (13), Hansen (17), Aston (28, 68), Halafihi (48), Wood (61), Dawson-Jones (65);
Goals: Aston 6/7.
Sin bin: Welham (52) - fighting.
THUNDER: 6 Alex Donaghy; 5 Alex Clegg; 3 Marcus Walker; 11 Alex Foster; 20 Gideon Boafo; 13 Connor Bailey; 27 Jack Miller; 8 Jay Chapelhow; 9 Curtis Davies; 15 Ted Chapelhow; 22 Jake Anderson; 12 Brad Gallagher; 10 Mitch Clark. Subs (all used): 14 Denive Balmforth; 17 Rob Tuliatu; 18 Jake Lightowler; 23 Connor Moore.
Sin bin: Clark (52) - fighting; Davies (52) - dissent.
Rugby Leaguer & League Express Men of the Match:
Eagles: Cory Aston; *Thunder:* Jack Miller.
Penalty count: 5-5; **Half-time:** 18-0;
Referee: Michael Smaill; **Attendance:** 879.

Saturday 24th June 2023

TOULOUSE OLYMPIQUE 52 BRADFORD BULLS 14

OLYMPIQUE: 23 Robin Brochon; 5 Paul Marcon; 4 Mathieu Jussaume; 18 Guy Armitage; 19 Benjamin Laguerre; 6 Josh Ralph; 7 Jake Shorrocks; 8 Lambert Belmas; 9 Calum Gahan; 27 Dimitri Biscarro; 10 Harrison Hansen; 11 Maxime Stefani; 13 Anthony Marion. Subs (all used): 20 Greg Richards; 16 Joe Bretherton; 15 Sitaleki Akauola; 14 Eloi Pelissier.
Tries: B Laguerre (3, 70), Ralph (20, 47, 57), Armitage (30, 68), Brochon (65), Maxime Stefani (80);
Goals: Shorrocks 8/9.
BULLS: 31 Jack Walker; 2 Ben Blackmore; 3 Joe Arundel; 4 Kieran Gill; 5 David Foggin-Johnston; 29 Lee Gaskell; 6 Dec Patton; 8 Jordan Baldwinson; 7 Jordan Lilley; 10 Michael Lawrence; 13 Bodene Thompson; 12 Chester Butler; 18 Keven Appo. Subs (all used): 14 Ebon Scurr; 23 James Segeyaro; 11 Brad England; 21 Fenton Rogers.
Tries: Blackmore (36), Gaskell (48), Gill (73);
Goals: Patton 1/3.
Dismissal: England (66) - punching.
Rugby Leaguer & League Express Men of the Match:
Olympique: Josh Ralph; *Bulls:* Dec Patton.
Penalty count: 7-4; **Half-time:** 16-4;
Referee: Liam Rush; **Attendance:** 4,211.

Sunday 25th June 2023

BATLEY BULLDOGS 18 LONDON BRONCOS 20

BULLDOGS: 21 Aidan McGowan; 22 Dale Morton; 4 Josh Hodson; 18 George Senior; 15 Elliot Kear; 14 James Meadows; 6 Ben White; 19 Tom Lillycrop; 24 Ben Kaye; 30 Martyn Reilly; 11 Dane Manning; 3 Kieran Buchanan; 17 Luke Blake. Subs (all used): 9 Alistair Leak; 16 Michael Ward; 26 Nyle Flynn; 29 Greg Johnson.
Tries: Morton (45, 50), Hodson (68); **Goals:** Meadows 3/5.
BRONCOS: 1 Alex Walker; 2 Paul Ulberg; 35 Kyle Evans; 39 Harry Stevens; 5 Iliess Macani; 6 Oliver Leyland; 38 Kieran Tyrer; 33 Rob Butler; 14 Bill Leyland; 12 Marcus Stock; 11 Will Lovell; 36 Jacob Gannon; 13 Dean Parata. Subs (all used): 9 Sam Davis; 24 Jensen Monk; 34 Matthew Davies; 37 Harvey Makin.
Tries: Parata (3), Macani (20), B Leyland (60);
Goals: O Leyland 4/4.
Rugby Leaguer & League Express Men of the Match:
Bulldogs: James Meadows; *Broncos:* Rob Butler.
Penalty count: 8-4; **Half-time:** 2-14;
Referee: Tom Grant; **Attendance:** 1,372.

HALIFAX PANTHERS 48 BARROW RAIDERS 20

PANTHERS: 1 James Woodburn-Hall; 2 Lachlan Walmsley; 35 Ben Crooks; 4 Ben Tibbs; 5 James Saltonstall; 6 Louis Jouffret; 14 Kyle Wood; 16 Will Calcott; 34 Adam O'Brien; 10 Dan Murray; 11 Ben Kavanagh; 12 Matty Gee; 13 Jacob Fairbank. Subs (all used): 20 Tom Inman; 29 Dan Fleming; 19 Ryan Lannon; 8 Adam Tangata.
Tries: Walmsley (24, 41, 65, 78), O'Brien (34), Kavanagh (48, 55), Fleming (61), Woodburn-Hall (69);
Goals: Jouffret 6/9.
Sin bin: Saltonstall (12) - professional foul.
RAIDERS: 24 Luke Broadbent; 5 Ryan Shaw; 18 Brett Carter; 2 Shane Toal; 27 Andrew Bulman; 6 Jarrod Sammut; 7 Ryan Johnston; 15 Ellis Gillam; 22 Josh Wood; 20 Ben Evans; 11 Danny Langtree; 17 Charlie Emslie; 10 Anton Iaria. Subs (all used): 9 Nathan Mossop; 28 Ellis Archer; 8 Greg Burke; 16 Sam Brooks.
Tries: Gillam (2), Shaw (10), Bulman (14), Johnston (75);
Goals: Shaw 2/4.
Dismissal:
Sammut (38) - dangerous challenge on Woodburn-Hall.
Rugby Leaguer & League Express Men of the Match:
Panthers: Lachlan Walmsley; *Raiders:* Ryan Shaw.
Penalty count: 11-9; **Half-time:** 12-16;
Referee: Cameron Worsley; **Attendance:** 1,744.

KEIGHLEY COUGARS 28 WHITEHAVEN 18

COUGARS: 21 Lloyd Roby; 2 Alix Stephenson; 3 Charlie Graham; 23 Robbie Storey; 5 Mo Agoro; 20 Brad Walker; 14 Harvey Spence; 10 Toby Everett; 13 Kyle Kesik; 32 Jack Bibby; 19 Ellis Robson; 27 Sadiq Adebiyi; 38 Joe Hird. Subs (all used): 8 Dan Parker; 9 Billy Gaylor; 12 Aaron Levy; 36 Cole Oakley.
Tries: Stephenson (13), Agoro (17), Roby (27), Robson (60), Gaylor (74); **Goals:** Spence 0/3, Walker 4/5.
WHITEHAVEN: 23 Josh Rourke; 2 Dave Eccleston; 3 Chris Taylor; 4 Curtis Teare; 26 Oscar Doran; 19 Ryan King; 14 Jamie Doran; 22 Lucas Castle; 15 James Newton; 28 Ross Ainley; 11 Connor Holliday; 12 Lachlan Lanskey; 16 Lasarusa Tabu. Subs (all used): 13 Dion Aiye; 18 Perry Singleton; 24 Daniel Spencer-Tonks; 27 Jake Carter.
Tries: Eccleston (32), King (66), Rourke (76);
Goals: Rourke 3/3.
Sin bin: King (80) - holding down.
Rugby Leaguer & League Express Men of the Match:
Cougars: Sadiq Adebiyi; *Whitehaven:* Dion Aiye.
Penalty count: 6-6; **Half-time:** 12-6;
Referee: Matt Rossleigh; **Attendance:** 2,106.

WIDNES VIKINGS 18 SWINTON LIONS 25

VIKINGS: 1 Jack Owens; 28 Ryan Millar; 26 Max Roberts; 29 Zach Eckersley; 5 Kieran Dixon; 18 Joe Lyons; 7 Tom Gilmore; 27 Anthony Walker; 14 Jordan Johnstone; 19 Olly Davies; 30 Jacob Jones; 11 Sam Wilde; 22 Aaron Brown. Subs (all used): 9 Matty Fozard; 12 Adam Lawton; 21 Lewis Hatton; 17 Shane Grady.
Tries: Walker (62), Davies (70), Lawton (78);
Goals: Gilmore 3/3.
Sin bin: Hatton (40) - fighting.
LIONS: 26 Joey Romeo; 4 Jayden Hatton; 3 Jake Spedding; - Ben Davies; 22 Andy Badrock; 31 Will Roberts; 36 Jamie Ellis; 8 Gavin Bennion; 30 George Roby; 13 Louis Brogan; 11 Rhodri Lloyd; 16 Gav Rodden; 6 Nick Gregson. Subs (all used): 14 Josh Eaves; 35 Lewis Hall; 34 George Delaney; 10 Kenny Baker.
Tries: Ellis (17), Roby (20), Lloyd (42), Hatton (46);
Goals: Roberts 3/3, Davies 1/2; **Field goal:** Ellis (73).
Sin bin: Rodden (40) - fighting.
Rugby Leaguer & League Express Men of the Match:
Vikings: Anthony Walker; *Lions:* Jamie Ellis.
Penalty count: 9-5; **Half-time:** 0-14;
Referee: Scott Mikalauskas; **Attendance:** 2,833.

YORK KNIGHTS 8 FEATHERSTONE ROVERS 24

KNIGHTS: 2 Joe Brown; 5 AJ Towse; 15 Myles Harrison; 33 Oliver Pratt; 25 Brad Ward; 6 Ata Hingano; 19 Josh Daley; 30 Brenden Santi; 9 Will Jubb; 21 Ukuma Ta'ai; 11 Chris Clarkson; 32 Oli Field; 14 James Cunningham. Subs (all used): 10 Conor Fitzsimmons; 13 Jordan Thompson; 17 Ronan Michael; 28 Adam Jones.
Tries: Hingano (10), Towse (29); **Goals:** Harrison 0/2.
ROVERS: 20 Mark Kheirallah; 2 Luke Briscoe; 21 Joey Leilua; 3 Chris Hankinson; 5 Gareth Gale; 23 Caleb Aekins; 25 Thomas Lacans; 10 James Lockwood; 14 Matty Wildie; 17 Gadwin Springer; 11 Brad Day; 13 Jack Bussey; 16 Junior Moors. Subs (all used): 9 Connor Jones; 27 McKenzie Yei; 15 John Davies; 18 Josh Hardcastle.
Tries: Leilua (23, 34), Kheirallah (52), Jones (78);
Goals: Kheirallah 4/5.
Rugby Leaguer & League Express Men of the Match:
Knights: Joe Brown; *Rovers:* Mark Kheirallah.
Penalty count: 4-3; **Half-time:** 8-10;
Referee: James Vella; **Attendance:** 2,554.

ROUND 15

Wednesday 28th June 2023

WHITEHAVEN 26 YORK KNIGHTS 24

WHITEHAVEN: 23 Josh Rourke; 2 Dave Eccleston; 3 Chris Taylor; 4 Curtis Teare; 26 Oscar Doran; 14 Jamie Doran; 27 Jake Carter; 22 Lucas Castle; 15 James Newton; 28 Ross Ainley; 11 Connor Holliday; 19 Ryan King; 13 Dion Aiye. Subs (all used): 8 Liam McAvoy; 16 Lasarusa Tabu; 17 Guy Graham; 18 Perry Singleton.
Tries: King (16), Aiye (22), Rourke (33), Teare (64), O Doran (74); **Goals:** Rourke 3/5.
KNIGHTS: 2 Joe Brown; 5 AJ Towse; 15 Myles Harrison; 33 Oliver Pratt; 25 Brad Ward; 6 Ata Hingano; 7 Liam

Championship 2023 - Round by Round

Harris; 30 Brenden Santi; 14 James Cunningham; 10 Conor Fitzsimmons; 11 Chris Clarkson; 12 Danny Kirmond; 13 Jordan Thompson. Subs (all used): 19 Josh Daley; 20 Jack Teanby; 21 Ukuma Ta'ai; 32 Oli Field.
Tries: Towse (5, 69), Kirmond (10), Santi (50), Pratt (78);
Goals: Harrison 2/5.
Rugby Leaguer & League Express Men of the Match:
Whitehaven: Dion Aiye; *Knights:* Josh Daley.
Penalty count: 5-2; **Half-time:** 16-10;
Referee: Michael Smaill; **Attendance:** 951.

ROUND 17

Saturday 1st July 2023

TOULOUSE OLYMPIQUE 40 WIDNES VIKINGS 28

OLYMPIQUE: 23 Robin Brochon; 5 Paul Marcon; 4 Mathieu Jussaume; 18 Guy Armitage; 19 Benjamin Laguerre; 6 Josh Ralph; 7 Jake Shorrocks; 8 Lambert Belmas; 9 Calum Gahan; 27 Dimitri Biscarro; 24 Pierre-Jean Lima; 11 Maxime Stefani; 13 Anthony Marion. Subs (all used): 20 Greg Richards; 16 Joe Bretherton; 26 Ramon Silva; 14 Eloi Pelissier.
Tries: Biscarro (4, 19), Gahan (9), Maxime Stefani (14), Marcon (44), Jussaume (52), Armitage (68);
Goals: Shorrocks 6/7.
VIKINGS: 20 Joe Edge; 28 Ryan Millar; 26 Max Roberts; 24 Ollie Brookes; 5 Kieran Dixon; 18 Joe Lyons; 7 Tom Gilmore; 19 Olly Davies; 14 Jordan Johnstone; 27 Anthony Walker; 11 Sam Wilde; 17 Shane Grady; 30 Jacob Jones. Subs (all used): 16 Callum Field; 9 Matty Fozard; 12 Adam Lawton; 23 Will Tilleke.
Tries: Millar (36, 38), Grady (47), K Dixon (57, 66), Wilde (80); **Goals:** Gilmore 0/2, Edge 2/4.
Rugby Leaguer & League Express Men of the Match:
Olympique: Josh Ralph; *Vikings:* Shane Grady.
Penalty count: 6-1; **Half-time:** 24-8;
Referee: Tom Grant; **Attendance:** 3,870.

Sunday 2nd July 2023

BARROW RAIDERS 6 BATLEY BULLDOGS 12

RAIDERS: 24 Luke Broadbent; 5 Ryan Shaw; 18 Brett Carter; 2 Shane Toal; 27 Andrew Bulman; 6 Jarrod Sammut; 7 Ryan Johnston; 8 Greg Burke; 22 Josh Wood; 16 Sam Brooks; 11 Danny Langtree; 17 Charlie Emslie; 4 Greg Worthington. Subs (all used): 9 Nathan Mossop; 30 Harvey Makin; 32 Tom Wilkinson; 1 Luke Cresswell.
Try: Broadbent (41); **Goals:** Shaw 1/2.
BULLDOGS: 32 Luke Hooley; 22 Dale Morton; 4 Josh Hodson; 18 George Senior; 15 Elliot Kear; 14 James Meadows; 7 Josh Woods; 13 James Brown; 6 Ben White; 20 Samy Kibula; 11 Dane Manning; 3 Kieran Buchanan; 30 Martyn Reilly. Subs (all used): 9 Alistair Leak; 10 Keegan Hirst; 16 Michael Ward; 26 Nyle Flynn.
Tries: Meadows (54), Hodson (78); **Goals:** Hooley 2/2.
Rugby Leaguer & League Express Men of the Match:
Raiders: Charlie Emslie; *Bulldogs:* James Meadows.
Penalty count: 4-3; **Half-time:** 0-0;
Referee: James Vella; **Attendance:** 2,096.

BRADFORD BULLS 74 KEIGHLEY COUGARS 12

BULLS: 27 Connor Wynne; 2 Ben Blackmore; 3 Joe Arundel; 4 Kieran Gill; 28 Jorge Taufua; 29 Lee Gaskell; 6 Dec Patton; 24 Masi Matongo; 7 Jordan Lilley; 10 Michael Lawrence; 12 Chester Butler; 15 AJ Wallace; 13 Bodene Thompson. Subs (all used): 11 Brad England; 14 Ebon Scurr; 18 Keven Appo; 23 James Segeyaro.
Tries: Blackmore (8, 67), Wallace (11, 28), Taufua (25, 49, 55), Scurr (44), Wynne (47, 80), Gill (51, 61, 78); **Goals:** Patton 9/11, Thompson 2/2.
COUGARS: 21 Lloyd Roby; 2 Alix Stephenson; 3 Charlie Graham; 36 Cole Oakley; 35 Phoenix Laulu-Togaga'e; 20 Brad Walker; 14 Harvey Spence; 32 Jack Bibby; 26 Thomas Doyle; 10 Toby Everett; 19 Ellis Robson; 27 Sadiq Adebiyi; 38 Joe Hird. Subs (all used): 9 Billy Gaylor; 12 Aaron Levy; 8 Dan Parker; 37 Luca Atkinson.
Tries: Levy (36), Graham (76); **Goals:** Spence 2/2.
Dismissal: Parker (80) - dissent.
Rugby Leaguer & League Express Men of the Match:
Bulls: Jorge Taufua; *Cougars:* Aaron Levy.
Penalty count: 7-3; **Half-time:** 22-6;
Referee: Scott Mikalauskas; **Attendance:** 4,879.

LONDON BRONCOS 56 NEWCASTLE THUNDER 10

BRONCOS: 1 Alex Walker; 2 Paul Ulberg; 17 Henry Raiwalui; 16 Ethan Natoli; 5 Iliess Macani; 6 Oliver Leyland; 20 Corey Norman; 10 Jordan Williams; 14 Bill Leyland; 33 Rob Butler; 11 Will Lovell; 36 Jacob Gannon; 13 Dean Parata. Subs (all used): 12 Marcus Stock; 8 Wellington Albert; 9 Sam Davis; 34 Matthew Davies.
Tries: B Leyland (2), Butler (4, 39), Ulberg (22), Walker (32, 73), Gannon (48), O Leyland (51), Raiwalui (55), Williams (63); **Goals:** O Leyland 8/10.
THUNDER: 6 Alex Donaghy; 5 Alex Clegg; 3 Marcus Walker; 11 Alex Foster; 20 Gideon Boafo; 27 Jack Miller; 7 Nikau Williams; 8 Jay Chapelhow; 9 Curtis Davies; 15 Ted Chapelhow; 13 Connor Bailey; 12 Brad Gallagher; 14 Denive Balmforth. Subs (all used): 10 Mitch Clark; 17 Rob Tuliatu; 40 Evan Simons; 18 Jake Lightowler.
Tries: J Chapelhow (16), Bailey (78); **Goals:** Miller 1/2.
Sin bin: Simons (34) - high tackle.
Rugby Leaguer & League Express Men of the Match:
Broncos: Corey Norman; *Thunder:* Denive Balmforth.
Penalty count: 3-5; **Half-time:** 30-6;
Referee: Nick Bennett; **Attendance:** 1,208
(at Kuflink Stadium, Ebsfleet).

SWINTON LIONS 30 SHEFFIELD EAGLES 22

LIONS: 26 Joey Romeo; 4 Jayden Hatton; 3 Jake Spedding; 22 Andy Badrock; 2 Mike Butt; 6 Nick Gregson; 7 Jordy Gibson; 8 Gavin Bennion; 30 George Roby; 13 Louis Brogan; 16 Gav Rodden; 34 Matthew Foster; 35 Lewis Hall. Subs (all used): 14 Josh Eaves; 10 Kenny Baker; 12 Mitch Cox; 15 Jordan Case.
Tries: Roby (9, 70), Butt (23), Gregson (49), Romeo (76);
Goals: Gregson 1/3, Gibson 4/4.
Sin bin: Case (36) - late challenge.
EAGLES: 29 Quentin Laulu-Togaga'e; 2 Ben Jones-Bishop; 3 Kris Welham; 23 Bayley Liu; 28 Matty Dawson-Jones; 32 Cory Aston; 19 Jack Hansen; 8 Brandon Douglas; 9 Vila Halafihi; 10 Tyler Dickinson; 18 Aaron Murphy; 27 Jesse Sene-Lefao; 13 Evan Hodgson. Subs (all used): 7 Anthony Thackeray; 12 Joel Farrell; 24 Oliver Roberts; 14 Titus Gwaze.
Tries: Dickinson (9), Dawson-Jones (12, 38), Thackeray (27);
Goals: Aston 3/4.
Sin bin: Dickinson (67) - late challenge.
Rugby Leaguer & League Express Men of the Match:
Lions: George Roby; *Eagles:* Kris Welham.
Penalty count: 10-8; **Half-time:** 10-22;
Referee: Liam Rush; **Attendance:** 1,094.

WHITEHAVEN 0 FEATHERSTONE ROVERS 60

WHITEHAVEN: 23 Josh Rourke; 2 Dave Eccleston; 3 Chris Taylor; 4 Curtis Teare; 26 Oscar Doran; 14 Jamie Doran; 27 Jake Carter; 17 Guy Graham; 20 George Hill; 28 Ross Ainley; 11 Connor Holliday; 6 Bailey Dawson; 19 Ryan King. Subs: 8 Liam McAvoy (not used); 16 Lasarusa Tabu; 18 Perry Singleton; 22 Lucas Castle.
Sin bin: J Doran (74) - dangerous challenge on Hankinson.
ROVERS: 20 Mark Kheirallah; 2 Luke Briscoe; 21 Joey Leilua; 3 Chris Hankinson; 5 Gareth Gale; 23 Caleb Aekins; 25 Thomas Lacans; 17 Gadwin Springer; 9 Connor Jones; 16 Junior Moors; 31 Arama Hau; 12 Elijah Taylor; 24 Mathieu Cozza. Subs (all used): 33 Logan Astley; 15 John Davies; 27 McKenzie Yei; 32 Daniel Smith.
Tries: Jones (8), Springer (14), Cozza (19, 45), Aekins (25, 73), Hau (37), Kheirallah (50, 68), Briscoe (60), Leilua (64); **Goals:** Kheirallah 8/11.
Rugby Leaguer & League Express Men of the Match:
Whitehaven: George Hill; *Rovers:* Connor Jones.
Penalty count: 7-12; **Half-time:** 0-28;
Referee: Cameron Worsley; **Attendance:** 841.

YORK KNIGHTS 28 HALIFAX PANTHERS 18

KNIGHTS: 2 Joe Brown; 5 AJ Towse; 11 Chris Clarkson; 4 Jesse Dee; 15 Myles Harrison; 14 James Cunningham; 7 Liam Harris; 17 Ronan Michael; 19 Josh Daley; 30 Brenden Santi; 32 Oli Field; 16 Bailey Antrobus; 13 Jordan Thompson. Subs: 10 Conor Fitzsimmons; 21 Ukuma Ta'ai; 33 Oliver Pratt (not used); 25 Brad Ward (not used).
Tries: Cunningham (9), Dee (27), Harrison (35, 75), Towse (57); **Goals:** Harrison 4/5.
PANTHERS: 1 James Woodburn-Hall; 2 Lachlan Walmsley; 35 Ben Crooks; 28 Mahe Fonua; 5 James Saltonstall; 6 Louis Jouffret; 14 Kyle Wood; 31 Kevin Larroyer; 34 Adam O'Brien; 16 Will Calcott; 11 Ben Kavanagh; 12 Matty Gee; 13 Jacob Fairbank. Subs (all used): 8 Adam Tangata; 3 Zack McComb; 19 Ryan Lannon; 20 Tom Inman.
Tries: Woodburn-Hall (6), Saltonstall (13, 21);
Goals: Jouffret 3/4.
Rugby Leaguer & League Express Men of the Match:
Knights: Myles Harrison; *Panthers:* Jacob Fairbank.
Penalty count: 5-4; **Half-time:** 16-16;
Referee: Michael Smaill; **Attendance:** 1,823.

ROUND 18

Saturday 8th July 2023

LONDON BRONCOS 22 TOULOUSE OLYMPIQUE 6

BRONCOS: 1 Alex Walker; 2 Paul Ulberg; 17 Henry Raiwalui; 16 Ethan Natoli; 5 Iliess Macani; 6 Oliver Leyland; 20 Corey Norman; 12 Marcus Stock; 9 Sam Davis; 33 Rob Butler; 11 Will Lovell; 36 Jacob Gannon; 13 Dean Parata. Subs (all used): 10 Jordan Williams; 14 Bill Leyland; 15 Lewis Bienek; 34 Matthew Davies.
Tries: Walker (10, 65), Ulberg (25), O Leyland (42);
Goals: O Leyland 3/5.
OLYMPIQUE: 22 Zac Santo; 5 Paul Marcon; 4 Mathieu Jussaume; 18 Guy Armitage; 19 Benjamin Laguerre; 6 Josh Ralph; 7 Jake Shorrocks; 8 Lambert Belmas; 9 Calum Gahan; 27 Dimitri Biscarro; 10 Harrison Hansen; 11 Maxime Stefani; 13 Anthony Marion. Subs (all used): 16 Joe Bretherton; 20 Greg Richards; 24 Pierre-Jean Lima; 26 Ramon Silva.
Try: Santo (52); **Goals:** Shorrocks 1/1.
Rugby Leaguer & League Express Men of the Match:
Broncos: Alex Walker; *Olympique:* Mathieu Jussaume.
Penalty count: 5-4; **Half-time:** 10-0;
Referee: Matt Rossleigh; **Attendance:** 1,089
(at Kuflink Stadium, Ebsfleet).

Sunday 9th July 2023

BATLEY BULLDOGS 42 HALIFAX PANTHERS 0

BULLDOGS: 32 Luke Hooley; 22 Dale Morton; 4 Josh Hodson; 18 George Senior; 5 Johnny Campbell; 14 James Meadows; 7 Josh Woods; 13 James Brown; 6 Ben White; 20 Samy Kibula; 11 Dane Manning; 3 Kieran Buchanan; 30 Martyn Reilly. Subs (all used): 8 Adam Gledhill; 9 Alistair Leak; 16 Michael Ward; 26 Nyle Flynn.
Tries: Hooley (17, 61, 75), Manning (38, 54), Senior (68), Hodson (70); **Goals:** Hooley 7/9.
PANTHERS: 1 James Woodburn-Hall; 2 Lachlan Walmsley; 35 Ben Crooks; 4 Ben Tibbs; 5 James Saltonstall; 6 Louis Jouffret; 14 Kyle Wood; 16 Will Calcott; 9 Brandon Moore; 31 Kevin Larroyer; 11 Ben Kavanagh; 12 Matty Gee; 13 Jacob Fairbank. Subs (all used): 8 Adam Tangata; 3 Zack McComb; 29 Dan Fleming; 34 Adam O'Brien.
Rugby Leaguer & League Express Men of the Match:
Bulldogs: Luke Hooley; *Panthers:* Kyle Wood.
Penalty count: 5-3; **Half-time:** 12-0;
Referee: Liam Rush; **Attendance:** 2,014.

FEATHERSTONE ROVERS 52 SWINTON LIONS 6

ROVERS: 20 Mark Kheirallah; 2 Luke Briscoe; 4 Craig Hall; 3 Chris Hankinson; 5 Gareth Gale; 23 Caleb Aekins; 33 Logan Astley; 17 Gadwin Springer; 14 Matty Wildie; 10 James Lockwood; 31 Arama Hau; 12 Elijah Taylor; 32 Daniel Smith. Subs (all used): 9 Connor Jones; 25 Thomas Lacans; 8 Craig Kopczak; 27 McKenzie Yei.
Tries: Hau (21, 41), Kheirallah (28), Briscoe (45), Hall (48, 58), Jones (67), Springer (71), Lacans (74);
Goals: Kheirallah 8/9, Hall 0/1.
Sin bin: Briscoe (33) - dangerous challenge on Hatton; Yei (35) - late challenge on Gibson; Hau (70) - fighting.
LIONS: 26 Joey Romeo; 4 Jayden Hatton; 3 Jake Spedding; 22 Andy Badrock; 2 Mike Butt; 23 Joe Lowe; 7 Jordy Gibson; 13 Louis Brogan; 30 George Roby; 8 Gavin Bennion; 34 Matthew Foster; 16 Gav Rodden; 35 Lewis Hall. Subs (all used): 14 Josh Eaves; 10 Kenny Baker; 12 Mitch Cox; 15 Jordan Case.
Try: Hatton (78); **Goals:** Gibson 1/1.
Sin bin: Hall (65) - holding down; Roby (70) - fighting.
Rugby Leaguer & League Express Men of the Match:
Rovers: Logan Astley; *Lions:* Louis Brogan.
Penalty count: 10-6; **Half-time:** 12-0;
Referee: Michael Smaill; **Attendance:** 2,845.

KEIGHLEY COUGARS 10 YORK KNIGHTS 50

COUGARS: 35 Phoenix Laulu-Togaga'e; 2 Alix Stephenson; 23 Robbie Storey; 21 Lloyd Roby; 3 Charlie Graham; 20 Brad Walker; 41 Jake Sweeting; 32 Jack Bibby; 26 Thomas Doyle; 10 Toby Everett; 19 Ellis Robson; 27 Sadiq Adebiyi; 11 Kyle Trout. Subs (all used): 37 Luca Atkinson; 38 Joe Hird; 13 Kyle Kesik; 12 Aaron Levy.
Tries: Stephenson (30, 48); **Goals:** Walker 1/2.
KNIGHTS: 2 Joe Brown; 15 Myles Harrison; 4 Jesse Dee; 11 Chris Clarkson; 5 AJ Towse; 14 James Cunningham; 7 Liam Harris; 30 Brenden Santi; 19 Josh Daley; 10 Conor Fitzsimmons; 32 Oli Field; 16 Bailey Antrobus; 13 Jordan Thompson. Subs (all used): 28 Jason Bass; 17 Ronan Michael; 21 Ukuma Ta'ai; 20 Jack Teanby.
Tries: Dee (17, 20, 34), Field (59), Fitzsimmons (65), Brown (71, 74), Towse (77), **Goals:** Harrison 9/9.
Rugby Leaguer & League Express Men of the Match:
Cougars: Thomas Doyle; *Knights:* Jesse Dee.
Penalty count: 6-4; **Half-time:** 6-18;
Referee: Nick Bennett; **Attendance:** 1,654.

NEWCASTLE THUNDER 30 WHITEHAVEN 12

THUNDER: 6 Alex Donaghy; 2 Alex Young; 3 Marcus Walker; 5 Alex Clegg; 20 Gideon Boafo; 27 Jack Miller; 13 Connor Bailey; 8 Jay Chapelhow; 9 Curtis Davies; 15 Ted Chapelhow; 12 Brad Gallagher; 17 Rob Tuliatu; 10 Mitch Clark. Subs (all used): 14 Denive Balmforth; 40 Evan Simons; 23 Connor Moore; 28 Tyler Walton.

Championship 2023 - Round by Round

Halifax's Zack McComb traps Newcastle's Gideon Boafo

Tries: J Chapelhow (15, 80), T Chapelhow (30), Boafo (46), Clark (76); **Goals:** Miller 5/6.
Sin bin: Clark (53) - dissent.
WHITEHAVEN: 23 Josh Rourke; 2 Dave Eccleston; 3 Chris Taylor; 11 Connor Holliday; 4 Curtis Teare; 14 Jamie Doran; 27 Jake Carter; 22 Lucas Castle; 15 James Newton; 28 Ross Ainley; 12 Lachlan Lanskey; 19 Ryan King; 13 Dion Aiye. Subs (all used): 20 George Hill; 16 Lasarusa Tabu; 18 Perry Singleton; 24 Daniel Spencer-Tonks.
Tries: Hill (53), Carter (55); **Goals:** Rourke 2/2.
Rugby Leaguer & League Express Men of the Match:
Thunder: Jay Chapelhow; *Whitehaven:* Jake Carter.
Penalty count: 8-8; **Half-time:** 14-0;
Referee: Ryan Cox; **Attendance:** 1,284.

SHEFFIELD EAGLES 36 BARROW RAIDERS 18

EAGLES: 29 Quentin Laulu-Togaga'e; 2 Ben Jones-Bishop; 33 James Glover; 23 Bayley Liu; 28 Matty Dawson-Jones; 32 Cory Aston; 7 Anthony Thackeray; 8 Brandon Douglas; 9 Vila Halafihi; 10 Tyler Dickinson; 27 Jesse Sene-Lefao; 12 Joel Farrell; 14 Titus Gwaze. Subs (all used): 4 Ross Oakes; 16 Blake Broadbent; 17 Liam Kirk; 19 Jack Hansen.
Tries: J Farrell (3), Dawson-Jones (22), Thackeray (43, 80), Sene-Lefao (47, 63), Oakes (69); **Goals:** Aston 4/7.
Dismissal: Halafihi (27) - high tackle on Emslie.
RAIDERS: 24 Luke Broadbent; 5 Ryan Shaw; 25 Zach Eckersley; 2 Shane Toal; 27 Andrew Bulman; 28 Ellis Archer; 7 Ryan Johnston; 20 Ben Evans; 22 Josh Wood; 30 Harvey Makin; 11 Danny Langtree; 17 Charlie Emslie; 32 Tom Wilkinson. Subs (all used): 1 Luke Cresswell; 8 Greg Burke; 23 Connor Saunders; - Kavan Rothwell.
Tries: Johnston (17), Burke (74), Cresswell (77);
Goals: Shaw 3/4.
Sin bin: Broadbent (62) - dissent.
Rugby Leaguer & League Express Men of the Match:
Eagles: Anthony Thackeray; *Raiders:* Josh Wood.
Penalty count: 10-7; **Half-time:** 8-6;
Referee: Cameron Worsley; **Attendance:** 1,011.

Monday 10th July 2023

WIDNES VIKINGS 31 BRADFORD BULLS 14

VIKINGS: 20 Joe Edge; 5 Kieran Dixon; 26 Max Roberts; 3 Matty Fleming; 24 Ollie Brookes; 18 Joe Lyons; 7 Tom Gilmore; 16 Callum Field; 9 Matty Fozard; 12 Adam Lawton; 11 Sam Wilde; 17 Shane Grady; 19 Olly Davies. Subs (all used): 31 Tom Forber; 27 Anthony Walker; 23 Will Tilleke; 8 Owen Farnworth.

Tries: Fozard (4), K Dixon (21, 52), Lawton (71), Brookes (77); **Goals:** Gilmore 1/1, Edge 4/6;
Field goal: Gilmore (64).
BULLS: 27 Connor Wynne; 2 Ben Blackmore; 3 Joe Arundel; 4 Kieran Gill; 28 Jorge Taufua; 29 Lee Gaskell; 6 Dec Patton; 24 Masi Matongo; 7 Jordan Lilley; 10 Michael Lawrence; 12 Chester Butler; 15 AJ Wallace; 16 Brad Foster. Subs (all used): 14 Ebon Scurr; 18 Keven Appo; 27 Jason Baitieri; 23 James Segeyaro.
Tries: C Butler (8), Gill (16); **Goals:** Patton 3/3.
Sin bin: Gaskell (38) - high tackle.
Rugby Leaguer & League Express Men of the Match:
Vikings: Joe Edge; *Bulls:* Ebon Scurr.
Penalty count: 7-3; **Half-time:** 14-12;
Referee: James Vella; **Attendance:** 2,561.

ROUND 19

Saturday 15th July 2023

TOULOUSE OLYMPIQUE 34 BATLEY BULLDOGS 12

OLYMPIQUE: 22 Zac Santo; 5 Paul Marcon; 4 Mathieu Jussaume; 25 Matthieu Laguerre; 19 Benjamin Laguerre; 6 Josh Ralph; 7 Jake Shorrocks; 8 Lambert Belmas; 9 Calum Gahan; 10 Harrison Hansen; 24 Pierre-Jean Lima; 11 Maxime Stefani; 13 Anthony Marion. Subs (all used): 20 Greg Richards; 16 Joe Bretherton; 15 Sitaleki Akauola; 14 Eloi Pelissier.
Tries: Ralph (7), Marion (28), B Laguerre (47), Maxime Stefani (55), Santo (57, 73); **Goals:** Shorrocks 5/6.
BULLDOGS: 32 Luke Hooley; 22 Dale Morton; 4 Josh Hodson; 18 George Senior; 5 Johnny Campbell; 14 James Meadows; 7 Josh Woods; 13 James Brown; 6 Ben White; 20 Samy Kibula; 11 Dane Manning; 3 Kieran Buchanan; 30 Martyn Reilly. Subs (all used): 9 Alistair Leak; 26 Nyle Flynn; 16 Michael Ward; 8 Adam Gledhill.
Tries: Reilly (23), Meadows (38); **Goals:** Hooley 2/2.
Rugby Leaguer & League Express Men of the Match:
Olympique: Eloi Pelissier; *Bulldogs:* James Meadows.
Penalty count: 2-6; **Half-time:** 12-12;
Referee: Michael Smaill; **Attendance:** 3,557.

Sunday 16th July 2023

BARROW RAIDERS 10 FEATHERSTONE ROVERS 20

RAIDERS: 24 Luke Broadbent; 5 Ryan Shaw; 26 Zach Eckersley; 2 Shane Toal; 27 Andrew Bulman; 28 Ellis Archer; 7 Ryan Johnston; 20 Ben Evans; 22 Josh Wood; 30 Harvey Makin; 11 Danny Langtree; 12 Jarrad Stack; 32 Tom Wilkinson. Subs (all used): 23 Connor Saunders; 1 Luke Cresswell; 25 Kavan Rothwell; 8 Greg Burke.
Tries: Shaw (24), Bulman (33); **Goals:** Shaw 1/3.
ROVERS: 20 Mark Kheirallah; 2 Luke Briscoe; 4 Craig Hall; 3 Chris Hankinson; 5 Gareth Gale; 23 Caleb Aekins; 34 Dane Chisholm; 17 Gadwin Springer; 14 Matty Wildie; 10 James Lockwood; 12 Elijah Taylor; 31 Arama Hau; 32 Daniel Smith. Subs (all used): 9 Connor Jones; 8 Craig Kopczak; 15 John Davies; 24 Mathieu Cozza.
Tries: Gale (6), Hall (18), Briscoe (46), Hau (55);
Goals: Kheirallah 2/4.
Rugby Leaguer & League Express Men of the Match:
Raiders: Danny Langtree; *Rovers:* James Lockwood.
Penalty count: 6-7; **Half-time:** 10-10;
Referee: Liam Rush; **Attendance:** 2,361.

HALIFAX PANTHERS 50 NEWCASTLE THUNDER 12

PANTHERS: 18 Brandon Pickersgill; 2 Lachlan Walmsley; 3 Zack McComb; 35 Ben Crooks; 5 James Saltonstall; 6 Louis Jouffret; 20 Tom Inman; 16 Will Calcott; 34 Adam O'Brien; 10 Dan Murray; 11 Ben Kavanagh; 12 Matty Gee; 13 Jacob Fairbank. Subs (all used): 9 Brandon Moore; 19 Ryan Lannon; 29 Dan Fleming; 31 Kevin Larroyer.
Tries: Crooks (9), Walmsley (34, 54), Gee (37, 40), Murray (57), McComb (68), Kavanagh (71), Moore (77);
Goals: Jouffret 7/9.
THUNDER: 6 Alex Donaghy; 2 Alex Young; 3 Marcus Walker; 5 Alex Clegg; 20 Gideon Boafo; 27 Jack Miller; 13 Connor Bailey; 8 Jay Chapelhow; 9 Curtis Davies; 15 Ted Chapelhow; 17 Rob Tuliatu; 12 Brad Gallagher; 10 Mitch Clark. Subs (all used): 14 Denive Balmforth; 29 Nick Staveley; 28 Tyler Walton; 40 Evan Simons.
Tries: J Chapelhow (43, 49); **Goals:** Miller 2/2.
Sin bin: Gallagher (61) - professional foul.
Rugby Leaguer & League Express Men of the Match:
Panthers: Tom Inman; *Thunder:* Jay Chapelhow.
Penalty count: 6-1; **Half-time:** 22-0;
Referee: Cameron Worsley; **Attendance:** 1,453.

KEIGHLEY COUGARS 22 WIDNES VIKINGS 38

COUGARS: 1 Lewis Young; 2 Alix Stephenson; 23 Robbie Storey; 42 Junior Sa'u; 3 Charlie Graham; 35 Phoenix Laulu-Togaga'e; 21 Lloyd Roby; 32 Jack Bibby; 13 Kyle Kesik; 10 Toby Everett; 19 Ellis Robson; 12 Aaron Levy; 20 Brad Walker. Subs (all used): 39 Aidan Scully; 26 Thomas Doyle; 11 Kyle Trout; 43 Matty Laidlaw.

Championship 2023 - Round by Round

Tries: Sa'u (21), Roby (45), Robson (70), Graham (80);
Goals: Walker 3/4.
VIKINGS: 20 Joe Edge; 5 Kieran Dixon; 26 Max Roberts; 3 Matty Fleming; 24 Ollie Brooks; 18 Joe Lyons; 7 Tom Gilmore; 16 Callum Field; 9 Matty Fozard; 12 Adam Lawton; 11 Sam Wilde; 17 Shane Grady; 19 Olly Davies. Subs (all used): 8 Owen Farnworth; 31 Tom Forber; 27 Anthony Walker; 30 Jacob Jones.
Tries: Lawton (14), Fozard (30), Lyons (36), Gilmore (44), Roberts (53, 66), Wilde (62);
Goals: Edge 0/2, K Dixon 5/5.
Rugby Leaguer & League Express Men of the Match:
Cougars: Lewis Young; *Vikings:* Kieran Dixon.
Penalty count: 3-5; **Half-time:** 6-14;
Referee: Scott Mikalauskas; **Attendance:** 1,267.

SWINTON LIONS 6 LONDON BRONCOS 12

LIONS: 1 Dan Abram; 26 Joey Romeo; 22 Andy Badrock; 3 Jake Spedding; 4 Jayden Hatton; 19 Ollie Olds; 7 Jordy Gibson; 13 Louis Brogan; 14 Josh Eaves; 8 Gavin Bennion; 11 Rhodri Lloyd; 12 Mitch Cox; 35 Lewis Hall. Subs (all used): 30 George Roby; 10 Kenny Baker; 34 Matthew Foster; 15 Jordan Case.
Try: Baker (43); **Goals:** Abram 1/1.
Sin bin: Hall (67) - fighting.
BRONCOS: 1 Alex Walker; 2 Paul Ulberg; 17 Henry Raiwalui; 3 Jarred Bassett; 5 Iliess Macani; 6 Oliver Leyland; 20 Corey Norman; 33 Rob Butler; 9 Sam Davis; 12 Marcus Stock; 11 Will Lovell; 16 Ethan Natoli; 13 Dean Parata. Subs (all used): 14 Bill Leyland; 15 Lewis Bienek; 10 Jordan Williams; 36 Jacob Gannon.
Tries: Macani (8, 27); **Goals:** O Leyland 2/3.
Sin bin: Gannon (67) - fighting.
Rugby Leaguer & League Express Men of the Match:
Lions: Jake Spedding; *Broncos:* Iliess Macani.
Penalty count: 10-8; **Half-time:** 0-10;
Referee: Matt Rossleigh; **Attendance:** 940.

WHITEHAVEN 18 BRADFORD BULLS 44

WHITEHAVEN: 23 Josh Rourke; 2 Dave Eccleston; 3 Chris Taylor; 4 Curtis Teare; 9 Will Groves; 27 Jake Carter; 13 Dion Aiye; 22 Lucas Castle; 15 James Newton; 28 Ross Ainley; 12 Lachlan Lanskey; 11 Connor Holliday; 19 Ryan King. Subs (all used): 20 George Hill; 16 Lasarusa Tabu; 18 Perry Singleton; 24 Daniel Spencer-Tonks.
Tries: Holliday (4), Aiye (6), King (22); **Goals:** Rourke 3/3.
BULLS: 27 Connor Wynne; 2 Ben Blackmore; 30 Jayden Myers; 4 Kieran Gill; 28 Jorge Taufua; 29 Lee Gaskell; 6 Dec Patton; 10 Michael Lawrence; 23 James Segeyaro; 24 Masi Matongo; 15 AJ Wallace; 12 Chester Butler; 37 Jason Baitieri. Subs (all used): 7 Jordan Lilley; 18 Keven Appo; 14 Ebon Scurr; 40 Daniel Okoro.
Tries: Segeyaro (13), Blackmore (31), Appo (47), Gill (63), Matongo (66), C Butler (70), Wallace (72), Patton (79);
Goals: Patton 6/8, Lilley 0/1.
Sin bin: Patton (24) - high tackle on Rourke.
Rugby Leaguer & League Express Men of the Match:
Whitehaven: Curtis Teare; *Bulls:* Ebon Scurr.
Penalty count: 4-6; **Half-time:** 18-10;
Referee: Nick Bennett; **Attendance:** 1,257.

YORK KNIGHTS 23 SHEFFIELD EAGLES 18

KNIGHTS: 2 Joe Brown; 5 AJ Towse; 11 Chris Clarkson; 4 Jesse Dee; 29 Jason Bass; 14 James Cunningham; 7 Liam Harris; 21 Ukuma Ta'ai; 9 Will Jubb; 10 Conor Fitzsimmons; 32 Oli Field; 16 Bailey Antrobus; 13 Jordan Thompson. Subs: 6 Ata Hingano; 17 Ronan Michael (not used); 20 Jack Teanby; 30 Brenden Santi.
Tries: Harris (12), Bass (50), Thompson (60), Dee (70);
Goals: Harris 3/4; **Field goal:** Harris (77).
EAGLES: 29 Quentin Laulu-Togaga'e; 2 Ben Jones-Bishop; 33 James Glover; 23 Bayley Liu; 28 Matty Dawson-Jones; 32 Cory Aston; 7 Anthony Thackeray; 8 Brandon Douglas; 9 Vila Halafihi; 14 Titus Gwaze; 12 Joel Farrell; 27 Jesse Sene-Lefao; 13 Evan Hodgson. Subs (all used): 4 Ross Oakes; 16 Blake Broadbent; 17 Liam Kirk; 19 Jack Hansen.
Tries: Jones-Bishop (14), Dawson-Jones (38), Sene-Lefao (74); **Goals:** Aston 3/3.
Rugby Leaguer & League Express Men of the Match:
Knights: Jordan Thompson; *Eagles:* Titus Gwaze.
Penalty count: 3-4; **Half-time:** 6-12;
Referee: James Vella; **Attendance:** 2,266.

ROUND 20

Friday 28th July 2023

SHEFFIELD EAGLES 32 HALIFAX PANTHERS 30

EAGLES: 29 Quentin Laulu-Togaga'e; 2 Ben Jones-Bishop; 33 James Glover; 4 Ross Oakes; 28 Matty Dawson-Jones; 32 Cory Aston; 7 Anthony Thackeray; 17 Liam Kirk; 19 Jack Hansen; 15 Mikey Wood; 11 Connor Bower; 27 Jesse Sene-Lefao; 13 Evan Hodgson. Subs: 8 Brandon Douglas; 14 Titus Gwaze; 16 Blake Broadbent; 22 Matty Chrimes (not used).
Tries: Dawson-Jones (34, 36), Hansen (49), Aston (61), Douglas (75), Jones-Bishop (77); **Goals:** Aston 4/6.
Sin bin: Kirk (72) - fighting.
PANTHERS: 18 Brandon Pickersgill; 2 Lachlan Walmsley; 22 Jake Maizen; 35 Ben Crooks; 3 Zack McComb; 6 Louis Jouffret; 1 James Woodburn-Hall; 16 Will Calcott; 34 Adam O'Brien; 10 Dan Murray; 11 Ben Kavanagh; 12 Matty Gee; 13 Jacob Fairbank. Subs (all used): 9 Brandon Moore; 19 Ryan Lannon; 29 Dan Fleming; 8 Adam Tangata.
Tries: Woodburn-Hall (2), Fairbank (13, 46), Jouffret (28), Lannon (79); **Goals:** Jouffret 5/5.
Sin bin: Calcott (72) - fighting.
Rugby Leaguer & League Express Men of the Match:
Eagles: Cory Aston; *Panthers:* Jacob Fairbank.
Penalty count: 4-3; **Half-time:** 12-18;
Referee: Scott Mikalauskas; **Attendance:** 1,327.

Saturday 29th July 2023

TOULOUSE OLYMPIQUE 64 KEIGHLEY COUGARS 0

OLYMPIQUE: 22 Zac Santo; 5 Paul Marcon; 4 Mathieu Jussaume; 18 Guy Armitage; 19 Benjamin Laguerre; 6 Josh Ralph; 7 Jake Shorrocks; 8 Lambert Belmas; 9 Calum Gahan; 10 Harrison Hansen; 24 Pierre-Jean Lima; 11 Maxime Stefani; 13 Anthony Marion. Subs (all used): 20 Greg Richards; 16 Joe Bretherton; 15 Sitaleki Akauola; 12 Dominique Peyroux.
Tries: Marion (5, 69), Ralph (9), Maxime Stefani (11, 31, 57), B Laguerre (16), Bretherton (37), Armitage (42, 74), Marcon (61); **Goals:** Shorrocks 10/11.
COUGARS: 1 Lewis Young; 5 Mo Agoro; 3 Charlie Graham; 42 Junior Sa'u; 2 Alix Stephenson; 9 Billy Gaylor; 21 Lloyd Roby; 43 Matty Laidlaw; 13 Kyle Kesik; 32 Jack Bibby; 19 Ellis Robson; 29 Joe Gibbons; 20 Brad Walker. Subs (all used): 26 Thomas Doyle; 45 Tom Nicholson-Watton; 38 Joe Hird; 11 Kyle Trout.
Rugby Leaguer & League Express Men of the Match:
Olympique: Anthony Marion; *Cougars:* Junior Sa'u.
Penalty count: 2-5; **Half-time:** 34-0;
Referee: Liam Rush; **Attendance:** 3,250.

FEATHERSTONE ROVERS 28 BATLEY BULLDOGS 8

ROVERS: 23 Caleb Aekins; 2 Luke Briscoe; 21 Joey Leilua; 3 Chris Hankinson; 5 Gareth Gale; 34 Dane Chisholm; 25 Thomas Lacans; 17 Gadwin Springer; 14 Matty Wildie; 10 James Lockwood; 31 Arama Hau; 12 Elijah Taylor; 32 Daniel Smith. Subs (all used): 9 Connor Jones; 15 John Davies; 24 Mathieu Cozza; 35 Ellis Longstaff.
Tries: Taylor (7), Wildie (19), Smith (47), Hau (55, 67);
Goals: Hankinson 4/5.
BULLDOGS: 32 Luke Hooley; 22 Dale Morton; 4 Josh Hodson; 18 George Senior; 21 Aidan McGowan; 14 James Meadows; 6 Ben White; 8 Adam Gledhill; 17 Luke Blake; 10 Keegan Hirst; 3 Kieran Buchanan; 11 Dane Manning; 30 Martyn Reilly. Subs (all used): 9 Alistair Leak; 16 Michael Ward; 20 Samy Kibula; 26 Nyle Flynn.
Tries: McGowan (36), Morton (61); **Goals:** Hooley 0/2.
Sin bin: Blake (78) - dissent.
Rugby Leaguer & League Express Men of the Match:
Rovers: Elijah Taylor; *Bulldogs:* Alistair Leak.
Penalty count: 7-7; **Half-time:** 12-4;
Referee: Ben Thaler; **Attendance:** 3,145.

Sunday 30th July 2023

LONDON BRONCOS 10 YORK KNIGHTS 24

BRONCOS: 1 Alex Walker; 2 Paul Ulberg; 3 Jarred Bassett; 19 Dean Whare; 5 Iliess Macani; 17 Henry Raiwalui; 20 Corey Norman; 15 Lewis Bienek; 9 Sam Davis; 33 Rob Butler; 11 Will Lovell; 36 Jacob Gannon; 13 Dean Parata. Subs (all used): 10 Jordan Williams; 12 Marcus Stock; 16 Ethan Natoli; 34 Matthew Davies.
Tries: Parata (4), Ulberg (40); **Goals:** Norman 1/2.
KNIGHTS: 2 Joe Brown; 29 Jason Bass; 4 Jesse Dee; 11 Chris Clarkson; 5 AJ Towse; 6 Ata Hingano; 7 Liam Harris; 30 Brenden Santi; 14 James Cunningham; 17 Ronan Michael; 32 Oli Field; 12 Danny Kirmond; 10 Conor Fitzsimmons. Subs (all used): 9 Will Jubb; 13 Jordan Thompson; 20 Jack Teanby; 21 Ukuma Ta'ai.
Tries: Field (7), Fitzsimmons (22), Bass (45), Jubb (75);
Goals: Harris 4/6.
Rugby Leaguer & League Express Men of the Match:
Broncos: Dean Parata; *Knights:* Ata Hingano.
Penalty count: 4-4; **Half-time:** 10-12;
Referee: Michael Smaill; **Attendance:** 957.

NEWCASTLE THUNDER 25 SWINTON LIONS 19

THUNDER: 6 Alex Donaghy; 2 Alex Young; 5 Alex Clegg; 3 Marcus Walker; 20 Gideon Boafo; 7 Nikau Williams; 27 Jack Miller; 8 Jay Chapelhow; 9 Curtis Davies; 10 Mitch Clark; 17 Rob Tuliatu; 12 Brad Gallagher; 13 Connor Bailey. Subs (all used): 40 Evan Simons; 14 Denive Balmforth; 23 Connor Moore; 18 Jake Lightowler.
Tries: Boafo (30, 80), Moore (39), Bailey (48);
Goals: Miller 4/5; **Field goal:** Williams (78).
Sin bin: Gallagher (36) - fighting.
LIONS: 26 Joey Romeo; 2 Mike Butt; 22 Andy Badrock; 3 Jake Spedding; 4 Jayden Hatton; 31 Will Roberts; 7 Jordy Gibson; 8 Gavin Bennion; 30 George Roby; 35 Lewis Hall; 11 Rhodri Lloyd; 12 Mitch Cox; 6 Nick Gregson. Subs (all used): 14 Josh Eaves; 15 Jordan Case; 16 Gav Rodden; 10 Kenny Baker.
Tries: Eaves (43), Hall (67), Butt (74); **Goals:** Gibson 3/3;
Field goal: Gibson (77).
Sin bin: Lloyd (36) - fighting.
Rugby Leaguer & League Express Men of the Match:
Thunder: Alex Donaghy; *Lions:* Jordy Gibson.
Penalty count: 7-6; **Half-time:** 10-0;
Referee: Matt Rossleigh; **Attendance:** 889.

WIDNES VIKINGS 36 WHITEHAVEN 28

VIKINGS: 20 Joe Edge; 5 Kieran Dixon; 26 Max Roberts; 3 Matty Fleming; 24 Ollie Brookes; 18 Joe Lyons; 7 Tom Gilmore; 16 Callum Field; 9 Matty Fozard; 12 Adam Lawton; 11 Sam Wilde; 17 Shane Grady; 19 Olly Davies. Subs (all used): 31 Tom Forber; 22 Aaron Brown; 8 Owen Farnworth; 27 Anthony Walker.
Tries: Edge (1, 22), Brookes (25), Farnworth (47), Grady (61), Davies (65); **Goals:** K Dixon 6/7.
WHITEHAVEN: 23 Josh Rourke; 2 Dave Eccleston; 3 Chris Taylor; 4 Curtis Teare; 26 Oscar Doran; 27 Jake Carter; 14 Jamie Doran; 22 Lucas Castle; 15 James Newton; 16 Lasarusa Tabu; 11 Connor Holliday; 19 Ryan King; 17 Guy Graham. Subs (all used): 13 Dion Aiye; 9 Will Groves; 12 Lachlan Lanskey; 24 Daniel Spencer-Tonks.
Tries: Castle (6), Eccleston (30, 39), King (52), Graham (80); **Goals:** Rourke 4/5.
Rugby Leaguer & League Express Men of the Match:
Vikings: Joe Edge; *Whitehaven:* Ryan King.
Penalty count: 9-4; **Half-time:** 16-16;
Referee: James Vella; **Attendance:** 2,785.

Monday 31st July 2023

BRADFORD BULLS 10 BARROW RAIDERS 14

BULLS: 1 Tom Holmes; 2 Ben Blackmore; 30 Jayden Myers; 4 Kieran Gill; 28 Jorge Taufua; 6 Dec Patton; 29 Lee Gaskell; 24 Masi Matongo; 9 George Flanagan; 10 Michael Lawrence; 3 Joe Arundel; 15 AJ Wallace; 37 Jason Baitieri. Subs (all used): 18 Keven Appo; 21 Fenton Rogers; 14 Ebon Scurr; 7 Jordan Lilley.
Tries: Myers (54), Blackmore (75); **Goals:** Gaskell 1/2.
Dismissal: Taufua (32) - biting Stack.
RAIDERS: 24 Luke Broadbent; 5 Ryan Shaw; 26 Zach Eckersley; 2 Shane Toal; 27 Andrew Bulman; 31 Adam Jackson; 7 Ryan Johnston; 8 Greg Burke; 22 Josh Wood; 30 Harvey Makin; 11 Danny Langtree; 12 Jarrad Stack; 4 Greg Worthington. Subs (all used): 1 Luke Cresswell; 17 Charlie Emslie; 25 Kavan Rothwell; 32 Tom Wilkinson.
Try: Shaw (58); **Goals:** Shaw 5/8.
Rugby Leaguer & League Express Men of the Match:
Bulls: Ebon Scurr; *Raiders:* Ryan Johnston.
Penalty count: 9-17; **Half-time:** 0-8;
Referee: Cameron Worsley; **Attendance:** 2,862.

ROUND 21

Saturday 5th August 2023

NEWCASTLE THUNDER 6 WIDNES VIKINGS 50

THUNDER: 6 Alex Donaghy; 2 Alex Young; 3 Marcus Walker; 5 Alex Clegg; 20 Gideon Boafo; 13 Connor Bailey; 27 Jack Miller; 8 Jay Chapelhow; 9 Curtis Davies; 10 Mitch Clark; 29 Paddy Burns; 12 Brad Gallagher; 17 Rob Tuliatu. Subs (all used): 40 Evan Simons; 14 Denive Balmforth; 23 Connor Moore; 18 Jake Lightowler.
Try: Balmforth (59); **Goals:** Donaghy 1/1.
VIKINGS: 20 Joe Edge; 5 Kieran Dixon; 26 Max Roberts; 3 Matty Fleming; 24 Ollie Brookes; 18 Joe Lyons; 7 Tom Gilmore; 16 Callum Field; 9 Matty Fozard; 12 Adam Lawton; 11 Sam Wilde; 17 Shane Grady; 22 Aaron Brown. Subs (all used): 31 Tom Forber; 27 Anthony Walker; 21 Lewis Hatton; 19 Olly Davies.
Tries: Roberts (10, 29), Lyons (18), Wilde (27, 52), K Dixon (39), Gilmore (44), Field (62), Brookes (69), Fleming (76); **Goals:** K Dixon 5/10.
Rugby Leaguer & League Express Men of the Match:
Thunder: Denive Balmforth; *Vikings:* Max Roberts.
Penalty count: 2-5; **Half-time:** 0-26;
Referee: Michael Smaill; **Attendance:** 2,206.

YORK KNIGHTS 14 TOULOUSE OLYMPIQUE 18

KNIGHTS: 2 Joe Brown; 5 AJ Towse; 33 Oliver Pratt; 4 Jesse Dee; 29 Jason Bass; 6 Ata Hingano; 7 Liam Harris; 17

Championship 2023 - Round by Round

Ronan Michael; 9 Will Jubb; 10 Conor Fitzsimmons; 32 Oli Field; 12 Danny Kirmond; 13 Jordan Thompson. Subs (all used): 20 Jack Teanby; 21 Ukuma Ta'ai; 30 Brenden Santi; 35 Toby Warren.
Tries: Bass (30, 44), Santi (56); **Goals:** Harris 1/3.
OLYMPIQUE: 22 Zac Santo; 19 Benjamin Laguerre; 18 Guy Armitage; 4 Mathieu Jussaume; 5 Paul Marcon; 13 Anthony Marion; 7 Jake Shorrocks; 16 Joe Bretherton; 9 Calum Gahan; 27 Dimitri Biscarro; 11 Maxime Stefani; 12 Dominique Peyroux; 10 Harrison Hansen. Subs (all used): 14 Eloi Pelissier; 15 Sitaleki Akauola; 20 Greg Richards; 25 Ramon Silva.
Tries: Armitage (15), Richards (36), Marion (71);
Goals: Shorrocks 3/3.
Rugby Leaguer & League Express Men of the Match:
Knights: Oliver Pratt; *Olympique:* Jake Shorrocks.
Penalty count: 3-3; **Half-time:** 4-12;
Referee: Ben Thaler; **Attendance:** 1,483.

Sunday 6th August 2023

BARROW RAIDERS 6 LONDON BRONCOS 26

RAIDERS: 24 Luke Broadbent; 5 Ryan Shaw; 3 Rio-Osayomwanbo Corkill; 2 Shane Toal; 27 Andrew Bulman; 31 Adam Jackson; 7 Ryan Johnston; 8 Greg Burke; 22 Josh Wood; 30 Harvey Makin; 17 Charlie Emslie; 12 Jarrad Stack; 4 Greg Worthington. Subs (all used): 1 Luke Cresswell; 32 Tom Wilkinson; 20 Ben Evans; 21 Jack Billington.
Try: Corkill (54); **Goals:** Shaw 1/1.
BRONCOS: 1 Alex Walker; 4 Dalton Grant; 3 Jarred Bassett; 19 Dean Whare; 5 Iliess Macani; 6 Oliver Leyland; 20 Corey Norman; 15 Lewis Bienek; 14 Bill Leyland; 33 Rob Butler; 11 Will Lovell; 16 Ethan Natoli; 13 Dean Parata. Subs (all used): 10 Jordan Williams; 12 Marcus Stock; 23 Daniel Hoyes; 34 Matthew Davies.
Tries: Norman (4), Whare (9, 60), Bienek (24), Grant (32);
Goals: Norman 3/5.
Rugby Leaguer & League Express Men of the Match:
Raiders: Charlie Emslie; *Broncos:* Corey Norman.
Penalty count: 7-6; **Half-time:** 0-20;
Referee: Matt Rossleigh; **Attendance:** 1,786.

BATLEY BULLDOGS 6 BRADFORD BULLS 42

BULLDOGS: 21 Aidan McGowan; 22 Dale Morton; 4 Josh Hodson; 18 George Senior; 15 Elliot Kear; 14 James Meadows; 7 Josh Woods; 8 Adam Gledhill; 6 Ben White; 13 James Brown; 11 Dane Manning; 3 Kieran Buchanan; 30 Martyn Reilly. Subs (all used): 9 Alistair Leak; 26 Nyle Flynn; 16 Michael Ward; 20 Samy Kibula.
Try: McGowan (32); **Goals:** Meadows 1/1.
BULLS: 1 Tom Holmes; 2 Ben Blackmore; 30 Jayden Myers; 4 Kieran Gill; 28 Jorge Taufua; 29 Lee Gaskell; 7 Jordan Lilley; 10 Michael Lawrence; 9 George Flanagan; 21 Fenton Rogers; 3 Joe Arundel; 15 AJ Wallace; 37 Jason Baitieri. Subs (all used): 23 James Segeyaro; 18 Keven Appo; 14 Ebon Scurr; 24 Masi Matongo.
Tries: Taufua (2), Blackmore (21, 62), Wallace (55, 70), Appo (57), Scurr (65), Lawrence (80); **Goals:** Lilley 5/8.
Rugby Leaguer & League Express Men of the Match:
Bulldogs: Samy Kibula; *Bulls:* Ben Blackmore.
Penalty count: 6-6; **Half-time:** 6-10;
Referee: James Vella; **Attendance:** 2,780.

SWINTON LIONS 18 KEIGHLEY COUGARS 10

LIONS: 1 Dan Abram; 2 Mike Butt; 11 Rhodri Lloyd; 3 Jake Spedding; 4 Jayden Hatton; 32 Robbie Butterworth; 7 Jordy Gibson; 8 Gavin Bennion; 30 George Roby; 35 Lewis Hall; 34 Matthew Foster; 12 Mitch Cox; 6 Nick Gregson. Subs (all used): 31 Cain Robb; 25 Scott Parnaby; 10 Kenny Baker; 17 Dane Windrow.
Tries: Foster (13), Abram (59), Butterworth (77);
Goals: Abram 3/4.
COUGARS: 1 Lewis Young; 3 Charlie Graham; 42 Junior Sa'u; 23 Robbie Storey; 5 Mo Agoro; 46 Oscar Thomas; 20 Brad Walker; 24 Mark Ioane; 26 Thomas Doyle; 11 Kyle Trout; 19 Ellis Robson; 27 Sadiq Adebiyi; 13 Kyle Kesik. Subs (all used): 21 Lloyd Roby; 8 Dan Parker; 32 Jack Bibby; 45 Tom Nicholson-Watton.
Tries: Young (35), Robson (68); **Goals:** Thomas 1/2.
Sin bin: Young (42) - high tackle on Abram.
Rugby Leaguer & League Express Men of the Match:
Lions: Dan Abram; *Cougars:* Oscar Thomas.
Penalty count: 6-3; **Half-time:** 8-6;
Referee: Nick Bennett; **Attendance:** 1,179.

WHITEHAVEN 32 SHEFFIELD EAGLES 20

WHITEHAVEN: 23 Josh Rourke; 2 Dave Eccleston; 3 Chris Taylor; 4 Curtis Teare; 26 Oscar Doran; 19 Ryan King; 14 Jamie Doran; 22 Lucas Castle; 15 James Newton; 16 Lasarusa Tabu; 11 Connor Holliday; 12 Lachlan Lanskey; 17 Guy Graham. Subs (all used): 13 Dion Aiye; 18 Perry Singleton; 20 George Hill; 24 Daniel Spencer-Tonks.
Tries: Teare (26), Rourke (37), Eccleston (44), O Doran (52), Spencer-Tonks (56), King (74); **Goals:** Rourke 4/6.
EAGLES: 29 Quentin Laulu-Togaga'e; 2 Ben Jones-Bishop; 4 Ross Oakes; 33 James Glover; 28 Matty Dawson-Jones; 32 Cory Aston; 7 Anthony Thackeray; 17 Liam Kirk; 19 Jack Hansen; 15 Mikey Wood; 11 Connor Bower; 27 Jesse Sene-Lefao; 13 Evan Hodgson. Subs (all used): 9 Vila Halafihi; 14 Titus Gwaze; 23 Bayley Liu; 8 Brandon Douglas.
Tries: Thackeray (2), Hansen (10), Dawson-Jones (20), Liu (61); **Goals:** Aston 2/4.
Rugby Leaguer & League Express Men of the Match:
Whitehaven: Dion Aiye; *Eagles:* Jack Hansen.
Penalty count: 6-2; **Half-time:** 12-14;
Referee: Scott Mikalauskas; **Attendance:** 720.

HALIFAX PANTHERS 25 FEATHERSTONE ROVERS 22

PANTHERS: 18 Brandon Pickersgill; 2 Lachlan Walmsley; 22 Jake Maizen; 35 Ben Crooks; 5 James Saltonstall; 6 Louis Jouffret; 1 James Woodburn-Hall; 16 Will Calcott; 9 Brandon Moore; 10 Dan Murray; 11 Ben Kavanagh; 12 Matty Gee; 31 Kevin Larroyer. Subs (all used): 8 Adam Tangata; 19 Ryan Lannon; 29 Dan Fleming; 34 Adam O'Brien.
Tries: Woodburn-Hall (7, 47), Gee (18), Maizen (22);
Goals: Jouffret 4/5; **Field goal:** Woodburn-Hall (73).
ROVERS: 20 Mark Kheirallah; 2 Luke Briscoe; 21 Joey Leilua; 3 Chris Hankinson; 5 Gareth Gale; 23 Caleb Aekins; 33 Logan Astley; 17 Gadwin Springer; 14 Matty Wildie; 10 James Lockwood; 31 Arama Hau; 35 Ellis Longstaff; 12 Elijah Taylor. Subs (all used): 8 Craig Kopczak; 9 Connor Jones; 24 Mathieu Cozza; 32 Daniel Smith.
Tries: Springer (3), Kheirallah (11), Kopczak (28), Briscoe (78); **Goals:** Kheirallah 3/4.
Sin bin: Kheirallah (15) - professional foul.
Rugby Leaguer & League Express Men of the Match:
Panthers: James Woodburn-Hall; *Rovers:* Luke Briscoe.
Penalty count: 5-5; **Half-time:** 16-18;
Referee: Liam Rush; **Attendance:** 1,609.

ROUND 22

Friday 18th August 2023

SHEFFIELD EAGLES 10 FEATHERSTONE ROVERS 38

EAGLES: 29 Quentin Laulu-Togaga'e; 2 Ben Jones-Bishop; 33 James Glover; 23 Bayley Liu; 28 Matty Dawson-Jones; 32 Cory Aston; 7 Anthony Thackeray; 15 Mikey Wood; 9 Vila Halafihi; 10 Tyler Dickinson; 11 Connor Bower; 27 Jesse Sene-Lefao; 14 Titus Gwaze. Subs (all used): 13 Evan Hodgson; 16 Blake Broadbent; 17 Liam Kirk; 19 Jack Hansen.
Tries: Jones-Bishop (6), Dawson-Jones (36);
Goals: Aston 1/2.
ROVERS: 20 Mark Kheirallah; 2 Luke Briscoe; 21 Joey Leilua; 3 Chris Hankinson; 5 Gareth Gale; 23 Caleb Aekins; 34 Dane Chisholm; 8 Craig Kopczak; 14 Matty Wildie; 10 James Lockwood; 31 Arama Hau; 12 Elijah Taylor; 32 Daniel Smith. Subs (all used): 9 Connor Jones; 15 John Davies; 16 Junior Moors; 17 Gadwin Springer.
Tries: Hau (12, 29), Aekins (33), Moors (39), Hankinson (47), Chisholm (54), Gale (63); **Goals:** Kheirallah 5/7.
Rugby Leaguer & League Express Men of the Match:
Eagles: Titus Gwaze; *Rovers:* Arama Hau.
Penalty count: 4-3; **Half-time:** 10-24;
Referee: James Vella; **Attendance:** 1,709.

Saturday 19th August 2023

TOULOUSE OLYMPIQUE 26 SWINTON LIONS 6

OLYMPIQUE: 22 Zac Santo; 5 Paul Marcon; 24 Pierre-Jean Lima; 18 Guy Armitage; 19 Benjamin Laguerre; 13 Anthony Marion; 23 Robin Brochon; 8 Lambert Belmas; 9 Calum Gahan; 27 Dimitri Biscarro; 16 Joe Bretherton; 11 Maxime Stefani; 10 Harrison Hansen. Subs (all used): 14 Eloi Pelissier; 20 Greg Richards; 15 Sitaleki Akauola; 26 Ramon Silva.
Tries: Brochon (36, 66), Bretherton (61), Marion (76), Akauola (79); **Goals:** Brochon 3/5.
Sin bin: Akauola (28) - dangerous challenge on Case.
LIONS: 1 Dan Abram; 5 Richard Lepori; 22 Andy Badrock; 4 Jayden Hatton; 26 Joey Romeo; 32 Robbie Butterworth; 7 Jordy Gibson; 13 Louis Brogan; 30 George Roby; 8 Gavin Bennion; 12 Mitch Cox; 16 Gav Rodden; 6 Nick Gregson. Subs (all used): 31 Cain Robb; 15 Jordan Case; 11 Rhodri Lloyd; 10 Kenny Baker.
Try: Abram (7); **Goals:** Abram 1/1.
Sin bin: Roby (78) - holding down.
Rugby Leaguer & League Express Men of the Match:
Olympique: Robin Brochon; *Lions:* Jordy Gibson.
Penalty count: 8-4; **Half-time:** 4-6;
Referee: Nick Bennett; **Attendance:** 2,430
(at Stade Albert Domec, Carcassonne).

Sunday 20th August 2023

BRADFORD BULLS 36 NEWCASTLE THUNDER 8

BULLS: 1 Tom Holmes; 2 Ben Blackmore; 30 Jayden Myers; 4 Kieran Gill; 5 David Foggin-Johnston; 29 Lee Gaskell; 7 Jordan Lilley; 10 Michael Lawrence; 9 George Flanagan; 21 Fenton Rogers; 3 Joe Arundel; 15 AJ Wallace; 37 Jason Baitieri. Subs (all used): 20 Billy Jowitt; 18 Keven Appo; 14 Ebon Scurr; 41 Eribe Doro.
Tries: Flanagan (12, 78), Holmes (16), Arundel (30), Lilley (43), Gill (66); **Goals:** Lilley 6/6.
THUNDER: 6 Alex Donaghy; 1 Jack Johnson; 26 Mac Walsh; 3 Marcus Walker; 20 Gideon Boafo; 7 Nikau Williams; 14 Denive Balmforth; 8 Jay Chapelhow; 9 Curtis Davies; 23 Connor Moore; 5 Alex Clegg; 17 Rob Tuliatu; 13 Connor Bailey. Subs (all used): 40 Evan Simons; 18 Jake Lightowler; 28 Tyler Walton; 21 Evan Lawther.
Tries: Tuliatu (23), Clegg (52); **Goals:** Williams 0/2.
Rugby Leaguer & League Express Men of the Match:
Bulls: Jordan Lilley; *Thunder:* Evan Simons.
Penalty count: 4-1; **Half-time:** 18-4;
Referee: Kevin Moore; **Attendance:** 2,685.

KEIGHLEY COUGARS 26 BATLEY BULLDOGS 20

COUGARS: 46 Oscar Thomas; 5 Mo Agoro; 23 Robbie Storey; 42 Junior Sa'u; 3 Charlie Graham; 40 Kieran Rush; 21 Lloyd Roby; 24 Mark Ioane; 26 Thomas Doyle; 11 Kyle Trout; 27 Sadiq Adebiyi; 19 Ellis Robson; 13 Kyle Kesik. Subs (all used): 45 Tom Nicholson-Watton; 32 Jack Bibby; 8 Dan Parker; 14 Harvey Spence.
Tries: Kesik (8), Robson (29), Agoro (57, 67);
Goals: Thomas 5/5.
Sin bin: Storey (20) - professional foul.
BULLDOGS: 21 Aidan McGowan; 22 Dale Morton; 4 Josh Hodson; 3 Kieran Buchanan; 29 Greg Johnson; 14 James Meadows; 7 Josh Woods; 8 Adam Gledhill; 6 Ben White; 13 James Brown; 11 Dane Manning; 12 Lucas Walshaw; 30 Martyn Reilly. Subs (all used): 9 Alistair Leak; 26 Nyle Flynn; 16 Michael Ward; 20 Samy Kibula.
Tries: McGowan (18, 52), Morton (63), Meadows (77);
Goals: Meadows 2/4.
Rugby Leaguer & League Express Men of the Match:
Cougars: Oscar Thomas; *Bulldogs:* Aidan McGowan.
Penalty count: 4-6; **Half-time:** 14-6;
Referee: Scott Mikalauskas; **Attendance:** 1,468.

LONDON BRONCOS 26 HALIFAX PANTHERS 12

BRONCOS: 1 Alex Walker; 4 Dalton Grant; 3 Jarred Bassett; 19 Dean Whare; 5 Iliess Macani; 6 Oliver Leyland; 20 Corey Norman; 15 Lewis Bienek; 14 Bill Leyland; 33 Rob Butler; 11 Will Lovell; 16 Ethan Natoli; 13 Dean Parata. Subs (all used): 8 Wellington Albert; 10 Jordan Williams; 12 Marcus Stock; 34 Matthew Davies.
Tries: Bienek (11), Walker (16, 29), Macani (47, 59);
Goals: Norman 2/4, O Leyland 1/1.
Sin bin: Norman (21) - late challenge.
PANTHERS: 18 Brandon Pickersgill; 2 Lachlan Walmsley; 22 Jake Maizen; 35 Ben Crooks; 5 James Saltonstall; 6 Louis Jouffret; 1 James Woodburn-Hall; 16 Will Calcott; 9 Brandon Moore; 10 Dan Murray; 11 Ben Kavanagh; 12 Matty Gee; 13 Jacob Fairbank. Subs (all used): 8 Adam Tangata; 19 Ryan Lannon; 33 Alex Sutcliffe; 34 Adam O'Brien.
Tries: Maizen (1), Walmsley (37); **Goals:** Jouffret 2/2.
Rugby Leaguer & League Express Men of the Match:
Broncos: Alex Walker; *Panthers:* Louis Jouffret.
Penalty count: 3-2; **Half-time:** 18-12;
Referee: Liam Rush; **Attendance:** 859.

WIDNES VIKINGS 30 YORK KNIGHTS 40

VIKINGS: 20 Joe Edge; 5 Kieran Dixon; 26 Max Roberts; 3 Matty Fleming; 24 Ollie Brookes; 18 Joe Lyons; 7 Tom Gilmore; 16 Callum Field; 9 Matty Fozard; 12 Adam Lawton; 11 Sam Wilde; 17 Shane Grady; 22 Aaron Brown. Subs (all used): 8 Owen Farnworth; 19 Olly Davies; 21 Lewis Hatton; 31 Tom Forber.
Tries: Wilde (14), Brookes (22), Farnworth (39), Edge (70), K Dixon (79); **Goals:** K Dixon 4/6, Gilmore 1/1.
KNIGHTS: 2 Joe Brown; 5 AJ Towse; 11 Chris Clarkson; 4 Jesse Dee; 29 Jason Bass; 6 Ata Hingano; 7 Liam Harris; 30 Brenden Santi; 9 Will Jubb; 10 Conor Fitzsimmons; 32 Oli Field; 12 Danny Kirmond; 13 Jordan Thompson. Subs (all used): 17 Ronan Michael; 33 Oliver Pratt; 34 Taylor Pemberton; 35 Toby Warren.
Tries: Dee (7), Pemberton (33), Pratt (50), Field (53, 65), Towse (56), Fitzsimmons (61); **Goals:** Harris 6/7.
Rugby Leaguer & League Express Men of the Match:
Vikings: Matty Fozard; *Knights:* Liam Harris.
Penalty count: 6-3; **Half-time:** 20-12;
Referee: Michael Smaill; **Attendance:** 3,008.

Monday 21st August 2023

WHITEHAVEN 22 BARROW RAIDERS 23

WHITEHAVEN: 23 Josh Rourke; 2 Dave Eccleston; 3 Chris Taylor; 4 Curtis Teare; 26 Oscar Doran; 27 Jake Carter; 14 Jamie Doran; 22 Lucas Castle; 15 James Newton; 28 Ross Ainley; 11 Connor Holliday; 19 Ryan King; 17 Guy Graham.

Championship 2023 - Round by Round

Subs (all used): 13 Dion Aiye; 18 Perry Singleton; 20 George Hill; 24 Daniel Spencer-Tonks.
Tries: O Doran (10), Holliday (34), Carter (39), King (59); **Goals:** Rourke 3/5.
RAIDERS: 24 Luke Broadbent; 5 Ryan Shaw; 18 Brett Carter; 2 Shane Toal; 27 Andrew Bulman; 31 Adam Jackson; 7 Ryan Johnston; 8 Greg Burke; 22 Josh Wood; 4 Greg Worthington; 17 Charlie Emslie; 12 Jarrad Stack; 32 Tom Wilkinson. Subs (all used): 1 Luke Cresswell; 3 Rio-Osayomwanbo Corkill; 20 Ben Evans; 21 Jack Billington.
Tries: Stack (2), Bulman (23), Wilkinson (47), Evans (59); **Goals:** Shaw 3/4; **Field goal:** Johnston (80).
Rugby Leaguer & League Express Men of the Match: *Whitehaven:* Ryan King; *Raiders:* Adam Jackson.
Penalty count: 7-6; **Half-time:** 14-10;
Referee: Matt Rossleigh; **Attendance:** 1,176.

ROUND 23

Friday 25th August 2023

BATLEY BULLDOGS 6 SHEFFIELD EAGLES 49

BULLDOGS: 14 James Meadows; 22 Dale Morton; 4 Josh Hodson; 3 Kieran Buchanan; 15 Elliot Kear; 6 Ben White; 7 Josh Woods; 20 Samy Kibula; 24 Ben Kaye; 30 Martyn Reilly; 11 Dane Manning; 12 Lucas Walshaw; 26 Nyle Flynn. Subs (all used): 9 Alistair Leak; 16 Michael Ward; 17 Luke Blake; 18 George Senior.
Try: Meadows (13); **Goals:** Morton 1/1.
EAGLES: 29 Quentin Laulu-Togaga'e; 2 Ben Jones-Bishop; 4 Ross Oakes; 33 James Glover; 28 Matty Dawson-Jones; 32 Cory Aston; 7 Anthony Thackeray; 15 Mikey Wood; 9 Vila Halafihi; 10 Tyler Dickinson; 11 Connor Bower; 23 Bayley Liu; 14 Titus Gwaze. Subs (all used): 13 Evan Hodgson; 16 Blake Broadbent; 18 Aaron Murphy; 19 Jack Hansen.
Tries: Liu (7), Oakes (29, 71), Jones-Bishop (44, 56), Thackeray (54, 61, 80); **Goals:** Aston 6/7, Hansen 2/2;
Field goal: Thackeray (79).
Sin bin: Halafihi (12) - dangerous challenge.
Rugby Leaguer & League Express Men of the Match: *Bulldogs:* Samy Kibula; *Eagles:* Anthony Thackeray.
Penalty count: 3-2; **Half-time:** 6-12;
Referee: Liam Rush; **Attendance:** 1,209.

NEWCASTLE THUNDER 6 YORK KNIGHTS 20

THUNDER: 6 Alex Donaghy; 1 Jack Johnson; 26 Mac Walsh; 3 Marcus Walker; 20 Gideon Boafo; 14 Denive Balmforth; 7 Nikau Williams; 8 Jay Chapelhow; 9 Curtis Davies; 23 Connor Moore; 5 Alex Clegg; 17 Rob Tuliatu; 13 Connor Bailey. Subs (all used): 40 Evan Simons; 18 Jake Lightowler; 28 Tyler Walton; 10 Mitch Clark.
Try: Boafo (45); **Goals:** Williams 1/1.
KNIGHTS: 2 Joe Brown; 5 AJ Towse; 11 Chris Clarkson; 33 Oliver Pratt; 29 Jason Bass; 4 Jesse Dee; 7 Liam Harris; 30 Brenden Santi; 9 Will Jubb; 10 Conor Fitzsimmons; 32 Oli Field; 12 Danny Kirmond; 13 Jordan Thompson. Subs (all used): 15 Myles Harrison; 17 Ronan Michael; 34 Taylor Pemberton; 35 Toby Warren.
Tries: Jubb (9), Harrison (52, 80); **Goals:** Harris 4/4.
Rugby Leaguer & League Express Men of the Match: *Thunder:* Gideon Boafo; *Knights:* Myles Harrison.
Penalty count: 5-3; **Half-time:** 0-6;
Referee: Ryan Cox; **Attendance:** 788.

Saturday 26th August 2023

TOULOUSE OLYMPIQUE 34 BARROW RAIDERS 10

OLYMPIQUE: 22 Zac Santo; 5 Paul Marcon; 24 Pierre-Jean Lima; 25 Matthieu Laguerre; 19 Benjamin Laguerre; 23 Robin Brochon; 7 Jake Shorrocks; 10 Harrison Hansen; 9 Calum Gahan; 16 Joe Bretherton; 12 Dominique Peyroux; 11 Maxime Stefani; 13 Anthony Marion. Subs (all used): 14 Eloi Pelissier; 20 Greg Richards; 15 Sitaleki Akauola; 26 Ramon Silva.
Tries: B Laguerre (9), Richards (20), Marion (38), Pelissier (53, 76), Santo (66);
Goals: Shorrocks 4/5, Brochon 1/1.
Sin bin: Marion (46) - dangerous challenge.
RAIDERS: 1 Luke Cresswell; 18 Brett Carter; 25 Keanan Brand; 2 Shane Toal; 27 Andrew Bulman; 31 Adam Jackson; 7 Ryan Johnston; 8 Greg Burke; 6 Jarrod Sammut; 4 Greg Worthington; 17 Charlie Emslie; 5 Ryan Shaw; 22 Josh Wood. Subs (all used): 23 Connor Saunders; 20 Ben Evans; 21 Jack Billington; 3 Rio-Osayomwanbo Corkill.
Tries: Bulman (16, 71); **Goals:** Shaw 1/2.
Rugby Leaguer & League Express Men of the Match: *Olympique:* Eloi Pelissier; *Raiders:* Ryan Johnston.
Penalty count: 4-4; **Half-time:** 18-6;
Referee: Michael Smaill; **Attendance:** 2,487 *(at Stade Mazicou, Albi).*

Sunday 27th August 2023

FEATHERSTONE ROVERS 36 KEIGHLEY COUGARS 6

ROVERS: 20 Mark Kheirallah; 2 Luke Briscoe; 3 Chris Hankinson; 21 Joey Leilua; 5 Gareth Gale; 23 Caleb Aekins; 34 Dane Chisholm; 10 James Lockwood; 9 Connor Jones; 8 Craig Kopczak; 31 Arama Hau; 12 Elijah Taylor; 32 Daniel Smith. Subs (all used): 6 Johnathon Ford; 15 John Davies; 16 Junior Moors; 24 Mathieu Cozza.
Tries: Kheirallah (13, 48), Gale (33, 80), Jones (35, 43), Leilua (67); **Goals:** Kheirallah 4/7.
COUGARS: 1 Lewis Young; 3 Charlie Graham; 42 Junior Sa'u; 23 Robbie Storey; 5 Mo Agoro; 46 Oscar Thomas; 40 Kieran Rush; 24 Mark Ioane; 13 Kyle Kesik; 43 Matty Laidlaw; 19 Ellis Robson; 27 Sadiq Adebiyi; 11 Kyle Trout. Subs (all used): 8 Dan Parker; 9 Billy Gaylor; 32 Jack Bibby; 45 Tom Nicholson-Watton.
Try: Adebiyi (74); **Goals:** Thomas 1/1.
Rugby Leaguer & League Express Men of the Match: *Rovers:* Mark Kheirallah; *Cougars:* Lewis Young.
Penalty count: 5-1; **Half-time:** 18-0;
Referee: James Vella; **Attendance:** 3,235.

HALIFAX PANTHERS 26 WIDNES VIKINGS 28

PANTHERS: 18 Brandon Pickersgill; 2 Lachlan Walmsley; 28 Alex Sutcliffe; 35 Ben Crooks; 5 James Saltonstall; 6 Louis Jouffret; 7 Joe Keyes; 10 Dan Murray; 9 Brandon Moore; 16 Will Calcott; 11 Ben Kavanagh; 12 Matty Gee; 13 Jacob Fairbank. Subs (all used): 3 Zack McComb; 8 Adam Tangata; 19 Ryan Lannon; 34 Adam O'Brien.
Tries: Crooks (17, 79), Tangata (32), Saltonstall (61);
Goals: Jouffret 5/5.
VIKINGS: 1 Jack Owens; 2 Ryan Ince; 3 Matty Fleming; 20 Joe Edge; 5 Kieran Dixon; 6 Danny Craven; 7 Tom Gilmore; 16 Callum Field; 9 Matty Fozard; 8 Owen Farnworth; 11 Sam Wilde; 17 Shane Grady; 22 Aaron Brown. Subs (all used): 31 Tom Forber; 19 Olly Davies; 32 Huw Worthington; 26 Max Roberts.
Tries: Ince (5, 10, 28), Craven (55), Owens (58);
Goals: K Dixon 4/7.
Sin bin: Craven (77) - late challenge on Jouffret.
Rugby Leaguer & League Express Men of the Match: *Panthers:* Louis Jouffret; *Vikings:* Ryan Ince.
Penalty count: 5-8; **Half-time:** 14-14;
Referee: Cameron Worsley; **Attendance:** 1,685.

LONDON BRONCOS 34 WHITEHAVEN 18

BRONCOS: 1 Alex Walker; 4 Dalton Grant; 3 Jarred Bassett; 19 Dean Whare; 5 Iliess Macani; 6 Oliver Leyland; 20 Corey Norman; 15 Lewis Bienek; 14 Bill Leyland; 33 Rob Butler; 11 Will Lovell; 16 Ethan Natoli; 13 Dean Parata. Subs (all used): 7 Rian Horsman; 8 Wellington Albert; 10 Jordan Williams; 12 Marcus Stock.
Tries: O Leyland (12), B Leyland (16), Whare (29), Bassett (32, 68), Grant (36, 52);
Goals: Norman 2/5, O Leyland 1/2.
WHITEHAVEN: 23 Josh Rourke; 2 Dave Eccleston; 3 Chris Taylor; 4 Curtis Teare; 6 Brad Holroyd; 27 Jake Carter; 14 Jamie Doran; 22 Lucas Castle; 15 James Newton; 24 Daniel Spencer-Tonks; 11 Connor Holliday; 12 Lachlan Lanskey; 17 Guy Graham. Subs (all used): 13 Dion Aiye; 16 Lasarusa Tabu; 18 Perry Singleton; 20 George Hill.
Tries: Eccleston (40), Lanskey (58), Rourke (79);
Goals: Rourke 3/3.
Rugby Leaguer & League Express Men of the Match: *Broncos:* Oliver Leyland; *Whitehaven:* Josh Rourke.
Penalty count: 1-3; **Half-time:** 24-6;
Referee: Nick Bennett; **Attendance:** 786.

SWINTON LIONS 26 BRADFORD BULLS 42

LIONS: 1 Dan Abram; 4 Jayden Hatton; 3 Jake Spedding; 2 Mike Butt; 5 Richard Lepori; 32 Robbie Butterworth; 7 Jordy Gibson; 13 Louis Brogan; 31 Cain Robb; 8 Gavin Bennion; 11 Rhodri Lloyd; 12 Mitch Cox; 6 Nick Gregson. Subs (all used): 30 George Roby; 15 Jordan Case; 35 Lewis Hall; 16 Gav Rodden.
Tries: Hatton (6), Lepori (18), Butt (55), Spedding (57), Rodden (72); **Goals:** Abram 3/5.
Sin bin: Spedding (31) - holding down.
BULLS: 1 Tom Holmes; 27 Connor Wynne; 30 Jayden Myers; 4 Kieran Gill; 5 David Foggin-Johnston; 29 Lee Gaskell; 7 Jordan Lilley; 10 Michael Lawrence; 9 George Flanagan; 21 Fenton Rogers; 3 Joe Arundel; 15 AJ Wallace; 37 Jason Baitieri. Subs (all used): 20 Billy Jowitt; 18 Keven Appo; 14 Ebon Scurr; 41 Eribe Doro.
Tries: Gill (2), Scurr (27), Appo (32), Lilley (38), Myers (45), Foggin-Johnston (51, 68), Rogers (78);
Goals: Lilley 5/8.
Rugby Leaguer & League Express Men of the Match: *Lions:* Louis Brogan; *Bulls:* Jordan Lilley.
Penalty count: 4-9; **Half-time:** 8-22;
Referee: Scott Mikalauskas; **Attendance:** 1,073.

ROUND 24

Saturday 2nd September 2023

NEWCASTLE THUNDER 16 TOULOUSE OLYMPIQUE 36

THUNDER: 6 Alex Donaghy; 1 Jack Johnson; 26 Mac Walsh; 3 Marcus Walker; 20 Gideon Boafo; 14 Denive Balmforth; 7 Nikau Williams; 8 Jay Chapelhow; 9 Curtis Davies; 10 Mitch Clark; 5 Alex Clegg; 17 Rob Tuliatu; 13 Connor Bailey. Subs (all used): 40 Evan Simons; 18 Jake Lightowler; 28 Tyler Walton; 23 Connor Moore.
Tries: Johnson (17, 39), Boafo (61); **Goals:** Williams 2/3.
OLYMPIQUE: 22 Zac Santo; 5 Paul Marcon; 24 Pierre-Jean Lima; 18 Guy Armitage; 19 Benjamin Laguerre; 23 Robin Brochon; 7 Jake Shorrocks; 10 Harrison Hansen; 9 Calum Gahan; 20 Greg Richards; 12 Dominique Peyroux; 11 Maxime Stefani; 13 Anthony Marion. Subs (all used): 14 Eloi Pelissier; 26 Ramon Silva; 28 Wail Skoundri; 25 Justin Tropis.
Tries: Marion (7), Silva (34), Santo (36, 72), Maxime Stefani (49), Richards (75); **Goals:** Shorrocks 6/6.
Rugby Leaguer & League Express Men of the Match: *Thunder:* Mac Walsh; *Olympique:* Zac Santo.
Penalty count: 5-7; **Half-time:** 10-18;
Referee: Matt Rossleigh; **Attendance:** 639.

Sunday 3rd September 2023

BRADFORD BULLS 8 FEATHERSTONE ROVERS 16

BULLS: 1 Tom Holmes; 30 Jayden Myers; 3 Joe Arundel; 4 Kieran Gill; 5 David Foggin-Johnston; 7 Jordan Lilley; 29 Lee Gaskell; 10 Michael Lawrence; 9 George Flanagan; 21 Fenton Rogers; 11 Brad England; 15 AJ Wallace; 37 Jason Baitieri. Subs (all used): 20 Billy Jowitt; 14 Ebon Scurr; 18 Keven Appo; 41 Eribe Doro.
Tries: Myers (24), England (55); **Goals:** Lilley 0/2.
ROVERS: 20 Mark Kheirallah; 4 Craig Hall; 21 Joey Leilua; 3 Chris Hankinson; 5 Gareth Gale; 23 Caleb Aekins; 34 Dane Chisholm; 17 Gadwin Springer; 14 Matty Wildie; 10 James Lockwood; 11 Brad Day; 35 Ellis Longstaff; 32 Daniel Smith. Subs (all used): 9 Connor Jones; 15 John Davies; 16 Junior Moors; 24 Mathieu Cozza.
Tries: Smith (13), Gale (49), Aekins (68);
Goals: Kheirallah 2/3.
Rugby Leaguer & League Express Men of the Match: *Bulls:* Ebon Scurr; *Rovers:* Gareth Gale.
Penalty count: 2-7; **Half-time:** 4-6;
Referee: James Vella; **Attendance:** 4,567.

KEIGHLEY COUGARS 26 BARROW RAIDERS 20

COUGARS: 1 Lewis Young; 3 Charlie Graham; 42 Junior Sa'u; 23 Robbie Storey; 5 Mo Agoro; 14 Harvey Spence; 40 Kieran Rush; 24 Mark Ioane; 26 Thomas Doyle; 45 Tom Nicholson-Watton; 19 Ellis Robson; 27 Sadiq Abebiyi; 11 Kyle Trout. Subs (all used): 46 Oscar Thomas; 8 Dan Parker; 16 Josh Lynam; 32 Jack Bibby.
Tries: Graham (26), Sa'u (34), Young (46), Parker (47), Bibby (57); **Goals:** Spence 1/3, Rush 2/2.
RAIDERS: 24 Luke Broadbent; 5 Ryan Shaw; 25 Keanan Brand; 2 Shane Toal; 27 Andrew Bulman; 6 Jarrod Sammut; 7 Ryan Johnston; 8 Greg Burke; 22 Josh Wood; 4 Greg Worthington; 17 Charlie Emslie; 12 Jarrad Stack; 32 Tom Wilkinson. Subs (all used): 1 Luke Cresswell; 20 Ben Evans; 18 Brett Carter; 21 Jack Billington.
Tries: Bulman (14, 27), Wood (38); **Goals:** Shaw 4/4.
Rugby Leaguer & League Express Men of the Match: *Cougars:* Sadiq Adebiyi; *Raiders:* Ryan Johnston.
Penalty count: 6-7; **Half-time:** 10-20;
Referee: Michael Smaill; **Attendance:** 1,828.

SHEFFIELD EAGLES 18 LONDON BRONCOS 26

EAGLES: 29 Quentin Laulu-Togaga'e; 2 Ben Jones-Bishop; 4 Ross Oakes; 33 James Glover; 28 Matty Dawson-Jones; 32 Cory Aston; 19 Jack Hansen; 15 Mikey Wood; 9 Vila Halafihi; 10 Tyler Dickinson; 18 Aaron Murphy; 23 Bayley Liu; 14 Titus Gwaze. Subs (all used): 13 Evan Hodgson; 16 Blake Broadbent; 24 Oliver Roberts; 27 Jesse Sene-Lefao.
Tries: Laulu-Togaga'e (42), Glover (50, 71);
Goals: Aston 3/3.
BRONCOS: 1 Alex Walker; 4 Dalton Grant; 3 Jarred Bassett; 19 Dean Whare; 5 Iliess Macani; 17 Henry Raiwalui; 20 Corey Norman; 15 Lewis Bienek; 14 Bill Leyland; 33 Rob Butler; 11 Will Lovell; 16 Ethan Natoli; 13 Dean Parata. Subs (all used): 6 Oliver Leyland; 8 Wellington Albert; 9 Sam Davis; 12 Marcus Stock.
Tries: Bassett (19), Walker (26, 67), Parata (64), Macani (80); **Goals:** Norman 3/5.
Rugby Leaguer & League Express Men of the Match: *Eagles:* James Glover; *Broncos:* Alex Walker.
Penalty count: 4-1; **Half-time:** 0-8;
Referee: Liam Rush; **Attendance:** 910.

Championship 2023 - Round by Round

WHITEHAVEN 8 HALIFAX PANTHERS 30

WHITEHAVEN: 23 Josh Rourke; 26 Oscar Doran; 3 Chris Taylor; 2 Dave Eccleston; 6 Brad Holroyd; 27 Jake Carter; 14 Jamie Doran; 22 Lucas Castle; 15 James Newton; 28 Ross Ainley; 11 Connor Holliday; 4 Curtis Teare; 13 Dion Aiye. Subs (all used): 12 Lachlan Lanskey; 18 Perry Singleton; 20 George Hill; 24 Daniel Spencer-Tonks.
Tries: Spencer-Tonks (36), O Doran (78); **Goals:** Rourke 0/2.
PANTHERS: 1 James Woodburn-Hall; 5 James Saltonstall; 3 Zack McComb; 35 Ben Crooks; 2 Lachlan Walmsley; 6 Louis Jouffret; 7 Joe Keyes; 16 Will Calcott; 34 Adam O'Brien; 8 Adam Tangata; 11 Ben Kavanagh; 12 Matty Gee; 13 Jacob Fairbank. Subs (all used): 20 Tom Inman; 19 Ryan Lannon; 28 Alex Sutcliffe; 29 Dan Fleming.
Tries: Woodburn-Hall (17), Jouffret (51, 55), Kavanagh (68), Gee (74); **Goals:** Jouffret 5/5.
Rugby Leaguer & League Express Men of the Match:
Whitehaven: Dave Eccleston; *Panthers:* Louis Jouffret.
Penalty count: 9-1; **Half-time:** 4-6;
Referee: Brad Milligan; **Attendance:** 1,056.

WIDNES VIKINGS 12 BATLEY BULLDOGS 4

VIKINGS: 1 Jack Owens; 2 Ryan Ince; 3 Matty Fleming; 20 Joe Edge; 5 Kieran Dixon; 6 Danny Craven; 7 Tom Gilmore; 8 Owen Farnworth; 9 Matty Fozard; 16 Callum Field; 11 Sam Wilde; 26 Max Roberts; 22 Aaron Brown. Subs (all used): 19 Olly Davies; 31 Tom Forber; 12 Adam Lawton; 32 Huw Worthington.
Tries: Field (16), Owens (74); **Goals:** K Dixon 2/2.
BULLDOGS: 21 Aidan McGowan; 22 Dale Morton; 4 Josh Hodson; 3 Kieran Buchanan; 15 Elliot Kear; 14 James Meadows; 7 Josh Woods; 8 Adam Gledhill; 6 Ben White; 13 James Brown; 11 Dane Manning; 12 Lucas Walshaw; 30 Martyn Reilly. Subs (all used): 9 Alistair Leak; 26 Nyle Flynn; 16 Michael Ward; 20 Samy Kibula.
Try: McGowan (39); **Goals:** Morton 0/1.
Rugby Leaguer & League Express Men of the Match:
Vikings: Jack Owens; *Bulldogs:* Samy Kibula.
Penalty count: 2-6; **Half-time:** 6-4;
Referee: Scott Mikalauskas; **Attendance:** 3,219.

YORK KNIGHTS 26 SWINTON LIONS 22

KNIGHTS: 15 Myles Harrison; 5 AJ Towse; 11 Chris Clarkson; 33 Oliver Pratt; 29 Jason Bass; 19 Josh Daley; 7 Liam Harris; 30 Brenden Santi; 9 Will Jubb; 10 Conor Fitzsimmons; 32 Oli Field; 4 Jesse Dee; 13 Jordan Thompson. Subs (all used): 17 Ronan Michael; 22 Pauli Pauli; 27 Harry Price; 34 Taylor Pemberton.
Tries: Thompson (17), Jubb (23), Pratt (43, 63);
Goals: Harris 5/5.
LIONS: 23 Joe Lowe; 26 Joey Romeo; 3 Jake Spedding; 22 Andy Badrock; 2 Mike Butt; 1 Dan Abram; 7 Jordy Gibson; 8 Gavin Bennion; 35 Lewis Hall; 13 Louis Brogan; 16 Gav Rodden; 12 Mitch Cox; 32 Matthew Foster. Subs (all used): 10 Kenny Baker; 15 Jordan Case; 25 Scott Parnaby; 30 George Roby.
Tries: Abram (9), Lowe (40), Roby (51), Brogan (76);
Goals: Abram 3/4.
Sin bin: Case (41) - dissent.
Rugby Leaguer & League Express Men of the Match:
Knights: Oliver Pratt; *Lions:* Dan Abram.
Penalty count: 7-9; **Half-time:** 14-10;
Referee: Cameron Worsley; **Attendance:** 2,114.

ROUND 25

Friday 8th September 2023

SHEFFIELD EAGLES 38 KEIGHLEY COUGARS 10

EAGLES: 29 Quentin Laulu-Togaga'e; 2 Ben Jones-Bishop; 33 James Glover; 4 Ross Oakes; 28 Matty Dawson-Jones; 32 Cory Aston; 7 Anthony Thackeray; 17 Liam Kirk; 19 Jack Hansen; 10 Tyler Dickinson; 18 Aaron Murphy; 27 Jesse Sene-Lefao; 13 Evan Hodgson. Subs (all used): 6 Izaac Farrell; 25 Joe Hird; 15 Mikey Wood; 16 Blake Broadbent.
Tries: Aston (19), Oakes (24), Glover (40), Sene-Lefao (44), Jones-Bishop (50), Murphy (69), Laulu-Togaga'e (75);
Goals: Aston 3/5, I Farrell 2/2.
COUGARS: 1 Lewis Young; 3 Charlie Graham; 42 Junior Sa'u; 23 Robbie Storey; 5 Mo Agoro; 14 Harvey Spence; 40 Kieran Rush; 24 Mark Ioane; 26 Thomas Doyle; 45 Tom Nicholson-Watton; 19 Ellis Robson; 27 Sadiq Adebiyi; 11 Kyle Trout. Subs (all used): 46 Oscar Thomas; 16 Josh Lynam; 32 Jack Bibby; 20 Brad Walker.
Tries: Young (3, 79); **Goals:** Spence 1/2.
Rugby Leaguer & League Express Men of the Match:
Eagles: Anthony Thackeray; *Cougars:* Mark Ioane.
Penalty count: 6-10; **Half-time:** 16-6;
Referee: Cameron Worsley; **Attendance:** 932.

NEWCASTLE THUNDER 22 FEATHERSTONE ROVERS 56

THUNDER: 6 Alex Donaghy; 1 Jack Johnson; 26 Mac Walsh; 3 Marcus Walker; 20 Gideon Boafo; 14 Denive Balmforth; 7 Nikau Williams; 8 Jay Chapelhow; 9 Curtis Davies; 15 Ted Chapelhow; 13 Connor Bailey; 29 Paddy Burns; 10 Mitch Clark. Subs (all used): 40 Evan Simons; 18 Jake Lightowler; 28 Tyler Walton; 41 Nathan Rushworth.
Tries: Balmforth (40), Boafo (54, 70), Williams (75);
Goals: Williams 3/4.
ROVERS: 23 Caleb Aekins; 4 Craig Hall; 35 Ellis Longstaff; 9 Connor Jones; 5 Gareth Gale; 25 Thomas Lacans; 34 Dane Chisholm; 8 Craig Kopczak; 14 Matty Wildie; 24 Mathieu Cozza; 11 Brad Day; 12 Elijah Taylor; 32 Daniel Smith. Subs: 20 Mark Kheirallah (not used); 15 John Davies; 16 Junior Moors; 17 Gadwin Springer.
Tries: Gale (7, 22, 29), Cozza (26), Hall (37, 50), Taylor (44), Day (48), Longstaff (59), Wildie (64);
Goals: Hall 8/10.
Sin bin: Chisholm (13) - trip.
Rugby Leaguer & League Express Men of the Match:
Thunder: Nikau Williams; *Rovers:* Gareth Gale.
Penalty count: 3-6; **Half-time:** 6-28;
Referee: Michael Smaill; **Attendance:** 747.

Saturday 9th September 2023

HALIFAX PANTHERS 26 TOULOUSE OLYMPIQUE 18

PANTHERS: 1 James Woodburn-Hall; 2 Lachlan Walmsley; 3 Zack McComb; 35 Ben Crooks; 5 James Saltonstall; 6 Louis Jouffret; 7 Joe Keyes; 16 Will Calcott; 9 Brandon Moore; 31 Kevin Larroyer; 11 Ben Kavanagh; 12 Matty Gee; 13 Jacob Fairbank. Subs (all used): 20 Tom Inman; 8 Adam Tangata; 19 Ryan Lannon; 28 Alex Sutcliffe.
Tries: Saltonstall (11), Woodburn-Hall (28), Kavanagh (46), Walmsley (65); **Goals:** Jouffret 5/6.
OLYMPIQUE: 22 Zac Santo; 5 Paul Marcon; 25 Matthieu Laguerre; 18 Guy Armitage; 19 Benjamin Laguerre; 23 Robin Brochon; 7 Jake Shorrocks; 8 Lambert Belmas; 9 Calum Gahan; 10 Harrison Hansen; 24 Pierre-Jean Lima; 11 Maxime Stefani; 13 Anthony Marion. Subs (all used): 14 Eloi Pelissier; 26 Ramon Silva; 28 Wail Skoundri; 12 Dominique Peyroux.
Tries: Brochon (2), Lima (17), Santo (62);
Goals: Shorrocks 3/3.
Rugby Leaguer & League Express Men of the Match:
Panthers: James Woodburn-Hall; *Olympique:* Zac Santo.
Penalty count: 4-3; **Half-time:** 12-12;
Referee: Marcus Griffiths; **Attendance:** 1,437.

Sunday 10th September 2023

BARROW RAIDERS 32 SWINTON LIONS 14

RAIDERS: 1 Luke Cresswell; 5 Ryan Shaw; 25 Keanan Brand; 24 Luke Broadbent; 27 Andrew Bulman; 6 Jarrod Sammut; 7 Ryan Johnston; 8 Greg Burke; 22 Josh Wood; 4 Greg Worthington; 17 Charlie Emslie; 12 Jarrad Stack; 32 Tom Wilkinson. Subs (all used): 18 Brett Carter; 3 Rio-Osayomwanbo Corkill; 20 Ben Evans; 21 Jack Billington.
Tries: Broadbent (15, 64), Brand (27, 62), Bulman (35), Shaw (48); **Goals:** Shaw 4/6.
LIONS: 23 Joe Lowe; 26 Joey Romeo; 3 Jake Spedding; 22 Andy Badrock; 2 Mike Butt; 1 Dan Abram; 7 Jordy Gibson; 13 Louis Brogan; 35 Lewis Hall; 8 Gavin Bennion; 11 Rhodri Lloyd; 12 Mitch Cox; 34 Matthew Foster. Subs (all used): 10 Kenny Baker; 15 Jordan Case; 30 George Roby; 16 Gav Rodden.
Tries: Abram (52), Badrock (75); **Goals:** Abram 3/3.
Sin bin: Roby (26) - dangerous challenge on Billington.
Rugby Leaguer & League Express Men of the Match:
Raiders: Keanan Brand; *Lions:* Dan Abram.
Penalty count: 2-9; **Half-time:** 16-2;
Referee: Liam Rush; **Attendance:** 2,117.

BATLEY BULLDOGS 25 WHITEHAVEN 12

BULLDOGS: 21 Aidan McGowan; 22 Dale Morton; 4 Josh Hodson; 3 Kieran Buchanan; 15 Elliot Kear; 14 James Meadows; 7 Josh Woods; 8 Adam Gledhill; 6 Ben White; 13 James Brown; 11 Dane Manning; 12 Lucas Walshaw; 17 Luke Blake. Subs (all used): 9 Alistair Leak; 16 Michael Ward; 20 Samy Kibula; 26 Nyle Flynn.
Tries: Meadows (23, 40), Morton (53, 59);
Goals: Morton 4/4; **Field goal:** Woods (69).
Sin bin: Flynn (72) - dangerous challenge.
WHITEHAVEN: 23 Josh Rourke; 2 Dave Eccleston; 3 Chris Taylor; 6 Karl Dixon; 4 Curtis Teare; 27 Jake Carter; 14 Jamie Doran; 22 Lucas Castle; 15 James Newton; 28 Ross Ainley; 11 Connor Holliday; 12 Lachlan Lanskey; 20 George Hill. Subs (all used): 9 Callum Phillips; 13 Dion Aiye; 18 Perry Singleton; 24 Daniel Spencer-Tonks.
Tries: Eccleston (65), Aiye (79); **Goals:** Rourke 2/2.
Rugby Leaguer & League Express Men of the Match:
Bulldogs: James Meadows; *Whitehaven:* Lucas Castle.
Penalty count: 2-1; **Half-time:** 12-0;
Referee: Matt Rossleigh; **Attendance:** 1,172.

BRADFORD BULLS 10 YORK KNIGHTS 20

BULLS: 27 Connor Wynne; 38 Liam Tindall; 3 Joe Arundel; 4 Kieran Gill; 5 David Foggin-Johnston; 1 Tom Holmes; 7 Jordan Lilley; 10 Michael Lawrence; 9 George Flanagan; 41 Eribe Doro; 12 Chester Butler; 15 AJ Wallace; 37 Jason Baitieri. Subs (all used): 11 Brad England; 14 Ebon Scurr; 18 Keven Appo; 20 Billy Jowitt.
Try: Wynne (16); **Goals:** Lilley 3/3.
KNIGHTS: 15 Myles Harrison; 33 Oliver Pratt; 4 Jesse Dee; 11 Chris Clarkson; 5 AJ Towse; 19 Josh Daley; 7 Liam Harris; 30 Brenden Santi; 9 Will Jubb; 21 Ukuma Ta'ai; 32 Oli Field; 12 Danny Kirmond; 13 Jordan Thompson. Subs (all used): 10 Conor Fitzsimmons; 17 Ronan Michael; 22 Pauli Pauli; 34 Taylor Pemberton.
Tries: Harrison (11), Towse (63), Fitzsimmons (79);
Goals: Harris 4/5.
Rugby Leaguer & League Express Men of the Match:
Bulls: Chester Butler; *Knights:* Conor Fitzsimmons.
Penalty count: 4-6; **Half-time:** 8-8;
Referee: Scott Mikalauskas; **Attendance:** 3,603.

LONDON BRONCOS 52 WIDNES VIKINGS 12

BRONCOS: 1 Alex Walker; 4 Dalton Grant; 17 Henry Raiwalui; 19 Dean Whare; 3 Jarred Bassett; 6 Oliver Leyland; 20 Corey Norman; 8 Wellington Albert; 9 Sam Davis; 33 Rob Butler; 11 Will Lovell; 16 Ethan Natoli; 13 Dean Parata. Subs (all used): 12 Marcus Stock; 10 Jordan Williams; 18 Emmanuel Waine; 14 Bill Leyland.
Tries: Albert (5), Stock (29), Whare (38, 68), Williams (52), Walker (59), Bassett (73), Raiwalui (76), O Leyland (80); **Goals:** Norman 8/9.
VIKINGS: 1 Jack Owens; 2 Ryan Ince; 3 Matty Fleming; 20 Joe Edge; 5 Kieran Dixon; 6 Danny Craven; 7 Tom Gilmore; 8 Owen Farnworth; 9 Matty Fozard; 16 Callum Field; 11 Sam Wilde; 17 Shane Grady; 22 Aaron Brown. Subs (all used): 19 Olly Davies; 31 Tom Forber; 12 Adam Lawton; 32 Huw Worthington.
Tries: Davies (45), K Dixon (63); **Goals:** K Dixon 2/2.
Sin bin: Lawton (27) - late challenge.
Rugby Leaguer & League Express Men of the Match:
Broncos: Corey Norman; *Vikings:* Kieran Dixon.
Penalty count: 4-3; **Half-time:** 18-0;
Referee: James Vella; **Attendance:** 1,062.

ROUND 26

Saturday 16th September 2023

NEWCASTLE THUNDER 36 BARROW RAIDERS 24

THUNDER: 6 Alex Donaghy; 1 Jack Johnson; 26 Mac Walsh; 3 Marcus Walker; 20 Gideon Boafo; 13 Connor Bailey; 7 Nikau Williams; 8 Jay Chapelhow; 9 Curtis Davies; 15 Ted Chapelhow; 17 Rob Tuliatu; 5 Alex Clegg; 28 Tyler Walton. Subs (all used): 29 Paddy Burns; 40 Evan Simons; 18 Jake Lightowler; 41 Nathan Rushworth.
Tries: Boafo (11, 53), Donaghy (36, 42), Clegg (40), Bailey (56), Burns (68); **Goals:** Williams 4/7.
Sin bin: J Chapelhow (23) - fighting; Tuliatu (27) - fighting.
RAIDERS: 1 Luke Cresswell; 5 Ryan Shaw; 2 Shane Toal; 24 Luke Broadbent; 27 Andrew Bulman; 6 Jarrod Sammut; 7 Ryan Johnston; 20 Ben Evans; 22 Josh Wood; 4 Greg Worthington; 17 Charlie Emslie; 12 Jarrad Stack; 32 Tom Wilkinson. Subs (all used): 18 Brett Carter; 31 Adam Jackson; 3 Rio-Osayomwanbo Corkill; 21 Jack Billington.
Tries: Bulman (50, 59), Broadbent (62), Jackson (77);
Goals: Shaw 4/4.
Sin bin: Broadbent (23) - fighting; Wood (32) - fighting.
Rugby Leaguer & League Express Men of the Match:
Thunder: Nikau Williams; *Raiders:* Andrew Bulman.
Penalty count: 4-4; **Half-time:** 14-0;
Referee: Cameron Worsley; **Attendance:** 904.

TOULOUSE OLYMPIQUE 16 FEATHERSTONE ROVERS 29

OLYMPIQUE: 22 Zac Santo; 5 Paul Marcon; 25 Matthieu Laguerre; 18 Guy Armitage; 19 Benjamin Laguerre; 23 Robin Brochon; 7 Jake Shorrocks; 8 Lambert Belmas; 9 Calum Gahan; 27 Dimitri Biscarro; 24 Pierre-Jean Lima; 11 Maxime Stefani; 13 Anthony Marion. Subs (all used): 14 Eloi Pelissier; 15 Sitaleki Akauola; 16 Joe Bretherton; 28 Wail Skoundri.
Tries: B Laguerre (23), Brochon (35), Akauola (38);
Goals: Shorrocks 2/3.
ROVERS: 20 Mark Kheirallah; 4 Craig Hall; 21 Joey Leilua; 3 Chris Hankinson; 5 Gareth Gale; 6 Johnathon Ford; 25 Thomas Lacans; 24 Mathieu Cozza; 14 Matty Wildie; 10 James Lockwood; 11 Brad Day; 12 Elijah Taylor; 32 Daniel Smith. Subs (all used): 9 Connor Jones; 13 Jack Bussey; 15 John Davies; 16 Junior Moors.
Tries: Lacans (4), Kheirallah (28), Taylor (50), Hall (61), Jones (77); **Goals:** Kheirallah 4/5; **Field goal:** Lacans (73).
Rugby Leaguer & League Express Men of the Match:
Olympique: Anthony Marion; *Rovers:* Thomas Lacans.
Penalty count: 2-7; **Half-time:** 16-12;
Referee: Michael Smaill; **Attendance:** 2,603
(at Stade des Minimes).

Championship 2023 - Round by Round

Sunday 17th September 2023

KEIGHLEY COUGARS 22 HALIFAX PANTHERS 23

COUGARS: 1 Lewis Young; 5 Mo Agoro; 23 Robbie Storey; 42 Junior Sa'u; 3 Charlie Graham; 14 Harvey Spence; 46 Oscar Thomas; 24 Mark Ioane; 9 Billy Gaylor; 13 Kyle Kesik; 19 Ellis Robson; 27 Sadiq Adebiyi; 11 Kyle Trout. Subs (all used): 40 Kieran Rush; 20 Brad Walker; 16 Josh Lynam; 32 Jack Bibby.
Tries: Agoro (1, 11), Graham (56), Ioane (74);
Goals: Thomas 3/6.
PANTHERS: 1 James Woodburn-Hall; 2 Lachlan Walmsley; 3 Zack McComb; 35 Ben Crooks; 5 James Saltonstall; 6 Louis Jouffret; 7 Joe Keyes; 31 Kevin Larroyer; 9 Brandon Moore; 10 Dan Murray; 11 Ben Kavanagh; 12 Matty Gee; 13 Jacob Fairbank. Subs (all used): 20 Tom Inman; 8 Adam Tangata; 19 Ryan Lannon; 33 Alex Sutcliffe.
Tries: Walmsley (19, 44), Sutcliffe (30), Woodburn-Hall (63); **Goals:** Jouffret 3/5;
Field goal: Jouffret (78).
Rugby Leaguer & League Express Men of the Match:
Cougars: Sadiq Adebiyi; *Panthers:* Louis Jouffret.
Penalty count: 5-5; **Half-time:** 10-10;
Referee: Nick Bennett; **Attendance:** 2,367.

LONDON BRONCOS 10 BRADFORD BULLS 12

BRONCOS: 1 Alex Walker; 4 Dalton Grant; 3 Jarred Bassett; 23 Daniel Hoyes; 5 Iliess Macani; 17 Henry Raiwalui; 20 Corey Norman; 8 Wellington Albert; 9 Sam Davis; 33 Rob Butler; 11 Will Lovell; 16 Ethan Natoli; 13 Dean Parata. Subs (all used): 6 Oliver Leyland; 10 Jordan Williams; 12 Marcus Stock; 14 Bill Leyland.
Tries: Raiwalui (27), Walker (70); **Goals:** Norman 1/2.
BULLS: 1 Tom Holmes; 2 Ben Blackmore; 30 Jayden Myers; 4 Kieran Gill; 38 Liam Tindall; 29 Lee Gaskell; 7 Jordan Lilley; 10 Michael Lawrence; 20 Billy Jowitt; 41 Eribe Doro; 12 Chester Butler; 3 Joe Arundel; 37 Jason Baitieri. Subs (all used): 9 George Flanagan; 18 Keven Appo; 14 Ebon Scurr; 21 Fenton Rogers.
Tries: Myers (15, 44); **Goals:** Lilley 2/4.
Rugby Leaguer & League Express Men of the Match:
Broncos: Alex Walker; *Bulls:* Jayden Myers.
Penalty count: 5-9; **Half-time:** 4-6;
Referee: Liam Rush; **Attendance:** 1,158.

SWINTON LIONS 21 WHITEHAVEN 20

LIONS: 1 Dan Abram; 26 Joey Romeo; 11 Rhodri Lloyd; 33 Wesley Bruines; 5 Richard Lepori; 34 Robbie Butterworth; 7 Jordy Gibson; 8 Gavin Bennion; 30 George Roby; 13 Louis Brogan; 12 Mitch Cox; 32 Matthew Foster; 35 Lewis Hall. Subs: 25 Scott Parnaby (not used); 10 Kenny Baker; 15 Jordan Case; 16 Gav Rodden.
Tries: Gibson (26, 43), Baker (39); **Goals:** Abram 4/5;
Field goal: Gibson (75).
WHITEHAVEN: 23 Josh Rourke; 2 Dave Eccleston; 3 Chris Taylor; 6 Karl Dixon; 4 Curtis Teare; 27 Jake Carter; 14 Jamie Doran; 22 Lucas Castle; 15 James Newton; 28 Ross Ainley; 11 Connor Holliday; 12 Lachlan Lanskey; 20 George Hill. Subs (all used): 13 Dion Aiye; 9 Callum Phillips; 18 Perry Singleton; 24 Daniel Spencer-Tonks.
Tries: Taylor (20), Teare (32), Aiye (37), Eccleston (55);
Goals: Rourke 2/4.
Rugby Leaguer & League Express Men of the Match:
Lions: Jordy Gibson; *Whitehaven:* Chris Taylor.
Penalty count: 5-6; **Half-time:** 12-16;
Referee: Aaron Moore; **Attendance:** 1,315.

WIDNES VIKINGS 18 SHEFFIELD EAGLES 38

VIKINGS: 1 Jack Owens; 2 Ryan Ince; 3 Matty Fleming; 20 Joe Edge; 5 Kieran Dixon; 18 Joe Lyons; 7 Tom Gilmore; 16 Callum Field; 9 Matty Fozard; 12 Adam Lawton; 11 Sam Wilde; 17 Shane Grady; 22 Aaron Brown. Subs (all used): 8 Owen Farnworth; 19 Olly Davies; 27 Anthony Walker; 26 Max Roberts.
Tries: Lawton (18), K Dixon (46, 64); **Goals:** K Dixon 3/3.
Dismissal: Brown (38) - high tackle on Gwaze.
EAGLES: 29 Quentin Laulu-Togaga'e; 2 Ben Jones-Bishop; 4 Ross Oakes; 33 James Glover; 28 Matty Dawson-Jones; 32 Cory Aston; 7 Anthony Thackeray; 17 Liam Kirk; 19 Jack Hansen; 10 Tyler Dickinson; 18 Aaron Murphy; 27 Jesse Sene-Lefao; 13 Evan Hodgson. Subs (all used): 14 Titus Gwaze; 15 Mikey Wood; 16 Blake Broadbent; 23 Bayley Liu.
Tries: Murphy (36, 49), Aston (53), Hansen (61), Thackeray (72), Hodgson (75); **Goals:** Aston 7/7.
Rugby Leaguer & League Express Men of the Match:
Vikings: Kieran Dixon; *Eagles:* Cory Aston.
Penalty count: 5-3; **Half-time:** 6-8;
Referee: Scott Mikalauskas; **Attendance:** 2,961.

Monday 18th September 2023

YORK KNIGHTS 15 BATLEY BULLDOGS 14

KNIGHTS: 2 Joe Brown; 5 AJ Towse; 11 Chris Clarkson; 33 Oliver Pratt; 15 Myles Harrison; 4 Jesse Dee; 7 Liam Harris; 21 Ukuma Ta'ai; 9 Will Jubb; 10 Conor Fitzsimmons; 32 Oli Field; 12 Danny Kirmond; 13 Jordan Thompson. Subs (all used): 17 Ronan Michael; 22 Pauli Pauli; 30 Brenden Santi; 34 Taylor Pemberton.
Tries: Pratt (24), Towse (36), Brown (39); **Goals:** Harris 1/3;
Field goal: Harris (79).
BULLDOGS: 21 Aidan McGowan; 22 Dale Morton; 4 Josh Hodson; 3 Kieran Buchanan; 15 Elliot Kear; 14 James Meadows; 7 Josh Woods; 8 Adam Gledhill; 17 Luke Blake; 30 Martyn Reilly; 11 Dane Manning; 12 Lucas Walshaw; 6 Ben White. Subs (all used): 16 Michael Ward; 18 George Senior; 26 Nyle Flynn; 28 Oli Burton.
Tries: Walshaw (8), Meadows (19), Morton (61);
Goals: Morton 1/3.
Rugby Leaguer & League Express Men of the Match:
Knights: Liam Harris; *Bulldogs:* Dane Manning.
Penalty count: 7-7; **Half-time:** 14-10;
Referee: Marcus Griffiths; **Attendance:** 2,377.

ROUND 27

Saturday 23rd September 2023

BATLEY BULLDOGS 32 NEWCASTLE THUNDER 18

BULLDOGS: 21 Aidan McGowan; 22 Dale Morton; 4 Josh Hodson; 18 George Senior; 15 Elliot Kear; 14 James Meadows; 7 Josh Woods; 24 Ben Kaye; 9 Alistair Leak; 17 Luke Blake; 11 Dane Manning; 3 Kieran Buchanan; 6 Ben White. Subs (all used): 28 Oli Burton; 16 Michael Ward; 12 Lucas Walshaw; 5 Johnny Campbell.
Tries: Leak (12), Meadows (28, 73), Manning (50), Kear (64), Campbell (69); **Goals:** Morton 4/6.
THUNDER: 6 Alex Donaghy; 20 Gideon Boafo; 3 Marcus Walker; 26 Mac Walsh; 1 Jack Johnson; 14 Denive Balmforth; 7 Nikau Williams; 8 Jay Chapelhow; 9 Curtis Davies; 15 Ted Chapelhow; 17 Rob Tuliatu; 5 Alex Clegg; 13 Connor Bailey. Subs (all used): 27 Jack Miller; 40 Evan Simons; 18 Jake Lightowler; 28 Tyler Walton.
Tries: T Chapelhow (15), Johnson (22), Williams (36);
Goals: Williams 3/3.
Sin bin: J Chapelhow (55) - interference.
Rugby Leaguer & League Express Men of the Match:
Bulldogs: James Meadows; *Thunder:* Nikau Williams.
Penalty count: 9-4; **Half-time:** 12-18;
Referee: Michael Smaill; **Attendance:** 1,070.

WHITEHAVEN 16 TOULOUSE OLYMPIQUE 26

WHITEHAVEN: 23 Josh Rourke; 2 Dave Eccleston; 3 Chris Taylor; 6 Karl Dixon; 4 Curtis Teare; 27 Jake Carter; 14 Jamie Doran; 22 Lucas Castle; 15 James Newton; 28 Ross Ainley; 11 Connor Holliday; 12 Lachlan Lanskey; 20 George Hill. Subs: 9 Callum Phillips; 13 Dion Aiye; 7 Will Groves (not used); 24 Daniel Spencer-Tonks.
Tries: J Doran (21), Teare (44), Dixon (56);
Goals: Rourke 2/4.
OLYMPIQUE: 1 Olly Ashall-Bott; 5 Paul Marcon; 24 Pierre-Jean Lima; 30 Justin Tropis; 19 Benjamin Laguerre; 22 Zac Santo; 6 Josh Ralph; 8 Lambert Belmas; 9 Calum Gahan; 27 Dimitri Biscarro; 16 Joe Bretherton; 11 Maxime Stefani; 13 Anthony Marion. Subs (all used): 14 Eloi Pelissier; 15 Sitaleki Akauola; 20 Greg Richards; 23 Robin Brochon.
Tries: Biscarro (5), Ashall-Bott (10), Santo (27, 72), Gahan (32); **Goals:** Santo 3/5.
Rugby Leaguer & League Express Men of the Match:
Whitehaven: Dion Aiye; *Olympique:* Calum Gahan.
Penalty count: 5-2; **Half-time:** 6-22;
Referee: Ryan Cox; **Attendance:** 997.

FEATHERSTONE ROVERS 62 WIDNES VIKINGS 10

ROVERS: 20 Mark Kheirallah; 4 Craig Hall; 21 Joey Leilua; 3 Chris Hankinson; 5 Gareth Gale; 23 Caleb Aekins; 25 Thomas Lacans; 24 Mathieu Cozza; 14 Matty Wildie; 10 James Lockwood; 11 Brad Day; 12 Elijah Taylor; 32 Daniel Smith. Subs (all used): 9 Connor Jones; 13 Jack Bussey; 16 Junior Moors; 27 McKenzie Yei.
Tries: Lacans (4), Hall (19), Moors (31), Gale (39, 65), Aekins (48, 77), Hankinson (52), Leilua (59, 70), Jones (74);
Goals: Kheirallah 9/11.
VIKINGS: 5 Kieran Dixon; 2 Ryan Ince; 3 Matty Fleming; 20 Joe Edge; 28 Ryan Millar; 18 Joe Lyons; 7 Tom Gilmore; 16 Callum Field; 9 Matty Fozard; 27 Anthony Walker; 11 Sam Wilde; 12 Adam Lawton; 22 Aaron Brown. Subs (all used): 1 Jack Owens; 8 Owen Farnworth; 19 Olly Davies; 26 Max Roberts.
Tries: Lyons (25), Ince (35); **Goals:** K Dixon 1/2.
Rugby Leaguer & League Express Men of the Match:
Rovers: Joey Leilua; *Vikings:* Ryan Ince.
Penalty count: 5-1; **Half-time:** 24-10;
Referee: Aaron Moore; **Attendance:** 3,874.

Sunday 24th September 2023

BARROW RAIDERS 18 YORK KNIGHTS 31

RAIDERS: 1 Luke Cresswell; 5 Ryan Shaw; 2 Shane Toal; 24 Luke Broadbent; 27 Andrew Bulman; 31 Adam Jackson; 7 Ryan Johnston; 21 Jack Billington; 22 Josh Wood; 4 Greg Worthington; 17 Charlie Emslie; 12 Jarrad Stack; 32 Tom Wilkinson. Subs (all used): 3 Rio-Osayomwanbo Corkill; 18 Brett Carter; 23 Connor Saunders; 6 Jarrod Sammut.
Tries: Johnston (52), Bulman (55), Wilkinson (66);
Goals: Shaw 3/3.
KNIGHTS: 2 Joe Brown; 29 Jason Bass; 15 Myles Harrison; 11 Chris Clarkson; 5 AJ Towse; 4 Jesse Dee; 7 Liam Harris; 30 Brenden Santi; 9 Will Jubb; 21 Ukuma Ta'ai; 32 Oli Field; 12 Danny Kirmond; 13 Jordan Thompson. Subs (all used): 34 Taylor Pemberton; 17 Ronan Michael; 10 Conor Fitzsimmons; 22 Pauli Pauli.
Tries: Field (28), Michael (33), Towse (44), Ta'ai (63), Santi (76); **Goals:** Harris 5/6; **Field goal:** Harris (74).
Rugby Leaguer & League Express Men of the Match:
Raiders: Greg Worthington; *Knights:* Liam Harris.
Penalty count: 2-4; **Half-time:** 0-12;
Referee: Liam Rush; **Attendance:** 2,292.

HALIFAX PANTHERS 12 SWINTON LIONS 22

PANTHERS: 1 James Woodburn-Hall; 2 Lachlan Walmsley; 3 Zack McComb; 35 Ben Crooks; 5 James Saltonstall; 6 Louis Jouffret; 7 Joe Keyes; 16 Will Calcott; 9 Brandon Moore; 10 Dan Murray; 11 Ben Kavanagh; 12 Matty Gee; 8 Adam Tangata. Subs (all used): 20 Tom Inman; 19 Ryan Lannon; 31 Kevin Larroyer; 33 Alex Sutcliffe.
Tries: Crooks (5), Walmsley (46, 64); **Goals:** Jouffret 0/3.
LIONS: 1 Dan Abram; 5 Richard Lepori; 22 Andy Badrock; 11 Rhodri Lloyd; 26 Joey Romeo; 33 Robbie Butterworth; 7 Jordy Gibson; 8 Gavin Bennion; 35 Lewis Hall; 13 Louis Brogan; 12 Mitch Cox; 32 Matthew Foster; 6 Nick Gregson. Subs (all used): 23 Joe Lowe; 15 Jordan Case; 10 Kenny Baker; 16 Gav Rodden.
Tries: Cox (18, 26), Gregson (35), Lloyd (50);
Goals: Abram 3/4.
Rugby Leaguer & League Express Men of the Match:
Panthers: Zack McComb; *Lions:* Mitch Cox.
Penalty count: 3-5; **Half-time:** 4-18;
Referee: Matt Rossleigh; **Attendance:** 2,122.

LONDON BRONCOS 24 KEIGHLEY COUGARS 16

BRONCOS: 6 Oliver Leyland; 4 Dalton Grant; 3 Jarred Bassett; 19 Dean Whare; 5 Iliess Macani; 17 Henry Raiwalui; 20 Corey Norman; 8 Wellington Albert; 9 Sam Davis; 33 Rob Butler; 11 Will Lovell; 16 Ethan Natoli; 13 Dean Parata. Subs (all used): 10 Jordan Williams; 12 Marcus Stock; 14 Bill Leyland; 18 Emmanuel Waine.
Tries: Whare (41, 54), Macani (50, 72), B Leyland (57);
Goals: Norman 2/5.
COUGARS: 46 Oscar Thomas; 3 Charlie Graham; 19 Ellis Robson; 42 Junior Sa'u; 2 Alix Stephenson; 1 Lewis Young; 14 Harvey Spence; 24 Mark Ioane; 13 Kyle Kesik; 43 Matty Laidlaw; 16 Josh Lynam; 27 Sadiq Adebiyi; 11 Kyle Trout. Subs (all used): 8 Dan Parker; 9 Billy Gaylor; 21 Lloyd Roby; 32 Jack Bibby.
Tries: Parker (34), Ioane (61); **Goals:** Thomas 4/5.
Rugby Leaguer & League Express Men of the Match:
Broncos: Dean Whare; *Cougars:* Mark Ioane.
Penalty count: 11-11; **Half-time:** 0-10;
Referee: Cameron Worsley; **Attendance:** 1,269.

SHEFFIELD EAGLES 16 BRADFORD BULLS 17

EAGLES: 29 Quentin Laulu-Togaga'e; 2 Ben Jones-Bishop; 3 Kris Welham; 33 James Glover; 28 Matty Dawson-Jones; 32 Cory Aston; 7 Anthony Thackeray; 8 Brandon Douglas; 19 Jack Hansen; 10 Tyler Dickinson; 18 Aaron Murphy; 27 Jesse Sene-Lefao; 13 Evan Hodgson. Subs (all used): 12 Joel Farrell; 14 Titus Gwaze; 16 Blake Broadbent; 23 Bayley Liu.
Tries: Laulu-Togaga'e (31), Jones-Bishop (56), Dawson-Jones (73); **Goals:** Aston 1/1, Hansen 1/3.
BULLS: 1 Tom Holmes; 2 Ben Blackmore; 3 Joe Arundel; 4 Kieran Gill; 38 Liam Tindall; 29 Lee Gaskell; 7 Jordan Lilley; 10 Michael Lawrence; 20 Billy Jowitt; 24 Masi Matongo; 12 Chester Butler; 15 AJ Wallace; 41 Eribe Doro. Subs (all used): 14 Ebon Scurr; 18 Keven Appo; 21 Fenton Rogers; 27 Connor Wynne.
Tries: Arundel (22), Tindall (40), Lilley (43);
Goals: Lilley 2/3, Gaskell 0/1; **Field goal:** Lilley (80).
Rugby Leaguer & League Express Men of the Match:
Eagles: Brandon Douglas; *Bulls:* Ebon Scurr.
Penalty count: 3-3; **Half-time:** 6-8;
Referee: Marcus Griffiths; **Attendance:** 1,976.

Championship 2023 - Round by Round

Eliminator action as Bradford's Jorge Taufua is halted by York's Brenden Santi, Jordan Thompson and Chris Clarkson

THE ELIMINATORS

Sunday 1st October 2023

SHEFFIELD EAGLES 0 LONDON BRONCOS 42

EAGLES: 29 Quentin Laulu-Togaga'e; 2 Ben Jones-Bishop; 4 Ross Oakes; 3 Kris Welham; 28 Matty Dawson-Jones; 6 Izaac Farrell; 7 Anthony Thackeray; 8 Brandon Douglas; 9 Vila Halafihi; 10 Tyler Dickinson; 18 Aaron Murphy; 27 Jesse Sene-Lefao; 14 Titus Gwaze. Subs (all used): 12 Joel Farrell; 15 Mikey Wood; 17 Liam Kirk; 19 Jack Hansen.
BRONCOS: 1 Alex Walker; 4 Dalton Grant; 3 Jarred Bassett; 17 Henry Raiwalui; 5 Iliess Macani; 6 Oliver Leyland; 20 Corey Norman; 33 Rob Butler; 9 Sam Davis; 8 Wellington Albert; 11 Will Lovell; 16 Ethan Natoli; 13 Dean Parata. Subs (all used): 10 Jordan Williams; 12 Marcus Stock; 14 Bill Leyland; 18 Emmanuel Waine.
Tries: Grant (7, 72), Bassett (11, 18), Williams (39), Walker (43), Lovell (62); **Goals:** Norman 7/7.
Rugby Leaguer & League Express Men of the Match: *Eagles:* Brandon Douglas; *Broncos:* Corey Norman.
Penalty count: 4-5; **Half-time:** 0-24;
Referee: James Vella; **Attendance:** 648.

BRADFORD BULLS 22 YORK KNIGHTS 8

BULLS: 1 Tom Holmes; 2 Ben Blackmore; 3 Joe Arundel; 4 Kieran Gill; 28 Jorge Taufua; 29 Lee Gaskell; 7 Jordan Lilley; 10 Michael Lawrence; 9 George Flanagan; 24 Masi Matongo; 12 Chester Butler; 15 AJ Wallace; 37 Jason Baitieri. Subs (all used): 18 Keven Appo; 21 Fenton Rogers; 27 Connor Wynne; 41 Eribe Doro.
Tries: Rogers (33), Appo (36), Holmes (44);
Goals: Lilley 5/5.
KNIGHTS: 2 Joe Brown; 5 AJ Towse; 11 Chris Clarkson; 12 Danny Kirmond; 29 Jason Bass; 4 Jesse Dee; 7 Liam Harris; 30 Brenden Santi; 9 Will Jubb; 21 Ukuma Ta'ai; 32 Oli Field; 10 Conor Fitzsimmons; 13 Jordan Thompson. Subs (all used): 17 Ronan Michael; 22 Pauli Pauli; 27 Harry Price; 34 Taylor Pemberton.
Try: Dee (20); **Goals:** Harris 2/2.
Rugby Leaguer & League Express Men of the Match: *Bulls:* Eribe Doro; *Knights:* Joe Brown.
Penalty count: 6-6; **Half-time:** 12-8;
Referee: Tom Grant; **Attendance:** 2,738.

SEMI-FINALS

Saturday 7th October 2023

TOULOUSE OLYMPIQUE 38 BRADFORD BULLS 20

OLYMPIQUE: 22 Zac Santo; 5 Paul Marcon; 25 Matthieu Laguerre; 18 Guy Armitage; 19 Benjamin Laguerre; 23 Robin Brochon; 6 Josh Ralph; 8 Lambert Belmas; 9 Calum Gahan; 10 Harrison Hansen; 24 Pierre-Jean Lima; 11 Maxime Stefani; 13 Anthony Marion. Subs (all used): 14 Eloi Pelissier; 15 Sitaleki Akauola; 16 Joe Bretherton; 12 Dominique Peyroux.
Tries: Santo (12), Maxime Stefani (21), Armitage (33), B Laguerre (37, 75), Ralph (42), Marcon (63);
Goals: Santo 1/2, Brochon 4/5.
BULLS: 1 Tom Holmes; 2 Ben Blackmore; 3 Joe Arundel; 4 Kieran Gill; 28 Jorge Taufua; 29 Lee Gaskell; 7 Jordan Lilley; 10 Michael Lawrence; 9 George Flanagan; 41 Eribe Doro; 12 Chester Butler; 15 AJ Wallace; 37 Jason Baitieri. Subs (all used): 20 Billy Jowitt; 21 Fenton Rogers; 18 Keven Appo; 40 Daniel Okoro.
Tries: Taufua (29), Arundel (47), Appo (73);
Goals: Lilley 4/4.
Sin bin: Baitieri (7) - high tackle.
Rugby Leaguer & League Express Men of the Match: *Olympique:* Josh Ralph; *Bulls:* Jordan Lilley.
Penalty count: 5-3; **Half-time:** 22-8;
Referee: James Vella; **Attendance:** 4,352.

Sunday 8th October 2023

FEATHERSTONE ROVERS 26 LONDON BRONCOS 36

ROVERS: 20 Mark Kheirallah; 2 Luke Briscoe; 21 Joey Leilua; 3 Chris Hankinson; 5 Gareth Gale; 23 Caleb Aekins; 6 Johnathon Ford; 24 Mathieu Cozza; 14 Matty Wildie; 10 James Lockwood; 11 Brad Day; 12 Elijah Taylor; 32 Daniel Smith. Subs (all used): 9 Connor Jones; 13 Jack Bussey; 15 John Davies; 16 Junior Moors.
Tries: Hankinson (27, 66), Leilua (32, 76), Briscoe (71);
Goals: Kheirallah 3/5.
Sin bin: Day (49) - dangerous challenge on Lovell.
BRONCOS: 1 Alex Walker; 4 Dalton Grant; 3 Jarred Bassett; 19 Dean Whare; 5 Iliess Macani; 17 Henry Raiwalui; 20 Corey Norman; 33 Rob Butler; 9 Sam Davis; 15 Lewis Bienek; 11 Will Lovell; 16 Ethan Natoli; 13 Dean Parata. Subs (all used): 10 Jordan Williams; 12 Marcus Stock; 14 Bill Leyland; 18 Emmanuel Waine.
Tries: Walker (5, 38), Whare (20), Macani (51), Grant (55), Raiwalui (63); **Goals:** Norman 6/6.
Rugby Leaguer & League Express Men of the Match: *Rovers:* Mark Kheirallah; *Broncos:* Corey Norman.
Penalty count: 6-6; **Half-time:** 12-18;
Referee: Tom Grant; **Attendance:** N/A (not given).

GRAND FINAL

Sunday 15th October 2023

TOULOUSE OLYMPIQUE 14 LONDON BRONCOS 18

OLYMPIQUE: 22 Zac Santo; 5 Paul Marcon; 4 Mathieu Jussaume; 18 Guy Armitage; 19 Benjamin Laguerre; 6 Josh Ralph; 7 Jake Shorrocks; 8 Lambert Belmas; 9 Calum Gahan; 10 Harrison Hansen; 12 Dominique Peyroux; 11 Maxime Stefani; 13 Anthony Marion. Subs (all used): 14 Eloi Pelissier; 15 Sitaleki Akauola; 16 Joe Bretherton; 20 Greg Richards.
Tries: Jussaume (3), Ralph (17); **Goals:** Shorrocks 3/3.
BRONCOS: 1 Alex Walker; 4 Dalton Grant; 3 Jarred Bassett; 19 Dean Whare; 5 Iliess Macani; 17 Henry Raiwalui; 20 Corey Norman; 33 Rob Butler; 9 Sam Davis; 15 Lewis Bienek; 11 Will Lovell; 12 Marcus Stock; 13 Dean Parata. Subs (all used): 8 Wellington Albert; 14 Bill Leyland; 10 Jordan Williams; 18 Emmanuel Waine.
Tries: Whare (25), Macani (59, 62);
Goals: Norman 1/4.
Rugby Leaguer & League Express Men of the Match: *Olympique:* Zac Santo; *Broncos:* Corey Norman.
Penalty count: 4-3; **Half-time:** 14-4;
Referee: Jack Smith; **Attendance:** 3,974.

Championship 2023 - Round by Round

London Broncos' Iliess Macani takes on Toulouse's Mathieu Jussaume during the Championship Grand Final

LEAGUE ONE 2023
Club by Club

League One 2023 - Club by Club

CORNWALL

DATE	FIXTURE	RESULT	SCORERS	LGE	ATT
19/2/23	Midlands Hurricanes (a)	L40-6	t:Slaney g:Rusling	9th	453
25/2/23	Rochdale Mayfield (h) (CCR2)	L14-20	t:Ashton,Brown,Aaronson g:Rusling	N/A	1,061
26/3/23	London Skolars (h)	W35-10	t:Carter(2),Cullen,Brown(2),Aaronson g:Rusling(5) fg:Rusling	6th	862
8/4/23	Doncaster (h)	L16-48	t:Rusling,Brown(2) g:Rusling(2)	7th	928
16/4/23	Dewsbury (a)	L78-10	t:Aaronson,Boots g:Rusling	8th	876
7/5/23	Oldham (a)	L36-16	t:Aaronson,Brown(2) g:Rusling(2)	8th	437
13/5/23	Hunslet (h)	L10-54	t:Brown,Ashton g:Rusling	8th	727
21/5/23	Rochdale (a)	L62-6	t:Weetman g:Brown	9th	496
28/5/23	North Wales (h)	L10-42	t:Weetman,Whitton g:Rusling	9th	1,008
4/6/23	Workington (a)	L54-0		9th	603
11/6/23	Dewsbury (h)	L6-30	t:Nichol g:Brown	9th	1,164
18/6/23	Hunslet (a)	L36-6	t:Weetman g:Brown	9th	433
8/7/23	London Skolars (a)	W14-30	t:Cullen,Ashton,I Badham,Weetman,Collins g:Rusling(5)	9th	281
16/7/23	Midlands Hurricanes (h)	W28-8	t:Nichol,Rusling,Brown(2),Whitton g:Rusling(4)	8th	957
23/7/23	Workington (h)	L16-34	t:Nichol,Brown,Rusling g:Rusling(2)	9th	1,204
30/7/23	North Wales (a) ●	W38-40	t:Boots,Brown(2),Cullen,Scurr,Rusling,Barraclough g:Rusling(6)	8th	649
6/8/23	Oldham (h)	L4-56	t:Mitchell	9th	891
20/8/23	Doncaster (a)	L60-0		9th	1,072
27/8/23	Rochdale (h)	W18-12	t:Brown,Mitchell,Whitton g:Brown(3)	9th	1,281

● *Played at Tynewydd Fields, Rhyl*

		APP		TRIES		GOALS		FG		PTS	
	D.O.B.	ALL	L1	ALL	L1	ALL	L1	ALL	L1	ALL	L1
Harry Aaronson	28/3/98	12	11	4	3	0	0	0	0	16	12
Callum Abbott	29/12/98	(1)	(1)	0	0	0	0	0	0	0	0
Tom Ashton	20/6/92	14	13	3	2	0	0	0	0	12	8
Ewan Badham	29/11/01	8(6)	8(6)	0	0	0	0	0	0	0	0
Ieuan Badham	29/11/01	(9)	(9)	1	1	0	0	0	0	4	4
Jaden Barraclough	10/7/03	(9)	(9)	1	1	0	0	0	0	4	4
Reece Boase	29/7/97	(3)	(3)	0	0	0	0	0	0	0	0
Charley Bodman	7/12/01	2(4)	2(4)	0	0	0	0	0	0	0	0
Paul Bolger	6/10/95	3(3)	3(3)	0	0	0	0	0	0	0	0
Harry Boots	15/12/96	10(6)	9(6)	2	2	0	0	0	0	8	8
Cameron Brown	8/4/00	17	16	14	13	6	6	0	0	68	64
Jordan Bull	14/12/99	(1)	(1)	0	0	0	0	0	0	0	0
Errol Carter	22/1/96	13	12	2	2	0	0	0	0	8	8
Luke Collins	7/12/97	15(2)	14(2)	1	1	0	0	0	0	4	4
Sean Croston	1/11/99	6	6	0	0	0	0	0	0	0	0
Nathan Cullen	24/11/02	17	16	3	3	0	0	0	0	12	12
Spencer Darley	25/9/98	(1)	(1)	0	0	0	0	0	0	0	0
Kaine Dimech	23/11/95	12(7)	11(7)	0	0	0	0	0	0	0	0
Josh Hartshorne	6/11/95	6(1)	5(1)	0	0	0	0	0	0	0	0
Brad Howe	21/12/95	1(2)	1(1)	0	0	0	0	0	0	0	0
Jake Lloyd	2/11/97	18(1)	17(1)	0	0	0	0	0	0	0	0
George Mitchell	22/5/97	4(3)	4(2)	2	2	0	0	0	0	8	8
Nathan Newbound	17/8/00	5	5	0	0	0	0	0	0	0	0
Coby Nichol	16/4/03	16(1)	15(1)	3	3	0	0	0	0	12	12
Jamie Prisk	31/1/93	(2)	(1)	0	0	0	0	0	0	0	0
Morgan Punchard	26/1/99	8	8	0	0	0	0	0	0	0	0
Jack Ray	8/10/98	5	5	0	0	0	0	0	0	0	0
Adam Rusling	25/5/03	13(1)	12(1)	4	4	31	30	1	1	79	77
Mackenzie Scurr	3/6/03	3	3	1	1	0	0	0	0	4	4
Louis Singleton	29/9/91	1(2)	1(1)	0	0	0	0	0	0	0	0
Nick Slaney	12/11/93	1	1	1	1	0	0	0	0	4	4
Leo Tennison	31/5/04	2(1)	2(1)	0	0	0	0	0	0	0	0
Decarlo Trerise	27/12/94	5(7)	5(7)	0	0	0	0	0	0	0	0
Tyler Walton	20/12/00	(1)	(1)	0	0	0	0	0	0	0	0
David Weetman	24/5/98	11(1)	11(1)	4	4	0	0	0	0	16	16
Harvey Whiteley	26/9/98	(1)	(1)	0	0	0	0	0	0	0	0
Liam Whitton	14/7/01	19	18	3	3	0	0	0	0	12	12

'L1' totals include League One games only; 'All' totals also include Challenge Cup

Liam Whitton

LEAGUE RECORD
P18-W5-D0-L13 (9th)
F257, A712, Diff-455, 10 points.

CHALLENGE CUP
Round Two

ATTENDANCES
Best - v Rochdale (L1 - 1,281)
Worst - v Hunslet (L1 - 727)
Total (excluding Challenge Cup) - 9,022
Average (excluding Challenge Cup) - 1,002
(Down by 43 on 2022)

CLUB RECORDS Highest score: 40-38 v North Wales, 30/7/2023 **Highest score against:** 78-10 v Dewsbury, 16/4/2023
Record attendance: 1,473 v Midlands Hurricanes, 10/4/2022
MATCH RECORDS Tries: 2 (7 players) Goals: 6 Adam Rusling v North Wales, 30/7/2023 Points: 16 Adam Rusling v North Wales, 30/7/2023
SEASON RECORDS Tries: 14 Cameron Brown 2023 Goals: 31 Adam Rusling 2023 Points: 79 Adam Rusling 2023
CAREER RECORDS Tries: 14 Cameron Brown 2023 Goals: 43 (inc 1fg) Adam Rusling 2022-2023 Points: 117 Adam Rusling 2022-2023 Appearances: 35 Liam Whitton 2022-2023

League One 2023 - Club by Club

DEWSBURY RAMS

DATE	FIXTURE	RESULT	SCORERS	LGE	ATT
19/2/23	North Wales (a) ●	W18-38	t:Restall(2),Greensmith,Jordan(2),Whiteley,Graham g:Sykes(5)	3rd	300
25/2/23	Ashton Bears (a) (CCR2) ●●	W8-38	t:R Dixon,Whiteley,Ferguson,Beckett,D Dixon,Jordan g:Sykes(5),Turner(2)	N/A	483
5/3/23	Midlands Hurricanes (h)	W50-10	t:Greensmith,Turner(2),Restall,Carr,Butterworth,Ferguson,Davies g:Sykes(9)	1st	771
12/3/23	Rochdale (h) (CCR3)	W38-18	t:Graham(3),Turner,Day,Davies,Greensmith g:Turner(5)	N/A	445
19/3/23	Workington (a)	W6-25	t:Whiteley,Jordan,Graham,Whiteley,R Dixon g:Sykes(2) fg:Sykes	1st	650
26/3/23	Rochdale (a)	W4-52	t:Carr,Greensmith,Ferguson(2),Restall(3),Whiteley,O'Connor g:Sykes(8)	1st	573
2/4/23	Widnes (h) (CCR4)	W32-12	t:Carr,Butterworth(2),Greensmith,R Dixon g:Sykes(6)	N/A	802
7/4/23	Hunslet (h)	W12-6	t:Turner,Carr g:Sykes(2)	1st	1,565
16/4/23	Cornwall (h)	W78-10	t:Whiteley(4),Beckett,D Dixon(3),Day(3),Summers,Frewin,Morris g:Turner(11)	1st	876
23/4/23	London Broncos (a) (CCR5) ●●●	L36-16	t:Carr(2),Graham g:Sykes(2)	N/A	353
29/4/23	London Skolars (a)	W16-48	t:Restall(3),Jordan(2),Carr(2),Greensmith,Garside g:Sykes(6)	1st	236
14/5/23	Doncaster (h)	W26-12	t:Turner,Frewin(2),Restall,Graham g:Sykes(2),Turner	1st	2,015
21/5/23	Oldham (a)	D26-26	t:Graham,Beckett,D Dixon,O'Connor g:Sykes(5)	1st	1,295
28/5/23	London Skolars (h)	W52-6	t:Restall(3),D Dixon(2),O'Connor(2),Garside,Collins g:Sykes(8)	1st	825
11/6/23	Cornwall (a)	W6-30	t:Beckett,Jordan(2),Graham,Carr g:Sykes(5)	1st	1,164
16/6/23	Rochdale (h)	W42-0	t:Collinson,Restall,Sykes,Gabriel,Graham,O'Connor(2) g:Sykes(7)	1st	811
23/6/23	Oldham (h)	W20-8	t:Graham,Sykes,Davies g:Sykes(4)	1st	1,650
2/7/23	Midlands Hurricanes (a)	W23-28	t:Greensmith(2),Day,Carr,R Dixon g:Sykes(2),Turner(2)	1st	423
23/7/23	North Wales (h)	W18-4	t:Whiteley,O'Connor g:Sykes(5)	1st	807
30/7/23	Hunslet (a)	L16-14	t:Graham(2),O'Connor g:Sykes	1st	1,064
6/8/23	Workington (h)	W38-8	t:R Dixon,Sykes,Gabriel(3),Restall g:Sykes(7)	1st	1,579
27/8/23	Doncaster (a)	L36-26	t:Garside(3),Restall,Greensmith g:Sykes(3)	1st	1,064

● Played at DCBL Stadium, Widnes
●● Played at FLAIR Stadium
●●● Played at The Rock, Roehampton

	D.O.B.	APP ALL	APP L1	TRIES ALL	TRIES L1	GOALS ALL	GOALS L1	FG ALL	FG L1	PTS ALL	PTS L1
Jimmy Beckett	29/8/99	22	18	4	3	0	0	0	0	16	12
Reiss Butterworth	7/12/98	22	18	3	1	0	0	0	0	12	4
Lewis Carr	11/8/00	17	14	10	7	0	0	0	0	40	28
George Collins	30/10/02	(1)	(1)	1	1	0	0	0	0	4	4
Louis Collinson	17/10/01	11	10	1	1	0	0	0	0	4	4
Jack Coventry	5/3/94	1(3)	1(2)	0	0	0	0	0	0	0	0
Connor Davies	17/1/97	13(5)	10(5)	3	2	0	0	0	0	12	8
Sam Day	12/6/94	1(11)	1(8)	5	4	0	0	0	0	20	16
Davey Dixon	31/5/97	6(1)	5(1)	7	6	0	0	0	0	28	24
Ronan Dixon	25/7/97	13(6)	10(5)	5	3	0	0	0	0	20	12
Oliver Farrar	8/6/02	(1)	(1)	0	0	0	0	0	0	0	0
Dale Ferguson	13/4/88	(11)	(10)	4	3	0	0	0	0	16	12
Simon Frewin	11/8/87	4	3	3	3	0	0	0	0	12	12
Andy Gabriel	21/12/93	3	3	4	4	0	0	0	0	16	16
Matt Garside	1/10/90	19	16	5	5	0	0	0	0	20	20
Brad Graham	1/9/01	19	15	13	9	0	0	0	0	52	36
Ollie Greensmith	3/12/99	20	16	9	7	0	0	0	0	36	28
Caelum Jordan	16/9/02	12	9	8	7	0	0	0	0	32	28
Luke Littlewood	7/11/00	1(7)	1(5)	0	0	0	0	0	0	0	0
Will Maher	4/11/95	4(1)	4(1)	0	0	0	0	0	0	0	0
Elliot Morris	4/1/96	2(19)	1(16)	1	1	0	0	0	0	4	4
Bailey O'Connor	29/5/02	13(4)	11(3)	8	8	0	0	0	0	32	32
Owen Restall	5/8/95	22	18	16	16	0	0	0	0	64	64
Joe Summers	7/11/99	1(4)	1(4)	1	1	0	0	0	0	4	4
Paul Sykes	11/8/81	19	16	3	2	89	76	1	1	191	165
Calum Turner	29/4/99	21	17	5	4	26	19	0	0	72	54
Jackson Walker	1/4/01	4(12)	3(9)	0	0	0	0	0	0	0	0
Perry Whiteley	22/2/93	16	13	10	9	0	0	0	0	40	36
Tom Wilkinson	3/10/02	(2)	(1)	0	0	0	0	0	0	0	0

'L1' totals include League One games only; 'All' totals also include Challenge Cup

Owen Restall

LEAGUE RECORD
P18-W15-D1-L2 (1st/Champions)
F623, A215, Diff+408, 31 points.

CHALLENGE CUP
Round Five

ATTENDANCES
Best - v Doncaster (L1 - 2,015)
Worst - v Rochdale (CC - 445)
Total (excluding Challenge Cup) - 10,899
Average (excluding Challenge Cup) - 1,211
(Up by 61 on 2022, Championship)

CLUB RECORDS	
MATCH RECORDS	**Highest score:** 90-5 v Blackpool, 4/4/93 **Highest score against:** 0-82 v Widnes, 30/11/86
	Record attendance: 26,584 v Halifax, 30/10/1920 *(Crown Flatt)*; 4,068 v Bradford, 6/4/2015 *(Tetley's/FLAIR Stadium)*
	Tries: 8 Dai Thomas v Liverpool, 13/4/1907
SEASON RECORDS	**Goals:** 13 Greg Pearce v Blackpool Borough, 4/4/93; Francis Maloney v Hunslet, 25/3/2007 **Points:** 32 Les Holliday v Barrow, 11/9/94
	Tries: 40 Dai Thomas 1906-07 **Goals:** 169 Barry Eaton 2000 **Points:** 394 Barry Eaton 2000
CAREER RECORDS	**Tries:** 144 Joe Lyman 1913-31 **Goals:** 863 Nigel Stephenson 1967-78; 1984-86 **Points:** 2,082 Nigel Stephenson 1967-78; 1984-86
	Appearances: 454 Joe Lyman 1913-31

League One 2023 - Club by Club

DONCASTER

DATE	FIXTURE	RESULT	SCORERS	LGE	ATT
19/2/23	Hunslet (h)	W18-16	t:Hall,McConnell,Halliday g:Robinson(3)	4th	1,251
26/2/23	Oldham (h) (CCR2)	W28-26	t:Sanderson(4),Ferres g:Robinson(4)	N/A	517
5/3/23	Rochdale (a)	W10-20	t:Robinson,Hall,Burns,Sanderson g:Robinson(2)	2nd	391
12/3/23	Workington (h) (CCR3)	W24-20	t:Halliday(2),Robinson,Hall g:Robinson(4)	N/A	485
19/3/23	North Wales (h)	W30-16	t:Halliday,Smeaton(3),Corion g:Robinson(5)	2nd	837
1/4/23	London Broncos (a) (CCR4) ●	L66-16	t:Hey,Corion,Ollett-Hobson g:Sanderson(2)	N/A	428
8/4/23	Cornwall (h)	W16-48	t:Smeaton(4),Hey,Hall,Ferres(2),Halliday g:Robinson(6)	2nd	928
16/4/23	Oldham (h)	W26-22	t:Hall(2),Hey,Halliday,Ferres g:Robinson(3)	2nd	1,308
7/5/23	Workington (h)	W46-6	t:Hall,Smeaton,McConnell(2),Sanderson,Tali(2),Johnston g:Robinson(7)	2nd	1,255
14/5/23	Dewsbury (a)	L26-12	t:Robinson,Tali g:Robinson(2)	2nd	2,015
21/5/23	London Skolars (h)	W60-30	t:Veacock,Robinson(2),Sanderson,Smeaton(2),Hall,Roberts,Johnston(2) g:Robinson(10)	2nd	1,158
4/6/23	Midlands Hurricanes (a)	W26-54	t:Cooper(3),Roberts(2),James,Robinson,Foster,Johnston g:Robinson(9)	2nd	273
11/6/23	Rochdale (h)	W42-20	t:Smeaton(3),Guzdek,Johnston,James,Robinson g:Robinson(6),Taulapapa	2nd	1,191
18/6/23	Oldham (a)	W22-28	t:Taulapapa(2),Smeaton,Hey,Johnston g:Robinson(4)	2nd	647
2/7/23	Hunslet (a)	L28-8	t:Hey,Taulapapa	2nd	767
23/7/23	Midlands Hurricanes (h)	L10-41	t:Smeaton,Butterworth g:Robinson	4th	864
30/7/23	Workington (h)	W19-22	t:Halliday,Guzdek,Smeaton(2) g:Robinson(3)	3rd	1,074
6/8/23	North Wales (a) ●●	L28-22	t:Sanderson,Robinson,Taulapapa,Johnston g:Robinson(3)	3rd	531
11/8/23	London Skolars (a)	W0-60	t:Taulapapa,Vete(2),Halliday,Boas(2),Holdstock,Robinson,Smeaton(2) g:Robinson(6),Boas(2)	3rd	509
20/8/23	Cornwall (h)	W60-0	t:Fonua(2),Johnston,Burns,Halliday(2),Boas,Corion(2),Ferres,Vete g:Robinson(8)	3rd	1,072
27/8/23	Dewsbury (h)	W36-26	t:Fonua(2),Boas(3),Johnston g:Robinson(6)	3rd	1,064
3/9/23	Oldham (h) (QPO)	W36-0	t:Fonua,Vete,Robinson,Holdstock,Halliday(2) g:Robinson(6)	N/A	615
10/9/23	Hunslet (a) (QSF)	W14-26	t:Fonua(2),Johnston,Boas,Smeaton g:Robinson(3)	N/A	897
24/9/23	North Wales (h) (ProF)	W18-6	t:Fonua,McConnell,Smeaton g:Robinson(3)	N/A	2,549

● Played at The Rock, Roehampton
●● Played at Hare Lane, Chester

Sam Smeaton

		APP		TRIES		GOALS		FG		PTS	
	D.O.B.	ALL	L1	ALL	L1	ALL	L1	ALL	L1	ALL	L1
Watson Boas	8/11/94	1(8)	1(8)	7	7	2	2	0	0	32	32
Greg Burns	25/3/95	20(2)	19(2)	2	2	0	0	0	0	8	8
Olly Butterworth	12/1/98	2	2	1	1	0	0	0	0	4	4
Max Clarke	1/1/00	(1)	(1)	0	0	0	0	0	0	0	0
Luke Cooper	28/7/94	10(3)	10(2)	3	3	0	0	0	0	12	12
Travis Corion	27/3/01	10	8	4	3	0	0	0	0	16	12
Bureta Faraimo	16/7/90	1	1	0	0	0	0	0	0	0	0
Brett Ferres	17/4/86	23	21	5	4	0	0	0	0	20	16
Mahe Fonua	24/12/92	5	5	8	8	0	0	0	0	32	32
Keelan Foster	26/1/00	11(8)	10(7)	1	1	0	0	0	0	4	4
Josh Guzdek	22/4/95	11	11	2	2	0	0	0	0	8	8
Elliot Hall	6/7/97	12	9	8	7	0	0	0	0	32	28
Tom Halliday	2/2/97	22	19	12	10	0	0	0	0	48	40
Brad Hey	4/9/94	22	20	5	4	0	0	0	0	20	16
Alex Holdstock	16/6/01	4(10)	1(10)	2	2	0	0	0	0	8	8
Matt James	26/3/87	6(13)	6(12)	2	2	0	0	0	0	8	8
Ben Johnston	8/3/92	22	20	10	10	0	0	0	0	40	40
Jose Kenga	3/5/95	5(8)	3(8)	0	0	0	0	0	0	0	0
Brad Knowles	31/7/93	10(7)	9(7)	0	0	0	0	0	0	0	0
Loui McConnell	21/11/99	19(1)	18	4	4	0	0	0	0	16	16
Aaron Ollett-Hobson	19/11/92	2(1)	(1)	1	0	0	0	0	0	4	0
Dave Petersen	6/3/92	1(3)	(3)	0	0	0	0	0	0	0	0
Jack Potter	12/6/04	1	0	0	0	0	0	0	0	0	0
Dean Roberts	19/8/96	1(13)	(11)	3	3	0	0	0	0	12	12
Connor Robinson	23/10/94	23	21	10	9	104	96	0	0	248	228
Jack Sanderson	18/3/98	12	9	8	4	2	0	0	0	36	16
Sam Smeaton	26/10/88	24	21	21	21	0	0	0	0	84	84
Jason Tali	7/7/89	9(1)	9	3	3	0	0	0	0	12	12
Misi Taulapapa	25/1/82	12(3)	11(2)	6	6	1	1	0	0	26	26
Josh Veacock	16/12/94	1(2)	1(2)	1	1	0	0	0	0	4	4
Albert Vete	24/1/93	6(2)	6(2)	4	4	0	0	0	0	16	16
Ross Whitmore	9/2/00	3(8)	2(6)	0	0	0	0	0	0	0	0
Brandan Wilkinson	7/9/97	1(2)	0	0	0	0	0	0	0	0	0

'L1' totals include regular season & play-offs; 'All' totals also include Challenge Cup

LEAGUE RECORD
P18-W14-D0-L4
(3rd/Promotion Final Winners)
F602, A352, Diff+250, 28 points.

CHALLENGE CUP
Round Four

ATTENDANCES
Best - v North Wales (L1-ProF - 2,549)
Worst - v Workington (CC - 485)
Total (excluding Challenge Cup) - 13,164
Average (excluding Challenge Cup) - 1,197
(Up by 198 on 2022)

CLUB RECORDS
MATCH RECORDS Highest score: 102-6 v West Wales, 15/7/2018 Highest score against: 4-90 v Widnes, 10/6/2007
Record attendance: 10,000 v Bradford, 16/2/52 *(York Road)*; 6,528 v Castleford, 12/4/2007 *(Keepmoat/Eco-Power Stadium)*
Tries: 6 Kane Epati v Oldham, 30/7/2006; Lee Waterman v Sharlston, 24/3/2012
Goals: 15 Liam Harris v West Wales, 15/7/2018
SEASON RECORDS Tries: 36 Lee Waterman 2012 Goals: 129 Jonny Woodcock 2002 Points: 306 Jonny Woodcock 2002
CAREER RECORDS Tries: 112 Mark Roache 1985-97 Goals: 850 David Noble 1976-77; 1980-89; 1992 Points: 1,751 David Noble 1976-77; 1980-89; 1992
Appearances: 327 Audley Pennant 1980-83; 1985-97

League One 2023 - Club by Club

HUNSLET

DATE	FIXTURE	RESULT	SCORERS	LGE	ATT
19/2/23	Doncaster (a)	L18-16	t:J Burton,Crossley,Render g:Sweeting(2)	7th	1,251
26/2/23	Heworth (h) (CCR2)	W68-6	t:York,Syme,Render,Ryder(2),Newbound,J Burton,Jordan-Roberts,McGrath,Watson,H Hallas,Barcoe g:Sweeting(10)	N/A	556
5/3/23	North Wales (h)	W22-8	t:Sweeting,Newbound,H Hallas,J Burton g:Sweeting(3)	5th	504
12/3/23	Keighley (h) (CCR3)	L14-16	t:Ryder,Wheeler,J Burton g:Knowles	N/A	519
18/3/23	London Skolars (a)	W22-66	t:Jordan-Roberts,Ryder(4),Knowles,S Hallas,Crossley,Conroy,Greenwood,Sweeting,Render g:Sweeting(9)	3rd	186
7/4/23	Dewsbury (a)	L12-6	t:Render g:Jordan-Roberts	5th	1,565
16/4/23	Midlands Hurricanes (h)	W48-6	t:Render(2),H Hallas(2),Syme(2),Conroy,Wheeler,Ryder g:Beharrell(6)	5th	358
13/5/23	Cornwall (a)	W10-54	t:Conroy,Ryder,Wray,Campbell,Syme,Goddard,Jordan-Roberts,J Burton,Barcoe,Render g:Knowles(6),Punchard	4th	727
21/5/23	Workington (h)	W22-18	t:Croston,Crossley(2) g:Beharrell(5)	4th	347
28/5/23	Rochdale (h)	W36-18	t:Conroy,Campbell(3),Jordan-Roberts,Beharrell,Render g:Beharrell(4)	4th	481
3/6/23	Oldham (a)	L40-20	t:Render,Conroy,Campbell g:Beharrell(4)	4th	361
18/6/23	Cornwall (h)	W36-6	t:Ryder,J Burton,Lawford(2),Jordan-Roberts,Watson g:Beharrell(6)	4th	433
25/6/23	North Wales (a) ●	W20-30	t:Render,S Hallas(2),Jordan-Roberts,Watson g:Beharrell(5)	4th	363
2/7/23	Doncaster (h)	W28-8	t:H Hallas,Lawford,Render(2) g:Beharrell(4)	3rd	767
9/7/23	Midlands Hurricanes (a) ●●	W22-54	t:Syme,Ryder(2),Goddard(3),O Burton,Wray,York g:Beharrell(8),Lawford	2nd	547
16/7/23	Oldham (h)	W21-8	t:Lawford,Render,J Burton g:Beharrell(4) fg:Knowles	2nd	726
30/7/23	Dewsbury (h)	W16-14	t:Campbell,Beharrell,Jordan-Roberts g:Beharrell(2)	2nd	1,064
6/8/23	Rochdale (a)	W22-35	t:H Hallas,Ryder,J Burton(2),Campbell(2),Render g:Beharrell(3) fg:Beharrell	2nd	344
20/8/23	London Skolars (h)	W56-14	t:Beharrell,Ryder,Crossley,Campbell(3),Syme,Lawford,J Burton,Wray g:Beharrell(7),Lawford	2nd	484
27/8/23	Workington (a)	L18-6	t:McGrath g:Beharrell	2nd	803
10/9/23	Doncaster (h) (QSF)	L14-26	t:Ryder,Campbell g:Beharrell(3)	N/A	897
17/9/23	North Wales (h) (FE)	L18-25	t:Watson,Goddard,Ryder g:Beharrell(3)	N/A	626

● Played at Hare Lane, Chester
●● Played at Haslams Lane, Derby

	D.O.B.	APP ALL	APP L1	TRIES ALL	TRIES L1	GOALS ALL	GOALS L1	FG ALL	FG L1	PTS ALL	PTS L1
Danny Barcoe	5/7/00	(7)	(6)	2	1	0	0	0	0	8	4
Matty Beharrell	29/3/94	15	15	3	3	65	65	1	1	143	143
Jordan Bull	14/12/99	5(3)	3(3)	0	0	0	0	0	0	0	0
Joe Burton	15/3/02	22	20	10	8	0	0	0	0	40	32
Oli Burton	15/3/02	(10)	(10)	1	1	0	0	0	0	4	4
Johnny Campbell	17/7/87	7	7	12	12	0	0	0	0	48	48
Liam Carr	10/11/02	(2)	(1)	0	0	0	0	0	0	0	0
Nathan Conroy	6/3/95	11(1)	10(1)	5	5	0	0	0	0	20	20
Steve Crossley	28/11/89	20	20	5	5	0	0	0	0	20	20
Sean Croston	1/11/99	2	2	1	1	0	0	0	0	4	4
Spencer Darley	25/9/98	1(4)	1(4)	0	0	0	0	0	0	0	0
Alfie Goddard	16/3/00	13	13	5	5	0	0	0	0	20	20
Marcus Green	27/3/03	(10)	(10)	0	0	0	0	0	0	0	0
Jamie Greenwood	27/10/98	(1)	(1)	1	1	0	0	0	0	4	4
Harvey Hallas	14/11/97	16(3)	14(3)	6	5	0	0	0	0	24	20
Sam Hallas	18/10/96	21	19	3	3	0	0	0	0	12	12
Josh Jordan-Roberts	26/8/98	22	20	7	6	1	1	0	0	30	26
Michael Knowles	2/5/87	18	17	1	1	7	6	1	1	19	17
Myles Lawford	9/9/03	10	10	6	6	2	2	0	0	28	28
Kieron Lawton	7/5/02	3	3	0	0	0	0	0	0	0	0
Jake Maizen	4/1/97	2	2	0	0	0	0	0	0	0	0
Dan McGrath	2/12/01	3	1	2	1	0	0	0	0	8	4
Nathan Newbound	17/8/00	1(7)	1(5)	2	1	0	0	0	0	8	4
Morgan Punchard	26/1/99	2	1	0	0	1	1	0	0	2	2
Jack Render	4/7/99	20	18	14	13	0	0	0	0	56	52
Adam Ryder	20/10/89	22	20	16	13	0	0	0	0	64	52
Fraser Stroud	12/4/99	2	2	0	0	0	0	0	0	0	0
Jake Sweeting	15/12/99	6(1)	5(1)	2	2	24	14	0	0	56	36
Jordan Syme	14/11/96	9(11)	7(11)	6	5	0	0	0	0	24	20
Jimmy Watson	9/9/91	1b	14	4	3	U	U	U	U	1b	12
Brad Wheeler	16/5/04	1(5)	1(4)	2	1	0	0	0	0	8	4
Harvey Whiteley	26/9/98	(2)	(1)	0	0	0	0	0	0	0	0
Lewis Wray	6/5/98	(19)	(17)	3	3	0	0	0	0	12	12
Aaron York	7/4/99	16(2)	14(2)	2	1	0	0	0	0	8	4

'L1' totals include regular season & play-offs; 'All' totals also include Challenge Cup

Adam Ryder

LEAGUE RECORD
P18-W14-D0-L4 (2nd/Final Eliminator)
F572, A284, Diff+288, 28 points.

CHALLENGE CUP
Round Three

ATTENDANCES
Best - v Dewsbury (L1 - 1,064)
Worst - v Workington (L1 - 347)
Total (excluding Challenge Cup) - 6,687
Average (excluding Challenge Cup) - 608
(Up by 55 on 2022)

CLUB RECORDS
MATCH RECORDS Highest score: 86-0 v West Wales, 27/5/2018; 86-6 v West Wales, 4/8/2018 Highest score against: 0-82 v Bradford, 2/3/2003
Record attendance: 24,700 v Wigan, 15/3/24 (Parkside); 2,454 v Wakefield, 13/4/98 (South Leeds Stadium)
Tries: 7 George Dennis v Bradford, 20/1/34 Goals: 13 Joe Sanderson v West Wales, 27/5/2018; Joe Sanderson v West Wales, 4/8/2018
Points: 30 Simon Wilson v Highfield, 21/1/96; Joe Sanderson v West Wales, 27/5/2018
SEASON RECORDS Tries: 34 Alan Snowden 1956-57 Goals: 181 Billy Langton 1958-59 Points: 380 Billy Langton 1958-59
CAREER RECORDS Tries: 154 Fred Williamson 1943-55 Goals: 1,044 Billy Langton 1955-66 Points: 2,202 Billy Langton 1955-66 Appearances: 579 Geoff Gunney 1951-73

League One 2023 - Club by Club

LONDON SKOLARS

DATE	FIXTURE	RESULT	SCORERS	LGE	ATT
18/2/23	Workington (h)	L16-58	t:O'Callaghan,Yates,Deery g:Ryan,Lee	10th	264
26/2/23	Rochdale (a) (CCR2)	L42-4	t:Ball	N/A	300
5/3/23	Oldham (a)	L62-18	t:Peut,Gale,Small g:Ryan(3)	10th	525
18/3/23	Hunslet (h)	L22-66	t:Small,Gale,O'Sullivan(2) g:Ryan(3)	10th	186
26/3/23	Cornwall (a)	L35-10	t:Yates,Cox g:Ryan	10th	862
29/4/23	Dewsbury (h)	L16-48	t:Bryan,Juma,Kaufman g:Ryan(2)	10th	236
7/5/23	Midlands Hurricanes (a)	L38-20	t:Yates,Juma,Kudangirana(2) g:Deery(2)	10th	239
13/5/23	Rochdale (h)	L24-28	t:Yates,Webb-Campbell,Deery,Ball,Wainwright g:Ryan,Deery	10th	209
21/5/23	Doncaster (a)	L60-30	t:Bryan,Deery,Dayes,Small,Juma g:Deery(5)	10th	1,158
28/5/23	Dewsbury (a)	L52-6	t:O'Callaghan g:Ryan	10th	825
3/6/23	North Wales (h)	L6-60	t:Small g:Thomas	10th	215
10/6/23	Oldham (h)	L14-62	t:Ball,Ross,Deery g:Deery	10th	338
18/6/23	Workington (a)	L34-6	t:Roberts g:Deery	10th	496
8/7/23	Cornwall (h)	L14-30	t:Ball(2),Deery g:Lyon	10th	281
5/8/23	Midlands Hurricanes (h)	L18-38	t:Porter,Juma,Ross g:Deery(3)	10th	204
11/8/23	Doncaster (h)	L0-60		10th	509
20/8/23	Hunslet (a)	L56-14	t:Allen,McDonald,Small g:Lyon	10th	484
27/8/23	North Wales (a)	L62-20	t:Juma,McDonald,Hughes,Ball g:Thomas,Lyon	10th	495

Handed 48-0 loss for Rochdale (a) game (unable to fulfil fixture)

		APP		TRIES		GOALS		FG		PTS	
	D.O.B.	ALL	L1	ALL	L1	ALL	L1	ALL	L1	ALL	L1
Max Allen	5/10/02	2	2	1	1	0	0	0	0	4	4
Leighton Ball	5/1/00	15	14	6	5	0	0	0	0	24	20
Sam Bardsley	28/1/00	(1)	(1)	0	0	0	0	0	0	0	0
Jason Bass	10/5/96	1	1	0	0	0	0	0	0	0	0
Delaine Bedward-Gittens	28/6/01	(2)	(1)	0	0	0	0	0	0	0	0
Luciano Bejanidze	3/12/02	12	11	0	0	0	0	0	0	0	0
Oliver Bloom	16/4/86	(1)	(1)	0	0	0	0	0	0	0	0
David Bofenda	10/8/99	1	1	0	0	0	0	0	0	0	0
Dan Bristow	22/8/95	8	8	0	0	0	0	0	0	0	0
Ed Brown	13/7/00	(4)	(3)	0	0	0	0	0	0	0	0
Lamont Bryan	12/4/88	8(3)	8(3)	2	2	0	0	0	0	8	8
Robbie Butterworth	7/6/02	2	2	0	0	0	0	0	0	0	0
Doug Chirnside	18/10/95	7(3)	7(3)	0	0	0	0	0	0	0	0
Anthony Cox	19/1/94	(5)	(5)	1	1	0	0	0	0	4	4
Henry Davetanivalu	6/2/98	(1)	(1)	0	0	0	0	0	0	0	0
Jaden Dayes	19/5/04	3	3	1	1	0	0	0	0	4	4
Alex Deery	24/2/02	9(5)	8(5)	5	5	13	13	0	0	46	46
Christian Gale	28/12/99	5(8)	4(8)	2	2	0	0	0	0	8	8
Josh Guzdek	22/4/95	2	2	0	0	0	0	0	0	0	0
Jack Harbridge	30/9/96	1(1)	1(1)	0	0	0	0	0	0	0	0
Jack Hughes	15/11/00	(3)	(3)	1	1	0	0	0	0	4	4
Shane Hurley	22/1/99	1	1	0	0	0	0	0	0	0	0
Elliott Hutchings	24/5/02	1(2)	1(1)	0	0	0	0	0	0	0	0
Lameck Juma	6/12/90	12	12	5	5	0	0	0	0	20	20
Harry Kaufman	20/12/91	2(2)	2(2)	1	1	0	0	0	0	4	4
Donald Kudangirana	23/5/95	8	8	2	2	0	0	0	0	8	8
Shane Lee	3/3/97	2(2)	1(2)	0	0	1	1	0	0	2	2
Malikhi Lloyd-Jones	29/8/94	13(1)	13(1)	0	0	0	0	0	0	0	0
Phil Lyon	21/3/92	4	4	0	0	3	3	0	0	6	6
Abevia McDonald	6/7/92	3	3	2	2	0	0	0	0	8	8
Jimmy Morgan	1/6/93	6	5	0	0	0	0	0	0	0	0
Liam O'Callaghan	24/9/94	9(2)	9(2)	2	2	0	0	0	0	8	8
Louis O'Sullivan	11/7/02	10	9	2	2	0	0	0	0	8	8
Todd Peut	27/4/88	9(9)	8(9)	1	1	0	0	0	0	4	4
Fraser Piercy-Farley	7/11/00	2(4)	2(3)	0	0	0	0	0	0	0	0
Tommy Porter	26/6/04	4(3)	4(3)	1	1	0	0	0	0	4	4
Ellis Roberts	12/11/03	(2)	(2)	1	1	0	0	0	0	4	4
Matt Ross	2/9/92	14(3)	13(3)	2	2	0	0	0	0	8	8
Jack Ryan	23/6/99	14	13	0	0	12	12	0	0	24	24
Joe Saunders	15/3/04	1	1	0	0	0	0	0	0	0	0
Aaron Small	28/10/91	16	15	5	5	0	0	0	0	20	20
Jacob Thomas	9/10/93	13	12	0	0	2	2	0	0	4	4
Jake Tilford	14/1/98	(1)	(1)	0	0	0	0	0	0	0	0
Ethane Wainwright	29/9/03	2	2	1	1	0	0	0	0	4	4
Sam Webb-Campbell	23/8/04	1(2)	1(2)	1	1	0	0	0	0	4	4
Sam Wellings	13/12/89	1(2)	1(2)	0	0	0	0	0	0	0	0
Jerome Yates	31/10/97	10	9	4	4	0	0	0	0	16	16

'L1' totals include League One games only; 'All' totals also include Challenge Cup

Alex Deery

LEAGUE RECORD
P18-W0-D0-L18 (10th)
F254, A897, Diff-643, 0 points.

CHALLENGE CUP
Round Two

ATTENDANCES
Best - v Doncaster (L1 - 509)
Worst - v Hunslet (L1 - 186)
Total (all home games included) - 2,442
Average (all home games included) - 271
(Down by 29 on 2022)

CLUB RECORDS
MATCH RECORDS — Highest score: 76-8 v West Wales, 7/4/2018; 76-6 v Hemel, 8/9/2018 Highest score against: 4-98 v Sheffield, 3/8/2003
Record attendance: 1,524 v Toronto, 4/3/2017
Tries: 5 Mark Cantoni v Gateshead, 27/6/2004; Omari Caro v West Wales, 29/5/2021
Goals: 12 Neil Thorman v West Wales, 7/4/2018 Points: 28 Dylan Skee v South Wales, 29/7/2012
SEASON RECORDS — Tries: 21 Mark Cantoni 2004 Goals: 100 Dylan Skee 2013 Points: 248 Dylan Skee 2013
CAREER RECORDS — Tries: 57 Austen Aggrey 2004-2012 Goals: 230 *(inc 1fg)* Dylan Skee 2011-2013 Points: 579 Dylan Skee 2011-2013 Appearances: 198 Gareth Honor 2003-2011

League One 2023 - Club by Club

MIDLANDS HURRICANES

DATE	FIXTURE	RESULT	SCORERS	LGE	ATT
19/2/23	Cornwall (h)	W40-6	t:Hallett,Martin,Flanagan,Wallis(2),Windley,M Welham g:Stead(6)	2nd	453
26/2/23	Hull Dockers (a) (CCR2) ●	W4-50	t:Bailey,Wallis,Dunne(2),M Welham(2),B Dawson,Hallett,L Welham g:Stead(7)	N/A	965
5/3/23	Dewsbury (a)	L50-10	t:M Welham(2) g:Stead	6th	771
11/3/23	Orrell St James (a) (CCR3)	W12-19	t:Dunne,Hill,M Welham g:Stead(3) fg:Coates	N/A	-
19/3/23	Rochdale (h)	L24-32	t:Flanagan,Bowring,Willis,Hallett g:Coates(4)	7th	384
26/3/23	Workington (h)	L28-38	t:B Dawson,M Welham,Hallett,Hill,Romeo g:Stead(4)	7th	324
2/4/23	Bradford (h) (CCR4) ●●	L18-66	t:M Welham,Moran,Dunne g:Stead(3)	N/A	1,003
16/4/23	Hunslet (h)	L48-6	t:Hallett g:Stead	6th	358
7/5/23	London Skolars (h)	W38-20	t:Freeman(3),Martin,M Welham,Johnson,L Welham g:Stead(5)	6th	239
21/5/23	North Wales (h)	L14-42	t:B Dawson,Hallett,Hill g:Stead	7th	321
28/5/23	Oldham (h)	L16-50	t:Beer,Cullimore,Freeman g:Stead(2)	8th	342
4/6/23	Doncaster (h)	L26-54	t:T Wilkinson,M Welham(3),Bass g:Stead(3)	8th	273
18/6/23	North Wales (a) ●●●	L62-24	t:Hill,Johnson,Stead,B Dawson g:Stead(4)	8th	205
25/6/23	Workington (a)	L60-10	t:Freeman,Richardson g:Stead	8th	843
2/7/23	Dewsbury (h)	L23-28	t:Horner,Bass,L Welham g:Stead(5) fg:Stead	8th	423
9/7/23	Hunslet (h) ●●●●	L22-54	t:Beardsworth,Clavering,Willis,Hallett g:Hookem(3)	8th	547
16/7/23	Cornwall (a)	L28-8	t:Johnson,Freeman	9th	957
23/7/23	Doncaster (a)	W10-41	t:L Welham(2),Barcoe,Oakes,Hookem,Bowring g:Hookem(8) fg:T Wilkinson	8th	864
30/7/23	Rochdale (a)	L37-22	t:Chrimes(2),L Welham,Bowring g:Hookem(3)	9th	334
5/8/23	London Skolars (a)	W18-38	t:M Welham(2),Turner(3),Sweeting,Chrimes g:Farrell(5)	8th	204
27/8/23	Oldham (a)	W10-18	t:Hookem,Turner,Levy g:Hookem(3)	8th	472

● Played at Sewell Group Craven Park ●● Played at Odsal Stadium ●●● Played at Nant Conwy RU Club ●●●● Played at Haslams Lane, Derby

		APP		TRIES		GOALS		FG		PTS	
	D.O.B.	ALL	L1	ALL	L1	ALL	L1	ALL	L1	ALL	L1
Matthew Bailey	1/12/91	4(8)	2(7)	1	0	0	0	0	0	4	0
Abdullah Balogun	16/1/03	1(1)	1(1)	0	0	0	0	0	0	0	0
Danny Barcoe	5/7/00	2(2)	2(2)	1	1	0	0	0	0	4	4
Jason Bass	10/5/96	3	3	2	2	0	0	0	0	8	8
Finley Beardsworth	16/1/04	4	4	1	1	0	0	0	0	4	4
Jacob Beer	20/10/02	3(4)	3(3)	1	1	0	0	0	0	4	4
Sam Bowring	1/7/91	5(8)	4(7)	3	3	0	0	0	0	12	12
Mekhi Bridgeman-Reaney	28/2/03	1	1	0	0	0	0	0	0	0	0
Adam Brook	29/9/94	4	4	0	0	0	0	0	0	0	0
Morgan Burgess	7/1/02	1	1	0	0	0	0	0	0	0	0
Matty Chrimes	2/11/97	3	3	3	3	0	0	0	0	12	12
Brad Clavering	14/3/98	10(2)	9(2)	1	1	0	0	0	0	4	4
Dan Coates	30/8/99	4	3	0	0	4	4	1	0	9	8
Jack Coventry	5/3/94	(1)	(1)	0	0	0	0	0	0	0	0
Chris Cullimore	13/2/93	13(6)	11(5)	1	1	0	0	0	0	4	4
Bailey Dawson	18/5/03	6(3)	5(2)	4	3	0	0	0	0	16	12
Jack Dawson	12/1/93	4(6)	3(4)	0	0	0	0	0	0	0	0
Callum Dunne	29/3/95	6	3	4	0	0	0	0	0	16	0
Izaac Farrell	30/1/98	2	2	0	0	5	5	0	0	10	10
Dom Flanagan	7/4/95	4	2	2	2	0	0	0	0	8	8
Hayden Freeman	20/8/97	10	10	6	6	0	0	0	0	24	24
Connor Gilbey	23/6/02	1(2)	1	0	0	0	0	0	0	0	0
Sam Hall	8/5/02	1	1	0	0	0	0	0	0	0	0
Macauley Hallett	27/11/95	17	14	7	6	0	0	0	0	28	24
Benn Hardcastle	4/1/90	1	1	0	0	0	0	0	0	0	0
Tyler Hepple	28/10/02	3	2	1	0	0	0	0	0	4	0
Nathan Hill	13/7/97	12	9	4	3	0	0	0	0	16	12
Ellis Hobson	30/11/03	2(4)	2(4)	0	0	0	0	0	0	0	0
Jacob Hookem	4/10/02	9	9	2	2	17	17	0	0	42	42
Todd Horner	19/3/04	7	7	1	1	0	0	0	0	4	4
Ryan Johnson	3/8/00	10(1)	10(1)	3	3	0	0	0	0	12	12
Kyle Kesik	3/6/89	2	2	0	0	0	0	0	0	0	0
Jon Luke Kirby	23/9/98	5	5	0	0	0	0	0	0	0	0
Aaron Levy	19/12/95	5	2	1	1	0	0	0	0	4	4
Brad Martin	6/2/01	3	3	2	2	0	0	0	0	8	8
Courage Mkuhlani	29/10/03	(2)	(2)	0	0	0	0	0	0	0	0
Kieran Moran	2/11/96	11(7)	8(7)	1	0	0	0	0	0	4	0
Anesu Mudoti	19/1/01	(2)	(1)	0	0	0	0	0	0	0	0
Scott Murrell	5/9/85	2	2	0	0	0	0	0	0	0	0
Ross Oakes	12/10/96	1	1	1	1	0	0	0	0	4	4
Jason Qaregare	26/1/04	2	2	0	0	0	0	0	0	0	0
Toby Richardson	5/6/96	5(2)	5(2)	1	1	0	0	0	0	4	4
Joey Romeo	28/9/99	1	1	1	1	0	0	0	0	4	4
Kavan Rothwell	1/2/03	(1)	(1)	0	0	0	0	0	0	0	0
Ben Stead	13/10/92	14	11	1	1	46	33	1	1	97	71
Jake Sweeting	15/12/99	2	2	1	1	0	0	0	0	4	4
Mackenzie Turner	30/1/03	3	3	4	4	0	0	0	0	16	16
Elliot Wallis	10/5/00	3	2	3	2	0	0	0	0	12	8
Liam Welham	11/11/88	15(2)	13(2)	6	5	0	0	0	0	24	20
Matt Welham	1/2/93	19	16	14	10	0	0	0	0	56	40
Richard Wilkinson	26/10/93	3(1)	2(1)	0	0	0	0	0	0	0	0
Tom Wilkinson	3/10/02	7(2)	7(2)	1	1	0	0	1	1	5	5
Aaron Willis	11/12/03	9(5)	8(4)	2	2	0	0	0	0	8	8
Elliot Windley	9/7/99	9(10)	7(9)	1	1	0	0	0	0	4	4
Max Wood	28/6/04	(1)	(1)	0	0	0	0	0	0	0	0
Mikey Wood	18/4/96	1	1	0	0	0	0	0	0	0	0

'L1' totals include League One games only; 'All' totals also include Challenge Cup

Macauley Hallett

LEAGUE RECORD
P18-W5-D0-L13 (8th)
F408, A647, Diff-239, 10 points.

CHALLENGE CUP
Round Four

ATTENDANCES
Best - v Hunslet (L1 - 547)
Worst - v London Skolars (L1 - 239)
Total (all home games included) - 3,306
Average (all home games included) - 367
(Up by 55 on 2022)

CLUB RECORDS Highest score: 64-6 v West Wales, 25/7/2018 Highest score against: 6-98 v Keighley, 6/5/2018
MATCH RECORDS Record attendance: 1,465 v Bradford, 30/6/2018 (Butts Park Arena); 453 v Cornwall, 19/2/2023 (Alexander Stadium)
Tries: 3 (13 players) Goals: 8 Connor Robinson v Hemel, 19/4/2015; Ben Stead v West Wales, 25/7/2018;
Ben Stead v Cornwall, 10/4/2022; Jacob Hookem v Doncaster, 23/7/2023 Points: 22 Dan Parker v London Skolars, 7/6/2015
SEASON RECORDS Tries: 17 Elliot Hall 2019 Goals: 61 Ben Stead 2018 Points: 141 Dan Coates 2021
CAREER RECORDS Tries: 58 Hayden Freeman 2016-2023 Goals: 163 (inc 1fg) Ben Stead 2018; 2022-2023 Points: 365 Ben Stead 2018; 2022-2023
Appearances: 115 Hayden Freeman 2016-2023

League One 2023 - Club by Club

NORTH WALES CRUSADERS

DATE	FIXTURE	RESULT	SCORERS	LGE	ATT
19/2/23	Dewsbury (h) ●	L18-38	t:Abel,Pemberton,Lynch g:Gibbons(3)	8th	300
25/2/23	Royal Navy (h) (CCR2)	W70-0	t:Reid(3),Gibbons(2),Barratt,Massam,Forster,Andrade(2),Abel,Taylor g:Billsborough(11)	N/A	255
5/3/23	Hunslet (a)	L22-8	t:Forster g:Billsborough(2)	8th	504
12/3/23	Thatto Heath (a) (CCR3)	W10-18	t:Andrade,Gibbons,Ellis g:Billsborough,Gibbons(2)	N/A	-
19/3/23	Doncaster (a)	L30-16	t:Abel,Barratt,Reid g:Moss(2)	9th	837
26/3/23	Oldham (h)	L4-18	t:Massam	9th	387
1/4/23	Keighley (a) (CCR4)	L36-14	t:Morley-Samuels(2),Taylor g:Abel	N/A	862
7/4/23	Workington (a)	L20-18	t:Andrade,Abel,Rainford g:Moss(3)	9th	603
7/5/23	Rochdale (a)	L32-18	t:Rainford,Lynch,Massam,Houghton g:Moss	9th	564
21/5/23	Midlands Hurricanes (a)	W14-42	t:Houghton,Lynch,Burns,Billsborough,Massam,Nash,Abel g:Billsborough(7)	8th	321
28/5/23	Cornwall (a)	W10-42	t:Houghton,Abel(2),Costello,Massam,Fletcher,Doolan g:Billsborough(7)	7th	1,008
3/6/23	London Skolars (a)	W6-60	t:Ellis,Forster,Hill(2),Massam(2),Billsborough,Holmes,Gibbons,Oakley g:Billsborough(10)	7th	215
18/6/23	Midlands Hurricanes (h) ●●	W62-24	t:Thewlis,Barratt,Ellis,Houghton,Andrade(2),Reid,Burns(2),Massam(2) g:Billsborough(9)	6th	205
25/6/23	Hunslet (h) ●●●	L20-30	t:Lynch(2),Taylor,Rainford g:Billsborough(2)	6th	363
2/7/23	Rochdale (h) ●●●	W32-24	t:Hill,Abel,Massam,Whitehead,Barratt g:Billsborough(6)	6th	375
9/7/23	Oldham (a)	L37-24	t:Andrade(2),Barratt,Lynch g:Billsborough(4)	6th	734
16/7/23	Workington (h) ●●●	L24-32	t:Fletcher,Ellis,Massam,Houghton g:Billsborough(4)	6th	340
23/7/23	Dewsbury (a)	L18-4	t:Abel	6th	807
30/7/23	Cornwall (h) ●●●●	L38-40	t:Massam,Eckley,Hayes,Wrench(2),Holmes(2) g:Billsborough(5)	6th	649
6/8/23	Doncaster (h) ●●●	W28-22	t:Rainford,Barratt,Ellis,Hayes g:Hayes(6)	6th	531
27/8/23	London Skolars (h)	W62-20	t:Massam,Houghton,Hughes,Reid(3),Lynch,Hayes(2),Gibbons(2) g:Hayes(9)	6th	495
3/9/23	Workington (a) (EPO)	W10-26	t:Forster,Taylor,Rainford,Reid g:Hayes(5)	N/A	611
10/9/23	Oldham (a) (ESF) ●●●●●	W12-13	t:Hazzard,Fletcher g:Hayes(2) fg:Hughes	N/A	836
17/9/23	Hunslet (a) (FE)	W18-25	t:Massam,Reid,Taylor,Oakley g:Hughes(3),Abel fg:Abel	N/A	626
24/9/23	Doncaster (a) (ProF)	L18-6	t:Hughes g:Hayes	N/A	2,549

● Played at DCBL Stadium, Widnes ●● Played at Nant Conwy RU Club ●●● Played at Hare Lane, Chester ●●●● Played at Tynewydd Fields, Rhyl ●●●●● Played at Boundary Park

Owain Abel

		APP		TRIES		GOALS		FG		PTS	
	D.O.B.	ALL	L1	ALL	L1	ALL	L1	ALL	L1	ALL	L1
Owain Abel	21/11/00	16(1)	13(1)	9	8	2	1	1	1	41	35
Jordan Andrade	24/1/92	6(16)	3(16)	8	5	0	0	0	0	32	20
Chris Barratt	7/2/93	23(1)	21	6	5	0	0	0	0	24	20
Lewis Baxter	1/6/02	1(4)	1(4)	0	0	0	0	0	0	0	0
Brad Billsborough	4/8/98	13(1)	11(1)	2	2	68	56	0	0	144	120
Jacob Bloxham	1/9/04	(2)	(1)	0	0	0	0	0	0	0	0
Brad Brennan	18/1/93	(10)	(7)	0	0	0	0	0	0	0	0
Wesley Bruines	25/6/03	3	3	0	0	0	0	0	0	0	0
McKenzie Buckley	3/12/03	6	6	0	0	0	0	0	0	0	0
Jake Burns	23/6/00	8	8	3	3	0	0	0	0	12	12
Shaun Costello	8/9/98	2(16)	1(14)	1	1	0	0	0	0	4	4
Aiden Doolan	5/9/03	1	1	1	1	0	0	0	0	4	4
Alex Eckley	25/8/99	2(1)	2(1)	1	1	0	0	0	0	4	4
Ryan Ellis	29/6/01	19	16	5	4	0	0	0	0	20	16
Matt Fletcher	15/2/00	17(8)	15(7)	3	3	0	0	0	0	12	12
Carl Forster	4/6/92	21(1)	19(1)	4	3	0	0	0	0	16	12
Matthew Foster	25/6/01	1	1	0	0	0	0	0	0	0	0
Dave Gibbons	27/11/00	13	11	6	3	5	3	0	0	34	18
Leon Hayes	4/3/04	8	8	4	4	23	23	0	0	62	62
Callum Hazzard	9/1/99	8(11)	6(11)	1	1	0	0	0	0	4	4
Daniel Hill	15/7/02	5	5	3	3	0	0	0	0	12	12
Jack Holmes	5/1/94	8(2)	7(2)	3	3	0	0	0	0	12	12
Jack Houghton	10/1/97	13(6)	13(4)	6	6	0	0	0	0	24	24
Toby Hughes	22/8/03	6	6	2	2	3	3	1	1	15	15
Declan Hulme	14/1/93	4	3	0	0	0	0	0	0	0	0
Brad Jinks	19/12/00	6	4	0	0	0	0	0	0	0	0
Ben Lane	2/9/03	2	2	0	0	0	0	0	0	0	0
Josh Lynch	8/11/03	19	19	7	7	0	0	0	0	28	28
Rob Massam	29/11/87	20	19	14	13	0	0	0	0	56	52
Alfie Matthias	19/1/99	(1)	0	0	0	0	0	0	0	0	0
Dante Morley-Samuels	22/11/98	2	0	2	0	0	0	0	0	8	0
Daniel Moss	23/11/02	4	4	0	0	6	6	0	0	12	12
Paul Nash	16/4/00	(7)	(7)	1	1	0	0	0	0	4	4
Cole Oakley	25/10/00	11	11	2	2	0	0	0	0	8	8
Taylor Pemberton	17/4/98	2(1)	2(1)	1	1	0	0	0	0	4	4
Pat Rainford	24/11/96	9(10)	7(9)	5	5	0	0	0	0	20	20
Matt Reid	16/9/92	14	11	10	7	0	0	0	0	40	28
Jono Smith	12/11/88	(1)	(1)	0	0	0	0	0	0	0	0
Kieran Taylor	8/10/02	22	19	5	3	0	0	0	0	20	12
Jake Thewlis	24/5/05	1	1	1	1	0	0	0	0	4	4
Tom Whitehead	7/11/02	5	5	1	1	0	0	0	0	4	4
Brandon Wood	31/7/00	3	1	0	0	0	0	0	0	0	0
Connor Wrench	4/10/01	1	1	2	2	0	0	0	0	8	8

'L1' totals include regular season & play-offs; 'All' totals also include Challenge Cup

LEAGUE RECORD
P18-W7-D0-L11
(6th/Promotion Final Runners-up)
F520, A437, Diff+83, 14 points.

CHALLENGE CUP
Round Four

ATTENDANCES
Best - v Cornwall (L1 - 649)
Worst - v Midlands Hurricanes (L1 - 205)
Total (excluding Challenge Cup) - 3,645
Average (excluding Challenge Cup) - 405
(Down by 119 on 2022)

CLUB RECORDS
Highest score: 84-4 v West Wales, 1/5/2012 Highest score against: 4-98 v Wigan, 15/4/2012
Record attendance: 1,562 v South Wales, 1/9/2013 (*Racecourse Ground*); 870 v Hunslet, 23/7/2022 (*Stadiwm Eirias*)

MATCH RECORDS
Tries: 5 Rob Massam v Rochdale, 30/6/2013; Jono Smith v Hemel, 16/5/2015 Goals: 12 Tommy Johnson v West Wales, 16/7/2022
Points: 30 Tommy Johnson v West Hull, 6/4/2013

SEASON RECORDS
Tries: 29 Rob Massam 2015 Goals: 110 Tommy Johnson 2022 Points: 276 Tommy Johnson 2022

CAREER RECORDS
Tries: 178 Rob Massam 2012-2016; 2019-2023 Goals: 740 Tommy Johnson 2012-2018; 2020-2022 Points: 1,800 Tommy Johnson 2012-2018; 2020-2022
Appearances: 209 Tommy Johnson 2012-2018; 2020-2022

League One 2023 - Club by Club

OLDHAM

DATE	FIXTURE	RESULT	SCORERS	LGE	ATT
26/2/23	Doncaster (a) (CCR2)	L28-26	t:Ferry,Paga,McNally,Makin g:Ridyard(5)	N/A	517
5/3/23	London Skolars (h)	W62-18	t:McNally(2),Paga(4),Sutton,Ah Van,Tyrer,Carr,Blagbrough g:Ridyard(9)	3rd	525
26/3/23	North Wales (a)	W4-18	t:Baker,Sutton,Astley g:Ridyard(3)	3rd	387
7/4/23	Rochdale (h)	W56-16	t:Ah Van,Astley(2),Sutton(2),Paga(2),Nelmes(2),Carr g:Ridyard(8)	3rd	824
16/4/23	Doncaster (a)	L26-22	t:Thornley,Baker,Slater,Paga g:Ridyard(3)	4th	1,308
7/5/23	Cornwall (h)	W36-16	t:Ah Van(3),Wilson,McNally(2),Hirst g:Tyrer(1),Slater,Ah Van(2)	3rd	437
14/5/23	Workington (a)	W18-28	t:Cameron,McNally,Brierley,Hartley(2) g:Ridyard(4)	3rd	1,010
21/5/23	Dewsbury (h)	D26-26	t:Ah Van,McNally,Hartley,Baker g:Ridyard(5)	3rd	1,295
28/5/23	Midlands Hurricanes (a)	W16-50	t:Meadows,Ah Van(2),Ridyard(2),Hirst,Paga,K Morgan,Newton g:Ridyard(7)	3rd	342
3/6/23	Hunslet (h)	W40-20	t:Wilkinson,Hartley,Carr,Ah Van(2),Baker g:Ridyard(8)	3rd	361
10/6/23	London Skolars (a)	W14-62	t:Paga,Ah Van(3),K Morgan,McNally,Baker,Kibula,Wilkinson,Nelmes,Slater g:Ridyard(5),Ah Van(4)	3rd	338
18/6/23	Doncaster (h)	L22-28	t:Wilson,K Morgan(2),Wilkinson g:Ridyard(3)	3rd	647
23/6/23	Dewsbury (a)	L20-8	t:Rawsthorne,Brierley	3rd	1,650
9/7/23	North Wales (h)	W37-24	t:Rawsthorne(2),Whittel,Carr,K Morgan,Tyrer g:Ridyard(6) fg:Ridyard	4th	734
16/7/23	Hunslet (a)	L21-8	t:Carr g:Ridyard(2)	4th	726
6/8/23	Cornwall (a)	W4-56	t:Carr(4),Hartley,Cameron,K Morgan,Hirst,Rawsthorne,Slater,Tyrer g:Ridyard(6)	4th	891
20/8/23	Rochdale (a)	W20-24	t:Rawsthorne(3),Wilkinson,K Morgan g:Ridyard(2)	4th	1,386
23/8/23	Workington (h) ●	W40-24	t:K Morgan,Nelmes,Paga,Rawsthorne(2),Ah Van,Tyrer g:Ridyard(6)	4th	1,238
27/8/23	Midlands Hurricanes (h)	L10-18	t:Rawsthorne,Paga g:Ridyard	4th	472
3/9/23	Doncaster (a) (QPO)	L36-0		N/A	615
10/9/23	North Wales (h) (ESF) ●	L12-13	t:Ah Van,K Morgan g:Ridyard(2)	N/A	836

● Played at Boundary Park

		APP		TRIES		GOALS		FG		PTS	
	D.O.B.	ALL	L1	ALL	L1	ALL	L1	ALL	L1	ALL	L1
Patrick Ah Van	17/3/88	18(1)	17(1)	15	15	6	6	0	0	72	72
Logan Astley	18/5/03	2	2	3	3	0	0	0	0	12	12
Zac Baker	1/3/92	17	16	5	5	0	0	0	0	20	20
Jack Blagbrough	18/1/94	5(3)	4(3)	1	1	0	0	0	0	4	4
Tommy Brierley	8/9/96	2(2)	2(2)	2	2	0	0	0	0	8	8
Callum Cameron	31/10/00	8(1)	8(1)	2	2	0	0	0	0	8	8
Connor Carr	27/2/03	15(4)	15(3)	9	9	0	0	0	0	36	36
Jacob Douglas	17/8/97	1	1	0	0	0	0	0	0	0	0
Jamie Ellis	4/10/89	1(1)	1(1)	0	0	0	0	0	0	0	0
Ethan Ferry	18/10/98	5	4	1	1	0	0	0	0	4	0
Tom Forber	22/5/03	(1)	(1)	0	0	0	0	0	0	0	0
Andy Gabriel	21/12/93	1	1	0	0	0	0	0	0	0	0
Joe Hartley	2/5/98	12	11	5	5	0	0	0	0	20	20
George Hirst	27/5/01	13(3)	13(3)	3	3	0	0	0	0	12	12
Josh Johnson	25/7/94	5(1)	5(1)	0	0	0	0	0	0	0	0
Samy Kibula	7/8/99	(4)	(4)	1	1	0	0	0	0	4	4
Harvey Makin	17/11/03	(2)	(1)	1	0	0	0	0	0	4	0
Gregg McNally	2/1/91	16	15	8	7	0	0	0	0	32	28
Deane Meadows	11/5/94	13(6)	12(6)	1	1	0	0	0	0	4	4
Pat Moran	2/4/98	3(12)	3(12)	0	0	0	0	0	0	0	0
Bob Morgan	10/10/99	(1)	(1)	0	0	0	0	0	0	0	0
Kian Morgan	11/5/00	19	19	9	9	0	0	0	0	36	36
Luke Nelmes	7/6/93	18(2)	17(2)	4	4	0	0	0	0	16	16
Dom Newton	24/12/92	1(11)	1(11)	1	1	0	0	0	0	4	4
Jordan Paga	23/5/01	16(1)	15(1)	12	11	0	0	0	0	48	44
Nick Rawsthorne	30/9/95	10	10	10	10	0	0	0	0	40	40
Martyn Ridyard	25/7/86	19(1)	18(1)	2	2	85	80	1	1	179	169
Sean Slater	3/10/01	2(16)	1(16)	3	3	1	0	0	0	14	14
Alex Sutton	23/9/02	4	3	4	4	0	0	0	0	16	16
Iain Thornley	11/9/91	1	1	1	1	0	0	0	0	4	4
James Thornton	30/9/95	(2)	(1)	0	0	0	0	0	0	0	0
Kieran Tyrer	24/10/02	6(2)	6(1)	4	4	1	1	0	0	18	18
Calvin Wellington	10/12/95	1	0	0	0	0	0	0	0	0	0
Emmerson Whittel	13/9/94	18	18	1	1	0	0	0	0	4	4
Matty Wilkinson	13/6/96	19(1)	19(1)	4	4	0	0	0	0	16	16
Harvey Wilson	31/1/04	2(6)	2(6)	2	2	0	0	0	0	8	8

'L1' totals include regular season & play-offs; 'All' totals also include Challenge Cup

Patrick Ah Van

LEAGUE RECORD
P18-W12-D1-L5
(4th/Elimination Semi-Final)
F605, A333, Diff+272, 25 points.

CHALLENGE CUP
Round Two

ATTENDANCES
Best - v Dewsbury (L1 - 1,295)
Worst - v Hunslet (L1 - 361)
Total (all home games included) - 7,369
Average (all home games included) - 737
(Up by 43 on 2022)

CLUB RECORDS
MATCH RECORDS Highest score: 102-6 v West Wales, 8/7/2018 Highest score against: 0-84 v Widnes, 25/7/99
Record attendance: 28,000 v Huddersfield, 24/2/1912 *(Watersheddings)*; 1,405 v Keighley, 20/9/2015 *(Vestacare Stadium)*
Tries: 7 James Miller v Barry, 31/10/1908 Goals: 14 Bernard Ganley v Liverpool City, 4/4/59; Martyn Ridyard v West Wales, 10/4/2022
Points: 34 Andy Ballard v London Skolars, 2/5/2009; Chris Baines v Hunslet, 20/9/2009; Lewis Palfrey v Hemel, 9/8/2015
SEASON RECORDS Tries: 49 Reg Farrar 1921-22 Goals: 200 Bernard Ganley 1957-58 Points: 412 Bernard Ganley 1957-58
CAREER RECORDS Tries: 174 Alan Davies 1950-61 Goals: 1,358 Bernard Ganley 1951-61 Points: 2,761 Bernard Ganley 1951-61 Appearances: 627 Joe Ferguson 1899-1923

313

League One 2023 - Club by Club

ROCHDALE HORNETS

DATE	FIXTURE	RESULT	SCORERS	LGE	ATT
26/2/23	London Skolars (h) (CCR2)	W42-4	t:Cooke(2),Purcell,O'Keefe,Else,Hewitt,Killan g:Hewitt(7)	N/A	300
5/3/23	Doncaster (h)	L10-20	t:O'Keefe,Tyrer g:Hewitt	7th	391
12/3/23	Dewsbury (a) (CCR3)	L38-18	t:Roden,Green,Brannan g:Hewitt(3)	N/A	445
19/3/23	Midlands Hurricanes (a)	W24-32	t:Else,Tyrer,Clarke(2),Boardman,Roden g:Hewitt(4)	6th	384
26/3/23	Dewsbury (h)	L4-52	t:Tyrer	8th	573
7/4/23	Oldham (a)	L56-16	t:Arnold,Holroyd,Else g:Hewitt(2)	8th	824
16/4/23	Workington (h)	L28-29	t:Arnold,Else(2),Nixon(2) g:Hewitt(4)	7th	588
7/5/23	North Wales (h)	W32-18	t:Purcell,Hanley(3),Else(2) g:Hewitt(4)	7th	564
13/5/23	London Skolars (a)	W24-28	t:Nixon,Peachey,Hanley,Tyrer,Killan g:Hewitt(4)	6th	209
21/5/23	Cornwall (h)	W62-6	t:Else(2),Arnold,Peachey,Smith,Hewitt,Tyrer,Brannan,Hanley,Purcell,O'Keefe g:Hewitt(9)	5th	496
28/5/23	Hunslet (a)	L36-18	t:Forber,O'Hanlon,Berry g:Hewitt(3)	6th	481
11/6/23	Doncaster (a)	L42-20	t:Berry,Brookes(2),Nixon g:O'Keefe(2)	6th	1,191
16/6/23	Dewsbury (a)	L42-0		7th	811
2/7/23	North Wales (a) ●	L32-24	t:Straugheir,A Jones,Tyrer,Else g:Hewitt(4)	7th	375
9/7/23	Workington (a)	L40-12	t:Boardman,Forber g:Hewitt(2)	7th	1,337
30/7/23	Midlands Hurricanes (h)	W37-22	t:O'Keefe,Else,Straugheir,Tyrer,Forster,Ratcliffe g:Hewitt(6) fg:Hewitt	7th	334
6/8/23	Hunslet (h)	L22-35	t:Roden,Forster,Straugheir,Smith g:Hewitt(3)	7th	344
20/8/23	Oldham (h)	L20-24	t:Else,Tyrer,Brierley(2) g:Hewitt(2)	7th	1,386
27/8/23	Cornwall (a)	L18-12	t:Brierley,Harrison,Brewin	7th	1,281

● Played at Hare Lane, Chester

48-0 win awarded for London Skolars (h) game (London Skolars unable to fulfil fixture)

		APP		TRIES		GOALS		FG		PTS	
	D.O.B.	ALL	L1	ALL	L1	ALL	L1	ALL	L1	ALL	L1
Jack Arnold	23/9/97	10(4)	10(2)	3	3	0	0	0	0	12	12
Connor Aspey	16/4/02	2	1	0	0	0	0	0	0	0	0
Ewan Badham	29/11/01	(2)		0	0	0	0	0	0	0	0
Cameron Berry	7/8/01	10(6)	8(6)	2	2	0	0	0	0	8	8
AJ Boardman	11/11/89	4(4)	3(4)	2	2	0	0	0	0	8	8
Zach Braham	14/1/95	5	3	0	0	0	0	0	0	0	0
Toby Brannan	27/11/02	2(11)	2(10)	2	1	0	0	0	0	8	4
Dan Brewin	15/11/02	17	15	1	1	0	0	0	0	4	4
Tommy Brierley	8/9/96	2	2	3	3	0	0	0	0	12	12
Ollie Brookes	19/6/01	3	3	2	2	0	0	0	0	8	8
Andy Clarke	14/2/99	4	3	2	2	0	0	0	0	8	8
Will Cooke	22/12/96	5	4	2	0	0	0	0	0	8	0
Lewis Else	30/3/00	19	17	12	11	0	0	0	0	48	44
Luke Forber	6/7/98	7(1)	7(1)	2	2	0	0	0	0	8	8
Ben Forster	27/12/00	14	14	2	2	0	0	0	0	8	8
Jacob Gannon	18/3/02	3	3	0	0	0	0	0	0	0	0
Jack Gatcliffe	5/10/98	(1)	(1)	0	0	0	0	0	0	0	0
Callum Green	27/9/99	1	0	1	0	0	0	0	0	4	0
Umyla Hanley	5/3/02	5	5	5	5	0	0	0	0	20	20
Dan Harrison	4/2/96	2	2	1	1	0	0	0	0	4	4
Sam Haynes	24/6/04	1	1	0	0	0	0	0	0	0	0
Dave Hewitt	4/11/95	18	16	2	1	58	48	1	1	125	101
Joe Hird	8/2/03	2	2	0	0	0	0	0	0	0	0
Brad Holroyd	15/4/00	1	1	1	1	0	0	0	0	4	4
Kyle Huish	11/9/02	(2)	(2)	0	0	0	0	0	0	0	0
John Hutchings	1/1/99	1	1	0	0	0	0	0	0	0	0
Adam Jones	11/1/03	2	2	1	1	0	0	0	0	4	4
Jacob Jones	15/2/99	2	2	0	0	0	0	0	0	0	0
Sion Jones	16/12/97	(8)	(8)	0	0	0	0	0	0	0	0
Ben Killan	13/5/03	12(4)	10(4)	2	1	0	0	0	0	8	4
Tom Nisbet	8/10/99	1	1	0	0	0	0	0	0	0	0
Dan Nixon	27/7/02	15	14	4	4	0	0	0	0	16	16
Ethan O'Hanlon	19/5/01	1(8)	1(7)	1	1	0	0	0	0	4	4
Ben O'Keefe	23/5/02	14(1)	12(1)	4	3	2	2	0	0	20	16
Lewis Peachey	25/3/01	9(2)	9(2)	2	2	0	0	0	0	8	8
Joe Purcell	22/8/99	9	8	3	2	0	0	0	0	12	8
Connor Ratcliffe	22/5/96	7(1)	6(1)	1	1	0	0	0	0	4	4
Nick Rawsthorne	30/9/95	1	1	0	0	0	0	0	0	0	0
Aiden Roden	4/6/00	9(8)	9(6)	3	2	0	0	0	0	12	8
George Senior	29/8/99	1	1	0	0	0	0	0	0	0	0
Aaron Smith	12/10/96	(6)	(6)	2	2	0	0	0	0	8	8
Daniel Spencer-Tonks	18/1/95	(3)	(3)	0	0	0	0	0	0	0	0
Duane Straugheir	29/9/89	9	7	3	3	0	0	0	0	12	12
Will Tilleke	18/11/99	1(3)	1(3)	0	0	0	0	0	0	0	0
Cian Tyrer	3/2/01	16	14	8	8	0	0	0	0	32	32
Nathan Wilde	29/12/99	(1)	(1)	0	0	0	0	0	0	0	0

'L1' totals include League One games only; 'All' totals also include Challenge Cup

Dave Hewitt

LEAGUE RECORD
P18-W6-D0-L12 (7th)
F425, A520, Diff-95, 12 points.

CHALLENGE CUP
Round Three

ATTENDANCES
Best - v Oldham (L1 - 1,386)
Worst - v London Skolars (CC - 300)
Total (excluding Challenge Cup) - 4,676
Average (excluding Challenge Cup) - 585
(Up by 64 on 2022)

CLUB RECORDS
Highest score: 120-4 v Illingworth, 13/3/2005 **Highest score against:** 0-106 v Castleford, 9/9/2007
Record attendance: 26,664 v Oldham, 25/3/1922 (Athletic Grounds); 8,061 v Oldham, 26/12/89 (Spotland)
MATCH RECORDS Tries: 5 Jack Corsi v Barrow, 31/12/1921; Jack Corsi v Broughton Moor, 25/2/1922; Jack Williams v St Helens, 4/4/33; Norman Brelsford v Whitehaven, 3/9/73; Marlon Billy v York, 8/4/2001 **Goals:** 18 Lee Birdseye v Illingworth, 13/3/2005 **Points:** 44 Lee Birdseye v Illingworth, 13/3/2005
SEASON RECORDS Tries: 31 Marlon Billy 2001 **Goals:** 150 Martin Strett 1994-95 **Points:** 350 Mick Nanyn 2003
CAREER RECORDS Tries: 103 Jack Williams 1931-37 **Goals:** 741 Walter Gowers 1922-36
Points: 1,497 Walter Gowers 1922-36; Paul Crook 2010-2016 **Appearances:** 456 Walter Gowers 1922-36

League One 2023 - Club by Club

WORKINGTON TOWN

DATE	FIXTURE	RESULT	SCORERS	LGE	ATT
18/2/23	London Skolars (a)	W16-58	t:Curwen,Anderson-Moore(2),J Burns,Steele,Kirkup(2),Marwood, Bickerdike,Barnes g:Walker(9)	1st	264
26/2/23	Ince Rose Bridge (h) (CCR2)	W68-6	t:Hurst(2),Henson,Sabutey,Steele(2),J Burns,Barnes(2),Key,Walker(2) g:Walker(10)	N/A	603
12/3/23	Doncaster (a) (CCR3)	L24-20	t:Walker,Sabutey(3) g:Walker(2)	N/A	485
19/3/23	Dewsbury (h)	L6-25	t:Sabutey g:Walker	5th	650
26/3/23	Midlands Hurricanes (a)	W28-38	t:J Burns,Sabutey(5) g:Walker(7)	5th	324
7/4/23	North Wales (h)	W20-18	t:Henson(2),Sabutey g:Walker(4)	4th	603
16/4/23	Rochdale (a)	W28-29	t:Thomson,Hurst,Bickerdike,Henson,Walker g:Walker(4) fg:Mallinson	3rd	588
7/5/23	Doncaster (a)	L46-6	t:Walker g:Walker	4th	1,255
14/5/23	Oldham (h)	L18-28	t:Henson,Reid,Thomson g:Walker(3)	5th	1,010
21/5/23	Hunslet (a)	L22-18	t:Walker,Sabutey(2) g:Walker(3)	6th	347
4/6/23	Cornwall (h)	W54-0	t:Bradley(2),Henson(2),Mossop,Sabutey,Reid,J Burns,Thomson,Walker g:Walker(7)	5th	603
18/6/23	London Skolars (h)	W34-6	t:J Burns(3),Walker,Terrill,Thomson g:Walker(5)	5th	496
25/6/23	Midlands Hurricanes (h)	W60-10	t:Steele(2),Charlton,J Burns,Sabutey,Holroyd,Forber,A Burns,Marwood(2) g:Walker(10)	5th	843
9/7/23	Rochdale (h)	W40-12	t:Bradley,A Burns,Walker(2),Bickerdike,Marwood,Sabutey g:Walker(6)	5th	1,337
16/7/23	North Wales (a) ●	W24-32	t:Bickerdike,Henson(2),J Burns,Kirkup,Stephenson g:Forber(4)	5th	340
23/7/23	Cornwall (a)	W16-34	t:Scholey,Steele,Sumner(2),Sabutey,J Burns,A Burns g:Walker(3)	3rd	1,204
30/7/23	Doncaster (h)	L19-22	t:Reid,Bickerdike,Forber g:Walker,Forber(2) fg:Walker	4th	1,074
6/8/23	Dewsbury (a)	L38-8	t:Walker g:Walker(2)	5th	1,579
23/8/23	Oldham (a) ●●	L40-24	t:Bickerdike,Kirkup,Marwood,Charlton g:Walker(4)	5th	1,238
27/8/23	Hunslet (h)	W18-6	t:Dawson,Henson,J Burns g:Walker(3)	5th	803
3/9/23	North Wales (h) (EPO)	L10-26	t:Forber,Bickerdike g:Walker	N/A	611

● Played at Hare Lane, Chester
●● Played at Boundary Park

Sean Sabutey

		APP		TRIES		GOALS		FG		PTS	
	D.O.B.	ALL	L1	ALL	L1	ALL	L1	ALL	L1	ALL	L1
Max Anderson-Moore	9/12/01	7	7	2	2	0	0	0	0	8	8
Caine Barnes	22/2/99	8	7	3	1	0	0	0	0	12	4
Ethan Bickerdike	15/2/01	19	17	7	7	0	0	0	0	28	28
Jake Bradley	29/4/01	11	11	3	3	0	0	0	0	12	12
Aaron Burns	15/12/99	6	6	3	3	0	0	0	0	12	12
Jordan Burns	2/9/95	20	18	11	10	0	0	0	0	44	40
Luke Charlton	29/3/95	(7)	(7)	2	2	0	0	0	0	8	8
Tom Curwen	15/8/89	1(2)	1	1	1	0	0	0	0	4	4
Hanley Dawson	25/5/96	12(1)	12(1)	1	1	0	0	0	0	4	4
Ethan Fitzgerald	4/10/03	1	1	0	0	0	0	0	0	0	0
Carl Forber	17/3/85	11	11	3	3	6	6	0	0	24	24
Matty Henson	31/10/94	16	14	10	9	0	0	0	0	40	36
Brad Holroyd	15/4/00	1	1	1	1	0	0	0	0	4	4
Earl Hurst	21/4/89	11	9	3	1	0	0	0	0	12	4
JJ Key	1/10/95	4(8)	2(8)	1	0	0	0	0	0	4	0
Joe Kirkup	25/5/95	1(11)	1(10)	4	4	0	0	0	0	16	16
Jack Mallinson	21/10/01	10(1)	9	0	0	0	0	1	1	1	1
Blain Marwood	23/1/98	(13)	(13)	5	5	0	0	0	0	20	20
Liam McAvoy	24/9/93	2(2)	2(2)	0	0	0	0	0	0	0	0
Liam McNicholas	14/1/97	6(7)	6(6)	0	0	0	0	0	0	0	0
Jason Mossop	12/9/85	18	16	1	1	0	0	0	0	4	4
Grant Reid	20/4/98	1(13)	1(11)	3	3	0	0	0	0	12	12
Sean Sabutey	16/1/99	20	18	17	13	0	0	0	0	68	52
Stevie Scholey	7/1/96	20	18	1	1	0	0	0	0	4	4
Fergus Simpson	7/10/01	6(6)	5(5)	0	0	0	0	0	0	0	0
Malik Steele	1/1/01	13	11	6	4	0	0	0	0	24	16
Jack Stephenson	4/9/01	7(8)	6(8)	1	1	0	0	0	0	4	4
Reagan Sumner	23/2/04	2	2	2	2	0	0	0	0	8	8
Connor Terrill	3/7/01	(5)	(5)	1	1	0	0	0	0	4	4
Jordan Thomson	23/1/93	19	17	4	4	0	0	0	0	16	16
Ciaran Walker	29/5/03	20	18	11	8	86	74	1	1	217	181

'L1' totals include regular season & play-offs; 'All' totals also include Challenge Cup

LEAGUE RECORD
P18-W11-D0-L7
(5th/Elimination Play-off)
F516, A385, Diff+131, 22 points.

CHALLENGE CUP
Round Three

ATTENDANCES
Best - v Rochdale (L1 - 1,337)
Worst - v London Skolars (L1 - 496)
Total (excluding Challenge Cup - 8,030
Average (excluding Challenge Cup - 803
(Down by 153 on 2022, Championship)

CLUB RECORDS
MATCH RECORDS Highest score: 94-4 v Leigh, 26/2/95 Highest score against: 0-92 v Bradford, 14/2/99 Record attendance: 17,741 v Wigan, 3/3/65
Tries: 7 Ike Southward v Blackpool, 17/9/55 Goals: 14 Darren Holt v Gateshead, 12/6/2011
Points: 42 Dean Marwood v Highfield, 1/11/92; Dean Marwood v Leigh, 26/2/95
SEASON RECORDS Tries: 49 Johnny Lawrenson 1951-52 Goals: 186 Lyn Hopkins 1981-82 Points: 438 Lyn Hopkins 1981-82
CAREER RECORDS Tries: 274 Ike Southward 1952-68 Goals: 937 (inc 5fg) Carl Forber 2007-2009; 2012-2023 Points: 2,141 Carl Forber 2007-2009; 2012-2023
Appearances: 419 Paul Charlton 1961-69; 1975-80

315

LEAGUE ONE 2023
Round by Round

ROUND 1

Saturday 18th February 2023

LONDON SKOLARS 16 WORKINGTON TOWN 58

SKOLARS: 1 Louis O'Sullivan; 5 Jerome Yates; 3 Alex Deery; 4 Aaron Small; 2 Leighton Ball; 6 Shane Lee; 7 Jack Ryan; 8 Lamont Bryan; 18 Liam O'Callaghan; 15 Todd Peut; 11 Luciano Bejanidze; 12 Jimmy Morgan; 13 Matt Ross. Subs (all used): 9 Elliott Hutchings; 21 Anthony Cox; 10 Delaine Bedward-Gittens; 19 Fraser Piercy-Farley.
Tries: O'Callaghan (18), Yates (42), Deery (78);
Goals: Ryan 1/2, Lee 1/1.
TOWN: 1 Jordan Burns; 19 Max Anderson-Moore; 4 Jason Mossop; 5 Ethan Bickerdike; 2 Sean Sabutey; 6 Ciaran Walker; 15 Fergus Simpson; 8 Jordan Thomson; 9 Matty Henson; 13 Tom Curwen; 12 Caine Barnes; 11 Malik Steele; 10 Stevie Scholey. Subs (all used): 16 JJ Key; 17 Joe Kirkup; 14 Blain Marwood; 20 Jack Stephenson.
Tries: Curwen (3), Anderson-Moore (10, 40), J Burns (13), Steele (26), Kirkup (38, 45), Marwood (48), Bickerdike (52), Barnes (65); **Goals:** Walker 9/10.
Rugby Leaguer & League Express Men of the Match: *Skolars:* Alex Deery; *Town:* Ciaran Walker.
Penalty count: 6-5; **Half-time:** 6-34;
Referee: Matt Rossleigh; **Attendance:** 264.

Sunday 19th February 2023

NORTH WALES CRUSADERS 18 DEWSBURY RAMS 38

CRUSADERS: 1 Owain Abel; 27 Josh Lynch; 3 Declan Hulme; 29 Wesley Bruines; 5 Rob Massam; 6 Brad Billsborough; 7 Dave Gibbons; 8 Callum Hazzard; 9 Brad Jinks; 17 Chris Barratt; 11 Alex Eckley; 25 McKenzie Buckley; 30 Matt Fletcher. Subs (all used): 10 Jordan Andrade; 15 Brad Brennan; - Shaun Costello; 28 Taylor Pemberton.
Tries: Abel (10), Pemberton (59), Lynch (80);
Goals: Gibbons 3/3.
Sin bin: Fletcher (74) - fighting.
RAMS: 1 Owen Restall; 4 Davey Dixon; 21 Caelum Jordan; 3 Ollie Greensmith; 23 Perry Whiteley; 6 Paul Sykes; 7 Calum Turner; 8 Jimmy Beckett; 9 Reiss Butterworth; 15 Ronan Dixon; 12 Matt Garside; 18 Brad Graham; 13 Louis Collinson. Subs (all used): 10 Dale Ferguson; 14 Sam Day; 17 Elliot Morris; 20 Jackson Walker.
Tries: Restall (17, 67), Greensmith (27), Jordan (32, 48), Whiteley (38), Graham (53); **Goals:** Sykes 5/7.
Sin bin: R Dixon (74) - fighting.
Rugby Leaguer & League Express Men of the Match: *Crusaders:* Owain Abel; *Rams:* Paul Sykes.
Penalty count: 3-4; **Half-time:** 6-22;
Referee: Scott Mikalauskas; **Attendance:** 300 *(at DCBL Stadium, Widnes).*

DONCASTER 18 HUNSLET 16

DONCASTER: 1 Elliot Hall; 2 Tom Halliday; 21 Brad Hey; 25 Jack Sanderson; 5 Travis Corion; 6 Ben Johnston; 7 Connor Robinson; 8 Keelan Foster; 9 Greg Burns; 17 Matt James; 11 Sam Smeaton; 27 Brett Ferres; 13 Loui McConnell. Subs (all used): 20 Brad Knowles; 16 Dave Petersen; 12 Aaron Ollett-Hobson; 18 Jose Kenga.
Tries: Hall (15), McConnell (38), Halliday (40);
Goals: Robinson 3/3.
HUNSLET: 1 Jimmy Watson; 2 Jack Render; 3 Adam Ryder; 4 Joe Burton; 5 Kieron Lawton; 6 Jake Sweeting; 7 Nathan Conroy; 8 Harvey Hallas; 9 Sam Hallas; 10 Steve Crossley; 11 Josh Jordan-Roberts; 12 Aaron York; 13 Michael Knowles. Subs (all used): 14 Danny Barcoe; 15 Nathan Newbound; 17 Lewis Wray; 26 Jordan Bull.
Tries: J Burton (4), Crossley (56), Render (73);
Goals: Sweeting 2/3.
Rugby Leaguer & League Express Men of the Match: *Doncaster:* Connor Robinson; *Hunslet:* Steve Crossley.
Penalty count: 5-3; **Half-time:** 18-6;
Referee: Brad Milligan; **Attendance:** 1,251.

MIDLANDS HURRICANES 40 CORNWALL 6

HURRICANES: 1 Nathan Hill; 24 Elliot Wallis; 3 Matt Welham; 4 Macauley Hallett; 25 Jason Qareqare; 23 Dan Coates; 6 Ben Stead; 8 Kieran Moran; 9 Elliot Windley; 13 Brad Clavering; 21 Bailey Dawson; 17 Dom Flanagan; 22 Brad Martin. Subs (all used): 10 Matthew Bailey; 11 Jack Dawson; 14 Chris Cullimore; 16 Anesu Mudoti.
Tries: Hallett (2), Martin (8), Flanagan (11), Wallis (15, 30), Windley (21), M Welham (75); **Goals:** Stead 6/7.
Dismissal: Wallis (71) - punching Bodman.
CORNWALL: 1 Liam Whitton; 2 Nick Slaney; 3 Errol Carter; 15 Tom Ashton; 5 Harry Aaronson; 9 Cameron Brown; 7 Adam Rusling; 8 Jack Ray; 16 Louis Singleton; 10 Paul Bolger; 11 Nathan Cullen; 12 Charley Bodman; 13 Jake Lloyd. Subs (all used): 4 Coby Nichol; 18 Harry Boots; 23 Jamie Prisk; 24 Kaine Dimech.
Try: Slaney (73); **Goals:** Rusling 1/1.
Rugby Leaguer & League Express Men of the Match: *Hurricanes:* Ben Stead; *Cornwall:* Jack Ray.
Penalty count: 1-5; **Half-time:** 34-0;
Referee: Kevin Moore; **Attendance:** 453.

ROUND 2

Sunday 5th March 2023

ROCHDALE HORNETS 10 DONCASTER 20

HORNETS: 1 Joe Purcell; 2 Cian Tyrer; 3 Will Cooke; 4 Ben O'Keefe; 5 Dan Nixon; 6 Lewis Else; 7 Dave Hewitt; 8 Zach Braham; 9 Cameron Berry; 10 Ben Killan; 11 Dan Brewin; 12 Duane Straugheir; 27 Toby Brannan. Subs (all used): 14 Aiden Roden; 18 Jack Arnold; 30 Luke Forber; 16 Ethan O'Hanlon.
Tries: O'Keefe (23), Tyrer (55); **Goals:** Hewitt 1/2.
DONCASTER: 1 Elliot Hall; 2 Tom Halliday; 25 Jack Sanderson; 21 Brad Hey; 5 Travis Corion; 6 Ben Johnston; 7 Connor Robinson; 17 Matt James; 9 Greg Burns; 18 Jose Kenga; 11 Sam Smeaton; 27 Brett Ferres; 13 Loui McConnell. Subs (all used): 20 Brad Knowles; 16 Dave Petersen; 22 Misi Taulapapa; 14 Dean Roberts.
Tries: Robinson (13), Hall (28), Burns (42), Sanderson (69);
Goals: Robinson 2/4.
Rugby Leaguer & League Express Men of the Match: *Hornets:* Zach Braham; *Doncaster:* Loui McConnell.
Penalty count: 4-3; **Half-time:** 4-8;
Referee: Matt Rossleigh; **Attendance:** 391.

DEWSBURY RAMS 50 MIDLANDS HURRICANES 10

RAMS: 1 Owen Restall; 2 Lewis Carr; 21 Caelum Jordan; 3 Ollie Greensmith; 23 Perry Whiteley; 6 Paul Sykes; 7 Calum Turner; 8 Jimmy Beckett; 9 Reiss Butterworth; 15 Ronan Dixon; 12 Matt Garside; 18 Brad Graham; 13 Louis Collinson. Subs (all used): 14 Sam Day; 17 Elliot Morris; 10 Dale Ferguson; 11 Connor Davies.
Tries: Greensmith (4), Turner (20, 22), Restall (34), Carr (47), Butterworth (53), Ferguson (58), Davies (70);
Goals: Sykes 9/9.
HURRICANES: 1 Nathan Hill; 25 Callum Dunne; 3 Matt Welham; 4 Macauley Hallett; 24 Jason Qareqare; 6 Ben Stead; 7 Richard Wilkinson; 8 Kieran Moran; 9 Elliot Windley; 13 Brad Clavering; 23 Bailey Dawson; 12 Liam Welham; 22 Brad Martin. Subs: 11 Jack Dawson; 14 Chris Cullimore; 18 Sam Bowring; 26 Matthew Bailey (not used).
Tries: M Welham (42, 76); **Goals:** Stead 1/2.
Rugby Leaguer & League Express Men of the Match: *Rams:* Calum Turner; *Hurricanes:* Ben Stead.
Penalty count: 5-6; **Half-time:** 26-0;
Referee: Luke Bland; **Attendance:** 771.

HUNSLET 22 NORTH WALES CRUSADERS 8

HUNSLET: 1 Jimmy Watson; 5 Kieron Lawton; 3 Adam Ryder; 4 Joe Burton; 27 Sean Croston; 24 Fraser Stroud; 6 Jake Sweeting; 8 Harvey Hallas; 9 Sam Hallas; 10 Steve Crossley; 11 Josh Jordan-Roberts; 12 Aaron York; 13 Michael Knowles. Subs (all used): 15 Nathan Newbound; 16 Jordan Syme; 17 Lewis Wray; 18 Harvey Whiteley.
Tries: Sweeting (31), Newbound (56), H Hallas (63), J Burton (67); **Goals:** Sweeting 3/4.
Dismissal: Wray (72) - fighting.
CRUSADERS: 1 Owain Abel; 27 Josh Lynch; 14 Kieran Taylor; 4 Matt Reid; 2 Jack Holmes; 6 Dave Gibbons; 7 Brad Billsborough; 8 Callum Hazzard; 9 Brad Jinks; 10 Jordan Andrade; 11 Alex Eckley; 26 Carl Forster; 17 Chris Barratt. Subs (all used): 13 Matt Fletcher; 15 Brad Brennan; 19 Shaun Costello; 20 Pat Rainford.
Try: Forster (5); **Goals:** Billsborough 2/2.
Dismissal: Gibbons (72) - fighting.
Sin bin: Andrade (61) - late challenge on Whiteley.
Rugby Leaguer & League Express Men of the Match: *Hunslet:* Harvey Hallas; *Crusaders:* Carl Forster.
Penalty count: 9-5; **Half-time:** 6-8;
Referee: Kevin Moore; **Attendance:** 504.

OLDHAM 62 LONDON SKOLARS 18

OLDHAM: 1 Gregg McNally; 5 Joe Hartley; 29 Alex Sutton; 4 Kian Morgan; 2 Patrick Ah Van; 6 Martyn Ridyard; 18 Jordan Paga; 17 Jack Blagbrough; 9 Matty Wilkinson; 8 Luke Nelmes; 11 Ethan Ferry; 12 Zac Baker; 10 Deane Meadows. Subs (all used): 28 Kieran Tyrer; 14 Sean Slater; 3 Connor Carr; 25 George Hirst.
Tries: McNally (2, 15), Paga (5, 12, 32, 73), Sutton (25), Ah Van (37), Tyrer (65), Carr (68), Blagbrough (78);
Goals: Ridyard 9/11.
SKOLARS: 1 Dan Bristow; 2 Leighton Ball; 3 Joe Saunders; 4 Aaron Small; 5 Louis O'Sullivan; 6 Alex Deery; 7 Jack Ryan; 8 Lamont Bryan; 9 Liam O'Callaghan; 10 Todd Peut; 11 Luciano Bejanidze; 12 Jimmy Morgan; 13 Matt Ross. Subs (all used): 14 Doug Chirnside; 15 Ed Brown; 16 Henry Davetanivalu; 17 Christian Gale.
Tries: Peut (17), Gale (54), Small (58); **Goals:** Ryan 3/3.
Sin bin: Peut (63) - use of the elbow.
Rugby Leaguer & League Express Men of the Match: *Oldham:* Jordan Paga; *Skolars:* Dan Bristow.
Penalty count: 11-3; **Half-time:** 38-6;
Referee: Brad Milligan; **Attendance:** 525.

ROUND 3

Saturday 18th March 2023

LONDON SKOLARS 22 HUNSLET 66

SKOLARS: 1 Jacob Thomas; 2 Louis O'Sullivan; 3 Dan Bristow; 4 Aaron Small; 5 Jerome Yates; 6 Alex Deery; 7 Jack Ryan; 8 Lamont Bryan; 9 Doug Chirnside; 10 Todd Peut; 11 Luciano Bejanidze; 12 Jimmy Morgan; 18 Liam O'Callaghan. Subs (all used): 14 Shane Lee; 15 Malikhi Lloyd-Jones; 19 Christian Gale; 22 Anthony Cox.
Tries: Small (37), Gale (42), O'Sullivan (66, 71);
Goals: Ryan 3/4.
HUNSLET: 1 Jimmy Watson; 2 Jack Render; 3 Adam Ryder; 4 Joe Burton; 36 Alfie Goddard; 6 Jake Sweeting; 7 Nathan Conroy; 8 Harvey Hallas; 9 Sam Hallas; 10 Steve Crossley; 11 Josh Jordan-Roberts; 16 Jordan Syme; 13 Michael Knowles. Subs (all used): 12 Aaron York; 22 Liam Carr; 23 Jamie Greenwood; 26 Jordan Bull.
Tries: Jordan-Roberts (4), Ryder (10, 22, 30, 59), Knowles (14), S Hallas (18), Crossley (49), Conroy (56), Greenwood (75), Sweeting (78), Render (80);
Goals: Sweeting 9/13.
Rugby Leaguer & League Express Men of the Match: *Skolars:* Christian Gale; *Hunslet:* Adam Ryder.
Penalty count: 4-5; **Half-time:** 6-34;
Referee: Luke Bland; **Attendance:** 186.

Sunday 19th March 2023

DONCASTER 30 NORTH WALES CRUSADERS 16

DONCASTER: 25 Jack Sanderson; 2 Tom Halliday; 21 Brad Hey; 22 Misi Taulapapa; 5 Travis Corion; 6 Ben Johnston; 7 Connor Robinson; 8 Keelan Foster; 9 Greg Burns; 17 Matt James; 11 Sam Smeaton; 27 Brett Ferres; 19 Ross Whitmore. Subs (all used): 14 Dean Roberts; 16 Dave Petersen; 18 Jose Kenga; 29 Max Clarke.
Tries: Halliday (21), Smeaton (35, 51, 64), Corion (67);
Goals: Robinson 5/5.
CRUSADERS: 25 Ben Lane; 2 Jack Holmes; 14 Kieran Taylor; 4 Matt Reid; 27 Josh Lynch; 1 Owain Abel; 28 Daniel Moss; 8 Callum Hazzard; 9 Brad Jinks; 17 Chris Barratt; 29 McKenzie Buckley; 26 Carl Forster; 13 Matt Fletcher. Subs (all used): 20 Pat Rainford; 10 Jordan Andrade; 19 Shaun Costello; 30 Lewis Baxter.
Tries: Abel (6), Barratt (56), Reid (78); **Goals:** Moss 2/3.
Rugby Leaguer & League Express Men of the Match: *Doncaster:* Sam Smeaton; *Crusaders:* Owain Abel.
Penalty count: 2-5; **Half-time:** 12-6;
Referee: Matt Rossleigh; **Attendance:** 837.

MIDLANDS HURRICANES 24 ROCHDALE HORNETS 32

HURRICANES: 1 Nathan Hill; 25 Callum Dunne; 4 Macauley Hallett; 3 Matt Welham; 21 Ryan Johnson; 23 Dan Coates; 7 Richard Wilkinson; 8 Kieran Moran; 9 Elliot Windley; 29 Sam Hall; 17 Dom Flanagan; 12 Liam Welham; 13 Brad Clavering. Subs (all used): 24 Chris Cullimore; 16 Jacob Beer; 18 Sam Bowring; 33 Aaron Willis.
Tries: Flanagan (16), Bowring (36), Willis (42), Hallett (69);
Goals: Coates 4/4.
Sin bin: Flanagan (38) - interference;
Clavering (59) - repeated team offences.
HORNETS: 24 Andy Clarke; 32 Ollie Brookes; 3 Will Cooke; 4 Ben O'Keefe; 2 Cian Tyrer; 6 Lewis Else; 7 Dave Hewitt; 18 Jack Arnold; 9 Cameron Berry; 10 Ben Killan; 11 Dan Brewin; 33 Joe Hird; 17 AJ Boardman. Subs (all used): 14 Aiden Roden; 27 Toby Brannan; 16 Ethan O'Hanlon; 31 Lewis Peachey.
Tries: Else (1), Tyrer (6), Clarke (23, 51), Boardman (63), Roden (66); **Goals:** Hewitt 4/7.
Rugby Leaguer & League Express Men of the Match: *Hurricanes:* Macauley Hallett; *Hornets:* Andy Clarke.
Penalty count: 5-11; **Half-time:** 12-14;
Referee: Andy Sweet; **Attendance:** 384.

WORKINGTON TOWN 6 DEWSBURY RAMS 25

TOWN: 1 Jordan Burns; 5 Ethan Bickerdike; 3 Earl Hurst; 4 Jason Mossop; 2 Sean Sabutey; 26 Jack Mallinson; 6 Ciaran Walker; 8 Jordan Thomson; 9 Matty Henson; 16 JJ Key; 12 Caine Barnes; 20 Jack Stephenson; 10 Stevie Scholey. Subs (all used): 15 Fergus Simpson; 17 Joe Kirkup; 18 Liam McNicholas; 25 Grant Reid.
Try: Sabutey (52); **Goals:** Walker 1/1.
Sin bin: Barnes (76) - dangerous challenge.

RAMS: 1 Owen Restall; 2 Lewis Carr; 21 Caelum Jordan; 3 Ollie Greensmith; 23 Perry Whiteley; 6 Paul Sykes; 7 Calum Turner; 8 Jimmy Beckett; 9 Reiss Butterworth; 15 Ronan Dixon; 12 Matt Garside; 18 Brad Graham; 11 Connor Davies. Subs (all used): 10 Dale Ferguson; 14 Sam Day; 17 Elliot Morris; 20 Jackson Walker.
Tries: Whiteley (2), Jordan (23), Graham (45), Whiteley (48), R Dixon (68); **Goals:** Sykes 2/5;
Field goal: Sykes (72).
Rugby Leaguer & League Express Men of the Match: *Town:* JJ Key; *Rams:* Dale Ferguson.
Penalty count: 4-8; **Half-time:** 0-12;
Referee: Brad Milligan; **Attendance:** 650.

ROUND 4

Sunday 26th March 2023

CORNWALL 35 LONDON SKOLARS 10

CORNWALL: 1 Liam Whitton; 2 Errol Carter; 4 Coby Nichol; 5 Harry Aaronson; 14 Decarlo Trerise; 6 Cameron Brown; 7 Adam Rusling; 8 Jack Ray; 9 Luke Collins; 10 Josh Hartshorne; 11 Nathan Cullen; 12 Kaine Dimech; 13 Jake Lloyd. Subs (all used): 15 Charley Bodman; 16 Harry Boots; 17 Brad Howe; 18 Paul Bolger.
Tries: Carter (8, 22), Cullen (16), Brown (32, 67), Aaronson (73); **Goals:** Rusling 5/7; **Field goal:** Rusling (34).
Sin bin: Hartshorne (12) - fighting; Ray (61) - late challenge.
SKOLARS: 1 Jacob Thomas; 2 Louis O'Sullivan; 3 Dan Bristow; 4 Aaron Small; 5 Jerome Yates; 6 Elliott Hutchings; 7 Jack Ryan; 8 Todd Peut; 9 Doug Chirnside; 10 Malikhi Lloyd-Jones; 11 Luciano Bejanidze; 12 Matt Ross; 13 Liam O'Callaghan. Subs (all used): 15 Shane Lee; 21 Lamont Bryan; 22 Anthony Cox; 16 Christian Gale.
Tries: Yates (57), Cox (64); **Goals:** Ryan 1/2.
Sin bin: Bejanidze (12) - fighting; Lee (78) - late challenge.
Rugby Leaguer & League Express Men of the Match: *Cornwall:* Cameron Brown; *Skolars:* Jack Ryan.
Penalty count: 4-4; **Half-time:** 25-0;
Referee: Ryan Cox; **Attendance:** 862.

ROCHDALE HORNETS 4 DEWSBURY RAMS 52

HORNETS: 2 Cian Tyrer; 5 Dan Nixon; 3 Will Cooke; 4 Ben O'Keefe; 24 Andy Clarke; 6 Lewis Else; 7 Dave Hewitt; 8 Zach Braham; 9 Cameron Berry; 10 Ben Killan; 11 Dan Brewin; 36 Luke Forber; 18 Jack Arnold. Subs (all used): 14 Aiden Roden; 31 Lewis Peachey; 16 Ethan O'Hanlon; 27 Toby Brannan.
Try: Tyrer (2); **Goals:** Hewitt 0/1.
RAMS: 1 Owen Restall; 2 Lewis Carr; 26 Bailey O'Connor; 3 Ollie Greensmith; 23 Perry Whiteley; 6 Paul Sykes; 7 Calum Turner; 8 Jimmy Beckett; 9 Reiss Butterworth; 15 Ronan Dixon; 12 Matt Garside; 18 Brad Graham; 11 Connor Davies. Subs (all used): 14 Sam Day; 17 Elliot Morris; 10 Dale Ferguson; 28 Luke Littlewood.
Tries: Carr (14), Greensmith (19), Ferguson (33, 39), Restall (51, 76, 79), Whiteley (55), O'Connor (74);
Goals: Sykes 8/9.
Rugby Leaguer & League Express Men of the Match: *Hornets:* Cian Tyrer; *Rams:* Dale Ferguson.
Penalty count: 5-4; **Half-time:** 4-24;
Referee: Brad Milligan; **Attendance:** 573.

NORTH WALES CRUSADERS 4 OLDHAM 18

CRUSADERS: 2 Jack Holmes; 27 Josh Lynch; 14 Kieran Taylor; 4 Matt Reid; 5 Rob Massam; 1 Owain Abel; 28 Daniel Moss; 30 Lewis Baxter; 9 Brad Jinks; 17 Chris Barratt; 29 McKenzie Buckley; 26 Carl Forster; 13 Matt Fletcher. Subs (all used): 20 Pat Rainford; 10 Jordan Andrade; 15 Brad Brennan; 19 Shaun Costello.
Try: Massam (76); **Goals:** Moss 0/1.
OLDHAM: 28 Logan Astley; 5 Joe Hartley; 29 Alex Sutton; 4 Kian Morgan; 2 Patrick Ah Van; 6 Martyn Ridyard; 18 Jordan Paga; 10 Deane Meadows; 9 Matty Wilkinson; 8 Luke Nelmes; 11 Ethan Ferry; 12 Zac Baker; 13 Emmerson Whittel. Subs (all used): 3 Connor Carr; 14 Sean Slater; 17 Jack Blagbrough; 25 George Hirst.
Tries: Baker (13), Sutton (29), Astley (63);
Goals: Ridyard 3/3.
Rugby Leaguer & League Express Men of the Match: *Crusaders:* Daniel Moss; *Oldham:* Emmerson Whittel.
Penalty count: 7-2; **Half-time:** 0-12;
Referee: Matty Lynn; **Attendance:** 387.

MIDLANDS HURRICANES 28 WORKINGTON TOWN 38

HURRICANES: 1 Nathan Hill; 26 Joey Romeo; 3 Matt Welham; 4 Macauley Hallett; 21 Ryan Johnson; 6 Ben Stead; 23 Dan Coates; 8 Kieran Moran; 24 Chris Cullimore; 18 Sam Bowring; 33 Bailey Dawson; 12 Liam Welham; 28 Morgan Burgess. Subs (all used): 7 Richard Wilkinson; 9 Elliot Windley; 10 Matthew Bailey; 33 Aaron Willis.
Tries: B Dawson (16), M Welham (30), Hallett (49), Hill (51), Romeo (64); **Goals:** Stead 4/5.
TOWN: 1 Jordan Burns; 19 Max Anderson-Moore; 5 Ethan Bickerdike; 3 Earl Hurst; 2 Sean Sabutey; 6 Ciaran Walker; 26 Jack Mallinson; 8 Jordan Thomson; 9 Matty Henson; 16 JJ Key; 12 Caine Barnes; 20 Jack Stephenson; 18 Liam McNicholas. Subs (all used): 15 Fergus Simpson; 17 Joe Kirkup; 25 Grant Reid; 30 Luke Charlton.
Tries: J Burns (2), Sabutey (7, 10, 47, 57, 78);
Goals: Walker 7/8.
Sin bin: Hurst (38) - fighting; Walker (68) - interference.
Rugby Leaguer & League Express Men of the Match: *Hurricanes:* Matt Welham; *Town:* Sean Sabutey.
Penalty count: 5-9; **Half-time:** 12-18;
Referee: Luke Bland; **Attendance:** 324.

ROUND 5

Friday 7th April 2023

DEWSBURY RAMS 12 HUNSLET 6

RAMS: 1 Owen Restall; 2 Lewis Carr; 26 Bailey O'Connor; 3 Ollie Greensmith; 23 Perry Whiteley; 6 Paul Sykes; 7 Calum Turner; 8 Jimmy Beckett; 9 Reiss Butterworth; 15 Ronan Dixon; 12 Matt Garside; 18 Brad Graham; 11 Connor Davies. Subs (all used): 14 Sam Day; 17 Elliot Morris; 10 Dale Ferguson; 28 Luke Littlewood.
Tries: Turner (24), Carr (38); **Goals:** Sykes 2/2.
HUNSLET: 1 Jimmy Watson; 2 Jack Render; 3 Adam Ryder; 36 Alfie Goddard; 5 Kieron Lawton; 4 Joe Burton; 7 Nathan Conroy; 10 Steve Crossley; 9 Sam Hallas; 15 Nathan Newbound; 11 Josh Jordan-Roberts; 16 Jordan Syme; 13 Michael Knowles. Subs (all used): 14 Danny Barcoe; 8 Harvey Hallas; 17 Lewis Wray; 28 Brad Wheeler.
Try: Render (45); **Goals:** Jordan-Roberts 1/1.
Rugby Leaguer & League Express Men of the Match: *Rams:* Jimmy Beckett; *Hunslet:* Jimmy Watson.
Penalty count: 3-7; **Half-time:** 12-0;
Referee: Kevin Moore; **Attendance:** 1,565.

WORKINGTON TOWN 20 NORTH WALES CRUSADERS 18

TOWN: 1 Jordan Burns; 2 Sean Sabutey; 3 Earl Hurst; 4 Jason Mossop; 5 Ethan Bickerdike; 6 Ciaran Walker; 26 Jack Mallinson; 8 Jordan Thomson; 15 Fergus Simpson; 10 Stevie Scholey; 12 Caine Barnes; 20 Jack Stephenson; 9 Matty Henson. Subs (all used): 14 Blain Marwood; 18 Liam McNicholas; 25 Grant Reid; 16 JJ Key.
Tries: Henson (40, 63), Sabutey (75); **Goals:** Walker 4/4.
CRUSADERS: 1 Owain Abel; 22 Brandon Wood; 14 Kieran Taylor; 29 Wesley Bruines; 5 Rob Massam; 25 Leon Hayes; 28 Daniel Moss; 8 Callum Hazzard; 20 Pat Rainford; 10 Jordan Andrade; 21 Ryan Ellis; 30 McKenzie Buckley; 13 Matt Fletcher. Subs (all used): 15 Brad Brennan; 16 Jack Houghton; 19 Shaun Costello; 26 Carl Forster.
Tries: Andrade (11), Abel (27), Rainford (33);
Goals: Moss 3/4.
Rugby Leaguer & League Express Men of the Match: *Town:* Ciaran Walker; *Crusaders:* Owain Abel.
Penalty count: 5-6; **Half-time:** 6-18;
Referee: Matty Lynn; **Attendance:** 603.

OLDHAM 56 ROCHDALE HORNETS 16

OLDHAM: 28 Logan Astley; 2 Patrick Ah Van; 4 Kian Morgan; 29 Alex Sutton; 32 Jacob Douglas; 6 Martyn Ridyard; 18 Jordan Paga; 8 Luke Nelmes; 9 Matty Wilkinson; 17 Jack Blagbrough; 11 Ethan Ferry; 12 Zac Baker; 13 Emmerson Whittel. Subs (all used): 3 Connor Carr; 14 Sean Slater; 15 Dom Newton; 30 Harvey Wilson.
Tries: Ah Van (4), Astley (9, 21), Sutton (18, 43), Paga (23, 62), Nelmes (65, 72), Carr (79);
Goals: Ridyard 8/10.
HORNETS: 2 Cian Tyrer; 5 Dan Nixon; 31 John Hutchings; 4 Ben O'Keefe; 30 Brad Holroyd; 6 Lewis Else; 7 Dave Hewitt; 8 Zach Braham; 9 Cameron Berry; 10 Ben Killan; 11 Dan Brewin; 32 Ben Forster; 13 Connor Aspey. Subs (all used): 14 Aiden Roden; 18 Jack Arnold; 33 Will Tilleke; 37 Sion Jones.
Tries: Arnold (30), Holroyd (51), Else (57);
Goals: Hewitt 2/3.
Sin bin: Forster (61) - high tackle.
Rugby Leaguer & League Express Men of the Match: *Oldham:* Patrick Ah Van; *Hornets:* Cian Tyrer.
Penalty count: 7-7; **Half-time:** 30-6;
Referee: Andy Sweet; **Attendance:** 824.

Saturday 8th April 2023

CORNWALL 16 DONCASTER 48

CORNWALL: 1 Liam Whitton; 2 Errol Carter; 4 Coby Nichol; 5 Harry Aaronson; 14 Decarlo Trerise; 6 Cameron Brown; 7 Adam Rusling; 8 Jack Ray; 9 Luke Collins; 10 Paul Bolger; 11 Nathan Cullen; 12 Kaine Dimech; 13 Jake Lloyd. Subs (all used): 15 Charley Bodman; 16 Harry Boots; 18 Louis Singleton; 26 Ieuan Badham.
Tries: Rusling (9), Brown (35, 59); **Goals:** Rusling 2/3.
Sin bin: Bodman (67) - high tackle.
DONCASTER: 1 Elliot Hall; 2 Tom Halliday; 21 Brad Hey; 4 Jason Tali; 5 Travis Corion; 6 Ben Johnston; 7 Connor Robinson; 29 Luke Cooper; 9 Greg Burns; 17 Matt James; 27 Brett Ferres; 11 Sam Smeaton; 13 Loui McConnell. Subs (all used): 15 Alex Holdstock; 18 Jose Kenga; 14 Dean Roberts; 19 Ross Whitmore.
Tries: Smeaton (13, 25, 44, 80), Hey (22), Hall (38), Ferres (51, 79), Halliday (75); **Goals:** Robinson 6/9.
Rugby Leaguer & League Express Men of the Match: *Cornwall:* Adam Rusling; *Doncaster:* Sam Smeaton.
Penalty count: 5-5; **Half-time:** 10-24;
Referee: James Jones; **Attendance:** 928.

ROUND 6

Sunday 16th April 2023

DEWSBURY RAMS 78 CORNWALL 10

RAMS: 1 Owen Restall; 19 Simon Frewin; 21 Caelum Jordan; 4 Davey Dixon; 23 Perry Whiteley; 26 Bailey O'Connor; 7 Calum Turner; 8 Jimmy Beckett; 9 Reiss Butterworth; 20 Jackson Walker; 12 Matt Garside; 11 Connor Davies; 14 Sam Day. Subs (all used): 28 Luke Littlewood; 22 Jack Coventry; 17 Elliot Morris; 24 Joe Summers.
Tries: Whiteley (3, 47, 57, 76), Beckett (12), D Dixon (15, 18, 79), Day (25, 35, 50), Summers (29), Frewin (32), Morris (45); **Goals:** Turner 11/14.
CORNWALL: 1 Liam Whitton; 16 Decarlo Trerise; 2 Coby Nichol; 4 Tom Ashton; 5 Harry Aaronson; 6 Cameron Brown; 7 Adam Rusling; 8 Jack Ray; 9 Luke Collins; 10 Paul Bolger; 11 Nathan Cullen; 12 Kaine Dimech; 13 Jake Lloyd. Subs (all used): 14 George Mitchell; 15 Harry Boots; 20 Ieuan Badham; 24 Ewan Badham.
Tries: Aaronson (38), Boots (70); **Goals:** Rusling 1/2.
Rugby Leaguer & League Express Men of the Match: *Rams:* Sam Day; *Cornwall:* Adam Rusling.
Penalty count: 5-5; **Half-time:** 46-4;
Referee: Matty Lynn; **Attendance:** 876.

DONCASTER 26 OLDHAM 22

DONCASTER: 1 Elliot Hall; 2 Tom Halliday; 21 Brad Hey; 4 Jason Tali; 25 Jack Sanderson; 6 Ben Johnston; 7 Connor Robinson; 29 Luke Cooper; 9 Greg Burns; 8 Keelan Foster; 11 Sam Smeaton; 27 Brett Ferres; 13 Loui McConnell. Subs (all used): 14 Dean Roberts; 15 Alex Holdstock; 17 Matt James; 19 Ross Whitmore.
Tries: Hall (6, 61), Hey (18), Halliday (30), Ferres (46);
Goals: Robinson 3/5.
OLDHAM: 4 Kian Morgan; 5 Joe Hartley; 32 Iain Thornley; 3 Connor Carr; 2 Patrick Ah Van; 6 Martyn Ridyard; 18 Jordan Paga; 8 Luke Nelmes; 9 Matty Wilkinson; 17 Jack Blagbrough; 11 Ethan Ferry; 12 Zac Baker; 13 Emmerson Whittel. Subs (all used): 10 Deane Meadows; 14 Sean Slater; 15 Dom Newton; 16 James Thornton.
Tries: Thornley (22), Baker (64), Slater (71), Paga (74);
Goals: Ridyard 3/4.
Rugby Leaguer & League Express Men of the Match: *Doncaster:* Jason Tali; *Oldham:* Iain Thornley.
Penalty count: 1-3; **Half-time:** 16-4;
Referee: Matt Rossleigh; **Attendance:** 1,308.

HUNSLET 48 MIDLANDS HURRICANES 6

HUNSLET: 4 Joe Burton; 2 Jack Render; 3 Adam Ryder; 28 Brad Wheeler; 36 Alfie Goddard; 13 Michael Knowles; 39 Matty Beharrell; 8 Harvey Hallas; 7 Nathan Conroy; 10 Steve Crossley; 11 Josh Jordan-Roberts; 16 Jordan Syme; 9 Sam Hallas. Subs (all used): 14 Danny Barcoe; 12 Aaron York; 17 Lewis Wray; 26 Jordan Bull.
Tries: Render (4, 59), H Hallas (11, 76), Syme (20, 44), Conroy (24), Wheeler (33), Ryder (75); **Goals:** Beharrell 6/9.
HURRICANES: 1 Nathan Hill; 23 Callum Dunne; 3 Matt Welham; 4 Macauley Hallett; 24 Elliot Wallis; 6 Ben Stead; 25 Benn Hardcastle; 8 Kieran Moran; 9 Elliot Windley; 18 Sam Bowring; 20 Aaron Willis; 12 Liam Welham; 14 Chris Cullimore. Subs (all used): 22 Ryan Johnson; 10 Matthew Bailey; 11 Jack Dawson; 16 Jacob Beer.
Try: Hallett (70); **Goals:** Stead 1/1.
Sin bin: Moran (76) - late challenge.
Rugby Leaguer & League Express Men of the Match: *Hunslet:* Matty Beharrell; *Hurricanes:* Nathan Hill.
Penalty count: 9-5; **Half-time:** 28-0;
Referee: Brad Milligan; **Attendance:** 358.

ROCHDALE HORNETS 28 WORKINGTON TOWN 29

HORNETS: 2 Cian Tyrer; 24 Andy Clarke; 29 George Senior; 4 Ben O'Keefe; 5 Dan Nixon; 6 Lewis Else; 7 Dave Hewitt; 18 Jack Arnold; 14 Aiden Roden; 31 Lewis Peachey; 11 Dan Brewin; 32 Ben Forster; 35 Connor Ratcliffe. Subs (all used): 9 Cameron Berry; 27 Toby Brannan; 33 Will Tilleke; 37 Sion Jones.

Tries: Arnold (6), Else (17, 30), Nixon (26, 68);
Goals: Hewitt 4/5.
Sin bin: Tilleke (21) - fighting, (36) - punching.
TOWN: 1 Jordan Burns; 5 Ethan Bickerdike; 4 Jason Mossop; 3 Earl Hurst; 2 Sean Sabutey; 6 Ciaran Walker; 26 Jack Mallinson; 10 Stevie Scholey; 15 Fergus Simpson; 8 Jordan Thomson; 12 Caine Barnes; 28 Jake Bradley; 9 Matty Henson. Subs (all used): 16 JJ Key; 17 Joe Kirkup; 20 Jack Stephenson; 25 Grant Reid.
Tries: Thomson (12), Hurst (36), Bickerdike (44), Henson (50), Walker (62); **Goals:** Walker 4/6;
Field goal: Mallinson (80).
Sin bin: Scholey (21) - fighting.
Rugby Leaguer & League Express Men of the Match:
Hornets: Lewis Else; *Town:* Ciaran Walker.
Penalty count: 7-7; **Half-time:** 22-8;
Referee: Kevin Moore; **Attendance:** 588.

ROUND 17

Saturday 29th April 2023

LONDON SKOLARS 16 DEWSBURY RAMS 48

SKOLARS: 1 Donald Kudangirana; 5 Leighton Ball; 3 Jerome Yates; 4 Aaron Small; 2 Louis O'Sullivan; 7 Jacob Thomas; 6 Jack Ryan; 15 Malikhi Lloyd-Jones; 9 Doug Chirnside; 8 Christian Gale; 12 Jimmy Morgan; 11 Lameck Juma; 13 Matt Ross. Subs (all used): - Alex Deery; 19 Todd Peut; 22 Lamont Bryan; 18 Harry Kaufman.
Tries: Bryan (52), Juma (58), Kaufman (80);
Goals: Ryan 2/3.
RAMS: 1 Owen Restall; 2 Lewis Carr; 3 Ollie Greensmith; 21 Caelum Jordan; 4 Davey Dixon; 6 Paul Sykes; 28 Luke Littlewood; 8 Jimmy Beckett; 9 Reiss Butterworth; 22 Jack Coventry; 12 Matt Garside; 18 Brad Graham; 13 Louis Collinson. Subs (all used): 20 Jackson Walker; 17 Elliot Morris; 25 Tom Wilkinson; 27 Oliver Farrar.
Tries: Restall (2, 8, 69), Jordan (11, 25), Carr (21, 40), Greensmith (36), Garside (77); **Goals:** Sykes 6/9.
Rugby Leaguer & League Express Men of the Match:
Skolars: Lameck Juma; *Rams:* Reiss Butterworth.
Penalty count: 6-4; **Half-time:** 0-36;
Referee: Luke Bland; **Attendance:** 236.

ROUND 7

Sunday 7th May 2023

OLDHAM 36 CORNWALL 16

OLDHAM: 1 Gregg McNally; 5 Joe Hartley; 3 Connor Carr; 4 Kian Morgan; 2 Patrick Ah Van; 28 Kieran Tyrer; 18 Jordan Paga; 8 Luke Nelmes; 9 Matty Wilkinson; 10 Deane Meadows; 25 George Hirst; 12 Zac Baker; 13 Emmerson Whittel. Subs (all used): 14 Sean Slater; 29 Harvey Makin; 30 Bob Morgan; 32 Harvey Wilson.
Tries: Ah Van (11, 15, 46), Wilson (35), McNally (38, 58), Hirst (53); **Goals:** Tyrer 1/2, Slater 1/3, Ah Van 2/2.
Sin bin: Meadows (31) - fighting.
CORNWALL: 1 Liam Whitton; 3 Errol Carter; 2 Coby Nichol; 18 Tom Ashton; 4 Harry Aaronson; 6 Cameron Brown; 7 Adam Rusling; 8 Jack Ray; 9 Luke Collins; 20 Ewan Badham; 11 Nathan Cullen; 12 Kaine Dimech; 13 Jake Lloyd. Subs (all used): 10 Leo Tennison; 15 Harry Boots; 16 Charley Bodman; 24 Decarlo Trerise.
Tries: Aaronson (61), Brown (71, 77); **Goals:** Rusling 2/3.
Sin bin: Ashton (31) - fighting;
Ray (57) - late challenge on Paga.
Rugby Leaguer & League Express Men of the Match:
Oldham: Patrick Ah Van; *Cornwall:* Cameron Brown.
Penalty count: 2-4; **Half-time:** 20-0;
Referee: Kevin Moore; **Attendance:** 437.

DONCASTER 46 WORKINGTON TOWN 6

DONCASTER: 1 Elliot Hall; 2 Tom Halliday; 21 Brad Hey; 4 Jason Tali; 25 Jack Sanderson; 6 Ben Johnston; 7 Connor Robinson; 8 Keelan Foster; 9 Greg Burns; 29 Luke Cooper; 27 Brett Ferres; 11 Sam Smeaton; 13 Loui McConnell. Subs (all used): 15 Alex Holdstock; 17 Matt James; 20 Brad Knowles; 28 Josh Veacock.
Tries: Hall (4), Smeaton (9), McConnell (19, 77), Sanderson (25), Tali (41, 49), Johnston (66);
Goals: Robinson 7/8.
TOWN: 1 Jordan Burns; 5 Ethan Bickerdike; 4 Jason Mossop; 3 Earl Hurst; 2 Sean Sabutey; 26 Jack Mallinson; 6 Ciaran Walker; 8 Jordan Thomson; 9 Matty Henson; 25 Grant Reid; 18 Liam McNicholas; 20 Jack Stephenson; 10 Stevie Scholey. Subs (all used): 27 Hanley Dawson; 16 JJ Key; 15 Fergus Simpson; 28 Connor Terrill.
Try: Walker (21); **Goals:** Walker 1/1.
Rugby Leaguer & League Express Men of the Match:
Doncaster: Jason Tali; *Town:* Fergus Simpson.
Penalty count: 1-3; **Half-time:** 22-6;
Referee: Nick Bennett; **Attendance:** 1,255.

MIDLANDS HURRICANES 38 LONDON SKOLARS 20

HURRICANES: 1 Nathan Hill; 23 Ryan Johnson; 3 Matt Welham; 4 Macauley Hallett; 5 Hayden Freeman; 25 Jacob Hookem; 6 Ben Stead; 8 Kieran Moran; 9 Elliot Windley; 20 Brad Martin; 11 Jack Dawson; 24 Bailey Dawson; 28 Kyle Kesik. Subs (all used): 18 Sam Bowring; 10 Matthew Bailey; 14 Chris Cullimore; 12 Liam Welham.
Tries: Freeman (15, 30, 57), Martin (23), M Welham (50), Johnson (62), L Welham (68); **Goals:** Stead 5/7.
Sin bin: Johnson (5) - delaying restart.
SKOLARS: 1 Donald Kudangirana; 2 Leighton Ball; 3 Jerome Yates; 4 Aaron Small; 5 Louis O'Sullivan; 7 Jacob Thomas; 6 Jack Ryan; 10 Malikhi Lloyd-Jones; 9 Doug Chirnside; 8 Christian Gale; 12 Jimmy Morgan; 11 Lameck Juma; 13 Matt Ross. Subs (all used): 14 Alex Deery; 18 Todd Peut; 21 Lamont Bryan; 15 Harry Kaufman.
Tries: Yates (2), Juma (44), Kudangirana (47, 52);
Goals: Ryan 0/1, Deery 2/3.
Rugby Leaguer & League Express Men of the Match:
Hurricanes: Ben Stead; *Skolars:* Donald Kudangirana.
Penalty count: 8-4; **Half-time:** 18-4;
Referee: Andy Sweet; **Attendance:** 239.

ROCHDALE HORNETS 32 NORTH WALES CRUSADERS 18

HORNETS: 1 Joe Purcell; 2 Cian Tyrer; 29 Umyla Hanley; 30 Nick Rawsthorne; 5 Dan Nixon; 6 Lewis Else; 7 Dave Hewitt; 18 Jack Arnold; 14 Aiden Roden; 10 Ben Killan; 11 Dan Brewin; 32 Ben Forster; 35 Connor Ratcliffe. Subs (all used): 9 Cameron Berry; 16 Ethan O'Hanlon; 37 Sion Jones; - Daniel Spencer-Tonks.
Tries: Purcell (2), Hanley (23, 39, 69), Else (50, 57);
Goals: Hewitt 4/6.
Sin bin: Arnold (76) - fighting.
CRUSADERS: 1 Owain Abel; 27 Josh Lynch; 14 Kieran Taylor; 3 Declan Hulme; 5 Rob Massam; 25 Leon Hayes; 28 Daniel Moss; 17 Chris Barratt; 20 Pat Rainford; 19 Shaun Costello; 21 Ryan Ellis; 29 McKenzie Buckley; 13 Matt Fletcher. Subs (all used): 7 Brad Billsborough; 8 Callum Hazzard; 15 Brad Brennan; 16 Jack Houghton.
Tries: Rainford (13), Lynch (19), Massam (44), Houghton (64); **Goals:** Moss 1/3, Billsborough 0/1.
Rugby Leaguer & League Express Men of the Match:
Hornets: Umyla Hanley; *Crusaders:* Owain Abel.
Penalty count: 4-5; **Half-time:** 16-8;
Referee: Ryan Cox; **Attendance:** 564.

ROUND 8

Saturday 13th May 2023

CORNWALL 10 HUNSLET 54

CORNWALL: 1 Liam Whitton; 3 Errol Carter; 2 Coby Nichol; 18 Tom Ashton; 4 Harry Aaronson; 6 Cameron Brown; 7 Adam Rusling; 8 Brad Howe; 9 Luke Collins; 26 Ewan Badham; 16 Charley Bodman; 12 Kaine Dimech; 13 Jake Lloyd. Subs (all used): 24 Reece Boase; 10 Harry Boots; 20 Paul Bolger; 15 Decarlo Trerise.
Tries: Brown (31), Ashton (36); **Goals:** Rusling 1/2.
HUNSLET: 4 Joe Burton; 2 Jack Render; 3 Adam Ryder; 20 Alfie Goddard; 36 Johnny Campbell; 13 Michael Knowles; 21 Morgan Punchard; 8 Harvey Hallas; 7 Nathan Conroy; 10 Steve Crossley; 11 Josh Jordan-Roberts; 16 Jordan Syme; 9 Sam Hallas. Subs (all used): 14 Danny Barcoe; 15 Nathan Newbound; 17 Lewis Wray; 28 Brad Wheeler.
Tries: Conroy (16), Ryder (23), Wray (44), Campbell (51), Syme (55), Goddard (59), Jordan-Roberts (62), J Burton (69), Barcoe (73), Render (78);
Goals: Knowles 6/8, Punchard 1/2.
Sin bin: S Hallas (38) - use of the forearm.
Rugby Leaguer & League Express Men of the Match:
Cornwall: Luke Collins; *Hunslet:* Nathan Conroy.
Penalty count: 4-5; **Half-time:** 10-12;
Referee: Matty Lynn; **Attendance:** 727.

LONDON SKOLARS 24 ROCHDALE HORNETS 28

SKOLARS: 1 Donald Kudangirana; 5 Leighton Ball; 3 Ethane Wainwright; 4 Aaron Small; 2 Jerome Yates; 6 Jack Ryan; 7 Jacob Thomas; 22 Lamont Bryan; 9 Doug Chirnside; 15 Malikhi Lloyd-Jones; 11 Jaden Dayes; 12 Lameck Juma; 13 Matt Ross. Subs (all used): 14 Alex Deery; 10 Christian Gale; 19 Todd Peut; 23 Sam Webb-Campbell.
Tries: Yates (30), Webb-Campbell (47), Deery (49), Ball (62), Wainwright (76); **Goals:** Ryan 1/2, Deery 1/3.
HORNETS: 1 Joe Purcell; 2 Cian Tyrer; 29 Umyla Hanley; 28 Luke Forber; 5 Dan Nixon; 6 Lewis Else; 7 Dave Hewitt; 31 Lewis Peachey; 9 Cameron Berry; 10 Ben Killan; 11 Dan Brewin; 32 Ben Forster; 35 Connor Ratcliffe. Subs (all used): - Jack Gatcliffe; 37 Sion Jones; 27 Toby Brannan; 30 Daniel Spencer-Tonks.
Tries: Nixon (8), Peachey (26), Hanley (29), Tyrer (53), Killan (71); **Goals:** Hewitt 4/5.
Rugby Leaguer & League Express Men of the Match:
Skolars: Doug Chirnside; *Hornets:* Lewis Peachey.
Penalty count: 1-4; **Half-time:** 4-16;
Referee: Matt Rossleigh; **Attendance:** 209.

Sunday 14th May 2023

DEWSBURY RAMS 26 DONCASTER 12

RAMS: 1 Owen Restall; 2 Lewis Carr; 21 Caelum Jordan; 3 Ollie Greensmith; 19 Simon Frewin; 6 Paul Sykes; 7 Calum Turner; 8 Jimmy Beckett; 9 Reiss Butterworth; 15 Ronan Dixon; 12 Matt Garside; 18 Brad Graham; 11 Connor Davies. Subs (all used): 26 Bailey O'Connor; 17 Elliot Morris; 10 Dale Ferguson; 20 Jackson Walker.
Tries: Turner (8), Frewin (53, 70), Restall (66, pen), Graham (68); **Goals:** Sykes 2/2, Turner 1/3.
Sin bin: Turner (45) - holding down.
DONCASTER: 1 Elliot Hall; 2 Tom Halliday; 21 Brad Hey; 4 Jason Tali; 22 Misi Taulapapa; 6 Ben Johnston; 7 Connor Robinson; 29 Luke Cooper; 9 Greg Burns; 18 Jose Kenga; 11 Sam Smeaton; 27 Brett Ferres; 13 Loui McConnell. Subs (all used): 15 Alex Holdstock; 17 Matt James; 20 Brad Knowles; 28 Josh Veacock.
Tries: Robinson (15), Tali (78); **Goals:** Robinson 2/3.
Rugby Leaguer & League Express Men of the Match:
Rams: Paul Sykes; *Doncaster:* Ben Johnston.
Penalty count: 6-4; **Half-time:** 6-4;
Referee: Brad Milligan; **Attendance:** 2,015.

WORKINGTON TOWN 18 OLDHAM 28

TOWN: 5 Ethan Bickerdike; 19 Max Anderson-Moore; 4 Jason Mossop; 3 Earl Hurst; 2 Sean Sabutey; 6 Ciaran Walker; 15 Fergus Simpson; 8 Jordan Thomson; 9 Matty Henson; 10 Stevie Scholey; 12 Caine Barnes; 11 Malik Steele; 27 Hanley Dawson. Subs (all used): 14 Blain Marwood; 17 Joe Kirkup; 25 Grant Reid; 16 JJ Key.
Tries: Henson (4), Reid (30), Thomson (57);
Goals: Walker 3/3.
OLDHAM: 1 Gregg McNally; 5 Joe Hartley; 25 George Hirst; 4 Kian Morgan; 2 Patrick Ah Van; 6 Martyn Ridyard; 18 Jordan Paga; 10 Deane Meadows; 9 Matty Wilkinson; 8 Luke Nelmes; 19 Callum Cameron; 12 Zac Baker; 13 Emmerson Whittel. Subs (all used): 14 Sean Slater; 17 Jack Blagbrough; 20 Tommy Brierley; 30 Pat Moran.
Tries: Cameron (8), McNally (38), Brierley (65), Hartley (69, 79); **Goals:** Ridyard 4/6.
Rugby Leaguer & League Express Men of the Match:
Town: Jordan Thomson; *Oldham:* Martyn Ridyard.
Penalty count: 2-4; **Half-time:** 12-10;
Referee: Kevin Moore; **Attendance:** 1,010.

ROUND 9

Sunday 21st May 2023

ROCHDALE HORNETS 62 CORNWALL 6

HORNETS: 1 Joe Purcell; 2 Cian Tyrer; 29 Umyla Hanley; 4 Ben O'Keefe; 5 Dan Nixon; 6 Lewis Else; 7 Dave Hewitt; 16 Ethan O'Hanlon; 9 Cameron Berry; 31 Lewis Peachey; 32 Ben Forster; 11 Dan Brewin; 18 Jack Arnold. Subs (all used): 25 Aaron Smith; 27 Toby Brannan; 30 Daniel Spencer-Tonks; 37 Sion Jones.
Tries: Else (3, 67), Arnold (12), Peachey (23), Smith (28), Hewitt (35), Tyrer (40), Brannan (55), Hanley (61), Purcell (64), O'Keefe (70); **Goals:** Hewitt 9/11.
CORNWALL: 1 Liam Whitton; 3 Errol Carter; 2 Coby Nichol; 4 Tom Ashton; 5 Harry Aaronson; 6 Cameron Brown; 7 Adam Rusling; 8 Leo Tennison; 9 Luke Collins; 10 Harry Boots; 11 Nathan Cullen; 12 Kaine Dimech; 13 Jake Lloyd. Subs (all used): 14 Harvey Whiteley; 16 Charley Bodman; 17 David Weetman; 22 Spencer Darley.
Try: Weetman (76); **Goals:** Brown 1/1.
Sin bin: Whitton (21) - dissent.
Rugby Leaguer & League Express Men of the Match:
Hornets: Dave Hewitt; *Cornwall:* Cameron Brown.
Penalty count: 8-6; **Half-time:** 34-0;
Referee: Brad Milligan; **Attendance:** 496.

DONCASTER 60 LONDON SKOLARS 30

DONCASTER: 1 Elliot Hall; 25 Jack Sanderson; 21 Brad Hey; 4 Jason Tali; 22 Misi Taulapapa; 6 Ben Johnston; 7 Connor Robinson; 8 Keelan Foster; 28 Josh Veacock; 17 Matt James; 11 Sam Smeaton; 27 Brett Ferres; 20 Brad Knowles. Subs (all used): 9 Greg Burns; 14 Dean Roberts; 19 Ross Whitmore; 29 Luke Cooper.
Tries: Veacock (8), Robinson (11, 22), Sanderson (25), Smeaton (29, 45), Hall (34), Roberts (49), Johnston (56, 61); **Goals:** Robinson 10/10.
SKOLARS: 1 Donald Kudangirana; 2 Leighton Ball; 3 Dan Bristow; 4 Aaron Small; 5 Shane Hurley; 6 Jack Ryan; 7 Jacob Thomas; 8 Lamont Bryan; 9 Doug Chirnside; 10 Malikhi Lloyd-Jones; 12 Lameck Juma; 11 Jaden Dayes; 13

Matt Ross. Subs (all used): 14 Alex Deery; 15 Sam Webb-Campbell; 19 Todd Peut; 22 Anthony Cox.
Tries: Bryan (51), Deery (65), Dayes (69), Small (72), Juma (80); **Goals:** Deery 5/5.
Sin bin: Small (61) - fighting.
Rugby Leaguer & League Express Men of the Match:
Doncaster: Connor Robinson; *Skolars:* Alex Deery.
Penalty count: 11-3; **Half-time:** 36-0;
Referee: Luke Bland; **Attendance:** 1,158.

HUNSLET 22 WORKINGTON TOWN 18

HUNSLET: 4 Joe Burton; 2 Jack Render; 3 Adam Ryder; 27 Sean Croston; 20 Alfie Goddard; 13 Michael Knowles; 39 Matty Beharrell; 8 Harvey Hallas; 7 Nathan Conroy; 10 Steve Crossley; 11 Josh Jordan-Roberts; 16 Jordan Syme; 9 Sam Hallas. Subs (all used): 14 Danny Barcoe; 15 Nathan Newbound; 17 Lewis Wray; 6 Jake Sweeting.
Tries: Croston (2), Crossley (6, 33); **Goals:** Beharrell 5/5.
TOWN: 1 Jordan Burns; 5 Ethan Bickerdike; 4 Jason Mossop; 3 Earl Hurst; 2 Sean Sabutey; 6 Ciaran Walker; 26 Jack Mallinson; 10 Stevie Scholey; 9 Matty Henson; 17 Joe Kirkup; 12 Caine Barnes; 11 Malik Steele; 27 Hanley Dawson. Subs (all used): 15 Fergus Simpson; 25 Grant Reid; 30 Luke Charlton; 16 JJ Key.
Tries: Walker (10), Sabutey (14, 66); **Goals:** Walker 3/5.
Sin bin: Kirkup (58) - dangerous contact.
Rugby Leaguer & League Express Men of the Match:
Hunslet: Steve Crossley; *Town:* Ciaran Walker.
Penalty count: 9-7; **Half-time:** 18-12;
Referee: Andy Sweet; **Attendance:** 347.

**MIDLANDS HURRICANES 14
NORTH WALES CRUSADERS 42**

HURRICANES: 1 Nathan Hill; 23 Ryan Johnson; 3 Matt Welham; 4 Macauley Hallett; 5 Hayden Freeman; 6 Ben Stead; 29 Adam Brook; 8 Kieran Moran; 14 Chris Cullimore; 18 Sam Bowring; 11 Jack Dawson; 24 Bailey Dawson; 28 Kyle Kesik. Subs (all used): 12 Liam Welham; 9 Elliot Windley; 10 Matthew Bailey; 22 Aaron Willis.
Tries: B Dawson (49), Hallett (64), Hill (74);
Goals: Stead 1/3.
CRUSADERS: 1 Owain Abel; 27 Josh Lynch; 14 Kieran Taylor; 3 Declan Hulme; 5 Rob Massam; 6 Dave Gibbons; 7 Brad Billsborough; 18 Jack Houghton; 25 Jake Burns; 17 Chris Barratt; 29 McKenzie Buckley; 11 Cole Oakley; 28 Carl Forster. Subs (all used): 10 Jordan Andrade; 13 Matt Fletcher; 18 Paul Nash; 19 Shaun Costello.
Tries: Houghton (2), Lynch (11), Burns (20), Billsborough (33), Massam (37), Nash (42), Abel (62);
Goals: Billsborough 7/8.
Rugby Leaguer & League Express Men of the Match:
Hurricanes: Bailey Dawson; *Crusaders:* Brad Billsborough.
Penalty count: 7-7; **Half-time:** 0-30;
Referee: Kevin Moore; **Attendance:** 321.

OLDHAM 26 DEWSBURY RAMS 26

OLDHAM: 1 Gregg McNally; 5 Joe Hartley; 25 George Hirst; 4 Kian Morgan; 2 Patrick Ah Van; 6 Martyn Ridyard; 18 Jordan Paga; 8 Luke Nelmes; 9 Matty Wilkinson; 10 Deane Meadows; 19 Callum Cameron; 12 Zac Baker; 13 Emmerson Whittel. Subs (all used): 14 Sean Slater; 20 Tommy Brierley; 30 Harvey Wilson; 32 Pat Moran.
Tries: Ah Van (8), McNally (14), Hartley (30), Baker (35);
Goals: Ridyard 5/7.
RAMS: 1 Owen Restall; 2 Lewis Carr; 26 Bailey O'Connor; 3 Ollie Greensmith; 19 Simon Frewin; 6 Paul Sykes; 7 Calum Turner; 8 Jimmy Beckett; 9 Reiss Butterworth; 15 Ronan Dixon; 12 Matt Garside; 18 Brad Graham; 11 Connor Davies. Subs (all used): 17 Elliot Morris; 10 Dale Ferguson; 20 Jackson Walker; 4 Davey Dixon.
Tries: Graham (18), Beckett (22), D Dixon (68), O'Connor (77); **Goals:** Sykes 5/5.
Sin bin: Sykes (51) - late challenge.
Rugby Leaguer & League Express Men of the Match:
Oldham: Martyn Ridyard; *Rams:* Calum Turner.
Penalty count: 9-5; **Half-time:** 20-14;
Referee: Matt Rossleigh; **Attendance:** 1,295.

ROUND 10

Sunday 28th May 2023

CORNWALL 10 NORTH WALES CRUSADERS 42

CORNWALL: 1 Liam Whitton; 3 Errol Carter; 2 Coby Nichol; 4 Tom Ashton; 5 Harry Aaronson; 6 Cameron Brown; 7 Adam Rusling; 8 Leo Tennison; 13 Jake Lloyd; 22 Harry Boots; 11 Nathan Cullen; 14 David Weetman; 12 Kaine Dimech. Subs (all used): 9 Luke Collins; 17 George Mitchell; 16 Reece Boase; 20 Ewan Badham.
Tries: Weetman (7), Whitton (30); **Goals:** Rusling 1/3.
CRUSADERS: 1 Owain Abel; 27 Josh Lynch; 14 Kieran Taylor; 11 Cole Oakley; 5 Rob Massam; 6 Dave Gibbons; 7 Brad Billsborough; 16 Jack Houghton; 25 Aiden Doolan; 17 Chris Barratt; 21 Ryan Ellis; 28 Tom Whitehead; 26 Carl Forster. Subs (all used): 29 Shaun Costello; 13 Matt Fletcher; 24 Jacob Bloxham; 18 Paul Nash.
Tries: Houghton (15), Abel (36, 52), Costello (39), Massam (47), Fletcher (55), Doolan (72);
Goals: Billsborough 7/7.
Sin bin: Gibbons (59) - professional foul.
Rugby Leaguer & League Express Men of the Match:
Cornwall: Adam Rusling; *Crusaders:* Owain Abel.
Penalty count: 7-10; **Half-time:** 10-18;
Referee: Andy Sweet; **Attendance:** 1,008.

HUNSLET 36 ROCHDALE HORNETS 18

HUNSLET: 4 Joe Burton; 2 Jack Render; 3 Adam Ryder; 20 Alfie Goddard; 36 Johnny Campbell; 30 Matty Beharrell; 6 Jake Sweeting; 9 Sam Hallas; 7 Nathan Conroy; 10 Steve Crossley; 11 Josh Jordan-Roberts; 12 Aaron York; 13 Michael Knowles. Subs (all used): 14 Danny Barcoe; 8 Harvey Hallas; 16 Jordan Syme; 17 Lewis Wray.
Tries: Conroy (18), Campbell (23, 32, 44), Jordan-Roberts (39), Beharrell (63), Render (66);
Goals: Beharrell 4/7.
HORNETS: 29 Umyla Hanley; 2 Cian Tyrer; 11 Dan Brewin; 36 Luke Forber; 5 Dan Nixon; 6 Lewis Else; 7 Dave Hewitt; 31 Lewis Peachey; 14 Aiden Roden; 10 Ben Killan; 33 Joe Hird; 32 Ben Forster; 18 Jack Arnold. Subs (all used): 30 Aaron Smith; 9 Cameron Berry; 27 Toby Brannan; 16 Ethan O'Hanlon.
Tries: Forber (53), O'Hanlon (74), Berry (80);
Goals: Hewitt 3/3.
Rugby Leaguer & League Express Men of the Match:
Hunslet: Johnny Campbell; *Hornets:* Lewis Else.
Penalty count: 5-5; **Half-time:** 22-0;
Referee: Matt Rossleigh; **Attendance:** 481.

DEWSBURY RAMS 52 LONDON SKOLARS 6

RAMS: 1 Owen Restall; 2 Lewis Carr; 26 Bailey O'Connor; 3 Ollie Greensmith; 4 Davey Dixon; 6 Paul Sykes; 7 Calum Turner; 8 Jimmy Beckett; 9 Reiss Butterworth; 17 Elliot Morris; 11 Connor Davies; 12 Matt Garside; 13 Louis Collinson. Subs (all used): 16 George Collins; 10 Dale Ferguson; 20 Jackson Walker; 24 Joe Summers.
Tries: Restall (11, 72, 78), D Dixon (18, 26), O'Connor (36, 56), Garside (60), Collins (70);
Goals: Sykes 8/9.
SKOLARS: 1 Donald Kudangirana; 2 Leighton Ball; 3 Josh Guzdek; 4 Aaron Small; 5 Jason Bass; 6 Jack Ryan; 7 Jacob Thomas; 8 Harry Kaufman; 9 Alex Deery; 10 Malikhi Lloyd-Jones; 11 Lameck Juma; 12 Luciano Bejanidze; 13 Matt Ross. Subs (all used): 14 Liam O'Callaghan; 15 Todd Peut; 16 Sam Wellings; 17 Anthony Cox.
Try: O'Callaghan (45); **Goals:** Ryan 1/1.
Rugby Leaguer & League Express Men of the Match:
Rams: Dale Ferguson; *Skolars:* Liam O'Callaghan.
Penalty count: 1-3; **Half-time:** 22-0;
Referee: Kevin Moore; **Attendance:** 825.

MIDLANDS HURRICANES 16 OLDHAM 50

HURRICANES: 1 Nathan Hill; 23 Ryan Johnson; 3 Matt Welham; 4 Macauley Hallett; 5 Hayden Freeman; 6 Ben Stead; 29 Adam Brook; 8 Kieran Moran; 9 Elliot Windley; 10 Matthew Bailey; 11 Jack Dawson; 16 Jacob Beer; 12 Liam Welham. Subs (all used): 14 Chris Cullimore; 27 Toby Richardson; 22 Jack Coventry; 28 Courage Mkuhlani.
Tries: Beer (3), Cullimore (32), Freeman (56);
Goals: Stead 2/4.
OLDHAM: 1 Gregg McNally; 20 Tommy Brierley; 3 Connor Carr; 4 Kian Morgan; 2 Patrick Ah Van; 6 Martyn Ridyard; 18 Jordan Paga; 10 Deane Meadows; 9 Matty Wilkinson; 8 Luke Nelmes; 19 Callum Cameron; 25 George Hirst; 13 Emmerson Whittel. Subs (all used): 14 Sean Slater; 32 Samy Kibula; 15 Dom Newton; 30 Pat Moran.
Tries: Meadows (16), Ah Van (38, 47), Ridyard (45, 52), Hirst (63), Paga (65), K Morgan (68), Newton (79);
Goals: Ridyard 7/9.
Rugby Leaguer & League Express Men of the Match:
Hurricanes: Macauley Hallett; *Oldham:* Martyn Ridyard.
Penalty count: 7-7; **Half-time:** 12-12;
Referee: Brad Milligan; **Attendance:** 342.

ROUND 11

Saturday 3rd June 2023

LONDON SKOLARS 6 NORTH WALES CRUSADERS 60

SKOLARS: 1 Josh Guzdek; 2 Leighton Ball; 3 Dan Bristow; 4 Aaron Small; 5 Donald Kudangirana; 6 Robbie Butterworth; 7 Jacob Thomas; 10 Harry Kaufman; 9 Jack Ryan; 15 Malikhi Lloyd-Jones; 11 Jaden Dayes; 12 Lameck Juma; 13 Luciano Bejanidze. Subs (all used): 8 Todd Peut; 17 Ellis Roberts; 18 Liam O'Callaghan; 19 Matt Ross.
Try: Small (68); **Goals:** Thomas 1/2.
CRUSADERS: 28 Daniel Hill; 27 Josh Lynch; 14 Kieran Taylor; 30 Cole Oakley; 5 Rob Massam; 6 Dave Gibbons; 7 Brad Billsborough; 16 Jack Houghton; 25 Jake Burns; 17 Chris Barratt; 21 Ryan Ellis; 29 Tom Whitehead; 26 Carl Forster. Subs (all used): 2 Jack Holmes; 10 Jordan Andrade; 13 Matt Fletcher; 19 Shaun Costello.
Tries: Ellis (3), Forster (11), Hill (13, 16), Massam (22, 80), Billsborough (29), Holmes (32), Gibbons (44), Oakley (53);
Goals: Billsborough 10/10.
Rugby Leaguer & League Express Men of the Match:
Skolars: Aaron Small; *Crusaders:* Carl Forster.
Penalty count: 4-5; **Half-time:** 0-42;
Referee: William Gilder; **Attendance:** 215.

OLDHAM 40 HUNSLET 20

OLDHAM: 1 Gregg McNally; 5 Joe Hartley; 3 Connor Carr; 4 Kian Morgan; 2 Patrick Ah Van; 6 Martyn Ridyard; 18 Jordan Paga; 8 Luke Nelmes; 9 Matty Wilkinson; 10 Deane Meadows; 25 George Hirst; 12 Zac Baker; 13 Emmerson Whittel. Subs (all used): 14 Sean Slater; 15 Dom Newton; 30 Pat Moran; 32 Samy Kibula.
Tries: Wilkinson (11), Hartley (25), Carr (32), Ah Van (54, 57), Baker (66); **Goals:** Ridyard 8/8.
HUNSLET: 4 Joe Burton; 2 Jack Render; 3 Adam Ryder; 20 Alfie Goddard; 36 Johnny Campbell; 6 Jake Sweeting; 30 Matty Beharrell; 9 Sam Hallas; 7 Nathan Conroy; 10 Steve Crossley; 11 Josh Jordan-Roberts; 12 Aaron York; 13 Michael Knowles. Subs (all used): 8 Harvey Hallas; 16 Jordan Syme; 17 Lewis Wray; 28 Brad Wheeler.
Tries: Render (6), Conroy (28), Campbell (44);
Goals: Beharrell 4/5.
Sin bin: S Hallas (72) - dangerous challenge.
Rugby Leaguer & League Express Men of the Match:
Oldham: Zac Baker; *Hunslet:* Adam Ryder.
Penalty count: 8-3; **Half-time:** 18-14;
Referee: Luke Bland; **Attendance:** 361.

Sunday 4th June 2023

MIDLANDS HURRICANES 26 DONCASTER 54

HURRICANES: 1 Ben Stead; 2 Jason Bass; 3 Matt Welham; 4 Macauley Hallett; 5 Hayden Freeman; 6 Jacob Hookem; 7 Adam Brook; 8 Toby Richardson; 9 Chris Cullimore; 10 Matthew Bailey; 11 Tom Wilkinson; 12 Jacob Beer; 13 Tyler Hepple. Subs (all used): 14 Elliot Windley; 15 Bailey Dawson; 16 Courage Mkuhlani; 17 Abdullah Balogun.
Tries: T Wilkinson (16), M Welham (20, 25, 78), Bass (79);
Goals: Stead 3/5.
DONCASTER: 1 Elliot Hall; 2 Tom Halliday; 21 Brad Hey; 25 Jack Sanderson; 5 Travis Corion; 6 Ben Johnston; 7 Connor Robinson; 29 Luke Cooper; 9 Greg Burns; 8 Keelan Foster; 11 Sam Smeaton; 27 Brett Ferres; 13 Loui McConnell. Subs (all used): 14 Dean Roberts; 17 Matt James; 18 Jose Kenga; 20 Brad Knowles.
Tries: Cooper (5, 9, 67), Roberts (37, 48), James (51), Robinson (61), Foster (64), Johnston (74);
Goals: Robinson 9/9.
Rugby Leaguer & League Express Men of the Match:
Hurricanes: Matt Welham; *Doncaster:* Dean Roberts.
Penalty count: 7-7; **Half-time:** 16-18;
Referee: Freddie Lincoln; **Attendance:** 273.

WORKINGTON TOWN 54 CORNWALL 0

TOWN: 1 Jordan Burns; 19 Max Anderson-Moore; 4 Jason Mossop; 3 Earl Hurst; 2 Sean Sabutey; 6 Ciaran Walker; 7 Carl Forber; 10 Stevie Scholey; 9 Matty Henson; 8 Jordan Thomson; 29 Jake Bradley; 11 Malik Steele; 27 Hanley Dawson. Subs (all used): 17 Joe Kirkup; 14 Blain Marwood; 25 Grant Reid; 18 Liam McNicholas.
Tries: Bradley (4, 44), Henson (14, 29), Mossop (24), Sabutey (31), Reid (39), J Burns (53), Thomson (72), Walker (74); **Goals:** Walker 7/10.
CORNWALL: 5 Harry Aaronson; 3 Errol Carter; 2 Coby Nichol; 4 Tom Ashton; 15 Decarlo Trerise; 6 Cameron Brown; 1 Liam Whitton; 8 Harry Boots; 13 Jake Lloyd; 10 Ewan Badham; 11 Nathan Cullen; 14 David Weetman; 12 Kaine Dimech. Subs (all used): 9 Luke Collins; 7 Adam Rusling; 16 Reece Boase; 15 Jordan Bull.
Rugby Leaguer & League Express Men of the Match:
Town: Jordan Burns; *Cornwall:* Jake Lloyd.
Penalty count: 6-9; **Half-time:** 32-0;
Referee: Elliot Burrow; **Attendance:** 603.

ROUND 12

Saturday 10th June 2023

LONDON SKOLARS 14 OLDHAM 62

SKOLARS: 1 Donald Kudangirana; 2 Leighton Ball; 3 Dan Bristow; 4 Aaron Small; 5 Jerome Yates; 6 Jack Ryan; 7

Jacob Thomas; 8 Christian Gale; 18 Liam O'Callaghan; 15 Malikhi Lloyd-Jones; 11 Luciano Bejanidze; 12 Lameck Juma; 13 Matt Ross. Subs (all used): 9 Alex Deery; 19 Todd Peut; 16 Tommy Porter; 10 Sam Wellings.
Tries: Ball (23), Ross (26), Deery (53);
Goals: Ryan 0/1, Deery 1/2.
OLDHAM: 1 Gregg McNally; 5 Joe Hartley; 3 Connor Carr; 29 Kian Morgan; 2 Patrick Ah Van; 6 Martyn Ridyard; 18 Jordan Paga; 8 Luke Nelmes; 9 Matty Wilkinson; 10 Deane Meadows; 25 George Hirst; 12 Zac Baker; 13 Emmerson Whittel. Subs (all used): 14 Sean Slater; 30 Samy Kibula; 15 Dom Newton; 32 Pat Moran.
Tries: Paga (5), Ah Van (13, 34, 60), K Morgan (38), McNally (40), Baker (45), Kibula (56), Wilkinson (63), Nelmes (67), Slater (80); **Goals:** Ridyard 5/6, Ah Van 4/5.
Sin bin: Paga (48) - holding down.
Rugby Leaguer & League Express Men of the Match:
Skolars: Matt Ross; *Oldham:* Zac Baker.
Penalty count: 5-6; **Half-time:** 10-28;
Referee: Andy Sweet; **Attendance:** 338.

Sunday 11th June 2023

CORNWALL 6 DEWSBURY RAMS 30

CORNWALL: 1 Liam Whitton; 3 Errol Carter; 2 Coby Nichol; 4 Tom Ashton; 5 Harry Aaronson; 6 Cameron Brown; 7 Morgan Punchard; 8 Harry Boots; 13 Jake Lloyd; 10 Josh Hartshorne; 11 David Weetman; 12 Kaine Dimech; 15 Ewan Badham. Subs (all used): 23 Paul Bolger; 14 Jaden Barraclough; 16 Decarlo Trerise; 20 Ieuan Badham.
Try: Nichol (48); **Goals:** Brown 1/1.
Sin bin: Brown (32) - fighting; Punchard (36) - fighting.
RAMS: 1 Owen Restall; 2 Lewis Carr; 21 Caelum Jordan; 4 Davey Dixon; 23 Perry Whiteley; 26 Bailey O'Connor; 7 Calum Turner; 8 Jimmy Beckett; 9 Reiss Butterworth; 15 Ronan Dixon; 18 Brad Graham; 24 Joe Summers; 13 Louis Collinson. Subs (all used): 28 Luke Littlewood; 17 Elliot Morris; 20 Jackson Walker; 10 Dale Ferguson.
Tries: Beckett (20), Jordan (55, 79), Graham (61), Carr (74);
Goals: Turner 5/6.
Sin bin: D Dixon (32) - kicking Whitton.
Rugby Leaguer & League Express Men of the Match:
Cornwall: Coby Nichol; *Rams:* Caelum Jordan.
Penalty count: 4-8; **Half-time:** 0-6;
Referee: William Gilder; **Attendance:** 1,164.

DONCASTER 42 ROCHDALE HORNETS 20

DONCASTER: - Josh Guzdek; 2 Tom Halliday; 21 Brad Hey; 4 Jason Tali; 22 Misi Taulapapa; 6 Ben Johnston; 7 Connor Robinson; 29 Luke Cooper; 9 Greg Burns; 8 Keelan Foster; 11 Sam Smeaton; 27 Brett Ferres; 13 Loui McConnell. Subs (all used): 14 Dean Roberts; 17 Matt James; 18 Jose Kenga; 19 Ross Whitmore.
Tries: Smeaton (27, 51, 79), Guzdek (42), Johnston (47), James (58), Robinson (63);
Goals: Robinson 6/6, Taulapapa 1/1.
HORNETS: 1 Joe Purcell; 31 Ollie Brookes; 36 Luke Forber; 4 Ben O'Keefe; 5 Dan Nixon; 29 Umyla Hanley; 6 Lewis Else; 33 Will Tilleke; 9 Cameron Berry; 10 Ben Killan; 11 Dan Brewin; 32 Ben Forster; - Jacob Gannon. Subs (all used): 14 Aiden Roden; 37 Sion Jones; 16 Ethan O'Hanlon; 27 Toby Brannan.
Tries: Berry (7), Brookes (21, 56), Nixon (36);
Goals: O'Keefe 2/5.
Rugby Leaguer & League Express Men of the Match:
Doncaster: Sam Smeaton; *Hornets:* Umyla Hanley.
Penalty count: 4-3; **Half-time:** 6-16;
Referee: Brad Milligan; **Attendance:** 1,191.

ROUND 13

Friday 16th June 2023

DEWSBURY RAMS 42 ROCHDALE HORNETS 0

RAMS: 1 Owen Restall; 5 Andy Gabriel; 21 Caelum Jordan; 3 Ollie Greensmith; 23 Perry Whiteley; 6 Paul Sykes; 7 Calum Turner; 8 Jimmy Beckett; 9 Reiss Butterworth; 34 Will Maher; 12 Matt Garside; 18 Brad Graham; 13 Louis Collinson. Subs (all used): 11 Connor Davies; 15 Ronan Dixon; 17 Elliot Morris; 26 Bailey O'Connor.
Tries: Collinson (10), Restall (24), Sykes (31), Gabriel (49), Graham (62), O'Connor (68, 73); **Goals:** Sykes 7/7.
HORNETS: 1 Joe Purcell; 26 Ollie Brookes; 36 Luke Forber; 11 Dan Brewin; 5 Dan Nixon; 6 Lewis Else; 7 Dave Hewitt; 18 Jack Arnold; 9 Cameron Berry; - Jacob Gannon; 17 AJ Boardman; 32 Ben Forster; 31 Lewis Peachey. Subs (all used): 4 Ben O'Keefe; 14 Aiden Roden; 33 Will Tilleke; 37 Sion Jones.
Rugby Leaguer & League Express Men of the Match:
Rams: Reiss Butterworth; *Hornets:* Dan Brewin.
Penalty count: 3-2; **Half-time:** 18-0;
Referee: Kevin Moore; **Attendance:** 811.

Sunday 18th June 2023

NORTH WALES CRUSADERS 62
MIDLANDS HURRICANES 24

CRUSADERS: 28 Daniel Hill; 27 Jake Thewlis; 14 Kieran Taylor; 4 Matt Reid; 5 Rob Massam; 7 Brad Billsborough; 13 Matt Fletcher; 16 Jack Houghton; 25 Jake Burns; 17 Chris Barratt; 21 Ryan Ellis; 29 Tom Whitehead; 26 Carl Forster. Subs (all used): 2 Jack Holmes; 10 Jordan Andrade; 15 Brad Brennan; 19 Shaun Costello.
Tries: Thewlis (6), Barratt (17), Ellis (22), Houghton (27), Andrade (32, 39), Reid (45), Burns (56, 60), Massam (78, 80); **Goals:** Billsborough 9/11.
HURRICANES: 1 Nathan Hill; 5 Hayden Freeman; 16 Ryan Johnson; 23 Jason Bass; 2 Mekhi Bridgeman-Reaney; 6 Ben Stead; 7 Jacob Hookem; 17 Aaron Willis; 14 Chris Cullimore; 15 Toby Richardson; 18 Jacob Beer; 24 Tom Wilkinson; 13 Liam Welham. Subs (all used): 9 Elliot Windley; 10 Matthew Bailey; - Brad Clavering; 11 Bailey Dawson.
Tries: Hill (35), Johnson (45), Stead (50), B Dawson (55);
Goals: Stead 4/4.
Rugby Leaguer & League Express Men of the Match:
Crusaders: Brad Billsborough; *Hurricanes:* Ben Stead.
Penalty count: 5-6; **Half-time:** 34-6;
Referee: Luke Bland; **Attendance:** 205
(at Nant Conwy RU Club).

WORKINGTON TOWN 34 LONDON SKOLARS 6

TOWN: 1 Jordan Burns; 5 Ethan Bickerdike; 4 Jason Mossop; 3 Earl Hurst; 2 Sean Sabutey; 6 Ciaran Walker; 7 Carl Forber; 10 Stevie Scholey; 15 Fergus Simpson; 8 Jordan Thomson; 29 Jake Bradley; 11 Malik Steele; 27 Hanley Dawson. Subs (all used): 14 Blain Marwood; 17 Joe Kirkup; 28 Connor Terrill; 18 Liam McNicholas.
Tries: J Burns (6, 57, 79), Walker (45), Terrill (53), Thomson (70); **Goals:** Walker 5/7.
SKOLARS: 1 Robbie Butterworth; 20 Jerome Yates; 3 Ethane Wainwright; 4 Aaron Small; 5 Dan Bristow; 6 Jack Ryan; 7 Jacob Thomas; 8 Sam Webb-Campbell; 9 Alex Deery; 15 Malikhi Lloyd-Jones; 12 Lameck Juma; 11 Luciano Bejanidze; 13 Matt Ross. Subs (all used): 14 Tommy Porter; 19 Todd Peut; 18 Ellis Roberts; 10 Christian Gale.
Try: Roberts (28); **Goals:** Deery 1/1.
Sin bin: Small (75) - dissent.
Rugby Leaguer & League Express Men of the Match:
Town: Jordan Burns; *Skolars:* Malikhi Lloyd-Jones.
Penalty count: 10-7; **Half-time:** 6-6;
Referee: Brad Milligan; **Attendance:** 496.

HUNSLET 36 CORNWALL 6

HUNSLET: 1 Jimmy Watson; 2 Jack Render; 3 Adam Ryder; 4 Joe Burton; 20 Alfie Goddard; 18 Myles Lawford; 30 Matty Beharrell; 8 Harvey Hallas; 7 Nathan Conroy; 10 Steve Crossley; 11 Josh Jordan-Roberts; 12 Aaron York; 9 Sam Hallas. Subs (all used): 37 Oli Burton; 16 Jordan Syme; 17 Lewis Wray; 19 Marcus Green.
Tries: Ryder (3), J Burton (27), Lawford (33, 65), Jordan-Roberts (42), Watson (72); **Goals:** Beharrell 6/6.
CORNWALL: 1 Liam Whitton; 3 Errol Carter; 13 Nathan Cullen; 4 Tom Ashton; 16 Decarlo Trerise; 6 Cameron Brown; 5 Harry Aaronson; 8 Harry Boots; 9 Luke Collins; 10 Josh Hartshorne; 11 David Weetman; 12 Kaine Dimech; 15 Ewan Badham. Subs (all used): 14 Jaden Barraclough; 20 Ieuan Badham; 17 Tyler Walton; 7 Jake Lloyd.
Try: Weetman (9); **Goals:** Brown 1/1.
Sin bin: Whitton (38) - professional foul.
Rugby Leaguer & League Express Men of the Match:
Hunslet: Myles Lawford; *Cornwall:* Tom Ashton.
Penalty count: 9-7; **Half-time:** 18-6;
Referee: Andy Sweet; **Attendance:** 433.

OLDHAM 22 DONCASTER 28

OLDHAM: 1 Gregg McNally; 28 Nick Rawsthorne; 3 Connor Carr; 29 Kian Morgan; 2 Patrick Ah Van; 6 Martyn Ridyard; 18 Jordan Paga; 8 Luke Nelmes; 9 Matty Wilkinson; - Harvey Wilson; 10 Deane Meadows; 12 Zac Baker; 13 Emmerson Whittel. Subs (all used): 14 Sean Slater; 15 Dom Newton; 30 Samy Kibula; 32 Pat Moran.
Tries: Wilson (3), K Morgan (23, 31), Wilkinson (43);
Goals: Ridyard 3/4.
DONCASTER: 23 Josh Guzdek; 2 Tom Halliday; 21 Brad Hey; 4 Jason Tali; 22 Misi Taulapapa; 6 Ben Johnston; 7 Connor Robinson; 29 Luke Cooper; 9 Greg Burns; 8 Keelan Foster; 11 Sam Smeaton; 27 Brett Ferres; 13 Loui McConnell. Subs (all used): 14 Dean Roberts; 20 Brad Knowles; 18 Jose Kenga; 19 Ross Whitmore.
Tries: Taulapapa (12, 70), Smeaton (46), Hey (65), Johnston (73); **Goals:** Robinson 4/5.
Rugby Leaguer & League Express Men of the Match:
Oldham: Jordan Paga; *Doncaster:* Ben Johnston.
Penalty count: 3-3; **Half-time:** 16-6;
Referee: Nick Bennett; **Attendance:** 647.

ROUND 14

Friday 23rd June 2023

DEWSBURY RAMS 20 OLDHAM 8

RAMS: 1 Owen Restall; 2 Lewis Carr; 21 Caelum Jordan; 3 Ollie Greensmith; 23 Perry Whiteley; 6 Paul Sykes; 7 Calum Turner; 8 Jimmy Beckett; 9 Reiss Butterworth; 34 Will Maher; 12 Matt Garside; 18 Brad Graham; 13 Louis Collinson. Subs (all used): 11 Connor Davies; 15 Ronan Dixon; 17 Elliot Morris; 26 Bailey O'Connor.
Tries: Graham (11), Sykes (30), Davies (39);
Goals: Sykes 4/4.
OLDHAM: 1 Gregg McNally; 28 Nick Rawsthorne; 3 Connor Carr; 2 Patrick Ah Van; 20 Tommy Brierley; 6 Martyn Ridyard; 18 Jordan Paga; 8 Luke Nelmes; 9 Matty Wilkinson; 30 Harvey Wilson; 10 Deane Meadows; 12 Zac Baker; 13 Emmerson Whittel. Subs (all used): 15 Dom Newton; 25 George Hirst; 29 Tom Forber; 32 Pat Moran.
Tries: Rawsthorne (26), Brierley (51); **Goals:** Ridyard 0/2.
Rugby Leaguer & League Express Men of the Match:
Rams: Paul Sykes; *Oldham:* Martyn Ridyard.
Penalty count: 3-8; **Half-time:** 18-4;
Referee: Brad Milligan; **Attendance:** 1,650.

Sunday 25th June 2023

NORTH WALES CRUSADERS 20 HUNSLET 30

CRUSADERS: 1 Owain Abel; 27 Josh Lynch; 28 Daniel Hill; 4 Matt Reid; 5 Rob Massam; 13 Matt Fletcher; 7 Brad Billsborough; 16 Jack Houghton; 25 Jake Burns; 17 Chris Barratt; 21 Ryan Ellis; 14 Kieran Taylor; 26 Carl Forster. Subs (all used): 20 Pat Rainford; 10 Jordan Andrade; 15 Brad Brennan; 8 Callum Hazzard.
Tries: Lynch (13, 80), Taylor (22), Rainford (38);
Goals: Billsborough 2/3, Abel 0/1.
Sin bin: Billsborough (76) - fighting.
HUNSLET: 1 Jimmy Watson; 2 Jack Render; 3 Adam Ryder; 4 Joe Burton; 20 Alfie Goddard; 30 Matty Beharrell; 18 Myles Lawford; 8 Harvey Hallas; 9 Sam Hallas; 10 Steve Crossley; 11 Josh Jordan-Roberts; 12 Aaron York; 13 Michael Knowles. Subs (all used): 37 Oli Burton; 29 Spencer Darley; 19 Marcus Green; 16 Jordan Syme.
Tries: Render (10), S Hallas (43, 64), Jordan-Roberts (52), Watson (72); **Goals:** Beharrell 5/5.
Rugby Leaguer & League Express Men of the Match:
Crusaders: Owain Abel; *Hunslet:* Sam Hallas.
Penalty count: 1-2; **Half-time:** 16-6;
Referee: Nick Bennett; **Attendance:** 363
(at Hare Lane, Chester).

WORKINGTON TOWN 60 MIDLANDS HURRICANES 10

TOWN: 1 Jordan Burns; 21 Aaron Burns; 4 Jason Mossop; 2 Sean Sabutey; - Brad Holroyd; 6 Ciaran Walker; 7 Carl Forber; 8 Jordan Thomson; 9 Matty Henson; 10 Stevie Scholey; 29 Jake Bradley; 11 Malik Steele; 27 Hanley Dawson. Subs (all used): 14 Blain Marwood; 18 Liam McNicholas; 28 Connor Terrill; 30 Luke Charlton.
Tries: Steele (6, 75), Charlton (19), J Burns (22), Sabutey (30), Holroyd (38), Forber (50), A Burns (58), Marwood (61, 64); **Goals:** Walker 10/10.
Sin bin: McNicholas (45) - professional foul.
HURRICANES: 1 Ben Stead; 2 Abdullah Balogun; 3 Liam Welham; 4 Ryan Johnson; 5 Hayden Freeman; 6 Adam Brook; 7 Tyler Hepple; 8 Toby Richardson; 9 Chris Cullimore; 10 Aaron Willis; 11 Finley Beardsworth; 12 Tom Wilkinson; 13 Brad Clavering. Subs (all used): 14 Elliot Windley; 15 Kavan Rothwell; 16 Max Wood; 17 Matthew Bailey.
Tries: Freeman (47), Richardson (69); **Goals:** Stead 1/2.
Sin bin: Brook (70) - fighting.
Rugby Leaguer & League Express Men of the Match:
Town: Ciaran Walker; *Hurricanes:* Ben Stead.
Penalty count: 8-7; **Half-time:** 30-0;
Referee: Ryan Cox; **Attendance:** 843.

ROUND 15

Sunday 2nd July 2023

NORTH WALES CRUSADERS 32
ROCHDALE HORNETS 24

CRUSADERS: 28 Daniel Hill; 27 Josh Lynch; 2 Jack Holmes; 4 Matt Reid; 5 Rob Massam; 13 Matt Fletcher; 7 Brad Billsborough; 16 Jack Houghton; 20 Pat Rainford; 17 Chris Barratt; 14 Kieran Taylor; 29 Tom Whitehead; 26 Carl Forster. Subs (all used): 1 Owain Abel; 8 Callum Hazzard; 10 Jordan Andrade; 30 Lewis Baxter.
Tries: Hill (28), Abel (30), Massam (45), Whitehead (62), Barratt (80); **Goals:** Billsborough 6/6.
HORNETS: 1 Joe Purcell; 3 Will Cooke; 29 Adam Jones; 4 Ben O'Keefe; 2 Cian Tyrer; 6 Lewis Else; 7 Dave Hewitt; 31 Lewis Peachey; 14 Aiden Roden; 18 Jack Arnold; 17 AJ

Boardman; 32 Ben Forster; 12 Duane Straugheir. Subs (all used): 26 Nathan Wilde; 25 Aaron Smith; 10 Ben Killan; 16 Ethan O'Hanlon.
Tries: Straugheir (9), A Jones (24), Tyrer (55), Else (69); **Goals:** Hewitt 4/5.
Sin bin: Straugheir (73) - high tackle on Rainford.
Rugby Leaguer & League Express Men of the Match: *Crusaders:* Owain Abel; *Hornets:* Lewis Else.
Penalty count: 8-10; **Half-time:** 12-14;
Referee: Andy Sweet; **Attendance:** 375
(at Hare Lane, Chester).

HUNSLET 28 DONCASTER 8

HUNSLET: 1 Jimmy Watson; 2 Jack Render; 3 Adam Ryder; 4 Joe Burton; 5 Jake Maizen; 30 Matty Beharrell; 18 Myles Lawford; 8 Harvey Hallas; 9 Sam Hallas; 10 Steve Crossley; 11 Josh Jordan-Roberts; 12 Aaron York; 13 Michael Knowles. Subs (all used): 37 Oli Burton; 17 Lewis Wray; 19 Marcus Green; 29 Spencer Darley.
Tries: H Hallas (11), Lawford (23, 78), Render (25, 49);
Goals: Beharrell 4/6.
Sin bin: Jordan-Roberts (30) - fighting.
DONCASTER: 30 Josh Guzdek; 2 Tom Halliday; 11 Sam Smeaton; 21 Brad Hey; 22 Misi Taulapapa; 24 Watson Boas; 7 Connor Robinson; 29 Luke Cooper; 9 Greg Burns; 8 Keelan Foster; 27 Brett Ferres; 13 Loui McConnell; 20 Brad Knowles. Subs (all used): 17 Matt James; 18 Jose Kenga; 14 Dean Roberts; 19 Ross Whitmore.
Tries: Hey (35), Taulapapa (38); **Goals:** Robinson 0/2.
Sin bin: Smeaton (30) - fighting.
Rugby Leaguer & League Express Men of the Match: *Hunslet:* Matty Beharrell; *Doncaster:* Tom Halliday.
Penalty count: 7-3; **Half-time:** 16-8;
Referee: Matt Rossleigh; **Attendance:** 767.

MIDLANDS HURRICANES 23 DEWSBURY RAMS 28

HURRICANES: 1 Todd Horner; 2 Jason Bass; 3 Matt Welham; 4 Ryan Johnson; 5 Hayden Freeman; 6 Ben Stead; 7 Jacob Hookem; 8 Toby Richardson; 9 Chris Cullimore; 10 Brad Clavering; 11 Finley Beardsworth; 12 Liam Welham; 13 Aaron Willis. Subs (all used): 14 Elliot Windley; 15 Tom Wilkinson; 16 Sam Bowring; 17 Kieran Moran.
Tries: Horner (2), Bass (11), L Welham (62);
Goals: Stead 5/6; **Field goal:** Stead (68).
RAMS: 1 Owen Restall; 2 Lewis Carr; 26 Bailey O'Connor; 3 Ollie Greensmith; 23 Perry Whiteley; 6 Paul Sykes; 7 Calum Turner; 20 Jackson Walker; 9 Reiss Butterworth; 34 Will Maher; 12 Matt Garside; 8 Jimmy Beckett; 13 Louis Collinson. Subs (all used): 14 Sam Day; 15 Ronan Dixon; 17 Elliot Morris; 11 Connor Davies.
Tries: Greensmith (8, 64), Day (54), Carr (58), R Dixon (74);
Goals: Sykes 2/3, Turner 2/2.
Sin bin: Sykes (52) - dissent.
Rugby Leaguer & League Express Men of the Match: *Hurricanes:* Ben Stead; *Rams:* Ollie Greensmith.
Penalty count: 4-1; **Half-time:** 16-4;
Referee: Luke Bland; **Attendance:** 423.

ROUND 16

Saturday 8th July 2023

LONDON SKOLARS 14 CORNWALL 30

SKOLARS: 1 Jacob Thomas; 2 Donald Kudangirana; 3 Jerome Yates; 4 Dan Bristow; 5 Leighton Ball; 6 Jack Ryan; 7 Phil Lyon; 8 Lamont Bryan; 9 Alex Deery; 15 Malikhi Lloyd-Jones; 11 Luciano Bejanidze; 12 Sam Wellings; 18 Liam O'Callaghan. Subs (all used): 16 Tommy Porter; - Matt Ross; 10 Todd Peut; 14 Sam Bardsley.
Tries: Ball (20, 43), Deery (80); **Goals:** Lyon 1/2, Deery 0/1.
Sin bin: Deery (17) - delaying restart;
Bryan (40) - fighting, (68) - fighting; Yates (79) - fighting.
CORNWALL: 1 Liam Whitton; 3 Errol Carter; 15 Sean Croston; 4 Tom Ashton; 18 George Mitchell; 6 Morgan Punchard; 7 Adam Rusling; 8 Harry Boots; 9 Luke Collins; 16 Nathan Newbound; 11 Nathan Cullen; 17 David Weetman; 13 Jake Lloyd. Subs (all used): 14 Jaden Barraclough; 12 Kaine Dimech; 10 Ewan Badham; 20 Ieuan Badham.
Tries: Cullen (5), Ashton (12), I Badham (30), Weetman (48), Collins (69); **Goals:** Rusling 5/6.
Sin bin: Carter (79) - fighting; Punchard (79) - fighting.
Rugby Leaguer & League Express Men of the Match: *Skolars:* Phil Lyon; *Cornwall:* Adam Rusling.
Penalty count: 6-9; **Half-time:** 6-16;
Referee: Matty Lynn; **Attendance:** 281.

Sunday 9th July 2023

MIDLANDS HURRICANES 22 HUNSLET 54

HURRICANES: 1 Todd Horner; 2 Hayden Freeman; 3 Matt Welham; 4 Macauley Hallett; 5 Ryan Johnson; 6 Izaac Farrell; 7 Jacob Hookem; 8 Toby Richardson; 9 Chris Cullimore; 10 Brad Clavering; 11 Liam Welham; 12 Finley Beardsworth; 13 Aaron Willis. Subs (all used): 14 Elliot Windley; 15 Sam Bowring; 16 Kieran Moran; 17 Ellis Hobson.
Tries: Beardsworth (2), Clavering (5), Willis (34), Hallett (66); **Goals:** Hookem 3/4.
Dismissal: Freeman (80) - punching.
Sin bin: Hookem (72) - fighting.
HUNSLET: 4 Joe Burton; 2 Jack Render; 3 Adam Ryder; 5 Jake Maizen; 20 Alfie Goddard; 30 Matty Beharrell; 18 Myles Lawford; 8 Harvey Hallas; 9 Sam Hallas; 10 Steve Crossley; 11 Josh Jordan-Roberts; 12 Aaron York; 16 Jordan Syme. Subs (all used): 37 Oli Burton; 19 Marcus Green; 28 Brad Wheeler; 17 Lewis Wray.
Tries: Syme (10), Ryder (31, 53), Goddard (40, 50, 77), O Burton (41), Wray (43), York (61);
Goals: Beharrell 8/8, Lawford 1/2.
Sin bin: Beharrell (72) - fighting.
Rugby Leaguer & League Express Men of the Match: *Hurricanes:* Jacob Hookem; *Hunslet:* Myles Lawford.
Penalty count: 7-7; **Half-time:** 18-18;
Referee: Andy Sweet; **Attendance:** 547
(at Haslams Lane, Derby).

OLDHAM 37 NORTH WALES CRUSADERS 24

OLDHAM: 1 Gregg McNally; 28 Nick Rawsthorne; 3 Connor Carr; 29 Kian Morgan; 2 Patrick Ah Van; 6 Martyn Ridyard; 20 Kieran Tyrer; 8 Luke Nelmes; 9 Matty Wilkinson; 32 Pat Moran; 19 Callum Cameron; 25 George Hirst; 13 Emmerson Whittel. Subs (all used): 14 Sean Slater; 10 Deane Meadows; 30 Harvey Wilson; 15 Dom Newton.
Tries: Rawsthorne (10, 40), Whittel (43), Carr (46), K Morgan (55), Tyrer (76); **Goals:** Ridyard 6/6;
Field goal: Ridyard (74).
CRUSADERS: 28 Daniel Hill; 27 Josh Lynch; 14 Kieran Taylor; 2 Jack Holmes; 5 Rob Massam; 6 Dave Gibbons; 7 Brad Billsborough; 8 Callum Hazzard; 20 Pat Rainford; 17 Chris Barratt; 21 Ryan Ellis; 13 Matt Fletcher; 26 Carl Forster. Subs (all used): 16 Jack Houghton; 18 Paul Nash; 10 Jordan Andrade; 30 Lewis Baxter.
Tries: Andrade (32, 49), Barratt (37), Lynch (58);
Goals: Billsborough 4/4.
Rugby Leaguer & League Express Men of the Match: *Oldham:* Martyn Ridyard; *Crusaders:* Carl Forster.
Penalty count: 7-3; **Half-time:** 12-12;
Referee: Brad Milligan; **Attendance:** 734.

WORKINGTON TOWN 40 ROCHDALE HORNETS 12

TOWN: 1 Jordan Burns; 21 Aaron Burns; 2 Sean Sabutey; 4 Jason Mossop; 5 Ethan Bickerdike; 6 Ciaran Walker; 7 Carl Forber; 10 Stevie Scholey; 9 Matty Henson; 8 Jordan Thomson; 29 Jake Bradley; 11 Malik Steele; 27 Hanley Dawson. Subs (all used): 14 Blain Marwood; 30 Luke Charlton; 28 Connor Terrill; 20 Jack Stephenson.
Tries: Bradley (4), A Burns (13), Walker (22, 75), Bickerdike (29), Marwood (66), Sabutey (68);
Goals: Walker 6/8.
HORNETS: 29 Adam Jones; 2 Cian Tyrer; 23 Sam Haynes; 4 Ben O'Keefe; 5 Dan Nixon; 6 Lewis Else; 7 Dave Hewitt; 31 Lewis Peachey; 14 Aiden Roden; 18 Jack Arnold; 36 Luke Forber; 32 Ben Forster; 12 Duane Straugheir. Subs (all used): 9 Cameron Berry; 17 AJ Boardman; 10 Ben Killan; 27 Toby Brannan.
Tries: Boardman (32), Forber (47); **Goals:** Hewitt 2/2.
Rugby Leaguer & League Express Men of the Match: *Town:* Ciaran Walker; *Hornets:* AJ Boardman.
Penalty count: 3-7; **Half-time:** 20-6;
Referee: Kevin Moore; **Attendance:** 1,337.

ROUND 17

Sunday 16th July 2023

CORNWALL 28 MIDLANDS HURRICANES 8

CORNWALL: 1 Liam Whitton; 5 Cameron Brown; 4 Sean Croston; 2 Coby Nichol; 18 George Mitchell; 6 Morgan Punchard; 7 Adam Rusling; 8 Harry Boots; 9 Luke Collins; 10 Nathan Newbound; 11 Nathan Cullen; 17 David Weetman; 13 Jake Lloyd. Subs (all used): 14 Jaden Barraclough; 12 Kaine Dimech; 3 Decarlo Trerise; 20 Ewan Badham.
Tries: Nichol (14), Rusling (55), Brown (59, 65), Whitton (74); **Goals:** Rusling 4/5.
Sin bin: Brown (45) - professional foul.
HURRICANES: 1 Todd Horner; 5 Hayden Freeman; 3 Matt Welham; 4 Macauley Hallett; 23 Ryan Johnson; 25 Jacob Hookem; 9 Elliot Windley; 22 Jon Luke Kirby; 14 Chris Cullimore; 10 Brad Clavering; 12 Liam Welham; 16 Finley Beardsworth; 20 Aaron Willis. Subs (all used): 15 Ellis Hobson; 8 Kieran Moran; 17 Tom Wilkinson; 24 Jacob Beer.
Tries: Johnson (24), Freeman (34); **Goals:** Hookem 0/2.
Sin bin: M Welham (63) - professional foul.
Rugby Leaguer & League Express Men of the Match: *Cornwall:* Adam Rusling; *Hurricanes:* Ryan Johnson.
Penalty count: 13-3; **Half-time:** 4-8;
Referee: Luke Bland; **Attendance:** 957.

NORTH WALES CRUSADERS 24 WORKINGTON TOWN 32

CRUSADERS: 25 Ben Lane; 27 Josh Lynch; 2 Jack Holmes; 29 Wesley Bruines; 5 Rob Massam; 13 Matt Fletcher; 7 Brad Billsborough; 8 Callum Hazzard; 20 Pat Rainford; 17 Chris Barratt; 14 Kieran Taylor; 21 Ryan Ellis; 26 Carl Forster. Subs (all used): 10 Jordan Andrade; 16 Jack Houghton; 18 Paul Nash; 30 Lewis Baxter.
Tries: Fletcher (25), Ellis (37), Massam (57), Houghton (72);
Goals: Billsborough 4/4.
TOWN: 1 Jordan Burns; 23 Reagan Sumner; 24 Ethan Fitzgerald; 5 Ethan Bickerdike; 21 Aaron Burns; 26 Jack Mallinson; 7 Carl Forber; 10 Stevie Scholey; 9 Matty Henson; 8 Jordan Thomson; 18 Liam McNicholas; 11 Malik Steele; 27 Hanley Dawson. Subs (all used): 17 Joe Kirkup; 15 Fergus Simpson; 28 Connor Terrill; 20 Jack Stephenson.
Tries: Bickerdike (4), Henson (9, 54), J Burns (12), Kirkup (32), Stephenson (52); **Goals:** Forber 4/6.
Rugby Leaguer & League Express Men of the Match: *Crusaders:* Jack Houghton; *Town:* Matty Henson.
Penalty count: 7-7; **Half-time:** 12-22;
Referee: Brad Milligan; **Attendance:** 340
(at Hare Lane, Chester).

HUNSLET 21 OLDHAM 8

HUNSLET: 1 Jimmy Watson; 2 Jack Render; 3 Adam Ryder; 4 Joe Burton; 20 Alfie Goddard; 30 Matty Beharrell; 18 Myles Lawford; 8 Harvey Hallas; 9 Sam Hallas; 10 Steve Crossley; 11 Josh Jordan-Roberts; 12 Aaron York; 13 Michael Knowles. Subs (all used): 37 Oli Burton; 17 Lewis Wray; 19 Marcus Green; 16 Jordan Syme.
Tries: Lawford (35), Render (38), J Burton (44);
Goals: Beharrell 4/4; **Field goal:** Knowles (73).
OLDHAM: 1 Gregg McNally; 28 Nick Rawsthorne; 3 Connor Carr; 25 George Hirst; 24 Andy Gabriel; 6 Martyn Ridyard; 4 Kian Morgan; 8 Luke Nelmes; 9 Matty Wilkinson; 21 Josh Johnson; 12 Zac Baker; 19 Callum Cameron; 13 Emmerson Whittel. Subs (all used): 11 Harvey Wilson; 10 Deane Meadows; 14 Sean Slater; 32 Pat Moran.
Try: Carr (55); **Goals:** Ridyard 2/2.
Sin bin: Meadows (61) - delaying restart;
Nelmes (68) - late challenge on Beharrell.
Rugby Leaguer & League Express Men of the Match: *Hunslet:* Matty Beharrell; *Oldham:* Matty Wilkinson.
Penalty count: 5-2; **Half-time:** 12-2;
Referee: Kevin Moore; **Attendance:** 726.

ROUND 18

Sunday 23rd July 2023

CORNWALL 16 WORKINGTON TOWN 34

CORNWALL: 1 Liam Whitton; 5 Cameron Brown; 15 Sean Croston; 4 Tom Ashton; 2 Coby Nichol; 6 Morgan Punchard; 7 Adam Rusling; 8 Josh Hartshorne; 9 Luke Collins; 10 Nathan Newbound; 11 Nathan Cullen; 17 David Weetman; 13 Jake Lloyd. Subs (all used): 14 Jaden Barraclough; 12 Kaine Dimech; 23 Ieuan Badham; 20 Ewan Badham.
Tries: Nichol (17), Brown (44), Rusling (54);
Goals: Rusling 2/3.
Sin bin: Brown (68) - professional foul;
Whitton (71) - fighting.
TOWN: 1 Jordan Burns; 23 Reagan Sumner; 2 Sean Sabutey; 5 Ethan Bickerdike; 21 Aaron Burns; 6 Ciaran Walker; 7 Carl Forber; 8 Jordan Thomson; 26 Jack Mallinson; 10 Stevie Scholey; 29 Jake Bradley; 11 Malik Steele; 20 Jack Stephenson. Subs (all used): 14 Blain Marwood; 17 Joe Kirkup; 22 Liam McAvoy; 18 Liam McNicholas.
Tries: Scholey (7), Steele (26), Sumner (31, 59), Sabutey (34), J Burns (47), A Burns (72); **Goals:** Walker 3/7.
Sin bin: J Burns (17) - fighting.
Rugby Leaguer & League Express Men of the Match: *Cornwall:* Jaden Barraclough; *Town:* Ciaran Walker.
Penalty count: 4-6; **Half-time:** 4-20;
Referee: Ryan Cox; **Attendance:** 1,204.

DEWSBURY RAMS 18 NORTH WALES CRUSADERS 4

RAMS: 1 Owen Restall; 2 Lewis Carr; 26 Bailey O'Connor; 3 Ollie Greensmith; 23 Perry Whiteley; 6 Paul Sykes; 7 Calum Turner; 8 Jimmy Beckett; 9 Reiss Butterworth; 34 Will Maher; 12 Matt Garside; 18 Brad Graham; 13 Louis Collinson. Subs (all used): 24 Joe Summers; 15 Ronan Dixon; 20 Jackson Walker; 11 Connor Davies.
Tries: Whiteley (23), O'Connor (39); **Goals:** Sykes 5/6.
Sin bin: Beckett (28) - high tackle on Andrade.
CRUSADERS: 1 Owain Abel; 27 Josh Lynch; 3 Cole Oakley; 14 Kieran Taylor; 5 Rob Massam; 13 Matt Fletcher; 6 Dave Gibbons; 16 Jack Houghton; 25 Taylor Pemberton; 17 Chris Barratt; 29 Matthew Foster; 21 Ryan Ellis; 26 Carl Forster. Subs (all used): 18 Paul Nash; 10 Jordan Andrade; 19 Shaun Costello; 8 Callum Hazzard.
Try: Abel (66); **Goals:** Abel 0/1.

Rugby Leaguer & League Express Men of the Match:
Rams: Paul Sykes; *Crusaders:* Carl Forster.
Penalty count: 12-4; **Half-time:** 14-0;
Referee: Kevin Moore; **Attendance:** 807.

DONCASTER 10 MIDLANDS HURRICANES 41

DONCASTER: 1 Elliot Hall; 25 Jack Sanderson; 21 Brad Hey; 4 Jason Tali; 3 Olly Butterworth; 6 Ben Johnston; 7 Connor Robinson; 29 Luke Cooper; 9 Greg Burns; 8 Keelan Foster; 11 Sam Smeaton; 27 Brett Ferres; 13 Loui McConnell. Subs (all used): 17 Matt James; 20 Brad Knowles; 22 Misi Taulapapa; 24 Watson Boas.
Tries: Smeaton (6), Butterworth (80); **Goals:** Robinson 1/2.
Dismissal: Ferres (67) - dangerous challenge.
HURRICANES: 1 Todd Horner; 3 Matt Welham; 4 Macauley Hallett; 16 Ross Oakes; 10 Matty Chrimes; 6 Jacob Hookem; 21 Scott Murrell; 13 Brad Clavering; 14 Chris Cullimore; 20 Jon Luke Kirby; 12 Liam Welham; 22 Tom Wilkinson; 17 Mikey Wood. Subs (all used): 23 Danny Barcoe; 18 Sam Bowring; 15 Ellis Hobson; 8 Kieran Moran.
Tries: L Welham (14, 32), Barcoe (36), Oakes (43), Hookem (73), Bowring (76); **Goals:** Hookem 8/8;
Field goal: T Wilkinson (40).
Rugby Leaguer & League Express Men of the Match:
Doncaster: Elliot Hall; *Hurricanes:* Jacob Hookem.
Penalty count: 5-7; **Half-time:** 6-19;
Referee: Matty Lynn; **Attendance:** 864.

ROUND 19

Sunday 30th July 2023

NORTH WALES CRUSADERS 38 CORNWALL 40

CRUSADERS: 1 Owain Abel; 2 Jack Holmes; 29 Connor Wrench; 3 Cole Oakley; 5 Rob Massam; 25 Leon Hayes; 7 Brad Billsborough; 10 Jordan Andrade; 14 Taylor Pemberton; 17 Chris Barratt; 24 Tom Whitehead; 21 Ryan Ellis; 26 Carl Forster. Subs (all used): 20 Pat Rainford; 11 Alex Eckley; 8 Callum Hazzard; 13 Matt Fletcher.
Tries: Massam (28), Eckley (43), Hayes (45), Wrench (58, 67), Holmes (61, 75); **Goals:** Billsborough 5/7.
Sin bin: Eckley (49) - use of the elbow.
CORNWALL: 1 Liam Whitton; 5 Cameron Brown; 15 Sean Croston; 2 Coby Nichol; 3 Mackenzie Scurr; 6 Morgan Punchard; 7 Adam Rusling; 8 Harry Boots; 9 Luke Collins; 10 Nathan Newbound; 11 Nathan Cullen; 17 David Weetman; 13 Jake Lloyd. Subs (all used): 14 Jaden Barraclough; 12 Kaine Dimech; 23 Ieuan Badham; 20 Ewan Badham.
Tries: Boots (7), Brown (9, 26), Cullen (15), Scurr (18), Rusling (22), Barraclough (39); **Goals:** Rusling 6/7.
Rugby Leaguer & League Express Men of the Match:
Crusaders: Carl Forster; *Cornwall:* Adam Rusling.
Penalty count: 6-7; **Half-time:** 4-40;
Referee: John Lincoln; **Attendance:** 649
(at Tynewydd Fields, Rhyl).

HUNSLET 16 DEWSBURY RAMS 14

HUNSLET: 1 Jimmy Watson; 2 Jack Render; 3 Adam Ryder; 4 Joe Burton; 36 Johnny Campbell; 30 Matty Beharrell; 18 Myles Lawford; 8 Harvey Hallas; 9 Sam Hallas; 10 Steve Crossley; 11 Josh Jordan-Roberts; 12 Aaron York; 13 Michael Knowles. Subs (all used): 37 Oli Burton; 17 Lewis Wray; 19 Marcus Green; 16 Jordan Syme.
Tries: Campbell (2), Beharrell (37), Jordan-Roberts (55);
Goals: Beharrell 2/3.
Sin bin: Lawford (77) - holding down.
RAMS: 1 Owen Restall; 2 Lewis Carr; 26 Bailey O'Connor; 3 Ollie Greensmith; 23 Perry Whiteley; 6 Paul Sykes; 7 Calum Turner; 8 Jimmy Beckett; 9 Reiss Butterworth; 20 Jackson Walker; 12 Matt Garside; 18 Brad Graham; 11 Connor Davies. Subs (all used): 14 Sam Day; 17 Elliot Morris; 15 Ronan Dixon; 34 Will Maher.
Tries: Graham (21, 62), O'Connor (45); **Goals:** Sykes 1/3.
Sin bin: Restall (78) - delaying restart.
Rugby Leaguer & League Express Men of the Match:
Hunslet: Matty Beharrell; *Rams:* Reiss Butterworth.
Penalty count: 3-5; **Half-time:** 10-6;
Referee: Nick Bennett; **Attendance:** 1,064.

ROCHDALE HORNETS 37 MIDLANDS HURRICANES 22

HORNETS: 4 Ben O'Keefe; 2 Cian Tyrer; 29 Tom Nisbet; 36 Luke Forber; 5 Dan Nixon; 6 Lewis Else; 7 Dave Hewitt; 30 Jacob Jones; 14 Aiden Roden; 31 Lewis Peachey; 11 Dan Brewin; 32 Ben Forster; 12 Duane Straugheir. Subs (all used): 9 Cameron Berry; 10 Ben Killan; 17 AJ Boardman; 35 Connor Ratcliffe.
Tries: O'Keefe (9), Else (32), Straugheir (36), Tyrer (45), Forster (61), Ratcliffe (79); **Goals:** Hewitt 6/7;
Field goal: Hewitt (40).
HURRICANES: 1 Todd Horner; 10 Matty Chrimes; 3 Matt Welham; 4 Macauley Hallett; 2 Mackenzie Turner; 6 Jacob Hookem; 21 Scott Murrell; 20 Jon Luke Kirby; 14 Chris Cullimore; 18 Sam Bowring; 22 Tom Wilkinson; 12 Liam Welham; 13 Brad Clavering. Subs (all used): 8 Kieran Moran; 15 Ellis Hobson; 17 Aaron Willis; 23 Danny Barcoe.
Tries: Chrimes (50, 72), L Welham (67), Bowring (79);
Goals: Hookem 3/4.
Rugby Leaguer & League Express Men of the Match:
Hornets: Dave Hewitt; *Hurricanes:* Jacob Hookem.
Penalty count: 5-7; **Half-time:** 21-0;
Referee: Brad Milligan; **Attendance:** 334.

WORKINGTON TOWN 19 DONCASTER 22

TOWN: 1 Jordan Burns; 21 Aaron Burns; 2 Sean Sabutey; 4 Jason Mossop; 5 Ethan Bickerdike; 6 Ciaran Walker; 7 Carl Forber; 10 Stevie Scholey; 27 Hanley Dawson; 8 Jordan Thomson; 29 Jake Bradley; 11 Malik Steele; 20 Jack Stephenson. Subs (all used): 14 Blain Marwood; 30 Luke Charlton; 25 Grant Reid; 22 Liam McAvoy.
Tries: Reid (31), Bickerdike (75), Forber (79);
Goals: Walker 1/1, Forber 2/2; **Field goal:** Walker (36).
Sin bin: Walker (70) - dissent.
DONCASTER: 30 Josh Guzdek; 2 Tom Halliday; 21 Brad Hey; 22 Misi Taulapapa; 3 Olly Butterworth; 6 Ben Johnston; 7 Connor Robinson; 17 Matt James; 9 Greg Burns; 20 Brad Knowles; 11 Sam Smeaton; 27 Brett Ferres; 13 Loui McConnell. Subs (all used): 15 Alex Holdstock; 18 Jose Kenga; - Albert Vete; 24 Watson Boas.
Tries: Halliday (26), Guzdek (41), Smeaton (45, 67);
Goals: Robinson 3/4.
Rugby Leaguer & League Express Men of the Match:
Town: Carl Forber; *Doncaster:* Ben Johnston.
Penalty count: 7-7; **Half-time:** 7-6;
Referee: Andy Sweet; **Attendance:** 1,074.

ROUND 20

Saturday 5th August 2023

LONDON SKOLARS 18 MIDLANDS HURRICANES 38

SKOLARS: 1 Louis O'Sullivan; 2 Leighton Ball; 3 Luciano Bejanidze; 4 Lameck Juma; 5 David Bofenda; 6 Alex Deery; 7 Liam O'Callaghan; 10 Todd Peut; 9 Tommy Porter; 15 Malikhi Lloyd-Jones; 11 Max Allen; 21 Lamont Bryan; - Matt Ross. Subs (all used): 14 Doug Chirnside; 19 Jack Hughes; 8 Christian Gale; 12 Fraser Piercy-Farley.
Tries: Porter (5), Juma (13), Ross (80); **Goals:** Deery 3/3.
HURRICANES: 1 Todd Horner; 2 Mackenzie Turner; 3 Matt Welham; 4 Macauley Hallett; 10 Matty Chrimes; 6 Jake Sweeting; 7 Izaac Farrell; 20 Jon Luke Kirby; 23 Danny Barcoe; 15 Ellis Hobson; 24 Tom Wilkinson; 21 Aaron Levy; 17 Aaron Willis. Subs (all used): 9 Elliot Windley; 8 Kieran Moran; 22 Toby Richardson; 11 Jack Dawson.
Tries: M Welham (2, 45), Turner (16, 55, 70), Sweeting (32), Chrimes (40); **Goals:** Farrell 5/8.
Rugby Leaguer & League Express Men of the Match:
Skolars: Tommy Porter; *Hurricanes:* Matt Welham.
Penalty count: 4-4; **Half-time:** 12-22;
Referee: Luke Bland; **Attendance:** 204.

Sunday 6th August 2023

CORNWALL 4 OLDHAM 56

CORNWALL: 1 Liam Whitton; 4 George Mitchell; 15 Sean Croston; 2 Coby Nichol; 3 Mackenzie Scurr; 13 Jake Lloyd; 7 Morgan Punchard; 8 Nathan Newbound; 9 Luke Collins; 10 Ewan Badham; 11 Nathan Cullen; 17 David Weetman; 12 Kaine Dimech. Subs (all used): 14 Jaden Barraclough; 19 Callum Abbott; 22 Decarlo Trerise; 20 Ieuan Badham.
Try: Mitchell (6); **Goals:** Punchard 0/1.
Sin bin: Nichol (75) - high tackle.
OLDHAM: 1 Gregg McNally; 37 Nick Rawsthorne; 3 Connor Carr; 12 Kian Morgan; 5 Joe Hartley; 6 Martyn Ridyard; 28 Kieran Tyrer; 10 Deane Meadows; 9 Matty Wilkinson; 38 Josh Johnson; 25 George Hirst; 19 Callum Cameron; 13 Emmerson Whittel. Subs (all used): 14 Sean Slater; 2 Patrick Ah Van; 32 Pat Moran; 17 Jack Blagbrough.
Tries: Carr (4, 23, 75, 79), Hartley (10), Cameron (15), K Morgan (28), Hirst (38), Rawsthorne (46), Slater (56), Tyrer (62); **Goals:** Ridyard 6/11.
Sin bin: Carr (32) - dangerous challenge on Nichol.
Rugby Leaguer & League Express Men of the Match:
Cornwall: Luke Collins; *Oldham:* Connor Carr.
Penalty count: 3-9; **Half-time:** 4-32;
Referee: Aaryn Belafonte; **Attendance:** 891.

NORTH WALES CRUSADERS 28 DONCASTER 22

CRUSADERS: 6 Dave Gibbons; 27 Josh Lynch; 14 Kieran Taylor; 3 Cole Oakley; 5 Rob Massam; 25 Leon Hayes; 28 Toby Hughes; 16 Jack Houghton; 20 Pat Rainford; 17 Chris Barratt; 13 Matt Fletcher; 21 Ryan Ellis; 26 Carl Forster. Subs (all used): 8 Callum Hazzard; 10 Jordan Andrade; 18 Paul Nash; 19 Shaun Costello.
Tries: Rainford (5), Barratt (25), Ellis (28), Hayes (65);
Goals: Hayes 6/6.
DONCASTER: 30 Josh Guzdek; 2 Tom Halliday; 22 Misi Taulapapa; 4 Jason Tali; 25 Jack Sanderson; 6 Ben Johnston; 7 Connor Robinson; 29 Luke Cooper; 19 Ross Whitmore; 18 Jose Kenga; 11 Sam Smeaton; 27 Brett Ferres; 15 Alex Holdstock. Subs (all used): 8 Keelan Foster; 9 Greg Burns; 14 Dean Roberts; 31 Albert Vete.
Tries: Sanderson (2), Robinson (47), Taulapapa (69), Johnston (77); **Goals:** Robinson 3/4.
Rugby Leaguer & League Express Men of the Match:
Crusaders: Leon Hayes; *Doncaster:* Connor Robinson.
Penalty count: 5-7; **Half-time:** 18-4;
Referee: Brad Milligan; **Attendance:** 531
(at Hare Lane, Chester).

DEWSBURY RAMS 38 WORKINGTON TOWN 8

RAMS: 1 Owen Restall; 5 Andy Gabriel; 26 Bailey O'Connor; 3 Ollie Greensmith; 23 Perry Whiteley; 6 Paul Sykes; 7 Calum Turner; 8 Jimmy Beckett; 9 Reiss Butterworth; 15 Ronan Dixon; 11 Connor Davies; 18 Brad Graham; 13 Louis Collinson. Subs (all used): 20 Jackson Walker; 14 Sam Day; 17 Elliot Morris; 10 Dale Ferguson.
Tries: R Dixon (19), Sykes (59), Gabriel (63, 65, 79), Restall (76); **Goals:** Sykes 7/8.
TOWN: 1 Jordan Burns; 5 Ethan Bickerdike; 4 Jason Mossop; 2 Sean Sabutey; 19 Max Anderson-Moore; 6 Ciaran Walker; 7 Carl Forber; 22 Liam McAvoy; 26 Jack Mallinson; 10 Stevie Scholey; 29 Jake Bradley; 18 Liam McNicholas; 27 Hanley Dawson. Subs (all used): 14 Blain Marwood; 25 Grant Reid; 20 Jack Stephenson; 30 Luke Charlton.
Try: Walker (11); **Goals:** Walker 2/3.
Sin bin: Scholey (3) - holding down.
Rugby Leaguer & League Express Men of the Match:
Rams: Andy Gabriel; *Town:* Ciaran Walker.
Penalty count: 5-6; **Half-time:** 8-8;
Referee: Kevin Moore; **Attendance:** 1,579.

ROCHDALE HORNETS 22 HUNSLET 35

HORNETS: 4 Ben O'Keefe; 25 Dan Harrison; 11 Dan Brewin; - Jacob Gannon; 2 Cian Tyrer; 6 Lewis Else; 7 Dave Hewitt; 30 Jacob Jones; 14 Aiden Roden; 31 Lewis Peachey; 35 Connor Ratcliffe; 32 Ben Forster; 12 Duane Straugheir. Subs (all used): 29 Aaron Smith; 17 AJ Boardman; 27 Toby Brannan; 10 Ben Killan.
Tries: Roden (26), Forster (41), Straugheir (49), Smith (61);
Goals: Hewitt 3/4.
HUNSLET: 1 Jimmy Watson; 2 Jack Render; 3 Adam Ryder; 4 Joe Burton; 36 Johnny Campbell; 30 Matty Beharrell; 18 Myles Lawford; 8 Harvey Hallas; 9 Sam Hallas; 10 Steve Crossley; 11 Josh Jordan-Roberts; 12 Aaron York; 13 Michael Knowles. Subs (all used): 37 Oli Burton; 17 Lewis Wray; 19 Marcus Green; 16 Jordan Syme.
Tries: H Hallas (3), Ryder (6), J Burton (11, 69), Campbell (38, 80), Render (72); **Goals:** Beharrell 3/7;
Field goal: Beharrell (78).
Rugby Leaguer & League Express Men of the Match:
Hornets: Jacob Gannon; *Hunslet:* Joe Burton.
Penalty count: 3-2; **Half-time:** 4-20;
Referee: Ryan Cox; **Attendance:** 344.

ROUND 14

Friday 11th August 2023

LONDON SKOLARS 0 DONCASTER 60

SKOLARS: 1 Louis O'Sullivan; 5 Abevia McDonald; 3 Lameck Juma; 4 Aaron Small; 2 Leighton Ball; 18 Liam O'Callaghan; 7 Phil Lyon; 10 Todd Peut; 9 Tommy Porter; 15 Malikhi Lloyd-Jones; 11 Luciano Bejanidze; 21 Lamont Bryan; - Matt Ross. Subs (all used): 14 Doug Chirnside; 19 Jack Hughes; 8 Christian Gale; 12 Fraser Piercy-Farley.
DONCASTER: 30 Josh Guzdek; 2 Tom Halliday; 21 Brad Hey; 22 Misi Taulapapa; 5 Travis Corion; 6 Ben Johnston; 7 Connor Robinson; 20 Brad Knowles; 9 Greg Burns; 31 Albert Vete; 11 Sam Smeaton; 27 Brett Ferres; 13 Loui McConnell. Subs (all used): 24 Watson Boas; 8 Keelan Foster; 14 Dean Roberts; 15 Alex Holdstock.
Tries: Taulapapa (3, 32), Vete (12, 74), Halliday (14), Boas (46, 75), Holdstock (55), Robinson (60), Smeaton (65, 71); **Goals:** Robinson 6/8, Boas 2/3.
Rugby Leaguer & League Express Men of the Match:
Skolars: Todd Peut; *Doncaster:* Connor Robinson.
Penalty count: 3-3; **Half-time:** 0-24;
Referee: Matt Rossleigh; **Attendance:** 509.

ROUND 21

Sunday 20th August 2023

DONCASTER 60 CORNWALL 0

DONCASTER: 30 Josh Guzdek; 2 Tom Halliday; 21 Brad Hey; 3 Mahe Fonua; 5 Travis Corion; 6 Ben Johnston;

7 Connor Robinson; 31 Albert Vete; 9 Greg Burns; 20 Brad Knowles; 11 Sam Smeaton; 27 Brett Ferres; 13 Loui McConnell. Subs (all used): 24 Watson Boas; 15 Alex Holdstock; 17 Matt James; 8 Keelan Foster.
Tries: Fonua (4, 23), Johnston (16), Burns (38), Halliday (39, 48), Boas (63), Corion (67, 77), Ferres (70), Vete (75); **Goals:** Robinson 8/11.
CORNWALL: 1 Liam Whitton; 2 Coby Nichol; 15 Sean Croston; 4 Tom Ashton; 5 Mackenzie Scurr; 6 Cameron Brown; 7 Morgan Punchard; 8 Josh Hartshorne; 9 Luke Collins; 10 Ewan Badham; 11 Nathan Cullen; 17 David Weetman; 13 Jake Lloyd. Subs (all used): 14 Jaden Barraclough; 12 Kaine Dimech; 20 Ieuan Badham; 22 Decarlo Trerise.
Sin bin: Brown (39) - dissent.
Rugby Leaguer & League Express Men of the Match: *Doncaster:* Connor Robinson; *Cornwall:* Luke Collins.
Penalty count: 9-4; **Half-time:** 28-0;
Referee: Andy Sweet; **Attendance:** 1,072.

HUNSLET 56 LONDON SKOLARS 14

HUNSLET: 1 Jimmy Watson; 2 Jack Render; 3 Adam Ryder; 4 Joe Burton; 36 Johnny Campbell; 30 Matty Beharrell; 18 Myles Lawford; 29 Spencer Darley; 7 Nathan Conroy; 10 Steve Crossley; 11 Josh Jordan-Roberts; 16 Jordan Syme; 26 Jordan Bull. Subs (all used): 37 Oli Burton; 15 Nathan Newbound; 17 Lewis Wray; 19 Marcus Green.
Tries: Beharrell (2), Ryder (5), Crossley (18), Campbell (25, 45, 74), Syme (56), Lawford (69), J Burton (77), Wray (79); **Goals:** Beharrell 7/9, Lawford 1/1.
Sin bin: Beharrell (9) - late challenge on Lyon.
SKOLARS: 1 Louis O'Sullivan; 2 Abevia McDonald; 3 Lameck Juma; 4 Aaron Small; 5 Leighton Ball; 6 Alex Deery; 7 Phil Lyon; 10 Todd Peut; 9 Tommy Porter; 15 Malikhi Lloyd-Jones; 11 Max Allen; 21 Fraser Piercy-Farley; 13 Liam O'Callaghan. Subs (all used): 19 Matt Ross; 8 Christian Gale; 12 Jack Harbridge; 18 Ed Brown.
Tries: Allen (11), McDonald (36), Small (60);
Goals: Lyon 1/3.
Rugby Leaguer & League Express Men of the Match: *Hunslet:* Johnny Campbell; *Skolars:* Phil Lyon.
Penalty count: 3-3; **Half-time:** 22-10;
Referee: Matty Lynn; **Attendance:** 484.

ROCHDALE HORNETS 20 OLDHAM 24

HORNETS: 4 Ben O'Keefe; 5 Dan Nixon; - Tommy Brierley; 11 Dan Brewin; 2 Cian Tyrer; 6 Lewis Else; 7 Dave Hewitt; 18 Jack Arnold; 14 Aiden Roden; 10 Ben Killan; 35 Connor Ratcliffe; 32 Ben Forster; 12 Duane Straugheir. Subs (all used): 24 Aaron Smith; 17 AJ Boardman; 27 Toby Brannan; 29 Kyle Huish.
Tries: Else (6), Tyrer (40), Brierley (43, 57);
Goals: Hewitt 2/4.
Sin bin: Hewitt (20) - holding down.
OLDHAM: 1 Gregg McNally; 28 Nick Rawsthorne; 3 Connor Carr; 29 Kian Morgan; 5 Joe Hartley; 6 Martyn Ridyard; 11 Kieran Tyrer; 36 Josh Johnson; 9 Matty Wilkinson; 8 Luke Nelmes; 25 George Hirst; 19 Callum Cameron; 13 Emmerson Whittel. Subs (all used): 14 Sean Slater; 32 Pat Moran; 10 Deane Meadows; 15 Dom Newton.
Tries: Rawsthorne (18, 33, 65), Wilkinson (48), K Morgan (79); **Goals:** Ridyard 2/5.
Rugby Leaguer & League Express Men of the Match: *Hornets:* Dan Nixon; *Oldham:* Nick Rawsthorne.
Penalty count: 3-4; **Half-time:** 10-8;
Referee: Brad Milligan; **Attendance:** 1,386.

ROUND 15

Wednesday 23rd August 2023

OLDHAM 40 WORKINGTON TOWN 24

OLDHAM: 18 Jordan Paga; 28 Nick Rawsthorne; 3 Connor Carr; 29 Kian Morgan; 2 Patrick Ah Van; 6 Martyn Ridyard; 7 Kieran Tyrer; 8 Luke Nelmes; 9 Matty Wilkinson; 30 Josh Johnson; 25 George Hirst; 12 Zac Baker; 13 Emmerson Whittel. Subs (all used): 14 Sean Slater; 10 Deane Meadows; 32 Pat Moran; 21 Harvey Wilson.
Tries: K Morgan (9), Nelmes (13), Paga (32), Rawsthorne (38, 55), Ah Van (41), Tyrer (49);
Goals: Ridyard 6/7.
Sin bin: Johnson (66) - late challenge.
TOWN: 1 Jordan Burns; 5 Ethan Bickerdike; 4 Jason Mossop; 2 Sean Sabutey; 21 Aaron Burns; 6 Ciaran Walker; 7 Carl Forber; 8 Jordan Thomson; 9 Matty Henson; 10 Stevie Scholey; 29 Jake Bradley; 11 Malik Steel; 27 Hanley Dawson. Subs (all used): 14 Blain Marwood; 17 Joe Kirkup; 20 Jack Stephenson; 30 Luke Charlton.
Tries: Bickerdike (18), Kirkup (29), Marwood (55), Charlton (68); **Goals:** Walker 4/4.
Sin bin: Thomson (60) - dissent; J Burns (79) - fighting.
Rugby Leaguer & League Express Men of the Match: *Oldham:* Emmerson Whittel; *Town:* Jake Bradley.
Penalty count: 4-6; **Half-time:** 22-12; **Referee:** Ryan Cox;
Attendance: 1,238 *(at Boundary Park).*

ROUND 18

Wednesday 23rd August 2023

ROCHDALE HORNETS 48 LONDON SKOLARS 0
(match postponed due to London Skolars being unable to fulfil fixture, 48-0 win awarded to Rochdale)

ROUND 22

Sunday 27th August 2023

CORNWALL 18 ROCHDALE HORNETS 12

CORNWALL: 1 Liam Whitton; 3 Errol Carter; 2 Coby Nichol; 4 Tom Ashton; 18 George Mitchell; 7 Cameron Brown; 6 Morgan Punchard; 8 Harry Boots; 9 Luke Collins; 10 Ewan Badham; 11 Nathan Cullen; 17 David Weetman; 13 Jake Lloyd. Subs (all used): 14 Jaden Barraclough; 12 Kaine Dimech; 22 Decarlo Trerise; 15 Josh Hartshorne.
Tries: Brown (23), Mitchell (48), Whitton (80);
Goals: Brown 3/3.
Sin bin: Whitton (63) - delaying restart.
HORNETS: 1 Joe Purcell; - Tommy Brierley; 5 Dan Nixon; 11 Dan Brewin; 25 Dan Harrison; 6 Lewis Else; 7 Dave Hewitt; 27 Toby Brannan; 14 Aiden Roden; 10 Ben Killan; 35 Connor Ratcliffe; 32 Ben Forster; 12 Duane Straugheir. Subs (all used): 24 Aaron Smith; 29 Kyle Huish; 37 Sion Jones; 9 Cameron Berry.
Tries: Brierley (5), Harrison (12), Brewin (72);
Goals: Hewitt 0/3.
Rugby Leaguer & League Express Men of the Match: *Cornwall:* Tom Ashton; *Hornets:* Tommy Brierley.
Penalty count: 1-4; **Half-time:** 6-8;
Referee: William Gilder; **Attendance:** 1,281.

NORTH WALES CRUSADERS 62
LONDON SKOLARS 20

CRUSADERS: 6 Dave Gibbons; 27 Josh Lynch; 3 Cole Oakley; 4 Matt Reid; 5 Rob Massam; 25 Leon Hayes; 28 Toby Hughes; 16 Jack Houghton; 20 Pat Rainford; 17 Chris Barratt; 21 Ryan Ellis; 13 Matt Fletcher; 26 Carl Forster. Subs (all used): 8 Callum Hazzard; 12 Jono Smith; 18 Paul Nash; 19 Shaun Costello.
Tries: Massam (3), Houghton (20), Hughes (24), Reid (27, 55, 61), Lynch (29), Hayes (39, 63), Gibbons (57, 70); **Goals:** Hayes 9/11.
SKOLARS: 1 Jacob Thomas; 2 Abevia McDonald; 3 Lameck Juma; 4 Aaron Small; 5 Leighton Ball; 6 Tommy Porter; 7 Phil Lyon; 8 Christian Gale; 9 Doug Chirnside; 10 Todd Peut; 11 Fraser Piercy-Farley; 12 Jack Harbridge; 13 Matt Ross. Subs (all used): 14 Jake Tilford; 15 Jack Hughes; 18 Oliver Bloom; 19 Ed Brown.
Tries: Juma (7), McDonald (34), Hughes (43), Ball (76);
Goals: Thomas 1/1, Lyon 1/3.
Sin bin: Lyon (2) - holding down.
Rugby Leaguer & League Express Men of the Match: *Crusaders:* Carl Forster; *Skolars:* Phil Lyon.
Penalty count: 4-3; **Half-time:** 34-10;
Referee: Andy Sweet; **Attendance:** 495.

DONCASTER 36 DEWSBURY RAMS 26

DONCASTER: 30 Josh Guzdek; 2 Tom Halliday; 21 Brad Hey; 3 Mahe Fonua; 5 Travis Corion; 6 Ben Johnston; 7 Connor Robinson; 31 Albert Vete; 9 Greg Burns; 20 Brad Knowles; 11 Sam Smeaton; 27 Brett Ferres; 13 Loui McConnell. Subs (all used): 8 Keelan Foster; 15 Alex Holdstock; 17 Matt James; 24 Watson Boas.
Tries: Fonua (20, 76), Boas (51, 60, 72), Johnston (57);
Goals: Robinson 6/6.
Sin bin: Ferres (66) - dangerous challenge.
RAMS: 1 Owen Restall; 2 Lewis Carr; 26 Bailey O'Connor; 3 Ollie Greensmith; 5 Andy Gabriel; 6 Paul Sykes; 7 Calum Turner; 8 Jimmy Beckett; 9 Reiss Butterworth; 15 Ronan Dixon; 12 Matt Garside; 18 Brad Graham; 11 Connor Davies. Subs (all used): 28 Luke Littlewood; 17 Elliot Morris; 24 Joe Summers; 22 Jack Coventry.
Tries: Garside (33, 46, 66), Restall (38), Greensmith (50);
Goals: Sykes 3/5.
Sin bin: Greensmith (78) - fighting.
Rugby Leaguer & League Express Men of the Match: *Doncaster:* Watson Boas; *Rams:* Matt Garside.
Penalty count: 3-2; **Half-time:** 6-10;
Referee: Brad Milligan; **Attendance:** 1,064.

OLDHAM 10 MIDLANDS HURRICANES 18

OLDHAM: 28 Nick Rawsthorne; 5 Joe Hartley; 3 Connor Carr; 29 Kian Morgan; 2 Patrick Ah Van; 18 Jordan Paga; 7 Kieran Tyrer; 15 Dom Newton; 14 Sean Slater; 17 Jack Blagbrough; 19 Callum Cameron; 12 Zac Baker; 32 Pat Moran. Subs (all used): 8 Luke Nelmes; 9 Matty Wilkinson; 30 Josh Johnson; 6 Martyn Ridyard.
Tries: Rawsthorne (62), Paga (74); **Goals:** Ridyard 1/2.
HURRICANES: 1 Todd Horner; 5 Hayden Freeman; 12 Liam Welham; 3 Matt Welham; 2 Mackenzie Turner; 6 Jake Sweeting; 7 Jacob Hookem; 20 Jon Luke Kirby; 23 Danny Barcoe; 15 Ellis Hobson; 22 Aaron Levy; 24 Tom Wilkinson; 21 Aaron Willis. Subs (all used): 9 Elliot Windley; 8 Kieran Moran; 18 Sam Bowring; 17 Brad Clavering.
Tries: Hookem (28), Turner (47), Levy (77);
Goals: Hookem 3/4.
Rugby Leaguer & League Express Men of the Match: *Oldham:* Jordan Paga; *Hurricanes:* Jacob Hookem.
Penalty count: 9-4; **Half-time:** 0-6;
Referee: Matty Lynn; **Attendance:** 472.

WORKINGTON TOWN 18 HUNSLET 6

TOWN: 1 Jordan Burns; 5 Ethan Bickerdike; 4 Jason Mossop; 19 Max Anderson-Moore; 2 Sean Sabutey; 6 Ciaran Walker; 7 Carl Forber; 8 Jordan Thomson; 9 Matty Henson; 10 Stevie Scholey; 18 Liam McNicholas; 29 Jake Bradley; 27 Hanley Dawson. Subs (all used): 16 JJ Key; 14 Blain Marwood; 25 Grant Reid; 20 Jack Stephenson.
Tries: Dawson (19), Henson (48), J Burns (66);
Goals: Walker 3/3.
HUNSLET: 1 Jimmy Watson; 25 Dan McGrath; 3 Adam Ryder; 4 Joe Burton; - Alfie Goddard; 30 Matty Beharrell; 18 Myles Lawford; 26 Jordan Bull; 9 Sam Hallas; 10 Steve Crossley; 11 Josh Jordan-Roberts; 12 Aaron York; 13 Michael Knowles. Subs (all used): 37 Oli Burton; 17 Lewis Wray; 19 Marcus Green; 16 Jordan Syme.
Try: McGrath (60); **Goals:** Beharrell 1/1.
Rugby Leaguer & League Express Men of the Match: *Town:* Matty Henson; *Hunslet:* Dan McGrath.
Penalty count: 7-7; **Half-time:** 6-0;
Referee: Kevin Moore; **Attendance:** 803.

QUALIFYING PLAY-OFF

Sunday 3rd September 2023

DONCASTER 36 OLDHAM 0

DONCASTER: 30 Josh Guzdek; 2 Tom Halliday; 21 Brad Hey; 3 Mahe Fonua; 22 Misi Taulapapa; 6 Ben Johnston; 7 Connor Robinson; 31 Albert Vete; 9 Greg Burns; 20 Brad Knowles; 11 Sam Smeaton; 27 Brett Ferres; 13 Loui McConnell. Subs (all used): 24 Watson Boas; 15 Alex Holdstock; 17 Matt James; 8 Keelan Foster.
Tries: Fonua (5), Vete (19), Robinson (29), Holdstock (40), Halliday (64, 80); **Goals:** Robinson 6/8.
OLDHAM: 1 Gregg McNally; 28 Nick Rawsthorne; 3 Connor Carr; 29 Kian Morgan; 2 Patrick Ah Van; 6 Martyn Ridyard; 18 Jordan Paga; 10 Deane Meadows; 9 Matty Wilkinson; 8 Luke Nelmes; 25 George Hirst; 12 Zac Baker; 13 Emmerson Whittel. Subs (all used): 33 Jamie Ellis; 32 Pat Moran; 15 Dom Newton; 19 Callum Cameron.
Sin bin: Ah Van (37) - professional foul; McNally (54) - professional foul.
Rugby Leaguer & League Express Men of the Match: *Doncaster:* Connor Robinson; *Oldham:* Jamie Ellis.
Penalty count: 7-5; **Half-time:** 24-0;
Referee: Kevin Moore; **Attendance:** 615.

ELIMINATION PLAY-OFF

Sunday 3rd September 2023

WORKINGTON TOWN 10
NORTH WALES CRUSADERS 26

TOWN: 1 Jordan Burns; 5 Ethan Bickerdike; 4 Jason Mossop; 19 Max Anderson-Moore; 2 Sean Sabutey; 6 Ciaran Walker; 7 Carl Forber; 8 Jordan Thomson; 27 Hanley Dawson; 22 Liam McAvoy; 29 Jake Bradley; 18 Liam McNicholas; 10 Stevie Scholey. Subs (all used): 16 JJ Key; 25 Grant Reid; 14 Blain Marwood; 20 Jack Stephenson.
Tries: Forber (17), Bickerdike (29); **Goals:** Walker 1/2.
CRUSADERS: 6 Dave Gibbons; 27 Josh Lynch; 14 Kieran Taylor; 4 Matt Reid; 5 Rob Massam; 28 Toby Hughes; 25 Leon Hayes; 16 Jack Houghton; 9 Jake Burns; 17 Chris Barratt; 21 Ryan Ellis; 3 Cole Oakley; 26 Carl Forster. Subs (all used): 8 Callum Hazzard; 10 Jordan Andrade; 13 Matt Fletcher; 20 Pat Rainford.
Tries: Forster (9), Taylor (52), Rainford (59), Reid (69);
Goals: Hayes 5/5.
Rugby Leaguer & League Express Men of the Match: *Town:* Carl Forber; *Crusaders:* Leon Hayes.
Penalty count: 7-7; **Half-time:** 10-8;
Referee: Ryan Cox; **Attendance:** 611.

League One 2023 - Round by Round

A jubilant Loui McConnell heads for the line during Doncaster's Promotion Final victory against North Wales

ELIMINATION SEMI-FINAL

Sunday 10th September 2023

OLDHAM 12 NORTH WALES CRUSADERS 13

OLDHAM: 1 Gregg McNally; 28 Nick Rawsthorne; 3 Connor Carr; 29 Kian Morgan; 2 Patrick Ah Van; 6 Martyn Ridyard; 33 Jamie Ellis; 32 Pat Moran; 9 Matty Wilkinson; 30 Josh Johnson; 25 George Hirst; 12 Zac Baker; 13 Emmerson Whittel. Subs (all used): 15 Dom Newton; 8 Luke Nelmes; 10 Deane Meadows; 18 Jordan Paga.
Tries: Ah Van (10), K Morgan (16); **Goals:** Ridyard 2/2.
Dismissal: Baker (77) - fighting.
CRUSADERS: 6 Dave Gibbons; 27 Josh Lynch; 14 Kieran Taylor; 4 Matt Reid; 5 Rob Massam; 28 Toby Hughes; 25 Leon Hayes; 16 Jack Houghton; 9 Jake Burns; 17 Chris Barratt; 21 Ryan Ellis; 3 Cole Oakley; 26 Carl Forster. Subs (all used): 8 Callum Hazzard; 10 Jordan Andrade; 13 Matt Fletcher; 20 Pat Rainford.
Tries: Hazzard (42), Fletcher (52); **Goals:** Hayes 2/3;
Field goal: Hughes (79).
Dismissal: Gibbons (77) - fighting.
Rugby Leaguer & League Express Men of the Match:
Oldham: Patrick Ah Van; *Crusaders:* Carl Forster.
Penalty count: 5-8; **Half-time:** 12-0;
Referee: Kevin Moore; **Attendance:** 836
(at Boundary Park).

QUALIFYING SEMI-FINAL

Sunday 10th September 2023

HUNSLET 14 DONCASTER 26

HUNSLET: 1 Jimmy Watson; 2 Jack Render; 3 Adam Ryder; 4 Joe Burton; 36 Johnny Campbell; 30 Matty Beharrell; 18 Myles Lawford; 8 Harvey Hallas; 9 Sam Hallas; 10 Steve Crossley; 11 Josh Jordan-Roberts; 12 Aaron York; 13 Michael Knowles. Subs (all used): 16 Jordan Syme; 17 Lewis Wray; 29 Spencer Darley; 37 Oli Burton.
Tries: Ryder (1), Campbell (48); **Goals:** Beharrell 3/4.
DONCASTER: 30 Josh Guzdek; 2 Tom Halliday; 21 Brad Hey; 3 Mahe Fonua; 22 Misi Taulapapa; 6 Ben Johnston; 7 Connor Robinson; 31 Albert Vete; 9 Greg Burns; 20 Brad Knowles; 11 Sam Smeaton; 27 Brett Ferres; 13 Loui McConnell. Subs (all used): 8 Keelan Foster; 17 Matt James; 24 Watson Boas; 29 Luke Cooper.
Tries: Fonua (6, 26), Johnston (55), Boas (63), Smeaton (77); **Goals:** Robinson 3/6.
Rugby Leaguer & League Express Men of the Match:
Hunslet: Matty Beharrell; *Doncaster:* Connor Robinson.
Penalty count: 4-7; **Half-time:** 10-8;
Referee: Nick Bennett; **Attendance:** 897.

FINAL ELIMINATOR

Sunday 17th September 2023

HUNSLET 18 NORTH WALES CRUSADERS 25

HUNSLET: 1 Jimmy Watson; 2 Jack Render; 3 Adam Ryder; 4 Joe Burton; 20 Alfie Goddard; 30 Matty Beharrell; 24 Fraser Stroud; 26 Jordan Bull; 9 Sam Hallas; 10 Steve Crossley; 11 Josh Jordan-Roberts; 12 Aaron York; 13 Michael Knowles. Subs (all used): 7 Nathan Conroy; 19 Marcus Green; 16 Jordan Syme; 29 Spencer Darley.
Tries: Watson (5), Goddard (23), Ryder (56);
Goals: Beharrell 3/3.
CRUSADERS: 1 Owain Abel; 27 Josh Lynch; 14 Kieran Taylor; 4 Matt Reid; 5 Rob Massam; 13 Matt Fletcher; 28 Toby Hughes; 16 Jack Houghton; 9 Jake Burns; 17 Chris Barratt; 21 Ryan Ellis; 3 Cole Oakley; 26 Carl Forster. Subs (all used): 8 Callum Hazzard; 10 Jordan Andrade; 20 Pat Rainford; 19 Shaun Costello.
Tries: Massam (1), Reid (14), Taylor (67), Oakley (77);
Goals: Hughes 3/5, Abel 1/1; **Field goal:** Abel (73).
Rugby Leaguer & League Express Men of the Match:
Hunslet: Matty Beharrell; *Crusaders:* Owain Abel.
Penalty count: 2-6; **Half-time:** 12-14;
Referee: Matt Rossleigh; **Attendance:** 626.

PROMOTION FINAL

Sunday 24th September 2023

DONCASTER 18 NORTH WALES CRUSADERS 6

DONCASTER: 30 Josh Guzdek; 2 Tom Halliday; 21 Brad Hey; 3 Mahe Fonua; 32 Bureta Faraimo; 6 Ben Johnston; 7 Connor Robinson; 20 Brad Knowles; 9 Greg Burns; 31 Albert Vete; 11 Sam Smeaton; 27 Brett Ferres; 13 Loui McConnell. Subs (all used): 8 Callum Hazzard; 15 Alex Holdstock; 17 Matt James; 24 Watson Boas.
Tries: Fonua (14), McConnell (66), Smeaton (76);
Goals: Robinson 3/4.
CRUSADERS: 1 Owain Abel; 27 Josh Lynch; 3 Cole Oakley; 14 Kieran Taylor; 4 Matt Reid; 25 Leon Hayes; 28 Toby Hughes; 16 Jack Houghton; 9 Jake Burns; 17 Chris Barratt; 21 Ryan Ellis; 13 Matt Fletcher; 26 Carl Forster. Subs (all used): 8 Callum Hazzard; 10 Jordan Andrade; 19 Shaun Costello; 20 Pat Rainford.
Try: Hughes (72); **Goals:** Hayes 1/1.
Rugby Leaguer & League Express Men of the Match:
Doncaster: Connor Robinson; *Crusaders:* Matt Reid.
Penalty count: 4-8; **Half-time:** 8-0;
Referee: Nick Bennett; **Attendance:** 2,549.

CHALLENGE CUP 2023
Round by Round

ROUND 1

Saturday 11th February 2023
Brentwood Eels 34 Bedford Tigers 24
British Army 12 Ashton Bears 28
Distington 4 Orrell St James 16
Doncaster Toll Bar 24 RAF 36
Edinburgh Eagles 20 Saddleworth Rangers 30
Featherstone Lions 6 Great Britain Police 20
Fryston Warriors 38 Thornhill Trojans 22
Hammersmith Hills Hoists 8 Dublin City Exiles 42
Hull Dockers 54 Rhondda Outlaws 10
London Chargers 38 North Herts Crusaders 12
Royal Navy 28 Barrow Island 16
Skirlaugh 16 Wests Warriors 26
Stanningley 38 Milford 4
West Bowling 30 Waterhead Warriors 12
Westgate Common 36 Crosfields 18
Wigan St Patricks 22 Ince Rose Bridge 30

Sunday 12th February 2023
Heworth 22 Oulton Raiders 6
Jarrow Vikings 26 Myton Warriors 40

ROUND 2

Saturday 25th February 2023

CORNWALL 14 ROCHDALE MAYFIELD 20

CORNWALL: 1 Liam Whitton; 2 Errol Carter; 4 Coby Nichol; 15 Tom Ashton; 5 Harry Aaronson; 6 Cameron Brown; 7 Adam Rusling; 26 Josh Hartshorne; 9 Luke Collins; 10 Harry Boots; 11 Nathan Cullen; 12 Kaine Dimech; 13 Jake Lloyd. Subs (all used): 14 Louis Singleton; 17 George Mitchell; 22 Brad Howe; 23 Jamie Prisk.
Tries: Ashton (15), Brown (69), Aaronson (72);
Goals: Rusling 1/3.
MAYFIELD: 1 Lewis Butterworth; 2 Jordan Parr; 3 James McDaid; 4 Dakota Tolhurst; 5 Wayne English; 6 Sam Wright; 7 Devlin Long; 8 Jarred Dash; 9 Sean Penkywicz; 10 David Mills; 11 Travis Long; 12 Ben Metcalfe; 13 Seta Tala. Subs (all used): 14 Dec Sheridan; 15 Nick Hargreaves; 16 Harry Sheridan; 17 Joe Taira.
Tries: Wright (9), English (38), T Long (41), H Sheridan (74);
Goals: D Long 2/4.
Rugby Leaguer & League Express Men of the Match:
Cornwall: Harry Aaronson; *Mayfield:* Sean Penkywicz.
Penalty count: 3-4; **Half-time:** 4-10;
Referee: Matt Rossleigh; **Attendance:** 1,061.

ASHTON BEARS 8 DEWSBURY RAMS 38

BEARS: 1 Matty Smith; 2 Alex Ashby; 3 Chris Rothwell; 4 Joe Pilling; 5 Tyler Pilling; 18 Rob Sexton; 7 Tom Hopkins; 8 Adam Jones; 9 Martyn Greaves; 19 Lee Jones; 11 Jordan Green; 10 Andy Thornley; 13 Ollie Smith. Subs (all used): 6 Kee Greenhalgh; 12 Matty Ireland; 15 Dec O'Donnell; 16 Kian Hampson.
Try: Smith (2); **Goals:** Sexton 2/2.
RAMS: 1 Owen Restall; 4 Davey Dixon; 21 Caelum Jordan; 3 Ollie Greensmith; 23 Perry Whiteley; 6 Paul Sykes; 7 Calum Turner; 8 Jimmy Beckett; 9 Reiss Butterworth; 15 Ronan Dixon; 18 Brad Graham; 12 Matt Garside; 13 Louis Collinson. Subs (all used): 10 Dale Ferguson; 17 Elliot Morris; 20 Jackson Walker; 26 Bailey O'Connor.
Tries: R Dixon (15), Whiteley (34), Ferguson (57), Beckett (71), D Dixon (73), Jordan (77);
Goals: Sykes 5/5, Turner 2/3.
Rugby Leaguer & League Express Men of the Match:
Bears: Adam Jones; *Rams:* Dale Ferguson.
Penalty count: 6-6; **Half-time:** 8-14;
Referee: Elliot Burrow; **Attendance:** 483
(at FLAIR Stadium).

NORTH WALES CRUSADERS 70 ROYAL NAVY 0

CRUSADERS: 1 Owain Abel; 2 Jack Holmes; 14 Kieran Taylor; 4 Matt Reid; 5 Rob Massam; 6 Dave Gibbons; 7 Brad Billsborough; 8 Callum Hazzard; 9 Brad Jinks; 10 Jordan Andrade; 26 Carl Forster; 21 Ryan Ellis; 13 Matt Fletcher. Subs (all used): 15 Brad Brennan; 17 Chris Barratt; 19 Shaun Costello; 27 Pat Rainford.
Tries: Reid (4, 25, 77), Gibbons (12, 72), Barratt (32), Massam (46), Forster (50), Andrade (57, 60), Abel (74), Taylor (80); **Goals:** Billsborough 11/12.
Sin bin: Rainford (68) - fighting.
NAVY: 1 Danny Dainty; 2 Joey Sugden; 3 Jack Bartlett; 14 Gavin Duffy; 20 Eddie Holland; 6 Charlie Mattison; 7 Matt Gaskell; 8 Jack Ray; 9 Eli Steinberg; 10 James Parry; 11 James Teixeira; 12 Brodie-Lee Butler; 13 Ben Taylor. Subs (all used): 15 Louis McKenna; 16 Eden Quantock; 17 George Hannan; 24 Tyler Leighton.
Sin bin: Hannan (68) - fighting.
Rugby Leaguer & League Express Men of the Match:
Crusaders: Owain Abel; *Navy:* Jack Ray.
Penalty count: 9-3; **Half-time:** 22-0;
Referee: John Lincoln; **Attendance:** 255.

Brentwood Eels 4 Wath Brow Hornets 58
Fryston Warriors 12 Stanningley 28
Hunslet ARLFC 66 Pilkington Recs 0
Lock Lane 22 West Bowling 30
Myton Warriors 22 Leigh Miners Rangers 34
Orrell St James 68 Dublin City Exiles 14
RAF 10 York Acorn 12
Saddleworth Rangers 4 Thatto Heath Crusaders 18
Siddal 14 West Hull 8
Wests Warriors 18 London Chargers 14

Sunday 26th February 2023

ROCHDALE HORNETS 42 LONDON SKOLARS 4

HORNETS: 1 Joe Purcell; 2 Cian Tyrer; 3 Will Cooke; 4 Ben O'Keefe; 5 Dan Nixon; 6 Lewis Else; 7 Dave Hewitt; 8 Zach Braham; 9 Cameron Berry; 10 Ben Killan; 11 Dan Brewin; 12 Duane Straugheir; 17 AJ Boardman. Subs (all used): 14 Aiden Roden; 16 Ethan O'Hanlon; 18 Jack Arnold; 19 Ewan Badham.
Tries: Cooke (12, 53), Purcell (17), O'Keefe (30), Else (39), Hewitt (51), Killan (70); **Goals:** Hewitt 7/7.
Sin bin: Arnold (62) - fighting.
SKOLARS: 1 Jacob Thomas; 2 Leighton Ball; 3 Jerome Yates; 4 Aaron Small; 5 Louis O'Sullivan; 6 Alex Deery; 7 Jack Ryan; 8 Christian Gale; 9 Shane Lee; 10 Todd Peut; 11 Luciano Bejanidze; 12 Jimmy Morgan; 13 Matt Ross. Subs (all used): 14 Elliott Hutchings; 15 Ed Brown; 19 Fraser Piercy-Farley; 21 Delaine Bedward-Gittens.
Try: Ball (8); **Goals:** Lee 0/1.
Sin bin: Yates (62) - fighting.
Rugby Leaguer & League Express Men of the Match:
Hornets: Dave Hewitt; *Skolars:* Shane Lee.
Penalty count: 5-11; **Half-time:** 24-4;
Referee: Matty Lynn; **Attendance:** 300.

WORKINGTON TOWN 68 INCE ROSE BRIDGE 6

TOWN: 1 Jordan Burns; 5 Ethan Bickerdike; 4 Jason Mossop; 3 Earl Hurst; 2 Sean Sabutey; 6 Ciaran Walker; 15 Fergus Simpson; 8 Jordan Thomson; 9 Matty Henson; 16 JJ Key; 12 Caine Barnes; 11 Malik Steele; 10 Stevie Scholey. Subs (all used): 13 Tom Curwen; 18 Liam McNicholas; 25 Grant Reid; 26 Jack Mallinson.
Tries: Hurst (7, 41), Henson (20), Sabutey (27), Steele (34, 46), J Burns (39), Barnes (52, 64), Key (74), Walker (78, 80); **Goals:** Walker 10/12.
ROSE BRIDGE: 1 Peter Valentine; 2 Kallum Rodgers; 3 Jamie Mallone; 4 Ben Tootle; 5 Ben Holcroft; 16 Keiran Eccleston; 7 Ben Cotterill; 8 Reece Cunningham; 20 Kieran Mallone; 15 Kyle Mallone; 11 Harry Penny; 12 Ben Fisher; 13 Robbie Valentine. Subs (all used): 6 TJ Boyd; 10 Andy Collier; 14 Mason Fillingham; 18 Jack Morrison.
Try: Holcroft (69); **Goals:** R Valentine 1/1.
Rugby Leaguer & League Express Men of the Match:
Town: Malik Steele; *Rose Bridge:* Keiran Eccleston.
Penalty count: 3-9; **Half-time:** 28-0;
Referee: Brad Milligan; **Attendance:** 603.

HULL DOCKERS 4 MIDLANDS HURRICANES 50

DOCKERS: 1 Dan Suddaby; 4 Dylan Rawlings; 3 Chris Heil; 5 Tim Heil; 2 Danny Patrick; 18 Dave Scott; 7 Matty Beharrell; 8 Paul Fletcher; 9 Aaron Pickering; 10 Chris Lyth; 11 Steve Mills; 12 Tom Whur; 13 Louis Sherriff. Subs (all used): 19 Kallum Birch; 17 Callum Taylor; 16 Josh Hamilton; 21 David Bade.
Try: C Heil (20); **Goals:** Suddaby 0/1.
Sin bin: Bade (57) - fighting.
HURRICANES: 1 Nathan Hill; 25 Callum Dunne; 3 Matt Welham; 4 Macauley Hallett; 23 Elliot Wallis; 6 Ben Stead; 7 Richard Wilkinson; 8 Kieran Moran; 14 Chris Cullimore; 10 Matthew Bailey; 24 Bailey Dawson; 12 Liam Welham; 13 Brad Clavering. Subs (all used): 11 Jack Dawson; 18 Sam Bowring; 16 Connor Gilbey; 17 Elliot Windley.
Tries: Bailey (4), Wallis (11), Dunne (14, 77), M Welham (43, 73), B Dawson (45), Hallett (52), L Welham (63); **Goals:** Stead 7/10.
Rugby Leaguer & League Express Men of the Match:
Dockers: Matty Beharrell; *Hurricanes:* Ben Stead.
Penalty count: 8-7; **Half-time:** 4-16;
Referee: Andy Sweet; **Attendance:** 965
(at Sewell Group Craven Park).

DONCASTER 28 OLDHAM 26

DONCASTER: 1 Elliot Hall; 2 Tom Halliday; 21 Brad Hey; 25 Jack Sanderson; 5 Travis Corion; 6 Ben Johnston; 7 Connor Robinson; 18 Jose Kenga; 16 Dave Petersen; 14 Dean Roberts; 11 Sam Smeaton; 27 Brett Ferres; 15 Alex Holdstock. Subs (all used): 10 Brandan Wilkinson; 17 Matt James; 19 Ross Whitmore; 22 Misi Taulapapa.
Tries: Sanderson (27, 39, 53, 75), Ferres (64);
Goals: Robinson 4/5.
OLDHAM: 1 Gregg McNally; 2 Patrick Ah Van; 22 Calvin Wellington; 29 Alex Sutton; 5 Joe Hartley; 6 Martyn Ridyard; 18 Jordan Paga; 8 Luke Nelmes; 14 Sean Slater; 17 Jack Blagbrough; 11 Ethan Ferry; 12 Zac Baker; 10 Deane Meadows. Subs (all used): 3 Connor Carr; 16 James Thornton; 28 Kieran Tyrer; 32 Harvey Makin.
Tries: Ferry (3), Paga (7), McNally (13), Makin (47);
Goals: Ridyard 5/6.
Sin bin: Thornton (52) - interference.
Rugby Leaguer & League Express Men of the Match:
Doncaster: Jack Sanderson; *Oldham:* Martyn Ridyard.
Penalty count: 7-7; **Half-time:** 12-20;
Referee: Kevin Moore; **Attendance:** 517.

HUNSLET 68 HEWORTH 6

HUNSLET: 1 Jimmy Watson; 2 Jack Render; 3 Adam Ryder; 4 Joe Burton; 25 Dan McGrath; 6 Jake Sweeting; 7 Nathan Conroy; 8 Harvey Hallas; 9 Sam Hallas; 26 Jordan Bull; 11 Josh Jordan-Roberts; 12 Aaron York; 16 Jordan Syme. Subs (all used): 14 Danny Barcoe; 15 Nathan Newbound; 17 Lewis Wray; 22 Liam Carr.
Tries: York (10), Syme (19), Render (23), Ryder (26, 59), Newbound (39), J Burton (41), Jordan-Roberts (46), McGrath (50), Watson (68), H Hallas (70), Barcoe (74);
Goals: Sweeting 10/12.
HEWORTH: 1 Adam Dent; 2 Will Sturdy; 3 Harrison Briggs; 4 George Elliott; 5 George Atang; 6 Danny Allan; 7 Liam Jackson; 8 Joe Hemmings; 9 Jack Earl; 10 Tom Clarke; 14 Tyler Craig; 11 Liam Watling; 13 Liam Richmond. Subs (all used): 12 Jack Sadler; 15 Tom Barron; 16 Joe Fish; 22 Liam Sharples.
Try: Allan (15); **Goals:** Allan 1/1.
Rugby Leaguer & League Express Men of the Match:
Hunslet: Lewis Wray; *Heworth:* Danny Allan.
Penalty count: 4-2; **Half-time:** 28-6;
Referee: Luke Bland; **Attendance:** 556.

Great Britain Police 18 Westgate Common 22

ROUND 3

Saturday 11th March 2023

ORRELL ST JAMES 12 MIDLANDS HURRICANES 19

ST JAMES: 1 Sean Findlow; 2 Liam McLoughlin; 3 Callum Taylor; 4 Owen Morris; 5 Jack Gallagher; 6 Bradley Kelk; 7 Chris Wilson; 8 Tom Whittle; 9 Callum Wood; 10 Kye Siyani; 11 Josh Wilde; 12 Dave Kennedy; 13 Jake Williams. Subs (all used): 14 Tom Derbyshire; 15 Sam Wilson; 16 Adam Ball; 17 Bruce Johnson.
Tries: C Wilson (17, 32); **Goals:** Kelk 2/2.
Dismissal: Williams (78) - retaliation.
Sin bin: Wilde (67) - dangerous challenge;
Williams (67) - dangerous challenge.
HURRICANES: 1 Nathan Hill; 25 Callum Dunne; 3 Matt Welham; 4 Macauley Hallett; 5 Connor Gilbey; 6 Ben Stead; 23 Dan Coates; 8 Kieran Moran; 9 Elliot Windley; 10 Matthew Bailey; 11 Dom Flanagan; 12 Liam Welham; 13 Jack Dawson. Subs (all used): 14 Chris Cullimore; 22 Anesu Mudoti; 16 Jacob Beer; 17 Aaron Willis.
Tries: Dunne (23), Hill (47), M Welham (50);
Goals: Stead 3/4; **Field goal:** Coates (78).
Dismissals: Moran (64) - headbutt;
Flanagan (78) - late challenge on C Wilson.
Sin bin: J Dawson (67) - retaliation.
Rugby Leaguer & League Express Men of the Match:
St James: Chris Wilson; *Hurricanes:* Nathan Hill.
Penalty count: 6-8; **Half-time:** 12-4;
Referee: Matty Lynn; **Attendance:** N/A (not given).

LONDON BRONCOS 32 WHITEHAVEN 10

BRONCOS: 1 Alex Walker; 2 Paul Ulberg; 3 Jarred Bassett; 23 Daniel Hoyes; 4 Dalton Grant; 7 Rian Horsman; 6 Oliver Leyland; 12 Marcus Stock; 9 Sam Davis; 10 Jordan Williams; 11 Will Lovell; 16 Ethan Natoli; 13 Dean Parata. Subs (all used): 14 Bill Leyland; 15 Lewis Bienek; 24 Jenson Monk; 22 Max Allen.
Tries: Bassett (4, 26, 47), B Leyland (33), Stock (35), Horsman (53); **Goals:** O Leyland 4/6.
WHITEHAVEN: 23 Josh Rourke; 2 Dave Eccleston; 3 Chris Taylor; 18 Perry Singleton; 4 Curtis Teare; 1 Sam Freeman; 14 Jamie Doran; 22 Lucas Castle; 15 James Newton; 17 Guy Graham; 11 Connor Holliday; 12 Lachlan Lanskey; 8 Liam McAvoy. Subs (all used): 13 Dion Aiye; 20 Jake Bradley; 21 Marcus O'Brien; 28 Ross Ainley.
Tries: Teare (64), Taylor (72); **Goals:** Freeman 1/2.
Rugby Leaguer & League Express Men of the Match:
Broncos: Jarred Bassett; *Whitehaven:* Sam Freeman.
Penalty count: 4-5; **Half-time:** 22-0;
Referee: Liam Rush; **Attendance:** 347.

Challenge Cup 2023 - Round by Round

WESTS WARRIORS 4 WIDNES VIKINGS 80

WARRIORS: 1 Blake Nahu; 2 Mitch Ingram; 3 James Robertson; 4 Mitch Large; 5 Dan Munt; 6 Peter Henshall; 7 Jack Payne; 8 Louis Robinson; 9 Jake Ritchie; 10 Dom Stock; 11 Sam Griffiths; 12 Mitch Cairns-Nelson; 13 Chris Watkins. Subs (all used): 16 Ben Yerby; 18 Kyle Tucker; 19 Ryan Couch; 24 Aaron Lewis.
Try: Nahu (46); **Goals:** Nahu 0/1.
VIKINGS: 3 Matty Fleming; 24 Ollie Brookes; 2 Ryan Ince; 20 Joe Edge; 25 Brad Holroyd; 6 Danny Craven; 18 Joe Lyons; 16 Callum Field; 14 Jordan Johnstone; 23 Will Tilleke; 19 Olly Davies; 12 Adam Lawton; 22 Aaron Brown. Subs: 1 Jack Owens (not used); 9 Matty Fozard; 11 Sam Wilde; 27 Anthony Walker.
Tries: Edge (10, 79), Holroyd (15, 64), Brookes (19, 53), Field (24), Brown (27, 56), Davies (31), Fleming (34, 74), Ince (39, 60), Walker (50); **Goals:** Edge 10/15.
Rugby Leaguer & League Express Men of the Match: *Warriors:* Jack Payne; *Vikings:* Joe Lyons.
Penalty count: 1-1; **Half-time:** 0-42;
Referee: Ryan Cox; **Attendance:** 843 *(at DCBL Stadium)*.

Leigh Miners Rangers 10 Rochdale Mayfield 38
Westgate Common 12 Hunslet ARLFC 15

Sunday 12th March 2023

STANNINGLEY 16 NEWCASTLE THUNDER 58

STANNINGLEY: 1 Adam Butterill; 2 Dylan MacAndrew; 3 Nathan Currie; 4 Dean Parker; 5 Carl McGuigan; 6 Harris Davison; 7 Will Baker; 8 Jamaine Ruan; 9 Josh Adams; 10 Sam Savage; 11 Jack Sykes; 12 Sam Moorhouse; 13 Jack Flanagan. Subs (all used): 15 Danny Salkeld; 16 Nathan Simpson; 17 Glenn Metcalfe; 20 Stephen Welton.
Tries: Sykes (56, 66), Simpson (71); **Goals:** Parker 2/3.
Sin bin: Sykes (2) - fighting.
THUNDER: 1 Jack Johnson; 5 Alex Clegg; 11 Alex Foster; 21 Evan Lawther; 2 Alex Young; 27 Jack Miller; 7 Nikau Williams; 8 Jay Chapelhow; 9 Curtis Davies; 10 Mitch Clark; 13 Connor Bailey; 12 Brad Gallagher; 23 Connor Moore. Subs (all used): 25 Max Flanagan; 15 Ted Chapelhow; 16 Rhys Clarke; 17 Rob Tuliatu.
Tries: Moore (5), Foster (8), Clegg (13, 27, 29), Johnson (15, 32), Bailey (40), Miller (62), Lawther (74), Flanagan (80); **Goals:** Williams 2/5, Miller 5/6.
Rugby Leaguer & League Express Men of the Match: *Stanningley:* Jack Sykes; *Thunder:* Brad Gallagher.
Penalty count: 9-13; **Half-time:** 0-40;
Referee: Luke Bland; **Attendance:** N/A (not given).

**THATTO HEATH CRUSADERS 10
NORTH WALES CRUSADERS 18**

THATTO HEATH: 1 Ryan Wood; 2 Dan McGahan; 3 Adam Saunders; 4 David Pike; 5 Nathan Taylor; 6 Jack Jones; 7 Harry Reardon; 8 Max Dudley; 9 Sean Kenny; 10 Jamie Tracey; 11 Reece Sumner; 12 Connor Dwyer; 13 Adam Hesketh. Subs (all used): 14 Josh Crehan; 15 Tom Yates; 16 Adam Carr; 17 Robbie Ascroft.
Tries: Carr (51), Pike (71); **Goals:** Jones 1/2.
NORTH WALES: 1 Owain Abel; 24 Dante Morley-Samuels; 4 Matt Reid; 3 Declan Hulme; 22 Brandon Wood; 6 Dave Gibbons; 28 Brad Billsborough; 10 Jordan Andrade; 20 Pat Rainford; 17 Chris Barratt; 14 Kieran Taylor; 21 Ryan Ellis; 26 Carl Forster. Subs (all used): 13 Matt Fletcher; 15 Brad Brennan; 16 Jack Houghton; 19 Shaun Costello.
Tries: Andrade (3), Gibbons (45), Ellis (77);
Goals: Billsborough 1/1, Gibbons 2/3.
Rugby Leaguer & League Express Men of the Match: *Thatto Heath:* David Pike; *North Wales:* Carl Forster.
Penalty count: 7-7; **Half-time:** 0-6;
Referee: Scott Mikalauskas; **Attendance:** N/A (not given).

BATLEY BULLDOGS 60 WATH BROW HORNETS 0

BULLDOGS: 21 Aidan McGowan; 22 Dale Morton; 4 Josh Hodson; 3 Kieran Buchanan; 5 Johnny Campbell; 6 Ben White; 14 James Meadows; 8 Adam Gledhill; 24 Ben Kaye; 30 Martyn Reilly; 11 Dane Manning; 12 Lucas Walshaw; 26 Nyle Flynn. Subs (all used): 28 Oli Burton; 19 Tom Lillycrop; 25 Toby Richardson; 20 Samy Kibula.
Tries: Gledhill (15), Kaye (20), Morton (25, 53), Hodson (27, 32, 60, 67), White (45), Buchanan (70), Burton (80); **Goals:** Meadows 7/10, Morton 1/1.
HORNETS: 1 Cole Walker-Taylor; 2 Morgan McCourt; 4 Greg Howland; 3 Jay Weatherill; 5 Sam Curwen; 6 Fran King; 7 Dan Burns; 10 Jake Pearce; 9 Owen McCartney; 8 Callum Farrer; 11 Jake Moore; 12 Clarke Riley; 13 Charlie Tomlinson. Subs (all used): 20 Dave Bradley; 24 James Dixon; 23 Sam Fulton; 17 Greg Rooney.
Rugby Leaguer & League Express Men of the Match: *Bulldogs:* Josh Hodson; *Hornets:* Callum Farrer.
Penalty count: 2-2; **Half-time:** 26-0;
Referee: Brad Milligan; **Attendance:** 493.

DEWSBURY RAMS 38 ROCHDALE HORNETS 18

RAMS: 1 Owen Restall; 2 Lewis Carr; 21 Caelum Jordan; 3 Ollie Greensmith; 19 Simon Frewin; 26 Bailey O'Connor; 7 Calum Turner; 8 Jimmy Beckett; 9 Reiss Butterworth; 20 Jackson Walker; 11 Connor Davies; 18 Brad Graham; 17 Elliot Morris. Subs (all used): 14 Sam Day; 15 Ronan Dixon; 22 Jack Coventry; 25 Tom Wilkinson.
Tries: Graham (4, 22, 26), Turner (16), Day (50), Davies (68), Greensmith (77); **Goals:** Turner 5/7.
HORNETS: 20 Callum Green; 2 Cian Tyrer; 4 Ben O'Keefe; 11 Dan Brewin; 24 Andy Clarke; 6 Lewis Else; 7 Dave Hewitt; 8 Zach Braham; 9 Cameron Berry; 10 Ben Killan; 35 Connor Ratcliffe; 12 Duane Straugheir; 13 Connor Aspey. Subs (all used): 14 Aiden Roden; 18 Jack Arnold; 27 Toby Brannan; 19 Ewan Badham.
Tries: Roden (46), Green (58), Brannan (63);
Goals: Hewitt 3/3.
Sin bin: Killan (52) - high tackle;
Roden (56) - late challenge.
Rugby Leaguer & League Express Men of the Match: *Rams:* Calum Turner; *Hornets:* Jack Arnold.
Penalty count: 9-7; **Half-time:** 20-0;
Referee: Cameron Worsley; **Attendance:** 445.

SIDDAL 12 SHEFFIELD EAGLES 34

SIDDAL: 1 Benjamin West; 2 Jamie Stringer; 3 Alex Chatterton; 4 Henry Turner; 5 Ethan Bush; 6 Richard Pogson; 7 Christian Ackroyd; 8 Daniel Williams; 9 Daniel May; 10 Toby Muscat-Baron; 11 Conner MacCallum; 12 Oliver Waite; 13 Josh Milnes. Subs (all used): 14 Edward Ainley; 15 Keenan Ramsden; 16 Canaan Smithies; 17 Mark Boothroyd.
Tries: Turner (23), Pogson (44); **Goals:** Pogson 2/2.
EAGLES: 1 Josh Guzdek; 22 Matty Chrimes; 21 Ryan Johnson; 23 Bayley Liu; 5 Jason Bass; 32 Cory Aston; 19 Jack Hansen; 16 Blake Broadbent; 13 Evan Hodgson; 10 Tyler Dickinson; 11 Connor Bower; 27 Jesse Sene-Lefao; 14 Titus Gwaze. Subs (all used): 4 Ross Oakes; 20 Lewis Peachey; 24 Oliver Roberts; 25 Joe Hird.
Tries: Johnson (19), Peachey (28), Bass (57, 63, 74), Hansen (66); **Goals:** Aston 5/6.
Rugby Leaguer & League Express Men of the Match: *Siddal:* Richard Pogson; *Eagles:* Jason Bass.
Penalty count: 5-3; **Half-time:** 6-12;
Referee: Kevin Moore; **Attendance:** N/A (not given).

BARROW RAIDERS 32 SWINTON LIONS 14

RAIDERS: 24 Luke Broadbent; 2 Shane Toal; 4 Greg Worthington; 3 Rio-Osayomwanbo Corkill; 5 Ryan Shaw; 7 Ryan Johnston; 6 Jarrod Sammut; 8 Greg Burke; 23 Connor Saunders; 10 Anton Iaria; 21 Tom Hopkins; 11 Danny Langtree; 13 Jack Wells. Subs (all used): 14 Jake Carter; 20 Ben Evans; 15 Ellis Gillam; 16 Sam Brooks.
Tries: Langtree (20), Shaw (24), Johnston (44), Evans (48), Broadbent (73); **Goals:** Shaw 6/6.
LIONS: 1 Dan Abram; 28 Callum Hughes; 11 Rhodri Lloyd; 22 Andy Badrock; 4 Jayden Hatton; 23 Joe Lowe; 7 Jordy Gibson; 15 Jordan Case; 6 Nick Gregson; 18 Liam Cooper; 10 Kenny Baker; 12 Mitch Cox; 13 Louis Brogan. Subs (all used): 9 Luke Waterworth; 20 Morgan Burgess; 25 Scott Parnaby; 35 Lewis Hall.
Tries: Lloyd (2, 12), Baker (79); **Goals:** Abram 1/3.
Sin bin: Lloyd (37) - holding down.
Rugby Leaguer & League Express Men of the Match: *Raiders:* Luke Broadbent; *Lions:* Louis Brogan.
Penalty count: 6-5; **Half-time:** 14-10;
Referee: James Vella; **Attendance:** 1,161.

BRADFORD BULLS 62 YORK ACORN 6

BULLS: 26 George Flanagan Jr; 30 Jayden Myers; 3 Joe Arundel; 4 Kieran Gill; 5 David Foggin-Johnston; 25 Myles Lawford; 6 Dec Patton; 18 Keven Appo; 9 George Flanagan; 17 Josh Johnson; 12 Chester Butler; 15 AJ Wallace; 16 Brad Foster. Subs (all used): 8 Jordan Baldwinson; 32 Marcus Green; 14 Ebon Scurr; 21 Fenton Rogers.
Tries: Foster (3), Flanagan Jr (12), Gill (15, 37, 57), Scurr (34, 50), Lawford (53), Appo (63), Myers (74), Patton (78); **Goals:** Patton 5/6, Flanagan Jr 4/5.
Sin bin: Rogers (39) - use of the elbow.
ACORN: 19 Josh Parker; 5 Ben Tenge; 3 Jordan Myers; 4 Ryan Gallagher; 2 Ben Dale; 6 Anthony Chilton; 7 Nathan Conroy; 8 Tim Stubbs; 9 Nick Speck; 10 Elliot Bulmer; 11 George Hunt; 12 Jordan Hyde; 13 Tom Holder. Subs (all used): 14 Danny Byworth; 18 Chris Rushworth; 15 Jack Byrnes; 21 Matt Wood.
Try: Stubbs (10); **Goals:** Chilton 1/1.
Rugby Leaguer & League Express Men of the Match: *Bulls:* Ebon Scurr; *Acorn:* George Hunt.
Penalty count: 6-3; **Half-time:** 30-6;
Referee: Aaryn Belafonte; **Attendance:** 1,143.

DONCASTER 24 WORKINGTON TOWN 20

DONCASTER: 1 Elliot Hall; 2 Tom Halliday; 11 Sam Smeaton; 22 Misi Taulapapa; 25 Jack Sanderson; - Jack Potter; 7 Connor Robinson; 8 Keelan Foster; 9 Greg Burns; 15 Alex Holdstock; 27 Brett Ferres; 12 Aaron Ollett-Hobson; 20 Brad Knowles. Subs (all used): 10 Brandan Wilkinson; 13 Loui McConnell; 14 Dean Roberts; 19 Ross Whitmore.
Tries: Halliday (38, 80), Robinson (40), Hall (63);
Goals: Robinson 4/4.
TOWN: 1 Jordan Burns; 5 Ethan Bickerdike; 4 Jason Mossop; 3 Earl Hurst; 2 Sean Sabutey; 6 Ciaran Walker; 26 Jack Mallinson; 8 Jordan Thomson; 9 Matty Henson; 16 JJ Key; 20 Jack Stephenson; 11 Malik Steele; 10 Stevie Scholey. Subs (all used): 13 Tom Curwen; 15 Fergus Simpson; 17 Joe Kirkup; 25 Grant Reid.
Tries: Walker (15), Sabutey (17, 51, 67); **Goals:** Walker 2/4.
Rugby Leaguer & League Express Men of the Match: *Doncaster:* Connor Robinson; *Town:* Sean Sabutey.
Penalty count: 4-7; **Half-time:** 12-12;
Referee: Nick Bennett; **Attendance:** 485.

FEATHERSTONE ROVERS 18 HALIFAX PANTHERS 22

ROVERS: 4 Craig Hall; 2 Luke Briscoe; 21 Joey Leilua; 18 Josh Hardcastle; 5 Gareth Gale; 25 Thomas Lacans; 14 Matty Wildie; 17 Gadwin Springer; 9 Connor Jones; 24 Mathieu Cozza; 11 Brad Day; 13 Jack Bussey; 12 Elijah Taylor. Subs (all used): 15 John Davies; 16 Junior Moors; 22 Dan Fleming; 27 McKenzie Yei.
Tries: Hardcastle (9), Lacans (44), Springer (63);
Goals: Hall 3/3.
Dismissal: Hardcastle (75) - kicking.
PANTHERS: 1 James Woodburn-Hall; 2 Lachlan Walmsley; 22 Jake Maizen; 3 Zack McComb; 5 James Saltonstall; 6 Louis Jouffret; 7 Joe Keyes; 15 Will Maher; 9 Brandon Moore; 10 Dan Murray; 11 Ben Kavanagh; 12 Matty Gee; 13 Jacob Fairbank. Subs (all used): 8 Adam Tangata; 16 Will Calcott; 20 Tom Inman; 21 Eribe Doro.
Tries: Gee (15), Walmsley (21), Inman (55), Jouffret (73);
Goals: Keyes 0/2, Jouffret 3/4.
Rugby Leaguer & League Express Men of the Match: *Rovers:* Gadwin Springer; *Panthers:* Louis Jouffret.
Penalty count: 8-7; **Half-time:** 6-10;
Referee: Liam Moore; **Attendance:** 1,487.

HUNSLET 14 KEIGHLEY COUGARS 16

HUNSLET: 1 Jimmy Watson; 2 Jack Render; 3 Adam Ryder; 4 Joe Burton; 25 Dan McGrath; 13 Michael Knowles; 21 Morgan Punchard; 8 Harvey Hallas; 9 Sam Hallas; 26 Jordan Bull; 11 Josh Jordan-Roberts; 12 Aaron York; 16 Jordan Syme. Subs (all used): 15 Nathan Newbound; 17 Lewis Wray; 18 Harvey Whiteley; 28 Brad Wheeler.
Tries: Ryder (40), Wheeler (64), J Burton (71);
Goals: Punchard 0/2, Knowles 1/1.
Sin bin: S Hallas (35) - kicking.
COUGARS: 1 Lewis Young; 5 Mo Agoro; 23 Robbie Storey; 3 Charlie Graham; 17 Keenan Dyer-Dixon; 2 Alix Stephenson; 9 Billy Gaylor; 15 Brenden Santi; 26 Thomas Doyle; 24 Mark Ioane; 28 Keenen Tomlinson; 8 Dan Parker; 13 Kyle Kesik. Subs (all used): 4 Nathan Roebuck; 10 Toby Everett; 12 Aaron Levy; 14 Harvey Spence.
Tries: Stephenson (7), Storey (37), Levy (55);
Goals: Young 2/2, Spence 0/1.
Dismissal: Young (50) - punching.
Rugby Leaguer & League Express Men of the Match: *Hunslet:* Michael Knowles; *Cougars:* Billy Gaylor.
Penalty count: 7-4; **Half-time:** 4-12;
Referee: Matt Rossleigh; **Attendance:** 519.

YORK KNIGHTS 52 WEST BOWLING 12

KNIGHTS: 2 Joe Brown; 25 Brad Ward; 11 Chris Clarkson; 15 Myles Harrison; 5 AJ Towse; 1 Matty Marsh; 7 Liam Harris; 16 Bailey Antrobus; 19 Josh Daley; 24 Ben Barnard; 4 Jesse Dee; 12 Danny Kirmond; 17 Ronan Michael. Subs (all used): 9 Will Jubb; 20 Jack Teanby; 21 Ukuma Ta'ai; 27 Harry Price.
Tries: Harris (5, 39), Towse (9), Marsh (13), Ward (23, 52), Brown (27), Antrobus (48, 76), Kirmond (73);
Goals: Harris 6/11.
WEST BOWLING: 1 Max Trueman; 2 Lewis Taylor; 3 Bradley Wright; 4 Daniel Gregory; 5 Owen Simpson; 6 Harry Williams; 7 Liam Coe; 8 Josh Lynam; 9 Kyle Carter; 10 Oliver Bartle; 11 Richard Lumb; 12 Jack Milburn; 13 Elliott Cousins. Subs (all used): 14 Liam Darville; 15 Nathaniel Light; 16 Ben Heald; 17 Lewis Galtress.
Tries: Trueman (16), Bartle (63); **Goals:** Williams 2/2.
Sin bin: Trueman (66) - high tackle.
Rugby Leaguer & League Express Men of the Match: *Knights:* Bailey Antrobus; *West Bowling:* Oliver Bartle.
Penalty count: 6-3; **Half-time:** 32-6;
Referee: Andy Sweet; **Attendance:** 1,040.

ROUND 4

Saturday 1st April 2023

ROCHDALE MAYFIELD 12 NEWCASTLE THUNDER 22

MAYFIELD: 1 Lewis Butterworth; 2 Jordan Parr; 3 James McDaid; 4 Dakota Tolhurst; 5 Wayne English; 6 Sam Wright; 7 Devlin Long; 18 Luke Fowden; 9 Sean Penkywicz; 10 Seta Tala; 11 Travis Long; 19 Ben Metcalfe; 13 Callum Ogden. Subs (all used): 14 Dec Sheridan; 15 Nick Hargreaves; 17 David Mills; 20 Joe Taira.
Tries: Metcalfe (7), Parr (76); **Goals:** D Long 2/2.
THUNDER: 25 Max Flanagan; 1 Jack Johnson; 5 Alex Clegg; 3 Marcus Walker; 2 Alex Young; 6 Alex Donaghy; 27 Jack Miller; 15 Ted Chapelhow; 9 Curtis Davies; 17 Rob Tuliatu; 13 Connor Bailey; 12 Brad Gallagher; 16 Rhys Clarke. Subs (all used): 8 Jay Chapelhow; 10 Mitch Clark; 22 Jake Anderson; 23 Connor Moore.
Tries: Johnson (12), Young (14), T Chapelhow (20), Moore (38); **Goals:** Miller 3/4.
Rugby Leaguer & League Express Men of the Match: *Mayfield:* Lewis Butterworth; *Thunder:* Alex Donaghy.
Penalty count: 1-7; **Half-time:** 6-22;
Referee: Nick Bennett; **Attendance:** N/A (not given).

KEIGHLEY COUGARS 36 NORTH WALES CRUSADERS 14

COUGARS: 1 Lewis Young; 17 Keenan Dyer-Dixon; 8 Dan Parker; 23 Robbie Storey; 5 Mo Agoro; 2 Alix Stephenson; 9 Billy Gaylor; 15 Brenden Santi; 26 Thomas Doyle; 24 Mark Ioane; 12 Aaron Levy; 29 Joe Gibbons; 14 Harvey Spence. Subs (all used): 10 Toby Everett; 13 Kyle Kesik; 19 Ellis Robson; 27 Sadiq Adebiyi.
Tries: Dyer-Dixon (2, 34), Agoro (20, 77), Gaylor (24), Doyle (52), Young (67); **Goals:** Parker 2/5, Spence 2/2.
CRUSADERS: 1 Owain Abel; 22 Brandon Wood; 14 Kieran Taylor; 4 Matt Reid; 24 Dante Morley-Samuels; 9 Brad Jinks; 13 Matt Fletcher; 10 Jordan Andrade; 20 Pat Rainford; 8 Callum Hazzard; 17 Chris Barratt; 21 Ryan Ellis; 19 Shaun Costello. Subs (all used): 16 Jack Houghton; 15 Brad Brennan; 29 Jacob Bloxham; 28 Alfie Matthias.
Tries: Morley-Samuels (16, 56), Taylor (72); **Goals:** Abel 1/3.
Sin bin: Hazzard (51) - dissent.
Rugby Leaguer & League Express Men of the Match: *Cougars:* Lewis Young; *Crusaders:* Owain Abel.
Penalty count: 4-1; **Half-time:** 18-6;
Referee: Michael Smaill; **Attendance:** 862.

LONDON BRONCOS 66 DONCASTER 16

BRONCOS: 1 Alex Walker; 2 Paul Ulberg; 3 Jarred Bassett; 4 Dalton Grant; 5 Iliess Macani; 6 Oliver Leyland; 7 Rian Horsman; 8 Wellington Albert; 14 Bill Leyland; 10 Jordan Williams; 11 Will Lovell; 16 Ethan Natoli; 13 Dean Parata. Subs (all used): 12 Marcus Stock; 18 Emmanuel Waine; 26 Euan Parke; 27 Ramon Silva.
Tries: B Leyland (5), O Leyland (9, 53), Ulberg (23, 72), Grant (45), Macani (50), Waine (55), Horsman (60), Parata (63), Silva (75), Albert (77); **Goals:** O Leyland 9/12.
DONCASTER: 1 Elliot Hall; 2 Tom Halliday; 21 Brad Hey; 25 Jack Sanderson; 5 Travis Corion; 13 Loui McConnell; 6 Ben Johnston; 18 Jose Kenga; 19 Ross Whitmore; 10 Brandan Wilkinson; 12 Aaron Ollett-Hobson; 11 Sam Smeaton; 15 Alex Holdstock. Subs (all used): 4 Jason Tali; 8 Keelan Foster; 14 Dean Roberts; 24 Luke Cooper.
Tries: Hey (14), Corion (17), Ollett-Hobson (35);
Goals: Sanderson 2/3.
Rugby Leaguer & League Express Men of the Match: *Broncos:* Oliver Leyland; *Doncaster:* Sam Smeaton.
Penalty count: 3-3; **Half-time:** 16-16;
Referee: Scott Mikalauskas; **Attendance:** 428
(at The Rock, Roehampton).

Sunday 2nd April 2023

YORK KNIGHTS 24 SHEFFIELD EAGLES 22

KNIGHTS: 2 Joe Brown; 15 Myles Harrison; 29 Connor Barley; 3 James Glover; 5 AJ Towse; 1 Matty Marsh; 7 Liam Harris; 16 Bailey Antrobus; 9 Will Jubb; 10 Conor Fitzsimmons; 32 Oli Field; 12 Danny Kirmond; 13 Jordan Thompson. Subs (all used): 17 Ronan Michael; 19 Josh Daley; 20 Jack Teanby; 21 Ukuma Ta'ai.
Tries: Harrison (3), Kirmond (7, 10), Fitzsimmons (22), Towse (57); **Goals:** Glover 2/6.
Dismissal: Kirmond (30) - late challenge on Aston.
EAGLES: 2 Ben Jones-Bishop; 22 Matty Chrimes; 3 Kris Welham; 4 Ross Oakes; 5 Jason Bass; 32 Cory Aston; 7 Anthony Thackeray; 8 Brandon Douglas; 9 Vila Halafihi; 10 Tyler Dickinson; 24 Oliver Roberts; 27 Jesse Sene-Lefao; 14 Titus Gwaze. Subs (all used): 15 Mikey Wood; 23 Bayley Liu; 12 Joel Farrell; 13 Evan Hodgson.
Tries: Welham (50), Aston (53), Bass (64), Chrimes (75);
Goals: Aston 3/4.
Rugby Leaguer & League Express Men of the Match: *Knights:* Bailey Antrobus; *Eagles:* Cory Aston.
Penalty count: 3-5; **Half-time:** 20-0;
Referee: James Vella; **Attendance:** 832.

HUNSLET ARLFC 6 BATLEY BULLDOGS 80

HUNSLET ARLFC: 1 Jake Dearden; 2 Tyler Dargan; 3 Tom Daley; 4 Omar Alrawi; 5 Will Cohen; 6 Jordan Gale; 7 Josh Perkins; 17 Moris Kamano; 20 Matthew Scott; 10 James Mulvany; 11 Dewi Billingham; 12 Micky Hoyle; 13 George Clarke. Subs (all used): 14 Thomas Boardman; 15 Joe Taylor; 16 Jack Briggs; 8 Elliot Morgan.
Try: Billingham (54); **Goals:** Gale 1/1.
BULLDOGS: 21 Aidan McGowan; 22 Dale Morton; 4 Josh Hodson; 15 Elliot Kear; 5 Johnny Campbell; 14 James Meadows; 6 Ben White; 8 Adam Gledhill; 9 Alistair Leak; 13 James Brown; 3 Kieran Buchanan; 12 Lucas Walshaw; 30 Martyn Reilly. Subs (all used): 7 Josh Woods; 19 Tom Lillycrop; 20 Samy Kibula; 26 Nyle Flynn.
Tries: McGowan (2, 35), White (11, 16), Hodson (14, 24, 46, 75), Morton (19, 67, 70), Flynn (29), Meadows (59, 62), Woods (80); **Goals:** Meadows 10/15.
Rugby Leaguer & League Express Men of the Match: *Hunslet ARLFC:* Jordan Gale; *Bulldogs:* James Meadows.
Penalty count: 4-6; **Half-time:** 0-44;
Referee: Brad Milligan; **Attendance:** 579
(at Fox's Biscuits Stadium).

DEWSBURY RAMS 32 WIDNES VIKINGS 12

RAMS: 1 Owen Restall; 2 Lewis Carr; 26 Bailey O'Connor; 3 Ollie Greensmith; 23 Perry Whiteley; 6 Paul Sykes; 7 Calum Turner; 8 Jimmy Beckett; 9 Reiss Butterworth; 15 Ronan Dixon; 12 Matt Garside; 18 Brad Graham; 11 Connor Davies. Subs (all used): 14 Sam Day; 17 Elliot Morris; 20 Jackson Walker; 28 Luke Littlewood.
Tries: Carr (27), Butterworth (37, 58), Greensmith (45), R Dixon (74); **Goals:** Sykes 6/6.
VIKINGS: 3 Matty Fleming; 2 Ryan Ince; 11 Sam Wilde; 20 Joe Edge; 5 Kieran Dixon; 1 Jack Owens; 18 Joe Lyons; 16 Callum Field; 9 Matty Fozard; 27 Anthony Walker; 12 Adam Lawton; 17 Shane Grady; 13 Liam Bent. Subs (all used): 8 Owen Farnworth; 10 Kyle Amor; 22 Aaron Brown; 24 Ollie Brookes.
Tries: Fozard (17), Lawton (43); **Goals:** Owens 2/3.
Sin bin: Lyons (69) - professional foul.
Rugby Leaguer & League Express Men of the Match: *Rams:* Reiss Butterworth; *Vikings:* Shane Grady.
Penalty count: 6-4; **Half-time:** 12-8;
Referee: Liam Rush; **Attendance:** 802.

HALIFAX PANTHERS 24 BARROW RAIDERS 18

PANTHERS: 1 James Woodburn-Hall; 4 Ben Tibbs; 22 Jake Maizen; 3 Zack McComb; 5 James Saltonstall; 6 Louis Jouffret; 7 Joe Keyes; 15 Will Maher; 9 Brandon Moore; 10 Dan Murray; 11 Ben Kavanagh; 12 Matty Gee; 8 Adam Tangata. Subs (all used): 20 Tom Inman; 21 Eribe Doro; 16 Will Calcott; 24 Cole Oakley.
Tries: Saltonstall (2, 69), Maizen (10), Jouffret (30), Doro (60); **Goals:** Keyes 2/5.
RAIDERS: 1 Luke Cresswell; 27 Andrew Bulman; 4 Greg Worthington; 3 Rio-Osayomwanbo Corkill; 2 Shane Toal; 14 Jake Carter; 6 Jarrod Sammut; 15 Ellis Gillam; 22 Josh Wood; 10 Anton Iaria; 11 Danny Langtree; 12 Jarrad Stack; 13 Jack Wells. Subs (all used): 26 Hanley Dawson; 17 Charlie Emslie; 16 Sam Brooks; 20 Ben Evans.
Tries: Langtree (42, 78), Corkill (73); **Goals:** Sammut 3/3.
Sin bin: Wood (29) - dangerous challenge on Doro.
Rugby Leaguer & League Express Men of the Match: *Panthers:* Will Calcott; *Raiders:* Danny Langtree.
Penalty count: 7-4; **Half-time:** 14-0;
Referee: Tom Grant; **Attendance:** 1,474.

MIDLANDS HURRICANES 18 BRADFORD BULLS 66

HURRICANES: 1 Nathan Hill; 25 Callum Dunne; 3 Matt Welham; 4 Macauley Hallett; 23 Joey Romeo; 6 Ben Stead; 14 Chris Cullimore; 8 Kieran Moran; 9 Elliot Windley; 18 Sam Bowring; 17 Dom Flanagan; 22 Aaron Willis; 15 Tyler Hepple. Subs (all used): 16 Connor Gilbey; 24 Bailey Dawson; 11 Jack Dawson; 10 Matthew Bailey.
Tries: M Welham (8), Moran (24), Dunne (66);
Goals: Stead 3/3.
BULLS: 20 Billy Jowitt; 2 Ben Blackmore; 3 Joe Arundel; 30 Jayden Myers; 5 David Foggin-Johnston; 25 Myles Lawford; 1 Tom Holmes; 8 Jordan Baldwinson; 7 Jordan Lilley; 14 Ebon Scurr; 18 Keven Appo; 12 Chester Butler; 16 Brad Foster. Subs: 39 Jansin Turgut; 17 Josh Johnson; 21 Fenton Rogers; 15 AJ Wallace (not used).
Tries: Holmes (12, 76), C Butler (34, 40, 41), Arundel (43), Jowitt (50, 59), Lawford (55), Rogers (66), Appo (79);
Goals: Lawford 11/11.
Rugby Leaguer & League Express Men of the Match: *Hurricanes:* Ben Stead; *Bulls:* Tom Holmes.
Penalty count: 4-9; **Half-time:** 12-18;
Referee: Cameron Worsley; **Attendance:** 1,003
(at Odsal Stadium).

ROUND 5

Friday 21st April 2023

YORK KNIGHTS 22 NEWCASTLE THUNDER 18

KNIGHTS: 1 Matty Marsh; 2 Joe Brown; 3 James Glover; 16 Bailey Antrobus; 5 AJ Towse; 14 James Cunningham; 7 Liam Harris; 8 Jon Luke Kirby; 9 Will Jubb; 21 Ukuma Ta'ai; 11 Chris Clarkson; 32 Oli Field; 13 Jordan Thompson. Subs (all used): 15 Myles Harrison; 17 Ronan Michael; 19 Josh Daley; 20 Jack Teanby.
Tries: Brown (17), Towse (45), Marsh (47), Harris (64);
Goals: Glover 3/4.
THUNDER: 6 Alex Donaghy; 1 Jack Johnson; 3 Marcus Walker; 26 Mac Walsh; 5 Alex Clegg; 7 Nikau Williams; 27 Jack Miller; 8 Jay Chapelhow; 9 Curtis Davies; 23 Connor Moore; 17 Rob Tuliatu; 13 Connor Bailey; 16 Rhys Clarke. Subs (all used): 15 Ted Chapelhow; 18 Jake Lightowler; 24 Daniel Okoro; 25 Max Flanagan.
Tries: Walker (24), Miller (34), Walsh (53);
Goals: Williams 3/3.
Rugby Leaguer & League Express Men of the Match: *Knights:* AJ Towse; *Thunder:* Alex Donaghy.
Penalty count: 3-2; **Half-time:** 4-12;
Referee: Nick Bennett; **Attendance:** 1,100.

Saturday 22nd April 2023

HALIFAX PANTHERS 26 BRADFORD BULLS 0

PANTHERS: 1 James Woodburn-Hall; 2 Lachlan Walmsley; 22 Jake Maizen; 4 Ben Tibbs; 5 James Saltonstall; 6 Louis Jouffret; 7 Joe Keyes; 16 Will Calcott; 9 Brandon Moore; 10 Dan Murray; 11 Ben Kavanagh; 12 Matty Gee; 13 Jacob Fairbank. Subs (all used): 3 Zack McComb; 8 Adam Tangata; 19 Ryan Lannon; 20 Tom Inman.
Tries: Jouffret (3, 16), Saltonstall (35, 49), Maizen (38);
Goals: Keyes 3/5.
BULLS: 31 Jack Walker; 2 Ben Blackmore; 30 Jayden Myers; 4 Kieran Gill; 37 Jason Qareqare; 1 Tom Holmes; 6 Dec Patton; 21 Fenton Rogers; 7 Jordan Lilley; 14 Ebon Scurr; 18 Keven Appo; 12 Chester Butler; 13 Bodene Thompson. Subs (all used): 16 Brad Foster; 17 Josh Johnson; 20 Billy Jowitt; 29 Rob Butler.
Rugby Leaguer & League Express Men of the Match: *Panthers:* Louis Jouffret; *Bulls:* Billy Jowitt.
Penalty count: 3-2; **Half-time:** 22-0;
Referee: Tom Grant; **Attendance:** 2,146.

Sunday 23rd April 2023

BATLEY BULLDOGS 34 KEIGHLEY COUGARS 16

BULLDOGS: 21 Aidan McGowan; 22 Dale Morton; 4 Josh Hodson; 3 Kieran Buchanan; 15 Elliot Kear; 6 Ben White; 7 Josh Woods; 19 Tom Lillycrop; 24 Ben Kaye; 13 James Brown; 26 Nyle Flynn; 12 Lucas Walshaw; 30 Martyn Reilly. Subs (all used): 14 James Meadows; 8 Adam Gledhill; 16 Michael Ward; 10 Keegan Hirst.
Tries: Walshaw (10, 55), Hodson (36), Morton (40), McGowan (49, 62), Meadows (58);
Goals: Morton 0/1, Meadows 3/6.
COUGARS: 1 Lewis Young; 25 Ben Crooks; 2 Alix Stephenson; 23 Robbie Storey; 3 Charlie Graham; 21 Lloyd Roby; 31 Luke Gale; 15 Brenden Santi; 26 Thomas Doyle; 24 Mark Ioane; 12 Aaron Levy; 27 Sadiq Adebiyi; 14 Harvey Spence. Subs (all used): 20 Brad Walker; 10 Toby Everett; 8 Dan Parker; 13 Kyle Kesik.
Tries: Storey (17), Ioane (68), Parker (75); **Goals:** Gale 2/3.
Rugby Leaguer & League Express Men of the Match: *Bulldogs:* Aidan McGowan; *Cougars:* Mark Ioane.
Penalty count: 4-6; **Half-time:** 14-4;
Referee: James Vella; **Attendance:** 923.

LONDON BRONCOS 36 DEWSBURY RAMS 16

BRONCOS: 1 Alex Walker; 2 Paul Ulberg; 3 Jarred Bassett; 23 Daniel Hoyes; 5 Iliess Macani; 6 Oliver Leyland; 17 Henry Raiwalui; 8 Wellington Albert; 9 Sam Davis; 15 Lewis Bienek; 12 Marcus Stock; 16 Ethan Natoli; 13 Dean Parata. Subs (all used): 14 Bill Leyland; 18 Emmanuel Waine; 26 Euan Parke; 10 Jordan Williams.
Tries: Macani (5, 65), O Leyland (30), Bienek (50), Albert (63), Stock (72), Bassett (80); **Goals:** O Leyland 4/7.
RAMS: 1 Owen Restall; 2 Lewis Carr; 21 Caelum Jordan; 3 Ollie Greensmith; 23 Perry Whiteley; 6 Paul Sykes; 7 Calum Turner; 8 Jimmy Beckett; 9 Reiss Butterworth; 15 Ronan Dixon; 12 Matt Garside; 18 Brad Graham; 11 Connor Davies. Subs (all used): 14 Sam Day; 17 Elliot Morris; 20 Jackson Walker; 28 Luke Littlewood.
Tries: Carr (7, 43), Graham (50); **Goals:** Sykes 2/3.
Sin bin: Whiteley (72) - dissent.
Rugby Leaguer & League Express Men of the Match: *Broncos:* Dean Parata; *Rams:* Lewis Carr.
Penalty count: 3-2; **Half-time:** 10-6;
Referee: Liam Rush; **Attendance:** 353
(at The Rock, Roehampton).

ROUND 6

Friday 19th May 2023

HALIFAX PANTHERS 6 ST HELENS 26

PANTHERS: 1 James Woodburn-Hall; 2 Lachlan Walmsley; 4 Ben Tibbs; 3 Zack McComb; 5 James Saltonstall; 6 Louis Jouffret; 7 Joe Keyes; 16 Will Calcott; 9 Brandon Moore; 10 Dan Murray; 19 Ryan Lannon; 12 Matty Gee; 13 Jacob Fairbank. Subs (all used): 20 Tom Inman; 21 Eribe Doro; 8 Adam Tangata; 31 Kevin Larroyer.
Try: Fairbank (73); **Goals:** Jouffret 1/1.
SAINTS: 1 Jack Welsby; 2 Tommy Makinson; 3 Will Hopoate; 21 Ben Davies; 25 Tee Ritson; 6 Jonny Lomax (C); 7 Lewis Dodd; 8 Alex Walmsley; 14 Joey Lussick; 13 Morgan Knowles; 11 Sione Mata'utia; 12 Joe Batchelor; 19 James Bell. Subs (all used): 5 Jonathan Bennison; 17 Agnatius Paasi; 18 Jake Wingfield; 30 George Delaney.
Tries: Lussick (6, 68), Wingfield (25), Makinson (28), Welsby (44); **Goals:** Makinson 3/5.
Dismissal: Knowles (79) - high tackle on Inman.
Rugby Leaguer & League Express Men of the Match: *Panthers:* James Woodburn-Hall; *Saints:* Jack Welsby.
Penalty count: 4-6; **Half-time:** 0-16;
Referee: Aaron Moore; **Attendance:** 4,693.

WAKEFIELD TRINITY 12 LEIGH LEOPARDS 40

TRINITY: 33 Will Dagger; 5 Tom Lineham; 6 Lee Gaskell; 30 Oliver Pratt (D); 2 Jorge Taufua; 7 Mason Lino; 20 Morgan Smith; 17 Renouf Atoni; 24 Harry Bowes; 16 Josh Bowden; 19 Kevin Proctor; 13 Jay Pitts; 14 Jordan Crowther (C). Subs (all used): 9 Liam Hood; 8 Eddie Battye; 25 Sam Eseh; 26 Dane Windrow (D).
Tries: Pitts (51), Dagger (65); **Goals:** Dagger 2/2.
LEOPARDS: 17 Gareth O'Brien; 2 Tom Briscoe; 1 Zak Hardaker; 4 Ricky Leutele; 5 Josh Charnley; 15 Ben Reynolds; 7 Lachlan Lam; 8 Tom Amone; 9 Edwin Ipape; 10 Robbie Mulhern; 16 Oliver Holmes; 24 Kai O'Donnell; 13 John Asiata (C). Subs (all used): 6 Joe Mellor; 27 Ava Seumanufagai; 18 Matt Davis; 25 Nathan Wilde.
Tries: Briscoe (2, 26), Asiata (10), O'Donnell (33, 55), Leutele (61), Charnley (75); **Goals:** Reynolds 6/7.
Rugby Leaguer & League Express Men of the Match: *Trinity:* Oliver Pratt; *Leopards:* Kai O'Donnell.
Penalty count: 8-6; **Half-time:** 0-22;
Referee: Ben Thaler; **Attendance:** 1,568.

HULL KR 50 BATLEY BULLDOGS 0

HULL KR: 2 Ethan Ryan; 24 Sam Wood; 4 Shaun Kenny-Dowall (C); 3 Tom Opacic; 5 Ryan Hall; 20 Mikey Lewis; 29 Phoenix Laulu-Togaga'e; 22 Dean Hadley; 14 Jez Litten; 15 Rhys Kennedy; 16 James Batchelor; 12 Kane Linnett; 13 Elliot Minchella. Subs (all used): 17 Matty Storton; 18 Jimmy Keinhorst; 26 Sam Luckley; 27 Yusuf Aydin (D).
Tries: Linnett (1, 13), Ryan (7, 19, 72), Kenny-Dowall (22, 33), Lewis (45), Luckley (58); **Goals:** Lewis 5/7, Wood 2/2.
BULLDOGS: 21 Aidan McGowan; 29 Greg Johnson; 3 Kieran Buchanan; 4 Josh Hodson; 5 Johnny Campbell; 6 Ben White; 7 Josh Woods; 8 Adam Gledhill; 24 Ben Kaye; 19 Tom Lillycrop; 11 Dane Manning; 12 Lucas Walshaw; 30 Martyn Reilly. Subs (all used): 14 James Meadows; 16 Michael Ward; 17 Luke Blake; 26 Nyle Flynn.
Rugby Leaguer & League Express Men of the Match: *Hull KR:* Ethan Ryan; *Bulldogs:* James Meadows.
Penalty count: 4-5; **Half-time:** 32-0;
Referee: Tom Grant; **Attendance:** 5,143.

Saturday 20th May 2023

LEEDS RHINOS 14 WIGAN WARRIORS 18

RHINOS: 1 Richie Myler; 23 Liam Tindall; 3 Harry Newman; 4 Nene Macdonald; 16 Derrell Olpherts; 20 Morgan Gannon; 7 Aidan Sezer; 8 Mikolaj Oledzki; 14 Jarrod O'Connor; 18 Tom Holroyd; 12 Rhyse Martin; 19 James McDonnell; 13 Cameron Smith (C). Subs (all used): 15 Sam Lisone; 17 Justin Sangare; 25 James Donaldson; 26 Corey Johnson.
Tries: Holroyd (9), Newman (32); **Goals:** Martin 3/3.
WARRIORS: 2 Bevan French; 23 Abbas Miski; 3 Toby King; 4 Jake Wardle; 5 Liam Marshall; 32 Ryan Hampshire (D2); 7 Harry Smith; 16 Ethan Havard; 9 Sam Powell; 10 Liam Byrne; 13 Morgan Smithies; 12 Liam Farrell (C); 19 Joe Shorrocks. Subs (all used): 15 Kaide Ellis; 20 Patrick Mago; 22 Brad O'Neill; 27 Junior Nsemba.
Tries: French (36, 41), Nsemba (53), Wardle (66); **Goals:** Smith 1/4.
Rugby Leaguer & League Express Men of the Match: *Rhinos:* Tom Holroyd; *Warriors:* Jake Wardle.
Penalty count: 4-4; **Half-time:** 14-4;
Referee: Chris Kendall; **Attendance:** 7,103.

CATALANS DRAGONS 14 WARRINGTON WOLVES 16

DRAGONS: 1 Arthur Mourgue; 19 Arthur Romano; 11 Matt Whitley; 21 Matt Ikuvalu; 24 Tom Johnstone; 7 Mitchell Pearce; 29 Sam Tomkins; 8 Mike McMeeken; 9 Michael McIlorum; 23 Jordan Dezaria; 26 Manu Ma'u; 12 Paul Seguier; 13 Benjamin Garcia (C). Subs: 10 Julian Bousquet; 16 Romain Navarrete; 22 Sio Siua Taukeiaho; 31 Tanguy Zenon (not used).
Tries: Romano (32), Johnstone (53), Ikuvalu (66);
Goals: Mourgue 1/3.
Sin bin: McIlorum (59) - holding down.
WOLVES: 1 Matt Dufty; 2 Josh Thewlis; 3 Peter Mata'utia; 4 Stefan Ratchford (C); 5 Matty Ashton; 6 George Williams; 7 Josh Drinkwater; 19 Joe Bullock; 9 Daryl Clark; 10 Paul Vaughan; 11 Ben Currie; 13 Josh McGuire; 8 James Harrison. Subs (all used): 14 Sam Kasiano; 15 Joe Philbin; 16 Danny Walker; 17 Gil Dudson.
Tries: Ashton (16, 78), Dufty (25); **Goals:** Ratchford 2/3.
Rugby Leaguer & League Express Men of the Match: *Dragons:* Mitchell Pearce; *Wolves:* Matty Ashton.
Penalty count: 4-5; **Half-time:** 6-12;
Referee: Jack Smith; **Attendance:** 5,014.

SALFORD RED DEVILS 42 HUDDERSFIELD GIANTS 40

RED DEVILS: 1 Ryan Brierley; 22 Rhys Williams; 28 Deon Cross; 24 Matthew Costello; 5 Joe Burgess; 6 Brodie Croft; 7 Marc Sneyd; 10 King Vuniyayawa; 14 Chris Atkin; 18 Alex Gerrard; 12 Sam Stone; 3 Kallum Watkins (C); 25 Ben Hellewell. Subs (all used): 13 Oliver Partington; 15 Danny Addy; 16 Tyler Dupree; 20 Ellis Longstaff.
Tries: Costello (4), Gerrard (7), Watkins (19), Williams (23, 64), Burgess (53), Sneyd (67);
Goals: Sneyd 7/7.
GIANTS: 32 Will Pryce; 5 Jake Bibby; 4 Kevin Naiqama; 3 Esan Marsters; 24 Sam Halsall; 1 Jake Connor; 7 Theo Fages; 8 Chris Hill; 19 Adam O'Brien; 20 Oliver Wilson; 29 Sam Hewitt; 21 Leroy Cudjoe; 16 Harry Rushton. Subs (all used): 6 Tui Lolohea; 10 Joe Greenwood; 13 Luke Yates (C); 18 Sebastine Ikahihifo.
Tries: Hewitt (29), Yates (32, 46, 79), Bibby (39), Lolohea (70), Naiqama (75); **Goals:** Connor 6/7.
Rugby Leaguer & League Express Men of the Match: *Red Devils:* Marc Sneyd; *Giants:* Luke Yates.
Penalty count: 6-6; **Half-time:** 24-16;
Referee: Marcus Griffiths; **Attendance:** 2,872.

Sunday 21st May 2023

CASTLEFORD TIGERS 8 HULL FC 32

TIGERS: 17 Jack Broadbent; 4 Mahe Fonua; 15 Alex Sutcliffe; 3 Jordan Turner; 39 Will Tate; 13 Joe Westerman; 9 Paul McShane (C); 14 Nathan Massey; 8 George Lawler; 23 Suaia Matagi; 25 Brad Martin; 12 Alex Mellor; 28 Sam Hall. Subs (all used): 10 George Griffin; 24 Cain Robb; 20 Muizz Mustapha; 30 Jacob Hookem (D).
Tries: Fonua (36), Tate (68);
Goals: McShane 0/1, Hookem 0/1.
HULL FC: 1 Tex Hoy; 2 Adam Swift; 4 Liam Sutcliffe; 3 Carlos Tuimavave (C); 17 Cameron Scott; 6 Jake Trueman; 7 Jake Clifford; 13 Brad Fash; 9 Danny Houghton; 10 Tevita Satae; 23 Josh Griffin; 12 Jordan Lane; 15 Joe Cator. Subs (all used): 20 Jack Brown; 33 Brad Dwyer; 31 Nick Staveley (D); 27 Will Gardiner.
Tries: Griffin (8), Swift (23, 28, 60), Brown (31), Lane (44);
Goals: Clifford 4/6.
Sin bin: Griffin (74) - dissent.
Rugby Leaguer & League Express Men of the Match: *Tigers:* Paul McShane; *Hull FC:* Jake Clifford.
Penalty count: 6-5; **Half time:** 4-22;
Referee: Liam Moore; **Attendance:** 4,249.

YORK KNIGHTS 36 LONDON BRONCOS 12

KNIGHTS: 2 Joe Brown; 5 AJ Towse; 3 James Glover; 4 Jesse Dee; 23 Olly Butterworth; 14 James Cunningham; 19 Josh Daley; 13 Jordan Thompson; 9 Will Jubb; 17 Ronan Michael; 11 Chris Clarkson; 32 Oli Field; 12 Danny Kirmond. Subs: 8 Jon Luke Kirby; 15 Myles Harrison (not used); 20 Jack Teanby; 21 Ukuma Ta'ai.
Tries: Butterworth (2, 37, 67), Daley (44), Brown (50), Thompson (54), Dee (78); **Goals:** Glover 4/8.
BRONCOS: 1 Alex Walker; 2 Paul Ulberg; 3 Jarred Bassett; 18 Emmanuel Waine; 5 Iliess Macani; 6 Oliver Leyland; 17 Henry Raiwalui; 15 Lewis Bienek; 9 Sam Davis; 12 Marcus Stock; 11 Will Lovell; 16 Ethan Natoli; 13 Dean Parata. Subs (all used): 7 Rian Horsman; 8 Wellington Albert; 10 Jordan Williams; 14 Bill Leyland.
Tries: Walker (6), Bassett (20); **Goals:** O Leyland 2/2.
Rugby Leaguer & League Express Men of the Match: *Knights:* Olly Butterworth; *Broncos:* Alex Walker.
Penalty count: 4-4; **Half-time:** 8-12;
Referee: James Vella; **Attendance:** 951.

QUARTER FINALS

Saturday 17th June 2023

HULL KR 28 SALFORD RED DEVILS 10

HULL KR: 35 Tanguy Zenon (D); 23 Louis Senior; 3 Tom Opacic; 4 Shaun Kenny-Dowall (C); 5 Ryan Hall; 20 Mikey Lewis; 21 Rowan Milnes; 10 George King; 14 Jez Litten; 26 Sam Luckley; 22 Dean Hadley; 12 Kane Linnett; 13 Elliot Minchella. Subs (all used): 9 Matt Parcell; 15 Rhys Kennedy; 17 Matty Storton; 27 Yusuf Aydin.
Tries: R Hall (5), Zenon (22), Linnett (39), Kenny-Dowall (62), Hadley (68); **Goals:** Milnes 4/5.
Sin bin: Minchella (33) - high tackle.
RED DEVILS: 1 Ryan Brierley; 2 Ken Sio; 28 Deon Cross; 4 Tim Lafai; 5 Joe Burgess; 6 Brodie Croft; 7 Marc Sneyd; 16 Tyler Dupree; 14 Chris Atkin; 10 King Vuniyayawa; 3 Kallum Watkins (C); 12 Sam Stone; 13 Oliver Partington. Subs (all used): 21 Amir Bourouh; 8 Jack Ormondroyd; 19 Adam Sidlow; 25 Ben Hellewell.
Tries: Lafai (44), Burgess (78); **Goals:** Sneyd 1/2.
Rugby Leaguer & League Express Men of the Match: *Hull KR:* Shaun Kenny-Dowall; *Red Devils:* Oliver Partington.
Penalty count: 9-5; **Half-time:** 18-0;
Referee: Ben Thaler; **Attendance:** 6,289.

HULL FC 18 ST HELENS 32

HULL FC: 25 Davy Litten; 2 Adam Swift; 4 Liam Sutcliffe; 3 Carlos Tuimavave (C); 5 Darnell McIntosh; 6 Jake Trueman; 1 Tex Hoy; 13 Brad Fash; 9 Danny Houghton; 30 Scott Taylor; 23 Josh Griffin; 11 Andre Savelio; 15 Joe Cator. Subs (all used): 8 Ligi Sao; 10 Tevita Satae; 12 Jordan Lane; 33 Brad Dwyer.
Tries: Griffin (16), Savelio (25), Trueman (66);
Goals: Sutcliffe 3/3.
Dismissal: Griffin (40) - dissent.
SAINTS: 1 Jack Welsby; 2 Tommy Makinson; 23 Konrad Hurrell; 4 Mark Percival; 25 Tee Ritson; 6 Jonny Lomax; 7 Lewis Dodd; 8 Alex Walmsley; 9 James Roby (C); 10 Matty Lees; 16 Curtis Sironen; 12 Joe Batchelor; 13 Morgan Knowles. Subs (all used): 11 Sione Mata'utia; 14 Joey Lussick; 17 Agnatius Paasi; 19 James Bell.
Tries: Batchelor (7), Hurrell (34), Sironen (45), Dodd (58), Welsby (70), Bell (77); **Goals:** Makinson 2/2, Lussick 2/5.
Rugby Leaguer & League Express Men of the Match: *Hull FC:* Danny Houghton; *Saints:* Jack Welsby.
Penalty count: 5-6; **Half-time:** 12-12;
Referee: Chris Kendall; **Attendance:** 8,127.

Sunday 18th June 2023

WIGAN WARRIORS 14 WARRINGTON WOLVES 12

WARRIORS: 1 Jai Field; 23 Abbas Miski; 3 Toby King; 4 Jake Wardle; 5 Liam Marshall; 2 Bevan French; 7 Harry Smith; 16 Ethan Havard; 22 Brad O'Neill; 10 Liam Byrne; 19 Joe Shorrocks; 12 Liam Farrell (C); 15 Kaide Ellis. Subs (all used): 6 Cade Cust; 8 Brad Singleton; 13 Morgan Smithies; 26 Harvie Hill.
Tries: King (10), Miski (58); **Goals:** Smith 3/3.
Dismissal: Ellis (7) - headbutt.
WOLVES: 1 Matt Dufty; 2 Josh Thewlis; 20 Connor Wrench; 4 Stefan Ratchford (C); 5 Matty Ashton; 3 Peter Mata'utia; 6 George Williams; 17 Gil Dudson; 16 Danny Walker; 10 Paul Vaughan; 11 Ben Currie; 8 James Harrison; 14 Sam Kasiano. Subs (all used): 9 Daryl Clark; 15 Joe Philbin; 19 Joe Bullock; 35 Lucas Green.
Tries: Bullock (53), Thewlis (73); **Goals:** Ratchford 2/2.
Rugby Leaguer & League Express Men of the Match: *Warriors:* Harry Smith; *Wolves:* Josh Thewlis.
Penalty count: 5-4; **Half-time:** 8-0;
Referee: Liam Moore; **Attendance:** 9,302.

YORK KNIGHTS 14 LEIGH LEOPARDS 34

KNIGHTS: 2 Joe Brown; 5 AJ Towse; 15 Myles Harrison; 28 Adam Jones; 25 Brad Ward; 6 Ata Hingano; 19 Josh Daley; 21 Ukuma Ta'ai; 9 Will Jubb; 10 Conor Fitzsimmons; 32 Oli Field; 11 Chris Clarkson; 14 James Cunningham. Subs (all used): 8 Jon Luke Kirby; 17 Ronan Michael; 20 Jack Teanby; 34 Reagan Sumner.
Tries: Brown (18), Harrison (34); **Goals:** Harrison 3/4.
Sin bin: Teanby (78) - dangerous challenge on Mulhern.
LEOPARDS: 17 Gareth O'Brien; 2 Tom Briscoe; 1 Zak Hardaker; 26 Umyla Hanley (D); 5 Josh Charnley; 6 Joe Mellor; 7 Lachlan Lam; 10 Robbie Mulhern; 18 Matt Davis; 8 Tom Amone; 24 Kai O'Donnell; 22 Tom Nisbet; 13 John Asiata (C). Subs (all used): 3 Ed Chamberlain; 19 Aaron Smith; 25 Nathan Wilde; 27 Ava Seumanufagai.
Tries: Mellor (25), Amone (57), Charnley (61, 72), Briscoe (67, 80); **Goals:** O'Brien 2/3, Hardaker 3/3.
Dismissal: O'Donnell (5) - dangerous challenge on Daley.
Sin bin: Hardaker (17) - dangerous challenge on Towse.
Rugby Leaguer & League Express Men of the Match: *Knights:* AJ Towse; *Leopards:* Gareth O'Brien.
Penalty count: 4-7; **Half-time:** 14-6;
Referee: Jack Smith; **Attendance:** 2,412.

Challenge Cup 2023 - Round by Round

Lachlan Lam wins the Challenge Cup for Leigh despite the despairing dive of Hull KR's Sam Luckley

SEMI-FINALS

Saturday 22nd July 2023

LEIGH LEOPARDS 12 ST HELENS 10

LEOPARDS: 17 Gareth O'Brien; 2 Tom Briscoe; 1 Zak Hardaker; 3 Ed Chamberlain; 5 Josh Charnley; 15 Ben Reynolds; 7 Lachlan Lam; 10 Robbie Mulhern; 9 Edwin Ipape; 8 Tom Amone; 12 Jack Hughes; 16 Oliver Holmes; 13 John Asiata (C). Subs: 6 Joe Mellor; 14 Ben Nakubuwai; 18 Matt Davis; 25 Nathan Wilde (not used).
Tries: Holmes (43), Hardaker (53); **Goals:** Reynolds 2/3.
SAINTS: 1 Jack Welsby; 2 Tommy Makinson; 23 Konrad Hurrell; 3 Will Hopoate; 25 Tee Ritson; 6 Jonny Lomax (C); 7 Lewis Dodd; 8 Alex Walmsley; 14 Joey Lussick; 10 Matty Lees; 11 Sione Mata'utia; 19 James Bell; 13 Morgan Knowles. Subs: 15 Louie McCarthy-Scarsbrook; 17 Agnatius Paasi; 21 Ben Davies (not used); 30 George Delaney.
Tries: Lussick (18), Lomax (79); **Goals:** Makinson 1/3.
Sin bin: Mata'utia (62) - high tackle on Reynolds.
Rugby Leaguer & League Express Men of the Match:
Leopards: Zak Hardaker; *Saints:* Joey Lussick.
Penalty count: 2-4; **Half-time:** 0-6;
Referee: Chris Kendall; **Attendance:** 12,113
(at Halliwell Jones Stadium, Warrington).

Sunday 23rd July 2023

HULL KR 11 WIGAN WARRIORS 10
(after golden point extra-time)

HULL KR: 20 Mikey Lewis; 23 Louis Senior; 3 Tom Opacic; 4 Shaun Kenny-Dowall (C); 2 Ethan Ryan; 21 Rowan Milnes; 37 Brad Schneider; 15 Rhys Kennedy; 14 Jez Litten; 10 George King; 16 James Batchelor; 12 Kane Linnett; 13 Elliot Minchella. Subs (all used): 9 Matt Parcell; 17 Matty Storton; 18 Jimmy Keinhorst; 26 Sam Luckley.
Tries: Senior (11), Ryan (62);
Goals: Milnes 0/1, Schneider 1/1; **Field goal:** Schneider (82).
Sin bin: Kenny-Dowall (49) - professional foul.
WARRIORS: 1 Jai Field; 23 Abbas Miski; 3 Toby King; 4 Jake Wardle; 5 Liam Marshall; 2 Bevan French; 7 Harry Smith; 15 Kaide Ellis; 22 Brad O'Neill; 10 Liam Byrne; 11 Willie Isa; 12 Liam Farrell (C); 13 Morgan Smithies. Subs: 17 Kai Pearce-Paul; 19 Joe Shorrocks; 20 Patrick Mago; 26 Harvie Hill (not used).
Try: Field (23); **Goals:** Smith 3/3.
Dismissal: Shorrocks (42) - shoulder charge on Lewis.
Rugby Leaguer & League Express Men of the Match:
Hull KR: Mikey Lewis; *Warriors:* Jai Field.
Penalty count: 4-4; **Half-time:** 4-8;
Referee: Liam Moore; **Attendance:** 10,926
(at Headingley, Leeds).

FINAL

Saturday 12th August 2023

HULL KR 16 LEIGH LEOPARDS 17
(after golden point extra-time)

HULL KR: 20 Mikey Lewis; 2 Ethan Ryan; 3 Tom Opacic; 4 Shaun Kenny-Dowall (C); 5 Ryan Hall; 21 Rowan Milnes; 37 Brad Schneider; 15 Rhys Kennedy; 14 Jez Litten; 10 George King; 16 James Batchelor; 12 Kane Linnett; 13 Elliot Minchella. Subs (all used): 9 Matt Parcell; 17 Matty Storton; 22 Dean Hadley; 26 Sam Luckley.
Tries: Litten (15), Parcell (79); **Goals:** Schneider 4/4.
Sin bin: Minchella (31) - late challenge on Reynolds.
LEOPARDS: 17 Gareth O'Brien; 2 Tom Briscoe; 3 Ed Chamberlain; 1 Zak Hardaker; 5 Josh Charnley; 15 Ben Reynolds; 7 Lachlan Lam; 8 Tom Amone; 9 Edwin Ipape; 10 Robbie Mulhern; 24 Kai O'Donnell; 12 Jack Hughes; 13 John Asiata (C). Subs (all used): 6 Joe Mellor; 14 Ben Nakubuwai; 16 Oliver Holmes; 18 Matt Davis.
Tries: Lam (26), Briscoe (66); **Goals:** Reynolds 4/5;
Field goal: Lam (84).
Rugby Leaguer & League Express Men of the Match:
Hull KR: Mikey Lewis; *Leopards:* Lachlan Lam.
Penalty count: 3-4; **Half-time:** 8-10;
Referee: Chris Kendall; **Attendance:** 58,213
(at Wembley Stadium).

1895 CUP 2023
Round by Round

SEMI-FINALS

Saturday 22nd July 2023

LONDON BRONCOS 6 HALIFAX PANTHERS 10

BRONCOS: 1 Alex Walker; 2 Paul Ulberg; 17 Henry Raiwalui; 3 Jarred Bassett; 5 Iliess Macani; 6 Oliver Leyland; 20 Corey Norman; 12 Marcus Stock; 9 Sam Davis; 15 Lewis Bienek; 11 Will Lovell; 36 Jacob Gannon; 13 Dean Parata. Subs (all used): 10 Jordan Williams; 14 Bill Leyland; 34 Matthew Davies; 19 Dean Whare.
Try: Stock (77); **Goals:** O Leyland 1/2.
PANTHERS: 18 Brandon Pickersgill; 2 Lachlan Walmsley; 22 Jake Maizen; 3 Zack McComb; 5 James Saltonstall; 6 Louis Jouffret; 1 James Woodburn-Hall; 16 Will Calcott; 34 Adam O'Brien; 10 Dan Murray; 11 Ben Kavanagh; 12 Matty Gee; 13 Jacob Fairbank. Subs (all used): 8 Adam Tangata; 9 Brandon Moore; 19 Ryan Lannon; 31 Kevin Larroyer.
Try: Walmsley (64); **Goals:** Jouffret 3/3.
Rugby Leaguer & League Express Men of the Match: *Broncos:* Dean Parata; *Panthers:* Brandon Pickersgill.
Penalty count: 4-6; **Half-time:** 0-0;
Referee: Liam Rush; **Attendance:** 417
(at The Rock, Roehampton).

Sunday 23rd July 2023

YORK KNIGHTS 8 BATLEY BULLDOGS 22

KNIGHTS: 2 Joe Brown; 5 AJ Towse; 11 Chris Clarkson; 4 Jesse Dee; 29 Jason Bass; 14 James Cunningham; 7 Liam Harris; 21 Ukuma Ta'ai; 9 Will Jubb; 10 Conor Fitzsimmons; 32 Oli Field; 16 Bailey Antrobus; 13 Jordan Thompson. Subs: 6 Ata Hingano; 12 Danny Kirmond; 17 Ronan Michael (not used); 20 Jack Teanby.
Tries: Towse (54), Harris (60); **Goals:** Harris 0/2.
BULLDOGS: 32 Luke Hooley; 22 Dale Morton; 4 Josh Hodson; 15 Elliot Kear; 21 Aidan McGowan; 14 James Meadows; 7 Josh Woods; 8 Adam Gledhill; 6 Ben White; 13 James Brown; 11 Dane Manning; 3 Kieran Buchanan; 30 Martyn Reilly. Subs (all used): 9 Alistair Leak; 16 Michael Ward; 20 Samy Kibula; 26 Nyle Flynn.
Tries: Hodson (19), Gledhill (24), Leak (51);
Goals: Hooley 5/5.
Rugby Leaguer & League Express Men of the Match: *Knights:* Oli Field; *Bulldogs:* Josh Woods.
Penalty count: 7-10; **Half-time:** 0-14;
Referee: James Vella; **Attendance:** 1,646.

FINAL

Saturday 12th August 2023

BATLEY BULLDOGS 10 HALIFAX PANTHERS 12

BULLDOGS: 32 Luke Hooley; 22 Dale Morton; 4 Josh Hodson; 15 Elliot Kear; 21 Aidan McGowan; 14 James Meadows; 7 Josh Woods; 8 Adam Gledhill; 6 Ben White; 13 James Brown; 11 Dane Manning; 3 Kieran Buchanan; 30 Martyn Reilly. Subs (all used): 9 Alistair Leak; 16 Michael Ward; 20 Samy Kibula; 26 Nyle Flynn.
Tries: Morton (68), Kear (80); **Goals:** Hooley 1/2.
PANTHERS: 18 Brandon Pickersgill; 5 James Saltonstall; 3 Zack McComb; 22 Jake Maizen; 2 Lachlan Walmsley; 6 Louis Jouffret; 1 James Woodburn-Hall; 16 Will Calcott; 9 Brandon Moore; 10 Dan Murray; 11 Ben Kavanagh; 12 Matty Gee; 13 Jacob Fairbank. Subs (all used): 8 Adam Tangata; 19 Ryan Lannon; 31 Kevin Larroyer; 34 Adam O'Brien.
Try: Moore (2); **Goals:** Jouffret 4/4.
Rugby Leaguer & League Express Men of the Match: *Bulldogs:* Josh Hodson; *Panthers:* Louis Jouffret.
Penalty count: 5-6; **Half-time:** 0-8;
Referee: Jack Smith. *(at Wembley Stadium).*

Adam Tangata savours Halifax's 1895 Cup Final victory against Batley

Batley's Alistair Leak beats York's Joe Brown and Ukuma Ta'ai to score

Halifax's Lachlan Walmsley dives over against London Broncos

2023 SEASON
Stats round-up

ATTENDANCES

SUPER LEAGUE CLUBS - AVERAGES

	2023 Avg	2022 Avg	Diff
Leeds Rhinos	13,805	12,941	+864
Wigan Warriors	13,616	12,314	+1,302
St Helens	12,856	11,896	+960
Hull FC	12,355	10,763	+1,592
Warrington Wolves	10,894	8,721	+2,173
Catalans Dragons	9,239	8,172	+1,067
Hull KR	8,808	7,789	+1,019
Leigh Leopards	7,254	3,244	+4,010
		(Championship)	
Castleford Tigers	7,186	7,508	-322
Salford Red Devils	5,293	4,639	+654
Huddersfield Giants	5,244	5,233	+11
Wakefield Trinity	4,319	4,634	-315
2023 Average	9,239		
2022 Average	8,298		
Difference	+941		

CHAMPIONSHIP CLUBS - AVERAGES

	2023 Avg	2022 Avg	Diff
Bradford Bulls	3,665	3,491	+174
Toulouse Olympique	3,374	4,968	-1,594
		(Super League)	
Featherstone Rovers	3,155	3,051	+104
Widnes Vikings	2,922	2,860	+62
Barrow Raiders	2,195	2,324	-129
York Knights	1,998	1,984	+14
Keighley Cougars	1,962	1,652	+310
		(League One)	
Halifax Panthers	1,879	1,801	+78
Batley Bulldogs	1,580	1,330	+250
Sheffield Eagles	1,140	669	+471
Swinton Lions	1,093	892	+201
		(League One)	
Newcastle Thunder	1,089	1,065	+24
London Broncos	1,019	935	+84
Whitehaven	974	1,086	-112
2023 Average	2,003		
2022 Average	1,853		
Difference	+150		

LEAGUE ONE CLUBS - AVERAGES

	2023 Avg	2022 Avg	Diff
Dewsbury Rams	1,211	1,150	+61
		(Championship)	
Doncaster	1,197	999	+198
Cornwall	1,002	1,045	-43
Workington Town	803	956	-153
		(Championship)	
Oldham	737	694	+43
Hunslet	608	553	+55
Rochdale Hornets	585	521	+64
North Wales Crusaders	405	524	-119
Midlands Hurricanes	367	312	+55
London Skolars	271	300	-29
2023 Average	719		
2022 Average	711		
Difference	+8		

BEST ATTENDANCES

		Round	Date
58,213	Hull KR v Leigh	CCF	12/8/23
	(at Wembley Stadium)		
58,137	Catalans Dragons v Wigan	SLGF	14/10/23
	(at Old Trafford, Manchester)		
24,275	Wigan v St Helens	SLR8	7/4/23
20,985	Hull FC v Hull KR	SLR8	7/4/23
17,088	St Helens v Wigan	SLR15	9/6/23
16,140	Leeds v Hull FC	SLR2	24/2/23
15,383	Hull FC v Castleford	SLR1	19/2/23
15,377	Wigan v Leigh	SLR20	29/7/23
15,166	Leeds v Warrington	SLR22	20/8/23
15,162	Wigan v Hull KR	SLSF	7/10/23
15,148	St Helens v Leeds	SLR3	3/3/23
15,109	Leeds v Castleford	SLR27	22/9/23
15,026	Warrington v Wigan	SLR9	14/4/23
14,866	St Helens v Warrington	SLR10	20/4/23
14,590	Leeds v Huddersfield	SLR16	23/6/23
14,321	Leeds v Catalans Dragons	SLR6	25/3/23
14,161	Leeds v St Helens	SLR13	26/5/23
14,036	St Helens v Hull FC	SLR27	22/9/23
13,873	Penrith Panthers v St Helens	WCC	18/2/23
13,801	St Helens v Warrington	SLE	30/9/23

2023 Season - Stats round-up

LEADING SCORERS

Lachlan Walmsley

Connor Robinson

CHAMPIONSHIP *(Regular season & play-offs)*

TRIES

#	Player	Club	
1	Lachlan Walmsley	Halifax Panthers	36
2	Gareth Gale	Featherstone Rovers	30
3	Guy Armitage	Toulouse Olympique	22
4	Connor Jones	Featherstone Rovers	21
	Ben Jones-Bishop	Sheffield Eagles	21
6	Alex Walker	London Broncos	19
7	Kieran Gill	Bradford Bulls	18
	Iliess Macani	London Broncos	18
	Matty Dawson-Jones	Sheffield Eagles	18
10	Kieran Dixon	Widnes Vikings	17

GOALS

#	Player	Club	
1	Jake Shorrocks	Toulouse Olympique	105
2	Cory Aston	Sheffield Eagles	96
3	Dec Patton	Bradford Bulls	74
4	Ryan Shaw	Barrow Raiders	68
5	Louis Jouffret	Halifax Panthers	62
6	Josh Rourke	Whitehaven	60
7	Mark Kheirallah	Featherstone Rovers	59
8	Oliver Leyland	London Broncos	58
9	Dan Abram	Swinton Lions	48
10	Nikau Williams	Newcastle Thunder	44

POINTS

#	Player	Club	T	G	FG	Pts
1	Jake Shorrocks	Toulouse Olympique	4	105	0	226
2	Cory Aston	Sheffield Eagles	8	96	0	224
3	Josh Rourke	Whitehaven	11	60	0	164
4	Ryan Shaw	Barrow Raiders	6	68	0	160
5	Mark Kheirallah	Featherstone Rovers	9	59	0	154
6	Dec Patton	Bradford Bulls	1	74	0	152
7	Louis Jouffret	Halifax Panthers	6	62	1	149
8	Kieran Dixon	Widnes Vikings	17	39	0	146
9	Lachlan Walmsley	Halifax Panthers	36	0	0	144
10	Oliver Leyland	London Broncos	6	58	0	140

LEAGUE ONE *(Regular season & play-offs)*

TRIES

#	Player	Club	
1	Sam Smeaton	Doncaster	21
2	Owen Restall	Dewsbury Rams	16
3	Patrick Ah Van	Oldham	15
4	Cameron Brown	Cornwall	13
	Jack Render	Hunslet	13
	Adam Ryder	Hunslet	13
	Rob Massam	North Wales Crusaders	13
	Sean Sabutey	Workington Town	13
9	Johnny Campbell	Hunslet	12
10	Jordan Paga	Oldham	11
	Lewis Else	Rochdale Hornets	11

GOALS

#	Player	Club	
1	Connor Robinson	Doncaster	96
2	Martyn Ridyard	Oldham	80
3	Paul Sykes	Dewsbury Rams	76
4	Ciaran Walker	Workington Town	74
5	Matty Beharrell	Hunslet	65
6	Brad Billsborough	North Wales Crusaders	56
7	Dave Hewitt	Rochdale Hornets	48
8	Ben Stead	Midlands Hurricanes	33
9	Adam Rusling	Cornwall	30
10	Leon Hayes	North Wales Crusaders	23

POINTS

#	Player	Club	T	G	FG	Pts
1	Connor Robinson	Doncaster	9	96	0	228
2	Ciaran Walker	Workington Town	8	74	1	181
3	Martyn Ridyard	Oldham	2	80	1	169
4	Paul Sykes	Dewsbury Rams	3	76	1	165
5	Matty Beharrell	Hunslet	3	65	1	143
6	Brad Billsborough	North Wales Crusaders	2	56	0	120
7	Dave Hewitt	Rochdale Hornets	1	48	1	101
8	Sam Smeaton	Doncaster	21	0	0	84
9	Adam Rusling	Cornwall	4	30	1	77
10	Patrick Ah Van	Oldham	15	6	0	72

2023 Season - Stats round-up

LEADING SCORERS

Abbas Miski

Stefan Ratchford

SUPER LEAGUE *(Regular season & play-offs)*

TRIES

1	Abbas Miski	Wigan Warriors	28
2	Tom Johnstone	Catalans Dragons	27
	Josh Charnley	Leigh Leopards	27
4	Liam Marshall	Wigan Warriors	24
5	Tommy Makinson	St Helens	23
6	Adam Swift	Hull FC	19
7	Matty Ashton	Warrington Wolves	18
	Jai Field	Wigan Warriors	18
9	Bevan French	Wigan Warriors	17
10	Tom Davies	Catalans Dragons	15
	Jake Wardle	Wigan Warriors	15

GOALS

1	Stefan Ratchford	Warrington Wolves	98
2	Harry Smith	Wigan Warriors	97
3	Marc Sneyd	Salford Red Devils	84
4	Rhyse Martin	Leeds Rhinos	77
5	Ben Reynolds	Leigh Leopards	76
6	Adam Keighran	Catalans Dragons	73
7	Mark Percival	St Helens	58
8	Jake Clifford	Hull FC	50
9	Arthur Mourgue	Catalans Dragons	41
10	Oliver Russell	Huddersfield Giants	40

GOALS PERCENTAGE

			G	Att	%
1	Will Dagger	Wakefield Trinity/ Hull KR	35	39	89.74
2	Stefan Ratchford	Warrington Wolves	98	114	85.96
3	Marc Sneyd	Salford Red Devils	84	98	85.71
4	Arthur Mourgue	Catalans Dragons	41	48	85.41
5	Mark Percival	St Helens	58	68	85.29
6	Ben Reynolds	Leigh Leopards	76	95	80.00
	Paul McShane	Castleford Tigers	8	10	80.00
8	Brad Schneider	Hull KR	35	44	79.54
9	Rhyse Martin	Leeds Rhinos	77	97	79.38
10	Lachlan Coote	Hull KR	26	33	78.78

(10 minimum attempts to qualify)

POINTS

			T	G	FG	Pts
1	Harry Smith	Wigan Warriors	4	97	2	212
2	Stefan Ratchford	Warrington Wolves	2	98	0	204
3	Adam Keighran	Catalans Dragons	13	73	0	198
4	Rhyse Martin	Leeds Rhinos	10	77	0	194
5	Marc Sneyd	Salford Red Devils	3	84	4	184
6	Ben Reynolds	Leigh Leopards	5	76	0	172
7	Mark Percival	St Helens	9	58	0	152
8	Tommy Makinson	St Helens	23	29	0	150
9	Jake Clifford	Hull FC	6	50	0	124
10	Abbas Miski	Wigan Warriors	28	0	0	112

CHALLENGE CUP

TRIES

1	Josh Hodson	Batley Bulldogs	9
2	Dale Morton	Batley Bulldogs	6
3	Tom Briscoe	Leigh Leopards	5
	Jarred Bassett	London Broncos	5

(11 players tied on 4)

GOALS

1	James Meadows	Batley Bulldogs	20
2	Oliver Leyland	London Broncos	19
3	Paul Sykes	Dewsbury Rams	13
	Ben Stead	Midlands Hurricanes	13
5	Ben Reynolds	Leigh Leopards	12
	Brad Billsborough	North Wales Crusaders	12
	Ciaran Walker	Workington Town	12

POINTS

			T	G	FG	Pts
1	James Meadows	Batley Bulldogs	3	20	0	52
2	Oliver Leyland	London Broncos	2	19	0	46
3	Josh Hodson	Batley Bulldogs	9	0	0	36
	Ciaran Walker	Workington Town	3	12	0	36
5	Myles Lawford	Bradford Bulls	2	11	0	30

2023 Season - Stats round-up

LEADING SCORERS

Jake Shorrocks

ALL COMPETITIONS

TRIES

1	Lachlan Walmsley	Halifax Panthers	38
2	Josh Charnley	Leigh Leopards	30
	Gareth Gale	Featherstone Rovers	30
4	Abbas Miski	Wigan Warriors	29
5	Tom Johnstone	Catalans Dragons	28
6	Tommy Makinson	St Helens	24
	Liam Marshall	Wigan Warriors	24
8	Adam Swift	Hull FC	22
	Guy Armitage	Toulouse Olympique	22
10	Dale Morton	Batley Bulldogs	21
	Kieran Gill	Bradford Bulls	21
	Connor Jones	Featherstone Rovers	21
	Iliess Macani	London Broncos	21
	Ben Jones-Bishop	Sheffield Eagles	21
	Sam Smeaton	Doncaster	21

GOALS

1	Jake Shorrocks	Toulouse Olympique	105
2	Harry Smith	Wigan Warriors	104
	Cory Aston	Sheffield Eagles	104
	Connor Robinson	Doncaster	104
5	Stefan Ratchford	Warrington Wolves	102
6	Marc Sneyd	Salford Red Devils	92
7	Paul Sykes	Dewsbury Rams	89
8	Ben Reynolds	Leigh Leopards	88
9	Ciaran Walker	Workington Town	86
10	Martyn Ridyard	Oldham	85

POINTS

			T	G	FG	Pts
1	Connor Robinson	Doncaster	10	104	0	248
2	Cory Aston	Sheffield Eagles	9	104	0	244
3	Harry Smith	Wigan Warriors	4	104	2	226
	Jake Shorrocks	Toulouse Olympique	4	105	0	226
5	Ciaran Walker	Workington Town	11	86	1	217
6	Stefan Ratchford	Warrington Wolves	2	102	0	212
7	Marc Sneyd	Salford Red Devils	4	92	4	204
8	Rhyse Martin	Leeds Rhinos	10	80	0	200
9	Adam Keighran	Catalans Dragons	13	73	0	198
10	Ben Reynolds	Leigh Leopards	5	88	0	196

FIELD GOALS

1	Marc Sneyd	Salford Red Devils	4
	Josh Woods	Batley Bulldogs	4
3	Gareth O'Brien	Leigh Leopards	3
	Jordy Gibson	Swinton Lions	3
	Liam Harris	York Knights	3

FINAL TABLES

SUPER LEAGUE

	P	W	D	L	F	A	D	Pts
Wigan Warriors	27	20	0	7	722	360	362	40
Catalans Dragons	27	20	0	7	722	420	302	40
St Helens	27	20	0	7	613	366	247	40
Hull KR	27	16	0	11	589	498	91	32
Leigh Leopards	27	16	0	11	585	508	77	32
Warrington Wolves	27	14	0	13	597	512	85	28
Salford Red Devils	27	13	0	14	494	512	-18	26
Leeds Rhinos	27	12	0	15	535	534	1	24
Huddersfield Giants	27	11	0	16	473	552	-79	22
Hull FC	27	10	0	17	476	654	-178	20
Castleford Tigers	27	6	0	21	323	774	-451	12
Wakefield Trinity	27	4	0	23	303	742	-439	8

CHAMPIONSHIP

	P	W	D	L	F	A	D	Pts
Featherstone Rovers	27	25	0	2	1079	295	784	50
Toulouse Olympique	27	19	0	8	832	385	447	38
Bradford Bulls	27	16	1	10	677	572	105	33
Sheffield Eagles	27	16	0	11	780	560	220	32
London Broncos	27	16	0	11	600	552	48	32
York Knights	27	15	0	12	557	557	0	30
Batley Bulldogs	27	15	0	12	506	519	-13	30
Halifax Panthers	27	14	1	12	690	572	118	29
Widnes Vikings	27	13	0	14	619	652	-33	26
Swinton Lions	27	9	0	18	426	739	-313	18
Barrow Raiders	27	8	1	18	471	672	-201	17
Whitehaven	27	8	0	19	481	809	-328	16
Keighley Cougars	27	8	0	19	506	837	-331	16
Newcastle Thunder	27	5	1	21	415	918	-503	11

LEAGUE ONE

	P	W	D	L	F	A	D	Pts
Dewsbury Rams	18	15	1	2	623	215	408	31
Hunslet	18	14	0	4	572	284	288	28
Doncaster	18	14	0	4	602	352	250	28
Oldham	18	12	1	5	605	333	272	25
Workington Town	18	11	0	7	516	385	131	22
North Wales Crusaders	18	7	0	11	520	437	83	14
Rochdale Hornets	18	6	0	12	425	520	-95	12
Midlands Hurricanes	18	5	0	13	408	647	-239	10
Cornwall	18	5	0	13	257	712	-455	10
London Skolars	18	0	0	18	254	897	-643	0